CRUCIBLE

CRUCIBLE

The Long End of the Great War
and the Birth of a New World,
1917–1924

CHARLES EMMERSON

PublicAffairs

New York

For E. W

All else is folly

PublicAffairs
Hachette Book Group
1290 Avenue of the Americas, New York, NY 10104
www.publicaffairsbooks.com
@Public_Affairs

Printed in the United States of America

Originally published in 2019 by Bodley Head in the United Kingdom

First U.S. Edition: October 2019

Published by PublicAffairs, an imprint of Perseus Books, LLC, a subsidiary of Hachette Book Group, Inc. The PublicAffairs name and logo is a trademark of the Hachette Book Group.

The Hachette Speakers Bureau provides a wide range of authors for speaking events. To find out more, go to www.hachettespeakersbureau.com or call (866) 376-6591.

The publisher is not responsible for websites (or their content) that are not owned by the publisher.

Print book interior typeset in Perpetua Std by Integra Software Services Pvt. Ltd, Pondicherry.

Library of Congress Cataloging-in-Publication Data has been applied for.

ISBNs: 978-1-61039-782-7 (hardcover), 978-1-61039-783-4 (e-book)

LSC-C

10 9 8 7 6 5 4 3 2 1

CONTENTS

Preface   vii

1917   I
1918   85
1919   179
1920   283
1921   365
1922   453
1923   527

Epilogue: 1924   595

Acknowledgements   611
Notes and Sources   613
Index   723

PREFACE

No one believed a modern war could last this long. But by 1917 Europe has already been at war for three years. The fabric of the Continent has been torn up. Now it begins to collapse from the inside. This book tells the story of that collapse, and the energies unleashed which made a new world to replace the old.

In Petrograd a fire is lit. People crowd the streets. The Romanov realm begins its journey into oblivion. The Tsar is packed off to the Urals, to spend more time with his family, his wood-chopping and his God. A Russian exile crosses war-torn Europe to make a triumphal entry into Petrograd at the Finnish railway terminus. 'Peace now!' the crowds cry. They cannot expect what happens next: another offensive, another revolution, anarchy and a civil war loosed across Eurasia.

November 1918: an armistice is signed to end the Great War on the Western Front. The shell-shocked begin their journey home. Yet even as the ink is drying on this promise of an end to Europe's nightmare, fresh conflicts and upheavals are in preparation elsewhere. True peace does not return for years to come. Risings in the Middle East are crushed. A massacre in India tarnishes Britain's imperial prestige. In Europe, new militia armies arise, unbound by the old rules of conflict. The peacemakers of Versailles draw lines on maps. Meanwhile, the Continent slips out of their control. Politics takes a violent turn. Modernity and barbarity develop side by side.

Defeated German soldiers return from the front and are sent to suppress a Communist rising in Berlin. Bodies bob along the river Spree. A dismal period in German history now begins, punctuated by plots, coups and foreign occupation. The country swings wildly from economic depression to boom to immiserating inflation. Nothing is solid any more; old hierarchies are upended. A lowly army field-runner is trained to give rousing speeches to the masses to prevent a slide to Bolshevism. Soon he is mixing with the generals who lost the war, and railing against the Jews.

The established order is swept away. Women are given the vote. Emperors, Kings and generals depart furtively on midnight trains or submarines. People who were nothing are catapulted into prominence. Europe explodes into a frenzy of creative energy. The real becomes sur-real. Marching tunes are syncopated into jazz. A former patent clerk from Switzerland becomes an instant celebrity when his theory of relativity is proven to be true. Time and space lose their fixedness.

Civilisation is released from its pre-war moorings. People search for meaning in the wreckage. Agitprop trains criss-cross Russia, spreading the gospel of revolution. A playful Italian prone to grand flourishes takes a train to Rome to proclaim a new era for his country. The city runs out of flowers to strew in front of its saviour. In the back streets, fascist violence ensures the socialists understand who is now in charge.

Paris bustles with new arrivals. Armenians from the Ottoman Empire and Russian aristocrats seek refuge. Americans armed with dollars live it up in Montparnasse for a pittance. A boy from Chicago who set out to see the world as a reporter starts writing literary sentences in a Paris attic – the shorter the better. There is a surge in Frenchwomen taking vows as nuns – there are no husbands left to be had. The government plans for the next war while its people mourn the last.

In Central Europe, the hole left by the Austro-Hungarian Empire is filled with plebiscites and martinets. The father of psychoanalysis advises his disciples to withdraw their libido from the Habsburg cause: seven centuries of their rule come to an end. In Budapest, a muckraking journalist becomes a fiery Red commissar, only to be ousted by an admiral without a fleet. An Italian writer marches into an Adriatic seaside town at the head of a ragtag band of troops. A soldier-revolutionary released from a German jail becomes leader of a resurrected Poland. Vienna survives on starvation rations.

Having saved the Continent from the overweening ambitions of the Kaiser, America turns its back on old, warring, disease-ridden Europe. The President, welcomed as a hero abroad for his vision of a new era of peace, loses the fight at home to take the United States into the League of Nations. The country turns its mission inwards – from saving the world, to saving itself. Red scares spread from New York to Los Angeles. The sale of alcohol is prohibited. Black American soldiers who have done their duty in France return to an uneasy welcome. Lynching carries on across the South. The black fight against injustice gears up.

And at opposite ends of Europe conflict continues unabated. In Ireland, atrocity and reprisal mar a nation's struggle for independence. The price of freedom from British rule is civil war and a divided island. In the east, a tangle of peoples fight for their share of what was once the Ottoman Empire. A heartbreaking, raki-drinking army officer crushes Greeks and Armenians who claim a historic homeland in Anatolia. He renames himself 'father of the Turks' and sets his country on a new path for the future.

It is seven years since the fire was lit in Petrograd before the crucible burns out. No new wars are fought in 1924: a decade since the Great War began, six years since the armistice, five since Versailles. The Russian exile who wanted to paint the globe red and the American President who wanted to make the world safe for democracy are both dead. New figures have arisen to take their place. Dreams of renewal are twisted into new fantasies of power. The Furies of war fade back into the past.

An uneasy peace settles over the European Continent, scarred by its experiences and purged of its old certainties. The world is forged into the shape of the twentieth century.

1917

The Earth shivers
         starving .
         stripped.
Mankind is vaporised in a blood bath
              only so that
                    someone
                    somewhere
                         can get hold of Albania

Vladimir Mayakovsky

WINTER

Petrograd, Russia: It is a lurid affair. The press, though heavily censored, have a field day. A popular hate figure – a holy man accused of hijacking the imperial family, cuckolding the Tsar and leading Russia to ruin – has been murdered by one of Russia's most prominent aristocrats. Rasputin's mutilated body is laid to rest in the foundations of a new church at Tsarskoye Selo, the Tsar's estate just outside Petrograd. Nicholas Romanov is there, his German-born wife Alexandra, and their four daughters (their son Alexei is too ill to attend). Boards are placed on the ground to protect their clothes from the frozen mud. Alexandra is in tears.

Russia is in crisis. The price of bread – and apples and cabbage and underwear and everything else – keeps going up. The soldiers' boots are worn out. There are rumours of a possible palace coup. The French Ambassador is told of plans to assassinate the Tsarina.

Nicholas is tired. He prays fervently for salvation.

Zurich, Switzerland: A man with narrow eyes, hobnail hiking boots, and clothes that smell faintly of sausage – he lives with his wife above a butcher's shop – fills in a questionnaire from the city authorities. Name and profession: 'Ulyanov, lawyer and writer'. Wealth: none. Ulyanov confirms that he is not a deserter from one of Europe's armies, nor a draft-dodger. Not entirely untruthfully he reports his income as coming from 'literary and journalistic work for a Petrograd publisher'. The authorities grant the Ulyanovs leave to remain until the end of 1918.

Vladimir Ulyanov – whose wife Nadya, former lover Inessa and political intimates call him by his patronymic Ilyich – is a familiar face in the narrow streets of Zurich. A little eccentric, perhaps, but no more than any of the other foreigners in the city. The Ulyanovs' neighbours include a former German soldier and an Austrian actor with a marmalade cat.

All seem to be escaping something. Zurich is full of writers and performers and cranks and crackpots looking for a safe haven in the middle of a war.

The Russian couple live a spartan existence. They eat horsemeat to save money. To judge by Vladimir's daily routine alone – to the library at nine in the morning, home for a quick lunch between midday and one, and then back to the library again till six – one might at first mistake him for being an academic (albeit on forced sabbatical, apparently). Pretty much the only time Ulyanov is not in the library is Thursday afternoon, when it closes early. On those days, the Russian couple are to be seen walking up the Zürichberg, the low, wooded mountain outside town. Vladimir purchases hazelnut chocolate bars wrapped in blue paper to share with Nadya. On the way down, in season, the two carry mushrooms and berries foraged from the mountainside.

But is he really so harmless? Look closer. The hobnail boots suggest a rougher past than a university lecture hall or the well-appointed offices of a publishing house. There is something quite worldly about him, quite physical, perhaps even a little coarse. His clothes are made of thick material, as if they might be his only set. And then there are those occasional flashes of intensity – those eyes, again – when Vladimir exudes a sense of inner purpose, unfathomable to the outsider, quite magnetic. He is always in a great hurry to get wherever he is going, even when just walking through town. His wife calls him her 'Arctic wolf', prowling within the bounds of polite society but always striving for the wilderness. He rarely seems fully relaxed, even when tucked up at home. The slightest sound can set him off. He can be tyrannically impatient with the world at times. When he goes to the theatre, which is not often, he and Nadya tend to leave after the first act.

As a younger man, Vladimir Ulyanov was quite a sportsman: a walker, a swimmer, a hardy (if not particularly skilled) fisherman prepared to wade perilously deep into Siberian rivers to try and catch a few small fish, a mountain hiker and keen hunter, a skater and skier. He is still a man who finds a winter without snow and ice not a real winter at all. And winter is his favourite season. He likes the Swiss mountains because the cold frosty air reminds him of Russia. He believes in *mens sana in corpore sano* – a healthy mind in a healthy body. He once thought that ten minutes' gymnastics every morning was the key. More recently he has turned to cycling to keep fit and burn off his excess energy. But his body is less cooperative than it used to be. He has headaches now; he sleeps badly. He is often short-tempered.

'It's the brain', a doctor tells him, when asked where the trouble lies. Vladimir is forty-seven. His father Ilya – hence Ilyich – was dead at fifty-four. What restless, anxious thoughts fill that bare skull of his?

The more one looks at this Vladimir Ulyanov, the more one digs into his past and certainly the more one listens to what he has to say, the less innocent he becomes. On the city's registration questionnaire, he writes that he is a 'political émigré'. Well, Russia produces plenty of those. But what kind of émigré? In revolutionary circles, he is known by the pseudonym Lenin, a name he picked up after returning from a stint in internal Russian exile in Siberia. Is he a paper tiger, or could Vladimir Ulyanov, aka Lenin, be dangerous? There is perhaps something a little sinister about him when he pulls his face into that leering half-smile of his, full of subtly demonic charm. Then there is the chilling way he narrows his gaze into a squint when he looks at people sometimes, as if he were actively sizing them up for the revolutionary judgement day. Then again, it could just be short-sightedness.

At the Zurich public library, Vladimir terrorises the staff with prodigious requests for works of German philosophy, revolutionary socialist theory and economic history. He admires the organisational efficiency of the Swiss in meeting his demands through their extraordinary system of inter-library loans. This would never work in Russia, Lenin sighs. There, one could not get hold of such books at all. He piles them on his desk like a barricade, warily eyeing anyone who might take them away from him. He fills note-book after notebook with agitated observations on what he has read. Occasionally, the scribbling stops and the squinty Russian mutters something inaudible under his breath.

The muttering generally happens when Vladimir thinks he has caught out some fellow Marxist in a misinterpretation of the theories of Karl Marx. For the man his political followers call Lenin, this is a frequent enough occurrence and an infuriating one. He feels himself to be in constant battle with those who do not understand Marxist theory the way he does. Lenin's own theoretical-historical-economic postulates, which his library studies serve to buttress and to elaborate, boil down to three. First, capitalism must eventually collapse in social revolution and reform attempts are, at best, a distraction and, at worst, a betrayal of the workers. Second, the majority are stupid and need a correctly indoctrinated minority to lead them: not a stance calculated to win many friends perhaps, but certainly consistent with Vladimir's own ability to be outnumbered even in avowedly socialist gatherings – Lenin has always been a splitter amongst splittists. Third, the world war – understood as an expression of the inherent tendencies of capitalist business interests – has created a revolutionary situation ripe for exploitation: so long as middle-class pacifists don't screw it up by settling for a bourgeois peace, and as long as the proletariat stop listening to patriotic socialists and start turning their weapons against their masters, rather than against each other. In the glowing embers of the imperialist-capitalist conflict, Lenin spies the spark needed for a European civil war, a class war, and with it: *revolution!*

The first step to victory is defeat all round – defeat for the French with their colonial empire across North Africa, defeat for the British with their imperialist designs across the globe, defeat for the autocratic regime of the Russian Tsar, defeat for the German Kaiser, defeat for the American business interests inexorably pushing their country further into the cauldron. Can a lose–lose scenario be arranged from which social revolution might spring? Vladimir's ears prick up at any sign that his message is getting through. Every encounter is an opportunity to make his case for the revolutionary necessity of defeat all round. Over the summer he is, in his wife Nadya's memorable phrase, like a 'cat after lard' when he identifies a soldier recovering from tuberculosis staying in the same small guesthouse, halfway up a mountain near St Gallen. He tries repeatedly to engage the patient in political chit-chat, asking him leading questions such as whether he agrees about the predatory character of the war. In Zurich, Vladimir is delighted when his wife relates to him the comment of one of the other women huddled around a gas stove that maybe soldiers should start attacking their own governments.

A flow of insistent questions and hectoring demands issue constantly from Vladimir's pen to his followers (not many, these days). His letters to fellow Bolsheviks – the name Lenin gives to his faction of the Russian left – are generally brief and unembellished, written in the shorthand of someone who expects his correspondent to immediately grasp their correctness, importance and urgency. They overflow with snap judgements on the shortcomings of others. To Lenin, the world is full of hypocrites. He is particularly disdainful of a group of former political associates known as the Mensheviks and a man called Kautsky, Marx's literary executor, who Lenin thinks has gone soft. For Lenin, calling someone a 'Kautsky-ite' is the highest term of abuse. He has no time for what he calls, with visceral hatred, opportunists. He considers the mainstream socialist movement to be full of them.

His correspondence is full of frustration about the state of things: there is not enough money, not enough translators, not enough of anything to do a proper job of revolution. In January, Vladimir suggests his former lover Inessa Armand have a dress made with a special pouch in which the last remaining Bolshevik party funds in Switzerland can be hidden and transported abroad if need be. Conspiracy is a way of life. He is hungry for information – from Russia, from Germany, from anywhere. In Zurich, he has made himself an authority on the factional struggles within the Swiss socialist movement. When a Russian prisoner of war escapes from Germany by swimming across Lake Constance, Lenin is keen to pump him for his impressions. Impatient, insistent exclamation marks pepper his letters like gunshot pellets.

Occasionally, summoning all his prestige as Lenin, the veteran of the Russian revolution of 1905, Vladimir gathers together Zurich's anti-war socialists in one of the city's bars. Naturally, he tends to dominate such events, speaking for an hour or so himself and then announcing that there is no time left for questions. Moderates accuse Vladimir of running head first into a brick wall with his revolution-at-any-cost approach. His embrace of violence as a political necessity strikes some as overdone. Who does Ulyanov speak for anyway? His Russian networks are largely blown (a couple of senior Bolsheviks turn out to be informants for the Tsar). Lenin is hardly a household name amongst the Petrograd proletariat. Who is he to lecture the socialists of Western Europe? After some initial success – as many as forty men and women crammed into the bar – Nadya notes a thinning-out in subsequent meetings, until there are just a couple of Poles and Russians left staring morosely into their beers.

In January, Vladimir gives a talk to a group of young Swiss socialists at the Zurich Volkshaus, twelve years to the day since the outbreak of revolution in 1905. He tries to arouse their enthusiasm, and instruct them in the lessons to be drawn from his experience. Yet there is an ambivalence here. 'The monstrous horrors of the imperialist war', he says, 'engender a revolutionary mood.' But when will that erupt into revolution? In six months? A year? Ten years? 'We of the older generation may not live to see the decisive battles of the coming revolution', Vladimir admits, 'but I can, I believe, express the confident hope that the youth which is working so splendidly in the socialist movement of Switzerland, and of the whole world, will be fortunate enough not only to fight, but also to win.' Will revolution happen within his lifetime? The impatient revolutionary sounds uncertain.

THE FRONT LINE: It used to be simple to draw. A line on the map from the North Sea to the Alps in the west, slicing through Europe in the east, and dividing Italy and Serbia from Austria in the south. Things get more complicated in Africa, and in the Middle East, of course, where the Ottoman Empire fights as ally to the Germans and the Austrians.

But where is the front line now? In this war, it is everywhere. It runs through towns and cities, across rivers, and through mountains. The front line is on the factory floor and in the fields. It is in the chemistry laboratories where scientists develop new ways of making stretched resources go a little further and invent new products to kill the enemy or prevent disease. The front line is in Europe's tax offices, in war bonds departments, and in the marketplaces of global finance, where money is borrowed to fund the war (increasingly, in America). It is in recruiting centres from Bombay to Brisbane, where Europe's empires try to persuade their subject peoples to join their struggle, shipping thousands off from Asia and Africa to fight the enemy. The front line is in the human mind, where the horror of war is in continual combat with the dream of victory. This war is constant. It never stops. Everyone is involved. Armies and navies are just the leading edge of whole societies in conflict.

There is little fighting of the old-fashioned variety this winter. Long periods in the trenches with nothing to do are punctuated by sudden, shocking violence. An Italian soldier sitting on the front line with Austria–Hungary just north of Trieste writes in his diary: 'snow, cold, infinite boredom'. Rations have been cut again. Stewed salt cod and potatoes for supper on Christmas Day; and a miserly half a dozen *panettone* to share amongst over two hundred soldiers. Cholera is spreading. The soldiers have fleas. Men returning from leave mutter about chaos back home. 'A government of national impotence'.

BUDAPEST, THE AUSTRO-HUNGARIAN EMPIRE: In the first days of 1917 the city of Budapest nurses an imperial hangover. It is a week since the newly elevated head of the Habsburg line, Emperor Charles I of Austria, was rushed from Vienna to be crowned a second time, as King Charles IV of Hungary, adding another royal title to the gazette of lesser honorifics inherited from his dead great-uncle, the bristly Franz Joseph.

Amidst the toasts to tradition and the oaths of blood fealty from Charles's varied subjects – Hungarians, Slovaks, Poles, Austrians, Romanians, Croatians – journalists huddle around field telephones to call in their latest coronation story. Film cameras whirr and click, recording the scene for the empire's newsreels, while a Hungarian Jew who will later make his name in Hollywood directs the film crews this way and that to catch the essence of the moment. One camera's gaze settles for an instant on the lolloping figure of a plump bishop, mounted uneasily on horseback, clinging on to his crozier for dear life while a soldier draws his horse past the cheering crowds. Another captures an undulating sea of hats – top hats, bowler hats, felt hats, fur hats, Tyrolean hats, fedoras, military caps and unseasonal straw boaters – as varied as the peoples of the empire. The war wounded are nowhere to be seen. For half an instant, it feels like 1914 all over again. Charles trots on horseback through the streets of Budapest, his moustache clipped in the modern fashion, smiling and nodding brightly in all directions, followed by a posse of slouching nobles with short legs and thick fur mantles, looking for all the world as if they have just stepped out of a Holbein group portrait. He swears to uphold the constitutional bargains at the heart of the old empire, whereby the Hungarians manage one half of his estate and Vienna manages the other half, and the Emperor sits on top trying to hold the whole thing together.

Budapest's streets are quieter now. The clip of cavalry hooves on cobblestone has been replaced by the more familiar sounds of daily life. The decorations which festooned the procession route, prepared in great haste by the scenery department of the Budapest opera, have been taken down. Police reports on the public response have come back: 'too much pomp', the citizens of Vienna grumble. Plans for a huge statue of Franz Joseph to be cast from captured Russian cannons proceed slowly for lack of funds. The dignitaries who travelled to Budapest to see the Austrian Emperor's second coronation as King of Hungary have now returned home. They are bombarded with questions about the new King-Emperor. One question above all: will he bring peace?

Charles is twenty-nine years old: a handsome man, but with a weak face, more like a character from Proust than a leader of an empire at war. (His wife Zita is not quite twenty-five.) It is three years since the assassination of his cousin Franz Ferdinand in Sarajevo unloosed this war. It was never meant to last this long. Charles now proclaims his desire for peace with honour to save his creaking empire, the product of several hundred years of dynastic accumulation, an unwieldy structure in which a kaleidoscope of nationalities live in moderate happiness under the Habsburg Crown, and which people have been trying to reform for years, but cannot quite work out how.

But peace cannot just be wished. Success depends on the willingness of others to play along – both one's enemies and one's allies. Yet Charles's most powerful ally, the German Kaiser Wilhelm, feels no deference to his junior partner-in-war. With each passing month, Austria's fate is bound tighter and tighter to that of Germany. Without a negotiated peace, what started as Austria–Hungary's war is likely to end up either as Germany's victory – with Austria reduced to vassal status – or with the collapse of both. Charles fears the possibility of imperial break-up or revolution amongst his peoples. Demands for independence have been growing for years. The war has made them louder.

There is a second current of revolution running through Charles's empire in the first days of 1917: an intellectual revolution, a revolution of the mind. For now, that revolution is self-proclaimed. It exists on paper, amongst the initiated. The inner cabal – somewhere between a study group and a secret society (their leader thinks of them as his 'adopted children') – denote their cause symbolically: with the Greek letter Ψ, or psi. More widely – which is not widely at all outside the hospital ward and the university – this revolution is known as 'psychoanalysis'. The revolution's father figure, based in Vienna, refers to the cause as a *Geistesrichtung*, a spiritual movement.

His disciples exchange a constant stream of letters, gossiping about patients and swapping insights. Topics of enquiry are varied. Karl Abraham, a German army doctor serving at a Prussian military hospital, takes time between tending to the war wounded to finish his paper on premature ejaculation and its relationship to early childhood. In Budapest, Sándor Ferenczi struggles with a study of the symbology of castration. Last winter a series of public lectures were organised in Vienna on the subject of psychoanalysis. It is said one of Emperor Charles's cousins popped in to hear a few.

In January, the revolution's latest front is opened in an article in Budapest's leading literary periodical entitled 'An Obstacle in the Path of Psychoanalysis'. It makes for uncomfortable reading for the city's literati. Their pupils dilate. Their synapses flash. Ink smudges onto sweaty fingertips. The chief impediment to the spread of psychoanalysis, the article proclaims accusingly, is *ourselves*. It has always been thus. It is our self-love, our narcissism, which makes us refuse the genius of the greatest of our scientists. First it was Copernicus, who had the temerity to tell humans that the sun and stars did not turn around us, but us around them. Then it was Darwin, who upturned the aggrandising idea that God made humans in His image to rule the earth, but showed rather that we are mere animals, super-brained monkeys in three-piece suits, evolved but not separated from our genetic forebears.

Now is the hour of the third revolution against which human narcissism rages, blindly and in vain. And this revolution is the most disturbing blow of all to human self-regard, for it shows that we are not masters even of ourselves. A deep breath, a sip of water. Budapest's trams scrape and rumble by outside, unheard. The readers' pulses race. The mind, they learn, is a 'labyrinth of impulses, corresponding with the multiplicity of instincts, antagonistic to one another and incompatible'. There is no coronation ceremony in the world which can change the facts: control is an illusion, order is fleeting. 'Thoughts emerge suddenly without one's knowing where they came from' and, once brought to mind, these 'alien guests' cannot be so easily removed. Such is the terrifying image conjured into life by the article's author, the man most closely associated with the psychoanalytic creed: the conscious and unconscious are held in constant tension, our minds are forever simmering with psychical revolt. This is a conflict that no earthly peace deal can resolve.

STOCKHOLM, SWEDEN: The Nobel Prize Committee receives a letter from an Austrian physicist recommending a former patent clerk in Switzerland, now working at one of the German Kaiser's most prestigious scientific institutes in Berlin, for the award of the Nobel Prize in Physics. Over the next few days, several more letters pile up suggesting the young Albert Einstein, still only in his mid-thirties, for the award.

PLESS CASTLE, SILESIA, THE GERMAN REICH: The German Kaiser is in no mood for compromise. 'The war', he explains, 'is a struggle between two Weltanschauungen, the Teutonic-German for decency, justice, loyalty and faith, genuine humanity, truth and real freedom; against the worship of mammon, the power of money, pleasure, land-hunger, lies, betrayal, deceit.' He blames his enemies for the war's continuation. They have rejected his latest (thoroughly disingenuous) peace initiative. He writes to nervous Emperor Charles: 'before God and before humankind the enemy governments will carry alone the awful responsibility for whatever further terrible sacrifices may now come to pass'. The matter is out of his hands.

In a conference room deep in a medieval castle the Kaiser and a few military men take a fateful step. Germany is suffering a slow suffocation at the hands of a British naval blockade. Its children are starving. Yet Britain is free to receive imports of food and weapons from around the world, both from the empire but also from supposedly neutral countries such as the United States. As the generals see it, Germany could disrupt this flow and force the war to an end in months by using submarines.

There is a catch. For maximum effectiveness of the campaign, submarine captains must be empowered to strike without warning and without mercy when they spot a target on the high seas. Fire first, ask questions later. They cannot wait to check the ship's nationality or the content of its hold. Law and morality must be set aside. To engage in such a war will spark condemnation. It will upset American public opinion. But it is a calculated risk. 'Things cannot be worse than they are now', the group is told by Field Marshal Hindenburg, who, with General Ludendorff, runs Germany's war.

Wilhelm has hesitated for months. He plays at being the decisive war leader. The truth is that he is never sure what he should do until he has done it. The generals try to sideline him as much as possible, leaving him to flitter-flutter around in his bubble of hunting excursions, meetings with foreign leaders and road trips along the Rhine. But on this issue, the Kaiser cannot be ignored. The generals resort to another technique: seducing him with the promise of a great victory achieved by the Kaiser's very own navy, and simultaneously dropping broad hints that they will resign if he does not do what they ask. It works.

There is one final obstacle: the Kaiser's appointee as the nation's civilian leadership, Chancellor Bethmann Hollweg. But once the Kaiser has been persuaded, the Chancellor is presented with a *fait accompli*. This is Germany's 'last card', he warns the generals. What if it goes wrong? The military men push back: 'energetic' and 'ruthless' methods are now needed to bring about victory before the Austrians start to fall apart. 'We must spare the troops a second battle of the Somme', Ludendorff tells the Chancellor. And if America joins the war? Hindenburg is confident: 'we can take care of that'. The war will be over before any Americans arrive.

The Kaiser signs the order that evening. He affects a strange insouciance as to its likely consequence: America's entry into the war. The order will come into effect on the first day of February. It will not be made public until the day before, the last day of January. Even the Austrians are not told of the final decision until it is too late to rescind.

VIENNA, THE AUSTRO-HUNGARIAN EMPIRE: Outside a few learned societies and the local Jewish welfare organisation, the name Sigmund Freud signifies little in the Austrian capital in 1917. Though a true son of the Habsburg Empire – a Moravian-born Jew who has made it in the capital – Freud's fame, as he himself puts it laconically, begins at the border. The first time he feels he might really one day be famous is in 1909, when he catches a cabin steward reading one of his books on an ocean liner crossing from Europe to America.

Freud's outward style of life is that of an ever-so-slightly eccentric *gentilhomme* of his generation (university class of 1881) and milieu (a medical professional). His daily schedule is regular: writing, hourly slots with patients, a light lunch, a brisk walk, and letter-writing before bed. Like Lenin, he lives above a butcher's shop, though his spacious family apartment at Berggasse 19 compares quite favourably with Vladimir and Nadya's spartan digs in Zurich. Freud has achieved sufficient prosperity to be able to spend reasonably freely on a few particular private passions: books, his family, holidays in Italy or in the Alps, cigars, ancient artefacts. But, generally, he is careful with money. He invests his savings in Austro-Hungarian state bonds and life insurance. He rarely drinks. He never goes to the opera, preferring silent contemplation in his study to the noise of music. (There is no piano in the Freud apartment and the doctor's study is situated as far as possible from the rooms of his musically inclined sister-in-law, 'Tante' Minna.) Though an avid card-player, Freud sticks to what he knows: the classic establishment game of *tarock*. The value he most admires, and demands, is loyalty.

Freud is far from being a political firebrand. He takes pleasure from the coincidence that Victor Adler, the leader of the Austrian socialists and one-time correspondent of Lenin, used to live at the same address as the Freuds. The fact that Victor's son Friedrich is currently in police custody, charged with assassinating the Austrian Minister-President at a popular Viennese restaurant the previous autumn, adds a certain frisson to the connection. But Freud's own radical heroes are of the past. His son Oli is named after Oliver Cromwell, leader of the Parliamentary forces in England's Civil War. Wide-eyed modern revolutionaries – too certain of their right to remake the world in the reflection of their ideals, too unforgiving of human nature – are foreign to Freud's sensibilities. The concept of the revolutionary masses scares him. He calls the French 'the people of psychical epidemics, of historical mass convulsions, unchanged since Victor Hugo's *Notre Dame*'. Freud prefers the English.

Not that he is immune to the gusts of the popular mood. In the emotional atmosphere of the summer of 1914, as his daughter Anna rushed back from an unfortunately timed trip to England, Freud briefly meta-morphosed from a Viennese man of the world into an Austro-Hungarian patriot. As Austrian soldiers tramped off to face the Russians and the Serbs, Freud declared himself willing to donate his libido to their fight.

(For a Freudian, there is no greater gift.) That was three years ago. These days Freud ruminates daily on the savage impulses war has unloosed. He takes no pleasure in having been proved correct: the war has set the stage for humankind's psychic dramas to play out *en masse*. Individuals have been transformed into stampeding hordes, the surface of civilisation has been peeled back. The sickness is deeper than even he had feared.

In photographs, Freud often appears rather severe. Perhaps it is the war which has made him that way: the lack of food, the cold. Or perhaps it is just age. His face is so much gaunter than it used to be, the skin drawn tightly over his bony features, the all-seeing eyes peering out with such intensity. (Some think Freud looks like Moses, a conceit in which he secretly delights, and occasionally plays up to.) Even in these difficult times, however, a smile can often be seen playing on Freud's lips, in the expectation of the punchline of some new joke or other. (Like most Viennese he considers humour an essential attitude to take towards a world at once tragic, comic and absurd.) Conscientious on matters of physical appearance, Freud dresses neatly in sober fashions that would once have marked him out as a man of style, but which now reveal him only as a man of substance. When seeing patients, he appears, rather stiffly, in a frock coat. It is on holidays in the mountains that Freud truly lets himself go, donning shorts, braces and a Tyrolean feathered hat.

Freud's eccentricities are a combination of the daft, the amusing and the superstitious: he hates umbrellas, is fascinated with porcupines, finds railway timetables impossible to understand and wonders if there is something in numerology (as a result of which he fears he will die at the age of sixty-one, or else in the month of February 1918). He is at his happiest when mushroom-picking; he is reputed to be able to pick out particularly promising patches of forest from a fast-moving train. When asked to recommend a good read Freud plumps for Rudyard Kipling's *The Jungle Book*. When Freud decides to initiate a select few of his closest associates as guardians of the sacred flame of psychoanalysis – the 'inner circle', some call it – he uses the gift of ancient seal rings to consummate the arrangement. Here is a man who does not shy away from the symbolic gesture.

Somewhere in the artefacts of the ancient world he senses the outlines of the basic drives and fears and beliefs which inhabit us all, which modern civilisation has tried so hard to suppress. He is an inveterate hoarder. Every surface of his study is covered with Roman busts, clay pots, ancient Chinese figurines or statuettes of winged Greek deities, primed for flight. His study is his private *imaginarium*, a place to commune with the past. It is also, of course, the room where Freud's patients are psychoanalysed, the doctor making infrequent notes and odd remarks and asking occasional questions while his patients lie on a rather elegant chaise longue and empty their minds at a hefty rate of Austrian crowns an hour. High on one wall, and almost always in Freud's line of sight, hangs a lithograph of the great French neurologist Charcot, under whom Freud studied in the 1880s, demonstrating hypnosis to a class at La Salpêtrière. There is a brass spittoon on the floor. On Freud's desk sits a curious porcupine paperweight he was given in America.

America. Now there's a conundrum to break one's head against, as much of a conundrum for Freud as for the Kaiser and his men. In many ways Freud would be most happy if America could be somehow made to disappear, sinking like the *Titanic* into the icy Atlantic, never to be heard from again. If physical removal is impossible, Freud would like it very much if he himself could just forget the existence of that brash, rich, uncivilised country (and the place where he had the worst attack of indigestion he has ever experienced in his life). And yet, like a disturbing thought one cannot quite shake off, America is always there lurking at the back of Freud's mind, and occasionally brought to the fore by news from family members across the Atlantic. Like many complex relationships in life, this one began with childhood infatuation: a visit to the American pavilion at the Vienna World Fair in 1873 and an intense curiosity in the facsimiles of the letters of President Lincoln on display. The young Freud, it is said, learned the Gettysburg Address by heart. As a newly minted graduate, he briefly considered moving there. It was only much later, well into middle age, that Freud finally consummated things by visiting the country. In 1909 he spent an entire week-long Atlantic crossing to America joyfully psychoanalysing his fellow passenger and erstwhile friend, Carl Jung.

Both relationships have since soured. Jung is an apostate, a Judas, these days. As for America, Freud has taken a violent dislike to it. He views Americans' love of money as a misdirection of natural human sexual urges. He worries that if psychoanalysis ends up being viewed as a sham medicine, it will be because of the New York hucksters simply *calling* themselves psychoanalysts – and then trying to make a quick buck from fleecing gullible Americans with the kind of voodoo remedies that would make a witch doctor blush. In America, Freud finds, his work is either crudely and inaccurately popularised in breathless articles in *Good Housekeeping* and *Everybody's Magazine* or else puritanically condemned, even by well-known physicians and psychologists, as 'filth' liable to corrupt public morality.

The whole business of 'filth' pains him. For, whatever his theories as to the origins of neurosis in childhood sexuality or the primordial role of what he terms the *Lustprinzip*, the pleasure principle, in driving human behaviour, Freud is far from being a bohemian or a sex addict. Rather he is a devoted middle-class family man, a good son to his ageing mother and a self-conscious patriarch to his children. Though the physical passions of youth have long subsided, Freud is rarely separated for long from his wife Martha, except in the holidays. (When a student in Paris, Freud found himself constantly turning around on street corners at the imagined sound of his beloved Martha calling out his name, so ever-present was she in his thoughts.) Some say Sigmund has eyes for her sister Minna, but the tittle-tattle doesn't seem to bother him. Freud is forever publicly anxious and privately solicitous of his children's health and safety. His letters to them often consist of little more than brief expressions of affection, followed by hungry demands for information.

In early 1917 it is the twenty-one-year-old Anna Freud, sick with the flu, who most exercises the doctor's paternal instincts. Freud organises her dispatch to a clinic in the nearby Wiener Wald, cross at himself for not being able to secure a room in a more salubrious sanatorium in the mountains. Freud's other daughters – Mathilde and Sophie – give no cause for concern. A greater worry are the three boys of the Freud family, all engaged in the Austro-Hungarian war effort in one way or another. 'It is better not to think in advance about the painful experiences that this spring will bring for the world', Freud writes to his friend Karl Abraham, imagining the next offensive which must surely come. But, for the moment, Freud's sons all seem to be out of harm's way: Martin in Vienna, Ernst recovering from tonsillitis in the Tyrol and Oli, a tunnel engineer, still in training in Cracow. (Earlier in the war, a dream of his son Martin's death at the front troubled Freud deeply, sparking bouts of furious self-analysis as the theorist of wish fulfilment tried to uncover what hidden desires his dream revealed.) Freud keeps photos of all his children in his study. A group portrait of the proud father with his soldier-sons hangs on one wall. Nothing could be more *bürgerlich*.

Freud's critics accuse him of manipulation of his patients, or even dabbling in the dark arts of the occult. It is true that Freud has tried out hypnosis (as taught by his teachers in Paris). The technique of free association, essentially persuading patients to blurt out the first thing that comes into their head when Freud gravely utters some such word as *Schnurrbart* (moustache) or *Eisenbahntunnel* (railway tunnel), strikes many as too suggestive. But how else to discover the secrets the conscious mind seeks to keep under lock and key? As for Freud's curiosity in the paranormal, his interest is not so uncommon, even for men of science. When quizzed on such matters as telepathy, he is fond of misquoting *Hamlet*: 'There are more things *between* heaven and earth, Horatio, than are dreamed of in your philosophy'.

Freud's lifetime has shown how previously fantastical ideas can turn into great discoveries or technological innovations: the transmission of radio signals through the empty air, the harnessing of invisible rays to peer inside the human body. In 1913, Freud's natural inquisitiveness into the possibilities of unseen communication led him to host a seance in his own home, led by a man claiming power as a medium, Professor Roth. The medium proved a dud. Fear of embarrassment prevented Freud from asking for the return of his brown envelope stuffed with Austrian crowns. But open-mindedness should be no crime, Freud pleads. For the scientist, it should be a duty, however apparently odd the theory proposed.

In a time of peace and plenty, the theories of such an unlikely revolutionary might get no further than the private consulting rooms of Mitteleuropa's larger cities and a handful of American universities. But war has changed all that. What was once outlandish now appears prophetic. The world is out of joint: the unconscious is the accepted culprit. Jabbering, spasmodic soldiers tumble into military hospitals across the Continent by the truckload every day, with disorders of the mind and body immune to rest or surgery – or even to electric shocks. As Freud himself might have remarked, people are more receptive to new gods when their old gods have proved false. And so it is that at the very moment when Freud himself feels most isolated, when his psychoanalytic associates are cut off from him by war and when his list of patients in Vienna has dwindled, Freud's ideas begin to take on a life of their own, spreading from the consulting couch to the hospital bed and into the cultural ether of the age.

THE BRONX, NEW YORK, UNITED STATES OF AMERICA: A Jewish dairy restaurant on Wilkens Avenue in the East Bronx. A regular customer – late thirties, medium height, black hair, glasses, moustache, slightly wild look about the eyes, dreadful English – shuffles in off the street. That man again! He comes in almost every day. He *never* tips. (The waiters occasionally spill hot soup on him by way of suggesting he should.) It is against his political beliefs, he says.

As a revolutionary agitator in wartime Europe the principled non-tipper attended the same political gatherings as his rival Vladimir and called, like him, for unflinching class struggle. But Lenin has never really trusted him, with regular spectacular fallings-out on ideological matters; he is too *obstinate*, too *capricious*, too *individual*. Vladimir once wrote to Inessa describing him as 'always the same, evasive cheating, posing as a leftist but *helping* the right while he can'. As a journalist – his off-again on-again profession – the principled non-tipper once interviewed the shadowy figure behind the Sarajevo murders. 'My young friend never thought his heroic bullet would provoke the current world war', Gavrilo Princip's mentor explained, 'and believe me, when I read the war reports, a horrible thought goes through my mind: did we indeed incite all this?'

The principled non-tipper's entry papers into the United States – off a ship from Barcelona called the *Montserrat*, on which he travels first class – list his profession as 'author'. The customs officials who let him into the country without a second look that rainy day note down his name, incorrectly, as Zratzky. Others pay closer attention. A local Yiddish-language newspaper prints a photograph of the new arrival on its front page by way of welcome. The principled non-tipper wears a three-piece suit for the shoot.

The new arrival soon finds a reasonably priced apartment for which his wife Natalya pays the rent three months in advance and where his children are fascinated by the telephone. Natalya has lost count of the number of homes they have had since they married, shortly after her husband's escape from exile in Siberia. Since then they have lived in Petrograd (where her husband made his name in the 1905 revolution), Vienna, Paris. Her husband was even briefly in Cádiz in Spain after the French tired of his presence and decided to unceremoniously deport him.

In America, Leon Trotsky is given a job writing for a Russian-language newspaper, *Novy Mir*. Typically, his first article is headlined 'Long Live Struggle!' When not writing, he tours around making fiery speeches about revolution and getting into arguments with local socialists about the direction their own movement should take. Particularly if war should come.

THE VATICAN: The Pope writes an early birthday card to Kaiser Wilhelm offering his warmest wishes and the rough outlines of a peace proposal he has been working on. 'First, we have to win', Wilhelm scribbles on the Vatican letter. How 'unworldly and utopian' of the Pope to think of future arms control at a time like this. Peace will only come, the Kaiser writes in the margins, 'through a German victory brought about with the help of God'.

WASHINGTON DC, THE UNITED STATES OF AMERICA: There is something of the romantic crusader spirit about this upright man – suspicious of emotion, yet highly emotional himself – who carries a poem by Rudyard Kipling in his breast pocket and who now sits behind his desk in the Oval Office, working on a speech.

He wants so badly to be a peacemaker, this man, who remembers the fires of America's Civil War from his childhood in Confederate Virginia. He wants so much to be the world's friend (except to Republicans, whom he despises). He wants to show the world the shining path to righteousness which he fervently believes it is America's destiny to light up. ('America First' is one of his political slogans.) Perhaps he, Thomas Woodrow Wilson, the son of a Presbyterian pastor, can personify that moral righteousness. Perhaps history will offer him, in his sixty-first year on earth, the opportunity to bring to worldwide fruition the political principles he has spoken about all his life. Perhaps his own blessings – and those of America – can be made universal. Would it not be a wonderful thing if the world could be made more American? Would not humanity benefit from a healthy dose of American-style self-government or from America's spirit of commercial enterprise?

Woodrow knows his Bible: 'blessed are the peacemakers, for they shall be called the children of God'. America must keep out of the war. It would be a 'crime against civilization', he tells his friend and adviser Colonel Edward House, for the last of the 'great White nations' to ruin itself in a contest between German and British ambitions. His concern with race is unexceptional. Many Americans view the European fighting as a white civil war, selfishly endangering the future security of the race itself. Last year, Madison Grant, chairman of the New York Zoological Society, described the war as race 'suicide on a gigantic scale'. Woodrow worries about a future war of the white nations against the Japanese.

America must keep itself chaste. It must prepare for the time when Europe's 'mechanical slaughter' has ceased and a new crusade for peace can begin under American tutelage. Woodrow understands his own particular authority in this regard. An American President, directly elected leader of the world's most populous white republic, burnished by the prestige of its wealth and power and not engaged in the war's present butchery, can speak directly to the peoples of Europe, over the heads of their leaders, man to man, as it were. An American President can speak to the world. He can speak *for* the world. There is a moral force in the affairs of humankind, that only the truly far-sighted can perceive. He must be that force.

Thinking through America's duty to itself and to the world, a noble idea takes root in Woodrow's mind: a plan not just to end this bloody war, but to end all wars. He writes and rewrites his text. He tosses around different versions of it with his confidants. And finally, when he is ready, he summons the elected representatives of America's forty-eight states to the Capitol to hear his shining vision for the future: a cooperative league of nations for world peace, with America its chief backer. No more the temporary truces and unstable alliances of the past, but a perpetual peace built on common democratic principles, enforced by common action. 'These are American principles, American policies', he tells the law-makers of the republic, 'they are the principles of mankind and must prevail'. One Democrat Senator declares it 'the greatest message of the century'. Another commends 'a fine literary effort'. Most Republicans find the peroration woolly, arrogant, even dangerous. 'The President thinks he is president of the world', notes a Senator from Wyoming. 'Ill-timed and utterly impossible of accomplishment', remarks his colleague from New Hampshire.

The speech is circulated to Europe's capitals. There is one phrase in particular which angers many: 'peace without victory'. A lasting peace, Woodrow lectures, as if back at Princeton, cannot be built on an equilibrium of terror but only on the equality of nations. An end to the present war which leaves one European power crowing triumphantly over the carcass of another would be a temporary expedient. 'Victory would mean peace forced upon the loser', the President explains, 'accepted in humiliation, under duress, at an intolerable sacrifice, and would leave a sting, a resentment, a bitter memory upon which terms of peace would rest, not permanently, but only as upon quicksand'. True peace will only come when both sides exchange the mirage of victory for something greater.

Easy for an American to 'sell so cheaply the interests and sacrifices of others', says a French newspaper. What insufferable arrogance.

LA SALPÊTRIÈRE HOSPITAL, PARIS, THE FRENCH REPUBLIC: A man stands naked in a room, one leg contorted and at rest, the other jacking up and down spasmodically against the parquet floor. His eyes are as vacant as the dead.

In front of him, a table, and on the table an array of objects: a cushion stuffed with pins, a reflex hammer, two batteries and a tuning fork. Not instruments of torture, but tools of diagnosis. On the other side of the table stands Dr Babinski, one of France's most famous neurologists (Marcel Proust's mother was once a patient) and a former student of Charcot (he is one of the students depicted in the engraving on Freud's wall in Vienna). The doctor raises his eyes to assess the patient, a soldier recently returned from the front. The doctor's notes fall from the table and land flat against the floor. A report echoes through the room.

Suddenly, the soldier's eyes come alive. He speaks, he raves, he rants. It is gibberish: associations, memories, stories that stop and start, a terrifying cannon burst of words. For Babinski's new assistant, a handsome plump-lipped boy newly arrived from Verdun, it is poetry. He watches enraptured as if the wounded man's speech were a transmission from another world. He searches for meaning in the torrent of words. Is the soldier describing what happened to him at the front, or a dream of what will happen if he is sent back? In his head perhaps he is there already, hot steel hurtling towards him from every side. And who, in this moment, can say which is more real: the hospital or the front, the memory or the fear, the inner or the outer experience?

Though only twenty, and uncertain yet whether he will be a doctor or a writer, Babinski's assistant is by now a seasoned observer of the ravages of war. He has seen the shell-shocked, those with lost limbs, the half mad and, most fascinating of all, those who deny there is a war at all and claim the whole thing is make-believe. His life has become a litany of whirlwind encounters with the wounded, assimilating their experiences into his own, drawing him deeper and deeper into a fascination with the unruly mind. Last spring it was Jacques Vaché, a wounded soldier at a military hospital in Nantes, whose mocking views on art and life had an almost magnetic attraction for the young André Breton. For a couple of months, the two young dandies rattled around Nantes in a fury of fun-making, jeering at the rules of bourgeois society and running from one cinema to the next to avoid seeing anything as boring as an entire film.

Last summer it was Lieutenant Guillaume Apollinaire, the literary standard-bearer of the French avant-garde – and correspondent of Breton's since the age of nineteen – wounded in the head by a piece of shrapnel which cut right through his helmet. Breton pronounced the great man's character irretrievably 'changed'. Last July he transferred to a neuro-psychiatric hospital where he interviewed victims of shell shock about their dreams and tried to free himself from his obsession with poetry. (The head doctor at the hospital introduced young Breton to untranslated German texts and suggested he write a doctoral thesis on Freud.) Now André is in

Paris, working where Charcot once hypnotised his patients as Freud stood back to admire.

The soldier's speech becomes steadier as the minutes pass. Babinski continues the investigation of his patient, tapping a reflex hammer here, then moving on almost without stopping to another body part, as if chasing the soldier's malady across the landscape of his body. Breton is fascinated at Babinski's technique, the diagnostic trance which seems to take hold of him. He stands back to admire the two of them – patient and doctor – the one uttering strings of words as if at random, the other diagnosing him, as if at random, both driven by unseen forces operating in the background of their minds.

Is this soldier mad, or is he the sanest of us all? Breton muses. How much more truthful – yes, how much freer – are this shell-shocked soldier's words, these ecstasies of the unconscious mind, than anything that passes for poetry or writing. And how impossible to fake.

UNDER THE ATLANTIC OCEAN – GERMANY – WASHINGTON: Silent and unseen, German submarines slip past the British Isles and into the open waters beyond. The ambassador in Washington begs Berlin to delay launching them against the world's shipping, fearing the consequences on relations with America. 'Regret suggestions impracticable', comes back the answer. The boats are beyond recall. They are out of radio contact.

The mood in Germany is jubilant when news breaks of the imminent resumption of unrestricted submarine warfare. A few more months of war, people think, then there will be peace. Not many parents have a son in the U-boat fleet. Millions have a son serving at the front. A shortened war might just save their lives. The Kaiser spends the evening at a banquet with Emperor Charles's brother, as if unaware of all the excitement that news of the decision has created. (Perhaps he is fearful of its consequences.) Later he gathers together his staff and reads aloud a paper he has come across by a German university professor on the vital subject of the eagle as a heraldic beast. 'A gruesome evening!' notes the Kaiser's naval attaché in his diary.

In Washington, the White House telephone rings incessantly. Woodrow feels betrayed. But he does not now want emotion to push him to take any rash decisions. 'Not sure of that', he says to the suggestion of an immediate diplomatic break with Germany. His friend Edward House finds him depressed. His vision of America as the neutral peacemaker above the fray is now in tatters. Germany is a 'madman that should be curbed', the President says. But his mind struggles with how to respond. Woodrow paces his study, nervously rearranging his books. He worries about the consequences of war on the 'white race', and wonders if the Japanese might take advantage. His wife Edith suggests a round of golf. House warns against 'anything so trivial at such a time'. The two men shoot a game of pool instead.

Relations with Germany are broken off, but war is not declared. Maybe the Germans will not follow through. Then an unarmed British vessel is sunk off Ireland, with several Americans on board. Perhaps American ships can be armed to defend themselves, satisfying considerations of immediate security, but stopping short of outright war. Then a top-secret German telegram is leaked, showing that Berlin has offered to give Mexico chunks of American territory in return for an alliance in the event of conflict. The country is enraged.

VIENNA: Doctor Freud writes a letter to a psychoanalytic colleague in Budapest. His mood is grave: 'I would have written you long ago, if there had been something positive to report. But everything is negative, everything is inhibition, limitation, renunciation, at most, stifled expectations'. The cold and dark make serious work impossible. The price of cigars is up. Across the Habsburg Empire, flour is mixed with ground chestnuts and coffee with ground acorns to make limited supplies go further. Freud finds himself preoccupied with submarines: 'so, everything is waiting until the U-boats have restored order in the world – if they succeed'.

MOGILYOV, RUSSIA: At Russia's military headquarters, the Stavka, five hundred miles south of Petrograd, Tsar Nicholas writes a letter home to his German-born wife, in English. Alexandra is his *lovebird*; the Tsar is her *huzy*. He so misses their time together, working away diligently on a jigsaw before bed. He finds barracks life unproductive. It is much less fun to play games by oneself. 'I think I will turn to dominoes again', he writes: 'of course there is no work for me'.

Elsewhere in Russia, the national crisis deepens. Cold shuts down the capital's transport system. The bakeries are out of bread. There are rumours that huge food supplies elsewhere are being wasted for lack of organisation. Caspian fishermen, it is said, have taken to burying their catch rather than letting it rot in the open air while waiting for a train to take it to the cities. A bishop blames the proliferation of cinemas and the army morphine for the chaos. The Interior Minister holds seances with Rasputin's ghost.

THE ITALIAN–AUSTRIAN FRONT LINE: An Italian soldier commits the events of the day to his diary. 'This morning, at dawn, I sent the Germans my best wishes for the day', he writes: a grenade launched against the enemy. 'The little red point of a lighted cigarette disappeared,' he notes, 'and probably also the smoker.' The next day it is the Italian's turn to suffer. A grenade is accidentally set off in the Italian trenches, ripping him through with shrapnel.

The wounded soldier's name is Benito, a journalist and former revolutionary agitator in the mould of Lenin who once founded a newspaper called *La Lotta di Classe*, or Class War. (At an event where the two men crossed paths in Switzerland before the war, Benito even gave a little speech ending with 'Long live the Italian proletariat! Long live socialism!') More recently he has acquired a passionate belief in the importance of the war splitting Italian socialism between spineless pacifists and noble, nationally minded warriors like himself. He also has a fondness for duelling. At the field hospital where he is now treated after his mishap with a grenade, the doctors notice something else about Benito's health – syphilis, perhaps?

In March, the King of Italy himself is amongst the visitors to the hospital. He stops by the corporal's bedside.

'How are you, Mussolini?' he asks.

'Not so well, master', the soldier answers valiantly.

PETROGRAD: The revolution begins on a radiant morning, warmer than it has been for weeks. A festive atmosphere for International Women's Day. Students and nurses link arms with the enlightened women of the bourgeoisie, marching down Nevsky – Petrograd's central thoroughfare – with banners above their heads demanding equal rights and bread.

In the city's industrial Vyborg district, on the other side of the wide Neva river, the mood is more militant. Women textile workers, tired of the queues for food and their treatment by the bosses, decide to come out on strike. They shout to their brothers and husbands to join them. At the munitions works, managers tell them not to play the Germans' game by striking in the middle of a war. 'The Empress herself is a German spy', comes the reply. The mutinous mood spreads. By afternoon, the workers have invaded Petrograd's commercial centre in force, evading squadrons of Cossacks on horseback. A few trams are rocked onto their side. The Siberian Trade Bank is robbed.

But no one is killed. As the sun goes down the city centre is quiet again. A searchlight scans the empty Nevsky with its electric beam. The French Ambassador holds a dinner party with the city's *beau monde* where there is a fierce debate about which of Petrograd's famous ballerinas deserves to win this year's award for best dancer. Alexandra writes a letter to Nicholas passing on news of the measles situation in the imperial family and of revolutionary informality entering the Romanov household: the Tsarevich's English tutor, it is reported, read to him 'in a *dressing gown*'.

Over the next few days, the crisis does not dissipate; it deepens. Strike action spreads. As the weekend approaches, the number of demonstrators increases. The workers' demands become more political: justice and an end to police intimidation. While Petrograd's revolutionaries still hesitate to call for an armed insurrection, the demonstrations are turning into a trial of strength. One day, a woman watching a demonstration is shot dead. The police deny they have started using guns. The next day, the chief of police is himself shot. Alexandra blames hooligans for the trouble. 'If it were very cold they would probably stay indoors', she writes.

The foundations of autocracy are creaking. Yet the military authorities in Petrograd convince themselves, and the absent Tsar, that the situation can be saved with a little traditional firmness. Even when the soldiers begin to refuse orders – and the mutineers are then caught in a gun battle with loyal police – the military authorities in Petrograd assure the Tsar that order will soon be restored in the city. The country's leading politician sends him a more alarmist message, talking of 'elemental and uncontrollable anarchy'. The disbelieving Nicholas sighs to an aide: 'I will not even reply'. Parliament, the Duma, is dissolved. Nicholas plays dominoes.

The next day, all hell breaks loose in Petrograd. A regiment previously ordered to fire on protesting civilians now shoots its commanding officer instead. Whole regiments go over to the rebellion. The Petrograd arsenal is attacked, and forty thousand rifles are captured. Police snipers on roof-tops pick off targets in the streets until they are hunted down and thrown to their deaths. Commandeered automobiles career around the city's streets, bristling with bayonets like hedgehogs. The regime disintegrates. The Tsar's brother Michael, the one man in Petrograd who might be able to rally troops to the Romanov cause, orders soldiers out of the Winter Palace when he finds them gathering to defend it – he is worried they might break things. Facing an inevitable assault of the rebels, the Tsar's ministers resign in a panic. Two hide in a photographic darkroom to try to avoid arrest. Others simply flee into the night.

The contest for power now switches to the Tauride Palace. Though the Duma has been formally dissolved by the Tsar, this is where members of Russia's parliament now meet to work out what to do. (The meetings are characterised as private in order to keep the semblance of constitutionality.) They must move quickly. The Tauride Palace swarms with soldiers. There are piles of looted goods everywhere. A dead pig adorns one patch of floor. And, in one of the palace wings, a council of workers' delegates has been established, calling themselves a Soviet. It is impossible to verify who voted for them; at first, most members are intellectuals, later most are soldiers.

The Soviet leaders debate whether, following Marxist dogma that bourgeois democracy precedes socialism, they should now take power themselves. To forestall that eventuality, a provisional committee of the Duma declares itself in charge of restoring order. Sheer anarchy reigns outside. Plain-clothes policemen are hunted down and lynched. In one instance a humble chimney sweep on a rooftop is mistaken for an escaping police sniper and shot by a trigger-happy rebel in the streets below. Isolated pockets of regime resistance are crushed. When the Astoria Hotel – a favourite with Russia's officer class – is raided, its cellars are flooded with broken bottles of cognac. Butter is handed out on the end of a sabre. Shooting between different factions of the same regiment – some for the Tsar and others against – is briefly stopped to allow the British Ambassador to get through to the still half-operational Russian Foreign Office to discuss the war with Germany. The French Ambassador, following his usual route to the same destination, runs into one of the Tsar's old Ethiopian guards, now dressed as a civilian, his eyes full of tears. In Tsarskoye Selo, Alexandra notes her children's temperatures. The palace lift is out of service.

Down at Stavka the imperial train is readied to bring the Tsar back to his capital. Lusty hymn-singing accompanies his departure. He never makes it to Petrograd. Instead, his train is directed and redirected around western Russia in the search for a safe route back to the capital. Much of his time is spent sleeping, or looking out of the window at the static landscape, or waiting for others. Finally, after a day and night of such pointless activity, the Tsar arrives in Pskov, still more than a hundred miles from Petrograd.

Again, he is left waiting. Now, the message from his army commanders is blunt: if he is to have any chance of saving the Russian Empire, he must abdicate in favour of his son with his brother Michael as regent. Nicholas lights up one cigarette after another. 'What else can I do when all have betrayed me?' he says to an aide.

Two politicians from Petrograd arrive with a draft abdication proclamation. As they are ushered into the Tsar's immaculate presence one of them is acutely aware that his own shirt is creased and he has not had time to shave. Nicholas wears a grey *chokha*, the Cossack national dress. He tells the delegation that he accepts the necessity of his own abdication, but that he intends to abdicate not only on his behalf but also on behalf of his son. Nicholas treats the throne as a gift he is free to assign. His brother Grand Duke Michael, who has not been asked his own view on the matter, is to become Tsar directly. The politicians question the constitutionality of it all. But what time is there for that when the country is in chaos?

In Petrograd, while the Duma and the Soviet negotiate the form of the next government, one figure emerges astride both: Alexander Kerensky, a Socialist Revolutionary who shares the same home town on the Volga as Vladimir Lenin. His days are spent in a delirious whirl of activity, surviving on coffee and brandy, using charisma and oratory to get what he wants.

'Comrades! Do you trust me?' he asks the soldiers of the Soviet, to gain their approval to become a minister. They roar approval. It is Kerensky who now phones up Grand Duke Michael to inform him of his brother Nicholas's decision, after leafing through the Petrograd telephone directory to find the right number. But Michael abdicates in turn. He will not accept such a poisoned chalice. Russia is now a republic. 'Slept long and soundly', Nicholas Romanov writes in his diary. He reads a lot about Julius Caesar, the Roman leader betrayed by his closest associates.

Across Russia there is hope: of freedom, land, bread. Censorship is removed. Statues of the Tsars are pulled down. Wherever the revolution arrives, officials of the old regime are arrested, local Soviets are formed and political prisoners set free. (A Georgian bank-robber and conspirator bearing the revolutionary pseudonym Stalin – man of steel – is released from exile in Siberia and travels back to Petrograd with a typewriter on his knee.) 'Festivals of Freedom' re-enact the events of the last week like latter-day mystery plays. The French Ambassador, touring Petrograd's churches the first Sunday after the revolution, notes that even in these citadels of Orthodoxy, which used to venerate the Tsar as God's anointed, everyone seems to sport a red cockade or armband. Though the new government reaffirms its commitment to uphold Russia's wartime alliances, there is also hope for peace.

One of the first orders of the new regime is to find the secret burial place of the murdered monk Rasputin – a symbol of Holy Russia or of Tsarism's ultimate decadence depending on your point of view – and destroy his bodily remains for ever. The furnaces of a local engineering school do the job. The ashes are then scattered and a false story told to prevent anyone building a shrine.

BERLIN, GERMANY: The Kaiser's naval attaché urges Wilhelm to consider cutting down on palace expenses, noting that some of the language used against the Romanovs might equally apply to the Hohenzollerns. 'Degenerate and basically egotistical dynasty' are the specific words he has in mind.

SPRING

ZURICH: Nadya has just finished washing up the dishes after lunch. Vladimir is preparing to return to the library. A young Russian barges in. 'Haven't you heard the news?' he asks. He is blabbering something about revolution in Petrograd. Excited but a little sceptical, the Ulyanovs hurry down to the lakeside, where the special editions of the newspapers are pasted up for the public. Lenin scans the reports. 'It's staggering', he exclaims to his wife: 'it's so incredibly unexpected'.

Joy soon gives way to scepticism and impatience. Already Vladimir can see that the Petrograd revolutionaries are screwing things up. 'It's simply shit', he shouts when he reads about the proceedings of the Petrograd Soviet, 'I repeat: shit'. There should be no discussion of supporting a provisional government which includes landlords and capitalists, he splutters. There should be no question of continuing a war of national defence. The workers must be armed. Soviets must be given full power everywhere. The revolution must be carried through to its finish and exported. 'All our slogans remain the same', he writes to a comrade in Oslo. But how can he correct the errors of those idiots in Petrograd while stuck in Switzerland? Vladimir telegraphs instructions to any Bolsheviks planning to return to Russia: 'no trust in and no support of the new government; Kerensky is especially suspect'. He is desperate to get home himself: but how?

Lenin's fervid imagination is full of madcap schemes. 'I can put on a wig', he writes to a comrade a little desperately. One day he sees himself travelling to Russia via steamer to England. The next he fixes on the fanciful notion that the Kaiser's government might let a group of Russian revolutionaries travel home through Germany – it might work *if* the idea were to appear to come from émigré circles in Geneva, or 'fools', as Lenin calls them. Perhaps an aeroplane could be chartered to fly across Eastern Europe. Maybe a fake Swedish passport could be obtained and the journey completed overland. One would not need to know much Swedish to trick the authorities. Even better to pretend to be deaf and unable to speak. Nadya points out the plan's fatal flaw: 'You will fall asleep and see Mensheviks in your dreams and you will start swearing, and shout, scoundrels, scoundrels! and give the whole conspiracy away'.

Vladimir storms down to the local police station, assuring the Zurich authorities that he is going to leave Switzerland very soon, and demands they return the one-hundred-franc administrative deposit he gave them when he arrived.

HALIFAX, DOMINION OF CANADA, BRITISH EMPIRE: Scurrying back from the United States to Russia to take part in the greatest event in the history of the world, the principled non-tipper runs into a problem: a telegram from British naval intelligence.

'FOLLOWING ON BOARD KRISTIANIAFJORD AND SHOULD BE TAKEN OFF AND RETAINED PENDING INSTRUCTION', it reads. The name Trotsky is one of those listed. He is alleged to be carrying ten thousand dollars, provided by 'socialists and Germans'. The principled non-tipper kicks and screams as some burly mariners carry him off the ship. His son, aged eleven, punches a British naval officer on the arm. Once ashore, Trotsky is strip-searched and taken to a prisoner-of-war camp for processing. Natalya and the children are housed in the Prince George Hotel.

Leon is held in the Amherst camp for several weeks. While there, he agitates for social revolution amongst the other Russian internees (some of whom prove to be excellent craftsmen, whose handiwork Trotsky admires keenly). It is the end of April before he is released. A whole month wasted.

ZURICH: Vladimir has more luck. His idea of a train through Germany turns out not to be so crazy after all.

With the help of mediation from Swiss socialists and the embassy in Bern, the German authorities agree to let a single carriage of revolutionaries transit their territory, travelling secretly from Switzerland to the Baltic. From thence, they will be put on a boat to Sweden. If they make trouble for the new Russian government in Petrograd – still Germany's enemy – then all the better. Lenin stipulates a range of conditions for his travel, including confirmation that the train carriage will be granted extra-territorial status – so he will be travelling *over* but not *through* Germany, technically speaking. News of these bizarre negotiations buzzes around

Zurich's expat community. An Irish short-story writer named James Joyce hears about it in a café.

When news comes through of German acceptance of Lenin's terms – the last time this will happen for a while – the Ulyanovs rush to pack up their apartment. There is just enough time to return Vladimir's books to the library. Lenin puts in a final telephone call to the American embassy in Bern, seeking a meeting with a diplomat there in the hope of getting American support for his return so as to make him appear less wholly dependent on the Germans. But it is a Sunday. The young American diplomat who picks up the phone is on his way to a tennis date with the daughter of a prominent Swiss family. He tells Lenin to call back. Tomorrow will be too late, Lenin tells the twenty-four-year-old Allen Dulles.

A strange and mutually antagonistic bunch of revolutionaries board a local service to the Swiss border. One couple have brought their children. The mood is tense. Much of the food the passengers have brought for the trip – sausage, of course – is confiscated by Swiss customs at the border. On the train journey through Germany, Vladimir tries hard to work. But he is disturbed by the constant shouting and debating and joking going on in the next-door compartment. When he can't take it any more, he goes in to remonstrate, blaming two troublemakers, Ravich and Radek, for the fuss. Another argument breaks out over people smoking cigarettes in the carriage toilet. Lenin proposes a ticketing system, provoking a debate about whether the need to smoke or to empty one's bladder is the greater human require-ment. At the Baltic port of Sassnitz, where a steamer – the *Queen Victoria* – awaits the revolutionaries, those leaving Germany for Sweden are asked to fill in departure forms. It seems a little pointless. Lenin is suspicious. He suggests that his group agree to fill in the forms, but use false names.

Most are seasick on the way across the Baltic.

WASHINGTON – NEW YORK: Two months after the beginning of Germany's unrestricted submarine warfare campaign, America's peacemaker becomes a war leader.

'We have no quarrel with the German people', Woodrow Wilson tells Congress and the world, announcing the declaration of war on Germany. The enemy is the Kaiser and autocracy. 'The world must be made safe for democracy', Woodrow says. The address takes exactly thirty-two minutes to deliver. Thousands of supportive telegrams arrive to congrat-ulate him. Woodrow signs orders permitting the government to remove from employment anyone whose loyalty they suspect. Mrs Wilson stands by his side, blotting his papers to dry the ink, and occasionally filling in the date of approval in her own hand.

There is little opposition to the war. In Congress a pacifist and a few Republicans vote against it. Outside it, Harvard-educated radical John Reed tells a so-called People's Council: 'this is not my war, and I will not support it'. Generally, the national mood is for unity. One immediate question is whether black soldiers should be deployed. Southern whites worry about upsetting the balance of power in the South if blacks are given military training. Many blacks see the war as an opportunity to prove themselves, in the hope that the government will repay black America's patriotism at the war's end.

In New York City, an all-black Harlem-based National Guard regiment – the 15th Infantry Regiment – draws in additional recruits. Its white commander aims to boost its attractiveness by persuading James Reese Europe – famous on the city's ragtime scene – to become the regiment's band leader.

MILAN, ITALY: Nowhere is excitement at America's entry into the war as palpable as in Italy.

Gabriele D'Annunzio, the overactive Italian poet, pilot and propagandist, a man who leads a bombing raid before lunch and takes part in a land battle before supper, sends his own message from Milan, where he is resting after his mother's death. Words are weapons in this war and D'Annunzio, a rather short, balding and unattractive fifty-four-year-old, with goggle eyes, thick lips and an increasingly hunched back, is not shy of turning his oratorical skills to the advantage of his country – or himself. His language is as flamboyant as the man. 'Now the group of stars on the banner of the great Republic has become a constellation of the Spring, like the Pleiades', the poet writes, 'a propitious sign to sailors, armed and unarmed alike, a spiritual token for all nations fighting a righteous war.' What are the confused masses of America to make of such wordiness? 'Propitious Sign to Sailors', runs the uncertain sub-headline in the *Chicago Tribune*.

'Our war is not destructive; it is creative', the poet writes, his words ascending into flights of passion and conviction. It is a battle for the human spirit against German barbarism. (He does not mention the territory that Italy has been promised as the price of joining the war on the Allied side.) He describes America's entry into the war as a metamorphosis. 'You were an enormous and obtuse mass of riches and power', the Italian writes, 'now you are transformed into ardent, active spirituality.' It is meant as a compliment.

BERLIN: In Germany, the Kaiser's American dentist is caught out by Woodrow's declaration, finding himself now an enemy alien, required to present himself daily to the police and not leave home between 8 p.m. and 6 a.m.

Amongst Wilhelm's entourage, Woodrow's declaration is received calmly. There are other matters to attend to, not least the question of how to reduce any impression of extravagance by the imperial household. Wilhelm protests his own personal consumption is already quite spartan: he eats neither sweets nor potatoes, he points out, and has only a few slices of bread and butter each afternoon with his tea.

To show his understanding of the national mood he decides to offer an 'Easter egg' to the nation: a promise to do away with the unequal Prussian voting system after the war. Electoral reform will be the people's victory prize. 'Never before have the German people proved so unshakable', runs the Easter proclamation, asking for patience while the U-boats finish the job.

WRONKE, SILESIA, GERMANY: On the same day the Kaiser gives the people their Easter present, a prisoner locked up in one of his jails receives a bouquet of flowers from Berlin.

Rosa Luxemburg, a Polish-Jewish-Marxist intellectual of diminutive stature, with one leg a little shorter than the other and a very slight humpback, is a woman who divides opinion. Some think her brilliant and principled. Others think her a fanatical ideologue. Estranged from the mainstream Social Democratic Party whose leaders she once taught how to think at the party's training academy, Rosa now leads a revolutionary splinter group known as the Spartacus League, named after the Roman slave rebel. Her police dossier includes a stint in jail before the war, a marriage of convenience in Germany which ended in divorce, and political connections with citizens of foreign states, including through her role as one of the founder members of the Polish Socialist Party.

She and Lenin go way back. There was a time before the war when, in between competitive bouts of Marxist theorising, Vladimir would cradle Rosa's cat flirtatiously in his lap, claiming suavely not to have seen such a majestic beast anywhere outside Siberia. Over black tea, they would argue the finer points of revolutionary theory: him insisting on the necessity for a strong party to dictate the course of revolutionary events and keep strict order; her countering that centralism could only stifle the essentially organic nature of a true social revolution.

In Wronke, Rosa is 'on leave from World History', as she puts it. She observes Russia's convulsions from afar and waits for the bigger explosion which Marxism dictates must now occur in a more advanced industrial economy – most critically, in Germany. She has few friends in Berlin to argue for her release. In 1914, her relationship with the Social Democrats ended in a fury of recrimination when they meekly supported the war rather than a general strike. Only one Social Democratic deputy, Rosa's fellow Spartacist Karl Liebknecht, voted against credits for the army. Rosa briefly considered suicide. Then she proposed a new slogan for the Social Democrats: 'workers of the world unite, in peacetime – in wartime, slit each other's throat!' The tongue lashings have not stopped since.

In prison, Rosa is tireless in her analysis of events in Russia and the coming revolution. 'I regard what has happened there so far as only a small overture', she writes to her friend Clara Zetkin, 'things are bound to develop into something colossal ... and an echo throughout the world is inevitable'. She writes of the 'unseen, plutonic forces' which Nicholas's overthrow has unleashed. She scans the papers for hints that the German proletariat are waking to their responsibilities. She is delighted by news of strikes in the German munitions industry: some three hundred factories are temporarily shut; several hundred thousand workers walk out. Anxious and excited, Rosa notes down key events in her pocket diary (alongside her falling weight: barely forty-six kilos this spring). How glorious it is to know that world revolution is on its way. How awful it is to have to wait.

She distracts herself with the great works of European literature, which she reads in the original, and cute letters to her friends. 'Sonyusha, my dear little bird!' begins one; 'I send you a kiss and a hearty squeeze of the hand', ends another. She becomes a keen amateur prison botanist. She looks out of her cell window, willing the trees in the garden to burst into colour and life: 'two young sycamores, one large silver poplar, one "acacia" (or that's what people call it, in reality it's: *Robinia*), two ornamental cherry trees, several snowberries and in addition a lot of lilacs'. She has nothing but goodwill towards the local fauna. She leaves out what food she can spare for a chaffinch who drops by every morning at seven. She asks her friend not to send more birdseed as the birds are simply too fussy for it. A mouse finds its way into her room, feasts on a dress in her closet – and promptly dies (from some chemical in the dye in the dress, Rosa surmises). 'I can't do anything about it', she writes, 'but I feel so awful when I find one of these charming little creatures lying there as a corpse.'

Occasionally Rosa smuggles out an article to be passed around by the Spartacus League and printed in its newsletter. 'For three years', reads one, 'Europe has been like a musty room, almost suffocating those living in it; now all at once a window has been flung open, a fresh, invigorating gust of air is blowing in, and everyone in the room is breathing deeply and freely of it.' She worries that what has started in Petrograd will lose momentum if the German proletariat does not rise at once. She rails against Social Democrats who, having failed to stop the war in the first place, are now calling for peace on bourgeois terms, leaving capitalism intact and returning the world to how it was before the war. This must not happen. No! The choice is clear: 'Imperialism or Socialism! War or Revolution! There is no third way!'

VIENNA – BERLIN: Emperor Charles receives a gloomy assessment of his empire's prospects. Though more British ships are being sunk than ever, the Kaiser's wild promises of a quick victory by submarine warfare are not believed. The Habsburg Empire is at breaking point. After the events in Russia, the monarchic principle that has dominated Europe for a thousand years is at risk: 'The world is not the same as it was three years ago.' Without peace there will be revolution. Charles urges Wilhelm to redouble his efforts to find an equitable peace. In fact, Charles has secretly made his own behind-the-scenes endeavours via his wife's brother, an Italian aristocrat serving in the Belgian army.

Wilhelm takes a month before even bothering to respond. The German position is plain. 'The outcome of the war is a question of nerves', comes the message from army headquarters. Peace overtures suggest weakness. Only by showing determination to fight to the last will the enemy become convinced of one's will to victory. It is a matter of psychology.

Germany's military leaders draw up their war aims. The richest mining regions of France, along with Luxembourg, are to be simply absorbed into the Reich. Belgium will be made, in effect, a German colony. The Flemish North Sea coast will be leased to Germany for a period of at least ninety-nine years, as the British lease Hong Kong from China. In the Baltic, Latvia and Lithuania will come under permanent German control, and the region's German minorities will be put in charge. The precise extent of any new independent Polish state to be set up after the war will depend on how far that state can be made practically subservient to Berlin from the outset. The Habsburgs will be granted Serbia, Montenegro and Albania. The oilfields of Romania are to be secured for German use.

Wilhelm decides this list is incomplete. The British must suffer and Germany must be a world power. He draws up his own wish list for the generals.

PETROGRAD: Smelling to high heaven from their days of non-stop travel, Lenin and his associates arrive back in Russia. A telegram sent from Finland to Vladimir's sisters alerts *Pravda* to his imminent arrival and produces a crowd of Bolsheviks (and various other well-wishers) to greet him at Petrograd's Finland station. He is in a foul mood. The latest reports suggest Bolshevik leaders in the capital – Stalin and so on – are willing to tolerate the rule of the new government despite its intention to continue the war (with the endorsement of those numbskulls in the Petrograd Soviet). Has no one read his messages? No trust and no support, etc.

Clambering onto an armoured car in front of the station, the returning exile gives a fiery speech against any hint of accommodation. He is against alliances with anyone at all, it seems. He tells the crowd of Bolsheviks that Russia's other supposed revolutionaries – the Mensheviks and the Socialist Revolutionaries – are betraying the workers by kowtowing to the bourgeoisie. In his impatience, Lenin seems ready to break with the traditional Marxist dogma of the two-stage journey to socialism, and telescope it into a single proletarian seizure of power. 'Long live the world socialist revolution!' he proclaims. For women and men who treat the words of Marx as the word of God, Lenin's apparent deviation from the scriptures – at least from their traditional interpretation – is breathtaking. Is the man unhinged?

The next day Vladimir visits the graves of his mother and sister, before dropping in on the Petrograd Soviet in the Tauride Palace to give them a piece of his mind. He makes it clear he will never – 'never!' – work with those who have gone soft by cooperating with the new government. He claims he alone understands the logic of the revolution (a bit rich for someone who was in Switzerland when it started). His strategy is to be proved right by events. As the fiercest opponent of conciliation, he will be best positioned to pick up the pieces when conciliation fails, as he believes it must. Can a bourgeois government really make good on the hopes and dreams the revolution has unleashed? Lenin thinks not. A leopard cannot change its spots. The bourgeoisie will always defend capitalism before the interests of the workers.

Lenin's plague-on-both-your-houses approach is challenged on the pages of the Bolshevik newspaper *Pravda*, airing the leadership's internal huffing and puffing in front of its supporters. Hitherto, Marx's two-stage theory of revolution – *first* bourgeois capitalism, *then* workers' regime – has been sacrosanct. Yet one must concede a certain dismal political logic to Lenin's strategy. The odds are surely against the new government functioning effectively.

And therein lies the Bolsheviks' opportunity. For how long will the soldiers continue to fight when they could be at home claiming land? The question of what they are even fighting for has been fudged. Some ministers are still wedded to the aggressive war aims of the Tsar – a far cry from the 'peace without annexations and indemnities' demanded by the Petrograd Soviet. The food situation is dire, and a two-headed power structure – the Soviets and the government – is a recipe for instability. Perhaps it is worth giving Lenin's plan a little time.

CHICAGO, ILLINOIS: News of events in Russia reaches the prosperous suburbs of Chicago. On the day Lenin gives the Petrograd Soviet the benefit of his insights, a young American girl, nineteen years of age, is moved to write a poem to celebrate the liberation of the Russian people:

> Out from the ice-bound desolation,
> Siberia's heart-eating waste,
> Out from the gloom of desperation,
> From dank foul cells they haste,
> Out from the rule of despotism,
> To the freedom of life they spring,
> They have double their might,
> Since their souls can fight,
> For the people of Russia are king!

Her younger brother Ernest is still a schoolboy at the local high school, keen on boxing, debating, athletics, and writing articles for the school newspaper, in which he positively reviews his own performances. He is in favour of the war, if he can be a part of it. (Not yet, his father tells him.) He scours the papers for news from the front, perhaps he even reads D'Annunzio's missive from Italy. Despite his brash self-confidence and clumsy youthfulness, the girls like him (and the boys, too). And no one doubts his brains. His English teacher, Miss Dixon – a breathless fan of Woodrow Wilson – considers him her precocious star pupil.

Whatever he is going to do in life, Ernest Hemingway knows it will be big. He intends to start by leaving Oak Park, Illinois, as soon as the school year is over.

VIENNA: Sigmund Freud worries about raised expectations of victory. 'If the overpowering effect of the U-boats hasn't become evident by September', he writes to a friend, 'there will be an awakening from illusion in Germany, with frightful consequences.' Anyhow, there are other disappointments to contend with. 'No Nobel prize 1917', he notes sadly in his diary.

THE WESTERN FRONT: French attack. German counter-attack. Poison gas. French counter-counter-attack. Stumble. Fall. Many dead. Many more wounded. No breakthrough. *Désastre* is the word they use in Paris.

Amongst Russian expeditionary units in France, soldiers' committees have now been formed. They refuse to swear loyalty to the provisional government in Petrograd. A full-scale Russian mutiny seems to be under way, on French soil. And it is catching. French soldiers refuse orders to make for the front. They start singing the Internationale. Revolutionary tracts circulate through their ranks. In a few cases guns are fired in the air. 'Shoot me if you like, but I will not go up to the trenches', one soldier tells his superior, 'the result is the same.' The French authorities are alarmed.

PETROGRAD: Trying to put to bed those stupid rumours about his being a German spy, Vladimir starts writing his autobiography. 'I was born in Simbirsk on 10 April 1870', he begins. His brother's execution for an attempt on the life of Nicholas Romanov's father merits a single sentence. Within a few lines he is already in 1895, the year of his arrest for spreading revolutionary propaganda in St Petersburg (as Petrograd was then called).

He stops. What foolishness this is! Why should he justify himself? His enemies in the Petrograd Soviet can make all sorts of wild accusations – but who cares? *He* knows the truth. And sooner or later, *they* will be history.

Bolshevik party membership has tripled since the revolution. This is the fact that matters. This is the tidal wave coming to sweep away the Mensheviks and Socialist Revolutionaries and all the other 'filthy scum on the surface of the world labour movement'. That is to say, the German Social Democrats and their ilk.

At a Bolshevik conference that spring, Lenin asserts himself as leader of his party, and imposes his views of the future. Conciliation is nonsense. The revolution cannot be allowed to atrophy in coalition with the bourgeoisie. But he admits that the majority of workers are not yet won around to the Bolshevik view. He demands tactical flexibility. 'To shout about violence now is senseless', he warns, 'what we need in the present situation is caution, caution, caution'. The future is coming: a proletarian-peasant republic of Soviets, without a police force or a standing army or even a bureaucracy. Everyone will be paid the same. It sounds wonderful. The state, in some form or other, will be required in a transitional period, of course. But not for long.

Lenin recalls the speech of a coal miner who explained how he and his comrades just seized control of their mine and then set about ensuring that it worked. 'Now that is a real programme of the revolution, not derived from books', says the terror of the Zurich public library.

HOMBURG PALACE, GERMANY: Wilhelm has received a letter from a German corn merchant who used to live in Argentina. He takes on some of his suggestions for the country's war aims. An aide worries that these would make negotiated peace impossible. Wilhelm is truculent. 'Yes', the Kaiser replies, '*but* those *are* my peace terms'.

A long list is sent to the German foreign office. Malta is to be German. Gibraltar will be given to Spain. The Azores, Madeira, Cape Verde and all Britain's assets in the eastern Mediterranean and the Middle East are to be turned over to Germany or her allies. The Kaiser imagines a German empire in Africa carved out of French and British possessions. He envisages reparations running into tens of billions of dollars too, and something like a German economic dictatorship over much of the globe. America will send its nickel and copper, Australia its wool, Russia its corn and oil – the list goes on.

That the war drags on is all the fault of the British, the Kaiser complains. The sooner they accept their defeat the better. 'Every week will be more expensive for them.'

THE WESTERN FRONT – SUSSEX, ENGLAND: Winston Churchill is sent to France on a fact-finding mission by the Prime Minister, bumping along rutted roads to the front line. (A few days at the Ritz prepare him for the ordeal.) He meets French generals who keep schtum about the disciplinary trouble they have been having. He meets the top brass of the British army and listens humbly to their views of the military situation before giving his own. He is out of office at the moment and in keen listening mode.

On return to England, at his new country house in Sussex (three German prisoners of war work on the farm), he can relax a little. He enjoys a new game he has recently devised with the help of his children. It is called the bear game. It involves Winston playing a bear while chasing the children around the garden – or, if it is raining, through the house. The man is indefatigable. The children love it.

TSARSKOYE SELO, RUSSIA: The horizons of the imperial family steadily narrow. In April, the children's use of the palace pond is revoked. There are no unauthorised guests. The guards scrawl lewd graffiti on the wall. One casually sticks his bayonet through Nicholas's bicycle wheel when the ex-Tsar is out getting a little exercise.

But Citizen Romanov does not complain. 'Am spending more time with my sweet family than in more normal years', he writes in his diary. He reads detective stories out loud to his children and diligently makes notes about the weather. As temperatures begin to rise, he decides to plant a little vegetable garden, sowing seeds for a summer harvest. He finds time to teach his children geography. (Alexandra is in charge of religious education.) The ex-Tsar celebrates his forty-ninth birthday with a jigsaw.

PETROGRAD: The provisional government broadens its membership to include more Socialist Revolutionaries and Mensheviks as ministers. The Petrograd Soviet's objective of 'peace without annexations or indemnities' becomes government policy. Kerensky becomes War Minister.

He tours the front to try and restore morale in Russia's shattered armies. A women's only battalion is formed under a Siberian peasant named Maria Bochkareva in an attempt to shame men into doing their duty. Kerensky insists military discipline is restored and gives rousing speeches to the soldiers, promising them that they are now fighting for peace and not empire: 'Not a single drop of blood will be shed for a wrong cause'. Those who want to give up now are traitors who would dishonour Russia's name by making it abandon its allies. Revolutionary Russia will only be able to demand peace of others if it proves its own mettle. Peace through strength will be the revolution's gift to the world. One final assault to make the Germans come to their senses.

Lenin is cutting: 'this is the sum and substance of the new government's "programme"', he writes in *Pravda*, 'an offensive, an offensive, an offensive!'

SUMMER

PARIS: In the midst of this strange war, an echo of 1913. The Ballets Russes put on a performance at the Théâtre du Châtelet. They call it *Parade*.

Russian dancers leap to French music. The stage designer is a Spaniard from Barcelona named Pablo. The story is eclectic, featuring a Chinese magician and an American child star. The orchestra includes a typewriter. All the ingredients, then, for a *succès de scandale* to match the premiere of *Rite of Spring* four years before, when Nijinsky pulsated his way across the stage and the audience hissed its disapproval. It is almost like old times (minus the Germans).

The wounded literary critic Guillaume Apollinaire coins a new word to describe the ballet, calling it 'a sort of Sur-realisme'. He enjoys the plasticity of the term. 'Surrealism does not yet exist in the dictionaries', he writes to a poet friend, 'it will be easier to manipulate than Supernaturalism, which is already in use by the philosophers.'

VIENNA: The following morning, at 9 a.m. precisely, a spectacle of quite a different kind gets under way in Vienna's central criminal court: a sensational murder trial involving the assassination of the Austrian Premier in one of the city's finest restaurants last year by Friedrich Adler, the son of the leader of the Austrian Social Democrats, Victor Adler.

All Vienna's attention is riveted on proceedings. Albert Einstein writes a personal letter to Emperor Charles pleading for the actions of his friend Friedrich – who is a physicist as well as a revolutionary – to be treated as a tragic accident rather than a crime. Freud writes to a friend: 'our inner conflict here is perhaps nowhere so plainly revealed as it is by the extremely notable trial of Fr. Adler'. Victor Adler defends his son by describing the stifling atmosphere in Vienna since 1914 with political debate curtailed by war conditions and state censorship. 'The very air in Austria had become suffocating', he declares dramatically to the court, casting his son's act as the desperate last resort of a man of intense convictions pushed to the edge of a nervous breakdown (and beyond). Before the trial he goes so far as to try and have his son declared insane.

Friedrich Adler shows no remorse. He bought the murder weapon, it turns out, as long ago as 1915, in Zurich, thus leaving no doubt that the crime was premeditated: 'I know only that I did what I had to do', he tells the court. He despises the hypocrisy of those who order men to certain deaths at the front every day but invoke the Ten Commandments when one of their own is killed. 'We live in a time when battlefields are covered with hundreds of thousands of the dead, and tens of thousands more fill the seas', he cries, 'and we are told: this is war, this is necessity.' Revolution also has its necessity. After Petrograd, will Vienna be next? A wave of strikes hits Vienna in the early summer.

At seven in the evening the judgement of the court is read out. Friedrich Adler is found guilty as charged. As he is taken down, there are cheers in the courtroom to Adler and the Socialist International. Adler himself is able to shout: 'Long live revolutionary international social democracy!' before he is bundled off by the police. Eight demonstrators are arrested inside the court, and another six on the street outside.

TSARSKOYE SELO: 'It's exactly three months since I came from Mogilyov and since we have been sitting here like prisoners', Nicholas writes in his diary. Occasionally War Minister Kerensky visits. The hardest thing to get used to is the lack of news from his mother.

One night there is a commotion when a shot is fired in the palace garden. A guard sees what appears to be a light being switched on and off repeatedly in the room of one of the Romanov children, as if sending a coded signal for help. Further investigation reveals the cause: Anastasia has been doing needlework late into the night, her head occasionally moving between the electric lamp and the window.

LEEDS, ENGLAND: The spirit of Petrograd reaches the north of England in June. A convention is called bringing together socialist, women's and trades union organisations in the Gothic splendour of the Leeds Coliseum. The organisers call it a Convention. It looks not unlike a Soviet. 'Let us lay down *our* terms, make *our* own proclamations, establish *our* own diplomacy', says pacifist Labour MP Ramsay MacDonald. The workers are now rediscovering their voice after three years when patriotism kept them silent.

A resolution in support of the Russian revolution passes easily. A second resolution calling for an immediate peace 'without annexations or indemnities' – the formula of the Petrograd Soviet – passes less easily. One delegate asks who will pay the pensions of merchant seamen killed by German submarines if not the German government. 'The shipowners', a few shout. An Irishman decries the double standards of those who celebrate the revolution in Russia, but ignore the failed independence rising in Dublin last year, 'where the leaders were taken out and shot like dogs'. The third motion is the most radical. It calls for the immediate establishment of workers' and soldiers' councils across the country. The speaker introducing the motion is quite clear that this means revolution. Another declares his support for Lenin's phrase: the dictatorship of the proletariat. The suffragette Sylvia Pankhurst calls the motion a 'straight cut for the Socialist Commonwealth we all want to see'.

The Leeds resolutions are published in *Pravda*. The King of England is informed.

LEWES, SUSSEX, ENGLAND: A few days later, word gets through the Lewes jail that an Irish maths professor lucky to have escaped the hangman for his role in the Easter Rising is to be released along with other Irish political prisoners held in British prisons. They say it is a gesture towards American opinion.

Before 1916, Éamon de Valera was not a figure of particular importance. His role in the rising and his time in prison have given him a new stature, as the most hard-line leader in the movement for Irish independence still around. The other Irish prisoners look up to him. He calmly ignores the third-class ticket in his hand when he boards the boat home at Holyhead and marches his men up the first-class gangplank.

In Dublin he is greeted as a hero and made the Sinn Féin candidate for the parliamentary seat of East Clare, vacated because of the death of its previous holder, an Irish patriot who decided to demonstrate his patriotism in a very different way: by fighting in the King's army in France. In the weather-beaten villages of western Ireland de Valera campaigns in the uniform of an Irish Volunteer, the force that launched last year's rising. He makes halting speeches to forgiving crowds. He curries favour with local priests by saying he is opposed to any further uprisings for the moment. He talks of his dream that Ireland will one day be not just a dominion of the British Crown but, perhaps, a republic.

THE WESTERN FRONT: 'The spring has been stretched too long', reports a French army officer, 'now it has broken.'

A wave of mutinies spreads through the French army. 'Even within the most reliable units, even amongst the best elements, there is moral as well as physical exhaustion', the officer writes: 'I repeat, the spring is broken, it has been kept taut for too long.' On one occasion four hundred soldiers abandon their posts and start marching towards Paris before being surrounded by cavalry units and persuaded to return. Another day, two thousand soldiers gather in Ville-en-Tardenois carrying a red flag and singing the Internationale.

Leave is improved. Pay is increased. Military repression is accelerated – but its severity is limited. The French army strains but does not shatter.

VIENNA: Freud flees the city for the summer. In the capital, black market-eers hoard food and government posters urge people to collect bones, lest they go to waste. The Hungarian countryside seems a different world. 'Friendship and loyalty are taking the form of generosity', Freud writes to a friend, 'with the result that we are able to wallow in the abundance of bread, butter, sausages, eggs and cigars, rather like the chief of a primitive tribe'. The Hungarians are 'unmannerly and noisy'. But amidst such plenty, he hardly cares. He knows it cannot last.

EAST ST. LOUIS, ILLINOIS: The town of East St. Louis on the Mississippi has a reputation for easy alcohol, easy women and politicians on the take. State after state has gone dry in recent years but East St. Louis is an oasis of vice. The licensing of saloons provides an income for local officials. 'Irrigation juries' from local bars ensure no one is ever acquitted except as required by the Mayor. Dance halls provide cheap thrills. Aunt Kate's Honkytonk advertises the Chemise-She-Wobble, where girls perform an Americanised version of the belly dance.

The city has a new reputation by 1917: for racial tensions between whites and blacks. White workers in the city's booming war industries protest that new black immigrants fleeing poverty and violence in the rural South are holding down wages and introducing crime into the city. In May, a white man is shot by a black man during a hold-up, prompting a downtown riot. Soon after, black labourers at a meat-packing plant are beaten up as they leave work. Whites move out of the neighbourhoods where black families move in. The city is ghettoised.

One Sunday in July, the tensions explode. In the course of a sweltering day, a string of assaults take place. White youths in a Ford motor car cruise along Market Avenue, unloading a gun at random into black houses and shops as they drive by. That night, a police automobile, perhaps mistaken for the same Ford, comes under fire from black residents. Two white officers, Samuel Coppedge and Frank Wadley, are killed. The shops and saloons of East St. Louis are closed the next day. Whites descend on the city's black neighbourhoods to terrorise the new arrivals and force them to leave.

Black men are pulled off streetcars and beaten to a pulp. Black homes are set alight. Josephine, an eleven-year-old black girl who likes to dress up and dance, runs through the flames to safety on the other side of the Mississippi, where she huddles with her friends and stares back in terror at her home town glowing with the fire of racial hatred. A fourteen-year-old white boy is killed when two black men, trapped in a burning barber's shop, try to disperse the angry crowd outside with bullets. A black man is lynched on Broadway. 'Get hold, and pull for East St. Louis!' bellows a man in a straw hat. The police are powerless to stop the violence. Some join in. The city descends into bloody lawlessness. 'Look at that', a rioter says that evening, flashing a torch in the face of a barely breathing black man: 'not dead yet'. A gunshot echoes around the shuttered streets. Grim order is eventually restored by the National Guard. Forty-eight men, women and children have been killed. Press photographs of the carnage are not allowed. 'East St. Louis doesn't want that kind of advertising', reporters are told.

Marcus Garvey, a Jamaican race activist living in Harlem, pours forth his anger in New York. He thunders against American hypocrisy: 'America that has been ringing the bells of the world, proclaiming to the nations and the peoples thereof that she has democracy to give to all and sundry, America that has denounced Germany for the deportations of the Belgians into Germany, America that has arraigned Turkey at the bar of public opinion and public justice against the massacres of the Armenians, has herself no satisfaction to give twelve million of her own citizens.' His solution is revolutionary: the world's blacks must unite around the world as the workers have, to throw off their enemies.

The Federal government declines to get involved in investigating the East St. Louis riot, just as it declines to intervene against lynching across the American South, where white mobs string up blacks in the name of rough justice for crimes real and imagined. The government seems prepared to let such violence occur, and leave it to the states to sort out. A few weeks after the riots, a silent parade in New York claims the nation's attention. Several thousand blacks march down Fifth Avenue, the women and children all dressed in white, protesting for justice. It is the first parade of its kind. A banner asks: 'Mr. President, why do you not make America safe for democracy?'

The East St. Louis riots put America on edge. Later that summer, in Houston, Texas, a mutiny breaks out amongst black soldiers when they hear false rumours that a rampaging white mob is on its way to their army camp. Twenty are killed in the ensuing violence, mostly whites. A court martial leads to the execution at dawn of thirteen black soldiers and forty-one sentences of life imprisonment. A second court martial results in sixteen more death sentences. A petition for clemency is prepared.

PETROGRAD: The leader of the Czech independence movement, Tomáš Masaryk long in exile from Habsburg Prague, meets two guests from Britain off their train. The famous suffragette Emmeline Pankhurst and her assistant Jessie Kenney are on a mission to make sure Russia does not drop out of the war. The Czech gentleman has a *droshky* waiting.

After a quick tour of the sights, the gallant Czech drops the ladies at their hotel and offers two pieces of advice for how to get on in revolutionary Russia: avoid big crowds and get your own cook. If they do not do the former, he says, they may get stuck between two rival mobs – one for and one against the war, for example. If they not do the latter, Masaryk explains cheerily, their choice in Russia will be between starvation or food poisoning. Emmeline refuses the offer of a Czech bodyguard to protect them.

Mrs Pankhurst is granted an audience with the Russian premier within days of her arrival and filmed for the newsreels. One evening, Emmeline and Jessie dine with Rasputin's aristocratic murderer (and are shown exactly where the grisly deed was done). They are in Petrograd when, on 19 June, the British House of Commons endorses the right to vote of several million more men – and, for the first time, eight million British women. The achievement of Emmeline's life's work is crowded out by the situation in Russia.

By day, she gives rousing speeches, in English, to women workers in Petrograd's munitions factories, urging them not to be misled by siren calls for an immediate and separate peace. She visits hospitals run by foreign aid workers. She attends fundraisers for Maria Bochkareva's women's 'battalion of death', admiring their strength and dedication to their cause. ('It is the men, principally, who are leading on to anarchy', Jessie notes in her diary.) Emmeline falls sick from overwork, with a recurring stomach complaint dating from her various hunger strikes as a suffragette. She rejects an offer to visit the ex-Tsar and his family. It would compromise her mission, she explains.

Petrograd is full of words, words, words. Liberals book up theatres and music halls to give patriotic lectures to their supporters. The city Soviet is packed with workers' representatives declaring their positions on everything from land reform to Ukraine's latest bid for autonomy from Russia. War Minister Kerensky, the provisional government's most dynamic and recognisable leader, never stops talking. But the most stunning newcomer on the speaking circuit is the principled non-tipper Leon Trotsky, with his wild gesticulations, mordant wit, quivering pince-nez and rousing speeches against the war. He revels in the 'human electricity' at his speeches at the Cirque Moderne. He has not quite thrown in his lot with Lenin, but is moving his way.

The impatient revolutionary himself is more comfortable with a pen. He castigates the Mensheviks and Socialist Revolutionaries for consenting to serve the provisional government and blames capitalist 'predators' for the ongoing food and industrial crisis. His position on the war remains: no separate peace with Germany, but no alliances with anyone else. In the First All-Russian Congress of Soviets, Lenin declares that the Bolsheviks, though only a small minority of the delegates present, are ready to take power by themselves 'at any moment': a boast greeted with fear and laughter in equal measure. Kerensky is highly irritated when he sees the Bolshevik leader, whom he has just met for the first time, grabbing his briefcase and slipping out before the end of his own peroration.

The city is bursting with nervous energy. Every rally seems to have the potential to turn into a riot; and every riot has the potential to become an uprising. The workers are losing faith in the Socialist Revolutionaries and Mensheviks. The Bolsheviks are suspected of using political agitation as cover for a coup. Their opponents consider banning them. 'What they are engaged in now is not propaganda', warns an anti-Bolshevik member of the Petrograd Soviet, 'it is a plot'. Lenin calls this an 'insinuation'. In truth he is trying to keep his own followers motivated, while at the same time ensuring they do not strike too early, giving their political enemies an excuse to suppress them. On the one hand he says that 'peaceful processions are a thing of the past'. On the other, 'we must give them no pretext for attack'.

A French diplomat hears about a revolutionary meeting at the Cirque Moderne where some joker shouted: 'here come the Cossacks', just to see what would happen. 'In a second', he writes, 'both speakers and audience vanished into thin air.'

SARAJEVO, BOSNIA, THE AUSTRO-HUNGARIAN EMPIRE: Three years to the day since the assassination of Archduke Franz Ferdinand and his wife Sophie, priests dedicate a huge iron and bronze cross to the site of their murder in the centre of Sarajevo.

Charles and Zita are on an official visit to Munich and unable to attend.

THE RUSSIAN FRONT: War Minister Kerensky ignores the generals who warn him that the army will not fight. He issues an order to attack. 'Let not the enemy celebrate prematurely his victory over us!' it reads. 'Let all nations know that when we talk of peace, it is not because we are weak! Forward!'

Success comes easily at first. Thousands of enemy soldiers are taken prisoner in the advance. At Tsarskoye Selo, a service of thanks is conducted before breakfast. The Tsar spends the rest of the day chopping down trees and working in the vegetable garden until interrupted by rain. News remains good for several days. A French diplomat wonders if somehow the Russian army, thought to be riddled with Bolshevik defeatism, is undergoing a glorious resurrection out there at the front. 'Anything is possible in this country', he notes. Nicholas and his son joyously saw up fir trees. He finishes *Le Comte de Monte Cristo* and hungrily starts a new detective novel: *Arsène Lupin contre Sherlock Holmes*.

The truth at the front is less rosy. Early victories are bought at a heavy price in desertions, dead and wounded. A British military observer reports that many of those missing are simply hiding in the woods and that a large proportion of wounds appear to be self-inflicted. Some of the best fighting is done by units that are not Russian at all, such as the Czechs inspired to fight on the Russian side against the Habsburgs in the hope of securing independence after the war. (The Czech presence on both sides can have ugly consequences: in one case a father shoots his own son in battle.)

Kerensky's offensive begins to peter out. On the Russian side, desperate appeals for reinforcements to be sent to the front to replace those who have fallen or run away produce no result. Soldiers in Petrograd are said to be selling cigarettes in the street or offering their services as railway porters rather than heeding the call to arms. The German army pulls soldiers from the Western Front to launch a counter-attack. The only bright spot for the Russians is the headlong advance of their troops into Austrian Galicia under a general named Kornilov. (A Siberian Cossack with authoritarian tendencies, the general has a mounted phalanx of Turkmen bodyguards to protect him and writes poetry in Tajik for relaxation.)

When Maria Bochkareva's women's battalion arrives at the front, she finds an army on the brink of collapse. 'What devil brought you here?' the soldiers jeer. 'We want peace!' That evening a band of deserters stone the women's barracks and thrust their hands through its broken windows to grab their hair. Maria has a vision of three hundred women marching into no man's land, and a million Russian men rising up behind them, shamed into becoming proper soldiers again by the women's example. They attack the next day. Several enemy machine guns are seized. Thirty-six of the battalion are wounded; Maria herself suffers concussion. (In the midst of battle she finds two soldiers having sex behind a tree: she promptly bayonets the girl, and sends the man running away in terror.)

The battle – and Kerensky's offensive – end in heroic failure.

TSARSKOYE SELO: 'There has been bad news from the south-western front in recent days', Nicholas Romanov notes in his diary: 'many units, infected throughout with base, defeatist teachings, not only refused to go forward but in some places retreated even without any pressure from the enemy'. Now, Kornilov's advance has been halted too. The Germans and Austrians are breaking back through the Russian lines: 'What disgrace and despair!'

That day the Tsar cuts down three trees, and saws up two more. Then he tidies his room.

ACROSS EUROPE: There is much talk of peace over the summer months: peace formulas, peace declarations, peace resolutions, peace terms. All over Europe, there are meetings, conventions and conferences to discuss it. Charles Habsburg prays for it. Workers strike for it. Diplomats send letters and messages around the Continent trying to figure out what will make the other side stop. At Fátima in Portugal, where young children have seen an apparition of the Virgin Mary, they ask her when the soldiers will come home.

At times, peace seems close, like a white dove appearing suddenly through the fog of war. For a moment over the summer, hope settles on the prospect of an international conference in Stockholm where socialists will hammer things out in a spirit of common humanity. But then the little bird disappears again as if it was just a trick of the light. The time is never right for everyone. What's more, peace has many meanings. Yes, peace – but *which* peace? *Whose* peace? Security for Germany or freedom for Belgium? Respect for borders or a plebiscite in Alsace-Lorraine? Arguments flare between those who think it worth talking to the enemy, and those who think it is betrayal while their countries are still occupied.

And all the while, the war goes on. In the west, the French army is in no position to launch a fresh offensive. A series of limited British assaults are launched to take out German naval bases on the Belgian coast, reducing the risk to cross-Channel troop transports and the danger of German submarines sailing from Ostend. Thousands killed and wounded as a result. An open letter by a soldier in the Royal Welch Fusiliers is read out in the British House of Commons. 'I believe the war is being deliberately prolonged by those who have power to end it', runs one line. The soldier is sent for psychiatric treatment by a follower of Freud in a hospital outside Edinburgh. In the meantime, the daily horrors of war increase. A new weapon is deployed which the German army calls *Gelbkreuz*: a poison gas which sinks into the trenches, getting inside even the most well-secured gas mask, burning any skin exposed to it, and lingering in the soldiers' clothes, and in the soil, for days. Even battle-hardened German soldiers find the conditions of 1917 more awful than the year before. Constant bombardment makes sleep impossible. The soldiers' nerves are shattered. Rates of desertion are on the rise.

In Germany, a mood of mutiny swells backwards and forwards between the soldiers at the front and the civilians left behind in the fatherland. Tentative dreams of peace clash with the army high command's demand for the full mobilisation of society. The people are exhausted. In July, when Kerensky's offensive is looking threatening, the situation takes a dramatic turn when a leading Catholic politician warns his fellow Reichstag members that they must now end their submission to the Kaiser and the generals. They must express their desire for a European peace of reconciliation negotiated by civilians, rather than pursue the fantasies of a military clique. The submarine war has failed. The Reichstag has been deceived. Peace cannot wait. If it does not come soon there will be a winter of unequalled suffering. Nineteen-eighteen will be even worse. Germany cannot win. Will peace now spring from the German Reichstag?

The relatively moderate German Chancellor demands that immediate electoral reform be introduced and that Reichstag representatives – many of whom are Social Democrats – are brought into government. For conservatives and nationalists, this confirms their belief that democracy and defeatism go hand in hand. Ludendorff and Hindenburg force out the Chancellor, threatening the Kaiser with their resignation if he objects. 'I might as well abdicate straight away', Wilhelm declares petulantly, before giving in to his generals' demands. A new Chancellor is soon appointed: quite out of his depth in matters of foreign and military policy. (Up until now, he kept himself abreast of world events 'by reading the newspapers', he explains.) Everyone knows he is little more than Ludendorff and Hindenburg's puppet.

A peace resolution still passes the Reichstag. But the tone is ambiguous. It calls for a 'peace of understanding' without territorial acquisition 'by force' – a major caveat – while affirming that the German people will fight on to the death until their rights to national 'life and development' are guaranteed. Perhaps it is a matter of timing. The resolution passes the Reichstag on the same day Kerensky's offensive collapses and Petrograd seems on the brink of yet another revolution. Peace negotiations suddenly do not seem quite so urgent in Berlin. The new Chancellor says he accepts the resolution *as I interpret it* – weasel words which ensure the motion will have no practical effect on government policy.

Despite its apparent desire for peace, the Reichstag nonetheless votes more money for the war. The Stockholm peace conference never takes place.

PETROGRAD: Nadya never sees her husband any more. They take no walks. Vladimir is too busy. She throws herself into the Bolshevik cause in her own way, getting elected to the Vyborg district council and conducting educational work. She notices how useful sellers of sunflower seeds are for conducting agitation amongst the troops. This is how the party grows: garrison by garrison, factory by factory, Soviet by Soviet. As living conditions worsen, the factories grow more militant. As inflation rises, so do the Bolsheviks.

Nadya organises a youth league that, amongst other things, proposes everyone should learn to sew. At first, the young male recruits laugh it off, noting that surely sewing is a woman's job. They are quickly corrected. 'Do you want to uphold the old slavery of women? The wife is her husband's comrade, not his servant!' Things are changing.

EAST CLARE, IRELAND: The public call the Sinn Féin candidate 'The Spaniard' or their 'Man with the Strange Name': Éamon de Valera. The Irish Volunteers hold marches in his support. On election day, 'The Spaniard' crushes his opponent, a more traditional Irish patriot and a lawyer who is said to have 'defended one half of the murderers in Clare, and is related to the other half'.

It is clear that de Valera's strain of nationalism is on the up: the militant, rebellious kind, the kind which refuses British rule entirely and honours the dead of the Easter Rising rather than the Irish dead in France.

NEIVOLA, FINLAND – PETROGRAD: A train chugs its way from Petrograd along the coast of the Gulf of Finland. A pale middle-aged man sits next to his sister, who talks at him non-stop as the carriage rocks from side to side. Occasionally the man holds his head in his hands, as if trying to rid himself of a headache. He looks tired.

For several days at a friend's dacha in the Finnish village of Neivola, not two hours from Petrograd, Vladimir walks, eats and swims. He spends long hours sitting on the veranda staring at the blue sky. He feels himself regaining his strength after all the scheming and scribbling of the last months. Then, early one morning, a messenger arrives with urgent news. In Lenin's absence, an insurrection has broken out amongst industrial workers in Vyborg and soldiers about to be sent to the front. It is unclear who, if anyone, is behind it.

Jessie Kenney hears armoured vehicles screaming through the streets of Petrograd. The Belgian Ambassador's Rolls-Royce is stolen by the mob, and then adorned with a machine gun and a red flag to flutter beside the Belgian tricolour. War Minister Kerensky is visiting the front, though said to be rushing back. The front page of *Pravda* is blank. A debate in the Petrograd Soviet about whether to support, reject or suppress the revolt does not begin until one in the morning. Lenin rushes to the capital by the first train. He is back at Bolshevik headquarters by midday. Those hothead fools! Too soon, too soon! 'You ought to be given a good hiding for this', he tells his over-eager comrades in private, furious that they have let an insurrection take place. Such undisciplined action is fraught with danger.

Twenty thousand armed sailors arrive from the Kronstadt garrison that morning, with their cap ribbons turned inside out so that no one can identify them by the name of their ship. Their purpose in the city is uncertain. The insurrection lacks leadership. Addressing a crowd from the balcony of Bolshevik headquarters, Lenin pointedly refuses to provide it. He even gets a stand-in to finish his speech. The uprising was rotten from the beginning, Lenin decides: this is going nowhere. Riderless horses are seen cantering through the streets. Sheets of paper from a ransacked office float downstream along the Neva. A Frenchman notes spilled face powder and ribbons from a looted shop.

The fair-weather revolutionaries amongst the Kronstadt sailors are cleared off the street by a torrential downpour in the afternoon. A hard core marches to the Tauride Palace. 'Take power you son of a bitch when it's handed to you', a worker shouts at a leading Socialist Revolutionary member of the Soviet who is also a minister. Leon Trotsky stands up on a car bonnet and requests that the man be released. The crowd are confused. Trotsky comes to Kronstadt regularly urging the need for the revolution to continue. Now he seems to be rejecting it. Has he lost his nerve? 'You've come to declare your will and show the Soviet that the working class no longer wants to see the bourgeoisie in power', Leon says. Their devotion to the revolution is not in doubt, he tells the rebels, but 'individuals are not worthy of your attention'. Trotsky stretches out his hand to one of the sailors: 'Give me your hand, Comrade! Your hand, brother!' The minister is released. There will be no revolution today. Pictures of War Minister Kerensky reappear on the walls of the city's apartments and cafés the next morning.

Despite their protestations of innocence, the Bolsheviks are blamed for the insurrection. The offices of *Pravda* are raided and Bolshevik headquarters turned inside out in the search for proof of the impatient revolutionary's German contacts and general Bolshevik perfidy. A warrant is issued for Lenin's arrest. The fugitive moves from apartment to apartment, from safe house to safe house. 'Now they are going to shoot us', he confides knowingly to Trotsky. 'We may not see each other again', he tells Nadya when she comes to visit him in one of his hideouts. He raises the possibility of giving himself up – there may be some propaganda benefit to a public trial. The Georgian bank-robber Stalin argues against it. Vladimir's mind turns to his intellectual legacy, and all the writing he was doing in Zurich before the revolution interrupted him. '*Entre nous*', he writes to a trusted comrade, 'if they do me in, I ask you to publish my notebook *Marxism and the State* (it got left behind in Stockholm)'.

The manhunt for the Bolshevik leader continues. Nadya is closely interrogated when the house in which she is staying is ransacked by a military search party. 'Look in the oven, someone may be sitting there', the servant girl tells the soldiers conducting the raid a little tartly. As the net closes in, Vladimir decides he must get out of the city. He has Stalin shave off his moustache and beard before catching a local train filled with summer holidaymakers heading up the Gulf of Finland, getting off not far outside the city and trudging to a property owned by an old Bolshevik party member.

The principled non-tipper Leon Trotsky is arrested and incarcerated in the Kresty jail, where he writes furious articles for *Pravda* expressing solidarity with Lenin. The Petrograd Soviet is moved to the Smolny Institute, formerly a private girls' school, full of long corridors and bare classrooms – a significant demotion from the grandeur of the Tauride. Kerensky takes over the formal leadership of the provisional government and moves into the Winter Palace.

UPSTATE MICHIGAN: An American summer at Walloon, the Hemingway family cottage near the Canadian border, five days of dusty driving from Chicago, not so different from Lenin's hideaway in Finland. Young Ernest the high-school graduate, no longer a boy exactly but not quite a man either, spends the summer fixing things up, helping out his father, going fishing, and pondering the greatness of his future, somehow about to begin.

Time passes slowly. The world is far away. Even the rest of America – where German-Americans are being hounded, suspect newspapers closed and socialists locked up – seems far away. Ernest's grandfather sends over the Chicago papers for his grandson to read, several days late, but always hungrily consumed. Ernest replies with the latest from Walloon, which isn't much: a visit by Uncle Tyler and his wife, worries about the potato crop this year, the condition of Clarence Hemingway's automobile ('Dad's Ford is running fine now that the cylinders are clean'.) The most exciting news concerns fishing, and Ernest's claim to have made 'the largest catch of trout that has ever been made' in Horton's Bay.

As the summer wears on, and the trout tally mounts at Walloon, Ernest begins to wonder whether his future will begin at all. He might stay up at the cottage until October, he writes. Or he might visit one of his uncles, or he might try and get a job at the *Chicago Tribune*, his newspaper of choice ...

THE VATICAN: The Pope tries another peace initiative, issuing an invitation to the warring parties to discuss a peace without annexations or indemnities, but with Belgium's independence guaranteed.

In Milan, the war-wounded newspaper editor Benito Mussolini calls the Pope a traitor to his country, and advocates total war against the Austrians. (At that very moment, the Italian army is preparing for yet another assault, hoping to crack open the Austrian defences in the mountains north-east of Venice.) To make peace now would be to give up on the nationalist dream of turning the Adriatic Sea into an Italian lake and building an extended empire in Africa. The British demand German withdrawal from Belgium before negotiations can begin. Woodrow Wilson writes that a return to the status quo before the war is impossible now that the Germans have covered Europe in a 'tide of blood'.

WILHELMSHAVEN, GERMANY: Wilhelm decides to conduct what he considers to be a morale-boosting visit to his fleet. The weather is balmy – 'Hohenzollern weather', they call it – and so is the political temperature aboard.

The mood amongst the sailors is poor. Germany's giant surface fleet has not ventured out onto the high seas in force since 1916. They hear that the submarine war has stalled, and that Germany is now losing U-boats faster than they can be replaced. They read in the newspapers from Berlin about the political crisis there, the calls for peace, and the instability in Russia. 'The entire world is a madhouse', one sailor writes in his diary that summer, 'the oldest dynasties have fallen or now hide fearfully from an increasingly restless and fuming volcano . . .' The sailors organise themselves into committees to present their complaints. Some are arrested for passing around socialist tracts or for refusing to attend drill practice. News that Russian sailors have taken matters into their own hands at Kronstadt over the summer is greeted warmly in Wilhelmshaven: 'we Germans ought to imitate them'.

A report on socialist agitation is delivered to Wilhelm in person. He listens approvingly as he is told of the death sentences expected to be handed down to the ringleaders. That evening before supper, Wilhelm addresses the naval chiefs with his own personal perspective on matters. Keen to emphasise his credentials as a far-sighted moderniser, the Kaiser suggests that the German navy should adopt an American-style naval jacket in the future. The senior officers demur: they prefer the old-fashioned cut.

WASHINGTON DC: America gears up for war. Like Tsar Nicholas at Tsarskoye Selo, Edith Wilson plants a vegetable garden at the White House. Across the country, the mines produce more coal. Steelworks produce more steel. Shipyards clank out new vessels.

American businesses, more profitable than ever, promise great feats of additional productivity to meet the fresh demands of war. (The Detroit automobile manufacturer Henry Ford, having apparently given up on his earlier peace efforts, promises to produce one thousand midget submarines and three thousand aeroplane engines *every day*.) American savers are encouraged to lend money to the government through new Liberty Bonds. The financial wealth of the country is pressed into national service. The first American soldiers reach Europe – though not yet the front – over the summer.

After the Houston mutiny, the army temporarily halts the draft for black Americans. Most existing black recruits are assigned to labour battalions or guard duty. (One activist notes that all the guards at the White House are black.) It is decided that only a handful of all-black combat units will be formed and sent to France.

TSARSKOYE SELO: On a warm and beautiful Friday morning towards the end of summer, just after breakfast, Nicholas Romanov is informed that he and his family are to be moved. Not to Crimea as they had hoped – 'and we were still counting on a long stay in Livadia!' he notes sadly in his diary – but somewhere out east. They are not told their exact destination. Nicholas engages in a final bout of chopping and sawing in the forest: eleven fir trees are felled in three days. On Sunday, the family celebrates the Tsarevich's thirteenth birthday.

Nicholas's brother Michael is brought to Tsarskoye Selo by Kerensky late one night. 'It was very pleasant to meet', Citizen Romanov writes in his diary: 'but to talk in front of strangers was awkward.' The next morning, the imperial party boards a train marked as belonging to the Red Cross and flying the Japanese flag. A few days after that, they are already in the middle of Siberia, where they pass the native village of their old holy man, Rasputin. They gather on the viewing platform to look at his house standing out amongst the meagre log cabins around it. Rasputin told them that they would come here one day.

Their final destination is Tobolsk. They are put up in the former governor's mansion. There is a fence to keep them in, and armed guards on the door.

MOSCOW, RUSSIA – RAZLIV, NEAR PETROGRAD: The villages outside Russia's second city are rather like the English county of Surrey, Jessie Kenney decides. In Moscow, Jessie and Emmeline enjoy a vegetarian dinner with two charming English bachelors who have taken up residence in the city. They talk about the Cossack shawls Emmeline so admires. They buy records of Russian folk songs to take home. The mood is lighter here than in Petrograd.

They are disappointed not to be able to get into the Bolshoi Theatre to see the main show playing in town: a political gathering called by Kerensky to assert his personal authority as leader of the provisional government and present himself as the only man capable of welding together Russia's fractured polity. Two thousand representatives from across the spectrum of Russian society and politics meet in Moscow – right and left, town and country. But without the Bolsheviks, of course, who declare Kerensky's national gathering to be counter-revolution dressed up as democracy and call for protest resolutions (but not street demonstrations) against it. Eventually Jessie and Emmeline are able to secure two tickets to view proceedings from the British box. They are delighted to recognise the odd Russian word they have learned: '*democratzie, revolutzie, organizatie*'.

The attempt to demonstrate Kerensky's power and indispensability to Russia's political renewal meets with only partial success in Moscow. The precautions necessary to protect the Bolshoi, with a triple cordon of police and militia, tell their own story. Kerensky seems fractious and exhausted: yesterday's favourite. He is upstaged at the gathering by General Kornilov, the new commander-in-chief of the army, who is greeted by one half of the meeting as a saviour and by the other as a Napoleon-in-waiting.

The army is falling apart, Kornilov explains: 'men have become like animals'. While he claims not to be against soldiers' committees in the army *per se*, he insists they should focus on issues of welfare and supply, on combating the spread of disease and hunger. They must not be allowed to elect officers or dictate tactics. Kornilov is blunt about the military situation: 'The enemy is knocking at the gates of Riga.' If the city falls, the road to Petrograd will be open. The next speaker, another army general, goes much further, calling for the Soviets to be abolished. He is applauded on the right. On the left, there is a feeling of unease. Are the generals preparing to take power and roll back the changes of the last six months?

While all this is happening in Moscow, the impatient revolutionary is still in hiding outside Petrograd, in a wooden hut with a thatched roof which leaks when it rains. The mosquitos are terrible. 'Power has passed into the hands of counter-revolution', he warns in a riposte to some Bolsheviks who clearly have not grasped the full magnitude of events, the full scale of betrayal which has occurred. The Mensheviks and Socialist Revolutionaries are 'butcher's aides'. Armed insurrection will now be needed against them. *All power to the Soviets* is no longer a suitable slogan now that the Soviets have proven themselves mere 'puppets' of the provisional government under Menshevik and Socialist Revolutionary influence. The slogan of the February revolution should be scrapped, Lenin demands.

He decides the time has come to move to a new, and safer, hideout. But to move anywhere at all these days, he needs a disguise. A Bolshevik comrade acquires a wig on the pretext that a troupe of amateur dramatics is being organised. A photographer comes out from Petrograd to take Lenin's picture for false identity papers. Because there is no tripod available, Vladimir is forced to kneel in the mud while the photo is taken. On the day of departure, the impatient revolutionary and his group get lost in the forest on the way to the railway station and are forced to run across a still-burning peat-bog. They then find they have come to the wrong station anyway. Two trains, a carriage, a change of clothes and an adhesive face mask later, Lenin arrives in the Finnish city of Helsinki, where he is put up in the safest place imaginable: the home of the elected local police chief.

RIGA, RUSSIA – PETROGRAD: A week after Kornilov's warning, Riga falls to the Germans in a lightning strike combining new tactics on the ground with poison gas and aeroplanes. 'Today's news is hateful', a French diplomat writes in his diary. For Russia, it spells disaster. Petrograd will soon be in range of German bombing raids. Only winter can save the city from German occupation now.

French citizens in the capital turn up at their embassy to ask whether they should leave for home. Petrograd's railway stations are crowded with those who need no such advice. Women sit on suitcases with their children, surrounded by bags. Trunks are tied up with rope. There are samovars, rolled-up mattresses, gramophone horns. The only winners from the latest crisis are the Bolsheviks.

Jessie Kenney is one of those who goes to the railway station that day, to see her friend Maria Bochkareva off to the front again. At the station, there is a ruckus as some try to prevent the women from boarding their train. Jessie finds herself caught between two opposing mobs – one for and one against the war – just as the gallant Czech gentleman had warned. Her ribs are crushed. She can hardly breathe. Her scarf gets caught, pulling tighter around her neck. Jessie raises one hand into the air, still bearing some flowers given to her by members of Maria's battalion, in the hope of attracting attention. A soldier on horseback makes his way into the crowd and rescues her.

Jessie has to hold back her tears when she returns to the hotel. She does not want Emmeline to see her this way. To cry in public is against suffragette etiquette. Suffragettes must smile while they bleed.

AUTUMN

Petrograd: Anatoly Lunacharsky, one of Lenin's fellow Bolsheviks, and undoubtedly one of the most cultured, is giving a lecture on Greek art to a group of workers in the Cirque Moderne. Afterwards, a group of his friends chat about aesthetics and culture. It is only towards evening, over tea, that they hear the news. A phone call from the Petrograd Soviet's new headquarters in the Smolny Institute: Kornilov is marching on Petrograd. The counter-revolution has begun.

The reality is more devious. Kerensky has been in touch with Kornilov for some time, sounding him out about the ideas he expressed in Moscow for giving Russia the strong government it needs. Messages shoot between Petrograd and army headquarters at Mogilyov. Kornilov believes his ideas for restoring order are being supported by Kerensky. Loyal troops are to be moved up to Petrograd in anticipation of a Bolshevik revolt should the scheme be put into action. But Kerensky has begun to have second thoughts. He now senses an opportunity to recast himself as the revolution's hero by framing the unwitting Kornilov.

Kerensky asks for the general's preference on a future structure of the government: a dictatorship led by Kerensky with the general as a minister, a collective *directoire* of some sort on the French revolutionary model, or a dictatorship with Kornilov in charge and Kerensky as his minister. The last, the guileless general answers. One night, over a special telegraph machine which records the conversation, Kerensky encourages the general to repeat his earlier unwisely expressed preference. Armed with this artfully manufactured evidence appearing to show Kornilov's perfidy against the regime, Kerensky demands his cabinet grant full powers to himself to counter the threat. 'I will not give them the revolution', he declares defiantly. The trap is sprung. Kerensky sings operatic arias in his study in celebration of his Machiavellian brilliance.

But there is a catch. Kornilov is informed he has been dismissed, but the order is ignored, and his official replacement refuses to take over his command. The general's troops are already on their way to Petrograd. Having conjured the fake threat of a military takeover to secure full powers for himself, Kerensky now has a real insurrection on his hands. A radio telegram informs the country that the general has conspired to establish 'a regime opposed to the conquests of the revolution', and must be stopped. Kornilov angrily denies this version of events. 'A *great provocation* has taken place which jeopardizes the fate of the motherland', his counterblast declares.

The troops march on. Reading the messages from Petrograd, the general suspects foul play. Perhaps the Bolsheviks have already captured the government and are now working hand in glove with the Germans. His duty, then, is clear: 'the heavy sense of the inevitable ruin of the country commands me in these ominous moments to call upon all Russian people to come to the aid of the dying motherland'. If he fails, the Russians will be made German slaves. Kerensky and Kornilov's budding alliance has turned into a contest. 'Kornilov has chosen a moment of deathly danger for his homeland to set the fire of a civil war', reads one paper.

The Petrograd Soviet, which Kerensky previously sought to sideline, is thrust back to prominence as the command centre of resistance against Kornilov. The Bolsheviks, who have long warned of counter-revolutionary machination, are rehabilitated. They demand Petrograd's workers be armed. While the Kronstadt sailors sweep into town to defend the revolution, Kornilov's troops are slowed down by sabotage. Agitators from Petrograd are sent out to win over the rank and file. The soldiers are told the truth: there is no Bolshevik rebellion to repress. If they continue their march into town they will be killing the revolution, not saving it. Kornilov's revolt – if that is what it ever really was – crumbles in fraternisation and confusion. The general is arrested not long afterwards.

'Is it a farce or a Shakespearean tragedy?' writes a French diplomat. Lenin is so surprised by the course of events, he proposes something quite unlike him: a compromise with his former enemies whereby the Bolsheviks forgo the possibility of taking power themselves for the time being, as long as all power now resides with the Soviets. Trotsky is released from jail and a little later becomes chairman of the Petrograd Soviet.

News reaches Nicholas Romanov in Tobolsk. 'It seems there is a vast muddle in Petrograd', he writes in his diary. At the front, the Russian army is collapsing faster than ever. 'She's a *Kornilovka!*' a mob shout at Maria Bochkareva. She is very nearly lynched.

SPARTANBURG, SOUTH CAROLINA: White locals didn't want black soldiers from New York training in their town – it's 'like waving a red flag in the face of a bull', Spartanburg's mayor writes to the War Department – but here they are.

One Saturday evening, the band of New York's 15th Infantry Regiment plays a concert in the town square, where a bandstand has been erected for the purpose. Lieutenant Jim Europe leads the band in playing rousing martial music. It's a huge success. 'When do they play again?' asks one of Spartanburg's white citizens when the band have finished their concert. Perhaps things will work out all right in South Carolina after all.

The feeling of patriotic unity does not last. In Spartanburg, black soldiers from New York are expected to follow the segregation laws of South Carolina without a word of complaint, are barred from certain shops, and are considered uppity should they so much as decide to walk on the pavement rather than the road. Abuse is common. Tensions soon boil over. One morning soldiers in camp hear that one of their number has been lynched after a fight with the local police. On investigation, it turns out that the story is nothing more than a malicious rumour, and a riot is averted.

On another occasion, one of Europe's band colleagues is physically assaulted by the manager of a whites-only hotel when he goes in to buy a copy of a New York newspaper. This time, white soldiers from New York are so enraged by the behaviour against one of their black colleagues that they seem ready to burn the hotel to the ground – until an officer arrives to calm things down.

The 15th Regiment are in town for just two weeks. Then the orders come: back to the city, then France.

THE EASTERN FRONT – KREUZNACH: The good news from Russia reaches Kaiser Wilhelm on board a train on his way back from a tour of Bulgaria. Emperor Charles joins his German ally for some of the journey, and bothers him with his latest thoughts on solving the conundrum of Poland's future status if the war is won. Wilhelm holds forth on Wagner and his operatic genius. 'The Kaiser's knowledge on this subject is astounding', notes an aide in his diary.

Back in Kreuznach it is a return to the regular drill: the odd drive along the Rhine, meetings on Germany's latest crisis (which the Kaiser dismisses as just the usual fluff), after-dinner films about the war and lectures about the latest subjects to pique Wilhelm's fancy. In early October, it is the history and folklore of Transylvania. Later in the year, the Kaiser is off again: this time to Macedonia and Constantinople.

HELSINKI, FINLAND: Vladimir writes to Nadya asking her to come and visit. His letter is, as usual, written in invisible ink. It is accompanied by a map. Nadya accidentally singes a corner of it while reading the letter by a gas lamp.

Shortly afterwards, she smuggles herself across the border and walks several miles through a forest to a Finnish railway station. In Helsinki, she struggles to find her husband's street with only the half-burned map as a guide. It is late by the time she arrives. Two weeks later, she makes the same trip again. The talk on the train to Finland is all political, Nadya reports to Vladimir when she reaches his hiding place. Soldiers openly boast of their willingness to rebel. At first he is delighted – and then alarmed at the news. This is it. The insurrectionary moment has arrived, quite suddenly. There is no more time to lose.

Only days ago, Vladimir was flirting with ideas of compromise with other socialist parties. Now, he has swung around entirely. The time for such tactical flexibility has passed. The Mensheviks and Socialist Revolutionaries cannot be trusted to break their links with the bourgeoisie. Kerensky will do anything to cling on to power. In the summer, Lenin considered insurrection premature. Now he thinks it urgent.

From his Finnish exile, Lenin writes a sharp letter to party leaders in both Petrograd and Moscow (he is not fussy about which group acts first): 'The Bolsheviks, having obtained a majority in the Soviets of Workers' and Soldiers' Deputies of both capitals, can and must take state power into their own hands', he insists. They are left with no choice as to the means to use: 'the present task must be an armed uprising'. There is no time to lose. What if there is a separate peace between Britain and Germany? he wonders. (This is a little fanciful.) What if the Kaiser's troops march into Petrograd? (This is a more likely.) 'History will not forgive us if we do not assume power now', Lenin declares. 'We shall win *absolutely and unquestionably*.'

In Petrograd, there is incredulity amongst Bolshevik leaders. Has Lenin lost his mind? Just at that moment, the Bolsheviks are trying out the previously agreed policy of limited compromise, attending a new conference bringing together all parties on the left, from the Bolsheviks to the Mensheviks and Socialist Revolutionaries. What if Lenin's latest missive fell into the wrong hands? The letter is burned.

TOBOLSK, SIBERIA: Three hundred and thirty-seven soldiers guard Nicholas Romanov and his family. They attract the curiosity of the townsfolk, who occasionally peep through the fence at them up on the balcony of the governor's house.

Nicholas does not ask for much: walks out of town (refused), a saw for cutting wood (accepted) and trips to the local church (allowed). He receives English and French newspapers as well as the Russian ones. A steady stream of hate mail is burned. The revolutionary commissar in charge tells the children stories about his travels in the far east of Siberia. He is surprised how little educated they are.

PETROGRAD: A boisterous, playful Harvard man, full of strong opinions about the world and how to make it better, a man who has seen and written about war in Europe and revolution in Mexico, arrives in Petrograd stoked with radical enthusiasm. He carries a notebook carefully inscribed with his name, address and profession in his best newly learned Cyrillic script – джон ридъ, 23 троитская, петроград, американски журналист.

John Reed – everyone calls him Jack – soaks up all he can of the revolutionary atmosphere in Petrograd that autumn. He jots down his observations ('Russians trust any foreigner – could kill Kerensky easily') and phrases he overhears in the street ('as long as capitalism in Europe, can have no socialism in Russia'). Conditions of life are poor. 'The bread is black and soggy', he writes to a friend back in America. There is no sugar. Milk is watery and arrives every ten days or so. He observes people queueing with fake babies in their arms to secure food.

But these details matter less than the intensity of life in Petrograd, the sense of possibility and the openness of the future. 'There is so much dramatic to write that I don't know where to begin', he gushes, 'for color and terror and grandeur this makes Mexico look pale'. Jack and his journalist wife Louise Bryant are having the adventure of their lives.

The American embassy keep an eye on Reed. A few weeks after his arrival he is reported speaking at a rally at the Cirque Moderne attended by some six thousand in which he denounces the supposedly free republic of the United States for its treatment of radicals at home. A protest resolution is passed, and a greeting sent across the ocean to those fighting for social revolution in North America. Reed is turning from reporter into participant.

In a private conversation with an embassy agent, Reed gives his assessment of the various factions in Petrograd politics. Apart from the liberals who want parliamentary order to be restored, he says, 'the Bolsheviks are the only party with a program'.

ROSENBERG FORTRESS, KRONACH, BAVARIA: In the middle of a storm, on an almost moonless night, five dark figures huddle at the bottom of the inner rampart of Rosenberg Fortress in northern Bavaria, now a prisoner-of-war camp. French soldiers are disguised as German civilians. This is the night of their escape. They check they have everything they need to get across a six-metre rampart, over another, and then down a rocky escarpment and into the forest below: a disassembled ladder made from bits of wood acquired from their jailers on the pretext of building a cupboard, a thirty-metre rope fashioned from strips of bedsheet and some crude skeleton keys.

One escapee has to be left behind on a ledge halfway down the escarpment when it turns out the rope is not long enough. The four remaining fugitives enter the forest at the edge of the castle grounds and start walking in the direction of Switzerland. Day after day, night after night, they continue along their way. Living off the land, forced to sleep rough during the day and travel by night, and with the weather turning cold, exhaustion is inevitable. On the tenth day after their escape from Rosenberg, the Frenchmen decide to give themselves a treat, and take refuge in a pigeon loft, not far from a German village.

They are out of luck. Some locals overhear them. They surround the pigeon loft at dusk, along with a nervous German soldier carrying an old rifle. While being led off, two of the four Frenchmen make a dash for it and manage to get away. The other two are returned to Rosenberg. One of them is Charles de Gaulle of the 33rd Infantry Regiment of the French army, taken prisoner during the battle of Verdun in 1916.

LONDON: Since the summer there has been a new dynamo at the heart of the British government, throwing off electricity and light, and sometimes a little heat as well.

Winston Churchill, now the Secretary of State for Munitions, is interested in everything this autumn. And war supply, it turns out, really *does* touch on everything at once. 'This is a steel war', he tells businessmen in the metal trade in September. The next day he is looking into the problem of spare parts for motor transport. Later in the month it is

poison gas. In early October: 'I have been giving a good deal of attention
to the Tanks lately' – without forgetting the essential importance of
ensuring that munitions factories have better air-raid shelters, or the
need for more shells from American factories. In the middle of the month
Winston is asking about the supply of chemicals and trying to find a way
to pay some crucial workers more without setting off a general increase
in wages which the country cannot afford. He demands experimental
work to neutralise the threat from German Zeppelin bombers which can
now fly at six thousand metres above sea level, far above the reach of
Britain's air defences.

One day Winston receives a letter from a friend in the army in Flanders
about the wars of the future. 'I am sure that *bombing from the air* – now
really only in its infancy – is going to make it impossible for the weaker
side in the air to fight', the correspondent writes. Churchill replies with a
missive on 'bombing machines' two weeks later (he had hoped to respond
in person on a visit to the Continent): 'I can assure you I shall do everything in my power to emphasize this development'.

VYBORG, FINLAND: What is taking them so long? Insurrection! Now! Is it
so hard to understand? He writes another letter to the Bolshevik leadership.
'Procrastination is becoming positively criminal', he tells them. It does not
matter where the revolution starts. In Moscow, even: 'victory is certain,
and the chances are ten to one that it will be a bloodless victory'.

Lenin decides he can wait no longer. He returns to Petrograd in secret
dressed as a Finnish priest. He meets the rest of the Bolshevik leadership
in a private flat – the owner's wife has a party connection. For an hour,
Vladimir harangues his comrades. He has become convinced that the
moment of revolution has arrived. Wait any longer and peace might cut
the momentum from the Bolsheviks, and the workers might lose their
appetite.

Eventually, the impatient revolutionary prevails. A vote is taken: 10–2
in favour of insurrection. Technical planning will now begin. The question
of precise timing is left open for the moment. The sooner the better,
Vladimir asserts. Trotsky has other plans. A national congress of Soviets
is planned in two weeks. Perfect cover. Lenin is given the job of preparing
the manifesto for the insurrection and what follows from it. He goes
back into hiding in Petrograd. The police are still searching for his whereabouts.

WASHINGTON DC: A New York businesswoman, the well-named Vira Whitehouse, addresses Woodrow: 'We have come to you as the leader of our country's struggle for democracy', she tells him.

This is America, the shining city up on a hill, a beacon to the world. And yet, outside some of the western states, women do not have the vote. She reminds the President of the role that women play every day in the war effort: selling war bonds door to door, stitching uniforms for the Red Cross and working in factories across the land. They are ready, if called, to bring in next year's harvest from the fields. Is it not illogical that while a woman sits in the US House of Representatives (a Republican from Montana), most states deny women the right to select who is sent to Washington?

In the United States, the most recent suffrage battle is under way in the state of New York, America's most populous, where the vote was denied women in a referendum in 1915, but where a new opportunity to win it now presents itself. 'We have come to you to ask you', Vira tells Woodrow, 'to send to the voters of New York State a message so urgent and so clear that they cannot fail as patriotic men to place the women of their State on an equal footing with the women of the Allied Countries'.

The President, not always the firmest friend of America's suffragists, issues a public statement. As two great ideas of political authority – democracy and autocracy – clash across the world at war, America must live up to its founding principles. Two weeks later, New York votes. Women's suffrage wins. It cannot be long now before the rest of the United States follows.

DUBLIN, IRELAND: What is an independent Ireland to be? The founder of Sinn Féin favours an Irish monarchy, along Austro-Hungarian lines – one monarch, two kingdoms. Others prefer a total break, a republic. The question threatens to split Irish nationalism.

At negotiations in a house on the outskirts of Dublin, the hard men, the men with guns who will settle for nothing less than a full-blown republic in honour of the martyrs of 1916, are ready to walk out and catch the last tram home. Michael Collins is one of these: a blustery Easter veteran who knows the inside of an English jail as well as anyone, is steeped in the secret societies of Irish nationalism, and who believes that only force will secure Ireland's freedom. De Valera talks them back inside. The nationalist cause has no hope of victory without an army. But an army without a popular movement has no legitimacy. The two must march forward together, arm in arm: Sinn Féin and the Volunteers.

That evening, de Valera drafts a politician's compromise. 'Sinn Féin aims at securing the international recognition of Ireland as an independent Irish republic', it reads, but 'having achieved that status the Irish people may by referendum freely choose their own form of Government'. Republic first — then let's see. In formulating the compromise to keep Irish nationalism together, Éamon demonstrates his own indispensability: he is the only soldier-politician available who can straddle both the bomb and the ballot box. He is more convinced than ever that leadership is his destiny.

In late October, in the effete surroundings of Dublin's Mansion House where Queen Victoria once visited her loyal subjects, the MP for East Clare and former inmate of His Majesty's Prisons at Dartmoor, Maidstone, Lewes and Pentonville is elected president of Sinn Féin (the party's founder is persuaded to step down over a coffee in Grafton Street). Two days later, in the rather more basic surroundings of the Gaelic Athletic Association — hay bales and bare wooden planks — the same man is made leader of the Irish Volunteers (with Michael Collins looking on). Thus Éamon unites two thirds of the nationalist Holy Trinity in himself. The last third of course is God. His loyalty is assumed.

PETROGRAD: The treasures of the Hermitage are packed up and sent out on barges. There are rumours that the government plan to quit the capital. One day news reaches town that German soldiers have landed on the islands off Estonia's coast. The Petrograd Soviet sets up a Military Revolutionary Committee to organise the popular defence of the city. Packed with Bolsheviks, many suspect it is planning a coup.

Everyone is talking about it. 'The moment has finally arrived when the revolutionary slogan *All power to the Soviets!* must finally be realised', one newspaper writes that October. 'The Bolsheviks are getting ready for action — that is a fact', says another two days later. The Smolny Institute is full of cigarette smoke and muttering. 'It is the inevitable *lutte finale*', Leon Trotsky explains languidly to John Reed.

The principled non-tipper is the public face of Bolshevism in these weeks. He is rarely at home, sleeping on a sofa at the Smolny and spending his days racing around Petrograd talking to the garrisons and to mass meetings at the Cirque Moderne. Trotsky explains the benefits of a Soviet regime in plain and simple terms. 'The Soviet government will give everything the country contains to the poor and to the men in the trenches', he promises.

All goods will be redistributed: 'You, bourgeois, you have got two fur caps!
– give one of them to the soldier who's freezing in the trenches. Have you
got warm boots? Stay at home. The worker needs your boots.'

Internal Bolshevik arguments about whether they should issue the call
for insurrection spill into the open. A senior Bolshevik, Lev Kamenev, writes
an article warning that an uprising in the next days would be 'a fatal step'.
Leon is forced into a denial, claiming: 'we have still not set a date for the
attack'. Lenin responds to those who publicly discuss the imminence of
insurrection with the worst insult he can muster: 'strike-breaker'.

Stalin attacks the 'general croaking' amongst intellectuals who used to
speak about revolution so warmly over the table but now are suddenly
afraid. Soon, he says, such 'celebrities' will be consigned to the 'museum
of antiquities'.

ROSENBERG FORTRESS: De Gaulle attempts escape from Rosenberg for the
second time in two weeks. This time he is only out of German captivity
for a few hours. The local police pick him up when he tries to board the
5 a.m. train from Lichtenfels to Aachen, on the German–Dutch border,
planning to make good his escape via the Netherlands. De Gaulle tells the
police exactly what he thinks of them when they arrest him – a lapse in
manners which will come back to haunt him later.

KARFREIT, THE AUSTRO-HUNGARIAN EMPIRE – MILAN: At the northern end
of the Western Front, the British, Canadians and Australians launch attacks
against the Germans. Advances are measured by who controls which farm
outhouse, who dominates which hill, who holds such-and-such a ridge. The
Canadians eventually capture Passchendaele, at the loss of several thousand
casualties. There is no knockout blow.

The real action, it turns out, is far to the south-east, around the village
of Karfreit – the Italians call it Caporetto – on the Isonzo river, where the
Austrians launch a major attack backed by battle-hardened German divisions. From the beginning, almost everything goes their way. Fog and rain
hide their artillery from the Italians. Forward units storm through the valleys
of Plezzo and Tolmino, west of the Isonzo, bypassing Italian defensive positions on the hills above.

Within a few days, German and Austrian troops are advancing towards
Venice. Italian generals blame dissent behind the lines for the military
collapse. Nearly three hundred thousand soldiers are taken prisoner and

the same number of civilians flee their homes. British and French forces are rushed to the Italian front line, their planes restoring control of the skies. Austrian and German forces continue to advance until their supply lines are too extended for them to carry on. The Italians secure a new defensive line on the Piave, dangerously close to Venice.

Caporetto becomes a symbol of everything that is wrong with Italy: the weakness of the state, the haughty attitude of the generals, the lack of national cohesion. Nationalists like Mussolini or D'Annunzio blame the corrupting influence of internationalism. They rage against the peaceniks who want to sell Italy short just at the moment when the country is on the point of becoming southern Europe's great power. The disaster of Caporetto does not kill Italian nationalism – it provides it with martyrs to honour, and new domestic enemies to defeat.

Benito Mussolini is in no doubt what is needed: Italy must dedicate itself once more to war. Cafés, concert halls and theatres should be shut. Order must be re-established. The Socialists, Mussolini's old comrades until they took the path of pacifism, must be locked up. Radical social change should be introduced to give soldiers something to fight for: land reform for the peasants and better conditions for the workers. But this is socialism *for* the nation, to strengthen its living force, not socialism *against* it. After Caporetto, it is clearer than ever to Mussolini that Italy must defeat two enemies to win this war: the Austrians at the front, and the pacifist-internationalist tendency behind it. War abroad and war at home are two sides of the same nationalist revolutionary coin. 'It is blood which moves the wheels of history', Benito once told a crowd in 1914. The war must be won for Italy to remake itself.

Perhaps the soldiers should take over, Mussolini writes, those who have felt the heat of war and know the price. True warriors understand commands, leadership, the cruel equality of death. Is it not just that those who sacrifice most for the nation's future should determine its path? Trenchocracy – *trincerocrazia* – will replace democracy. The new division in society, Benito decides, is between 'those who have fought and those who haven't; those who have worked and the parasites'. So then, a soldiers' council – in essence, a nationally minded Soviet – should run Italy.

But better still, how about a single leader, a nationalist socialist vanguard in the living flesh of one man? It would cut out the bickering. Allow things to move faster. The Russian experiment is hardly a model to take in a time of war. Occasionally glancing at his own rather striking visage in the mirror, Mussolini lovingly describes the kind of leader he has in mind: 'A man who has both the delicate touch of an artist and the heavy fist of a warrior. A man who is sensitive and yet strong-willed. A man who knows and loves the people, and who can direct and bend them with violence if required.' A modern leader, Benito explains on the pages of *Il Popolo*, should be an artist, a conjuror, a mind-reader, a man of magnetic appeal, a man who instinctively understands the impulses of human nature explored by Freud and who is able to respond and shape them through his own leadership, turning the docile and idiotic masses into an army of renewal.

Such a leader must be a visionary. He must be virile, yet sensitive. He must be sensual in his exercise of power, yet have no fear of embracing brutality when required. Mussolini looks at himself in the mirror again and runs his eyes over his own strong features: the jutting chin, the Roman nose, the bullet-smooth dome of the forehead, the fierce black eyes and the luscious lips which seem to form themselves naturally into a pout, ready to deride, or order, or even to kiss. They will make marble busts of this head one day, he thinks.

BERLIN: 'In all my life, Davis', Wilhelm tells his American dentist, 'I have never suffered so much pain.' The first panicked telephone call to Davis comes in at three-thirty in the morning. A limousine is sent to pick him up, complete with an outrider carrying a bugle. By the time they get back to the Neues Palais in Potsdam the palace is gearing up for the day ahead. Davis cannot believe his luck: real coffee, real white bread, butter, marmalade and cold meats await him in the antechamber to Wilhelm's apartments. The dentist leaves a single slice of bread by way of politeness. The Kaiser's manservant tells him not to be so foolish. 'Even here', he says, 'we don't get too much of that.'

The Kaiser is placed in a chair looking out over the palace grounds while the dentist gets to work. Wilhelm's rowing machine, with a special attachment for the Kaiser's unusable left hand, stands to one side. 'Look here', he tells Davis, 'I can't fight the whole world, you know, and have a toothache!' It is not long before the American is able to solve the problem. And not long before the Kaiser's braggadocio has returned to its usual gale-force levels. He boasts about Caporetto: 'Italy will never get over this defeat', he brags. '*Now, we've got the Allies*'.

A week or so later Wilhelm visits the Italian front with Charles. The emperors hand out medals. There is a spat between them about the apparent Habsburg lack of generosity towards German soldiers. Wilhelm catches a chill and has to return home early.

PETROGRAD: 'I don't understand them', Lenin cries on receiving another note from the Smolny. 'What are they afraid of?' He throws it on the floor. A hundred loyal soldiers, he says, is all he would need to finish off the provisional government. And the Petrograd Soviet's Military Revolutionary Committee, with Trotsky at the helm, already have the support of the city's garrison.

Still cooped up in an apartment, unable to leave for fear of being arrested on the street, Vladimir waits. He issues impatient notes to his fellow Bolsheviks, urging them to action, action, action where once he recommended caution, caution, caution. Have they lost their nerve? 'We must not wait!' he writes in one missive. 'We may lose everything!' Then he decides he must go to the Smolny himself, where the All-Russian Congress of Soviets is due to open in a day or so. He must herd the Bolsheviks towards insurrection. The congress will be presented with a *fait accompli*. Vladimir throws caution to the wind. He leaves a note for his hostess: 'I have gone where you did not want me to go. Ilyich.' He wears a wig, of course. And a bandage wrapped around his head.

At the Smolny, to his surprise and relief, Lenin finds the uprising already under way. Kerensky has finally been provoked into an ineffective crackdown: the printing presses of two papers, including one edited by Stalin, are smashed up. This gives the Bolsheviks their excuse to act – defensively, of course – to take over key points in the city. In no time, they have seized the railway stations, telephone exchange, an electricity generation plant and the post and telegraph offices. Kerensky's regime is melting away. Lenin insists the Bolsheviks push harder. They must plan their moves for when the congress opens, and proclaim their own government. (It is Trotsky who comes up with the vigorous title of 'People's Commissar' to replace that old-fashioned 'minister': 'smells terribly of revolution', Lenin says enthusiastically.) Everyone is tramping through the Smolny to get a taste of what is going on. The building is lit up day and night. John Reed gives up his ballet tickets to hang out there.

The vice is closing on the provisional government. Kerensky escapes in a car belonging to the American embassy. A Bolshevik proclamation is issued claiming, a little prematurely, that the government itself has been overthrown. 'We must now set about building a proletarian socialist state in Russia', Lenin thunders. 'Long live the world socialist revolution!' The Petrograd Soviet passes a resolution stating its conviction that 'the proletariat of the West European countries will help us to achieve a complete and lasting victory for the cause of socialism'. Can it really be this easy? Vladimir admits he finds it all quite dizzying: '*es schwindelt*', he says in German, circling his hand around his head. Exhausted by all his agitation over the last few weeks, Leon suffers a blackout from lack of food.

That evening, the Smolny is full of tobacco smoke and bayonets of the Red Guards. But not everyone is happy at their *putsch*. The Bolsheviks must explain themselves. Why did they not wait? Why did they not work with others? Trotsky is uncompromising: the Bolsheviks represent historical destiny. 'A rising of the masses of the people', he says, 'needs no justification.' What happened is not a conspiracy, it is a popular insurrection. 'And now we are told: renounce your victory', Trotsky snorts. Those who do not like it can leave. Some factions in the Soviet walk out. This merely increases the Bolshevik majority.

But their power is not completely cemented yet. There is a final act still to play out. The ministers of the government remain holed up in the Winter Palace, anxiously waiting to be arrested or killed. There are few soldiers left willing to defend them: one hundred and forty members of a women's battalion, the boys from the military academy, and a special bicycle unit amongst them. An attack is bound to come. At the British embassy candles and torches are distributed. In the palace, the electricity is cut off. Then the phone lines. Calls for reinforcements are tapped out by a sole loyal telegrapher at the war office. The palace is taken that very night. A deafening blank fired from a frigate signals the start of the assault. A clatter of soldiers across cobblestones. The whistle of gunshots. Later, there are reports of some of the women soldiers being thrown out of windows – or worse. They do not stand a chance.

In the depths of that freezing night, to waves of applause, a new government of commissars is proclaimed at the Smolny, with Lenin at its head and Trotsky made responsible for foreign affairs (after being denied the job of commissar for the press, and refusing responsibility for interior affairs on the basis that anti-Semitic Russians would not like a Jew in that position). Stalin is made responsible for nationality issues. There is cheering: they have done it. A decree on peace is passed demanding an immediate armistice on all fronts, between all belligerents, and announcing the abolition of secret diplomacy. 'We shall send out our appeal everywhere, it will be made known to everybody', Lenin announces, 'it will be impossible to hush up our workers' and peasants' revolution, which has overthrown the government of bankers and landowners'. He calls the war a 'bloody shambles', a 'nightmare of slaughter'. Private land ownership is to be abolished. Theory is to be put into practice.

Ludendorff sends a telegram to his generals on the Eastern Front. 'ACCORDING TO INTERCEPTED RADIO TRANSMISSIONS', he reports, 'A REVO-LUTION HAS BROKEN OUT IN PETROGRAD IN WHICH THE WORKERS' AND SOLDIERS' COUNCIL IS SUPPOSED TO HAVE BEEN VICTORIOUS.' This is 'DESIR-ABLE FROM OUR POINT OF VIEW'. Ludendorff asks that the events in Petrograd be used for propaganda purposes.

Curious visitors inspect the Winter Palace the next day. The British Ambassador observes that while there are thousands of bullet holes in one side of the building, there are only three larger marks where artillery shrapnel has struck. The damage from looting is much worse inside – a French diplomat heads to the Petrograd flea market in the hope that he may be able to pick up some imperial antiques. Michael Romanov, the ex-Tsar's brother, sees the damage for himself when he is escorted back to Petrograd after a failed escape to Finland. He spends a couple of days visiting his old haunts before returning to Gatchina, where he is held under house arrest and spends his time playing the guitar.

In Moscow the fighting around the Kremlin lasts for a week. There are wild rumours of Kerensky gathering a Cossack army to take back Petrograd. Even without such a push from the outside, how long will it be before the Bolshevik insurrection collapses? Informed observers give it a week or two at most.

VIENNA: Freud smokes his last cigar, and immediately suffers the ill effects of its absence. 'Since then I have been grumpy and tired, got heart palpita-tions and an increase in the painful swelling of my gums (carcinoma? etc.)', he writes to a colleague. But Freud is lucky. Help is at hand: 'Then a patient brought me fifty cigars, I lit one, became cheerful, and the gum irritation rapidly abated'.

In between puffs Freud works on a new idea, to prove the role of the unconscious in shaping the process of evolution, giving a psychological basis to evolutionary biology, and making thought the ultimate master of genetics. 'The idea', Freud writes a few days later, 'is to put Lamarck entirely on our ground and to show that his "need", which creates and transforms organs, is nothing but the power of unconscious ideas over one's own body, of which we see remnants in hysteria, in short the "omnipotence of thoughts"'.

Freud's patients talk of nothing but guilt. Sigmund himself begins to wonder out loud whether he will last the war, and worries for his son Martin, involved in the fighting in Italy. In correspondence with Karl Abraham, who still believes in German victory and the triumph of psychoanalysis with it, Freud is pessimistic. 'I do not believe that the events in Russia and Italy will bring us peace', he writes; 'one should admit the U-boat war has not achieved its object. Our future is pretty dim.' Both sides stink.

Freud's latest paper is finally released, about mourning and melancholia. Other unfinished papers lie on his desk, the building blocks of what he has called metapsychology. Somehow, they trouble him. These papers must be 'silenced', Freud writes to a friend. Eventually he decides to burn them, watching the words turn to cold ash.

SIBERIA: The Bolshevik revolution is not instantaneous across the entire country. It spreads by railway and by telegraph wire. It reaches some places in a few hours. In other parts of Russia, the news takes days or even weeks to get through. 'Can it be that Kerensky cannot stop this wilfulness?' Nicholas Romanov asks when the tidings from his old capital finally penetrate the Siberian isolation of Tobolsk.

It is several days before news gets another thousand miles east to Tomsk, where the Hungarian socialist Béla Kun is busy in the local library learning Russian and writing pieces for the local newspaper, the *Siberian Worker*. The next revolution, he declares, will take place in Germany.

BRESLAU, SILESIA, GERMANY: Rosa writes her usual letters to her friends. She tells them about a fuchsia plant which blossomed for a second time in October. She fulminates against the spineless German Social Democrats. How pathetic they have been to not take advantage of the sailors' mutiny in Wilhelmshaven over the summer! How weak in their response to the government crackdown which followed! Is the Russian proletariat to be left to 'bleed to death', she asks?

But she believes in the inevitability of history. 'Lenin and his people will not of course be able to win out against the insuperable tangle of chaos', she writes, 'but their attempt, by itself, stands as a deed of world-historical significance.' What Lenin has started on the fringes of the capitalist system – in backward Russia – will inevitably spread to Britain, France and Germany, the only places where the struggle for world revolution can finally be won. 'In a few years, everything, all around, will have to change', she explains; 'the more the general bankruptcy takes on gigantic dimensions and steadily persists, the more it will become obvious in an elementary way that appropriate measures must be taken against it.'

History is taking its course, she tells herself. It must be observed, with 'the calmness of a research scientist'.

BERLIN: Albert Einstein writes to a friend. 'Would it not be good for the world if degenerate Europe were to wreck itself totally?' he asks. 'All of our exalted technological progress, civilisation for that matter, is comparable to an axe in the hand of a pathological criminal.' The Chinese, he says, would do a better job.

He survives on food parcels sent from Switzerland (to which he is entitled as a Swiss citizen). On Thursdays, he lectures on statistical mechanics and the latest theories from the world of physics. Amongst the tiny group of European intellectuals familiar with reports of his work, Einstein is either the budding prophet of a new philosophical order or a dangerous charlatan, another harbinger of the universal derangement of society. To most of the world, he is an unknown quantity. His name means nothing.

PETROGRAD: Lenin and his closest allies work day and night at the Smolny to secure control of what remains of the Russian state. It is an uphill struggle. They have never really run anything before. Most are writers and professional revolutionaries, with backgrounds in Marxist theory and Siberian exile. The ministries are resistant to such freelancing outsiders.

One day, the old state will be smashed, of course. But first, it must be mastered. The secretive habits of revolutionaries in exile are not designed for smooth and efficient government. They have no cash. Lenin wires to Stockholm: 'Urgently find and send here three highly skilled accountants to work on reform of the banks. Knowledge of Russian is not essential. Fix their remuneration yourself in accordance with local conditions.'

The Smolny is a tip. Trotsky's wife notes Lenin's dirty collar and reminds his sister to get him a new one. Everyone eats and sleeps irregularly. A cleaner catches a furtive figure helping himself to bread and herring in the Smolny canteen late one night. 'I felt very hungry, you know', Vladimir says sheepishly when challenged. The impatient revolutionary's first official automobile is stolen from outside the Smolny's front gate by members of the fire brigade hoping to sell it across the border in Finland. Are the Bolsheviks in power or are they merely squatting?

In such a hothouse atmosphere, relationships are forged and broken in an instant. One day, Leon Trotsky and Joseph Stalin arrive at the same time to a meeting of Lenin's cabinet – the Sovnarkom – to hear the sound of a lusty twenty-nine-year-old sailor seducing the beautiful forty-six-year-old Alexandra Kollontai (an old associate of Lenin, and leading expert on the relationship of sex and love to socialism). Hearing the muffled sounds of amorous embrace, Joseph nudges Leon: 'That's Kollontai! That's Kollontai!' Trotsky is not amused by such backwater crudeness. 'That's their affair', he snaps back unsmilingly. Mutual prejudices are re-enforced. Trotsky is a cosmopolitan intellectual, who speaks several languages effortlessly and is conversant in all the latest literary debates. Stalin speaks even Russian with a Georgian accent. His mother, embarrassingly enough, does not speak the language at all. The Georgian bank-robber overcompensates with a dose of Russian chauvinism as a result.

A flurry of proclamations declare an eight-hour work day, the right of workers to oversee the management of their workshops and factories, the nationalisation of the banks, the removal of religious privilege, the equal-isation of pay for intellectual workers and labourers. Whether any of these will become reality is quite unclear. Petrograd is a revolutionary island; Russia is another country. Workers are one thing; peasants quite different. Vladimir and Leon work as one, with offices at either end of a long corridor in the Smolny. A young sailor runs with messages between them. Sometimes they use the telephone. They correct each other's texts. Several times a day Leon strides up the corridor to see Vladimir personally. Lenin jokingly suggests he get a bicycle for the journey.

Leon does not take his work as commissar for foreign affairs entirely seriously. 'What diplomatic work are we apt to have?' he asks one comrade. 'I will issue a few revolutionary proclamations to the peoples of the world, and then shut up shop.' Worldwide revolution will do the job for him. John Reed joins the Bureau of International Revolutionary Propaganda to help the process. A more junior official is sent to the German-held citadel of Brest-Litovsk to negotiate an armistice with the representatives of Germany and her allies. Leon prefers to stay in Petrograd, where he can exercise a more freewheeling influence on events. He sends out radio messages exhorting the world to revolution, to counter the critical ones that are being broadcast from the Eiffel Tower in Paris.

There is a distinct turn to dictatorial methods even in these first weeks. The ends justify the means. 'As soon as the new order becomes consolidated, all administrative pressure on the press will be terminated', it is promised. In the meantime, opposition newspapers are deemed counter-revolutionary. The expansive theory of all power to the Soviets is honoured in principle.

But the practical reality is that decision-making authority lies increasingly in small committees – or, to be precise, in an exclusively Bolshevik cabal at the very top. The line between state and party is blurred. Theory and practice collide.

Lenin answers his critics with platitudes. 'Socialism cannot be decreed from above', he says comfortingly; 'living, creative socialism is the product of the masses themselves.' And yet formalities cannot be observed right now: any delay would be a disaster. He wonders whether calling the Constituent Assembly – long promised by everyone including the Bolsheviks as the sovereign body to choose a government for the Russian people – is such a good idea at this particular juncture. Alarmingly, elections show the Socialist Revolutionaries are far more popular across the country than the Bolsheviks.

Vladimir appoints a thin and gloomy Pole with shifty grey eyes and an intellectual's beard to run a new security outfit to fight against the spies and saboteurs he imagines everywhere. He calls it the All-Russian Extraordinary Commission for Combating Counter-Revolution, Profiteering and Corruption – or Cheka, for short. 'The bourgeoisie are prepared to commit the most heinous crimes; they are bribing the outcast and degraded elements of society and plying them with drink to use them in riots'. Such things must be stopped.

The impatient revolutionary applies his personal experience in other matters of essential importance. Library policy, for example. 'The following changes, based on principles long practised in the free countries of the West, especially Switzerland and the United States, must be made immediately and unconditionally', Lenin writes: networks to exchange books must be introduced (particularly with Finland and Sweden); forwarding books between libraries must be made free; libraries should be open from eight in the morning to eleven at night. In other words, like Zurich – but better.

KANSAS CITY, MISSOURI: Riding around in squad cars, chasing ambulances, getting 'the latest dope', describing almost anything as 'jazzy', chatting man-to-man with hard-bitten police officers who have seen it all – this is the life!

Within a few weeks of starting as a cub reporter with the *Kansas City Star* – a job acquired with Uncle Tyler's help, the *Chicago Tribune* firmly forgotten – Ernest, barely eighteen years of age, has reported on a conference of black religious leaders, talked his way into the trust of an American army captain to enquire about confidential troop movements, made friends with a guy called Ted fresh back from France, and become the mascot of the local police. 'All cops love me like a brotherhood', Ernest writes excitedly to his sister Marcelline.

And he has other news a few days later. 'I intend to enlist in the Canadian Army soon', Ernest scribbles to his sister in early November, in strictest confidence: 'Honest kid I cant stay out much longer'. It takes just three months, he explains, from signing up to arriving in France. He has already discussed the whole thing with his friends at the Canadian recruitment office. They are, Ernest writes, 'the best fighters in the world, and our troops are not to be spoken of in the same breath'. He feels his place is with them. 'I may wait until the summer is over', he explains, 'but believe me I will go not because of any love of gold braid glory etc. but because I couldn't face anybody after the war and not have been in it.'

A week later Ernest Hemingway signs up with the Missouri National Guard and uses a large portion of his reporter's salary to buy himself a second-hand khaki uniform and an overcoat for training in the woods outside the city ('we marched and skirmished and had bayonet charges and sent out spies and all'). 'We will get our winter uniforms soon', Ernest reassures his parents, 'and then I will get snapped and send to you'.

One night in December, Ernest spots an unusual sight at Kansas City railway station: three train-cars full of black American soldiers sentenced to life imprisonment for their part in the Houston riots that summer.

JERUSALEM, THE OTTOMAN EMPIRE: After several weeks of fighting nearby, in mid-December the British receive the surrender of the Holy City, ending centuries of Ottoman rule. Where the Kaiser rode in on horseback on a state visit nearly twenty years before, the British General Allenby now enters Jerusalem on foot. The event is filmed. Allenby makes a short proclamation. It is then read out to the population of the city in the languages spoken there: Arabic, Hebrew, French, Italian, Greek and Russian.

'A Christmas present to the British people', they call it in London, particularly welcome after the bloody grind of news from Flanders and the narrowly averted disaster at Caporetto. 'Jews Here Jubilant', runs the headline in the New York Times. It is only a few weeks since the British declared their support, in principle, for a Jewish homeland in Palestine. Now they run the place.

On a cold Sunday in Vienna, Freud is in a rotten mood – angry at Germany for the war (he warns he may never go there again), angry at himself for a bad bout of writer's block, frustrated that the latest edition of his psychoanalytic journal cannot be circulated for lack of wrapping paper, and pessimistic about the future. 'The only thing that gives me any pleasure', he writes, 'is the capture of Jerusalem, and the British experiment with the chosen people.'

In Istanbul, there is horror. Mecca, Medina and Baghdad have already fallen. Now Jerusalem. How long can the Ottoman Empire and its Sultan – who doubles as Islam's Caliph – survive this shame? The triumvirate of pashas who run the empire – Grand Vizier Talaat, Navy Minister Djemal and War Minister Enver – are downcast. They entered this war on the German side – even to the point of accepting German army commanders – in order to reunite the Turkic peoples of the world (Enver's particular dream), and to save the empire. They might end up ruining it. Djemal is reported to be in tears.

A fourth man, a general named Mustafa Kemal – the man who defeated Winston's grand plans at Gallipoli and is now a Turkish national hero – is plunged into despair. He paces up and down in his suite at the Pera Palace hotel in Istanbul, where he is taking a period of leave after a bruising run-in with his German superior officer (personally he has always preferred the French). There are reports that Kemal went to see Enver after the Jerusalem debacle to remonstrate against the management of the war and that things got so heated that both men drew their guns.

To calm him down, War Minister Enver offers Kemal a place on a diplomatic trip to Europe, accompanying the Sultan's younger brother and heir apparent, Crown Prince Vahdettin, on a trip to visit the German Kaiser. Kemal's initial impression of the fifty-six-year-old Ottoman Prince is unpromising: he seems a nice enough man, but a little unsure what day it is and perhaps in some kind of trance. The first stage of the trip to Europe continues in that vein. A communications cock-up in Istanbul means that when the imperial delegation arrive in Vienna there is no one there to greet them, and the party are forced to sleep on board their stationary train.

Things get better in Bad Kreuznach, where Wilhelm welcomes Mustafa Kemal as the hero of Gallipoli and his visit is reported in the German papers. He goes to see Strassburg, where he is embarrassed to be asked whether the gruesome stories of the mass deportation and starvation of the empire's Armenian population – allegedly ordered from the top – are true. He breaks away from the imperial party to explore a little bit of the front line by himself, climbing a tree to get a better view. He concludes the Germans cannot be relied upon to win the war.

BREST-LITOVSK: The Germans and Austrians anticipate peace negotiations with the Russians along traditional lines, cementing their military triumph in the east on terms of their choosing. The Bolsheviks see the negotiations rather differently: as an opportunity to propagandise for wider revolution around the world, as a short and painless interlude before their own ultimate victory. Berlin and Vienna must be made to understand: the future is theirs.

An awkward dinner party is held in December, hosted by Prince Leopold of Bavaria. 'I hope we may be able to raise revolution in your country as well', a Russian delegate looking for an ice-breaker tells the Austrian Foreign Minister. A Russian peasant picked up off the streets of Petrograd at the last minute to ensure the peace delegation represents the full spectrum of Russian society enquires of the wine, 'Which is the stronger? Red or white? – it makes no difference to me which I drink, I'm only interested in the strength'.

Over lunch one day a German general casually informs the Russians that German acceptance of the peace-without-annexations formula does not imply German withdrawal to the borders of 1914 given the vast areas in the east which have already declared independence from Russian control. Whatever visions of worldwide revolution may dance before the eyes of the Bolsheviks, the Germans expect to impose *their* conception of peace in the east in the meantime. And quickly.

INGOLSTADT, BAVARIA: As the end of the year approaches, a French prisoner in German captivity laments his powerlessness. Escape is impossible. The snow is too deep. 'My heartache will only end with my life', Charles de Gaulle writes in a letter home to his mother. 'It is the cruellest fate one could imagine', he tells her, 'to be so totally and irredeemably useless in such times as these.'

BRESLAU: A few hundred miles away, another prisoner, Rosa Luxemburg, lies awake one night. She listens out for the rumbling of a train passing somewhere in the night, the distant whispering of the prison guards, and the crunch of their boots on the gravel as they walk under her window.

She recalls the recent arrival of a wagonload of bloodstained German army coats and shirts at the jail, sent there to be patched up and returned to the army for further use. Such wagons are not pulled by horses any more. They are too valuable at the front. Instead, water buffalo from Romania are used. Rosa observes these beautiful, strong, bewildered creatures being beaten into service. Their thick skin is broken by the soldiers' cudgels. Their hair becomes matted with blood. Rosa fancies she sees a tear roll down one animal's cheek. Don't the troops have any pity for these poor animals? one of the prison guards asks. 'No one has pity for us humans', the soldier replies.

She waits for the revolution to spread.

WASHINGTON DC: On New Year's Eve, the President is at work. He writes letters. He annotates a statement about America's progress in the war. A million problems bear down upon him: the oil situation in California, the railways, Russia, an amendment to prohibit the sale of alcohol. A journalist writes him a memorandum warning that the war is turning into a 'class war', even in America, setting town against country. Woodrow seems distracted, as if his mind were far away, in the mud and snows of Europe. One evening, he reads aloud a poem by Wordsworth, describing Britain under threat of invasion from Napoleon:

> Another year! Another deadly blow.
> Another mighty Empire overthrown.
> And we are left, or shall be left, alone,
> The last that dare to struggle with the Foe.

How swiftly the world changes sometimes. A week, a month, a year. For a moment, Woodrow Wilson feels quite alone, an enormous weight of responsibility resting on his soul. More than any other political leader, the outcome of this war now depends on the inner workings of Woodrow's spirit and Woodrow's mind. He must ensure the peace is worthy of the sacrifice.

1918

Order = disorder; ego = non-ego; affirmation = negation
Dada Manifesto

*Revolutions do not stand still. The law of all living things drives
them to advance and to outgrow themselves.*
Rosa Luxemburg

WINTER

BREST, FRANCE: After a tense voyage across the Atlantic spent worrying about a U-boat attack – even smoking a cigarette on deck at night is forbidden in case the ship is spotted by a German submarine – on New Year's Day, a contingent of black American soldiers lands in the port of Brest. The regimental band led by Jim Europe strikes up the Marseillaise for the crowd assembled to meet them. At first, the audience do not recognise their own national anthem played New York-style. Then they do, and break into cheering.

STOCKHOLM: Albert Einstein is nominated again for the Nobel Prize in Physics. Six nominations this year. No award yet.

In Berlin, the physicist is bedridden with the effects of a stomach ulcer. His cousin Elsa nurses him back to health on a diet of rice cooked in milk and sugar. Albert wishes he could be married to her, rather than to his wife Mileva in Zurich. He sends Mileva his latest divorce proposal, promising her the proceeds of a Nobel Prize, if he ever wins one. 'Why do you torment me so endlessly?' she writes back. 'I would never have thought it possible that anyone, to whom a woman who had devoted her love and her youth, and to whom she had given the gift of children, could do such painful things as you have done to me.'

KANSAS CITY: A new year, a new plan for getting into the war – or several. Ernest tells his parents of his latest plan to join the Marines, 'unless I can get into aviation when I am 19 and get a commission'. He toys with going to France with the army medical corps. His father Clarence should join up too, he insists in letters home to his parents. 'He could get a captain's commission ... all you have to do is apply for one', he writes encouragingly. 'There are a bunch that are married and fat and a lot older than Pop too'.

In letters to his mother, Ernest reassures her he is still a Christian, despite the temptations of the city. His letters to his sister cover more terrestrial matters: a crush on film star Mae Marsh, trips to the theatre and a new-found ability to distinguish between different kinds of wine 'sans the use of the eyes'. It is his last hurrah before coming face to face with death, Ernest reasons: one way or another he will be in Europe before the year is out.

WASHINGTON DC: At 10.30 on a Saturday morning in January Woodrow and his friend House sit down to remake the world. They pore over maps of Europe. They start to draft the practical essentials of what America expects from the war, and what America wants from the peace. By the end of the day, the two men have them down: fourteen points, bashed out on the President's typewriter.

Sunday is spent tinkering. On Tuesday, after a morning round of golf, the President goes to the Capitol – at short notice, again – and stands before Congress to deliver a speech. 'The moral climax of this the culmin-ating and final war for human liberty has come', he tells them, more like a prophet than ever before.

Belgium is to be restored. France will have Alsace and Lorraine. Insofar as clear lines of nationality can be drawn, Italy's borders will be readjusted in her favour. The peoples of Austria–Hungary and the Ottoman Empire will have opportunities for 'autonomous development', which sounds a lot like independence. Poland will be free – and have access to the sea. An association of independent nations is to be set up to guarantee it all.

The fourteen points ricochet around the world. Woodrow's intention is now plain. Inspired by God – and by the principles of America – he intends to remake the world.

BREST-LITOVSK: In the first days of 1918 it is not obvious the Russians will return to Brest-Litovsk at all. They ask for the conference to be moved to Stockholm where it will be easier to turn proceedings into a megaphone for world revolution. The request is refused.

When the parties do return to the fortress of Brest-Litovsk the mood is different from before. The preliminaries are over. The notion that the conference's remit might be expanded to encompass peace in both east and west has been crushed. A suicide has taken place amongst the delegates. It is bitterly cold. The Austrian Foreign Minister returns in the middle of a blizzard in a train in which the heating system is frozen solid. The top

German military representative, General Hoffmann, arrives from difficult consultations in Berlin where tempers flare between the Kaiser and Ludendorff over how Europe's borderlands should be rearranged. (Wilhelm presents a map showing modest direct annexations of territory to Germany so as to minimise the number of Poles added to Germany's population; not enough territory for Ludendorff.) A new delegation has arrived from the Ukrainian Rada – the national parliament – anxious to use the imprimatur of the conference to confirm their independence from Petrograd. The exact status of their delegation is fudged.

But the greatest change is the arrival of the new head of the Russian delegation, Leon Trotsky, persuaded by Lenin that he is the man to hold up negotiations while revolution is given time to break out across Europe. While passing through the front lines on the way to Brest, the principled non-tipper strikes a defiant pose. 'The Russian revolution will not bow its head before German imperialism', he tells the soldiers. 'It was not for this that Russian peasants, soldiers and workers deposed the Tsar.' He assures them he will sign only an honourable peace. In truth he intends to turn the negotiations into a drawn-out revolutionary tribunal on the imperialists, with a revolutionary war at the end if all else fails.

Trotsky bristles with self-righteousness in Brest-Litovsk. He condemns a proposed preamble to the peace treaty declaring Russia's intention to live in peace and friendship with the German and Austro-Hungarian empires as unnecessarily decorative. It will be revolution which draws the Continent together, he notes, not empty promises of good neighbourliness. He bans the habit of the delegations dining together which developed the previous year. The Soviet delegation to be an example of revolutionary self-reliance.

The principled non-tipper is repulsed by attempts to soften him up with bourgeois charm. On the day he arrives, the German Foreign Minister, Richard von Kühlmann, greets him while he is hanging up his coat and tells him how glad he is to be finally dealing with the master rather than his emissary. Trotsky answers this unfortunate turn of phrase with a show of revolutionary *froideur*, stepping away without a word. When his Austrian counterpart offers to look into the return of the personal library Trotsky left behind in Vienna when he was forced to leave in haste in 1914, Leon is about to express gratitude – until the Austrian links it to the question of some prisoners in Russia (officers, of course) who are said to have been badly treated. Leon tells the Austrian flatly he would be happy to have the books back and he personally abhors ill-treatment of prisoners, but that the two issues are quite unconnected. He will not be bribed.

The new Russian chief negotiator makes hay from the German and Austrian rejection of the Russian proposal to move the conference to more neutral ground. To be incarcerated, in effect, at 'the fortress of Brest-Litovsk, at the Headquarters of the enemy armies, under the control of the German authorities, creates all the disadvantages of an artificial isolation which is in no way compensated for by the enjoyment of a direct telegraph wire'. Nonetheless, Trotsky declares, Russia accepts the 'ultimatum' because it wishes to provide no technical excuse to the other side to restart the war. Between negotiating sessions, Trotsky dictates a history of the Russian revolution that is barely three months old.

Alone amongst the delegates on the other side of the table, Leon does eventually develop a grudging intellectual respect for German Foreign Minister von Kühlmann. Here at least is a man with whom he can have a proper argument about matters of principle, wasting a little more time in the process. The two spend days in non-stop debate about the precise meaning of self-determination and the extent of its application to parts of the former Russian Empire now under German occupation which the Bolsheviks would like them to vacate. The German minister notes that the Bolsheviks have declared themselves in favour of self-determination, 'even going so far as complete separation' for territories of the former Russian Empire. They have formally allowed the independence of Finland. The situation in Ukraine is more complex but, in principle, independence has been promised there as well should a legitimate authority demand it. (In practice, the Bolsheviks intend that this could only happen under a Soviet regime – not a Ukrainian nationalist one – which would in any case be joined to Bolshevik Russia at the hip.)

Kühlmann argues that the areas of the Baltic now under German occupation are no different. Through various locally based institutions, they have declared their desire for separation. They have already *self-determined*. Germany is no longer a conqueror in these lands, but a protector. German soldiers cannot be asked to leave. Trotsky questions the validity of the bodies which voted for separation. They are the product of feudalism, he declares; only true workers' Soviets can express real self-determination. At times the debates become quite philosophical. This suits Trotsky fine. 'I am taking part with much interest in the debates on these questions, which, thanks to the kindly forethought of the President of the German Delegation, are reaching such ever-increasing proportions', he says at one point.

As time goes on, the onlookers to this game of diplomatic cat and mouse become more frustrated. General Hoffmann is infuriated when the

Bolshevik delegation, active proponents of revolution throughout Europe, have the gall to insist that the Germans and Austrians must agree to refrain from any interference in the former territories of the Russian Empire and forgo any annexations whatsoever. Only once German and Austrian occupation forces have left can the future status of these lands be determined, they contend. 'I must first protest against the tone of these proposals', Hoffmann says. He reminds the Soviets that 'the victorious German army stands in your territory'.

The Austrian Foreign Minister winces at such Prussian aggressiveness. Vienna urgently needs grain from Ukraine. If these roundabout negotiations go on much longer, Vienna will be forced to consider the possibility of a separate peace with the Rada Ukrainians – though any recognition of Ukrainian independence implied by such an agreement is bound to raise problems with the empire's existing Polish and Ukrainian populations, which have their own aspirations and claims to territory.

After blustering and blathering for days on end, Trotsky manages to secure a ten-day break for consultations with Petrograd.

VIENNA: Cold is everywhere in the Habsburg capital these days. The walls seem to exhale it. Women stamp their shoes to try to keep warm while queueing up in the hope of getting their hands on the latest supply of vegetables. The flour ration falls early in the year, prompting furious strikes (and an expectant headline in *Pravda*: 'On the Eve of the Austrian Revolution'). There is no meat. Thought becomes slow, movement painful. Freud's hand shakes over a letter to a friend. 'Cold shivers', he heads the letter, by way of explanation for his writing. An old superstition haunts him: that he will die in his sixty-first year, or in February 1918.

BERLIN: The Kaiser is in one of his exultant moods. The turnaround in the south and in the east, he writes in the margins of an article he is reading, is just a taste of things to come. 'The same must now be done in the west!' scribbles the imperial hand. 'First victory in the west with the collapse of the Entente, then we will impose our terms which they will simply have to accept!'

Outside the imperial cocoon, a dog goes missing in Berlin. The next day the owner finds the dog's skin, quite cleaned of any flesh, with a crude sign attached: 'Died for the Fatherland'.

PETROGRAD: What good is Russia to the European proletariat if the revolution does not survive where it has started?

The Bolsheviks face challenges from all sides. There is more violence on the streets this winter and less food. Factories are closed. Street lamps are barely lit. Lenin is angry at striking workers. How self-indulgent of them, he thinks, wondering how they can be forced back to work. One evening, Vladimir makes a rousing speech to Red Guards about to head off to fight a Cossack rebellion which has flared up in the south, led by General Kornilov. He calls them the 'first heroic volunteers of the socialist army' and promises, on somewhat slim evidence, that 'our army's ranks will soon be swelled by the proletarian forces of other countries and we shall no longer be alone'. On the way back to the Smolny, his limousine comes under fire. Lenin is unharmed. A Swiss socialist travelling with him is injured. The impatient revolutionary's old rivals the Socialist Revolutionaries are blamed for the attack.

Another challenge to Lenin's power is posed by the imminent meeting of the elected Constituent Assembly. Its creation had been one of the key demands of Russia's revolutionaries in 1917. But that was before the coup. Now that Lenin has power, the assembly – in which Bolsheviks will be a minority – represents a threatening alternative source of legitimacy. The impatient revolutionary is concerned that the meeting of the assembly might be used to launch a counter-coup, which is, after all, what he would have done if the situation were reversed. Loyal security forces are brought in to prevent this. Red Guards are stationed at important junctions. Barricades are put up. It is made clear that disturbances will be dealt with harshly. Martial law is proclaimed. Lenin worries about the loyalty of the city garrison. The day before the assembly is due to meet, an American journalist notes in his diary: 'Eve of a battle or collapse of a bluff, which?'

In early January, the great day arrives. Tens of thousands of pro-assembly demonstrators gather in central Petrograd singing the Marseillaise. Red Guards fire a few volleys in the air to disperse the crowds. The message from Bolshevism's shock troops is clear: they will not shrink from the use of extreme violence, as the Tsar's forces did until it was too late. 'Ex-poachers make the best gamekeepers', a French observer comments in his diary; if there had been a Tsarist Lenin or Trotsky the Romanovs would still be in power. No one is hurt in these first encounters. Later, several marchers who persist in demonstrating in favour of the assembly and against the Bolshevik regime wind up dead. Red blood colours the snow.

At the Tauride Palace, where the Constituent Assembly is due to meet, Red Guards with machine guns and fur hats pace up and down behind a huge wooden barricade. Occasionally they remove a piece and burn it to keep warm, the fire lighting up their faces. In the early afternoon, a side door to the palace opens for the members of the assembly to file in, passing a security cordon to check their credentials. The Socialist Revolutionary delegation, despite being the largest, are given a small room at the back in which to meet before the opening. Here they nervously fine-tune their plans to establish their legitimacy as the true voice of the Russian people through a wave of proposed legislation.

The Bolsheviks, despite being the smaller group in the assembly, are given a grand room at the front of the palace in which to meet. Their deliberations mostly boil down to tactics: how long should this masquerade be allowed to go on? Socialist Revolutionary delegates carry candles in case the Bolsheviks turn out the lights. In accordance with revolutionary tradition, the tea rooms at the Tauride are out of food. Wisely, most delegates come armed with sandwiches. It is dark outside by the time the members of the assembly are fully gathered inside. Lenin looks at them and sees a company of corpses, the walking dead. The red-and-gold chamber is decorated in funereal black.

Foreign observers take up position in the gallery. 'It's going to be a real Wild West show', the Mayor of Stockholm whispers in John Reed's ear. 'Everyone seems to be carrying a gun.' A moment of excitement comes early when a group of Bolsheviks storms the stage and gets everyone to sing the Internationale. Lenin turns white in anger at this overly precipitate action. Certain formalities must be followed. Appearances are important. He does not want this to just look like another coup.

In a recess while votes are being counted for the election of the chairman of the assembly, Reed is over the moon to be introduced to his idol, who dispenses advice on learning Russian. 'You must go at it systematically', the impatient revolutionary says, 'you must break the backbone of the language at the outset.' One must learn all the nouns, then the verbs, then the adverbs and adjectives, leaving grammar and syntax till last, he explains. Then *practise, practise, practise*. Vladimir jabs a finger towards the ceiling to emphasise this last point.

As expected, Viktor Chernov, a leading Socialist Revolutionary, is elected chairman of the assembly. Several speeches are made which are critical of the Bolshevik regime. 'You promised bread for all the people but can you now say hand on heart that Petrograd is guaranteed against starvation even for the next few weeks?' one speaker asks. On matters of war and peace he wonders: 'Do you really believe the Germans will take account of you in the way they would inevitably have to respect a universally representative and recognised supreme authority, not dependent on an extended civil war for its survival?' Louise Bryant is impressed by the speaker. 'He has that majestic air', she says. John Reed is not pleased at his wife's softness for an anti-Bolshevik. 'And you'll be given the air if you keep that up', he rejoinders.

Enough talk! The Bolsheviks bring matters to a head by demanding a vote on a motion calling for the assembly to rubber-stamp the rule of the Soviets from now on, making itself essentially irrelevant. The motion is voted down. The Bolsheviks storm out of the room, declaring proceedings counter-revolutionary. Meeting his caucus behind closed doors, Lenin is adamant that the assembly cannot be allowed to continue sitting indefinitely. But his strategy is to let it fade out rather than benefit from the martyrdom of any great clash with Bolshevik forces. Now that the delegates have rejected the supremacy of the Soviets they have signed the assembly's death warrant anyway. 'Let them just go home', he says. After some discussion, the party agrees his approach. The Bolsheviks formally withdraw and Lenin goes back to the Smolny.

For the moment, the assembly continues its discussions. Long-winded speeches are made to a half-empty chamber. Two o'clock in the morning passes. Then three. Then four. Eventually the captain of the loyal Bolshevik troops on duty, a reliable Kronstadt man, decides to call time. 'The guards are tired', he announces. 'I suggest you vacate the premises.' The chairman frantically puts everything he has proposed to the vote – land reform, statements on peace, the federalisation of Russia. All these measures are adopted overwhelmingly. At five in the morning the remaining delegates go home. 'Perhaps this is not the end', one delegate says to another hopefully.

The next morning the delegates of the Constituent Assembly are refused access to the Tauride Palace. Russia's democratic experiment is over.

THE WESTERN FRONT: Ludendorff visits the troops, checking on morale, ensuring fresh supplies of munitions are going where they are needed, speaking to the officers in the field. (One day, he attends a field exercise involving the 16th Bavarian Reserve Infantry Regiment; he takes no note of a mangy Austrian field-runner called Adolf Hitler.)

Back at headquarters, Ludendorff puts the finishing touches to plans for the final assault against the British and French. With troops now freed up from operations against Russia, the Germans have a numerical advantage on the Western Front for the first time in years. Ludendorff runs the battle plans through his mind again. Preparations are meticulous.

The tactical scheme is bold. Battle-hardened soldiers, trained in the latest storm-trooper tactics, will smash the enemy's death grip in a series of concentrated hammer blows (particularly against the British, in the hope of breaking their army and putting intolerable strain on relations with the French). Rather than setting final objectives for each assault, a degree of flexibility will be maintained. German troops will be sent wherever they can best exploit a weakening of enemy resolve. In this way, a new war of movement will be unleashed, confusing an enemy grown used to static warfare.

A German Prince asks Ludendorff what will happen if things go wrong. 'Then Germany will have to go under', he responds gruffly.

PETROGRAD: Fighting a revolutionary war of defence against the Germans may sound good – it 'might perhaps answer the human yearning for the beautiful, dramatic and striking', Lenin writes. But in reality, it makes no sense. The army is not ready. The peasants would not support it. 'It would totally disregard the objective balance of class forces and material factors at the present stage of the socialist revolution now under way', he concludes. If the German proletariat start a revolution in the next few months the point can be revisited. In the meantime, concluding peace with Germany and Austria – on their terms – is essential.

At a meeting of the Bolshevik inner cabal, Vladimir tries to persuade Leon and the others of the new position he has come to. They are shocked. How can they give in to imperialist blackmail? It would turn the Bolsheviks into German tools – just as some have always said they are. The whole thing is a 'dirty stable', Vladimir admits. But what is the choice?

Leon comes up with his latest wheeze: to neither wage war, nor sign a peace treaty. Neither war, nor peace. If that does not confuse the monocles at Brest-Litovsk, what will? Vladimir is sceptical. An 'international political demonstration', he calls it mockingly – and a pointless one. The terms the Germans will exact will only get harder over time, he says. The Bolsheviks should sign now for fear of being forced to accept worse later. Vladimir is out-voted. Leon Trotsky's suggestion of neither peace nor war wins the day, as a final measure should there be an ultimatum from the Germans and no other way out. It is agreed he will try and delay getting to that point for as long as possible.

On the home front, Lenin is constantly in and out of meetings to try and keep his shaky regime on track. 'We can't expect to get anywhere unless we resort to terrorism', the impatient revolutionary yells at leaders of Russia's food supply organisation. There can be no mercy. Revolutionary justice means that 'speculators must be shot on the spot'. Compulsory searches should be carried out. The wealthy should have food taken from them.

PARIS – LONDON: Guillaume Apollinaire, still recovering at the Villa Molière, writes a letter to his young admirer André Breton, in anticipation of the latter's imminent visit (a previous visit having been cancelled on account of the Italian War Minister dropping by Apollinaire's hospital room). 'Would you mind bringing me that book of the theories of Freud?' Apollinaire asks.

The same day, in London, a telephone rings in a small flat above an office in Knightsbridge. Jessie Kenney answers. News just in. Royal assent has been granted to the Representation of the People Act. The final stage of Britain's constitutional process has been completed. All men now have the vote in Britain, and eight million women.

TOBOLSK: Nicholas saws up wood, reads philosophy and starts a new thriller: *The Garden of Allah*. Some days, the Tsar sits on the greenhouse roof to warm himself. Inside the house the temperature in the bedrooms is often barely above freezing. Alexandra spends a lot of time thinking about God, suffering and her children's health. She writes postcards to friends signed with an eastern religious symbol she is fond of: a left-facing swastika.

News of the latest Soviet reform reaches the Romanovs one day. The old calendar, used in Orthodox Russia for centuries, and strongly associated with the Church, is to be replaced with that in use in Western Europe. 'In other words', Nicholas writes in his diary on the first day of pre-revolutionary February, 'today already turns out to be 14 February'. Whatever will they think of next? 'There will be no end of misunderstandings and mix-ups', he notes.

BREST-LITOVSK: A patriotic Ukrainian from the Rada delegation engages in a long harangue against Petrograd trying to prevent Ukraine from slipping out of Russian control. 'The noisy declarations of the Bolsheviks regarding the complete freedoms of the peoples of Russia are simply a mean demagogic trick', the young man rages. 'The government of the Bolsheviks, a government whose power rests on the bayonets of hired Red Guards, will never elect to apply in Russia the very just principle of self-determination.' Just look at their methods, he goes on: 'They disperse assemblies, they arrest and shoot politically active personalities'. They have introduced not self-determination but 'anarchy and devastation'.

Sweat trickles down Trotsky's forehead at these accusations of Bolshevik hypocrisy. The Austrian Foreign Minister even feels a twang of sympathy for the principled non-tipper at his obvious discomfort at being upbraided in such terms. But by the end of the Ukrainian's speech Trotsky has suffi-ciently recovered his composure to try to verbally reoccupy the moral high ground. 'I can only thank the President', he says, 'that he, in harmony with the dignity of this assembly, has not opposed in any way the free-speaking of the preceding orator.' The Austrians and the Germans now declare that they recognise the full independence of Ukraine. The old Russian Empire is drifting from Bolshevik control.

Trotsky's attempts to delay and confuse proceedings grow more desperate. He requests a visa for Vienna so as to speak with the Austrian working classes directly. The suggestion is refused. On the question of admitting Polish representatives to the conference, he opens up a new Pandora's box by asking whether the proto-kingdom which Berlin and Vienna have estab-lished to try and keep the Poles on their side – without definite borders and without a sovereign – can be considered a state at all. 'The negotiating powers have not come here to engage in intellectual combat', Kühlmann notes curtly. Trotsky's tricks are wearing thin.

In Berlin, the Austrian and German Foreign Ministers are confronted by Ludendorff over the delays in signing a final peace treaty with Russia. He is incensed that it is taking so long to reach a deal which will allow him to transfer troops west, and even crosser at apparent Habsburg willing-ness to countenance a peace unlikely to give Germany every little scrap of territory she wants. 'If Germany makes peace without profit, then Germany has lost the war', he rants. Back in Brest-Litovsk, and above Trotsky's protest that it is an interference in internal Russian affairs, the Austrians agree peace with the Rada Ukrainians and get the promise of the grain they need. Whether any of this will work remains to be seen. 'I wonder if the Rada is really sitting at Kiev', the Austrian Foreign Minister writes in his diary the day the peace is signed. Their claim to rule is fragile.

Trotsky is down to his final card. He plays it with aplomb. 'The war ceased long ago to be a defensive war', he tells the conference at Brest-Litovsk. 'When Great Britain takes African colonies, Baghdad and Jerusalem, then that is certainly not a defensive war. When Germany occupies Serbia, Belgium, Poland, Lithuania and Romania, that is a struggle for the partition of the globe.' Russia wants no further part in this war, he says. Russia's aim is to build socialism. 'Our peasant soldiers must return to their land to cultivate in peace the field which the revolution has taken from the landlords and given to the peasants.' In anticipation of worldwide revolution, Bolshevik Russia is leaving the war, its forces are returning home but – it is not going to sign a peace. No war, no peace. Trotsky allows no further discussion on the matter. His team get up to leave. '*Unerhört, unerhört!*' General Hoffmann exclaims: 'Unheard-of, unheard-of!' The German minister asks how the Russian delegation can be contacted in future. There is always the wireless radio, Trotsky suggests.

'So, what is going to happen now?' a German major asks his Russian counterpart. 'Do we have to go back to war with you?' The Russian shrugs his shoulders. On the train home, the Bolsheviks are jubilant. Trotsky seems confident the Germans will not start a war again. Lenin is not so sure.

PETROGRAD: Anarchy reigns in the Bolshevik capital. The Italian Ambassador is robbed blind in the middle of the street (they even take his snow boots). A former colonel in the army begs the head waiter at the Hôtel d'Europe to give him a bowl of soup. He used to be a regular customer, he explains. The Patriarch of the Orthodox Church declares all Bolsheviks to be anathematised. 'Hell's fire awaits you in the next life beyond the grave', he warns those who do not repent.

John Reed decides to head back to America. He spends several weeks at a loose end in Norway while American officials debate whether to grant him a passport or not. He begins to write a book about the Russian revolution of October 1917.

HASKELL COUNTY, KANSAS: A windswept, poor, empty kind of place. Far from the war, far from anything. But beautiful in its way, with all that sky to look at. There are few roads in this part of the country. People get around on horseback, mostly. The railway is a recent arrival. It gets cold in the wintertime.

The local doctor is a large, well-educated man who passes his evenings reading the classics in ancient Greek. He also tries to keep up with the scientific literature. His wife, from a wealthy Kansas landowning family, is head of the Red Cross Women's Work Committee. And the doctor is busy this February. Everyone seems to be sick. It almost seems as if God – whom Dr Loring Miner is not particularly fond of anyway – has sent a plague upon the people of Haskell County.

Not just the old, but the young as well, are falling ill. This is influenza, but more virulent than anything he has seen before. It spreads quickly. It kills. 'Most everybody over the county is having la grippe or pneumonia', a local paper reports. At Camp Funston, over near Kansas City, where soldiers are trained up for France, a thousand young men fall sick over the next few weeks.

BREST-LITOVSK: If the Russians want to denounce war *and* peace, fine, the Germans decide. But then the armistice must be considered to be over as well.

'Tomorrow we are going to start hostilities again against the Bolsheviks', General Hoffmann writes in his diary. 'No other way out is possible, otherwise these brutes will wipe out the Ukrainians, the Finns and the Balts, and then quietly get together a new revolutionary army and turn the whole of Europe into a pigsty.' He does not expect much resistance: 'the whole of Russia is no more than a vast heap of maggots – a squalid, swarming mess.'

When Lenin hears of the German plans, he proposes to his comrades that the enemy be given whatever he wants – immediately. Trotsky is against it. Again, Lenin is outnumbered. Only when the Germans actually begin their advance – virtually unopposed – does the penny drop. Stalin is blunt: 'The Germans are attacking, we have no forces, the time has come to say that negotiations must be resumed.'

This time it is the Germans who want to delay proceedings. When a message comes in from Petrograd requesting another armistice, Hoffmann asks for it in writing. He wants German troops in Estonia at least before calling a stop to the advance. 'It is the most comical war I have ever known', he writes in his diary. 'We put a handful of infantrymen with machine guns and one gun on a train and push them off to the next station; they take it, make prisoners of the Bolsheviks, pick up a few more troops and go on.' Petrograd is wide open. Some in the capital are delighted at the prospect of a return to order (even if it wears a German jackboot). 'Everyone is radiant with joy', a Frenchman writes in his diary.

Panicking that his revolution is about to be swept away, Vladimir writes a spiky article in *Pravda* castigating those who would hide behind slogans rather than look reality in the face. 'The slogans are superb, alluring, intoxicating', he writes, 'but there are no grounds for them.' The expectation that the German proletariat will prevent an attack by the enemy has been disproved. He dismisses the argument that, just as in the revolution in October 1917, the struggle itself will produce the means to victory as 'so childishly ridiculous that I should never have believed it possible if I hadn't heard it with my own ears'. He threatens to resign.

VIENNA – BAY OF KOTOR: February is over, and Sigmund Freud is still alive. He sighs. His long-held superstition that he would die in February 1918, in his sixty-first year, can now be buried. Or can it? Perhaps it was only the month that was incorrect. It is another nine weeks before he will escape the age of sixty-one entirely. Freud remains in a state of nervous apprehension waiting for his birthday.

In February, a mutiny breaks out in the Austro-Hungarian navy. For two long days, the red flag flutters over the mutineers' vessels in the Bay of Kotor. The rebels demand not only more cigarettes – such requests Charles Habsburg can understand – but an immediate end to the war and self-determination for all the empire's nationalities (several ringleaders are Czech). Loyal units crush the uprising. A Hungarian naval captain named Horthy is promoted. A news blackout means that the public know nothing of what has happened.

The promise of grain from Ukraine brings some prospect of alleviation in the food situation, but the political price – a peace deal with the Ukrainians – infuriates the empire's Poles who hoped to win territory now accepted by Vienna as Ukrainian. The contradictions of the Habsburg realm are becoming harder and harder to contain.

PETROGRAD: Lenin wins. An extraordinary congress of the party – renamed the Communist Party (Bolsheviks) – ratifies the punishing German peace terms. The Russia of the Bolsheviks is a shadow of its former imperial extent. Trotsky refuses to go to Brest-Litovsk and sign the peace himself, but he accepts that the revolution has no choice.

Another decision is taken which will change the character of the revolution: to move the capital to Moscow. The regime calls it a temporary measure. The vague possibility is raised that perhaps Petrograd will be redesignated a free city, an economic boomtown open to the world; one newspaper suggests it will become a 'second New York'. In the meantime, government offices are stripped. Anything that can be moved is taken away: books, curtains, ashtrays, stoves, mirrors, blankets, furniture.

Foreign embassies are not long behind in planning their departure, burning diplomatic papers and settling accounts. Old retainers are laid off. Foreign diplomatic staff leaving the country altogether in expectation of Bolshevik collapse face tense passport checks at the border. When a French diplomat gets through to Finland he is thrilled at the order and cleanliness which appears to prevail there – despite a bloody civil war between Finnish Reds and Whites – and enjoys the refreshing taste of a glass of fresh milk. One of the last acts of the regime in Petrograd is to send the Tsar's brother Michael into exile to Siberia. He is sent to Perm in a first-class carriage with all the windows missing. A journey that once took two days now takes eight.

When the time comes for the Bolsheviks to leave the cradle of the revolution, they do so in the dead of night and in total secrecy. Crates marked with the Sovnarkom stamp are conspicuously loaded onto a train at the city's main railway station. Meanwhile, the rail convoy that will actually carry the Bolshevik leadership to Moscow is prepared far from public view, in a disused siding south of the city. Vladimir, Nadya and his sister Maria travel in the first train to set out that night, with the electric lights switched off to avoid any unwanted attention. Other trains follow at regular intervals behind. The head of the Cheka travels with a single briefcase. The case files follow separately, leaving some prisoners locked up in Petrograd with no paperwork to indicate what they have been incarcerated for.

In Moscow, there is a scrum for office and living space when the Bolshevik leadership and their officials arrive. Some move into the city's hotels. The National Hotel is renamed the House of the Soviets No. 1. The Cheka find lodgings on the Lubyanka (and later acquire an imposing building around the corner which used to be an insurance company headquarters). Lenin and Trotsky move into the Kremlin, where the clock tower still rings 'God Save the Tsar' and dinner is served on plates adorned with the double-headed eagle of the Romanovs. The only food available is tinned meat and caviar that is no longer exported. On the wall of Trotsky's office hangs an allegorical painting of classical love between Cupid and Psyche.

The Georgian bank-robber is less fortunate in the lodgings he is assigned. Joseph Stalin arrives in Moscow with his new wife Nadya, an innocent girl twenty-two years his junior whom he has known since childhood – Joseph is rumoured to have had an affair with her mother – and who still addresses her husband with the formal *vy* rather than the informal *ty*. The newly-weds are given a noisy apartment in a Kremlin outbuilding to live in while Stalin has to make do with some offices the Cheka did not want to continue his work on the nationalities question.

Lenin promises that things will get better for the Bolsheviks now. Moscow is less vulnerable than Petrograd. But the regime must be adaptable. 'History is moving in zig-zags and by roundabout ways', he writes. The revolution must learn from its enemies. He expresses admiration for the 'scientific American efficiency' of the Taylorist system, and the German genius for 'modern machine industry, and strict accounting and control'.

In spreading revolution, the Bolsheviks must work with what they have to hand. How many million prisoners of war are there still in Russia who can be turned against their homelands? 'Béla Kun', Lenin observes, naming one Hungarian who has recently come to his attention, 'should be a dark spy.' At home, the Bolsheviks must show no mercy. A rumour starts in Moscow that the government has decided to kill anyone younger than seven years old so that no child of these painful years will grow up in ineradicable resentment of the harshness of the regime of the time (whereas adults are expected to understand its necessity). A Muscovite writer asks his doorman whether such a thing could really happen. 'Anything can happen', the man replies. 'Anything is possible.'

German armies continue their advance through Ukraine. First Kiev, then Odessa are occupied. But this is a military sideshow now. With Russia defeated, German troops are now available for transfer to the west.

NANTES, FRANCE: There is a new musical sound in France in the winter of 1918, first heard on the quayside at Brest back in January and now travelling across the country.

It hits Nantes, where Jim Europe's band plays outside the opera house, working its way from French military marches to Southern 'plantation' melodies and finally to the uninhibited syncopation and instrumental experimentation that some call jazz. Elsewhere in France, the band plays railway stations and town squares as it tours the country before winding up in an American army rest-and-recuperation centre in the Alpine spa town of Aix-les-Bains, where French civilians come along to listen. When the band finally receives orders to move out to rejoin their regiment – now renamed the 369th Infantry Regiment, US Army, and allocated to serve behind the front line within a French division – their departure is met with fond farewells from the local population and parting gifts of champagne. Europe reaches Connantre, just behind the front line with Germany, on 20 March 1918.

Around the same time, in Washington, Woodrow Wilson receives a delegation of black leaders with a petition carrying twelve thousand signatures and requesting that the soldiers sentenced for their part in the Houston affair receive a presidential pardon. Under the circumstances, Woodrow seems amenable to such an act of grace.

SPRING

The Western Front: The middle of the night. German soldiers are in high spirits. This is the moment they have been waiting for. The bombardment begins at 4.20 a.m. It is 21 March 1918.

Over the course of the next five hours, a million shells rain down on British positions. There are rumours among German troops that a new type of grenade is being used today, containing a powerful substance previously forbidden by the Kaiser on humanitarian grounds. The soldiers smell bitter almonds, the smell of gas – or is it their minds playing a trick on them? They wait in the trenches for the signal to attack. A soldier whose account of his storm-trooper days will catapult him to fame after the war takes a final swig from a friend's field flask. The alcohol tastes like water. He is so taut from the waiting that it takes him three matches to light a single cigarette. Then, over the top. The officers behind the line watch the action through telescopes. 'It looks like a film', one of them writes in a letter home.

Winston Churchill, ever the man in the right place at the wrong time, over from London on another fact-finding mission, hears the German artillery cannonade for himself. The fire of the guns lights up his sleeping quarters like a magic lantern. He cannot make out the sound of the replying British guns, so overwhelming is the Teutonic fury. In Kansas City, Ernest Hemingway's newspaper office goes mad with phones ringing and fresh bulletins every hour. 'The German push looks awful', he writes back to his family in Oak Park; 'we just got a bulletin that they were shelling Paris'. In Vienna, Freud cannot summon up such a young man's interest. 'Beginning of the German offensive in the West', he notes flatly in his diary, blaming Austria's food supply problems for his sullen mood. 'Perhaps, as I have always been a carnivore', he writes to a friend, 'the unaccustomed diet contributes to my listlessness.'

The Kaiser races up and down the front. A disappointing first day. A better second day. On the third day, a breakthrough. Wilhelm is jubilant.

'The battle is won, the English have been utterly defeated', he shouts to a bewildered guard on the station platform when the imperial train pulls into Avesnes that evening. Champagne is served at dinner. There are loyal toasts and patriotic speeches. (In London, there is discussion of evacuating British forces through the Channel ports, raising the conscription age to fifty-five and sending King George V to the front to raise morale.) The German military issue an official communiqué proclaiming a great victory of German arms, achieved under the Kaiser's personal leadership. Wilhelm is suitably flattered, until he begins to wonder whether it was right to specify his leadership role in this particular battle, as if all the others had nothing to do with him.

While the corks fly around the Kaiser's dinner table, Ludendorff feels the pressure mounting. His youngest stepson, an airman, has gone missing, shot down over Flanders. The attack on the ground is losing momentum. The general decides to double up, taking on the British and French at the same time. It is a mistake which weakens the impulse of attack by spreading it across two foes. Belatedly, Ludendorff decides to refocus his forces and aim straight for Amiens, a crucial railhead for Allied supply. The enemy falls back, but cannot be dislodged.

German soldiers have advanced, but the territory they have conquered is a wasteland: no target of significant strategic value has been captured. The British replenish their ranks with fresh soldiers from England. The French do not abandon their allies, as Ludendorff had hoped. The Americans make their presence felt, taking up the slack in quieter sections of the front, and releasing more experienced troops for service elsewhere. In April, Jim Europe's regiment is given responsibility for defending a section several miles long in the Argonne forest. Within a few weeks Jim is crawling through no man's land with French soldiers – fortified by a bottle of wine – to raid outlying German positions.

Increasingly it is the German army that is breaking apart. Attack after attack has left the men exhausted. There are not enough troops to replace those that have fallen. The bountifulness of the food and drink found in captured British and French supply depots not only holds up the advance as German soldiers gorge themselves on American bacon and French wine – but also gives the lie to German propaganda that the Allies' supply lines are at breaking point.

Winston attends a meeting in Beauvais town hall where the French commander of Allied forces in the west, Marshal Foch, gives a presentation on the weakening German advance. He marks out enemy gains on a large map with coloured pencil. At first, he draws an expansive bulge. 'Oh! Oh! Oh! How big!' he exclaims sarcastically. Now there are only some pathetic protuberances, not worth anything strategically. The consequence is clear. 'Stabilisation', Foch tells his audience, 'sure, certain, soon.'

And then? 'Ah, afterwards!' the field marshal sighs. 'That is my affair.'

ZURICH AND BERLIN: Albert and Mileva exchange letters about their divorce: what the financial terms should be, shares or cash; whether it is best for the process to be completed in Switzerland or in Germany. Albert favours Germany. It is quicker, he explains. And, in any case, were he to admit to adultery with cousin Elsa in Switzerland he would be banned from remarrying for two years, which would defeat the purpose of the exercise. Eventually, the two agree on how to settle things.

VIENNA: The imperial government is in a state of panic. The French have hinted they are in possession of a secret Austrian letter entrusted by Charles to his brother-in-law Sixtus last year, in the hope of using him as an intermediary to start peace negotiations with France. The letter is political dynamite, suggesting Vienna's willingness to help Paris recover Alsace-Lorraine from Germany as part of a general peace. What would the Germans say if they knew? A frantic search is made of Empress Zita's bedroom desk to try and find a draft of the letter that was sent to check the actual wording. It turns out no copy was taken of the original. Do the French actually have the letter or are they bluffing?

Vienna denies its existence, and then is embarrassed when the letter is published. Charles suffers a minor heart attack. Some suggest that the Emperor should stand aside. His Foreign Minister threatens suicide, and then is persuaded to take the fall. The result of the dynastic peace attempt and botched cover-up is to further reduce Vienna's freedom of action. The future of the Habsburg Empire will be decided in Paris, London and Washington or, most frighteningly of all, in Berlin.

A few weeks later Charles travels to German military headquarters – now moved from Kreuznach to Spa, in Belgium – to pay his respects to the Kaiser and sign an agreement on military coordination. In the wake of the embarrassment of the Sixtus affair, the Germans present a draft outlining complete economic and effective political unity between the two empires, to remain in force until 1940. When the Austrians say they need time to think, Wilhelm is incredulous. 'What's wrong about it?' he cries.

'Bavaria has already signed the same convention with us, and is quite happy with it', seemingly forgetting that Bavaria is already part of the German Reich. The direction is clear: *Anschluss* by another name.

MAYNOOTH, CO. KILDARE, IRELAND: There is one great reserve of manpower in the British Isles not yet fully tapped for war. As ministers in London wonder how to replace British losses in France and fight back against the German surge, they look hungrily across the Irish Sea. Why should Ireland shirk the responsibilities that England, Wales and Scotland bear so manfully?

'I have not met one soldier in France who does not think we shall get good fighting material from Ireland', Winston tells his cabinet colleagues in April. Fifty thousand men under the age of twenty-five might be raised in Ireland – maybe more. But there is Irish opposition to the idea. Across the board. And it is fierce. Much of the island is already seething. The carrying of arms has already been outlawed. 'The fit resting place for an Irish bullet is in an English heart', an Irish priest from County Clare declares that spring.

Ireland's bishops are less colourful, but no less firm. Meeting in the gabled glory of the seminary at Maynooth – the former schoolmaster Éamon de Valera feels right at home when he pays a visit to make his case directly to the men in purple – the bishops release a statement entitling Catholics to resist conscription into the British army by all means 'consonant with the laws of God'. An anti-conscription Mass is organised. London's mistake makes Ireland's unity.

A few weeks later, de Valera is arrested while on his way home, one of many Sinn Féin leaders picked up that evening. (Typically, Michael Collins evades the net.) They are accused of plotting with Germany – a well-watered Irishman has recently been picked up in a pub after arriving home on a German submarine. Back to England. Back to jail.

RUSSIA: 'We have taken Kharkov', Hoffmann writes in early April; 'I could never have dreamt a while ago that German troops would enter that little hole.' In the south, German forces penetrate deeper into Ukraine. In the north, they are fighting with White Finns against Red Finns in a vicious civil war. The British and French worry that their former ally Russia is about to become a German satellite, with their access to the central Eurasian landmass blocked by German soldiers on its northern and southern fringes and their ability to both influence Russian affairs and enjoy its natural resources correspondingly diminished. They consider sending a military force into the White Sea port of Archangel to try to keep the country open, and leave themselves the option of fuller military intervention in the Russian heartland later if required.

Over the spring, senior Allied diplomats either leave Russia entirely or move to the medieval city of Vologda, which the American Ambassador anoints 'the diplomatic capital of Russia' to the delight of the local mayor. A French diplomat describes the place more truthfully as a big village – 'a little monotonous but full of charm' – and spends evenings at the theatre marvelling at local attempts to put on classical opera to impress the visitors. There is not much work to do but try and make sense of garbled reports of the situation from across the country, probably long out of date by the time they arrive. Fed up, the Belgians decide to leave. Given the situation in European Russia they opt to exit Eurasia via the Pacific port of Vladivostok, where Allied Japanese troops have just landed.

In Moscow, the Bolsheviks are clinging on to power by their bare teeth, fighting a triple war: for grain to feed the cities, against Socialist Revolutionaries disgusted by the peace of Brest-Litovsk; and against the military threat of counter-revolutionary White armies gathering in the Cossack heartlands of southern Russia under General Kornilov, the would-be strongman of 1917. Leon Trotsky, the former war correspondent, is made war commissar. He takes to the job of turning the Red Guards into a proper army with a dictatorial zeal for order and authority which many old Bolsheviks find distasteful.

Transforming himself from red-hot revolutionary intellectual into military supremo, Trotsky gives an interview to *Pravda* declaring that 'discipline must be discipline, soldiers must be soldiers, sailors sailors and orders orders'. Soldiers' committees are formally abolished. The cosmopolitan war commissar is even prepared to accept the services of former Tsarist officers – 'military experts' is the euphemism used – to boost the army's fighting capacity. Stalin is disgusted by such Napoleonic attitudes. Army officers are class enemies. He suspects Trotsky is not building a revolutionary army, but a personal one.

A culture of diplomatic intrigue pervades Moscow, where the Allied military missions left behind by their ambassadors engage in an exhilarating game of plot and counter-plot to try and prevent further German encroachment. Spies are everywhere. Information is sold and loyalties purchased on the intelligence black market. Danger is ever-present. At a meeting where

Trotsky is due to talk about the new Red Army, a British operative briefly considers liquidating Bolshevism the old-fashioned way by shooting the new war commissar. The Bolsheviks are knee deep in intrigue themselves, trying to play the Allies and the Germans off each other in a desperate effort to keep them both at a safe distance. In early March, when the German military threat is at its height, Trotsky even considers allowing a small British force of marines to land at Murmansk.

'We can say with confidence that in the main the civil war is at an end', Lenin tells a political gathering towards the end of April, after hearing that General Kornilov has been killed trying to take the city of Ekaterinodar. (He claims Kornilov was murdered by his own soldiers, when in fact he was killed by artillery fire.) 'There will be some skirmishes, of course, and in some towns street fighting will flare up here or there', he says, 'but there is no doubt that on the internal front reaction has been irretrievably smashed by the efforts of the insurgent people.' Nonetheless, Lenin admits that the revolution is not strong enough to wage war against foreign imperialists, 'armed to the teeth and possessing a wealth of technical equipment'. Anyone who suggests otherwise is an 'agent provocateur'. The revolution will only be truly safe when the workers have risen up elsewhere. In the meantime, the regime must turn its energies against enemies who are even more dangerous than Kornilov: the merchants and the peasants who prefer to stock what little food they have rather than sell it to the towns. 'Furious struggle' against them lies ahead.

Towards the end of April, while German and Austrian armies are completing their occupation of Crimea, a new German Ambassador arrives in Moscow, setting up a full embassy in the mansion of a former sugar merchant (outshining the lower-level Allied missions). Count Mirbach insists on presenting his credentials formally to the Bolshevik regime, and has to be dissuaded from doing so in uniform, or at least in evening dress. He leaves the Bolsheviks in no doubt as to who he thinks is in charge under the circumstances. The German Count goes to see the Commissar of Foreign Affairs at least once a day, generally throwing his stick and hat onto a chair in the waiting room and simply barging into his office without knocking. After Brest-Litovsk, he sees his role as an enforcer of the German will, not as a friend to the Russian people.

The Kaiser is delighted at the firm approach his new man in Moscow is taking towards Lenin's regime – 'a thieving rabble of proles', Wilhelm writes in the margins of one of Mirbach's reports. The Count describes a sad city. Even the relatively prosperous wear drab clothes to avoid standing out. The factories have stopped working – 'signature of the socialist future!'

Wilhelm scrawls – and the shops have nothing to sell. What the country is going through is not just a change of leadership but a total collapse. The former ruling classes feel powerless. According to the Count, they look to Germany as a potential saviour. 'We'll see', writes Wilhelm, in English, after this report.

Faced with growing German influence in Russia, the question of a counterbalancing Allied military intervention becomes more pressing. Woodrow has never liked the idea, worried that American troops entering Russia uninvited would make America look like just another grasping imperialist power. In January, an American diplomat in Archangel suggests other means. 'The tremendous advertising power of a few shiploads of food is well worth weighing and can hardly be exaggerated', he writes. In late April, he proposes another scheme: a new railway from Siberia to Archangel to act as a giant 'suction pump' drawing the wealth of Siberia away from the existing railway routes heading west towards Germany and, instead, directing it towards the Allies. Such a plan, he writes triumphantly, 'would be more important in the world's economic history than the Baghdad railroad', the iron link intended to weld together Berlin and the Middle East.

Such grand schemes ignore the immediate necessity for action. 'I think time is fast approaching for Allied intervention, and Allies should be prepared to act promptly', the American Ambassador writes from Vologda to Washington. But with what forces?

THERESIENSTADT FORTRESS, THE KINGDOM OF BOHEMIA, THE AUSTRO-HUNGARIAN EMPIRE: Weakened by tuberculosis, malnutrition and blood loss from an amputated arm, a Bosnian Serb boy of twenty-four – the young idealist Gavrilo Princip whose bullets killed Archduke Franz Ferdinand in 1914 – dies in an Austro-Hungarian prison cell.

TOBOLSK: For months, false stories have been circulating of the escape of Nicholas Romanov or members of his family from Siberia. There are rumours the Tsar's daughter has left for America, where she is said to give public lectures on Russian subjects. Questions are being asked about the adequacy of the guard assigned to the Romanovs. There is rivalry between different Soviets in Siberia about who can best ensure they stay under lock and key. Moscow's intentions are viewed with mistrust. Some fear a dirty diplomatic deal to release them.

The tensions swirling around the Romanovs' situation do not go unnoticed in the imperial household. They are instructed to economise. Nicholas asks the children's French tutor to help with the accounts and forms a committee to look into possible spending cuts. Since everyone else appears to be creating Soviets, the Tsar jokes, we might as well form our own. As many as ten loyal servants may have to be let go, it is concluded. Butter and coffee drop off the menu at the imperial dining table. 'Our last chance of escape has been snatched from us', the children's French tutor writes in his diary shortly after an unruly contingent of two hundred Red Guards arrive from Omsk, quickly staking *their* Soviet's claim to determine the Romanovs' future. Nicholas notes in amazement how they sing songs and play the balalaika for seven hours straight one day. They must be very bored, he decides.

One day, a new man arrives from Moscow, tasked with clearing up the semi-anarchy which has been allowed to develop in Tobolsk. He bears instructions that the Romanovs are to be removed without delay to the city of Ekaterinburg in the Ural Mountains, a place renowned for its strongly anti-monarchist politics. The Tsarevich is too sick to travel. At first, the Tsar protests that therefore he cannot go either. But the man from Moscow leaves him no choice. (In messages to Moscow the Tsar is referred to as 'the baggage'.) Alexandra is forced to choose between travelling with her husband or staying with her son. Distraught, she chooses Nicholas. Perhaps the Bolsheviks want him to endorse the peace they made at Brest-Litovsk, Nicholas speculates. 'I'd rather cut off my own hand.'

The imperial party led by the man from Moscow leaves in the middle of the night. Conditions along the way are dreadful as the ice and snow begin to melt and the roads turn to freezing mud. Neither Nicholas nor Alexandra have been told their destination.

Moscow: A decree is issued. Russia is to be cleansed. Statues of the Tsars and their cronies – barring those considered to have particular artistic merit – are to be removed from public places. A competition of revolutionary artists will be held to determine what to replace them with. Coats of arms and other emblems of the old regime are to be removed. Street names are to be changed. The new Soviet Commissariat of Enlightenment will be in charge. Money will be provided. No expense must be spared.

Spa, German-occupied Belgium: Ludendorff's nerves are shot. The death of his stepson affects him deeply. 'It has taken away my will to live', the general writes. When the young man's body is recovered, the general commands that he be buried in the grounds of the high command's head-quarters, so he can visit his grave whenever he wants. He makes excuses to his wife Margarethe for not sending the body back to Berlin to be buried next to another of Ludendorff's stepsons, who was killed last September. 'I would gladly give up my so-called fame if I could get the two boys back in return', he writes to the grieving mother in Berlin.

In early May, a lieutenant visits Ludendorff to provide the latest report from the front. The general taps his pen incessantly, impatient at the bad news he is receiving. Finally, he explodes. 'What do you want from me?' he shouts. 'Should I make peace at any price?' The lieutenant tries to calm the general down. He is only doing his job, he says, telling Ludendorff that the troops cannot be pushed further. 'If the soldiers' morale is getting worse, if discipline is breaking down, that is *your* fault, and that of all the other officers at the front', Ludendorff screams. The blame game has started.

AMERICAN FRONT LINE, NEAR MALMY, FRANCE – NEW YORK: Two soldiers of Jim Europe's 369th Regiment hear the sound of barbed wire being cut. Then a squad of Germans rushes towards them from the darkness. One of the American privates, Needham Roberts, is wounded badly by a German grenade. The other, Private Harry Johnson, now fights for both their lives. He knocks one German to the ground with his rifle butt. As another tries to drag away the wounded Roberts to enemy lines, Johnson plants his knife in the German's head. He then rips open the stomach of the soldier he has knocked to the ground. The remaining attackers flee. Johnson flings some grenades after them. By the time the relief party arrives he has fainted.

The French, under whose command the 369th Regiment is serving, immediately cite Johnson and Roberts for outstanding bravery: they will be awarded the French Croix de Guerre. The US army is more miserly at first, but once the story is reported in the American press they recognise both the American soldiers' valour, and their propaganda potential.

After months of training, and waiting, the first American soldiers have started fighting and dying in this war. Stories of real-life heroism are important. The army newspaper, the *Stars and Stripes*, runs a long story on the two men. The bravery of black American soldiers in the Civil War and the Spanish–American War is well known, goes the piece. 'Now the slaves of a century ago are defending their American citizenship on a larger battlefield', it continues. 'Now is their first chance to show themselves before the whole world as good and brave soldiers, all.' Johnson becomes the first black American hero of the war.

In America, William Du Bois writes an article in *The Crisis*, the magazine of the National Association for the Advancement of Colored People. 'For all the long years to come', he predicts, 'men will point to the year 1918 as the great Day of Decision, the day when the world decided whether it would submit to military despotism or whether they would put down the menace of German militarism and inaugurate the United States of the World'.

CHELYABINSK, RUSSIA: An orphan Czechoslovak army, raised to fight on the Russian side in the war, and now stranded by revolution and Brest-Litovsk, travels slowly by train across Russia towards the Pacific port of Vladivostok.

Hundreds of freight cars, spread out over hundreds of miles of the trans-Siberian line, are pulled east by the locomotives. Each car is equipped with bunk beds and a central stove, which has to be constantly fed with scavenged wood. The interiors are decorated with paintings of the Charles Bridge in Prague. The soldiers make weather vanes in the shape of the Kaiser. The wagons smell of smoke, human waste, sweat, half-washed clothes. Forty thousand members of the Czechoslovak Corps are travelling this way, the best-trained force in Russia, viewed with envy and suspicion by supporters of the revolution. They are on their way home – and then to the front in France to continue the fight against Germany and Austria and ensure that when peace comes a new Czecho-Slovak state will arise from the destruction of the old empires.

In Chelyabinsk, a train carrying Czech soldiers meets a train going the other way bearing Austro-Hungarian prisoners of war. One of the Austro-Hungarian soldiers throws an iron bar, wounding a Czech. An Austro-Hungarian soldier is lynched in revenge. The Soviet authorities detain the Czechs responsible for the killing and take them into town. Hours pass. Officers are sent to check what is going on. They are put in jail as well. The Czechs are furious. Eventually, they take matters into their own hands. They occupy the main points in Chelyabinsk, taking the city over with ease and helping themselves to local weapons stocks.

Ekaterinburg, where Nicholas and Alexandra are now being held, is only a few hundred miles up the line.

NEW YORK: Down Fifth Avenue from the Upper East Side to Downtown, well-wishers crowd the sidewalk, craning their necks to catch a glimpse of the largest parade ever organised through the city: seventy thousand women and men of the American Red Cross and similar organisations engaged in the national war effort.

A cacophony of music and cheers, and the steady tramp, tramp, tramp of new leather boots – and then, between 67th and 68th Streets, a surprise. The parade is halted. For a moment, a ripple of concern runs through the crowd. A black car appears from nowhere, surrounded by a motorcade. From it emerges a tall man in tails and top hat, blinking into the sun. As the marchers start up again, Boy Scouts are sent ahead to spread the news. For forty blocks, Woodrow Wilson, a picture of healthful manhood, leads the Red Cross volunteers through New York, raising his top hat in polite greeting to the cheering crowds, bowing this way and that, and waving occasionally as if he has spotted some long-lost friend in the throng.

Towards the back of the parade marches a young man from Oak Park, Illinois, freshly commissioned as a second lieutenant, with a thousand-dollar life insurance policy in his pocket and the view of the Atlantic from the top of the Woolworth Building still fresh in his mind's eye. A few days later Ernest Hemingway is aboard the *Chicago*, a French Line steamer bound for Bordeaux. It is a 'rotten old tub', he writes, 'but we travel 1st class'.

There is a collective sigh of relief back at home that Ernest did not get married in New York, as he jokily threatened to do. But then, a wave of fresh anxiety overcomes his parents: an Atlantic crossing in the midst of a U-boat war (though Hemingway himself is over the moon at the possibility of spotting a German submarine), then France, then front-line duty in Italy – Grace and Clarence worry about their boisterous, brave, foolish son. Will he be sensible over there, will he look after himself, or will he do something stupid and get himself killed?

CHELYABINSK: The leaders of the Czechoslovak Corps meet at the railway station to discuss their position. Most want to press on to Vladivostok.

A telegram from Moscow to the Soviets along the trans-Siberian railway, intercepted at Chelyabinsk, gives orders that the Czechoslovak Corps should be taken off their trains, and drafted into labour units or the Red Army. A misunderstanding, the Russians now say. Czechoslovak representatives in Moscow try to calm things down, ordering the troops to give up their weapons and rely on the Soviets for security. The soldiers refuse, swearing that they will not surrender their arms till they reach Vladivostok. 'The assurances of safe transportation cannot satisfy us', they telegraph Moscow.

Then an order from war commissar Trotsky: 'Every armed Czechoslovak found on the railway is to be shot on the spot; every troop train in which even one armed man is found shall be unloaded, and its soldiers shall be interned in a war prisoners' camp.' Delay in carrying out these orders will be counted as treason. Any Russian assisting the Czechoslovaks, even under threat of violence, is to face severe punishment. When local authorities question Moscow's orders, Trotsky thunders that they are to do what they are told.

More fighting breaks out along the line between members of the Czechoslovak Corps and German and Austro-Hungarian prisoners of war. Arms dumps and railway stations are seized.

THE WESTERN FRONT: The Germans launch an unexpected attack across the Chemin des Dames ridge, the same ground Nivelle sent the French army over last year. As with the March offensive, the initial phases go well. Several bridges are captured without the Allies having had time to blow them up. Communication lines are severed. Confusion reigns. A captured British general is taken to meet the Kaiser.

'Does England wish for peace?' Wilhelm enquires, breaking off from his lunch.

'Everyone wishes for peace', the general replies. The Kaiser nods and makes his exit.

The Allied line is close to buckling over the next few days. American soldiers are thrown into battle. The French still fear an attack elsewhere. The Germans surge forward to the river Marne, and are less than fifty miles away from Paris. They hope to either punch through to the French capital here or draw so many French troops south that they can launch a final attack against the British through Flanders.

Amongst the Allies, the military crisis begins to metastasise into a political one. The British cabinet discuss evacuating the army. French charities issue urgent requests for help to deal with the latest wave of refugees fleeing from the German onslaught. Those who can afford to leave the capital now do so. 'Paris is a city of the dead', writes the British Ambassador. But then, slowly, very slowly, the German advance of 1918 grinds to a halt a second time.

PETROGRAD: Lenin writes a letter to the workers of what is now Russia's second city. He blames the bourgeoisie for the lack of bread in Petrograd. Wealthy peasants are hoarding grain to force up prices, he explains, and profit from the hunger of others.

He proposes a new maxim for Soviet Russia: 'He who does not work, neither shall he eat.' A food dictatorship must be enforced. Peasants will be compelled to deliver grain at a fixed price. The state will control who is given what to eat. There will be no private buying and selling. The proletariat must not be tempted to return to the market; instead it must lead a crusade against bribe-takers and profiteers. 'Every particle of surplus grain must be brought into the state stores', Lenin writes. 'The whole country must be swept clean'.

Occasionally over the spring, his driver takes him out hunting for wood grouse in the countryside.

EKATERINBURG: The Romanov family are reunited again. They let go the French tutor and their old retainers. Now it is just them and their guards.

SUMMER

LINCOLN, ENGLAND: Late one evening a group of prisoners arrive in the cathedral city of Lincoln. They sing a song as they are driven through the prison gates. 'Isn't it fine when you come to think of it', one of them says, 'the generations of Irishmen who have gone into prison singing as we are now.'

Back inside, de Valera returns to the study of mathematics. He becomes an altar server in the prison chapel. He tries to stay fit playing rounders in the prison yard, and handball – just by himself. Éamon sends to Sinéad for his old raincoat, and tenderly imagines little Brian following her around the house as usual. His wife is pregnant again. He teaches Irish to the prisoners but wishes he could be teaching his children geometry. For his own edification, he reads Niccolò Machiavelli's *The Prince* and reacquaints himself with the finer points of Spanish grammar.

MADRID, THE KINGDOM OF SPAIN: 'For several days, Madrid has been affected by an epidemic, which fortunately is mild', *El Liberal* reports, 'but which, from what it appears, intends to kill doctors from overwork.' Some suspect the illness must originate from the construction of the new metro and repairs on the city's sewers.

It is highly infectious, positively social. It spreads through the parties held during the holidays to celebrate Madrid's patron saint, San Isidro. A hundred thousand are believed to have been infected in just a few days. King Alfonso is declared to have fallen sick. Debates in parliament are cancelled.

But there is little panic. The disease seems mild. In Spain, they call it the three-day fever. A British report suggests that although the disease has already reached millions – yes, millions – of the Spanish population, not a single fatality has yet been recorded. 'Alarmist suggestions' of a pandemic are dismissed. But the new strain is certainly virulent. By early summer it has shown up in all the armies of Europe, from American troops training near Bordeaux to soldiers from French Indochina being taught how to drive. It has spread out along the world's trade routes to Bombay and Shanghai. But it is not yet a cause for undue alarm. People fall ill. They recover. The world does not stop.

PARIS: Early June. A city under attack, still just within range of the most powerful guns of the German artillery, seventy-odd miles away. Two Americans turn up at the Gare du Nord and accost a taxi driver, asking him to take them to where the shells are bursting. The driver refuses. 'Offer him more money', the younger of the two Americans suggests. So begins an impromptu tour of the French capital, taking them all over town in the hope of seeing some historic facade or other blown into smithereens by German shells.

And so begins Ernest Hemingway's European war: the Folies Bergère ('hot poppums'), Napoleon's tomb, first-class train travel to Milan and then on to the front. From Italy, Ernie sends a postcard back to the gang at the *Kansas City Star*. 'Having a wonderful time!!!' he scrawls eagerly. 'Had my baptism of fire my first day here, when an entire munition plant exploded … I go to the front tomorrow. Oh, Boy!!! I'm glad I'm in it.'

SAMARA, RUSSIA: An arc of insurrection faces the Bolsheviks from the south and east, from the Black Sea to the Urals and Siberia.

The Czechoslovak Corps, lately bound for Vladivostok, finds it easy to pick off one town after another along the trans-Siberian line: Novo-Nikolaevsk, Penza, Omsk. Austrian and German prisoners of war are prevented from travelling to rejoin their armies in the west. Soviet authority crumbles along the way. The Czechoslovaks are greeted as liberators. In June, they take the city of Samara on the Volga, south-east of Moscow, and hand it over at once to Socialist Revolutionary politicians who claim to speak in the name of the Constituent Assembly, dissolved by Lenin at the beginning of the year. In July, the boom of Czechoslovak artillery can be heard in Ekaterinburg, in the Urals, where the Tsar and his family are held.

Bolshevik control of the entire Volga region is now threatened. Joseph Stalin is sent to secure food supplies for Moscow and Petrograd, establishing his base of operations in the city of Tsaritsyn, where he orders a local cobbler to make him some black leather boots, dons a collarless tunic like

Kerensky in his golden days, and takes up residence in a train carriage with his wife Nadya, who doubles as his secretary.

Further south, anti-Bolshevik Cossacks are in control of the Don region and a White army is being raised by General Denikin. 'Götterdämmerung' is about to break out, Count Mirbach writes in June. He spends more time meeting with opposition figures and trying to figure out the consequences of a Bolshevik overthrow for Germany.

VIENNA: Freud has survived his sixty-first year. 'There is indeed no relying on the supernatural', he writes to a friend, as if he had never been worried at all.

Planning for the all-important annual summer break is well under way. It is much harder than in peacetime. All the decent guesthouses are full of convalescing soldiers, it seems. Civilian postal communications across the empire are worse than usual. Freud outsources the whole wretched business to a colleague in Budapest, requesting that he arrange a return visit to the mountainous Csorba region which Freud enjoyed the year before. Warm weather (but not too hot), Hungarian food supplies and time to think: this is all that Freud asks for.

Emperor Charles is forced to write a begging letter to Wilhelm around this time. He asks for at least two thousand freight cars full of grain, warning that the Austrian army will starve without them.

PERM, SIBERIA: Michael Romanov is abducted from his hotel in Perm by members of the local Cheka.

In a forest outside town, the Tsar's brother is shot at close range with a Browning pistol. The rumour is spread that he has escaped. Over the next few weeks, he is variously reported to be living in the governor's house in Omsk from where he leads a monarchist campaign or else doing something similar in Turkestan.

The vagueness suits the Bolsheviks. A dead man cannot lead a real rebellion. But rumours he is alive will stop a rival from seeking to claim the mantle of the Romanovs.

GIZAUCOURT, FRANCE: Noble Sissle hears that Jim Europe has been caught up in a German gas attack, and taken to a hospital a few miles behind the lines. He rushes to see him.

He is shocked by what he finds: men gasping for breath, mouths covered in sores, bleeding scabs instead of eyes. Lieutenant Europe himself seems fine. He is coughing quite a bit, of course, and there is no way of knowing whether there may be further damage to his insides. (Poison gas is tricky like that – less honest than a bullet or a bomb.) He is in fine spirits, in any case. He has a new idea for a song, with a syncopated chorus. He shows it to the boys.

> Alert! Gas! Put on your mask
> Adjust it correctly and hurry up fast
> Drop! There's a rocket for the Boche barrage
> Down! Hug the ground close as you can
> Don't stand! Creep and crawl
> Follow me, that's all
> What do you hear, nothing near
> Don't fear, all's clear
> That's the life of a stroll
> When you take a patrol out in No Man's Land
> Ain't life great out in No Man's Land

AHRENSHOOP, THE GERMAN REICH: Albert spends the summer holidays with Elsa on the Baltic. 'No telephone, no responsibilities, absolute tranquillity', he writes to a friend; 'I am lying on the shore like a crocodile, allow myself to be roasted by the sun, never see a newspaper, and whistle at the so-called world.' He reads Kant for relaxation.

In Zurich, his son Hans-Albert is disappointed that his father has abandoned him for the summer. 'Wasn't it nice last year?' he asks. Fourteen now, he fills his time accompanying the ladies in the apartment block on the piano and dreaming up plans for an aerial tramway.

PETROGRAD – MOSCOW: Russia's cities are starving. People struggle to stand up straight from hunger. Skin becomes translucent, as if made of wax. The question of how to fill one's stomach dictates everything else. A new rationing system is introduced, dividing Petrograd's population into four categories: the industrial proletariat, white-collar employees such as doctors and teachers, the intelligentsia and artists, and the scum of the earth: the bourgeoisie. Categorisation determines survival.

Items once considered valuable are now worthless; things commonplace are now priceless. All is for sale on the street: old rugs from imperial campaigns in Turkestan, gold-framed mirrors which once reflected the gay dancing of the cavalry officers and their belles, pianos, pillowcases, individual lumps of sugar. In one case, a single boot is offered for sale. 'Are there so few one-legged people around?' the vendor retorts when challenged. Local Chekas proliferate around the country, bands of heavies motivated by the thrill of power and opportunities for extortion as much as any revolutionary zeal for social cleansing. Gangster criminality is dressed up as class warfare. Support for the Bolsheviks within the Soviets falls. The country slips further into civil war. Lenin's rivals start to circle. Moscow is full of plotters.

'Today, after two months' close observation I can no longer give a positive diagnosis to Bolshevism', Count Mirbach writes to Berlin. 'The patient is dangerously ill and in spite of occasional improvements, his fate is preordained.' While it should remain on good terms with the Bolsheviks until the last minute, Germany must prepare for their collapse. There is a risk the Socialist Revolutionaries will come to power, repudiate Brest-Litovsk and relaunch the war. Mirbach recommends that he seek to improve relations with pro-Germans on Russia's political right to counter this. The map drawn at Brest-Litovsk may have to be redrawn. 'Nothing can be had for absolutely free', he warns.

A short while later Count Mirbach is murdered in broad daylight at the German embassy. The details of the assassination plot are unclear. The killer appears to be a Cheka agent. But operating on whose orders? Within minutes of learning of the atrocity, Lenin firmly points the finger of blame at the Left Socialist Revolutionaries, the group which splintered from the Socialist Revolutionaries after the coup of 1917 to support the Bolsheviks, but whom Lenin has now fallen out with over his acceptance of the Carthaginian peace of Brest-Litovsk. He claims that the ambassador's assassination was the signal for a long-planned Left Socialist Revolutionary uprising. Whether that assertion is true or not, Lenin spies an opportunity to strike hard against his enemies in response.

There is the small matter of diplomatic etiquette to attend to first. Vladimir Lenin, enemy of capitalism, scourge of imperialism, unflinching promoter of the worldwide dictatorship of the proletariat, goes to the imperial German embassy to sign the condolence book for the slain aristocrat. In private, the impatient revolutionary jokes with his associates about the appropriate German word to use in such circumstances. In public, he pulls his face into a mask of horror at what has happened to ensure that the diplomatic telegrams sent back to the Kaiser report no trace of *Schadenfreude*. Once this painful task has been completed, Vladimir can return to domestic affairs. Soviet delegates from across Russia and from across the revolutionary spectrum are currently in session in the Bolshoi Theatre. Lenin orders loyal troops to cordon off the building. Bolshevik supporters inside are allowed to leave by the back door. The rest – Lenin's political opponents – are kept prisoner.

Left Socialist Revolutionaries protest their incarceration. Their operatives outside the Bolshoi take the head of the Cheka hostage in response. Several buildings are occupied. But such actions are isolated, reactive, uncoordinated. If this is an insurrection, it is a very poorly executed one. The last redoubt of Left Socialist Revolutionary rebels is soon under siege by Latvian troops loyal to the Bolsheviks. Artillery shells smash through the walls of the old mansion where the rebels are holed up. Later that day, the impatient revolutionary himself comes to inspect the damage, crushing pieces of broken glass under the soles of his shoes.

Opposition parties are suppressed. The Congress of Soviets becomes a Bolshevik-only institution.

FOSSALTA DI PIAVE, ITALY: In early July, the inevitable happens: Hemingway gets his war wound, while handing out chocolate, cigars and postcards to Italian troops along the front line.

One soldier beside him is killed by the explosion of an Austrian mortar. Another has both legs blown off. Ernest, furthest away from the blast, is peppered with shrapnel, knocked unconscious and buried under a pile of earth. But he isn't dead. Not even close. Not Hemingway. Instinct kicks in. Ernest struggles back to the first-aid station, under fire, carrying an Italian soldier in his arms. There, he is given a shot of morphine to ease the pain. Just a few weeks into the war, and Oak Park's brightest son is awarded one of Italy's highest medals of honour. His photograph appears in the *Chicago Daily Tribune*, although the article misspells his name (not for the last time) as Hemenway. Ernest's grandfather, a veteran of the American Civil War, pastes it all into his scrapbook.

Now things get even better. Ernest is sent to recuperate in Milan, in a small, rather luxurious hospital occupying a single floor of a grand mansion in the best part of the city. Hemingway can see the dome of the cathedral from the porch; the offices of *Il Popolo d'Italia* are not far away. The shrapnel wounds he has received – over two hundred perforations – and a few bullet injuries turn out to be nothing serious for the young man, medically speaking. A long period of recuperation is advisable, but no amputations are necessary. Hemingway is able to dig some of the shrapnel out of his legs himself, using a penknife. While in hospital, he keeps himself well stocked with cognac, and contrives to fall in love with one of the nurses looking after him, an American called Agnes. She thinks Ernie rather a sweet boy, and takes the night shift so that she can talk to him more. Later they go to the opera and the races together, and write to each other furiously – sometimes a letter every day – claiming to be deeply in love.

To the folks back home, Ernest writes in the same jocular tone as always. And why not? For the price of what amounts, in relative terms, to a few scratches, he finds himself a war hero. Rather than denting his pride, or giving him a sense of his own mortality, the incident has made young Ernest feel more invincible than ever. Not like the rest of the poor bastards left on the front line, he reflects. He tells his family about the souvenirs he has managed to collect: 'Austrian carbines and ammunition, German and Austrian medals, officers' automatic pistols, Boche helmets, about a dozen bayonets, star-shell pistols and knives and almost everything you can think of.' The only limit to what he could take, Ernest explains to his family, is what he could carry with him: 'There were so many dead Austrians and prisoners, the ground was almost black with them.'

Hemingway is in no hurry to get home. He hopes to be driving ambulances by the end of the summer.

KARLSBAD, BOHEMIA, THE AUSTRO-HUNGARIAN EMPIRE: A striking-looking Turkish gentleman with a kidney complaint arrives in the society spa town of Karlsbad, sent there by Professor Zuckerkandl of Vienna, a member of one of the empire's best-connected Jewish medical families. Karlsbad is one of those places where Europe's *beau monde* used to congregate before the war. It is full of grand hotels. There is a faint smell of sulphur in the air.

Mustafa Kemal gets off on the wrong foot with Dr Vermer, the local doctor he has been assigned. The Turkish national hero complains that the apartment rented for him and his servant at the Rudolfshof is a little small. He preferred the look of the Grandhotel Pupp. Vermer replies, a little testily: 'Have you come here for a serious cure, or to enjoy and tire yourself in splendour?' Not a good start. The doctor asks Kemal if he has brought his own flour supply with him and when the confused Turk answers in the negative, Vermer informs him that in Austria the authorities are only required to hand out flour to locals, not foreigners. He will have to do without bread. Turkish hospitality, Kemal retorts, means that foreigners consume *more* than locals. If he is not to have bread in Karlsbad he will return to Istanbul at once and advise the Sultan to curtail the bread given to foreign guests.

There is a pause. Kemal is a proud man. He is not used to being treated this way. Vermer tries to smooth things over by asking his new patient if there are other generals as young as him in Turkey. The brigadier general replies gracefully that it is the war conditions in his country which require one so young to fulfil a post so elevated. At last, a little *politesse*. The entire conversation takes place in French.

It is not the only awkward encounter in Kemal's first few days in Karlsbad. By rights, of course, he should feel quite at home. He has travelled with an Ottoman Prince to meet the German Kaiser. He has lived the high life in Bulgaria. He knows French. He has worn fancy dress. Though of a somewhat authoritarian disposition, he regards himself as a social liberal. He considers himself a European gentleman as well as a proud Turk. And yet he lives in fear of putting his foot wrong somehow, of embarrassing himself in front of Europeans who may see only the Turkish and not the European side of his identity. On one of his first nights in town Kemal finds himself sitting down for dinner at the Imperial Hotel, a little early, perhaps. As more people start coming into the restaurant than there are tables available, he begins to panic. 'A distress, a sadness, a freak invaded my soul', he admits to his diary. Is he allowed to be there? Should he have reserved? Is the restaurant only for hotel guests? The general takes up the matter confidentially with his doctor the next day. He is reassured: the dining room has a free-seating policy.

Kemal settles into a routine. His daytime treatments involve a mud bath (every day) and a compress (every second day). He is required to drink large quantities of mineral water from the springs; his servant has the bright idea of filling up thermoses so his master can drink the stuff in bed. In the time when he is not horizontal, the general starts taking German lessons and reads improving books, including a critique of Marx's *Das Kapital*, in French. He soon finds the other Turks in the resort. In the course of his first week, he runs into the wife of Djemal Pasha, an army colonel and his wife, and an old friend from the military academy in Salonika. He compares rooms with his friend and, having ascertained that his is better, Kemal invites him over for a cup of coffee.

One evening, after exchanging war stories with the Turkish colonel and his wife over dinner, and discussing what makes a good general – the will to win, the ability to make decisions and then take responsibility for them, rather than blaming everything on one's subordinates – the group stroll onto the veranda and watch young European ladies dancing with their male suitors, dressed in dinner jackets. (Kemal, who generally wears his military uniform or a dark suit in the evenings, makes a mental note of the attire.) The colonel's wife comments how difficult it is for such modern European attitudes to take root back home. The general turns on his heels: 'I always say that if I one day obtain great authority and power I think I will be able to implement the desired revolution in our social life by a coup – in an instant.' He does not believe in gradualism, he declares, or pandering to popular prejudices or so-called Islamic rules. There can be no compromise: 'Why should I lower myself to the level of the ignorant when I received higher education for many years?' No, he insists, 'I shall bring their levels to mine; I won't be like them, they will be like me.' Women, he says, should be better educated: 'Let us ornament their minds with science and knowledge'.

On another occasion, Kemal finds himself arguing with a Turkish woman who tells him that daughters should be kept illiterate so they cannot challenge their mother's authority. If the generations are not more educated from one to the next, the general angrily ripostes, how will progress ever occur? Asked about his attitude to marriage, the bachelor war hero rather daringly quotes the French playwright Marcel Prévost: '*Le mariage est une chose, l'amour est une autre chose*' – marriage is one thing, and love another. He will not get married until he is sure that he knows which is which. Perhaps he is already too old anyway, he says. Mustafa Kemal is thirty-seven. (For years he has had an on–off relationship with the daughter of his step-father's brother: a romantic young woman named Fikriye.)

It is in Karlsbad that Kemal learns that the Sultan has died in Istanbul and Prince Vahdettin, whom he accompanied to Germany last year, has succeeded him. Immediately, Kemal's mind is onto politics. He jots down the main questions in his diary. How does Djemal get his money? What is the relationship between Djemal and Talaat? What is Enver's attitude towards himself, Mustafa Kemal? What is the new Sultan's approach likely to be? He kicks himself for not having paid a courtesy call to Vahdettin before he left.

But he does not return home immediately. Mustafa Kemal is beginning to enjoy himself in Karlsbad. He starts avoiding his daily mud-bath treatments (without telling Dr Vermer). On the first day of Ramadan he takes a car trip with his German teacher, Mademoiselle Brandner, to visit a china factory. A few days later, his landlady invites him to a concert. He takes French lessons from a blind Swiss woman, although he asks his diary what on earth has motivated him to agree to lessons from a lady who can neither read nor correct anything he writes.

On another trip out of town with Miss Brandner, she asks him about the Ottoman army, expressing surprise that there are enough men to fill its ranks after all the wars it has had to fight: against the Italians in Libya back in 1911, against the Bulgarians, the Greeks and others in the Balkans, and now the current war against the Russian Empire, the British, and recently the Armenians in the Caucasus. Kemal praises Enver Pasha for getting rid of, as he puts it, 'the old pieces of cloth' in the Ottoman army. He has made things much more efficient, he explains, more modern.

Without the Ottoman army, Kemal boasts, Germany would not be standing now and the British and the French would already be victorious. He bemoans the fact that the Turkish contribution is so little understood – even at home.

SPA: Once more German troops are sent forward into battle by their masters. But the French have the measure of Ludendorff's new storm tactics by now. They understand how to counteract its impact: by absorbing the blow with a system of deep defence. The French even know the time of the planned attack, having learned it from prisoners. A few minutes before the German bombardment is due to begin, at the very moment that the German trenches are most crowded, the French artillery opens up. The impact is devastating. The subsequent German attack is stopped within hours.

And here's another innovation for 1918: a combination of American and French divisions (including one from North Africa) spearheads a well-planned and well-executed counter-attack. There is no artillery barrage to signal Allied intentions. This time, the assault relies not on the weight of munitions fired at the enemy, but on the element of surprise. The night before the counter-attack, a heavy thunderstorm covers the gathering of men and munitions in the village of Villers-Cotterêts (before the war, Baedeker recommended 'pleasant excursions' in the village forest). On the morning of the attack, smoke shells are fired into the fields through which French and American troops will move forward. Allied tanks, hidden under camouflage, suddenly come out of nowhere.

There is confusion amongst the Germans. A lieutenant on Ludendorff's staff writes home that he has heard that 'several thousand tanks' participate in the French attack; in fact, there are only a few hundred. Ludendorff's mind is wracked with indecision. What to do? Pull back to another line of defence, or deny reality, stay in position and hope for a miracle? Faced with such an unpalatable choice, emotion overwhelms the Prussian general.

Ludendorff blames his subordinates for the situation. When, two days after the beginning of the Franco-American counter-attack, a trusted officer suggests that it is still not too late to order a tactical retreat, the general replies that while he agrees that such a course of action is advisable, he cannot bring himself to issue the order. He worries about the impact on the mood at home. Ludendorff threatens to resign if anyone disagrees with him.

His reasons are not hard to fathom. An order to retreat would mean abruptly waking the German nation from the dream of victory. And it would mean a personal admission: that Ludendorff, the man who was supposed to bring Germany its greatest military triumph, has instead become chief author of its downfall. This is something the general cannot allow.

PRESSBURG, THE AUSTRO-HUNGARIAN EMPIRE: The Emperor Charles and his wife Zita take a steamer down the Danube to the city of Pressburg for the harvest festival. The enthusiasm of the crowds that greet them seems real enough. 'Is it all a dream?' Zita asks herself. Her husband warns against any illusions. The flour ration in Vienna has been reduced again. The soldiers at the front are famished and underweight. Suicides are becoming more frequent.

EKATERINBURG: The Czechoslovak Corps is expected in the city in a matter of days.

The Romanov family are woken up in the middle of the night. They are told they are to be moved to a place of greater safety. Nicholas carries his son Alexei down to the cellar in his arms. The rest of his family follow, ready for a trip ahead. A hand-picked firing squad awaits them. A death sentence is read out. Nicholas tries to ask a question. Trucks outside rev their engines to try and drown out the sound of gunfire.

SPA: A quiet evening at headquarters. No banqueting tonight. Everyone knows the truth: the offensive towards Reims has failed and the German army has no strength to launch another attack. The Kaiser turns in soon after supper.

But Wilhelm cannot find escape in sleep. His mind is haunted by visions of what might have been – and by the bitter disappointment of what is. He imagines a parade of onlookers marching slowly past him, shaking their heads as if he were a condemned prisoner about to be sent to the gallows. He sees his wife, whose health has been a constant worry these last few months. He sees Ludendorff and the other generals. He sees his British and Russian cousins, too. They laugh at him as they pass, mocking his grandiose ambitions and how far he has fallen short of them. How ridiculous he is, their faces seem to say. He who wanted so much to be the master of the European Continent. He who wanted to finally show the world what he was truly made of . . .

The same evening, Ludendorff meets one of his senior officers. He is dejected. Superstition has overcome him. The date of the latest attack was wrong, he says, flicking through his prayer book to show his colleague the entry for 15 July. 'I shouldn't have trusted that date', Ludendorff says. The biblical texts on the dates of previous attacks were all good, he insists. This one was not. It seems clear that higher forces are involved in Germany's fate. 'May God not forsake us now', says the general before shuffling off.

PARIS: *Le Matin* is jubilant. The Germans are falling apart. Influenza has played its part. 'In France, it is benign; our soldiers are able to resist it quite effortlessly', the newspaper reports, quite unlike the German troops, who are said to be laid low in their thousands, their tens of thousands, perhaps even their hundreds of thousands: 'Is this a symptom of the weakness and failure of organisms whose resistance has finally been crushed?'

WÜLZBURG: A month since his last attempt, Charles de Gaulle tries to escape again. Getting out of the German camp is the easy bit: he hides in a laundry basket and is carried out of Wülzburg on the back of a lorry. His problems come later, on the open road, when he has already tasted the sweetness of freedom for a day or two. The German police ask him for his papers during a routine check on the Frankfurt express. There is nothing he can do.

Back in camp, a gust of optimism sometimes fills Charles's sails: the end of the war is in sight, and with it the prospect that he will see his family once more. This is good. But then again, Charles considers, a premature end to the conflict will scupper his chances of redeeming the dishonour of being captured through a heroic escape from German custody. This is not good. 'I've been buried alive', he complains to his mother. She writes that he must read, he must work – for the sake of his future career if nothing else. 'What future?' de Gaulle writes back, angrily. 'For any ambitious officer of my age to have any serious future in the army he must have been in the thick of it all along.'

NEW YORK: Over the summer, Marcus Garvey submits the necessary papers to incorporate a new association: the Universal Negro Improvement Association and African Communities League, or UNIA for short.

For anyone unhappy with Du Bois's patriotic embrace of the war and his constitutionalist, integrationist approach to changing America, Garvey is the alternative. In place of integration with white society, Garvey advocates race pride and independence. Where Du Bois talks of improving the lot of black Americans through enforcing full legal rights and the high-minded example of an enlightened elite, Garvey emphasises the power of mass organisation and people doing it for themselves. But it is his vigorous personality as well as the radicalism of his politics which draws some to the chubby-faced, tub-thumping activist. He is a world away from the slim, pale, patrician Du Bois.

The organisation he creates lies somewhere between an African government-in-waiting, a fraternity and a business. It provides embossed membership certificates to those who pay a monthly subscription. Its funds may be invested in black enterprises. Local divisions are to help those in need with loans and jobs. In anticipation of statehood UNIA also has a lengthy constitution, a flag and an anthem – 'From Greenland's Icy Mountains'. It aims to represent all black people around the world, be they middle class and educated like William Du Bois (who can count the universities of both Harvard and Berlin as his alma maters) or poor and illiterate. Its structure of infinitely replicable local chapters is designed to work for a city, a country or a continent. All the divisions must maintain a band or orchestra. UNIA has its own newspaper, the *Negro World*.

It is a flamboyant enterprise. Its organisational chart overflows with magnificent titles borrowed from the traditions of black Freemasonry and the British Empire of which Garvey is a subject: High Chancellor, Chaplain-General, President-General. (In this, it is perhaps not very different from a recently refounded white supremacist organisation known as the Ku Klux Klan, with its knights and wizards.) Grandest of all, the supreme leader is known as the Potentate. A Moses to his people, he is entitled to rule over

them for life. The constitution stipulates that he must be of 'Negro blood
and race' and may only marry a 'lady of Negro blood and parentage'. After
each UNIA convention, the Potentate is to hold a 'Court Reception', which
is off-limits to convicted felons, anyone of dubious morality, men under
twenty one and women under eighteen.

MOSCOW: In the midst of civil war, the Soviet Commissariat of Enlightenment
issues its list of individuals deemed worthy of a statue in the new Russia.
Sculptors are commissioned to produce these monuments by the time of
the anniversary of the revolution in November – an almost impossible task
with only three months left but one which will get the young artists out
of their 'attics and dark rooms'.

Most of the names on Vladimir Lenin's list (compiled with the help of
others, but signed off by him) are familiar. There is little new blood. Tolstoy
sits atop the writers' section: he remains one of Lenin's favourites, despite
the old man's weird descent into radical Christianity towards the end of
his life. The great chemist Mendeleev is included, as is the medieval icon
painter Andrei Rublev, the writers Dostoyevsky and Pushkin, and of course
the major Russian revolutionary figures of the last century – the dead ones,
that is: those who cannot challenge Comrade Lenin to a debate about his
interpretations of their work.

There are very few women on the list. One who does make the cut is
Sophia Perovskaya, an aristocratic lady with the face of an angel who was
involved in the assassination of the Tsar in 1881 and then executed as a
terrorist. She is Vladimir's kind of heroine. The only other woman deemed
suitable for memorialisation is well-known actress Vera Komissarzhevskaya,
who starred in Chekhov's plays and was close to the revolutionary set in
Petrograd before the war.

Then there are the foreigners. A more disparate bunch, these. Marx and
Engels are there, of course. After them, the French revolutionaries whom
Lenin obsesses over: Robespierre, Marat and Danton. But there is also
Spartacus, the rebel slave of the ancient Roman world; Brutus, a great role
model for stabbing Julius Caesar in the back; the Polish composer Frédéric
Chopin; and Giuseppe Garibaldi, the nationalist father of modern Italy and
boyhood hero of the Bolshevik leader.

MILAN: *Il Popolo d'Italia*, the influential Milanese newspaper edited by the
war veteran Benito Mussolini, changes its masthead. The newspaper is no

longer described as socialist, as it has been since its foundation, but dedicated to the nation's soldiers and productive forces. Socialism without nationalism leads to chaos and terror, Benito has decided. A people must come before a class. He has already scrapped two hero-worship quotes which used to flank the paper's title and which now seem a little too much: 'he who has steel, has bread' by the French theorist of revolution, Blanqui; and 'revolution is an idea that has found bayonets' by Napoleon.

Italy is not immune from the threat of Bolshevism, Benito writes. The events of the last few months (including riots in Turin last year) have shown it can happen here too. Italy must save herself from disaster, by whatever means. If the internationalist scum try anything here, violence will be met with violence. 'Today is not a time for angels, it is a time for devils', he declares. 'Either that, or Russia.'

Benito takes no chances himself. He is almost always armed. He warns colleagues that he will shoot anyone who interrupts him while he is at work writing his latest column for the paper. No one can be entirely sure if he is joking.

ACROSS RUSSIA: August. Civil war is in full flow. Bolshevism's enemies close in from all sides.

Russia's old agricultural heartland along the Volga river is aflame with anti-Bolshevik rebellion. In Samara, a government claiming to represent the disbanded Constituent Assembly is formed. Ukraine is now ruled by a nationalist overlord, while the Kaiser's army scours the place for supplies to sustain its hungry soldiers fighting a thousand miles to the west. Ukraine's Communists (mostly Russian-speaking) are reduced to holding a congress in Moscow. Towards the Caucasus, General Denikin's White army is regrouping in Don Cossack territory, from which it strikes out to capture Ekaterinodar and the port of Novorossiysk on the Black Sea. Everywhere, opposition forces try to raise popular armies to fight the Bolsheviks. But mobilisation is patchy and slow. Russia's peasants may not like the Bolsheviks but are they prepared to leave the land to fight against them?

To the east, the Czechs take Ekaterinburg, where an investigation begins into the fate of the Tsar and his family. In Siberia, the green–white flag of independence has been raised. An American expeditionary force is dispatched to join the Japanese in Vladivostok. Now, in high summer, a small British military contingent lands at Archangel on the White Sea. An anti-Bolshevik of impeccable revolutionary credentials – in an earlier life he set up a socialist commune in Kansas and in 1917 he was a member of the Petrograd Soviet – becomes the city's ruler.

For the foreign powers, the objectives of intervention are strategic: to grab land, secure resources, or else ensure that whoever assumes power after the Bolsheviks have been swept away takes their side in the great world war being fought to the west. Russians take up arms for more visceral reasons: to save the nation they love or the revolution they have waited their whole lives for. Various anti-Bolshevik tendencies arise, from conservative and liberal to Socialist Revolutionary. All seek a return to order in place of the chaos of civil war. They hate Lenin. Hardly any want the Romanovs back. The Bolsheviks define them all indiscriminately as counter-revolutionaries. Yet many of those taking up arms against Vladimir Lenin and his rule feel it is he who has betrayed the spirit of 1917, not they. Some fight for honour, or to reignite the war against Germany. Others fight to return the revolution to its true course.

For the Bolshevik leadership, this war is one of survival – but it is also a chance to accelerate the pace of history, just as the imperialist-capitalist war did before it. Violence must be embraced as a purgatory. Lenin sends out orders demanding the brutal suppression of those moderately prosperous peasants, known as the kulaks, whom he blames for withholding grain from hungry Moscow and starving Petrograd. Examples must be made of them. Rural Russia must see there is no going back. Surpluses are to be confiscated. Peasants who resist are to be left with nothing. 'Hang no fewer than one hundred known kulaks, rich men, bloodsuckers', the impatient revolutionary demands. 'Do it in such a way that the people will see, tremble, know, shout: they are strangling and will strangle to death the bloodsucker kulaks.' Mercy is worse than foolishness. 'You are committing a great crime against the revolution', Lenin warns one official accused of 'softness'.

In Bolshevik eyes, there is no standard of morality above the victory of the revolution. Moral codes devised by the bourgeoisie are mere fairy tales, told to keep the people placid. In an age of revolutionary war, the ends justify the means. To allow humanitarian relief to one's enemies is bourgeois, outdated thinking. It is unacceptable that aid steamers sail along the Volga under a Red Cross flag, war commissar Trotsky writes: 'the receipt of grain will be interpreted by charlatans and fools as showing the possibility that agreement can be made'. Military necessity is all; the sooner that is understood, the better. Commanders of retreating Red Army units are to be shot. Captured Whites may join the Reds – but their families will be killed if they defect. Aircraft and artillery are ordered to set fire to the bourgeois districts of enemy-controlled cities. There is no concern for the civilian deaths or refugees this will generate. Military setbacks multiply, however. The ancient Tartar city of Kazan, the jewel of the Volga, falls to the Whites in early August.

In his own little corner of southern Russia, in Tsaritsyn, the Georgian bank-robber oversees a bloody reign of terror. Stalin makes himself dictator, acquiring a taste for independent action and rule by fear. Under his watch, the local Cheka gains a reputation for cutting through human bones with hacksaws. So-called military specialists – former officers from the Tsar's forces whom Trotsky wants to integrate into the new Red Army – are arrested, held on a river barge and left to rot.

Trotsky sees this as interference in military affairs, putting Tsaritsyn's defence at risk. Stalin ignores the cosmopolitan war supremo's protests. He makes the town's bourgeoisie build trenches around the city instead. Mass arrests continue. Summary execution becomes the norm. Stalin crushes White plots – imaginary or real – with exemplary violence. Tsaritsyn's fate hangs by a thread.

CROYDON, ENGLAND: A glorious English summer's day, and the countryside spread out like a picnic. From his plane flying above it all Winston Churchill can clearly make out the road from Croydon, just south of London, to Caterham, on the South Downs. He fancies he can almost see as far as his own house, at Lullenden. By the evening he is in a French chateau – 'filled with the sort of ancient wood-carved furniture that you admire', he writes to his wife.

Winston has come hotfoot from London to see the beginnings of a British offensive against the Germans, in preparation for final victory – it is hoped – in 1919. The advantage the Allies have in men and materiel – increasing every month – now shows itself on the battlefield. British aeroplanes dominate the air and are able to spot with ease the location of the enemy's artillery battalions, making it more likely that they can be put out of action early on in the battle. More tanks are deployed than ever before. These material advantages make a preliminary artillery bombardment – effectively, a warning of impending assault – less necessary. When British, Canadian and Australian soldiers go over the top in Amiens they are more heavily armed than ever before. Each battalion is now half the size they were at the Somme, but has ten times as many machine guns.

The success of the combined Allied forces is immediately apparent. The Germans are forced out of their positions. The following morning, on his way towards Amiens, Churchill finds the road clogged with German prisoners of war. Over ten thousand have given themselves up. 'A sturdy lot', Winston writes home, 'though some of them were very young'. He feels a wave of pity. And then something more positive: could the war *really* be over by Christmas?

VIENNA: At first it sounds almost like a small and particularly persistent insect, a large mosquito perhaps. But the buzzing is too constant to be natural. Soon it is too loud, as well. From a good vantage point on the outskirts of the city, a few can make out the true source of the noise. In the far distance, coming in from the south, a biplane bumps through the air towards Vienna. A little later, spectators can make out not one, but eight or nine planes, flying towards the city in formation. An aerial acrobatics display perhaps?

Swooping down over the Habsburg capital, at last we can see who is flying one of the planes: Gabriele D'Annunzio. He grabs a fistful of leaflets in the colours of the Italian flag. They flutter to the ground like confetti. A camera on board one of the planes captures the moment on film. The citizens of Vienna come out to watch. They should be terrified. Some almost cheer.

Some leaflets are written in Italian in D'Annunzio's own flowery prose. 'We didn't come except for the delight of our own audacity, except to prove what we dare to do and what we can do, whenever we want', one of them reads. 'Long live Italy!' A few bear the poet's signature. The leaflets in German are cruder. 'Do you want to continue the war?' the Viennese are asked. 'Do so, if you wish to commit suicide'. Next time, we will be back with bombs. There will be two million American soldiers in France by next month, they warn. Your destiny is defeat.

The press in Vienna puts a brave face on it. The Italians were actually *over* Vienna for only a few minutes, one journalist writes. One plane was forced to land outside the city as a result of engine trouble. They never could have actually bombed the city, as the weight of the ordnance would have made it impossible for the planes to cover the distance to and from Vienna safely. Still an impressive display of modern aviation, and how wonderfully theatrical. Austria could do with a bit of Italian flair. 'Where are our D'Annunzios?' the *Arbeiter-Zeitung* asks.

MOSCOW: A dark night in the Red capital. The impatient revolutionary gives a rousing speech at a factory – his third of the evening – railing against the evils of bourgeois democracy and offering his listeners a stark choice for the future of the revolution: 'victory or death'. Leaving the factory, without bodyguards, he is attacked.

Lenin's chauffeur initially mistakes the sound of gunfire for a motor car backfiring. Then he realises. The crowd scatters. The boss is lying face down on the ground. He is rushed to the Kremlin, his driver constantly turning around to check his condition. Vladimir's face grows paler and paler. 'Lenin!' his driver shouts at the guards to make them open the Kremlin gate. The Bolshevik leader is helped inside and his coat taken off. What is to be done? There are no proper medical facilities on hand in the Kremlin. In a panic, Vladimir's sister suggests someone go out and buy a lemon – but then worries that the grocer could be part of the plot as well. A doctor is called. Someone is sent to the pharmacy to get whatever medical supplies they can. A Bolshevik comrade's wife with medical training comes in, checks the leader's pulse and calmly administers morphine.

What has happened? Eyewitness testimony is confused. Was the assassin a man or a woman? How many shots? One shooter or several? Were there accomplices? A half-blind woman, a Socialist Revolutionary, is picked up and interrogated by the Cheka overnight. She claims that she is solely responsible. Her bag is searched: cigarettes, a brooch, hairpins – but no gun. Within days she is executed and her body burned. The case is closed; the mystery remains. Who ordered the hit? The Socialist Revolutionaries are soon blamed – they deny it – alongside their puppet-masters, the British and the French. A more awful thought is left unexpressed: that the enemy comes from within. Why was Lenin without bodyguards when, that very morning, the head of the Petrograd Cheka had been gunned down? Scores are being settled, people are being moved out of the way – but by whom? Is a power struggle under way within the regime?

The Bolshevik leadership crowd anxiously around the patient's bed. It might be convenient for some if he were now to die. Some wonder if they could do a better job without him, this disputatious, difficult and intransigent man, this perpetual, impatient schemer. Yet at this moment, far from the public eye, everything is done to keep Vladimir Lenin alive. Nadya is picked up from a conference on education she has been attending. She is driven home to the Kremlin in silence to find her husband fading fast. She cannot bear to watch his agony, taking refuge in the room next door. 'What are we going to do?' she asks those around her in desperation.

Vladimir urges her to make arrangements in case he does not pull through. Later, and to her consternation, he asks to see Inessa Armand, his old flame from years ago. When she arrives, Nadya discreetly takes Inessa's sixteen-year-old daughter on a tour of the Kremlin to give her husband and his former lover some privacy.

The telephone rings incessantly. No one sleeps that night. Across Russia, the outcome of the civil war is on a knife edge. But tonight, its cockpit is Moscow, where a man in late middle age fights for his life behind the walls of the Kremlin. Blood-soaked dressings are removed and washed in the leader's private bathtub. 'What's there to look at?' the impatient revolutionary asks when he sees the frightened expressions on his followers' faces. The doctors are concerned his gullet may be punctured. He is denied all liquids. He tries to persuade Nadya to get him a cup of tea. She refuses. Press bulletins announce that an assassination attempt has taken place. Within twenty-four hours, in prisons around the country, hundreds of prisoners have been executed by way of crude retaliation.

Trotsky is telegrammed to return to Moscow at once: 'ILYICH IS WOUNDED; IT'S UNCERTAIN HOW DANGEROUS THINGS ARE'. He rushes to the capital, not knowing whether his old rival will live or die. As in 1917, he turns his talents to propaganda. The epoch of Europe's bourgeois development, when society's contradictions could accumulate quite peacefully and blood flowed only in the colonies, is over, Leon Trotsky proclaims. He declares Lenin the man for the new tumultuous age into which the world has been thrown, an era of 'blood and iron'. Of course, the victory of the proletariat does not depend on one person, Trotsky says – and yet he praises Vladimir's personality as if it did. 'Any fool can shoot through Lenin's skull', he declares, 'but to recreate that skull is a difficult task even for nature itself.' Trotsky is not alone in transforming Lenin from the obstreperous political operator of real life into the semi-divine figure of myth. Another Bolshevik leader compares the writings of Lenin with the Bible and calls him 'the greatest leader ever known by humanity, the apostle of the socialist revolution'. At times like this, it pays to be seen to praise the leader – all the more if one intends to bury him.

From Tsaritsyn, Stalin has an earthier message to deliver after the assassination attempt. What is needed, he writes, is 'open, mass, systemic terror against the bourgeoisie'. Even as his life hangs in the balance, the impatient revolutionary's mind turns in the same direction. No crisis can be allowed to go to waste in the struggle for the revolution: 'it is necessary secretly – and urgently – to prepare the terror'. Now that a pretext for extreme measures has been helpfully provided, nothing must be held back.

FORT GIRONVILLE, FRANCE: At five in the morning, the first major American offensive of the war begins, to try and flatten the front and force the Germans out of the Saint-Mihiel salient. The US Secretary of War is on hand to observe the opening attack. Jim Europe is doing his duty in Paris, where his band plays in hospitals and army camps and even in the theatre where Stravinsky's *Rite of Spring* was premiered back in 1913.

The second wave of the attack is launched three hours later, the sun now rising over the battlefield. Pershing watches from his command post, trying to make out what is going on through the rain and the mist. By the time he leaves Fort Gironville, at nine o'clock, there are the first signs that the American offensive is successful: thousands of German prisoners are brought in. By early afternoon it is clear that the objectives set for the attack have been achieved and, in places, exceeded. 'The boys have done what we expected of them', Woodrow writes to his general. 'We are deeply proud of them and of their Chief.'

America savours the victory. 'Pershing Leads Army in First Big Drive', runs the headline in the *New York Times*: 'Gain of Five Miles; 8,000 Prisoners Taken'. A new chapter in American history – and at least a paragraph in world history – has just been written in France, one journalist writes: 'This operation far and away transcends anything that our troops have previously attempted.'

American soldiers are still arriving in France by the thousand every day.

MOSCOW – KAZAN: 'Recovery proceeding excellently', Lenin telegraphs to Trotsky. He urges the war commissar to be ruthless in suppressing 'kulak extortioners'. He cracks jokes with his doctors, while impatiently cross-examining them about the attempt on his life. (He has not yet been informed that the woman accused of shooting him has been put beyond further questioning.) He is eager to return to work.

On 10 September, *Pravda* announces that the Bolshevik leader is out of danger. Kazan is retaken by the Reds the same day. 'Comrades, it is no accident that it was yesterday that the doctors detected such a marked improvement that they allowed him to sit up in bed', the atheist Trotsky tells his troops, asserting a mystical connection between the leader's health and the military situation. A few days later, Lenin's home town of Simbirsk is retaken. The military situation, while still dire, is at least stabilising. The scattered regiments of Red Guards with which Trotsky began the year – essentially, revolutionaries with guns – are slowly being welded into something more substantial.

By the middle of September, two weeks after the attempt on his life, the Bolshevik leader is back at his desk, dictating, cajoling and threatening in his usual manner, as impatient with the pace of change as ever. Faster, faster, more, more. The impatient revolutionary demands that newspaper articles are made shorter and punchier. They should be charge sheets against the forces holding back the revolution, not long-winded political analysis. 'Fewer highbrow articles; closer to life', he commands. Class enemies should be identified in print. Inefficient military officers should be named and shamed. 'Where is the blacklist with the names of the lagging factories?' Lenin demands to know. A prominent German Marxist theoretician has written a pamphlet criticising the Bolshevik dictatorship. Vladimir fires off a furious note to his representatives in Berlin, Berne and Stockholm demanding it be sent to him – *as soon as it appears*'.

Another day, the impatient revolutionary writes to the commissar in charge of education to express his fury that there is no bust of Marx on public display in Moscow yet. And another thing: why is there not more revolutionary propaganda on the streets? 'I reprimand you for this criminal and lackadaisical attitude, and demand that the names of all responsible persons should be sent me for prosecution', Lenin writes: 'Shame on the saboteurs and thoughtless loafers.'

When he finds out that the Kremlin lift has still not been fixed after three days out of action, Lenin writes an angry note asking for a list of those in charge and demanding that 'penalties' be imposed. 'There are people suffering from heart disease' – his wife Nadya is one of them – 'for whom climbing the stairs is harmful and dangerous', the Bolshevik leader writes. 'I have pointed out a thousand times that this lift must be kept in order and one person should be responsible for it'.

The bullets may have weakened Vladimir Lenin's body; but his mind is still sharp. On matters large and small, there can be no let-up. No one else can be trusted but him to get things done. The pressure must remain firmly on.

AVESNES-SUR-HELPE, FRANCE: A psychiatric doctor arrives at German army advance headquarters, sent for by the army's medical staff to speak to one of its most senior officers: Ludendorff himself.

As the German army is on the brink of collapse, senior officers worry about their military leader's state of mind. Some say Ludendorff has burst into tears on more than one occasion. Others report his worrying inability to make decisions, or the shortness of his temper when faced with further bad news; an independent peace démarche sent by Austria–Hungary to the Allies without telling Wilhelm first; the dire situation in Bulgaria; further British and French attacks. The general is said to stay up late into the night telephoning front commanders at random. One doctor has already tried to convince the general to alter his habits, without effect. Now, with Hindenburg's approval, a doctor has been sent for whom Ludendorff knows and trusts, a man with experience of nervous disorders from his clinic in Berlin. He arrives unannounced one morning at the general's door.

Ludendorff freely admits to this familiar face that he has not felt himself for some time. As Dr Hochheimer describes it in a letter to his wife, 'he hasn't spared a thought for the well-being of his soul for years'. The doctor advises more regular sleep and exercise. He prescribes breathing exercises and massages. He places flowers in Ludendorff's room to remind him of the beauty of nature. Finally, he suggests the general adapt his speaking voice from its usual military bark. The general seems to take well to the treatment over the next few days. He asks after the doctor's family. His mood seems to lighten.

Occasionally, he expresses optimism that a heroic defence of Germany can be organised. Perhaps the army can hold out despite everything. Hope dies last.

THE BRONX, NEW YORK: Friends suggest he should lay low for a while back in America. That is not John Reed's style. He has a story to tell, he must tell it, he must be part of it.

In July, he is in Chicago to witness the trial of over a hundred members of the radical trades union the Industrial Workers of the World, arrested for hindering the draft and encouraging desertion. Reed praises the 'hardrock blasters, tree fellers, wheat binders, longshoremen, the boys who do the strong work of the world', noting that though their union representatives are just now facing judgement in an American courtroom, he sees in the faces before him the same proud, unquenchable revolutionary fire which set Petrograd alight. In September, he gives a fierce pro-Bolshevik speech in Harlem, recounting his Russian experiences. He has started to write a book about them.

The next day, Reed is arrested for sedition. The third time since his return.

GORKI, OUTSIDE MOSCOW, RUSSIA: Finally accepting the need for a little rest – while not being too far from the Kremlin – Lenin agrees to take a working holiday in a mansion just outside town which used to belong to one of Moscow's leading families.

Vladimir and Nadya are greeted by the guards with a large bunch of flowers and a little speech before being shown around the house, built in the classical style with a splendid portico (a good place to read, Lenin notes), electric lighting throughout and countless bathrooms. The large grounds in which the house is situated vaguely remind Lenin of Switzerland – a public park in Zurich, perhaps. It is quite unlike anywhere they have actually lived before.

A trifle overwhelmed, Vladimir chooses the smallest bedroom (even that has three huge standing mirrors on the floor, Nadya notes). One evening, when it begins to get chilly, the champion of proletarian dictatorship asks one of the guards to light a fire in one of the house's many fireplaces. Too late they discover that that particular fireplace was only decorative. It has no chimney – what a ridiculous bourgeois conceit! The attic catches fire. The flames have to be doused with pails of water. Lumps of plaster fall off the ceiling onto the floor below. They get over the embarrassment soon enough.

BUDAPEST: In the magnificent surroundings of the Gellért Hotel and a hall in the Hungarian Academy of Sciences, an international Psychoanalytic Congress is held in Budapest. Sigmund Freud is beaming.

For the first time in a psychoanalytic congress, participants include senior government officials, keen to understand how psychoanalysis may help war-wounded soldiers get back from the Continent's psychiatric hospitals to where they are most needed: the front. Officers in Austrian and German uniforms sit stiffly behind student desks, as if back in training school. Someone spots a general. There are no French or British or American participants, of course. A few hardy Dutchmen have made their way across Germany, bearing gifts from neutral Holland. There is an official reception with the mayor. A banquet is laid on. Despite Freud's warnings to Ferenczi not to let the generosity of psychoanalysis's benefactors make things too lavish, lest this should detract from the more serious matters at hand, he cannot but be pleased with the result. At last, a proper congress, with all the trappings. At last, psychoanalysis seems socially acceptable – *hoffähig*, presentable at court, as the stuck-up Viennese would say. Food appears from nowhere, as if the war were a million miles away rather than a few hundred. Spirits rise at such unexpected largesse. The trip, it seems, has been worth it.

The proceedings of the business part of the congress are more dour. Speaker after speaker addresses the immediate problems of the war. The symptoms of shell shock are described and methods of treatment discussed, including the one of using strong electric currents to try and force patients out of their mental state. Other world events are mentioned. Ferenczi jokes about the hard-pressed Bolsheviks. They are just beginning to realise, he suggests, that it is psychoanalysis and not Marxism which is the key to understanding human behaviour, as he boasts of a steady stream of Bolsheviks asking questions about Freud. The soldiers in the audience nod along, or nod off. Civilian officials cross their arms and assume a look of intense concentration, while their minds wander off elsewhere. Freud sits in the front row, loudly sucking a lump of sugar, his thoughts inevitably drifting towards nicotine. Eventually he can contain himself no longer. He lights up, and as he does – as if driven by some unconscious group urge of imitation for their leader – Freud's disciples follow suit and search inside pockets for their pipes and cigars. Soon smoke billows through the hall in oily puffs. A red-faced building caretaker comes in to protest. No one listens. A Budapest hack writes up the congress in an article for a local magazine under the headline 'Freud's Cigar'.

When Freud's turn comes to speak he plays the father-preacher to his flock. He looks beyond the war to the peace which must follow. 'There are only a handful of us', he intones severely, reminding his audience of the importance of their role: 'Compared to the vast amount of neurotic misery which there is in the world – and perhaps need not be – the quantity we can do away with is almost negligible.' Unless ... And here Freud makes his pitch. He summons up a picture of the future where, with state support, psychoanalytic treatment is no more unusual than treatment for toothache or tuberculosis. He envisages a time when psychoanalytic clinics flourish across the world, providing free services for all those who need it. 'It may be a long time before the State comes to see these duties as urgent', Freud tells his audience. 'Some time or other, however, it must come to this.' These are revolutionary times, after all.

Back in Vienna, Freud counts the congress a success: 'I am swimming in satisfaction, I am light-hearted to know that my problem child, my life's work, is protected and preserved for the future.' As late summer turns to autumn, and as the situation of the Central Powers becomes more and more desperate, for the first time in months Freud allows a little uncharacteristic optimism to creep into his correspondence: 'I will see better times approaching, if only from a distance.'

BRESLAU: Rosa Luxemburg is worried. The old argument she used to have with Vladimir – whether a revolution is led by a party or operates through the energy that it releases in society – is now being played out in real time in Russia. Lenin's revolution looks increasingly like a coup d'état, rather than a genuine revolution of the masses. The Bolsheviks are allowing their tactics to become their ideology. If this continues, Rosa fears, then 'socialism will be decreed from behind a few official desks by a dozen intellectuals'. To overthrow the rotten Kerensky regime was one thing; to build socialism, another. 'The negative, the tearing down, can be decreed', Rosa writes; 'the building up, the positive, cannot.'

Rosa's own conception of what a socialist revolution must be – a spontaneous swelling-up of proletarian consciousness, and a dynamic, continuous process of reordering society by and for the masses – seems to be in jeopardy. She warns of the alternative: 'Freedom only for the supporters of the government, only for the members of one party – however numerous they may be – is no freedom at all.' Terror cannot bring lasting social change and will besmirch the image of the revolution. An uncomfortable question animates Rosa's concerns: will the Russian example launch world revolution, or kill it dead? 'Yes, dictatorship!' she agrees. 'But this dictatorship must be the work of a class and not of a little leading minority in the name of the class – that is, it must proceed step by step out of the active participation of the masses, it must be under their direct influence.'

Lenin and Trotsky are not miracle-workers, of course. They have acted as they think fit, beset by enemies on all sides. Whatever errors they have made, they must be thanked for trying. They have been far braver than the German Social Democrats – 'spineless jellyfish' – whose chief concern seems to be maintaining imperial order under the Kaiser. But in this latest phase of world affairs, nine months after the Bolshevik seizure of power, Rosa sees the risk of a dreadful strategic error being made in Moscow.

'The flames of the world war are leaping across Russian soil and at any moment may engulf the Russian revolution', she writes in a letter to the Spartacists. She worries that her old sparring partner Vladimir Ilyich may be tempted to save himself and his regime through an alliance of convenience with the German generals. Such a pairing would be grotesque, a Frankenstein accommodation between revolution and reaction, between Moscow and Berlin. The moral credibility of the workers' revolution would be destroyed. The most reactionary state in Europe would be helped to military victory. Even if the Bolsheviks clung on in Moscow, world revolution would be stillborn.

Vladimir has always been more of a politician than Rosa, ready to make sharp deviations if he thinks they are needed. Rosa believes the revolution must be kept pure. However difficult the situation, the Bolsheviks must resist further German pressure. As for the German workers, Rosa is exasperated. When will they finally be compelled to rebel?

'Four weeks ago, it looked as though big things were underway in the Rhineland', Rosa writes angrily to a friend, 'but of course our blockheads didn't accomplish anything politically and the movement collapsed'. Where are the German soldiers and workers' councils? Where is the Berlin Soviet? Everything depends on the German workers now.

Sofia, the Kingdom of Bulgaria: Grand Vizier Talaat, returning from a trip to visit the Ottoman Empire's allies in Germany, stops briefly in Sofia. The news there is bad. The Bulgarian King Ferdinand (the one whom Wilhelm made such fun of) is seeking an armistice. The game is up. 'We've eaten shit', Talaat tells his compatriots as he boards the train to Istanbul.

Mustafa Kemal is in the Ottoman province of Syria, where he is given a fresh command. British and Arab forces are driving further north every day.

Spa: In moments of lucidity he sees the position is hopeless – Germany can no longer win this war. Yet still he tries to find a way out. 'I am like a drowning man clutching at straws', Ludendorff admits to senior officers when he tells them of the latest rumours he has picked up: that lung infections are ravaging the French army and that the plague has hit Milan.

The general's entourage decide to go above his head, sending a message to Berlin that the military position is now untenable. Peace must be made at all costs. 'His Excellency is still desperate enough to fight', one of Ludendorff's aides writes in his diary. 'He does not have the courage to make an end of it; he won't do it unless forced.' On a Saturday evening at the end of September, the German war leader finally cracks.

THE WESTERN FRONT: Boats arriving from America have tens, then hundreds, of dead or dying soldiers on board by the time they have crossed the Atlantic and dock in Brest, where Jim Europe and his band arrived nine months ago. The influenza victims' lungs are blue and swollen. Nothing can be done for them. Local hospitals are overwhelmed. The disease starts spreading amongst the civilian population.

Woodrow calls a conference in Washington. Should the troop transports be stopped? Is shipping troops to Europe doing more harm than good, sending ill men in cramped conditions to a Continent already on the point of starvation? The army recommends the ships be equipped with more coffins and embalming fluid instead.

MUNICH, BAVARIA: A secret society is formed in the Bavarian capital. It calls itself the Thule Society, in reference to the supposed ancient origins of the Germanic peoples in the far north. It is animated by a witches' brew of beliefs: worship of the sun and various other life forces; a belief in the superiority of the so-called Aryan race; a conviction in the importance of blood; a cultish fondness for neo-medieval ritual, Nordic rune-writing and faux-historic initiation ceremonies. Ardent anti-Semitism is *de rigueur*.

A man who calls himself a baron (he is in fact the son of a Silesian train engineer) leads the society. Others drawn into its strange orbit include the German translator of Ibsen's *Peer Gynt* and a sports journalist called Harrer. Most are outsiders in the Catholic high society of Bavaria. Several are Protestants. Some have spent time living in Turkey. All wear swastikas – bronze pins for the men, gold brooches for the women. Every Saturday the society's men and women meet in the club rooms of one of the city's grand hotels, the Vier Jahreszeiten, either to initiate new members into the society or to listen to lectures from fellow Thule members on their latest theories and pet subjects. One early talk is on the subject of divining rods.

Over the summer, the society acquires a long-established newspaper and gives it a radical twist. 'Race purity', the *Münchener Beobachter* declares, 'is the basis of national well-being.' *Kultur* is carried in the blood. The claim is based in shadowy theories of historical evolution, quite popular in America. 'New research has shown', the *Beobachter* asserts, 'that northern Europe, northern Germany in particular, is the cradle of all those bearing *Kultur* and who, since the dawn of time, have sent wave after wave of people to bring *Kultur* to all the world and fertilised it with their blood.'

AUTUMN

CHICAGO: For a few seconds he is there right in front of her. A moment later he is gone. In the middle of a Pathé newsreel about the war, Marcelline Hemingway spots the jerky black-and-white figure of her kid brother, all grown up now in his military uniform, being pushed about in a wheelchair by a pretty nurse on a sun-drenched porch in a foreign land.

In the foreign land itself, Hemingway tries one last time to get back into the action before the whole show is over. He makes for the front. But jaundice catches up with him. By the beginning of November, he is back in hospital in Milan again, further away from danger than if he were in Chicago, where influenza closes everything except the city's churches for weeks.

Ernest Hemingway's war is over. For the rest of the world, it limps on.

SPA: On the first day of autumn, Ludendorff calls his staff officers together to a meeting.

The Western Front could break at any moment, he tells them. Germany's allies have already folded, or will soon be forced to surrender. A combination of Arab and British Empire forces captures Damascus the same day; Istanbul is wide open after the collapse of Bulgaria; Austria–Hungary is a spent force militarily. The German army, 'poisoned with Spartacist and socialist ideas', cannot be relied upon. The real enemy now is revolution.

In consequence of this, the general tells his staff, the German high command has recommended to the Kaiser that Germany sue for peace immediately. Having resisted such a decision for weeks, Ludendorff is now adamant it must happen immediately. (In the Reichstag, there is surprise at the sudden change of heart; and the Kaiser, while accepting that a cease-fire may be the only way of saving his throne, worries about the widows who will now blame him for all the blood which has been spent when, of course, he wanted none of it.)

At Ludendorff's announcement that morning, some begin to weep. A few find themselves holding each other's hands so tightly they feel they might break. The general has only a few final words left to add. But these are political. They will weigh heavily in the future. He has recommended to Wilhelm that any new German government be made up of 'those responsible for putting us where we are today'. The socialists and pacifists will be forced to make the peace. 'They must be made to drink the soup they have brewed', he tells his officers.

A lieutenant grabs the general's arm. 'Is this the last word? Am I alive or am I dreaming?' he asks. 'God has wished it so', replies the general. 'I see no other escape.' In private, he tries to soften the blow. A direct approach to Wilson, bypassing the British and French, may yet produce an armistice on honourable terms. 'The fourteen points are not so absolute', the general suggests. With a new Chancellor in Berlin – the liberal Prince Max von Baden – perhaps Woodrow will soften his position. But if acceptable terms cannot be secured, 'believe me, we will fight on to the bitter end'. Two possibilities, then: an honourable peace or glorious annihilation.

That evening, a birthday party for Hindenburg goes ahead as planned at Spa. As is traditional, there are drinking songs and dancing. But all those present know that they are witnessing the end of an era. 'You and I will be hanged some day', one of Ludendorff's close associates whispers in the general's ear. Some say Ludendorff has lost his nerve.

GORKI: Reports come in every day about anti-government protests spreading through Germany. The unpopularity of the Kaiser's war is finally turning the people against his regime. Nadya and Vladimir are beside themselves. At last! The revolution is spreading. From his country retreat the impatient revolutionary fires off a note instructing Trotsky and another top Bolshevik to set up a meeting the very next day, in Moscow, to discuss matters in committee. He commands that an automobile be sent the following morning to pick him up. Only a one-word confirmation by telephone, he insists: *agreed*. One cannot be too careful.

'Things have so "accelerated" in Germany that we must not fall behind either', the impatient revolutionary writes to his Moscow comrades, 'but today we are already behind.' There will be no alliance with the Kaiser (or with the Social Democrats for that matter). Instead, the German workers must be given encouragement to revolt. The Bolshevik leadership should declare themselves ready to die to help them. An army of three million must be raised as soon as possible. The moment must be seized: 'The international revolution has come so close in one week that it has to be reckoned with as an event of the next few days.'

In the midst of all this, Lenin finds time to be infuriated about the work of a German Marxist he used to worship – someone who actually *knew* Karl Marx – and who has now published a pamphlet criticising the Bolsheviks for their turn towards the methods of dictatorship. There is a lot at stake for Lenin here: the question of who is the better interpreter of Marx – the man chosen to be his literary executor or the terroriser of the Zurich library staff. While Europe seems on the cusp of actual revolution, Vladimir's mind is on the paper war.

Lenin cannot let it rest. He decides to write a counterblast and sits up every night till the early hours venting his spleen against a man he now describes as a 'despicable renegade', whose distortions of Marx, in Lenin's reading, make Marx himself into a kind of soggy liberal. His irritation is immense. But getting it all into shape takes longer than he expected. 'To analyse Kautsky's theoretical mistakes in detail would mean repeating what I have said in *The State and Revolution*', Lenin writes. But he cannot resist: 'I must mention, in passing, a few gems of renegacy ...'

It is as if he is back in Zurich in 1917, arguing it out over a beer with some dimwit or other.

WASHINGTON – BERLIN – PARIS – LONDON: A German diplomatic note is sent to Washington requesting that Woodrow take the initiative to bring about peace. It asks for an immediate armistice 'in order to prevent further bloodshed'. A parallel Austrian note adds a few lines about Charles's peace attempts in the hope that this will soften the President's approach to Austria–Hungary now. In Istanbul, the three pashas resign. But it is much harder to end a war than to start one.

There are complex calculations to be made. A balance must be struck between what the public wants, what the army can bear, and the higher interests of the state (by which those in charge generally mean themselves). For those on the losing side, political survival and national honour are major concerns. For those who feel things going their way, there is the question of how far to push: whether to exact righteous revenge, or be magnanimous. Make peace too soon, or on the wrong terms, and the sacrifices will have been in vain. Make peace too late, and more lives will be lost for no good reason. So much depends on timing.

No one knows when exhaustion will result in breakdown – of their side, or the enemy's. Within days of insisting that a ceasefire is the only way of avoiding Germany's total collapse, Ludendorff seems suddenly quite chipper about the ability of the army to hold out, suggesting that perhaps Germany should fight on after all. For the Allies, it is perhaps easier to continue fighting than agree the precise terms on which to stop. Some argue that the only way to crush Prussian militarism is to push on all the way to Berlin; others want an armistice, but only after a few more victories have been secured, particularly for their own armies, so as to increase their national prestige when it comes to making peace.

Woodrow Wilson sends his own reply to Berlin, without first bothering to consult his partners. He trusts only himself to give the world the peace it needs.

THE WESTERN FRONT: As the German army retreats, farms are pillaged and houses burned. Whether the intention is to slow down the Allied advance, or simply to feed off the land, is unclear. Allied officers warn their soldiers to be careful when inspecting seemingly abandoned buildings. There may be snipers. Or hidden machine-gun posts. Improvised explosive devices are left behind for the careless to touch: books rigged up to grenades and pianos filled with explosives.

There are few solid defensive lines left for the Germans to fall back on. Neither is there time to dig proper trenches and there are few concrete pillboxes in which to take cover. There are only hills, and rivers, and a sea of mud. One night, near the small village of Wervik, right on the border between France and Belgium, three German dispatch runners from the 16th Bavarian Reserve Infantry Regiment find themselves caught up in a British gas attack. They are taken to a field hospital at Oudenaarde. Within a few hours they can barely see from the effects of the gas. Slowly, steadily, their world gets darker. Then it turns black. Nothing left but themselves to contemplate. The horror of the void.

MOSCOW – THE SOUTHERN FRONT: The telegrams fly. War commissar Trotsky accuses Stalin of amateurism and interference in military matters he does not understand; Stalin accuses Trotsky of being all mouth and no trousers.

'The point is, Trotsky generally speaking cannot get by without noisy gestures', the Georgian bank-robber writes. 'At Brest-Litovsk he delivered a blow to the cause by his far-fetched "leftist" gesturing', he continues. His treatment of the Czechs caused them to revolt. 'Now he delivers a further blow by his gesturing about discipline, and yet all that this Trotskyite discipline amounts to in reality is the most prominent leaders on the war front peering up the backsides of military specialists from the camp of "non-party" counter-revolutionaries'. Stalin asks Vladimir Ilyich to intervene to bring the unruly Trotsky to heel. He is 'no lover of noise and scandal' himself, the Georgian writes.

The war correspondent turned military supremo bristles. 'I categorically insist on Stalin's recall', he wires to Moscow in October. It is a matter of military necessity: 'There remains only a short while before the autumn weather makes the roads impassable, when there will be no through road here either on foot or horseback.' Trotsky wins this round – in part. Military specialists are to be encouraged (or forced) to join the Red Army. Any captured White officer joining the Reds must sign a paper agreeing that their family will be arrested if they desert. 'By this means we shall lighten the load on the prisons and obtain military specialists', Trotsky explains: justifying his approach as a simple matter of military necessity. The Georgian bank-robber is called to Moscow and given a different job. But then he is sent back to Tsaritsyn with the task of smoothing things over.

The city is saved from the Whites, just. In later years it will be called Stalingrad.

VIENNA: 'The bankruptcy of the old state is now a fact', Victor Adler tells parliament.

Emperor Charles tries to win American favour and buy some time by promising wide constitutional reform within the empire. It looks like desperation. The nationalities of the Habsburg realm are already taking matters into their own hands. The empire's Poles look forward to an independent Polish state. In Prague, the double-headed eagle starts disappearing from the streets, and the police do not know which way to jump. Slovenes, Croats and Serbs – collectively known as the southern or *yugo*-Slavs – have already set up their own national council in Zagreb. Autonomy is no longer enough, Woodrow Wilson responds. Benito Mussolini calls Woodrow the 'magnificent *Duce* of the peoples' for his stance.

In Budapest, the capital of the other half of his failing empire, Charles's reform proposals are taken to represent the liquidation of the constitutional bargain he swore to uphold in 1917. There are calls for Hungarian troops to come home now rather than keep fighting for Austria. At the opening of a new university, the imperial anthem is hissed. No one will take the Emperor's instructions any more. 'It's always difficult to find a crew for a sinking ship', he comments to Zita on a trip to sell his reforms in Budapest. When the imperial couple return to Vienna they leave the children behind in the Hungarian capital to demonstrate that their departure is only temporary.

BERLIN: Woodrow's latest diplomatic note blows away any last illusions of an armistice of equals. It proposes what amounts to capitulation. The Allies' present military superiority will be guaranteed. The submarines will have to return to port. Arbitrary power – the Kaiser, that is – will have to be curbed. In other words, the Americans are demanding regime change as the price of peace.

In meetings with top civilian and military officials in the German capital, Ludendorff is evasive as to the consequences of rejecting Wilson's demands. When asked whether another six months of fighting, with twenty thousand to twenty-five thousand casualties a month, would earn Germany a better peace he answers breezily: 'Maybe it would, maybe it would not.' (He orders that his stepson's body, buried in the grounds at Spa, be dug up and sent home just the same.) The general asks a Social Democrat politician if he can somehow boost the people's morale again. 'It's a question of potatoes', the politician responds. With the army unwilling to provide assurances, the civilians take charge. The desire to perish in honour may be suitable for an individual, the new German Chancellor writes, 'but the responsible statesman must recognise that a people in its entirety has the right to demand with all due sobriety that they live, rather than die in beauty'.

VENICE, ITALY: Gabriele D'Annunzio confesses to a friend: 'I love the war'. To another, he writes that 'for you and me, and for those like us, peace is a disaster'.

MOSCOW: Lenin gives his first public speech since the attempt on his life in August.

'Comrades, this is the fifth year of the war and the universal collapse of imperialism is as plain as can be', the impatient revolutionary tells a meeting in Moscow. 'Everyone can now see revolution must come in every country in the war'. Bolshevism is on the march across Western Europe, in Italy, France,

Britain and Spain. The workers are giving up on spineless social democratic types and veering left. 'Bolshevism has become the worldwide theory and tactics of the international proletariat!' Lenin thunders. For or against the Bolsheviks: that is the only dividing line which matters now in socialist parties around the world.

'Three months ago, people used to laugh when we said there might be a revolution in Germany', the impatient revolutionary says. 'They said that only half-crazy Bolsheviks could believe in a German revolution.' Times have changed: 'In these few months Germany, from a mighty empire, has become a rotten hulk.' And the same forces operating in Germany are at work elsewhere, in America, Britain and France. 'This force will loom larger and larger and become even more formidable than the Spanish flu', Lenin declares.

And yet it is precisely at this moment that Bolshevism is most in danger. The enemy is waking up. 'The more the revolution develops, the more the bourgeoisie rally together', Lenin warns. The capitalist powers have already intervened in Russia, directly and indirectly. But the Czechs, Cossacks and Whites are only pawns in a wider struggle. Once world capitalism fathoms the seriousness of its predicament German capitalists may strike some kind of bargain with the British, French and the Americans – and then all turn east.

'The workers are mature enough to be told the truth', the impatient revolutionary avers. The revolution is going to have to fight for its life, on many fronts, maybe for years. The army must be everyone's top priority. Sacrifice and discipline are needed for the struggle ahead.

Lenin is still working on his pamphlet day and night.

VIENNA: The Habsburg Empire still exists on paper. Each day brings evidence that it will not last long.

In most places, the transition is peaceful. In the Adriatic port of Fiume, Croats disarm Hungarians without a fight, and the navy is transferred into the hands of the locals. In Prague, the Czechs pretend that a declaration of independence on 28 October is simply a loyal echo of Charles's reform promises – and, to avoid any unpleasantness, the Habsburg authorities pretend to believe them. The troops are kept in their barracks.

In Vienna, the empire's German-speaking parliamentarians, including those from the Czech kingdom of Bohemia, set themselves up as the self-declared provisional German-Austrian National Assembly. The groundwork is laid for a new country called German-Austria. In Budapest, a local army commander orders soldiers to fire on a student demonstration. A former premier is murdered in his home by those who blame him for the war. A playboy liberal is appointed Hungarian Minister-President by a popular Habsburg Archduke.

Charles is a spectator to this historical unfurling of his inheritance. He tries to prevent further bloodshed at the front by asking the Pope to intervene with the Italians to stop them from launching a last offensive. To no avail. Italian artillery begins firing one year to the day since the beginning of Austria's Caporetto offensive. Rome wants a stunning victory now to erase the memory of that defeat.

On the seven hundredth day of his troubled reign Charles breaks definitively with Kaiser Wilhelm by making clear that his government will now negotiate a separate peace. Wilhelm is scathing of the betrayal: 'We have had to endure this war in order not to leave Austria in the lurch, and now she does so to us'. Germany now stands alone against the world.

Sigmund Freud, who had greeted the outbreak of war with enthusiasm, is now caught up in the excitement of its end. It is 'terribly thrilling', he writes to a friend, to live through days where 'the old has died, but the new has not yet replaced it'. He will shed no tears for '*this* Austria or *this* Germany'. To Ferenczi in Budapest he advises the most dramatic course of action: 'Withdraw your libido from your fatherland in a timely fashion and shelter it in psychoanalysis.' Apparently it is the only safe place for it.

PASEWALK, THE GERMAN REICH: Amongst the new arrivals at a Prussian military hospital by the Baltic Sea is one of the dispatch runners from Flanders, temporarily blinded by British poison gas, in abject pain, his eyelids swollen, hysterical from shock. He lies powerless in hospital, separated from his regiment, from the few he might call friend. He hears whispers of retreat, collapse, betrayal. Adolf Hitler burns with indignation.

MUDROS, THE OTTOMAN EMPIRE: Aboard a British warship named after an ancient Greek hero, the Ottomans sign an armistice. Talaat, Djemal and Enver Pasha escape Istanbul aboard a German ship.

BERLIN – SPA: Ludendorff issues an order to the army stating that the peace terms on offer from Woodrow Wilson cannot be squared with military honour.

At a royal palace in Berlin, the man who told Wilhelm to start peace negotiations now tells him he should break them off. He loses his temper with the monarch. 'You seem to forget that you are talking to a King', the Kaiser reminds him. Ludendorff's offer to resign is accepted. (Hindenburg keeps his mouth shut and remains in his post.) 'The Kaiser thinks he can build an empire with the Social Democrats', he bellows at his adjutant. 'Mark my words: there will be no Kaiser within two weeks.' Members of his staff are already weighing up emigration options, with Chile and Argentina most popular.

Wilhelm decides to return to headquarters in Spa.

WASHINGTON DC: Discussions begin about the possible location of the future peace conference. The French push for Paris. Though it is still under German occupation, the Belgians suggest Brussels as a symbolic choice. Woodrow writes to Colonel Edward House: 'Much as I should enjoy Paris I think a neutral place of meeting much wiser, care being taken not to choose a place where either German or English influence would be too strong.' His preference is for Lausanne, Switzerland.

SPA: The Prussian Interior Minister is sent to military headquarters to persuade the Kaiser to abdicate. Wilhelm is having none of it: 'It would be incompatible with my duties as successor to Frederick the Great, towards God, the people and my conscience.' He seems convinced that if he were to go then the army would disintegrate. He will not give up his throne, he writes to a friend, 'on account of a few hundred Jews or a thousand workers'. He will answer troublemakers with machine guns.

THE AUSTRO-ITALIAN FRONT LINE: Carrying a flag of surrender and heralded by a trumpet signal, an Austrian captain tries bravely to make his way across enemy lines to hand a formal peace overture to the Italians. The messenger is shelled. Austrian commanders try an open radio transmission to get their message across. The Italians question the credentials of a proposed peace commission. They are in no hurry to halt their advance.

The town of Vittorio Veneto is reconquered by Italian troops. Austro-Hungarian forces collapse. On the last day of October an Austrian general is finally allowed through the lines to sue for peace. He is sent to the villa of an Italian Senator near Padua and told to wait.

Moscow: News from Austria is garbled. The impatient revolutionary speculates on the course of events. 'Friedrich Adler is very likely on his way to Vienna after his release from prison', Lenin tells a rally. 'The first day of the Austrian workers' revolution is probably being celebrated on the squares of Vienna.' In fact, Adler is still in jail and Charles is still at Schönbrunn. But details hardly matter at times like these. What *must* happen *will* happen.

'Hard as it was for us to cope with famine and our enemies,' Lenin says, 'we now see that we have millions of allies'.

The Austro-Italian front line – Vienna: The peak of the highest mountain in Habsburg territory is abandoned by its Austrian guardians, who leave the imperial flag flying at half-mast. The Italians surge forward over the Isonzo river, occupying all the land they failed to gain in the previous three years of war. Several hundred thousand Austro-Hungarian troops are taken prisoner. Amongst them is Sigmund Freud's son Martin.

Monday 4 November 1918, 3 p.m. The armistice comes into force. Gabriele D'Annunzio writes a macabre Lord's Prayer: 'O dead who are in earth, as in heaven, hallowed be your names'. He swears to keep alive their 'sacred hatred' and continue their fight. He warns against political compromises which might, in his words, mutilate the soldiers' victory. The territory promised to Italy must be handed over in full.

In Vienna, ministers gather in St Stephen's cathedral to celebrate the Emperor's name day. Across the empire, the troops head home. Barracks are plundered for food. A trainload of Austrian soldiers arrives at one station stark naked. Their clothes were stolen by Hungarians along the way.

London: 'A drizzle of empires falling through the air', Winston tells his assistant. He decides to visit the front one last time.

Kiel, Germany: Mutiny breaks out in the imperial fleet. The sailors call each other comrade. A wave of revolutionary fervour spreads from ship to ship. 'There is no turning back any more', a proclamation reads. A Social Democrat sent up from Berlin to calm the situation is elected chairman of the sailors' council. The sound of gunshot echoes around the city. No one knows whether the shots are intended to celebrate the people's victory, or whether they are the sound of loyal imperial forces trying to put the mutiny down. The hussars are said to be on their way from Hamburg.

Spa: Officers at headquarters look at the map to find a good spot where the Kaiser could lead some soldiers into a final battle and thereby earn himself a hero's death. 'Whoever wants to can sign up', one writes in his diary. The Kaiser is not informed of the plan.

The Ghent road, Belgium: The front line has become supple again. Allied troops are advancing at pace. Winston's car takes a wrong turning into the battle zone. 'I was puzzled', he writes after the event, 'to see a peasant suddenly throw himself down behind the wall of a house; something seemed to be very odd about his gesture'. The sound of a shell burst a moment later explains his behaviour. Winston still makes it to Bruges in time for lunch. 'All's well that ends well', he writes cheerfully.

Berlin: Mutiny leaps from Kiel to other cities along Germany's northern coast. Red sailors stream into Berlin by train. Workers and soldiers' councils spring up across the country. The Russian embassy, whose staff are suspected of coordinating events, is raided by government forces. The German revolution has begun.

Petrograd – Moscow: Great armies have been destroyed on Europe's battlefields. Europe's old kingdoms are being swept away. Even at this very moment, magnificent empires are crumbling under the pressure of the war. And yet that motley crew of wide-eyed revolutionaries, once mocked and told they could never mount a successful workers' revolt in backwards Russia, are still standing. In spite of invasion, civil war, disease, hunger and assassination their regime, the Bolshevik regime, has survived its first year in power. Surely that is something to celebrate.

A small fortune is set aside to prepare Petrograd and Moscow for the festivities. Millions of roubles are available. Seventy-one sites around the old capital are chosen to be specially decorated. Bands play from balconies. Children are taught revolutionary songs. Mobile cinemas show stirring movies. The people of Petrograd are told that the events of October 1917 were *their* revolution: a popular uprising, not a party coup. They must be made to understand the scale of what has happened, the permanence of the change. Terror shows them there is no going back; mass propaganda is intended to push them forward.

The Bolshevik Party takes pride of place, of course. Non-Bolsheviks involved in the revolution last year are excluded from the commemoration: they do not fit with the story the choreographers of the new regime want to tell. The fact that some prominent Bolsheviks vigorously (and publicly) opposed Lenin's coup last year is conveniently forgotten.

This is a time for new stories to be told – stories that make the regime's triumph appear inevitable and its leadership look united. It is a time for warring revolutionaries to make peace with each other, at least on the surface. The Georgian bank-robber writes an article for *Pravda* praising the role of a man he despises. 'All the work regarding the practical side of organising the uprising was carried out under the direct management of the Chair of the Petrograd Soviet, Comrade Trotsky', Comrade Stalin writes (imagine the pain of putting that down on paper). 'It can be said, without doubt, that the defection of the garrison to the Soviet and the organisation of the Military Revolutionary Committee depended above all on Comrade Trotsky's contribution.'

One year later, and Petrograd has become holy ground. The revolution has been sacralised. As the anniversary date approaches, Petrograd's bridges and public spaces are renamed, with such catchy new nomenclature as Dictatorship of the Proletariat Square. Tsarist symbols are removed or covered up. Carpenters and construction workers on other projects are simply commandeered to work on the celebrations. Potential troublemakers are put in jail.

A special news sheet is produced. 'Shortly the revolution will pass from Austria to Italy', it crows. The red flag will fly over Berlin and Paris soon. London might hold out a couple of years 'but from the moment when socialism in Russia, Austria, Germany, France and Italy becomes a fact, English capitalism will have reached its end'. The world is following where Petrograd has led. The mood of the true believers is triumphant, euphoric. For nearly three days there are marches, fireworks and speeches. 'We are strong and can do anything we wish', says one speaker.

In Moscow, the Bolsheviks' new capital, food rations are increased for the day. The buildings are lit up with red-tinted electric lights. Even the grass is painted red. Portraits of the great Communist leaders of past and present are hung in the streets: Marx, Lenin and Trotsky. (The war commissar's sister is one of the organisers of the Moscow events.) Fireworks scream into the air. 'It seemed as if the edifice of capitalism itself were being blown up', *Pravda* reports, 'with the exploiters and the abusers buried under its rubble.' A scarecrow representing a kulak is doused in paraffin and set alight. The city is

covered in slogans: 'Peace to the Peasantry; War on the Palaces', 'The Proletariat
has Nothing to Lose but Its Chains; It Has a Whole World to Win'. 'Revolution
is the locomotive of history' is the slogan assigned to the city's railway workers.

The seal of the new Russian Soviet Republic – the hammer and the
sickle – is printed on everything. At last, Lenin gets busts of Marx and
Engels on the streets of Moscow. The sculpture designs are mostly conservative. One with Marx atop four elephants is dismissed as a little whimsical.
Other artwork on display follows a more radical, modern aesthetic, not
the kind of thing Vladimir likes at all – all cubes, planes and geometric
shapes. The designs of the Futurists are too close to Dada for some people's
taste – and if the workers do not like it, how can it be considered proper
proletarian art?

Lenin unveils a monument to those who fell in the Bolshevik revolution
last year: a white-winged figure bearing a wreath of peace. 'The best sons
of the working people laid down their lives in starting a revolution to
liberate nations from imperialism,' he intones, 'to put an end to wars among
nations, to overthrow capital and to win socialism.' Now that revolution
has spread all over the globe. But the imperialists of the world are uniting
to suppress Russia's Soviet Republic. 'Comrades, let us honour the memory
of the October fighters by swearing before their memorial that we shall
follow in their footsteps', the impatient revolutionary demands. 'Let their
motto be our motto, the motto of the rebelling workers of the world:
victory or death!'

As part of the anniversary celebrations, Vladimir pays a special visit to
Cheka headquarters to congratulate them on all their hard work suppressing
counter-revolutionaries, finding saboteurs, eliminating the enemy. Mistakes
have been made, Lenin admits. But then, what do they really matter in the
broader scheme of history? 'People harp on individual mistakes Cheka
makes, and raise a hue and cry about them', the impatient revolutionary
says. 'We, however, say that we learn from our mistakes.' And anyway, is it
not better to kill a few innocents, than let a counter-revolutionary run
free? As someone who has experience of how the Tsarist security services
used to work, Vladimir has plenty of advice and expertise to offer, even of
a practical nature. Searches should be sudden, unexpected, he tells the
Chekists. Arrests should be carried out at night.

THE WESTERN FRONT: A brief interruption in the fighting allows the
German peace delegation to cross the front line. They have been sent by

Berlin to agree an armistice on whatever terms they can get. At three in the morning they board a train which takes them to a railway siding in the middle of the forest of Compiègne. Autumn leaves float to the ground. Everything is damp. The following morning the armistice conditions are read out to them in French. The terms are harsh. 'Then we are lost', a German delegate protests. 'How are we going to be able to defend ourselves against Bolshevism?'

A request for a temporary ceasefire is rejected.

SPA – GERMANY: Friday.

The Kaiser's train is readied with machine guns to return to Berlin.

Rosa Luxemburg is released from jail and travels to the capital on an overcrowded train, sitting on her suitcase all the way.

The King of Bavaria flees Munich and a sixty-one-year-old theatre critic called Kurt Eisner takes over as chairman of a workers' and soldiers' council. He sports a biblical beard, pince-nez glasses and an untested conviction in the possibility of non-violent revolution.

A German diplomat named Count Harry Kessler dodges revolutionary roadblocks to release from jail a Polish nationalist military leader currently imprisoned in Magdeburg. His instructions are to send the Pole post haste to Warsaw, where it is hoped that Józef Piłsudski will put himself at the head of a new regime friendly to Berlin (or at least friendlier than any led by his French-backed rivals). Piłsudski asks the German aristocrat if he can find him a sword – even a Prussian one will do – so that he will be able to look the part of returning warrior when he arrives in Warsaw. All Berlin's swords have been impounded. Kessler gives Piłsudski his sidearm instead. Under current circumstances, it may be more useful.

VIENNA: 'So much is now going on in the world that one doesn't know about', Freud writes to a friend. 'What one does know about is strange enough. Would you have thought a republican rising in Munich conceivable?'

Adler is released from jail. Thousands of Austrian refugees are said to be trying to get into Switzerland. Jewish property is being plundered in Budapest, Freud hears. He predicts a 'frightful dawning' in Germany which he expects the Kaiser to resist: 'Wilhelm is an incurable romantic fool. He is miscalculating the revolution just as he did the war. He doesn't know that the age of chivalry ended with Don Quixote.'

There is no word of the whereabouts of Martin Freud. His father begins to contemplate the worst.

SPA – GERMANY: Saturday.

The Kaiser wakes from his medicated slumber at the Villa Fraineuse in Spa. He sketches out plans to reconquer Berlin. Only one of his senior officers believes sufficient soldiers can be found to follow the Kaiser back to Germany. They will not start a civil war for him. Wilhelm decides to semi-abdicate – giving up his imperial title, but not that of Prussian King. He asks for the documents to be drawn up and sits down for lunch.

That very moment, in the Reichstag canteen in Berlin, Philipp Scheidemann, a senior Social Democrat, breaks off from his soup. The situation in the capital is tense. The Spartacist Karl Liebknecht is expected to proclaim a German Soviet Republic any minute from the balcony of the royal palace. A crowd has gathered at the Reichstag. Scheidemann goes to the window and makes a speech. The monarchy has collapsed, he proclaims. *Long live the German Republic!* A few words which change everything.

At Spa, tears rolling down his cheeks, an old general brings in the radio message from the capital with news of the declaration of the republic. 'Betrayal, shameless, disgraceful betrayal!' the Kaiser declares. He chain-smokes cigarettes furiously in front of the fire, then spends the afternoon ordering that Villa Fraineuse be stocked with weapons.

The army tells him that his security cannot be guaranteed. The Kaiser is put on the imperial train. He demands it stay put on occupied Belgian soil for one more night. He leaves occupied Belgium for the neutral Netherlands at five the following morning.

In Berlin, Friedrich Ebert, the Social Democrat leader who had assumed the title of Imperial Chancellor just hours before his colleague's unexpected proclamation of the republic, now struggles to form a new regime of People's Commissars with the support of the workers' and soldiers' councils. *Ordnung muss sein.* There must be order.

EIJSDEN, THE NETHERLANDS – FOREST OF COMPIÈGNE: Sunday.

Just before seven in the morning, two motor cars arrive at the Belgian–Dutch border. A startled sentry is informed by a party of mysterious Germans that they would like to cross. His sergeant makes a phone call to his superiors. An hour later the Germans are admitted to the Netherlands and ordered to wait at the train station while the Dutch Queen and her government figure out what to do. The ex-Kaiser is amongst the fugitives.

The German imperial train, having been abandoned during Wilhelm's flight, pulls into Eijsden station sometime later. The Kaiser paces the platform, smoking. A local crowd begins to jeer. Wilhelm decides he would be better off inside.

It takes some time for the Dutch government to decide how to deal with the unexpected guest. The problem of finding him suitable board and lodgings is compounded by the fact that the Dutch telephone network only functions at certain hours on Sundays. After everyone else has refused, a good-natured Dutch Count is finally persuaded to house Wilhelm and his entourage for a period of no longer than three days.

While arrangements are being made for his temporary accommodation, the German Ambassador to The Hague goes to Eijsden to formally greet the Kaiser-in-exile. 'How can I start again in life?' Wilhelm complains. 'There is no hope left for me and nothing remains for me save despair.' The ambassador tentatively suggests the Kaiser should find a new occupation for himself, perhaps writing his memoirs. Wilhelm's eyes light up. 'I'll start tomorrow', he cries.

That evening, at Count Bentinck's home in Amerongen, dinner is served for twenty-six. Wilhelm makes a little speech. 'My conscience is clear', he says. 'As God knows, I never wanted this war.'

The same night, on a stationary train in the Forest of Compiègne, a letter is read out in German protesting the harshness of the Allied armistice terms: 'the German people, which has held its own for fifty months against a world of enemies, will in spite of any force that may be brought to bear upon it, preserve its freedom and unity.'

Très bien, responds Marshal Foch. The armistice is signed. It is not yet dawn.

THE WESTERN FRONT: Monday.

A German machine-gunner fires his last ammunition into the sky, then emerges from the trenches and bows at the enemy. British soldiers break into song. The French sing the Marseillaise. Then a strange silence.

The unnaturalness of peace.

Peace

PEACE

PEACE

PEACE

PEACE

PEACE

PEACE!

PARIS: In amongst the crowds celebrating the armistice, Guillaume
Apollinaire's funeral cortège winds its way towards Père Lachaise. André
Breton is depressed. The man who was once his hero is dead, murdered by
the influenza which is still killing three hundred Parisians every week.

The ceremony is simple. André lays white flowers on the poet's grave.
Pablo Picasso looks on, ashen-faced. Apollinaire's last diary entry recalled
a visit to the Spaniard's new apartment on the Rue de la Boétie. That was
just a week ago.

VIENNA: In the days following the revolution in Berlin, sympathetic visitors
turn up at Schönbrunn Palace to see Emperor Charles. Some come out of
curiosity. Others offer advice. One old lady claims to be the daughter
of Prince Metternich, the man who masterminded the Congress of Vienna
in 1815 and was overthrown in the liberal revolutions of 1848. She bears
a message from another age: 'Tell the Emperor, he shouldn't worry too
much', she says. 'Revolutions are like floods – they do not last for ever.'

The day of the German armistice, Charles makes a public declaration
that he will no longer play a part in the affairs of state: 'May the people of
German-Austria, in unity and in tolerance, create and strengthen the new
order!' He does not renounce the crown. It is not quite an abdication. A
German-Austrian Republic is confirmed the next day and, despite the
ongoing crisis across the border, provisionally declares itself part of Germany.

It is time to leave Vienna. Charles and Zita bundle up their family in the back of a car and are driven off to a hunting lodge at Eckartsau forty miles away, where Franz Ferdinand used to go hunting before he was shot in Sarajevo. The imperial party leave Schönbrunn by the back gate. Charles dresses as a civilian. Later that night, thieves break into the palace and find it empty but for a single chambermaid.

On the cusp of seeing the first stage of revolution, the Austrian Social Democrat leader Victor Adler has a heart attack and dies. The newspapers report his final conversation with his son Friedrich, newly released from jail. 'Did they excuse me at the parliament sitting?' he asks weakly. 'What is happening in Germany?' He enquires about the armistice conditions laid down for the Kaiser.

'Very difficult', Friedrich replies.

His father murmurs something impossible to understand. Then: 'Well, I'm afraid I won't be able to go on – you will have to excuse me.'

EUROPE: There are many comings and goings in these first few days of peace. Some want to go home. Others want to escape.

Four days after the armistice, a Finnish diplomat with a beard and blue glasses arrives in Copenhagen. His passport declares him to be one Ernst Lindström. His luggage carries the monogram E. L. Thank God no one tries to speak to him in Finnish. Under the fake beard is the face of a fugitive: Erich Ludendorff. The Social Democrats in Berlin let him go. He would have hanged them if the situation were reversed. 'If I come back to power one day, there will be no pardons', he tells his wife Margarethe. He expects the Spartacists to be in power in Berlin in a few weeks. 'Everything is like a bad dream', he writes. His lodgings in Copenhagen are small. The tram runs just outside his window. He is anxious all the time.

The same moment Ludendorff arrives in Copenhagen, another traveller, also in thick disguise, arrives at an Austrian military post in occupied eastern Ukraine. He claims to be Dr Emil Sebastyen, a Hungarian gentleman returning from the front. The eyes of his fellow officers widen in horror over dinner when he shares his tales of Bolshevik bloodthirstiness. They agree to help him get back home as quickly as possible, facilitating his journey westwards via Kiev. The last section is completed in the back of a Red Cross truck.

The doctor's ultimate destination is Budapest, where he can reveal his true identity: Béla Kun, son of a Transylvanian notary and an ardent convert to the Bolshevik cause, on a mission from Moscow. In the Hungarian capital, he visits

Russian prisoners of war, gives speeches at a locomotive factory and attempts to recruit the city's sheet-metal workers to the notion that the proletariat should seize power for itself. He settles into a loft apartment in one of the city's northern suburbs, which he shares with an artist and his wife. There he hosts the founding meeting of the Hungarian Communist Party.

MILAN: Benito senses one of those rare times in history when the world is cracked open and what matters is not position, but energy and vision. 'If, in a certain sense, the war was ours', he writes, 'so the post-war must be ours'. He has plans for the future.

D'Annunzio has spontaneity and bravado, admirable qualities in a propagandist. Mussolini, the former Socialist Party political organiser, has a more ordered cast of mind. While Gabriele expects to dominate others by sheer force of personality – through pure spirit, as it were – Benito is a materialist in his politics. Spirit must be allied with structure. He imagines creating a national association of like-minded men, not a political party exactly but something more organic, comprising the strongest and most energetic elements of the nation. He pictures a club in every Italian town, where glorious veterans can meet their comrades-in-arms, and where the spirit of the war will live on. This will be an organisation which is as Milanese as it is Venetian as it is Roman. Benito already has a name for it: he calls it the *Fasci*. Together they will remake Italy.

BERLIN: With the Kaiser gone, the contest for Germany's future moves to the streets. For some, the country has entered a period of moral and spiritual collapse, a retreat from *Kultur* into barbarism with a Bolshevik twist. The old virtues of respect, duty and hard work are melting away. Servants have started answering back. Peasants refuse to work as they used to. Criminality is widespread. But the elemental qualities of revolution can unleash creative as well as destructive forces. Revolutions can both terrify and inspire. On his way back to Munich after release from hospital Adolf Hitler passes through Berlin and is drawn to a socialist rally. He finds himself overwhelmed by the power and energy of the sea of red flags and red flowers which surrounds him.

The question with revolution is knowing when to stop. 'Germany has completed its revolution', announces Friedrich Ebert after his six-man directorate of People's Commissars is given the formal support of the workers' and soldiers' council in Berlin. Everyone over the age of twenty – men and women – is given the vote. There is an amnesty for political crimes. The new rulers announce they will solve the housing problem by simply requisitioning empty houses while, at the same time, in a sop to the bourgeoisie, promising that personal freedom and private property will be protected. An eight-hour day is to be introduced by 1919. A constituent assembly is to be elected. In the meantime, Ebert pleads for unity and order to manage the deep economic crisis into which Germany has been plunged. Pending a final peace treaty, the country is still under Allied blockade. The troops are returning from the front, bedraggled and without discipline. Should all of Germany's six million soldiers try to return home at once there will be 'chaos, hunger and misery', a government circular warns. *Ordnung muss sein!*

But Ebert's position is delicate. The workers' and soldiers' councils which have lent their support to the People's Commissars have not disbanded. They still claim to represent the spirit of the revolution. Hard-line radical sailors from Kiel occupy the royal palace. Ostensibly they are there to prevent further plunder in the capital. But their loyalty to the People's Commissars cannot be taken for granted. Their message to Ebert is clear: they will decide when the revolution is over, not him. Ebert tells the workers to stay off the streets so the government can do its job. The Spartacists say they must stay on the streets to ensure that the revolution forges ahead with thoroughgoing economic and social change. The workers cannot let their future be decided in the palaces of the aristocracy or the parliaments of the bourgeoisie, where they will be betrayed just as they were tricked into war in 1914.

Rosa Luxemburg has never been more tired in her life. 'All of us over our ears in turmoil and travail', she writes to a friend. The European proletarian revolution must be encouraged, not put to sleep with talk of constituent assemblies and limited social reform. A new world beckons. 'And it is coming!' Rosa writes. The Spartacists must show the way forward. Momentum must not be lost. *Agitate, agitate, agitate.*

ISTANBUL: Forty-two Allied ships, led by the vessel on which the armistice was signed, the HMS *Agamemnon*, sail through the Dardanelles and into the heart of the Ottoman Empire. Allied biplanes fly overhead to complete the picture of mastery. (British planes have already landed at Gallipoli, a place they could not take in months of fighting in the war.)

For many of Istanbul's Christians – Greek and Armenian – this is a moment to savour. An Armenian bishop, deported in 1915 and now returned, crosses the Bosphorus in disguise to observe the arrival of the victors, before returning to complete his account of all the horrors perpetrated against his people in the war – a million massacred, maybe more. There is feasting in the city's Christian-owned restaurants. Greeks wonder if the ambitious Athenian scheme of a new trans-Aegean empire might now be possible, reversing centuries of Ottoman domination.

For Istanbul's Muslims – Turks, Circassians, Kurds – the sight of foreign troops marching through the city is bitter. The Ottoman Empire has been at war almost continuously since 1911. The people of Istanbul have seen armies trudge out to the Balkans to defend Ottoman territory against Greeks, Bulgarians and Serbs. They know the price of defeat: refugees, retribution, submission to foreigners. Property taken from deported Greeks and Armenians will have to be returned. Impoverishment is certain. Meanwhile, Anatolia is in ferment. 'Turkey Overrun by Brigands', runs a headline in a British newspaper.

Mustafa Kemal arrives at Haydarpaşa station that morning. He puts up briefly at the Pera Palace Hotel, but finds it is too expensive for him now. He rents a house from an Armenian gentleman. Like all Turks, Kemal must now decide how far to cooperate with the foreigners, and how far to resist them. Perhaps the Ottoman Empire needs a military man at the helm. The Sultan demurs. Not him.

VIENNA, GERMAN-AUSTRIA: Ten days since Austria's removal from the war and still no news of Martin Freud. His anxious father tries to explain his son's silence. Perhaps he has been taken prisoner with his unit but, through some dreadful injury or other, is unable to write. Perhaps he is on his way home now, waiting somewhere for the next train. Perhaps Martin has escaped and been accidentally shot by his own side. To survive four years of war and to die at the end – what could be crueller?

In Vienna, only the railway stations are still working. Everything else is *kaputt*. 'Limitations and deprivation are worse than ever', Freud writes. 'The Habsburgs have left nothing behind but a pile of shit', he tells a friend. Charles and Zita lie low in Eckartsau, where they struggle to get their hands on a single bar of soap or even a single match to light a fire.

Some tell Freud he should emigrate. But where to? Switzerland? Hungary? America?

WASHINGTON DC: Since the summer, a document has been circulating in the corridors of power in Washington. It is a neatly typed-up English translation of a Russian book published in Kiev around 1917. Nicholas was reading it last winter. *The Protocols of the Elders of Zion* purports to be an account of a meeting between various prominent Jews, the 'Elders' of the title, in which they discuss a stupendously complex and daring conspiracy to take over the world through endless chaos and manipulation.

The document is a typical example of Tsarist-era anti-Semitic *provokatsiya* – a provocation – of a piece with various made-up stories intended to cement support for the Russian Orthodox Romanovs and encourage pogroms by the peasantry. But the translation is now being used in an attempt to persuade the West to intervene in Russia to prevent the spread of Bolshevism which, the *Protocols* would suggest, is in fact one tentacle of a much wider conspiracy masterminded by this alleged secretive Jewish cabal.

In the fevered anti-Bolshevik, anti-German atmosphere in Washington, some believe the document to be an astonishing revelation. Initial credence is given by the fact that the Russian monarchist circulating it is a sometime source of American intelligence. Others see right through it. A Jewish Supreme Court judge – a Woodrow appointee – is called into the Justice Department in November to take a look at the so-called 'Zionist Protocols'. He can barely believe his eyes at the poisonous nonsense that is presented to him.

SOUTHERN RUSSIA – MOSCOW: 'We have been given a breathing space', Trotsky admits, but it will not last for long.

In the autumn, Leon Trotsky's train roars around Russia so the war commissar can dispense iron discipline and provide encouragement wherever it is required. His train is well equipped: it has a library, a printing press, a radio transmitter which can capture and receive signals from as far away as the Eiffel Tower in Paris, and a bathtub for the commissar's private use. Like an old-fashioned Russian aristocrat touring his estate, Trotsky packs his train with presents to hand out to the people along the way: cash and cigarette cases, mostly. But like a modern political leader, he often has a photographer or film crew in tow to capture his munificence. Two engines pull the train. One is always under steam, ready to move on at a moment's notice.

Trotsky has no friends aboard. The commissar has no need of them. Instead he has a squad of leather-jacketed bodyguards – leather always seems to impress people, he decides – and a bunch of stenographers who somehow manage to type up his dictation without error, even as the train bumps over loose tracks at breakneck speeds. Away from his family for months on end, Leon is master of everyone and everything. His word is law. When a drunk staff member gets into a fight and tries to shoot his head of security, it is Trotsky who decides whether the man should live or die. When the train stops in some godforsaken town and commissar Trotsky commands that food be brought, no one is likely to refuse. Lenin takes to telegraphing the commissar 'at his present whereabouts'. It is impossible to know where he might be at any given hour of the day or night. For the purposes of both propaganda and discipline (as well as the small matter of the commissar's security), surprise is of the essence.

At one stop in his perpetual peregrinations this autumn, along the shaky Southern Front, Trotsky makes a speech. 'Revolution, the daughter of war, is advancing,' he announces encouragingly, 'shod with iron sandals, as they used to say in olden times'. People mocked the Bolsheviks once, he recalls; now they are terrified of them. 'In the last analysis it was we who were right, we who relied on the sound materialist method of investigating historical destinies', Trotsky declares. The inevitability of revolution is an established scientific fact.

Germany, as yet uncertainly, has started down the path lit up by the Russian workers. Soviets have been established. 'There can be no doubt that these councils will for a certain time – let us hope, only for a short time – waver from one side to the other, limping and hobbling', Trotsky admits. 'They are still headed by compromisers, those very same men who bear an immense share of guilt before the German people for the misfortunes and humiliations into which Germany has fallen.' But Ebert in Germany is like Kerensky in Russia – a fake, a charlatan, an impostor. The workers will find him out eventually.

France has a revolutionary tradition that will soon catch fire. Italy as well. Britain may be a harder nut to crack, with its patriotic working-class traditions, but Leon detects the first distant rolls of thunder there as well. As for America – well, here Leon can talk from direct experience. The country is a strictly for-profit enterprise, he explains. The President has become a Tsar, with capitalist bosses pushing him this way and that. The war was fought in their interests, on the backs of American workers. But there are revolutionary elements amongst them, immigrants from Europe in particular: 'all this in combination will undoubtedly cause the American revolution to assume American dimensions.'

This is all fine and dandy, but what the soldiers want to hear is what is in it for them. And here Trotsky's message is blunt. The end of the war in Europe does not mean the end of the war in Russia. The world is now divided into two camps: the Bolsheviks and the rest. A fight to the death between them has begun. 'That is not just an agitational phrase, comrades, it is an actual reality', Trotsky tells the hungry, disease-ravaged troops. After a flurry of success, the Red Army is on the back foot. It must hold out. There are only two possible outcomes: the world revolution secured, or the world revolution delayed by a quarter-century or more.

'History is working now not with small, finely sharpened instruments, but with a heavy steam-hammer, with a gigantic club', Trotsky says. 'A formidable blow may still fall upon us, too, comrades'. The imperialists are trying to regroup. The Whites may argue amongst themselves at least as much as the Bolsheviks do – but they are dangerous. In the south, Denikin's well-fed, well-equipped and well-led armies have inflicted a series of defeats on the Reds. In the north, close to Petrograd, another White army has formed under General Yudenich. Meanwhile, two thousand miles east of Moscow, a conservative young admiral named Kolchak has imposed himself on the anti-Bolshevik factions in Siberia to declare himself supreme ruler of all Russia with his capital at Omsk. Moderate Socialist Revolutionaries denounce Kolchak's assumption of power in Siberia as a coup, an unacceptable lurch to the right in the anti-Bolshevik camp. The British and French are more supportive. Conservative Russians are jubilant. Finally! A White Russian military leader at three points of the compass.

The war commissar warns that until the world revolution takes off, Soviet Russia is on its own. And so the Bolsheviks must be as ruthless as their enemies. Every town must be a fortress. Mobilisation must be total. 'Comrades, all history is now condensed for us in this question', Trotsky tells his men: 'shall we be able to do this, shall we succeed in it?' The period of tactical retreat is over; the period of the offensive must now begin.

In Moscow, Vladimir finally finishes the pamphlet he has been working on these last few weeks, even while Europe has been going through the revolution he seeks to theorise. Lenin's retort to his ideological enemy is peppered with abusive language. 'Like a blind puppy sniffing at random first in one direction and then in another, Kautsky accidentally stumbled upon one true idea', he writes at one point. 'Kautsky has made himself particularly ridiculous', he notes at another. His pamphlet is a 'sheer mockery of Marxism'. The man himself is a Judas and a sycophant. Vladimir has never taken well to criticism. And the German's crime is as great as it can be: he has dared to question the impatient revolutionary's interpretation of Marx, and criticise the Bolshevik regime as undemocratic, instead wishing for some kind of 'pure democracy', achieved without violence.

What a fantasy! It amounts to a revolution without revolution. Has the German understood nothing of the world? Has he not seen oppressive bourgeois democracy in action? It oppresses. Has he not heard of lynching in America? Does he not know about the situation of Ireland and Britain? The revolutionary dictatorship of the proletariat can be won and maintained only through the use of force against the bourgeoisie, 'unrestricted by any laws'. It is impossible – *impossible!* – to do things in any other way.

As for democracy: 'proletarian democracy is *a million times* more democratic than any bourgeois democracy; Soviet power is a million times more democratic than the most democratic bourgeois republic'. As far as Lenin is concerned, the case is closed.

BLODELSHEIM, ALSACE-LORRAINE – NEW YORK: By the time Thanksgiving 1918 comes around, the boys from Harlem are on the Rhine. German troops withdraw in fulfilment of the armistice terms. Jim Europe writes a letter to his sister in America, warning her to stay away from big crowds until the influenza epidemic has passed. 'I am so tired of the army life now that I do not know what to do', he writes. 'I want to get home and get to work and make some money.'

Back in New York, the cover of *The Crisis* shows a black American soldier planting the Stars and Stripes in no man's land, staking a double claim: to victory and its spoils. 'The nightmare is over', Du Bois tells his readers: 'we were cold and numb and deaf and blind, and yet the air was visioned with the angels of Hell; the earth was a vast groan; the sea was a festering sore, and we were flame'. Now, he writes, 'suddenly we awake!' He prepares himself to travel to Europe to remind Woodrow of the meaning of democracy at the peace conference.

LINCOLN: One Sunday late in 1918, Éamon de Valera slips off from the chapel during Mass on the pretext of fetching some religious article or other from the sacristy. He uses his few moments there to try and make an impression of the prison chaplain's key in the melted wax of church candles. But by the time he gets to it, the wax which melted before the service has turned solid from the cold. Éamon returns to the chapel, a look of innocent religious devotion on his face, without his absence being noted by the prison wardens in the congregation.

He gets a second chance a little later, when clearing up after the service. Éamon's assistant, trained by him in the various bits of Latin required for the job of sacristan and now employed for rather more illicit purposes, distracts the chaplain with questions of a religious nature. Meanwhile, the Sinn Féin leader tries to get an impression of the clergyman's key in the sacristy, warming up bits of candle wax in an old tobacco tin by rubbing his hands against it. This time, it works.

THE ATLANTIC: It is almost like a cruise, now that the U-boats have gone. Edith Wilson has a set of invitation cards made so that she and Woodrow can invite people for dinner on the boat over to Europe. In the mid-Atlantic the weather is positively balmy.

The President is in a boisterous mood on board the *George Washington*, freed from the bickering of Washington DC, where the Democrats are reeling from poor election results and the Republicans are furious at the President leaving the country without a single member of their party amongst his top team. On the way to France, Woodrow feels that he is his own man again, free to pursue his purpose in life and that of the war: to enforce a just and permanent peace, with his League of Nations to secure it. Mr and Mrs Wilson take long walks on deck, strolling arm in arm like two lovebirds (he calls her 'sweetheart' incessantly). The President, who has no particular fondness for the press, is found chatting amiably to newspaper reporters. On Sunday, he attends chapel with the sailors below decks; one night, he sings with them. In the evenings, he is a regular in one of the saloons, set up as a movie-theatre. He becomes rather fond of ice cream, though asks for it without the rich sauces the French (and the ladies) seem to like. There is a Victrola phonograph aboard in the music room, and records of popular operatic melodies and even the odd bit of jazz.

The President is more relaxed, and more at ease, than he has been for months. He freely shares his favourite limericks. Amongst those he knows well, he cracks off-colour jokes about the guile of Irish-Americans or puts on the accent of Southern blacks. There will be several weeks of touring Europe before the serious business of negotiation begins. Brooks, Wilson's black valet, checks that he has all the clothes the President needs to ensure that no European clothing protocol is broken and America thereby shamed for its backwardness. Edith, horrified at the prospect of her own black maid being treated as an equal to the white staff at Buckingham Palace, declares she will 'let her have her sandwich in her room and lock her in' to prevent her being spoilt. (At the same time, Du Bois is on his way to Paris on board another ship, the *Orizaba*, hoping to turn the contributions of America's black troops in the war abroad into better rights at home, while advocating the equality of races across the globe and accelerated self-government in Africa.)

Woodrow looks forward to meeting the leaders of Britain, France and Italy and 'letting them know what sort of a fellow I am and giving myself the opportunity of determining what sort of chaps they are'. Wilson is in no doubt of America's right to shape a new world order, a revolution in international affairs to counterbalance (and perhaps to confound) those who seek more violent social revolution. American power and prestige are at their height. Only the American dollar has any credibility around the world now. Everyone owes the country money. It is only a matter of time before Wall Street, rather than the City of London, becomes the centre of world finance.

And then there are the contributions made by Pershing's army. Woodrow boasts, predictably enough, that it was American troops who turned the tide of the war. ('It is not too much to say that at Château Thierry we saved the world', he tells his team, 'and I do not intend to let those Europeans forget it'.) He brushes off foreign ambassadors – the Italian Ambassador, in particular – who seek to use the opportunity of an ocean crossing with the President to influence him. Instead, he busies himself with maps and reports written by the experts he has brought along from America. He muses over whether the world's new League of Nations should be head-quartered in The Hague (where the steel magnate Andrew Carnegie built his Peace Palace before the war) or in Bern, the Swiss capital.

On Friday 13 December, the *George Washington* docks in Brest. Woodrow considers the date a good omen: thirteen is his lucky number. The crowds in Paris are overwhelming as they welcome the American prophet. He takes up residence in a mansion owned by the family of Napoleon.

AMERONGEN, THE NETHERLANDS: Things are not quite up to the palatial standards that Wilhelm is used to – his retinue is down to as little as two dozen – but the ex-Kaiser soon develops a new routine for his life under semi-house arrest, as guest of unlucky Count Bentinck.

The days begin with morning prayers at nine o'clock, for which the Count's daughter plays the organ. After breakfast, Bentinck is generally subjected to Wilhelm's harangues about the world for an hour or two. After lunch, perhaps a stroll in the park or a visit to a nearby castle and some more discussion of the iniquities of fate. ('Now I know who carries the blame for all this', the Kaiser tells a German aide one afternoon. 'It's

Ludendorff'.) All this under the watchful eyes of the Dutch police, who are there both to protect the ex-Kaiser from assassination and to ensure that he does not stray too far.

In the evenings, Wilhelm talks some more – often family reminiscences, such as his memories of his grandmother Queen Victoria. Occasionally he reads out a letter from a well-wisher. 'Dear Kaiser,' reads one from a young Dutch girl, 'I would like to give you a kiss. Mother is neutral, but I am pro-German.' Wilhelm is delighted.

But neither the rhythm of these first few days of exile nor the odd piece of fan-mail can hide the general precariousness of the situation for both the Kaiser and his family. Wilhelm's wife, Auguste Viktoria, is more or less held hostage by the new German government, unable to join her husband until the end of November. The Crown Prince is housed by the Dutch government on the island of Wieringen, in a remote and modest house, fitted with neither proper plumbing nor electricity. There is no guarantee that Wilhelm will not be shipped off somewhere similar.

In Paris and London, people demand the Kaiser's blood. He should be hanged, some say. At the very least, he should stand trial for what he has brought upon the world. Faced with the headache of what to do with this unwelcome guest, in December the Dutch government tell Wilhelm that while they will not expel him forcibly, they would very much like it if he were to leave their territory of his own accord. Wilhelm fulminates at this latest betrayal. He blames the Queen of the Netherlands for disloyalty towards a fellow royal in letting her government request his departure. How poorly he is repaid for choosing not to invade the country in 1914!

In the drawing room at Amerongen Wilhelm's alternatives are weighed up. Of course, one option is simply to ignore the government's request, stay in Holland and see what happens. Another is to find a way of Wilhelm giving himself up to the Americans, thereby avoiding the wrath of the British and the French. Conversation soon turns to a more dramatic possibility: escaping to some more friendly country – or even returning to Germany.

This will not be easy. For a start, Count Bentinck's house is surrounded by two moats. These can only be crossed either by using the castle rowing boat, or else by waiting for a cold snap to freeze the ice thick enough to cross on foot. (Wise to this possibility, the Dutch police regularly break up any ice formations.) Beyond the moats lie the grounds of Count Bentinck's estate, which are patrolled. And even if an escape party were to succeed and get onto a public road, that's when the real problems start. As Charles de Gaulle knows to his cost, travelling incognito in a foreign country is no easy matter. Wilhelm's advisers suggest the Kaiser shave off his moustache, dye his hair and acquire a pince-nez. 'What about my damn arm?' he asks. A suitable disguise is devised.

Taking a train after his escape could become very undignified if Wilhelm were recognised by other passengers. Perhaps he could hide out on a pleasure-steamer on the Rhine, one adviser suggests, and then make a dash for Scandinavia, like Ludendorff. Someone else proposes that a small aeroplane fly the Kaiser to a farm in East Prussia or a chalet in the Black Forest. (The problem of how to actually get hold of a plane proves insuperable.) A final, and more realistic, suggestion involves Wilhelm feigning illness. Such an option has three substantial merits. First, the Kaiser's nervous state is already very poor, so additional illness will be easily believed. Second, illness will likely increase Dutch popular sympathy for the poor man (and thus make it less likely that the government will turn its request that he leave into a deportation order). Third, a sick Kaiser could be sent to a sanatorium on medical grounds, from which it might then be easier to escape than from Amerongen.

To play his part, the Kaiser takes to bed. His head is bandaged, and word spread about an ear infection. For six weeks, he takes meals only in his room rather than at the family dining table. A friendly German-Swiss doctor with a background in psychiatry is called in from Antwerp to both treat the Kaiser's nerves, and stand witness to the reality of his illness.

So in the final weeks of 1918, Wilhelm stews in his room, with a view out over the moat and to a world which suddenly seems very far away. He considers the enormity of the betrayal he has suffered. He starts to write his memoirs.

BERLIN: German soldiers return home to find cold hearths and hungry mouths. The discharge suits never fit. Some are just given the cloth and told to make the suits themselves. Ebert worries about their morale, concerned they will fall in with the Spartacists.

In Berlin, he greets them in person in a speech. 'Comrades,' he begins, 'welcome back to your homeland which has so longed for your return and for which you have experienced such anguish.' He lavishes praise on the 'super-human deeds' of the rank and file. 'You have kept the murder and fire of war away from your wives, your children, your parents', Ebert says. In some parts, it sounds almost like a victory speech – 'no enemy has overcome you', the

German leader declares – in others, it sounds like a plea for help. The task
now is to hold the country together: 'Germany's unity lies in your hands'.

The country has never been more divided. The German Reich, less than
fifty years old, could easily break up. A current of separatism runs through
the politics of Germany from Bavaria to Silesia and the Rhineland. In the
German-occupied east, schemes are hatched for a Baltic imperium run by
the region's German minority. Revolutionaries in Munich are unwilling to
take orders from Berlin. Conservative Bavarians wonder if it might be
possible to create a new southern German state incorporating Catholic
German-speakers from the Rhine to the Danube, as a counterweight to
Prussian domination.

'We have one enemy above all we must fight', the Social Democratic
leader tells one journalist, 'the attempts of individuals to overthrow the new
order through armed putsches'. The country is awash with enough weaponry
to start a civil war. The Spartacists are accused of agitating for a coup in
Berlin. They, in turn, declare Ebert's regime a counter-revolutionary front
and demand that the workers be armed against it. Enterprising right-wing
officers form volunteer militias, the Freikorps, to intervene as required.

Moscow: As usual, the impatient revolutionary's mind darts between the big
picture and the mundane, between theory and practice, between the grand
course of world revolution and petty administrative matters which seem to
be holding everything up at home.

It is all so frustrating. Orders are issued, and people do not follow them.
Decrees are published, then nothing happens. Lenin gives instructions but
has to repeat them two or three times and then check to see if they have
been understood. Why is it all not working better? 'Any worker will master
any ministry within a few days', he said in 1917, just before the coup. It
does not seem to be panning out that way.

In food matters, Vladimir can blame the kulaks for hoarding grain – how
else to explain the poor results of his requisitions policy? In more general
matters of daily administration, he blames 'bureaucracy', a legacy of the old
world, for holding things up. But how is one supposed to run the country
without bureaucracy? There is so much to do. The nationalisation of all big
companies has swollen the state's responsibilities. Accurate information has
to be collected so they can be properly managed (Vladimir has a mania for
accounting, imagining an economic system where information will take the
place of human choice). The chaos on the railways must be sorted out.

True socialism – an economy run by the people for the people – cannot be built in a day. In the interim, the state will rule on the proletariat's behalf. Someone needs to decide how many galoshes have to be produced, whether to feed horses oats or wheat. Under war conditions, centralisation is essential. A Council of People's Commissars is set up for the job.

Councils and committees grow like weeds in the brave new Soviet Republic. The number of state officials keeps creeping up. More and more people join the Communist Party simply as a means to advance their careers in the various branches of administration established since the revolution. A new bureaucratic class is being created, a class of managers, like in the big capitalist enterprises that Lenin so admires for their feats of production and efficiency. But whereas capitalist managers seem able to make things work in the West, in revolutionary Russia, the lifts in the Kremlin still break down on a daily basis. Moscow is perpetually on the brink of starvation.

Lenin himself works from dawn till dusk with the blinds drawn up. His office is deliberately maintained at a Siberian temperature. He keeps his feet warm with a sheepskin mat under his desk, and protests at the luxury when somebody replaces it with polar bear. He always turns off the light when he leaves, normally late at night. Reports from subordinates pile up on his desk; his secretaries learn what they are allowed to touch (a pair of scissors on a pile of papers means: do not dare). He always reads the ends of the reports first, leaving out what he calls the 'literature'. A register is kept of those who are late for meetings. And yet despite all these attempts to promote efficient working practices Lenin feels himself in constant struggle against the most insidious, evil, invisible enemy – red tape.

And then there is the big job of educating the masses. Nadya, staying for a while to recuperate from illness in a children's school on the outskirts of Moscow, where the crisp air smells of pine, shows Vladimir the letters she receives from peasants in the provinces. No one out in the sticks has a clue what is going on in the Bolshevik capital. The peasants ask stupid questions about the meaning of government decrees. One could try sending newspapers to make them better informed – but then again, Nadya points out, there is not enough paper and the peasants cannot read. Vladimir suggests setting up enquiry offices in every village in the land. He drafts rules about how such desks should be managed: a book must be kept in which every enquiry, and the person responsible for dealing with it, is jotted down. Personal responsibility is key.

War commissar Trotsky sends more immediate complaints back to the Red capital. There is no grease for the guns, and no hay for the horses. Factories have stopped producing shells and guns. How is he supposed to win a war under such circumstances? In December, dreadful news arrives in Moscow that the Ural city of Perm, the gateway between Siberia and central Russia, has fallen to Kolchak's army. Comrade Stalin is sent to investigate.

The vice is tightening again. In 1919, it will either snap shut or break.

TRAUNSTEIN-IM-CHIEMGAU, BAVARIA: Adolf settles into a new job working at a prisoner-of-war camp by the Austrian border. The camp is being wound down. The French POWs are nearly all gone. The Russians remain. Adolf works in the clothing distribution section, keen to demonstrate his reliability and usefulness. To most he is virtually invisible: he has just one friend in the camp. Local newspapers report Woodrow Wilson's arrival in Paris. There is still hope for a final peace on honourable, American terms. The white tops of the Alps shimmer in the distance.

ZURICH: In Switzerland, that wartime haven for Europe's oddballs, draft-dodgers, revolutionaries and spies, Tristan Tzara and his friends greet the war's end with the publication, in *Dada* magazine, of a manifesto for their movement.

What is this strange, chaotic, rambling document? Is it a call to arms? A mirror to a world gone mad? A provocation? A joke? 'Dada means nothing', the manifesto tells its readers halfway through. But no one is fooled by that. In the hands of a showman such as Tzara, self-contradiction is a technique as much as a position. Even an anti-manifesto is a manifesto. And all manifestos, whether written by an American President, a Russian revolutionary or a Romanian poet, demand the same thing from the world: attention. If only Tzara had an aeroplane to distribute the tract from the skies, like that showman D'Annunzio over Vienna.

For Dada, at this minute, nothing could be more urgent than publicity. Zurich has had its day. As the city's temporary cosmopolitans pack up their bags to return home and the city fades back into its normal peacetime obscurity, Tzara knows that his Dada, the Dada of Zurich, must reach out to the world – or else become as charming and irrelevant as a cuckoo clock. In the scramble for peacetime attention, Zurich Dada cannot be left behind. After four years of war there are plenty of others – radical nationalists, Futurists, Communists – who are rivals in the race for relevance. The manifesto is a shout, a cry, a demand to be heard. Look at me!

Incendiary phrases swarm across the page, each line a tightly bound packet of dark Dadaist energy, a heavy mass of contradictions and conundrums, like a universe collapsed in on itself, incapable of resolution. 'Order = disorder; ego = non-ego; affirmation = negation', the manifesto claims. 'Each man must shout: there is work to do – destructive and negative. To sweep, to clean.' Sentimentality is bourgeois. Logic is bunk. Art must be free to be what it wants to be – or not be art at all. The individual is all. Spontaneity is life. 'We are a furious wind', the manifesto declares, 'tearing up the fabric of clouds and prayers, preparing the great spectacle of disaster, fire, decomposition.' This is the news from Zurich's Dadaland: angry, exhilarating, funny, determined. (In Berlin, where Dada has now gained a second foothold, they are more political, but no less self-contradictory: 'To be against this manifesto is to be a Dadaist!' the Berlin lot wrote in their own manifesto earlier in the year.)

As Tzara proclaims it, after four years of bloody and purposeless carnage, the only adequate response to the sanctimony and hypocrisy of bourgeois society is energy, activity, spectacle, provocation. 'How can one contemplate ordering the chaos of humankind's infinite, formless variation?' the manifesto asks. How indeed? And so Dada proposes not a practical programme for how to remake the world, so much as an impulse to shake it from its torpor. Tzara is no dialectical materialist. Disaster, and chance, are to be embraced for their own sake. 'Freedom: DADA DADA DADA', the manifesto cries, 'howl of taut colour, interweaving of opposites and contradictions, grotesques and in-consequences: LIFE.' To those who have been so close to death these past few years, this fulsome appeal to life – violent and unruly – has an unmistakeable appeal.

A copy of the magazine makes its way to Paris a few weeks later and into the hands of a young man searching for a cause: André Breton.

BERLIN: On Christmas Eve, Berliners are woken by the boom of artillery. Troops loyal to Friedrich Ebert's regime launch an assault to dislodge radical sailors from the royal palace in Berlin.

Incredibly, they fail. The palace stables are used to stack the dead. Ebert fears for his life. Several members of his government of People's Commissars resign in disgust at his decision to launch the attack. On the day of the sailors' funerals demonstrations are held on both sides. There are daily rumours of a Spartacist coup. 'We are on the edge of the abyss', report the newspapers.

During these weeks of unrest and uncertainty, Rosa Luxemburg works long hours on the Spartacist newspaper, the *Rote Fahne*. She discusses, watches, debates. 'Can you tell me why I constantly live like this?' she asks her friend Mathilde one evening, walking to the Berlin metro just before midnight. 'I would like to paint and live on a little plot of land where I can feed and love the animals', she says: 'but above all to live peacefully and on my own, not in this eternal whirlwind.' Mathilde worries for her friend. Is she exhausting herself? Is she living too intensely? Is she perhaps too revolutionary? One of Rosa's former lovers tells Mathilde not to worry: 'If Rosa lived differently she would be even less satisfied', he says. 'She *cannot* live differently.'

VIENNA: Sigmund Freud finally gets word that his son Martin is alive. He has washed up in an Italian military hospital. Information is scant, but his injuries do not appear to be serious.

Just before the end of the year more definite news arrives: Martin is now in a convalescent hospital in Teramo, a town in the Apennine mountains not far from Italy's Adriatic shore. Freud, looking out of his frosty window at Berggasse 19, imagines the view his son Martin must have from his hospital bed. A few weeks later and Martin has moved again, this time to a barracks in Genoa, in the north of Italy, with a view of a lighthouse and the Mediterranean.

DOUAI, FRANCE: From the soil of a French artist's garden, a resurrection. French soldiers are commandeered to do the job. She was buried in the garden five years ago, when German soldiers came storming through, looking for loot. Now she is free again. Rodin's *Eve*. In bronze.

MOSCOW: Vladimir receives a message from an old friend, alongside a very special Christmas gift: the latest publication of the German Spartacist League. 'God grant that the coming year will bring us great fulfilments', the letter reads. It is signed: *Roza*.

1919

Victory attained by violence is tantamount to a defeat, for it is momentary.
Mohandas Gandhi

Proletarians, to horse!
Leon Trotsky

WINTER

A ROAD OUTSIDE MOSCOW: The former territory of the Russian Empire is a dangerous place to be this winter. All is upheaval. In the capital of the Soviet Republic, ice bursts open all the water pipes. No one repairs them. In five years, someone says, all the buildings will have fallen down. In ten, we will be running around on all fours like animals, another jokes.

War stalks the land. Bandit units prowl the borderlands of Russia and Mongolia, led by a man who claims to be either a new Genghis Khan or a new Napoleon. The Muslim population of Central Asia is in a state of insurrection. Lawless Ukraine is torn in every direction as the Germans pull out. A wave of pogrom violence intensifies. In Siberia the new darling of the Whites, Kolchak, tries to persuade the world they should lend him their support so he can restore law and order. (Meanwhile, he crushes moderate Socialist Revolutionaries who cannot decide who they dislike more: Kolchak or Lenin.) The conquest of Perm in the Urals gives him a new base from which to attack Bolshevism's citadel in central Russia.

Who wouldn't want to escape this maelstrom if they could? With the war over in Europe and their country's independence won, most Czech troops in Russia can now think only of how to get home. The Russian conundrum is a mess that they cannot solve; there is no love lost between them and Kolchak. They are told to wait a little longer, and assigned guard duties along the trans-Siberian railway. The first boatload of Czech troops – sick with tuberculosis – is finally allowed to leave Russia via the Japanese-occupied port of Vladivostok. A long journey around Asia and Africa awaits them. But what is two months at sea compared to three years in the Russian soup?

Is nowhere safe? Vladimir Ilyich and his sister Maria are on their way to visit Nadya at the forest school she is staying at on the outskirts of Moscow. A traditional Russian Christmas party is in store. A fir tree has been specially decorated by the children with whom Nadya has made friends. The impatient revolutionary's motor car bumps over the wintry road out of town. And then, unexpectedly, it skids to a halt. A hold-up. The outlaws take everyone's papers and money, and make off with the car. A member of the Cheka travelling with the boss is left standing in the middle of the road holding a giant pail of milk which was to have been delivered to Nadya as a special gift. The car is recovered later that night, with a policeman and a soldier shot dead next to it.

A thousand miles to the south of Moscow, the ragged, typhus-riddled Red Army of the North Caucasus launches a New Year's attack on the White army led by General Denikin. Their advance is quickly stopped. A sweeping White counter-offensive begins soon after, led by a dashing cavalry officer named Wrangel. Town after town falls as the Whites clear the more numerous Reds out of the area. Though still miles away from Moscow and separated from each other by huge swathes of territory under Bolshevik control, the White forces of Kolchak and Denikin are on the move again.

PARIS: The stained-glass windows of Notre-Dame are still in storage. Yellow replacement glass fills the unheated cathedral with a weak northern European light. 'As cold as Greenland', shivers an American history professor. The Seine is swollen with the winter rains, and the city filled with refugees from northern France. Everyone seems to have a cold. Woodrow's friend Colonel House falls ill with influenza for the third time in a year; some newspapers prematurely pronounce him dead.

Paris is a little tattier than before the war, but it still intends to put on a show for its foreign guests. Restaurants lay in additional supplies. Dance halls rehearse their latest acts. Visitors in need of historical edification visit the *Panthéon de la Guerre*, a painting over a hundred metres long which shows portraits of the war's main characters. Two black American soldiers, one of whom is supposed to be Harry Johnson, peep out from one of the panels alongside Pershing, Wilson, Foch, Pétain and the rest.

For the next few months, Paris is to become the capital of the world. Anyone who is anyone is there. Here is their chance to lay their claims before the world. Here is their chance to circulate whatever particular piece of gossip, rumour or story they wish to have widely believed. (*The Protocols of the Elders of Zion* make the rounds, inevitably.) Alongside the British, American and Italian delegations there are Japanese and Chinese representatives, Indian princes dressed in British uniform, Czechs and Poles, Albanian warlords, delegates from Persia, Armenians and Arabs.

The Hotel Crillon becomes the United-States-on-the-Seine. A lieutenant who used to manage the Vanderbilt Hotel in New York is put in charge. American soldiers man the lifts and guard the building. Keeping the focus of the American delegation on preparations for the conference, rather than on the attractions of Paris, falls to a bunch of rather humourless security officials. They are horrified when they discover a secret trapdoor between the American offices on the Place de la Concorde and the private rooms of Maxim's restaurant, famous around the globe as the meeting place of the world's courtiers and courtesans. The restaurant is declared out of bounds, and a padlock purchased to keep the trapdoor closed. It lasts less than two weeks.

HÄSSLEHOLM, SWEDEN: Ludendorff has moved on to Sweden, where he is living as a guest of the Swedish horse-riding champion Ragnar Olson. In conversation, his lips quiver with half-muttered accusations of who is to blame for Germany's defeat: Bolsheviks, socialists, Jews – everyone but him. He compares himself to the Carthaginian general Hannibal. 'He, too, was stranded shortly before reaching his goal, because the home front did not provide the army with what it needed', he tells a visiting Swedish military officer. 'In fact, it stabbed him in the back.' The country lacked charismatic civilian leadership. Lessons must be learned.

Wild rumours circulate in Sweden as to the general's whereabouts. One paper reports that Ludendorff was only travelling through and is now in Russia, where Lenin has asked him to command the Red Army. Local Swedish socialists threaten to burn down Olson's house when they find out that the general is living in their district.

BERLIN: Better Sweden than Germany. Here, everything is in flux. Former intimates of the Kaiser now line up to tell embarrassing stories about their former patron – the more salacious the better – in the hope of currying favour with the new regime. Social Democrats who claim to be the true inheritors of Karl Marx huddle in dark corners with revanchist army officers, to discuss how to prevent revolutionary insurrection from the left. Conspiracy is everywhere. Einstein decides to clear out of town with his cousin Elsa, taking the train to Switzerland to visit his ailing mother. He asks the university in Zurich to bring forward a planned lecture series about relativity.

For weeks now, Berlin has been rocked by demonstrations, each faction in Germany's fractured politics trying to claim the mantle of the people.

Funerals are political events. Liebknecht turns every street corner into a tribune. *Agitation, agitation, agitation.* Even as the election of a national assembly approaches, the question remains: will Germany's future be decided in parliament or on the streets? Lenin's revolution shows you do not have to be a majority to win power. All you need is courage, conviction and a bit of luck.

The hope of socialist unity is gone. 'We have been awakened from our dreams', Rosa Luxemburg tells the founding congress of the new Communist Party of Germany. She jokes that Ebert, her former student at the Social Democratic academy years ago, would like to be King if the capitalists let him. German soldiers are already serving world imperialism by fighting the Bolsheviks in the Baltic. But she tells new Spartacist recruits to be patient: 'The conquest of power will not be effected with one blow.' Reprising her old argument with Lenin, she imagines a progressive revolution from below, rather than a centrally dictated one from above. The German proletariat's 'school of action', Rosa declaims, will be the daily struggle in each factory, in each village, in each municipality.

There is a rustic charm to the idea of a landscape blooming with social revolution. Events intervene. When Ebert fires Berlin's far-left police chief – a former telegraphist at the Russian embassy who got the job during the confusion when the Kaiser fell – renegade Social Democrats decide to call an anti-government demonstration. Not wanting to be left behind, the Spartacists rally on Berlin's Alexanderplatz. After the police chief declares he will not be pushed out without a fight, Liebknecht makes a speech. His words carry weakly through the cold air. But his gestures convey the point. One observer is reminded of a religious prophet worked up into a righteous fury. That evening, a group of armed revolutionary youths occupy the offices of the Social Democrat newspaper – *Vorwärts*, or *Forward* – for the second time in as many weeks.

Suddenly, almost by accident, the revolution seems to be happening. The masses have not waited for instructions. The revolutionary moment, it appears, has materialised by itself. It is a question of seizing the moment or losing momentum. Meeting late at night in Berlin's police headquarters, the Spartacists and their allies try to piece together what is happening on the ground. Their information is imperfect. But it is encouraging. Worked up by their revolutionary agitation and exhausted by the day's events, Liebknecht and his comrades decide to go all in. They call on the proletariat to take power. The government has to be toppled. An improvised revolutionary plan of action is put into effect. Newspaper and telegraph offices are occupied. For a moment, to Spartacist eyes at least, Berlin looks like Petrograd in 1917.

Over the next couple of days, pro and anti-government demonstrations – both flying red flags – confront each other in the city's streets. Rival mobs – who can tell from which side? – look for enemies to beat up. Soldiers bark orders across empty streets. A machine gun is mounted on the Brandenburg Gate. Women and children are told to stay indoors. Government offices shut their doors. 'There will be further loss of blood', a pro-government speaker predicts. The Spartacists seem ready to oblige.

The dandy and diplomat Harry Kessler books a room at the Hotel Kaiserhof to observe the action at close quarters. When the machine guns and grenades start – difficult to know who fires the first volley – he goes downstairs, speaks to some soldiers bracing for an imminent Spartacist assault and decides he might be better at home after all. 'Berlin has become a witches' cauldron', he writes in his diary that night. 'Not since the great days of the French Revolution has humanity depended so much on the outcome of street-fighting in a single city.'

The mood is ugly. Some say Ebert has already fled. Others say government shock troops are preparing to storm the city. (Over a thousand Freikorps volunteers arrive by train over the next few days.) A wave of panic convulses Berlin following claims that the central bank has been emptied by the rebels. Both sides accuse the other of poisonous alliances: the Social Democrats with Prussian landowners, the Freikorps and the British; the German Communists with the Russian Bolsheviks. The time for talking is over. Germany's fate will be decided in the next few days. Perhaps the fate of the world.

MILAN: After London (where he meets the King), Scotland (where he visits his grandmother's birthplace and sermonises in a local Presbyterian church), Rome (where he pays his respects to the Pope) and Genoa (birthplace of Christopher Columbus), Woodrow finds himself in Milan.

Amongst the smartly dressed guests at a banquet at La Scala opera house sits the editor of a local newspaper: Benito Mussolini. He wonders if the American President has read the editorial he wrote a few days before, in language as colourful as D'Annunzio's. 'We do not intend to flatter only the President of the great Republic of the stars', the article reads, 'if we say that today he is our guest and that Italy, by spirit, tradition and temperament is the most Wilsonian nation of all'. The love seems to be mutual.

In answer to a toast proposed by a Milanese lawyer at the banquet, Woodrow declares that 'the heart of America has gone out to the heart of Italy', before exclaiming 'Viva l'Italia!' in a moment of un-Presbyterian abandon. On a Sunday, as well.

Mussolini and his friends are to be disappointed if they think their charm offensive will convince the American President to support Italy's territorial claims: south Tyrol, Dalmatia (including the town of Fiume, now added to the list), and various colonial baubles so Italy can stand tall in the world. On the issue of Italy's claims to land once ruled by the Habsburgs (but where Italians are in a minority) Woodrow is unmoved. He takes the cheering crowds as evidence that he has the Italian people on his side – or can put them on his side, if he needs to. Whatever promises were made to Italy during the war by the British and the French, these are not Woodrow's promises. The United States is not bound to honour them. The time for secret treaties is gone. Things are different now.

A week after Woodrow's visit to La Scala, Benito is back at the opera house to hear a speech from a leading Socialist – once a frequent correspondent of Mussolini's – about the upcoming negotiations in Paris. He counsels compromise. He warns that the country must face up to the reality that the Americans will never accept Italian national aggrandisement at the expense of the principles of self-determination, and Italy should be prepared to settle for far less in territorial gains than was once promised by the British and the French to get Italy into the war in the first place. The dream of the Adriatic as an Italian sea must be abandoned. Ownership of the Dodecanese islands between Greece and Turkey should be renounced. Italy must demonstrate reasonableness and modesty. The speaker is shouted down. Is this what the war was fought for?

Gabriele D'Annunzio feared as much, even before the end of the war. Weeks after the armistice lost him his role as the Italian army's top propagandist, he steels himself for a new campaign. His incendiary 'Letter to the Dalmatians' is published in the main newspapers. The mutilation of Italy's wartime victory – that evocative word again – is not acceptable. 'Not only has our war not ended', he writes, 'it has only now reached its climax.' He rejects the idea of an Italy 'made stupid by the transatlantic care packages of Dr Wilson' or a country 'amputated by the transalpine surgery' of the peacemakers in Paris. Italy's claims to Dalmatia must be respected.

'We will confront the new conspiracy', D'Annunzio proclaims in an article reported as far away as New York, 'with a bomb in either hand, and a knife between the teeth!'

PARIS: First Apollinaire, now something even worse. Breton's old friend Vaché, the wounded soldier whose mocking attitudes he so admired back in 1917, is found dead in a hotel room in Nantes. Alongside him lies the naked body of another French soldier. The newspapers report the cause of death: an overdose of opium pellets.

But what really happened? The question haunts Breton. A celebration gone wrong? An accident? This seems the most likely hypothesis. Two other men took opium with Vaché that evening and survived, including an American soldier who raised the alarm on waking up and finding the others comatose on the bed. Then again, perhaps there was more to it than that. Could it have been a double suicide? Like so many others, Vaché had seemed adrift since the end of the war. Perhaps he could not live without it.

But maybe it was something else entirely, something positive: an extravagant *coup de théâtre*, to die as remarkably as one has lived, and certainly before life gets too dull. Breton will never know. The words of his friend's last letter run through his mind, now an instruction from beyond the grave: 'I rely on you to open the way ... it'll be such fun, you see, when this true NEW SPIRIT is unleashed!' What a responsibility! Uncertain that he can ever live up to his dead friend's expectations of him, André spends the days walking around Paris. In the evenings he sits alone on a bench in the Place du Châtelet, quite oblivious to the peace conference, with all its hangers-on.

Then, as if called upon by providence, a new hero turns up in young Breton's life to show him the way. Tristan Tzara, the Dadaist bard of Zurich, writes to Breton to ask him for a poem for his magazine. It takes two weeks for Breton to write back. But when he does, it is to declare a new loyalty – to Dadaism. 'What I loved most in the world has just disappeared', he writes; 'today all my attention is turned toward you.' So begins a stormy love affair.

BUDAPEST, HUNGARY: A letter is smuggled from Budapest to Kiev by a former Hungarian prisoner of war, identifying himself as a member of a Red Cross delegation (that old trick). In Kiev, the letter is passed into the hands of a Russian courier and thence transported to Moscow and onto the desk of Lenin himself.

Béla Kun's report is encouraging. The new regime in Budapest is close to collapse, unable to defend the country from dismemberment. Communist agitators have infiltrated French army units in the region and made their way into Romania. But Kun is under no illusions as to the next stage of development for any prospect of a Hungarian revolution. 'We know very well that our fate is decided in Germany.'

BERLIN: While the peacemakers gather in Paris to talk of a new world, in Berlin the words on everyone's lips are terror, famine, blood, chaos.

But still the newspapers come out each morning and the cafés on Potsdamer Platz remain open. While the shots ring out in Berlin's central district, street vendors wander around selling cigarettes. 'King' Ebert has not budged. Within seventy-two hours of the launch of the Spartacist uprising, an adviser sent from Moscow, Karl Radek – who accompanied Lenin on his train journey in 1917 – privately declares it has failed.

Defeatist talk is rejected at Spartacist headquarters. A week ago, Rosa warned her Communist comrades to be patient, advocating a methodical approach to revolution, conducted with steady resolve through the education of the working classes and brought about with their overwhelming support. She has since thrown caution to the wind. 'In the fiery atmosphere of the revolution, people and things mature with incredible rapidity', she now says. Who is she to hold back history? From the current vantage point it would be 'spineless' to seek negotiations with the Social Democrats, as some fair-weather revolutionaries are suggesting. What has been started must now be finished. No retreat from destiny. 'Disarm the counter-revolution, arm the masses, occupy all positions of power', she commands the readers of the *Rote Fahne*. 'Sweeping measures must be undertaken immediately.' In a revolution, each hour is like a month, each day a year: 'Act quickly!'

If Rosa Luxemburg's words were all it took, Berlin would already be in Spartacist hands by now. Red flags would adorn every balcony. Vladimir would arrive from Moscow to inspect the city's proletarian legions, and everyone would embrace as comrade-brothers. But fiery words are no substitute for machine guns. The Spartacists are outnumbered and outgunned, and their position is unlikely to improve. Ebert's government have called in the assistance of Freikorps units who see the war as unfinished business and the Spartacists as the latest enemy.

As the days wear on, only the most dedicated revolutionaries remain behind to fight for the Spartacist cause. Gunfire become sporadic and localised. The snow muffles its echoes. The violence becomes almost theatrical – as if a revolution scene was being filmed for a movie, but someone forgot to tell the public or put up a cordon. As a result, spectators are quite often killed.

Atrocities are alleged on both sides. The Spartacists accuse the government of shooting unarmed civilians and then cynically claiming they were provoked, in order to allow them to justify further crackdowns. The gulf between Social Democrats and Spartacists hardens into hatred. As the insurrection fails, thoughts turn to revenge against the perpetrators, to teach them a lesson once and for all. 'The sick body of the German people needs an operation', a Catholic paper now tells its readers. 'It may be painful, but it appears to offer the only solution to restore our health.' Operating under licence from government – and now God, it would appear – the Freikorps are released to do whatever they want.

Six days into their occupation of the *Vorwärts* offices, the Spartacists barricade themselves into their last redoubt. Freikorps assault troops are brought up to deliver the *coup de grâce*. When they begin their attack, they are surprised, at first, by the ferocity of the rebels' resistance. A single machine gun seems to be the problem. Word spreads that Rosa Luxemburg herself is firing it, perhaps a knife between her teeth, D'Annunzio-style.

Within three quarters of an hour the gun has been silenced. By late morning the newspaper offices have been cleared. Seven Spartacists taken prisoner are killed in an army barracks shortly afterwards – neither the first, nor the last, to face such an end. The right-wing Social Democrat in charge of operations, Gustav Noske, personally leads a column of troops through Berlin to show who owns the streets. 'The psychosis of the days of August 1914 appears to have been re-awoken', reports one far-left journalist.

And what of Rosa Luxemburg? On the morning the *Vorwärts* building is stormed some soldiers see a woman emerging from the rubble. They think it is Rosa and are on the point of shooting her when an officer intervenes. A case of mistaken identity, it turns out. So where is she, then? Has she fled the capital, in disguise, like Ludendorff and Lenin before her? Not a bit of it. Rosa may not be a front-line fighter, but nor can she leave Berlin: that is where the printing presses are. And what is Rosa without a printing press? As the Spartacist uprising crumbles, she is holed up in the working-class district of Neukölln, the guest of an increasingly nervous Spartacist-supporting family. Covert visitors besiege her to seek advice. 'I wish I were back in jail', she tells her friend Mathilde. 'In prison, I had my peace.' One evening Karl Liebknecht turns up and the assembled company read a fairy tale by Tolstoy and then a little Goethe before trying to catch an hour or two of sleep. Soon after, Rosa and Karl move to a new hiding place in the middle-class district of Wilmersdorf. Safer, they think.

Rosa can sense that her time is running out. The bloodhounds are on her trail. Each hour brings news of the arrest or death of former friends or lovers. She knows that information leading to her capture will earn a pretty penny for whoever is ready to spill the beans. She cannot hide for ever. At least her writing has lost none of its energy. If anything, the uprising has made it more strident. 'Future victories will spring from this defeat', she thunders in the *Rote Fahne*, citing the failed uprisings of 1848 and 1871 which nonetheless provided both education and revolutionary experience for the masses. History cannot be halted. Luxemburg is scathing of government claims to have restored order in Berlin. 'You foolish lackeys!' she writes. 'Your "order" is built on sand. Tomorrow the revolution will rise up again clashing its weapons and to your horror it will proclaim with trumpets blazing: I was, I am, I shall be!'

The following day, acting on a tip-off, members of the local Wilmersdorf militia break into the apartment where the Spartacist leaders are hiding. Liebknecht is taken into custody immediately. (He protests that he is a Mr Marcussen, until the initials sewn into his clothing give him away.) Rosa Luxemburg is picked up a little later that evening. After some debate as to what to do with the prisoners – a call is made to government headquarters – they are handed over to a nearby military unit with a strong anti-Spartacist reputation. They are taken to the Casino-Hotel Eden, not far from the Kurfürstendamm, the temporary headquarters of the Guards Cavalry Division, where a man named Waldemar Pabst is in charge. No direct orders are required for a nationalist soldier who has seen action on both the Eastern and Western Fronts and whose unit was involved in the retaking of the *Vorwärts* building a few days before. Pabst will know what to do.

While Liebknecht is questioned by Pabst and then beaten up by a group of soldiers, Rosa awaits her turn in a nearby room. She leafs through Goethe's *Faust*, a tale rich in bloody pacts and devilish betrayals. A little after eleven, on the pretext of driving their prisoner to jail, the soldiers haul Liebknecht off to the Tiergarten park in central Berlin where they stop the car, take out their bloodied passenger, and shoot him dead. Returning to the Eden, they frogmarch Rosa Luxemburg through the hotel lobby and shove her through the swing doors onto the street outside, where she is set upon with rifle butts. Beaten unconscious, her limp body is thrown into a waiting open-top car. In the kerfuffle one of Rosa's shoes and her handbag are left on the pavement. The engine revs. The car drives off. They have not got far before a soldier decides to finish the job with a shot, at point-blank range, into Rosa's head. Her body is dumped in a nearby canal.

The next day, the Guards Cavalry Division release their sanitised version of events. Liebknecht's guards took a detour through the Tiergarten to avoid the crowds, they pretend, stopped because of a puncture and only shot the Spartacist leader when he tried to escape after first knifing one of his guards and ignoring several orders to halt. The official story claims that Rosa was shot by an unknown assailant and her body dragged off to God-knows-where by an angry crowd gathered outside the Eden. A public investigation is launched – but to be conducted under military rather than civilian law. Ebert is silent about the deaths. (Pabst later claims he met Ebert the day after the killings and was thanked for his service.) Scheidemann, the man who declared the German republic barely two months ago, tells a rally in Kassel that the Spartacist leaders were 'victims of their own bloody terror tactics'. The suppression of the uprising, he bellows, was an 'act of deliverance'.

Berlin carries on as if the uprising never happened – like an 'elephant stabbed with a penknife'. Elections are held as planned. The Social Democrats are triumphant. The National Assembly meets in Weimar, far from any revolutionary unpleasantness. For now, at least, it looks as if Ebert's Faustian pact with the Freikorps has paid off. But how long will the lull last?

PARIS: Woodrow, suffering from an almighty cold, stays in bed all morning. The rain falls constantly outside. When he finally makes his way to the French Foreign Office for the official opening of the peace conference, trumpets and kettle-drums greet his car and film cameras record his arrival. Inside, the President rambles on about how welcoming the French have been. He terms the meeting 'the supreme conference in the history of mankind'.

The French premier, elected to the role of chairman, is not to be outdone. Clemenceau calls upon his fellow leaders to conduct themselves in the next few weeks not just as friends, but as brothers. He talks about the need for heavy enemy reparations, to restore northern France to its former glory before the Kaiser's army turned it into a wasteland. This, he says, is a matter of justice. But hoping to win over the Americans, he also talks about Wilson's favourite subject. 'The League of Nations is here', says Clemenceau solemnly, looking around the room: 'it is in yourselves; it is for you to make it live; and for that it must be in our hearts'.

SOLOHEADBEG, CO. TIPPERARY, IRELAND: They have been drilling young republicans for months, training them to fire a rifle or how to blow up a railway line. There have been confrontations. There have been deaths. But in January the Irish Volunteers truly go to war. Armed with a single rifle and a few pistols, a group of Volunteers – acting on their own initiative, it is said, but in the militant spirit of their organisation – raids a delivery of explosives to a quarry in south Tipperary. Two members of the Royal Irish Constabulary are shot dead.

That same day, Sinn Féin delegates elected to the Westminster parliament last year – those not languishing in British jails, that is – meet together publicly for the first time in Dublin. They declare themselves the parliament of Ireland, the Dáil – the one true voice of all the people of the island. A Catholic priest intones a prayer to convey an appropriate solemnity to it all. Though not everyone can understand its cadences, the Irish language is used throughout the meeting – except when the audience is asked to quieten down, an injunction delivered, apologetically, in English. The number of elected Irish delegates actually present – a mere twenty-seven out of a total of one hundred and five Irish MPs – is exceeded many times over by the number of spectators craning their necks around marble sculptures to catch sight of the formal proceedings.

That morning there was a luncheon at the Mansion House to celebrate the return of several hundred Irish soldiers from service with the British army in France. Now, as the roll is called for the Dáil, the response to over thirty names – including that of Éamon de Valera – is 'Fé ghlas ag Gallaibh': imprisoned by the foreigner, those same British. Other Irish parliamentarians elected to Westminster are simply declared 'as láthair' – absent. (This includes Unionist MPs who view the Dublin gathering as a nationalist stunt and reject the invitation to take part.) There is a little subterfuge when the name Michael Collins is read out, and someone pretending to be him declares him present. In fact, Collins is across the water in Manchester, putting the final touches to an escape plan for his boss.

Such play-acting can be forgiven. For the moment the Dáil has a single purpose: to reveal, by its very existence, that Ireland's independence is a reality, dependent on no one else's say-so, its legitimacy drawn from the innate right of nations to rule themselves – the principle that Woodrow has proclaimed. It is a parliament for declarations and proclamations, not one for debate and argument. That will come later. On this Tuesday afternoon, the members present rise as one when called upon to hear a solemn declaration formally ratifying the establishment of an Irish republic, backdated to Easter 1916. A message is then read out for the benefit of the outside world – first in Irish, then French and finally in English: 'To the nations of the world, greeting!'

But what are words without deeds? Over the coming weeks and months, the Volunteers acquire a new name: the Irish Republican Army, or IRA for short. The Dáil has declared the will of Ireland, a Volunteer newspaper reads; but 'the most drastic measures against the enemies of Ireland' will be required to enforce it. People talk about a new rising in the making.

Moscow: 'Our enemy today is bureaucracy and profiteering', the impatient revolutionary tells a conference convened to discuss relations between Moscow and the provinces. 'We are being ground down by red tape', he warns. Localism is a 'quagmire'. For the moment, centralism must prevail. The following day he speaks at a rally to protest the murder of Karl Liebknecht and Rosa Luxemburg. Germany's Social Democrats have again revealed their true face, he declares: imperialist stooges and counter-revolutionaries, all. 'Death to the butchers!' he cries.

The news from the Caucasian front, in Russia's deep south, is bad. In late January, Lenin receives a telegram telling him that Red forces there have collapsed. 'The eleventh army has ceased to exist; the enemy occupies cities and cossack villages almost without resistance.' From Moscow, war commissar Trotsky blames the persistence of ineffective partisan methods amongst the Reds for their defeat, calling the Red Caucasian army an unruly horde. The collapse reveals the need for the disciplined modern soldiering he has been advocating all along, led by professionals.

With the Caucasus now secure behind them, Denikin's White forces are free to advance towards Ukraine, where departing German forces have left a chaotic contest for power in their wake which the Red Army is rapidly exploiting. A race is on. Who will win: revolution across Europe or the White armies marching to decapitate Bolshevism in its lair?

Berlin: Nervous of a repeat attempt at a German Bolshevik revolution, Ebert's government bars a funeral procession for Liebknecht and thirty other Spartacists in the centre of Berlin at the end of January. Machine guns and artillery pieces guard the republic's citadels. At a hastily rearranged gathering on the outskirts of Berlin, Rosa Luxemburg is represented by an empty coffin. Her body has not yet been found. Marchers carry signs on which the word 'murderer' is scrawled. Her transfiguration into revolutionary martyr is complete.

Over the next few weeks, as the newly elected National Assembly assembles in Weimar to deliberate the new constitution, Germany awaits the next explosion at home. In this, at least, Rosa Luxemburg was right: the crushing of the revolution in Berlin does not end matters. Instead, remarks one Communist, 'hills of corpses' now mark out its road ahead. A Soviet-style republic is put down in Bremen. On the Ruhr, the miners go on strike, organise themselves into workers' councils, thumb their noses at government demands to disband and threaten to flood the mines. Across Germany, the ranks of the Freikorps swell with fresh recruits itching for a chance to fight the next Rosa or the next Karl, or else seek fame and fortune further east.

The middle classes quake with rumours of Bolsheviks everywhere, with their sinister methods and Russian backing. A volunteer army is raised to secure the country's northern ports. On the Ruhr, howitzers are used to subdue the miners: seventy-two are killed in a single bombardment. German cities fill with restless legions of the unemployed, while in the countryside, no one can be found to till the fields. Food aid from America is promised – but only if Germany first hands over its entire commercial shipping fleet.

In Munich, Kurt Eisner's political authority is obliterated by elections in which his party wins hardly any seats at all. And yet, for weeks, he clings on to power, trying to square the circle of Bavarian politics by mediating between those who demand that parliament's full authority be restored and those who see this as a bourgeois plot to disempower the workers' councils and turn back the clock. After the closure of the Traunstein camp, Adolf is sent back to Munich to take up guard duty for Eisner's increasingly beleaguered regime.

Back in Berlin, the dandy Kessler lunches with both former diplomatic buddies apoplectic at Germany's international situation, and also with young intellectuals who see no future but with the Communists. But he is also drawn to the furious energy of the new Berlin. 'In the evening friends abducted me to a bar where dancing goes on until morning', Harry confides in his diary. 'There are hundreds of such places now.' In the first few months of 1919, doctors note a spike in cases of venereal disease.

VIENNA: As the long first winter of peace bites deep, a visitor arrives for Sigmund Freud, from the peace conference in Paris. An American who claims to work for President Wilson. In the circumstances, Freud's immediate interests in the man are basic. 'He came accompanied by two baskets of provisions', Freud writes to an astonished colleague, and was happy to swap the food for two signed copies of one of his books. Freud's estimation of Woodrow immediately rises. In the Austrian capital, newspapers carry reports of animal hooves being boiled up and ground down to serve as ingredients for sausages to make up for the lack of meat.

Not long afterwards, a second visitor from Paris arrives at Freud's door. This time, a friend of his nephew, New York publicity man Edward Bernays, turns up with an even more valuable cargo than food: a box of Corona cigars from Havana. Freud lights up. Even at a time when survival seems to have replaced pleasure as the principle of life, all is perhaps not lost, Sigmund reflects warmly, cigar smoke curling up through the heavy coldness of his study. Freud sends back his nephew's emissary with a book, in German, of the lectures he gave in Vienna in that bitter third winter of the war. 'In grateful acknowledgement of a nephew's thought of his uncle', he writes by way of dedication.

LINCOLN, ENGLAND: A cake baked by a Mrs O'Sullivan of Manchester is delivered to Lincoln jail by a young Irish teacher, Kathleen Talty. It is the fourth cake received by the Irish prisoners in recent weeks. And baked inside is the fourth attempt at a key to open the prison's doors, fashioned according to de Valera's imprint of the chaplain's key, its outline drawn on a Christmas card.

Seven-forty in the evening. From a field outside the prison grounds an electric torch lights up. Inside the prison, nervous hands light matches and extinguish them by way of a response. The message is conveyed: all clear. The escape takes place tonight.

This time, the key works. Like a beauty, it turns through the locks from cell to corridor, and from corridor to the last door between the prison and the outside world. Michael Collins and another comrade from Ireland wait on the other side, impatiently stuffing their own duplicate key in the door to open it from the outside. Then panic. 'I've broken a key in the lock, Dev.' Hot words are uttered into the cold air. What now? Somehow the broken-off stub is pushed out. Divine intervention. Another key is inserted. Turn. Pray. A long, loud screeching sound as the gate swings open. Freedom.

AMERONGEN: Security around Wilhelm is tightened up. At the beginning of the year, a former Senator from Tennessee takes part in a clumsy freebooting attempt to kidnap Wilhelm and present him to the American army on the Rhine as a belated Christmas present. A little later, warnings are received of a Belgian pilot's plan to bomb the castle, leading the government to ban flying over Count Bentinck's estate. Dutch public opinion has shown some sympathy to Wilhelm since the story of his illness was spread around. The government seems unwilling to turn him over. But what if the British and the French demand extradition, and back up their demand with the threat of force? The former Kaiser's position cannot be guaranteed.

The nearby village now swarms with police. Passport checks are common. Journalists cannot get beyond the castle gates. 'He remained in the open air more than an hour', writes one journalist after observing the Kaiser from a distance, 'and talked to his aide while making rapid gestures.' The Dutch suggest Wilhelm move to a more remote part of the country, where his security and privacy can be more easily guaranteed (but they veto a large house near the German border).

On the Kaiser's birthday, Count Bentinck presents Wilhelm with a painting of William the Silent, their common ancestor. Bentinck's daughter remarks on the number of beautiful flower arrangements which arrive that day, and wonders how the local postman is getting on with the new burden of all the postcards and letters (some supportive, some not). That evening at dinner, the table is decorated with white lilacs and red tulips.

PARIS: At teatime on most days, the leaders of the victorious powers gather in the French Foreign Office and, like magnificent potentates of old, receive representations from the four corners of the earth. A British chemist named Weizmann makes a plea for a Jewish homeland in Palestine. One afternoon, a particularly long-winded presentation by a Syrian – in French – is cut short when it is realised that he has not actually lived in the land he professes to represent for more than thirty years. The Greek premier impresses with his recitations of Homer and announces that Greece is prepared to forgo its historic claims to Constantinople, as long as it is granted Smyrna, the Christian-majority city on the Aegean coastline of Anatolia which the Turks call İzmir.

Much of the real work is done behind the scenes, by the thousand or so delegates to the conference: in the meeting rooms of grand hotels or over supper in the city's restaurants. Once-intractable problems are again deliberated: the Polish question, the opium question, the labour question, the Arabian question, the League of Nations question. A kaleidoscope of expert committees, commissions and conclaves is formed to answer them. Predictably, Woodrow chairs one on the League of Nations. Fact-finding missions are sent out. Coal production statistics and population pie charts are used to adjudicate where Europe's new borders should lie. A team of Americans roves Paris ensuring that the best libraries are at their disposal.

The Italians care mostly about the territory promised them for joining the war. The French are mostly concerned with regaining Alsace-Lorraine and keeping Germany down (for a while they even think of breaking up the fifty-year-old Reich entirely, and maybe pushing the French border to the Rhine). The British have wider horizons: the freedom of the oceans, the security of the empire, and the future of everything in between. The Americans, some of them at least, aspire to something greater still: a permanent peace, a just peace, a scientific peace, a peace based on principles and facts. But which facts? Whose principles? Diplomats in a position of influence find themselves hot property in Paris. A twenty-six-year-old American diplomat, Allen Dulles, is taken out for a slap-up private dinner by the Foreign Minister of Czechoslovakia. 'And so it goes', the well-fed diplomat writes home to his mother.

Russia perplexes everyone. 'Europe and the world cannot be at peace if Russia is not', Woodrow notes in January. But who is willing to sort out the mess? Having made a separate peace with the Germans and Austrians in early 1918, whatever now constitutes 'Russia' can hardly be invited to the conference as one of the victors a year later. On the other hand, surely Russia's war sacrifices up to 1917 demand some kind of recognition. The brutal victors' peace of Brest-Litovsk cannot be allowed to stand.

So what to do about the Bolsheviks? Some in Paris urge a policy of containment: trying to hold back the Bolshevik tide from the rest of Europe through the imposition of what amounts to a militarised quarantine. A *cordon sanitaire*, as the French call it. Others demand a more muscular approach, arguing for striking at the heart of the beast where Lenin's regime is weak. The Red Army is on its last legs. In February, a British military assessment concludes that Trotsky's army has no winter boots or gloves left and its political capital is spent.

The forces for a more energetically interventionist approach are already in place, contend its advocates, Winston Churchill chief amongst them. Eurasia is dotted with contingents of Allied troops – from the British in Archangel to the French in Odessa, and Americans, Canadians, Japanese, Romanians and Italians elsewhere. The Czechs, though less willing than before, are still a serious factor in Siberia. Piłsudski's Poles have been probing east to see how far they can push Poland's border before the Reds push back. The Royal Navy is the dominant factor in the Caspian and the Baltic, where it has provided support to local anti-Bolshevik forces. There are still German troops in the region, not to mention Yudenich's White army in Estonia. The British have already given support to Kolchak, sending tons of ammunition along the trans-Siberian railway. In Siberia, the Whites joke that they get their uniforms from Britain, their boots from France, their bayonets from Japan and their orders from Omsk.

The material is to hand, the interventionists argue, and the situation ripe. As the peacemakers gather in Paris, Denikin's White forces are romping through southern Russia. Kolchak is rallying for an offensive. Why not go all out now and settle things? When Winston hears that Woodrow may return home without a proper decision on the subject one way or the other he races to Paris to put his case to the Allied leaders (shattering his car windscreen along the way). He arrives just as everyone is getting ready to pack up.

Attempts to talk to the Bolsheviks directly are botched. Early in February, a plan is hatched to meet their delegates in Turkey. An invitation is transmitted by short-wave radio to the Kremlin, suggesting Prinkipo, near Istanbul, as a suitably private venue for the parley. The answer from Moscow is one long sneer, skirting the demand for a ceasefire. A couple of weeks later, a junior American diplomat is sent to Russia on a fact-finding mission. The self-assured twenty-eight-year-old manages to convince himself that his real job is far grander: to broker the outlines of a comprehensive peace deal with the Bolsheviks. He has a wonderful time in Moscow, dining with Lenin and attending the opera in the Tsar's box. The Bolsheviks consider him a useful messenger to the Western powers; they do not take him seriously as a negotiator.

When it comes to the League, Woodrow seems to score complete success, a justification of his decision to come to Paris in person. On St Valentine's Day, to a packed gathering, he presents a draft constitution of the League – called, somewhat religiously, a covenant – so far hashed out in private. 'Many terrible things have come out of this war, gentlemen,' Woodrow says after reading out the sacred text line by line, 'but some very beautiful things have come out of it' too. Edith, without a ticket for the presentation, is smuggled in by the President's doctor and hides behind a curtain to watch her husband speak. Several hundred copies of the covenant are printed and distributed among the politicians and diplomats in Paris.

That very evening, after two months in Europe, Woodrow sets sail for a brief trip home to convince America about its new role in the world. He leaves House in charge for the period of his absence from the peace conference. House promises to have the whole thing – the German peace deal, mostly – wrapped up by the time Woodrow gets back.

WASHINGTON DC: A Senate inquiry, originally set up to look at German subversion during the war, now turns its attention to the latest menace: Bolshevism. A general strike in Seattle in which sixty thousand workers take part causes panic in America in February. The city's mayor calls in the troops and claims it is a revolution averted.

One witness talks about Trotsky's time in New York. He is 'very radical looking in appearance as well as in speech', the subcommittee is told, and rather shorter than is normally thought. Another witness reports on the role of Soviet legations in foreign countries as fronts for agitation and the use of foreign journalists as financial couriers for shadowy international revolutionary networks (the name John Reed is mentioned). Others describe the conditions in Russia itself. One witness terrifies – or fascinates? – the Senators with stories of just how far the Bolsheviks are prepared to go in upending the norms of civilised society:

Senator OVERMAN (D-N.C.): Do they have as many wives as they want?

Mr. STEVENSON (*a witness*): In rotation.

Maj. HUMES: Polygamy is recognized, is it?

STEVENSON: I do not know about polygamy. I have not gone into the study of their social order quite as fully as that.

Senator NELSON (R-Minn.): That is, a man can marry and then get a divorce when he gets tired and get another wife?

STEVENSON: Precisely.

NELSON: And keep up the operation?

STEVENSON: Yes.

OVERMAN: Do you know whether they teach free love?

STEVENSON: They do.

It is said Russian women have been nationalised by the state like everything else.

Over the course of a whole day in mid-February, while Woodrow Wilson is still on his way back from Paris, the subcommittee hears from a Methodist missionary about conditions in ungodly, degenerate Bolshevik Russia. Ancient monasteries have been robbed by the revolutionary heathens, Reverend Simons reports. Churches have become dance halls. He suggests that most Bolshevik agitators in Petrograd are foreign Jews rather than Christian Russians (he claims a black American is the sole exception in one district of the city). Many hail from New York's Lower East Side. 'Shortly after the great revolution of the winter of 1917 there were scores of Jews standing on the benches and soap boxes and what not, talking until their mouths frothed', the missionary reports: 'I often remarked to my sister "Well, what are we coming to anyway? This all looks so Yiddish" '.

The reverend raises the subject of a text he came across in Russia entitled *The Protocols of the Elders of Zion*, and which he clearly views as representing some sort of game-plan for Jewish world domination. 'Now, I have no animus against the Jews but I have a great passion for the truth', Mr Simons says: 'if there is anything in it, I think we ought to know.' The President of the American Jewish Committee writes a stiff letter of complaint to the committee for the slanderous equation of Jews and Bolsheviks.

The committee faces its slipperiest witnesses towards the end of the month: Louise Bryant, and her husband, the journalist and revolutionary rabble-rouser John Reed.

Senator OVERMAN (D-N.C.): Miss Bryant, do you believe in God and in the sanctity of an oath?

Miss BRYANT: Certainly, I believe in the sanctity of an oath.

Senator KING (D-Utah): Do you believe there is a God?

BRYANT: I suppose there is a God. I have no way of knowing.

Senator NELSON (R-Minn.): Do you believe in the Christian religion?

BRYANT: Certainly not. I believe all people should have whatever religion they wish because that is one of the things—

NELSON: You are not a Christian then?

BRYANT: I was christened in the Catholic Church.

NELSON: What are you now, a Christian?

BRYANT: Yes; I suppose that I am.

NELSON: And you do not believe in Christ?

BRYANT: I did not say that I did not believe in Christ.

NELSON: But do you believe in Christ?

BRYANT: I believe in the teachings of Christ, Senator Nelson.

OVERMAN: Do you believe in God?

BRYANT: Yes; I will concede that I believe in God, Senator Overman.

KING: This is important, because a person who has no conception of God does not have any idea of the sanctity of an oath, and an oath would be meaningless.

Senator WOLCOTT (D-Del.): Do you believe in punishment hereafter and a reward for duty?

BRYANT: It seems to me as if I were being tried for witchcraft.

Louise admits to carrying certain documents out of Russia as a messenger for the Bolsheviks, but insists that was the only way of leaving the country. Contrary to what other witnesses have alleged, she saw no one killed in Russia. (It was dark when the October revolution took place, she says.) One Senator asks if she saw beggars in Bolshevik Russia. 'No more than I see here in the United States', she shoots back. And as to whether she ever met any black Americans in Russia, as suggested by Reverend Simons in his testimony, Louise replies that she met just one: 'He was a professional gambler.' Senator Nelson enquires as to whether Louise would like a Bolshevik government set up permanently in Russia. 'I think the Russians ought to settle that', she responds. 'I said I believed in self-determination.'

Bryant is quite clear what she is against: American intervention. The Russians should be allowed to work things out amongst themselves, even at the point of a gun, just as Americans did in their civil war. She does not imagine that a Soviet regime would fit America 'at the present time'. Yes, Russia is currently a dictatorship – but a dictatorship of the majority, and only temporarily. She defends the head of the Cheka as 'an idealist, a very aesthetic young man, not the kind of man who is a real butcher'. Perhaps there has been Red terror in Russia, she admits: but then there has been White terror as well.

Bryant expresses particular anger at the idea that Russian women have been 'nationalised', explaining that they are 'even more belligerent' than the men and would never allow such a thing. Her own belligerence as a witness before the committee goes down badly. When her husband John appears in order to give evidence the following afternoon the atmosphere is more genial. He is a Harvard man after all (albeit one recently suspended from the Harvard Club in New York for being behind on paying his club-house bill). He charms everyone. The subcommittee and Mr Reed engage in long exchanges on the nature of law and a friendly discussion about land reform. Jack pleasantly admits being in favour of revolution, but without violence.

Reed and the Senators part on pleasant terms, with Jack recommending other potential witnesses to balance the subcommittee's proceedings.

By then, America's political attention has turned again to the Atlantic, and to the imminent arrival of Woodrow Wilson, carrying the draft covenant of the League of Nations back from Paris. (His ship is forced to dock in Boston rather than New York, owing to a longshoremen's strike.) The newspapers no longer carry stories about John Reed, but about Senator Reed, a Democrat from Missouri, who declares the League of Nations 'infamous' and anti-constitutional, putting power in the hands of foreign delegates.

NEW YORK – PARIS: 'A triumphal epoch in the history for the colored population of New York', the New York Age calls it. The 369th Regiment is back in town. Others have a jazzier name for them: the Harlem Hellfighters.

They did not have a parade when they left. They make up for it now. Sixteen abreast, the soldiers turn from 25th Street into Fifth Avenue. Jim Europe's band beats out the steady time of military marches (syncopation is banished for the downtown part of the parade). Harry Johnson, the little man from Albany who disembowelled a German soldier with his bolo knife and killed another with a single blow to the head, is carried in an automobile at the rear, standing to take the salute of the crowds. (The same day, an impostor claiming to be Johnson draws a crowd of ten thousand in St. Louis, Missouri.) At 110th Street, the regiment enters Harlem and the formation is relaxed. Jim switches to ragtime and jazz. Marcus Garvey is moved to tears.

An ocean away, Du Bois is taken on a tour of the French battlefields. He searches out material for a book he is writing on the black contribution to the war effort, arguing that 'the black soldier saved civilization in 1914–1918'. On the margins of the peace conference, he attends the first Pan-African Congress in nineteen years, with fifty-seven delegates from around the world. A declaration demands that 'wherever persons of African descent are civilized and able to meet the tests of surrounding culture, they shall be accorded the same rights as their fellow-citizens'. If these rights are denied, the League of Nations must be asked to intervene.

Garvey would not be satisfied with such a statement, with the rights of blacks made conditional on someone else's assessment of whether they are 'civilized'. But for Du Bois, it is a start: 'the world-fight for black rights is on!'

LIBAU, LATVIA: A Freikorps unit led by a German general lands in Latvia.

Some are here for honour, to show the Germans still have some fight left in them. Some have come to the defence of the ancestral ethnic German population of the Baltic, imagining themselves reincarnations of the Teutonic Knights and recalling when this part of Latvia was named Courland (as the Kaiser and Ludendorff still call it). Others fight to resist the tide of Bolshevism – and better to do so on Baltic soil than in Prussia. (By way of thanks, the Latvian government which has invited them in offers soldiers full Latvian citizenship after four weeks' service.) A few join up to keep the German northern flank in play, in preparation for the next war and the inevitable final showdown against Russia. These are the kind of men who fancy themselves as far-sighted strategic thinkers, who spend time in beer halls with maps of Europe rolled out on trestle tables, a stein holding down each corner.

But not all Freikorps volunteers have such highfalutin ambitions. Some fight to win land for themselves and their families: 'excellent colonisation opportunities' are promised. Some fight for the lack of anything better to do back in Germany. One Freikorps commander recruits by simply sitting outside a country pub near Berlin and offering passing men a chance of eastern glory. Amongst those who journey to Latvia this winter is Captain Pabst, the officer in charge at the Eden Hotel when Liebknecht and Luxemburg were killed. There are plenty such men in Germany now, their mercenary instincts fired by patriotism and the lure of booty to continue the war in the east.

Fighting their way through Latvia, proclaiming themselves as the vanguard of German *Kultur* against eastern barbarism, these volunteer soldiers dispense entirely with regular army discipline. The Hamburg Freikorps let their beards grow long, sing old pirate songs and recognise no one's will but their own – and that of whoever they have chosen as their *Führer*. Normal rules of warfare break down. Summary judgement and gruesome collective punishment are common. Latvians accused of helping the Bolsheviks are skewered on German bayonets. Entire families, and some-times whole villages, are murdered by Freikorps troops this way.

For these men – some of whom spent four years in the trenches, others who were too young now making up for lost time – it is as if a psycho-logical dam has been broken. In the Baltic, they are free to live out their most bloody fantasies, against enemies they are told are everywhere. Nothing is too brutal. Everything is possible. To burn down a village: a mere baga-telle. To string up a farmer who gave food to a Bolshevik: simple justice. This is violence meted out face to face, not like the huge, mechanical artillery bombardments of the war on the Western Front. For some, it is intensely liberating. It is as if these soldiers, freed from all restraint, some of them only teenagers, have become Nietzschean supermen, endowed with super-powers over their fellow humans. The aftertaste of such power will linger long after they have left the Baltic far behind. (In some cases, it propels them to the obscenity of Auschwitz.)

Occasionally, news from the rest of Europe breaks through the Baltic fog to reach the Freikorps and their leaders. Some celebrate at the news that Kurt Eisner, Bavaria's hapless revolutionary premier, has been shot dead by a right-wing radical (who is immediately killed himself), throwing Munich into a new bout of unrest, as the parliamentary left and the revolutionary far left compete for power. (A member of the Thule Society decides to mark the place of Eisner's assassination by sprinkling it with the urine of a bitch on heat, ensuring it will attract the attention of other dogs.) Towards the end of winter, Berlin too explodes in violence once more when a general strike turns sour. ('The dead are rising up again', declares Rosa Luxemburg's old paper, the *Rote Fahne*, with blood-curdling glee.) Communist militias are accused of murdering sixty policemen in cold blood. Government soldiers are given permission to execute suspects on the spot. Aeroplanes bombard pockets of resistance.

Many cheer such decisive action. Others worry about the consequences. 'During the past week', writes Kessler, 'thanks to its wanton lies and bloodshed, the government has caused a breach in the nation which decades will not suffice to mend.'

Paris: While not entirely relinquishing the possibility of a medical career and not yet fully demobilised from his military duties, André Breton decides to develop a sideline in the literary magazine business, in emulation of his new hero Tristan Tzara. He assembles a group of like-minded co-conspirators. But what to call their publication? *Dada* is too obvious, and too derivative. *Ciment armé* (Reinforced Cement) is rejected. Breton's idea of *Le Nouveau Monde* (The New World) is adopted but then dropped when it is discovered a magazine of the same name has been around since 1885.

Eventually they settle on the rather dry-sounding *Littérature*, without the pizzazz of *Dada* (no typographical experimentation at all), but with a seriousness of intent that is the proper preserve of the young (Breton is not quite twenty-three). Put together at great speed in a flurry of excitement, the first edition of *Littérature* appears in March. Breton is the magazine's co-editor. Tristan Tzara is asked to contribute to the following month's publication. If only they could meet in person.

MUNICH: Now that he is dead, the assassinated left-wing leader Kurt Eisner is transformed in the public standing from Marxist anti-patriot to a good man in hard times, doing his best to tame the wild beasts unleashed by war and revolution. The coachman who drives the hearse on the day of his funeral wears his Wittelsbach best, as if a Bavarian King were being laid to rest, rather than a Jewish theatre critic from Berlin. Public buildings fly the white-and-blue of the Bavarian flag at half-mast.

Tens of thousands turn out to join the procession: socialists, trades unionists, representatives of all the regiments stationed in Munich. A former field-runner is one of those caught in a snapshot of the procession, amongst the sea of other soldiers with their blank faces and worn-out boots and uncertain political opinions. When not on guard duty or attending beer hall meetings, Adolf has very little to do back at barracks. He and a friend earn some extra money by taking apart and reassembling old army gas masks.

Far from turning back the revolution as intended by his murderer, Eisner's assassination has radicalised it. A new workers' council proclaims it is in charge now, as the true successor to the revolution of 1918. Social Democrats in the Bavarian parliament scramble to assert their counter-claim to power based on the January elections. Munich swings between compromise and chaos.

VENICE: A message arrives at the Hotel Danieli, one of D'Annunzio's old haunts, with orders for one of the hotel's British guests. The recipient, a certain Colonel Lisle Strutt, is told to proceed at once to a place called Eckartsau to offer his personal protection to the Austrian Emperor and his family. The colonel, one of Europe's finest mountaineers, has no idea where Eckartsau is. He heads first for Vienna, and asks around.

A few days later, the colonel arrives at Eckartsau hunting lodge, where he is greeted warmly by Charles and Zita. Looking around, he spots a photograph of himself before the war, taken at St Moritz with Franz Ferdinand. He ponders if such a house could be adequately defended if marauding revolutionaries decided to attack.

DUBLIN: In the last weeks of winter, wild speculation flourishes as to the whereabouts of Éamon de Valera.

His photograph is circulated by the authorities. His description – sallow complexion, scar on the top of his head, mole on his forehead – is given to ports and police stations. Some say he has been espied wandering the hills of Kilkenny, deep in southern Ireland. Others have spotted him in the port of Grimsby, on the North Sea coast of England. A British commercial traveller on the overnight train from Paris to the Alps claims he caught sight of Ireland's rebel leader, clean-shaven and dressed as a Roman Catholic priest, on his way to Rome, masquerading as an Irish-American. In Paris, an Irishman struggling to get the attention of the peacemakers drops a broad hint to a journalist of the *Daily Mail* that de Valera could be in the French capital in a couple of hours if called upon to make Ireland's case. A French paper suggests he is there already, having been smuggled across the English Channel to Holland. British intelligence notes an unsubstantiated rumour in the Cork area that de Valera is dead.

All quite false. After a few weeks in the care of a friendly priest in Manchester, de Valera is shipped back to Dublin, where he spends a night in a whiskey factory before reaching the blessed safety of his final destination: a gatekeeper's lodge in the grounds of the Archbishop of Dublin's house. Back on Irish soil, Éamon is reunited with his wife Sinéad, and with his Sinn Féin comrades-in-arms. He has bad news for all of them. While things are hotting up in Ireland, de Valera has decided he will be most useful to the Irish cause abroad. He is going to America.

WASHINGTON DC: It is worse than Woodrow thought. He is fighting on two fronts at once – in Europe and in America – for the same glorious cause: his peace, his League.

The Republicans do not like the covenant he has brought back from Paris and are coming out against it. It would turn the United States into a sub-state of a new world state, some say. It would force America to enter any future war, others warn. There seem plenty of reasons to dislike it, whatever the high motives that may have inspired it. It would spell the end of the Monroe Doctrine – a venerable American foreign policy ordinance which declares that Europeans should play no role in the affairs of Latin America – by potentially giving the League of Nations a role in America's back yard. Far from freeing subject peoples in the British Empire, it would commit all states to respect the existing borders of the United Kingdom – thus sidestepping the question of self-determination for the island of Ireland – and give an international imprimatur to London's role around the globe.

At a gala dinner in New York, a delegation from Clan na Gael, an Irish-American organisation dedicated to Irish independence, declares its intense distrust of Woodrow's League, viewing it as a British trick. One Senator at the same dinner warns starkly that the League could end up destroying democracy in America, for 'the government of the world will be despotic, and it will inevitably be in the hands of Europeans or Asiatics'. The other powers in the League will try to open America's borders against the national will. They will swamp the country with fresh immigrants. America will be internationalised. By this reckoning, Woodrow Wilson is virtually a Bolshevik himself.

SPRING

MOSCOW: Leon Trotsky embarrasses poor Stalin once again. The war commissar notices that the special Kremlin shop catering for the Bolshevik leadership stocks wine from the Caucasus, which is otherwise banned for sale across the land. (The Tsar banned vodka when Russia went to war in 1914, and it has been all downhill from there.) Leon suggests to Vladimir that the bottles be removed from sale at once to prevent a scandal.

'What would happen if news got to the front that they are carousing in the Kremlin?' the high-minded war commissar asks pointedly.

'What will happen to us Caucasians?' the Georgian bank-robber responds. 'How can we live without wine?'

The matter is dropped.

OAK PARK, ILLINOIS: The conquering hero is home again at 600 North Kenilworth Avenue. But boy, is he bored. 'It's hell – Oh gosh but it's hell', the young Mars writes to an old friend. Back in America, where all the women seem to be his mother's age and all the men, too old to have fought in the war themselves, are 'crying for second-hand thrills to be got from the front'. Ernest tells his friends still in Italy to stay put in Taormina or wherever they happen to be that week, asking them to look up Agnes, who he still expects to marry, despite rumours of an Italian aristocrat with other ideas.

In March, Hemingway, still just nineteen years old, is asked to give a talk at his high school, less than a year after leaving it. The students learn a rousing song to greet him.

> Hemingway, we hail you the victor,
> Hemingway, ever winning the game,
> Hemingway, you've carried the colors,
> For our land you've won fame.

Hemingway, we hail you the leader,
Your deeds – every one shows your valor,
Hemingway, Hemingway, you've won
Hemingway!

But the young Hemingway is not to be outdone. With his family all
around him he sings, in Italian, the marching song of the Arditi – the black-
shirted crack troops of the Italian army whose valour and toughness he
admires so much. Ernie then tells a fanciful tale about one of their number
who, having been shot in the chest, fights on by using cigarettes to plug
the bullet holes in his lungs. Hemingway slides over the detail that his own
mission to the front line was to distribute chocolate, not to fight. The story
matters more than the truth. (In an interview on the quayside in New York
earlier in the year he allowed a reporter from the *New York Sun* to believe
he stayed at the front until the armistice, whereas in fact he was back in
Milan by then.)

Ernest gives the whole talk dressed in full uniform, carrying all his field
equipment. He even manages to slip in a description worthy of D'Annunzio
or the leader of the Italian Futurists, Filippo Marinetti. 'A machine gun',
the high-school wordsmith announces portentously, 'resembles closely a
crazy typewriter'. (Around the same time, Harry Johnson gives a talk at
the St. Louis Coliseum, for which he is paid over $2,000, and where he
manages to offend most of the whites in the audience by claiming white
soldiers were cowards and that if he himself were white, he would be the
next governor of New York.)

A few days later, Ernest receives the bad news he has been dreading. 'She
doesn't love me Bill. She takes it all back. A "mistake" one of those little
mistakes you know ... And the devil of it is that it wouldn't have happened
if I hadn't left Italy'. Agnes has called the whole thing off. The young veteran
is heartbroken. 'I love Ag so much', he writes, and then, plaintively, 'Write
me Kid, Ernie'. This wasn't the future Hemingway had in mind.

Moscow: The Spartacists may have been crushed in Berlin, and Rosa
Luxemburg thrown to a watery grave, but Lenin has not given up on international proletarian revolution. In January, an invitation is issued to the
foundation of a new International – an association of the world's socialist
parties – dedicated to the overthrow of capitalism and the proletarian
seizure of state power across the globe.

In March, the delegates meet – in secret, at first – in a Moscow court-house. An entire room is painted red for the occasion (including the floor). Flimsy chairs are set up, with little writing tables for the delegates. Given wartime travel conditions – and the short notice – the number of inter-national delegates is limited. Some are prisoners of war or radicals who happen to be in Russia anyhow. Vladimir opens proceedings by asking the delegates to stand in memory of Rosa Luxemburg and Karl Liebknecht. War commissar Trotsky, once one of Europe's great anti-militarists, appears in a leather coat and military breeches. It is bitterly cold. Only the Finnish delegate is able to walk around outside without a hat and coat. 'Spring is coming', he explains.

Though the language of the conference is German, it is quite clear that the Russian hosts are in charge. They act as the secretariat of the congress and decide who is eligible to speak and vote. Lenin has too much experience of being outgunned in such gatherings in the past not to make sure things are different on home turf. A motion is formally moved for a new, Third International to be formed to replace the worn-out Second International (whose internationalist pacifist principles were betrayed by the social demo-crats at the outbreak of war in 1914). The German delegate present considers such a move premature. Should they not wait for matters to settle in Europe before launching a new organisation? It is explained to him by one of the Russians present that to dither now would confuse the workers and make the revolutionaries look weak, particularly in the eyes of the capitalists who are trying to destroy them. The formation of the Communist International is, quite simply, a 'historical imperative'. The German is overruled. The Internationale sung in a dozen, clashing languages.

Over the next couple of days, the foreign delegates are subjected to a barrage of theses, declarations and manifestos. Civilisation is on the brink of annihilation, they are told. Chaos must be met with order: but 'genuine order, communist order'. The revolution is not yet safe. Capitalism is regrouping: 'under the cloak of the League of Nations, pouring out torrents of pacifist words, it is making its last efforts to patch together again'. All through Europe, the workers are under attack: 'indescribable is the terror of the white cannibals'. Trotsky makes a scathing attack on Paris peace-makers, unable to see that it is they who caused the 'debris and smoking ruins' in the first place.

Alexandra Kollontai puts forward a resolution on the role of working women, noting that at least half the wealth of the world is produced by female labour and that capitalism can only be destroyed by men and women working together as equals. Lenin launches a fierce attack on social democratic stooges like that bloody German Marxist Kautsky who have the temerity to call the Soviet system a *dictatorship* while extolling the virtues of what they call *democracy*. What fools and dissemblers! Bourgeois democracy is simply the rule of the property-owners dressed up with the odd vote, Vladimir thunders. It is the dictatorship of the proletariat which opens the way to real, workers' democracy. What is capitalist freedom? It is the freedom for the rich to make profits and for the poor to starve. What is press freedom so long as the printing presses are owned by the capitalists? What is freedom of assembly, so long as the bourgeoisie have the best buildings and most leisure time in which to meet?

Now that it has been formally established the question remains how the Communist International, or Comintern, should be run. This is where Lenin's conference tactics come into their own. An Executive Committee will need to be elected and headquarters chosen. But with so few properly accredited foreign representatives present in Moscow, Vladimir simply offers for the host-country representatives to do the job. 'Does anyone wish to discuss this?' he asks the delegates. A short pause. It is hard to object to such apparent generosity. 'The proposal is therefore carried'. The Russian Communist Party thus asserts its central role as the creator and master of the new International. 'The victory of the proletarian revolution on a world scale is assured', the impatient revolutionary crows, 'the founding of an international Soviet republic is on the way'.

A Comintern group photograph is called to capture the moment. War commissar Trotsky, always haring off somewhere before the official farewells, is ordered back on stage to take part. 'Dictatorship of the Photographer', someone says, laughing. For once, Leon plays along. Despite the mixed situation at the front, with the Red Army's recapture of Kiev from Ukrainian nationalists balanced by the launch of a new offensive by Kolchak in the east and Denikin's successes in the south, the mood in Moscow is festive. That evening there is a public rally to celebrate the Bolsheviks' new tool of worldwide revolution. Trotsky calls the Comintern meeting 'one of the greatest events in world history'.

The next day Lenin collars a sympathetic English journalist to have a chat about the prospect for an upcoming revolution in Britain. He remembers his time in London all those years ago, hanging out in the British Museum and attending earnest socialist meetings; all talk and no action. 'Pitiable, pitiable', the Bolshevik leader spits: 'a handful at a street corner, a meeting in a drawing room'. But the war has changed things. 'If Russia today were to be swallowed up by the sea, were to cease to exist altogether, the revolution in the rest of Europe would go on', Lenin tells his wide-eyed British friends: 'England may seem to you to be untouched, but the microbe is already there'.

Comintern couriers will soon be running around the world with suitcases full of cash to finance revolution across the globe.

ECKARTSAU, AUSTRIA: In between trips to Vienna to relay messages back to London and sniff the political atmosphere, Colonel Lisle Strutt becomes an honorary Habsburg. He eats with the family, plays bridge with them and shares their hopes and fears for the future.

Vienna is an unhappy city these days, Charles complains. The Bolsheviks are circling like hungry vultures and may swoop at any moment. The *Volkswehr* people's militia are said to be confiscating food from private houses and hustling restaurant diners for money at the end of a bayonet. British intelligence notes the fury of the Viennese at occupying Italian forces carting off truckloads of old master paintings – for 'repatriation', the Italians say. Insult on top of injury.

'I am still Emperor', Charles declares to Lisle Strutt one day. If he were given just a few thousand good Allied troops – not French and Italian, whom he despises – he insists he could be back in charge in Vienna in a trice. Charles begs the colonel to pass on this message to the King of England.

The two men talk about everything. Charles reveals he does not think the Serbs were truly responsible for the assassination of his cousin in Sarajevo after all. He asks whether the flags of any great Austrians still hang inside the Royal Chapel at Windsor, to which his British companion is too polite to reply. The name D'Annunzio crops up in conversation. On a walk down by the Danube one afternoon two peasants doff their caps to Charles and the colonel and offer their sovereign three fish they have just caught. The Emperor is forced to borrow two hundred crowns from the British officer to pay them.

BOSTON, MASSACHUSETTS: The 369th Regiment has been disbanded. Its men are free to do as they please. Jim Europe heads out on tour, to bring to America the musical style it has already brought to France.

The band's playlist ranges widely. There are military marches to get the audience warmed up and then medleys of popular Broadway tunes to give audiences that comforting sense of being up to date with the leading edge of the nation's musical tastes. Some of the music played is daringly original, including a syncopated arrangement of the Russian composer Rachmaninov's Prelude in C sharp minor. And then, at the most liberated and most inventive end of the spectrum, there is the jazz. A snare drum duet, for example. Or a rendition of 'On Patrol in No Man's Land', with Jim Europe singing along with his army buddy Noble Sissle, accompanied by effects to replicate the rat-a-tat-tat of the machine guns in France.

In Boston, not exactly a city where one would expect the metronome to bend, the band plays at the opera house. Then it's Albany, Buffalo, Cleveland, Pittsburgh and a couple of days in St. Louis, where Josephine, now nearly thirteen, works as a waitress in a musicians' hang-out called the Old Chauffeur's Club. In Terre Haute, Indiana, a picket line enforces a black boycott of the opera house when the manager announces the concert will be held with the same segregated seating rules as usual. Jim Europe's band ends up playing to an audience of two hundred whites and two blacks.

VIENNA: Sigmund writes to a friend. Word has come in of just how far Austria will be reduced. It will even lose some of the territory where the locals speak German. 'Today we learn that we are not permitted to join Germany but must yield up south Tyrol', he complains: 'To be sure I'm not a patriot, but it is painful to think that pretty much the whole world will be foreign territory.'

MOSCOW: *Long Live Ilyich!* The representatives of the vastly expanded Communist Party – who wouldn't want to join a ruling party that offers a shortcut to the top? – meet in the Red capital. A huge coloured map reminds delegates of the difficult military situation at the front (and why, therefore, they must back their leaders). After a bitter and public spat about how the army is run – Stalin's behaviour in Tsaritsyn is brought up again – a compromise is secured, with Lenin's support, backing the use of military experts. The idea that the foundations of a new society can be built without the help of bourgeois experts is, Vladimir says, simply 'childish'. Trotsky's unpopular policy is upheld.

The party rank and file are forced to hold their noses at the decision. Many are nonetheless out of joint over Trotsky's conduct of the war. They dislike the way his sense of iron military discipline seems unable to discriminate between party members – good Communists whose minor infractions should be overlooked – and non-party members, who should be punished more vigorously. Trotsky is gaining a reputation as a super-propagandist, yes – but also as an arrogant disciplinarian, a Napoleon-in-waiting, a military strongman with designs on power. The war commissar is not there in Moscow to make his case in person. That tends to increase the animus against him: distant, haughty, petulant, not really a party man at all.

Lenin rams through a few more small details, correcting the errors of others as he goes. (Proofreading a draft of the party programme the impatient revolutionary notes the persistent misspelling of the word 'exploitation' and takes it upon himself to personally explain the word's origins to the poor typesetter who keeps messing it up.) The centralisation of Bolshevik power is confirmed by the formal creation of a small Politburo as the party's top decision-making body (and therefore, over time, the centre of effective state power as well). In theory, the five-member Politburo – including both Stalin and Trotsky – works collectively. But given Trotsky's frequent absences from Moscow and Lenin's personal prestige he is unquestionably the man in charge.

At the same time, a new inspectorate is set up to oversee the burgeoning structures of state administration and root out corruption and bureaucracy. Now here's a job for Comrade Stalin: reliable, salt of the earth, understands the party. The Georgian bank-robber may not have the war commissar's flair. But he knows how to make the machinery work. Perhaps more than that, he knows how to make the machinery work for him.

Paris: Woodrow returns to Paris and to disappointment. House has not kept his promises. The German peace terms have not been finalised. The reparations question is unresolved. The French have become bolder in demands for German territory to ensure their security. To make matters worse – hard not to sense a snub here – the Wilsons have been moved into smaller lodgings, much less comfortable that those they had before. Edith makes the best of the change, noting a nice garden, an enormous bath and gold taps.

Despite all the rage and fury from Republicans in America, Woodrow thought at least he left the League covenant in good shape in Paris. Yet it turns out that there remain two major obstacles to its completion, both rather trickier than he had anticipated. The Japanese demand that a clause on racial equality be inserted into the text (something the white powers are unwilling to concede). Meanwhile, Woodrow is enraged to find opposition to his polite request that the covenant should explicitly recognise America's Monroe Doctrine. The French see the American desire to exclude Europeans from Latin America as something of a one-way street given America's intention to dictate what happens in France's back yard in Europe.

Russian affairs remain a quagmire. The young man sent to Moscow on a fact-finding mission just before Woodrow left for America has now returned with what he believes is the outline of a grand deal with the Bolsheviks. But in Paris, he is greeted with a wall of scepticism. Most experienced hands think the young diplomat has fallen prey to Bolshevik game-playing: Brest-Litovsk tactics. Woodrow is too busy to sit down with his diplomatic envoy. But he is leery of alternative means of grappling with the Bolshevik challenge. To try and stop a revolutionary movement with a line of armies, Woodrow lectures his fellow leaders, is like trying to use 'a broom to stop a great flood'.

'The only way to act against Bolshevism is to make its causes disappear', he says: 'this is, however, a formidable enterprise; we do not even know exactly what its causes are'.

MILAN: Lies, lies and more lies. In Italy, demobilised soldiers returning home find one broken promise after another. Jobs are scarce. Land reform is stalled. The old men are still in charge.

Nationalists are furious that the territorial gains they were promised by the British and the French to join the war are about to be sold out from under them by the politicians and the diplomats in Paris. The country is rocked by strikes and up to its eyeballs in debt. The Socialists are turning further to the revolutionary left, scaring the wits out of Italy's business owners, farmers and the Church.

Some begin to look beyond the old formulas of Italian politics to combat this new threat. Perhaps a more muscular figure is needed, with the smartly dressed Arditi at his back. Maybe it takes a street-fighter to re-establish order in the streets. There seem several candidates for the job, ready to reform the country, give the soldiers their due and save Italy from Bolshevism. D'Annunzio is the obvious choice, of course. But then again, he is a propagandist rather than a pugilist. His instincts are libertarian – does he have the cynicism to be a politician? He could be a figurehead of some new movement, but could he really organise one? How about that newspaper editor, Benito Mussolini? His background as one of Italy's most prominent Socialist Party activists gives him a certain credibility as a man of substance. He certainly seems keen to get stuck in, however dirty things may get. The battle against chaos is urgent, Mussolini writes in *Il Popolo*. 'As for the means,' he warns, 'we have no preconceptions, we accept what will be necessary: both legal and so-called illegal means.' Such moral flexibility may be just what is required. Mussolini is a man who makes a virtue out of it.

Benito assembles his fellow discontents in the elegant offices of the local employers' federation in Milan. There are conservatives who have lost faith in the methods of the old right, dislike the arrogance of the ruling classes and want strict measures to ensure order is returned. There are socialists who have lost faith in the Socialist Party the moment it opposed Italy's entry into the war. Marinetti is there as the representative of the newly founded Futurist Party (daily gymnastics features amongst its manifesto commitments). There is a sprinkling of men who refer to themselves as anarchists, syndicalists or anarcho-syndicalists and who expect everyone to know the difference. Then there are the veterans, of course, with their particular claim to moral leadership of Italy, based on the lost futures of the country's war dead and an energetic sense of camaraderie forged in the trenches.

Under Mussolini's watchful eye, this rather eclectic group establish a new organisation, the Fasci di Combattimento. A manifesto is agreed. Its defining characteristic – besides nationalism – is opportunism. Women are to be given the vote. The voting age for men is to be dropped to eighteen in a nod to young soldiers returning home and hungry for something better. Workers are to be given an eight-hour day, the totemic socialist demand. In a gesture to the traditions of Italian anti-clericalism, the Church is to be expropriated. The manifesto is ideologically anti-ideological. It is Dadaism as politics. Reality comes from struggle, not from books. The energy of war is to be channelled into social revolution.

If this group were to have a spiritual leader, his name would surely be Gabriele D'Annunzio. But D'Annunzio is a busy man. He has better things to do than to attend what is, at first glance, an administrative gathering of his tribe. He doesn't make time to meet Benito until June, when the two finally get together over drinks at the Grand Hotel in Rome.

BUDAPEST: A diplomatic note is delivered to Hungary's Minister-President by France's military representative in Budapest. Hungarian soldiers, already far inside the old borders that Charles Habsburg swore to defend, are now required to vacate an additional swathe of Transylvania, to become a neutral zone opposite occupying Romanian forces. Why not occupy the whole country right now, the Minister-President asks: 'make it a French colony, or a Romanian colony, or a Czechoslovak colony'? The Frenchman shrugs.

The government collapses. The country is close to being dismembered. America has proved unfriendly. The British and the French seem no better. As the Red Army carries all before it in neighbouring Ukraine after the fall of Kiev, some begin to wonder if Hungary's national salvation may lie through an alliance with Soviet Russia. After a half-hearted attempt to suppress them over the last few weeks, Hungary's Communists now march out of jail and straight into a leading role in a new Revolutionary Governing Council alongside more mainstream Social Democrats. Béla Kun is made Foreign Minister. The Hungarian Soviet Republic is proclaimed.

At first, Moscow is not entirely sure whether to support this new enterprise. Who is really in charge? Two attempts at communication between Lenin and Kun prove abortive: once when Kun is in a meeting and cannot come to the receiving post, and another time when Lenin is uncertain that the person on the other end is who he claims to be. It is several days before Kun is able to convince Moscow that he is the real boss. 'My personal influence in the Revolutionary Governing Council', he writes reassuringly, 'is such that the dictatorship of the proletariat is firmly established.'

Lenin is delighted – it will be far easier to promote world revolution with an avant-garde in Budapest. The Comintern issues a statement declaring events in Hungary 'the first flash of lightning splitting the threatening clouds'. *Long live the international Communist republic!*

ECKARTSAU: Even in times of revolutionary upheaval, news about the Habsburgs travels fast around Austria. Supposedly secret news spreads even faster.

By 9 a.m. on 23 March 1919 (the same day Mussolini's Fascists are meeting in Milan) the spectators have already begun to gather at Eckartsau to observe the latest chapter in the seven-hundred-year saga of the Habsburgs: their journey into exile. The imperial train stands ready at the small station of Kopfstetten, a few miles away.

In Vienna, the republican government looks the other way. The Chancellor knows full well that Charles's departure is imminent, having been warned of the fact. But what can he do? An attempt to stage-manage matters to the new republic's advantage – by forcing the Emperor to abdicate before he goes – is prevented by a little subterfuge from Colonel Lisle Strutt, who ostentatiously waves before the terrified Chancellor's nose a fake telegram suggesting Austria will be subject to an immediate British blockade if the Emperor's departure is interfered with in any way. The Chancellor appears to buy this outrageous bluff. But Lisle Strutt is apprehensive. One half of the former Habsburg Empire has just gone Red. If Austria follows, a new Chancellor may come to power who is not so easily fobbed off.

The chapel at Eckartsau is packed to the rafters that Sunday. The organist plays passages from Wagner to keep the punters happy. Afterwards, the imperial cook distributes any remaining food amongst spectators who have come from Vienna. British trucks arrive that afternoon to ferry the Habsburgs' luggage to their train. At nightfall, Lisle Strutt marches out to cut down a nearby intersection of telegraph wires to stop any orders being sent from Vienna for the Emperor to be arrested at the border – or worse.

A little after 6.30 p.m., Charles and Zita (who is pregnant with the couple's sixth child) appear at the top of the stairs at the Eckartsau hunting lodge. Behind them follows the Emperor's mother, Maria-Josefa, dripping in jewels and holding two collie dogs on their lead. Lisle Strutt, revolver in hand, accompanies the family in a motorcade to Kopfstetten and the waiting train. A few thousand well-wishers are there to see them off, and to hear the Emperor's faint '*Auf Wiedersehen*'. 'After seven hundred years', Charles sighs to his family as the train pulls away into the gathering darkness.

In the middle of the night, at a place called Amstetten, Colonel Lisle Strutt takes the precaution of redirecting the train onto a subsidiary line, and telling local officials he is accompanying members of a British food commission back from Budapest. The following morning, when the Habsburgs wake, they find themselves in the Alps, a changing picture-postcard view through every window: the frozen lake at Zell am See, the old-world charm of Kitzbühel. Occasionally, they pass a curious villager or two. Once, they see Italian cavalrymen on horseback, tramping heavily through the snow. Some British soldiers salute as the train crawls through a mountain pass.

How different Charles's arrival in Switzerland to that of Wilhelm's in Holland the previous November! In Buchs, Charles is greeted as the representative of an ancient and noble dynasty, rather than as an unwanted guest. A Swiss diplomat is already there to officially pass on the best wishes of the government. Some Swiss soldiers stand to attention. Charles, in civilian clothes now, is allowed to continue with his family to a house belonging to Zita's family, on the southern shores of Lake Constance.

Lisle Strutt can make out the shapes of the houses on the opposite shoreline, in Germany. (Lenin once met an escaped Russian prisoner of war who swam across this lake.) There is rioting on the other side, the colonel is told. Bolsheviks. They are everywhere, it seems.

Moscow: In a high-pitched, somewhat hectoring voice, Lenin makes a series of recordings of his speeches for wide distribution.

The records are short; so are his speeches. Some are lectures delivered in short phrases and slogans; others are straightforward appeals for popular support. In one, he commemorates a leading Bolshevik comrade who has just died from influenza. (The comrade is granted a lavish state funeral; when his personal safe is opened a decade later it is found to contain a small fortune in Tsarist-era gold coins and jewels, as well as no fewer than nine passports.) In another, Lenin explains why it was essential to form the Comintern after the mainstream socialist betrayal of 1914. 'They helped to prolong the slaughter, they became enemies of socialism, they went over to the side of the capitalists', he instructs the recording horn.

One record takes on the question of anti-Semitism. This has become an acute issue in Ukraine in particular, where the bitter struggle between the Red Army and Ukrainian nationalists has been accompanied by a renewed surge in pogrom violence against the Jews. 'Only the most ignorant and downtrodden people can believe the lies and slander that are spread about the Jews', Lenin tells listeners. Under the Tsars, he explains, false rumours were spread and pogroms incited in order to distract the workers from the truth of their own exploitation. But most Jews are workers. And as for those Jews who *are* exploiters and capitalists, they are no different from rich Russians, or the rich anywhere else in the world who are 'in alliance to oppress, crush, rob and disunite the workers'. What matters is class, not religion.

Down at his Gorki retreat, meanwhile, Lenin tries to get the estate manager to understand his ideas for how state farms should be run now, as models of collectivisation for the peasants, and as propaganda to show them how much better things can be under Communism. The feeling in the Russian countryside is not warm towards the Bolsheviks. Yet it must be won over. Lenin asks the manager what he is doing to help the local peasantry.

'We sell seedlings', the manager replies.

'He doesn't understand the very question', Vladimir says dispiritedly to Nadya.

Around the same time, Nadya experiments with a kitchen garden where peasants work without hired labour to grow cabbages. The cabbages are misappropriated. Vladimir gets the Cheka to investigate. Things are not working out as hoped at all.

AMRITSAR, PUNJAB, BRITISH INDIA: Against a background of economic dislocation, Muslim fury at Britain's supposed enmity to Islam and the

Caliphate, and a passive resistance campaign led by the Hindu leader Mohandas Gandhi, a wave of pent-up Indian anger at the iniquities of British rule explodes into life. The Raj is beset by riots. Europeans fear for their lives. Some consider a full-blown insurrection to be imminent.

The British response is to lock up Gandhi and other political leaders, further inflaming the situation. In Amritsar, matters come a head when a British general takes it upon himself to order indiscriminate shooting into a crowd of Indian protestors in order to teach them a lesson. Hundreds are killed; the wounded are left to fend for themselves. Order is restored, but there is widespread revulsion at the brutality of the measures taken to achieve it. British prestige in India plummets.

Anti-British riots in Egypt reveal a similar reality: despite winning the war in Europe (with assistance from the empire), Britain's hold over its possessions and protectorates around the globe is increasingly fragile. The empire is in crisis.

PARIS: He has pushed himself too hard. In April, Woodrow is confined to bed for several days with influenza. Europe thought it had seen the end of the disease but Woodrow gets caught up in its last convulsions. A young aide on the American delegation who falls ill at the same time is dead in days, aged just twenty-five.

The President is exhausted. Most of all, he is frustrated with the slowness of progress towards his cherished peace and the lack of vision of his interlocutors. His temper seems to fray quite easily these days. Some say his brush with flu has made it worse. There are those who say the disease makes people nervy, or that it even makes them mad. 'Influenzal psychoses', they call it in an Italian journal.

The larger meetings of the conference are scrapped. Instead, the four main players – the leaders of the United States, Britain, France and Italy – gather twice a day in Woodrow's study (or his bedroom, if he is too ill) to work things out. Reports from various commissions come in almost daily. The leaders bicker. Privately, Clemenceau compares Woodrow to Jesus Christ, with his preachy morality. Woodrow asks for the USS *George Washington* to be prepared in case he needs to break off negotiations and walk out of the conference entirely. The British become alarmed that the French are making the terms too harsh for Germany. The Italians see their own demands slowly slipping down the agenda. The peacemakers disagree about what to do with the Kaiser. 'He has drawn universal contempt upon himself, is that not the worst punishment for a man like him?' Woodrow argues. The French want him brought to trial.

Wilson does little to relax himself. He plays no golf. Occasionally he manages a night-time drive with Edith. He is almost never alone. His diary is an endless round of meetings. On a single day in April, he receives a delegation from China and representatives of the Assyrian–Chaldean Christians, the Women Workers of America, the patriarch of Constantinople, the Albanian leader, the former premier of Portugal and an Irish-American from Kansas City who berates him for not doing more to support a united Ireland. He is also awarded the honorary citizenship of San Marino, a tiny republic entirely surrounded by Italy.

'After all this ocean of talk has rolled over me,' Woodrow sighs to his doctor, 'I feel that I would like to return to America, and go back into some great forest, amid the silence, and not hear any argument or speeches for a month.'

AMERONGEN: The Kaiser finds a new hobby for himself on Count Bentinck's estate. Like the Russian Tsar, he takes to wood-chopping. Every thousandth log is signed and dated by Wilhelm and given away as a present. One journalist is said to have paid one hundred Dutch guilders for the honour of possessing one.

As the Count's trees start falling one by one, the days begin to blur. The archaeologist who used to manage Wilhelm's digs in Corfu pays an extended visit, and for several days the assembled company at Amerongen are regaled with endless stories about the pair's various excavations. (One of the Kaiser's old retainers is so bored that he decides to move into a hotel.) A steady stream of visitors arrive from Germany. Amerongen becomes a mini-court, albeit a court in someone else's house, someone else's country.

Some ask Wilhelm if he would not like to go back to Germany, now that the threat of imminent Bolshevik revolution seems to have passed. Not until the people call him back, the Kaiser says proudly. He cherishes the image of his return, and how his enemies will suffer for their sins. He will be ruthless, he assures his guests. But also wise. He writes to Ludendorff, his one-time foe, and offers him the job of Chief of the General Staff once he has been restored.

VIENNA: In the Austrian parliament, a new law is passed. The Habsburgs are banned from ever setting foot in Austria again. From one of the city's publishing houses, a pamphlet appears to diagnose this state of affairs in psychological terms: *On the Psychology of Revolution*. A 'fatherless society' has been created, writes its author, a close associate of Sigmund Freud. Without Kings, without Emperors, perhaps even without God, society has been orphaned.

But just as an orphan may look for a new family, so now society as a whole is engaged in a quest to make sense of its own place in the world, in search of new leaders, new idols, new gods. Some proclaim the brotherhood of man as the new model for society, where brotherly solidarity replaces filial duty, where the vertical axis of power is flattened into a horizontal line of equality. Such is the psychology of socialism, Paul Federn writes.

But he fears another alternative, more rooted in the traditions of a society in which order and authority have always been cardinal virtues, where people expect to be told what to do. Having lost one symbolic father, Federn warns, the masses will create another. From the demise of Kings will emerge a new type of father figure, a populist leader borne aloft on the shoulders of the masses, better able to harness their desires than a King, better able to channel their angers and their hope. Federn has a name for such a man. He calls him a *Volksführer*.

MUNICH: The mangy field-runner feels the end of his army career approaching fast. In desperation to avoid being demobilised against his will, he gets himself elected as the *Vertrauensmann* of his left-leaning army company: a role which makes him both spokesman for his unit and servant of the Social Democrat-led regime, expected to distribute government circulars and report on troublemakers. For the moment, the axe of demobilisation will fall elsewhere.

But events are moving fast. While the leader of a caretaker Bavarian government, Johannes Hoffmann, is in Berlin trying to drum up support from his fellow mainstream Social Democrats at the national level, a Soviet Republic led by more radical elements is proclaimed behind his back in Munich. Bavaria's Communists at first oppose this Soviet regime as insufficiently proletarian. Munich's garrisons declare themselves neutral.

Ernst Toller, a twenty-five-year-old playwright currently working on a play about the traumatic effects of war, is catapulted into the leadership of the new republic. For a flickering moment, Munich seems the world capital of radical chic. Students are put in charge of the universities and empty lofts are handed over to artists; banks are to be nationalised and free money issued to destroy the basis of capitalist exploitation. Newspapers are required to print poems on their front pages. Toller gives great orations, speaking in ecstatic tones, shaking feverishly as if quite possessed by the spirit of the age. The formation of a Red army is announced, starting with the Munich garrisons. Adolf Hitler's barracks is renamed after the slain Communist leader Karl Liebknecht.

Cultural revolution does not feed the people. Lexicologists are worked up into a furious debate about whether the German word for Bavaria should henceforth be spelt *Baiern*, rather than *Bayern*, thus overturning a royal preference – from the early nineteenth century – for using the Greek 'y'. Toller's new Foreign Minister sends a furious telegram to Lenin – copied to the Pope – complaining that his predecessor has absconded with the key to the ministry loo. (He is later revealed as the recent inmate of a mental asylum.)

Meanwhile, Johannes Hoffmann puts the city under an economic blockade and establishes a new base in northern Bavaria. Within days, he is ready to retake the city, preferring to do so with his own republican security forces rather than wait for Berlin or the Freikorps to do the job for him. Tipped off by an anonymous phone call, Toller takes refuge in a friend's apartment and then escapes in a soldier's uniform he borrows in return for a strange promise to let the soldier 'fly to the North Pole and marry an Eskimo girl' as soon as this latest crisis has been resolved.

The farce is over. The tragedy begins. Hoffmann's forces are strong enough to destroy Toller's credibility, but not strong enough to secure Munich. Bavaria's hard-line Communists now leap into the gap. Eugen Leviné, a tweed-cap-wearing, Russian-born law graduate of Heidelberg University who holds the Leninist principle that terror is essential to revolution, takes power. Class warfare is not a by-product of revolution, it is an objective. There is no attempt to win over the bourgeoisie. Confiscation raids turn nasty. That Leviné happens to be Jewish – like Kun in Budapest and Trotsky in Moscow – strengthens a public perception that Bolshevism is a Jewish phenomenon.

The day after assuming power, the Munich Bolsheviks decide on new elections in the Munich garrison to ensure its loyalty to the revolution. Despite the new regime in charge, Adolf stands for election a second time. He gets nineteen votes, which is enough to make him deputy battalion councillor.

MILAN: The Futurist leader Marinetti meets with a colleague at a fashionable pastry shop in the Galleria, the splendid glass-and-wrought-iron shopping mall in the heart of the city. Together, they head off to cause some trouble. Breaking into the offices of *Avanti*, the Socialist newspaper which Mussolini himself used to work for, they smash up some machines and furniture before escaping back onto the street. Who can stop them? Certainly not the police. They can do as they like. Even some in the government seem to like this approach to dealing with the threat of revolutionary socialism.

Two days later, a newspaperman from Rome interviews Benito Mussolini about the incident. The attack was 'spontaneous, absolutely spontaneous', Mussolini insists, throwing up his hands and denying any involvement of his own group while accepting 'moral responsibility' as if it were his own doing. (He does not mention Marinetti at all.) The atmosphere in Italy was bound to break somehow, Benito tells the journalist. Perhaps this incident will come to be seen as the first battle of a civil war, he suggests darkly. The Fasci di Combattimento, Mussolini boasts, now have fifteen thousand members.

THE URAL MOUNTAINS – MOSCOW – LONDON: Throughout the first weeks of spring, Admiral Kolchak's White army races west, sledging across the snow and ice towards Moscow.

In March, Kolchak's forces take the city of Ufa, west of the Urals. By the end of April, they are two hundred miles beyond their start line, closing in on the mighty Volga river. The Ural mountain range has been breached. Vast territory has fallen under Kolchak's sway. The mines and factories of the Urals are now available to him and the admiral has an additional civilian population of five million from which to supplement his army (though this is a mere fraction of the population under Bolshevik control). For a moment – and from a distance – it seems possible that his army, roaring in from the east, may be able to connect with General Denikin's forces in the south. Tsaritsyn, the city saved by the Reds last autumn, stands halfway between the two. Yet the more Kolchak advances, the more his supply lines are stretched. He is counting on the Red collapse coming before his own.

In Moscow, there is panic. Lenin calls for total mobilisation. Women should go into the offices; men should be sent to the front. He demands registers be taken to catch those shirking their responsibilities. Yet it seems that for every man conscripted, another soldier deserts. Trotsky gives rousing speeches. Last year the war commissar said the struggle would be won or lost in the south. Now he declares the east the decisive front. Next week it may be the west, where the Poles have occupied swathes of land and Piłsudski dreams of forming a Polish–Ukrainian–Lithuanian federation as a permanent bastion against Muscovy.

In London, in the calmer surroundings of a luncheon club, Winston tries to drum up support for Britain's continued backing for the Whites. Despite Kolchak's lightning advance, the cause is shaky. Intervention looks to some like Winston's personal crusade, an adventure Britain cannot afford. (The *Daily Express* accuses him of being a 'military gamester' with a clear streak of megalomania.) Where does intervention begin and end? British nurses' uniforms are being appropriated by the daughters of the Russian bourgeoisie and weapons shipments being 'taxed' by Siberian bandits long before they reach their proper destination. The French have already yanked their forces from Odessa. A French naval mutiny is blamed on the Bolshevik virus.

There are rumours in London that some kind of diplomatic accommodation is being sought between the British and the Bolsheviks. The Prime Minister fiercely denies that any such idea has crossed his mind. But there are limits to what can be done. Lloyd George compares Russia to an erupting volcano, where the best one can do is 'provide security for those who are dwelling on its remotest and most precipitous slopes, and arrest the devastating flow of lava so it may not scorch other lands'. Winston has no time for such passivity. 'The British nation is a foe of tyranny in every form', he tells his luncheon club: 'that is why we fought Kaiserism; that is why we are opposing Bolshevism.' He is in no doubt which enemy is worse. The Germans were honourable enough to stick with their allies; the Bolsheviks betrayed them. 'Every British and French soldier killed last year', Winston says, 'was really done to death by Lenin and Trotsky'. The Bolsheviks are 'the worst tyranny in history'. In private, his language is still more colourful. 'After having defeated all the tigers and the lions I don't like to be defeated by baboons', he is reported as saying – baboons being Winston's favourite word to describe his least-favourite people.

As Western capitals debate the merits of Kolchak's cause and the extent to which they can support him, the weather changes in Russia. The ground under Kolchak's feet thaws. The roads turn to mud. Within a few weeks of Winston's speech in London, the admiral's offensive has petered out. By summer, he is back at the Urals with the Reds in fierce pursuit.

VIENNA: 'The next months will be, I expect, full of dramatic movement', Freud writes to a friend. 'But we are not spectators, not actors, in fact not even chorus – but merely victims!'

A sense of unaccustomed powerlessness sweeps over Freud. What is one to do? One cannot survive on thought alone, he tells himself. To feed oneself and one's family by whatever means, that is the highest duty. Freud fumbles for a letter recently arrived from England, from his cousin Sam, a businessman in Manchester. He resolves to write for help.

BUDAPEST: On paper, Hungary's Bolshevik revolution is proceeding just as planned.

Titles and ranks are abolished. All forms of transport are commandeered by the state. Motor cars are handed out to government commissars. Apartments and houses are redivided. Kitchens are shared. Ambitious plans for the future are prepared. British intelligence gets hold of the regime's housing policy, and reports to London a scheme to 'cover the hills around Budapest with workmen's villas and picture palaces'. One of Freud's acolytes is made the world's first professor of psychiatry. Meanwhile, counter-revolutionaries – supposed or real – are arrested. A group known as the 'Lenin Boys', dressed head to toe in black leather, roam the countryside tracking down anyone they suspect of harbouring anti-revolutionary tendencies, killing merrily as they go.

Given Hungary's geographic location, Kun and the other commissars know their regime will either be a revolutionary dagger pointed at the heart of bourgeois Europe or else a lonely outpost, vulnerable to invasion. In other words, what happens outside Hungary will determine their fate as much as what happens inside. At first, the news looks good. Kun draws courage from events in Munich. 'Your example shows that the international proletarian revolution is gaining ground and winning', he writes to the revolutionaries there. A diplomatic mission sent from the Paris peace conference briefly raises the prospect of the Hungarian Soviet Republic receiving official recognition. In the event, it comes to nothing: the delegates do not even leave their train.

More concrete hopes for the Hungarian revolution's survival are placed in the possibility of spreading contagion to Vienna, thus creating an impregnable Bavarian–Austrian–Hungarian revolutionary core. The Hungarians send a few dozen experienced agitators to Vienna to stir things up. Kun himself tries to get a visa to travel there through official channels. To no avail. A demonstration of soldiers, workers and disabled war veterans in front of the Austrian parliament in April ends in the building being set on fire. Several policemen are killed. But the government still stands. Amongst those who call for calm is Friedrich Adler.

Towards the end of the month, with the Czechs and Romanians poised to invade and claim slices of formerly Hungarian territory for themselves, Kun sends a comrade to ask Lenin for his advice. 'You don't need instructions', comes back the helpful reply.

PARIS – ITALY: Another crisis for the peacemakers, this time amongst their own. The Italian premier breaks down in tears as he tries one final time to persuade Woodrow to grant his country's demand for the port of Fiume alongside the lands promised Italy when she joined the war. Rejected, the premier returns to Rome.

Italians erupt in anger. In Turin, students tear down the street signs on the recently renamed Corso Wilson and replace them with ones daubed Corso Fiume. Mussolini dips his pen in their fury. He wonders if Italy should now support the Irish guerrilla campaign to overthrow the British, 'the fattest and most bourgeois nation in the world'. The Americans have revealed themselves as mere plutocrats, he says, not at all the idealists he took them for. What a change from a few months ago.

In St Mark's Square in Venice, D'Annunzio pops up again. 'A tragic gargoyle', one observer notes. D'Annunzio suggests Venetians form a militia to march into Dalmatia and save it from the Slavs. In a series of speeches in Rome, he turns his poetic invective against Woodrow, accusing him of being a mask rather than a man, a 'Croatified Quaker'. Italians should not be blinded by the American President's flashing white smile. It is nothing more than a shop display of the wares of modern American dentistry, D'Annunzio cries. The teeth are as false as the man who wears them.

SEATTLE – NEW YORK: A suspicious parcel arrives at the office of the Seattle strike-breaker, Mayor Ole Hanson. It leaks acid. Closer inspection reveals a home-made bomb inside. In Atlanta, a bomb of the same type explodes in the home of a former Senator, blowing off the hands of a maid.

Reading a description of the parcels on his way home, a postal clerk recalls a series of others he handled, all with the same return address. An alert is sent out. Over thirty packages are recovered. It would appear that the intention was for the bombs to go off on the first of May, International

Labour Day. The list of addressees reads like a card index of America's high officials, anti-Bolshevik crusaders and capitalist plutocrats: the new Attorney General, Mitchell Palmer; John D. Rockefeller; J. P. Morgan Jr.; Lee Overman, the Senator who led the subcommittee on Bolshevik propaganda. Someone is running a terrorist campaign. Is America infected with the same revolutionary bug as Europe?

A malicious rumour is spread that some of the bombs were posted from the offices of Marcus Garvey's newspaper, the *Negro World*. Garvey angrily denies it. Spring for him has been taken up with a quite different activity: raising money for a brand-new business venture, a black-owned shipping line to be called the Black Star Line. To potential investors amongst the UNIA membership he paints a picture of a profitable and purposeful enterprise to match the white-owned White Star Line, with its glamorous multi-funnelled steamers plying the waterways of the world. The Black Star Line, Garvey says, will light up the path to black economic emancipation. Black travellers will no longer be made to feel second class on the high seas. The line's destinations, linking America, Africa and the West Indies, will create a new sense of common destiny amongst the black peoples of the world. To buy a share in the Black Star Line is to buy a share in the future of the race.

MUNICH – BUDAPEST: 'What measures have you taken to fight the bourgeois executioners?' the impatient revolutionary asks Munich's Bolsheviks in a letter at the end of April. 'Has the six-hour working day with two- or three-hour instruction in state administration been introduced?' he enquires. 'Have you taken hostages from the bourgeoisie?'

Leviné's Bavarian Soviet Republic is close to collapse. Hoffmann continues to blockade the city. Leviné's regime declares the manufacture of cheese to be sabotage in an attempt to save milk stocks. Support for the hardliners is drying up even amongst revolutionaries. Ernst Toller accepts a plea to lead a Red army unit in the last-ditch defence of Dachau. ('All you've got to do is wear a pretty hat', he is told.) Shortly afterwards he warns against the 'magic lustre' of Lenin's compatriots. 'We Bavarians are not Russians', the Munich workers' council declares after a stormy session in the Hofbräuhaus. In upper Bavaria, horror stories from the capital stiffen the spines and swell the ranks of Hoffmann's forces. Right-wing radicals join up in droves. One has a dog named Putsch. A true White army is created.

The campaign to retake Munich is bloody. Unarmed Red army medical orderlies are slaughtered. In return, a Bavarian Communist orders the execution of bourgeois hostages held in a local high school, including several members of the Thule Society, an unfortunate Jewish painter caught up in the violence and an innkeeper denounced by a waiter he had to let go. A rumour that the hostages were horrifically mutilated before their deaths starts when their corpses are found amongst piles of half-recognisable body parts (the inedible portions of freshly slaughtered pigs, it turns out).

Leviné is caught and shot. Toller evades arrest for several weeks by various means, including donning a top hat, growing a moustache, peroxiding his hair and sleeping in a cupboard behind a false wall in a Munich apartment. The Catholic Church – including the Pope's diplomatic envoy to Bavaria, himself a future pontiff – demands that Munich be spiritually cleansed. It is common to associate the latest revolutionary convulsions with the Jews, despite the fact that anti-Bolshevik Freikorps have their fair share of Jewish members too. The public mood is for retribution.

The same day the Whites take Munich a thunderstorm shreds May Day street decorations in Budapest. The omens are gloomy: the Czech army is in Slovakia, the Romanians are on the Tisza river, Trotsky's Red Army is tied up in Ukraine, and now the Bavarian Soviet Republic has been smashed. The vice around Red Hungary is tightening. Béla Kun throws the magic cloak of Hungarian nationalism around his Bolshevism, declaring that he is defending not just revolution but Hungary's very existence.

At a rally in Budapest, an overexcited worker demands a St Bartholomew's night: the liquidation of the country's entire bourgeoisie. For once, Kun demurs. In the current circumstances, he says, 'mass killing at the front' is preferable to 'mass murder at home'.

BOSTON – NEW YORK: During the interval at one of Jim Europe's concerts in Boston, there is an altercation backstage. One of the brothers involved in the snare duet claims Europe does not respect him as a musician, always criticising him rather than his brother when it is his brother who screws something up on stage. Jim Europe is stabbed and dies within hours. 'Jim Europe Killed in Boston Quarrel', says the *New York Times*, on the front page: 'Won Fame by "Jazz" Music'. The *Chicago Defender* praises Europe for 'jazzing away the barriers of prejudice'.

In Harlem, thousands turn out for a public procession when Europe's coffin takes its last journey. St. Mark's Church is packed for his funeral. The French army is represented. A bugler from the old regiment plays. The following day, Lieutenant James Reese Europe – the 'jazz king', some call him – is buried with military honours. 'He was not ashamed of being a Negro or being called a Negro', says the *New York Age*. 'He was the Roosevelt of Negro musicians – a dynamic force that did things – big things.' He was, in other words, a leader.

There is a new edge to race relations in America. The time for standing together with white Americans was 1918. Now is the time for standing up for your rights. The soldiers have been changed by what they have seen and experienced in France. A new battle faces them in America. 'We *return*', William Du Bois writes. 'We *return from fighting*. We *return fighting*.' Several thousand copies of *The Crisis* are confiscated from New York's central post office while the authorities consider whether such sentiments should be allowed. In the current febrile atmosphere, it takes a couple of days before it is decided that Du Bois's aim is racial equality, not the overthrow of the American government.

PARIS: The spell of winter at last is broken. In early May, the city's lilacs and chestnut trees begin to bloom. To Edith's delight, Woodrow follows his doctor's advice to take advantage of the weather to take her to the horse races at Longchamp. The Italian premier who tearfully stormed out of the conference a few weeks ago now returns so as to be there for the first presentation of the proposed peace terms to the Germans.

The terms are an unwelcome shock to those who first see them. Several American diplomats resign, dismayed by the harshness of what Woodrow has agreed, so far removed from the 'peace without victory' of 1917. The British fear that the terms will turn Germany into a permanently embittered enemy, and stall Europe's economic recovery.

French concerns run the other way: that the treaty puts long-term French security at risk and does not do enough to keep the Germans down. As it stands, the text confirms the current, temporary, Allied occupation of the Rhineland, with a right to extend the occupation further into Germany should reparations not be paid. But this is not enough for some. Marshal Foch makes a last-ditch appeal for a permanent Franco-German border on the Rhine. 'The next time, remember, the Germans will make no mistake', the Frenchman says; 'they will break through into

Northern France and seize the Channel ports as a base of operations against England'.

Only the Rhine, he says, will make France safe.

WEIMAR, GERMANY: In the National Assembly, a fist slams down. *'Deutschland verzichtet – verzichtet – verzichtet'*. These are the words one politician picks out from the treaty text: 'Germany renounces – renounces – renounces'. Germany renounces – itself. The loss of colonies is painful enough. But to be occupied, humiliated, forced to take the blame for the war in its entirety? This is not peace, it is a 'bath of steel', it is a 'murder plan'. Wilsonism was an illusion. Reparations represent 'merciless slavery for our children, and for our children's children'. The proposed peace terms treat people as animals.

The speaker raises his eyes. 'When I look around your ranks', he says, 'the representatives of the German lands and their peoples, from the Rhineland to the Saar, from East and West Prussia, Posen, Silesia, Danzig and Memel … in the gravity and sanctity of this hour, when our opponents intend us to be meeting for the last time as Germans amongst Germans, my heart knows only one commandment: we belong together'. Roars of approval. 'We are one flesh and blood, and those who try to separate us cut with assassins' knives into the living flesh of the German *Volk*.' He does not forget Austria: 'We greet you, we thank you, we are one with you'.

The speaker is no radical nationalist: he is the Social Democratic Chancellor Philipp Scheidemann, the man who broke off his soup to declare a republic six months before. 'Today it almost seems as if the bloody battlefield from the North Sea to Switzerland has been brought back to life in Versailles,' he says, 'as if ghosts have risen from the mounds of bodies to fight again a last battle of hate.'

A delegation is sent from Germany to France to try to soften the terms and turn a dictated peace into a negotiated one. Their train is directed through the devastated regions of Belgium to make a point. They arrive in Paris armed with crates of documents and work away in a damp hotel, playing loud music on a gramophone to prevent the French from listening in, and trying to find arguments for the peace terms to be changed.

SMYRNA, THE OTTOMAN EMPIRE: Following a decision made in Paris, Greek forces are given permission to land in the Aegean city of Smyrna, and occupy it on behalf of the Allies. (This is to prevent the difficult Italians from taking it.) One morning Greek ships are suddenly there in the harbour, blowing their whistles in celebration of their bloodless victory, and disgorging troops onto the shore.

The new arrivals are greeted warmly by the city's Greek population, almost as large as that of Athens. The church bells clang. Local Turks are downcast. The Ottoman garrison is ordered to offer no resistance so the Turkish civilian population protest in the street instead. Things soon take a turn for the worse. As Greek soldiers decide to take a victory march through town, shots are fired. The Greek standard-bearer is hit. The looting of Muslim houses begins not long after. Hundreds of Turks and a hundred Greeks are killed. Foreign observers are horrified at the sight of fezzes ripped off the heads of Ottoman soldiers and wanton violence committed by ill-disciplined Greek troops. News of the occupation of Smyrna (or İzmir, as the Turks know it) is greeted with horror in what remains of the Ottoman Empire.

Anatolia is in a state of disorder this spring. Malnutrition and disease stalk the land. Grass grows instead of wheat. The central state is weak or non-existent. Bandit armies take what they can. Everyone has an axe to grind. Armenians returning to their villages reclaim the houses taken from them, turfing out Turkish families and making them refugees in turn. By the Black Sea, a sort of Turkish Freikorps emerges to terrorise local Greeks and stop them getting any grand ideas from events in Smyrna. Further east, there are rumblings that elements of the old Ottoman army may take matters into their own hands.

A French general ceremoniously enters Istanbul on a white horse in February, like a Christian potentate symbolically reversing the conquest of 1453. In London, the idea is mooted that perhaps the Turkish should be permanently ejected from their capital, the Sultan moved to Konya, and the city's main mosque turned back into a church. The Greek Patriarch begins to issue followers of the Greek Orthodox Church with their own passports. The Armenian Patriarchate does the same.

Meanwhile, an Ottoman tribunal deliberates the fate of those accused of responsibility for the Armenian massacres of the war. In April, a provincial governor is executed. (The Sultan confirms the sentence only once he has a *fetva* pronouncing it acceptable under Islamic law.) The governor's funeral turns into a nationalist protest. A young medical student standing at the graveside with a bunch of flowers clutched tightly in one hand demands nothing less than an uprising against the foreign occupiers. 'This is our duty', he declares, his voice breaking with anger. 'With the help of God we will soon be able to crush their heads'. The three Pashas – Enver, Djemal and Talaat – are put on trial *in absentia* for their role in the hope that if enough of the blame for the Armenian massacres can he shifted onto them perhaps the empire as a whole will be spared retribution. As the evidence piles up – telegrammed orders, testimony from witnesses – there is no doubt they will be found guilty.

The morning after the taking of Smyrna, Mustafa Kemal embarks for the Black Sea port of Samsun, some three days from Istanbul by ship, aboard the rather sluggish Bandırma. He has a new job: Inspector of the 9th Army in Erzurum, with the civil administration of central and eastern Anatolia subordinate to his command. Before leaving port, troops check the Bandırma for contraband. 'The fools', Kemal mutters. 'We are not taking contraband or arms, but faith and determination'.

From Samsun, where British troops are responsible for security, and keep an eye out for the possibility of organised rebellion, Mustafa proceeds – for medical reasons, he says – to the spa town of Havza. (He teaches his party a Swedish marching song when their open-top Benz breaks down.) In Havza, the patient sends a large number of telegrams: to other army commanders, to old friends, to rebels who have already declared themselves unhappy with the Sultan's appeasement. Istanbul becomes suspicious. He is recalled. He does not go.

BERLIN: The Guards Cavalry Division takes over the central criminal court in Moabit for a court martial. A huge portrait of Kaiser Wilhelm hangs on one of the walls.

The defendants, charged with involvement in the murder of Karl Liebknecht and Rosa Luxemburg, do not seem concerned. They enter the courtroom through the same door as the judges. The death of Liebknecht is easily dealt with. Testimony that he was shot trying to escape is accepted without question and the defendant allowed to go free.

The events surrounding the disappearance of Rosa Luxemburg are harder to elucidate. The sequence of events is difficult to get straight. And, without a body, how can one really know how she died? A bullet or a blow to the head? It is not even clear exactly who was present at Rosa's death. Short custodial sentences are handed down to the minor players; sentences of two years for those convicted of causing bodily violence to Rosa and then misreporting their actions.

The impression of a stitch-up is not easily shaken off. Nor is it helped when one of those incarcerated manages to escape from jail. (A brother officer – one of the judges from the trial, in fact, and later a spy chief for the Nazis – arrives with a faked release order and a false passport, allowing the lieutenant to flee to Holland.) The German left are apoplectic. Some suspect Pabst, the Freikorps inquisitor and Baltic freebooter, of organising things behind the scenes. Others blame the government.

After the last of the winter ice has broken on the city's canals, a woman's body is found in the Landwehr canal that May. It has to be prised free from a lock gate. The army take it to a military base outside Berlin. A friend of Rosa Luxemburg's is called in to inspect a few objects found with the body. Mathilde Jacob thinks she recognises a gold clasp, a scrap of velvet dress and some gloves which she once bought herself. She cannot bring herself to look at the corpse itself, or even photographs of the body. Others confirm it is Rosa Luxemburg. An inconclusive autopsy is carried out. At the funeral – Rosa's second – the banners recall her last article for the (now-underground) *Rote Fahne*: 'Our Rosa – she was, she is, she will be again'.

BELÉM, BRAZIL: Sometime towards the end of spring, a British ship, the *Anselm*, arrives at the mouth of the Amazon. Aboard are a British scientific team, armed with huge telescopes several metres in length, and various bits of inexplicable, scientific-looking machinery.

Weeks early for their mission – the observation of a solar eclipse – the astronomers, led by Dr Andrew Claude de la Cherois Crommelin, decide to take the boat further into the rainforest. (A second British expedition heads simultaneously to the tropical island of Principe to observe the eclipse from a different vantage point.) The scientists wonder at the coffee and pineapples growing everywhere. Crommelin is particularly fascinated by armies of leaf-cutting ants which march along the ground carrying foliage many times their size.

Arriving in the city of Belém, the Britishers are quickly inducted into the Anglo-American Club, hungry for new recruits. To honour their presence, a local newspaper publishes a Portuguese translation of one of their articles, an attempt to explain Einstein's theory of relativity in layman's terms: ideas which would suggest that space is somehow curved, that time is slippery, and that light itself is bent by the gravitational pull of large objects (such as the sun). The eclipse, they explain, is a test. Einstein's theories predict a certain amount of deflection of distant starlight caused by the pull of gravity. The theories of Isaac Newton predict a much lower deflection. Assuming the equipment is good enough, photographs of the eclipse, coupled with other astronomical data about the location of the stars and some mathematical wizardry, should allow scientists to decide between the two theories. The self-appointed intellectual caste of Belém grapple with the philosophical consequences of relativity. Are there no absolutes left anywhere, no certainties? What about God?

After a couple of weeks wowing the locals, Crommelin and his crew continue on a coastal steamer to Camocim, and then by train to the inland town of Sobral – considered one of the best spots in the world to observe the eclipse – where they are greeted by the only two English-speakers in town. A local factory owner puts them up in his villa. The scientists decide to set up their equipment on the racecourse. A Brazilian team of astronomers arrive from Rio de Janeiro (accompanied by their families, on a sort of astronomical jamboree). They bring an automobile with them – the first ever seen in Sobral – and use it to drive the British up into the mountains to escape the heat.

On the day of the eclipse, clouds cover the sky above the town. (The team on Principe are similarly worried when their day begins with a tremendous rainstorm.) But as the day heats up, the clouds disperse. By the time the moon first crosses the sun over Sobral, they have gone entirely. Locals watch the eclipse through improvised lunettes, using panes of smoked glass to shield their eyes. For a while, it is as if the day has reversed itself to a few moments before dawn, when the world is still sleeping. A few strange, unearthly minutes. Animals and birds fall silent. Three hundred and two seconds of totality.

The British scientists take photographs as quickly as they can, barely looking skyward, worried at all the things which could go wrong: the telescope might be out of focus, the rotation of the earth might blur the photographs, the change in temperature caused by the disappearance of the sun might cause distortion on the photographic plates. Nothing is certain. Two maddeningly inconclusive telegrams are sent back to London from Sobral and Principe. 'ECLIPSE SPLENDID'. 'THROUGH CLOUD. HOPEFUL'.

Crommelin and his fellow astronomers retire for a month to the coastal town of Fortaleza, where they are put up in a seminary, returning only briefly to Sobral to take a second set of reference photographs from which to make their measurements of the deflection of light, as predicted by Einstein and Newton. That summer, they return to Britain aboard the *Polycarp*.

MUNICH: To save his skin from the backlash against those suspected of involvement with the Bavarian Soviet regime, Adolf turns informant. 'In regimental meetings, he always advocated the most radical positions and agitated for the dictatorship of the proletariat', he testifies about a fellow *Vertrauensmann* to whom he takes particular exception. He joins an investigative commission to weed out such politically unsuitable characters.

The political situation in Munich remains fluid. The military command decide to train a group of patriotic agitators to help deradicalise those who still remain in the army.

MILAN: Nationalism, socialism, Wilsonism. 'Disappointment only lights the lamp of new illusions', Mussolini writes. Perhaps *something* can be extracted: a hope, a vision, an energy, an impulse. 'Mirages of distant horizons are the ones providing the strength to go forward to the unattainable goal,' he writes. Will the ends, and the means will appear.

DUBLIN: They try everything to make him stay in Ireland rather than travel to America. To delay his departure across the sea, in March they organise a homecoming parade (which has to be cancelled at the last minute, facing a British ban). In April, they make him President of the Dáil, effectively proclaiming him president of the Irish republic. But de Valera's conviction is unshaken: if the world will not listen, it must be made to listen. If Wilson will not hear him, he will speak over his head.

All the while, the Irish state which de Valera and his comrades have dared to imagine is being willed into more elaborate and more solid form. It is still just words, of course – but how long will it be before words become facts? De Valera's Sinn Féin comrades are now glorified as ministers. Though they have no one fixed place where they can assemble and their meetings are kept short so to reduce the likelihood of being raided, these ministers meet as a cabinet, in the British style. De Valera's envoys abroad, who travel under watchful British eyes and find more doors shut than open, anoint themselves ambassadors. Michael Collins, the Volunteer organiser turned Finance Minister, attempts to raise a loan of a million pounds – bonds for an Irish republic which no other state yet recognises.

And as de Valera's imagined republic builds up the nominal accoutrements of statehood, so the current instruments of Irish order are declared invalid and illegitimate. Members of the Royal Irish Constabulary – Ireland's police force – are pronounced guilty of treason. Sinn Féin, the Dáil, the

IRA: they are to be the law in Ireland now. If the British will allow it. The confrontation is turning darker. Raids are up, arrests are up, an explosion seems on the cards.

Some say de Valera is escaping to America to keep himself above the fray, to keep his hands clean. 'I trust you will not allow yourself to be lonely', he writes to Sinéad. 'It will be only for a short time'. Dressed as a sailor, he makes his way across the Atlantic.

AMERONGEN: The Kaiser's total now stands at four thousand eight hundred and twenty-four logs chopped from Count Bentinck's trees. A respectable total for any man. 'At least I'm doing something useful', Wilhelm tells his equerry.

He has not left Amerongen since December. Some suggest the Kaiser might make a gift of himself to the peacemakers, as a way of trying to get them to soften Germany's peace terms. The idea is dismissed out of hand.

SUMMER

Petrograd – Moscow: A sharp thrust towards the old imperial capital of Petrograd from the third (and much the smallest) White army still in action, led by the rotund Yudenich, a former Tsarist general. The White troops, many of them Estonian, number only a few thousand. The Bolsheviks are engulfed in a fresh wave of panic. Is Russia's second city about to fall? The Georgian bank-robber is sent to stiffen resolve, seek out the bad apples and report back to the boss in the Kremlin. Lenin issues a fierce proclamation (co-signed by the leader of the Cheka) warning of saboteurs waiting to blow up every bridge or give up every Red position to the enemy. 'Death to spies!' it reads. 'Every man should be on the watch'. A shortage of firewood to burn means trains carrying troops from Moscow cannot get through to Petrograd. One Bolshevik suggests an innovative solution: 'well, they can chop down wood on the way'.

The expected White assault on the city never materialises. But on its outskirts a small naval fort called Krasnaya Gorka mutinies against the Reds in early June. Stalin tries to claim credit for its recapture and put the boot into Trotsky and his military experts by telegraphing Lenin that he personally came up with the plan to assault from the sea. The professionals said it was impossible. 'The swift capture of Gorka was due to the grossest interference in the operations by me and civilians generally', the Georgian bank-robber boasts: 'I consider it my duty to declare that I shall continue to act in this way in future, despite all my reverence for science'.

Lenin scrawls '???' on the telegram and then the observation: 'Krasnaya Gorka was taken by *land*'. He seems amused at Stalin's attempts to impress him.

Washington DC: On a summer's evening in June a bomb explodes on the front steps of a town house in the capital's most elegant district. The house belongs to the Attorney General, Mitchell Palmer. He stepped out of the residence's library moments before. The bomb destroyed it. The Palmers – Mitchell, his wife and his young daughter – are unharmed. Their neighbour, another Democrat named Franklin D. Roosevelt, goes to check up on them and drives the Attorney General's wife and daughter to a friend's house where she hopes they can be safe.

There is glass everywhere on the street. Body parts belonging to the unfortunate bomber are spread over a wide area by the force of the blast. Pamphlets blow about in the warm air. 'Now that the great war, waged to replenish your purses and build a pedestal to your saints, is over,' they read, 'do you expect us to sit down and pray and cry?' The proletariat has been suffocated, the pamphlet reads. But, in language which would make D'Annunzio proud, 'we mean to speak for them with the voice of dynamite, through the mouths of guns.' Class war is declared on America: 'Long live social revolution! Down with tyranny! THE ANARCHIST FIGHTERS.'

Eight more explosions take place that night. Most blame the Bolsheviks. John Reed fingers provocateurs, hoping to encourage a crackdown against the unions. Mitchell Palmer promises to crush the criminals behind these acts with all the power at his disposal.

ADINKERKE, BELGIUM: Woodrow and Edith arrive by train. The Belgian King and Queen fly in by aeroplane. Over the next two days the party travels around the country by automobile on a kind of history tour, to show Woodrow how its people suffered under the German war-machine, and convince him not to go soft on the Germans at the last minute.

The group visits the locks on the Ypres canal which the Belgians opened in 1914 to flood their own farmland and slow down the German advance towards the sea. They eat a hasty battlefield picnic, with the sun-bleached skeletons of dead war horses for a view, and flies for company. They drive through the fields where Canadian troops fell by the thousand and the Germans first used poison gas, past the empty hulks of British tanks and clusters of crosses marking the final resting places of the dead.

German prisoners clearing debris occasionally raise their eyes from the ground to look at the motorcade as it speeds past them, lifting up clouds of dust and ash behind it. Woodrow wears a golf cap to protect his head. A linen duster covers his clothes. In Charleroi, he sees factories picked clean, the machinery carted off to Germany, the chimneys smokeless. In

Louvain, he is awarded an honorary doctorate in the ruins of the medieval library, burned down on German orders within the first weeks of the war.

Meanwhile, the Germans play for time, unable to form a government that can agree the peace terms as they are and yet divided as to what alternative there is to acceptance. The peacemakers bicker to the last. The French keep up the pressure. The British are accused of losing their nerve in now asking for concessions for Germany. Woodrow, once the advocate of a generous peace, is quite intransigent. What's done is done, he tells a meeting of the American delegation.

TEREZÍN FORTRESS, CZECHOSLOVAKIA: A group of Yugoslav students gather with Czech patriots in the old Austro-Hungarian fortress of Theresienstadt. Guided by the map of a patriotic Czech prison guard, they find and exhume the bodies of the assassins of Sarajevo, Gavrilo Princip's amongst them.

A Czech journalist gives an oration. He calls the murders in Sarajevo 'a purgative bolt of lightning into a stifling atmosphere'. The war brought suffering, but also independence: for the Czechs in the new state of Czechoslovakia, for the Serbs and other south Slavs in the new Yugoslavia.

The fortress of Theresienstadt, he declares, is no longer 'our mutual prison', but 'a symbol of our common liberation'.

NEW YORK: One evening in June, Éamon de Valera appears at a press conference in the presidential suite of the Waldorf Hotel.

He parries enquiries about how he got to America – 'that's a secret' – but says he has seen a Cardinal and 'several Senators' since his arrival, as well as his half-brother and mother (a white-haired lady in Rochester who stonewalled resolutely the previous day when asked her son's whereabouts). The newspapers remark on his accent: 'when he used the word "merchant", for example, it sounded like "mare-chint" and when he said "reduced" it sounded like "re-juiced"', the *Tribune* reports.

De Valera compares Ireland today to the American colonies in 1776. Had they waited for unanimity before declaring independence, they would still be colonies. But American patriots chose to fight; so have the Irish. 'They were called traitors and murderers', he says, and 'so are we'. America's founding fathers looked to France as their ally; the Irish look to America, confident in the strength of the principles which animate the American people. The Poles and others have already relied on these principles, de Valera says, to secure their independence. 'Ireland, the one remaining white nation in the slavery of alien rule, will similarly be free unless Americans make scraps of paper of their principles and prove false to the tradition their fathers have handed down to them'.

Éamon de Valera's plan is clear: to fight for Ireland on Woodrow's turf, claiming the moral high ground from the preacher's son and shaming him into supporting Ireland's cause, even to the point of persuading Irish-Americans to reject the League of Nations, if necessary. 'We shall fight for a real, demo-cratic League of Nations,' de Valera says a few weeks later, 'not the present unholy alliance.' Irish politics is to become American politics is to become world politics. On his continental tour, De Valera speaks to a crowd of seventy thousand in the hallowed Fenway Park baseball arena in Boston.

'I am thinking of you and the children always', he writes, somewhat hurriedly, to Sinéad: 'you know I will fly back as ever I can'. When asked why his wife does not simply join him in America, de Valera has a ready reply: 'Six at home'. Back in Ireland, violence flares sporadically. A police raid here, an assassination there. Tit for tat. A strange and intimate war. The Volunteers parade defiantly under the eyes of the Royal Irish Constabulary, not strong enough to intervene. Michael Collins forms a hit squad to intimi-date and murder anyone who crosses Sinn Féin's path. The limits of London's rule – and the strength of its resolve – are being tested all the time.

PARIS: *Littérature* is humming along. The establishment literati seem to like it – which young André Breton is not sure is such a good thing for his reputation as a provocateur, let alone a Dadaist. In the early summer Breton and Philippe Soupault, a friend who works at the French petrol commis-sariat, decide to try something new: a writing experiment they have been discussing non-stop for the last few months, but have been too afraid to give a go. One evening, a little uncertain of where the experiment will lead them, they begin.

Slowly at first, then faster, and then faster still, Breton and Soupault jot down in their *cahiers* whatever word comes into their heads, and then the next, and then the next. They urge spontaneity and chance to guide their pens across the page, and by so doing put into words the deep undercurrents of the human mind, as if taking dictation from their Freudian unconscious.

It is a technique Breton knows from psychiatry, of course: a means of unlocking patients' inner conflicts by encouraging them to speak or write without boundaries, without conscious supervision, leaping from one association to the next. It has been tried for predominantly spiritualist purposes. Sherlock Holmes's creator, Arthur Conan Doyle, is a fan. The poet W. B. Yeats and his wife have been experimenting with it for their own personal use. But Breton intends to write – just write.

At first, it is hard work. To write without a purpose – indeed to write with deliberate purposelessness – feels fake. It feels contrived. Their conscious mind holds Breton and Soupault back, as if warning them against the madness of the whole enterprise. Stop before it is too late! For a moment, they pause, wondering if they should turn back from the precipice, close up their notebooks, and head out to a local café for a Picon *citron*, Breton's favourite cocktail (in emulation of Apollinaire). They could stop now: no harm done, no one need ever know.

But they don't. Urging each other on, Breton and Soupault press further into the unknown, uncertain of how far they can – or should – go. And bit by bit, word by word, they find that the more they write, the easier the writing becomes: the more automatically the words flow onto the page, straight from the unconscious source, uninterrupted by conscious interference. Faster and faster sentence follows sentence and association follows association, a mash-up of thoughts and ideas and images. Like feverish scribes possessed by unseen spirits Breton and Soupault write on into the night until their arms ache from overwork.

Eventually they can write no more, so they compare notes. And they laugh joyously at what they have written. 'Prisoners of drops of water, we are but perpetual animals', runs one line. 'Our mouths are as dry as the lost beaches', goes another. 'True stars of our eyes, how long do you take to revolve around our heads?' asks a third. This is it! This is what the world has been waiting for! For hours, for days, Breton and Soupault barely leave the room, convinced that they have made a great discovery: a new literature for the times in which they live, a literature that writes itself, a literature from the unconscious mind, set down automatically. What Freud is doing for the understanding of the human mind, Breton and Soupault will do for the advancement of human literature.

But will anyone appreciate this great discovery? Will anyone understand? Should it be published? Who can they rely on to help them decide? One morning Breton and Soupault arrange to meet a poet they trust in a nearby café. Soupault, his anxieties getting the better of him, decides to take a walk. Breton is left alone to recite the first lines of the notebooks out loud for the first time. Louis Aragon's response – silently spellbound as the summer rain begins to fall – tells Breton everything he needs to know.

SCAPA FLOW, SCOTLAND – AMERONGEN: Off the coast of Scotland, the huge naval fleet built up by Germany over the course of the Kaiser's rule is scuttled. A desperate act. The British Royal Navy tries to stop the vandalism (they are hoping for the ships themselves). German organisation prevails. The ships sink to the depths.

In Amerongen, Wilhelm's wife expresses her satisfaction. 'It really is most pleasing to know', she tells an equerry, 'that the work of the Kaiser should not fall into the hands of the enemy, but now find its resting place on the sea floor.'

WASHINGTON DC: Woodrow is far away. The threat to America is close at hand. Mitchell Palmer considers a new line of attack to deal with the people who blew up his home. If not the *actual* people, then at least the *kind* of people: radicals. He has a new idea of how to do it.

What if, instead of only locking up those who committed actual crimes – hard to prove, time-consuming – one could just make these people, all of them, disappear? Most radicals, it is believed, are foreigners. That makes things easier. Their rights are more limited. Corners can be cut. The 1918 immigration law allows the government to deport any foreign anarchist, or anyone who belongs to an association advocating the violent overthrow of the government. All that is required is a signature from the Secretary of Labor. 'Round up these men and upon proper proof rush them back to Europe', a Bureau of Investigation official tells the newspapers. 'You will find this situation subside very rapidly'.

VERSAILLES, FRANCE: The day has arrived. The day the Germans sign.

An American businessman hitches a lift with a few diplomats to Versailles, and blags his way through the security cordon by showing the guards a Pall Mall cigarette case, emblazoned with a golden coat of arms. French lancers in sky-blue uniforms line the avenue leading to the palace, their horses perfectly still. Inside, cuirassiers wearing gilded helmets line the staircases. The Hall of Mirrors fills with representatives from around the world. The guests are made to sit on red velvet benches. Edward House signs souvenir programmes. Attendants hiss for quiet.

Then, through a side door, two Germans, one tall and one short, are marched into the room: a wine-dealer's son from Saarbrücken and a Catholic notary from Essen. Everything is calculated to humiliate the Germans, to demonstrate the cruel twist of fate. The room is the same room in which the

German Empire, now defunct, was declared in 1871. The table on which the current treaty is to be signed is the one on which France's earlier defeat was sealed. When one German comes up to sign the treaty, he finds his pen does not work and is handed a fountain pen by a secretary. It is five years to the day since the Archduke Franz Ferdinand was murdered in Sarajevo.

The French guns boom as the last of the powers sign the document. The windows tremble. In private, a last-minute push is made to try and settle the question of Italy's claims on the Adriatic before Woodrow catches the train to Normandy and the boat home. But such unresolved matters are considered entirely secondary to the German peace treaty and the creation of the League.

A separate settlement for Austria and Hungary does not require the presence of the President of the United States. The details can be hashed out amongst lesser mortals. (Within a few weeks the French are sending notes to the British on such essential issues as the urgent need for the return of the stained glass from Colmar Cathedral, which the Habsburgs carried off in 1815 when they helped defeat Napoleon.) As for the Ottomans, there is no doubt the empire will be severely pruned. Woodrow declares he has 'never seen anything more stupid' than an Ottoman presentation in Paris asking that its borders in Thrace and Anatolia be retained. But exactly how much the map of Anatolia will be redrawn is still uncertain.

Woodrow sleeps late each morning on the boat back to America. Every evening he attends the movies. He shares gossip from the peace conference, recalling one time Clemenceau told the Belgian premier, 'the best thing you can do for Belgium is to die or resign'. On Independence Day, he makes a speech to the American soldiers on board, telling them that 'this is the most tremendous Fourth of July that men ever imagined, for we have opened its franchise to all the world', and praising the role of immigrants in building the United States.

One day on board, Woodrow is handed a list of names of thirty-two Senators who will oppose ratification of the treaty unless certain American reservations can be lodged, including one which would absolve the United States of some of its key responsibilities to the League. Thirty-two, as near as damn it to a blocking minority. Woodrow will have to fight.

MODLIN, POLAND: A young French military officer, currently serving with the Polish army outside Warsaw, expresses his doubts about Versailles. He knows the Germans well. Too well, perhaps. 'They will do nothing, give up nothing, pay nothing', Charles de Gaulle writes to his mother, 'unless we make them do something, give up something or pay something – and not just through the use of force, but through the use of the utmost brutality.'

In Poland, Charles feels that he is at last doing something useful for his country. It is good to be a soldier again, to be an active participant in the fates of nations, rather than a prisoner of the enemy, trapped behind barbed wire. As part of the French military mission to Poland, de Gaulle dedicates himself to the task at hand: creating a strong and unified Polish army as a bulwark against both the Bolsheviks and the Germans. For the moment the French-trained contingent of the Polish army is, as de Gaulle tells his mother, 'the only serious military force between Prussia and Siberia'.

Unlike some of his compatriots, Charles has no time for carousing around Warsaw, exploiting the status of French officers as the country's heroic saviours. He judges the capital 'without any cachet'. He is positively disgusted by White Russian émigrés who continue to live their lives as if they were in St Petersburg in 1913. Most of all, he hates the 'insolent and useless' soldiers of other Allied countries – America, Britain and Italy – who he accuses of being only interested in making money. 'Like most of my compatriots', he writes, 'I've ended the war with a generalised dislike of foreigners'.

De Gaulle spends his time in camp preparing his lectures, including a particularly well-received lesson on how a breakdown in morale brings about defeat, based largely on his close reading of German newspapers in 1918. He lives in expectation of fresh disaster at any minute: another war, an invasion, a revolution. 'You see, our generation is the generation of catastrophes', Charles tells a Polish officer.

Personal catastrophe strikes in July when he returns to his room after supper to find that the lock to his chalet has been broken and some money stolen from inside his tunic pocket. Two pairs of shoes and the young captain's bedsheets have also been taken. 'I am furious, humiliated and very embarrassed', Charles writes home.

URALS – TSARITSYN – MOSCOW: After his rapid advance westwards in the spring, Admiral Kolchak is now being chased back towards the Urals. In Paris, the powers hesitate as to whether to grant him diplomatic recognition. They send him a political questionnaire instead.

The real danger to the Bolsheviks is now in the south. At first the threat is underestimated. 'I think that Kharkov stands in no greater danger than Tver, Penza, Moscow or any other city of the Soviet Republic', Trotsky says in June. Within days of the war commissar's confident assessment the city is in the hands of Denikin's White army, which continues to thrust deeper into Ukraine on its left and towards the Volga on its right. At the end of the month, using British tanks on the ground and supported by a volunteer squadron of British aircraft from the air, Wrangel's forces sweep into Tsaritsyn, the city where Stalin made his bloody mark the year before. The lower reaches of the Volga, much of southern Russia, the Cossack steppe and rich industrial region of eastern Ukraine are again in White hands. The commander of the Red Army – Leon Trotsky's choice for the job, a reliable Latvian – is replaced. Trotsky, ill and exhausted, storms out of a meeting to discuss the issue, proudly offering his own resignation as war commissar. It is refused.

Consolidate or capitalise? Denikin weighs up his options. Foreign support is running thin. The French have withdrawn from the Russian mess; the British plan to pull out their troops soon. The Whites are outnumbered. They have little hope of recruiting as quickly as the Red Army. Time is not on Denikin's side. If he does not strike now, he may lose his chance to land the fatal blow. His thoughts are full of grand, old-fashioned ideals: honour, motherland, duty, fortitude, redemption.

At headquarters in freshly conquered Tsaritsyn, a large map is spread out. Denikin points out the railway lines radiating from Moscow like the spokes of a bicycle wheel. He proposes that his White armies spread out over a broad front and then fight their way north along three lines of axis, until they converge victoriously upon their final goal. The order is called Directive Moscow. Wrangel objects. Dividing the army into three forces is a mistake. Why not let it advance along a narrower front, as one? Denikin slaps him down. 'I see!' he exclaims. 'You want to be the first man to set foot in Moscow.'

Lenin issues another of his furious instructions. 'All Soviet officials must *pull themselves together like soldiers*', he demands. The impatient revolutionary declares war on 'organisational fuss': 'speechifying must be prohibited, opinions must be exchanged as rapidly as possible and confined to information and precisely formulated practical proposals.'

MT. CLEMENS, MICHIGAN: For several weeks over midsummer, the American public is treated to the spectacle of America's most successful industrialist, Henry Ford, claiming one million dollars in libel damages from a Chicago newspaper that dared to call him an ignorant idealist for his apparent pacifism early in the war.

The quiet Michigan town is overrun with reporters. Ford's legal and media team take over the floor of a downtown office building. A wall is covered with a map of the United States dotted with different flags showing the location of friendly and hostile news reports on the case. Various professors take the stand to argue that Ford's views on war are in line with those of such great luminaries as Martin Luther and Victor Hugo.

Then Ford takes the stand. When asked the year of the American Revolution, he answers 1812. He does not seem to understand the basic principles of the constitution. Ford describes anarchy as 'overthrowing the government and throwing bombs'. An idealist, he says, is 'anyone who helps another make a profit'. He is made to look a simpleton. He does not seem to mind.

> HENRY FORD: I admit I am ignorant about most things.
> OPPOSITION ATTORNEY: You admit it?
> HENRY FORD: About most things ... I am not ignorant about all things.
> ATTORNEY: You know about automobiles, of course?
> FORD: No, I don't know a great deal about—
> ATTORNEY: You know about business?
> FORD: I don't know about business. Know just a little.
> ATTORNEY: But you don't know very much about history?
> FORD: Not very much about history.
> ATTORNEY: And you don't believe in art?
> FORD: I am coming to like it a little better than I did.
> ATTORNEY: Since when?
> FORD: Because I was criticized for saying what I did about art.
> ATTORNEY: You don't care anything about music?
> FORD: I never said that.
> ATTORNEY: You like the banjo and the fiddle?
> FORD: I like the banjo, yes.

A jury of farmers find in favour of Ford. They award him six cents in damages. But America loves him. 'You are my ideal of a self-made man whose opinions are sincere and justly righteous', writes one admirer.

MUNICH: Escaping demobilisation again, the pale Austrian with the trim moustache enrols in a propaganda course organised by the army to train up patriotic political agitators.

One instructor, a member of the Thule Society, provides a furious critique of international capitalism, describing the way that Anglo-American finance controls the whole world through the instrument of financial interest, enslaving productive capital in the process. Another identifies Britain as Germany's long-term geopolitical enemy. There is consensus around the injustice of Versailles and much loose talk about the Jews. Political pamphlets are shared around. This jumble of ideas converges on the essential notion that Germany is surrounded by enemies and that its rebirth lies within. To the former dispatch-runner it is intoxicating.

One day at the end of a class, one of the lecturers finds him holding a small group of fellow soldiers in thrall with his repetition of what he has learned, delivered in a thick Austrian accent. His fervour rises as he speaks, as if he has just discovered the explanation for world events that he was looking for, and needs to communicate it to the world. Adolf Hitler has found a talent.

ERZURUM, EASTERN OTTOMAN EMPIRE: Who does Mustafa Kemal represent? The Sultan, the Turkish people, the army, or just himself? He has made clear his scorn for the government in Istanbul, declaring them incapable of defending the nation's integrity and unity while under occupation. Yet he still wears the gold cordon of an aide-de-camp to the Sultan and, despite ill-temperedly resigning his commission some weeks ago, he still wears the uniform of a general in the Sultan's army.

Over the last few weeks, his calls for resistance to schemes of foreign domination have grown louder and, to the ears of the British and French, more dangerous. They have found an echo across the country, where Greek units have already clashed with Ottoman soldiers. They have attracted attention in other countries too. Nationalists in Germany celebrate Kemal as a man prepared to fight against a 'Turkish Versailles'.

In Erzurum, it is time to weld disparate acts and vague words together into something more solid: a movement. Representatives of patriotic organisations from the Black Sea region and eastern Anatolia gather in Erzurum in a low, dark stone building, once an Armenian school, built with thick walls to keep it cool in the region's baking summers and warm in its harsh winters. The town is sparsely built: a stop on the railway line, an outpost in the empire's eastern highlands, a garrison town eight hundred miles east of the capital. The plains around are treeless. Some locals remember a pogrom here against the Armenians in 1895; nearly all remember the town's bloody occupation by the armies of the Russian Tsar in 1916. This is where General Yudenich made his name.

A sheep is sacrificed in a religious ceremony as the nationalist congress opens. Prayers are recited. There are only a few dozen delegates. Kemal is immediately elected chairman. Loyalty to the Sultan is declared. But there is no doubting that the new organisation is a challenge to the authority of his government. It does not take a devious mind to see that Mustafa Kemal is bidding for the leadership of something grander than the East Anatolia Society for the Defence of National Rights. Another general in Erzurum – and potential rival – ignores an order from Istanbul to arrest him.

One delegate questions whether an officer in uniform should preside over what is supposedly a loyal, democratic upswelling of the people. Kemal, ever aware of the importance of appearance, borrows morning dress from the local governor. A step is taken in his transformation from loyal Ottoman general to Turkish patriotic leader. In private, Mustafa Kemal admits his true ambition: the establishment of a republic. It is far too early to admit to such a thing in public.

THE UPPER REACHES OF THE VOLGA AND KAMA RIVERS: Nadya is sent on a propaganda mission aboard a steamboat named *Krasnaya Zvezda*, Red Star. The boat is equipped with a cinema, a printing press and, of course, a well-stocked library. It is to travel to villages and cities recently abandoned by Admiral Kolchak's Whites and ensure that they understand the Bolshevik view of things. Vladimir Ilyich gives Nadya strict instructions about what to say and then sees her off at the railway station.

Nadya hears stories from Russian peasants about the horrors of White rule. Most of the professional kind have left with Kolchak's forces. In the middle of her tour she meets an old school friend who stayed behind. Nadya gives thirty-four speeches, according to the ship's newspaper. One agitator attached to the Red Army turns out to be a former priest, who calls the Bolsheviks 'today's apostles'. When someone asks him about baptism, he responds: 'that would take a couple of hours to explain, but briefly it's pure eyewash'. Nadya has a quiet laugh when one of the Red Army commanders claims that Soviet Russia is unconquerable on account of its 'squarity and sizeability'.

Vladimir Ilyich writes to her from the Kremlin, reporting on a pleasant Sunday spent down in Gorki – 'our country house', he calls it now. He asks

Nadya to telegraph more often and not work too hard: 'Eat and sleep more, then you will be fully fit for work by winter'. A few days later, he has cause to write again. Nadya's health has taken a turn for the worse: 'you must stick strictly to the rules and obey the doctor's orders absolutely', he warns. His brother has been visiting in Gorki. The lime trees are in bloom.

News from the Eastern Front is good. Kolchak's Whites have been pursued beyond the Urals, Ekaterinburg has been taken. The news from the south is less good. 'There is still no serious turn for the better', he writes, 'I hope there will be'.

FIUME: A young Italian woman walks along a street in Fiume. Tucked into her blouse she wears a cockade in the green, white and red of the Italian flag, to demonstrate her attachment to the cause of reunification with the homeland across the water.

A couple of bored French soldiers decide to have some fun. Harassing the young woman as she walks, they grab at the cockade on her blouse, and make off with it. (The soldiers later claim the lady was a prostitute, and that the cockade fell to the ground by accident.) Word goes around that Italian womanhood has been insulted. Do the French think they can simply do as they please?

An angry crowd gathers in Fiume's main public square. Some French soldiers are beaten up. A few others are chased away, and the chairs of a nearby café thrown at them. An American diplomat is pushed around a bit. The window of a hotel is broken when the crowd hears a French officer is dining in its restaurant. A club for the local Croatian population is sacked as well. Italian soldiers do little to intervene. Some stand around and laugh. Posters proclaiming 'Italy or Death' appear around the city.

A few nights later there is more rioting. This time the windows of shops with Slovenian and Croatian owners are smashed, and two more French soldiers are injured. An Italian general claims that while he tried to calm the crowds, more direct action taken by his soldiers would have sparked worse violence. The very next evening, a French storehouse at the end of the sea defences comes under gunfire. Italian sailors are said to be involved, while civilians are reportedly armed with rifles. Again, the Italian army does not get involved. A French battleship is sent.

Later in the summer it is agreed in Paris that Fiume will be permanently internationalised and Dalmatia given to the new Yugoslavian Kingdom (a merger of the Kingdom of Serbia with former Austro-Hungarian territories in the Balkans). In Fiume, tension continues to rise.

CHICAGO: It has already been a hot and sultry summer. There have been race riots in Charleston, South Carolina, in Bisbee, Arizona, and in Washington DC (where local boy Edgar Hoover of the Bureau of Investigation searches for evidence to connect unrest amongst American blacks to the Bolsheviks).

Then this. Sunday by the South Side Beach, Chicago. Mid-afternoon. The sun just past its zenith, but still beating down in fury. The kind of weather where ice cream melts in seconds. The kind where fights start a little too easily. Some black Chicagoans step onto that part of the beach that, by some unwritten rule, white Chicagoans consider theirs. Stones are thrown at the unwelcome arrivals. Blacks retaliate. Stones become rocks and rocks become bricks. Some black boys out on a raft on the lake think it is some kind of game. Then one of them gets hit in the head and drowns. Before long, guns are used and gangs arrive, both white and black. The papers embellish the incident as best they can, fanning the flames with additional rumour and prejudice.

On Tuesday, gangs of whites are reported to be making their way through the Loop of Chicago on a hunt for black employees in the city's restaurants. Chicago's chief of police cordons off City Hall with riflemen. Pawnshops are looted for guns. Newspapers talk of armed black men taking up strategically elevated positions near the stockyards. Their pages read like wartime casualty lists: 'Croft, William, white, shot in left wrist; Smith, Thomas, colored, lacerations of head and body; Unknown Negro, skull fractured at Thirty-Sixth and Cottage Grove Avenue; Virden, Henry, white, shot, wounded in abdomen, will die'.

Several veterans are involved. A white man decorated with the Croix de Guerre is reported to have been injured in the shoulder when he stopped a black man threatening a lady on a streetcar with a knife. A thirty-three-year-old black soldier with three years' service in the Canadian army, still suffering from the after-effects of poison gas, is knocked on the head while walking down South State Street. 'I don't see why they want to bother a fellow like me', he tells the *Tribune*. 'I did all I could to help make this old country safe for just such men as these.'

On Wednesday night, over six thousand troops are finally called in to stop the fighting. Rain helps to dampen the violence. But calm only fully returns on Friday. By now, twenty-three blacks and fifteen whites are dead. One thousand Chicagoans, mostly black, have lost their homes to fire. Yet it could have been worse. At least an East St. Louis-style disaster has been avoided. Some see a silver lining in the determination of blacks to fight rather than run. 'As regrettable as are the Washington and Chicago riots,' writes a leading officer of the National Association for the Advancement of Colored People, 'I feel that they mark a turning point in the psychology of the whole nation regarding the Negro problem'. The war has changed America. Resistance, not submission, is the new attitude.

VIENNA: On holiday high in the mountains, news reaches Sigmund Freud of the suicide of a Viennese psychoanalyst, Victor Tausk, by simultaneous hanging and gunshot. 'He swore undying loyalty to psychoanalysis etc.', writes Freud uninterestedly, referring to the farewell letters Tausk sent to him before he died. The suicide is put down to the horrors of war, and the pressures of peace. Freud's own reaction is cold: 'I confess I do not really miss him'.

Every day when the weather is good Freud walks up alone into the hills, picking orchids one day, strawberries the next, and seeking out mushrooms. He receives letters from his daughter Anna, in which she reveals her (often violent) dreams and informs him of her latest holiday adventure. 'Most of the time we do nothing, climb up a little to pick alpine roses and lie in the heather and feel the time passing', she writes. Occasionally Freud hears an echo of what is happening in Hungary. But mostly he works on the outlines of a new theory. 'There is a lot of death in it', he admits to Anna.

At the end of the month, he finds distraction in a new book, sent to him from Switzerland: *The Erotic Motive in Literature*. 'Freud is a genius whose performances astonish one as do those of a wizard', notes the book's introduction. 'After his discoveries, literary interpretation cannot remain the same.' How pleasing it is to have the importance of his work recognised. Perhaps these are the first intimations of something he once hardly dared to believe in: celebrity.

BUDAPEST: There are celebrations in the Hungarian capital in June when, reconquered by Hungarian soldiers, a Soviet Republic is set up in next-door Slovakia. Pretzels are handed out to children at school. Women are given half a kilo of white flour in additional rations. A gypsy band plays revolutionary songs for Béla Kun's delight. The Jewish Bolshevik former prisoner of war is celebrated as a national hero.

But times are fickle. The promise of joining forces with the Soviet Red Army has not come off. Food remains scarce. Hungary's conservatives have never liked him, of course, but now the workers are starting to waver. Kun catches wind of a plan by hardliners in his own camp to overthrow him. He holds two Ukrainians responsible. They are thrown into the Danube with rocks tied around their necks.

In July, an international strike called to show support for Soviet Russia and Soviet Hungary fails to rally the workers of the world. Kun still issues orders – on the number of shirts and pieces of underwear a citizen of the Soviet Republic is allowed to own, for instance – but the tide is turning strongly against him now. Lenin regrets Soviet Russia is unable to help in any material way. He sends his 'warmest greetings and a firm handshake'. At the end of July, the Romanians cross the Tisza river.

The Hungarian Social Democrats who supported Kun in spring abandon him in August. He is forced to flee to Austria with his family and a handful of associates. Their money is confiscated and they are kept incommunicado – and as far away as possible from Vienna – to prevent them from causing a new revolution. The Romanians march into Budapest a few days later. The experiment of the Hungarian Soviet Republic is over. From being Europe's capital of revolution Budapest becomes the Continent's capital of reaction. Hungary emerges from the war more reduced in territory than any other country. The bitterness lasts.

UPSTATE MICHIGAN: Now it is Ernest's turn to commiserate with an old friend, unlucky in love. 'There's something wrong with us Bill – we're idealists', he writes. 'If you do want to keep the old ideals straight and cut loose from the damned dirty money grubbing for a year I'm your man.' Hemingway proposes a trip to Hawaii and the South Pacific: 'And we'll live Bill! We'll live.'

In the end, a fishing trip in the Charlevoix region is organised instead with a group of old school friends. One hundred and eighty trout are caught in four days. When his father visits, Ernest asks him to bring his Italian medal to remind him of those glorious days. At the end of the summer, he moves into accommodation in Petoskey, sleeps with a woman for the first time in his life, and begins work on a couple of short stories about the war. The rejections mount.

Russia: Kolchak, the shooting star of the spring, is pushed back further east. In June, the city of Ufa, which he took at the beginning of his offensive, is retaken by the Reds. Trotsky fleetingly suggests doubling down on Bolshevism's eastward advance. A revolutionary training academy should be set up in Turkestan. Perhaps the revolution will reach Paris and London not through Europe after all, but through 'the towns of Afghanistan, Punjab and Bengal'. Leon's fertile mind imagines a dramatic turn towards Asia.

And yet there is real danger much closer to hand. Trotsky's grand eastward vista may hold promise for tomorrow, but only if it survives the threat building in the south. Denikin's armies roam across a broad front stretching almost from the Urals to the Black Sea. Over the summer, Wrangel's army marches up the Volga from Tsaritsyn before being forced halfway back. Ukraine crumbles into savage anarchy, torn between peasant warlords, nationalists seeking to free Ukraine for ever from the Russian yoke, Reds who see its future as a brother proletarian republic of Soviet Russia, and Whites who view it as an integral part of the conservative greater Russia of the future. Piłsudski's Poles hover on the sidelines, opposed to Lenin's Bolshevism and Denikin's Russian nationalism alike.

In Ukraine, all sides operate according to the same principle: today's ally may be tomorrow's enemy (and usually is). All sides officially repudiate anti-Semitism – but all sides, including the Reds, are involved in pogroms against the Jews. Techniques of mass violence and torture are routine. One Cossack method is to tie a rope around a householder's neck, a sturdy soldier pulling on either end to tighten the noose, and choke him until his family give up everything they own. The procedure can be repeated several times until the requisite sum is provided, or the man is dead (or both). Synagogues are torched. Women are raped. Copies of *The Protocols of the Elders of Zion* circulate freely. (It is said to be Admiral Kolchak's favourite book.)

Out of chaos arises opportunity. White forces swoop into the Black Sea port of Odessa, where the cosmopolitan war commissar went to school all those years ago, and towards which his train now imperiously steams. Denikin's men on the ground search out anyone with the surname Bronstein. Everywhere, the Reds are forced back. At the end of August two rival flags fly over Kiev: the flag of imperial Russia under which Denikin's Whites fight, and the nationalist flag of the Ukrainian republic. Denikin promptly pushes out the nationalists, bans the Ukrainian language and orders the arrest of Ukrainian intellectuals. In Russia itself, a roving contingent of

White cavalry pierce the Red lines and strike a hundred miles behind them towards Moscow, conquering town after town, causing havoc along the way.

'It is true, comrades, that we are facing an unpleasantness,' Trotsky admits a little primly on a trip back to Moscow, 'not a military failure, but an unpleasantness in the full sense.' He devises a new slogan: 'Proletarian, to horse!'

WASHINGTON DC: A new confidential memorandum arrives on the desk of the Director of Military Intelligence: 'Beyond a doubt, there is a new negro to be reckoned with in our political and social life.' The memo notes the proliferation of 'defense funds' amongst American blacks and a new slogan animating the community: 'Fight for your rights'. It warns that the doctrines of radical socialists are gaining ground. The experience of black soldiers in France has also played its role. Then there is the propaganda of the NAACP: 'They have become more sensitive than ever to the practice of lynching'.

J. Edgar Hoover is made chief of the new Radical Division of the Department of Justice around the same time. Within two months he has compiled an index of fifty thousand names, cards that can be cross-checked against radical organisations, and against the files in the Bureau's archive, just like at the Library of Congress. To prepare himself for the next part of his mission to clean up America he reads the *Communist Manifesto* and studies the workings of the Comintern. He tries to get inside the Bolshevik mind.

MUNICH: Within a month, the students have become teachers. Towards the end of August, Adolf is sent as part of an army propaganda squad to a camp for returning POWs, where they give political lectures to keep up morale and ensure the soldiers' political soundness before they are released back into civilian life.

The squad leader lectures on war guilt, Goethe, the rise of Germany in the nineteenth century, as well as his own experiences during the Bavarian Soviet Republic. Hitler lectures on peace and reconstruction.

The soldiers consider the mangy field-runner a natural. He speaks from personal experience, capturing the audience's imagination with his turns of phrase and passion for his subject. In a lecture on capitalism, he gets a little carried away talking about the Jews, raising concern that his talks might be considered anti-Semitic.

For the first time in his life, Adolf Hitler basks in the warm glow of public appreciation.

VIENNA: The Austrians try one final diplomatic manoeuvre to avoid being tarred with the same brush as imperial Germany. Since Austria–Hungary has ceased to exist, they argue, and entirely new states have been born from the ashes of the empire, the new Austria should be considered a partner for the future, rather than a historic enemy. It should not be made to bear the sins of its former imperial bosses.

The victorious powers in Paris are having none of it. 'The people of Austria, together with their neighbours, the people of Hungary, bear in a peculiar degree the responsibility for the calamities which have befallen Europe in the last five years.' The crowds on the streets of Vienna in 1914 are proof enough of popular complicity with the Habsburg regime – 'an ancient and effete autocracy' – in conducting the war. The Austrian and Hungarian people are particularly damned for their domineering rule over other nationalities, nothing less than a 'policy of racial ascendancy and oppression' over Czechs, Slovaks, Poles and the rest.

The plight of the Sudeten Germans in the new state of Czechoslovakia, the Austrian parliament warns, will be a stain on the consciences of the victorious powers. Nevertheless, bitter and defeated, they recommend the treaty be signed all the same.

CHICAGO: A national convention of the American Socialist Party takes place in Machinists' Hall at 113 S. Ashland Avenue, in the industrial Lower West Side. The party has been engaged in a vicious organisational civil war for months. In Chicago, only those with a white card issued by the national executive, the moderates, are to be allowed into the hall. Those without such credentials, delegates from local associations excluded for being too left-wing, are to be kept out. A government spy reports that 'John Reed had about 50 husky Russians and Finns lined up to "start something"'. Chicago police are on hand to enforce the white card rule.

A small group of renegades, including Reed, decide to meet in the basement of the same building and set themselves up as the Communist Labor Party, the only party, they claim, that really gets revolution. A different group of renegades, including a large number of Russian-speakers, establish themselves as the rival Communist Party of America. The two parties agree that capitalism should be overthrown, and power conquered. But they hate each other. Both seek sanction as official representatives of the worldwide Communist movement from Moscow. Reed plans to return there to make his case.

BERLIN: At the beginning of September, a minister of the Prussian government signs a release form for a number of items – furniture, paintings, silver plate, a motor boat and the tobacco-box of Frederick the Great – to be sent to the former Kaiser in Holland. The manifest covers seventy-one pages. The goods fill sixty-two railway carriages.

All this will help with the decoration of Huis Doorn, the estate the Kaiser has just purchased for himself and his family, a few miles from Amerongen. Count Bentinck's joy when informed of the imperial departure – at least some trees will be left standing – is cut short when told renovations at the new residence will take at least six months. Central heating must be installed, as well as a lift and electric lighting for the garden. The Kaiser discusses all these issues at length with the local mayor.

At the same time, Germany is barely holding together. Ebert's government sends German soldiers, reinforced by right-wing Freikorps, to suppress an incipient Polish uprising in the economically vital, coal-rich province of Silesia, where the Versailles Treaty calls for a plebiscite to determine its future status.

FIUME: There is at least one man in Europe who consistently shuns the mediocre, who thumbs his nose at the Great Powers, who proclaims only me, me, me and Italy, Italy, Italy. And why not? Are they not one and the same?

Gabriele D'Annunzio, recently promoted to lieutenant colonel, decides to bite the bullet. For a long time, Italy's various nationalist groups have been pressing him to lead an expedition to Fiume. What is needed, they tell him, is a demonstration that Italians will not give up their Adriatic dreams, whatever the weakling government in Rome agrees. A theatrical act with a bit of military muscle behind it. A propaganda coup. In early September, Gabriele writes to Mussolini complaining of a temperature. And yet, he announces, he will nonetheless rouse himself from his sickbed and do his duty. D'Annunzio instructs Mussolini to provide vigorous journalistic support from Milan. Although Benito later presents himself as Gabriele's equal in this endeavour, their letters suggest that his role is closer to that of unpaid publicist.

Tension in Fiume has been rising again since the summer riots. Protests against the town's imminent internationalisation and against Dalmatia being handed to Yugoslavia have turned violent. The Italian military has done little to calm the feelings of Italians amongst the local population. They make ostentatious preparations for the winding down of operations in accordance with instructions. And yet an American diplomat catches soldiers pasting up posters promising Fiume will never be abandoned. The security situation goes from bad to worse. A French soldier is murdered. It is reported that a number of children thought to be local Croats are shot by Italian police when they refuse to shout *Viva Italia* on returning to town from a picnic in the countryside. The city seems primed for a takeover by the time D'Annunzio sets out one morning in a Fiat Tipo 4, at the head of a column of trucks stolen from a nearby barracks.

Along the short drive to Fiume, the poet and his band of legionnaires pick up support from regular army units. The black-shirted Arditi so admired by Hemingway, bored with peace and keen to add a touch more swagger to their reputation, prefer to join in Gabriele's fun than follow half-hearted instructions to stop him. When an Italian general orders D'Annunzio to turn back or else, the hero of Vienna simply offers up his medal-covered chest and suggests the general shoot him. He knows the threat is empty. Mussolini's paper reports that the general sent Gabriele on his way with the words: 'Great Poet, I hope that your dream will be fulfilled, and that I may shout with you "Viva Fiume Italiana"'.

By midday, D'Annunzio and his legionnaires – swollen to about two thousand men (and a few schoolboys) – have arrived in the city. Church bells welcome them. Not a shot is fired. Over the next days, the British and the French decide to withdraw. 'There is nothing to show whether this is a revolution in the Italian army or an attempt to seize the town for Italy', reads an urgent telegram to London. Allied forces do not want to be stuck in the middle when Rome sends troops to restore order – by force, if necessary – against apparently rebellious units of its own army, led by the rubber-faced poet-aviator.

Mussolini writes an editorial in *Il Popolo d'Italia* applauding Gabriele's work (and rather wishing, like with the attack on the *Avanti* offices earlier in the year, that it was his own). 'It is the first act of revolt' against the coalition of Versailles, he thunders. But D'Annunzio wants action, not just words. Why, he asks in an angry letter to Milan, have the Fasci not risen to support the cause of Fiume? Indeed, why are the premier and his government in Rome still in office at all? 'I am astonished at you and the Italian people', he tells Benito: 'Any other country – even Lapland – would have overthrown that man, those men.' While boasting about his own exploits – 'I have risked all, I have accomplished all, I have gained all' – Gabriele upbraids his factotum for his inaction. 'Where are the combatants, the shock troops, the volunteers, the Futurists?' he rants. 'At least prick the belly which weighs you down, let some of the air out'. Mussolini publishes the letter in his newspaper with the unflattering bits taken out.

Meanwhile, the Italian government does nothing, or next to nothing. A blockade on Fiume is announced. But not enforced. The trains still run in and out of the station as they ever did, often carrying fresh recruits from Italy ready to serve the nationalist cause. The boat service to nearby Abbazio is uninterrupted. The army drops pamphlets from aeroplanes over the city – a nice D'Annunzian touch – warning soldiers they will be considered deserters if they do not surrender. But is that really what the Italian authorities want? The British are uncertain whether an admiral sent in to secure the Italian naval vessels in Fiume harbour is Gabriele's prisoner or his guest. D'Annunzio himself remarks on the 'comic element' in the whole situation.

Vast sums of money are raised in Italy and sent to the nationalist camp in Fiume. Patriotic speeches and processions are organised in the city's squares. The physically unimposing D'Annunzio puffs himself up into right-eous anger, struts out onto the balcony of his new headquarters, and proceeds to cast his spell over the locals in high-blown language they can barely understand. All the desperadoes in Italy make a beeline for the city to glorify themselves with the title of legionnaire. Fiume overflows with ill-shaven men with big ideas. That old rabble-rouser Marinetti, now very much second fiddle to D'Annunzio, turns up. The city has become 'truly Futurist', he decides. It is like a dream come true.

MUNICH: On the day D'Annunzio strides into Fiume, Adolf Hitler takes his place in the back room of a brewery restaurant, the Sterneckerbräu. A meeting of the German Workers' Party – a small political group, loosely associated with the Thule Society – is under way. The former *Vertrauensmann* is there to take notes for his boss in the army propaganda department. The main speaker at the event is one of his old lecturers from the propaganda course, delivering a talk on 'How and By What Means Can Capitalism Be Eliminated?' It is a small gathering, rather like one of Vladimir's group harangues in Zurich in 1917.

A second speaker, a teacher who has previously written a book about the need for a German-based rival to Esperanto, begins his own contribution to the evening's proceedings with a talk on Bavarian separatism. He argues that Bavaria should split from the rest of Germany and join with Austria so as to protect it from the revolutionaries in Berlin. Hitler is appalled. Germany cannot be broken up. He stands up to interrupt the speaker and launches into such a vehement denunciation of him that the separatist teacher takes his hat and leaves.

The leader of the German Workers' Party invites Adolf to return the following week.

BERLIN: After months of waiting, a sign. Not quite certainty, but an indication. 'Joyous news', Einstein writes on a postcard to his sick mother in Switzerland: 'English expeditions have actually measured the deflection of starlight from the Sun.' But how much? Enough to confirm Einstein's value and change the world? The news of the provisional calculations – received third-hand from England via two Dutch intermediaries – is maddeningly inconclusive. The results need to be properly interpreted. It could go either way.

MUNICH: His success from the Sterneckerbräu still ringing in his ears, Adolf is tasked by his army boss with responding to a letter asking about the proper attitude to take towards the Jews. He jumps at the opportunity to show what he has learned.

'Anti-Semitism is too lightly characterised as a merely emotional phenomenon', he writes: 'This is incorrect'. The Jews, Adolf insists, are not a religious community but a race, sustained in their difference by 'a thousand years of in-breeding'. Germany's Jews are no more German than a Frenchman who speaks German. Hitler portrays Jews as the enemy of higher values, driven only by money and power. They are a 'racial tuberculosis' on the nation.

The answer to the Jewish problem does not lie with random pogrom emotions, but with systematic exclusion of Jews from society by legal means: 'the end goal must be the Jews' complete and total removal'.

SOUTHERN RUSSIA – LONDON: General Denikin issues the order to march on Moscow. A last throw of the dice. A final assault on the heart of the beast.

In London, Winston makes endless suggestions about how to help. 'You will see in my memo how much I have tried to harmonise my views with yours, as it is my duty to do while I serve you', he writes to the Prime Minister with characteristic bonhomie, a threat of resignation not very well concealed. Lloyd George is exasperated. 'You confidently predict in your memorandum that Denikin is on the eve of some great and striking success', he responds. 'I looked up some of your memoranda and your statements made earlier in the year about Kolchak, and I find that you use exactly the same language in reference to Kolchak's successes'.

Britain has honoured her commitments to friends old and new. Tens of millions of pounds have been spent. No government could do more: 'I wonder if it is any use my making one last effort to induce you to throw off this obsession, which, if you will forgive me for saying so, is upsetting your balance.'

ORLY, FRANCE: André Breton is sent by the military to be an auxiliary doctor at the Aviation Centre at Orly, just south of Paris. It is a welcome respite from the city. The experiment with Soupault has exhausted him. The first chapters of the pair's automatic writing are published in *Littérature* in September. A book is planned for 1920 (a couple of hundred copies will suffice). André's mood is as flat as the landscape. 'I'm not working', he writes to a friend. 'I happily ponder the vast airfield, deserted and silent.'

Paris itself is quieter now that the Austrians have signed their own peace treaty at Saint-Germain-en-Laye (not quite as harsh as that for the Germans). The French capital winds down as the world's diplomatic epicentre. 'It is almost impossible to rally a foursome for golf', complains Allen Dulles, 'and absolutely impossible to get four for bridge.'

AUTUMN

MOSCOW: Vladimir speaks to a conference of working women. War commissar Trotsky has already lectured the group on the situation at the front, now only a few hundred miles from the Bolshevik capital. Others have been drafted in to talk about the food crisis. Lenin allows himself to talk about higher matters.

The regime has made great advances since the revolution, he begins, abolishing the old laws on divorce or on children born out of wedlock. But yes, he recognises, this is not enough. Equality before the law? Well, even bourgeois states can do that. But, as every good Bolshevik knows, law is one thing and power another. Women 'still remain factually downtrodden because all housework is left to them', Lenin sighs. In the new communist society which, one day, will be built, women will be emancipated from such 'petty, stultifying, unproductive work'. Canteens will be established and nurseries for children set up. Yes, women will be involved in politics, just like any other worker. That is the goal, Lenin says, but it will take many years to achieve.

He has frequently discussed these ideas with Inessa Armand, his former lover. The two once fell out over Vladimir's pedantic, prudish, entirely theoretical response to free love — bourgeois, he calls the idea (a little steep given his own status as an adulterer). But that was long ago. Inessa is a frequent visitor to see him and Nadya in the Kremlin these days. Together, they talk about everything: the past and future. Sometimes Inessa brings her young daughter Varya with her, nearly killed in an anarchist bomb attack on the headquarters of the Moscow Communist Party that September. Vladimir enjoys having such a young and receptive audience around to listen to his stories about his exile past and his musings about the future.

Other times this autumn, when he is not out lecturing, or else dictating telegrams in his Kremlin office, Vladimir sits in his kitchen with the Ulyanovs' housekeeper — a former factory worker from the Urals. He daydreams about the imminent victory of world revolution, even as Denikin's armies approach Moscow from the south.

ISTANBUL: 'MUSTAPHA KEMAL'S INFLUENCE CONTINUING TO SPREAD', warns a secret British telegram on the first day of October. The general's pronouncements from Ankara are still barely consistent with a constitutional Sultanate. A long-distance power struggle is under way. New parliamentary elections have been called. Kemal considers moving west.

FIUME – FLORENCE: Better late than never. Benito Mussolini flies to Fiume to congratulate Gabriele D'Annunzio on his taking of Fiume, with the hope of recouping some of the glory for himself.

Two days afterwards, and out of his flying gear for once this autumn, Benito is in Florence for an election rally of his Fasci di Combattimento. The Fascists, he proclaims elliptically, are 'not republican, not socialist, not democratic, not conservative, not nationalist'. They are all of these and none, he says, taking a leaf out of Dada. They are a party and anti-party, 'the sum of all negations and affirmations' representing 'all those who feel uncomfortable with the old categories and the old way of thinking'.

VIENNA: Having lost contact for the duration of the war, Freud meets again one of his English colleagues, who has travelled through war-torn Europe to Vienna and is staying at the Hotel Regina. Like long-lost friends, they talk of everything: how each has aged in the war, how bad things are in Austria these days, and of course they talk of psychoanalysis.

Gingerly, they broach the situation of their two countries, and of the world. Freud admits that he has become half a Bolshevist during the last few weeks. In a recent discussion with an ardent Bolshevik, he was told that the revolution will bring a few years of misery and chaos and then eternal peace and prosperity. 'I told him I believed the first half', Freud says.

When it comes to President Wilson, Freud is more serious. 'He should not have made all those promises', he insists. An awkward silence hangs between the two men.

AMERICA: For the next few weeks the White House will be wherever Woodrow is. He departs on a tour of America to sell the League of Nations to the country.

As befits a modern, American-style agitprop train, twenty journalists are invited along for the ride and, as the newspapers put it, 'five moving picture men'. (Colonel House, the President's adviser from Paris, with whom relations are now strained, is not invited.) If the Senate does not have the sense to ratify the treaty as he signed it, Woodrow believes, he must go directly to the people – as he did in Europe – so that they can put pressure on their representatives to do the right thing. Woodrow has faith in the people. All he asks is that they, and God, have faith in him.

Arriving in Ohio for his first big speech, Woodrow is already exhausted, his head aching, the blood pumping around his nerve-racked frame. 'The terms of the treaty are severe', he admits, 'but they are just.' No humiliation or retribution is sought. 'This treaty is an attempt to right the history of Europe', he declares: 'in my humble judgement, it is a measurable success.' It will not please everyone, of course. Some Italians think the Adriatic coast essential to their security. But why should Italians need to rule over Slavs for their security when the League will assure the security of all? 'If they were going to claim every place where there was a large Italian population', he jokes, 'we would have to cede New York.'

He talks about Silesia, and the role of referendums in making sure people get the government they want. He talks about a new deal for workers within the treaty's provisions: a 'Magna Carta of labor'. All this is necessary to make the world a safer place. 'Revolutions don't spring up overnight', he tells the businessmen of Ohio, but are born from the failure of governments to understand their people. The best antidote to Bolshevism is freedom, democracy and sound social protection. 'I used to be told that this was an age in which mind was monarch', Woodrow says in the most philosophical passage of his speech. Now we know better. The mind 'reigns, but does not govern'. Passion is what drives us. And this treaty represents the triumph of humanity's higher passions – for justice and civilisation – over its baser ones. It promises the elevation of the whole world to the higher plane that America already inhabits.

How, then, can America, a country of strong passions for what is right and just, reject it? 'The only country in the world that is trusted at the moment is the United States', Woodrow declares: it must not fail. In Kansas City, he appeals to the crowd's patriotism, urging the ratification of the treaty as the completion of what the soldiers fought and died for in France. 'The men who make this impossible or difficult', he snarls, 'will have a lifelong reckoning with the men who won the war'.

As Woodrow travels further west in his jolting, swelteringly hot train, an Old Testament tone enters his perorations. 'Do you not know that the whole world is all now one single whispering gallery?' he asks the crowd in Des Moines, Iowa, with all the evangelical fury of a preacher's son. 'All the impulses of mankind are thrown out upon the air and reach to the ends of the earth', the President warns. 'With the tongue of the wireless and the tongue of the telephone, the suggestions of disorder are spread through the world'. The treaty and the League will lead the world to its holy destiny: 'those distant heights upon which will shine at last the serene light of justice, suffusing a whole world with blissful peace'. The President's doctor watches anxiously from the sidelines. He urges more breaks, fewer speaking engagements, shorter speeches. He insists that the President not shake so many hands.

The tour is relentless, yet the President seems to relish it. As the train crosses the prairies from Omaha, Nebraska, to Sioux Falls, South Dakota, Woodrow and Edith sit out on the rear platform of the presidential train carriage and wave to the small farmers and ranchers who have come out to greet them. The speeches continue, day after day. At every station, the President's remarks are printed and distributed to the local newspapers, thus magnifying his audience a thousandfold and allowing him to hog the national limelight for weeks. (Henry Ford, the automobile manufacturer, peace advocate and former Democratic Senatorial candidate, provides the funding for this particular propaganda effort.) In the north-western states, old frontiersmen turn out to greet the President alongside Native American chiefs, forty years after the annexation of their lands to the United States. (Men younger than Woodrow died at Custer's Last Stand.) The President thinks he can feel the country turning his way.

Yet there is an unease in America which no amount of presidential glad-handing can overcome. This has been a year of riots and bombings. Warnings against Bolshevism run through the President's speeches. 'There are disciples of Lenin in our own midst', he tells one assembly, who long for nothing more than 'night, chaos and disorder'. Woodrow is in Montana when news arrives that police have gone on strike in Boston after the refusal of their request to affiliate with America's largest trades union. The city immediately descends into looting. 'Lenin and Trotsky are on their way', the *Wall Street Journal* shudders. Boston's entire police force is eventually fired, and Governor Coolidge becomes a national hero for putting the National Guard on the streets instead.

The news from Washington is no prettier. Giving evidence to a Senate inquiry, a disgruntled former diplomat causes a media storm by revealing the Secretary of State's private view of the treaty. 'If the American people could really understand', he is reported to have said in Paris, 'it would unquestionably be defeated.' A Senate committee recommends a long list of reservations and amendments. Both sides bait each other in speeches across the floor of the Capitol. Several Senators fan out across the country on their own anti-treaty tour, often speaking in the same cities that Woodrow has just visited and to crowds almost as large. The President's inflexibility on the treaty – demanding that it be ratified without anything more than interpretative reservations – makes negotiation impossible.

Passing west through the Rockies, Woodrow has difficulty breathing. (He has to sleep sitting up to prevent congestion, with pillows plumped up in a chair.) A long loop through the forests of Oregon and California provides an opportunity for rest. In San Diego, he makes one of his best speeches, standing in a glass box equipped with electric amplifiers to project his voice across a crowd of over thirty thousand. In Los Angeles, Edith and Woodrow even sleep in a hotel for once. But as they make their way back east into the mountains the President's headaches return, sometimes so powerful he can hardly see. In Salt Lake City, Wilson speaks to fifteen thousand in an unventilated hall (Edith Wilson dabs a handkerchief in lavender and has it taken to her husband to help him through the ordeal). His temper frays. In Wyoming a local paper reports a look of 'inexpressible weariness – the weariness of a nation' on his face.

Twenty miles outside Pueblo, Arizona, the President's doctor stops the train and Woodrow and Edith are sent on an evening stroll to get some fresh air (a farmer recognises the President and presents him with cabbages and apples for his supper). That evening, Wilson seems full of optimism. 'Now that the mists of this great question have cleared away', he tells his audience for that night, 'I believe that men will see the truth, eye to eye, and face to face.' America will rise to the challenge of peace as it rose to the challenge of war: 'We have accepted that truth, and we are going to be led by it, and it is going to lead us, and through us, the world, out into pastures of quietness and peace such as the world never dreamed of before.'

Late that night, Woodrow knocks timidly on Edith's door. He cannot sleep. His head is splitting. The doctor is called. The President's face twitches uncontrollably. He feels he is about to be sick. It is hours before he drifts off to sleep. The next morning, he dresses and shaves as usual. But something inside of him has gone, as if he were suddenly no longer himself, but another, lesser man; a mere mortal, rather than President of the United States. 'I just feel like I am going to pieces', he admits weakly. A talk in Wichita, Kansas, is cancelled. The railway lines to Washington DC are cleared.

A telegram is sent to both his daughters: 'Returning to Washington. Nothing to be alarmed about. Love from all of us. Woodrow Wilson'.

OMAHA, NEBRASKA – PHILLIPS COUNTY, ARKANSAS: A riot breaks out in Omaha the same day Woodrow returns to Washington. A black man accused of raping a white woman is pulled from jail by a mob of several thousand, shot, set on fire, and then dragged through the streets of the city. Soldiers have to restore order.

A few days later in Arkansas there are rumours of a radical-inspired revolt by black sharecroppers against white plantation owners. (In fact, the sharecroppers are simply trying to organise a union to get a better price for their cotton.) Whites are trucked in from Mississippi and Tennessee to teach the uppity workers a lesson. No one knows how many blacks are killed. Their bodies are dumped in the river.

Afterwards it is only blacks who are indicted, on charges of killing a white man. The trial is a farce. Black witnesses called for the prosecution are forced to provide false testimony. The defence offers no case: the lawyer does not meet his clients before the trial and calls no witnesses. Even the testimony of the defendants is not sought. Though a white mob surrounds the courthouse, threatening to lynch the black defendants unless they swing, no legal attempt is made to move the trial to safer and more neutral ground. A white jury decides the case in minutes. The blacks are sentenced to death.

NEW YORK: 'Once more the white man has outraged American civilization', Garvey writes. Lynching proves that America is no place for blacks. A fine and great democracy, but one built and run for whites. A race war is on its way – and blacks must organise, Garvey writes. America does not deserve their effort. It is Africa that must be redeemed, a splendid continent 'kept by God almighty for the Negro'.

In the meantime, Garvey tells his readers: 'let me remind all of you, fellow men, to do your duty to the Black Star Line Steamship Corporation'. The shares now cost five dollars each, he reports: 'and I now ask you to buy as many shares as you can and make money while the opportunity presents itself'. A ship has now been found and part purchased. A black captain has been hired (and receives a kickback from the vendors of the rusty hulk for his help in negotiating the inflated price of the vessel). The sum of fifty thousand dollars has been raised.

Not everyone is convinced by Marcus Garvey. In Chicago, a local community leader accuses him of being just the latest in a long line of foreign con men – Nigerians are said to be particularly blameworthy – who take the hard-earned money of black Americans and provide nothing in return. Du Bois warns his uncle not to invest. In New York, Garvey survives an assassination attempt by a disgruntled investor in an earlier UNIA enterprise.

MOSCOW – LONDON – PETROGRAD: A last line of defence is designated by the Bolsheviks and a huge area of European Russia placed under martial law. Though outnumbered two to one, the Whites soon breach the Red perimeter. Denikin's army races forwards. In London, Winston plays with the idea of going out to Moscow to help the Whites write a new Russian constitution. He feels an awesome sense of having been proven right.

In the Kremlin plans are made to move the seat of Bolshevik government from Moscow to the Urals. Cheka officials sift through their current hostage list – ten thousand names – and mark out who should be killed first. Trotsky and Stalin argue about the right military strategy to deflect the danger from Denikin's troops. Lenin receives anonymous letters threatening him with all kinds of horrible retribution when he falls.

Vladimir has no intention of letting that happen. He barely leaves his office during the day. When he cannot sleep in the middle of the night the impatient revolutionary phones his subordinates, to check that his orders in some vital matter have been obeyed. When things are really bad, he even stops going on his walks with Nadya. And he worries: what if the Finns were to decide to join the White offensive? What if the Poles throw their armies into the fray?

In the middle of October, while matters are reaching a climax outside Moscow, Yudenich's northern army launches towards Petrograd. The White general declares he stands for the eight-hour day and against the restoration of the Tsars. Within days his forces have reached Tsarskoye Selo. The British provide naval and air support. The prospect of an attack by British-made tanks terrifies Petrograd's Red defenders. Evacuation plans are prepared. The top Bolshevik in the city has a nervous breakdown. He retires to the sofa, as Trotsky crushingly puts it.

Lenin is ready to abandon Petrograd to its fate and focus instead on crushing Denikin. Trotsky gets him to change his mind. 'Very well, let us try', Vladimir says, at last. The war commissar is sent north. There, he finds chaos, panic, dissolution. Trotsky may not be much of a general, but this is a situation which requires bravura – and he has plenty of that. Tanks, Leon tells a troop of Red soldiers, are nothing but 'metal wagons of a special construction'. He laughs in the face of danger and encourages others to do the same.

To achieve his goal of destroying Yudenich's army Trotsky is prepared to consider every eventuality. He toys with the idea of letting the White army into Petrograd, and then turning the 'stone labyrinth' of streets into their mausoleum by flattening the whole city with powerful artillery. He accepts that such an approach would 'destroy a certain number of inhabitants, women and children'. But it would be effective. It is only on reflection that the war commissar is persuaded the cost in 'accidental victims and the destruction of cultural treasures' would be too high. He opts for a more classical course of action. Mounted on horseback, like Napoleon crossing the Alps, the Jewish farmer's son from Ukraine rallies the fleeing Red Army at the very gates of the city, persuading the troops to turn back against the enemy. The counter-attack succeeds. The Whites fall back in disarray.

By this time Denikin's advance on Moscow has ground to a halt. There is no popular upsurge to carry him on to victory as he had hoped. And the Bolshevik regime has not collapsed as expected. The White army of 1919 is well equipped and well led – but it is not the popular force the anti-Bolshevik rebel armies of 1918 seemed set to become and is far outnumbered by the Red Army. A long, slow retreat begins.

MANCHESTER, ENGLAND: A letter from Vienna arrives at 61 Bloom Street. Sam Freud, a local businessman, tears open the battered envelope. As expected, it is from Uncle Sigmund, the family success. 'Life is hard with us', Freud writes. 'I don't know what the English papers tell you – maybe they don't exaggerate.'

Much of what Sigmund writes, Sam already knows: that the Austrian crown is worthless these days and the city unable to feed itself. The railways that once connected Vienna to the rest of the world are now like the pathetic stumps of an amputee, cut clumsily by the bloody surgeons of Paris. A once-peaceful Continent seems perpetually torn between revolution and reaction. 'Which rabble is the worst?' Freud asks another correspondent. 'Surely the one just on top.'

But it is the news of family which affects Sam most. 'We are living on a small diet', he reads, 'the first herring some days ago was a treat to me. No meat.' Whoever can leave Austria has already left. 'My own family is dissolving rapidly', Freud writes. 'Ernst has got a job in Berlin in the Palestine settling business, Oli looks forward to an engagement in the Dutch colonial government, ready to go to the East Indies ... Anna will be the only child left to us.' Sam fingers a photograph sent with the letter. His uncle Sigmund looks sterner than he used to, he thinks.

'You know I have a big name and plenty of work', Freud writes, but never enough to make ends meet. (He does not mention Edward Bernays, his American nephew, who at that very moment is finishing off the translation of some of Freud's lectures for publication in America, in spite of a cable from Vienna countermanding the project.) Sigmund writes out a list of necessities which, if sent post-haste from Manchester, might make it through to Vienna unharmed: fat, corned beef, cocoa, tea and English teacakes ...

PRANGINS, LAKE GENEVA: Charles and Zita Habsburg take a different tack. In October, a pair of emerald bracelets and a ruby brooch are put up for sale. Later in the autumn, a set of emerald pieces earns the family a little over one million Swiss francs, enough to keep them in imperial style for a few more months at least.

WASHINGTON DC: For weeks, no one outside Woodrow's immediate family, his valet Brooks and the White House servants see the President. Edith allows no outside visitors. (An exception is made for the King of the Belgians, Woodrow's host from the battlefield tour in June.) The President's chief of staff is kept out. Even Colonel House is left to wonder what is going on. The first outsider to see Woodrow properly, a month after his return to the White House, is Attorney General Mitchell Palmer, currently leading a crackdown against a coal miners' strike he has declared to be as deadly as an invading army and probably Bolshevik-inspired.

Edith decides what correspondence reaches the President, and what is ignored. She is his gatekeeper, his avatar. Much of the daily work of presidential government – such as the appointment of ambassadors – simply grinds to a halt. The rest is left to cabinet secretaries to sort out as best they can. Some measures taken sail close to constitutional impropriety. In consultation with Woodrow's advisers, Edith goes so far as to deploy the presidential veto against a wide-ranging law on the enforcement of the Eighteenth Amendment, defining what 'intoxicating liquor' is to mean in practice and how prohibition is to be applied. Rabbis and priests, for example, are allowed to make sacramental wine, but not allowed to sell it to anyone other than other rabbis and priests; doctors may prescribe liquor, but must keep a list of the patients who have received it, for examination at any time. Edith's veto is overridden by Congress the same day. The clock to nationwide prohibition ticks down to 1920.

Woodrow's doctor is evasive about the President's condition. He laughs off suggestions of a cerebral lesion. 'Nervous exhaustion' is the preferred terminology. But the signs are there of a more serious illness. A draft of the President's annual Thanksgiving proclamation is returned without a single word altered – very unlike the President – and with a signature, scrawled in pencil, that is virtually illegible. Edith Wilson, people joke, has become America's first woman President.

The truth is that there is a power vacuum. Nature abhors such things. Ambitious politicians rather like them.

MUNICH: 'Are we citizens or are we dogs?' the mangy field-runner asks his audience. While keeping his day job as a member of the army's propaganda team, Adolf is making a name for himself as a rising star on Munich's far-right political scene and the newest member of the German Workers' Party.

His speeches rage at those in power. They tell a story of hopes dashed and dreams betrayed. Germany has been cheated, Adolf declares. Never in the whole history of the earth has such a shameful peace been signed. 'Instead of the understanding we hoped for, we have deceit', he says: 'instead of reconciliation, we have violence'. He shakes his fists and slices the air with his hand, copying the gestures he has picked up from other political orators. One student compares his technique to that of the playwright revolutionary Ernst Toller.

Adolf is connecting with his public and becoming the chief recruiting officer for the German Workers' Party. At the end of one of his speeches, the chairman of the meeting – the slick-haired Thule Society member Karl Harrer – urges the audience of students, soldiers and shopkeepers to bring three friends each to the next event. At another party meeting, the police note a new energy, with three hundred in the audience now. To keep up the momentum, a further Christmas meeting is planned, despite the ban on heating public rooms so as to conserve coal and wood through the winter.

The mangy field-runner finds that his talent as a speaker opens doors to people he would never have dreamed of talking to before. He latches on to the German translator of Ibsen's *Peer Gynt*, another Thule Society member, as someone who understands Hitler as he sees himself: as an artist.

LONDON: The teams that travelled to observe the eclipse in Brazil and Principe earlier in the year finally present their findings to the public. The Royal Astronomical Society is packed. A portrait of Isaac Newton hangs on one wall.

Rumours of the results have been circulating in the physics community for a few weeks now – Einstein and his colleagues have already exchanged celebratory poems. But it falls to Britain's Astronomer Royal, the successor to Newton – and a mild sceptic of relativity as a theory – to announce the results to the wider world. 'A very definite result has been obtained', he tells the gathering. The deflection of light shown by the Sobral and Principe expeditions corresponds – within reasonable bounds of error – to the values predicted by Einstein. The Astronomer Royal calls the result 'part of a whole continent of scientific ideas affecting the most fundamental principles of physics'. A sceptic present points to Newton's portrait and warns against accepting all of Einstein's ideas on the basis of a few photographs. His voice is soon drowned out.

For outside the room, a popular craze erupts. The rule of the absolutes has fallen, in science as in politics. 'Revolution in Science', runs the headline in *The Times*: 'New Theory of the Universe. Newtonian Ideas Overthrown.' Suddenly, everyone is grappling to understand Einstein's ideas – and their implications for everything else. For if time and space are not as straightforward as they seem, what else might prove to be just an illusion, a trick of the mind? People who have never given a thought to why up is up, and down is down, now find themselves perturbed – or invigorated. Occultists wonder if talk of an Einsteinian 'Fourth Dimension' holds, at last, the secret to telepathy or communication between the dead and the living. Painters and poets see relativity as the portal to a new world view where – of course – they can act as the true interpreters of a shattered reality. The bewildered public find relativity blaring at them alongside news of war and revolution across the world. The *New York Times* runs a gargantuan headline: 'Lights All Askew in the Heavens. Men of Science More or Less Agog Over Results of Eclipse Observations. Einstein Theory Triumphs. Stars Not Where They Seemed or Were Calculated to Be, but Nobody Need Worry'. What does it all mean?

In Berlin, Albert is besieged by well-wishers, many of them foreign. A scientist from Yorkshire writes asking for a signed photograph to add to his collection of Austrian, Hungarian and German scientists. Albert fields invitations to speak from around the world and the Prussian government jacks up his salary by fifty per cent to make sure he returns to Germany. He is asked to write popular articles about relativity for the masses. In *The Times* he illustrates relativity by joking that now that he is considered a success Germans claim him as a German and the British call him a Swiss Jew – but if he were ever to fall out of favour Germans would certainly refer to him as a Swiss Jew and the British as a German. Einstein complains to his friends that he can't get any work done these days, that his life is now just 'telegrams, ringing telephones, stacks of letters'. 'I can hardly breathe anymore', he complains to one correspondent.

Fame has arrived. And with it controversy. Some are uneasy at yet another success of German science so soon after the war. There are scientists who dislike the over-hasty elevation of a fellow scientist into a demigod. They demand more proof (and rather better photographs) before succumbing to the craze. Some wonder if relativity – and the rush with which it has been embraced – connects to some deeper strain of sickness in the world. 'For some years past,' an American professor writes, 'the entire world has been in a state of unrest, mental as well as physical'. Is it so far-fetched to imagine that all the symptoms of this unrest – war, Bolshevism, relativity, even jazz – are linked somehow? Perhaps they have a common psychological root, as if the whole world were suffering from the same neurosis.

For those who liked the world as it was – or as they imagined it was – Einstein is not a scientist so much as a sorcerer, a necromancer, a hypnotist of the masses. His theory must be squashed.

ACROSS THE UNITED STATES OF AMERICA: Mitchell Palmer sees his chance to act. Two years to the day since Lenin's coup in Petrograd, the Bureau of Investigation lashes out at Bolshevism – real or imagined – in the United States. The borders are sealed. The raids begin around nine in the evening.

In Detroit, agents surround a major theatre showing a Russian play. A Russian-speaker is sent in to announce to the audience that some of them will not be going home that evening. A pool hall popular with Russians is raided near Pittsburgh. Boarding houses are stormed in Bridgeport, Connecticut. The main hit is at the Russian People's House in New York where over two hundred are rounded up as members of the Union of Russian Workers, an organisation suspected of anti-American treachery (its constitution contains a line about socialistic revolution, making all foreign members liable for deportation). American citizens, who it would be illegal to hold without charge, are quickly released, as are those who do not appear in Hoover's card index. But by the following morning nearly forty others have been identified as worthy of deportation. They are marched to Battery Park and put on boats to Ellis Island. 'We're going back to Russia – that's a free country', one shouts. Some have black eyes. It is the history of the United States in reverse.

The press has a field day. The *New York Tribune* describes how a communist meeting in Yonkers was broken up by a priest leading his parishioners in singing the national anthem. 'Russian Plot Nipped in the Bud', shouts the *Wausau Daily Record* in Wisconsin. Days later, on Armistice Day, an American Legion march in the mining town of Centralia, Washington, is fired upon from a building belonging to the local chapter of a radical trades union. Four are killed. Rage against the Reds notches up another level.

America is fighting back, and it is Palmer, not Wilson, who is leading the crusade. The *Brooklyn Daily Eagle* runs a cartoon of Uncle Sam striding across the land, picking up tiny gesturing figures marked 'Reds' – one looks like Lenin, a worker's cap atop his head and a single hand raised in exhortation. The 'Reds' are placed in a sack marked 'Deportation'. But there is a particular detail to the cartoon. A few of the prisoners manage to escape the sack through a hole at its bottom marked 'Legal Technicalities'.

IRELAND: The Dáil is suppressed, and operates in the shadows. In the nationalist south and west, brigandage is rife. Military zones are declared. In County Clare, there are attacks on police posts, and ambushes on their patrols. Rifles and ammunition are stolen. In County Cork, attacks on post offices aim to disrupt police operations and steal their correspondence (armoured cars are used from now on).

The Royal Irish Constabulary, barely ten thousand strong, finds it hard to keep up its strength. Irish constables tread carefully or retire from fear, warned by their neighbours that they are now in danger of their lives should they be too zealous in their duties. In some rural parts, IRA volunteers patrol the lanes with impunity.

Once a week, Michael Collins visits Sinéad de Valera to hand over her husband's salary.

MILAN: Benito wins just five thousand votes in elections in Milan (out of some quarter of a million cast). Neither a victory, nor a defeat, he claims in public. In private, he is bitterly disappointed. The Socialists, the most popular party across the country, organise a mock funeral march for Benito, passing by the front door of his apartment building and terrifying his wife Rachele trapped inside.

Mussolini takes stock. He needs more money, he concludes. He needs to distinguish himself as a man who understands the politics of compromise, rather than just being perceived as a subspecies of the crazy liberators of Fiume or a has-been like Marinetti (or an ex-socialist, which is what he really is).

His profile is lifted when he is arrested for illegally hoarding weapons. But the government opts not to prosecute. It may need Mussolini in the future, and Italy already has enough martyrs.

LONDON – SIBERIA – MOSCOW: By December, even Winston is ready to accept the bitter truth. 'The last chances of saving the situation are passing away', he writes. 'Very soon there will be nothing left but Lenin and Trotsky, our vanished 100 millions, and mutual reproaches.'

Denikin's troops are in full flight from Moscow towards the south. In the east, along a single railway line, Admiral Kolchak, his army, and supporters and their families struggle to make good their own escape. Rebellions against his rule flare up along the way. White refugees freeze to death in railway carriages; others try to trudge through the Siberian winter on horse or foot. In Moscow, war commissar Trotsky is the hero of the hour.

At a ceremony in the Bolshoi he is awarded the Order of the Red Banner. To smooth things over between the two rivals, the Georgian bank-robber is given the same award. 'Can't you understand?' one old Bolshevik mutters to another. 'This is Lenin's idea – Stalin can't live unless he has what someone else has.'

WASHINGTON DC: The Senate is deadlocked on the treaty. Yet Woodrow does not answer his opponents' letters and will hear of no compromise. He will not see his treaty, his League, mutilated. He comes up with fantastic schemes to try and save it: challenging fifty-six Senators to stand for immediate re-election, as a kind of referendum on the treaty. When visitors come to see him he hides his paralysed left arm under the covers and arranges state papers by his bed in an attempt to show that his bedroom is a hive of government activity – before relapsing exhausted when they have gone.

AMERONGEN: Wilhelm reaches the twelve thousand mark in November. By early December his total stands at thirteen thousand logs. Some days the ex-Kaiser only breaks his labours for an occasional glass of port, or a rambling discussion with his adjutant about the state of Europe while sheltering from the rain in the children's playhouse. 'Aged and Melancholy, the War Lord in Exile', runs the headline in the *Dearborn Independent*, Henry Ford's newspaper, above a picture of Wilhelm in civilian clothes, snapped illicitly by a Dutch photographer. There are rumours that Wilhelm offered to buy the plates in order to have them smashed.

Wood-chopping seems the only thing to stop the ex-Kaiser from chain-smoking and fantasising about bloody revenge in his room. His wife, physically fragile, worries about the 'dark musings' her husband has become prone to. There are particular reasons for Wilhelm's mood. The newspapers have got hold of some of his marginalia on diplomatic reports going back to 1914 which make it look as if the Kaiser actively wanted war. Wilhelm's entourage worry about the effect on public opinion. The Dutch might hand him to the French and British after all.

Wilhelm's mind wanders freely over past, present and future. He talks extemporaneously to anyone within earshot about his pet subjects: the war, Germany's need for a strong *Führer*, the situation in Russia, or his grandmother, Queen Victoria. He tells Count Bentinck's daughter that the Queen died in *his* arms, and that it was a Union Jack from *his* yacht which lay on her coffin at her funeral, because her English family – how typical! – had forgotten to arrange it themselves.

Earlier that autumn the Kaiser explains to a bewildered guest how he has been fighting a shadow war with the Catholics and Jews all along, who have been conspiring to replace the Hohenzollerns with the Habsburgs. He goes on to explain that the parlous economic situation in Britain and France means Germany has won the war not lost it, and that all that is needed now is an alliance with Russia to finish the job. In the board-game of world politics, Wilhelm seems to have things sewn up in a trice. 'Japan I will attach to Russia in the east', he explains, 'and then we'll march together with Russia against England!' The French will eventually feel obliged to attack England too, the Kaiser insists. Such imperial fantasies leave his young guest quite shaken. Has Wilhelm always been this way?

Occasionally one of his sons drops by. Wilhelm takes little interest in them. He expresses positive disgust for August Wilhelm, whose wife has run off with one of the servants. He blames the moody temperament of Prince Joachim on Jewish influence. Indeed, he blames the Jews for his wife's illness too. In December, he writes to one of his most trusted generals to explain that it is the Jews who carry the responsibility for pretty much everything which has befallen him and his country. 'Let no German ever forget this, nor rest until these parasites have been destroyed and exterminated from German soil!' Wilhelm writes. He calls the Jews a 'poisonous mushroom on the German oak-tree'. He thirsts for revenge.

As the wet winter weather causes the Rhine to flood the meadows on his estate, Count Bentinck wonders whether the imperial couple might move temporarily to another house. Impossible, as the only option available would require the Kaiser and his wife to share a dressing room, which apparently they cannot do. In The Hague, some wish the waters of the Rhine would force Wilhelm out of Holland altogether. 'If, indeed, by some act of Providence, this self-invited and embarrassing guest could be sunk without a trace,' a diplomat reports, 'such a solution would be hailed with unmitigated relief.'

SAGUA LA GRANDE, CUBA – NEW YORK: After a journey which the ship's captain describes euphemistically as 'adventurous' – including running aground on a sandbank – the first Black Star Line vessel arrives in Cuba from New York. The captain blames saboteurs amongst the (mostly British) crew for problems along the way. 'The passengers', he writes, 'are behaving splendidly.'

'The Eternal has happened', Garvey tells his faithful readership. This is a moment to savour, a moment of regained self-confidence, the firing of the starter's gun in a struggle between the races. 'We black folks believe so much in the omnipotence of the white man that we actually gave in all hope and resigned ourselves to the positions of slaves and serfs for nearly five hundred years', he writes. 'But, thank God, a new day has dawned'. He beseeches his readers to 'steel their souls' for the revolution to come and buy as many shares in the Black Star Line as they can.

MODLIN, POLAND: Captain de Gaulle has one more course to teach. One hundred officers of the Polish army attend his lectures on how morale makes the difference between victory and defeat, and why France must stand by Poland to the end.

He prepares to leave before the spring. 'The Polish army will have been what I intended it to be for me: a military restoration', he tells his mother.

He has been awarded the Légion d'honneur for his bravery prior to his capture in 1916. The shame of being a prisoner of war has been erased.

Moscow: 'Our banking on the world revolution, if you can call it that, has on the whole been fully justified', the impatient revolutionary declares in his end-of-year report to an All-Russia Congress of Soviets. Nonetheless, 'from the point of view of the *speed* of its development we have endured an exceptionally difficult period', he admits. Developments have been, for want of a better word, full of 'zigzags'.

'I think we may say without exaggeration that our main difficulties are already behind us', Vladimir reassures the Soviet representatives. The Whites have been chased away like children. The foreigners have pulled out. Kiev is Red Kiev once again, and the Ukrainian nationalist leader has gone into exile. The imperialists have been caught out by their hypocrisy. They call themselves democrats but lock up opponents. They say they stand for the rights and freedoms of small nations, but try to bribe them to fight their wars. The workers are waking up to such tricks; they will not be duped by propaganda: 'the lie being spread about us is fizzling out'. In the frightened Western capitals they call the Bolsheviks terrorists, Vladimir snorts indignantly: 'We say terror was thrust upon us.' He quotes a Swedish newspaper suggesting Churchill had expected to be in Moscow by now: 'just try it, gentlemen!'

Life in Russia is hard. The population of the cities has collapsed. Those that remain eat in collective canteens to avoid starvation. Wooden fences are burned so the people can keep warm. But it won't be long now, the impatient revolutionary declares, before the Bolsheviks will be able to turn from fighting wars to building socialism. 'Comrades, the task which now confronts us is to transfer our war-time experience to the sphere of peaceful construction.'

It is already happening. Look around you, Vladimir exhorts: the workers' state is coming into existence, the old bureaucrats are being pushed out. Efforts are already being redirected to the struggle against cold and hunger, how to provide the people with grain and fuel. To allow peasants to sell their produce in the market, like before the war, is no solution: 'if you want free sale of grain in a ruined country, go back, try out Kolchak and Denikin!' No, the challenges now are organisation and distribution, keeping up socialist self-sacrifice, continuing the fight against plotters and saboteurs.

And then there is the battle against disease. The scourge of typhus must be subdued. 'Either the lice will defeat socialism', Vladimir thunders, 'or socialism will defeat the lice!'

KIRŞEHİR, OTTOMAN EMPIRE: Struggling west through mud and snow to reach Ankara, the hilltop city he has chosen as his new base of operations, Mustafa Kemal stops one night in the small town of Kırşehir.

He has carried all before him in the elections. The nationalists are triumphant. A new Ottoman parliament is to assemble in Istanbul, where patriotic demonstrations against foreign occupation are now gathering pace. After dinner, Kemal gives a campaign speech to the notables of Kırşehir. He quotes a few lines of poetry: 'The enemy has pressed his dagger to the breast of the motherland / Will no one arise to save his mother from her black fate?'

Kemal answers his question with a smile. Surely they can see that he is the saviour they have been waiting for.

MUNICH: Wearing black trousers, white shirt, black tie and an old jacket he bought years ago in Vienna, Adolf Hitler opens a meeting of the German Workers' Party in December.

Adolf is still fed and housed at the expense of the army, unable to stand on his own two feet. But now that he has found his calling as a speaker he is growing more confident in his own ideas. Anti-capitalism, German nationalism, a hatred of the Versailles Treaty, and a firm belief in German unity rather than Bavarian particularism still form the bedrock of his speeches, alongside popular anti-Semitism. Occasionally he allows himself to range more widely. In December, he talks expansively about how Britain's colonisation of India and the opium war with China expose the hypocrisy of the Great Powers and demonstrate the fundamental truth that legitimacy is ultimately derived from power, not the other way around. 'Is right possible without might?' Adolf asks. America does not wish to join the League of Nations because it believes itself too strong to need it. The strong do not want constraints on their action.

Hitler divides the world into two. There are temporary enemies with whom Germany may be drawn into occasional conflict but with whom a future alliance cannot be ruled out. Russia falls into this category. And then there are Germany's permanent and perpetual enemies, of which the most prominent are the British and Americans, who think only of money 'even if it is soaked in blood'. Adolf Hitler does not mention Bolshevism once.

International capitalism rather than international socialism is the chief focus of his anger.

VIENNA: As the year shivers towards its end Sigmund Freud is busy corresponding with his British and American nephews.

Sam has dutifully dispatched a food parcel from Manchester to Austria as requested. But nothing has yet arrived in Vienna. Perhaps the goods are lost in a railway siding somewhere, or making a feast for a hungry postmaster and his wife, or waiting unclaimed in an Austrian customs office. 'You seem not to be aware of the whole amount of governmental stupidity', Sam reads in the latest missive from his uncle. Permits are required for everything these days, Sigmund explains. Hopes for the parcel being recovered grow slighter with each passing day.

Around the same time, Sigmund finally hears back from his American nephew Edward, the publicity man. Edward blames strike conditions for his silence over the last few months. But he has good news: despite Sigmund's second thoughts about the whole business, the American translation of one of his books is now nearly ready. A first instalment of one hundred dollars is on its way. Edward suggests that a well-paid lecture tour could be arranged, as well: 'America would listen eagerly to what you would say.' Flattery, and money, he hopes, will soothe his uncle's nerves.

Edward even suggests that Freud write a public appeal for the American people to come to the aid of the suffering population of Austria, which would make his name better known in the United States. Freud politely declines the offer. 'I do not consider myself a person of public notoriety such as may be entitled to appeal to the American people on behalf of the Austrian people', he writes, 'and in my own country at least I am in the dark.'

Where is Freud's country now anyhow? Fear of revolution and civil war stalks the streets. The Habsburgs are banished. Prague and Budapest are now foreign capitals, where German is the dirty language of a defeated, humiliated power. Freud's homeland is no more. Even his thoughts about psychoanalysis tend to darkness. 'I have finished sowing', he writes gravely to a colleague. 'I shall not see the harvest.'

NEW YORK – RUSSIA: One cold morning in December the USAT *Burford*, an old naval ship from the Spanish–American War, slips past the Statue of Liberty into open water, carrying the first wave of foreign radicals deported from the United States away from American shores.

'This is the beginning of the end for the United States', shouts the famous anarchist Emma Goldman, as the ship pulls away. Another deportee's words are more menacing: 'we're coming back – and we'll get you.' On board, the passengers share out clothing with those who did not have time to pack before they were forced to leave. Someone strikes up a Russian folk song.

John Reed is already in Russia waiting for them, having worked his way across the Atlantic to Norway as a stoker under false papers and then making the last leg of his journey by sleigh and on foot.

In the Kremlin, the latest recipient of a personal copy of *Ten Days that Shook the World* is writing a note on the Russian language. It is being spoiled by too many foreign words, Lenin tells his colleagues. His attention has been drawn to the increasingly common use of *defekty* – meaning defect, fault, imperfection, shortcoming. He points out that Russian already has three <u>perfectly good</u> words for that.

1920

*Here was a new generation grown up to find all Gods dead,
all wars fought, all faiths in man shaken.*
F. Scott Fitzgerald

*The old family, in which the man was everything and the woman nothing,
the typical family where the woman had no will of her own, no time
of her own, no money of her own, is changing before our very eyes.*
Alexandra Kollontai

WINTER

Paris – Washington: The Great War is over.

The Versailles Treaty comes into effect. The League of Nations council meets for the first time in Paris, in the same room where Woodrow read his draft of the covenant a year ago. A new world order has begun. The American chair is empty, for now.

'It probably would be better if I'd died last fall', Woodrow Wilson tells his doctor. His reputation is under fire. A book by a British economist who was at Versailles, called John Maynard Keynes, describes Woodrow as a 'blind and deaf Don Quixote', tragicomically tilting at windmills, bamboozled by the French. Woodrow's advisers urge him to compromise to let the treaty pass the Senate. Wilson refuses.

Hamburg, Germany – Vienna: In northern Germany, influenza claims its latest victim: a young mother named Sophie Freud. Sigmund learns of Sophie's death the same afternoon, in Vienna. 'We had been worried about her for two days', he writes to an old friend, 'but were still hopeful. From a distance it is so difficult to judge'. It is not possible for Sigmund to travel to his daughter's funeral. There are no available trains. 'The undisguised brutality of our times weighs heavily upon us'.

In the depths of melancholy Freud finds, at last, a new word – *Todestrieb*, or death-drive – to describe the fantastical idea growing in his mind: that there is in life an instinct not only to seek pleasure, but also for self-destruction. Death now takes its rightful place alongside sex in Freud's model of the mind.

America: By midnight on the second day of the year, over two and a half thousand have been arrested in anti-radical raids across America. Mitchell Palmer is said to be considering a run for President in 1920.

No community, large or small, is untouched. Eighteen are arrested in Oakland, six in Denver and twenty in Portland, Oregon. In New York the total stands at seven hundred. In Los Angeles, a thirty-three-year-old Lithuanian machine worker named Benjamin Ling is hauled in, accused of being the organiser of a local Communist cell. A search of his apartment turns up revolutionary song books, in Spanish. A newspaper in Utah applauds the 'Greatest Raid in History of U.S.; Tons of Literature Taken will Prove Guilt of 4,500 Anarchists'.

But the initial impression of efficiency and organisation soon frays. There are not enough warrants for those detained. Nor are there enough police to separate the Americans from the rest, meaning that US citizens are held without charge for days. In Boston, prisoners are herded into unheated cells. In Chicago, a group of Italians protest that the only reason they joined the Communists was to play music and learn English. (Their story is confirmed when the minutes of the local party's meetings are finally translated – but by then the Italians have been incarcerated for several weeks.)

The public mood begins to shift. 'There is a danger in the dragnet methods of rounding up alleged revolutionists', the *Chicago Daily News* editorialises. 'Not every radical is a "red" and not every "red" is a criminal anarchist, bomb manufacturer or advocate of physical force.'

MUNICH: The sports journalist has been pushed out of the party leadership. A man called Drexler is now its chairman. Hitler increasingly sees the party as his.

In January, he speaks at a huge event convened by a number of different right-wing organisations in Munich's largest beer hall on the Jewish question. It is an opportunity for Adolf to fly the flag of the German Workers' Party. 'We fight against the Jew', he says, 'because he stands in the way of the struggle against capitalism.' A few days later, he calls the Versailles Treaty nothing more than the tool of capitalists to keep the workers down, enslaved by taxes and interest. 'Every drop of our sweat flows not for us but for enemies', he declares. But this cannot last: 'The day will come when the eyes of the workers will be opened and their leaders will go to hell.'

Adolf begins to sketch out ideas for a manifesto, to lead Germany out of darkness and into the light. He found a party last year. Now he has found a mission.

Sunderland, England – The Urals – Irkutsk, Siberia: 'Was there ever a more awful spectacle in the whole history of the world than is unfolded by the agony of Russia?' Winston asks a rally in the north of England. Europe's grain factory is now starving. Wolves roam through Russian villages: 'and this is progress, this is hope, this is Utopia!'

En route to the Urals to spread his latest idea – the militarisation of the labour force; compulsory work in the service of building socialism – Trotsky's train is derailed in a snowstorm. The train is left in the snow for a whole day. No one comes to help.

In Irkutsk, in Siberia, Admiral Kolchak is betrayed, arrested and interrogated. He is not put on trial. Execution by firing squad. His body is shoved through the ice in a Siberian river.

The United States of America: Nationwide prohibition comes into effect.

New York's saloon bars shut their doors just after midnight. Liquor stores are emptied in a last rush to beat the cut-off. Protestant churches across the country hold prayer meetings to celebrate. In rural areas, and in states where the sale of alcohol has been banned for years already, there is particular jubilation at the thought of big-city types finally brought to heel by this latest triumph in the morality crusade.

Off the east coast boats piled high with liquor depart for the Bahamas and Cuba to avoid the risk of their cargo being impounded on American soil. One of these is the Black Star Line's only vessel, the *Yarmouth* – though it heaves and rolls so much in a storm that five hundred cases of whiskey have to be unceremoniously dumped overboard before the ship has even reached the high seas.

In Chicago, the first major crime of the prohibition era is committed that very night when one hundred thousand dollars' worth of whiskey is stolen from a freight-yard where the now-illicit substance was being stored. Crime and alcohol have always gone together in America. Prohibition simply raises the stakes.

Berlin: Enver Pasha, the dynamo of the triumvirate which ruled the Ottoman Empire during the war, resurfaces in the German capital. A lady calls on a British military officer late one evening with a message from a Monsieur Enver, asking if he is able to meet at an undisclosed location on the morrow. The British officer is duly taken to an address in Grunewald, on the western side of the city. 'He fully understood my surprise,' the officer writes of Enver, 'firstly at his being in Germany at all and secondly at his wanting to get in touch with the British government.'

Enver, sentenced to death in Istanbul last year, explains that he is a simple patriot and that as such he is prepared to deal even with the English to try and save his country. He proposes a long-term alliance, in return for only limited border adjustments for Turkey. (It is at this moment that both men realise neither of them has a map.) Of course, his old political party would have to be resurrected, allowing him to regain power.

He tells the British officer that the Italians and French are also keen to make some kind of deal with him if London will not, and helpfully points out that he has recently returned from discussions in Moscow. He asks that his proposition be put directly to the one man he considers to have the kind of wild imagination required to see the brilliance of such an alliance: Winston Churchill.

London declines the offer. At a subsequent meeting the following week Enver offers a fresh incentive: to use his influence to douse the problems the British are having amongst the Muslim populations of Egypt, the Middle East, India and Central Asia, turning his wartime advocacy of anti-British *jihad* on its head. The British will have no trouble pacifying Afghanistan with him on board, Enver says. He suggests that an independent Turkestan stretching from the Caspian to the Himalayas is created as a buffer between Russia and British India.

Enver avers that the new strongman of Anatolia, Mustafa Kemal, will work under him 'as a sergeant' if needed. The British officer is impressed by his chutzpah. 'The fact that he led Turkey into a disastrous war, that he should presumably be a discredited man in consequence, that he has been condemned to death and is a fugitive in hiding does not cause him the slightest misgiving as to his influence and power'.

Moscow: The impatient revolutionary's approach to solving administrative problems – pester, prod, cajole, check, double-check – remains the same. In January, he finds himself looking through the Russian dictionary and deciding it is out of date. 'Is it not time to produce a dictionary of the real Russian language', he wonders: 'a dictionary, say, of words used nowadays and by the classics, from Pushkin to Gorky?' He suggests thirty scholars be put on to it, with generous soldiers' rations as the ultimate incentive.

Vladimir is increasingly frustrated by red tape and corruption. The thought that he himself might be part of the problem does not cross his mind. The

Kremlin is a Bolshevik village these days. The Communist Party is like one big and rather unhappy family, with Vladimir Ilyich as its slightly autocratic father: indulgent to those closest to him, but a man who, in the end, expects to be obeyed. Those closest to the leader enjoy the benefits of his position. Vladimir's brother regularly visits to go on hunting trips or joins Lenin down in Gorki, where the two men play skittles together. His younger sister lives in the Ulyanovs' apartment. Inessa is given a place nearby, connected by special telephone to the closed-circuit Kremlin system (once, her daughter Varya impresses her friends by calling up Lenin directly). In time, both Stalin and Trotsky will be given country houses outside Moscow; Stalin's is a Gothic dacha, Trotsky's a palace. The Kremlin elite enjoy special privileges. The administration's chief inspector is none other than Comrade Stalin.

Naturally, jobs are handed out on the basis of loyalty, party service, personal connection. This is only logical: loyalty to the revolution should be rewarded and party members are surely more trustworthy than others. Older party members, those who were Bolsheviks when the movement was little more than a sect, are considered particularly worthy. Stalin's wife is one of Lenin's secretarial staff: a useful way for the Georgian bank-robber to keep tabs on the boss. The Commissariat of Enlightenment, responsible for education and culture, employs half the wives of the Bolshevik top brass, including Trotsky's wife Natalya (museums and ancient monuments department), Vladimir's sister Anna and his wife Nadya (in charge of deciding what books to remove from Soviet libraries).

Opportunities for favouritism run right through the system from top to bottom. In February, Vladimir wants his wife's nephew be accepted onto a course for naval commanders. 'The answer should come to me', the impatient revolutionary writes to the appropriate department overbearingly. 'If there are any obstacles what are they?'

NEW YORK: A few weeks after prohibition comes into effect a novel named *This Side of Paradise* is published, granting its author instant fame as the fashionable interpreter of the sexual mores and alcoholic indulgence of America's upper crust – the kind that small-town folk despise and envy at the same time. Both the author and his wife come from smallish American cities themselves (his blue-blooded friends think her a trifle tacky when they first meet). F. Scott and Zelda now set out to live the big-city life as fully as possible, whirling their way through prohibition's party scene in New York. There will always be whiskey for those who can pay.

Moscow: Inessa Armand is ill. Vladimir wants to speak to her on the telephone he arranged to have installed for her, but it is out of order. The impatient revolutionary pesters her to see a doctor. 'Please write me what is the matter', he orders. 'The times are bad: typhus, influenza, Spanish flu, cholera.' A few hours later, he checks to see whether the doctor has been. She must tell her children – 'from me' – to not let her leave the house.

When Inessa does not immediately recover, Vladimir insists that Varya call him every day between the hours of twelve and four with an update on her mother's situation. Does she have wood? Who is making the fire for her? Does she even have food? The shortages in Moscow are still bad. Has her telephone been fixed yet? 'You are evading my questions', Vladimir writes to Inessa. 'Answer immediately on this sheet, answer *all my points*'.

Berlin: 'Since the light deflection result became public', Einstein writes to a friend, 'such a cult has been made out of me that I feel like a pagan idol'.

Einstein's handsome mug graces magazine covers. 'A New Great Man of World History', runs the caption under one in Germany. A Prague philosopher becomes so obsessed with relativity that he talks about it non-stop in his sleep, waking up his wife and turning both into virulent anti-relativists. Albert receives petitions from all over, asking him to lend his prestige to new campaigns for international friendship, on the future of European libraries or for German food relief. Men of the cloth ask for Einstein's guidance on the impact of relativity on religion. (Fed up of such pseudo-philosophical nonsense, he curtly tells the Archbishop of Canterbury that the two are separate domains, one of facts and the other of belief.) Inevitably, a journalist from the *Daily Mail* eventually gets around to asking Einstein's view on extraterrestrial life. Albert pronounces it quite likely, suggesting that if the aliens did want to get in touch, they would use the medium of light, rather than the wireless, to do so. A fund is set up to raise money for an Albert Einstein Tower, a new observatory outside Berlin. In Russia, the Futurist poet Vladimir Mayakovsky engages in serious-minded conversations about the meaning of it all. Einstein is everywhere. He is a gift to the media: friendly, not bad-looking, a touch eccentric, quotable.

As befits a modern celebrity, Albert is increasingly asked about his views on current affairs. His well-attested internationalism and pacifism make him suspect to many Germans, though he is at pains to point out to interviewers that he is neither the Bolshevik nor the anarchist some make him out to be.

To his friends Albert is more candid, confessing: 'the Bolsheviks are not so unappealing to me, however funny their theories are', expressing admiration for the effectiveness of their publicity machine, and rather wishing he could go to Russia to look at the Soviet system up close. Shocked at the rise of anti-Semitism, Einstein feels himself increasingly Jewish, and called upon to defend his people in public. For the first time in his life, he expresses strong public support for the Zionist cause. He accuses old-fashioned assimilationists – *Kaiserjuden*, or Kaiser-Jews, such as Fritz Haber or Walther Rathenau, the industrialist – of being both naive and selfish, concerned more about their position in Western European societies than with welcoming in their poor brethren from the East. As in almost every year since 1910, Einstein is nominated for the Nobel Prize. If Haber can get one, why not him? Will 1920 be his year? (Not yet – the anti-relativists scupper it.)

In January, there is uproar at the university when hundreds of people swarm in off the street to see this Einstein for themselves. The crowd is broken up by students crying abuse at the uninvited masses. Some blame nationalist anti-Semites for trying to disturb the lectures of the most famous Jew in Germany. Others blame Einstein himself for the uproar, claiming he more or less invited the crowds to occupy the university. They accuse him of being a self-publicist looking for a little *succès de scandale* to keep his name in the headlines and distract from the hollowness of his theories. The more famous Einstein becomes, the more some people seem to hate him for it.

Around the same time, a first German edition of *The Protocols of the Elders of Zion* is published in Berlin, complete with a picture of one of Kaiser Wilhelm's illustrious forebears on the inside cover, and a line expressing the hope that one day a saviour may arise from the bones of the dead to avenge the evil calumnies of the present. The introduction reads like a breathless true-life spy story, recounting how the top-secret *Protocols* fell originally into the hands of the Russians, and then made their way to Germany, despite attempts to suppress and denounce them along the way. The Jews are blamed for starting the war. The book immediately becomes popular in nationalist circles. The poison is spreading.

PETROGRAD: Having secured Moscow's blessing for the newly created United Communist Party of America, John Reed is to return home. To disguise himself, he grows a moustache. The Comintern provides one hundred and two small diamonds to take as a nest-egg for the new, merged party. Jack travels once more under the assumed identity of stoker Jim Gormley, making his exit with letters from the *Burford* deportees in his pocket and a personal endorsement of *Ten Days that Shook the World* from Lenin. He is only halfway to the Baltic before he is forced to turn back. War intervenes.

THURLES, CO. TIPPERARY, IRELAND: A policeman is shot on his way home. The town in which he died is smashed up by security forces in reprisal. 'It is clearly established that four hand grenades were thrown into houses,' the *Manchester Guardian* reports, 'fortunately with no more effect than the destruction of glass and furniture'. The offices of a local Sinn Féin-supporting newspaper are particularly targeted.

A new vocabulary of violence emerges: of outrages and retaliation, each side calling the other terrorists, each side blaming the other for the disorder and for the growing number of the dead. Every attack is claimed as a counter-attack. No end and no beginning. Not quite war, but certainly not peace. Newly elected Irish councils – Sinn Féin wins even in parts of the north – announce that they recognise only the legitimate authority of the Dáil.

In America, de Valera's combination of sanctimony and deviousness has begun to test the patience of his hosts. The man takes on airs of such unconscionable grandeur, as if he were the mediator between an Irish God and the people of the world. In his own letters he refers to himself increasingly as 'we', not 'I'. He seems to think himself infallible. Irish-American leaders chafe under his presidential pomposity, his inflexibility, his presumption that he should be able to simply commandeer their organisations for his purposes, however obscure. They worry that his attempts to meddle in domestic American politics, calling upon Irish-Americans to only vote for candidates he endorses, may bring into question where the first loyalties of Irish-Americans lie. They start plotting ways to get him to leave.

PARIS: Let the klaxons sound! At long last, here he is. Having finally given up on Zurich, Tristan Tzara, Dada's great instigator-in-chief, steps off his train at the Gare de l'Est and looks around him at the French capital. A disappointment, he sniffs. What is to be done?

At first, the feeling in Paris is mutual. Having read Tzara's manifesto Breton and the others have imagined the Romanian prankster as not just a great writer but also as a magnetic physical presence, rippling with taut Dadaist energy, and with a commanding voice to match. In fact, when a small, short-sighted man with the complexion of candle wax turns up unannounced at the apartment of Francis Picabia – a senior member of the

Breton gang – the first reaction of the nanny who opens the door is to shoo this strange unhealthy-looking man away, as one might a suspected carrier of the flu or a travelling underwear salesman.

When the lady of the house comes to the door to see what is going on, Germaine Picabia tries to make the Romanian from Zurich understand that the apartment is quite full already: she has just had a baby and Francis has to sleep in the living room. But Tzara is not so easily put off. He cites a year-old invitation to Paris from Francis. He declines Germaine's offer to book him a room in a hotel. He has no money, he explains.

Soon Tzara is merrily unpacking his bags in the Picabias' rococo living room, emptying an arsenal of Dadaist publicity materials (and a large type-writer) onto their piano and Louis XV console. 'These things are too important for you to touch!' he hisses at the maid when she tries to help. Dada has arrived in Paris. It rather looks as if he intends to stay. Within days Tzara is cooing at the baby, proprietorially carrying him around in his arms and trying to teach him his first word: 'Dada', of course.

Tzara's arrival at this particular juncture is fortuitous. Breton and his group are planning a poetry reading in a few days as a way of giving *Littérature* a much-needed boost. But they need help to make the whole thing go off with a bang. Tzara looks at the plans for the event and thinks the Paris group are being far too timid. If they want the public's attention they have to do more than get a few well-meaning modernist poets to read out their latest work. They must provoke. It is the oldest avant-garde technique in the book, but provocation works. Tzara explains the stagecraft of Zurich Dada and demonstrates a few basic tricks of the trade: reciting several poems at once, whistling and shrieking at random, and so forth. The earnest young Parisians take notes. A rather more daring programme starts to take shape.

The audience that turns up at the Palais des Fêtes is larger than expected. Some have been lured there under false pretences: a public notice of the event advertises a lecture on France's present exchange-rate crisis, attracting the merchant community that works nearby. Others are drawn by the promise of good poetry, the presentation of some of the latest artists, and perhaps a little good-natured buffoonery. The presence of Tristan Tzara is kept secret.

At first, the show falls rather flat. Attempts at provoking the audience only serve to cause mild amusement. It is not long before spectators start to leave, asking for their money back at the door. A few heckles are raised in response to a couple of paintings which poke fun at the audience. But the whole thing is far from riotous. It hardly qualifies as Dadaist spectacle. Breton's own performance is not helped by him having a cold – and an attack of stage fright. By the time the musical interlude comes around, the whole thing looks like a failure.

But the second half goes better. First, Louis Aragon begins by declaiming a poem by Tristan Tzara, and, irritated at the poem's complete nonsense, the audience begins to stir. 'Good morning without a cigarette tzantzantza ganga', Aragon pronounces, 'boozdooc zdooc nfoonfa mbaah nfoonfa.' A few shout at him to get off stage. Aragon persists. At the end of the recital, there is a dramatic announcement: the poem's author will now appear in person. A ripple of expectation runs through the auditorium.

With the audience thus fired up, the surprise guest from Zurich finally makes his entry. Tristan Tzara walks on stage reading out loud a speech by Léon Daudet, a nationalist French politician and the founder of *Action française*, the kind of monarchist magazine one might easily finding lying around the de Gaulle family house, full of speculation on foreign plots to take over France. For some, this is too much. It is not just the speech to which they object. It is Tzara's delivery, too: murdering the French language with his thick Romanian accent. This is not literature, this is a mockery of literature. To top it all, Breton and Aragon start energetically ringing two bells they found that morning, filling the hall with ear-splitting cacophony.

Finally, the audience's patience breaks. 'Back to Zurich! Shoot him!' someone shouts. Breton and the others are pleased. It's a start.

FIUME: Tzara would fit right in here. The atmosphere in Fiume grows more piratical with each month that D'Annunzio is in charge. The city becomes a haven for chancers and thrill-seekers.

De Valera's Irish nationalists and Béla Kun's Hungarian Bolsheviks all think of visiting, hoping to find moral support or a stockpile of weaponry. Berlin Dada telegrams support. A Belgian poet sets up the League of Fiume, an anti-imperialist answer to the League of Nations. All the oppressed peoples of the world – from Catalans in Spain and Chinese labourers in California to Flemings in Belgium – will find a ready ally in Gabriele, it is claimed. There is even talk of a link-up with Moscow. A vibrant counter-culture is taking hold.

Rome tries hopelessly to rein in its former poet-propagandist. The longer Fiume is occupied by Italian irregulars, the greater the risk that the Yugoslavs decide to invade, possibly with French or British backing. But Gabriele is having too much of a good time playing the Renaissance despot to care very much about anything else. He orders Italian flags to be stitched with his personal slogan: *No me frego* – I don't give a damn. Rather than worrying about invasion, his court is full of wild schemes to actually foment civil war in Yugoslavia.

On the ground, the line between loyalist Italian army units outside the city and nationalist legionnaires within is blurred. On Valentine's Day the army holds a dance in the Quarnero Hotel, up the road in Abbazia. In contravention of the rules of the blockade, a special steamer service is laid on to carry D'Annunzio's gang there and back. A few days later a fancy-dress ball is held in Fiume in return. Army officers stream in by motorboat and automobile.

And why wouldn't they take the opportunity for a bit of fun? Fiume is, after all, a hedonist's delight. Orgies are common. Cocaine is abundant (Gabriele is said to be addicted). The patisseries are excellent. The wine flows freely. When D'Annunzio is not leading his favourite legionnaires on a mountain hike or haranguing the crowds with his latest speech, or seducing one of his female acolytes, he is to be found getting drunk in his favourite restaurant, the Golden Platypus. The name is the idea of Guido Keller, D'Annunzio's equally colourful deputy, a daring aviator with a penchant for public nudity which saw him arrested for indecent exposure several times before the war.

None of this is cheap. Ships in the Adriatic are raided and redirected towards Fiume to provide a source of income for the rebels. No crackpot moneymaking scheme is too wild. An aeroplane is sent to Paris with a cargo of contraband postage stamps to be sold on the black market. A tablecloth with a large ink stain said to have been the accidental result of one of Gabriele's literary effusions is put up for sale for one thousand lire. Kidnapping becomes an accepted way of raising money. D'Annunzio once orders Guido Keller's pet eagle to be briefly seized to make a more playful point about who is in charge.

Despite the perennial marches and speeches, popular support for D'Annunzio in Fiume fades as it becomes clear that the poet has no intention of reaching a reasonable deal with Rome to secure the city's future. He wants to stay in charge in Fiume until there is a wholesale change of regime in Italy. For him, the city is just a springboard, a bargaining chip. In the meantime, living conditions in Fiume deteriorate. Counterfeit money floods in. Honest trade virtually shuts down. In a patriotic gesture, Italian industrialists are persuaded to buy the city's shipyards to try and keep some activity going, but it is a hopeless task when no one knows what will happen even a week from now. In the meantime, the pleasure-seeking continues. A special hospital is set up for legionnaires whose sexual escapades have landed them with venereal disease.

In late February, hundreds of children are evacuated to Milan to be taken care of by ladies associated with Mussolini's Fasci di Combattimento. D'Annunzio turns their departure into a public-relations triumph, claiming that the children's forced departure shows the inhumanity of the Italian government's blockade.

VIENNA: At last some good news on the home front. After three months, Sam's parcels from Manchester have begun to arrive in Austria. A lifeline has opened up. On receiving one of the packages Anna Freud immediately writes a thank-you note. 'It needed all my good bringing up', she confesses in her somewhat German English, 'not to eat all the good chocolates on the spot.'

She requests a small amount of sugar for the future, if possible. Her father Sigmund is bolder. 'Dear Sam,' he writes at the end of February, 'I beg you to choose for me a soft Shetland cloth – pepper and salt, or mouse-grey or *tête de nègre* in colour, in sufficient quantity for a suit.'

MUNICH: It is a big risk for a party which used to fit all its followers in the back room of one of Munich's lesser restaurants. But one evening in late February, the German Workers' Party hires out the whole first floor of the Hofbräuhaus – big enough for a couple of thousand braying beer-swillers – for the launch of a manifesto cooked up over the last few weeks between Hitler, one of the lecturers from the political education course he took last year, his new father figure Dietrich Eckart (the *Peer Gynt* man), and Drexler, the party chairman.

Posters advertising the meeting are plastered up all over town, printed in red so as to grab the public's attention (and to annoy socialists who think they have a monopoly on the colour). They make no mention of the German Workers' Party and name only one speaker, a populist rabble-rouser called Johannes Dingfelder. Dingfelder's name will attract a good crowd. If a few hecklers come along, no harm done. As any avant-gardist knows, hecklers are good for a group trying to make a splash.

Only once Dingfelder has finished does Adolf stand to read out the party's new manifesto. He is met with cries of 'Get out!' by a few hecklers in one corner. The disturbance makes it hard for the rest of the audience to hear what the figure at the front of the room is saying, his forelock swinging up and down, his hand sawing, his little moustache neatly trimmed. From a distance, he looks like Charlie Chaplin.

Rather like Benito's manifesto in Milan last year, Adolf's twenty-five points veer between radical nationalism – all Germans must be united in a single country, Versailles must be revoked, Jews must be forbidden from German citizenship, only German newspapers are to be allowed – and a radical communitarian socialism. The public interest is to be put before any individual interest. Unearned income is to be banned (with the death penalty for those who lend money at interest) and war profits are to be confiscated. In the future, large companies will be required to share their profits with their workers. The pension system is to be overhauled to give workers greater security. Access to education will be improved for the poorest and public health boosted by mass calisthenics, as suggested by Marinetti in Italy.

The main newspapers barely report the party's manifesto. The day after Hitler's speech, even the Thule Society's newspaper has more important front-page news. Under the headline 'A Secret Jewish Document' it excitedly reviews a new German translation of the *Protocols*.

PARIS: After the moderate success of Dada's first Paris outing, planning gets under way for something more spectacular. At Tzara's instigation the story is spread – with the help of a couple of gullible newspaper journalists – that Charlie Chaplin himself will be speaking at this latest event, and that both Gabriele D'Annunzio and the Prince of Monaco have officially converted to Dadaism. It is nonsense, of course, but then what else is there these days?

It is not long before Breton and others start to have doubts. Where is this all leading? Who will have the last laugh? It is no surprise that *Action française* should pronounce Dada an 'inconsistent farce' produced by a bunch of spoiled children, inspired by a foreign German and Jewish culture. But it hurts when André Gide declares Dada a spent force: 'With this single word "Dada" they have expressed in one go everything they had to say.'

Breton begins to worry that all these Dadaist events are turning the group into little more than a troupe of music-hall entertainers. Tzara thinks André should lighten up. When Tzara receives a nasty anonymous letter written in the style of an insider, everyone is immediately put under suspicion of being a closet saboteur (something Tzara rather delights in).

Inevitably, *esprit de corps* suffers.

THE HAGUE: Informal discussions about what to do with the Kaiser continue. Some suggest his internment on the Dutch colonial islands of Java or Curaçao. But nothing comes of it. In the end the Dutch persuade the Kaiser to provide an undertaking to at least not leave the province of Utrecht without permission and to steer clear of politics.

Wilhelm explains to his aides that the coming months are bound to bring a turn of events in his favour. The Bolsheviks will invade Poland, Versailles will be smashed, and a new world order will take shape based on the defence of Europe against the barbarian hordes from Russia. Germany will need an experienced leader. Him.

NEW YORK: Marcus Garvey provides his latest update to UNIA members and Black Star Line shareholders on the progress of the *Yarmouth*. After the travails of January, the ship is now back in Havana, Cuba, he says, where more shares in the company are being sold and the ship's cargo is being unloaded as planned. In fact, various problems mean the unloading is delayed by a month, and the company's profit on the first leg of the trip reduced to nil.

A tone of injured pride runs through this meeting. Marcus Garvey and his organisation have come in for criticism: some black leaders think him too radical, too ambitious. Garvey accuses them of wanting an easy life. They seek approval from whites, rather than doing what it takes to reclaim their future for themselves. They talk; the UNIA acts. Without naming names – William Du Bois cannot be far from many people's minds – Garvey's warm-up speaker at the meeting notes that 'the New Negro is getting tired of the doubting Thomases and the pessimists'. All leaders of new movements from Jesus Christ to Abraham Lincoln have had to face down their critics before being recognised in the end for the greatness of their ideas.

Garvey defends his mission to take control of black people's future everywhere, pointing to what Zionists are doing for the Jewish people and Irish campaigners are doing for the cause of Irish freedom. What counts, he says, is results. 'Nine months ago, the UNIA did not have one nickel', he tells his followers. 'Today the UNIA is the richest Negro organization in the United States of America.' He provides the address of the association's bank in case anyone wants to check.

TORONTO, CANADA: A new face at the newspaper: a young man who claims to have seen action in Italy and to have worked as a journalist before.

Ernest gets the job at the *Toronto Star Weekly* through the most unlikely twist of fate. Among the audience at a war talk Ernest gave in Petoskey last autumn was the wife of a wealthy Canadian with publishing connections, Harriet Connable. By January, Ernest has moved to Toronto, going skating with the Connables' daughter Dorothy (to whom he presents a book by D'Annunzio) and spending time with the Connable boy, for whom he has been hired as a companion. By February, he is writing for the *Star*, earning the 'shekels' he needs to finance another summer by the lake, or else get him the train fare to San Francisco from whence he can work his way to Yokohama as a deckhand. His first signed article for the *Star* is about getting a free shave at the barber's college. Others follow, somewhat irregularly, mostly about boxing and trout-fishing.

In March, he writes an article rather closer to the bone, aimed at those Canadian slackers who dodged the draft during the war by taking well-paid work in the United States. Hemingway has advice for such men, who made a quick buck while others died, and who now want to pass themselves off as having done their bit. Buy a threadbare trench coat and worn-out shoes to look the part of the true war vet. Learn a few army songs to whistle absent-mindedly on the tram, as if remembering the good old days spent knee deep in mud. Buy a good history of the war, so you know what happened at Ypres better than those who were actually there. 'If anyone at the office addresses you as "major",' he suggests, 'wave your hand, smile deprecatingly, and say "No; not quite major".' This should do the trick: 'After that you will be known to the office as Captain.'

'Go to your room alone at night', Hemingway advises any draft dodgers amongst his readers, 'stand in front of your mirror and look yourself in the eye and remember that there are fifty-six thousand Canadians dead in France and Flanders. Then turn out the light and go to bed.'

ST. LOUIS: A failed marriage behind her and fed up with her job at the Old Chauffeur's Club, Josephine decides to try her luck singing and dancing. She falls in with the Jones Family Band, a local outfit that make their money playing restaurants around the city.

One day, a touring troupe called the Dixie Steppers arrive in town for a week's engagement at the Booker T. Washington Theater. Word gets around they are on the lookout for local talent to incorporate into their show. Josephine adds two years to her age to get an audition, saying she is fifteen, which is barely believable. But she impresses the manager so much he decides to give the girl with the funny smile a role in a short skit as part of the entertainment. Josephine is to play Cupid.

The role does not work out quite as intended. Her entrance is dramatic. But it soon goes wrong. Josephine, suspended from the ceiling on a rope and pulley, wearing pink tights and two little wings, and armed with a quiver and arrows, gets stuck in mid-air. The mechanism will not budge. While the lovers exchange their promises of evermore, Josephine is left to try and wiggle her way off stage as best she can. But the audience love her. She smiles at them with a big toothy smile, laughing along at her own misfortune. In later performances, Josephine is allowed to dance, and she does so with a vibrancy and energy that puts the other girls on stage in the shade. She shimmies and she shakes. It is almost unseemly how good she is, for a girl who is used to getting by stomping around on the pavements of St. Louis, or else in the city's restaurants. Perhaps her dancing is more funny than it is sensuous. Whatever it is, it works.

The Dixie Steppers hire her for a tour of the Southern states, leaving by train a couple of weeks later. The hotels are flea-bitten. The welcome from locals is not always warm. When she is not on stage – which is most of the time, at first – Josephine helps the leading lady of the troupe, a formidable singer named Clara Smith, get ready with her purple make-up and red wig. Clara repays the favour by buying Josephine sweets, and helping to teach her to read. She only gets to dance in the chorus line when another girl twists her ankle. She is considered good, but a little wild to perform with the others and certainly too pale-skinned, too white. At least she is no longer in St. Louis.

The troupe breaks up in Philadelphia and Josephine is on her own.

BERLIN: This is becoming a habit. A British military officer in the German capital is invited to an impromptu interview with another former military leader, out of office but eager to return: General Ludendorff. The German has a message to convey to London. Who he speaks for is unclear.

Ludendorff's request to the British, personal or otherwise, is for a new alliance against Bolshevism. 'It will mean a complete reconstruction of the people's ideas,' the general admits, 'almost a turning inside out of their minds, but it will have to be.' The Bolsheviks are already slowing the Polish advance east, he points out. Soon the advance will stop. And then what? The Reds will move west. Ludendorff hints that some of his own former colleagues are ready to make a deal with the Russians. The implication is clear enough: help us now, or face a Bolshevik Germany in a year's time.

The general proposes a new Germano-Franco-British army. Of course, he adds, the Germans would need some incentives in order to fight: perhaps the cancellation of Versailles and a slice of Poland. When the British officer asks who would lead this international force it becomes painfully obvious that Ludendorff has himself in mind. He could accept a British commander, he says, but certainly not a French one: 'I – don't – think – that – could – be done', reads the British officer's report to his superiors. When the question is raised of whether the general's plan has the support of the government in Berlin, Ludendorff brushes the query aside. 'There will be a big change in the government soon.'

One final request, man to man, anti-Bolshevik to anti-Bolshevik: 'Can you get Mr Churchill to come over here, even for a few days, incognito if he likes?' A senior official in London is dismissive: 'Really these Huns are very impudent.' Winston does not go to Berlin.

DUBLIN: A furtive campaign is waged in the back streets and alleyways of Ireland's capital. The thirty-year-old Michael Collins develops a network of secret agents to turn against the security operatives of Dublin Castle loyal to Britain and the King.

They meet in pubs, in upstairs rooms and darkened saloons thick with smoke and the smell of beer. Suspected informants are played back against the other side to test their loyalties. Murder is the price of betrayal. No one can be trusted. A former soldier in the Irish cause is found to be working for Collins's capture. The hall porter of the Wicklow Hotel is shot dead one morning for giving information to the British. 'It is a question of our nerves', Michael Collins explains. 'There is no doubt a great deal of punishment ahead of us. It is a question of the body wearing longer than the lash.'

At night, Collins smashes furniture in his room at the back of Devlin's pub to calm himself. By day, he invites new recruits to the races at Phoenix Park. He takes enormous risks, and takes them in his stride. He becomes a hero of the cause.

MOSCOW: Whenever he gets the chance – and the occasions are rarer and rarer – Vladimir goes off on hunting trips. It is the only time he can get away from the incessant telephone calls and messages and letters. He goes hunting with old and new comrades. He invites himself along on others' trips. He arranges to go hunting with Trotsky several times, but the war commissar always cancels at the last minute. (It's probably for the best: Leon is convinced he is the better shot.)

Vladimir notices changes about himself on these excursions. He has worried about his health for years. He has always been nervy. But more recently, over the last six months or so, he has begun to feel that he is getting old. All the agitation, all the reading, all the late nights, the bad food, the stress, the arguments, and then the bullets – the years of permanent revolution have tired him out. Nothing too alarming yet. He has long suffered from bad headaches. In conversation with him in the Kremlin, Trotsky occasionally notices that Lenin's voice is not quite as strong as it used to be. One day out on a hunt Vladimir is forced to tell his companions to slow down, complaining of pins and needles in his legs.

Since his youth, the impatient revolutionary has been a keen hunter, if not a particularly skilled one. He is frustrated when he misses – and indeed when others do, too – which is most of the time. But somehow these days it is just being outdoors that matters most. He is still game enough to make bird noises in the middle of frozen forests. He still tramps through snow, miles from Moscow, driven out there by his chauffeur on a Sunday at the drop of a hat. He still gets the old revolutionary's thrill from sleeping in haylofts, dropping in on villages without prior announcement and then delivering his catch – usually the result of someone else's shooting – anonymously at the door of a Bolshevik comrade from the olden days. (Once, on a hunting trip for grouse with his brother, Lenin passes himself off as a locksmith from Moscow.) But it is all a lot harder than it used to be. Vladimir can feel his breathing more. He hears his bones creaking.

One day, someone arranges an old-fashioned Russian *battue* for Lenin, the kind of hunt the aristocracy used to enjoy before the revolution: a circle is formed by the servants and the fox beaten into the middle, where the chosen hunter waits to shoot it. That day, when the circle closes, the fox appears momentarily, looks Vladimir straight in the eyes, and then darts off. Lenin is too slow off the mark.

'Why on earth didn't you fire?' Nadya asks him afterwards.

'Well, he was so beautiful, you know', her husband replies, a little sheepishly.

ÅBO, FINLAND: A seaman bearing papers with the name Jim Gormley is found in the coal bunker of a Swedish-bound freighter in a Finnish port. The diamonds and letters in English give John Reed away. Finnish police take him off for questioning.

SPRING

Montreux – Berlin – Amerongen: Harry Kessler is in a bookshop in Montreux, Switzerland, when he hears the news. An old German lady wanders into the shop in a state of some excitement. The counter-revolution has begun in Berlin, she splutters: Hindenburg is to be head of state.

Harry rushes to the newspaper displays. It is a Saturday. There is little fresh from Germany; but at first glance it looks as if a coup has taken place in Berlin. A Prussian nationalist politician called Wolfgang Kapp – known for his links to the old regime, Russian émigrés and the Freikorps – has declared himself Chancellor. Telephoning Zurich, Harry learns that several leading centrist German politicians have been arrested and the Social Democrats have called a general strike. The country seems on the brink of civil war. Foreign intervention cannot be ruled out. Harry strongly suspects Ludendorff's involvement.

In Berlin, Kapp's troops have no difficulty taking over government buildings. Ebert's ministers flee to Dresden. A quick-thinking civil servant is said to have absconded with as many government stamps as possible to prevent the impostor Chancellor from issuing official-looking decrees.

In Amerongen, Wilhelm calls for champagne. Surely it is only a matter of time before he is summoned back. He always knew his people would do the right thing in the end.

Prangins, Lake Geneva, Switzerland: Wilhelm is not the only Emperor who thinks that 1920 may be the year of his restoration. Charles Habsburg is no less expectant.

Charles's hopes rest on the Hungarian Admiral Horthy, a guest at Charles and Zita's wedding in 1911 and a man who, with tears in his eyes, swore his personal loyalty to the Habsburg cause in 1918 even as the imperial family fled Vienna. Now that Horthy has re-established order in Budapest, surely it is only a matter of time before a full-scale restoration takes place.

Yet something is not quite right. Charles issues royal proclamations to his Hungarian subjects from Prangins, sending them on to Horthy for publication. For some inexplicable reason, however, the admiral decides these proclamations are best kept secret. Charles sends letters asking Horthy when, in his estimation, would be the most propitious moment for his return to the royal palace in Budapest. Horthy replies evasively, or not at all.

The Habsburg family keep themselves afloat selling their jewellery. Some rubies are sold in January, a jewel-encrusted hairpin in March.

AMERONGEN – BERLIN: The situation in the German capital turns out to be more complicated than Wilhelm imagined. The coup has stalled.

On the one hand, Kapp's putsch cannot be easily put down. The army high command is unwilling to order troops to open fire, fearing that the soldiers will refuse to shoot Freikorps comrades they have fought with to rid Munich of the Bolsheviks, crush a Polish rising in Silesia and defend German interests in the Baltic. On the other hand there is no evidence of widespread popular support for Kapp. His coup is more bluster than substance.

A young American diplomat whose weekend plans to visit Warsaw are spoiled by the events expects the government back in charge before long. 'If you want a tame revolution instead of the opera,' he writes to his friend, 'you may have to come soon.'

CORK, CO. CORK, IRELAND: 'Thomas MacCurtain prepare for death', reads the letter to the new Lord Mayor of Cork and local IRA commandant: 'You are doomed'. A few days later, armed men with blackened faces enter his home. 'All right, I'll be out', the Lord Mayor says as he appears on the landing, his trousers quickly pulled on, his shirt half open. He is killed in front of his wife.

Though the British authorities in Dublin blame dissident republicans – the threatening note is on Dáil notepaper – a local jury in Cork places the blame for the murder at the feet of the British government. The evidence is circumstantial. The killers are said to have spoken with English accents.

The police do not bother to investigate. The law is crumbling. British civilian administration is halfway to collapse. The hunters have become the hunted.

BERLIN: Coups, like revolutions, depend on momentum: either they establish themselves before anyone can crush them or they fail. The Kapp putschists hoped their action in Berlin would spark copycat uprisings across Germany. Within days, it is clear the would-be masters of Germany's counter-revolution are alone.

A messenger sent from Berlin to Munich to try and enlist high-level army support in Bavaria is met with frosty rejection. No one wants to risk association with a failed coup. Except the desperate. Encouraged by an officer in the army's propaganda department, two informal emissaries fly to Berlin to see if some kind of link can nonetheless be established between the putschists in the capital and like-minded circles in Munich.

They travel in disguise, as a paper merchant and his accountant visiting Berlin on business. Dietrich Eckart, whose nationalist and anti-Semitic propaganda Kapp once supported financially, plays the paper merchant. The role of junior accountant goes to the mangy field-runner, who dons a Lenin-style fake beard. Terrified of heights and unused to flying, Adolf throws up constantly on the bumpy ride north over the frozen forests of Bavaria. By the time he and Dietrich get to Berlin, it is obvious Kapp's coup cannot possibly succeed. They travel home by train.

ISTANBUL – ANKARA – SAN REMO, ITALY: A guerrilla campaign has begun against the French in the south, and the Greeks in the west. Mustafa Kemal has become the focus of nationalist resistance in Ankara. The newly elected parliament in Istanbul, filled with nationalists, stakes out the borders it expects from the final peace. It declares its opposition to any foreign encroachment. The Ottoman Empire seems to be slipping from submission to resistance.

British soldiers shut down the Ottoman parliament. High-ranking opponents of the occupation – and those intellectuals and journalists deemed a danger to it – are detained and shipped off to Malta. The Sultan is powerless to prevent it. He seems dreamily unaware of the consequences of these events for his own prestige. Cocooned from reality by the thick carpets of the palace, he declares the Turkish people but a flock of sheep, and himself their eternal, divinely appointed shepherd. When his choice of a new Grand

Vizier is disputed, Vahdettin responds that 'if I wanted I could give the office of grand vizier to the Greek or the Armenian Patriarch, or the Chief Rabbi'.

In Ankara, Kemal follows developments by telegraph. He issues a circular ordering that there be no retribution against non-Muslims for the British action. Then he issues another proclamation. 'The forcible occupation of Istanbul today has destroyed the seven-centuries-old existence and sovereignty of the Ottoman Empire', reads the text. 'Consequently the Turkish nation is compelled today to defend its rights, its independence and its entire future.' It is not an appeal to Ottoman loyalty but to the Turkish people. The implication is clear: that legitimacy derives from the nation, not from the dynasty. Nationalists now flock to Ankara not just to escape arrest, but to form a new national assembly, free from foreign influence. The Istanbul parliament is dissolved.

The Sultan, in his religious role as Caliph, orders a *fetva* to be issued against Kemal and his associates. They are declared infidels. Ankara's senior mufti responds with his own *fetva*, backed by the clerisy of Anatolia, declaring Vahdettin a hostage of hostile powers. Revolution is in the air. But Kemal must be careful. He is not a general now. As a politician – and diplomat – he must weave and wind, he must charm and convince. Turkey is a conservative country. At the opening of the new national assembly in Ankara, Kemal swears – in the name of God and the Prophet – that he is no rebel to the Sultan-Caliph. He simply wishes Turkey to avoid the fate of India and Egypt, both under the thumb of foreigners. The next day, a fraternal greeting is sent from Ankara to Moscow, suggesting cooperation against the common imperialist enemy. Mustafa must be everything to everyone: radical, traditionalist, conservative, revolutionary, loyalist, Bolshevik.

Meanwhile, a world away, in a seaside town in Italy, representatives of the Allied powers meet to finalise the shape of the peace they wish to impose on the Ottoman Empire. It has taken them this long. For the Arab lands, the powers agree a combination of Arab kingdoms under foreign protection and a series of League of Nations mandates. The French take Syria (including Lebanon). The British are granted Mesopotamia and Palestine, where their mandate includes the promise of a Jewish national homeland. Anatolia is to be partitioned. The Ottoman Empire is to become the Hungary of the Middle East, a shadow of its former self, weak and surrounded.

Drawing lines on a map is one thing, policing vast territories another. Jerusalem has already been shaken by violence between Arabs and Zionist Jews, newly arrived from Europe, schooled in the need for self-defence by Russian pogroms, and determined to carve out their own destiny in dusty Palestine. Tribal revolt is brewing in Mesopotamia. In Syria, a national congress echoes the Istanbul parliament in declaring its independence. Considerable numbers of men and guns will be needed to quell all these trouble-spots at the same time.

Anatolia is one problem amongst many. Only the Greeks seem to have the appetite for it.

Moscow: The bloom is coming off the old revolutionary dream. And it is the workers who are unhappy now. There are strikes across the country.

Down with the commissar! That is a charge heard more often now. The workers' state seems to have grown new bosses, not much different from the old. The tendency from collective decision-making to one-man rule is hardening across state, party and factory floor. The old Soviets have been hollowed out; party officials run the show these days. They are the ones who make appointments and issue orders. Very few of them are proper workers. And who guards against corruption within the party? Why, the party itself, of course. (This is one of Comrade Stalin's jobs, the omnipresent party mechanic.) In everything, power seems to flow one way now: down, not up.

Perhaps this was right for wartime, but is it really needed now the civil war is over? A simple question of good management, Lenin explains. Nothing personal. 'The will of a class may sometimes be carried out by a dictator, who sometimes does more alone and is frequently more necessary.' He wrote about this in 1918. Was no one paying attention? Trotsky wants to go further. Workers should be treated as if they were in the army – conscripted into labour battalions, made to follow orders and then shot if they desert. They 'must be appointed, rerouted and dispatched in exactly the same way that soldiers are'. The workers must grasp that the party understands their interests better than they can themselves. The man who joined the Bolsheviks so late now demands absolute submission to party rule. To some this all looks like a new serfdom, a dictatorship of bureaucrats.

Washington DC: A final vote in the US Senate. American ratification of the Treaty of Versailles is dead. 'The President strangled his own child', one

Senator remarks. Next day's papers agree. 'If I were not a Christian', Woodrow remarks, 'I think I should go mad.'

ACROSS GERMANY: In the chaos surrounding Kapp's coup, leftist radicals spy an opportunity to rekindle the workers' council movement and return Germany to the path of full-on revolution.

The Communists demand that the strikes first launched in resistance to the putsch are now used to launch Germany leftward towards Bolshevism. They are sickened at the idea of negotiations between the putschists and the Social Democratic government. 'The strike must continue until the clique of officers have been totally defeated, and until the workers and employees have been armed against any possible further aggression', reads a Communist Party statement.

In western Germany, the industrial Ruhr region is convulsed with political and social unrest. In the city of Duisburg, where the Rhine and the Ruhr rivers meet, a workers' council proclaims the 'dictatorship of the proletariat'. The mines are closed. A volunteer Red army is formed. Fighting breaks out. The region is spinning out of control again. After attempts to break the deadlock through political negotiation fail, Freikorps units join the regular army to restore order.

In the south, the conservative right in Bavaria present their region as a bulwark against revolution. While Kapp flees to Sweden, Ludendorff moves to Munich. The city that once seemed the capital of Marxist radical chic now becomes a magnet for Europe's counter-revolutionaries: militarist Prussians and Baltic Germans who feel that Berlin has betrayed them, and White Russians who dream of a return to power in Petrograd.

The left bank of the Rhine remains under Allied occupation.

PARIS: Breton's mother turns up unannounced in Paris at the end of March, brandishing a newspaper account of the various Dadaist japes her son has been getting up to. She issues an ultimatum: either he will give up Dada or his financial support will be stopped. André very nearly buckles. His allowance is cut off the following day.

MUNICH: Around the same time, Adolf finally leaves the army. A party supporter finds him a small, cheaply furnished room to rent. He sleeps late and reads a lot.

One day he talks himself into the home of the former director of the Bavarian Royal Opera House, a Baron. Hitler turns up wearing gaiters, a large hat, and carrying a riding crop in one hand, dressed as his idea of a Bavarian country gentleman. He sits awkwardly in his chair, not quite able to relax. He stays for more than an hour – well beyond the time he is welcome. He tries to make conversation but ends up making a speech. The noise brings the servants rushing in, thinking their master is being attacked.

SEBASTOPOL, CRIMEA: Following all the other commanders who have come and gone in Russia's kaleidoscopic civil war, General Denikin decides to leave the scene. The Western powers have abandoned him. His forces have been pushed back to the shores of the Black Sea. An evacuation to Crimea is a disaster. There is much intriguing amongst the generals. There have been a number of suicides among the rank and file. 'God has not given my troops victory', Denikin writes.

After being blessed with an icon of the Virgin Mary, a new and much younger soldier, the forty-two-year-old General Wrangel, takes over as commander-in-chief of the Armed Forces of Southern Russia. The position is quite hopeless. There is hardly any coal or oil for the ships, no horses for the cavalry, no petrol for the aeroplanes and no proper equipment for the troops. 'I have shared the honour of its victories with the Army', Wrangel writes, 'and cannot refuse to drink from the cup of humiliation with it now.'

The general – tall, aristocratic, the very model of the dashing White officer, a man most often seen in a Circassian tunic and fur hat, with a string of bullets around his neck – sets about trying to reform those areas still under White Russian control in order to turn them into a solid base from which to continue the war against the Bolsheviks. At the same time, he sets out to win over the French and the British, to persuade them that he is not as hopeless as his predecessor (nor as anti-Semitic). 'I'm struggling', Wrangel writes to his wife Olga, already in exile in Istanbul. He thanks her for the icon she has sent him. He is so busy, so tired. 'I go to bed at two or two thirty in the morning and wake up at 7', he writes. 'I only have a rest at lunch time and dinner time, but even then, I'm distracted incessantly.' He travels up to the front: 'If only God helped me and gave me the time to finish the job'.

COLÓN, REPUBLIC OF PANAMA – BOSTON – PHILADELPHIA: The Black Star Line's *Yarmouth* is renamed the *Frederick Douglass*, in honour of the great

American abolitionist and former slave. It sails, quite slowly, through the Caribbean, meeting with local adulation (and British colonial suspicion) wherever it weighs anchor.

There is little business value to the voyage. There are few cargoes to pick up or drop off. Passenger numbers vary hugely. Though there are hints that Cuban sugar exporters would be prepared to switch to the Black Star Line if enough good ships were available, the current voyage has more the character of a royal progress than a serious commercial venture.

In Cuba, the President throws a party for the crew at the presidential palace. In Colón, Panama, thousands greet the *Frederick Douglass*, carrying baskets of fruit and vegetables as gifts to the heroic (and somewhat dazed) arrivals, while five hundred black workers cram aboard to escape the appalling conditions of servitude under which they suffer in the country. In Kingston, Jamaica, the captain decides to take seven hundred tons of ripe coconuts on board in the hope that their prompt arrival in America might allow the Black Star Line to turn at least some minor profit from the ship's Caribbean peregrination.

But Garvey abrogates the commercial imperative to get the cargo home as fast as possible and orders the *Frederick Douglass* to make a courtesy call in Costa Rica instead. The ship is then sent to call at Boston and Philadelphia – where UNIA meetings are being planned – rather than head straight for New York. By the time the vessel arrives at its final destination, the coconuts are spoiled.

Back in the United States, Garvey works up his audiences with fresh vistas of black empowerment, with the Black Star Line as a symbol and advert of that process. The impression of successful enterprise trumps the reality. His self-confident self-help message is being heard. In Boston, Garvey talks of how it is the human will which is the deciding factor in the history of the world these days. Power is a psychological question, he says. Whites are born with the consciousness of what they can achieve; blacks have been told that they can do nothing. And therein lies the perniciousness of those who talk down the Black Star Line, he says. Naysayers, black or white, are as bad as each other. (A cartoon in the *Negro World* suggests that 'white interests' are the puppet-masters behind some so-called black community leaders.) It is self-belief that matters most. That is what Garvey is there to provide.

His own self-belief is not in doubt. His oratory is grandiose. His vision scopes the widest horizons of the future. His speeches are immoderate, intemperate affairs. In the last war, Garvey tells his supporters, the Kaiser wanted a place in the sun. 'Now we also want a place in the sun', he proclaims, noting that if sixty million Germans could last five years of war, 'four hundred million ought to be able to do it a little longer'. Africa must be reclaimed. A race war must be fought and won.

The British were Roman slaves once, Garvey notes, and now they rule the world. He imagines a new black aristocracy arising from the present struggle, a Duke of the Nigerias and an Earl of Lagos ennobled by the fight ahead just as Arthur Wellesley became the Duke of Wellington after Waterloo. Garvey lacerates the lies of whites who have led blacks to believe they must serve and never rule. In front of a crowd of six thousand in Philadelphia, he promises that 'no power on earth can stop the great onward rush of the UNIA'. 'The black men of the world have fought the last war for others', he says. The next war will be one for freedom.

He promises a convention will be held in New York in August to elect a leader for the black race. Garvey may be bombastic and he may be vain, but to many blacks he tells it like it is. He makes them proud. He does not pull his punches. He stands up for what he believes in. He is willing to shake things up – and maybe that is just what is needed.

WASHINGTON DC: In the spring of 1920, the League fight over, Woodrow Wilson meets his cabinet for the first time since the summer of 1919.

The President looks tired. He seems distracted. His voice is scratchy. As the meeting drags on, Woodrow's doctor looks meaningfully at the door to indicate things should be drawn to a close. It is Edith who finally breaks things up, bustling into the room and suggesting it is time to go. 'This is an experiment, you know', she tells the cabinet as she ushers the men out.

Woodrow hears about Attorney General Mitchell Palmer's raids for the first time. It is unclear how much he understands of them. He pronounces himself neither in favour, nor against. He asks only that Palmer not let the country 'see red'.

MOSCOW: Vladimir protests at the fuss everyone is making over his birthday. Still, he does not stop them, all the same.

The newspapers are full of stories of peasants going to visit the Kremlin, and Vladimir greeting them like a father. Trotsky, travelling across Russia trying to sort out the railway network, writes an article declaring his old rival the unquestioned leader of the proletariat, comparing him favourably to Marx. The poet Mayakovsky composes a poem honouring the great leader: '*like a bomb the name explodes: Lenin! Lenin! Lenin!*' (Vladimir *hates* Mayakovsky.) Not just one but two celebratory biographies are published. Two hundred thousand copies are printed.

Celebrations are organised by the party leadership. The Georgian bank-robber makes a speech praising Vladimir for his modesty, his willingness to correct his mistakes. The birthday boy arrives after all the speeches are over and then scolds the party, warning it against getting a big head. That only contributes further to the growing cult around Lenin, a man who virtually no one had heard of three years ago: Lenin the simple toiler in the Kremlin, Lenin the people's servant (no grand titles, *please!*), even Lenin the worker (despite his minor aristocratic heritage).

There are other matters he has to think about: such as the imminent arrival of an eclectic delegation of British leftists – a Labour parliamentarian, a trades unionist, a famous suffragette, a philosopher, a Quaker – sent to investigate true conditions in Soviet Russia. The purpose of their trip is to help the British left take a view on the issue which has split Europe's socialist movement in two: whether or not to join the Comintern. Anticipating difficulties with some of these mushy-minded middle-of-the-road types, Vladimir instructs their interpreters to stick to them like glue. He secretly proposes a newspaper campaign to discredit the least pro-Soviet and a variety of old tricks – the usual planted questions – so the whole event can be stage-managed for propaganda. He has not forgotten the lessons of Potemkin.

There is bad news at the end of April. Marshal Piłsudski's Poles cut a deal with nationalist Ukrainians and invade Red Ukraine, beating Lenin to the punch he had intended to land on them. A city for a city: Polish troops will recapture Kiev on their behalf and, in return, the Ukrainians will renounce their claim to the mixed city of Lviv and the surrounding prov-ince of eastern Galicia. The Red Army is in retreat again. Trotsky calls for 'drastic measures'. The Poles advance with barely a shot fired. The birthday celebrations sour.

DOORN, THE NETHERLANDS: Count Bentinck sighs deeply. The wonderful day has at last arrived: Wilhelm and his entourage move out of Amerongen and into their new house down the road.

Wilhelm's personal taste is in ample evidence at Huis Doorn. He surrounds himself with family treasures. 'Busts, paintings and etchings of

Fredrick the Great, Grosspapa and Papa' line the walls, he writes enthusiastically, 'and pictures of the Prussian army in the moments of its greatest
triumphs'. He even gets his old writing chair back, in the form of a saddle.
It is almost as if he were still really Kaiser.

He has already got to work on the estate's forest over the last few months
while overseeing the renovations. Some four hundred and seventy imperially felled logs lie in a pile before the Kaiser and Kaiserin even move in.

WASHINGTON: Mitchell Palmer is an angry man. Most of the alleged
dangerous radicals picked up in January have now been released for lack
of evidence. The raids are beginning to look like a fiasco. He blames a liberal
magazine editor named Louis Post, the Assistant Secretary of Labor, whose
department is responsible for enforcing immigration law. He will only issue
deportation orders with proof of intent to harm America. Palmer tries to
get him impeached.

In April, Palmer publicly warns that he has knowledge of a wave of
assassinations to occur on 1 May. Leave is cancelled for the nation's police
forces. Public buildings are put under heavy guard. In Chicago, a further
three hundred and sixty suspected radicals are locked up for twenty-four
hours as a security measure. Then – nothing happens.

Palmer is made to look foolish. 'Everybody is laughing at A. Mitchell
Palmer's May Day "revolution", says the *Boston American*. During the first
step in his impeachment hearings, Post points out that despite the arrest
of several thousand supposed radicals in January, only three handguns have
been found.

PETROGRAD – MOSCOW: While nothing much is happening in America, on
May Day in the birthplace of the revolution a stupendous agitprop performance takes place on the steps of the former stock exchange in Petrograd.

The world is shown in the state it was before the war, with Kings and
Queens feasting up above, and the enslaved masses toiling below, staggering
under the weight of huge boulders. A red flag appears and disappears, waved
by a solitary agitator. Then August 1914 arrives, to the strains of 'God Save
the King' and the abandonment of the working classes by its socialist representatives. Now comes 1917, red flags everywhere, the storming of the
Winter Palace, peals of joy as a new world is created.

Across Russia, brightly painted agitprop trains spread the gospel of
Bolshevism, armed with pamphlets, film projectors and posters. In Moscow,

Lenin speaks to Red Army soldiers about to be sent off to Ukraine to fight Piłsudski's Poles. He calls the rumour that the enemy is on the outskirts of Kiev the 'sheerest fabrication', remarking that he was on the telephone to the local Red commander only hours ago.

Kiev falls to the Poles the following day.

VIENNA: Anna Freud and her cousin Mausi are in torment. Summer is fast approaching, the time of year when two twenty-something young girls should be enjoying themselves. But in Vienna there is nothing to do. The shops are empty of goods. The theatres may close at any minute. In January a fuel shortage and a ban on lighting after three in the afternoon prevents any evening entertainment at all for a week.

Then Anna and Mausi hit on an idea. It is healthy, cheap and fun. It is an activity for two, or more, depending on how it is played. It requires only sunlight, something which even the government of Austria cannot ration. They are going to play tennis. But there is one problem. There are no tennis balls in Vienna, or none which Anna and Mausi can afford. Anna composes a letter to Sam in Manchester. 'I know that it must sound rather bad of us', she writes, in the perfect script of a schoolteacher, 'our wanting superfluous things like tennis balls when things are as bad and as serious as they are now.' But then, 'there is so very little pleasure to be had for young people in Vienna now.' She asks Sam to send a dozen balls. But only if they are not more than one pound. Six would do.

Two weeks later Anna countermands her order. It is too frivolous. 'Mausi and I decided to give up tennis', she explains.

MUNICH: Adolf hones his speaking technique. He tries out different lines on the disillusioned who gather at party meetings, turning from anti-British remarks to anti-capitalist ones before testing out anti-Bolshevism on his audiences, talking gravely about Russia's economic collapse and the mass murder of the intelligentsia. Invited to give a talk in Stuttgart, he savages the Versailles Treaty. In Munich, he talks about interest slavery and launches a bitter attack on the British Empire and its subjugation of India.

When he senses the audience drifting away, Adolf shifts gears from a simulacrum of analysis to an accusatory and finally a messianic tone. 'The day will come', he exclaims, 'when the sun will shine through once more.' He calls for a new kind of leader. 'We need a dictator', he says bluntly, 'who is at the same time a genius'. There are echoes of Mussolini here. Adolf increasingly singles out one root cause for Germany's ills, something for his audiences to focus on: the Jews. This always seems to get a warm reaction.

Even in Munich's crowded political market, where politics has become a blood sport, civility is long gone, wild conspiracies find willing believers and the so-called 'Jewish question' is widely discussed, the vociferousness of Hitler's anti-Semitic rants marks him out. Adolf decides not just to ride Munich's wave of anti-Semitism, but to make himself its most ardent exponent. His fanaticism becomes part of his brand.

A Hitler speech without reference to the Jews is simply not a Hitler speech. Building on a public perception during the war, but without any basis in fact, Adolf denounces German-Jewish soldiers for having shirked their patriotic duty at the front and then conspired to bring about revolution behind it. He accuses Jews of using finance and the media to control society. Some of this is familiar. The Thule Society newspaper, now renamed to take account of its role in the ethno-nationalist *völkisch* movement as the *Völkischer Beobachter*, runs excerpts of the *Protocols* this spring, suggesting it should be published in the millions and made essential reading for patriotic Germans.

When it comes to dealing with this imagined, conspiratorial, ever-present influence Hitler urges followers of the German Workers' Party – now renamed the National Socialist German Workers' Party, the Nationalsozialistische Deutsche Arbeiterpartei, or Na-zis – to think strategically about the future. 'We do not want to be the kind of sentimental anti-Semites who create a pogrom atmosphere', he tells his followers: 'we want to grasp at the very root of this malignancy and eradicate it, stump and stalk.' These slogans become the defining feature of the party, the tools with which to activate the crowds. 'All means are justified in reaching this goal,' the mangy field-runner says, 'even if it means making a pact with the devil himself.'

LONDON: An English version of the *Protocols* is printed in London, causing quite a stir. *The Times* does not pronounce on the authenticity of the document. Instead it asks a leading question which resounds amongst its readership. If not true, 'whence comes the uncanny note of prophecy, prophecy in parts fulfilled, in parts far gone by way of fulfilment?' The forgery continues its world tour.

BERLIN: Will Einstein stay in Germany, or will he leave? In Germany's fevered atmosphere, where morality and sound money seem both to have gone up the spout, the question takes on political proportions. Departure might be seen as a betrayal of Germany at its moment of weakness. It might reflect badly on Germany's Jews.

Yet with a dirty campaign against him, must Einstein just put up with it? He could make more money and have more peace elsewhere: in Britain perhaps, maybe even in America or (worst of all) in France. As much as he loves the beautiful world of German science – and supports it as much as he can by acting as its unofficial representative – there is his own well-being to think about, and that of his family. 'My situation is like that of a man who is lying in a beautiful bed, tortured by bed bugs', Albert explains one day. 'Nevertheless, let us wait and see how things develop.'

In early summer, he departs with Elsa on a Nordic tour, to lecture in Oslo and in Copenhagen.

DEARBORN: Henry Ford is not an educated man, but he is a highly successful businessman. He believes in what he calls 'facts'.

A fact, Ford writes, is like granite: 'winter will not freeze it, summer will not melt it, rains will not wash it away'. The key is finding one's own facts and then sticking to them. Ford is fascinated by theories about what happened in the past, but we are missing the right facts to prove. He is quite taken with the idea that Abraham Lincoln's assassin did not die in a shoot-out as everyone thinks, but escaped to become a saloon keeper in Texas and then a house painter in Oklahoma. Ford is a superficially inquisitive man, but not discriminating in what he draws on to back up his feelings about things. He believes what he wants to, and takes attempts to persuade him otherwise as propaganda. He is a contrarian who believes in his own truths. He trusts his instincts rather than the views of others. He is primed for conspiracy theories.

Henry Ford's magazine, the *Dearborn Independent*, is not making as much money as he would like. It is distributed through his Ford dealerships, and they are everywhere across America, but he is persuaded that an attention-grabbing campaign of some sort might help him to reach a wider readership. In the summer of 1920, Ford's prejudices and credulity combine with the sharp pen of a journalist and the influence of Ford's German secretary, well acquainted with the Russian who hawked the *Protocols* around America two years ago. Henry Ford launches an anti-Semitic campaign on the pages of the *Dearborn Independent*.

The campaign presents itself as an inquiry into why Jews are persecuted. In pretending to simply ask why this might be, the magazine explores and repeats any anti-Semitic slander it can find. 'Persecution is not a new experience to the Jew', says the *Independent*, 'but intensive scrutiny of his nature and super-nationality is'. The magazine claims that it is revealing a necessary truth which others want to hide: 'efforts will be made to hush it up as impolitic for general discussion'. Anyone disclaiming the conspiracy must clearly be part of it.

Ford's own brand of anti-Semitism springs from personal experience. He believes that financiers on Wall Street are making things difficult for his business. And everyone *knows* that Wall Street is run by Jews. He blames the embarrassment of his peace attempts during the war on a Jewish associate. He concludes that the Jews must have wanted the war to continue so as to line their pockets with the profits to be made. And then, of course, there is the popular association of the Jews with Bolshevism. In Ford's mind, this all seems to fit together.

A hired journalist writes up Ford's prejudices into long, superficially researched articles, finding new angles when the old ones get tired, playing on concerns about immigration, jobs and terrorism. After a few weeks, the *Independent*'s campaign is being picked up by other newspapers and magazines, just as planned. The spark has been provided. Now the fire is catching. Disinformation thrives on repetition. In July, the case of *The Protocols of the Elders of Zion* is raised.

Some Jews wonder if Ford himself can be personally involved in spreading such stuff, imagining that someone behind the scenes must be taking advantage of him. A few send in protest telegrams, hoping Ford will realise what is being perpetrated in his name. 'These articles shall continue', replies the *Independent* to one complainant. 'When you have attained a more tolerable state of mind we shall be happy to discuss them with you.' The magazine blames Jews for 'supersensitivity'. The campaign seems to have hit a nerve; the truth must be close at hand.

Ford seems genuinely surprised when, in June, a local rabbi returns a special Model T the car manufacturer gave him recently, with a letter hoping the mogul will realise the 'enormity of the injury' he is causing. Ford telephones the rabbi and asks him what is wrong. 'Has something come between us?' He seems to think it is a personal matter.

Meanwhile, the campaign continues. Sales of the *Independent* begin to rise. It all seems to be a great success.

PETROGRAD: Dressed in their oldest clothes — so as not to embarrass their Russian hosts — the British Labour Delegation arrives in Russia. A special train is laid on for them, decorated with red bunting, Communist slogans and pine sprigs. As it crosses the border, the most ardent members of the delegation break out into the Internationale. They have reached the promised land. They have heard so much about the great experiment. At last they can see it for themselves. One of the travellers, the suffragette Ethel Snowden, describes the sensation of peering behind an iron curtain.

ÅBO: John Reed is finally released from his Finnish jail after payment of a fine for smuggling (and a campaign by Louise). Unable to travel to America — the State Department will not issue him a passport — he returns to Petrograd and is put up in the Hotel International to recover from his ordeal. He is not a well man, after being fed on a diet of dried fish. He is much thinner than he used to be. His eyes are sunken.

Further east, in Siberia, after several Cheka interrogations, Maria Bochkareva is executed.

PARIS: Three friends are walking through the Jardin du Luxembourg. They run into a girl one of them knows. She is introduced to the others. 'I'm not a Dadaist, you know', Simone Kahn tells André Breton. 'Neither am I', André replies, with a smile which suggests that he may or may not be telling the truth.

SUMMER

Kiev: The Poles are thrown back. Barely a month after they conquered Kiev, the city has changed hands again. Locals have lost count of how many times their city has been trampled through by competing armies these last three years. The Bolsheviks present themselves as Russian patriots fighting against the historic foe. The Tsar's former commander-in-chief appeals for all patriotic officers to join the Red Army.

Now, with Piłsudski's armies in retreat, the question is no longer how to save Bolshevism, but how far to extend it. Europe's populations have not risen up in revolution as Vladimir had hoped. Might Red Army bayonets in Warsaw help to concentrate their minds?

Stalin argues that Wrangel should be knocked off first. Trotsky, for once, urges caution. But Lenin is impatient. A young aristocrat who is appointed as the commander of the Red Army in the west shares his ambitions. He is the same age as Napoleon when he conquered Italy – just twenty-seven.

Washington DC: In January, Mitchell Palmer was untouchable, a crusader for American values against the Bolsheviks. By summer, he is under fire for abuse of power, accused of terrorising thousands with an illegal witch-hunt and then trying to ruin those who stand in his way. 'I declare these charges are outrageous and unconscionable falsehoods', he tells a Congressional committee looking into the matter. He is just doing his job. For two days straight he rebuts his critics. His political career is on the line. The Democratic convention is just weeks away.

'The world is on fire', Palmer warns, and the arsonists in Moscow are doing all they can to spread the conflagration. The flames of revolution are leaping across western Asia from the Caspian Sea to the Suez Canal. They have reached 'the huts of Afghanistan'. Americans must understand what it is that they are up against. Those who oppose his methods are playing the Bolshevik game. They are either knaves or fools. Honest American workers are being manipulated. Palmer furiously attacks 'our so-called "liberal press"' and the 'parlor Bolsheviki' who cannot see what is happening outside their book-lined studies.

He invites members of the committee to come down to the offices of the Justice Department to look at the photographs of the foreign Bolshevik agitators that have been compiled. 'Out of the sly and crafty eyes of many of them leap cupidity, cruelty, insanity and crime', he says. 'From their lopsided faces, sloping brows and misshapen features may be recognized the unmistakeable criminal type.'

PARIS – BERLIN: Paris Dada takes off on summer holiday. Tzara heads to the Balkans; André recovers from his Dadaist activities in Brittany, writing letters to Simone almost every day.

Fun and games may suit the Paris lot. Berlin has no time for dilettantes and dandies. The mood is different there. Berlin Dada is serious, anti-war, political. It celebrates the arrival of summer with an art fair, closer in spirit to Moscow than to the Latin Quarter. 'Dada is Fighting on the Side of the Revolutionary Proletariat', reads one slogan. 'DADA is the Voluntary Destruction of the Bourgeois World of Ideas', shouts another. 'Dadaist Man is the Radical Opponent of Exploitation', declares a third.

A life-size model of a German soldier with a pig's head hangs from the ceiling. (It is called *Prussian Archangel*.) A painting shows three war-wounded soldiers playing cards, one with his mouth crudely stitched up and a black hole for an eye, another with a prosthetic nose, a third with a metal plate holding his skull together.

PETROGRAD – MOSCOW: Wherever they go, they are treated like royalty.

In the old imperial capital, the British Labour Delegation tour the great revolutionary sites of 1917 and are treated to several outings to the ballet and opera. In Moscow, they are given an hour and a half with Lenin in person (who as usual pretends to be quite frank, while saying very little). At the Bolshoi Theatre, they sit in the imperial box. Hearts pound a little faster when war commissar Trotsky joins them for the opera one evening dressed in a tight-fitting Red Army uniform and bearing news of Russian success in pushing back the Poles from Red Ukraine. During the second half, when a lovemaking scene takes place on stage, Leon turns to the suffragette sitting by his side, gestures towards the actors and murmurs in broken English: '*There* is the great international language.' Some delegates go to see a Futurist performance as well. Their minders never leave their side. A sleek Comintern representative is assigned to answer questions. She is horrified when Ethel Snowden seems concerned about the whereabouts of the former owners of the palace in which they are staying.

The consequences of three years of war and revolution are everywhere to see on the streets of Petrograd and Moscow. The suffragette asks why so many women on the streets have short hair. Typhus makes the hair fall out, she is told. When Ethel gives a woollen jacket to the maid who has been looking after her, the girl falls to her knees and kisses the generous British lady's hand. The Bolsheviks have destroyed the old economy – but its replacement has not yet arrived. In parts of the Russian countryside, peasants reportedly eat moss. Even Trotsky admits that rations are now weighed on 'the chemist's scales'. In the cities, illegal markets sell shoddy goods at inflated prices. A rouble note with lots of zeroes is referred to on the streets as a *limon*, a sour reflection of all it can buy. Factory workers are paid in goods they do not want and then resort to barter, with matches exchanged for glasses of milk, and overcoats bought with firewood. Commissars get their lemons hand-delivered from abroad.

Perhaps money could be abolished entirely? For what are banknotes but coloured paper, the symbol of capitalist oppression? Lenin gives Marx's dictum that each should be provided for according to their need a little twist: for each according to their work. An economist proposes a system based on units of work-energy with a giant centralised ledger keeping everything in balance. Realism intervenes. The tools are not yet ready and the economy is not prepared for such a shock. Some have more blasphemous thoughts. Trotsky, while demanding the extension of military discipline to the industrial workforce, simultaneously suggests that the wartime policy of simply requisitioning grain from the peasantry should now be softened to encourage them to grow more. Vladimir shoots him down. *Heresy!*

While debates rage in the Kremlin, Russia shivers and the peasants do not plant for the year ahead. A summer tour of villages near Moscow inspires John Reed to start work on a new play with the working title *Hunger*. In Petrograd, Ethel meets one of Russia's most famous singers and spots his bare toes poking through his worn-out shoes. Another delegate asks about the fashion for women wearing socks rather than stockings. 'Socks use up less wool than stockings', comes back the answer. 'Most have neither'. But, ultimately, who is to blame for these material conditions: the

Bolsheviks or the enemies they have been forced to fight for the last three years? Meeting Vladimir in the Kremlin, one of the British delegates compares Soviet Russia to a patient recovering from a serious illness: sick, but on the mend. Yes, Lenin pounces, that's it. And the revolution is like a severe but vitally necessary operation.

The delegates arrive in Russia wanting to believe in the great experiment, or at least wanting to approach it with an open mind. They leave it disappointed. The commissars are worse than the old Etonians they have to deal with back home. The intellectual inflexibility of the Bolsheviks grates. Is poetry, art, love, all just a subset of Marxist theory? On a long cruise down the Volga, even the philosopher attached to the British delegation grows a little tired of interminable discussion of the materialistic conception of history. Many of his fellow delegates fall sick at some point during their time in Russia, mostly with digestive trouble. One very nearly dies from pneumonia. Colleagues nurse him back to life, no thanks to Bolshevik doctors who give him two days to live. The delegates dine a little too much on fish heads – and never fish. (That part goes to the commissar, they joke.) Abject poverty is less romantic when looked at up close.

The delegates leave Russia with the belief that it should be given a chance to work out its difficulties without outside intervention. London and Paris should keep their hands off. But they do not think the great experiment would work at home.

TEREZÍN FORTRESS, CZECHOSLOVAKIA – SARAJEVO, YUGOSLAVIA: The coffins of the Sarajevo martyrs are laid out on a long black dais. There are flowers everywhere. A crucifixion scene is placed in the middle. For the Serbians in attendance these bodies are holy relics. Their nerves tremble with patriotic energy. Gavrilo Princip's body is reburied in Sarajevo's Koševo cemetery a few days later. A new cult of Serbian heroism is born to justify their domination of the new kingdom of Yugoslavia.

MOSCOW: The impatient revolutionary involves himself in all details of Soviet Russia's ongoing crisis.

The authorities must act firmly to confiscate the surplus produced by people growing food on allotments outside Moscow and Petrograd, he writes. Muscovites must be mobilised to forage for firewood – '*by hand*' – in the forests within a twenty-mile radius of the city and dump it at railway stations. Each man should be required to haul one cubic metre of wood every three months ('the experts can figure it out more exactly', Vladimir writes, 'I mention a figure as an example'). Failure will result in arrest and execution: 'inactivity and negligence cannot be tolerated'. At the same time, he orders that the estate manager at his Gorki country house – he prefers to use the more proletarian-sounding term *sanatorium* in public – should be imprisoned for a month for cutting down a fir tree. The charge is 'causing damage to Soviet property'.

No matter is too small to demand Vladimir's personal attention. Everything is important. Everything is urgent. One day he finds himself leafing through a pamphlet produced in the dark days of 1918 called *Cooking Food Without Fire*. He asks the relevant official to update him as to whether anything ever came of a competition for a new kind of thermos vessel mentioned therein. In late June, he orders the state publishing house to 'publish quickly' the book of the British economist John Maynard Keynes. When he discovers that the Commissariat of Enlightenment has no film with which to record the trial of Kolchak's ministers, Vladimir personally orders the foreign ministry to buy some abroad immediately.

While trying to keep the revolution on the road at home, Vladimir's attention is increasingly drawn to the situation with the Poles. He pesters his subordinates daily for more news from the front. A Red cavalry division is harassing the Poles towards the line they held before they launched their offensive. But no final decision has been taken as to what to do when the task of clearing the area has been completed.

The twenty-seven-year-old commander of the Red Army in the west, Mikhail Tukhachevsky, is keen to push on. At the beginning of July, he issues an order of the day to all his units.

> The time of reckoning has come.
> In the blood of the defeated Polish army we will drown the criminal government of Piłsudski.
> Over the corpse of White Poland lies the road to World Conflagration.
> On our bayonets we will bring peace and happiness to the toiling masses of mankind.
> On to Wilno, Minsk, Warsaw – Forward!

The road west is open. All that is needed is the order from the top to fire the starter's pistol.

Vladimir is surrounded by voices urging caution. Despite all the stirring speeches in Moscow about a proletarian war against the Polish landlord class, in private many Bolshevik leaders fear that the workers of Warsaw may not welcome the Red Army as liberators. The British offer to mediate a ceasefire in order to save the Poles and hold back the Reds in Russia. Trotsky urges Lenin to take the offer up.

But the impatient revolutionary will not be held back. Visions of sweeping conflagration dance before his eyes: the defensive turned into the offensive again. A Red empire stretching from Moscow to Berlin – or further. 'It is time to encourage revolution in Italy,' he wires to Stalin. 'Hungary must be sovietised, and maybe also the Czech lands and Romania.' (The loyal Georgian replies that it would indeed be 'sinful' not to promote revolution in Rome.) The prestige of military victory will surely knock any moderate socialist doubters off their perches, and push the international workers' movement Moscow's way.

Confident of success, throwing all caution to the wind, Vladimir demands an acceleration of the military campaign. A timetable is set: six weeks to conquer Poland.

MUNICH – SEBASTOPOL: 'The fate of Poland today should be a warning sign to the Entente', Adolf tells an audience in Rosenheim, where a new party chapter has been opened by a local railway administrator and his wife. Germany's salvation, he says, will not come in the west. It will come in the east. Once Lenin has been overthrown, he sees a match made in heaven of agrarian Russia and industrial Germany. Grain for iron. 'We must seek an *Anschluss* with national, anti-Semitic Russia', Adolf declares, a new geo-political grouping to take on the world: an unbeatable, Eurasian bloc.

At that very moment, a far-right delegation of Germans, Austrians and Hungarians arrives in Crimea to explore the possibilities of an alliance with like-minded Russians.

BAD GASTEIN: The sacred summer break has arrived. Freud is in the mountains again, this time with his sister-in-law Minna, as far away as possible from Vienna. 'The peace is delightful,' Freud writes to Anna, 'not even an organ grinder.' There is a waterfall nearby. Every day after lunch, while Minna takes her siesta, Freud settles down to work. And in this high solitude, far from the city, Freud decides to turn his mind to that most salient feature of his age: the crowd.

It is a subject that Freud knows he must address. Everyone is writing about it. Everyone has views on it. Psychoanalysis cannot be left behind.

And it is a matter of which Freud has some experience. After all, he has seen the infectious power of crowds. He remembers well the Parisian crowds he wandered through as a student, astounded by the volatility of their moods, so easily manipulated by the martinets and mountebanks of French politics, a type Freud profoundly despises. He has experienced for himself the exhilaration which can go with feeling part of a group united for a single purpose: he remembers 1914.

Freud fears the tendency of his age to discount the individual in favour of the group. He reads about its vicious consequences every day: in wars, pogroms, revolutions and riots from Petrograd to Munich to East St. Louis. He knows the strange influence which the masses exert on the individual – and vice versa. He worries about those rabble-rousers who seem to want to exploit matters further rather than calm them down, who celebrate the collective against the individual, and in so doing make the baying crowd (or the lynch-mob) the only true source of legitimacy. The cult of the masses – whether that of the faceless proletariat or the millions of war dead or the identikit consumer – is all around these days.

What are the masses, psychologically speaking? What is it that makes humans seek sublimation in a group? By what means of hidden communication does a group of individuals cohere into a group, as if possessed of a single will and a single mind? These are not simple problems. Nor are they dry and academic. What makes an army follow its commanders to the death? What makes a revolutionary mob act as one? By what strange power does a leader direct a crowd? And by what craven instinct of submission does a crowd decide to follow? To answer these questions is to unlock the public mind. It is to expose the hidden, subterranean workings of society. And it turns the person who can read them into a god.

What Sigmund seeks to analyse, others are already trying to apply. The notion that the whims and fancies of the masses can be understood in scientific terms fascinates those with the ambition to convert such knowledge into power. Sigmund's nephew Edward hopes to turn crowd psychology into a marketable business proposition: the management of the public mind for private ends. Benito Mussolini reads the same texts on crowd psychology as Freud in his Austrian hideaway – Gustave le Bon, in particular – looking to improve his political technique. The plasticity of human emotions which so terrifies Sigmund is, for Benito, a thrilling fact, an incredible opportunity. For those who know the workings of the public mind will be those best placed to control it. Politics can become a science and individuals mere cells within the greater body of society, all directed by a fascist super-brain.

Mussolini knows he is not the only one to have picked up on the idea of a leader conjuring the masses to follow his will. There is one other European leader whose methods he admires above all others. 'Lenin is an artist who has worked with human beings as other artists work with marble or metals', Benito gushes. It is just a pity that the artwork he has produced has not lived up to his promise.

In Bad Gastein, high up in the mountains, the nightmares of the modern world crowd into Freud's makeshift study.

WARSAW: Having returned to France to an administrative job which bored him, Charles de Gaulle is back in Poland. He has been here now almost as long as he served on the Western Front in the war.

He left in April, when Poland was thrilled by reports of constant victory. By July, the news is all of defeat. The currency has collapsed; the queues for bread have grown longer. The mood is less one of anger than one of Slavic resignation. 'The more the danger approaches, the less they react,' Charles writes in his diary, 'which explains why, throughout history, a handful of barbarians have been able to dominate such huge territory.' This is the captain's own pet theory, of course, that wars are won or lost on the question of popular morale.

Occasionally, he catches sight of a flash of resistance. One Sunday, after a solemn Catholic Mass in what was once a Russian Orthodox cathedral, he attends a parade of volunteers, mostly students. They carry imitation guns. 'What tragic destiny that the energy and spirit of these people's elites has never been equal to the virtue and readiness of the masses', de Gaulle jots down. His own students from last year are now all at the front. Several have been killed. His military acquaintances in Warsaw — Charles has made no real friends here — ask him what the French will do to help. De Gaulle chafes under the restrictions of neutrality. Once again, he is a bystander to great historic events. It is particularly vexing that the young commander of the Red Army, Mikhail Tukhachevsky, is a man de Gaulle remembers from their time in the same German prisoner-of-war camp. (Mikhail was called Misha then and, unlike Charles, he managed to escape.)

But this war is quite unlike the last one. Then, for three years, the Western Front barely moved. Its symbol was Verdun. This war is fought on horseback, like a Napoleonic campaign, with a front line that moves this way and that with the speed of a cracking whip. Cavalry emerge from huge dust clouds, scattering their foes, sabres slashing through the air. The open borderlands are like an ocean: empty and immeasurable, the enemy hidden in its vastness. The Red Army survives off the land and the promise of rapid conquest. Horse-drawn wagons are mounted with machine guns. Where will they come to rest?

The fate of Western civilisation seems to hang by a thread.

NEW YORK: The bare-faced cheek.

Marcus Garvey sends William Du Bois a free pass for the upcoming UNIA convention and asks if he would like to throw his hat into the ring as candidate for 'accredited spokesman of the American Negro People', a subsidiary position to that of the worldwide leader.

Du Bois bristles. He takes a week to respond to the Jamaican upstart. He wants his name put forward 'under no circumstances'. Instead he requests that Garvey answer a series of basic questions about the UNIA so *The Crisis* can provide a 'critical estimate' of the organisation and its leader in an upcoming issue. 'I expect only such answers as you are willing to divulge and to have the public know', he writes.

LONDON: 'It is late in the day to consider all these matters after so many opportunities and resources have been thrown away with both hands through all these disastrous months', Winston writes. But it is not too late. Churchill demands the suspension of trade talks with Soviet Russia and more aid to Wrangel. British supplies and aircraft should be sent to Warsaw and arms provided to Finland, Romania and Serbia to help them intervene on the Polish side. All the material, in other words, to fight a new world war.

PETROGRAD – MOSCOW: In an atmosphere of intense excitement, two hundred delegates meet in Petrograd for the opening of the second congress of the Comintern. They arrive on false passports from around the world.

It is a far more impressive gathering than the year before, when delegates were rounded up from whoever happened to be in Moscow and the entire conference barely filled a single room. Last year the congress was over in a few days. This year, it takes three weeks, divided between Petrograd and Moscow. The invitation to attend is answered by delegates from far and wide. A raucous contingent of Italians represent Benito Mussolini's old Italian Socialist Party. They bring their own Chianti, and share it nightly in one of the Comintern leader's hotel rooms. Serious-minded delegations arrive from Germany (Rosa Luxemburg's lawyer amongst them) and France (including a former stretcher-bearer from Verdun with a new book out entitled *Revolution or Death*). Several Asian delegates arrive in Soviet Russia by various routes in the weeks leading up to the congress. A group of Irish delegates register at the congress under code names, and use their presence to advertise support for the Irish cause as an opportunity for world communism to strike a hammer blow against British imperialism. There is one Pole: he soon leaves for the front.

Amongst the more familiar figures, one can spot John Reed, still recovering from his Finnish ordeal, his skin pale and his cheeks sunken. His romantic ideas about Lenin and his regime are wearing thin. But the Comintern still fires his imagination: as a gathering of like-minded spirits, united by the cause of world revolution, free to debate and argue their way to the victory of the proletariat. One such spirit, Sylvia Pankhurst – Emmeline's militantly left-wing daughter – decides to make the journey to Russia in spite of an ongoing dispute with Lenin about the correct tactics to use in the struggle in Britain. (Incredibly, Vladimir considers Sylvia's approach to be *too radical* and deals with the disagreement in his usual way, writing a pamphlet accusing her and others of being 'infantile' and making sure every delegate gets a copy as soon as they arrive.) Amongst the Russian delegates, by far the most numerous, are both Vladimir's wife Nadya and his former lover Inessa, who is given the job of organising a women's conference on the margins of the main affair.

No expense is spared to impress the foreign delegates. They feast in the colonnaded grandeur of the Smolny, the epicentre of the revolution in 1917. A six-hour open-air agitprop performance is put on with thousands of conscript soldiers, even grander than the May Day show. A Red Mass commemorates fallen comrades, accompanied by the music of Wagner. Monuments are erected to the Paris Commune of 1871 – from which Communism derives its name – and to Rosa Luxemburg. A special commemorative plate is produced. Despite paper and ink shortages, a Comintern bulletin is produced in four languages.

At the congress opening, a huge orchestra plays the Internationale to specially composed new music. All delegates then rise for a funeral march in memory of the martyrs of the revolution. Vladimir gives the opening speech. He declares that Versailles has turned Germany into a colony of the American banks. He quotes approvingly from a new book by the British economist John Maynard Keynes, *The Economic Consequences of the Peace*. He talks encouragingly about the possibility of communist revolution in otherwise 'backward' colonies, forgetting his earlier insistence that socialism could only follow a period of capitalism. But these are heady days. Revolution is on the march again in Europe – and soon in Asia too. A painter is commissioned to capture the moment for posterity.

In Moscow, the congress reassembles a few days later in the coronation hall of the Kremlin. The golden eagles atop the building have been especially regilded for the occasion, for the first time since the revolution. (Some delegates take the opportunity to test the springs of the imperial mattresses in a nearby bedchamber.) A huge map is set up with little red flags to show the daily advance of Red Army troops towards Warsaw. The scent of victory on the battlefield a thousand miles to the west permeates proceedings in the Kremlin. The world is going Moscow's way.

DUBLIN: A new force appears in Ireland, screeching down country lanes in speeding lorries, stomping through towns and villages. They are not quite soldiers, but not quite policemen either. London's answer to the IRA. Winston's answer, too.

Their accents are estuary English, rather than the familiar Irish of the police or the cut-glass accents of the British officer class. They wear a jumble of khaki and green and black leather, topped with a Scottish military beret, rather than the dark bottle green of the Royal Irish Constabulary, the force with which they are supposedly associated. They become known to locals as the Black and Tans after a well-known fox hunt in Limerick. And it is to hunt that they have come to Ireland: to hunt down the IRA, and neutralise them by whatever means most expedient. They arrive in Ireland in dribs and drabs, a few dozen every month at first, then a few hundred.

There is a coarse swagger to these battle-hardened men, men who have come to expect no kindness or sweetness in their lives but what is bought and paid for with blood and money, former British soldiers operating under military law when they feel like it, and outside the law when it suits them. They wear their pistols strapped onto their thighs, or one on each hip, for easy shooting. They are careless about how much ammunition they use, or who they use it on. They have little stake in Ireland's future and little care for Ireland's woes. They hunt for King and Empire – and for the sake of a job when no work is on offer back home. They hunt as a pack, travelling around in lorries with machine guns poking out the back. A pound a week and no questions asked. The IRA fights dirty, and so they will fight dirty too, outrunning and outgunning them where they can.

The rhythm of outrage and reprisal continues, of assassination and counter-assassination. In Tuam, County Galway, it is Irish police who lead reprisals against the town for an IRA ambush on the road to Dunmore which leaves two officers dead. In what has become the pattern now, houses and shops are burned to the ground in retaliation. The town hall is torched. A visitor is reminded of the war-scarred villages of Belgium and France.

Sinéad de Valera visits her husband in America that August. (Michael Collins provides her with a false passport for the journey.) Éamon is not best pleased to see her. He is overworked with his fight for control of Irish America, he explains. He cannot spare her much time. There are rumours that he is having an affair with his secretary.

UPSTATE MICHIGAN: The greatest soldier-journalist-fisherman Horton Bay has ever seen (currently unemployed, having left the *Star*) is at it again: Hemingway is back by the lake.

He seems happy enough to those who meet him, the same chipper character, the same attitude. He has picked up the habit of shadow-boxing when he speaks, as if constantly sparring with an imaginary opponent. On his extended holiday in the country, Ernest fishes and plays tennis nearly every day. (Occasionally he gambles at roulette – and loses.) But something is eating him up inside, the same thing which has been gnawing at him since he got back from the war, just as it gnaws at thousands of other young Americans who have seen a glimpse of the wider world and then had it snatched away. The war has opened up their minds. Peace seems dull. America seems dull. Life seems dull. Ernest Hemingway's parents seem particularly dull. The war boom has turned into the peace slump. Metaphorically, and in every other way. (Share prices on Wall Street drop almost one third this August; a get-rich-quick scheme dreamed up by a man named Ponzi shuts down around the same time.)

'I'm for a job in New York', Ernest writes to Grace Quinlan, a fourteen-year-old schoolgirl he has befriended in Petoskey, 'but then I'm also for the open road and long sea swells, and an old tramp steamer hull down on the oily seas.' Open warfare breaks out with his mother, who warns Ernest to 'cease your lazy loafing and pleasure seeking'. For a while the prodigal son becomes the black sheep.

The plan to go to Yokohama withers on the vine. Hemingway moves to Chicago instead.

MOSCOW: The Russians dominate. At a football match organised to celebrate the gathering of the Comintern, a team made up of international delegates including John Reed is soundly beaten by a local Moscow squad. The winners are given prizes of outstanding current value: a jar of fruit and a bag of flour each.

In the Comintern meeting the same pattern prevails. There is no doubt the Russians are in charge. Everyone uses the word 'comrade'; that does not mean that they are always comradely themselves. Procedures are manipulated, debate curtailed, bully tactics employed. At one point, John Reed is called a liar when he points out how his own words are being misrepresented. (His threat to resign from the Comintern is laughed off as petit-bourgeois indulgence.) Sylvia Pankhurst, arriving late, is cut off when she speaks for too long in a direction of which Lenin disapproves. Rosa Luxemburg might have received a better hearing, but she is long gone. Vladimir scuttles in when necessary to make sure the delegates are kept in line. His prestige is critical. A Scottish delegate accepts correction from Lenin 'as a child accepts the rebuke of a father'.

Dissent turns to deference. The Moscow line is pushed through: the dictatorship of the proletariat conducted by the dictatorship of the party. The organisational principles of Russian Bolshevism become the principles to be adopted by all communist parties the world over: unity, hierarchy, 'iron proletarian centralism'. Rules are drawn up to ensure that all future decisions of the Comintern will be binding for its member parties. Moscow rule.

The rattle of typewriters fills the air. The bells of the Kremlin clock tower which used to play the anthem of the Tsars play the Internationale three times a day. And still the news from the western front remains good.

NEW YORK: 'We are here because this is the age when all peoples are striking out for freedom, for liberty and for democracy', Marcus Garvey thunders. 'We have entered this age of struggle for liberty at the same time with the people of Ireland, the people of Egypt, of India, and the people of the Eastern states of Europe.' The UNIA is the only truly black organisation in the United States that that meets 'not as cringing sycophants, but as men and women standing erect and demanding our rights from all quarters'.

For the whole month of August, the UNIA holds its convention in New York. Jim Europe's old band plays marching tunes and jazz in UNIA parades. Placards reading 'Africa for the Africans' and 'Negroes Helped Win the War' are waved aloft in marches through Harlem. Twenty-five thousand are reported to attend a rally in Madison Square Garden, where Garvey trumpets a telegram of support from a leading Californian Zionist: 'no peace in this world until the Jew and the Negro both control side by side Palestine and Africa', it proclaims. Garvey reads out another telegram that he intends to send to his hero Éamon de Valera.

Through the stiflingly hot summer, hope, pride and anger intermingle in the airless Liberty Hall. Grievances from around the world are shared. Redress is demanded. A long UNIA Declaration of Rights is agreed, noting the multiple ways blacks are discriminated against and demanding rectification, from a requirement to teach black history in schools to an end to unequal treatment on the world's railways and steamships. One clause states that blacks must seek the approbation of their leader – that is, whoever Garvey's organisation chooses – before fighting in any war. Opposition to such a move, on the basis that it suggests the split loyalties of black Americans, is voted down.

'This movement, let me tell you, has already swept the world', he tells his audience on the fourth Sunday of the convention, comparing it to the global spread of Bolshevism (a comparison from which he backtracks when he realises the danger in associating himself with the global outlaws Lenin and Trotsky). Garvey preaches the doctrine of African redemption, warning the colonial powers that 'we are coming, and this we will continue to do for another fifty years if need be'. He is just as fierce in his censure of his critics in America, those black leaders 'comfortably resting back in cushioned chairs in their editorial rooms'. He plugs the shares of the Black Star Line whenever the opportunity arises.

Outside the hall, Garvey's radicalism horrifies as much as it inspires. The Bureau of Investigation receives daily updates from its informants, each one more lurid than the last, accusing Garvey of inciting race hatred and playing on the crowd's emotions and prejudices. Other black community leaders accuse Garvey of being a 'fool or a rogue'. Du Bois, more quietly, goes about collecting evidence of financial misconduct on the part of the UNIA. In July, he writes in a private letter of his suspicion that 'Garvey is financially more or less a fraud'. In August, he forms a still more disagreeable opinion. 'I do not believe that Marcus F. Garvey is sincere', he tells an interviewer: 'I think he is a demagogue and that his movement will collapse in a short time'.

At the close of the convention, Garvey appears at the New Star Casino in scarlet robes, wearing a turban with a large gold tassel. He is confirmed as President-General of the UNIA at a salary of ten thousand dollars a year. In a self-conscious nod to de Valera's aggrandisement, the *Negro World* terms Garvey the 'Provisional President of Africa'. He is acclaimed as 'the ablest statesman of his race, and its acknowledged greatest orator'.

Garvey signs off his latest editorial letter in the usual fashion. 'Those who have not already bought shares send in to the office of the Black Star Line, 56 West 135th Street, New York, U.S.A., and purchase them now'. The Black Star Line has not yet made one cent in profit.

THE POLISH FRONT: Captain de Gaulle is driven out to the front, crossing lines of trenches from 1915 and 1917. The hastily erected wooden crosses which mark the burial sites of these earlier campaigns have begun to rot. 'For the sixth year in a row,' Charles writes in his diary, 'there will be no harvest from these fields.' The next day, he rides with the Polish cavalry in headlong retreat.

The Red Army enters Brest-Litovsk, where the Germans forced the young Soviet Republic to accept such bitter terms of peace two years before. Warsaw is just one hundred miles away. A Polish Revolutionary Committee is formed to take control of the city when the Reds get there. (In the meantime, it takes up residence in a grand palace to the east.) In Germany, while some worry that the Red Army's approach will spark a Communist coup in Berlin, others welcome it as a chance to smash the hated Versailles Treaty. (Lenin himself is not averse to a temporary alliance between German nationalists and the Bolsheviks; it will all be resolved in civil war in the end.) In between sessions of the Comintern, Vladimir commends 'a beautiful plan' to hang priests and landowners along the line of the Red Army's advance and then blame it on a peasant uprising as a way of further stirring up animosity between different groups in Polish society. He suggests a reward of one hundred thousand roubles for every person hanged.

The central spearhead of the Red Army, the western armies commanded by Charles de Gaulle's erstwhile fellow POW Misha, thrust forward towards Warsaw. The Polish peasants do not rise in revolution. The flanks of the advance are exposed. An order is issued for the armies of the south-western front, to which Stalin is attached, to provide cavalry in support, breaking off from its own assault on Lviv. The Georgian bank-robber bristles at the suggestion. Misha is about to take Warsaw in any case. Why should Comrade Stalin give up his own prize of Lviv to help him?

In Warsaw, Piłsudski shuts himself in a room of the Belvedere Palace to consider what to do. Everything depends on his next move. He pulls back his armies as far as he dares. A few days later he departs for the front.

SÈVRES, FRANCE: In a Parisian suburb famous for its breakable porcelain the Sultan's envoys sign a devastating peace to end the Ottoman Empire's six-year war.

The Sultan will retain Istanbul – under temporary foreign occupation – and a small portion of the old empire in Anatolia. Zones of influence are delineated for the European powers. The Armenians, Greeks and Kurds will gain more than they could have dreamed of. Greek troops have already marched two hundred miles from Smyrna to occupy the territory they plan to annex. The Ottoman Grand Vizier resigns in shame and travels to the Czech spa town of Karlsbad to recuperate.

Enver Pasha plays with the idea of a new role for himself at the head of a league of Turkic-speaking peoples from Europe to middle Asia, backed by Moscow. In the baking heart of Anatolia, Mustafa Kemal makes his own gestures to Soviet Russia, congratulating the Bolsheviks on their latest victories and declaring that 'Bolshevism includes the sublime principles and laws of Islam'. He still ends his speeches with praise for Allah.

DEARBORN: The *Independent* continues its anti-Semitic campaign. Henry Ford's own voice remains that of the Olympian observer, dispensing common wisdom from his factory throne. Over the summer, he opines innocently on the nature of the presidency, casually reigniting the thought that he might run for the highest office in the land.

WARSAW: The sound of artillery bombardment can be heard in the Polish capital. The churches are crammed with the faithful at prayer. Grenades are stockpiled to mount a last and surely hopeless stand should the Red Army break through. Inexperienced Polish volunteers are sent forward through the villages and orchards around the capital to face the onrush of the enemy.

When a Catholic chaplain is killed in the first line of defence, he is instantly considered a martyr of the faith, and a symbol of the spirit of national self-sacrifice. 'This is a battle for life and death, a crusade against modern heathens, a fight against the devil himself', the priest at his funeral declares. 'At the gates of Warsaw rages a battle for Poland's existence, at the gates of Warsaw the fate of all Europe and all humanity is being determined at this very moment.'

But the truly decisive battle is about to be fought elsewhere. While the Red Army, its supply lines stretched to breaking point, advances on Warsaw, Piłsudski manoeuvres a strike force far to the south and east of the spearhead of the Red advance. This now wheels hard against the Red Army's exposed flank. Surprise is complete. Russian supply and communication lines are cut. The Red Army collapses in retreat.

'Our Poles have grown wings!' de Gaulle writes in his diary. Out of the jaws of defeat, the Poles have managed to pluck victory. Lenin's revolutionary bayonets have missed their target.

MUNICH: Hitler's anti-Semitic ramblings acquire a mystical tone over the summer. For two hours one evening in the Hofbräuhaus, a regular meeting ground for the Nazi membership now, he declaims on the genesis and future of the Aryan race.

It was born in the far north, he declares, where harsh environmental conditions forced Aryans to be both particularly creative and possessed of great inner strength. The Ice Age pushed them south, the mangy field-runner explains, sweeping his hand to demonstrate the vastness of his conception of things. They were cold, he says, which is why they all worshipped the sun – of which the swastika is one symbol. Then they spread out. 'We know that Egypt's cultural flowering was brought about by the arrival of Aryan immigrants', he continues, 'and it was the same for the Persians and the Greeks.' They were all blonde with blue eyes, the dark-haired speaker asserts confidently.

In this racial recasting of world history, Jews are viewed as the eternal opposite of Aryans. 'I could not survive without work', Adolf claims. He accuses the Jews of an inborn aversion to proper work, illustrated by their alleged use of Assyrian stonemasons to build their temple in Jerusalem.

Hitler's anti-Semitic speeches now fuse the kind of traditional prejudices that circulated around the Vienna of his youth with eccentric racial and historical theories picked up from his new acquaintances in Munich and the toxic notion of a worldwide Jewish conspiracy manifested in international finance capitalism and global political chaos. The Spartacists, Hitler says, have been led astray: behind Vladimir Lenin, it is Jewish millionaires who are pulling the strings. True socialism can only be built *against* the Jews, not with them: 'if we are socialists, then we must be anti-Semites'. The Zionist project, he says, is nothing less than a plan to establish a training academy for world domination.

The mangy field-runner spices this poisonous brew with his own personal anxieties and hatreds. In amongst his sweeping statements about the history of the Aryan race, he rants furiously against the success of the operettas of the Austro-Hungarian composer Franz Léhar, adducing his commercial success to Jewish preponderance amongst music critics. He claims all pimps are Jewish, 'always ready to rip up a happy marriage, if there are thirty shillings' profit to be made'.

The police report lively and enthusiastic crowds.

MILAN: At the airfield of Arcore, not far from Monza, the newspaper editor Benito Mussolini starts taking flying lessons. If D'Annunzio can do it, why not him?

Somewhat awkwardly he turns up for his first lesson wearing a bowler hat and spats. But he takes to the new pursuit with vigour over the following months, inviting his family along to watch. His newspaper starts running a regular page on flying, with the command '*Volare!*' at its top. Benito takes to donning flying gear to impress his followers. Nothing could be more fascist, he tells them, than the will to conquer the skies. He considers participating in an aeronautical marathon from Rome to Tokyo as a way of burnishing his credentials.

In Rome, the political carousel turns ever faster. One government replaces another. Over the summer, Italy experiences a wave of factory occupations, with hundreds of thousands downing tools and demanding workers' control. The Italian flag is desecrated and the Red flag raised instead. Catholic priests are beaten up, accused of being the representatives of the old order which must be swept away (on this point, socialists and some Fascists agree). Political violence – both by and against the Socialists – proliferates. Dozens are killed. Physical assault becomes an accepted means of making a political point. The weakness of the central state is self-evident.

Out of this violence, local anti-socialist militias emerge – a sort of Italian Freikorps – sometimes little more than gangs of friends from school or university. They become known as the *squadristi*. Fired up on whatever local booze they can find – cherry brandy in Ferrara – these gangs see themselves as the only true patriots left in a country on the brink of a foreign-inspired Bolshevik takeover. Their leaders, men who idolise D'Annunzio and his panache, award themselves the extravagant title of *ras*, in emulation of the tribal leaders of Ethiopia. Landowners and industrialists are only too willing to provide them with trucks and money if they turn their energies to strike-breaking. Thus enriched with potential new supporters – albeit with their own leaders, their own local power bases and a taste for independent action – the Fascist movement which Mussolini purports to lead becomes both more powerful and more unruly.

Benito is skilful in riding this wave of violence and discontent. He flatters whomever he needs to. He cultivates his image as a man who flies planes, but also reads books (some call him Professor Mussolini). He espouses a fascist creed of constant readiness and permanent mobilisation against all threats, from wherever they may come. He talks about violence, without getting caught up in it himself. He expresses an understanding for the plight of the workers. (After all, he is a working man himself, he claims, who sleeps in his underwear rather than in the pyjamas of the bourgeoisie.) But he rails against the socialist doctrines of class war he once espoused.

In print and in speeches, he reminds his readers of the Socialists' attitude to the war. They are to be blamed for Caporetto. They, and the old-fashioned politicians in Rome, mutilated the soldiers' eventual victory. Now they are trying to destroy Italy from the inside and impose their internationalist ideology on Italy, Europe and the world.

In contrast, Mussolini presents himself as a practical man, ready to fight against the Socialists as violently as the situation demands but – and this is crucial – also prepared to reach accommodation with whoever he must in order to serve the national interest. This disappoints those who, like Marinetti, like the idea of simply demolishing the old to make way for the new (whatever that may be). But Benito is savvier. He must appeal to more than just the Futurist fringe. There are many more potential Fascists out there who must be won over with an open hand as well as a clenched fist.

As D'Annunzio's regime in Fiume begins to flounder, Mussolini's credit rises. For all his skills as a master of public relations, Gabriele's faults are all too obvious: his personal weaknesses, his disdain for authority, his unpredictability, his love of extravagance. Mussolini seems a man whom one can do business with.

Moscow: Warsaw has not been captured. The Red Army is in retreat again. John Reed pesters Vladimir for an urgent meeting to protest his treatment by the Comintern. Lenin is preoccupied with a personal matter: Inessa Armand is ill again.

She wants to travel to the South of France to see the sea. Vladimir worries that she might be arrested. He suggests alternative destinations – Norway, Holland, Germany – where she might be able to go without so much risk, travelling as a Frenchwoman or as a Russian or perhaps even passing herself off as Canadian. Then there is the possibility of a sanatorium much closer to home, in the Caucasus. Vladimir writes to the appropriate authorities insisting they take care of Inessa and her son.

The sanatorium at Kislovodsk is run-down. There is no electric lighting in her room. When the local party officials check up on Inessa, on Lenin's insistence, her principal request is that they get her a pillow. She is given three. Inessa sunbathes and gets bored. Her son plays croquet.

Berlin: The anti-relativists strike. Outside the Berliner Philharmonie young men sell swastika lapel pins. Inside, a new organisation called the Study Group of German Scientists for the Preservation of Pure Science holds a public meeting. The organisation's founder, an undistinguished engineer called Paul Weyland, stands to address the audience, and starts the attack which has been brewing these past few months.

There is not much science in his speech. Its tone is angry, its contents are personal. Relativity, Weyland tells them, is a hoax, a publicity stunt by a sensation-seeking manipulator. Einstein is accused of 'scientific Dadaism', of plagiarism, of taking the German people for a ride. The relativity craze is an offence against common sense, he cries, and a menace to the German spirit. To begin the fightback, he announces a series of anti-relativist lectures to prove the matter scientifically (including one, impressively enough, by the Nobel Prize-winning German physicist Philipp Lenard). After Weyland, an actual physicist takes to the stage: Ernst Gehrcke, a long-time critic of Einstein whom Albert has (unwisely perhaps) chosen to ignore. Gehrcke's pince-nez quivers with indignation as he lists his deeply felt objections to relativity. But just as he gets into the stride of his lecture, another name is heard rising from the audience. Just a murmur at first and then, unmistakeably: 'Ein-stein, Ein-stein, Ein-stein'.

And there he is. The scientific Dadaist himself. Sitting in a box. Grinning at the hateful idiocy of the proceedings, surrounded by a phalanx of scientific friends (and his stepdaughter, who is now also his secretary). At each statement made against his person and his theory Einstein bursts into prolific laughter, his cackles echoing through the hall. He mock-claps his way through Gehrcke's speech. At its end, he turns to his friends with a broad smile. 'Most amusing', he tells them loudly as they leave.

In truth, he is livid. A few days later, he takes up his pen and writes an article, returning fire with fire. To Weyland and Gehrcke he directs withering sarcasm, referring to his opponents as the Anti-Relativity Company Ltd. Such men are hardly worth responding to, Einstein claims: why waste the ink? Their arguments – if any can be perceived – are nonsense. They themselves are nonentities. Einstein also turns his anger on Lenard – who wasn't even there – proclaiming him a good experimental physicist but having produced nothing of worth in the theoretical domain. Such men must be driven by hatred, or envy, or some combination of the two. 'If I were a German nationalist with or without a swastika, instead of a Jew', Einstein writes, they would have nothing to rail against, these poor fools. Would I be treated so badly in Britain or in Holland, he asks?

A flood of letters urges him not to leave Germany. (His friend and colleague Fritz Haber begs that this swastika-wearing 'entente of mediocrity cannot appear to counterbalance the shared respect all serious scientists have for you' and promises to look into Einstein's salary again – a serious matter for a man who has to pay alimony to an ex-wife with two children in expensive Switzerland.) Friends warn against further intemperate articles, suggesting Einstein leave to others the dirty work of defending relativity against such lowlifes. 'Don't let yourself get cross!' a friend urges him. 'Stay the holy man in the temple – and stay in Germany.'

'This world is a curious madhouse', Albert writes to a friend, where 'coachmen and waiters debate the correctness of the theory of relativity', and where their convictions on the subject seem to depend on their politics more than anything else. He challenges his detractors to a proper scientific debate, at a conference of physicists in a few weeks' time.

WALL STREET, NEW YORK: Men and women are knocked off their feet when the bomb explodes outside the offices of J. P. Morgan, the most famous finance house in America. A sheet of flame stretches from one sidewalk to the other. The sound of broken glass tumbling onto the road below reminds one man of Niagara Falls. A young financier who works on the unregulated, creative fringes of the market – father of a three-year-old boy called John Fitzgerald Kennedy – is knocked to the ground by a wave of hot air.

The streets fill with the smell of blood and burned rubber and acid and dust. Papers flutter in the air. Body parts are everywhere: hands on window ledges, feet still inside warm shoes. War veterans take care of the wounded with makeshift tourniquets. The stock market shuts. A ripple of fear resonates out from Wall Street around the world. 'Bodies are rent asunder and crushed to pulp', reports the *Philadelphia Enquirer*.

And yet, by the next morning, the scene has been cleared. Bloodstains have been removed with bleach. The stock market reopens earlier than expected. There are rumours that Mitchell Palmer is planning a fresh raid against radicals. But the public mood is weary of such panics now. While commiserating with the families of the victims, the *Wall Street Journal* warns against any political overreaction. 'The relations between capital and labor will not be changed,' the paper says in its first comment on the attack: 'not even for the worse as regards labor.' Stocks surge when trading begins again. Capitalism is more resilient than expected.

BAKU, AZERBAIJAN: 'Don't you know how Baku is pronounced in American?' John Reed asks. 'It's pronounced *oil!*'

The Comintern launches its latest front in the oil town in the Caucasus where Stalin perfected his bank-robbing techniques in the last days of the empire. The purpose of the gathering is to spread the word of Moscow to the peoples of the east. The British have only just left Baku. Reed travels there across typhus-ravaged southern Russia. He is not given a choice: 'Comintern has made a decision. Obey.' He takes it as punishment for the difficulties he caused in Moscow. His wife Louise is expected to arrive from America within weeks. Jack is not well. But he cannot refuse. A special train is laid on. All requirements are taken care of.

The conference takes place mostly at night, when the heat of the day has begun to wear off. Speeches have to be translated and retranslated from English to Russian, Russian to Turkish or Turkish to Persian – and then into Urdu, Pashto, Kalmyk and a dozen other languages. (To speed things up the organisers resort to asking the two thousand delegates to huddle in linguistic groups so interpretation can take place simultaneously.) A band keeps playing the Internationale, sometimes striking up several times in a single speech. The delegates cheer, often at the wrong time, waving their swords and rifles in the air. British and French speakers attack their countries' imperialism. Don't expect anything better from American capitalists, Reed warns: 'No, comrades, Uncle Sam is not one ever to give anybody something for nothing.'

In his latest swerve towards whoever may be able to help him realise his ambitions, a proclamation by Enver Pasha is read out at the conference. (He has too many enemies to be allowed to speak in person.) He apologises for his support of German imperialism during the war, saying he now hates the Germans as much as the British: 'If we fell into a false situation, that was our bad luck.' Had Soviet Russia existed in 1914 he would have fought by Lenin's side, Enver insists. A British spy files a report to London on proceedings.

The Bolsheviks have been defeated at the gates of Warsaw. Moscow now wants to open a new front. The war has expanded Europe's colonial empires but it has also weakened them. National liberation movements such as Mustafa Kemal's, or the Muslim Khalifat campaign in India, are growing. Even if these movements are not strictly speaking socialist, let alone prole-tarian, this must be exploited. Marxist theory must adapt.

In Baku, the words of the Communist Manifesto are updated: 'workers of all lands and *oppressed peoples of the whole world*, unite!' A new holy war is called for: not under the green flag of Islam, but under the Red banner of Communism: 'Sweep away with fierce will the evil shamelessness of buying and selling!' There are only two centres of power in the modern world, a Chechen from Grozny explains: 'the centre of bourgeois domin-ation, Versailles, and the centre of proletarian struggle, Red Moscow.' 'Blow up Europe!' runs one slogan. Effigies of the French, British and American leaders are burned on the streets. The Hungarian Béla Kun conjures up a picture of the delegates meeting next year and swapping stories on how they overthrew the colonisers.

THE HAGUE: An early evening in late summer. A group of revellers walk arm in arm along the beach by the Dutch capital, singing snippets from *Carmen*.

Next morning, a more serious tone is adopted at the first psychoanalytic congress since the war. Freud, returning to his pet subject, talks about dreams. A German colleague gives a rambling presentation on how various illnesses of the eye – a bleeding retina, myopia and the like – are simply the body's way of reflecting the mind's attempt to suppress hidden desires.

There are no soldiers attending the congress as there were in Budapest in
1918. Instead, there is a welcome smattering of foreigners: a few Americans,
some British, one delegate from Poland. Not quite full peacetime conditions, perhaps, but a sign that psychoanalysis is to be spared the opprobrium
of too close an association with defeated Germany and Austria. There was
some discussion of holding the congress in Berlin. Too soon, wiser voices
counselled.

For the emaciated visitors from German-speaking Europe, Holland is a
paradise. Anna Freud spends the pocket money her father has given her on
bananas. At lunch one day she worries about the consequences of the rich
food on her father's health.

'I hope you are eating sparingly,' Anna writes on a note passed under
the table.

'I am only making an exception for champagne, which is not wine',
Freud replies jauntily.

'Do you eat pineapple?' Anna asks in another note.

He does.

It is not possible for the Freuds to make it to England. Sigmund sends
the briefest of apologies to Sam. Instead they are conducted on a whistle-
stop tour of Holland, including a canoe trip on the waterways of the Zeeland
region.

KISLOVODSK, RUSSIA: On the other side of the Caucasus from Baku, Inessa
feels herself a 'living corpse'.

She thinks of dear Vladimir Ilyich. But she is tired, 'as if having given up
all my strength, all my passion to V. I. and the work, all the springs of love
have dried up in me, all my sympathy for people'. She catches herself. Of
course, 'personal relationships are nothing compared to the needs of the
struggle'.

She plays the piano for guests after dinner one night. The security situation in the Caucasus is getting worse again. They are told they will have
to leave.

AUTUMN

VIENNA: A woman opens the door of her apartment. A strange man stands in the doorway. There is no initial flicker of recognition. She has not seen him since she was a child. She did not know whether he was dead or alive. Now, suddenly, out of nowhere, he has turned up. To Paula Hitler's delight, Adolf takes his sister out shopping.

He leaves again. They promise to stay in touch.

BAD NAUHEIM, GERMANY: The cream of Germany's scientists gather in a spa resort to discuss the matter troubling the peace of German science: Einstein's relativity.

Everything has been done to prevent a riot. Armed police guard the building where the discussion is to take place. Only registered participants – some five hundred of them – are allowed inside Bathhouse Number 8. A mathematician and a physicist jointly check people's credentials. There is to be no trolling by unscientific outsiders. Politics is banned. Most of the discussion of relativity is taken up with presentations – four hours in total – full of mathematical formulae, counted on to suppress (or exhaust) the kind of emotions that were on display in the Berlin outrage, and to put things on a purely scientific plane.

Philipp Lenard, the victim of Einstein's acid pen, and nearly a generation older than him, is quite courteous when his turn to speak eventually comes around. His objections to relativity, he says, are those of a simple scientist appealing to common sense. But he is not given much time to make his case. Einstein, equally polite, is brief and to the point. The chairman of the meeting calls an end to the debate after just fifteen minutes: 'Since the relativity theory unfortunately has not yet made it possible to extend the absolute time interval that is available for the meeting, our session must be adjourned.' Lenard believes he has been cut short, dismayed that the anti-relativists have been smothered by procedure. Though he has undoubtedly won the encounter, Einstein feels uncomfortable at the course of events. At dinner that evening, after a calming walk in the park, Einstein and his party avoid the other physicists. His wife Elsa is confined to bed with nervous exhaustion.

Albert spends the next two weeks relaxing in the hills around Stuttgart with his boys, Hans-Albert and Eduard. 'Best greetings from the most romantic point of our expedition', he writes on a postcard to an old friend. 'Here even consciousness hasn't made an appearance yet – so it seems.' When Einstein is not talking with his sons, or dozing, or calculating how many rapidly depreciating German marks he must earn to send to Mileva in Switzerland, his mind wanders towards a new idea quite unconnected with physics. The experiences of war and economic crisis, he writes to a colleague, 'have made minds so malleable that a real statesman could achieve grand things: I am thinking of a union of European states'.

NALCHIK, RUSSIA – MOSCOW: Two romantics of the revolution, Inessa Armand and John Reed, die within days of each other in the autumn of 1920, one from cholera and the other from typhus. Or is it from disappointment? The disappointment that their beloved revolution, now that it has been realised, is not quite everything they imagined. The reality is never as bright as the dream.

Inessa is evacuated from her Caucasian sanatorium, and contracts cholera somewhere in southern Russia as she tries to escape the disease-ravaged, bandit-ridden regions of the borderlands of the Soviet Republic, sleeping in her railway car and being shunted this way and that as the security situation demands. Her body is taken back to Moscow in a zinc-lined coffin. Vladimir and Nadya greet it at the station. Lenin walks bare-headed behind the funeral cortège. He is distraught.

Jack makes it back from Baku to Moscow where his wife Louise is waiting for him. They go to the ballet. He introduces her to Lenin and Trotsky. But he is not himself. The doctors cannot figure it out. Eventually they diagnose typhus. (Some blame a watermelon picked up en route from Baku in a market in Dagestan, not far from where Inessa died.) In the end, Jack is delirious. He is caught in a trap, he says. The Harvard revolutionary dies in a Moscow hospital.

Reed's coffin stands on display for several days surrounded by flowers and palm fronds and the slogans of the revolution he loved. 'The leaders die, but the cause goes on', reads one in gold lettering. Under a thin and freezing rain, his body is buried in the Kremlin wall. There are speeches in several languages. Louise collapses. 'John was a real American', she tells a reporter later. He would have wanted to be buried at home.

VIENNA: The luxuries of Holland seem a world away. A new parcel from Manchester arrives. Chocolate. Freud greedily unwraps it. He places a tiny piece inside his mouth to let it melt slowly. Quite suddenly a taste of mouldy cheese overwhelms the sweetness. Freud writes a stern letter to Sam advising sackcloth to wrap things up next time. And to send meat extract, coffee and cinnamon.

Sam sends a comic poem about Freud and Jung that he found in an old copy of *Punch* magazine lying around in his dentist's waiting room. Sigmund is not amused. He is quite indifferent to 'popularity in itself'. But he pronounces the poem 'silly'. Freud is angry the editors of *Punch* do not properly understand who he is. He reminds Sam that his name can be found in the *Encyclopaedia Britannica* in 'the supplement to it of the year 1913'.

The dutiful nephew scans the British newspapers for more positive mentions of his uncle.

MOSCOW: History repeats itself, first time as tragedy, the second time as farce. The day after John Reed's untimely death, a new Western visitor is ushered into the presence of Bolshevik greatness. The visitor is Clare Sheridan, an adventurous Englishwoman in her thirties with two children, whose husband was killed in the war. Winston Churchill is her cousin, a fact she does not need to be prompted to reveal. Clare has taken up sculpture since her husband's death and discovered a talent for it. (She has already done Winston; the person she would really like to do is D'Annunzio.)

It is sculpture which has brought Clare to Moscow. Sculpture and adventure. 'Artists are the most privileged class' in Soviet Russia, she was told in London. Lenin and Trotsky will sit for her, she is promised. The offer of such a commission is not easily refused. So Clare braves a ferry across the Baltic to the new independent republic of Estonia, and then a train east. She crosses the front line where White troops fought their last engagement with the Reds after failing to take Petrograd last year. The war has moved on now, and so has the world. London is abuzz with talk of trade deals with the Bolsheviks, in spite of the war with Poland. Of the White armies which once threatened Lenin's regime, only Wrangel's forces are left, holding out in southern Russia.

Clare finds that promises made in London by a Soviet representative intent on seducing her do not match reality in Moscow. The schedule of the impatient revolutionary this autumn does not easily accommodate a few hours of sitting for a sculpture. The Warsaw catastrophe hangs over a disputatious Communist Party conference in Moscow. Only a redacted version of Vladimir's speech can be published in *Pravda*. 'I absolutely in no way in the slightest pretend to knowing military science', he admits. The invasion of Poland was an error, some say. Lenin holds up his hands: what would you have done? Private tensions spill out into the open. Trotsky blames Stalin for holding back troops at the crucial moment; the question of who actually supported the timing of the revolution in 1917 is dragged up again. There is criticism that the party apparatus is getting too strong, too centralised. A week later Vladimir gives a rambling speech to a Communist youth congress. 'The generation of people who are now at the age of fifty cannot expect to see a communist society', he admits, 'but the generation of those who are now fifteen will see a communist society, and will itself build this society.' The period of construction will be long.

While Clare waits for the call from the Kremlin, she is put up in a guesthouse for foreign dignitaries alongside an American capitalist seeking concessions from the Bolshevik regime and the popular British writer H. G. Wells, who has already been honoured with an interview with Lenin during which the Bolshevik leader talks mostly about his latest scheme for Russia's electrification. (Wells is given a film of the Baku conference to take back home with him.) Clare finds herself an observer rather than a participant. There are awkward encounters. At the ballet, a minor official asks how she can wear a red star on her lapel *and* bourgeois white gloves. Clare responds winsomely that what truly matters is what is in one's heart. The apparatchik is unmoved. The days go by. Clare sees Trotsky from a distance. She meets John Reed before he falls ill. Once, she is mistaken for Sylvia Pankhurst. But there is no hot water to take a bath and no newspapers from home. She starts to become a little lonely.

Finally, things start to move. A studio in the Kremlin is assigned to her. A sack of clay is delivered (later a carpet from Turkestan and a gaudy sofa) so she can prepare herself to sculpt the Bolshevik leader. The good and the great start dropping by. Word gets around the Bolshevik village. Soon everyone wants to be sculpted by the English lady: the Comintern chief, the Cheka boss, Béla Kun (whom Clare finds repulsive). Finally, she is taken to see the impatient revolutionary. Vladimir is hard to sculpt, as he *cannot* keep still. He harangues Clare over her cousin Winston, whom he accuses of being the acme of Western capitalism. But she is delighted when he hands her some British newspapers – several weeks old – which have been piling up on his desk. She is particularly interested in news from Ireland, where her father has a large estate.

It is war commissar Trotsky who sweeps Clare Sheridan off her feet. For starters, he speaks French. While setting up and trying to figure out how best to rearrange the furniture in his office for the sitting, she finds herself looking at him for a little too long.

'I hope you don't mind being looked at', Clare says.

'I don't mind', Trotsky replies. 'I have my *revanche* in looking at you, and it is I who gain'. He seems much less busy now the war with Poland is over and the Red Army is closing in on Wrangel's Crimean lair. He is quite prepared to flirt. '*Tout ce que vous voudrez*', he says, when Clare asks if he would mind if she measured his face. 'You are caressing me with tools made of steel', he tells her when she takes out her callipers. Trotsky innocently points out to Clare that his face is somewhat asymmetric, snapping his jaw shut to prove a point. There is still dash about the man. He is only forty, after all.

Clare feels that she is making a connection at last. They talk about poetry. Trotsky claims Shakespeare's existence justifies the existence of England – even if the country is now Soviet Russia's greatest geopolitical enemy. They read the newspapers together. Clare works deep into the night, adjusting and readjusting the bust she is making, while Leon dictates letters to his secretary or else just stands staring at her. He tells her that even when she is toiling with her clay, '*vous êtes encore femme*'. One night, at Clare's request, he unbuttons his shirt to reveal his neck and chest – so that she can better convey his energy and vitality, she says.

Leon warns her against writing bad things about the Soviet experiment when she returns to England. If she betrays him, he warns, he will come to London in person to punish her. 'Now I know how to get you to England', Clare replies.

New York: It all seems to have gone to his head.

Marcus Garvey returns from a speaking and fundraising tour of Pennsylvania, Delaware, New Jersey, Maryland and Ohio, bathing in the acclamation he has received. 'The masses of the race', he writes, 'absorb the doctrines of the UNIA with the same eagerness with which the masses in the days of the supremacy of imperial Rome accepted Christianity.'

William Du Bois continues his enquiries. He writes to the shipping registers to ask if they can provide detail on the legal ownership of ships claimed publicly by the UNIA as belonging to the Black Star Line. He asks for any information on their movements.

Patiently and methodically he builds his case.

RIGA, LATVIA – SEBASTOPOL – MOSCOW: A preliminary peace is agreed between the Bolsheviks and the Poles.

In Crimea, General Wrangel issues an order to his army. 'We are now alone in the struggle which will decide the fate not only of our country but of the whole of humanity', he writes. 'Let us strive to free our native land from the yoke of these Red scum who recognise neither God nor country, who bring confusion and shame in their wake.' Wrangel's forces take refuge behind a defensive line of trenches, barbed wire and artillery pieces dug into the ground. The temperature is falling now. Freezing fog engulfs the troops.

In Moscow, war commissar Trotsky issues an order to annihilate them: 'We need peace and manpower! Soldiers of the Red Army! Destroy Wrangel! Wipe his gangs from the face of the earth!' Leon and Vladimir send a joint telegram to the front telling the Red commanders that letting Wrangel escape would be 'the greatest crime'. The war commissar's train is prepared. He heads to the front again.

VIENNA: Freud is called to give evidence to an inquiry set up to investigate the brutal methods of various doctors during the war, particularly the use of electric shocks. 'I would have done it differently', Sigmund tells them, accidentally reminding the panel that, despite his reputation, he himself did not treat a single case of shell shock throughout the war. He describes the wartime role of psychiatrists, often called upon to catch malingerers and frighten men into returning to duty as soon as possible, as being like a 'machine gun behind the front line'.

The whole affair of the inquiry – the feeling of being put on the stand, as it were, if only as a witness rather than as one of the accused – leaves a bad taste in his mouth. 'I could once more see the mendacious spitefulness of the psychiatrists here', Freud writes to one of his German colleagues. 'But naturally they dared to come out only after I had left. In my presence they were *scheissfreundlich* [shit-friendly] as one says in the language of the erogenous zone.'

WASHINGTON DC: There's a new word in America this autumn. In the towns and villages outside the big cities with their psychoanalysts and their vegetarians and their League-fanatics, the word has a homespun, no-nonsense quality to it which people seem to like: normalcy.

Americans are fed up with grand visions of the wide blue yonder. They are tired of the riots and the raids and endless high drama in the nation's capital. They crave something more straightforward, more American, more calm, perhaps even more boring. Normalcy it is. So, the country turns from Woodrow Wilson to someone very few had heard of before the autumn: Warren Harding, the Republican candidate for President, and Mr Normalcy himself. His running mate is Calvin Coolidge, the man who beat the Boston police strike last year.

Their promise is simple: to put America first. The economy is not doing well. The country needs leaders who understand American business and promote it unashamedly, not distant professors who seem more concerned with the situation in Silesia and Siberia than in Sioux Falls and Saratoga. Normalcy stands for law enforcement, for sound but not overweening government, for more businesslike management of the country's railroads, for balancing the books. While promoting world peace and supporting the independence of small states, America should not seek to meddle in global affairs too much. Nor should it drift too far from its roots.

Wilson's name is not on the ballot paper in this election. (The idea of a third term dies in the Democratic convention in San Francisco, where James Cox and Franklin D. Roosevelt edge out Mitchell Palmer.) But Wilson is not absent entirely. He is a brooding offstage presence: the Republicans' political piñata doll. Woodrow makes no campaign appearances, and when he eventually issues his message to the nation, a few days before the actual vote, he fails to mention the Democratic candidates by name. Instead, he talks about the League. 'The whole world will wait for your verdict in November,' his message reads, 'as it would wait for an intimation of what its future is to be.'

Mr Normalcy wins almost every state. The anti-war Socialist Eugene Debs, still in prison, garners nearly a million votes. (The veteran-turned-writer Hemingway casts his vote that way.) The prospect of his departure from the White House depresses Woodrow. He worries he will be forgotten. Why is it, he mutters to an aide, that the streets of Washington are numbered or lettered, or named after states? Should they not instead be named after the country's leaders?

His supporters write in to comfort him. 'The people have just stopped to get their breath', one suggests.

'Your crown will be one of glory', writes another, likening Woodrow to a wise prophet: 'The heathen who have imagined vain things, will someday creep penitently to touch the hem of your garments'.

'I *know* that this is not a repudiation of the League', Woodrow's daughter Eleanor writes. 'Nothing can destroy what you have done – nothing in the whole wide world.'

The letters and visitors soothe the pain. Woodrow announces to his brother-in-law that he has not lost faith in the American people because they have elected Harding: 'They will realise their error in a little while.'

The next day the President makes his first public appearance in a year, in a wheelchair on the White House lawn. A band plays a song about Virginia, the President's home state, to which it is assumed he may now return as a plain citizen. (Edith has other places in mind, which she ranks according to 'Climate', 'Friends', 'Opportunities', 'Freedom' and 'Amusements'.) Woodrow grimaces. Three weeks later he is awarded the Nobel Peace Prize.

SEBASTOPOL – ISTANBUL: In the cold Crimean autumn of 1920, a salt marsh which normally never freezes begins to harden and ice over. Wrangel's defensive line is suddenly extended. There are not enough troops to man it. As the Red Army marches across the ice, the Whites fall back into Crimea. After that, there is nowhere left to go but the open sea. The Bolshevik military commander offers generous terms to those who surrender – but who can believe a Bolshevik promise? Wrangel gives the order to evacuate. The objective now becomes to get out as many soldiers and sailors as possible. But where can they go?

Istanbul is the obvious choice. The city is just across the Black Sea and under international control. A British admiral questions whether this is such a good idea. 'If these ships filled with refugees arrive in this port what provision is to be made for them?' he asks. 'They cannot be landed here as the town is already overcrowded with refugees from Asia Minor, Thrace, and with returned Turkish prisoners of War.' In other words, Istanbul is full. But where else can the refugees be taken? Conditions in Bulgaria or Serbia are only slightly better. The situation in Greece is just as bad.

THE FORMER BATTLEFIELDS OF NORTHERN FRANCE: In each of the nine French military districts along the old Western Front, soldiers are sent out into the mud and cold and rain on a grim mission.

Each district has been ordered to produce from the earth of the battle-fields the body of a French soldier – clearly identifiable as to his nationality, but otherwise unknown and unknowable. Not a simple matter. Some are too decomposed. Others too fresh, or too easily identified. In one district, it is impossible to produce a single body definitely French (some of the unearthed corpses might be British or Canadian) yet otherwise anonymous. In another, the officer in charge orders his men to dig up one corpse after another until one that meets all the criteria can be found. (Two are discarded because they belong to troops from French North Africa.) The chosen body is placed in a wooden coffin and transported to the underground citadel of Verdun, the supreme symbol of French wartime resistance, to join other, identical coffins from the other military districts.

Lying side by side in a low-ceilinged room, the coffins are covered in flags and flowers. The walls are covered in the colours of the French flag. Soldiers stand guard over the bodies. At dawn on 10 November 1920, the schoolchildren of Verdun process past. The local clergy kneel to pray before the coffins. That afternoon, a French minister, André Maginot, arrives for the ceremony to designate one of the eight as the symbol of France's war dead: the country's Unknown Soldier. Auguste Thin, a young soldier, is asked to make the final choice, placing a bouquet of flowers from the battlefield on one of the coffins. That night, the Unknown Soldier is loaded on a train and taken to Paris.

The following morning, on Armistice Day, in the fiftieth year of the French Third Republic, the nation unites in mourning. From an overnight resting place in the south of Paris, the Unknown Soldier is carried first to the Panthéon, a symbol of republican tradition. Then, along the boulevards of Paris, lined with veterans, the procession winds its way to the symbol of the French nation's military might: the Arc de Triomphe. Along the way, the Unknown Soldier is blessed by the Archbishop of Paris. The crowds, dressed in black, gather around.

One young Frenchman, a soldier himself, and a good Catholic, chooses Armistice Day to become engaged to a young woman from the provinces. On leave from Poland, Charles de Gaulle has been courting Yvonne Vendroux for the last month under the watchful eyes of her family. (One date involves a group trip to a Paris art exhibition on the pretext of seeing a new painting by Kees van Dongen, a friend of Picasso.) The two make plans for a spring wedding.

SEBASTOPOL — ISTANBUL: Papers and maps are packed away or burned. Commercial vessels are commandeered: barges, tugs, anything that floats. There is panic amongst the civilian population of Crimea: what will their fate be if they are abandoned to the Bolsheviks? Long queues form outside Sebastopol's banks. The quayside is cluttered with people and their possessions. Shots are fired in the air to prevent disorder. Wrangel tries to exude calm as he makes the final arrangements for departure. One of his generals dies of a heart attack. The French offer their protection to the White flotilla. In return, the Russian ships of the line are offered as security to defray France's costs in helping with the evacuation.

On the day the flotilla sets sail from Sebastopol, the cold weather breaks and the sun comes out. A motorboat takes Wrangel out to the cruiser *General Kornilov*, named after a previous leader of the White cause. Wrangel tries to look as dignified as possible as he clambers aboard. He makes a short speech. A band plays some music.

There are last-minute delays. The officer on the *Kornilov* responsible for the sailors' health is missing; a search party is sent ashore to find him. The senior French civilian representative in Sebastopol requests that the White authorities produce a formal letter with details of the Russians about to be shipped to Istanbul. There is panic amongst Wrangel's officials as they consider how they can best meet the French demand, and in particular how they should number any letter responding to it, having destroyed or stowed away most of their other administrative correspondence and files. Marking a letter 'No. 1' would look amateurish, it is decided, giving the unforgivable impression that the White administration has no numbering system at all. A general solves the problem by asking for the brand of one of his junior officers' eau de cologne. The letter is duly sent marked 'No. 4711'.

An eerie calm descends over Sebastopol when the last of Wrangel's boats pulls away from the quay – those strange hours between one army leaving and the next army arriving to take its place. With the Crimean coast still in sight, the radio cabin on board the *General Kornilov* intercepts a wireless message from the Reds crowing about their victory. It is easy for the Whites to imagine the doors being kicked in: the shouts, the orders, the screams. (Béla Kun is put in charge of the reprisals and clean-up operation.) Then the last of Russia disappears over the horizon. The Whites have left. The Reds have won.

Conditions at sea are awful. There is not enough food or water. On one torpedo boat, a thousand men, women and children are crammed all along the deck, and in every nook and cranny below. On another ship, several women give birth during the journey. Their babies are stillborn. In order to conserve fuel, the ships travel slowly. Some take several days to cover the few hundred miles across the Black Sea. Some hundred thousand Russian soldiers and sailors and another fifty thousand civilians make it across. Nearing Istanbul, French flags are raised on the Russian warships and the remnants of the imperial fleet are redesignated as a mere squadron. Wrangel's sick and defeated armies are placed in quarantine. They are sent to build their own camps at Gallipoli and on the island of Lemnos. For the first few nights they sleep on the ground.

In the heady days of 1914, patriotic Russians imagined arriving in Constantinople as conquerors. Now they have come as refugees.

DUBLIN: A Sunday morning in November. Small teams of IRA men appear at addresses across the city.

A dozen British officers – all suspected members of the intelligence services – are shot dead where they sleep. Two are killed in their rooms at the Gresham, Dublin's finest hotel. The manager finds a copy of *Irish Field* next to one of the dead men's beds. He always thought the late-sleeping officer was nothing more than a bored army veterinary surgeon with a fondness for horse-racing. He suspects a bad mistake has been made by Collins and his gang. Others die alone in their lodgings across southern Dublin, or in front of silent, tearful wives or screaming, terrified girlfriends. Remembering that he has missed Mass that day, one of the killers slips off to church to pray for the departed when the deed is done. Michael Collins, the man who has sent the killers to their prey, waits for news, beside himself with worry at his assassins' fates. 'Any casualties?' he shouts at one of the scouts sent out to gather up information about the morning's cull. None, so far.

Blood revenge comes that afternoon at a Gaelic football match between a Dublin team and one from Tipperary. The stadium is surrounded by the army and the Black and Tans. Shooting breaks out inside. It is claimed that the IRA fired first. The dead tell a different story: all civilians, all killed by British bullets. Three minutes of firing, one hundred and eighty seconds, and a round for each one of those seconds. An Amritsar-style massacre, albeit with much smaller casualties, on Irish soil. The vicious circle continues a week later, when British forces on patrol in an open lorry are ambushed on a rainswept road in County Cork. A few weeks after that, half the high street in Cork is burned down.

'A Devil's competition' is what the Bishop of Cork calls it, criticising both sides for their violence. He condemns the killing of men of the Royal Irish Constabulary as plain 'murder', contrary to God's teaching, and declaring the destruction of property, by whichever side, to be pure vandalism. He further infuriates nationalists by issuing a pastoral letter to his flock noting that Ireland is not yet an independent sovereign state – whatever the Dáil may have said in 1919 – and that consequently acts of violence in the republic's name enjoy no special legitimacy or religious sanction. It is not just the control of Ireland's streets that is at issue in this struggle. It is the moral authority of those who seek to rule them, killing both British and Irish in Ireland's holy name.

'People speak quite calmly of a large part of Europe sinking back into barbarism & compare it to the break-up of civilization at the fall of the Roman Empire', William Butler Yeats notes to a friend. Martial law is declared in the autumn in the most rebellious southern provinces of Ireland (though not yet in Dublin). Michael Collins is the most wanted man in the country. Yet he slips through British fingers like a phantom.

NEW YORK – VIENNA: As royalties begin to flow more regularly from America to Vienna, the stiff relationship between Sigmund and his nephew Edward loosens up a little. Freud suggests at last that he may indeed be willing to write a few popular articles for the American public. The doctor from Vienna proposes a title for his first: 'Don't Use Psychoanalysis in Polemics'. The New York publicity man suggests they try something a little catchier: 'The Wife's Place in the Home', for instance.

REVAL, ESTONIA – MOSCOW: Exhilarated, transformed and convinced that Bolshevism is a wonderful experiment in new living – whatever nasty things Cousin Winston might have to say about it – Clare Sheridan prepares to leave Russia. She hands out her spare stockings, soap, shoes, gloves and hat to her new friends. To one she donates a particularly valuable item: her hot-water bottle. Boarding her ship home on the Baltic coast, Clare begs the captain to be particularly careful with the oversized packing cases she has brought from Moscow. 'They contain the heads of Lenin and Trotsky', she explains. The captain looks impressed. 'Plaster heads and breakable', she adds.

Back in the Kremlin, Vladimir receives an old friend from Germany, a woman he has not seen since the revolution: Clara Zetkin. They are joined by Nadya – and a cat, which reminds them of the times Rosa Luxemburg's cat used to purr contentedly in the impatient revolutionary's lap. The old comrades drink black tea together. Someone goes off in search of jam as a special treat. They talk about life and art. Vladimir admits to feeling somewhat out of touch when it comes to artistic matters. 'We don't understand the new art any more, we just limp behind it', he says. He admits to even being something of a 'barbarian' in such matters.

The tendency towards artistic experimentation leaves him cold: 'I cannot value the works of expressionism, futurism, cubism, and other isms as the highest expressions of artistic genius. I don't understand them. They give me no pleasure.' Art for art's sake? A bourgeois idea. Over the autumn, Vladimir orders that the organisation responsible for all this cultural experimentation be reined in, with the party placed firmly in charge and class war made the cultural lodestar for the future.

In the end, what really matters, of course, is not whether people go to the theatre or the opera – landlord culture, Vladimir calls it, though he used to hum arias after going to the opera as a young man in Kazan – but whether the great broad masses of the people can read. 'Don't complain so bitterly of the illiteracy', Comrade Clara objects. The illiteracy of the masses helped the revolution: 'It prevented the mind of the workers and peasants from being stopped up and corrupted with bourgeois ideas and conceptions'. Vladimir nods. Yes, he says, but what about bureaucracy? If the people can read, they can do more things for themselves and require less supervision. The path to communist utopia lies through literacy. Nonetheless, there remains an important question of *what* people read – which is why it is essential to ensure that libraries stock the right books. People must not be led astray.

Another time, Clara comes to Vladimir's office in the Kremlin to talk business: whether Germany is ripe for another revolutionary attempt, how women's organisations should relate to the Communist Party and so forth. They end up talking about sex. Vladimir upbraids her. He has been told that in Communist Party circles in Germany, women spend most of their time debating marriage and sex. 'What a waste!' he exclaims. Everything that needed to be said on that score was said years ago. He is particularly cross about the Viennese, with their pseudoscientific pamphlets and dissertations on the matter. 'Freudian theory is the modern fashion', Vladimir complains. Personally, he dislikes all this 'poking about in sexual matters'. It is a hobby of the intellectuals. It distracts people from the proletarian revolution – and that is all that matters in the end. Class war is more urgent than 'marriage forms of Maoris or incest in olden times'.

Worse, all this Vienna stuff is getting at the young, Vladimir says. It is positively unhealthy. He worries about the 'over-excitement and exaggeration in the sexual life of some of them'. All these ideas that sex should be as simple as drinking a glass of water. Nonsense! A thought straight from the bourgeois gutter! All this so-called 'living to the full' is rubbish. Vladimir tells the story of one young comrade he knows who seems to stagger from one love affair to the next. And how is that going to help the revolution? 'The revolution demands concentration, increase of forces,' he tells Clara; 'it cannot tolerate orgiastic conditions, such as are normal for the decadent heroes and heroines of D'Annunzio.' What young people need is sport, fresh air and a good dose of Karl Marx. Healthy bodies, healthy minds!

There is hardly time to discuss the other matter Clara came to talk about: bringing more women over to the revolutionary cause. If only Comrade Inessa were here! Vladimir gives Clara a lecture on the subject. Working women should understand that the root of their problems is capitalism. Their freedom can only be achieved under communism. He is all in favour of more agitation amongst women – 'working groups, commissions, committees, bureaus or whatever you like'. But that is not feminism. It is simply 'practical, revolutionary expediency'. There can be no special organisations outside the party. Vladimir warms to his theme; Clara cannot get a word in edgeways. Male workers must be taught to help with the housework, rather than act as if they were a factory boss at home. The problem is bourgeois mentality. Proper communism will change that, he explains.

There is a knock at the door. The impatient revolutionary's next meeting. Ten minutes later there is another knock. Lenin is late. He tells Clara he will blame it on women who talk too much. He helps her with her coat: 'You must dress more warmly. Moscow is not Stuttgart. Don't catch cold. *Auf wiedersehen!*'

VIENNA – NEW YORK: The truce between the old-world Viennese and the New Yorker trying to help him to his share of American-style fame and fortune does not last so far as the end of the year. Edward conjures up the possibility of a well-paid lecture tour, detailing it in a long cable. Freud's initial reply is brusque: 'NOT CONVENIENT', an Austrian telegraphist taps out. It is some weeks before Freud gets around to composing a letter on the subject to send to his nephew.

A lecture tour would make the American analysts jealous, Freud explains. And the money on offer – a guarantee of at least ten thousand dollars – is not enough. There is a psychological element to this for Sigmund. 'The outcome of this undertaking would be that the New York people had got the better of me', he complains. 'They could get my treatment cheaply while I would get nothing out of them.' His fee should be five or ten times higher. After all, 'it is not much in America'.

DEARBORN: The *Independent* has become a machine, a production line spewing out anti-Semitism every week. The hack who has to write all this stuff – a sometime preacher who believes Anglo-Saxons are the Bible's 'chosen people' and that Britain and North America are the true Holy Land – starts taking to the bottle. The articles published between May and October are collected in a book entitled *The International Jew* that is sent out to influential community leaders, for free. Hundreds of thousands of copies are produced.

ISTANBUL – BIZERTE, TUNISIA: The first of the Russian ships offered to France as security set sail again for Bizerte naval base in the French protectorate of Tunisia.

There, the Russian sailors are treated with suspicion, as if infected with the virus of Bolshevism. (It does not help that they are penniless too, relying on a French wage of ten francs a day.) The authorities in Tunisia suggest that the Russians be sent on immediately to the neighbouring French colony of Algeria.

Wrangel's refugee army has become a problem no one wants.

MUNICH: Adolf declares that he is against Germany joining the League of Nations. Would it be right for young Germans to be sent to defend someone else's land? Has the League ever done anything to help the Irish in their national struggle, he asks, or the Indians in their fight against the British? Even in America, the country of the League's originator, it is viewed as a 'crazy utopia, yet amongst our own enslaved people you still find people willing to defend it'. The only strength any country can rely on is the strength of their own people, the solidarity of the *Volk*. This is the national in national socialism.

'We want to build', the mangy field-runner declares on another occasion, 'not just smash everything up like the Bolsheviks in Russia.' Germany's productive forces – from the business managers to the workers – must function as one national unit. The needs and interests of the community must predominate over the individual. Every German citizen – every person, that is, whom the NSDAP determines is worthy of membership in the German *Volk* – must have equal rights and bear equal responsibilities in the collective. Work must be upheld as a cardinal virtue. The young must be educated and protected. This is the socialism in national socialism.

Hitler's events are sold out. But is progress quick enough for the party to break free from its beer-hall origins and become a serious political player? The number of fee-paying party members, though double what it was in the summer, is still less than a single Hofbräuhaus audience. In order to give an impression of greater scale, numbered membership cards start at 500.

In December, a unique opportunity arises. The Thule Society's *Völkischer Beobachter* comes up for sale. In the past, though not controlled by the Nazi Party, the newspaper has been favourable to it. If ownership were to fall into the wrong hands now, the party might lose that thin oxygen of publicity on which it survives. The *Beobachter* has only a few thousand readers, nothing like Henry Ford's *Dearborn Independent*. But as Ford himself has shown, readership can expand with the right editorial line. Adolf persuades Dietrich Eckart to mortgage his home to find the money to buy the paper. A Freikorps general agrees to get hard cash from an army slush fund. Within twenty-four hours the newspaper is secured.

The first edition of the *Völkischer Beobachter* after the change of ownership is much the same as before. In between advertisements for hot chocolate and requests for subscribers to send in their fees early for the year 1921 it includes a helpful primer on the swastika and the announcement of the publication of an address book for non-Jewish businesses, allowing *völkisch* consumers to exercise the power of their wallet.

By the end of the year the newspaper has become a purely party paper, advertising Nazi meetings and finding an anti-Semitic slant to every story. Adolf Hitler can add articles to speeches in his propaganda armoury, reaching out to a far larger potential audience than can be accommodated in a beer hall.

PARIS: Breton takes odd editing and consultancy jobs to keep off the bread-line. Despite the support of Marcel Proust, he loses out on a major literary prize. Yet not everything is gloomy. Simone Kahn has agreed to marry him. André feels like a changed man.

Tzara and Breton avoid each other. Paris Dada descends further into spectacle: high jinks, jazz, and a lot of self-indulgent laughter. Over the course of the year, Tzara produces no fewer than four Dadaist manifestos. His tricks are starting to wear thin.

'Hold on to your overcoat', André writes in the December edition of *Littérature*, 'Dada is not dead'. But who is in charge?

LUDWIGSHÖHE, BAVARIA: Travelling through Germany from the Netherlands on the occasion of his honeymoon, Kaiser Wilhelm's equerry pays a visit to a large villa on the outskirts of Munich. The villa's owner is a rather portly man, given to conspiracy theories. He hopes a new volume of his wartime documents, some hundreds of pages long, will 'fill the German people with renewed national will and open their eyes to the truth'. They will prove his own blamelessness for Germany's wartime defeat once and for all. As Wilhelm's equerry is ushered in, General Ludendorff shows off a statuette of the Kaiser sitting on his desk, and a portrait of Wilhelm on the wall. No hard feelings, it would appear.

Conversation quickly turns to the chances of Wilhelm's restoration. Ludendorff proclaims himself in favour of the Hohenzollerns but, he warns, perhaps the Kaiser's sons might be better placed to take over the reins. Other German dynasties – he mentions the royal houses of Baden and Hanover – might stand in the way of the Hohenzollerns by asserting their rights as co-creators of the empire if Wilhelm were to propose simply returning to the post of Kaiser himself.

On his return to Huis Doorn, the equerry finds a dark mood. The Kaiserin is sick. It is uncertain whether she will recover. As usual, Wilhelm takes refuge outside. 'The park looks ever barer', an aide writes. 'One tree falls after another'. Occasionally the Kaiser shares his latest insight on the world situation, predicting war between America and Japan, or war between Russia and China against Japan, or war by Russia, China and Japan against all of Europe. Such a race war cannot be far off. Europe must prepare for it.

NEW YORK: William Du Bois launches his broadside in the direction of uptown Harlem.

Marcus Garvey's first commercial scheme, Du Bois writes, was for a farm school in Jamaica which ran into financial difficulties and failed, causing Garvey to come to America. His political projects in the United States were similarly unsuccessful until a sufficient number of his Jamaican compatriots

had moved to New York to provide him with a solid base in the city. Du
Bois provides a short history of the Black Star Line. The convention of
August 1920 is covered in a few lines.

Then come the questions on matters of honesty, businesslike attitude
and practical chances of success. On the first of these, Du Bois is generous
to Garvey, a man he has never met. His tone is patronising – that of an
upper-crust patrician looking down on a West Indian peon – but not unkind.
'He has been charged with dishonesty and graft,' Du Bois writes, 'but he
seems to me essentially an honest and sincere man with a tremendous
vision, great dynamic force and an unselfish desire to serve.'

There, the compliments end. The list of defects William Du Bois finds
in his rival is long. He is 'dictatorial, domineering, inordinately vain and
very suspicious', Du Bois writes. He mentions the breakdown of his marriage,
as well as various lawsuits in which Garvey has had to make an account of
himself. Worse, 'he has absolutely no business sense, no *flair* for real organization'. Du Bois is highly doubtful of the back-to-Africa movement.

A tone of mockery enters into the article when the editor of *The Crisis*
describes the personality cult which Garvey seems to have encouraged
within the UNIA: all the grandiose titles and gowns and pretensions to
nobility. 'He has become to thousands of people a sort of religion.'

A second instalment of the article is promised for January.

FIUME: D'Annunzio is now officially Regent of his mini-state, Canaro. A
constitution is promulgated. Postage stamps emblazoned with his profile
appear. Men shave their heads in emulation of Gabriele's baldness. Some
go so far as to imagine that Fiume will now annex Italy, rather than the
other way around.

On the surface, the Fiume experiment seems as lively as ever. The legionnaires take to wearing an extraordinary range of self-designed military
uniforms, complete with feathers and Roman daggers. When the Italian
conductor Toscanini (once an election candidate for the Fascists) comes to
Fiume with his orchestra, a mock battle with live weapons is staged for the
orchestra's entertainment, leading to several injuries amongst the musicians
(a few of whom get so excited they decide to take part themselves). Several
musical instruments are shattered by shrapnel.

But, in truth, D'Annunzio's adventure is reaching a dead end. When
Gabriele learns of a treaty about to be signed by the Italian and the Yugoslav
governments which will make Fiume a self-governing Free State, never to

be incorporated into either Italy or Yugoslavia, he flies into a rage. This is not the ending he wanted. The fact that Mussolini and others view the treaty as a great success makes it worse. Public attention shifts elsewhere. In November, three hundred Fascists interrupt the swearing-in of the new Socialist administration in Bologna. Several are killed in the ensuing fracas. This is the front line now.

D'Annunzio withdraws into seclusion. The Italian government issues an ultimatum for him to leave. Some of his closest followers urge him to clear out now and accept the laurels that must come his way for saving Fiume from the Yugoslavs. Gabriele's response is blistering: 'I have to consider you as deserters to the Cause in the face of the enemy.'

He waits for the ultimatum to pass. Surely the Italian army will not attack its own.

CHICAGO: Ernest Hemingway's latest from the seamy underside of prohibition-land. American gunmen from the big cities are being shipped across to Ireland – the 'Red Island' – to carry out contract killings. The going rate, Ernest reports, is four hundred dollars: enough to then go to France and have a good time blowing it all on the horses. 'They say that if you throw a stone into a crowd at the famous Longchamps racecourse outside of Paris, you would hit an American gunman, pickpocket or strong-arm artist', he reports. So much for American hoodlums. On the other hand, bootlegging business is bad. Too much booze is just being made right here under the noses of the police.

ANKARA: Mustafa Kemal's twenty-three-year-old female admirer Fikriye plays the piano at his hillside villa. He knocks back raki late into the night with his army buddies. The Armenians have been defeated in the east – crushed between the Bolsheviks and the Turks. The Greek nationalist government in Athens has fallen.

Kemal dashes off two diplomatic telegrams to new friends. 'We know how vital it is that the European proletariat and the enslaved and colonised peoples fight against the common enemy', he writes to the Bolshevik nationalities' commissar, Comrade Stalin. He thanks him for his work bringing Bolsheviks and Muslims closer together. He notes the importance of smashing imperialism to achieve the 'demolition of capitalism'.

Then one to Lenin greeting the Bolsheviks' recognition of the independence of Dagestan in the north Caucasus, referring to Moscow's new tendency to establish autonomous republics in its unruly extremities. 'Autonomy does not mean independence', Stalin is at pains to point out when he travels there himself. The language has changed but the territorial ambitions remain. The Russian Empire is being recreated under another name.

Moscow: 'We are now passing through a crucial period of transition,' Lenin announces, 'something of a zigzag transition from war to economic development'. Transition! Zigzag! Those words again.

Each year, things are supposed to get better. But somehow events conspire to make them worse. Peace and plenty are always just around the corner. Now, peace has arrived, but plenty is still very far away. The economy is in a dreadful state. Industry has virtually closed down: Russia produces one fifth of the goods manufactured before the war. The cities survive on hunger rations. The countryside is starving. Factories feel like prison camps. Now the Bolsheviks do not even have a foreign enemy to pin their misery on. Out of desperation, the call to strike is going up again. Peasant rebellions are swelling across the land. Trotsky is making trouble in the party. Something in the mechanism of government is faulty, Lenin admits. Decrees are signed 'and then we ourselves forget about them and fail to carry them out'. Communism isn't working.

Vladimir struggles for answers to the crisis. He is caught between purity and practicality, between the ideals he came to power with, and the need to cling on now. He tries to find a middle course, to split the difference, and dress it up as revolutionary statesmanship. The revolution – *his* revolution, that is – will only be truly safe once it is strong economically, he concludes. To achieve that, it must trade with the outside world. Foreign businesses – German ones, in particular – should be encouraged to invest. The impatient revolutionary becomes an advocate of extensive concessions to foreign capitalists – land for tractors, oil for investment. Many Bolsheviks are appalled. Was this what the revolution was for? Only weeks before, on the third anniversary of the revolution, the largest agitational spectacle yet was put on in Petrograd, with banker capitalists in top hats carrying huge sacks marked with dollar signs and a cast of eight thousand storming the Winter Palace – a far greater number than were involved in the real thing in 1917. 'Lenin! Lenin!' they cry at one point. The whole thing has been made into a film.

'There is no question of selling out Russia to the capitalists', the impatient revolutionary reassures them. He tries to turn the horror of most Bolsheviks at his proposals into an argument in their favour: it proves that

Russia is already ideologically inoculated against capitalism and can therefore survive the presence of a few foreign capitalists in their midst without fear of contamination. Anyway, the ends justify the means. The situation is desperate. Adjustments are necessary.

But how far will the impatient revolutionary go? He promises he has no intention of letting the poison of the market back into Russia in a broader sense: no private trading, no capitalist mentality. As a testament to this, Vladimir points to the recent suppression of the Sukharevka, a large Moscow street market where speculators thrive (but also where people go to try and buy the food they cannot get from the rations or the canteens). But we must go further, the impatient revolutionary demands. After all, the true danger is not on the street. It is 'the *Sukharevka* that resides in the heart and behaviour of every petty proprietor'. 'This is the *Sukharevka* that must be closed down.'

In any case, the present adjustments are temporary. The key to the future is scale: big factories, big farms, nationwide electricity. Vladimir has a new slogan for it: 'Communism is Soviet power plus the electrification of the whole country.' A plan is being drawn up to achieve it over the next decade. But the people are hungry now. And they are getting hungrier.

FIUME: When the assault to recover Fiume comes, fifteen months after D'Annunzio marched in and took over the city, the whole of Italy is preparing itself for the festivities of Christmas. People have more important things to worry about than politics.

Though defensive preparations have been made, with fishing nets slung across the streets and barricades built up, Lieutenant Colonel D'Annunzio (Retd) can hardly believe it when the attack begins. Soldiers shout over their lines to the defending legionnaires, warning them to get out now. No one wants to shoot. Can this really be happening?

After three days of intermittent fighting, Italian against Italian, a shell fired from a battleship whistles through an open window of D'Annunzio's headquarters. If he does not surrender now, the poet is warned, more will follow. Italy's famous Great War hero ponders for a while, and then makes his decision. Negotiations begin for the safe passage of him and his men. The adventure is over.

DUBLIN: A stormy crossing of the Irish Sea from Liverpool. Éamon de Valera acts the drunk when challenged by the ferry's captain as to his identity. By Christmas Eve he is in a Dublin safe house owned by a gynaecologist. Sinéad visits him but does not stay.

The new returnee blasts Michael Collins's guerrilla tactics in the war fought during his prolonged American absence. Too much violence, too little distinction between Irish and British. 'This odd shooting of a policeman here and there is having a very bad effect, from the propaganda point of view, on us in America', Éamon de Valera sermonises to his Irish courtiers. 'What we want is, one good battle about once a month with about 500 men on each side.' Collins is incensed. Open battle means certain, bloody, glorious defeat. Another waste of heroes' blood. More martyrs for the cause. Which will it be: glorious defeat or bloody victory?

Everyone knows the war must be ended, somehow. But when, and on whose terms? Who will tire first? Each act of violence ratchets up the pressure on the other side. Openings for negotiation are narrow, fleeting. Possible intermediaries come and go: an Australian archbishop, an Irish businessman. The day de Valera returns from America, a British law officially splits Ireland into two, with a self-rule parliament to be established in each part, north and south, in Belfast and Dublin, and elections held next year. Vague hopes for peace are shrouded in mutual mistrust and blackened by daily, tangible acts of murder and retribution. The time is never right.

One night at the end of the year, like on so many nights before in other Irish towns and villages, a Black and Tan patrol in Midleton, County Cork, comes under fire. IRA men appear from nowhere, emerging from the laneways. For twenty minutes, the main street becomes a shooting gallery. Taken by surprise, several Black and Tans are badly wounded and later die in hospital. An IRA man takes a bullet in the wrist, but nothing serious. He and his comrades escape into the mountains with a haul of weapons, and later occupy an abandoned farmhouse outside the village of Clonmult.

Three days later reprisal comes to Midleton: not in the heat of battle, as before, but now as a matter of official policy, an instrument of British martial law. Half a dozen houses near the ambush site are selected, somewhat randomly. The inhabitants are given an hour to clear out. They are allowed to take their valuables with them but not their furniture. Then the houses are burned to the ground.

It is the first day of 1921.

1921

The man with a gun who was the terror of the working people in the past is no longer a terror for he is now the representative of the Red Army and is their protector.
Vladimir Lenin

Prejudices have become grotesque.
Albert Einstein

WINTER

DUBLIN: Back safely on Irish soil, Éamon de Valera ventures a suggestion: perhaps Michael Collins, his hotheaded rival, would like to go to America on a fundraising tour.

The pill is sugared as much as possible. The break would do him good. Collins is tired out. He looks ten years older than the man of thirty he is. It would be a chance to travel, and to use his reputation in the Irish cause without worrying for his safety every minute of the day. And it would infuriate the British.

'The Long Whoor won't get rid of me as easily as that' is the furious reply. Michael Collins is staying put.

CHICAGO: After a few false starts (including lying on an application form to work in advertising), Ernest is made the assistant editor of a magazine for the American cooperative movement. It's not for ever, Hemingway tells himself, and it's a job.

But that's not all that is new in his life. The young hero has met a woman he likes, a far more serious proposition than the Petoskey girls he has been hanging out with: a tall, limber, well-educated girl called Hadley, eight years his senior, with no parents to call her own, but with a trust fund to her name instead. Ernest and Hadley – or Hash, as he likes to call her – write slightly tortured letters to each other and worry about who loves whom more. He gives her a book by D'Annunzio to show his worldliness, just as he did to Dorothy Connable last year.

On cold dark evenings in Chicago, Ernest flicks through the poems of Siegfried Sassoon, which leave him feeling bitter about the war. A journalist fresh back from Moscow – the man who ghost-wrote Maria Bochkareva's autobiography in 1918 – comes over for supper. Isaac Don Levine brings with him 'the cold dope on Rooshia', as Ernest types it up for his mother.

Poor Hemingway feels a little sorry for himself that he is not closer to the action in Europe. For a while in January, he entertains the notion of jacking it all in and going to Italy for a few months with a friend. Then he has another idea: perhaps he should get married.

LONDON: The President of the British Phrenological Society, whose members believe measurements of the skull can give insights into the character of their owners, visits the studio of sculptor Clare Sheridan.

He has brought his tools to measure the sculptures Clare did in the Kremlin as one would measure an actual human head. Lenin, he says, is clearly a thinker and a planner. He has great ideals which he wishes to put into effect on a grand scale. He is secretive and ambitious. He is gracious towards women, but fails to understand the views of others. Turning to the bust of Trotsky he states that the measurements of his head suggest greater intuition, though with a tendency towards brusqueness. He has a strong self-preserving instinct and high self-esteem. The shape of his cranium shows that his amorousness is greater than his powers of concentration.

GORKI: Vladimir spends nearly three weeks at his country house. He finds it hard to relax.

The country is in permanent economic crisis. And it is spreading to the political. He is worried about the party. Too much debate. Too many arguments. Too many factions, says the arch-factionalist of yesteryear. 'The party is sick,' Vladimir writes, 'the party is down with the fever.' Some are saying the party has got too far away from the workers – there are not many in its leadership. They want the trades unions to control the economy and the party hacks reined in. 'Syndicalist deviation,' Lenin calls it, 'which will kill the Party unless it is entirely cured of it.'

Trotsky has stirred things up the other way, saying the unions should be nationalised: who needs to represent the workers *against* the state when you have a workers' state already? And all this being discussed in public! Lenin is appalled. Why does Comrade Trotsky not know when to stop? So reckless. So irresponsible. So individualistic. Lenin's own line is that the whole Soviet system should be viewed as an arrangement of cogwheels, with the unions as 'transmission belts' running between the party and the workers. Unfortunately, the machine has stopped working.

In the cities, bread rations are cut again this January. Factories shut down for lack of fuel. In the countryside, the Cheka estimates one hundred and eighteen peasant uprisings. Vladimir receives maps showing the vast areas of the country in rebellion. He personally speaks to peasants from the affected areas. They cannot *all* be class enemies. They cannot *all* be put down either. Something will have to give. A new zigzag starts forming in Lenin's mind.

FIUME: In January, D'Annunzio leaves the city-state he once ran with such extravagance. He will face no trial or punishment for insubordination. Those who died in Fiume's defence will be his personal martyrs. His conquest of Fiume, however badly it ended, makes him an icon for the nationalist right. Many consider him a demigod. The poet now travels to a new house by Lake Garda, reclaimed from a German art historian (Wagner's wife once played on its piano). He is delighted to have a new project of Italianification on his hands.

His legionnaires split up. Some retire from their nationalist pursuits. Others drift to Milan, where Mussolini is making his name. Some lend their services to the Fascist gangs roaming central and northern Italy, seeing a reflection of Fiume in their habits of strange, exotic violence: using dried cod heads as weapons and force-feeding castor oil to their foes.

PRAGUE, CZECHOSLOVAKIA: A man with something of the look of a travelling violin player arrives at the railway station, his hair swept back dramatically, an impish grin on his face. Though he has been here before, he acts like a tourist, asking to be taken by his guide to different cafés to get a good look at the population of Prague these days – Czech nationalists in one, German nationalists in another, Jews, Communists and actors in a third. For lunch, Einstein eats calf's liver cooked over a Bunsen burner in the apartment of a scientist friend.

As is common wherever Einstein comes to speak these days, the lecture hall at the Urania Association is crammed. After the lecture, he avoids in-depth questioning by offering to play a Mozart violin sonata instead. As he is leaving Czechoslovakia on his way to Vienna, he is accosted by a young man talking gibberish about how the energy contained within an atom could some day be used to create the most extraordinary explosion. Einstein tells him to abandon such foolishness.

His mood seems quite playful this wintertime. Perhaps it is his hope that this year – surely – will be the year he finally gets his Nobel Prize. Perhaps it is just the effects of being amongst friends – and Prague seems a rather happier place than Berlin right now. Perhaps it is the prospect of a trip to

America. Einstein has demanded fifteen thousand dollars from Princeton and Wisconsin universities for a short lecture tour – one way to solve the problem of how to make his alimony payments – and now awaits their response. Or perhaps it is just the acclaim which seems to greet him wherever he goes these days. The anti-relativists have been silenced. The fan-mail keeps on piling up. His theory – however misunderstood – seems to reign supreme.

Yet, in some quarters, a different and darker mood is building. The day Albert arrives in Prague, Adolf gives a speech in a Munich beer hall entitled 'Stupidity or Crime', claiming that a Jewish conspiracy is at work in the world of science, aiming at the 'deliberate poisoning of our national soul, and thereby bringing about the inner collapse of our people'. Such manipulators, Hitler says, are prepared to work for years and decades before they achieve their final objective: 'psychological illness of the masses'.

The day Albert leaves Prague an extremist hack suggests that Einstein should be murdered. He is fined a small sum by a Berlin court for incitement to violence.

DEARBORN: On week thirty-five of Ford's campaign it is the world of American entertainment which the *Independent* has in its sights. The theatre has been taken over by Jews, and turned from a place of refinement where Americans can be instructed in sound virtues into a money machine. It is now 'show business'. Commercialism trumps everything else and vulgarity reigns supreme. The *Independent* provides a list of actors operating under innocent-sounding 'cover names'. Such as Charlie Chaplin.

In January, over one hundred Christians – including Woodrow Wilson, his predecessor, several bishops and William Du Bois – sign a letter attacking Ford's campaign of 'prejudice and hatred'. They call it un-American. America's moral majority is at last finding its voice. It is all far too late. Henry Ford's *Independent* has given worldwide credibility to anti-Semitic slander; *The International Jew* has been translated. Henry Ford is now an idol to anti-Semites around the world. And still the articles are churned out like automobiles.

INÖNÜ, THE OTTOMAN EMPIRE: Greek troops advance into Anatolia, probing deeper and deeper into the interior. A reconnaissance mission, they claim. The Turks suspect the incursion is the prelude to a general assault, with the objective of smashing Turkish resistance, safeguarding Smyrna from attack

and enforcing whatever they can of the Sèvres peace – signed but unrati-
fied, and already falling apart. Nearly a hundred Turks are killed in battle
and Turkish troops repair to a new line. But the Greeks turn back as well.
Who has won, who has lost?

MUNICH: 'Before the war', the *Völkischer Beobachter* recalls, 'Turkey was
called the "sick man".' That has changed since Kemal. His war of resistance
against the Sèvres peace terms has given his country back its sense of pride.
National solidarity has been revived. The 'sick man' has returned to vigorous
health. Could not Germany manage something similar if it opposed
Versailles? Could Bavaria be a second Anatolia? 'One day', the paper says,
'Germany may have to resort to Turkish methods.'

MOSCOW: It is bitterly cold.

Nadya and Vladimir pay a visit to young Varya Armand, staying in a
commune for art-school students. They sleep on bare wooden boards; they
have neither bread nor salt. But they do have cereals. The students make
the impatient revolutionary and his wife a bowl of porridge. They show
them their drawings. Vladimir looks confused. One has a locomotive in it.

'Dynamic!' Lenin calls it. He asks them whether they read Pushkin.

'Oh no,' the students reply, 'we read Mayakovsky.'

Bloody Mayakovsky! Nadya remembers one time at a Red Army concert
when Vladimir was confronted with an actress declaiming a Mayakovsky
poem almost in front of his nose – 'Speed is our body and the drum our
heart!' Her husband breathed a deep sigh of relief when another actor came
on and started reading a short story by Chekhov. Vladimir pauses before
responding to young Varya. 'I think *Pushkin* is better', he says eventually.

Back at the office, he takes comfort in a new project, more attuned to
his own literary tastes: to build up a library collection of the works of Marx
and Engels. Perhaps, Vladimir wonders, they could go one better. 'Could
we *buy* the letters of Marx and Engels, or photographs of them?' Vladimir
asks. They must be in Germany: 'You know, this dirty lot will sell anything.'

CLONMULT, CO. CORK: Twenty IRA men, some involved in the Midleton
ambush of last year, are surprised by the army while hiding out in a farmhouse just beyond the isolated village of Clonmult. Twelve of them are
killed in the ensuing battle.

Whole provinces of southern Ireland have become battlefields in a bitter guerrilla war. 'The area of active lawlessness is extending to counties which have hitherto been comparatively free from the more violent kinds of crime', reads the weekly report to the British cabinet. There are thirty-two British casualties in Ireland for that week alone. Attacks are reported against the distribution of the mail. London is informed of the case of a thirteen-year-old girl found in possession of a machine gun and three revolvers, sentenced to detention in a Catholic reformatory.

The war divides, building walls of mistrust between communities and individuals. The longer the violence continues, the more impossible it is to stand above the fray. Ireland's people find themselves in one camp or the other. Friend or enemy. Patriot or traitor. These are the only categories left. There is no middle ground – or at least none that is safe.

Over the winter weeks, an Irish woman in County Cork – a Presbyterian landowner – is kidnapped by the IRA. Her offence is to have passed on information about a planned IRA ambush when advised by a local grocer not to take a particular road one day. She pleads for her life and is shot as a spy. In Cork itself, the houses of Protestant businessmen suspected of loyalty to the old regime are burned down. British reprisals are now met with IRA counter-reprisals. Six civilians are caught in the crossfire when a train carrying British soldiers is shot up. The house in which Michael Collins was born – now occupied by his brother Johnny – is destroyed. Eight children of the Collins family are left without a home.

In those areas under martial law, life is lived with the constant threat of disruption and arrest, and of intimidation by friends and foes alike. New weapons are devised to try and shift the odds of victory. Empty shell cases fired by the British into the sea to test their artillery are recovered by fishermen and filled with a home-made explosive known as 'Irish cheddar' and turned into road mines. Normal daily life has been sabotaged by war. Nothing escapes it.

MUNICH: The NSDAP is still in start-up mode. It is growing fast – and yet never quite fast enough. It must compete for attention and support with plenty of other more established organisations. The Freikorps and nationalist and patriotic associations of Bavaria have fifty or a hundred times as many members as Hitler and Drexler's party. They look askance at the upstart on the fringes of Munich's patriotic scene, with no substantial links to the Bavarian establishment but plenty of Protestants and non-Bavarians. At a nationalist anti-Versailles congress where all these groups are represented and which Adolf hopes to hijack, his attempt at a speech is drowned out by a brass band.

There are those who think that, if it wants to grow, the NSDAP needs to merge with other like-minded groups. Adolf is against it. Some even propose trying to get close to the Communists as a means of siphoning off their support amongst the workers. The party's financial situation is disastrous. The *Beobachter* makes no money. The NSDAP survives from speech to speech. The bigger the audience at Hitler's events, the greater the fees. In February, Adolf speaks to a crowd of six thousand at the Zirkus Krone at an entry price of one mark per person: war wounded go free, Jews not allowed.

Adolf himself relies on the kindness of strangers to provide him with enough money and food to get by, never much worrying where it comes from. He has a sweet tooth, it turns out. Cakes home-baked by the party faithful are a favourite. He wears the same blue suit and trench coat almost every day. In between his speaking engagements, and meetings with the inner circle of the party, he hangs around in cafés. In these months, he often only gets out of bed at midday. One might almost mistake him for a Bohemian.

PARIS: A new play is about to begin at the Théâtre Deux Masques. The curtain rises on the office of Madame de Challens, aristocratic headmistress of a private girl's school in Versailles called Les Fauvettes. Preparations are under way for prize-giving, an event marked the previous year by the unexplained death of one of the school's pupils.

The plot of *Les Détraquées*, or 'The Crazed Women', is clunky. Its themes are both racy and gruesome: sex, murder and the power of mind over matter (and occasionally mind over mind). The school, it turns out, is little more than a playground for the predatory lesbianism of Madame de Challens and her lover Solange, a Parisian dance teacher with a taste for heroin. Both are drawn to Lucienne, the prettiest girl in the school, who obeys de Challens as if controlled by telepathy. 'I've never met anyone with such a passive nature', Madame de Challens tells Solange excitedly. 'She obeys my thoughts.' An unequal *ménage à trois* is formed.

In the play's second half, Lucienne has disappeared. The local police are stumped. Ultimately it is a doctor with experience of psychiatric patients who unravels the mystery. Solange is a 'femme fatale', he declares – something that the unimaginative police believe to be nothing more than a cinematic invention. The doctor insists that such characters really exist and they are more common after the war than ever before: women whose psychiatric sickness drives them to seek ever greater nervous stimulation. When opium and cocaine are not enough, he explains, they seek still more risky highs. Why not sex and murder? 'Everyone poisons themselves their own way, no?' the doctor asks, before offering a cigarette to a policeman. At the end of the play, Lucienne's body is found in a cupboard, evidently tortured to death in a sexual game by the two older women.

For André Breton, the whole affair is captivating. His enjoyment is no doubt enhanced by knowing the true identity of one of the play's authors. Referred to in the programme simply as Olaf, he is none other than André's former teacher and Freud's former colleague the great neurologist Babinski. For André, *Les Détraquées* is not a spectacle, but an act of literary bravery: a serious attempt to embrace the latest theories of the mind – even where these are shocking. The psychological mechanisms to which the play alludes – telepathy, mind control, addiction, unseen drives – all echo Breton's own obsessions, adventures and experiences. The play speaks to a world coming to terms with its own neuroses, confronting it with the realities it would prefer to cover up.

Why can't Dada be more like this?

Moscow: The latest zigzag takes definite form in the impatient revolutionary's mind. Some people will not like it. But then again, the ends – if anyone can remember what they were – will surely justify the means.

Vladimir is still pushing for concessions for foreign businesses, a little too eagerly for several of his party colleagues. His latest concern is that the oilfields of Baku will collapse without the involvement of foreign enterprise. 'Disaster is *imminent*', Vladimir writes: 'The working out of the terms must be speeded up.' Now he is thinking of something even more radical: allowing peasants to sell whatever surplus they produce individually, upending several years when the policy has been for the state to requisition it and private commerce was declared anathema. The change is a matter of political and economic common sense, Vladimir has come to believe. The peasants must be brought onside. More grain must be produced. A regime that cannot feed its people is not long for this world, as Lenin knows, and no one denies that profit can be an incentive. Lenin can already hear the clamour of opposition from the old Bolshevik believers.

Unthinkable! Preposterous! Letting the very seed of capitalism back into the bosom of the Soviet Republic. Giving in to the backward peasants. Giving up on state monopoly. Turning back the clock. Vladimir Lenin turned into a shopkeeper.

Well, yes. But maybe it is the only way to save the regime – and nothing is more important than that. To give up power would be to give up on the revolution. And that is something that Vladimir will not do. Party, regime and revolution are all one in the end. What helps one, helps the other. 'The proletarian class = the Communist Party = Soviet Power', he wrote last year. When it comes to weighing up means and ends, Vladimir (and Leon too) have always thought that the latter justifies the former. There is a certain devious charm to using the market to save its supposed antithesis. That appeals to Lenin's mind, a sort of intellectual one-upmanship over the capitalists. If it works, that is. The emergency is acute. Last year was dry, this year has been little better, and if the weather does not change and the peasants do not plant, Russia will face famine. There are peasant risings in the Volga region, protest marches in Moscow. Now the rot has even spread to Petrograd, birthplace of the revolution.

How bad will it get? Some sense a dangerous mood in Russia's second city resembling that of 1917. The authorities take away soldiers' shoes to prevent them from joining demonstrations. Strikers are locked up. There are rumours that the Kronstadt sailors are ready to revolt, not to defend the Bolsheviks but to destroy them, saying they do not represent the will of the people. Already in February, newspapers in Paris and New York report that the Kronstadt batteries are trained on Petrograd. At the end of the month, a proclamation spread around the streets of Petrograd calls for freedom of assembly for workers, new elections to the Soviets, the release of political prisoners – another revolution, in other words. Isn't this what the Bolsheviks once stood for themselves? That was then. Now it sounds like dangerous talk.

Party, country, all at sea. 'My nerves are *kaput*', Vladimir writes to Comrade Clara. He starts putting his zigzag down on paper.

BERLIN: In February, Einstein gets his answer from the Americans. He asked for too much money. But then, almost immediately, another opportunity arises: to go to the United States at the invitation of the Zionist organisation to raise money for a new university planned for Jerusalem. This appeals to Albert. How could it not? A charitable mission with a political purpose.

Plans are made. The *Rotterdam* will sail from Plymouth in the spring. Chaim Weizmann, the British chemist and leader of the Zionist movement, will host Albert and Elsa aboard.

Albert's German friends cannot believe the news. For any German to travel to America while a state of war still exists between the two countries, and just as a schedule for the payment of German reparations is being prepared – well, the optics, as they say, are bad. 'The whole world looks on you as the most important German Jew', Albert's friend Fritz Haber tells him. 'If, *at this moment*, you ostentatiously cosy up to the British and their friends, people in this country will see that as evidence of Jewish faithlessness.'

Einstein responds the same day. He has made up his mind. No argument will deflect him. 'I am not needed for my abilities, of course, but only for my name', he admits. 'Its promotional value is anticipated to reap considerable success amongst our rich tribespeople in Dollaria.' In the name of internationalism, he is bound to do his duty: to spread the word of science and to link arms with like-minded people across the ocean.

In any case, Einstein writes, 'I must go . . . the steamship seats have already been booked'.

CHICAGO – CINCINNATI – NEW YORK: 'There is nothing in the wide world – in the great universe – to intimidate Marcus Garvey', Garvey says in a pit stop in Chicago. He tells police spies in the audience not to worry: he doesn't mind them taking notes of what he says, as long as they understand he is not a Bolshevik.

Look how few statues there are to black men and women in the United States, he tells an audience in Cincinnati. 'All that we have done was to carry mortar for the other fellow when he was building up his property', he says. 'The time has come for us to build up in Africa'. (Garvey is at this time trying to develop a business relationship with Liberia through the good offices of the mayor of its capital, Monrovia.)

Back in New York, he prepares his departure for a tour of the Caribbean. He obtains a new British passport and secures an apology from *The Crisis* for a misstatement of fact in one of their articles on Garvey, the UNIA and the Black Star Line. The correction reads: 'Our statement that the *Yarmouth* is a wooden vessel is incorrect, as it is in fact steel.'

Before he leaves, the Provisional President of Africa gives a speech to the faithful at Liberty Hall. He takes aim at those who call Africa the 'dark continent', noting rather the diamond-and-gold brilliancy of its future, its mineral wealth waiting to be tapped by its rightful owners. And he launches a verbal assault on the new British Secretary of the Colonies, just moved sideways from his post at the War Office. 'This temperamental, unscrupulous, and audacious and irresponsible person', Garvey contends, 'has done more than any ten men in the British Empire to bring disrepute and bad credit morally and financially upon the British government.' He is referring, of course, to Winston Churchill.

VIENNA: Freud writes to a Russian psychoanalyst who has recently fled the Bolsheviks. He promises to help him settle in Prague, fast becoming one of the centres of Russian émigrés in Europe. 'Your wishes that your great fatherland may soon awaken again, and come out of its crisis', Freud writes, 'find in us the strongest sympathetic response.'

There seems little chance of Freud visiting Russia. 'How much would I have liked – protected by powerful connections – to see your magnificent Moscow', he confides. It is not to be: 'All gone! There will be no change in my lifetime.'

KRONSTADT FORTRESS – MOSCOW: Across the ice from Petrograd, the island fortress of Kronstadt, home of the Baltic Fleet and symbol of the revolution of 1917, is in open mutiny against Bolshevik rule. The local Soviet is deposed and Bolshevik leaders thrown in jail. New elections will be organised. In Paris, Prague and Istanbul there is rejoicing – Russia's exiled leaders offer what assistance they can.

The Communist Party has alienated itself from the workers, the mutineers declare. All they want is what the revolution promised them: freedom. Lenin calls the rebellion a White plot cooked up in Paris. The White generals, says *Pravda*, have 'bared their fangs'. Family members of sailors are taken hostage in Petrograd. Trotsky, the man who made Kronstadt his second home in 1917, is sent to smash the uprising. Mercy will only be shown to those who give up unconditionally. 'Your clemency, Mr Trotsky, will not be needed', the mutineers respond. A pamphlet dropped from the air tells the sailors to surrender, or they will be 'shot like partridges'. De Gaulle's acquaintance Misha is sent to command the assault.

One ultimatum is ignored. A second passes also without surrender. At the beginning of March, the Red Army launches a first attack across the ice. The Kronstadt newspaper issues its own retort. The Communists have replaced the 'hammer and the sickle' with the 'bayonet and the barred

window'. They have stifled the creative spirit of revolution with bureaucracy, turned work into slavery. Now that they have won power, there is
nothing they will not stoop to in order to keep it: slander, violence, deceit.
But a third revolution is on its way: 'At last, the policeman's club of
Communist autocracy has been broken'. On the ground, a Red Army
attack is repelled.

Even as the guns are firing outside Petrograd, in Moscow Vladimir
commends his latest policy zigzag to a meeting of the Communist Party:
letting the peasants sell their grain, accelerating concessions to foreign
capitalists. He rips into his opponents from all sides. The splits and squabbles must stop. To some arguments – Kronstadt arguments, he calls them
– there is only one response: 'a gun'. He jibes Trotsky, accusing him of
grandstanding on the trades union business, of going too far in his call to
simply make them servants of the state, the shock troops of a militarised
labour force. But nor is Lenin going to tolerate the opposing tendency
advocating putting independent unions in charge of the economy, which
Vladimir considers a dangerous deviation towards syndicalism. Where would
the revolution be then? It needs a party vanguard. To simply hand things
over to the workers – many of whom are not even Bolsheviks – would be
an abdication of responsibility.

One must not make a 'fetish of democratic principles', as Trotsky puts
it with characteristic hauteur, after his own position has been rejected. No
one should forget the 'historical birth-right of the party', the war commissar
says, 'obliged to maintain its dictatorship regardless of temporary wavering
in the spontaneous moods of the masses, regardless of the temporary vacillations even in the working class'. Trotsky has a way with words. But he
uses them too much.

In Moscow, Vladimir alternates defence and attack. He acknowledges
that the state has 'bureaucratic distortions' – but these can be corrected.
He accepts that 'we may have made mistakes' in the past – but there was
'no alternative'. Perhaps we nationalised too much, too quickly. Perhaps
we abolished the market too readily. He is quite plain in admitting what
he now proposes: letting peasants sell their produce means 'turning back
towards capitalism'. But it is expedient. He is vague about how it will work:
'I only wish to prove to you that theoretically it is conceivable.' There is
no alternative. Taxing *something* is better than trying to requisition *nothing*.
Vladimir wants to reassure his followers he has not gone soft on the peasants: 'The peasant must do a bit of starving so as to relieve the factories
and towns from complete starvation.' Proletarian dictatorship will not be

weakened. Compulsion will be used where necessary. Meanwhile, Kronstadt is bombed from the air.

Reconstruction will take perhaps a decade, perhaps more, Lenin says. The country has been beaten to within an 'inch of its life' for seven straight years: 'It's a mercy she can hobþle about on crutches.' Foreign concessions are such a crutch. He recalls being told by Clare Sheridan in the Kremlin last year that when the Bolsheviks came to power, British politicians called them crocodiles. Vladimir smarts: 'Crocodiles are despicable'. Now Britain wants to trade. See how far the Soviet Republic has come! (A trade agreement is signed the following day, including a promise to stop hostile propaganda against each other – a promise Moscow has no intention of abiding by.)

In the final minutes of the congress, when everyone is exhausted or beaten into submission, Lenin pulls off his masterstroke. A motion on party unity. Who can be against that? The odd voice raised in comradely enquiry as to the correctness of the party line – totally ineffectual, anyhow – will be permitted. But organised dissent against the party line will be met with expulsion. Factions are banned. Some sense that a Rubicon is being crossed, even if they cannot quite perceive the full significance of Lenin's move for themselves. (Trotsky has no conception it could be ever used against *him*.) The Soviets have already been hollowed out, and made the creatures of the Bolsheviks. Now party democracy is set aside. For all practical purposes, the leadership will rule over the party as it wishes, and the party will rule over everything. The structure is completing itself. All it needs is a mechanic to sit at the controls and make it work better. If only there was someone loyal and reliable who could do the job. Certainly not Trotsky. 'A temperamental man', Vladimir decides. 'As for politics, he hasn't got a clue.'

On Kronstadt island, the rebel sailors produce their last newspaper. 'Socialism in Quotation Marks' is the title of its main article. That evening, Misha prepares his final assault. The Kronstadt garrison have little ammunition left. Medical supplies have run out. The sailors survive on canned horsemeat. At three in the morning, Misha's troops start across the ice through freezing fog. No talking, no smoking. By five they are nearing the first of Kronstadt's defensive forts, approaching it on their bellies. Then an electric lamp is switched on. Blinding light. The firing begins. For nearly two days the battle for Kronstadt rages: house to house, street to street. The Bolsheviks consider using poison gas. Some sailors attempt to flee across the ice to Finland. In the days to come, the government in Helsinki asks Moscow to clear the corpses: it is feared they will cause a public health risk in the thaw. Captured rebel leaders are either shot or sent to a prison camp above the Arctic Circle.

The ideals of 1917 are very far away. All power to the Soviets! Who remembers that now? The day that Kronstadt is conquered is the fiftieth anniversary of the Paris Commune, notes one revolutionary exile in Petrograd, expelled from the United States last December. She came to Russia in hope, singing revolutionary songs. Now Emma Goldman is appalled. The revolution has murdered its children. Trotsky's hands are covered with their blood. Lenin's rule has become a dictatorship. Opposition to the Bolsheviks is repressed by the Cheka. John Reed is dead. World revolution is delayed. Dreams of new ways of living, new forms of organisation, new ideas of art and society, have been disappointed. Electrification is held up as the new ideal where freedom once stood.

NEW YORK: Clare Sheridan embarks on a lecture tour of the United States.

She talks passionately about Russia, and about Trotsky in particular. (One evening, playing charades, she has to act out his name, first imitating a horse trotting along, and then someone skiing down a mountain.) Clare excites audiences large and small with her devil-may-care attitude, feminine vivacity and vague radicalism. 'I worship force as an element, force and energy in humans, force and power in machinery', she tells one hall. She compares Pittsburgh steel mills to Bolshevism: 'something so tremendous that my mind cannot grasp it'. While in America, Clare exchanges a few letters with Winston Churchill, in which he says he is almost prepared to forgive her for consorting with the Bolsheviks – 'fiends in human form', as he calls them – while she suggests to him that, given the excellent high-level contacts she has established, she should now be made British Ambassador in Moscow.

In New York, there is an exhibition of Clare's work – mostly bronze busts of the leading figures of the Russian revolution. Some visitors come to ogle their political heroes, blinking reverently at the mute figures of Lenin and Trotsky. Others tell Clare to her face how much they hate them. 'I am always amused by people who want to kill off all Bolsheviks, all Sinn Féiners and all Jews', she writes in her diary. 'It would make for a wonderfully emptier world: anyway, it is very emblematic of the Christian spirit of today!'

The city fairly bubbles with concern for the situation in Ireland. Clare has been warned of an anti-British mood. One day she attends a public lecture by a loyalist British Catholic on the situation in Ireland which is interrupted by a group of hecklers waving Irish flags. On St Patrick's Day, her taxi ride across town is held up by a large Sinn Féin procession through the city. Her Russian cab driver is unsympathetic to all this protesting. It is action the Irish need, he tells Clare, not placards. The Russians rose up and killed the Tsar, he points out: why don't the Irish rise up and kill King George?

MOSCOW: The Bolshevik regime works overtime to downplay the significance of Kronstadt, and spreads rumours that it was nothing more than a final episode in Russia's long civil war. Red against White – and the Reds have prevailed.

'The Kronstadt affair is itself a very petty incident', Lenin tells a journalist from New York. 'It does not threaten to break up the Soviet state any more than the Irish disorders threaten to break up the British Empire.' People in America are foolish to imagine that if only the Bolsheviks were overthrown then some kind of admirably middle-of-the-road government would take over. Wrong! The only alternatives are 'butcher generals and helpless bureaucrats'. He is hoping for more trade with America: fur for tractors, timber for shoes.

Comrade Stalin is admitted for an operation to remove his appendix. Vladimir sends the Georgian four bottles of the best port wine to be found. He is ordered to go to a spa to recover. Stalin chooses Nalchik, the town in the Caucasus where Inessa died.

BERLIN – MUNICH – BERLIN: Germany lurches towards a new crisis.

In order to force the Germans to pay reparations as required, the French and their allies move in to take control of the German cities of Düsseldorf, Duisburg and Ruhrort. Over the next few weeks, trains carrying foreign soldiers arrive at the cities' main stations every day.

While the government in Berlin is reeling from that first blow to its authority, a wave of Communist-inspired strikes breaks out in the central German province of Saxony. Policemen are attacked, courthouses bombed and banks robbed – part of an 'offensive theory' backed by Béla Kun. He is keen to have a second go at revolution; local Communists are not sure the conditions are right. Three thousand striking workers occupy Germany's biggest chemical works. The Saxon crisis gives the police an excuse to crush the Communists. Kun returns to Moscow with his tail between his legs. Hitler starts a Bavarian tour under the question 'Statesmen or National Traitors?', blaming the politicians for the country's dire straits.

In amongst all the violence, a murder in Berlin goes almost unnoticed. Talaat Pasha, one of the triumvirate who ran the Ottoman Empire during the war, is shot dead one day while out walking with his wife. His assailant, a twenty-five-year-old Armenian student who survived the massacres, is hauled before a German court and acquitted on the grounds of mental trauma. Witnesses attest to the horrors perpetrated against Armenians during the war. Talaat's killing is deemed an understandable response.

PARIS: The latest edition of *Littérature* appears. Inside, a chart. And on the chart, a statistical ranking of the men and women of the age according to the opinions of the magazine's leading lights: André Breton, Tristan Tzara and the rest. The range is somewhat arbitrary, from −25 (representing total aversion) to +20 (representing something akin to hero-worship). A score of zero is taken to mean indifference. The purpose of the rankings, so *Littérature* claims, is not 'to grade, but to degrade'.

No surprises at the bottom end of the scale: Anatole France, John Stuart Mill, Émile Zola and Rodin all come off badly on the judges' score sheet. The Unknown Soldier, buried physically only a few months previously, is now buried figuratively on the pages of *Littérature:* both Breton and Tzara give him −25. (Pretty much the only positive score Tzara gives is to Breton, and even then, only a measly 12 out of a possible 20.)

Further up the rankings things are more ambivalent: a mild distaste for the Prophet Muhammad and Jesus Christ (an average across the board of −1.72 and −1.54 respectively), and a slightly more negative view of Lenin and Trotsky (−3.72 and −3.63). Kaiser Wilhelm comes in at −2.09, well above D'Annunzio (−7.36), and at the midpoint between Henri Matisse (−3.27) and Oscar Wilde (−1.45).

Jostling for position in the upper tier of the rankings are, amongst others, Einstein (+9.54), Freud (+8.63) and Shakespeare (+9.18, despite another −25 from the Romanian). At the very top of the chart — surprise, surprise — feature the contributors and editors of *Littérature* themselves: Breton in the lead (+16.85), Soupault just behind (+16.30) and Aragon (+14.10) snapping at their heels. Tzara is a little behind on +13.30. (Suppressing his doubts, André publicly awards Tzara 18 points, but, privately, there is an awkwardness about their relationship now, like two lovers who have learned too soon the other's imperfections.)

The surprise of the rankings, however, is amongst the runners-up. With a positive score across the board from every judge, in third place: the actor Charlie Chaplin.

ISTANBUL: The British Ambassador has an audience with the Sultan. Vahdettin is angry and depressed. The French and Italian Ambassadors are made to wait outside for over two hours.

The list of the Sultan's complaints is long. Ankara, he says, is a 'madhouse'. He is furious at the equal billing given to Kemal's representatives at a recent conference in London reopening the Sèvres terms. He distrusts the French, who are now thought to only have eyes for Syria and commercial opportunities in the wider Middle East. The Italians are said to be providing arms to Ankara on the side. Vahdettin dislikes even his own ministers. He pointedly threatens the British Ambassador with abdication. That way the British would have no one in Istanbul to negotiate with at all. He wonders aloud as to the true nationality of the cashiered general who once accompanied him to Berlin. 'A Macedonian revolutionary of unknown origin', the Sultan calls Mustafa Kemal spitefully. The Sultan decides he must be Serbian.

His fevered speculations are whirlpools in an Ottoman teacup now. Vahdettin is isolated. The Sultan-Caliph still has the trappings of imperial authority. He still appears to the faithful in the *selamlik* procession each Friday. But politically, he is a busted flush. Nationalists view him as a British puppet. Militarily, he has no power.

All the advantage now lies with Ankara. Anatolia has been largely pacified by Mustafa Kemal's forces. His position gets stronger by the day. Kemal's associates have finally signed a real treaty with Moscow. A trickle of Russian weapons becomes a flood. After the Turkish military successes of last autumn and the treaty with Moscow, Turkey's borders in the Caucasus are decided between Moscow and Ankara alone. Istanbul is cut out entirely. (The Armenians and Georgians – outnumbered, outgunned, and now theoretically part of their own Soviet Socialist Republic – have no choice but to accept Moscow's decision.)

There are now only the Greeks left to deal with. In late March, they attack again.

MUNICH: Adolf appears to be making headway with Munich's power-brokers. At the end of winter, one of the party's new acolytes introduces him to Erich Ludendorff, now engaged in defending his image, explaining the causes of Germany's defeat and plotting his return. Ludendorff looks at Hitler and sees the kind of effective propagandist he could have done with during the war; Hitler looks at Ludendorff and sees the political capital of his name (and the fundraising possibilities).

MILAN: The flying lessons continue. In March, Benito is involved in that most Futurist of events: a crash. He emerges unscathed. Another story to add to his legend. Another story to raise his profile. Someone writes a song about it. 'The airplane and the bomb wanted to oust you', it goes. 'You answered to Lady Death: come back another time.'

Across Italy, the tempo of political violence has not slackened even as the threat of a socialist takeover has diminished. The *squadristi* have become more brazen than ever. Socialist offices are ransacked with joyful abandon. Left-wing newspapers have their printing presses smashed. Socialist politicians live in fear of the sound of a truck pulling up outside their door. Local magistrates are too afraid to act. Many condone the Fascist violence. In Mantua, Fascists charged with six separate counts of murder all get off while sixteen socialists are awarded a collective century in jail for the murder of two *squadristi*. So successful have the gangs become that it now looks as if they and their leaders, the *ras*, are the true leaders of Italian fascism (particularly given D'Annunzio's retreat into writing books). Mussolini is worried. If he does not watch out, perhaps the *ras* will come to dominate the movement he helped to found.

In a speech in Trieste, he is forced to defend himself for not having come to the rescue of D'Annunzio in Fiume. What was he supposed to do? 'Revolutions are not jack-in-the-boxes which can be set off at will', he says. 'Revolutions are made with armies, not against them; with arms, not against them; with disciplined movements, not with amorphous masses called to attend a gathering in the town square'. Fiume tried to mix 'the devil and Holy Water', anarchists and nationalists. The army and navy did not switch sides. Fascism must be smarter in the future. It must think big, it must choose its time, and use tactics which will bring success rather than just adulation. 'I reject all forms of Bolshevism', Benito tells his audience, 'but if I was forced to choose one it would be that of Moscow and Lenin, if only because its proportions are gigantic, barbaric, universal.'

He looks to Rome and to the elections. The prestige of national office would surely help him against the pretenders for the Fascist throne. He makes friends with the political class and insinuates himself into an electoral alliance. On the principle of holding one's rivals close, and basking in reflected glory, Mussolini even pays a visit to that old roué D'Annunzio and asks him whether he would like to stand alongside him in the elections. The poet declines.

PARIS: A few days before Easter Sunday 1921 a Spanish diplomat wearing a pair of dark glasses arrives in the French capital on the night express from Strasbourg. There he picks up the Vienna train. Finally, after spending the night at a friend's apartment in the Austrian capital, the same man is driven westwards towards Hungary. But at the border, the Spanish diplomat has changed. A remarkable metamorphosis. Now he wears motoring goggles rather than dark glasses to hide his face. And he is no longer a diplomat but, according to his passport, a British representative of the Red Cross. The motor car is nodded through. Charles Habsburg keeps the goggles on.

The drive through the Hungarian–Austrian borderlands is picturesque. It is almost like old times: girls dressed in dirndls, and schnitzel and cucumber salad for lunch (paid for with French money). Afterwards, still in disguise, Charles and his party run into an Easter procession, at which sight the successor of the Holy Roman Emperors is moved to kneel down in the street to pray. It all seems to be going so well – until the car breaks down. The last few miles to Szombathely are completed in a horse and cart. There, Charles spends the night in the house of the local bishop, while the Minister-President, who happens to be on a shooting holiday nearby, is called over to give his advice on the situation with Horthy in Budapest.

The capital can only be reached the following day. Expecting Horthy to turn over power without a fight – after all, Horthy is only a regent, suppos-edly standing in for the Habsburgs during their absence – Charles dispenses with the idea of taking any soldiers with him to his capital. When Charles arrives at his old palace, there is no one there to greet him. There is no fanfare, no red carpet. When he meets the once-loyal admiral, Horthy is rather rude. He tells Charles to go back to Switzerland at once. The timing is wrong.

Charles has miscalculated. The French seemed willing to support a Habsburg back in Budapest – maybe even in Vienna. But not a Habsburg so witless as to conduct his own restoration without even a revolver. Conservative Hungarians might have sympathy – but are they willing to risk a civil war to have Charles back? Meanwhile, in Prague, Bucharest and Belgrade, there is outright fury. The governments there threaten military intervention.

Charles beats a hasty retreat from Budapest and holes up in Hungary's royalist west for a week or so, while recovering from the flu. He ponders his options. The international chorus telling him that a Habsburg restoration will not be accepted grows louder. Charles gathers around his closest followers and suggests a new tack: perhaps one of their number could return to Switzerland disguised as him, while he remains in Hungary. An embarrassed silence. No one volunteers. It is time to go into exile, again.

DOORN: Wilhelm has little time for *Schadenfreude* at the embarrassment of that ridiculous man Charles. At home at Huis Doorn, the atmosphere is heavy. The Kaiser is preoccupied with the state of his wife's health. And, increasingly, another subject which he has been reading up on: the Jews.

One evening, he breaks into an anti-Semitic diatribe over dinner. There will be a reckoning, he warns. All these people will have to give up their art collections and their houses. They will be banned from public office.

SPRING

MOSCOW: Vladimir has returned to his old habits. He cannot seem to help himself.

He sends a note to the head of the Commissariat of Enlightenment ordering a barrage of propaganda measures to emphasise the importance of developing the local peat industry, a source of fuel in which Russia is particularly rich. He demands 'leaflets, pamphlets, mobile exhibitions, films, publication of textbooks; teaching about the peat industry to be introduced as a compulsory subject in schools and higher technical colleges; textbooks must be written; study groups must be sent abroad annually'. A hundred thousand copies of the pamphlet *Peat* are to be printed within the week. Why are people so slow?

The same day, the impatient revolutionary fires off a note to Comrade Trotsky's deputy on military matters. His sister Maria has gone off to the Crimea with a few colleagues, Vladimir explains. They have a special coach on their train, of course. But he is worried about time. 'Could you not give orders that if the passengers ask, this coach should be attached to military trains *in order to speed it up?*' he asks. Vladimir adds in brackets: 'there and back'.

The impatient revolutionary is working himself to the bone with all this activity. But, then, can he trust anyone else to deal with these matters? Comrade Trotsky is quite sick; Stalin is recuperating. Vladimir himself is getting more and more tired. You mustn't work so hard, those closest to him say (as they have been saying for years). He finds it harder to concentrate for long periods, forced to pause even when writing short notes. His nerves flare more readily. He speaks to the doctors. They tell him he is a hypochondriac.

KINGSTON, JAMAICA: Marcus Garvey returns to the island of his birth. He faces criticism for not having returned the year before, when his father died.

In return, Garvey attacks local leaders and preachers for their lack of leadership on the island, declaring it the most backward country in the western hemisphere. 'You lazy, good-for-nothing Jamaicans, wake up!' he rails at one meeting, browbeating the population for their failure to secure their rights from the British.

He finds his onward journey delayed by problems with one of the Black Star Line ships – its boiler blows up, then it crashes into a pier – and American diplomatic officials who refuse Garvey a visa to travel to the American-controlled Canal Zone of Panama (on the basis that he could use this as a back door to the United States, from which he should be excluded as a dangerous agitator).

Eventually, he sets sail for Costa Rica.

INÖNÜ – ROME – MUNICH: Two victories for the Turks against the Greeks. 'Our army has reappeared on the stage of history in thunderous majesty', Mustafa Kemal avers, sending a message of congratulations from Ankara. Five thousand Turks have been killed but the Greeks have been stopped for now.

Benito Mussolini's *Il Popolo d'Italia* runs a series of breathless articles on the rise of the new strongman in the east. German papers celebrate the rebirth of Turkish power. The *Völkischer Beobachter* dismisses the idea that Kemal's dalliance with Moscow might amount to anything serious – to be a nationalist and a Bolshevik is as impossible as 'hot snow or wooden iron'.

PHILADELPHIA, PENNSYLVANIA: Noble Sissle, Jim Europe's friend and fellow musician from the days of the Harlem Hellfighters, is in Philadelphia looking for singers and dancers for a new all-black show he wants to stage – on Broadway. There is not much money to do it. Sissle can barely raise the funds to travel from one city to the next.

The show is to be called *Shuffle Along*, and tells the story of two men running for mayor in the fictional Jimtown in the American South, and their various loves, triumphs and experiences along the way. The original idea for the project comes when Sissle and his old friend the pianist and composer Eubie Blake meet two other black vaudeville stars at a fundraising event for Du Bois's NAACP in Philadelphia the previous year and discuss how to get black performers onto Broadway in their own musicals, rather than as comic turns in blackface.

Of course, anyone in Philly who has half an interest in the new sound in music knows Sissle and Blake, or at least a couple of their songs. Josephine decides to try her luck in an audition for the new show. She is told she looks too young. (She is still only fourteen.) And, this time, her skin is considered too *dark* for the look of the show. Josephine is furious.

NEW YORK: The *Rotterdam* pulls into the Battery on the island of Manhattan. On deck, a man in early middle age stands staring at the welcoming crowds. He wears a faded grey raincoat, and a floppy black hat. His tie is skewed. In one hand he holds a pipe, in the other a violin. An expression somewhere between bemusement and pride hovers over his face. Thousands are there to greet him, waving Jewish flags of white with two blue bars, or else wearing Zionist lapel pins. The refrain of the American national anthem makes its way up to his ears. It feels like a homecoming.

Special guests and the press are ferried aboard to meet Einstein before the passengers disembark. Albert and Elsa pose for photographs in front of the New York skyline. Film crews order the hapless professor about from one part of the ship to the next – getting him to point at things – to get some good footage for the newsreels. Einstein finally excuses himself, virtually running away from the movie men. At a news conference held in the captain's quarters, Albert speaks through an interpreter. The journalists are enchanted by his old-world charm. 'How long did you take to conceive your theory?' one asks him: 'I have not finished yet', he replies, laughing. Mrs Einstein confesses she does not understand relativity herself, explaining that 'it is not necessary for my happiness'. She paints a rather romantic picture of living with a genius such as Albert, describing a man inclined to pick up his violin at any moment of the day or night and who sometimes spends whole weeks just daydreaming. Someone asks Albert about the anti-relativists. 'No man of culture or knowledge has any animosity towards my theories', he says. 'Even the physicists opposed to my theories are animated by political motives.' He gives a name to these motives: anti-Semitism.

New York lies at Einstein's feet like a puppy-dog, just waiting to show affection to its master. Outside City Hall, Albert is lifted onto the shoulders of his colleagues and driven away in an open-top automobile. In a tour through the Lower East Side, the crowds show their love for the man by tooting horns out of windows. There is something 'psychopathological' about all these non-scientists and their new obsession with relativity, Einstein admits. An 'Einstein Made Easy' handbook is produced. Day after day, Albert's mere presence in America is front-page news. Some problem means he is not immediately awarded the freedom of the city. (It turns out that a city alderman opposes it, on which the official is congratulated by the *Dearborn Independent*.) In Albany, they award him the freedom of New York State instead.

There are daytime fundraisers, evening fundraisers, morning fundraisers. In the Metropolitan Opera House, every seat is filled with men and women keen to see Einstein – and to hear Weizmann and the New York rabbis make their pitch for Zionism. 'We are going to respond to every attack upon our people, to every libel and every slander', Rabbi Silver tells them, 'by more Jewishness, by more schools and synagogues, and by a more intensive and loyal work in Palestine.' Anti-Semitism, far from weakening these intentions, will only strengthen them. The land of Israel will become the land of the prophets once more. Albert nods along. He speaks barely a word of English. In fact, at such events, he barely speaks a word at all.

DUBLIN: Éamon de Valera looks at Michael Collins and sees a force of nature: wild and dangerous, perhaps a little feral. He must be tamed, this brilliant, boisterous, boyish rival of his. He has grown too big for his boots. A loose cannon. Popular with the women. He needs a father figure to steer him away from further trouble, and put him in his place. He swears too much. He smokes.

Michael looks at Éamon and sees a freedom fighter who has elbowed his way to the top, stepping over bodies along the way, and been transformed into the mirthless, bloodless politician he is today: all calculation, all angles, all abstraction, without any of the natural failings or stirrings of human flesh, a Holy Ghost for the nationalist movement. The armed struggle is now two years old. The republic's declaration of independence has grown stale. How is Ireland to advance its cause? By stealth or by spectacle? Through what combination of politics and force?

Collins laughs at de Valera behind his back, joking with the hard men from the provinces about the boss's shaky grasp of military tactics and the sheer bloody foolishness of his desire for the IRA to engage in large-scale battles with the British. But behind the laughter there is a worry, too: where might de Valera's meddling in military matters lead? Collins doubts his boss has the stomach to win the war for Ireland the way he thinks it must be fought. But he is quite sure de Valera has the arrogance to lose it.

But strategy and tactics discussed in Dublin matter little to the war at large. Across Ireland, the Furies have been unleashed. They follow no dictates but their own. The local hard men are in charge, and they know what's best for all concerned. Men and women marked out as spies and traitors are shot out of hand, or kidnapped to be murdered later, their bodies dumped as a warning to others. The grand country houses of Ireland's landowners, presumed to be supportive of the old regime, are burned to the ground. The British count their losses: forty-six casualties amongst army, Black and Tans and Royal Irish Constabulary in a single week over Easter – the highest since 1916. Reprisal and retribution are not working. The IRA is untamed.

A heavy atmosphere of paranoia descends – and with it, the inevitable fog of war. In County Clare, out-of-uniform constables of the Royal Irish Constabulary and auxiliaries of the same force mistake each other for members of the IRA at a hotel bar in Castleconnell. A Wild West shoot-out follows, all broken glass and flying bullets. A popular pub landlord dies in front of his customers. 'It shows how Nemesis may follow upon a policy of shooting first and asking questions afterwards', a British newspaper reports to its readers. Public opinion receives another jolt: a dirty colonial frontier war is being fought a day's journey from London and, what is worse, it is not going well.

JERUSALEM – LONDON: Fresh from a colonial conference in Cairo – and a camel ride amongst the Pyramids alongside T. E. Lawrence and Gertrude Bell – Winston travels to Jerusalem. There he defends the concept of a Jewish national home in Palestine and rejects the appeal of an Arab delegation to renege on the promises made to the Zionists by the British in 1917.

Jewish immigration will be slow and steady, Winston tells the Arab delegation. There will be benefits for all. It will take a very long time before full self-government in Palestine: 'All of us here today will have passed away from the earth and also our children and our children's children before it is fully achieved.' Another day he visits the site of the planned new Hebrew university. 'Personally', he says, 'my heart is full of sympathy for Zionism.' But he cannot ignore the fact that local Arabs do not feel the same way.

Churchill finds Emir Abdullah, Britain's choice to rule neighbouring Trans-Jordan, to be 'moderate, friendly and statesmanlike', willing to operate with British funds and military aid. Winston appreciates Abdullah's promise to try and rein in the various tribes raiding the French in Syria. He frets about the cost of Britain's continuing role in Iraq, where Abdullah's brother is in the frame to become King (his second kingdom in as many years). Churchill is against the Prime Minister's pro-Greek line in Anatolia (and not displeased that it is failing to work), rather favouring the Turks.

The Middle East seems full of problems and requirements and expense.

DOORN – BERLIN: One morning, a little after six, Kaiserin Auguste Viktoria's heart stops beating. The Kaiser is distraught. Inexplicably, he compares his own dear Kaiserin unfavourably to that young Empress Zita, Charles's wife. That afternoon, he spends an hour outside in the garden, by himself. Later, he lays fresh flowers on his wife's dead body.

Wilhelm's children try to persuade their father to let their mother be buried at Doorn, where he will be able to visit. But the Kaiser has other ideas. He has been planning it for months: her body must lie in Potsdam. There her grave will become a site of pilgrimage, he believes. Through her death, the Hohenzollern flame will be kept alive. He hears the low sobs of a nation deprived of their Mother Empress. Perhaps they will shed a tear for him too. Perhaps the German nation will at last realise the dreadful mistake that it has made in getting rid of him.

The German government accedes to the request to bury Auguste Viktoria at Sanssouci, Frederick the Great's palace at Potsdam, just outside Berlin. But Wilhelm will not be allowed to attend the ceremony. 'What every common worker can do, namely follow his wife's coffin to the grave, even that has been made impossible for me by my traitorous people', the Kaiser writes in fury. He is only allowed to accompany her coffin to the local railway station at Maarn.

When the train carrying Auguste Viktoria's coffin crosses the border it is met by a band of veterans of the war of 1870 playing a funeral march. Six thousand imperial officers accompany the procession in Potsdam. Ludendorff is there. American newspapers estimate a crowd of a quarter of a million in the streets, though it is hard to tell whether they have come to support the Hohenzollern cause, or to protest it, or simply out of curiosity. Workers in Potsdam threaten a flash strike unless the old imperial flag is taken down from public buildings.

The republican papers carry a quite different story during these days: the amount Germany will have to pay in war reparations and the strict schedule of these payments, as determined following intensive discussions between the Allies in London. Germany will be paying for the Hohenzollerns' folly for years.

Istanbul: 'If it weren't such a tragedy, it could be looked at just as a wonderful romance,' writes Clover Dulles to her family, 'such a turning up-side down of things that might have been written in a play and now has suddenly cropped up in real life.' Former Russian officers come door to door selling sausages. Sons of millionaires have become window-cleaners. The Russian embassy has been turned into a refugee camp. It smells, writes Clover, of a 'family menagerie'.

The refugee problem is acute – and political. The remnants of Wrangel's army cannot be left for ever encamped at Gallipoli and on various Aegean islands. Suspicion of the Allied authorities grows daily. The French army offers Wrangel three options: repatriation of his men to Russia, membership of the French Foreign Legion, or evacuation to Brazil or Peru. A French general travels to Lemnos to persuade the Cossacks that Russia is perfectly safe now and that an amnesty offered by the Bolsheviks will protect them. Wrangel's officers tell the Cossacks not to believe the French. Several thousand make the journey nonetheless, taking their chances on Bolshevik honour and finding themselves bitterly disappointed. Wrangel's attempts to unify Russian émigrés behind him and claim possession of foreign assets of the Tsarist state come to naught.

Clover gets involved in Red Cross work. She takes clothing, cigarettes, food parcels and Russian magazines to the refugees, sometimes in the company of Olga Wrangel, the general's wife. Her husband Allen meanwhile tries to make sense of what is going on in Russia by gathering intelligence from what remains of Wrangel's networks and intercepting short-wave radio transmissions between Russia and the Caucasus. He becomes fascinated with all the old books that poverty-stricken Russian civilians are trying to sell to make ends meet. He strikes up a friendship with a British journalist who shares this interest.

What is really happening on the other side of the Black Sea is shrouded in mystery. The stories coming out of Russia now are sparse, pitiful and confused. From recently arrived émigrés one can pick up only fragments: snippets of hearsay, hints of the truth. It is hard to know how reliable they are. The country is slowly starving, that much is clear. How long the Bolshevik regime will last is anyone's guess.

Berlin – Munich – Berlin: The French are not prepared to back down from their demands and they insist that Germany must pay up in coal and gold. In Berlin, the government totters. In Munich, Adolf Hitler rails against

the rapacious British and French, trying to enslave Germany with reparations, blaming Germany's political class for the disaster they have brought
upon the country since 1918 and accusing them of being too spineless to
now fight back.

A few days later, Polish nationalists in Silesia – where a vote has just
taken place to decide how much of the coal-rich region will remain in
Germany, and how much will be awarded to the revived state of Poland
– launch an uprising to wrest the entire region from German control.
Bridges are blown up. American newspapers report the sudden appearance of unidentified but well-armed Polish-speaking soldiers. Warsaw is
suspected of engaging in covert warfare against its neighbour. The integrity
of Germany's borders is in question again.

The French are sympathetic to the Poles, whom they need as a strong
eastern ally against the Germans; the British seem more minded to accept
the German point of view, noting the importance of Silesia to German
industry. The Wilsonian dream is very far away.

WASHINGTON DC: Woodrow spends a lot of time in the past these days.
Though he prefers not to be called Mr President, Edith ensures that he is
surrounded by reminders of his former position. His bedroom deliberately
echoes that which he occupied in the White House. His bed is a replica of
the Lincoln bed. The presidential doctor continues to serve Woodrow. The
couple often watch movies together, just as they did in the White House,
or on the boat over to France after the war. A downstairs solarium plays
the role of the old White House portico. The only off note in the new
set-up is a painting of a woman Woodrow insists on hanging prominently
over the mantelpiece in his room: the first Mrs Wilson.

Time passes. Woodrow has few visitors. He reads murder mysteries in
bed. Sometimes he does not come down all day; often he is read to, as he
finds it hard to hold a book for long periods. Like Freud's relationship with
America, Woodrow's relationship with politics veers between attraction and
repulsion. 'He seems not to want to know or think about what is going
on', a visitor notes, 'and yet broods on it.' Woodrow has a 'self-consuming
mind', his doctor explains: always active, never relaxed. Somewhat whim-
sically, Woodrow decides he will set himself up as a lawyer again, just as
he was in Atlanta, Georgia, four decades before. A business partner is duly
dispatched to find a Washington office for the two of them, and prepares
it for a grand summer opening.

Every Saturday, Edith and Woodrow go to the same theatre for the evening show. At three each afternoon, as regular as clockwork, the Pierce-Arrow automobile is brought around to the front and the couple are taken on a drive – always the same trip – out along the Potomac. So regular is this ritual that little crowds gather outside the house each afternoon to catch sight of the presidential couple, sometimes waving, sometimes cheering. The tourist buses come by too, the tour guides pointing out the house and making the same stale joke through a megaphone each time: 'On the left just below you will see the new home of Ex-President Wilson. He paid one hundred and fifty thousand dollars for it – or she did!'

PRINCETON, NEW JERSEY: At Wilson's alma mater a Marx Brothers comedy is enacted. When Albert Einstein is invited to stand up, he sits down. When he is invited to sit down, he stands up. When he is to be awarded his doctoral gowns, he turns the wrong way. Things go more smoothly that afternoon when Albert gives a lecture, in German, about the theory of relativity.

The triumphal tour continues to Boston (where Einstein is asked for the speed of sound and tells the impertinent journalist to look it up in a book), to Chicago (where he lectures at the university) and to Cleveland (where the entire city seems to shut down to greet the great physicist). One place not on Albert's itinerary is Dearborn, Michigan, where Henry Ford's *Independent* – now nearly one year into its anti-Semitic campaign – devotes an entire page to suggesting that the theory of relativity actually derives from the earlier work of a scientist known only as 'Kinertia'. (This week's cover reads: 'Is Einstein a Plagiarist? Jew admits Bolshevism'.)

'America is interesting,' Albert writes on the journey home, 'more easily aroused to enthusiasm than other countries I have unsettled with my presence.' He has been made to feel like a 'prize ox': yanked this way and that by his minders, slapped on the back by all and sundry and shown off. 'But now it is finished', he writes, 'and what remains is a wonderful sense of having done something truly good and having worked for the "Jewish matter" steadfastly in the face of opposition from Jews and non-Jews.'

Even his friend Fritz Haber admits the trip has not been quite the disaster he feared. It may have even done something for German–American friendship.

MUNICH: In May, the Bavarian premier – a patrician conservative with an authoritarian streak – calls in various NSDAP representatives for a meeting, to see if they can work together in preventing the kind of instability seen elsewhere in Germany from spreading to Bavaria.

Afterwards a student who has taken up the Nazi cause sends a letter to the premier, offering personal testimony of Adolf Hitler's character and learning. His understanding of history is 'way beyond the average', the student claims. His simple upbringing gives him a 'rare sensitivity for the public mood, keen political instincts and tremendous strength of will' – precisely what patrician politicians lack. Hitler's true political philosophy, the student explains, is straightforward national solidarity, underpinned by 'pragmatic, honest socialism' and the liberation of the masses from 'foreign race leaders'. (There is no mention of anti-Semitism, the Aryan race or anti-capitalism.) Oh, and he is also a good Catholic: 'Your Excellency can place total trust in him'.

ROME – IRELAND: A Papal letter is published about the war in Ireland, drafted by Irish priests. 'We do not perceive how the bitter strife can profit either of the parties,' it reads, 'when property and homes are being ruthlessly and disgracefully laid waste, when villages and farmsteads are being set aflame, when neither sacred places nor sacred persons are spared, when on both sides a war resulting in the death of unarmed people, even of women and children, is carried on.' The British authorities are furious, claiming the letter treats the forces of order and disorder the same way.

In Ireland two days later, a general election held by the British authorities reconfirms the virtual political monopoly of Sinn Féin in the south, and the strength of Unionism in the north. A day after that, against Michael Collins's advice, a spectacular attack of the kind de Valera likes is launched. The Custom House in Dublin – the centre of British financial administration and a symbol of London's rule – is occupied by a hundred-strong force of the local IRA. Petrol is spread through the building and set alight. Ireland's administrative records go up in smoke.

In military terms, the attack is an awful failure. The building itself is soon reoccupied. A large contingent of IRA men are captured by the Black and Tans. Collins's Dublin IRA is decimated. In de Valera's terms, none of this matters: headlines have been made and a symbol has been destroyed. Irish republican determination is reasserted. Britain's war is shown once more to be unwinnable. 'Truly the hills of Ireland could be levelled to the ground and all her children driven out upon the seas of the world before

England can conquer us', Michael Collins writes a few weeks later to the woman he loves, Kitty Kiernan. But must all Ireland become a wasteland before peace can return?

VIENNA: Sigmund Freud receives an unexpected birthday present: a sculpture of his head. He is horrified. 'A ghastly threatening bronze doppelgänger', he calls it. When he sat for the sculpture the year before, Freud had assumed it was for an admirer.

MOSCOW: The impatient revolutionary is furious. 'Aren't you ashamed?' he writes to the Commissar of Enlightenment, Anatoly Lunacharsky. On his watch Mayakovsky has been allowed to publish a new poem, entitled *150,000,000* (in reference to the population of Soviet Russia and its brother republics):

Today
      we rush Russia
               into paradise
through the rainbow coloured chinks in sunsets
Go, go
      go, go, go, go
             go, go!
Letsgoletsgo!
      Through the white guard of snows!

'It is nonsense, stupidity, double-eyed stupidity and affectation', Lenin rages. It should be printed, in a far smaller print run than proposed, 'for libraries and cranks'.

Instead of faith
      In our soul
             we've got steam
                  and electricity.
No beggars here!
      We'll pocket the wealth of all worlds!
If it's old, kill it.
      Use their skulls as ashtrays!

Everything
>   will be a joy
>   to our eyes –
>   the eyes of overgrown children!

Lunacharsky should be 'flogged for his futurism', Lenin writes a touch histrionically – to Lunacharsky. (The Commissar of Enlightenment defends himself by noting that the poem was very popular when it was read out in public.)

Mayakovsky imagines the people of Russia, personified as Ivan, arising like a whirlwind of revolutionary fervour, and throwing themselves into battle against a wealthy, powerful, imaginary America, bristling with skyscrapers and airships.

That's not the afternoon sun in your eyes,
But Wilson's gigantic top hat
rising up like Sukharev tower.
He spits dynamite
and belches,
red all over

As Ivan and Woodrow begin their final struggle for supremacy, inanimate objects suddenly come alive. Man, machine and nature meld into one. Hunger, disease and even ideas are weaponised.

Wilson's sabre screamed.
>   From Ivan's shoulder,
>   downward
People,
>   buildings,
>   battleships,
>   horses,
all clambered through the narrow incision.
They came out singing,
>   all in music.

'Can't we stop this?' Vladimir asks a senior official responsible for cultural affairs. The impatient revolutionary is in the midst of trying to get America to trade with Soviet Russia. Poems like this will not help.

It must not be allowed to happen again. 'Let's agree that these futurists are to be published not more than twice a year and not more than 1,500 copies', Lenin writes. He proposes a pincer movement, asking if reliable anti-futurists can be found to drown out Mayakovsky on the poetic front while demanding a progress report on his request for a new Russian dictionary from Pushkin onwards so as to put language itself back on an even keel. 'Is it being done?' the impatient revolutionary writes. 'What precisely? Find out and send me exact details.'

PARIS: Six months after being ceremoniously buried under the Arc de Triomphe, and two months after his poor showing on the pages of *Littérature*, the ghost of the Unknown Soldier appears in Paris: he is a character witness in a theatrical mock trial organised by André Breton. To the horror of French nationalists in the audience, the Unknown Soldier, played by one of Breton's friends, appears dressed in German army uniform and gas mask. The nationalists break into a rousing rendition of the Marseillaise in protest.

The figure in the dock – represented in proceedings as a stuffed dummy – is Maurice Barrès, a French nationalist author, activist and friend of Gabriele D'Annunzio. On the political right, Barrès is seen as a heroic, inspiring figure – an unflinching critic of anything German, the author of several novels about the grounding of national identity in blood and soil. Charles de Gaulle is an avid reader. To André and those like him, the days when Barrès could be considered an appropriate mentor to young French writers are gone. He now epitomises a bygone era and a failed generation: those self-satisfied nationalist bastards who led France into war and seem to think that they have the moral right to dictate the peace.

For André, the stakes are high. He intends the trial to be a serious affair, not just a spectacle. In the weeks before the trial he even takes to studying formal court procedure. Though the Dadaists have to be involved in the preparations – they are still his tribe, after all – André is very much the man in charge.

Led by Tzara, the hard-core Dadaists find André's earnestness laughable. What is justice, anyhow? A Dadaist should ridicule convention, not attempt to repurpose it in the service of one's pet cause. Tzara uses his time in the witness box as an opportunity to make a mockery of proceedings and put in his own performance. In answer to the question of whether he served in the war, he responds sarcastically in the affirmative: at the 'Verdun of Dadaism'. He ends his testimony with a Dadaist song:

The song of an elevator,
Which had Dada in its heart
Tired out its motor part
That had Dada in his heart

Tzara rather enjoys himself. Breton fumes. (Barrès is condemned in absentia to twenty years' hard labour.)

SAINT-CYR, FRANCE: Around the same time that the Unknown Soldier is being dressed up as a German in André's theatre of the absurd, the new history professor at France's officer training school at Saint-Cyr strides into the academy's lecture hall. He is wearing full dress uniform, complete with cap, gloves and a sabre hanging at his side. Before starting his lecture Charles de Gaulle ceremoniously removes the sword and cap. The gloves stay on.

The lecture lasts for two hours. Towards the end of his peroration, the young French captain – now married with a child on the way – comes to the subject of the battle of Verdun. 'Soldiers, stand up!' he roars. The officer cadets of Saint-Cyr rise as one, and salute in silence. This is what France needs more of, de Gaulle reflects: respect, order, leadership, military ideals.

ROME: After the embarrassment of 1919, the triumph of 1921. At the end of spring, Mussolini arrives in the capital as the leading light of a small phalanx of Fascist deputies elected to the Italian parliament as part of a more mainstream coalition (which the Fascists immediately dump). He takes up residence in a hotel not far from the Piazza di Spagna.

CROTON-ON-HUDSON, UNITED STATES: Clare Sheridan drops by the artists' colony at Croton-on-Hudson in upstate New York. The smell of summer is in the air. Clare notices one rather neglected-looking cottage. Some irises are growing nearby. She recognises the names on the post box: *Reed, Bryant.* Louise is not in. For just an instant, Clare is back in Moscow, amidst the excitement of a society making itself anew. America is less enthralling.

SUMMER

SMYRNA – ISTANBUL: The blonde-haired Greek King Constantine (his father was a Dane) lands at the port of Smyrna, the first Christian King to set foot in Anatolia since the Crusades. The entire Greek nation has been mobilised for this final fight. Troops are shipped over by the thousand. Kemal must be finished off. The summer campaign will be decisive. It is a heady gamble.

In Istanbul, foreign diplomats enjoy after-dinner dances on terraces overlooking the Bosphorus. There are only two topics of conversation: how far the British will back the Greeks, and whether the Bolsheviks will turn up to spoil the party.

MOSCOW: Vladimir does a quick calculation. Basic electrification will take 10 years, which will require 370 million days of work. That is, 37 million days a year. There are 1.5 million soldiers in the Red Army. 37 divided by 1.5 makes 24. That's it! '24 working days, i.e. *two days a month.*' That is all that is required from the Red Army to electrify the entire country as planned. Lenin asks that his back-of-the-envelope calculation be circulated widely. If only others would take the job as seriously as him.

There are still Bolsheviks ideologically unhappy with Lenin's policy of granting concessions to foreign capitalists and reintroducing elements of the market into the Russian economy. Vladimir makes no apologies. The peasants need 'a push' so they will grow more food, he argues at a special conference called to make the case for the new direction. As he speaks, central Russia is in full-blown famine conditions, with no buffer from previous years because of requisitioning.

Nor will the retreat from full-on economic socialisation, the kind of communism that used to make Vladimir's pulse race, last for just a year or two. Without quite putting a figure on it, he admits that the new direction will have to last for a 'long time'. 'The disintegration of the capitalist world is steadily progressing', of course, just as he always said – this is a matter of historical inevitability, a scientific fact established by Marx – but no one can deny that a sort of 'temporary, unstable equilibrium has been established' in the capitalist world. It is most unfortunate. But one must face up to it. 'Of course, if revolution occurs in Europe naturally we'll change the policy', Lenin promises, but 'we can make no conjectures on that score'.

In the hungry Tambov region of the Volga, Misha – defeated at Warsaw, victorious at Kronstadt – is sent to suppress the most dangerous of the Soviet Republic's home-grown peasant rebellions, still burning across Moscow's empire. The papers call the rebels 'bandits', but they are tens of thousands strong. In some places they have been in charge since last summer. They have even introduced conscription. Further from the prying eyes of the world than Kronstadt, Moscow does not shrink from harsh measures to eliminate the threat. Concentration camps are set up. Thousands are shot without trial. Whole villages are relocated. The Red Army threatens to use poison gas against its enemies. 'Massive terror' becomes policy. Lenin tells Trotsky to ensure such measures are properly enforced.

The rebels are put down. The hunger spreads.

WASHINGTON DC: Normalcy in action. The new President, Warren Harding, signs into law radical measures to restrict immigration into the United States. The Congressman whose name is attached to the law hails it as vital to stop the entry of those infected with what US diplomatic cables refer to as the 'perverted ideas' so prevalent in Europe. America must not let in 'economic parasites', with Bolshevist tendencies and deteriorated morality. (By this, the Congressman means Eastern Europeans and Jews.)

The new immigration restrictions are based on the national origins of the American population, as recorded in the census of 1910. For each hundred citizens of German origin in 1910, for example, only three will now be allowed to settle in the United States every year. The choice of the 1910 census is significant, before the latest wave of Italians, Eastern Europeans and Jews. In effect, the restrictions are an attempt to both slow total inward migration to the United States and prevent the make-up of the American population from shifting further away from the preponderance of those with north European roots.

The annual allowance from different countries based on the 1910 census is then divided by twelve to give the monthly maximum. For example, no more than twenty-two will be allowed in from Albania each month, sixty-nine from Syria or three from Fiume. In an attempt to game the system, ships laden with migrants now wait offshore and dash into harbour on the first of the month to make sure their passengers disembark before the quota is exhausted. The days when America was an open door to those fleeing Europe is over. America's relationship with the world has changed.

BERLIN – RÜGEN: Stop press. Twenty German newspapers report a startling new discovery derived from Einstein's relativity. Dancing couples waltzing in the direction of the earth's rotation will grow thinner over time. If they waltz in the opposite direction, they will grow fatter. 'According to this new theory, nothing else will be possible than for the dancing couples to pair up by weight', the newspapers report. 'It is to be feared that many a love affair will be disrupted by these unexpected effects of the theory of relativity.'

Einstein himself is to be found on the Baltic coast, near the island of Rügen, with his two sons – aged seventeen and eleven now – and a maid. They travel third class, and take rooms above a bakery. They go sailing together. The mind of the former patent-office employee is bursting with ideas for the practical application of science – for a new type of gyroscope or a new kind of refrigerator.

Over the summer Albert gets himself into trouble when he makes some rather reckless remarks to a Dutch journalist, venturing the opinion that women are the real rulers of America and that the men are nothing but 'toy dogs' working as their slaves. American science is something of a joke, Einstein declares. As for the American public's obsession with relativity: 'I believe quite positively it is the mysteriousness of what they cannot understand which places them under a magic spell.' The work of several weeks is undone in a few minutes. There is a flood of angry letters to the *New York Times*.

A German-American in Mexico addresses an anonymous letter direct to Professor Einstein, Berlin University. 'The sooner you, accursed Jew, vanish with all the other German Jewish professors to Jerusalem,' it reads, 'the better for Germany and German students.' (Another person in Mexico who reads about Einstein's faux pas, though with hardly the same reaction, is Clare Sheridan, who spends several weeks there over the summer, meeting the country's power-brokers, talking about Lenin and Trotsky, and attempting to bully the Mexican President into having his bust done.)

While Albert is on holiday on the Baltic, Adolf Hitler spends several weeks in the German capital on a fundraising drive. It is an opportunity to familiarise himself with radical nationalist circles in Berlin, and mix with the right kind of people for his political career. From his base at the Hotel Sanssouci, a basic bed-and-breakfast popular with nationalists – Waldemar Pabst, the former officer responsible for the death of Rosa Luxemburg, is one of the permanent guests – Adolf can attend secret meetings with right-wing German nationalists and strike out for the city's museums and galleries.

At the Arsenal, Hitler is disappointed to find that trophies from the war have been removed. 'Thank God, they will not be able to lie to history', he remarks.

ISTANBUL: A down-at-heel Russian offers a leather-bound volume, written in French, to a British newspaper correspondent with an interest in old books.

The Russian claims this particular book came from the private collection of a former Tsarist spy who fled to Istanbul after the revolution. It bears an uncanny resemblance to *The Protocols of the Elders of Zion*. The structure is the same. There are dialogues which seem identical, almost word for word. Yet while the French book is clearly not a factual account of anything – it is an imagined dialogue between two philosophers, Machiavelli and Montesquieu, whose lives were separated by more than a hundred years – the *Protocols*, which have now been published and read all over the world from Michigan to Munich, purport to be a historical document of an actual meeting.

The British journalist shows the book to his American diplomat friend. Allen Dulles is intrigued. He then sends the French book for verification to the British Museum in London. He asks for their help in identifying the title of the book and, crucially, the date of its publication.

NEW YORK: There's a new hit in town. A converted lecture hall on 63rd Street is not exactly Broadway, but who cares?

'If you chance to be in the market for a new pre-breakfast whistling tune, see "SHUFFLE ALONG"', says the *Morning World*. 'Love will Find a Way' and 'Honeysuckle Times' are great melodies. The chorus line is less mechanical than that at *Ziegfeld's Follies*. The *New York Times* reports a 'swinging and infectious score'. There is a midnight performance on Wednesdays when tickets cost as little as fifty cents. 'A breeze of super-jazz blown up from Dixie', the *Evening Journal* tells its readers.

Shuffle Along is thousands of dollars in debt by the time it gets to the metropolis, having been performed for weeks at smaller east-coast venues before the show is considered ready for the big time – and there are no profits from a try-out production in Trenton, New Jersey. But now *Shuffle Along* is in New York, the centre of the American entertainment industry, where shows can be turned into national triumphs or where they die within the week. It is here that Sissle and Noble will be made – or broken.

A black critic who saw the show when it swung through the Dunbar Theater in Philadelphia decides to see for himself how an influential white audience in New York reacts to seeing black singers doing more than acting up to old Southern stereotypes. 'Knowing the strange workings of the Caucasian mind,' he writes, 'I was curious to find if *Shuffle Along* would find its way into the category of what is known, in the language of the performer, as a "white folks' " show.' Having seen the audience reaction in New York, he rather thinks it will work. 'Speaking as a colored American,' the critic writes, 'I think *Shuffle Along* should continue to shuffle along at the 63rd Street Theatre for a long time.' White Americans are falling in love with jazz. They might just end up feeling they own it too.

Moscow: The entire Hotel Lux is taken over by the Comintern in June. The place crawls with Cheka agents. The Comintern congress, now an annual affair, opens with greetings sent to comrades behind prison bars around the world, in the United States, in Britain, in Czechoslovakia: 'They are with us in spirit.' A memorial is unveiled to the memory of John Reed.

Feeling his nerves stretched and his body tired, Lenin shuttles between days in Moscow and days in the peace and quiet of Gorki. A chauffeured limousine stands at the ready. When he does attend the congress, he always causes a stir. He bounds up to delegates to engage them in conversation. He asks a few perfunctory questions – then makes his own views known. War commissar Trotsky appears at the congress in a magnificent white uniform. He is as upright and short-tempered as usual. One day, he flies into a rage with a Spanish delegate and, holding him by his lapel, digs up from deep inside the worst insult he can muster: '*Petit bourgeois.*' Another time, after giving a speech, he descends the podium to speak to the French delegation, translating his own words for them to ensure they have understood him properly.

This is a meeting of retrenchment. Europe is growing Communist parties, but the workers are not going their way. Socialism is split. Plenty of time is spent attacking those who have not yet seen the advantages of joining the Comintern (or worse, who have left). The world situation is said to be 'developing' in a revolutionary direction – but is not necessarily 'ripe'. The usual exhortations sound thin compared to twelve months ago, when a map showed Red Army troops advancing on Warsaw, Berlin, Rome. A 'lengthy period of revolutionary struggles' now lies ahead. What is more, Lenin does not want anyone to launch a premature uprising anywhere which might upset his attempts at rapprochement with foreign powers. 'The world revolution does not develop in a straight line', the congress is told.

In a subterranean banqueting hall one day, the impatient revolutionary lets off a little steam about the antics of Béla Kun, trying to force the pace of revolution in Germany earlier in the year when the masses were not ready for it. '*Les bêtises de Béla Kun*' – the 'stupidities of Béla Kun' – he says, in French, repeating the phrase several times to make sure everyone has heard. (The official note-takers courteously pause their pens to save Kun's blushes.) But later, Vladimir does something he almost never does: he apologises. His language was perhaps intemperate. 'I was an émigré myself', he writes. He understands how it feels. He was also too keen once, he admits: in 1917.

Practicality and pragmatism are the watchwords now. 'Whoever arrives in Russia with the hope of finding a communist paradise here will be cruelly disappointed', Trotsky tells the Comintern during a debate on problems with the Italian party. Russia, he says, is 'very backward, still very barbaric'. But until revolution takes place elsewhere, it is the stronghold. Anyone who dares to take current imperfect conditions in Russia to mean that communism itself has failed is 'our open enemy'.

Famine has spread across the country now: the Volga, parts of Siberia, southern Ukraine. (Trotsky annoys Vladimir by refusing to travel there as commissar in charge of food supplies.) Under the baking summer heat, huge numbers of peasants make for the towns in search of sustenance. Moscow holds up the railways to prevent the spread of disease. Newspapers are forbidden from mentioning the crisis. The Volga turns to dust.

TULSA, OKLAHOMA: A black shoeshine boy, nineteen years old, is accused of assaulting a white girl in an elevator in town. An inflammatory article about the incident is published (the paper later admits it got essential details wrong). A white mob gather around the courthouse where the black boy is kept. The police tell them to clear out. Later, a group of blacks march into town, offering to assist the police in the boy's protection. They are told to disperse as well.

That evening, a few hundred whites go to the National Guard armoury to try to arm themselves. At the same time, three automobiles of blacks drive into town and surround the courthouse. Some of them fought in France; they are damned if they will let a lynching happen in their city. The war has changed things.

It is not long before a riot breaks out. The black section of town, Greenwood – local newspapers call it 'Little Africa' – is soon encircled. The National Guard is called in. Fighting soon gives way to burning and looting. Dozens are killed. Whites accuse a shadowy organisation called the African Blood Brotherhood of starting a race riot. But its representatives deny responsibility, asking instead: 'haven't negroes the right to defend their lives and property when they are menaced, or is this an exclusive prerogative of the white man?'

BELFAST, ULSTER, UNITED KINGDOM: The King comes to visit his loyal subjects in Ireland, to open a parliament for the six counties of the north, in Belfast.

A week after sectarian riots across the city, his message to the overwhelmingly Protestant gathering is one of peace and reconciliation. The King intends it to be heard in Dublin, and London, and every corner of the British Empire where Ireland's tragedy is a gaping, open wound. 'I appeal to all Irishmen to pause, to stretch out the hand of forbearance and conciliation, to forgive and to forget, and to join in making for the land which they love a new era of peace, contentment, and goodwill', the King says.

After all the tentative, failed peace efforts of the last few months, a truce is agreed in a matter of weeks. It is only a ceasefire and yet, in Ireland, it feels like victory. On the hot summer's day in July that the truce is announced in Dublin, there is euphoria. People stay out late. There is an unaccustomed feeling of lightness in the air. The nationalists have forced the most powerful empire the world has ever seen to the negotiating table. The people of Dublin savour the taste of peace, of normality.

MOSCOW: Comrade Lenin's latest calculation.

He takes the amount of grain he expects to be grown this year and divides it by twelve for a monthly figure of what will be available to distribute. This must be shared out – how? First, to the army. Next, to office employees. ('Drastic reduction', Lenin notes.) Third, to the workers. Vladimir suggests a quarter or a half of enterprises – 'stress *enterprises*' – should be shut down entirely with the remainder operating in two shifts for the rest of the year.

He orders that a state economic plan reflecting these priorities be drawn up in haste: 'Do this in rough outline, as a first approximation, immediately, in a month, no later.' Members of the economic planning commission are to work fourteen-hour days. 'Let science sweat a bit', the impatient revolutionary writes. 'We have given them good rations, now we must make them work.'

In the meantime, it is left to the public and to foreign organisations to provide relief for the starving peasants in the Volga. The day after the Comintern congress has finished, the writer Maxim Gorky – a sometime friend of Lenin's – issues a humanitarian appeal to Europe and America for bread and medicine for the country of 'Tolstoy, Dostoyevsky, Mendeleev, Pavlov, Mussorgsky, Glinka'. Vladimir's contribution to the situation is to write an angry note in response to information of food mismanagement and government corruption in southern Russia: 'everyone found guilty of plundering should be shot on the spot.'

He then departs to his country house at Gorki for a month to recover his health. His Kremlin apartment is to be repaired in his absence. Lenin insists the partition walls are made soundproof and the floors made absolutely free of squeaks, so he can sleep without disturbance when he returns. There will be three bedrooms: one for Vladimir, one for his sister Maria, and one for Nadya. No sitting room, so as to discourage guests.

LONDON: Éamon de Valera arrives in the capital of his former jailers for discussions on Ireland's future. He has not taken Michael Collins with him, citing his concern that the young man's face might be photographed, and thus become known to the British authorities. Collins is furious at the obvious snub, sensitive to being treated as de Valera's lackey, rather than as co-author of Ireland's military success. 'At this moment, there is more ill-will within a victorious assembly than ever could be found anywhere else except in the devil's assembly', he writes to a friend.

De Valera arrives at Number 10 Downing Street by Rolls-Royce. Hawkers sell Irish flags on the street outside. A crowd of well-wishers cheer. The British Prime Minister, David Lloyd George – fast-talking, theatrical and every bit as politically devious as de Valera himself – welcomes in the former mathematics teacher from Carysfort College. Hoping to impress upon de Valera the power relationship between them, the Prime Minister ushers him straight into a room with a huge map of the British Empire on the wall. Ireland is just a tiny speck in a sea of red. De Valera notes to himself that the map is of the Mercator type, flattering the scale of Britain's possessions. He will not let himself be impressed by British pomp, nor by Lloyd George's Welsh charm.

While the two men talk – the one florid and passionate, the other frigid and austere, both raised to see the divine in the everyday, and forthright defenders of their cause – it begins to rain outside. A London summer drizzle. Irishwomen kneel in the street and chant the rosary. De Valera slips out that evening without a word.

ROME: Benito is settling in nicely. The city, he discovers, is really not so bad after all. Being an elected politician makes him part of the establishment. It must be turned to his long-term advantage. He sees an opportunity to stamp his authority over the Fascist movement and to demonstrate that he is its indispensable leader.

In late July, he announces that the violence which has engulfed the country must stop. The Socialists are beaten (a few have hived off and founded a Communist Party). The young and over-eager *squadristi* have got ahead of themselves. The Fascist dogs of war are to be called off. Mussolini is even ready to make a deal with the Socialist unions in a so-called pact of pacification. He knows how unpopular this will be with some. An end to hostilities with the Socialists will spoil the fun of the *squadristi* and undermine the authority of the *ras*. No more racing around in trucks in search of the nearest left-wing activist to beat up. No more interrogations with the aid of castor oil, the great fascist laxative. But for every disgruntled blackshirt, Benito reasons, there will now be ten more Italians who will admire him for his moderation. To start a campaign is one thing. But to end a campaign – now that is the mark of a statesman. Fascism is to be made respectable.

On the pages of *Il Popolo d'Italia* Mussolini goes all out to stake his claim to sole leadership of the movement. It was he who first gathered the Fascists together at the Piazza San Sepolcro, he points out. It is his vision which has animated the movement from the start, and which will sustain it now. Only he can 'see the far horizon from the mountain-top, and take in a vista which extends beyond Bologna, Venice or Cuneo to Italy, Europe and the world'. Only he can 'assemble the full political and moral panorama from the thousands of local elements which make it up'. Only he can continue the war that never ended, and lead Italy to final victory. He would like nothing better than to be simply a humble member of the local Fascist association of Milan, he writes, but destiny has picked out a different course for him.

A couple of the *ras* travel up to Lake Garda to see if D'Annunzio can be persuaded to step up and oust the presumptuous Benito. But seeing the poet in the flesh and sensing his uncertainty – he is too busy writing books – the two are spooked and leave without an answer. Gabriele never was a man for parties, after all; at least not *that* kind of party. His leadership was always inspirational rather than organisational.

Mussolini spends the rest of his summer plotting a new structure to replace the Fasci di Combattimento. No more rivals, no more petty squabbling. Instead: iron discipline from the top down. The man who would be Duce must pretend, of course, to be more collegial than that. But since when was it a crime for a politician to pretend?

LONDON: For a whole week, Éamon de Valera and David Lloyd George probe the logic and limits of each other's positions.

The Welshman tries to encircle and entrap his prey in clever phrases, and half-innocent questions. He asks the Irishman to admit that Celtic languages have no word of their own for 'republic', as if an argument from linguistics could determine the freedom and rights of the Irish people. (He emphasises the authenticity of his own Celtic heritage by conversing with one of his advisers in Welsh, while de Valera speaks to his in English.) De Valera meanwhile lectures the British Prime Minister on all the wrongs done to Ireland by the British since the seventeenth century. Neither seems to make much progress with the other. Lloyd George is reminded of being on a circus horse on a merry-go-round as a boy, racing faster and faster round and round, but always finishing up the same distance behind the horse in front as at the beginning.

The two men assess each other's strengths and weaknesses: how badly the other needs peace, and who they are afraid of in their political hinterland. The British draw up a proposal to keep Ireland in the empire and, nominally at least, under the rule of the British King but with a full measure of practical independence on most matters, equivalent to the dominions of Canada, Australia and New Zealand. There are no concessions on the question of Ulster. De Valera storms out, leaving Britain's peace terms behind, lying on the table.

He recognises his mistake at once. The British cannot be given an excuse to launch open season on the IRA over the summer months. They cannot be allowed to present themselves to the world as the honest peacemakers, rejected in their quest for a reasonable settlement, and present the Irish as the fanatics, for whom only republican purity will do. De Valera asks for a copy of the British peace terms to be sent to his hotel – for further consideration, subject to consultation in Ireland. The door to negotiation – and peace – is left ajar. The truce is maintained. Back home in Dublin, and after discussion with his colleagues, de Valera writes to Lloyd George confirming his rejection of the British offer as it stands. He proposes a more tangential relationship between Britain and Ireland, the product of a mind steeped in mathematical theory and Trinitarian theology: that Ireland be *associated* with the empire, but not be *part* of it, touching it and yet still distinct.

His colleagues scratch their heads. De Valera draws a diagram to help them understand what he means.

ESKİŞEHİR, THE OTTOMAN EMPIRE: July. A fighting Turkish retreat in the face of superior Greek forces. The city of Eskişehir falls to the Greeks. Thousands of Turkish soldiers desert their posts. Their commanders quarrel as to what to do: to stand and fight, or turn and flee. Nationalists are in uproar. Ankara is threatened.

Kemal knows that a war cannot be won without an army. It must retreat to a more secure line. He is appointed supreme commander, virtually dictator of Anatolia – although for three months only. If he can win the war in that time he will be a hero; if he loses, he will be disposed of. (Enver travels from Moscow to the Caucasus to be close by, swearing he will do nothing to undermine Kemal – but ready to step in should he fail.) Ammunition supplies are transported to the front on the backs of women and camels. The Turks dig in.

NEW YORK: Garvey is back. He gives a boastful account of his trip to the Caribbean and beyond, forcibly extended by his difficulties in acquiring a new American visa.

He glides over more embarrassing episodes of his odyssey, such as the time his ship set sail for America with Garvey registered as its purser (in the hope that crew members would be able to slip into the country more easily than passengers). An ill-starred voyage, that, with the vessel's boiler constantly about to explode and the novice Garvey arguing with the captain as to what to do about it. The ship was forced to turn back for safety long before it could essay the unloading of the obstreperous purser on American soil.

Garvey focuses on the positive. In Costa Rica, a special train was laid on, he says. In Panama, he was carried by enthusiastic crowds from train to automobile. Everywhere he went, Garvey tells his devotees, thousands of dollars of shares were sold. Even the poorest wanted to buy some. In Jamaica, the largest public building on the island was filled with the biggest crowd in its history: thousands had to be turned back. 'We have already swept the world', he exhorts the crowd. 'All that is left for us to do is to conquer Africa.' Four years ago, policemen did not know who he was, says Garvey. Now governments are spending hundreds of dollars a day on anxious diplomatic cables just to try and find out where he will go next. Such expenditures are a measure of how significant the UNIA has become: 'You have become so powerful they cannot afford to ignore you'.

He does not blame whites for looking out for their race interests. But he fiercely denounces 'Negro traitors' who have turned their backs on his projects. They should beware: for 'when Marcus Garvey starts a fight he will not stop until he has finished completely'. One name in particular spells treachery amongst his supporters. William Du Bois is 'the exponent of the reactionary class of men who have kept Negroes in serfdom and peonage', Garvey says. They hide behind their university degrees and imagine themselves intellectuals. They proclaim the need for uplift of the black race – when what they actually mean to do is to keep themselves on top and everyone else below.

Garvey invites his rival to debate him, as if challenging him to a duel: 'at midnight, at noon time, or any time'. He has no doubts who will win. 'I will make you look', he tells Du Bois, 'like a piece of cotton.'

LONDON: Private grief intrudes on public life. Winston Churchill's American-born mother dies suddenly one early summer's day at the age of sixty-seven (her third husband is forty-four at the time). She trips on her high heels and falls down a staircase. A broken leg leads to infection and amputation below the knee. Amputation leads to haemorrhage. Letters of condolence pour in from his many friends.

Several weeks later, in August, Clementine and Winston are struck with another tragedy. Clementine is at a house party at the Duke of Westminster's northern pile near Chester. 'I arrived here last night about 11.30 and found dancing in full swing', she writes to Winston in London. The children are in the care of a French nanny by the sea in Kent.

Their youngest daughter, Marigold, aged just under three years, has a sore throat that seems to be getting worse. An infection develops. There are no antibiotics. A specialist is called. Clementine rushes down to Kent. Winston is called from London. (He has been meeting a Palestinian delegation, defending British policy against what they see as the undermining of Arab rights by the migration of European Jews.)

Both Winston and Clementine are by Marigold's bedside when, one evening, the little girl finally gives up her tenuous hold on life. Her parents are struck by an ocean of grief. They mourn in silence.

BERLIN – AUGSBURG – MUNICH: In between museum trips in the German capital, word reaches Adolf Hitler of conspiracy in Munich. Party chairman Drexler has been having merger discussions with other political groups. Hitler is alarmed to learn that, in his absence, the leader of one of these groups, a schoolteacher named Dickel, was invited to Munich to give a speech – Adolf's job – and was considered a great success. The mangy field-runner begins to worry whether Drexler is trying to sideline him. Drexler is now reported to be heading to Augsburg to discuss matters directly with Dickel and other *völkisch* leaders. Adolf rushes to Augsburg himself. When he does not manage to break up the discussions, he storms back to Munich. He resigns from the party the next day.

The struggle for the leadership of the NSDAP is now in the open. Adolf writes a six-page letter explaining his decision. He dislikes the idea of the party being diluted by others. He cites passages from one of Dickel's books. 'I leave it to the party leadership to check these quotes', Adolf writes, 'and these are only the most harmless.' He lays down the conditions under which he would rejoin the party. He wants to be given dictatorial power over it. Munich must be made the party's permanent headquarters 'now and for ever more'. Negotiations with other groups must be broken off and a meeting with like-minded Austrians cancelled. The party needs 'iron leadership', Hitler writes. It is clear he has come to believe only he can provide it.

There is civil war within the party. Adolf continues giving speeches at NSDAP events, proving himself the best draw the party has. Reality begins to sink in among the leadership: if its best speaker goes elsewhere, the NSDAP will disintegrate. Some members produce a pamphlet calling Hitler a traitor, accusing him of being an Austrian (which is undeniable) and a closet supporter of Charles Habsburg (which is more dubious). Hinting at anonymous, deep-pocketed supporters in the business world, the pamphlet asks where Adolf gets the money on which he lives and which he spends, they say, on a string of girlfriends. His manipulative methods are 'frankly Jewish'. The anti-Adolf contingent warns he is just a common 'demagogue' who will lead the German people astray. Drexler, meanwhile, is an 'oak'.

But it is Drexler who gives in. He is offered the post of honorary party chairman for life, without any real power. In return, he condemns the pamphlet, blaming it on a couple of disgruntled party employees, and makes up with Adolf in public. Hitler gets exactly what he wants. The party is his now. No more democracy. Only the leader and his followers. Shortly after assuming his new role as the party's dictator, Adolf decides to forms a party militia, his own private army. He replaces the editor of the *Völkischer Beobachter* with one of his own men.

DOORN: The Kaiser seems to be making a remarkable recovery from his wife's death. Summer is marked by a steady procession of female suitors beating their way to the door of Huis Doorn and so, they hope, into the affections of the imperial widower who resides within: two women from Hungary (described as 'very lively' by Wilhelm's doctor), a couple of German aristocrats and a Finnish lady doctor (who, perhaps alerted to her quarry's predilections, brings pine-tree cuttings as a gift).

Occasionally a more political visitor drops by and has to endure the latest rant. (The Kaiser has just received the racist anti-Semite Houston Stewart Chamberlain's latest book from Bayreuth, which seems to have made quite an impression.) To one of these visitors, the Kaiser makes a very special gift as he leaves: a silver brooch in the shape of a swastika. 'Now you have been admitted to the order of the decent people', he tells his guest.

In August, one of the men who signed the 1918 armistice, the Catholic politician Matthias Erzberger – against whom Hitler has been fulminating in his speeches for months – is assassinated while out walking in the Black Forest. The murderers, part of a shady Freikorps organisation based in Bavaria known as Organisation Consul, flee to Hungary.

ACROSS ANATOLIA: Far from the front line between the Turkish nationalist forces and the Greek army, the civilian population of Anatolia is the real victim of this war.

No one is safe. In the Black Sea region, Turkish nationalists deport Christians from their homes, chasing out communities older than Byzantium itself. In the west, native Turks flee Greek brigands. Shops are looted. Villages are burned to the ground. Door frames are removed to convey the message that there will be no going back for those who have been forced to leave their homes. Foreign observers accuse Greek authorities of being complicit in such ethnic cleansing, and of devising crude propaganda stunts to cover their tracks. There are rumours that they intend to exterminate the Turkish population around Smyrna.

'The "subconscious" pre-human animal had come to life', writes an eyewitness of these events shortly afterwards, a British professor of Greek and Byzantine history. It is as if a fount of suppressed violence has suddenly been released, exposing the violent depths of the human psyche. It is a metamorphosis of human into beast.

LONDON – DEARBORN – MUNICH: An answer has come back from the British Museum. The book the journalist friend of Allen Dulles was offered in Istanbul, and which bears such a striking resemblance to the *Protocols*, is a political tract published in the 1860s in Geneva. It predates the meeting of the so-called Elders of Zion of which the *Protocols* purport to be an account by thirty years. The *Protocols* are clearly plagiarised from the earlier book. Only historians will be interested in it now, *The Times* assures its readers: 'The legend can be allowed to pass into oblivion.'

The *Dearborn Independent* continues its anti-Semitic campaign as usual. It is now selling several hundred thousand copies a week. Adolf Hitler, who days before the rebuttal had thanked *The Times* for bringing the *Protocols* to light, ignores the revelation that it is a forgery entirely.

GORKI: 'I am so tired that I am unable to do a thing', Vladimir Lenin writes to Maxim Gorky.

With Lenin's permission, Gorky has set up an independent public body – the only such organisation in the Soviet Republic – to secure foreign aid. Remarkably, a former Tsarist minister and Tolstoy's daughter are allowed to join its board. The Americans have responded positively – as long as the American Relief Administration (just winding up its operation in the rest of

Europe) is given complete freedom of action in Soviet Russia. Vladimir worries that the ARA is a front for spies or, as he puts it, 'disguised interventionists'. But to refuse help would look bad – and anyway, help is needed. Perhaps Trotsky should handle the whole thing. 'He has a capacity for these things (both diplomatic experience and a military and political instinct)', Vladimir explains.

Gorky *certainly* has done quite enough. Vladimir now wants him to go abroad where he can cause no further embarrassment to the regime. Lenin suggests a sanatorium in Europe. 'Over here you have neither treatment, nor work – nothing but hustle,' he writes, 'plain empty hustle.' He urges Gorky not to be so stubborn.

DUBLIN – LONDON: An exchange of letters and telegrams across the Irish Sea – fifteen in all – continues David Lloyd George and Éamon de Valera's London discussions, now carried out with a wider audience in mind. Every word and phrase is weighed for hidden meaning. The British Prime Minister calls his cabinet to his Scottish holiday retreat to dissect de Valera's latest letter. Eventually, a vague formula is agreed as a basis for a final negotiation to be held in London in the autumn. Not a settlement yet, but a starting point for one. The final compromises will be made later.

And while all this goes on, the IRA swells with new recruits, eager to share in the glamour of Ireland's freedom fighters. The British public grows used to the idea that Ireland will never be fully British again. In the north, Protestants and Catholics snipe at each other. In the South, the Irish savour a summer's peace, and hope never to return to war. The Black and Tans take to the beaches and flirt with Irish girls. 'With the exception of Belfast, the country remains in a peaceful and undisturbed condition', reads the British cabinet report at the end of August. Hay-burning, cattle-stealing and the odd kidnapping replace outright murder and assassination as the chief issues of concern.

Michael Collins moves into new offices in the Gresham. Officially, he is Ireland's Finance Minister and Director of Intelligence, nominally subordinate to the Minister of Defence (a man who hates his guts). Unofficially, he is Ireland's second in command, a man with a reputation and a following – and with ambition. He works long hours: twelve-, sixteen-, eighteen-hour days. He drives others as hard as he drives himself, heedless to the damage done by his bruising commentary on their failings. He has many rivals. 'I find myself looking at friends as if they were enemies,' he writes one day, 'looking at them to make sure that they are really friends at all.' Having snubbed him in July, Éamon now suggests Michael be one of those to go to London to negotiate the peace with Britain. He must remain at home, Éamon explains, to keep the symbol of the republic pure. Collins smells a rat. He resists, fearful that if he goes he will be made to bear the blame for any compromises made in the name of peace.

The two men argue the matter late into the night. It is Michael's sacred duty to go, Éamon insists. He will not be required to lead the Irish delegation, but simply to give it the weight of a military man's authority. Finally, Collins succumbs. How can he refuse?

HORTON BAY, MICHIGAN: Eventually the bride arrives, her hair still slightly damp from an afternoon swim in a nearby lake. Her husband-to-be, just back from a few days' fishing, is already waiting at the church dressed smartly in white trousers, a dark jacket and a striped tie. He cannot kneel on account of his leg wounds. ('The first American *killed* in Italy', so his bride introduced him, by accident, at their engagement party earlier in the summer.) The church is strewn with flowers. The young couple, now Mr and Mrs Ernest Hemingway, make their getaway in a Ford automobile, and a rowing boat across the lake.

Ernest takes his new wife to meet his bevvy of female admirers in Petoskey by way of a backhanded compliment. But wider horizons than Michigan are opening up for them both now. For Hadley: the chance to see the world. For Ernest: an opportunity to return to it.

RIVER SAKARYA, THE OTTOMAN EMPIRE: For three weeks in late summer, the Greek and Turkish armies tussle around the river Sakarya. Mustafa Kemal is asked what he will do if the Greeks lunge for Ankara. 'I will attack them in the rear and they will perish in the wilds', he replies: '*Bon voyage, messieurs.*'

Greek aircraft buzz in the sky, outnumbering Turkish planes twenty to one. But on the ground, the summer heat exhausts Greek soldiers. Their supply lines are overextended, harassed by Turkish cavalry. Their advances become more modest, until their offensive comes to a halt. Eventually they turn tail, retiring to positions they held several months before.

Kemal's prestige has never been higher. He is proclaimed Gazi – hero, warrior of Islam.

NEW YORK – LONDON – BRUSSELS – PARIS – GENEVA: Two congresses take place in August, one on either side of the Atlantic. Both claim to represent the interests of the black peoples of the world. Both talk the language of empowerment. But it is not just the ocean which divides them. They represent two different philosophies of change and two different ideas of how the races must interact: one fighting, the other conciliatory; one hungry for immediate results, the other patient for incremental change; one predicting race war, the other advocating race cooperation; one seeking to bring about change by smashing the system, the other seeking compromise through diplomacy.

In New York, Garvey's annual convention is quieter than last year. There are still flourishes of the Garvey style, such as the composition of messages for various world leaders – Éamon de Valera, President Harding, the American Secretary of State, King George V, Mohandas Gandhi – containing words of support or warning from the four hundred million blacks the UNIA claims to represent. The *Negro World* acclaims the official court reception at the end of the convention – where shredded chicken and ice cream are served – as 'the greatest state social event that has taken place among black people in the last three hundred years' and an evocation of 'the splendour of Ethiopia in the days of the Queen of Sheba'. Garvey calls Du Bois's rival meeting across the ocean in Europe, worked out with the cooperation of colonial governments, a congress of rats presided over by a cat. 'I am surprised at the philosophy of Dr Du Bois', he says. 'Why, he is a disgrace to Harvard.'

But the UNIA dream is under fire. The organisation's Secretary-General has absconded with some of its funds. Wages are chopped in half. The Black Star Line stockholders' meeting is adjourned pending clarification of the accounts. There are unanswered questions about its latest ship. Garvey has a dramatic run-in with the African Blood Brotherhood, the group accused of involvement in the Tulsa riot, denouncing it for its secretiveness. Not long after, the brotherhood derides Garvey for turning the UNIA into a 'tinsel show'.

There are no rallies or marches at William Du Bois's Pan African Congress. Meetings take place, discreetly, at the edges of the great power centres of European colonialism, first in London, where Du Bois mixes with sympathetic British politicians, and then in Brussels, where Belgian colonial officials observe proceedings. The French Senegalese chair heads off any motions which might offend the hosts. (The horrors of King Leopold's exploitation of the Congo are not mentioned.) Garvey's scheme of Africa for the Africans is deemed 'Bolshevik talk' and its leader described as a black Lenin. In Paris, Du Bois is said to repudiate Garvey's back-to-

Africa ideas in his strongest language yet. 'The colored American cannot withstand the African climate', he reportedly says. 'We cannot oust the Europeans and do not desire to do so.' Later, he denies ever having spoken these words.

Du Bois carries on alone to Geneva, to speak with those who still see in the League of Nations the embryo of a new global order. The League has settled only one dispute so far: the ownership of a group of forested islands in the Baltic claimed by both Sweden and Finland. But Du Bois has a shimmering goal in sight: acceptance of the Pan-African Congress as the legitimate representative of black aspirations around the world. He takes up residence in the Hôtel des Familles, not far from Geneva railway station. An Englishwoman with a history of being helpful to worthy causes – in India, she once tried to find Gandhi an appropriate substitute for cow's milk – uses her contacts to help the editor of *The Crisis* get access to the people who matter on Geneva's diplomatic circuit. Du Bois pays social calls on possible supporters. He gives a talk to the English Conversation Club which goes down a storm. He presents the resolutions of the Pan-African Congress to the British Secretary-General of the League in person and counts this as a major success.

Moscow: The impatient revolutionary ploughs through books of statistics, makes recommendations for improvement, points out the errors of others – and sees virtually no one. He is too ill, he says. Not a word about the famine on the Volga.

Meanwhile, the Patriarch of the Orthodox Church donates all unconsecrated vessels to be sold to feed the hungry.

Hildesheim, Germany: After a summer darting around Germany and Austria almost as if the war had never happened – Bad Gastein, Seefeld, Hamburg, Berlin – in September Freud finds himself in the Harz mountains of central Germany with his most trusted colleagues on a group holiday.

In Hildesheim, the group check into the rather grand Hôtel d'Angleterre, and then explore the town. Together they traipse to the town's two main churches – one Romanesque and one Gothic – while Freud pontificates about the relevant qualities of the architecture. At a local museum with a fine collection of Egyptian antiquities Freud quizzes the curator about ancient burial rituals. Over the next few days this merry band of psychoanalysts explore the area by train, bus and on foot.

Much in the planning of their excursions is calculated to please the proclivities of the doctor from Vienna. On one day they walk past the house where Goethe stayed in the 1770s, and where he wrote an important section of *Faust*. On another day, the group ascend the Brocken, a local mountain larded with mystical associations as the annual meeting place of the world's witches (that is to say, women who have had sex with the Devil). Freud takes the opportunity to play a practical joke on the group, getting them all to stand at the top of a tall tower with their eyes closed and leaning forward over a rickety railing with their hands behind their backs – before telling them the railing has disappeared and watching their flailing responses.

In among the practical jokes and the camaraderie, Freud returns to one of his pet subjects: telepathy. It is impossible, he tells the group, to avoid investigation of what others might call 'occult' phenomena. Such is the spirit of the times, so to speak. 'It is a part expression of the loss of value by which everything has been affected since the world catastrophe of the Great War', Freud explains. It is also an indication of 'the great revolution towards which we are heading and of whose extent we can form no estimate'.

The discovery of radium and Einstein's theory of relativity have contributed to this trend of belief in unseen powers or hidden means of communication, Freud asserts. The war has for ever blown up any easy certainties. Earlier that summer Freud admitted to an English investigator of psychic phenomena that 'if I were at the beginning rather than at the end of my scientific career, as I am today, I might possibly choose just this field of research, in spite of all difficulties'.

Freud foresees a time when certain hypotheses currently derided as 'occult' are proved right. Psychoanalysis cannot afford to be left on the sidelines. His acolytes are split on the matter.

DOORN: The Hungarians and the Finn have moved on. A German aristocrat hangs around a little longer as company for the mourning Kaiser. Now it is a local Dutch aristocrat named Lili van Heemstra who catches Wilhelm's attention. Over the summer, she visits almost every day (eating considerably into the Kaiser's wood-chopping duties).

The two become inseparable. They whisper sweet nothings at each other during a movie night at Huis Doorn, to the obvious annoyance of everyone else. Wilhelm's aides describe the young lady as 'Baroness Sunshine', in reference to the Kaiser's own description of her as a delightful ray of sunlight in his dark world. (He takes her advice on financial matters, too, now that the money from Berlin seems to be drying up.)

Will Wilhelm actually marry her? He protests not. His wife has been dead less than six months, and Lili is nearly thirty years younger than him. But his mind is wandering in that direction. To the shock of some, he is certainly prepared to countenance the idea of marrying a non-royal in the future. After all, he tells an aide one day, 'if one considers that cousins and Catholics are out of the question, there is hardly anyone left'.

AUTUMN

STOCKHOLM: This is getting embarrassing. Riven by indecision, the Nobel Prize Committee decides not to award the physics prize to anyone at all in 1921.

MUNICH: Ludendorff finishes the manuscript of his latest magnum opus. 'International, pacifistic, defeatist thinking' is in the dock for the defeat of 1918. The same spirit can be detected everywhere. 'The un-German is within us and around us,' the general writes, 'principally in the form of insufficient race-consciousness.' The book ends with the words of an uplifting Dutch song about conquering evil through belief. 'God turns a pious people's enemy into its prey, however great the enemy's realm.' Erich's wife Margarethe increasingly takes refuge in morphine.

MOSCOW – PETROGRAD: Over the first weeks of autumn, the contradictions in Lenin's Russia become acute.

There is famine in the Volga region and in Ukraine. But in Moscow and in Petrograd, shops open up stocking imported goods no one has seen for years outside the Kremlin. A regime which has sworn itself to be the eternal enemy of capitalism receives its first delivery of food aid from capitalist America. (Much of the shipment is promptly stolen by dock workers while the guards look the other way.) A government ideologically committed to the principles of communism once again legalises private trading for anyone over the age of sixteen. The hustlers and the hucksters that the impatient revolutionary once condemned as parasites now come out of the shadows, with their leather jackets, shiny shoes and their creed of buying cheap and selling high. Bright new cafés for the rich appear alongside drab canteens for the workers and the first American-run soup kitchen for the destitute. The sweet smell of fresh pastries is in the air. But only for those who can pay.

Old Bolsheviks tear up their party cards in disgust.

VIENNA: The value of the Austrian crown collapses further every week. Visitors from abroad find that their foreign currency makes them virtual millionaires in crisis-hit Vienna. A young New York psychoanalyst who comes to the city to be analysed by Freud – the precondition for being considered a true Freudian – thinks nothing of hiring a pianist from the Vienna Philharmonic to play the entire score of Strauss's *Der Rosenkavalier* to a group of friends one evening, on a whim. Sigmund insists on charging ten dollars an hour for his services, to be paid in hard currency.

He is inundated with Anglo-Saxon student-patients, mostly budding psychoanalysts. What was once a quiet family apartment has been turned into a psychoanalytic assembly line – or a menagerie, perhaps. Freud's pupils debate and discuss amongst themselves. One gives a paper on the spider as the symbol of the female genitalia, another expounds on the interpretation of dreams, a third talks about sexual perversion. A man in his midthirties, whom the other patients call 'the imitation Freud' on account of his trimming his beard and smoking his cigar in exactly the same way as the great man himself, delivers lectures on Jewish mythology.

But it is Freud himself they all want to spend time with, to whom they want to pour out their dreams and their desires. For Freud's students he is the master. For him, they are material, and sometimes disappointing material at that. An American from Atlanta comes to see Freud with a dream of being in a carriage pulled by two horses, one black and one white, to an unknown destination. Sigmund, who fancies himself an expert on America on the basis of his journey there ten years before, tells him that the dream clearly means that his Southern patient cannot decide whether to marry a white or a black woman. The American dares to question this interpretation. The two men argue. Freud eventually cuts him off and tells him to leave. Why should he waste his time on those who do not understand their true predicament? Fools – American ones at that – should not be suffered gladly.

How times have changed. Before, it used to be that Freud had to convince others of psychoanalysis; his supporters were few and far between. Now, the problem is the other way around. He must ensure that *his* science, *his* psychoanalysis, is not distorted by his over-keen acolytes. There are many who parrot his work these days, but few who really understand it. He is surrounded by pygmies. There has not been anyone like Jung in years – and he, of course, was a traitor.

At the end of listening to a particularly long-winded paper from one of his students on chess and the Oedipus complex, an enraged Freud tells the presenter that it is such meaningless papers that will bring about the fall of psychoanalysis. 'Please desist from writing such papers again', he fumes. 'It is not productive and I do not want it.' On another occasion, when fellow psychoanalysts break into a dispute over whether some have plagiarised Freud's works – the worst epithet between them is to call each other 'unanalysed' – Freud smashes his fist on the table at the cheek of it all. Why have they not consulted *him*, he asks? 'I take this to be an insult', he tells the shocked group, 'because if this is what you do when I am still among you, I can imagine what will happen when I am really dead'.

MUNICH: If Hitler has learned one lesson from his political rise thus far it is this: extremism works. Provocation is an effective political technique. Violence now becomes the party's second calling card besides anti-Semitism. When Nazi thugs break up a rally of Bavarians who want to separate from Germany, Adolf is delighted. The Bavarian leader was literally 'dragged down from the podium by the outraged masses, and kicked out of the room', he writes gleefully. Hitler is briefly held in police custody for incitement.

The nineteenth-century Prussian theorist of war Carl von Clausewitz once wrote that war is the continuation of politics by other means. Hitler turns this famous dictum on its head, and suggests that the party needs to apply the tactics of Flanders in 1918 to the streets of Munich in 1921. 'Just as during the war we moved from a war of position to a war of attack, so it must be now', says the mangy field-runner when he meets members of the euphemistically named gymnastics and sports units of the party: 'You too will be trained as storm-troopers', he tells them. The Nazi militia is henceforward called the Sturmabteilung, or SA for short.

Adolf Hitler seeks to turn the national socialist movement into a political army: disciplined, regimented and uniformed. Local chapters are encouraged to sell swastika lapel pins at five marks each to be worn at all times. ('If any Jew takes offence', the party leader writes in an NSDAP circular, 'he is to be manhandled ruthlessly'.) Hitler personally designs new party armbands: ten centimetres wide, blood red, with a nine-centimetre-diameter white circle in the middle and a black swastika. 'The red is social, the white is national, and the swastika is anti-Semitic', he explains. 'Honour these colours.'

MOSCOW: *Go-siz-dat. Glav-kom-trud. Go-elro. Nar-kom-zem. Tsek-tran. Tsentro-soyuz.* The workers' republic has become a forest of acronyms. To enter it too deeply is to lose oneself amongst its trees, even if one has planted them oneself.

There are, of course, the acronyms that everyone in Moscow knows. *Sovnarkom*: the Council of People's Commissars, the state body of which the impatient revolutionary is chairman. *Politburo*: the Communist cabal at the top of the party structure where things really get decided. *Orgburo*: its slightly less grand operational twin. (Stalin serves on both.) *Comintern*: the body charged with making the revolution happen worldwide, based in a Moscow mansion, and with an almost unlimited budget for global troublemaking. ('Don't economise', Lenin instructs, 'spend millions, many millions'.) *Revoyensoviet*: the revolutionary military council, Comrade Trotsky's stomping ground. *Cheka* (soon to become the GPU): the ones you do not want to stop you in the street. *Narkompros*: the Commissariat of Enlightenment, charged with educating the masses and ensuring that they think the right way.

But those are just the tallest trees in the forest of acronyms. Then there are saplings like *Rabrkin*: the anti-bureaucracy commissariat set up by Lenin. Finally, there are the trees that are really more like weeds, the ones that grow in the shade, and do not seem to suffer from the lack of light. These carry acronyms most people have never heard of: *Orgotdel, Uchraspred*. They are the internal bodies of the Communist Party, the personnel department, the file keepers, the accountants, the administrative link between centre and periphery, those who assign jobs and shuffle people around the constantly growing *apparat* (the apparatus, as the Communist Party's organisation is charmingly known).

And, when he is not dealing with nationalities' issues for which he is also responsible, it is in amongst these obscure but powerful bodies that Comrade Stalin is to be found, toiling selflessly away in the forest under-growth – and just occasionally tweaking matters to serve his own inter-ests. (It is around this time that the Georgian gets his wife expelled from the party in the hope that this will persuade her to spend more time at home.) Stalin is perfect for these kinds of jobs. He remembers people's names; Trotsky never would. You want someone to organise an agenda for the next Politburo? Stalin is your man. Someone who knows his way around the acronyms, who understands how everything links up? Stalin, again.

And it is from within this forest of acronyms that another soon arises – the *nomenklatura*, the list of Communist Party members to whom the choicest jobs will be doled out, with the grandest privileges and the best future prospects. With these jobs come automobiles and telephones. And loyalty to whoever put them there.

DOORN: The Kaiser's entourage is split. Some think Lili a positive influence on old Wilhelm. (This group includes the Crown Prince, despite the fact that Lili used to be his mistress.) Others are more doubtful.

They worry about the press coverage if word should leak out that the Kaiser is now gallivanting around with a much younger woman. A recent book by an English guest at Amerongen paints a rather undignified and gossipy picture of the Kaiser's home life, after all. A story about a young admirer would not help to solidify Wilhelm's credentials as a heroic slave of the German nation, in mourning for both his country and his wife. And what if things with Lili go further? Wilhelm's hopes of restoration would surely suffer if he were to commit himself to a partner deemed unsuitable by conservative monarchists at home.

There is a collective sigh of relief when the Kaiser eventually suggests Lili go on a trip to Germany to bag herself a Prince from the royal house of Hesse. Lili spills out her heart to a friend. 'Best of all I'd like to marry the Kaiser', she confesses, 'as soon as possible really, seeing as he probably won't live much longer … but if that isn't possible, I'd be happy to take on one of the princes.'

LOS ANGELES, THE UNITED STATES: Clare Sheridan tours the stage sets of Hollywood's film studios, travelling from ancient China to Russia to the Wild West just by stepping around a corner.

Clare likes Los Angeles. It is warm and pleasant and full of creative people. She likes the fact that nobody here seems to mind the rules too much, particularly when it comes to the prohibition on alcohol. One evening, Clare finds herself drinking absinthe in a Californian speakeasy. Another, she is taken to Venice Beach, where she tastes chewing gum for the first time.

The name on everyone's lips in Los Angeles is Charlie Chaplin. People who have never met him talk about him quite intimately, as if they were close friends. That is the price of fame: everyone thinks they know you, everyone thinks they own you. Clare is delighted to learn that Charlie has apparently read her books on Russia and the Bolsheviks and pronounced them rather good. There is no better publicity.

After a few weeks in the sun – and a trip up to San Francisco – Clare hits the jackpot. Charlie Chaplin has just returned from England – his first trip home since becoming a star. (In London, he tries to visit his old school incognito but ends up being mobbed, and declares the city a much sadder

place than he remembers from before the war.) Clare is granted an audience with the hottest property in Hollywood. The two instantly become
friends. They talk about their childhood memories. They watch *The Kid*
together at a private screening, with Charlie occasionally tiptoeing up to
the harmonium to add in music when he thinks the movie needs it. They
discuss politics. Despite the rumours, Chaplin is not a Bolshevik, Clare
discovers, just an instinctive internationalist who sees a world made up of
millions of individual souls and wishes they would all get on. Winston's
cousin eventually persuades Charlie to sit for a sculpture of his head.

He dresses in a brown dressing gown for the occasion. When he gets
fidgety, he stands up and wanders around the room playing the violin for
a while, or the two of them break off for a cup of tea. Charlie examines
the work in progress. 'I find him very interesting, this fellow you have
made!' he tells her. 'It might be the head of a criminal, mightn't it?' (Chaplin
has a theory, Clare learns, that master criminals and artists have a similar
psychological make-up: a desire to be bound by their own rules, rather
than those of others.)

The two decide to set off on a camping trip along the Californian
coast. A chef, Charlie's secretary and some tents travel in a second automobile behind them. Chaplin is delighted to be referred to as 'brother'
by the waiter in a roadside restaurant along the way. (Clare sees this as
evidence that working men's comradeship is alive and well in the United
States.) They find a beautiful spot to camp and, for a day or two, an
atmosphere of freedom and playfulness descends. Charlie rolls down the
dunes with Clare's son. He does comic impressions of the great Russian
ballet dancers.

When they talk about the rather depressing world situation, Clare
suggests Charlie should go into politics to change things for the better. He
works himself up into the role of great political speaker, and harangues the
dunes, bellowing slogans at the imaginary masses. Clare is reminded of
Leon Trotsky.

Eventually, the press catch up with the happy troupe. Charlie gets that
hunted look on his face again. It is time to go.

Tarrenz bei Imst, Austria: In early October, a young French couple arrives
in the mountains of the Tyrol region. André and Simone Breton (née Kahn),
married about the same time as the Hemingways and a little after the de
Gaulles, are on their honeymoon. André has decided that they will spend

a part of it with Tristan Tzara in the small village of Tarrenz. Breton tries to rekindle that spark of friendship which he once felt was so strong. It is no use. Tzara is bored by the monkish André and does not try to hide it, only hanging around for a few days before flying the coop muttering something about renewing his visa. Breton and his wife leave soon after.

They travel on to Vienna, where Breton hopes to meet another hero of his, the one man who he thinks might understand the earth-shattering significance of Breton himself. It is nearly a year since that experiment in automatic writing with Soupault. Breton feels sure that Sigmund Freud will want to know about it.

For days, André prowls restlessly around Vienna with a press photograph of the great Austrian psychoanalyst in his jacket pocket, trying to summon the courage to ring the bell of Berggasse 19. He walks past Freud's building several times. But each time, his resolve to go inside cracks at the last minute. Eventually, frustrated at his cowardice, he writes a note to Freud from his hotel. He is promptly invited over the next day at three in the afternoon, during Freud's visiting hours. Simone waits in a nearby café while Breton heads off for what he hopes will be a great meeting of minds. Wait till Tzara hears about this!

Simone has barely had time to drink her coffee before André is back, in a huff. Yes, he met Freud and no, he doesn't want to talk about their encounter. The newly-weds march around Vienna in silence until dusk.

WASHINGTON DC: After four years, America and Germany are no longer at war. A peace treaty passes the Senate in October. Woodrow is furious. The treaty is the same as that he signed in 1919, he fulminates – but without the League. A 'national disgrace', he writes.

Woodrow is slowly getting used to the role of an ex-President. He works on a book about America's place in the world. He takes the odd phone call from the other partner in his law firm (though there is not much business Wilson is willing or able to accept). He corresponds with ex-servicemen, addressing them as 'comrade' in his letters. He insists on slowing down the automobile to exchange greetings when he sees wounded soldiers on the street.

The former President finds much to criticise, of course, in his successor. One day, he writes an angry note on how the Republicans abuse one of his own slogans – America First. He accuses them of interpreting it to mean America must act selfishly in the world, whereas he meant it as an expression of the nation's calling to lead it by example. These things rankle.

The newspapers are filled with concern for Woodrow's health when he misses his regular Saturday theatre outing. For a week, he is unable even to see visitors. He commiserates by letter with another man struck down by illness this autumn: that energetic New Yorker Franklin Delano Roosevelt.

MOSCOW: Trotsky receives a letter from the head of one of the more recent acronyms in Soviet Russia: *Istpart*, an organisation dedicated to writing the history of the Communist Party and the Bolshevik revolution, as demanded by Lenin. It has already started publishing the collected works of the impatient revolutionary.

Trotsky cannot fail to be flattered. 'Why not begin to prepare a complete collection of your writings?' the letter asks. Why not indeed? Trotsky may have had his fallings-out with Lenin in the past, he may have rubbed people up the wrong way, but no one can deny his prestige. The two men are so closely associated in people's minds that during the civil war children thought of them as one person: *Lenintrotsky*. 'It is high time it was done', the *Istpart* director writes. 'The new generation, not knowing, as it should, the history of the party, unacquainted with old and recent writings of the leaders, will always be getting off the track'.

LONDON: Michael Collins, scourge of the British secret service and the most famous Irishman yet to be snapped by the British paparazzi, arrives in town. His habits remain those of a fugitive. 'How did you get to Hans Place this morning without being discovered?' asks a reporter who catches up with him at the smart address where the Irish delegation are being housed. 'I always watch the other fellow instead of letting him watch me', Collins explains. 'I make a point of keeping the other fellow on the run, instead of being on the run myself.' He reminds the reporter that his newspaper, the *Daily Express*, once called him a murderer. It now refers to Michael Collins as the 'big, good-humoured Irishman' and comments on the softness of his voice.

He is no stranger to the city. He once shared a cramped flat with his sister in a boarding house in Shepherd's Bush. Working as a clerk like thousands of others come to make their way in the imperial metropolis, he attracted no particular attention during his stay. An Irish patriot, to be sure. A good-looking young man in a rough-and-tumble way, always ready for an argument about politics or an opinion on the latest playwrights. A regular in the local pubs. Times have changed. Now he has at his disposal a six-storey house not far from Harrods, complete with his own staff brought from Ireland. (It 'makes the place feel less strange', he explains in a letter home.) The boy from Cork has become a celebrity. Half proud, half appalled, he sends Kitty a package of newspaper clippings. 'What do you think of the enclosed?' he asks. 'Writing all bosh. I never said any of those things. Just a few remarks. Newspaper men are Inventions of the Devil.'

Collins feels the weight of responsibility upon his shoulders, to try and achieve for his people what thousands of Irishmen and -women, dead and alive, have struggled for in vain this past century and longer. He cannot sleep the night before the negotiations begin, and stays up writing a letter to Kitty. At eight o'clock in the morning, alone, he seeks out the Catholic church he used to go to all those years ago, and attends early-morning Mass. Two Rolls-Royce motor cars drive up to the black door of Number 10 Downing Street a few hours later. Tuesday, 11 a.m. Michael Collins, his hat tipped down firmly in front of his face, fairly dashes from the car into the residence of the British Prime Minister (to avoid being photographed, some speculate). Journalists look for any signs that members of the Irish delegation are carrying guns under their coats. A crowd was gathered outside, mostly made up of Irish well-wishers. They sing hymns to pass the time.

David Lloyd George glad-hands the Irish by the door, greeting them one by one as they come in. The rest of the British negotiating team, unwilling to shake hands with men they consider murderers – Collins most of all – are already upstairs, seated on one side of a long, imposing table. Winston Churchill is amongst them, taking time away from the rest of the empire's problems to try and hash out the Irish situation. 'In the past when England was in the mood for peace, Ireland was not, and when Ireland had been in the mood for peace, England was not', Lloyd George tells the gathering, suggesting that the desire for peace on both sides has created a window of opportunity which must not be missed. But there is a stiffness to these first meetings. Positions are laid out. Platitudes are exchanged. The leader of the Irish delegation, Arthur Griffith, scribbles a letter to de Valera that evening. 'The most difficult part has yet to be discussed'. He signs off, 'In haste'.

Over these first days, meeting sometimes in the morning, sometimes in the afternoon, the Irish and the British get the measure of each other. The talks roam widely. What should Ireland's future trading relationship with Britain be? How should financial issues be dealt with? What about defence? Subcommittees are set up to deal with particular issues (Michael Collins is the sole Irishman on several of these). For the Irish, these are not dry, impersonal matters; they are charged with emotion and experience. Collins expresses his fury at British police having the temerity to search passengers arriving in Ireland for weapons. 'I would certainly never allow myself to be searched in this way', he says. The Pope sends a telegram to the British King, wishing him success in bringing peace to his people. De Valera does not like this at all. He scolds the Holy Father, telling him the Irish are no one's people but their own. The atmosphere in London is not improved by news that an IRA arms shipment has been seized in Hamburg, Germany, and a cache of weapons discovered in Cardiff, Wales.

As usual, Lloyd George charms and bullies in equal measure – his own side as much as the Irish. 'Fertile in expedients, adroit, tireless, energetic and daring in ways which would be reckless apart from his uncanny intuition', reads a character study drawn up for the Irish team before their departure. In London, Arthur Griffith finds the British Prime Minister to be 'a humorous rascal'. Lloyd George extemporises one day on the sheer quantity of Irish produce sold in Britain, taking it as a token of the eternal bonds tying the two islands together, and which no man should rend asunder. 'You don't buy it for love of our beautiful eyes', Griffith replies to these flights of lyricism. 'No, on account of your beautiful butter', the Prime Minister parries good-naturedly in return.

Michael Collins blusters, dogged in pursuit of his arguments, infuriating in his tenacity, occasionally cavalier in his language but, on the whole, constructive. The British are impressed by his force of personality, his swagger – he appears to think he has defeated the British Empire single-handed – and the quickness with which he understands the essentials. He naturally tends to dominate on the Irish side. He has political imagination. But he is not a details man. 'Good feelings are better than good clauses', he says at one point, arguing that a generous settlement will be better for all than one which appears mean. De Valera is informed of the state of play by courier.

The talks edge quickly towards a dangerous precipice, the two issues on which war is most likely to reignite: the partition of Ireland into North and South, and its relationship with the empire. On partition the Irish are insistent: no man can rend asunder what God has put together. Ireland is one, to divide it is unnatural. The British respond that they cannot coerce loyal northern Protestants into Dublin rule. Collins shakes his head. 'It is you have made the position and you must repair it', he retorts. Still, he leaves open the possibility of some kind of compromise, a border commission perhaps.

The imperial question is more intractable. The problem is the Crown. The British see its acceptance as a matter of cardinal importance: the warrant of Ireland's future amity and guarantee of Ireland's permanent commitment to imperial defence. In most matters, they urge, the Crown would be just a symbol, reflecting Ireland's place in the evolving structure of the empire, as an admitted equal to the independent nations of Canada, Australia or New Zealand. But in Ireland, the Crown denotes obeisance, not collegiality. It seems to suggest that Ireland's statehood is a gift to be bestowed by an enlightened foreign monarch, rather than the inborn right of the ancient Irish nation. And, in any case, how can a British monarch now be accepted when an Irish republic has already been proclaimed? De Valera's idea – that Ireland be *associated* with the empire, but not be *part* of it – is kept in reserve for several days, and then presented by the Irish as a compromise. There ensues some discussion of the precise meaning of the word 'adhere' in the context of this proposal.

Much hinges on such wordplay: a people's fate, an empire's solidity. 'It is a matter of drafting', an Irish delegate argues. The Irish offer a permanent alliance. The British demand an oath of allegiance at the very minimum. The Irish baulk.

BOLOGNA: Albert's first lecture in Italian – a language he half learned as a teenager – goes down a storm. Like everywhere else he goes, the local university offers him a job.

After his German mangling of the Italian language, and with his son Hans-Albert in tow, Einstein embarks on a little rail trip around the country, making it as far as Fiesole, outside Florence, where Einstein *père et fils* visit old friends. Albert takes careful note of the exchange rate. The German mark is not what it once was (and it seems to be getting worse). He also notices a change in his physique, from the rakish physicist-about-town, a bundle of nervous energy and ambition, to the portlier middle-aged man of the people. (Einstein is forty-two.) 'My little paunch is taking on an ever-more threatening shape', he confesses in a letter to his step-daughter.

On their way back north, Albert stops in Zurich, where he plays music with his sons – 'intelligent, musical and still very childish', in their father's opinion – and dines most evenings with his ex-wife Mileva in the family apartment. (To forestall any nasty rumours – and avoid any unwelcome questions from Elsa – Albert takes a room in a nearby inn rather than spend the night on his ex-wife's sofa.) Then it's off again by overnight train to Holland, for a lecture series at the University of Leiden.

Albert has been invited to visit Japan next year. He cancels a planned appearance in Munich on account of concerns about politically motivated disturbances. Elsa writes about a new domestic assistant she has hired in Berlin. 'Another pretty housemaid!' Albert responds. 'Unlucky soul that I am: cover her in a veil when I get home'.

NEW YORK – RUSSIA – MOSCOW: 'Remember, these are the gray days of the revolution, everything has settled down into the monotonous, undramatic task of reconstruction', Louise Bryant writes in an article about her latest trip to Russia, quoting the Russian feminist Alexandra Kollontai: 'If you look for that high elation you saw here in 1917 you will be disappointed'. Advances have been made for Soviet women's education and childcare. But there are hardly any women in the political institutions of the regime. Men are less inclined to recognise their failings, Kollontai explains.

It is one year since John Reed's death. Louise tries to gather his papers together. There is talk of a movie of *Ten Days that Shook the World*. In October, a memorial service is held in the New York Central Opera House. Edgar Hoover has sent his men to observe. The two-thousand-strong audience sing the Internationale and the 'Red Flag', accompanied by an orchestra of Latvian immigrants. One of Louise's poems is read out:

> Three ikons
> And your photograph
> Hang on the Wall
> You've been there so long, dear
> With the same expression on your face
> That you've become an ikon
> With the rest

Louise recalls how Russia's grand drama caught her husband's imagination, how he went to 'fulfil the mission of the most humane government the world has ever seen'. She ends with a plea to help the millions starving in the country he came to love: 'today, Russia is being crucified for her ideals'.

As the operatives of the American Relief Administration fan out across Soviet Russia, they find devastation. Buildings have been stripped of floor-boards for firewood. In Kazan, the city's sewage system, left unattended, has flooded the city's basements. Communication is difficult: telegrams take two weeks from Moscow. In Tsaritsyn, the Americans are forced to rely on the services of a Baltic German who picked up a little English on a visit to Chicago years ago or else use two interpreters: an American and a Russian lady who both happen to speak French. In Orenburg, they find several thousand Polish prisoners of war living in an abandoned train.

Villages are silent, deserted. No one bothers to record who has died. By October, the Americans are feeding sixty-eight thousand Russians a day; by November, three times that. By December, the figure stands at half a million and the American relief workers have arrived at the shores of the Caspian Sea. As winter draws in, peasants resort to cannibalism. The soul has departed the body; the meat should be used. Children's flesh is considered especially sweet. A man murders his wife for supper. 'I had enough of her', he is reported to have said. Cemeteries are raided for corpses. The world is upside down.

The same day on which Louise addresses the mourners at the Central Opera House in New York, the impatient revolutionary lectures propaganda officers in Moscow. The new economic policy is, he admits, a 'strategical retreat'. But 'when the Red Army retreated, was its flight from the enemy not the prelude to its victory?' This is war fought by other and more devious means. A frontal attack would not work. The enemy must therefore be outflanked, and their weapons turned against them. We will let the capitalists re-enter Russia through the front door, Vladimir tells them – 'and even by several doors (and by many doors we are not aware of, and which open without us)' – in order to defeat them in time. They will profit, they will squeeze Russia. Let them! Meanwhile, 'you will learn from them the business of running the economy, and only when you do that will you be able to build up a communist republic'.

Vladimir's words are darker now. The promise of redemption is far off. The Bolsheviks thought their 1917 enthusiasm would make communism a reality with a commanding snap of the fingers, he admits. They were wrong. 'It appears that a number of transitional stages were necessary – state capitalism and socialism – in order to *prepare* – to *prepare* by many years of effort – for the *transition* to communism'. He predicts that a future capitalist war will kill twice as many as the last: twenty million rather than ten million will die. This is what makes the struggle so essential – and why it is so vital to focus on ends rather than means. Dreams of utopia cannot be allowed to get in the way of practicality. 'The proletarian state must become a cautious, assiduous and shrewd "businessman", a punctilious *wholesale merchant*'. There is no other way.

Lenin's headaches are getting worse. 'A mass of current work', he complains. 'I am becoming tired.' Will he live to see the day history proves him right? His father worked himself to an early grave at the age of fifty-four. Vladimir is fifty-one.

LONDON: Ten days in, and Michael Collins admits to Kitty that he is beginning to grow lonely, away from her and away from home.

In Dublin, he feels himself the master. In London, he feels himself oppressed, a servant amongst masters. He is being spied upon at Mass, he complains to Lloyd George. He has information that a photograph snapped in the British capital is now being circulated in Ireland. His anonymity has been compromised. One night he takes himself off for a drive alone to get things straight in his head. 'Rather funny – the great M.C. in lonely splendour', he writes self-consciously. The next afternoon he visits an old friend in jail, and makes a scene when the prison governor refuses to let in two other men he has brought with him. 'Mr Lloyd George won't thank you for being discourteous to me', he shouts, his breath heavy with the smell of whiskey. Collins ends up staying nearly four hours in discussion with the jail's Irish inmates.

Yet there are few such outings. Most of the time, Michael Collins is alone with his thoughts and his compatriots. He decides to grow a moustache.

NEW YORK: *Shuffle Along* is doing so well that Sissle and Blake decide to assemble a second cast to take the show on tour.

This time, Josephine – Josephine Baker since she married a Pullman porter called Willie Baker – is not leaving things to chance. She travels up to New York from Philadelphia (leaving Willie behind). She hangs around the theatre. She sleeps rough. And when the time for the audition comes, remembering what she was told a few months before, she borrows a friend's powder to lighten her skin the way northern audiences are said to like it. Sissle and Blake aren't there. The audition is run by the show's manager, Al Mayer. Once more, Josephine is told she looks too young and too thin. (She is fifteen and still growing.) But she gets a job as a dresser for the other girls. And soon enough, when one of them falls ill, Josephine Baker is put on the chorus line. Right on the end, where she can't make too much trouble with all her out-of-time, energetic gyrations.

But the audience seem to like that kind of thing. 'Is that cross-eyed girl in the show?' people ask, before deciding whether to come and see the show a second time. Word gets back to New York. The girl has got something.

DUBLIN – LONDON: No compromise, no concession. 'There can be no question of our asking the Irish people to enter into an arrangement which would make them subject to the Crown, or demand from them allegiance to the King', Éamon de Valera writes to the negotiators across the water. 'If war is the alternative we can only face it.' He refuses to go to London himself.

A furious row breaks out amongst the Irish negotiators in the capital. Collins sees de Valera's game more clearly than ever: to bind the hands of the peacemakers with an impossible task – peace on his terms, and his terms only – and blame them when they fail.

BIRMINGHAM, ALABAMA: The magic city of the South is celebrating its fiftieth birthday. The streets are awash with confetti. A daredevil pilot performs terrifying tricks in the air while his passenger swings from a rope attached to the plane, holding on only by his teeth. The city's hotels are swamped.

A crowd of a hundred thousand – blacks and whites stand separately – gather in the newly renamed Woodrow Wilson Park to hear a speech from Wilson's successor. The sun is high in the sky. A raised dais is draped with American flags. The mood is patriotic. As President Harding stands, he is greeted warmly, despite his party's generally poor showing in the South. The President warms up rather slowly, moving crabwise to the subject that he has really come to talk about: race.

Wars are great accelerators of change, he notes, and this last war has changed things around the world. 'Thousands of black men, serving their country just as patriotically as did the white men, were transported overseas and experienced the life of countries where their color aroused less of antagonism than it does here'. Their conception of their role as citizens has changed – and that must be reflected in Alabama, in the South, across the nation. 'I would say let the black man vote when he is fit to vote', Harding says. That is shocking enough for some. But it gets worse: 'Prohibit the white man voting when he is unfit to vote.' In the black section of the crowd there are great cheers.

Everyone knows how hard it is for blacks to register to vote in the South. When a young preacher and student named Michael King attempts to do so at City Hall, Atlanta, he is directed to an office on an upper floor which can only be accessed by an elevator for blacks which never works, or a staircase – which is for white use only. Some see such underhand techniques as the only means of keeping white supremacy intact, and quite defensible as a result. Harding has a different message. If Southern blacks do not believe they will be better treated, they will move north. The South's economy will slow. Society will atrophy. Birmingham's second half-century will be less bright than its first.

When it comes to equal political rights, the President is blunt: 'whether you like it or not, our democracy is a lie unless you stand for that equality', pointing at the silent whites in the crowd. But he is wary of the word being misconstrued. The right vote and to succeed economically should not be taken to mean equality of blacks and whites in society at large. Social equality is a dream. Harding advocates cooperation not integration: 'racial amalgamation, there cannot be'. He wishes black men to be the best black men they can be, 'not the best possible imitation of a white man'. Race pride, Harding says, is healthy. 'Natural segregation' is its consequence.

Reaction to the speech divides broadly on party and geographic lines. A Senator from Mississippi warns: 'if the President's theory is carried to its ultimate conclusion, namely, that the black person, either man or woman, should have full economic and political rights with the white man and white woman, then that means that the black man can strive to become President of the United States'. A Senator from Georgia, where half the population are black, is angered by the idea that a politician from Ohio 'should go down in the South and there plant fatal germs in the minds of the black race'. Supremacist assumptions run deep.

Marcus Garvey welcomes Harding's speech. He calls the President 'a sage, a man of great vision' for reframing the issue of black and white as a global issue, rather than as the special preserve of the Southern states. He views the speech as a vindication of his own approach. 'How long can Americans continue to lynch and burn Negroes?' he asks. For as long as it takes blacks to organise themselves around the world, he replies. He chides the Mississippi Senator who says he is in favour of justice for blacks yet cannot envisage the final consequence of political equality: a black President. 'If I cannot be President in the United States of America as I desire,' Garvey says, 'I am going to be President in Africa.'

Garvey likes one of the President's phrases in particular, about black men taking pride in being black rather than, in Garvey's words, 'trying to bleach up ourselves, straightening out our hair to make it look like the white man's'. That, he says, is 'a great slap at Dr Du Bois'.

LONDON: 'The weekend (notwithstanding my own unpleasantness) did me a great deal of good', Michael Collins admits to Kitty after a short break in Ireland in November. 'The constant and changing fresh air was a great tonic.' On the way back, he admires the autumn leaves falling off the trees, and the sun glimmering on an Irish lough. 'Really, I never thought things looked so lovely', he writes. 'Perhaps it is that I was happy'.

Duty pulls him back to London, and the hope of peace: one moment close enough to touch, at another as distant as the moon. The negotiations grow more hectic. Lloyd George tries to cajole the politicians of Northern Ireland (while privately informing the King that he will not order any more shots fired in southern Ireland). Collins shuttles between his London residence and meetings at the Grosvenor Hotel. During breaks in the talks, he consents to having his portrait painted. (There are rumours that he is having an affair with the artist's wife.) Collins sits facing the door, as if expecting a messenger to burst in with news at any moment, or in preparation for a quick escape.

Dübendorf airfield, Zurich: Two faintly familiar figures, Mr and Mrs Kowno, arrive at a private airfield just outside town to pick up a single-engine Junkers, chartered to take them to Geneva. Their pilots – two Hungarians and a Bavarian – are ready and waiting. There is little in the way of formalities to complete. Shortly after taking off, just after midday, the aircraft banks hard and makes a full turn. Not towards Geneva, then? Levelling out, a course is set due east.

Mr and Mrs Kowno are Charles and Zita Habsburg in disguise, off to claim the crown of Hungary once more – this time with a little more force and forethought. Though there is a some confusion amongst his allies over the exact date of the King's arrival – meaning loyalist forces are not quite fully mustered by the time Charles and Zita's plane touches down in western Hungary – the element of surprise is nonetheless maintained. The day after Charles's landing, troops loyal to the Habsburg Crown are entrained for Budapest. It is only once they are under way that Horthy learns of it. The admiral sends panicked orders to local garrisons to tear up the railway lines to impede the royal progress. The garrison commanders decide to leave themselves out of it. In desperation, Horthy spreads the rumour that the Czechs are invading. Budapest University students are raised into a defensive battalion.

But Horthy is a politician, and Charles is not. Deep down, Charles believes that honour goes with rank. So it is that, when his train gets to the outskirts of his capital, he decides to appoint as commander of his royal forces the most senior officer he can find, taking his loyalty for granted. And then tasks him with settling matters with his enemy. Charles halts outside Budapest, waiting for the obstacles in front of him to be cleared up by his subordinates. The result is predictable. A stand-off develops, giving Horthy all the time he needs to persuade Charles's freshly appointed commander to defect. Overnight, when Charles thinks a ceasefire has been agreed (ostensibly to give time for peace negotiations to take place the next day), the Habsburg positions are overrun without a shot.

Charles and Zita spend one last night on Hungarian soil, as guests of an aristocratic family that count their period of service to the Habsburg cause in centuries. Within a week Hungary's erstwhile King is on a British ship, heading down the Danube, bound for exile in a destination yet to be decided (but certainly further away than Switzerland). Within two weeks, they have passed Belgrade and are at the mouth of the Danube, emptying into the Black Sea. A few days further and they are passing through the Bosphorus. Docked in the occupied Ottoman capital, the Emperor is fitted out with a new set of civilian clothes, including clunky American shoes (which Zita hates). They are not allowed ashore. 'One could have imagined oneself back in the time of the Crusades', the Empress notes as the city she knows as Constantinople (or is it Istanbul these days?) slips by. It is a strange cruise, this final journey to God knows where.

Eventually, in Gibraltar, orders are received for the ship to make for the Portuguese island of Madeira, in the Atlantic. No one knows what government there is right now in Portugal. 'Not that it matters', remarks the British captain cheerfully; 'in a fortnight there will be a different one anyway.' The Portuguese republic has earned itself a reputation for instability. Bombs go off in Lisbon all the time. The premier was killed by one just a few weeks ago. It is to be hoped that Madeira will be more peaceful.

ROME: In November, Benito Mussolini gets back to basics. He fights a duel with a newspaper editor he has taken a dislike to. In a fencing bout lasting a little over an hour – ten minutes spent fighting, fifty minutes with the unhealthy newspaper editor recovering his breath – Mussolini is triumphant. The duel is reported as news in *Il Popolo d'Italia*. Such things matter in the macho world of Fascist politics.

A little over a week later, Mussolini engages in a more subtle duel, with his Fascist rivals. At a congress in Rome, Benito renounces his earlier pact of pacification with socialist unions and embraces the *ras* from Venice and Bologna.

In return for this shift in policy, the regional power-brokers now accept Benito as their Duce and agree to his programme of reform of the Fascist movement. A National Fascist Party is established, with a clear central command structure. Offices in the regions will provide a counterbalance to any centrifugal tendencies. The blackshirts will become a Fascist militia. What fascism itself means is left somewhat open: it is a movement, it is energy, it is a state of mind, it should not be bound by a single programme as such.

The contrast of the determined Fascist movement with the weakness of the state, and the vacillations of its traditional leaders, escapes no one. The *squadristi* are unleashed to drive the point home, and to warn against any attempts to suppress them by force.

Moscow: 'If, after trying revolutionary methods, you find they have failed and adopt reformist methods, does it not prove that you are declaring the revolution to have been a mistake in general?' Lenin asks. 'Does it not prove that you should not have started with the revolution but should have started with reforms and confined yourselves to them?' Absurd! One should not allow such defeatism. The kind of anti-revolutionary nonsense a German Social Democrat might come up with. How childish.

Vladimir imagines a day in the distant future when gold will be used to build public lavatories. What better way to show the workers that the capitalist age has finally bitten the dust, and that its gods no longer rule. But the capitalists are not quite finished yet. Even now they are preparing for a new war over gold, between themselves. It is inevitable. 'They intend to kill twenty million men and to maim sixty million in a war say, in 1925, or 1928,' he writes, 'between say, Japan and the USA, or between Britain and the USA, or something like that.'

Kansas City, Missouri – Arlington Cemetery, Virginia – Washington DC: The fighting has been over for three years. But it is still fresh in the memory of those who gather in their thousands to inaugurate a monument to their fallen comrades in the heartland of America, honoured by the presence of military commanders from Britain, France, Italy and Belgium. 'America Impresses the Allied War Chiefs with Youth, Hope, Bigness and Fairness', reports the *New York Times*. The most senior figure present is the Frenchman Marshal Foch.

In Indianapolis, the seventy-year-old French marshal watches a motor race where the winning car averages a hundred miles an hour. A quarter of a million gather on the streets to welcome him to their town. Across the Midwest, Foch kisses a lot of young ladies on the cheek, confirming ideas of French gallantry towards the fairer sex. The entire student body of the University of Michigan at Ann Arbor turns out to salute him as his train travels past to Detroit, where he visits an automobile factory. Foch's message to America is one of thanks – but with a political undertow. 'France did not want war in 1914', he tells one dinner audience. 'We don't want it now'. But to keep the peace, the alliances of war must be maintained. The two great republics must stand shoulder to shoulder.

As the French supreme commander is applauded on his travels across the United States, the American Unknown Soldier is borne across the Atlantic by a naval flotilla. On 11 November 1921, the two processions converge in Arlington Cemetery, where the Unknown Soldier is interred for ever. Woodrow and Edith Wilson travel to the cemetery in a carriage and are greeted by a roar of approval as they pass.

President Harding makes a speech, carried by telephone cable as far as San Francisco. He recalls a recent demonstration of modern weaponry: the 'rain of ruin from the aircraft, the thunder of artillery, mortars belching their bombs of desolation, machine guns concentrating their leaden storms'. He swears that the sacrifice of the Unknown Soldier, and that of millions of others, will not have been in vain. 'There must be, and there shall be, the commanding voice of a conscious civilization against armed warfare', he intones.

The next day, a naval disarmament conference gets under way across the Potomac, the first time such a conference has been held in America. For the American delegation the key aim is to restrain the Japanese and keep China open. Britain wants to prevent a financially crippling naval race with the United States. The French seek to maintain their position in the calculus of global power. The Italians hope to become masters of the Mediterranean. The Chinese want further recognition of their sovereignty. The US Secretary of State shocks the conference by suggesting that hundreds of tons of naval shipping be scrapped, starting with a list of vessels he calls out by name. He proposes a new ratio for the tonnage of the world's navies, putting America on a par with Britain, and the rest behind. It is a new ratio of global power.

BUKHARA, TURKESTAN: As Mustafa draws closer to his goal of unquestioned leadership of the Turks of Anatolia, his rival Enver moves further east, into the wilds of Turkestan, hoping to find redemption in a new struggle for the freedom of the Turkic peoples of central Asia — against the Russians, this time.

ROME: A few weeks after Albert Einstein's halting Italian lecture in Bologna, Benito weighs in with his own views on the subject of relativity. A debate is brewing in Italy about the new science. He does not want to be left out.

Some in Italy, including those associated with the Fascist movement, see relativity (and its linguistic cognate, relativism) as a German–Jewish plot to confound the world with the destruction of absolute truths. It is a philosophy of disorder. (Einstein himself is wary of over-interpreting the consequences of relativity for philosophy, preferring to view science as science, more or less insulated from other kinds of speculation.) A society without truth cannot have order; and a society without order at home cannot succeed in the global struggle for power abroad. In this light, relativity is a pernicious attempt to prevent the restoration of basic authority and stability necessary for the re-establishment of Italian national power. It is German philosophy, weaponised.

But Benito sees an opportunity to confound his enemies. Relativity has stirred things up. It seems clever, audacious, mould-breaking. Mussolini sees a mirror to his own movement, so slippery and hard to define according to the old-fashioned outdated political categories of the past. 'Fascism is a super-relativist movement', he declares, 'for it does not seek to dress up its complex and powerful states of mind as definitive programmes.' Instead, he writes in *Il Popolo d'Italia*, 'it proceeds by intuition and fragments'.

Unlike those who see relativity as a variant of Bolshevism — and therefore associate it with fascism's enemies — Mussolini views it as the final death knell for socialism's claims to scientific truth. If all is provisional, if all is contingent, all is relative, how can socialist theoreticians dare to claim a monopoly of knowledge about the past and future? With his usual flourish, Benito's intellectual gymnastics lead him to conclude that Italian fascism is, in fact, the 'most interesting phenomenon of relativist philosophy'. He does not mention Albert Einstein by name.

MOSCOW: Stalin's son from his first marriage arrives to stay in the Kremlin: a teenager who smokes and speaks bad Russian. Yakov's appearance sharpens one of his father's old gripes: the question of a decent place to live in Moscow.

The apartment that Stalin and his wife Nadya currently occupy, handed out in the division of spoils of 1918, is embarrassingly small. It hardly corresponds to Stalin's present status. These things matter. The Bolshevik leadership play a constant double game in such matters – greedily eyeing up others' accommodation and privileges, while simultaneously trying to impress upon Lenin their revolutionary frugality.

But there are limits. Stalin's apartment is in an outbuilding of the Kremlin. He complains to Vladimir about the noise from the communal kitchen in the morning. (This is something the super-sensitive boss should understand.) His living conditions are affecting his work, he says. He is not asking for his own sake, but for the sake of the revolution. Lenin is sympathetic. Vladimir relies on Stalin more and more. The two men are in constant contact over the telephone, by note, in person. Lenin worries about the Georgian's health. He must not fall sick.

With a little helpful prodding, a solution is suggested by the head of the Kremlin bodyguard. Perhaps Stalin could move into the palace itself? The Georgian already has his eye on rooms in the old Tsarist treasury building, with its high vaulted ceilings and commanding views. All it would take is a few false walls to divide the place up. If that does not work, surely space can be made for him elsewhere. It has become a matter of urgency. 'Cannot the vacating of the apartment, promised to Stalin, be speeded up?' Vladimir enquires of the Kremlin staff in November: 'I ask you particularly to do this and to *ring me up* ... whether you are being successful, or whether there are *obstacles*.'

There are. And they carry the name of Leon Trotsky's wife, Natalya. The problem is jurisdictional. The Kremlin treasury building is under the authority of the State Museum Directorate, Natalya writes in a personal letter to Lenin. And, unfortunately, it is already in use by them. It cannot just be commandeered by another department. The impatient revolutionary tries to persuade her, a little testily, to show some flexibility. To no avail. 'Naturally Comrade Stalin must have a quiet flat', Natalya replies, 'but he is a living man and not an exhibit in a museum.' He would not be happy there. And then there is the matter of heating. 'The Treasury is very cold, Vladimir Ilyich', Natalya explains. This appeals to Lenin's concerns about the Georgian's health. 'Only a single room can be heated', she writes, 'where the treasures to be sent to the mint are being selected.' If Comrade Stalin were allowed to move in then this vital work would come to a standstill and the Georgian might fall ill.

Stalin's search for a new apartment continues.

DUBLIN – LONDON – BELFAST – LIMERICK – DUBLIN: Ireland's leaders are split on the terms of a draft treaty brought back from London. A tense cabinet meeting at Dublin's Mansion House is inconclusive.

The lead Irish negotiator begs that this chance for peace not be lost: it is the best Ireland can hope for. Not enough for some. 'Don't you realise that if you sign this thing, you will split Ireland from top to bottom?' declares a naysayer. Hours pass in argument. Michael Collins rumbles. Éamon de Valera pontificates against any oath of allegiance to the British Crown at all – and then suggests a form of words which he might just be able to accept. (Whatever else happens, de Valera expects to have the final word.) The meeting breaks up in a hurry to allow the delegates to return to London that very night. They do not travel together. The weeks of intense pressure have taken their toll. Comradeship has been pushed to breaking point. Their return across the Irish Sea is filled with a foreboding sense that this is their last chance. 'There's a job to be done and for the moment here's the place', Michael Collins writes to Kitty when he arrives back in London. 'And that's that.'

It is December. The British are impatient. They have risked much to get this far. Their careers are on the line. They can wait no longer. Journalists are told the situation is 'very grave'. There are no more concessions to be wrung out. The substance of Irish freedom has been offered. An independent Ireland is to become the Irish Free State. Northern Ireland's Protestant leaders will be forced to either opt into this new state – in which they will be a minority – or else accept a commission to redraw the border. An Irish oath of allegiance to the King – in whatever form the Irish like – will seal the matter for ever. The British present their ultimatum. What is it to be: peace or war?

The leader of the Irish delegation announces that he is ready to sign the treaty – in a personal capacity. Not enough. They must all sign, Lloyd George demands, or face the consequences. A naval frigate is waiting to carry word of the decision to expectant Ulster. The British Prime Minister holds up two letters in his hands – one for war and one for peace: 'which letter am I to send?' No more prevarication. The Irish must return to Downing Street with their answer by ten o'clock, in two hours' time.

Michael Collins has made his decision. Already in the taxi back, the man who once ordered British agents be murdered in their beds now says he will sign the treaty and so must all the rest. To refuse peace now, on these terms, he argues, is to damn Ireland to an unending war with an uncertain outcome. Men and women will be slaughtered for nothing.

The cry of betrayal goes up from those who came to London to safeguard the Irish republic and for whom nothing less will do. They will be hung from the lamp posts if they plunge Ireland back into war, comes the reply. Slowly, regretfully, painfully, the others are won around to Collins's argument. How can they refuse? He is a military hero; they are mere politicians. No one thinks to refer the matter back to Dublin. It is their responsibility now.

It is 11 p.m. before the Irish return to Downing Street. Two more hours are needed to agree a few final changes. Another hour to type it all up. But, at a little after 2 a.m. on 6 December 1921, the Irish and the British sign. They have done it. All at once, the tension breaks. Like strangers who find themselves the unlikely survivors of a horrible calamity, and are now bound for ever by their fate, the British and Irish delegates clasp each other in congratulation. It is the first time they have shaken hands in two months. Lloyd George expresses the hope that the treaty will lead to permanent reconciliation. Winston lights a large cigar. (The following morning, he is already suggesting the Black and Tans be assigned a new role in Palestine.)

Michael Collins staggers out of Downing Street. Peace has been won, but at what cost? 'When you have sweated, toiled, had mad dreams, hopeless nightmares, you find yourself in London's streets, cold and dank in the night air', he writes that night, exhausted and in agony. His mind fills with anxious thoughts. Will the Irish people thank him for winning the country's freedom – as he thinks they should – or will they brand him a traitor for not getting all they ever wanted? 'Early this morning I signed my death warrant', he writes despondently. 'A bullet may just as well have done the job five years ago'.

It is not yet day in Ireland. News of peace has not yet arrived. Neither Dublin nor Belfast knows what has happened. The British envoy carrying the treaty to the north sleeps with the sacred text under his pillow. A special train takes him to Holyhead; then a naval vessel across the Irish Sea. He arrives in Belfast to discover he has no small change with which to make the phone call to announce his presence to Northern Ireland's premier, and inform him in person of the bargain that Ireland's Protestants must now accept. The treaty terms are read out in the premier's billiards room, where there is consternation, but acceptance of the deal.

Far to the south, in Limerick, Éamon de Valera sits with his entourage around the fireside. A phone call comes in with the news that a treaty has been signed – not just presented, mind you, but signed as well. What can it mean? De Valera refuses to go to the phone. The next morning, still unaware of exactly what has transpired, but with a rising sense that he has lost control of events and Michael Collins has done the deed without him, he travels by train back up to Dublin. Éamon's ego is bruised. He spends most of the afternoon closeted at home. That evening, he carries on as if nothing has happened, making no attempt to discover the details of events in London. He attends a university symposium on the life of the Italian poet Dante Alighieri. The text of the deal struck in Ireland's name has to be virtually forced upon him.

In Ireland's name. But not in his own.

NEW YORK: William Du Bois finally gives his view on the President's speech in Birmingham. He calls it 'sudden thunder in blue skies', which 'ends the hiding and drives us all into the clear light of truth'.

While approving of the President's words on political rights, he takes issue with his words on social equality. 'No one denies great differences of gift, capacity and attainment amongst individuals,' he writes, 'but the voice of science, religion and practical politics is one in denying the God-appointed existence of superior races, or of races naturally and inevitably and eternally inferior.' Human equality cannot be qualified.

As to the President's statement on racial amalgamation, Du Bois is shocked: is he not aware that there are already four million Americans of mixed heritage? Such racial amalgamation as exists does not, in general, arise from the wishes of the majority of black Americans. 'It has been forced on us by brute strength, ignorance, poverty, degradation and fraud', he writes. 'It is the white race, roaming the world, that has left its trail of bastards and outraged women and then raised its hands to high heaven and deplored race mixture.' It is quite wrong to suggest that two individuals, of whatever race, may not marry if they so desire.

A creed of race separateness can only lead to ghettoisation. It encourages the awful rise of the Ku Klux Klan. It encourages Garvey. 'The day black men love black men simply because they are black is the day they will hate white men simply because they are white', he writes: 'and then, God help us all!'

SFAYAT, TUNISIA – ISTANBUL: Over a year now since Wrangel's fleet left Crimea. On the north coast of Africa, a Russian community has been established.

One by one, the better ships of the Russian squadron are taken away, renamed and repurposed for the French fleet. Icebreakers become minesweepers. In Sfayat, the town by the port of Bizerte, a Russian priest celebrates the Orthodox Christian festivals. A naval academy is established, with three hundred cadets for a navy that no longer exists. Russians take jobs in Tunis as porters, house-cleaners, mechanics, cooks. Baked delicacies once popular in Tsarist Petrograd now reappear under African skies.

In Istanbul, Wrangel's yacht, the *Lucullus,* is rammed and sunk by an Italian vessel. It is taken as a bad omen. Though an accident is claimed, some suspect an assassination attempt directed from Moscow. Prince Yusupov, Rasputin's killer, dispatches a letter of sympathy from Rome. A British admiral conveys his condolences. 'The general is taller than I am', he writes, 'but my wardrobe is at his disposal'.

Wrangel is not ready to give up. He addresses a long letter to Henry Ford suggesting that they join together 'to crush the forces aiming at the destruction of the highest achievements of human culture made in the whole history of man'. He writes to Winston Churchill – receiving a warm but non-committal response. The world is moving on.

MUNICH: Adolf spends the autumn stirring up trouble, engaging in deliberate provocation of his enemies, basking in the attention of various legal disputes, and watching the membership numbers of the NSDAP tick up all the time.

One evening, he tells members of the SA that a professional boxer has now joined the ranks of the party and agreed to give boxing lessons two or three times a week to members. Another evening, on a secret trip to Berlin to meet nationalist circles there, he offers the suggestion that, if the party were ever to win power, special camps could be set up to concentrate Marxists and Jews in one place, removing them entirely from national life.

THE SS *LEOPOLDINA*, THE ENGLISH CHANNEL: Not far from Le Havre now, thank the Lord! There are a couple of over-exuberant young Americans on board – hard not to like them, but an earful none the less. They are heading to Paris, so they tell anyone who will listen. The wife plays the ship's white grand piano non-stop. Her husband, a journalist, hangs around the bar telling far-fetched stories about his time in the war and generally making a nuisance of himself. Somewhere in the middle of the Atlantic he challenges a professional boxer from Utah to a practice bout, to get him in shape, so he says. The two men clear a few tables from the ship's dining room to make a ring, and then go at each other full pelt for a few rounds, lashing this way and that while the ship heaves beneath their feet. The American lady towels off her young husband's brow between rounds, whispering encouragement in his ear. He acquits himself well, or at least so he tells his family in his letters back home.

At the Spanish port of Vigo things on board quieten down for a few hours while the energetic Americans insist on going ashore, heading straight for the town's fish market, where Ernest Hemingway takes a particular interest in the size of the local tuna – and the remarkable strength of the old fishermen who land them. Somehow Ernest manages to converse with the locals – or thinks he does – in a blend of Italian, Spanish and school French, spiced with American slang.

In their cabin, the couple's suitcases are mostly full of the kind of smart clothes that they think one is supposed to wear in the French capital. But one suitcase carries a more precious cargo: the addresses of a few Americans in Paris (a Miss Stein, a bookstore owner called Miss Beach, on whose younger sister André Breton once had a crush), the beginnings of a novel, some war tales set in Italy, some poems, and a couple of short stories set in upstate Michigan.

DEARBORN: 'As the Jewish propagandists in the United States cannot be trusted to give the people all the facts,' notes the *Independent* before launching into its latest tendentious diatribe, 'it devolves upon some impartial agency to do so.' The exposure of the *Protocols* as a forgery is batted away: 'The Jews still have time to repent and tell the truth.'

Another volume of anti-Semitic articles from the *Independent* is made available in book form, absolutely free to anyone who wants a copy, aside from the twenty-five-cent cost of postage. The magazine fingers Jews as being the associates of the famous traitor of the American War of Independence, Benedict Arnold, accuses them of fomenting war in Palestine, ruining the great American game of baseball and polluting young minds with jazz and its 'abandoned sensuousness of sliding notes'.

MANCHESTER: Letters from Vienna have thinned out since the summer. A postcard or two, the odd family update. Requests for food have stopped. The situation in Austria must be stabilising, Sam reflects. He scans the *Manchester Guardian* for news.

Shutting up shop at the end of December, Sam decides to pen a final letter to wish the Austrian branch of the family a happy New Year – a 'pre-war Happy New Year', as he puts it. 'I am sure we can all do with it and it must come sometime', he writes. 'Let us hope in 1922.'

DUBLIN: The world proclaims a great victory for peace. 'These are indeed fitting peace terms to mark the close of an age of discontent and distrust, and the beginning of a new era of happiness and mutual understanding', declare the editors of the London *Times*. 'This settlement we believe to be a fair one', reads Dublin's nationalist equivalent, 'and full of blessings for the Irish people.' 'Well done all', pronounces the *Daily Mail*.

There is rejoicing in Melbourne, Australia, where the premier issues a statement warmly welcoming the new treaty and greeting Ireland as a sister state. American Senators voice their support for the peace deal. Indian nationalists see Ireland's success as a harbinger of their own future independence and celebrate accordingly. Marcus Garvey sends a telegram of congratulations (and tells UNIA members that 'we have a cause similar to the cause of Ireland'). Dublin's stock market booms. Irish prisoners are released from British jails. Reconciliation has triumphed. Michael Collins appears the hero of the hour. His photograph is everywhere.

But Collins wants more reassurance than newspaper headlines. On landing back in Ireland, he grabs an ally by the shoulders. 'What are our own fellows saying?' he asks, hurriedly. 'What is good enough for you is good enough for them' is the reply. Collins tells an American journalist he anticipates resistance to the treaty from hardliners – those more hardline than him, that is – to be overcome through persuasion from the top. He expects de Valera's backing.

He will not get it. Éamon de Valera fumes at the treaty terms – not his terms, not his treaty. He feels personally betrayed. If there is no republic, he is no president – at least not in the sense he imagined it. Before Collins and the others have got back, de Valera calls together cabinet members currently in Dublin and angrily announces his intention to demand the immediate resignation of those who signed the treaty without referring it first to him. It is with the greatest difficulty that he is dissuaded from such a perilous course. It would look autocratic, he is told. It would break the cause in two. The men who signed the treaty should at least be allowed to defend themselves for their acts, in private. 'What a fiasco', de Valera's secretary writes in her diary. The President, she says, is in an 'awful state'.

When the full cabinet meets formally the following day, de Valera discovers his old authority no longer works. His presidential prestige no longer carries all before it. On the treaty, he is outnumbered. By four to three the cabinet votes to recommend ratification to Ireland's republican parliament, the Dáil. De Valera is unmoved. He repudiates the negotiators' work, claiming now that it is in violent conflict with the wishes of the nation. 'Mr de Valera steps between Ireland and her hopes', says the *Irish Times*. Peace will not win out so easily.

To settle the matter, the Dáil is called together for debate. A few days later, it meets in Dublin, with its full complement of members for the first time, IRA commandants and all. An attempt is made to keep the tone civil. But tempers soon fray. The atmosphere grows rowdy. Speakers interrupt each other constantly. Emotions run high. To save embarrassment, and to keep things under control, de Valera asks for the Dáil to meet behind closed doors, as if holding a secret court martial (which is more or less what he considers it). Michael Collins prefers the open court of public opinion. 'If I am a traitor, let the Irish people decide it or not', he says. He lays down a challenge: 'If there are men who act towards me as a traitor I am prepared to meet them anywhere, anytime, now as in the past.'

Collins proves a better politician than expected. Over several days of debate, he becomes the public figure he never was before, a man rather than a myth. He rises to the occasion. His prestige – and the loyalty of his associates – is thrown behind the treaty. 'Michael Collins – his name alone will make that thing acceptable to many people in the country', says one passionate republican, furious at the treaty and at the blind willingness of some to follow their leader into the abyss. 'If Mick Collins went to hell in the morning, would you follow him there?' she asks his supporters. Some cry: 'No'. But others cry: 'Yes'. His voice, his presence, is a factor of undeniable popular importance. It increases day by day. His speeches matter. So do his silences.

De Valera speaks at wearisome length in metaphors and riddles. He refuses to publish his alternative to the treaty he so violently rejects, fearful it will show just how little the two texts differ. Collins, meanwhile, speaks the straightforward language of an honest patriot. While de Valera talks as if he were above the people, Collins talks as one of them. He speaks for what is vital, not just for what is pure. The treaty 'gives us freedom', he says: 'not the ultimate freedom that all nations desire and develop to, but the freedom to achieve it'. Those who do not wish to seize this opportunity possess a 'slave mind', he says. They have no vision, they have no future. 'Deputies have spoken about whether dead men would approve of it, and they have spoken of whether children yet unborn will approve of it,' he tells the Dáil, 'but few of them have spoken as to whether the living approve of it.' The country's mood is for peace. Parliament must follow, whether its President approves or no.

In private and now in public session, Éamon de Valera grows more antagonistic. At times, he is quite incoherent in his anger. Arguments become denunciations. Those who signed the treaty are declared guilty of 'subverting the Republic'. The words fall heavily, bomb blasts to nationalist unity. 'When men are bitter', the Irish poet William Butler Yeats writes to a friend, 'death & ruin draw them on as a rabbit is supposed to be drawn on by the dancing of a fox.' Dublin's newspapers accuse their President of asking Irish men and women to give up the chance of freedom and peace to die for a 'grammarian's formula'. But that does not mean the grammarian will not win, marshalling the fury of those who have suffered under British rule behind yet more struggle for the cause. 'Yesterday was the worst day I ever spent in my life', Collins writes to Kitty after a long day of such speeches.

He expects to lose the treaty vote when it comes. But first a break for Christmas. A chance for Ireland's politicians to hear from Ireland's people.

ATLANTA, GEORGIA: Imprisoned during the presidency of Woodrow Wilson for agitating against the draft of Americans into the world war, the socialist candidate in five presidential elections from 1900 to 1920 walks free the day before Christmas, his sentence commuted by the Republican in the White House to time served. This is normalcy in action.

On his way back home to Indiana, the socialist Eugene Debs drops by Washington DC to meet the President. 'Mr Harding appears to be a kind gentleman,' he declares after the meeting, 'one who I believe possesses humane impulses.'

MOSCOW: A dictator's gift to his people.

The impatient revolutionary recalls the howls of Russian émigrés who 'can say the word *Cheka* in all languages, and regard it as an example of Russian barbarism'. No wonder! 'It was our effective weapon against the numerous plots and numerous attacks on Soviet power made by people who were infinitely stronger than us', he tells the Ninth All-Russian Congress of Soviets. He accuses the American Relief Administration of containing such plotters, even as they feed one million of Russia's starving people every day.

But everyone knows that times change, and that the zealous can occasionally overreach themselves. The Cheka will henceforth be reined in. It will be confined to political matters. 'The closer we approach conditions of unshakeable and lasting power and the more trade develops, the more imperative it is to put forward the firm slogan of greater revolutionary legality,' he promises, 'and the narrower becomes the sphere of activity of the institution which matches the plotters blow for blow.'

The Politburo grants Lenin six weeks' rest at Gorki, starting on 1 January 1922.

ZURICH – VIENNA: Eduard Einstein – youngest son of the great physicist Albert, theoretician of relativity and not quite a Nobel laureate – stays up to midnight writing a letter telling his father what presents he has received for Christmas: tabletop croquet, new pieces for his Meccano set, some books and a model steam engine. None of it is what he really wants, of course. 'It would be so nice if you could spend Christmas with us one time', little Eduard writes (aged eleven). 'I can't remember even when that last happened.'

The same evening in Vienna, one of Freud's American student-patients meets a pretty Austrian girl at the New Year's Ball. They go to the opera together. They laugh. Then – silence. He is Jewish, she discovers. The fledgling romance is broken off. The American student goes home alone through the cold streets, reverberating with anger and with shame.

1922

WINTER

DEARBORN: Suddenly, without any explanation, Henry Ford's campaign stops dead. There are no more articles about the Jews in the *Dearborn Independent*. A series on banking and finance starts instead. No one can quite explain what has happened.

KOSTINO, NEAR MOSCOW – GORKI – MOSCOW: For a few days, Vladimir rests on a state farm in the countryside. Then he travels to Gorki, where he moves into a room in one of the secondary properties on the estate. Nadya remains in Moscow. Vladimir travels back and forth irregularly.

Wherever he is, the impatient revolutionary is never far from a writing pad or a telephone (he has the local telephone line upgraded to ensure he can always get through to the Kremlin). He dictates messages and scribbles instructions. He urges the Politburo to speed up the process of granting foreign concessions. The latest idea is to lease a vast swathe of southern Russia to Krupp, the German industrial behemoth which produced most of Germany's artillery pieces in the war. He writes a directive for the Commissariat of Enlightenment on how the Soviet film industry should be organised, suggesting appropriate subjects for propaganda: 'Britain's colonial policy in India, the work of the League of Nations, the starving Berliners'.

In return, he receives government reports which invariably dissatisfy him. 'In a word, it is obvious that the struggle against red tape has not moved ahead one iota', he writes in response to an update on the anti-bureaucracy campaign he requested last year. He demands this issue be taken up again and conducted in the manner of a military campaign. A few days later, he receives a note from the Commissar of Foreign Affairs wondering whether some language about traditional representative institutions should be inserted into the Soviet constitution in order to secure a trade relationship with the United States. 'This is *madness*', Vladimir scribbles in the margin. The author of such a suggestion should be forced to go to a sanatorium '*right away*'.

DUBLIN: The debate in the Dáil goes on for several days more. The lives and beliefs of men and women long dead are brought into the university meeting hall, and presented as case studies for and against the treaty. Personal animosities are given public airing. More interruptions, more points of order, more amendments, more delays, more heartfelt speeches.

One speaker calls forth an image of a proudly Gaelic Ireland unshackled from British political and cultural tyranny blossoming – literally and figuratively – from the blessings of the sweet freedom now on offer. 'We can have our national theatres and municipal theatres, music halls and picture halls redolent of a national atmosphere', he insists. All this is within the nation's grasp. 'We can have our marshes and waste lands turned into plantations and our hillsides covered with trees.' Children will be instructed in the Gaelic language and local manufacturers will flourish once more. Are these tangible opportunities for national rebirth to be ruled out on a 'question of formulas'? Will those who reject this chance take responsibility for 'crushing this frail and beautiful thing in the chrysalis'?

Others urge Ireland to hold fast against temptation, and reject the current offer. 'Now you all know me,' says one of Ireland's most ferocious republicans, daughter of an Anglo-Irish Arctic explorer and wife of a Pole of dubious lineage. 'You know that my people came over here in Henry VIII's time, and by that bad black drop of English blood in me I know the English – that's the truth.' The British intend no good, she says. Ireland has been tricked. She repeats a strange rumour that Michael Collins is to be married to the sole daughter of the British King as part of the proposed bargain. The principle of the republic, a principle for which men and women have suffered and died, cannot be given up. What was declared in 1916 cannot be taken back. The treaty is typical British divide-and-rule. 'You can have unity by rejecting this thing', says another speaker. 'You cannot have unity by approving of it.'

On Saturday, the vote is held: sixty-four in favour and fifty-seven against. Too close to settle matters finally. Collins calls for unity behind the majority, declaring his respect for de Valera to be unchanged and that the vote is not personal. There is no echo from the defeated. 'Let there be no misunderstanding, no soft talk', spits a de Valera ally: 'This is a betrayal, a gross betrayal.'

Irish nationalism is rent asunder: 'I tell you here there can be no union between the representatives of the Irish Republic and the so-called Free State'. De Valera himself claims the republic exists and will continue to exist irrespective of the vote. He breaks off and sobs mid-speech.

The political manoeuvring continues. De Valera resigns as President on Monday, but is immediately proposed by his allies for re-election. He promises, if thus re-elected, to continue the fight against the treaty, against the majority who voted for it two days before. 'I say that is tyranny,' one Dáil member complains, 'that is dictatorship'. The risk of two separate Irish governments is raised: one for the treaty, one against. 'Mexican politics', grunts Collins. A vote is held on the presidency. It is closer than the treaty vote but de Valera loses again. 'You will want us yet', he tells Collins, suggesting his side will keep themselves apart for the present, serving as a kind of auxiliary army, ready to continue to fight for true republican purity against the foreign enemy whenever the need arises. 'We want you now', Collins replies.

Final, desperate ideas for unity are tossed around: a coalition government of some sort, a committee of public safety comprising both members who back the treaty and those who don't. Efforts at compromise are dismissed. De Valera's followers have backed themselves into a corner. There is no escape. There can be no cooperation on the treaty, for the treaty must lead to the Free State, and the Free State represents – in their eyes – the negation of the republic. The centre cannot hold.

Another man is elected President. De Valera walks out of the meeting hall in response. Others follow. 'Deserters all!' cries Michael Collins at the departing gang, nearly half the membership of the Dáil. 'Up the Republic!' one shouts back over his shoulder. 'Oath breakers and cowards!' shouts another. Collins repays this insult in like coin: 'Foreigners, Americans ... English!'

Munich: Adolf Hitler and his co-defendants are sentenced to three months' imprisonment – two thirds of which is suspended – for commissioning various acts of violence and disorder at the end of last year (such as using Nazi thugs to demonstrate the proper meaning of German unity and strength to a meeting of Bavarian separatists).

The case is reported in local newspapers. Ernst Toller, the playwright who briefly ran a Bavarian Soviet Republic during the crazy days of 1919 and who is now in prison for his pains, is told about the mangy field-runner by a fellow inmate. Hitler, *Hitler*? The name does not ring a bell, Ernst says. Another recalls that the Adolf Hitler he remembers from 1919 used to call himself a Social Democrat and gave the impression of someone who reads a lot of books without understanding them.

The prison sentence – which does not have to be served at once – adds to Hitler's personal allure as a man struggling against the discredited authorities, a man ready to suffer for his beliefs. At the NSDAP's first large-scale congress, held just days after the trial, delegates flock to Munich from all over Germany, Austria and even the Sudetenland, the border area of Czechoslovakia where German is the predominant language. Anton Drexler is allowed to say a few words. But there is no doubt as to who is really in charge. In their speeches, a string of party members declare outright loyalty to the party Führer. The party now has six thousand members and is growing all the time.

'If they lock us up and think that will stop our movement they are making a big mistake', Adolf thunders. 'We will go to prison as national socialists and come out of prison, enriched by the experience, as national socialists.' A police report suggests that, given the patriotic tone of his speeches, Hitler should be treated generously when it comes to the exact timing of his prison sentence and how long he should serve.

PARIS: Beginning to stake out his independence from Tzara, André Breton works on an idea for a new international artistic congress. Dada are invited along, but now only as one group amongst many. Recognising the affront, Tzara declines to attend.

Worried that the Romanian may now try to disrupt proceedings – as he did with the Barrès trial last year – Breton issues an ill-judged public warning against any engagement with 'a person known as the promoter of a "movement" that comes from Zurich, whom it is pointless to name more specifically, *and who no longer corresponds to any current reality*'. The language is incendiary. It is personal. It borders on the kind of anti-foreign rhetoric which Barrès and others are famous for. It is André who is made to look the fool when the Parisian artistic milieu sides with Tzara.

A few weeks later André drops a bombshell. In France's main entertainment newspaper, jammed between a notice for a fundraiser for actors killed in the war and another for Russian émigré writers stuck in Paris, appears a short article penned by Breton entitled 'After Dada'. It is strong stuff. André accuses Tzara of being a fraud. He did not even invent the name Dada, Breton claims. Nor did he write the 1918 manifesto. He predicts a

Paris funeral for Dada within a month or two, with a Dada effigy floating down the Seine.

Breton describes his own fling with Tzara's version of Dada as 'a bet gone wrong'. He dedicates himself to new ideas and experiences. He takes to the cafés and to the streets. He runs sessions of automatic writing and dream recitals. 'Leave everything, leave Dada, leave your wife, leave your mistress, leave your hopes and fears … take to the highways', Breton writes that spring. At last, he is free to be his own man. He is twenty-six years old.

NEW YORK: John Reed's *Ten Days that Shook the World* is reissued in the United States in a special famine relief edition with an endorsement by the impatient revolutionary himself written two winters ago:

'With the greatest interest and with never slackening attention I read John Reed's book, *Ten Days that Shook the World*. Unreservedly do I recommend it to the workers of the world. Here is a book which I should like to see published in millions of copies and translated into all languages. It gives a truthful and most vivid exposition of the events so significant to the comprehension of what really is the Proletarian Revolution and the Dictatorship of the Proletariat.'

The American Relief Administration in Russia is now feeding nearly one and a half million Russians every day.

DUBLIN – PARIS: On a cold day early in the year, a short ceremony is held at Dublin Castle, the seat of imperial authority in Ireland. Power is formally handed from the British Viceroy to the new provisional government. Collins is late, blaming his tardiness on a train strike. On a day such as this, it hardly matters. 'The castle has fallen!' Collins proclaims.

Newspapers show pictures of the Black and Tans, kitbags slung over their shoulders, marching to the boats which will carry them home. The provisional government spins the affair as British 'surrender'. Republicans are unconvinced. They see Collins as a man who has made a pact with the enemy and received power in return. This is no revolution. It is a sell-out.

A conference for the worldwide Irish diaspora opens at the Hotel Continental in Paris a few days later. Supposed to be a family reunion, it soon turns into a fight. The different factions barely talk to one another. William Butler Yeats gives a paper on 'The Plays and Lyrics of Modern Ireland'. Another Irish expatriate writer, James Joyce, is unable to attend. He is busy finishing a book, a few blocks away.

PARIS: Ernest Hemingway makes a discovery of major literary significance: a bottle of good French wine can be bought (and drunk) for just sixty French centimes, equivalent to eight American cents. The good news must be shared. 'The dollar', Hemingway informs Torontonians planning their next foreign adventure, 'is the key to Paris.' A single dollar will buy two good meals.

The city is fizzing. Anyone can be who they want to be – or claim to be: a champion boxer, a Grand Duchess, a great artist. All a young journalist has to do to make a living is head out to the nearest café, soak up some atmosphere, talk to a few blabbermouths (these are easily found), and write the whole thing up as Parisian colour. Not much work, and the folks back home love it.

In February, Hemingway files a piece about the charmingly innocent Russian émigrés who hang around the cafés of Montparnasse waiting for some sudden change of the political weather that will whisk them back to Petrograd. (A few waiters remember a different Russian crowd from before the war, led by a certain Trotsky; the real old-timers recall a man with a goatee called Vladimir.) In March, the Café de la Rotonde features in another Hemingway article as a hang-out for American poseurs – 'the scum of Greenwich Village, New York' – with their bleached hair, artists' smocks and foot-long cigarette-holders. 'They are nearly all loafers', the *Toronto Star*'s man in Paris tells his readers on the other side of the Atlantic. 'If the exchange ever gets back to normal they will have to go back to America.'

For Ernest, Paris seems a gateway to all that matters. Everything is available. Everything is fascinating, from the Senegalese soldiers in the Jardin des Plantes to the roaring crowds at the horse races to the one-legged war veterans, ghosts from another age. 'Paris is so very beautiful', he writes, 'that it satisfies something in you that is always hungry in America.' Within a couple of months, he has met the Idaho-born poet Ezra Pound, who decides that Hemingway is the man to teach him to box; a woman called Gertrude Stein who seems to know everyone in town ('She is about 55 and very large and nice', Ernest writes to his mother); and James Joyce, whose manuscript for a rather bulky book has only just been handed in to its Parisian publishers, on Joyce's fortieth birthday.

At last, people seem to take Ernest seriously not just as a fine journalist, or even as a fine boxer, but as a man of letters, an American *homme de lettres*. He rents a room, away from the apartment, away from Hadley, as his study. Here, crouched for hours over his Corona typewriter, he tries to distil his experiences of Paris into paragraphs, and then turn those paragraphs into single sentences. Ernest Hemingway feels that he is becoming a real writer at last.

> The mills of the gods grind slowly;
> But this mill
> Chatters in mechanical staccato,
> Ugly short infantry of the mind,
> Advancing over difficult terrain,
> Make this Corona
> Their Mitrailleuse

ISTANBUL: An envoy from Ankara is ushered into the perfumed presence of the Sultan. He declaims the loyalty of Mustafa Kemal to His Imperial Highness. The Sultan shuts his eyes and remains silent, lips pursed. He no longer believes such protestations.

The winter is harsh. The Greeks are in crisis. They can rely on no one but themselves, and their strength is at an end. In western Anatolia, the Greek army clings on to the territory it occupies, hungry and tired. If it leaves, the Christian population will have to go too.

Everyone awaits the Turkish offensive from the east.

MUNICH: Adolf rages against the nomination of Walther Rathenau, a patriotic Jewish industrialist who used to revere Kaiser Wilhelm, as Foreign Minister. 'Jewish pig!' shouts the crowd when Rathenau's name is mentioned at a Nazi rally. 'You're not allowed to say that these days', says Adolf, mockingly. 'He's a human being again now he's a minister.'

Hitler enjoys these exchanges. They show his mastery over his supporters. They complete his thoughts and he completes theirs. Insinuation is the game. Adolf makes an allusive remark about something, dropping a heavy hint about his own opinions – and then the audience answers out loud what he really means but cannot say in public. The speaker and the audience are entirely complicit. Adolf tests how far he can go, skirting close to the edge of Germany's laws on defamation and incitement to violence without crossing the line.

'Our young girls are being pursued by Jews', he declares in one speech. 'Every Jewish man caught with a German blonde', he says, 'should be ...' He lets the words breathe a little. 'Hanged!' shouts the crowd. 'I wouldn't say hanged', Adolf replies, as if appalled at the idea of a lynching, 'but a court of law should certainly condemn them to death.'

WASHINGTON DC: A federal anti-lynching bill conceived in the wake of the 1917 St. Louis massacre finally comes to a vote in the House of Representatives. If passed in both houses of Congress and signed by the President, counties where a lynching occurs may be fined ten thousand dollars; officers of the law who fail to prevent it may be imprisoned.

The bill's opponents call it unconstitutional. Criminal law is a matter for the states. To give the federal government a back-door means of intervening would turn America from self-government to tyranny ('from a democracy to a bureaucracy', says one Congressman). Some call it an assault on Southern chivalry. 'In Pennsylvania it may be possible for a black brute to lay his lecherous hands on the fair form of a virtuous white girl, deflower her youth, blacken and wreck her life, and by counting out a thousand filthy dollars walk out of the courtroom', says a Congressman from Georgia. Not in his state. In Georgia, the penalty is death – and no Act of Congress or Presidential proclamation will be allowed to alter it.

Such arguments cut little ice with Du Bois. Constitutionality can be no bar on justice and progress. Lynching is 'public debauchery'. It is a stain on America's reputation and a threat to domestic order. 'Either the United States can and will end lynching or lynching will end these United States.' The bill passes the House of Representatives by 230 to 119. An electric wave of jubilation radiates out from Washington to the black communities of America. To become law, the bill must still pass the Senate.

GORKI – MOSCOW: A note from Lenin to the boss of the Kremlin staff: 'Stalin's apartment. When? What *red tape!*'

Vladimir's irritation with the slow work of government is titanic. 'The departments are shit; decrees are shit', he writes to one functionary. 'To find men and check up on their work,' he tells him, 'that is the whole point.' Lenin demands show trials of those he considers to be enemies of the regime and scolds the Commissariat of Justice for its slow work. Abuses of the new economic freedoms should be met 'with every means, including the firing squad'. When the Tsars ruled the roost, prosecutors were simply removed if they did not get enough convictions, Lenin notes approvingly. 'We managed to adopt the worst of tsarist Russia – red tape and sluggishness – and this is virtually stifling us, but we failed to adopt its *good* practices.'

Vladimir feels tired all the time. He finds it harder to concentrate. He has dizzy spells. He tries to hide the seriousness of his illness. Doctors hover around him uncertainly.

A new acronym is created. The Cheka becomes the GPU, or State Political Directorate. Its headquarters and personnel are just the same as before.

WASHINGTON DC: 'I love you', reads Woodrow Wilson's Valentine note to his wife Edith. 'You are my inspiration and my constant joy.'

Woodrow seems more chipper this year than last. His personal correspondence is livelier. Though hardly back to his old self, his physical health improves. He is mentally less flexible than he used to be, but seems more upbeat about the world and his place in it. His chosen historian – and former press secretary – is working on a more favourable version of the Paris conference, to blast away those critical books already published. He contributes to 'The Document', a manifesto of Wilsonian principles being prepared by his supporters to reboot his vision of America. He declines to give his support to the anti-lynching bill now making its way towards the Senate, deeming its timing inopportune and its constitutionality questionable.

ACROSS IRELAND: The departure of the British from the south of Ireland is swift. Barracks are abandoned. Yard sales are held in former garrison towns. Within weeks, the old regime is gone (the least change is in Dublin, where British forces remain in strength). What will replace it is not yet clear.

The provisional government is weak. Rival centres of authority make claim to be the heirs of Ireland's historic struggle. The people's loyalties are split between Michael Collins and the treaty or Éamon de Valera and its repudiation – or whatever local figure has the influence (and guns) to sway them. Personality as much as principle determines who goes which way. Old friends fall out; new enmities are born. Collins and de Valera tour the country making speeches. Both warn against division, and blame the other side for bringing it about. They warn of further and still deeper splits to come. If the treaty is implemented and a new vassal state brought into existence, de Valera cries, real Irish freedom will only be achieved by the most tragic of all conflicts – a war between the Irish themselves. 'They will have to wade through Irish blood', he tells audiences in County Kerry and County Tipperary, full of men who have guns and are ready to use them. Incitement to civil war, declare Éamon de Valera's opponents. Just the facts, protest his allies.

Rival military forces form in southern Ireland: a new, regular army under the provisional government (small, at first) and an unruly bunch of irregulars (most members of the IRA go this way) dedicated to unsullied republican virtue. Having always preferred their own counsel to that of Michael Collins or Éamon de Valera, local warlords raid banks and post offices to raise money for the republican cause. They follow their own path to the republic. They fire gunshots in the air to intimidate pro-treaty gatherings. They threaten to disrupt a planned election, seen as the stamp of approval for the establishment of the Free State. They pursue vendettas against their enemies – real and perceived. Michael Collins goes to the republican section of a Catholic cemetery in his native County Cork. Men with guns bar his entry. He is no republican any more, they tell him.

Southern Protestants flee to Belfast to find safe haven in the north; Catholics terrorised by sectarian violence flee the other way. The north's regular police stand aside as loyalist militias – 'match-and-petrol men', some call them; others use the term *fascisti* – raid Catholic households in search of IRA weapons, smashing things up as they go. In Belfast, a Catholic pub owner and the male members of his family are murdered. 'You boys say your prayers', he is told as they are lined up to meet their maker. The police are implicated. This is not government but gang rule.

'Protective measures' directed from the south may be required, Michael Collins warns, burnishing his credentials as a man of force. Arms are shipped north for a coordinated offensive with the IRA.

GORKI – MOSCOW: Vladimir's headaches are worse than ever. He battles with depression. He finds himself thinking in riddles and metaphors. His mind is pulled this way or that by fleeting obsessions. Then he becomes listless again, as if he were losing his mind entirely.

One day, he imagines himself somewhere on a mountainside. He is walking up the mountain. The view is tremendous. He has conquered a string of obstacles behind him. He is higher than any man has ever been before. The peak is ahead, the summit is in sight – but it cannot be reached directly. It is impossible. There is a different path. But it too is dangerous to reach. One could slip. Hours must be spent cutting into the rock to get a good foothold. He has to tie a rope around himself to prevent himself from falling. He can half hear the voices of the people far below, peering up through their telescopes. They jeer. *He'll fall in a minute! Serve him right, the lunatic!* The mountaineer *must not give in* to despondency, he tells himself. He *must not* fall. He *must not let himself* be shaken.

Vladimir finds himself thinking about Rosa Luxemburg. He is annoyed at the delay in publishing her collected works – *unpardonable*. She made mistakes, of course. She was wrong in 1918 when she wrote that nasty letter worrying about dictatorship overpowering the force of revolution. But she corrected herself. Vladimir is reminded of the old Russian fable of the eagle and the hen. One day, after swooping and soaring high in the sky, the eagle decides to rest for a while atop a plain farm chimney, there being no impressive rock nearby. The hen notices and says: why, I could fly there, if I wanted to. Why are eagles considered better than hens? Ah, quite right, the eagle responds from the sky, eagles may sometimes swoop lower even than hens, but a hen can never soar into the sky like an eagle. Rosa Luxemburg, Vladimir decides, was an eagle.

In early March, Vladimir confides in one of his doctors his fears that he is finished. His nights are spent in anxious insomnia, worrying about the work he has to do the next day and that he knows he cannot manage. Thoughts of suicide cross his mind. Perhaps every revolutionary should be made to retire at fifty, he tells the doctor. The doctor tells him to stop worrying. There is no obvious disease of the brain. To get better, he needs rest. He must relax. He must give fewer speeches. He must go into the fresh air – another trip to the villages outside Moscow perhaps. He must not let himself get worked up. *Yes, yes, yes!*

Doctors are called in from Germany, at great expense, to investigate Vladimir's condition further.

BELGRADE – SOFIA – NEW YORK: White Russians were once considered grand, exotic creatures, forever on the point of returning home and reclaiming whatever fantastic wealth they had left behind. These days the Soviet Union looks here to stay. White Russians are left with the question of survival. General Wrangel tries to keep his men together by getting them jobs in construction squads building roads in Serbia or working in the mines and forests of Bulgaria.

In March, a one-eyed Russian admiral arrives in New York on a Greek steamer from Istanbul, alongside some refugee opera singers from Petrograd and former officers from Wrangel's army who have decided to start a new life in America. They are sent to Ellis Island for processing. And then they disperse: the admiral to his wife's family in Philadelphia, the officers to Gary, Indiana.

VIENNA: Sigmund Freud is upset. He misses his daughter Anna, who is visiting Berlin and Hamburg. 'I have long felt sorry for her for still being at home with us old folks', he writes to Lou Andreas-Salomé, 'but on the other hand, if she really were to go away, I should feel myself as deprived as I do now, and as I should do if I had to give up smoking!'... Given such conflicts,' Freud writes, 'it is good that life comes to an end sometime or other.'

Freud's spirits are lifted by news from the wider world. The steady global march of psychoanalysis since the dark days of the war continues apace. Despite last year's untimely death (suicide again) of a leading light of Russian psychoanalysis, Dr Rosenthal, a Russian Psychoanalytic Society has been formed in Moscow. The same week, Freud receives word from Calcutta of a new psychoanalytic group there – local Bengalis call it the Eccentric Club – founded by a long-time Indian correspondent of Freud's, Dr Girindrasekhar Bose.

From Calcutta, Freud is sent a portrait – supposedly of himself. It is called an 'Imaginative Portrait': 'a painting by someone', he notes, 'who is said to be a famous Indian artist, and which represents his idea of my person, of whom he has never seen a likeness'. The result is predictable: 'Naturally he makes me look the complete Englishman'.

Freud is blissfully unaware of a short and bitter article that appears that same month in the newly revamped *Littérature* by that young Frenchman André Breton, who visited him in Vienna last autumn. Breton makes Freud, the man he once hero-worshipped as a smasher of realities – just like him – look bourgeois and ridiculous. His apartment building is 'mediocre', Breton writes, located in an 'out of the way' corner of Vienna. Freud's collaborators, pictured in a photograph on his waiting-room wall, are said to be 'vulgar-looking'. His maid is 'not particularly pretty' either. Then there is Freud himself, a 'little old man without any particular charm' and the appearance of a small-town doctor.

Simone now understands her husband's foul mood that day in Vienna. He felt patronised. Freud's only interest in receiving the foreign visitor was the chance to boast about a translation of one of his works in some French-Swiss journal. He took no interest in Breton's own work, except as a means of furthering his cause in France. Freud's parting words while patting André on the back and guiding him towards the door still sting: 'We're counting on the young.'

QUINTA DO MONTE, MADEIRA, PORTUGAL: Charles Habsburg, the Emperor of Austria, the King of Hungary, a man who once counted his castles by the dozen, has been reduced to the status of a beggar. His money has run out. No one wants to look after him.

On Madeira, he is left relying on the generosity of a local Portuguese hotelier, who allows Charles, Zita and their family to stay for free in his summer retreat in the mountains above Funchal. In the hotter months of the year, such a place is a paradise: a view over the ocean, lush vegetation, a cooling breeze. In winter, it is cold and damp, surrounded by mists that seem never to clear up. The house is impossible to keep warm. The children's tutor lives in a hut at the bottom of the garden. There is not enough to eat. There is only cold water for washing. Zita is pregnant.

One day, returning from a walk to Funchal, Charles catches a chill. It seems nothing, at first. He is a young man, only thirty-four years old. But as the days go on, Charles finds he cannot shake off this particular cold. Eventually, a doctor is called up from town, and then another. Charles's lungs are infected. Linseed and mustard plasters are ineffective. His mind wanders into delirium. Once, he imagines some Austrians have come to visit, and Zita pretends to busy herself with the imaginary guests. Another time, he states that he is King of Hungary. A Hungarian priest is there at the end.

The news breaks soon after. The front pages of the newspapers in Vienna are edged with black. The *Neue Freie Presse* declares that Charles's passing represents the end of 'a piece of history that was once life ... a life we shared'.

Zita is alone now, the mother of seven children and her eighth on the way. It is a miracle her faith remains intact. Her husband is buried in the local church.

MUNICH: The question of another semi-stateless Austrian, only a year or so younger than Charles, is discussed at the highest political level in Bavaria: should the authorities let him stay in Germany, where he has become a nuisance to public order, or should they expel him to his homeland and let the Austrians figure out what to do with Adolf the troublemaker?

Deportation to Austria would surely make it impossible for him to continue leading the NSDAP. Worried that the Bavarian authorities might swoop in at any moment to deport him, Adolf avoids his apartment and takes up residence with the family of his bodyguard. At a meeting of the main Bavarian parties called to discuss Hitler's case only the leader of the Social Democrats opposes his deportation. It would be undemocratic, he says.

Moscow: Mayakovsky's latest contribution.

Every morning, at dawn, a man sees a stream of bureaucrats heading to their offices in the city, the forest of acronyms in which any normal person would get lost in an instant.

> Some to <u>Glav</u> –
> Some to <u>Com</u> –
> Some to <u>Polit</u> –

You try and get a meeting with one of the bureaucrats – but, unfortunately, they are at another meeting already, and who knows how long it might last. A hundred more staircases to see a second bureaucrat and then the same response: 'he's at a meeting concerning the purchase of a bottle of ink by the District Co-Op.' Come back in an hour. One hour later, neither the secretary nor the secretary's secretary is anywhere to be found. So you head back to bureaucrat no. 1: 'he's at a meeting of the A-B-C-D Commissariat.' In anger, you storm to the commissariat to find – not bureaucrats, but half-bureaucrats, their bodies sliced in two. The secretary explains: they were double-booked, so one half went to one meeting and one half to another. It's all quite normal. You should not be surprised.

This is a poem that Lenin likes. 'I am not an admirer of his poetical talent', Vladimir admits of Mayakovsky at the end of a speech at a metal-workers' congress he has decided to address (whatever the doctors might have to say about it), 'but I have not for a long time read anything on politics and administration with so much pleasure as I read this.' It hits a nerve. 'We have huge quantities of material, bulky works, that would cause the heart of the most methodical German scientist to rejoice', Lenin says. 'We have mountains of paper, and it would take *Istpart* fifty times fifty years to go through it all' – but what we need is efficiency, executive control, ruthless administration.

Throughout the winter Vladimir's notes and dictations are peppered with imprecations against the bureaucracy. Vladimir needs someone who can *lean* on others, club the bureaucrats into doing their jobs properly, keep the Politburo's more theatrical and individualistic members under control. Someone who gets things done. He knows such a man.

SPRING

BERLIN: An Italian arrives in the German capital on a fact-finding trip. Or is it tourism? Benito Mussolini, now one of the most powerful men in Italy, is taken on a guided tour of the city, affirms its title as 'the world capital of bad taste' and writes up his observations in *Il Popolo d'Italia*.

He takes in a play at one of the city's theatres and marvels at the Germans' appetite in its restaurants. 'It's incredible how much these people eat!' he writes, half-admiringly. He is impressed by Berlin's underground railway, and by the apparent prosperity of the city (despite being accosted by a number of war-wounded beggars). He wonders at the Germans claiming that they cannot pay reparations when there are so many motor cars on the street.

Mussolini enjoys being an observer. He hangs around the Brandenburg Gate for half an hour to verify whether it is true, even now, that no one dares go through its central arch – a privilege reserved for the Kaiser – and delightedly concludes that it is. He is unconvinced by claims of republican stability. The current form of German government, he notes, seems to please neither the militarists who want a return to the old regime, nor the extreme left who would like to see the country ruled by workers' Soviets. The majority accept the republic, maybe – but they certainly do not love it.

As part of his tour Benito visits the imperial palace – a huge, imposing but artistically 'mediocre' building, he tells his Italian readers. In one of the rooms hangs a portrait of a King, the canvas slashed with a knife. 'Bolshevik vandalism', his guide tells him. Looking at a portrait of Kaiser Wilhelm, with his moustache in its full, bristling, wartime glory, Mussolini asks the guide: 'Do you believe that the Kaiser will come back to this castle?' 'Never', the guide responds: 'Men like me who spent five years fighting in the war don't want that man back here.'

On his return to Italy, Benito prepares for the third anniversary of the foundation of the Fascist movement in Milan. There are rallies and marches, like those D'Annunzio used to hold in Fiume. But who cares about D'Annunzio now? Mussolini is the man to watch.

NEW YORK: Edward Bernays reports the latest sales figures of Freud's lectures in America. Over seven thousand books have been sold.

KORZINKINO VILLAGE, NEAR MOSCOW: Two and a half million Russians are being fed by the American Relief Administration every day. Vladimir decides it is time to strike at another Russian institution.

Plans have been prepared for churches and monasteries to be raided and stripped of their icons, their gold, their crosses. The peasants will be too hungry to protest, Lenin reasons, and the gold and silver can be sold abroad and the money used for electrification and other things (certainly not to buy food, though that will be the excuse). The campaign begins. But there is resistance. Lenin insists it must continue. 'It is precisely now and only now, when in the starving regions people are eating human flesh,' Lenin writes, 'that we can (and therefore *should*) carry out the confiscation of church valuables with the most savage and merciless energy.'

Resistance will be crushed. The Patriarch will be spared for the moment, but the GPU keeps an eye on his friends and acquaintances. The more priests who are executed, the better, Lenin writes. 'We must teach these people a lesson right now, so that they will not dare to even think of any resistance for several decades.' The letter is to be kept secret, he instructs. *No copies.*

DOORN: The park around Huis Doorn is looking rather bare from the Kaiser's tree-chopping exertions this spring. A visitor suggests he take a break. Wilhelm explodes in anger. How dare he! 'It's been like this my whole life!' he shouts. 'Whenever I've had a plan, someone else comes along who claims to know better and tells me to back off ... Those times are over'.

When not outside chopping things with an axe, the Kaiser wields his pen instead, writing angry notes in the margins of the slew of war memoirs now being published in Germany. He is livid at how his actions are so misrepresented. Wilhelm's own memoirs are published that year and slated as a transparent exercise in self-justification – though they sell rather well.

His ego is massaged by a visit from his Finnish lady-friend from the previous year. 'If German women were like Finnish women', she coos, 'they would have worked on their husbands to convince them to make sure of Your Majesty's return to the homeland'.

Surrounded by sycophants, unquestioning old retainers and those who share his conspiratorial world view, the Kaiser sinks deeper into the morass of his own prejudices. People are sensible chaps if they agree with him, and dunces if they do not. Exile strengthens his predispositions to believe what he wants to, and dismiss the rest. He imbibes the latest racist or anti-Semitic tracts from Germany or elsewhere – the works of Henry Ford in particular – with enthusiasm.

On the side, Wilhelm starts writing to a German Princess whose husband has recently died. This will be *his* secret, he determines. Neither his family nor his entourage are told of the burgeoning epistolary romance. They would probably tell him to stop it, if they knew.

WEXFORD, CO. WEXFORD, IRELAND: 'Our country is now in a more lawless and chaotic state than it was during the Black and Tan regime', Michael Collins admits in April. Wherever he goes, roads are blocked and railway lines torn up by those who hate the treaty he has signed. He is heckled when he speaks. The air is thick with recrimination. Would-be assassins weigh up their chances. Intimidation is rife.

In Dublin, a contingent of the anti-treaty IRA occupies the Four Courts, the heart of the Irish legal system, and fortifies it against recapture. 'We are absolutely independent of Mr de Valera's political organisation', their leader claims. De Valera welcomes their defiance nonetheless. He needs their support, he needs their fury. 'Yours is the faith that moves mountains', he tells a meeting of his followers, 'the faith that confounds cowardly reason and its thousand misgivings.' He treads a delicate path: one moment seeming to support outright insurrection against Michael Collins's provisional regime, the next proposing national unity – but on his terms. 'Ireland is yours for the taking', de Valera urges: 'Take it.' So the country slips and slides towards civil war – without quite slithering over into the abyss.

Any historic transition brings a certain amount of disorder, Collins tells an American journalist. 'In Poland, Germany, Estonia, Finland and in practically all of the European countries that underwent change as the result of the European war,' he notes, 'there were many months of fierce civil war which was only put down after vigorous fighting and appalling loss of life.' Nothing so bad has happened – or will happen – in Ireland: 'Our methods may be different but the results will be equally satisfactory.'

Neither side wants to take the blame for the fatal, final step towards a civil war. Collins and de Valera meet to try and paper over their divisions and give unity a second chance (and take the fight to the British in the north). Collins is frustrated with his erstwhile friends. 'We did nothing at the conference yesterday – except talk, talk, all the time', he writes to Kitty. 'And the country! But they never think of the country at all – they only think of finding favour for their own little theories, they only think of getting their own particular scheme accepted.' Nonetheless, in May a deal is struck. An election will be held. Both pro- and anti-treaty sides will participate. An electoral pact between them should mean that the outcome will give both sides roughly the share of the seats in the Dáil that they have currently. A Sinn Féin stitch-up, it is true, but one which keeps the possibility of party unity alive a little longer. (Churchill gets wind of the idea and warns of the 'worldwide ridicule and reprobation' such a deal would bring – so far removed from the principles of a democratic, open vote.)

An agreement here, a pact there, a statement somewhere else: Michael Collins has made too many promises to too many different people to keep all of them at bay. His promises are like a house of cards, waiting for a gust of wind to make them collapse. In London, the British worry whether he will ever be strong enough to enforce the treaty terms he signed half a year ago – or whether he intends to dishonour that agreement now, by preparing an Irish constitution which tries to circumvent it. They plan for the worst.

MUNICH: On balance, Munich's mainstream politicians conclude, it is better not to turn the scoundrel into anything more than he is. Hitler should not inadvertently be turned into a martyr by over-zealous suppression. It is better to ignore him. He is allowed to stay in Bavaria. But the political sages have not reckoned with Hitler's own view of himself. His martyr complex is fully formed. In the run-up to his thirty-third birthday, it turns into something even grander.

After a few weeks' absence, Hitler is back in public – giving speeches, choosing enemies, picking fights, slandering all and sundry. The audience in the Bürgerbräukeller laugh at the mention of Bavaria's current premier, who declared in a recent parliamentary debate that, 'as a human and as a

Christian', he could not be an anti-Semite. He has got it all wrong. Speaking for himself, Adolf explains that it is *because* he is a Christian that he must be an anti-Semite. 'My Christian faith', he announces gravely, 'tells me that my master and saviour was a fighter.'

'We have been called – no, decried – as rabble-rousers', Hitler tells party members. But what about Jesus Christ? Did he not chase the money-lenders out of the temple? 'Two thousand years on, I can see the true enormity of His struggle for this world, against Jewish poison,' Adolf announces, 'for which He had to bleed on the cross'. Just as Jewish leaders chose to denounce Christ two thousand years ago, Hitler shouts triumphantly, so they are denouncing anti-Semites today. Nothing has changed, the mangy field-runner cries: Jesus Christ was an anti-Semitic rabble-rouser who argued against the worship of money, and the Nazis are just the same.

On Adolf's birthday, a week or so later, a little surprise party is organised. He is delighted to receive one particularly special present: a German Alsatian dog, a replacement for the little canine friend he lost during the war. The dog is named Wolf. Hitler's bodyguard takes care of him for a while. There is not enough room for Adolf and his dog in the Führer's one-bedroom apartment.

Paris: As his train arrives from Belgium at the Gare du Nord, Albert Einstein is advised by a friendly French policeman that a crowd of journalists is waiting to ambush him. He escapes across the railway tracks and makes it to his hiding place – a fifth-floor flat on the Rue de Humboldt, near Montparnasse – without being intercepted. Albert has been entrapped by journalists too many times. A famous German scientist in Paris cannot be too careful. If his trip is to be a success, he must be disciplined.

As it turns out, Albert has a wonderful time in Paris. He lectures at the Collège de France – in French – to a carefully selected audience. The great Polish-French scientist Marie Curie is there, along with the cream of France's scientific elite and a former French War Minister. (No Germans are invited.) When, as he puts it, he has trouble 'extracting from his throat' a particular French word, he is prompted or else replaces it with an English one. Such liberties are excused, for the French find him nonetheless a captivating speaker, with the far-off look of a mystic seer in his eyes, talking without notes, his voice low and vibrating with energy, his hands constantly moving as if drawing out the invisible thread of his argument. There is no shortage of French scientists who want to show him the town: on his last night in Paris Einstein stays out till two in the morning. He is taken to the theatre to see Molière's *The Miser* and Marivaux's *A Game of Love and Chance* (the racy *Les Fauvettes* is long forgotten now). A caricaturist trawling the cafés of the Left Bank for business produces a comic portrait of Albert for free. A pretty young Frenchwoman asks Einstein whether it is true what she has read in the papers – that he has the most powerful mind in all of human history. It seems genius is an aphrodisiac.

To his new French friends, Albert admits to having felt apprehensive about the trip. The new nationalist French government is determined to ensure Germany pays its financial dues in full, and has little sympathy with German requests for leniency. In Germany, Einstein has been accused of disloyalty for visiting the land of his country's enemies. Albert takes the precaution of writing a letter to the German Academy of Sciences before he goes, emphasising that he has sought advice from Walther Rathenau himself. But by the end of his Parisian sojourn, he is sure he made the right decision. The French he meets seem open-minded and friendly. (A debate with the philosopher Henri Bergson, who sees philosophy as having some say in the interpretation of phenomena such as time, is civilised: both sides feel they have made their point.) The old spirit of internationalism seems alive and well in Paris. If his visit can help improve political relations between France and Germany, so much the better. Albert obviously does not come across Léon Daudet, editor of *Action française*, de Gaulle's paper, who writes a scathing series about the trip in which he refers to Einstein as 'our inter-stellar visitor' and 'the Moses of Calculus'. Daudet asks how many bombed-out houses will be restored by Einstein's visit: none. Anti-relativists exist in France, too.

But Daudet is too quick to judge. Before returning to Germany, Albert goes on a pilgrimage. Leaving Paris one morning at the crack of dawn, he is driven out to the region of Dormans. The scene is not quite the same as back in 1917, when Churchill drove up and down the front here, and saw nothing but a sea of ensanguined mud. Nor the summer of 1919, when Woodrow and Edith picnicked by the bleached skeleton of a war horse. Such remains have been cleared up by now, or nature has turned them to dust. In some places, the line of the trenches is only visible through the wheat as a continuous gentle dip in the landscape, as if tracing an ancient Roman road. It is the ruined buildings which are more shocking. And the sad trees, left bare by the lingering effects of poison gas. 'German students – no, students from all over the world – should be taken here to see how ugly war is', Einstein remarks to his French hosts. It is one thing to read about it, but you need to see it with your own eyes.

The cathedral at Reims is still missing its roof, blown off by German artillery in 1914. At lunch, Albert refuses wine. In the afternoon, travelling north across the landscape towards Saint-Quentin, where there are no trees at all any more, he is silent. That evening, Einstein is put on board a train to Cologne. 'I will tell everyone there what I have seen here', he shouts by way of a farewell as the train pulls out.

Moscow: Vladimir orders imported German sedatives from the special Kremlin pharmacy, off-limits to outsiders. 'My nerves are still hurting.'

He toys with the idea of going on holiday to the Caucasus as a rest cure. He enquires about a possible spot. Quiet, and not too high in the mountains would be best (Nadya's heart could not manage it, and they must go for walks). On the other hand, he worries about the goings-on in the capital which may have to draw him back. There is the upcoming diplomatic conference to worry about. He has given clear instructions for how it is to be handled: the goal is to secure a trade deal and ensure there is no rapprochement between Germany, France and Britain. But who can be trusted these days? Lenin and Trotsky are squabbling like hens again about reform. Why are they not more like eagles?

One of Vladimir's doctors proposes an operation to remove the bullets still lodged in the impatient revolutionary's body from that assassination attempt back in 1918. There are concerns he is suffering from lead poisoning. Some think that perhaps the bullets were dipped in some kind of slow-working poison, a fiendish idea cooked up by his political enemies. An operation is arranged for the day after Vladimir's fifty-second birthday. A German surgeon is brought in from Berlin.

At least the party is now in safer hands. Comrade Stalin is made General Secretary of the Communist Party in April, becoming its coordinator-in-chief, the man to cut through the chaos and make things *work*. A hard job, but someone has to do it. And he is virtually doing it already, with all the different posts he holds, with the way he is always there to help. Not like Trotsky, who has developed the annoying habit of ostentatiously studying English during Politburo meetings, only piping up irregularly to make the odd withering remark about how one or other of his fellow colleagues has screwed something up.

CHICAGO — GENOA, ITALY: A postcard arrives at the Hemingway family residence, with a picture of a European hilltop fort. 'If you've read the *Daily Star* you know all about this town', Ernest scribbles home to his father.

The town in question is Genoa, an industrial port in northern Italy, chosen as the venue for a major diplomatic conference, the first where the Soviets are invited to attend as a semi-recognised power. British ambitions in the lead-up to the conference are high. They hope that the United States, the new master of world finance, can be prevailed upon to financially underwrite the architecture of what would amount to a revised European peace. Germany will be brought in from the cold, and a moratorium placed on its reparation payments. The French will be kept sweet by Russia being forced to repay Tsarist-era debts. The Soviet presence at the conference is unpalatable but unavoidable: after all, how can the Bolsheviks be made to pay the debts of the Tsars if no one will speak to them?

It is a crowded agenda. It proves impossible to line up all sides behind a new deal. The French are unimpressed by what they see as a manoeuvre to let the Germans wiggle out of reparation payments while they are left to cover the cost of rebuilding their country (and remain on the hook for their debts to the Americans). Everyone knows that the Russians cannot be trusted and will make whatever mischief they can. In the end, the Americans do not even bother to attend the Genoa conference, dashing hopes that the United States will play a constructive role in resetting Europe's affairs.

The conference goes ahead anyway. For weeks Ernest is run off his feet trying to figure out what the hell is going on, attempting to get the right accreditations for the right meetings, gossiping with the other journalists over Chianti in a local trattoria and guessing who will do what next. The British and French delegations strive to keep things serious and dull. The Germans, though more desperate for some kind of breakthrough, seem no more exciting. Ernest finds the Russians most interesting to watch.

Some see the Soviet regime as little better than a gang of criminals. Stories of Soviet excesses — starvation, murder, repression — are common-place. It is well established that Soviet agents and sympathisers are actively working to overthrow the governments of Europe and America. To have even been invited to Genoa is, therefore, a magnificent Soviet propaganda coup. It gives legitimacy to Lenin's regime. It confirms the practical recognition — if not the formal acceptance — that the Communists are firmly in charge in Moscow. It also stirs the hornet's nest of Italian politics. Nervous soldiers patrol the city in pairs, a warning to leftist troublemakers to stay indoors. Hemingway notes the graffiti on the streets of the working-class parts of Genoa: Viva Lenin! Viva Trotsky! (The possibility of an assassination attempt – Polish agents, perhaps – is considered too great for Vladimir or Leon to attend in person.)

Ernest hangs around the villa housing the Soviet delegation – safely located some miles outside town – as much as possible. It may not be as magnificent or so well located as other residences, but the cast of characters is unbeatable. Take Louise Bryant's friend Alexandra Kollontai, the Bolshevik feminist who advocates sexual revolution as the necessary accompaniment to social and political revolution. Consider the case of Chicherin, the former anti-war activist turned Commissar of Foreign Affairs who once spent time in London's Brixton jail (and who later that year pays a visit to D'Annunzio at his new palace by Lake Garda). Then there is the businessman-turned-Bolshevik Krasin, a man as familiar with the techniques of bank-robbing as he is with German industrial management (and who was once sculpted by Clare Sheridan). 'Four years ago, they were hunted, fleeing men,' Hemingway writes enthusiastically; 'now they sit at the table with representatives of every great power, except the United States.' It is hard not to find these characters more interesting than the stuffed shirts down the road. (The young journalist's commentary on the attractiveness of Russian secretaries leads to the screaming headline back home, 'Russian Girls at Genoa'.)

In the end, it is the Russians and the Germans – the two outsiders at the conference – who manage to steal the show, by signing their own separate agreement, a few miles from Genoa in Rapallo. Germany formally recognises the Soviet regime and renounces any financial claims on Russia. Both sides proclaim their goodwill towards the other and their intention to cooperate on economic matters. (Inevitably, German nationalists call Foreign Minister Walther Rathenau a traitor for signing up to what they consider to be a Communist stitch-up, unaware of secret military protocols allowing for a new German army to be trained on Soviet soil and for a secret poison-gas facility to be built.) The British and French are taken by surprise. They had not expected such audacity. Their worst nightmare is now taking shape: the two enemies of the Versailles Treaty in alliance.

Though the main conference stumbles on, it is beginning to look like a fiasco. The British are embarrassed; the French are worried. 'What was the use of four years of war?' asks one French nationalist newspaper: 'What was the point of losing one and a half million French lives?' Having won the war, is the French government now losing the peace? Some blame the British, accusing London of failing to back up Paris sufficiently on the matter of reparations, and thus opening the way for German adventurism. The wartime alliance is looking a little rocky now. The French view the British as unreliable backsliders; the British worry that France's reparation anxieties are just a cover for their intention to establish the border on the Rhine which they had been unable to achieve at Versailles.

In a speech in the eastern province of Lorraine – directed as much at London as Berlin – the French premier makes clear his concerns. Poland is directly threatened by German–Russian rapprochement, he notes. The threat to France is more indirect, but no less real. 'France, which clearly sees the dangers of tomorrow, will try to convince our allies that the best way to avoid their realisation is to never answer intimidation with weakness', he says. 'As for us, we are resolved to do whatever it takes to keep what was given to us in a treaty paid for by our heroes' blood.' The message is clear. France is prepared to act alone, if necessary.

Meeting in the occupied Rhineland, French political and military leaders dust off old plans to occupy the valley of the Ruhr. If Germany cannot be made to pay, France will take what is hers by force.

Moscow: Vladimir's operation has been a success. The doctors congratulate the patient. One bullet was three millimetres from his carotid artery, it turns out. The course of history was almost very different.

Lenin's physical recovery is slow. The dictator's body is weak. He suffers relapses. But he will not let this keep him from his duties. There is always more work to do. His mind races. He writes a celebratory article for the tenth anniversary of *Pravda*, crowing that imperialism is now on the run all around the globe. The so-called Great Powers have been fatally weakened by the war. They are helpless to resist the awakening of the peoples of the world against their overlords. 'The present "victors" in the first imperialist slaughter have not the strength to defeat small – I might say, tiny – Ireland.' Rebellion in India and anti-imperialist revolt in China will be next. The 'not far distant' triumph of the world proletariat is a matter of historical inevitability, Lenin writes.

But there can be no let-up in the struggle just yet. Around the world, 'the bourgeoisie is still able freely to torment, torture and kill'. And enemies of the revolution are everywhere, plotting and scheming. Barely risen from his sickbed, the dictator's thoughts return to the need to eliminate potential sources of opposition at home. Traitors must be rooted out. No weakness and no remorse. A show trial of fifty Orthodox priests and laymen is organised in Moscow in front of an audience of two thousand to make the point. Eleven are condemned to death. A trial of Lenin's old socialist rivals is planned along the same lines.

One day, the dictator writes to the head of the GPU with a still-bolder proposition: the wholesale deportation of intellectuals deemed anti-regime. He suggests that each member of the Politburo spend two or three hours a week looking through periodicals and magazines to identify potential candidates for expulsion: economists, anyone with religious convictions, socialists who still seem to think that Bolshevism is up for debate. The charges against them need not be precise. What a person thinks may be just as dangerous as what they do.

Particular attention should be paid by the security services to collecting information on the personal lives of professors and writers. 'Assign all this to an intelligent, educated and scrupulous man at the GPU', Lenin instructs. Again, *no copies*.

VIENNA: Anna Freud becomes a member of the inner circle of psychoanalysis after the successful reading of a paper to the Vienna psychoanalytic society on 'Beating Fantasies and Day Dreams'. Vienna's first private psychoanalytic clinic – the 'Ambulatorium' – opens its doors around the same time.

AMERICA: Marcus Garvey is on tour again, speeding through the Midwest on his way to California, untroubled by the multiple crises he has left behind in New York.

In Washington, the anti-lynching bill is still stuck in Senate committee where Southern Democrats want to kill it dead and Republicans worry about its constitutionality, unwilling to pass a law which the Supreme Court may then slap down. Some blame the President for raising unrealistic expectations.

In Florida, a UNIA commissioner, sent to proselytise in the black churches of the South, is kidnapped in broad daylight by members of the Ku Klux Klan. 'I tried to let out a cry, but was struck in the mouth by a man weighing 200 pounds', he writes to Garvey. They horsewhip him to within an inch of his life then tell him to get out of town. Battered and bleeding, he struggles three miles to the nearest town. He can barely walk for weeks.

In Texas, three blacks are burned alive for the alleged murder of a seventeen-year-old white girl. The newspapers run the story for a day. Then it disappears. There is no investigation.

SUMMER

GORKI: Vladimir Ilyich Ulyanov, aged fifty-two, walks around the house at night like a ghost. He cannot sleep. He throws pebbles at a nightingale singing too loudly. Later, he falls asleep, only to be awoken feeling stranger than usual. His head swims. He grabs a nearby cupboard to steady himself. All right, all *right*. Nothing serious. Nothing *serious*! He gasps. He throws up. He falls. Doctors are called. Nadya is there. Vladimir is put back in bed. For a time, he cannot move one side of his body. Thoughts start forming in his mind, and then disappear as if into a heavy mountain fog. He tries to follow them into the mists, but then they are gone. Words that used to flow from him as if there was no gap between thought and expression at all now seem like strange-shaped objects in his mouth, which he cannot quite get his lips to fit around or his tongue to express. A neurologist is fetched from Moscow.

Speech returns, but it is slower, more forced. His language is impaired. ('Years, years', he says at one point, as if asking how long this will last.) He finds simple mathematical calculations difficult. He spends three hours trying to work out, by a painful process of arithmetic, the answer to the doctors' question of what's seven multiplied by twelve. For several weeks he cannot write properly. The doctors are stumped. A spinal tap reveals no particular disease. Vladimir's symptoms seem too broad for a single, agreed diagnosis. Epilepsy, perhaps? Or – this can be only whispered, and is soon rejected as a hypothesis – syphilis contracted in Paris many years ago? His eyes are inspected by a top ophthalmologist, to look for any signs of disease there. Perhaps there are several things going wrong at once. Neurologists suggest neurasthenia. Others diagnose a hardening of the arteries, believing Lenin may have suffered a stroke. Maria and Nadya are there at Gorki to look after him. So is Vladimir's brother Dmitri, a doctor.

Leon has just returned from a fishing trip, and is himself not well. He does not attend his old rival's bedside. Comrade Stalin is called instead. Lenin has a very particular job in mind for him: to procure cyanide so that the impatient revolutionary can kill himself in the proper fashion should the paralysis get worse. Vladimir has been reading up on his symptoms. There is something impressively unsentimental about suicide, he decides. Stalin is sent back in to persuade the dictator that he will make a full recovery. 'You're being sly', Vladimir tells the Georgian bank-robber. 'When did you ever know me to be sly?' Stalin responds.

Gorki buzzes with doctors, sworn to secrecy about the dictator's true condition. A famous specialist is flown in from Berlin. The public are told Lenin has a stomach complaint and will recover soon. He is quite at home at Gorki now, with his Rolls-Royce in the garage (with snow tracks for bad weather), lots of books, his personal chef and a film projector which he can use to watch newsreels of Henry Ford's assembly lines churning out new automobiles.

EICHHOLZ-IN-MURNAU, BAVARIA: A large house in the foothills of the Alps. Adolf is taking tea with the family of one of his party's major supporters: an engineer, co-author of the Nazi party's twenty-five-point programme of 1920 and one of Hitler's teachers from his army course in 1919. (He lectured Adolf on the pernicious nature of debt interest.)

An unexpected guest arrives, another one of Adolf's teachers, a historian who spotted his speaking talent when he found him haranguing the other students after class. The engineer hisses in the historian's ear as he crosses the threshold. 'Don't quote anything in Latin which he doesn't understand', he whispers. 'He'll never forgive you'.

The former field-runner of the 16th Bavarian Reserve Infantry Regiment has acquired a more dictatorial tone of voice since he last saw him, the historian notes. His voice has become more of a growl. Adolf prefers not to talk about politics over tea. Instead, he gives his forthright opinions on alcohol and nicotine (both of which he detests) before going to play with the children in the garden, rattling a sweet tin to get their attention and chuckling along like a merry infant.

The historian's son gives his opinion on the strange man. 'Fanatical', he says, 'but trivial'.

ATLANTA, GEORGIA: Marcus Garvey, self-proclaimed Provisional President of Africa, arrives in the capital of the South for a business meeting with someone he thinks could be useful to the UNIA: Edward Young Clarke, the head of the Ku Klux Klan.

The two men speak for hours. The KKK leader explains he has nothing against blacks, he just wants America to be reserved for whites. Garvey wants black Americans to move to Africa; so do the KKK. On this rather shaky ground, an alliance of sorts is built. Garvey invites Clarke to come to New York to the UNIA convention in the summer.

Garvey writes a public letter defending his action. To speak to the KKK is plain common sense: it is to negotiate with those who really run the country. 'In spirit and in truth America shall be a white man's country', he contends, however many anti-lynching bills are passed.

America offers comfort but Africa offers redemption. 'Will you forget just for a while the beautiful lights of Broadway, the comforts afforded by a 1920 or 1921 model Sedan, and the temptation of a well-furnished parlor with Persian rugs', Garvey asks, 'and go to Africa, even now, and help to fell trees, help to clear the land and build up the city, build up the nation and extend the bounds of the empire?'

The messianic tone is back. Men like Du Bois are 'living in the air', Garvey writes, 'as far from understanding the Negro problem of America and the western world as a monkey is in understanding how far Mars is from Jupiter'.

BERLIN: The anti-relativist physicist Ernst Gehrcke adds a new article to his anti-Einstein scrapbook: a review of the so-called Einstein Film, a two-hour educational movie about relativity taking Germany by storm.

More propaganda, as far as Gehrcke is concerned, full of clever trick shots and Dada-style splicing. (Eighty thousand pictures are taken in the course of making the film, and then cleverly cut in with the movie to create all kinds of illusions making the impossible appear real.) No better than advertising, really. The movie is shown at trade fairs, in research institutes, and wherever there is an audience willing to let themselves get thoroughly confused. 'The Film of Physical Nihilism', runs the headline of one review. German nationalists hate it.

MILAN – PARIS: Two journalists meet. Both are war veterans. One is the bull-headed editor of a national Italian newspaper, not yet quite forty years old. The other is an American newspaperman who has just hiked over the Alps with his wife (and a friend) on a kind of second honeymoon. Both believe in their destiny as great men. Both believe in the importance of having experienced war. Both love Italy, or at least their idea of Italy. Both know the power of words.

Mussolini sits behind a grand desk, lazily fondling the ears of a wolfhound puppy, and assessing the absurdly healthy-looking American who has come to pay him a visit. Then he languidly opens his big mouth and begins to talk very slowly to make sure his Italian is understood. 'We are not out to oppose any Italian government', Benito explains, with a hint of menace, 'but we have force enough to overthrow any government that might try to oppose or destroy us.' It is only a few weeks since several thousand black-shirts marched into Bologna and briefly occupied the city to force Rome to remove the region's top civil servant, considered unfriendly to the Fascists. 'The whole business', writes Hemingway, 'has the quiet and peaceful look of a three-year-old playing with a live Mills bomb.'

Later, with Hadley accompanying him, Ernest returns to the front line of 1918, to the place where he was wounded, the place that made him a hero for a while. Nothing is as he remembers it. The signs still say Fossalta, but to Hemingway the town which he passed through fifty times or more in his few months at the front line is now unrecognisable: 'All the shattered tragic dignity of the wrecked town was gone.' Instead of ruins, which might have conveyed to his wife the drama and pathos of what had happened nearby, they find 'a new, smug, hideous collection of plaster houses'. Even the people are new: there are migrants from Naples and Sicily living here now. 'I was here during the war', he tells a young woman, by way of explanation for the unlikely presence of a couple of American tourists. 'So were many others', she replies flatly.

Crestfallen, Ernest returns to Paris. 'Chasing yesterdays is a bum show', he advises the readers of Toronto's finest newspaper, 'and if you have to prove it, go back to your old front'. Gertrude Stein has a name for Hemingway and his type, the men who experienced the intensity of war and now feel that nothing else quite matches it, who carry around with them a secret anger. It is a phrase she picked up from the owner of a Parisian garage where her Ford was being fixed. 'That's what you are, that's what you all are,' she tells Ernest, 'you're all a lost generation'.

GORKI: A small room, simply furnished: a bed, a desk, a chair, a Persian rug on the floor. Two tall trees shade the room. A mosquito net prevents the flies from getting in. For two weeks, the patient hardly moves. He tries to read but, at first, finds that all the letters flow together. Mostly he rests. Newspapers are strictly banned. There are no visitors from the Kremlin to bother him – these too are banned. Still, Vladimir's mind cannot be kept completely free of political concerns. He asks about the ongoing show trial – tickets are only issued to reliable Communist Party members – of his political enemies, the Socialist Revolutionaries, just a month after the trial of the Moscow clergy ended. He asks about the harvest. Is there a threat from the locusts? He is made to drink carrot juice for his health.

In June the patient is moved back into the big house at the estate on a stretcher. He sits on the veranda in the sun. After a few days more he starts to feel mobile again, wandering from one balcony to another around the house. This will improve his digestion, he says. Vladimir asks that chairs be placed at regular intervals so that he can make it to one if he feels another spasm coming on (he calls these 'snakes'). He makes a joke of it. Question: 'When will the Commissar for such-and-such a department be assured of not falling?' Answer: 'When he is sitting in an armchair'. He starts reading a book about the artificial cultivation of mushrooms and asks why they are not doing more of it at Gorki.

Vladimir's sister Maria bans the playing of the piano so as not to jangle her sick brother's nerves.

MUNICH – BERLIN – LEIPZIG – KIEL: In late June, Adolf begins his deferred jail sentence for breaking up a Bavarian political meeting last year.

The same day in Berlin men in leather coats shoot up the car of Foreign Minister Walther Rathenau as he drives to work. A grenade finishes the job. The murderers are members of the Organisation Consul terrorist cell which killed Erzberger last year, who dislike Rathenau's reparations policy and believe their prey to be one of the latter-day Elders of Zion. They escape on foot. Two are eventually tracked down to a medieval fortress outside Leipzig, where they are killed in a police siege. The driver of the getaway car is turned in by a family member and sent for trial.

Germany reels. Is there any end to the upheavals the country must go through? The Rhineland is occupied by foreign powers, the question of reparations hangs over the country's future, stability is threatened from Communists and putschists of all stripes. There are tumultuous scenes in the Reichstag. Conservatives and nationalists are held responsible for Rathenau's murder by having so vehemently condemned his policy on reparations. That very evening, the Chancellor invokes a special provision of the German constitution – Article 48 – to push through emergency security measures. 'Rising terror and nihilism, frequently cloaked in the mantle of national sentiment, must no longer be looked upon with indulgence', he declares. 'We cannot go on as we did before.'

Rathenau's murder has wide implications. There is concern in Moscow that it may affect relations with Russia. Vladimir manages to hear of the murder despite the ban on newspapers at Gorki. ('Well, did Rathenau slip?' he slyly asks one of his interlocutors, unwilling to be drawn into a conversation about Germany.) After a period of relative stability, the German mark crashes against the American dollar. Rathenau's picture appears on the front page of the *New York Times* above reports of a royalist coup in the works. In Germany, university lectures are cancelled. There is one exception. In Heidelberg, the anti-relativist and anti-Semite Philipp Lenard decides to carry on as before in protest at the overreaction to a traitor's death. He is nearly thrown into the Neckar river as a result.

At Rathenau's funeral, held in the Reichstag, his mother sits on a red brocade throne in what used to be the Hohenzollern royal box. After a short oration, the coffin is carried out past a statue of Kaiser Wilhelm – it is said some republicans wanted it covered in black cloth during the ceremony – and then raced by motorised hearse to the cemetery to prevent a riot breaking out around the German parliament. Albert Einstein is prominent amongst the mourners. Sympathy marches are organised in cities across Germany.

Rumours circulate of further assassination lists. The name Einstein is said to be near the top. After the funeral, Albert goes to see a play by Ernst Toller, and laments how far Germany has fallen: 'O, people of poets and thinkers, what has become of you!' He cancels public-speaking engagements, including at a prominent gathering of German scientists in Leipzig. Rightwing newspapers accuse him of running away, either because he is worried about being unmasked as a fraud or simply to create yet more media attention. 'The Fugitive Relativity', runs one headline. Einstein blames it all on the English and their damned eclipse expedition in 1919 for having made him so famous in the first place.

'Where will this dangerous mental derangement lead us?' he asks a friend.

DUBLIN – LONDON: An Irish constitution – approved in London – is published in Ireland, and an election held the same day. The treaty side wins.

But before the final tally is announced, news comes in from London which may change everything. An Irish-born retired field marshal in the British army – much hated by the IRA as a security adviser to Belfast – is assassinated on the steps of his London home on his return from unveiling a memorial to the dead of the Great War. The killers wave down a taxi to try to escape the scene. A shoot-out follows in the streets of Belgravia, near where Michael Collins stayed while negotiating the treaty last year. Both men give false names when arrested, though their true identities are soon uncovered. Both served in the British army in the war. One lost a leg below the knee. In France, they fought for freedom, they explain. Yet that same freedom has not been given to Ireland.

'I do not approve, but I must not pretend to misunderstand', declares Éamon de Valera. The *Irish Times* mourns the loss of a great Irishman in Field Marshal Sir Henry Wilson. 'Our whole country ought to be in mourning', write its editors. Such an act can only further estrange north and south. 'It may provoke reprisals and counter-reprisals, until not only Belfast, but the whole country, runs with bloodshed.'

There is shock and panic in the British capital. Some believe that Collins, through weakness or intent, must bear the blame. But suspicion falls most heavily on the rebels in Dublin's Four Courts – the republicans who reject the treaty and want no Free State.

London demands immediate action be taken by the Irish government to dislodge the rebels, warning it will send in its own troops to do the job if not.

NEW YORK: *Shuffle Along* is coming to the end of its run in New York, after five hundred performances, and everyone wants a piece of its success. The fashion for black revues – or 'Negro Revues' as the newspapers call them – is spreading. In June, *Strut, Miss Lizzie* opens at the Times Square Theatre, a two-act musical entertainment (written by two white composers) that 'glorifies the creole beauty'.

In July, Josephine Baker turns sixteen – which makes it legal for the twice-married chorus girl to work in the state of New York – and *Shuffle Along* goes on a nationwide tour, with Josephine as one of the show's chief attractions, even if most people are more likely to remember her funny-girl antics than her name.

DUBLIN: Waving her credentials from an American newspaper, the intrepid Clare Sheridan talks her way into the Four Courts. Inside, she notes a

Rolls-Royce armoured car on which someone has painted the words 'The Mutineer'. The rebels are young. They have no proper uniforms. They do not stand a chance.

She interviews their leader. He arranges bullets on the table in front of him while he replies to her questions, clearly uncertain whether he should be talking to her at all. The republic is the only true cause, he says. The oath to the British Crown cannot be stomached. 'Irishmen will walk into English jails with their heads high,' he declares, 'but they never can hold their heads high as subjects of a British colony.' He calls Michael Collins an opportunist and a bully.

Guns open fire on the Four Courts the next morning, early Wednesday. It is not a very determined attack. Collins hopes the bombardment will persuade the anti-treaty IRA men to leave; he does not want to kill them all. Chunks of stone masonry crash down into the streets. Gunshots echo through Dublin. It is like 1916 again, but it is Irish fighting Irish now. Free State artillery pieces (borrowed from the British army) fire shells filled with shrapnel. Occasionally, they overshoot their target and the shells explode further afield. The British encourage the Irish to hurry up. Churchill offers British aeroplanes – painted in the colours of the Free State – to finish the job.

By Friday, the Four Courts are empty. The archive holding Ireland's public records going back centuries is lost to fire. Pockets of resistance remain in Dublin's central quarter. Several hotels are occupied. O'Connell Street becomes a battleground. De Valera joins the rebels, taking his oath of service just as he did six years ago. Provisional government soldiers slowly close the net. By the time the fighting stops, several dozen Irish have been killed – civilians, too – and civil war is beyond recall. Éamon de Valera – professor, prisoner, President and now fugitive again – escapes in a Red Cross ambulance.

DOORN: The Kaiser's secret female correspondent comes to stay at Huis Doorn. Within a matter of days, Princess Hermine and Wilhelm are engaged.

One of the Kaiser's sons warns his father that his remaining supporters in Germany will not look kindly upon remarriage so soon and suggests he think again before things are made public. (In response, Wilhelm calls him a good-for-nothing bum.) The Kaiser's daughter comes to Doorn to discuss what she calls 'The Subject'. She is convinced that her father has deluded himself and that Hermine will leave him as soon as she gets bored – which, she judges, won't be long.

The Kaiser will not be put off. For once, he tells himself, he is not going to be told what to do. 'I've given everything to the German people: my crown, my freedom, and yes, my wife', Wilhelm complains to his adjutant. 'My sacrifices stop with matters of the heart.' A wedding in November is planned. Affairs will be kept under wraps till then.

ISTANBUL: In the Ottoman capital, there is anxiety amongst the Sultan's supporters about his future, and squabbles amongst European diplomats over what to do should Mustafa Kemal and the nationalists lunge for Istanbul itself.

The French and Italians want a deal. Only the British seem willing to resist the rising star, their presence strengthened by the arrival of HMS *King George V*, the battleship on which Kaiser Wilhelm once hoisted the flag in celebration of Anglo-German friendship before the war.

Fearing they are about to be deserted, the Greeks threaten their British allies that they will occupy Istanbul themselves if necessary. The British Ambassador's wife is outraged: 'The cheek of them!'

Diplomats scurry around to give another chance to negotiation between Kemal and the Greeks. Venice is suggested as the venue for a peace conference, or perhaps the Italian-held island of Rhodes. It could even be held aboard a British naval ship. Time is short. The Turks will not wait for ever.

ACROSS SOUTHERN IRELAND: The fight moves out of Dublin and into the countryside. Michael Collins makes himself commander-in-chief of the Free State forces. He dons an army uniform and races around the country inspecting the troops and barking orders as he tries to end the conflict before it gets any worse. There can be no winners in such a war. The best end is a quick one.

'Of all things, it has come to this', he writes to an old friend, with whom he once jousted for the heart of Kitty, and who has now sided with the republicans against the government. 'You are walking under false colours', he continues, begging the recipient to change his mind.

The people are supporting the government. In much of the south, the republicans melt away. In Cork, they go out in an orgy of destruction and burning.

MOSCOW: For the inhabitants of the Kremlin, there is a strange absence over the summer months.

In place of the usual avalanche of telephone calls and memorandums and letters there is silence from the office of Vladimir Lenin. It is unprecedented. For some, it is not entirely unwelcome. But the absence of the leader slowly turns into a scramble for power. Émigré papers speculate as to the true state of the dictator's health. Some write of his 'retirement'. A deputy has taken over temporary duties of chairing the Sovnarkom, the cabinet. The Politburo is meeting without Lenin for the first time in years.

It is natural to have ideas about where this all might lead. The scheming has already begun. A bloc is formed that tries to sideline Trotsky. Stalin is its chief organiser, but not yet its leader.

OCCUPIED RHINELAND, GERMANY: Clare Sheridan discovers it is bloody hard to get a square meal in the Rhineland these days.

In the town of Aachen, under occupation by Belgian forces since 1918, she is told that there is no milk to be had. (The delivery of cows to France as war reparations-in-kind is blamed.) In Cologne, it is the British who are in charge, but the café along the way still has nothing to offer in the way of proper sustenance. In Koblenz, the Americans rule the roost, and here it is alcohol that is unobtainable. (Local children, Clare notes, have picked up the American word 'swank', which well describes the shiny new US Army uniforms compared to those of the clapped-out British.) In Wiesbaden, where Rhineland separatists tried to proclaim their own independent state in 1919 – with the rumoured backing of Paris – it is French soldiers who are in control. A bevy of tourists have followed in their wake, taking advantage of the fall in the value of the German mark.

To a person carrying foreign currency Germany is cheap – if you can find what you want, of course. Clare buys a pair of fine leather gloves for the princely sum of half a dollar. Germans with any money spend it as soon as they can. Who knows what it might be worth tomorrow?

FRINTON-ON-SEA, ESSEX, ENGLAND: August is bittersweet for Clementine.

One year since little Marigold Churchill fell ill and died, and only a few months until her and Winston's next child is due to be born. Clementine is still just about able to chase her elder children around the garden of the house they have rented for the summer holidays. The sea is not far away. The children compete in a tennis tournament at the local club. Winston is away in France – he tries to resist the casino at Biarritz and fails – but will be back before the end of the month, no doubt with plans for new sand-castles, as is his general inclination when on the beach.

'I feel quite excited about the arrival of a new kitten', Clementine writes to her husband: 'darling, I hope it will be like you.' Winston, in between corresponding with Michael Collins and Chaim Weizmann, recalls the awful sadness of the year before: 'A gaping wound whenever one touches it and removes the bandages and plasters of daily life.'

He, too, looks forward to 'a new darling kitten to cherish'.

GORKI: When the patient is feeling a little better, the doctors allow him into the garden to examine the flowers. He is deeply offended when one of the medical staff looking after him suggests he might be up to a game of draughts – but only with bad players. 'They think I'm a fool', he complains.

Dmitri brings his son to see Uncle Vladimir. Inessa Armand's children are also allowed to visit Gorki. Vladimir's sister Maria does not approve; but Nadya, his wife, does. There is a row, bringing on one of Lenin's headaches again. A dog is acquired, to whom Vladimir develops a strong attachment. The impatient revolutionary is given various tasks to improve his motor skills. He tries basket weaving, but finds it irritating and gives up after one basket. He scrawls a letter to Stalin – his writing is so bad that Maria has to countersign – asking him *please* to rid him of the two German doctors who have been assigned to him: 'extreme concern and caution can drive a person out of his mind'. At one point, Vladimir comes up with the idea that the Gorki estate tennis court should be used instead to breed rabbits.

There are pauses, obstacles, reverses – but as the weeks go by, the dictator's health continues to improve. He is sleeping better. His dreams are less troubled. 'You can congratulate me on my recovery', Vladimir writes in his own hand to his secretary in July: 'The proof is my handwriting, which is beginning to look human again.' He asks her to start preparing books for him, firstly of science, then fiction and lastly politics (he is not allowed that kind of book just yet). A few days later he is able to celebrate the next breakthrough. 'I have been permitted to read the papers!' he tells Stalin. 'Old papers from today, and new ones from Sunday.'

After an angry outburst against the ban on political visitors – it is the *lack* of politics which makes him ill, he tries to explain – the doctors allow Lenin to meet with fellow members of the Politburo. Leon Trotsky is invited, but does not come. Stalin travels down to Gorki. A bottle of wine is prepared to slake the Georgian's thirst.

One day, Lenin sends a note to Stalin enquiring about progress with the expulsion of intellectuals he proposed before he fell ill. Vladimir picks on the staff of some magazines he has decided he does not like. 'All of them must be chucked out of Russia', he writes. 'No explanation of *motives* – leave, gentlemen!' Lenin's note is immediately passed on to the GPU. At last Vladimir will be able to rid Russia of those annoying people who disapprove of him, the baying crowds he dreamed of earlier in the year, hoping for Lenin the mountain climber to fall from the snowy peaks to his death in the ravines below. *But he won't. Oh no.*

SEEFELD, AUSTRIA: A momentous decision. Members of the inner circle of psychoanalysis – the Committee – decide to address each other using first names and the informal German *Du*. Sigmund Freud will continue to refer to the Committee using surnames and the formal *Sie*.

On holiday in Berchtesgaden he has sad news from Vienna to report to his family – the suicide of his niece Mausi, Anna's prospective tennis partner, by poisoning.

EASTERN TURKESTAN: Enver Pasha, the last of the Ottoman Empire's three wartime leaders to remain alive, is run to ground in Turkestan. His intrigues have caught up with him. His plans for a Muslim rebellion against the British, against the Russians, against the world, have come to this: a small band of followers, tracked down to a hillside lair. He dies with a Koran in his hand.

LAKE GARDA: What a transformation! The humble villa which Gabriele D'Annunzio got his hands on in 1918 is now being turned into a dream of Italian glory in plaster, paint and gold. Gabriele acquires colonnades, tombs and statues to fill out the garden. He creates a throne for himself and surrounds it with seventeen columns to signify the greatest Italian victories of the Great War (and a broken half-column to represent Caporetto). He calls his new palace the Vittoriale degli Italiani – the Shrine of Italian Victories.

The poet has zigged and zagged a bit since his Adriatic adventure. He has written some successful books, and then spent the proceeds as quickly as he can. His talent for extravagance is undimmed. He refuses the opportunity to stand for election – parliament would not suit him – but, somewhat quixotically, accepts a role as leader of the Federation of the Worker of the Sea, a union often in competition with Fascist syndicates in Italy's main ports. Some whisper that drugs have got the better of him (cocaine, it is said). He is well known as something of a sex fiend, a condition he links to his creative passion. For most, however, Gabriele D'Annunzio is still the hero of Fiume. He declines to visit the town, despite the best efforts of his old legionnaires, who tell him he could take it over again whenever he wants.

As always, his attitude towards Mussolini is unclear. Should Benito consider him a risk? No doubt if Gabriele put his mind to it, he could be. But does he want the responsibility? His haranguing days appear to be over, at least in public. He prefers to communicate with his adoring fans in writing. Then, in Milan of all places, D'Annunzio is flattered into saying a few words in public – hardly a speech, and no one can quite understand what he is saying anyway. But the content hardly matters, for Gabriele is surrounded by a group of blackshirts while he talks. Though he does not even use the word, *Il Popolo d'Italia* proclaims this as D'Annunzio's formal coming out as a Fascist. This is NOT what he intended, he complains.

A few days later the poet falls out of the window of his house and bangs his head. Was he pushed or did he jump?

GORKI: By the time the summer heat reaches its peak in August, ten million Russians are being fed every day by the American Relief Administration. There are almost no reports of deaths from starvation now. The situation is improving.

In Gorki, Vladimir has the worst seizure he has had for a long time. All he can say is 'yes, yes', then 'no, no', and finally 'oh hell'. The right side of his body twitches. Doctors observe a reflex identified by Babinski – André Breton's teacher at La Salpêtrière all those years ago – and generally associated with a disease of the spinal cord or brain. It takes nearly two hours for him to recover.

Another morning, at breakfast, he feels so good that he could eat for a hundred people. Stalin comes to visit again, wearing an impressive white jacket. Maria experiments with taking photographs of her brother with the Georgian bank-robber in his weekend finest.

BERLIN – MUNICH: The public order measures introduced by emergency decree after the assassination of Walther Rathenau are now passed permanently into law.

In Munich, Adolf Hitler, newly released from his one-month prison sentence, vehemently criticises the legislation. He claims its purpose is not to stabilise Germany but simply to shut down healthy criticism, free debate and alternative points of view to that of the so-called moderate centre. It is a flat-out lie, he declares, to say that the republic is somehow under threat.

Meanwhile, in the shadows, Adolf works on an idea for a putsch to take control of the Bavarian government, with the expectation that success in Munich would spark nationalist uprisings elsewhere in Germany. He tries to make peace with the most important nationally minded organisation in Bavaria, whose leader claims to be able to mobilise forces across the whole of Germany through allies from Stuttgart to Stettin.

The excitement comes to nothing. There is no coup. Hitler feels let down by his supposed allies. He swears he will not let it happen again.

NEW YORK: Based on all its legal and financial travails of the last few months, William Du Bois publishes an in-depth *exposé* of the Black Star Line, every bit as detailed as the *New York World*'s dissection of the Ku Klux Klan last year, and every bit as damning.

There are excerpts from sworn testimony showing the cack-handed management of the shipping line. There are stories of bills unpaid and monies stolen. There are tales of cargoes wasted and losses hidden. There is no need for much commentary. The testimonies and the figures speak for themselves. The *exposé* covers five searing pages in *The Crisis* – in between an account of the difficulty *Shuffle Along* is having in finding a new permanent home (white entertainment monopolies are blamed), a report on the latest push for the anti-lynching law, and a review of a French novel by a black author from the Gabon who has just won the Prix Goncourt.

Up the road, Garvey presides over the latest convention of the UNIA. A full-blown cult of personality has grown up around its leader by now. Recordings of his speeches are available for purchase; large portraits of him grace the walls.

BÉAL NA BLÁTH, CO. CORK, IRELAND: Late August. A tour around an Irish constituency by its elected representative. The day plays out hazily: drinks in various country pubs, a visit to a former schoolteacher, an encounter with an old friend of his mother's, a meeting with his brother.

Michael Collins's advisers are against such a journey at a time like this. But he insists: 'Ah, whatever happens, my own fellow countrymen won't kill me'. Éamon de Valera is said to be in that part of the island too, holed up in a hut somewhere. Perhaps the two will meet. It is evening before Collins's convoy starts back to Cork, down a quiet valley, the light falling softly through a fine drizzle.

A cart blocks the road. Collins's car slows down. A small IRA ambush party, on the point of dispersing after a long day's wait, open fire. Another gunfight to add to hundreds before it these past few years. An hour of shooting. A bullet enters Michael Collins's skull. Ebbing life, his body is carried around the Cork countryside in desperate search of a priest. Collins's men get lost in the dark. They find blown-up bridges and rain-sodden fields barring their way.

The world's newspapers report the death of a hero, a paragon of virtue, the humble Irish peacemaker. The ambush is magnified out of its true dimensions, and raised from a gunfight into a full-scale battle, with two hundred IRA fighters imagined as the slayers of this single man, his detachment outnumbered ten to one, his last generous words reported as 'forgive them'.

How can Ireland ever recover from such a blow? Republican prisoners in Irish jails sink to their knees to recite the Rosary for their fallen enemy's soul. Churchill sends condolences. On the day of his funeral procession in Dublin, an Irish flag is draped over Collins's coffin, loaded on a gun carriage led by six black horses, priests and soldiers marching behind. A single flower, a white lily, rests upon it, too: sent by Kitty, Collins's fiancée. No innocence left in Ireland's war.

De Valera is still at large.

DUMLUPINAR, TURKEY: To divert the Greeks from the threat of an imminent attack, a false story is circulated that a tea party is to be held at Mustafa Kemal's house in Ankara on a particular day in late August 1922. The Turkish attack comes the following morning at dawn. The Greeks fall back in disarray. At last Kemal is able to issue the order for their wholesale expulsion: 'Armies! The Mediterranean is your immediate objective. Forward!'

Two hundred miles away, in Smyrna, word of the Turkish advance is met with surprise. But not yet with panic.

GORKI: Almost back to normal. One day, Vladimir is able to ride a horse for a mile or so. Nadya and Vladimir are taken out to hunt for mushrooms in a nearby forest. Vladimir jokes about an article by an English journalist referring to Nadya as the 'First Lady' of the Soviet republic. She is the 'First Ragdoll', he declares, a jovial comment on the poorness of her clothing.

Towards the end of the summer, Vladimir allows himself to entertain a truly delightful thought: a return to work in the autumn. He presses his case on his doctors. They see they have no choice. To prevent Vladimir Lenin from working would kill him just as surely as allowing him to work as hard as before.

Vladimir has plans for a reshuffle of his government. Perhaps things can be smoothed out between him and Trotsky. Leon is offered a position as one of his formal deputies (one of several). The principled non-tipper turned war supremo categorically refuses Lenin's offer as humiliating. He has his heart set on a grander job managing the planned economy. Anyway, he is about to go away on a month-long holiday.

BLACK FOREST, GERMANY – NEW YORK: On the search for the best fishing this side of Horton Bay, Michigan, the Hemingways head to southern Germany, where their dollars go even further than in Paris. Indeed, with the rate of German inflation ticking as it is, a dollar seems to go a little further every day. For the first time in his life, Hemingway decides to grow a moustache. Back in America, a book entitled *Tales of the Jazz Age* is published.

SMYRNA: Broken Greek troops and hungry refugees are pouring into Smyrna. The quayside heaves with soldiers. This is not a retreat, it is a rout. It is not a setback, it is a shocking defeat. The Greek commander himself has been taken prisoner. The harbour is crowded with boats trying to make good their escape. Smyrna is left without police, without protection.

For a few days, the mood of Smyrna's foreign and Christian communities hovers between despair and resignation. There is nothing to do now but wait. And what is there really to fear? Once the Ottomans ruled Smyrna, and it flourished. Now a different group of Turks will be in charge. Foreign ships lie at anchor, stern, iron-clad representatives of the Great Powers. Surely they will not allow the city to be punished. Kemal is not cut from the same cloth as Enver, Talaat and Djemal, and anyhow, Smyrna is not some remote and dusty Anatolian village. It is a key destination on Mediterranean shipping routes, famed for its Levantine cosmopolitanism, known to all the world. Besides the Europeans and

Americans who live here, many local Armenians and Greeks hold foreign passports.

On Saturday, with no police to stop it, the looting starts. Greek military warehouses are emptied out. Rival groups of Greek soldiers shoot at each other in the streets as the political tensions between them break into the open. Sensible civilians stay indoors. Turkish cavalry enter Smyrna that afternoon and, despite a few gunshots aimed at them, process along the quayside in perfect discipline. Here is admirable evidence that the optimists were right: rule by the Turkish nationalists will be no better or worse than life under the Ottomans. The Turks assure the public that they will maintain order in the city. They will not allow the mob, from whatever community, to take over. But by evening the disturbances have already returned. Broken glass, gunshots, the occasional explosion: the sound of ancient scores being settled and opportunities for personal enrichment taken.

An atmosphere of suppressed panic takes over the Christian parts of the city. There is a rush for places of supposed safety. Armenians shelter behind the walls of their church compound. Europeans take cover in foreign hospitals. Native-born Americans head to the protection of the consulate, while naturalised Americans are gathered in the Smyrna Theatre. Anyone not formally entitled to be there is thrown out.

AUTUMN

Moscow: An illustrated supplement of Pravda appears: *Comrade Lenin on Vacation*. There are several photographs of the dictator. In one he has picked up a cat and is cradling it in his arms. In another he is walking down a lane in the garden at Gorki. There are pictures of Vladimir with his wife Nadya. And a picture of him with Stalin, with the hale and hearty Georgian smartly attired in his bright white jacket while the clearly frail Lenin wears rumpled green-grey. This is an image which matters: the loyal Georgian by the master's side. (Trotsky has meanwhile just been reprimanded by the party for a breach of Communist discipline in refusing the job he was offered.)

Comrade Stalin writes an article to accompany the photographs. 'I have to do it, since the editors insist', he claims modestly. He describes two visits to Gorki, the first in July, the second in August. On the first, Lenin looked like an 'old fighter', his face creased with fatigue, but inquisitive as always. On the second, Stalin writes, he was a changed man: 'Calmness and confidence have fully come back to him.' The Georgian describes the range of weighty topics that Lenin wished to discuss with him – currency matters, foreign affairs, the harvest, America's position – which reflects well on both Lenin's acuity and Stalin's importance.

They even discussed rumours of Lenin's death. Lenin's response, the Georgian writes, was spiteful towards those who wish him ill: 'Let them lie and that way console themselves; there is no need to take away from the dying their last consolation.'

Smyrna: Outside the city, skirmishes continue between conquering Turkish troops and Greek stragglers trying to escape to the sea. The largely foreign-owned villas of Bournabat are ransacked. Churches are violated. The new Turkish governor – a general appointed by Mustafa Kemal, with a fearsome reputation for his activities against the Christian population in the Black Sea region – calls the Greek bishop of Smyrna to his headquarters, denounces him as a traitor and then sets him free on the streets of the city, where he is immediately lynched.

These are strange days in Smyrna. No one is sure who is in charge. No one is prepared to take responsibility for dealing with the nightly outbreaks of violence: not the foreign forces at anchor outside Smyrna, who are wary of being seen to intervene, nor the Turkish authorities who seem unable or unwilling to rein in their men. Accurate and impartial information is impossible to come by. Stories of resistance against the Turks circulate alongside rumours of imminent catastrophe for anyone seen as a threat to their grip on the city. A hysterical Armenian priest begs an American naval officer to save the lives of thousands of his co-religionists, said to be sheltering from Turkish sniper fire and bombings, fearful they will all soon be killed.

Christian refugees from the hinterland fill the waterfront and the city's parks. They will not be able to return home, insists the Turkish governor. Their houses and villages have been destroyed by Greek soldiers in their retreat. 'Bring ships and take them out of the country,' he tells a foreign delegation, 'it is the only solution'. He breaks off the conversation to greet the arrival of another unit of Turkish cavalry. 'Look at them,' he says proudly: 'five hundred kilometres in twelve days.' Greek prisoners of war are paraded through town. The city's bars are still open.

Visiting Smyrna for the first time since its reconquest, Mustafa Kemal meets a young Turkish lady, Lâtife, from a good family, just returned from legal studies in France, and promptly falls in love. Lâtife seems purer and more suitable as a mate than Fikriye, a cousin by marriage. Kemal is delighted to discover she wears a locket around her neck containing his picture. One afternoon, as the ransacking in the Armenian quarter of the city continues and as the foreign powers scramble to organise the departure of their own citizens, Kemal turns up at the Grand Hotel Kraemer Palace and orders a glass of *rakı*. He asks idly whether King Constantine ever did the same. On discovering the answer is negative, Kemal replies suavely: 'in that case, why did he bother to take İzmir?'

As the days wear on, Turkish military discipline breaks down. The city is engulfed in violence. Americans report casual murder in the street, daylight looting, back-alley executions. British sailors watch atrocities being committed on shore through their field glasses. Corpses float out to sea. A British reporter tracks down Kemal. The war with the Greeks is over, he tells the journalist, in French: 'There is nothing to fight about any more.' His aim now is to take back Istanbul. The foreign armies occupying the Ottoman capital must agree to leave. If not, he will be forced to march there too. His patience is not infinite, he warns.

On the day that the major powers start the full-scale evacuation of their citizens, Smyrna starts to burn. Turks are seen dousing the Armenian quarter in petrol to help the fire along. Black smoke billows into the air. Strong winds whip up the blaze. The city's firemen, paid for by foreign insurance companies, are powerless. Throughout the afternoon, American citizens gathered in the Smyrna Theatre are led to the quayside in small groups, where boats wait to take them to the battleships further off. Each group is protected by a double file of marines to prevent other refugees from insinuating themselves amongst the lucky few. As they shuffle towards the embarkation point, they hear the anxious pleas of those about to be left behind. Some claim their papers have been burned. A few manage to talk their way through to safety this way. Others drown in the sea trying to swim out to the ships. 'Without exaggeration, tonight's holocaust is one of the biggest fires in the world's history', a British journalist writes.

The fire leaps and licks its way down to the waterfront. Hundreds of thousands of Christian refugees are gathered on the quayside now, trapped between the hot fire behind them, the sea in front and Turkish troops in the side streets. A low wail of anguish rises. Men and women cling to each other in fear. Well past midnight, the British finally decide to intervene, sending all available boats in to pick up as many of the refugees as they can. Thousands of Armenians and Greeks are ferried to the American, British, French and Italian battleships that night, and over the next few days. But the relief effort is a reprieve, not a solution to the underlying problem. The old Smyrna is dead. The city's Christian population have been turned into refugees. Word spreads that the Turks intend to resettle any homeless Christians who remain to central Anatolia, within a month. Many fear another destination: a shallow grave or a funeral pyre somewhere. 'The final solution of the refugee problem', writes an American sailor helping with the relief operation, 'is wholesale evacuation.'

It takes several days for the fire to burn itself out. The world's attention shifts between awful stories coming out of Smyrna and concerns about Istanbul. Will a new war break out over the Ottoman capital? Kemal has made it clear that for him Turkey encompasses all of Anatolia, including Istanbul and eastern Thrace, the last remaining European portion of the Ottoman Empire. Will the Americans and Europeans really go to war to keep the Turkish national leader out of a city the Turks have called their capital for half a millennium? Will the alliances of the Great War hold firm to enforce a peace settlement agreed two years ago, in which no one believes any more?

'We are celebrating Smyrna, you must drink with us', Kemal tells the Turkish novelist Halidé Edib at a party on the day the fire finally goes out. He raises a glass of *rakı*. She prefers champagne, she says. Lâtife gazes at her hero, dressed in a crisp white suit, holding court. He engages in his favourite pastime: retelling old war stories for an appreciative audience. His advisers wonder whether Lâtife might make a good wife for their bachelor leader, by now the most powerful man in Turkey.

Mustafa Kemal is no longer a man in search of a role. His destiny has arrived.

NEW YORK: 'Mustapha Kemal has become the man of the hour, even as the Kaiser was in 1914', declares Garvey.

Just as Wilhelm laid the foundations for a changed Europe, so Kemal is now laying the foundations for a changed world. In the next war, he says, blacks will not fight for their colonial masters as they did in the past. They will fight for themselves. Garvey sees the uncertain situation in Turkey and the Middle East as the promise of something greater: 'We do not say a holy war; we said a race war, but a holy war may be the sign by which we shall see liberty through the race war that will follow.'

Garvey pummels the white governments of Europe and America: 'They tell us that Kemal is a barbarian and the Turks are barbarians and cannot be allowed even to live in Europe because they burned Smyrna.' But who are the real barbarians? In their colonial conflicts, the British bomb people from the air who have nothing but 'sticks and stones to fight with'. Who is more civilised: the man ordering the strikes in London from the comfort of an office with thick carpets and a telephone, or the men and women under attack, screaming for their lives?

SMYRNA: Towards the end of September, intrepid Clare Sheridan, fresh off the Orient Express to Constantinople, armed with her newspaper credentials and an old petrol can filled with clay, tracks Mustafa Kemal down to his new seaside headquarters for an interview.

He says a few words about his desire for peace (if it can be achieved). To satisfy Clare's curiosity, he affirms he is not a Bolshevik (and notes that

Bolshevism will never take root in Turkey, a country in which the peasants own the land they work). He evades questions about the Armenians, simply expressing Turkish tolerance for all non-Muslims. He gets cross when Clare suggests that there are no sculptors in Turkey as in Europe (representation of the human form is banned by Islamic teaching). Rather piqued at the implication of Turkish backwardness, Kemal points out that more than a decade of continuous war may be to blame for the current state of art and culture in the country.

Sheridan produces her trump card: photographs of various busts she has done of Lenin, Trotsky and Churchill. She proposes Mustafa Kemal be her next subject. Trapped, he accepts, before adding that he can only sit for her once he is in charge in Istanbul. But that might not be for ages, Clare protests. Kemal assures her that it will come sooner than she thinks. Turkish cavalry cross over into the neutral zone around Gallipoli a few days later.

The evacuations from Smyrna continue. By October, two hundred thousand people have left. Kemal heads back to Ankara. His new love Lâtife is told to stay where she is. 'Don't go anywhere. Wait for me. This is an order', Mustafa tells her. Fikriye – Kemal's unsuitable female admirer in Ankara – is meanwhile sent to a sanatorium in Germany, so as to recover from the ravages of tuberculosis (and get her out of the way). 'You will be well, and you will come back, my dear', a female friend tells her. '*Inshallah*', she responds.

BERLIN – MILAN: Kemal's success echoes through Europe. German nationalists treat his story as a parable for their own country. 'The man Mustafa Kemal rises and turns a seemingly helpless and unstable, disoriented and faltering mass into a unified nation', one propagandist writes excitedly: 'A *Führer* rises and shows the way'. Some admire the approach of the Turkish authorities – long before Kemal came to power – in ridding Anatolia of its potential enemies.

In Milan, Benito Mussolini declares that Turkey has now returned to Europe: 'all attempts to contain it in Asia have failed'. British prestige in the Islamic world has been crushed. The Versailles order hangs by a thread now that Sèvres has been disembowelled. 'All the other treaties, connected so intimately to one another, are now in peril', he writes. The Turkish war may have been 'peripheral'. But what if there is now a cascade of collapsing treaties? What if a revived Germany, backed by Bolshevik Russia, embarks on a similar revision of the European peace settlement through force?

Benito blames a 'Wilsonian mentality' for the current European mess: a frame of mind which tries to rationalise the world, to compartmentalise it into neat categories which do not exist, refusing to get to grips with the undercurrents of human emotion which govern the reality of power. 'A peace of the sword', he writes, would have been better than the dog's breakfast cooked up at Versailles.

But new war now would spell 'catastrophe for European civilisation', declares Mussolini. 'This is the challenge from Anatolia, illuminated by the glow of Smyrna's conflagration'.

PARIS: As late summer runs into early autumn, strange gatherings begin to take place at André Breton's studio on the Rue Fontaine. With the lights off, curtains drawn, eyes closed and hands outstretched around a table, Breton and his closest associates attempt to put themselves into a hypnotic trance, and from this trance to summon their inner voices to speak aloud.

Some find this easier than others. Two of Breton's rather more competitive friends seem to be particularly adept at falling into this dreamlike state, and then murmuring suspiciously well-crafted stories from the spirit-deep, or else answering questions, in writing, put to them by the other members of the group. Sometimes things get quite noisy. One of Breton's friends has a tendency to bang his head against the table and throw chairs around the room when under hypnosis. Simone is sent downstairs to calm the neighbours and promise not to summon any more evil spirits into the apartment block.

Breton writes up the seances in *Littérature* as long series of questions (from whoever happens to be leading the group that evening) and answers (from whoever happens to be in a trance):

Q: *Where are you going?*
A: *Where they take me.* (Then) *Where men fall dead, fall dead like snow.*
Q: *Where is this country?*
A: *There.* (Finger pointing)
Q: *Is it in Europe? In Asia?*
A: *No.*
Q: *Another planet?*
A: *Yes.*
Q: *Jupiter?*
A: *No. The furthest one from the earth.*
Q: *What do you see?*

A: *A big blue blade … a big blue blade … rolling, rolling …* (From now on Péret's face takes on a look of ecstasy which doesn't leave him until he wakes up. He seems astonished, he laughs uncontrollably.)

Q: *What is it used for?*

A: *Nothing.*

Q: *Are there animals?*

A: *An egg … an egg … an egg …*

Breton is excited. He is back on his own turf, adventuring into the world of the subconscious – other people's, this time – just as he did with Soupault three summers ago.

André searches for the right phrase to describe these adventures into the lost worlds of the human mind. Like Freud, Breton considers himself an explorer after the model of Columbus rather than purely a scientist, let alone an artist. He settles on surrealism, the word Apollinaire coined back in 1917, when André was still a medical auxiliary treating shell-shocked patients with poetic imaginations more vivid than his own.

Apollinaire liked the fluidity of surrealism – a term waiting to be properly defined. André has no hesitation now in appropriating it and giving it his own definition. 'By this word we mean a certain psychological automatism,' Breton writes, 'essentially the state of dreaming' – a condition it is harder than ever to distinguish from reality these days. Dada begins to seem a diversion. Tzara dismisses the whole exercise as nonsense.

In London, an American bank clerk publishes a rather depressing poem entitled *The Waste Land*.

PETROGRAD – MOSCOW: Over the first weeks of autumn, two of Vladimir Lenin's fondest wishes are realised.

First, two steamers leave Russian waters, carrying philosophers, academics, scientists, economists – the intelligentsia Vladimir does not like – into exile in Europe. In 1920, it was Wrangel's Whites from Crimea, sent packing, never to return. Now it is a group of people expelled not for the military risk they pose but for their dangerous ideas. Trotsky gives the expulsion a humanitarian glow. If these people had stayed in Russia, he notes, they probably would have wound up getting themselves shot as counter-revolutionaries.

But more significant is the realisation of Lenin's other wish: to return to work. In Moscow, his apartment still smells of paint from the additional renovations carried out while he was away. The Politburo meets the day after he gets back.

The dictator seeks to pick up where he left off before his incapacity. He soon finds himself squabbling with Stalin about the future form of the Soviet state. Lenin accuses the Georgian of being a Russian nationalist, seeking to sweep all the nationalities of the former empire into the Russian Soviet republic – rather than creating a federation of Soviet republics, across Europe and Asia, as Lenin himself would prefer. Stalin is forced to concede the point. But Lenin is perplexed. The loyal Georgian seems to have grown ideas of his own in his absence. He is not so pliable as before.

Vladimir tries to get back on top of the matters which Stalin and the others have grown accustomed to managing without him. His doctors are there at every turn. Within days of his return to work, inflammation of the gums keeps Vladimir awake for three nights in a row. He is ordered to cut down his working hours to 11 a.m. to 2 p.m. and 6 p.m. to 8 p.m, with regular days of rest. He tries to evade the rules, of course, coming to the office earlier than strictly allowed and, when his secretaries knock on the door, declaring innocently that he is 'not working, just reading'.

Lenin's world-famous scheming is reduced to trying to fool his doctors. He starts meetings fifteen minutes early to gain a bit more time from their regime. He brings forward Politburo meetings in the evening by half an hour to shorten his afternoon break. He always comes back from lunch with a list of comments on papers he has taken away with him, against instructions. His secretaries try to reduce stress by collecting the answers which arrive to his constant queries so he can look at them together in one go rather than in dribs and drabs. 'Are you plotting against me?' the impatient revolutionary asks: 'Where are the answers to my notes?'

The question is not so innocent. Political intrigue in Moscow is reaching fever pitch. One day someone suggests to Vladimir that maybe it is time to get rid of Trotsky once and for all. Lenin suspects they have been put up to it. But on whose behalf? Stalin perhaps, or one of the other Politburo members: Zinoviev, Kamenev? Vladimir calls the idea of dropping Trotsky 'the height of stupidity'.

But the dictator begins to sense a conspiracy forming against him. Increasingly, he feels himself out of the loop, slowly falling into the void, his authority slipping away. Who can he really trust?

MUNICH – MILAN: Adolf makes the acquaintance of a new disciple, perhaps even a new friend: a serial swindler from a good German family named Kurt Lüdecke.

Though in some ways the two men could not be more different – Lüdecke is a self-confident German who has experienced the world while Adolf is a provincial Austrian who just talks about it – they hit it off immediately. Perhaps it is the reflection of themselves they see in the other: both Kurt and Adolf lost their fathers when they were young, both have an uneasy relationship with the truth. Perhaps it is the overlap in their interests: Adolf is hungry for power, Kurt likes the thrill of risk. Perhaps it is just that each knows the other has something they lack: Adolf has a cause, Kurt has style.

Lüdecke regales Hitler with tales from his exotic past. How he gave up the cotton trade in Manchester to live as a professional gambler in France, falling in love with another man's wife along the way. How he reached his understanding of racial theories while working in a psychiatric hospital in Heidelberg during the war (thus avoiding the front, of course). How, after the great betrayal of 1918, he came up with a legally dubious scheme to sell impounded ships and surplus army aircraft in Latin America – and then treadless tyres in the Baltic. To Adolf, all this must sound like the work of a world-class operator.

Having heard the mangy field-runner give a rousing speech in Munich and deciding he is the man to save Germany, the serial swindler offers Adolf his services and his soul. As a first step, he suggests he go to Italy to make contact with the Fascists there. German radical nationalism seems to be going nowhere. It needs allies. Perhaps the dynamic Italian Benito Mussolini might be sympathetic. The Nazis have everything to gain and nothing to lose.

The serial swindler is sent off to Italy to try and meet Benito in person. (An introduction from Ludendorff is secured to help the process.) It is surprisingly easy to gain an interview. Lüdecke notes the Italian's bitten-down nails. Mussolini seems under pressure, though he waves away the idea that he is anything other than fully in control of the situation. The German and the Italian talk about the Jews. While Benito seems just as keen a critic of the pernicious role of international finance as the German National Socialists, he is unimpressed by Lüdecke's anti-Semitism. They talk about the status of the south Tyrol, won from Habsburg Austria–Hungary in the dying days of the war. Mussolini tells the German that the region is Italian, and must remain so despite the predominance of German-speakers. Lüdecke mentions the name Hitler. It barely registers with Benito.

The serial swindler asks the Fascist leader whether it is true that he is plotting a coup and, if so, whether the Italian King will be allowed to remain in office. Mussolini answers in French with a statement of typical forcefulness and ambiguity. '*Nous serons l'état*', he says, '*parce que nous le voulons!*' 'We will be the state, because we wish it so.'

Lüdecke comes back from Italy empty-handed. But the serial swindler's account of Mussolini's aggressive *squadristi* techniques catches Hitler's attention. There is something to this, Adolf decides: out of the beer hall and into the streets.

DEARBORN: Henry Ford's autobiography is now published as a book and immediately enters America's bestseller lists. Some people find it inspirational and visionary. Others find it confused. The *Wall Street Journal* reaffirms its support for a possible presidential bid.

ISTANBUL: 'There is a tight-drawn, electric tension in Constantinople', young Hemingway writes on his latest trip. He compares the mood in Istanbul to the expectation of the first ball game of the world's series, multiplied by the tension of a horse race – the 'Woodbine thrill', he calls it, after Toronto's most famous racetrack – with the addition of knowing a loved one is under the scalpel in a hospital somewhere, and you can do nothing to help. These are things the readers of the *Daily Star* will understand.

Ernest paints a picture of a city filled with 'cut-throats, robbers, bandits, thugs and Levantine pirates' – all ready to begin looting just as soon as Mustafa Kemal's armies march in. The Greeks and Armenians are busy arming themselves. The Greek owner of Hemingway's hotel tells him, 'I am not going to leave my life's work here just because the French force the allies to give Constantinople to that bandit'. The European quarters of the city are engaged in 'a sort of dance of death' – a last bacchanal in which the reputable nightclubs open at two in the morning and the disreputable ones at four. Russian refugees, worried that they will be left high and dry if the foreign powers leave, are preparing for yet another hasty exit. 'I would hate to be Kemal,' Hemingway writes, 'with all the dangerous prestige of a great victory behind me and these problems ahead.'

By day, Ernest attends press briefings by the senior American representative in Istanbul, a fan of Mustafa Kemal. He hears horrible stories of what happened in Smyrna, picking up his impressions from sailors and other journalists. By night he contends with bedbugs and comes down with malarial fever.

One day, Ernest scores an interview with Kemal's man in Istanbul, who tells him that Western fears of a massacre of Christians in the city are misplaced. He suggests reporters pay attention instead to stories of horrible violence being perpetrated against Turks by Greek troops still in Thrace, the Ottoman Empire's European toehold. 'That's why we must occupy Thrace now,' he says, 'to protect our people.' An armistice is agreed the next day between Kemal's representatives and the Great Powers. In Britain, David Lloyd George, Prime Minister since 1916, is chucked out of office by his Conservative coalition partners, his war-like stance against the Turks finishing him off. Another peace conference will be held in Switzerland in a few weeks' time. There is no doubt Kemal will get most of what he wants.

Despite not having met him, Hemingway writes a profile of Kemal, describing how he has been transformed in just a few months from a contemporary Saladin, prepared to lead the Muslim world in arms against the West, into 'Kemal the businessman', a deal-maker for peace. Ernest compares him to the late Michael Collins. 'As yet his de Valera has not appeared', he notes.

ACROSS IRELAND: The war takes a dark turn. A spirit of revenge inhabits it.

Sidelined by others who were always more soldierly than him, the man some still call 'the President' grows a beard. He is just a simple volunteer with no special influence, he tells Michael Collins's successor as commander-in-chief of the national army when they meet early that autumn, just a few weeks after his rival's death. He has not the power to make peace over the heads of the men of faith now fighting for the republic, he says. It might just be the truth.

The republican campaign returns to the old ways: assassinations and bombings. A pane of glass in the poet W. B. Yeats's new home in Dublin is cracked by a blast targeting a nearby Free State interrogation house. But the republicans are picked off one by one. The national army grows by the thousand. The Catholic Church stands behind the provisional government, declaring it alone has God's sanction. 'Vanity, perhaps self-conceit, may have blinded some who think that they, and not the nation, must dictate the national policy', reads the bishops' statement.

De Valera is furious. The Church has got it wrong. He will not attend Mass until such time as the clergy correct themselves.

BERLIN: Albert Einstein responds to a series of written questions from Henry Brailsford, editor of the British Labour Party's weekly magazine, about the current situation in Germany. With the decline in value of the German mark, he notes, salaries of academics are now worth one fifth of what they once were. Musicians are in dire straits. Artists are starving. Anyone with any money tries to get it out of the country. Even the spate of political murders can, in part, be blamed on personal destitution brought about by the country's uncertain economic conditions.

And then there is the psychological factor. 'People's energy is sapped by the consciousness that under present conditions it is impossible to provide for the future', Einstein writes. Without confidence in the future, people are adrift. They seek guidance from even the most extraordinary sources.

COBURG, GERMANY: A touch of *squadristi* flair in the Bavarian hinterland. Invited to attend a patriotic festival in Coburg, a pretty little town a couple of hundred miles to the north of Munich, Adolf decides to go all out to show that the Nazis mean business.

The name Hitler does not feature in the festival's official programme. The list of talks on offer includes such topics as 'New Work Methods for the Nationalist Campaign' and 'The Homeland Schooling Movement'. A gala planned for the end of the festival promises a short play by a well-known nationalist playwright called *The Consecration of the Sword*. The mangy field-runner intends to hijack this cosy get-together assembled under the patronage of a local aristocrat and turn it into a display of Nazi power.

A special train is commissioned to carry the Führer to Coburg from Munich – accompanied by his inner circle of advisers, and several hundred members of the SA with swastika armbands. Like a Soviet agitprop train, Hitler's locomotive blazes through the Bavarian countryside covered in Nazi flags, in open defiance of the law against such provocation. There is a marching band aboard. A thirty-minute halt in Nuremberg station provides the opportunity for a nationalist sing-along.

Word of the Nazis' impending arrival has been signalled ahead. A welcoming party awaits at the station, issuing the warning that, while SA members are free to join the festival celebrations, they are not to march through town in formation. The SA disobey and start out of the railway station through an underpass. There is a short but violent clash with workers who have gathered to show their opposition to the Nazis. The main Coburg newspaper gives the confrontation a few lines, describing it as a pitiful attempt by local socialists to disrupt the festival. Adolf and his supporters celebrate the punch-up as a great battle victory against the forces of inter-nationalism and glory in the black eyes and sore heads suffered by the enemy. 'After the ruthless punishment they just received,' reports the *Beobachter*, 'they'll remember this little moment for a month.'

In his speech at the festival that evening, Hitler rails against the 'demo-cratic poison' that is killing Germany. He talks about the importance of a political avant-garde, claiming that all real change throughout history comes from some kind of elite guiding the masses, rather than from the masses themselves. He calls for national rather than class consciousness to be the governing principle of society. He is dismissive of capitalists who fail to realise how crooked and corrupt capitalism has become. He pleads for the concept of the *Volk* – the ethno-national people of Germany – to be at the heart of building a new economy.

The local reception is positive. Hitler's speech is amongst the best received of the festival. He uses his moment in the limelight to make his pitch for ownership of the radical nationalist movement as a whole. 'Our symbol', he says, pointing to the swastika, 'is not the symbol of an asso-ciation; it is a victory banner'.

The German mark crashes further. Last Christmas, one dollar bought two hundred marks. Now it buys several thousand.

PARIS: The occupation of the Ruhr is no longer an abstract matter. Military plans are well developed. Politicians compete with each other to attach their names to the scheme. The more military action is talked about, the more impossible it becomes for Paris back down from their threats to make the Germans pay by force.

'We are living through an armistice – an unstable armistice – not a peace', says France's leading nationalist newspaper. Making more worthy speeches is a waste of time. The League of Nations is a 'deformed child': equipped with a huge tongue for the purposes of speaking, but with no arms for getting things done. If the British are too spineless to force the Germans to pay what they owe then France will have to act alone.

MOSCOW: A ripple of applause echoes through a grand state room in the Kremlin, still decorated with the gold double-headed eagle of the empire, ten gaudy chandeliers hanging from the ceiling, an empty throne at one end. The name *Lenin* is whispered amongst members of the All-Russian

Central Executive Committee – what passes for a parliament in the brave new one-party state. A small, parched figure appears through a side door. He is called up on stage. Yes, it's him. The assembly rises to its feet.

Lenin apologises that the doctors have allowed him to speak for only twenty minutes (and no time for questions). He starts by congratulating the Red Army on entering the port of Vladivostok in Russia's far east after the Japanese withdrawal, the last mopping-up operation of the civil war. Then he turns to domestic matters: the need to prevent abuse of the new economic policy he has instituted, the need for greater efforts in the sphere of industrialisation, his dissatisfaction with the inefficiency of the machinery of state and the 'deluge of paper' which he himself has done so much to create. It will take years before such things are fully worked out, Lenin admits. In the meantime, the central role of the Communist Party is essential. It is because the revolution's promise has not yet been fully realised that its self-appointed vanguard must remain in control indefinitely.

Back at his office, Vladimir frenetically fires notes in all directions. He throws his weight behind the construction of a paper factory in Karelia: 'If there are no special obstacles, please speed up the matter.' He enquires about the purchase of peat-digging machines to boost Russia's peat production and about the distribution of money for tractors and work animals in Armenia: 'The matter should be speeded up and checked.' He issues an order banning private conversations during Sovnarkom meetings (he needs complete calm to function). He requests an update on a new Soviet world atlas designed to show how much of the earth is controlled by the imperialists: 'we will translate it into all languages, make it into a textbook; add supplements every two years'.

Nadya persuades him to go to the theatre to try and relax. They see a play by Charles Dickens, *The Cricket on the Hearth*. Vladimir leaves after the first act. Such sentimentality!

NAPLES, ITALY: Late October. A Fascist rally in the metropolis of the Italian south. The *ras* are growing impatient again.

Mussolini has been in negotiations with Italy's main political leaders for months now. He has perfected the art of the bully-boy, warning the politicians of his violent henchmen, while assuring them that he personally would much rather reach a peaceful deal with them. He has tried out the same manoeuvre on the King, assuring him of his royalist (or at least not anti-royalist) inclinations while letting it be known he would be foolish to stand in the way of a Fascist role in government (and that other royals could easily replace him if he did). Appealing to people's desire for respect and recognition, while at the same time threatening the security of their position, is a winning combination for political success. Benito knows his Machiavelli.

But the Fascist rank and file want more than just the share of power that seems to be on offer. Increasingly they want it all. They want conquest. They want Rome. Real power is there for the taking. Why not take it? To a sea of blackshirts in Naples Mussolini now proclaims himself ready. They may not have long: D'Annunzio is due to make a speech in Rome on the fourth anniversary of the armistice with the Austro-Hungarian Empire. Perhaps he is about to throw his weight behind some kind of national reconciliation. That is the last thing the Fascists need.

The idea of a theatrical march on Rome has been circulating for months. Now, finally, it is put into action. Thousands of black shirts are ironed in preparation. Back in Milan, Benito strenuously attempts to give the impression that nothing dramatic lies ahead (perhaps also because he is not entirely sure it will succeed). He unplugs the phone. He goes to the theatre. He takes long drives into the countryside. He acts relaxed. (At the same time, D'Annunzio is promised a deal with his Federation of the Workers of the Sea to keep him sweet and dissuade him from taking any peremptory action which might spoil the Fascists' plans.)

Over the next few days, post and telegraph offices are taken over in the north of Italy. Outside Rome, thousands of Fascist blackshirts assemble (though neither as many as had been hoped nor as many as are claimed). Slowly, they walk towards the city. Their leaders know the truth: they are badly armed, badly fed and cold and wet from the stormy autumn weather. A few army battalions could stop them if they wanted to. Mussolini is nowhere to be seen.

At first, the country's political leaders cannot decide what to do. Their internal rivalries hold them back. The loyalty of the army is uncertain. Don't test us, the generals warn. The Vatican is silent. Then, around breakfast time on the morning of 28 October 1922, the Italian premier finally grows a spine. It is agreed that the King will announce a state of emergency. In Rome, the roads are blocked with barricades and barbed wire. Telegrams are sent to government officials across the country to prepare them for the crackdown. It looks as if the Fascist bluff will be called. There is even talk of killing Mussolini. But then the King decides not to sign the order. The political collapse is total.

The following day, Benito receives the royal summons to Rome. He takes a while to reply. He wants to give the press time to organise themselves.

'Wearing my black shirt, as a Fascist', and claiming that there are three hundred thousand *fascisti* ready to follow his orders (at least ten times greater than the actual number camped outside Rome), Mussolini gets on the 8.30 p.m. sleeper from Milan, insisting that it stop wherever there is demand for a speech. As the train makes its leisurely progress through the Italian countryside, Benito gives interviews deep into the night. The black-shirts are selfless, patriotic people, he says. They seek only to give Italy a new government and then return to their families and get back to work. Mussolini promises he will restore Italy's standing in the world. He will give the country some style.

He arrives in Rome the next morning, in bowler hat and spats, just before eleven. By the end of the day – after yet another change of clothing – he is Italy's new constitutionally appointed leader. Planes drop Fascist manifestos from the air. There is a crush of Mussolini's supporters around the Tomb of the Unknown Soldier. A flurry of Fascist-led violence breaks out in the streets. Old scores are settled. Communist Party offices are ransacked.

For many without much interest in the minutiae of politics, the mood is one of relief. The city's florists run out of flowers to strew upon the black-shirted victors. The King, it is reported, warmly embraces Benito after he has sworn him in as premier. How different from their first encounter back in the cold spring of 1917, when Mussolini lay in a hospital bed, and the King enquired after the wounded soldier's health.

Benito exchanges messages with Gabriele in the *Vittoriale*, keeping him up to date and, with an eye to history, inviting him to deliver a public statement of support of his subaltern-turned-superior. Instead, D'Annunzio makes obtuse replies and sends a copy of his wartime speeches to help Mussolini with his new duties. 'Victory has the clear eyes of Pallas,' Gabriele writes mysteriously; 'do not blindfold her'. Benito responds in similar style: 'the vigorous fascist youth which is restoring the nation's soul will not put a blindfold on victory.' As always, the two men dance around each other.

NEW YORK – LONDON – PARIS – DOORN – VIENNA – MOSCOW – ROSENHEIM: Around the world, people take stock of the news from Rome. It is like Fiume all over again.

The tone is mostly positive. 'Every window was filled with cheering, some showering flowers upon the passing blackshirts,' the *New York Times* reports from Italy, 'while those in the streets saluted straight-armed from the shoulder, with hands extended towards the west.' (The reporter notes a Fascist from Ancona who marches with a baseball bat.) Mussolini tells foreign journalists that he is their friend. He believes in the value of hard work so Italy can renew itself. 'The country had got tired', he explains, 'it had been running in a groove too long.' He seems to bring a new energy to the office of the premier. 'Mussolini's chin may become famous throughout the world for its squareness and force', Americans read over their breakfast.

Benito is an instant celebrity. On the right, he is applauded. On the moderate left, he is seen by many as a force of renewal. He does not seem to quite fit in the normal spectrum of politics. In London, conservative newspapers compare him to Garibaldi, the nineteenth-century unifier of Italy. Meanwhile, the liberal *Manchester Guardian* calls him a 'revolutionary' and an 'apostle of national regeneration', immediately bracketing him with de Valera and Mustafa Kemal. A Swiss newspaper applauds his 'extraordinary temperament, exceptional organisational strength and marvellous ability to dominate'.

In Paris, despite public concern about just how far Mussolini's revanchist attitudes will take him – does he really want to take back Nice? – *Action française* welcomes Benito's power grab as a sign of Europe's nationalist turn. Nationalism, writes the editor, is an 'irresistible reality', even if the Continent's liberal elites don't like it and the mainstream media don't understand it: 'The anti-democratic and anti-parliamentary success of Italian fascism won't surprise any reader of *Action française*, but they will horrify the readers of the so-called "big" newspapers.' The revolt against liberal orthodoxy has finally arrived. Only in Moscow is the tone more critical. The newspapers note Mussolini's past as a socialist, suggesting that social democrats and Fascists are cut from the same cloth.

In Vienna, Sigmund Freud is both fascinated and horrified by the super-energetic Italian. In Doorn, Wilhelm compares the nervous Germans with the ballsy Italians. 'What on earth are all those field marshals, generals, staff officers doing?' the Kaiser asks. 'What is keeping them?' Over the Alps in Bavaria, Hitler is cautious. The Italian model should be handled with care, the *Völkischer Beobachter* eventually declares. The ideology of Italian fascism is a muddle. Moreover, 'it is not the shadow of the Italian Blackshirts coming down off the Brenner Pass', but rather 'the words of Hitler that are inspiring German hearts'. Nonetheless, the comparison is irresistible. 'We have a Mussolini in Bavaria', announces a party hack at an event a few days later: 'his name is Adolf Hitler.'

ADRIANOPLE — ISTANBUL: The exodus continues. 'In a never-ending, stag-gering march the Christian population of Eastern Thrace is jamming the roads towards Macedonia', Ernest writes, on his way back to Paris from the east.

Shortly afterwards, another refugee leaves his homeland quite unob-served. Sultan Vahdettin, formally shorn of his political role by Ankara, decides Istanbul is no longer safe. The palace has emptied. He tries to pretend everything is normal when the British Ambassador comes to visit, making excuses for the absence of staff. He makes his own exit under a rainy sky a few days later. Two ambulances take the Sultan the short distance to the Bosphorus (one gets a puncture on the way). A British boat takes him into exile. It sets sail for Malta a little before nine in the morning.

The Sultan is gone. His heir, a keen nationalist and quite capable painter, is made Caliph, leader of the world's Muslims, a purely religious post. The Ottoman Empire has ceased to exist.

WASHINGTON DC: The anti-lynching bill dies on the Senate floor, killed by a filibuster of Southern Democrats. Activists blame Republicans for not pushing the matter hard enough. Republicans declare the numbers were not there and the bill's constitutionality was in doubt.

Garvey blames the NAACP. The organisation is, he says, 'nothing else but the trick of the white man to control the rising ambition of the Negro'. Hopes of democratic liberation can never be achieved in white America.

DOORN: A letter arrives from England from a Mrs Frances Pelly, who claims skill as a fortune-teller. She has looked into Wilhelm's future, she writes. She sees flowers and warns him to look after the seeds.

The Kaiser's entourage are not clear whether the message is intended as a good or bad omen. Are the flowers celebratory or funerary? Wilhelm has no doubts. He interprets the letter as meaning that his second marriage – symbolised by flowers, don't you see? – brings with it the prospect of additional positive developments – seeds, obviously! – which can only mean his return to power in Germany. Italy has led the way. 'Fascism will take over in Germany as well', Wilhelm insists confidently; 'that's how we'll get the monarchy back.'

The next day, a private wedding ceremony takes place at Huis Doorn. The world's paparazzi are kept at a safe distance. Some formal press photographs are released instead. Hermine wears a knowing expression and a mauve dress of her husband's design. She leans towards the Kaiser proprietorially. Wilhelm, his face all steely self-righteousness, chooses to be photographed in the uniform he wore crossing into Holland in 1918. This is to show that he is still at war, Wilhelm says by way of explanation. It is not long before Hermine starts taking long trips back to Germany, leaving her husband to himself.

Moscow: Vladimir speaks to a Comintern gathering, in German. One of his comrades from the train in 1917 prompts him with the right German word when he cannot find it.

He blames the famine on the civil war. The Soviet state has been guilty of mistakes, but he blames them on sabotage, poor education and the machinery of state inherited from the Tsars. Anyhow, 'I don't think it will be an exaggeration to repeat that the foolish things we have done are nothing compared with those done in concert by the capitalist countries', the Versailles Treaty in particular. He laughs off the notion that there is anything to worry about with all the money circulating in Russia now: 'The noughts can always be crossed out.' Lenin even recasts Benito's coup as good news: 'this will be very useful', he believes, a wake-up call to the Italian proletariat. He declares the prospects for world revolution as 'not only good, but excellent'. A bravura performance. Lenin's shirt is drenched in sweat. He cannot remember a word he has said.

Vladimir tries to convince his colleagues, Russia and the world that all is well. He is getting better, he is in charge. He gives interviews to foreign journalists, with the questions submitted in advance. Those who have not met him before think he is fine; others see a changed man. Lenin's once-overflowing natural dynamism – the revolutionary in hobnail boots stomping around Zurich as if racing to some goal no one else can quite see – now seems forced: it is an act. His mind is more brittle than it used to be. It requires long prompting to get to where it needs to go. Lenin is quickly irritated by criticism that his policies to allow private trade to return have allowed a new class of small-time merchants to emerge in Russia, the so-called NEP-men, 'New Economic Policy-men'. Only when talk turns to the subject of Mussolini does a flash of the old dog's wit return. 'A merry story', Vladimir chuckles.

A week later, he addresses a meeting at the Bolshoi. True socialism, he declares, 'is no longer a matter of the distant future, or an *abstract picture*, or an *icon*' but something which is now appearing in everyday life. But his words are hollow. His delivery is hesitant.

Lenin's doctors are never far away. The headaches are coming back. In Politburo meetings, Lenin loses his train of thought and repeats himself. Amongst the inner circle, Vladimir is fooling no one but himself. Around the Politburo table, his comrades look at him and see a man who is no longer the Lenin they used to know. Properly speaking, he is not Lenin at all.

He is becoming plain old Vladimir Ilyich Ulyanov again, a man like any other. A man who loses his temper too much. A man a little prone to ranting when things are not going his way. A man who, one day, will do what all men do eventually.

His colleagues look at him with a mixture of pity, respect, fear, trepidation – and anticipation.

BARCELONA, SPAIN – PARIS, FRANCE: In town for the opening of an exhibition by his friend Francis Picabia – Tristan Tzara's host in 1920 – André Breton gives a talk to a local group of Dadaists. They are eager to hear from one of the movement's figureheads. They are disappointed. With great solemnity, André tells them that, after a short illness, Dada is now dead. They look at each other in horror, not sure what to make of it. Is he out-Dadaing Dada? Or is he serious?

The next day there is a real death in the family. Two doctors are called to the Paris sickbed of author and one-time Breton supporter Marcel Proust. One of them is the neurologist Babinski, Breton's former teacher, Freud's colleague and Proust's doctor on matters neurological. Obsessed with the vagaries of memory and mind, Marcel has been consulting him on and off since 1918. Proust's sister asks for the doctor's reassurance. Is everything being done to cure Marcel's bronchitis? Babinski's answer is blunt: 'You must be brave', he says. 'It is all over.'

The American Dadaist photographer Man Ray – another soul who has found that Paris is the place to be for art and life – takes a picture of Proust on his deathbed. Vladimir Mayakovsky, who is in Paris visiting the impresario Diaghilev, Picasso and a few others, attends his funeral. So does James Joyce.

MARSEILLES, FRANCE: For six weeks, the sea will be Albert and Elsa Einstein's daily view. And not the cold Baltic, but the warm Mediterranean, the Indian Ocean and the Pacific. In the autumn, Albert takes a leave of absence from his post in Germany, and heads east at the invitation of a publishing house in Japan. They consider him one of the two most significant people alive, the other being Lenin, who is unavailable.

Given the situation in Germany, the trip could not have come at a better time. Albert will be gone for months. As the Japanese ship heads southward towards Suez and a warmer sun begins to beat down on him, Albert can feel, as he puts it, his *ego* and his *id* becoming reacquainted with one another. On board, he reads philosophy. One morning, he sketches the Italian volcano of Stromboli in his travel diary. He muses on the relationship between the climate in which a people live and their intellectual life. He spots sharks off the coast of Africa.

Though travelling on a Swiss passport, Einstein is everywhere counted a German. ('Deutschland, Deutschland über Alles' is played whenever the *Kitano Maru* comes into port; German associations open their doors to him to show off their famous countryman.) But Chaim Weizmann ensures that Albert's trip is useful to the Zionist cause as well. In Singapore, a banquet is given by the city's business community, with a Malaysian band playing Viennese waltzes and American jazz in, as Albert notes, 'the European schmaltzy coffee-house style'. At the end of the evening, an appeal is made for the Hebrew University of Jerusalem. In Hong Kong, where Einstein notes the segregation of Europeans and Chinese in the funicular railway journey to The Peak, he visits the Jewish clubhouse, where he feels suddenly connected to a Middle Eastern tradition hardly present in Europe. 'A sense of belonging together is strong', he writes.

In November, they reach Japan. Einstein visits the temples and the Kabuki theatres, and lectures about relativity. He is the centre of attention at the Tokyo chrysanthemum festival, where he is accosted by a Japanese admiral in full uniform. 'I admire you', the admiral tells the most famous man on the planet before respectfully withdrawing. In Osaka, Albert speaks in front of over two thousand. He takes the train to Hiroshima – a name he will recall in horror in 1945 – and hikes on nearby Miyajima island. Albert immerses himself in Japanese culture. He visits poets and artists. He is particularly fascinated by Japanese music – so different from that of Europe – and by its stylised interpretations of birdsong or the beating of the waves. The German embassy follows the visit closely, hoping it will foster more positive political and economic relations. If Germany is to be frozen out by its neighbours in Western Europe, it must search for friendship elsewhere. In Japan, an apparent victor in the Great War, there is some sympathy with the German predicament. Japan, a major power, but a late arrival on the international scene, is also facing a sort of union of Western powers seem-ingly arrayed against it.

While in Japan, in December, Einstein receives confirmation from Stockholm: at long last, he has been awarded the Nobel Prize in Physics. Better late than never. He is part of the establishment now. The Swedish Academy awards the prize retrospectively for the year 1921, to be handed out in 1922 alongside another award for the Danish physicist Niels Bohr. (Even then, the Academy tries to avoid the wrath of anti-relativists by awarding Albert his prize not for his theory of relativity but for a quite different contribution: the law of photoelectric effect.) There is a brief diplomatic tussle in Stockholm when the Swiss and German Ambassadors, both claiming Einstein as their own, demand the honour of representing him at the prize-giving ceremony.

The whole Nobel saga leaves a bitter taste for Albert. But the money will be welcome. With the German exchange rate as it is, the prize is worth fifty times all Einstein's German salaries combined. As per his divorce agreement with Mileva, the money will go to the children.

LAUSANNE, SWITZERLAND: Ernest Hemingway is off again. Switzerland, this time, to cover the latest international diplomacy: negotiations on a final deal with the Turks, now Kemal is in charge.

There is plenty of bluster and grandstanding on display. The world has grown familiar with it all. İsmet Pasha, the Turkish representative at the conference, takes a leaf out of Trotsky's playbook, pretending to be deaf when a subject comes up which he does not want to engage with and playing for time. The British, having dumped the Greeks, petulantly threaten to storm out of proceedings unless they get what they want, which is access to the Turkish Straits and control of the oil town of Mosul. The French talk about the historic role of France in the Near East – no change there. A delegation from Moscow turns up late and, ever conscious of the free publicity available whenever a few hundred journalists are gathered in one place and bored out of their minds, kicks up a fuss about not being invited for the entire conference. The Italians speechify at length about their historic rights to the Dodecanese islands in the Aegean, making clear their intention to hang on to them whatever anyone else might think.

Hemingway, by now the seasoned foreign correspondent, tries to gather what he can. (Later he writes a scathing poem: 'They All Made Peace – What is Peace?') One evening he runs into İsmet Pasha in a jazz bar in

Montreux, busily scoffing cakes, drinking tea and joking in bad French with the waitress. Another day he is summoned, along with the rest of the hungry press pack, to an audience with Italy's new leader. Mussolini takes a theatrically long time to look up from the book he is reading before acknowledging the existence of anyone else in the room. Such is the choreography of power. Hemingway later identifies Benito's book as a French–English dictionary held upside down – and begins to wonder whether the half-crazy Gabriele D'Annunzio might be the better option for Italy. He is annoyed to discover that his rival Clare Sheridan secures a private interview with Benito and accepts an invitation to follow him to Rome.

Ernest is getting bored. When can he get back to being a writer? Or at least have some decent fun? 'HUSTLE DOWN HERE SOON', he telegraphs to Hadley, left back in Paris. She does. Before travelling down to Switzerland Hadley packs up a suitcase with everything she will need – riding breeches for the skiing they will do, and so forth. At the last minute, she decides to pack a smaller valise with her husband's manuscripts – his unfinished novel, his short stories and his poems – so that he can work on them in the mountains. She so wants to be the good, supportive wife, even if Ernest is a bit of a beast sometimes. Then, on the platform at the Gare de Lyon, the suitcase is gone.

LONDON – DUNDEE – CANNES, FRANCE: It is that season of British politics when MPs return to their constituencies to seek the renewal of their mandate, and at last the people's voice is heard above the braying of the parliamentarians. Having got rid of that old Welshman Lloyd George, the Conservatives are now in power and expect the voters to confirm it. The venerable Liberal Party, of which Winston is one of the leading figures, is divided. The Labour Party, barely twenty years old, is growing stronger and stronger, drawing off Liberal support in industrial constituencies across the country.

Winston is sick in bed in his London home following an operation for appendicitis. Clementine is up in Dundee campaigning on his behalf, with their seven-week-old baby in tow. It is several days before he is well enough to join her. He is not his normal, ebullient self. Some see Winston as yesterday's man, from yesterday's party – and a warmonger to boot. On election day he comes in fourth behind a Scottish Prohibitionist, the Labour candidate and a fellow Liberal. Nationally, the Conservatives are triumphant.

Labour win four million votes and one hundred seats in parliament. They have become the main opposition party. Winston is bereft.

'What bloody shits the Dundeans must be', fumes T. E. Lawrence in a private letter to a friend, angry at the summary ejection of that great titan Churchill. Winston tries to be more forgiving. 'If you saw the kind of lives the Dundee folk have to live, you would admit they have many excuses', he writes. No one quite knows what the former Colonial Secretary will do next. One society lady tells everyone she knows that he is going to spend four months recuperating in Rome, where the British embassy is said to have rather good tennis courts. An immediate return to politics is not on the cards. 'Mr Churchill has had as many lives as the proverbial cat', notes the *Daily Mail*, 'but the indictment against him is a long one.'

In the end, Winston decides to go to France, where he has always felt himself at home. Clementine and Winston rent the villa Le Rêve d'Or, near Cannes, for six months. Before they go, Winston pays a visit to Buckingham Palace to see the King. 'His Majesty was very sorry about the Dundee election', the King's secretary writes to Winston afterwards. 'The Scotch electorate is rather an incomprehensible body!'

Winston Churchill is out. Gone, but not forgotten.

DUBLIN: The republican campaign, de Valera knows, is already lost. Militarily, the IRA are weak and isolated, constantly on the run. Politically, they are bereft. Assassinations are a dead end. 'The policy of an eye for an eye is not going to win the people to us', he writes in a letter to the IRA's military leadership, 'and without the people we can never win.'

The Free State comes into official existence in December. (Yeats is made a Senator.) Its leaders are determined to end Ireland's civil war by whatever means. The time for half-measures, pity or hope is gone. Four Irishmen – the leaders of the Four Courts' occupation – are shot by firing squad in an Irish prison, on the orders of an Irish cabinet.

One of the men shot was best man at the wedding of one of those who gives the order. Such wounds cut deep.

MOSCOW – GORKI: One day in late November: Lenin spends five minutes in his office and dictates three letters down the telephone line. Then he collapses in the corridor. His doctors tell him he must rest for a week at least. He comes back to the office the same evening.

The next day he is depressed. His legs feel weak. He receives medication from abroad. The doses are increased. A week or so later he goes to Gorki, taking his papers with him. He is there for five days. He sits on the terrace in a fur coat, sad and silent. He is having paralytic attacks every day. His limbs feel heavy. Over the telephone from Gorki, Vladimir issues new rules for the Politburo, to try to ensure that they do not meet without him, and that decisions are not taken late at night, when his health will not permit him to attend. He tries to follow up on a row he has been having with Stalin about rival Communist factions in Georgia.

Back in Moscow in the middle of December, Vladimir Lenin dictates a message over the telephone: 'Owing to a recurrence of my illness I must wind up all political work and take a holiday again'. His writing becomes illegible. A few days later, he has another stroke. Lenin is ordered by his colleagues in the Politburo – the dictator is *ordered* – to take a complete rest this time. Comrade Stalin is put in charge of his medical regime. Its primary rule is isolation.

MUNICH: A mania has taken hold of him. One night in November Adolf gives speeches in five different beer halls. In December, he appears in ten different venues over a period of four hours talking on the same theme: Jews, Marxists and other gravediggers of the Reich. Adolf is a creature of the night.

His hyperactivity pays off. His name starts to crop up in Italian diplomatic correspondence. Hitler's growing celebrity draws the Duke of Anhalt, a young and rather impressionable aristocrat, to see him in action. (The Duke, unused to being jostled by the sweaty crowds of a beer hall, soon makes a getaway in his white Mercedes.) In Berlin, rumours swirl that Henry Ford is now funding the Nazis. (The *New York Times* reports that there is a portrait of Ford in Hitler's study.) It is surely a backhanded compliment that the party has now been banned in large parts of Germany. Adolf claims there is a price on his head.

An American military attaché is sent to Munich to check up on the situation. He finds himself having an afternoon tête-à-tête with Adolf, eager for the chance to get his message out. Suiting his argument to his audience, Hitler presents the Nazi movement as fully dedicated to the payment of reasonable reparations – once a national dictatorship has been brought to power in Germany to defend the country against Bolshevism, hopefully with American financial help. Not entirely convinced, the attaché asks an old German friend to check up on Hitler at one of his events – to see whether the afternoon and evening versions match.

The tall German who now turns up at the attaché's request to see Hitler speak is certainly a cut above Lüdecke. At Harvard, he entertained rich Americans on the pianoforte, and crossed paths with both the red-hot revolutionary John Reed and the author of *The Waste Land*. During the war he ran a fashionable art shop in New York. He is on nodding terms with Franklin Roosevelt from his luncheons at the Harvard Club and claims both Charlie Chaplin and Henry Ford as former clients. He finds his old German homeland rather depressing these days. But in Adolf Hitler, he likes what he sees: a common man able to give the masses something to believe in. He does not seem to mind Hitler's rancid anti-Semitism. These are just words, after all.

The tall German introduces himself to the former field-runner after the talk. His friends call him Putzi. His real name is Ernst Hanfstaengl.

ROME: Around eight in the evening, a messenger arrives at Clare Sheridan's room in the Grand Hotel. Benito Mussolini will see her for a private interview.

There are the remains of a light meal on the table. He does not eat much, Benito explains, pushing the plate away. His expression is one of cold disdain, as if the world bores him. Clare notes that his room is filled with photographs, of himself. Benito talks grandiosely about his origins, his disillusionment with socialism during the war, and his devil-may-care attitude towards death. He offers to give Clare a Fascist uniform for her seven-year-old son. The black shirt and the death's head emblem, he explains, will teach him to despise death. His own heart is like a desert, he says. It is the only way for a leader to live, he rhapsodises: lonely, pure and strong. The only thing that means anything to him now is '*le pouvoir*' – 'power'. As he says this, he clenches his jaw and looks Clare long and hard in the eyes. The next night, he dares to kiss her hand. He seems determined to seduce her.

Clare suspects she is under Italian police surveillance during her time in Rome. The British Secret Intelligence Service considers her a person of interest too. Not much spying is required for the Rome station to make its report to London. At a party thrown for Clare by an Italian noblewoman, she publicly declaims the advantages of Bolshevism and free love in particular. Another night, in a restaurant where the British Ambassador is also dining she talks loudly – wishing to be overheard, clearly – about how Benito Mussolini has converted her from Bolshevism to fascism. She is already hard at work making a bust of the Fascist leader – for posterity, she claims.

The commission does not work out. Mussolini decides he has told Clare too much. She rejects his violent advances. He tells her not to write anything about him. He writes her a note in French asking her to return any preliminary work she has done on his bust. '*J'aime pas les monuments faits aux vivants*', he writes, '*leur résultat est de veillir*' – 'I do not like monuments of the living; it makes them look old.' Clare decides she does not like Italy, after all.

VIENNA: The work of Sigmund Freud is stopped by news from Egypt: the discovery of Tutankhamun's tomb. 'Such important things and so tangible', he writes to a friend in mid-December.

At home, things are rather less exciting. 'Our money is stable and worth nothing', Freud writes to his nephew Sam. 'Vienna is left quiet and lonely. All eyes are turned to Germany and the impending collapse there'. To Manchester Freud sends a photograph of himself with his latest grandson. From London he orders the latest volumes of the *Encyclopaedia Britannica*, in which psychoanalysis is fully detailed for the first time.

MOSCOW: Vladimir dictates a note to his wife Nadya, to be sent to Comrade Trotsky, thanking him for his recent support in the Politburo (against a position taken by Stalin). He begs Leon to continue such work. Finally, Lenin and Trotsky seem to be moving closer together again.

Stalin gets wind of Vladimir's actions. Furious, he rings up Nadya. He accuses her of going against the express wishes of the party that Lenin be isolated from politics from now on. She is sticking her nose in where it is not wanted. She is risking her own husband's health. Nadya is deeply upset at such treatment. She does not dare tell her husband what Stalin has said.

The impatient revolutionary is truly impatient again – desperate to get his thoughts on paper before it is too late, before the Politburo cabal takes over everything. It feels like that hurried departure from Zurich five years ago. So much to do. So little time. So many mistakes of others to be corrected. That sense of being the only man with the right answers – and yet far away from getting them through to where they matter.

He can only work in short bursts. He starts dictating a series of new notes to his secretary. He orders that they be kept strictly confidential. They are not. Stalin commands that the notes be burned. A new directive is issued limiting Lenin to five to ten minutes of dictation each day.

LAUSANNE: There is still no agreed draft treaty on the horizon. The victors of the Great War grow impatient. İsmet Pasha holds firm. He quotes Voltaire. The West has interfered with Turkey's national development for centuries, he says. That must now stop. Only full sovereignty will do. No special rights for foreigners on Turkish soil. No foreign oversight of national finances, railways or waterways.

Behind each abstract term raised for discussion – nation, state, citizen, rights – lie the hopes and interests of hundreds of thousands of huddled Greeks and Turks on either side of the Aegean Sea, fearful for their future as a minority in someone else's country. How can the problem be solved? An extraordinary solution is discussed: a compulsory trans-Aegean population exchange. Anatolia's remaining Greeks will be swapped for northern Greece's Muslims, ethnic cleansing sanctified by treaty and codified in law. The British Foreign Secretary calls it 'a thoroughly bad and vicious solution'. But who wants to guarantee the rights of a Greek minority in Turkey, or a Muslim minority in Greece? And why should either state accept the possibility of an enemy people residing in its midst?

As the year winds down, conversation moves from the conference table to the dining room. The head of the Russian delegation in Lausanne sweet-talks the Scandinavians and the Americans over caviar and vodka, discussing painting, literature and other countries' politics. 'Mussolini', Chicherin says, 'has a passion, not a program'. The Italians throw a dinner party at which İsmet Pasha indulges in his taste for champagne. But the Turks remain as obstinate as ever. 'You remind me of nothing so much as a music box', the British Foreign Secretary tells İsmet Pasha one day: 'you play the same old tune day after day until we are heartily sick of it – sovereignty, sovereignty, sovereignty.'

The holiday break is cancelled. The diplomats and politicians struggle on.

MOJI, JAPAN – BERLIN: The Nobel laureate Albert Einstein has another photograph taken of him. It must be the ten thousandth picture, he calculates. In Moji, he plays the violin at a children's Christmas party.

WASHINGTON DC: Woodrow instructs Dr Grayson in the pronunciation of the latest Italian word he has learned. The middle syllable, he insists, should be pronounced like 'cheese'. 'Fas-*chees*-ti', he repeats, for his doctor's edification. Has Grayson had time to study the photographs of Mussolini's face, he asks? Woodrow has already drawn his own conclusions. 'Shifty', he decides.

Moscow: On the last day of the year, a new state officially comes into being: the Union of Soviet Socialist Republics. As a consequence of war, disease and famine there are ten million fewer people in the Soviet Union than there were on the same territory in 1917.

1923

People are doing far too well. Only when things are going
really badly will more people come over to us.
Adolf Hitler

WINTER

DEARBORN: 'Today he looms a powerful and enigmatic figure on the political horizon', says the *New York Times*. Updated photographs of Henry Ford have been sent out to automobile dealerships around the country. Copies of his new autobiography have been procured. Estimates are made of the increase in sales the *Dearborn Independent* might expect if he were to announce his candidacy for the presidency. The campaign machinery is primed. 'Ford for President' associations have started sprouting up across the country. But no one knows whether he will run.

MOSCOW: Vladimir asks his secretary to retrieve from his safe the short secret notes on the future of the regime he wrote at the end of the year. He has a codicil to add. Perhaps he is fleetingly aware of the irony. It was supposed to be workers' rule, dictatorship of the proletariat. Now all that really matters is who is on top – who is in, who is out. Personality, it turns out, is essential.

Vladimir dictates: 'Stalin is too rude and this defect, while fully tolerable in the milieu and company amongst us Communists, becomes intolerable in the post of General Secretary'. The Georgian has accumulated too much power. He ought to be removed. Vladimir has left it very late.

ROME – LAKE GARDA: His picture is everywhere: on postcards, in newsreels, on bars of soap. Italy's illustrated magazines cannot get enough of him. Photographers follow him everywhere, whatever he is doing: arriving at a train station, going for a walk. The camera loves him; he loves the camera. No one knows what Adolf looks like, but pretty much everyone in Europe knows the face of Benito Mussolini.

Benito the former journalist – the management of *Il Popolo* now passes to his brother – knows the importance of getting his image right. He has read books about the psychology of the crowds, about how they need to be fed on illusions of omnipresence and omnipotence for a politician to become a cult figure. Benito is obsessed with the news (even the headlines that his own press office has created). His lieutenants claim he gets through dozens if not hundreds of newspapers a day. Every reporter in Italy is thus put on notice that they are being watched. Mussolini is the most written-about man in the country. Celebrity-watchers declare him magnetic. Church leaders call him providential.

And yet, as omnipresent as he is becoming on the pages of the newspapers, Benito's position as Italy's leader is not unassailable. He is still a politician rather than a dictator: he must still flatter to survive. His authority – even over the Fascist movement – cannot be taken for granted. If Mussolini falters, others may pounce. Fascism's regional bosses remain as difficult as ever – they have grown too used to deciding matters for themselves. And then there is the man Benito really worries about. Gabriele D'Annunzio, although a brooding offstage presence these days, is a potential lightning rod for opposition, a national icon beloved of millions of Italians. Out of sight, but not out of mind.

In early January, Benito writes Gabriele a long telegram, asking him to publicly disavow rumours that he is not one hundred per cent behind the new regime. Such stories are damaging to the hardest-working government Italy has seen in fifty years, Mussolini writes, a government that is 'restoring the spirit and the backbone of the nation'. D'Annunzio responds with an alarming boast. 'Is it not the case that the best of the so-called "fascist" movement was generated by my spirit?' he asks Benito: 'was today's national revanche not announced by me a good forty years ago?'

Such self-confidence is dangerous in a rival. The man must be watched.

OUTSIDE MUNICH: One weekend at the beginning of the year, a hundred men dressed in army-surplus gear march along forested country lanes outside Munich. They wear Austrian ski-caps and swastika armbands. They carry flags and beat drums. In bad weather they are given the use of an army drill-hall by a sympathetic officer.

The serial swindler Kurt Lüdecke supervises the drill, hoping to provide a great surprise for Adolf Hitler on a Nazi Party day planned for a few weeks hence: his own special troop of the SA professionals. He stores the uniforms and boots at home. He buys guns and grenades on the black market. All quite cheap for those with a bit of foreign currency.

New Orleans, Louisiana: Reverend Eason, a long-time thorn in Marcus Garvey's side, is shot leaving a political meeting in a Louisiana church. One bullet hits him in the back. A second enters his skull by his right eye. The reverend was shortly expected to testify against Garvey in a trial in which the UNIA leader stands accused of using the mail service for the purposes of selling stock in a fraudulent venture. Before he dies, Eason is able to make public his suspicions about who is responsible for the attack on his life. 'I am positive', a local newspaper reports him saying, 'that my assailants were acting on instructions to put me out of the way and prevent my appearing as a witness.'

Marcus Garvey announces a fresh speaking tour. Du Bois writes another piece in *The Crisis*, calculating the membership of the UNIA in thousands rather than the millions claimed. Harlem is more split than ever between the two men.

Cannes: Has Winston had his moment? Here is a forty-seven-year-old man with a somewhat chequered career and a reputation for warmongery to live down. He is out of office and his party is out of power.

The black dog gnaws at Winston. Over the winter, he throws himself headlong into other activities: painting and writing, in particular. He meets with his cousin Clare, now writing her memoirs of her life during the last year. She tells him how beastly Mussolini was to her. She gets her revenge by writing a rather comical piece for the American newspapers, comparing Benito's daily dress to that of a magician at a second-rate Christmas party (it becomes front-page news in California).

In January, under a familiar French sun, Winston's spirits begin to revive. One day he meets an old friend on a beach and enquires what he is up to. Painting, and trying to forget the war, the Frenchman replies – and you? Churchill explains that he is finishing the first volume of his memoirs of the Great War. His French friend finds the subject of the last war 'like digging up a cemetery'. 'Yes', replies Winston Churchill, a little twinkle in his eye, 'but with a resurrection.'

Smyrna: Mustafa Kemal's mother dies in İzmir. Her son hears the news while touring the country to drum up support for the political party he has founded. He sends others to arrange the funeral. His priority is the nation.

As Mustafa rides from town to town across barren Anatolia, he sells his vision of a modern, secular Turkey arising from a decade of war. He talks of the change he wishes to see, nothing less than the cultural revolution he spoke of in Karlsbad all those years ago, when he was just a humble servant of the Sultan. Now the Sultan is no more, and Kemal's radicalism has come of age. The country will no longer bow and scrape to anyone, he says. It will regain its national self-confidence. Turkish, rather than Arabic, will be the national language. The nation, rather than religion or class, will be the organising principle of society. The strength of Kemal's convictions is intoxicating.

Traditions that can be harnessed for national renewal will be embraced. Those that prevent the country's development will be discarded. Clare Sheridan will be proved wrong: Turkey will be a country filled with sculptures, he declares, unafraid to represent the human form in stone for fear the people will mistake them for false gods. Religion will be repurposed. 'I do not like the clerics', Kemal says frankly. A few weeks later he gives a sermon in a mosque, suggesting they should become agents of change rather than dead weights on society.

Change, Mustafa Kemal tells his rapturous audiences, is inevitable and irrevocable. 'The law of the revolution is above all existing laws', he announces, and the blood spilled in the wars of independence is proof of the people's vitality and determination. When he finally visits his mother's grave in İzmir, he swears he will give his own life for Turkish sovereignty if necessary. As negotiations continue on the country's final peace deal in Lausanne, such rhetoric carries particular meaning.

Two days later Mustafa Kemal does something he said he never would: he marries. The marriage ceremony is conducted by an Islamic cleric, but according to Mustafa's instructions. Lâtife is his joyous bride. There is no honeymoon. In Germany, Fikriye is distraught when she hears the news. To Kemal's fury, she decides to return to Turkey without his permission.

Moscow: Vladimir orders books to his bedside. The subjects vary: organisational theory by the American time-and-motion man F. W. Taylor, a history of the Russian cooperative movement, a book about imperialism in China. Nadya hovers around her husband. He succeeds in dictating a few articles for *Pravda* a few minutes a day over several weeks. It is hard work. His secretaries note his frustration. If he is interrupted in mid-sentence, he loses his train of thought entirely and has to start again.

The articles go over familiar ground. Vladimir dictates a review of a history of the revolution of 1917 (which he castigates for being pedantic in its interpretations of Marxism). He complains about bureaucracy and singles out the inspectorate of which Stalin has been commissar for particular criticism. (The Politburo, not wanting the public to have any idea of political disagreement at the top, consider blocking this article, or even producing a single dummy version of *Pravda* for Vladimir personally in order to make him believe it was published.) He returns to the promise of electrification. New power plants are being built, he writes. It is coming.

Stalin occasionally phones to ensure Lenin is not doing any work of a political nature, worried that he is preparing to ambush him at a party congress planned for March, perhaps with Trotsky's help. The great drama of the Russian revolution has turned into a three-sided palace farce: the sick Tsar Vladimir; the sly politicians Stalin and the other members of the anti-Trotsky bloc; and the arrogant soldier-prince Leon, who still expects things to go his way.

ESSEN, THE RUHR VALLEY, GERMANY: Using the pretext of the late delivery of a certain amount of timber and telegraph poles – part of Germany's in-kind reparations – French and Belgian troops enter the Ruhr valley, the industrial heartland of western Germany. British protests are overruled. The French parliament votes almost unanimous support.

In diplomatic correspondence with Berlin the occupation is presented by Paris as a civilian, purely technical matter. The presence of so many machine guns and tanks is explained as a matter of ensuring the security of the engineers needed to make Germany's coal mines fulfil the terms of the Versailles Treaty. French newspapers emphasise the moderation of the French approach, in strict conformity with the law, with no motive other than to enforce the treaty terms.

The Germans denounce French cynicism. The French premier, notes one of Germany's leading papers, 'gives the impression of a man who realises he and his country are falling into the most awful stupidity, and tries to salvage something at the last minute by claiming an invasion is not an invasion and an occupation not an occupation'. 'It would seem like a joke, were it not so ridiculous', the paper concludes. In London, the unilateral French move is considered a seismic shift in European relations 'as far reaching in its effects as the declaration of war in 1914 or the armistice of 1918'. Mussolini's attempts to play the peacemaker change nothing.

The streets of Essen, the Ruhr's main city, are quiet when the French cavalry ride in. A statue of Alfred Krupp, once owner of Europe's biggest

steelworks, surveys the occupation in silence. The Mayor of Essen refuses
to break off his wife's birthday party to greet the arriving French general.
When the two men meet the general is met with a protest speech against
the occupation and Versailles. In a message to the German people from
Berlin, President Ebert calls for passive resistance: 'The welfare or misery
of the whole depend upon the iron self-control of each individual.' He
admits he has no idea how long the occupation may last.

Over the next few days, the invasion proceeds in carefully planned stages.
The French make clear they expect the German police to keep doing their
job and public services to run as usual. French military law will be applied
if needed. A protest by a few hundred nationalist youths in Essen is broken
up by local police. One evening in Bochum a German civilian is killed when
a French guard-post comes under attack. The French want to keep down
the costs of the occupation. Apartments are requisitioned. Private houses
taken over for the higher ranks. In one case, French soldiers demand the
German local authorities provide a large quantity of barbed wire. The
demand is refused.

MUNICH: Adolf Hitler spits rage. He knows who to blame for the occupation
of the Ruhr: German politicians who have chosen to disarm the country rather
than resist. He harps back to the war. The roots of 1923, he argues at a meeting
in the Zirkus Krone on the day the French cross into the Ruhr, lie in 1918.

'Germany was unconquered' in that year, Hitler shouts, 'in four and a
half years, twenty-six enemies could not bring Germany to her knees'.
Defeat came only when the 'November criminals' – the Social Democrats
and revolutionaries – 'stabbed the old army in the back'. The country's
politicians have left Germany without weapons and without honour: 'France
treats our Germany as less than one of its African colonies'. The speech is
carried in all the main newspapers in Munich. It is even reported as far
away as Berlin. 'The National Socialists want to organise an army of revenge
for the Fatherland', one newspaper tells its readers. Adolf refuses to sign
up to the idea of national solidarity and passive resistance under the leadership of the current government in Berlin, the political heirs of the traitors
of 1918.

There are 'two fronts' on which patriotic Germans must fight now,
Hitler declares, one in the Ruhr and one behind the lines against the Jews.
'We know that if they get to power our heads will roll in the sand' – just
like the French aristocrats who went to the guillotine in the French

Revolution. 'But let me tell you something', screams the mangy field-runner, 'if we are at the helm it is their heads which will roll – and misery upon them'.

Copies of the German translation of Henry Ford's book, *The International Jew*, are piled high at Nazi headquarters.

VIENNA: Sigmund Freud, the eminent psychoanalyst, swallows hard. With his tongue he feels around the inside of his mouth. There! He is sure of it. There again! A roughness inside his mouth, a faint pressure, something swollen. Dark premonitions fill Freud's mind. He banishes them and keeps quiet. Inwardly, he wonders whether he will ever make it to Egypt.

He writes to Sam in Manchester with family news. 'Oliver had got a position at Duisburg on the Rhine and expected to enter on February first', Freud tells his nephew, 'but he could not get there as the French have broken all communications.' A family wedding is planned, 'but who can fix any date in such a time'?

ACROSS IRELAND: The government has learned its lesson: there is no hope of conciliation. An end to the civil war can only be brought about by the application of overwhelming – and if necessary, brutal – force. Military courts dispense summary justice. Anyone found with a weapon is liable to be shot. Reprisals are undertaken, both officially and unofficially. Old British methods are applied by Irish forces.

Republicans adopt a scorched-earth policy, blowing up bridges and sabotaging infrastructure. More grand houses are burned down in rural areas, to warn landowners against supporting the Free State. (In Dublin, Yeats's house receives an armed guard.) The IRA expand their list of legitimate targets, as if a greater whirlwind of destruction will yield better results. It is a strategy born from weakness and desperation. The facts are plain: the republicans hold no Irish towns and are outnumbered everywhere.

ESSEN – BERLIN – MUNICH: In the Ruhr, Berlin's call for passive resistance is being heeded. The directors of the Ruhr's main industrial concerns declare that they will not obey orders from the French, and are taken into custody. Civil servants receive instructions to ignore French commands. Everything is to be done to make the occupiers' task as hard as possible.

Company archives are hidden. Statistical records are destroyed and empty trains redirected to unoccupied Germany. Hotels and restaurants close their doors to foreigners. Newspapers refuse to publish French directives.

Sometimes passive resistance turns active. The signalling system of the Ruhr valley railway network is sabotaged. Telephone lines are cut. By early February, goods transport has frozen up entirely. A wave of strikes closes down mines and factories. No coal is sent to France and Belgium.

Berlin claims the invasion of the Ruhr is itself a breach of Versailles: Germany is not the aggressor, but the victim. German aid committees take out full-page appeals for help in American newspapers. In Copenhagen, Oslo and Stockholm sympathetic articles appear suggesting that the French are creating famine conditions in Germany. German papers portray the French as rapacious, mindless, evil, subhuman. The presence of African colonial troops in the French army of occupation in the Rhineland – though not in the Ruhr – is considered a particular source of shame by some in Germany, sharpening nationalist fury at the French occupation with a racial edge and giving rise to the casual use of racist imagery across the board. The cover of *Simplicissimus*, a liberal satirical magazine published in Munich, depicts a French trooper as a monkey with a dagger between its teeth and a blood-smeared sabre dangling by its feet.

Inside, the same issue of *Simplicissimus* sports a satirical ode 'To Adolf Hitler', mocking him and his followers for exploiting the crisis with their prophetic airs, rather than rallying around the government:

> He is the saviour! He is the prophet!
> So whisper the excited old-timers,
> Speaking of heavenly apparitions,
> And God's path marked out

The magazine costs two hundred and fifty marks these days. One year ago, it cost just thirty-six.

SAN SEBASTIAN, BASQUE COUNTRY, SPAIN: Zita Habsburg settles with her family in a little corner of paradise tucked between France and Spain, where the Pyrenees meet the Atlantic Ocean. Her house is bought for her by a local charitable committee. The family's private income – from its share of a Rhineland winery – does not meet the bills of the imperial household. In Paris, a submission is made to the representatives of the victorious wartime powers requesting a stipend for Zita of no less than seventy thousand Swiss francs a month.

A suite of tutors teach the Habsburg brood in exile. The older children receive Hungarian lessons – just in case. Little Otto's tenth birthday is celebrated by thousands in Budapest, Zita is informed by a Hungarian loyalist. He does not tell her that the church service was conducted by a junior priest, and that Horthy ostentatiously stayed away.

There is little immediate hope of restoration. Like Lenin in exile, Zita often uses code names in correspondence with the outside world. Little by little, anything Charles and Zita took with them into exile is sold.

ROME: What should a Fascist leader who has won power through a show of force, but then been appointed as premier serving a constitutional monarch, wear to work? Should he play to his base: the Fascist blackshirts and disappointed D'Annunzians? Or should he try to appeal to big business and the political centre?

When Benito meets the King, he generally opts for a morning suit and top hat, the clothes his respectful predecessors would have worn. This presents Mussolini as a pragmatic builder, not a wrecker. His quotidian attire is more workaday, a hint of radical chic coupled with the sobriety of a statesman: a starchy wing-collared shirt (Mustafa Kemal likes these too) and a black (or powder-grey) bowler hat. (This becomes his standard get-up until, years later, watching one of the American movies he so loves, Benito has the horrible realisation that the only people who still wear bowler hats these days apart from British stiffs are Laurel and Hardy, his favourite comedians.)

Sometimes he spices things up by wearing a black shirt – thus thrilling the hardcore Fascists and demonstrating that he is still really one of them, rather than a toady to the establishment. One day in January, having incorporated the blackshirts into a formal national volunteer force under the authority of the premier, Benito appears for the first time in military uniform – as a corporal of the militia.

LAUSANNE: İsmet Pasha plays billiards and drinks green chartreuse. He tells the Americans he would like to see the United States one day. Of course, State Department officials say – just as soon as he has signed the peace treaty. İsmet slaps his knee, laughs uproariously and takes another swig. The British Foreign Secretary, Lord Curzon, tries to reason with him, demanding he accept that foreigners in Turkey must retain their special status before the courts, given all the stories of mistreatment and abuse. Curzon ends up smashing his cane against the wall in making his point.

Finally, one Sunday afternoon, İsmet Pasha is called to Curzon's suite at the Hotel Beau Rivage for a make-or-break discussion. The Orient Express leaves on the dot of nine that evening, the Foreign Secretary announces, and he intends to be on it whatever the outcome. (The tactic worked for Lloyd George with the Irish, why not for Curzon with the Turks?) İsmet is presented with a final draft treaty for him to sign. He goes off to consult with his advisers. When he returns, he rejects the treaty. Nothing less than full sovereignty, he declares.

Curzon has his train held at Lausanne for half an hour in case the Turks regret their decision. The Americans work on İsmet to bring him round. He seems willing to concede a point or two, subject to further discussion. The Americans race to the station to try and haul the British back to the negotiating table. Five minutes too late. The Orient Express has gone.

MUNICH: The Nazis plan a series of *fascisti*-type events around town on what they call a 'Party Day'. The Bavarian authorities suspect the planned demonstrations are cover for a coup attempt. Some want the demonstrations (and the SA) banned. Others warn that a ban could backfire, giving the Nazis more free press coverage and making the government look afraid. The authorities draw up strict limitations instead. Adolf reacts badly, warning the police that the dedication of the SA's standards must be allowed to go ahead as planned and that if force is used to try to prevent it then he, Adolf Hitler, is willing to be killed on the spot defending his men. Such action by the government would only embolden the Communists. A single bullet against his SA men, Hitler warns, and Bavaria's government will be overthrown in two hours.

In Munich there is crisis meeting after crisis meeting to decide how to handle matters. The generals are asked their view. Bavaria's patriotic associations, energised by events in the Ruhr, are sounded out. A state of emergency is declared. The police hold a last-minute meeting with Hitler. It is too late now to cancel the event, he says: the guests are already on their way. But he promises – on his honour – that there will be no violence. The SA will not march through town in formation. He warns the Bavarian police of negative consequences should the event not be allowed to go ahead. Surely the authorities would not want to see several thousand angry citizens just let loose on the streets.

The party day goes ahead with few modifications. The government looks weak. Hitler gives a dozen triumphant speeches around Munich. The serial swindler and one-time Nazi ambassador Kurt Lüdecke does not hear any of them. Tipped off about his paramilitary training activities, the police take him in for questioning that morning. Lüdecke's apartment is turned upside down. Police find a Mexican passport and a stash of foreign currency. Adolf does not bother to visit or get in touch with him during the weeks he is in jail. The serial swindler is abandoned.

JERUSALEM, BRITISH MANDATE OF PALESTINE: Albert Einstein is ferried around in a chauffeur-driven motor car that used to belong to the Kaiser.

What a change there has been from the Palestine of 1898, when Wilhelm visited the place on an imperial tour, rode into Jerusalem on horseback in emulation of a medieval pilgrimage, declared his fondness for the absolute rule of the Ottoman Sultan, briefly raising and then dashing the hopes of the Zionist Theodore Herzl that Germany might throw its weight behind the idea of a semi-autonomous Jewish homeland in the ancient land of Israel. The German Empire is no more. The Ottoman Empire is defunct. The British are in charge now, and the promise of a Jewish homeland is underwritten in London rather than Berlin.

The British High Commissioner shows Albert around old Jerusalem, walking along the city's ancient battlements to point out the sights. Einstein is not sure he likes it much, at first. He describes Orthodox Jews praying at the Western Wall as 'people with a past but without a present'. He prefers the striking modernity of Tel Aviv, where he is taken to a power station and a brick factory. This is what excites Albert most: things being built, harmony through work, a certain egalitarianism of the classes and the sexes. 'The common people know no nationalism', he jots down in his travel diary after spending time first with a Jewish settler and his Arab friend, then with an Arab writer and his German wife. Surely this is reason for hope?

The highlight of Albert's visit to Palestine is a lecture on relativity in the auditorium of the British Mandate Police School on Mount Scopus, billed as the first scientific lecture in the temporary halls of the new Hebrew University. In order to ensure he is best understood by a mixed audience consisting of local Arabs and Jews as well as the British, Albert speaks in French. Towards the end of his trip he visits a kibbutz by Lake

Tiberias, set up by Zionists inspired by the principles of socialism. Will he come back? people ask him. 'My heart says yes but my reason says no', Einstein writes.

CHAMBY, SWITZERLAND: Up in the Alps, Ernest stops shaving. He lays off the journalism for a while. With the loss of the valise, he wonders what to do about his writing – his proper writing. A few of his poems are published over the winter in Chicago. That's it.

Ezra Pound calls the loss of the manuscripts an act of God. He advises Ernest to rewrite what he can remember. It will be better that way anyhow. 'Memory is the best critic', he explains. By way of thanks, the Hemingways decide to visit Rapallo, searching out Pound and his wife in the Hotel Riviera Splendide. Somewhere along the way, Hadley reveals that she is pregnant. Ernest feels trapped.

NEW YORK – WASHINGTON DC: The rivalry between Marcus Garvey and William Du Bois has now developed into bitter enmity. Garvey regularly calls Du Bois a traitor to the race, an 'unfortunate mulatto' who wishes he were French. In February, Du Bois describes Garvey as 'a little fat black man, ugly, but with intelligent eyes and a big head'. He declares that Garveyism is a 'bubble' which now finally has burst, however appealing the ideas behind the Black Star Line or the undoubted appeal of the back-to-Africa refrain. The two men have never even met.

Du Bois hears the same dismal message from all over the world, he writes: the warning that race war is inevitable and that segregation, ghettoisation, emigration and separation is the future. Racism has always been there, but now new and dangerous theories of race have arisen, to be exploited by the unscrupulous and the foolish, white and black, from the pavement pundits of Harlem to the beer-hall orators of Munich. Race superiority has become a cult, and its acolytes are everywhere. Two pathways now lie ahead. For a thousand years, Du Bois writes, 'from the First Crusade to the Great War', the barriers between nations and races have been breaking down. The reversal is recent, and can and must itself be reversed. Those who prophesy race war, Du Bois warns, will bring upon themselves 'a death-struggle whose issue none can surely foretell'. And yet every day, a different human story is under way: 'Races are living together,' he writes, 'buying and selling, marrying and rearing children, laughing and crying.' The struggle to break down barriers between the races may be long and weary. But that is the path that humanity must take.

In February, the Supreme Court reviews the trial of several black men accused of murdering a white railway guard in Arkansas in 1919, in the midst of what some call a massacre and others an insurrection. The black men were convicted within minutes, by an all-white jury, with a white mob baying for their blood outside. Now, four years later, the Supreme Court decrees: 'there never was a chance for the petitioners to be acquitted; no juryman could have voted for an acquittal and continued to live in Phillips County, and if any prisoner by any chance had been acquitted by a jury, he could not have escaped the mob'. Justice cannot be so abridged. Every American has a right to a fair trial under the constitution. Mob rule outside the courthouse cannot be allowed to so trample on legal due process inside. If the states do not guarantee the rights of their citizens, appeal may be made to federal courts.

In America, by this faint light, Du Bois's pathway is again lit up amidst the darkness of the world around.

MUNICH: While Lüdecke languishes in a prison cell, Adolf Hitler and Putzi Hanfstaengl get to know one another better. Adolf now seems to drop round Putzi's apartment almost every day for lunch or dinner.

The Hanfstaengl residence is not particularly grand: three rooms on Gentzstrasse and rather haphazardly furnished. But Hitler's place on Thierschstrasse has just one room, with a single bedhead which blocks out part of the window and a small collection of books. (When Putzi comes to visit he notices a book by Ludendorff, a biography of Wagner, some American thrillers and a well-thumbed *History of Erotic Art*.) By contrast, the Hanfstaengl home has life within its walls. There is a happy family at its core – very different from Adolf's own.

Hitler particularly enjoys the company of Helene Hanfstaengl, Putzi's elegant German-American wife. Adolf thinks her the most beautiful woman he has ever met. Helene likes his blue eyes, which flash so brightly when he starts telling stories about the past. He takes an immediate shine to little Egon, Helene and Putzi's son. One day, when the boy hurts his knee against a wooden chair leg carved into the form a lion, Adolf slaps the naughty wooden beast to stop it from 'biting' the child in future. Egon and Adolf become fast friends. 'Please Uncle Dolf, spank the naughty chair', the infant cries whenever Hitler turns up. Sometimes Helene, Putzi and Adolf go to the movies together. The mangy field-runner enjoys greatly a film about

Fredrick the Great, the Enlightenment-era King of Prussia who catapulted his kingdom from backwater to one of Europe's foremost military powers.

With Putzi, Adolf talks about history, politics, the Prussian war theorist Clausewitz – and America. He expresses fascination with its skyscrapers and admiration for both Henry Ford and the Ku Klux Klan. With Helene, Hitler is more relaxed. One day, he tells her of the time he dressed up in his mother's apron and mounted a stool in the kitchen as if giving a sermon from a pulpit. He wanted to be a preacher, Adolf explains. The one thing he will not talk about is his time in Vienna. Something must have happened to him there, Helene surmises. The Hanfstaengls often wonder about Adolf's sexuality. There are rumours he is having an affair with his driver's sister. Helene cannot believe it. 'I tell you,' she says to her husband one night, 'he is a neuter.'

Despite his success as a public speaker at the Zirkus Krone, where his common-man-as-messiah routine goes down so well, the thirty-three-year-old Adolf is still socially awkward. He feels uncomfortable in small groups, particularly amongst those of higher educational or social status where he is not the natural centre of attention. His fawning attempts at politeness to those for whom he feels a natural deference come off as gauche. His shaky understanding of dining etiquette is frequently remarked upon. Here is a man who heaps sugar in the finest Gewürztraminer wine to sweeten it. When confronted with an artichoke, he is totally stumped, having to ask his hostess – in hushed, embarrassed tones – how he should eat such a strange-looking thing.

Helene and Putzi introduce him to rich and powerful friends who may be useful to Adolf. They teach him social graces and educate him on the various distinctions within the upper classes, giving him the antennae to tell the difference between a man on the make such as Lüdecke – useful to the party, but not a true blue-blood – and men and women of real class, like themselves. Putzi also gives Adolf money to turn the *Völkischer Beobachter* from a weekly into a daily rag. Adolf feels he is going up in the world. The wife of a wealthy piano manufacturer from Berlin invites him to dinner in her hotel suite where only champagne is consumed, and where she prevails on the frumpish Nazi leader to purchase a dinner jacket and patent-leather shoes. For a brief period Adolf wears the shoes whenever he can.

Through the Hanfstaengl connection, Hitler makes the acquaintance of a Benedictine abbot of strongly nationalist and anti-Semitic views, who hopes Adolf, being Austrian, will somehow be able to help the Habsburg cause. The SA too starts attracting men of a different calibre from the normal roughnecks. A dashing Great War air ace named Hermann Göring joins the SA and is swiftly appointed to run it. (A period in Denmark after the war flying loop-the-loops for money and then selling planes in Sweden only seems to add to his cachet amongst the Nazis.) Hermann's Swedish-born wife Carin is as thick as thieves with Helene.

Before one of Adolf's trips to see the police, Putzi soothes the mangy field-runner's nerves by playing some Bach on the piano in the hallway outside Hitler's apartment. Adolf wants something more stirring. Putzi plays the overture to Wagner's *Die Meistersinger von Nürnberg*. Hitler hums along, marching up and down the corridor. Another time, Putzi entertains him with a rendition of various Harvard songs used to whip up the crowds before a football game, when the cheerleaders twirl their batons. 'This is it, Hanfstaengl, this is what we need for the movement', Adolf enthuses.

'*Rah, rah, rah!*' becomes '*Sieg Heil, Sieg Heil!*'

MOSCOW: At the beginning of March, against her better judgement, Nadya admits to her husband how Stalin treated her on the phone last year. Vladimir is livid. At once, he writes a sharp note requesting that the Georgian apologise to his wife, or else he will break off relations. It is the behaviour of a nineteenth-century gentleman, faced with a slight to his honour and an offence to *politesse*. But despite all the terror he has overseen over the years, such things still matter to Vladimir. He is punctilious that way. Nadya and Maria are in two minds whether they should allow this letter to be delivered to the General Secretary. They wait a day, then pass it on.

Stalin is shocked. He sends back a half-apology. 'If my wife were to behave incorrectly and you had to punish her, I would not have considered it my right to intervene', the Georgian writes, 'but inasmuch as you insist …' He says that he is willing to apologise if that will make Nadya and Vladimir feel better – but writes that he has no idea what it is he is really supposed to have done to provoke such a reaction.

The wily Georgian delays the upcoming congress of the Communist Party. Who knows what a few days more may bring for Comrade Lenin's health?

ST. LOUIS: She is dressed smartly. She knows herself. She knows the world (a little). In March 1923, Josephine Baker arrives back in her home town, three years after she left to tour America with the Dixie Steppers. Her return, as part of the line-up for *Shuffle Along* after successful runs in Boston and Chicago, earns a four-line entry under 'Negro News' in the *St. Louis Star*, next to reports that Woodrow Wilson may be back on the campaign trail in 1924.

She takes a taxi to her old home, where her family still live. Here, Josephine is still Tumpie. The light still comes from a kerosene lamp, not from electricity. The communal bathtub is in the middle of the kitchen. Josephine hands out tickets for the show at the American Theater (whites take the stalls, and blacks the balcony).

Josephine's mother is angry to see her daughter in a line-up with so much naked flesh. 'All you can see are their legs', Baker retorts to her mother's moralising. Her own role is more cross-eyed comedy than sex. The next day Josephine returns for a family celebration with a bottle of prohibition whiskey to fire things up. As she leaves that evening she promises to send money for clothes, and for the children's education.

MUNICH: There is no doubt that Henry Ford would get Hitler's vote for the American presidency – should he decide to throw in his hat. 'I wish I could send some of my shock troops to Chicago and other big American cities to help in the elections', a Chicago reporter is told: 'We look on Heinrich Ford as the leader of the growing *fascisti* movement in America.'

But, Hitler tells an American diplomat sent to investigate, Ford's financial largesse has not yet been extended to him. He hopes this will change in the future.

MONAVULLAGH MOUNTAINS, CO. WATERFORD, IRELAND: Like characters in an ancient Irish play, a group of warriors meet on a hillside to discuss their fate. They fear capture by the enemy at any moment. A tall bearded figure – he has travelled partway on horseback to this remote corner of the land – asks that he might be permitted to try negotiations with the enemy. The warriors split on the issue; they plan to meet again.

Éamon de Valera's journey back to Dublin is no easier than his journey out. Wind and rain make the going tough. 'Stuck my left leg in a boghole up to the groin', he writes in his diary. 'Arrived in the morning. Clothes and leather jacket all ruined.'

ESSEN: The situation in the Ruhr deteriorates sharply as winter turns to spring. There are conflicting stories of what is going on. In one incident in February, a German policeman reportedly refuses to salute two French soldiers and is shot in the street. The two Frenchmen are attacked in turn. A few days later there is another confrontation between local police and the French in Recklinghausen. The German police are now disbanded and disarmed – all filmed for the Paris newsreels – and their dependants told to clear out of the Ruhr entirely. There are reports that six French soldiers have raped a young girl about to be married. The Germans lodge an official protest with the French authorities – though with little expectation that any action will be taken.

Adolf rails against the policy of passive resistance. If nothing more is done, Germany will go under just like the ancient city of Carthage. 'It is perfectly clear what the French are planning', he tells a local party meeting. 'They are waiting for the warm season to send an African army of eight or nine hundred thousand in to complete Germany's violation.'

As passive resistance spirals up in the Ruhr, Paris responds with harsher and harsher measures to try and regain control. If German railwaymen refuse to do their jobs, they must be forced to work or else be replaced with French *cheminots*. If communication lines are cut, the saboteurs will be made to pay with their lives. German newspapers report the use of horsewhips against miners to get them to do their job. Viewed from the French capital, the principle at stake is non-negotiable: a defeated power cannot be allowed to rewrite the peace. Paris cannot afford to back down without prompting a crisis at home. And whatever the French or Belgian occupying forces do now in the Ruhr, it is no worse than what German forces did in Belgium and France during the war.

PARIS: At the Rue Fontaine, Breton's surrealist seances are getting out of hand. Some attendees seem addicted, turning up day and night begging to be put into a trance. One regular attendee, reportedly on drugs at the time, tries to stab Ezra Pound in a café one evening, mistaking him for someone else. As news of the soirées gets around, a number of Americans – the Greenwich-on-the-Seine expatriates that Hemingway so despises – ask if they can come along to watch. (Going the other way, one American on the fringes of Breton's group returns to New York that summer to take on an extremely Dadaist job full of promise: he becomes a stockbroker on Wall Street.)

When one of the frequent visitors of the club, supposedly in a hypnotic sleep, locks some other participants up in a room for several hours against their will, Breton decides to call a halt. Things have gone too far. André feels that he is at risk of repeating the mistakes of Dada and descending into pointless spectacle. For a while, he proclaims his intention not only to stop the seances but to stop writing altogether. 'Literary possibilities are no more interesting than political possibilities,' André tells a newspaper interviewer; 'only spontaneous forces interest me.'

It looks as if surrealism may be over before it has even begun.

LONDON – ROME: The latest diplomatic communication from the British Ambassador to Italy arrives in London.

Despite his occasional fits of temper, the ambassador believes that Benito Mussolini is an able statesman whose vaulting ambitions – whether to be the founder of a new Roman empire, or to be Europe's peacemaker – can be contained. Admittedly, he can be a little eccentric. He has recently been seen driving around the Italian capital at great speed in a two-seater automobile with a lion cub he has been given. 'The Italians seem to like this sort of thing', the diplomat notes wryly.

MOSCOW: Vladimir's headaches return. He sits with his sister Maria talking about the past. He recalls the time when he had to stay in a hut outside Petrograd in 1917, hiding out during the turbulent times when things could have gone either way. They reminisce about the assassination attempt in 1918.

He suffers another stroke. Vladimir's right side is paralysed. Doctors huddle around him. The Politburo summons a Swedish specialist at vast expense. Someone suggests a Tibetan doctor should be called in. It must be shown that everything possible is being done. As he sits at a table in his Kremlin apartment, a pen, spectacles and a paper-knife are arranged in front of Vladimir, who is no longer able to speak at all. He is asked to hand over the spectacles. He does. Good. He is asked to hand over the pen. He reaches for the spectacles again. Not good.

Stalin can breathe easily again. Lenin is kaput.

SPRING

Paris – Essen: In between articles about the health of Vladimir Lenin, and a story that Gabriele D'Annunzio has now bought a villa outside Rome which used to belong to the Kaiser, the French nation is told to keep calm and remain resolute. One journalist expresses his new-found love of the word '_Non!_' – a word he says France should use against both the Germans and the British who want to negotiate some kind of compromise. '"No" is a strong syllable; for the moment, it is the right syllable', the article reads. The war was ended too soon in 1918, when the Germans were on the run and the whole Rhineland could have been simply taken by France. 'If only on November 11th 1918 we had been smart enough to say – "_Non!_"'

In the Ruhr, the crisis risks becoming a humanitarian disaster. Food becomes a weapon. French authorities forbid the offloading of grain transported along the Rhine, insisting two hundred thousand children will have to be evacuated. The search begins for foster parents in the rest of Germany, or for empty rooms in private hostels. Local councils are left to decide who stays and who goes. Trains carry thousands away, identity tags around their necks and their eyes full of tears.

Berlin sends in money to try and keep the Ruhr afloat. The French confiscate it as soon as possible, to try and force the Germans to give up. Cash becomes an illicit commodity: it is smuggled in from unoccupied Germany as if it were a drug. French spies sniff it out and track it down. The army raids government offices and regional headquarters of the German central bank to seize hidden stocks. The supply of fresh banknotes struggles to keep pace. A new, financial front opens up in the struggle for the Ruhr. And as more money is printed, and Germany's gold reserves run down, inflation spirals up across the country. _Simplicissimus_ cost two hundred and fifty marks this February, in March it costs three hundred and fifty, by April, a staggering five hundred marks – a tenfold increase in just one year.

Pending the total collapse of the German economy – which surely must force Berlin to give in – the French authorities decide on a series of further measures to tighten the screws. Prominent local citizens are taken hostage or expelled. When two officers are shot in Buer, a French general declares the local mayor will be shot without trial if there is any more trouble. Passive resistance turns active. Reprisals follow. What was once intended to be a peaceful occupation degenerates into a low-level war. It feels like Ireland in 1920. At the end of March, a dozen German workers are shot dead by French soldiers pinned down in a Krupp factory they were searching.

Freikorps veterans flock to the Ruhr. Former comrades from the Baltic campaign or the struggle against the Munich republic regroup. One of these is Leo Schlageter, a twenty-something-year-old who gave up student life in Freiburg in 1919 to become, in succession, a Baltic Freikorps trooper, an anti-Bolshevik paramilitary in the Ruhr, a mercenary in Lithuania, a nationalist warrior against a Polish uprising in Silesia and finally an undercover putschist in Free State Danzig. Sent into the Ruhr from a guerrilla base in unoccupied Germany, he now runs a campaign of sabotage in the Essen region.

In March, he dynamites a railway bridge on the line between Düsseldorf and Duisburg. In April, he is arrested.

Moscow: Vladimir is too fragile to be moved to Gorki. He is attended by a legion of doctors and nurses day and night. He confuses 'yes' and 'no'. His conversation is reduced to the repetition of single words – 'here-here', 'congress-congress' – to which are added facial expressions to try and get his meaning across. Nadya is the best at interpreting Vladimir's wishes, followed by his sister. For everyone else, the man is an invalid. One can expect nothing from him. Certainly not a campaign to remove the General Secretary of the Russian Communist Party from his post.

Only a few weeks after his stroke, the authorities in Moscow create a Lenin Institute to collect anything he has ever written. Vladimir would surely approve of the thoroughness of the approach, if not perhaps the creation of a cult. He is being treated as if he were dead. Politically, he is already a corpse.

At the party congress in Moscow, Comrade Stalin gives a clever speech, accepting parts of Comrade Lenin's criticisms and assuring the party that the leadership is united. He retains his post as General Secretary with ease. Leon Trotsky does not strike. He turns down an offer to deliver the Congress report – the speech traditionally given by Lenin. He does not want to give the impression that he expects to rule in Lenin's place.

LONDON: 'I must confess myself more interested in the past than the present', Winston writes in a letter to a cousin. The first volume of his account of the Great War is published in the spring. It is an instant success. 'Remarkably egotistical', judges one reviewer.

AMERICA: Ford boosters are hard at work. In several Midwestern states where life has been transformed by the arrival of a tractor or a Model T automobile, petitions circulate to put Henry Ford's name on the ballot for the presidential primaries, without the man himself even declaring whether or not he wants to run. 'Let them go ahead with it and see what happens', the sage of Dearborn tells his secretary. 'We might have some fun with these politicians.'

At a patriotic congress in Washington his wife tries to set the record straight: 'Mr Ford has enough and more than enough to do to attend to his business in Detroit.' She then phones up Dearborn to berate her husband's staff. 'You got him into it,' she shouts at Henry Ford's secretary, 'so you can get him out of it.' If her husband goes to Washington, she announces, she will go to England. Henry Ford is not concerned. 'Oh well, don't pay any attention to Mrs Ford,' he says, 'she'll get over it.'

DELITZSCH, SAXONY, GERMANY: On the Berlin road, just north of Leipzig, left-wing militia are inspecting vehicles travelling north, looking out for conspirators against Saxony's socialist-led regional government.

Hitler's driver gulps when he sees them up ahead. Adolf grips the handle of his riding crop a little tighter. The Nazi Party is illegal in Saxony. The car's number plate has been smeared with oil to make it unreadable. But if he is identified, Adolf will not receive the kid-glove treatment he gets in Bavaria. As the motor car slows to a halt, one of the other passengers decides on a little play-acting. Putzi Hanfstaengl flourishes a Swiss passport in the faces of the militia and, putting on a deliberately awful German-American accent, claims loudly to be a paper manufacturer on a business trip to the annual Leipzig Fair. He points to the silent Adolf. 'This is my valet', says Putzi in a commanding foreign voice. They are waved through. Hitler looks up admiringly.

In Berlin, Adolf attends meetings with one of the party's main funders. In his free time, he takes Putzi round the military museum in the Zeughaus on Unter den Linden, showing off his in-depth knowledge of Prussian military campaigns. He admires a statue of Fredrick the Great. He is fascinated by the death masks of soldiers from earlier wars. Later Adolf leads Putzi through the national art gallery, triumphantly declaring Rembrandt an Aryan and misattributing a Caravaggio to Michelangelo.

That evening, at Luna Park, they watch some ladies' boxing (Adolf is fascinated, but does not approve). Someone recognises Hitler and snaps a photograph. He is outraged. Photographs are dangerous. If his likeness is published, travel through Germany will become ever more dangerous. Hitler tries to smash the camera. Eventually, the photographer agrees not to develop the film.

VIENNA: Freud is afraid. He visits a doctor friend to ask about the swelling in his mouth, who promptly tells him to give up smoking, an unwelcome recommendation. A second friend is consulted. 'Be prepared to see something you won't like', Freud warns him before opening his mouth wide to let himself be examined. The recommendation now is even worse: an operation, immediately, to remove the growth.

A few days later, without telling his family, Freud takes himself to hospital to be operated on by a well-known surgeon. The first Anna learns of it is a message received from the clinic, asking that Freud's family bring anything necessary for an overnight stay to the hospital at once. Anna finds her father sitting on a kitchen chair in a small room, covered in blood, unable to speak.

BERLIN – ESSEN – MUNICH: Albert Einstein resigns from the League of Nations' international committee on scientific cooperation, in protest at the League's failure to take action against the occupation of the Ruhr. (He also writes a letter to a friend suggesting a second motive: dislike of Henri Bergson, the French philosopher who chairs the committee and who has written a book containing 'serious blunders – may God forgive him' – on the subject of relativity.)

The German Communists are split on whether to blame capitalism or the French for the situation. The knee-jerk reaction of local Communists in the Ruhr to the Krupp shootings is to blame the firm's management and nationalist provocateurs for the tragedy. Party headquarters in Berlin – and the Comintern in Moscow – order a different course. German Communism cannot afford to look pro-French.

Adolf has a broader target in his sights. He blames democracy itself for the unacceptable situation in the Ruhr. He gives an interview to Spain's leading newspaper in which he argues that the parliamentary system should be abolished entirely. (The journalist also notes Hitler's opposition to unlimited press freedom and his demand for greater censorship of the theatre, cinema and women's clothing; no mention is made of his anti-Semitic agenda.) In the Zirkus Krone one evening in April, in front of ten thousand people, Adolf declares moderation to be the real crime. 'Whoever follows only the path of the golden mean will never reach their goal'. He embraces the idea of a popular uprising, the *Götterdammerung* that did not occur in 1918. What would the French do, Hitler asks, 'if faced with seventy million standing up to them in a life or death struggle?'

Fanaticism is no crime when the life of the nation is at stake. Paris wants to cut Germany's population down by another twenty million, he claims. They want the Rhineland for themselves. Moreover, if Germans do not fight now and recover their strength, they will soon find the Bolsheviks standing over the ruins of Germany's shattered culture. The choice has come to this: either the Nazi swastika or the red star of Communism.

Hitler now feels strong enough to challenge the Munich authorities directly. Germany's highest federal court has issued an order for the arrest of Hitler's mentor, Dietrich Eckart, for a violent verbal attack on President Ebert on the pages of the *Völkischer Beobachter*. Adolf challenges the Bavarian government to reject the arrest order. When the government does not follow the mangy field-runner's advice, he responds by threatening to hold another large-scale Nazi demonstration in Munich on the first of May – a date cherished by the right as the day of Munich's liberation from the Soviet in 1919 but celebrated by the left as the day of workers around the world. Should both left and right be allowed to march on the same day, bloodshed is inevitable.

On his birthday, towards the end of April, flowers and cakes are delivered to Adolf's sparse living quarters. The headline of the *Völkischer Beobachter* proclaims him Deutschland's Führer. Eckart contributes a poem:

> Five years of hardship, unequalled in human history!
> Five years of dirty excrement and mountains of sordid infamy!

The glow of pride and purity that great Bismarck left us –
Quite annihilated.

And yet – even as we are almost overcome with sickness,
A reminder:
Was this land not – unless the legends lie – a German land?
Can such a land be ended thus?
Have we no strength left to seize victory?

Lift up your hearts! Who wants to see, will see!
The strength is here before us, that will yet banish night!

Putzi drops by to congratulate his friend Adolf, having made the effort to look up beforehand all the other great men with whom the mangy field-runner shares a birthday, including Napoleon III and Oliver Cromwell, the king-slayer of the English Civil War. He finds Adolf in a state of some agitation. Hitler fears that his birthday cakes might be poisoned. He waits for Putzi to try them first, before launching himself onto the sugary peaks.

WASHINGTON DC: Woodrow sends an article he is writing to a friend. The friend responds to Edith instead. 'Speaking quite frankly, and from the bottom of my heart, the article is far from being what it should be', he writes. 'What the article lacks', as he puts it, 'is *body*'. It is unsuitable as the statement of Woodrow's return to public life. He asks Edith to destroy his letter before her husband sees it.

A few days later, on their daily drive along the Potomac, Edith brings up the subject. The article isn't quite good enough for publication, she tells Woodrow – yet. It might need to be expanded a little, she suggests (or edited down, another passenger chimes in unhelpfully). Woodrow loses his temper: 'I have done all I can, and all I am going to do.' Later, Edith is in tears: 'I just want to help and I just don't know how to help.'

THE OCCUPIED RUHR: On a mid-April morning not long after dawn, crowds gather in the streets of Essen to watch as the coffins of the Krupp workers shot by panicking French soldiers a few days before are paraded through the city. Flags with patriotic emblems flutter besides banners bearing socialist slogans. An image of the Virgin Mary is carried above the heads of the mourners. A group of men in top hats carry a five-pointed star adorned with a hammer and sickle. The capitalist Krupp, about to go on trial for his role in the incident, gives a speech lauding the patriotism of the men who died. The only sour moment comes at the cemetery, when one Communist agitator attempts to hijack proceedings to make a party-political speech on the grave of one of his fallen comrades.

'I have heard at least fifteen different accounts of what actually happened', Hemingway writes of the Krupp tragedy; 'at least twelve of them sounded like lies.' The most solid thing he finds in the Ruhr is the hatred. 'It is as definite', he writes, 'as the unswept cinder-covered sidewalks of Düsseldorf or the long rows of grimy black cottages.' No one is winning this war. 'France refused in 1917 to make peace without victory', Ernest writes. 'Now she finds she has victory without peace.'

In his prison cell near Düsseldorf, Leo Schlageter pens a letter to his parents telling them that if he is shot by the French for sabotage they should imagine it was just a sudden illness which carried him off. 'A few years earlier than expected', he writes, 'but it often happens that way.' He is ready to confront death. 'If I were alone on this earth, I truly do not know what could be more beautiful than to die for the Fatherland.'

DOORN: Worried that he will try to abscond, the Dutch government refuses permission for the Kaiser to visit the tulip fields of Haarlem (they are too near the open sea). Instead, he is allowed to take a road trip to the town of Tiel, the first time he has left the immediate vicinity of Doorn in months. Each time Wilhelm sees a pig in a field – and there are many in this particular part of Holland – he raises his hat to it, and bids it good day. It is a superstition, his equerry explains to a bewildered guest, supposed to bring good luck in foreign lands.

Back at Doorn the Kaiser alternates between rage at all those who have forsaken him and confident assertions of his imminent return to Germany. Visitors mention Hitler as a man to watch. They wonder about the possibility of a Mussolini-style dictator coming to power in Germany who will invite Wilhelm back as a symbol of continuity. From one of his guests, Wilhelm is delighted to learn of the commercial success of his memoirs in America. In Mexico, he is told, the effect is such that Germany is considered to be quite free of any responsibility for the war. 'What thanks do I get?' Wilhelm asks aloud. 'Filth and rubbish.'

MUNICH – BERCHTESGADEN: Paula Hitler leaves Austria for the first time in her life, to visit her brother Adolf in Bavaria.

Hasn't he done well? The party leader has a bright red car these days, and a driver. Paula briefly entertains the idea of working for Adolf, even living with him and taking care of his household. He does not seem so keen on the idea. He asks a party member to put his sister up while she is in town. She will not stay long.

Adolf invites his sister on an impromptu trip into the Alps, taking the car up to Berchtesgaden (one of Freud's favourite mountain hideaways). Once there, Paula discovers her brother has other plans. She is dumped in town with a female chaperone. Hitler heads further up into the mountains with his chauffeur.

His intention is to pay a surprise visit on Dietrich Eckart, currently on the run. After a strenuous climb up through the snow, Adolf and his chauffeur reach the Pension Moritz, a simple guesthouse run by a retired racing-car driver and his wife, a six-foot-tall blonde whom Adolf admires as a perfect specimen of Aryan womanhood.

'Diedi, the wolf is here', Hitler shouts through Eckart's door, identified by the lack of proper hiking boots outside. The poet appears in his nightgown, quite touched by his young protégé's decision to pay him a visit in his mountain hideout. Hitler wakes up early the next morning to see the sun rising over the mountains, and to enjoy the best view in Bavaria.

MOSCOW – GORKI: Nadya writes to Inessa Armand's daughter. 'I'm kept alive only by the fact that Volodya is glad to see me in the mornings, he takes my hand, and sometimes we talk about different things which anyway have no names.'

In May, the invalid is finally moved to Gorki. He is pushed around in a wicker wheelchair.

MUNICH: Hitler's threat to crush the socialists on May Day comes to nothing. In the event, the police warn that they are ready to shoot either way – left or right – should there be any trouble. The socialists march in strength and Communist flags are unfurled without permission (but also without trouble). But a few days later Hitler is on the attack again. 'The only thing that can save Germany is a dictatorship of national will and national purpose', he announces. There is no point trying to search for the saviour, Hitler says: he will come from the heavens, or he will not. 'Our job', he says modestly,

'is to make the people ready for the dictator, for when he comes.' That day
is near: 'German people, awake!'

VIENNA: A week after his operation Freud celebrates his birthday. 'Nothing
but visitors and celebrations', he writes to Lou Andreas-Salomé. 'I can now
inform you that I can again speak, chew and work, indeed even smoking
is permitted – to a certain moderate, cautious so to speak *petit bourgeois*
degree', Freud reports. The birthday itself is celebrated 'as though I were
a music hall star'. Or perhaps, he adds, 'as though it were to be my last'.
Freud's doctor gives him a new cigar-holder.

Uncertainty and anxiety now hover over Freud's whole existence. He is
treated with radium and X-rays. He has not been told the diagnosis of
cancer, but he suspects it. Then more calamity. Freud's grandson Heinz
Rudolf, the son of his daughter Sophie, visits from Hamburg, falls ill with
tuberculosis and is dead by June. 'I don't think I have ever experienced
such grief,' Freud writes; 'perhaps my own sickness contributes to the
shock.' For the first time in his life, he admits to full-scale depression.

DUBLIN: Ireland's civil war draws to its sad close. There are more
internments and executions; the killing of the IRA's chief commander
in the mountains of County Waterford; an order to dump arms (Yeats
initially suggests the Vatican look after the weapons); a grudging IRA
ceasefire.

'Soldiers of the Republic, legion of the rearguard,' Éamon de Valera
writes from hiding, 'the Republic can no longer be successfully defended
by your arms.' Bitter reality has spoiled the dream. Those loyal to the cause
will now be rewarded only with suffering. But therein lies redemption, de
Valera writes: 'What you endure will keep you in communion with your
dead comrades.' From defeat will spring a moral victory. The war is to be
continued – but by other means.

Ireland is a broken country. But it is, at long last, at peace. The soldier
becomes a politician again.

GOLZHEIMER HEATH, GERMANY: A little after four o'clock one morning at
the end of May, after a hurried Holy Communion, a final letter to his
parents, and a shot of rum to protect against the cold, the former Freikorps
trooper Leo Schlageter is blindfolded, forced to his knees and executed by

a French firing squad in a quarry outside Düsseldorf. He dies with a crucifix in his hands. The prison chaplain notes the sound of a lark singing in the morning air.

French newspapers report the accuracy of the French riflemen, their bullets guided to their target by their patriotism. No fewer than ten bullets hit Schlageter's heart, they say – he must have died instantly. German accounts suggest a far more messy execution, and that a French officer had to administer a final shot to the head from close range. Within twenty-four hours of his death a birch cross has appeared on Golzheimer Heath at the place of Schlageter's death. The man has become a martyr.

LAKE GARDA – VENICE: Gabriele D'Annunzio is smothered with gifts and surrounded by spies. Whatever he asks for, he gets. For the moment, Benito has no choice. He must indulge the myth of the hero of Fiume – or he must create his own. Only rarely does he dare push back. In May, Gabriele suggests a nearby hill should be flattened to make way for a private airstrip. To this, at least, Benito does not respond.

The Italian premier is too busy with the real stuff of politics: sidelining his enemies, setting Fascist rivals against each other, opening highways, and establishing himself as the only game in town. 'I am not so proud as to suggest that the man who speaks to you and fascism constitute only one identity,' Benito tells a congress of Fascist women in Venice, 'but four years of history have shown quite clearly that Mussolini and fascism are two aspects of the same nature, two bodies and one soul, or two souls and one body.'

He talks about destiny. He explains how, although he is descended from the labouring classes, his soul is that of an aristocrat, which is why he recoils from the double-dealing of parliamentary governments. He rejects those who suggest he compromise his values. 'I cannot abandon fascism', Mussolini says, 'because I created it, I brought it up, I protected it, sometimes I scolded it, and I still hold it within my fist: always!'

SUMMER

ACROSS EUROPE – NEW YORK: The Tsar's mother has returned to her native Denmark. Wrangel and his family take up residence in a rented villa by the Danube outside Belgrade. Denikin is in Budapest and Yudenich in the south of France. White Russians circulate in ever-smaller social circles, whirling with intrigue. Moscow has set up a fake monarchist organisation to make the whole thing spin faster into oblivion, wasting the émigré community's time on the chimera of anti-Communist resistance from within the Soviet Union.

In certain cafés in Paris and Prague, more Russian is spoken than French or Czech. 'New York has so many Russian nobles that they are in danger of losing their identity merely by force of numbers', the *New York Times* reports. Titled ladies take up new jobs as seamstresses. The former editor of Petrograd's leading newspaper is now said to be working in a hospital laundry uptown. Whatever they do, White Russians stick together: 'They gather in restaurants, pull down the shades, close the doors, dim the lights and are in Russia again – that lost, magical, mystical Russia of yesterday.'

MUNICH: 'What does Hitler look like?' asks the magazine *Simplicissimus* (price seven hundred and fifty marks, up by half since April). There are no photographs of him so people must use their imagination. Some imagine him fat, others imagine him thin. Some have heard about the fanatical gleam in his eyes, others about the prominence of his mouth. Does he have a jutting chin, or a prominent forehead? Not all these mental pictures can be accurate. When the magazine's cartoonist travels up to Berlin for a few days, he is asked all kinds of questions about the true appearance of Bavaria's new far-right *Wunderkind*.

In response, the cartoonist draws sixteen very different-looking pictures of Hitler, focusing on the attributes others ascribe to him. One depicts a well-defined mouth, in mid-rant, looming out of an otherwise faint and featureless face. Another shows a washed-out figure where the only notice-able feature is a pair of large ears: to better hear the voice of the people. The cartoons grow more absurd. One shows a man with a flowing beard dressed in a prophet's smock, reflecting one Berliner's question as to whether Hitler looks, in fact, a little bit like the Nordic god Wotan. 'Is it true', asks another, 'that he only ever appears in public wearing a black mask?'

'Hitler is not an individual at all', the cartoonist writes in the caption under his last representation of him: an abstract jumble of Bavarian beer mugs, a knife (about to plunged in an imaginary back, perhaps), a handgun, a swastika and black thunderclouds above: 'He is a condition – only the Futurists can draw him.'

PARIS: Trying to revive his flagging fortunes, his Parisian novelty value now well and truly worn off, Tristan Tzara decides to stage a new show. Banned from booking any theatres himself, he has to take on a few Russian partners for the enterprise.

The plans which emerge from this joint effort are for a rather tame avant-garde variety show, a far cry from the Dadaist *événements* of previous years: some light music by Stravinsky and a few readings. There is nothing here to shock a Parisian audience brought up on *The Rite of Spring*. Tzara does not bother to ask Breton's poet friends whether he can use their work; he puts them in the programme anyway. André is furious.

NEW YORK: One Friday in early summer, Marcus Garvey's trial for mail fraud finally gets under way.

The atmosphere is tense. Garvey supporters are said to have stockpiled weapons. The captain of one of the Black Star Line ships is said to have been intimidated with threats of violence to ensure his testimony is favour-able. After discovering that his own lawyer thinks he should plead guilty to secure a reduced sentence, Garvey opts to conduct his own defence. In his last speech to his followers before heading to his trial, Garvey name-checks himself fifty-six times, and compares his courage going into battle with that of Kaiser Wilhelm in 1914. 'I am saying to those who think they are getting even with Garvey, when Garvey dies a million other Garveys will rise up', he declares. 'Garvey goes to court like a man.' He claims it will be the biggest trial in American court history.

He is not as good a lawyer as he is an orator. Garvey is jailed for five years. There is no sympathy from William Du Bois. 'I think that Mr Marcus

Garvey had an unusually fair trial and that, all things considered, he got a very lenient sentence', Du Bois writes to a friend in Florida.

ESSEN – SCHÖNAU – MUNICH: Schlageter's body is transported back to his home town in the Black Forest. Wherever the train carrying his corpse stops it is greeted by processions of nationalist associations. The rector of Giessen University, just outside Frankfurt, announces that 'the name of Schlageter will be inscribed in our hearts, where he lives as a glorious example of love of the Fatherland, of unwavering belief in the future of the German people, and inspiring heroic loyalty to the death.' In the student town of Freiburg, thirty thousand people turn out. The family ceremony in Schönau is overwhelmed. Schlageter's name is mentioned even in Moscow, where the Comintern debates whether to treat him as a hero struggling against French profiteers.

In Munich, nationalist associations hold their own commemorative ceremony with Ludendorff in attendance. Hitler claims that Schlageter's death proves that freedom will only come through armed action. At the city's St Boniface church, a religious service honouring Schlageter is held and SA standards are sprinkled with holy water.

Schlageter becomes a Nazi icon. The *Völkischer Beobachter* publishes and republishes accounts of the martyr's last hours, emphasising his Christ-like composure in the face of death. An SA motorbike parade to pay homage in Schlageter's home town is organised. Schlageter trinkets are produced. Putzi contributes with a song. 'Our movement is a restless force', Hitler tells a crowd in the Bavarian town of Passau, after another flag-waving procession, 'and those who come to us are those ready for battle'. After the May setback, membership starts rocketing up again.

PARIS: On the night of Tzara's show, the spark that sets thing off is, strangely enough, the name of Spanish painter Pablo Picasso. As part of the spectacle, the artist's name is maliciously recited on stage as if he were a war victim: 'Pablo Picasso, dead on the field of honour'. Breton rushes up to defend the Spaniard from being treated this way and orders the reader to vacate the premises. When he refuses, Breton strikes out with his cane, breaking the poor man's arm.

Tzara, the anti-establishment, anti-everything founder of Dada, then does what any impresario would in such a situation: he calls the police. (He later instructs a lawyer to seek damages, too.) Breton and his companions are chucked out onto the street. But it is Tzara's reputation which is in tatters. He is no longer shocking. But nor is he commercial. The theatre owner cancels the show's second night. The Russians split. André takes himself on a well-deserved holiday to Brittany for a spot of fishing and ponders his next move.

Essen: A full-blown terrorist campaign is now under way in the Ruhr. Belgian soldiers are shot while checking passes. A curfew is introduced which forbids Germans from using their gardens at certain times of the day and requires them to keep their windows shut; curfew-breakers are liable to be shot. Later, locals are banished from the trams, and cafés are shut down. When two French adjutants are shot in Dortmund, six German civilians are summarily executed in return. On the last day of June another railway bridge is dynamited. Nine Belgian soldiers die. The morale of the occupying forces begins to crack.

Attempts at diplomatic resolution fail. Paris sticks to its guns, insisting it has no political goals in the Ruhr, while making plain that, whatever happens next, the mechanisms of economic control may remain there for a long while to come. The French are willing to negotiate, but only if German resistance ends first. Berlin cannot budge for fear of a nationalist backlash – and how can it call off a resistance movement it does not control? London tries to break the deadlock, calling for level heads and common sense. Such efforts are rebuffed. 'An eye for an eye, a tooth for a tooth', the French respond. Moreover, when it comes to reparations, 'the German government will never recognise any amount as just and reasonable, and if it does, will deny it on the following day.' They cannot be trusted.

An edict is announced requiring German officials be kept within the blast zone while improvised explosive devices are dismantled in the Ruhr. They are also required to be the first to physically investigate them, in case they are booby-trapped. Hostages are forced to ride the region's trains to discourage night-time attacks.

Gothenburg, Sweden: Seven months after the award of the Nobel Prize for his discovery of the law of photoelectric effect, Einstein finally gets around to giving his Nobel lecture in Sweden – on the subject of relativity. He also tells the audience about his ambition to formulate a unified field theory connecting electromagnetism to gravity, the strong and the weak forces of nature: the holy grail, in other words. It is a speculative quest, led by mathematics. A unified theory must, he intuits, be mathematically beautiful.

But there is not much time for such thoughts in the summer of 1923. Einstein is distracted. 'One nearly goes mad from all the visitors, the letters and the phone calls', he writes to a friend. Throughout the early summer, Einstein fights with Mileva and his sons about where the Nobel Prize money earmarked for them should be kept. Nineteen-year-old Hans-Albert tells him: 'You don't know how much you're always frustrating and upsetting Mama with this business, and I too find your handling of business affairs like this really inconsiderate.' And then there is politics. In July, he attends a pacifist rally in Berlin with a French friend, in support of Franco-German reconciliation and against the occupation of the Ruhr. (The police warn that the Frenchman's safety cannot be guaranteed if he tries to give a speech.)

It is only at the end of the summer that Albert is reconciled with his son. They travel to Kiel together and go sailing. It takes rather longer to settle matters with Mileva – three apartment blocks are eventually purchased in Zurich. But by then Albert has other family problems to manage.

LAKE GARDA – ROME: Gabriele D'Annunzio enjoys the latest addition to his palace garden: several large boulders from sites of Italian victories in the Great War. He has a new French mistress, over thirty years his junior.

In Rome, Benito continues his work to make his government impregnable against all challengers and prepare the way for the next stage of his conquest of power. He tightens up the country's media laws, making it easier for the government to close down newspapers. In June, he sets off on a nationwide tour. He is trailed by journalists who dutifully report on the adoring crowds at his speeches – and the black-shirted Fascist militias who turn out to be inspected by their leader.

Step by step, Benito wears down those who oppose him, making it harder and harder for them to regain the initiative. In July, under heavy intimidation, the Italian parliament passes a new electoral law providing for the party which wins one quarter of the vote in a future election to be automatically awarded two thirds of the seats in parliament. Men armed with daggers and guns sit in the public gallery to make sure all goes as planned.

All this is helpful, but Mussolini has another trick up his sleeve, something he learned from D'Annunzio. Benito needs to win a little theatrical war. He must have his own Fiume. The target is chosen as the Greek island of Corfu. Now all he needs is an excuse to invade it.

BERLIN: By the beginning of June, a copy of *Simplicissimus* costs one thousand marks. By the beginning of July its price is up by half again. Inflation distorts everything. No one knows how much things *should* cost. In spring, a woman working as a porter in Baden railway station charges Ernest Hemingway fifty marks to help him with his luggage; in Mannheim the same day, a porter charges him a thousand marks, protesting that it is barely the cost of a glass of schnapps. Factory workers demand higher and higher wages, to be adjusted monthly, weekly, daily so that their pay keeps pace with the rising cost of living. Factory owners either close down or comply. (The sharper ones turn inflation into profit, paying their workers in falling German marks, and selling goods abroad for hard currency.) Those with savings in marks are impoverished. Unemployment rockets up.

Government attempts to stop the fall in value of the mark are ineffective. The Reichsbank spends its remaining gold and foreign currency reserves achieving virtually nothing. New banknotes are produced: the old thousand-mark bill is retired, and a new series with denominations up to fifty million is produced. There are stories of Americans unable to change a five-dollar bill because no one could possibly provide so much money in German currency. Currency speculators thrive. The black market flourishes. Huge shipments of banknotes are required for employers to pay the workers. Riots break out if they haven't arrived. The state daily teeters on the edge of insolvency.

As in 1919, sometimes it is the very unity of the German nation which seems to be at stake in all these interlocking financial and political crises. On a Sunday at the end of July, in Koblenz in the Rhineland, occupied by the French since 1918, several thousand separatists gather to express their anger at still being shackled to the German basket-case. They demand a new currency for the Rhineland and popular self-determination. 'We are free citizens of the Rhineland; we do not want to be sold; we want to determine our own future', one speaker says. Prussia may want war, but the people of the Rhine want peace. French newspapers report the main slogan of the meeting: '*Los von Berlin!*' – 'Away from Berlin!'

In early August, the Chancellor makes a speech in the Reichstag on the crisis in the Ruhr. 'In a few days,' he starts – 'the dollar will be worth ten million', interrupt the Communists – 'it will be the end of seven months of occupation'. He counts the cost in lives lost, refugees, the number who have lost their homes. The French have earned the contempt of all true Germans, he says. In return they have got less than one fifth of the coal they could have received from free German labour. They have started a 'process of annihilation'. Discussions with London to help restrain the French have gone nowhere. 'We stand alone and must and will help ourselves', he says. In 1918, Germans hoped for a peace of understanding. There is no such hope now, 'and so the fight goes on'.

The Chancellor notes the rise of extremisms on the left and right. Both sides seem to have grown closer to each other in recent months, both willing the collapse of the centre so as to impose their vision of the future. 'The government is on guard', he declares, 'and will clamp down on unrest – *from whichever side it comes* – with all its force'. To stir up civil war at a time like this is criminal. 'For as long as you – the representatives of the people – place your trust in me, I will serve until the last day of my strength', the Chancellor concludes. He is gone within a week.

SAN FRANCISCO – WASHINGTON DC: President Warren Harding, the younger and more energetic man who succeeded Woodrow Wilson in March 1921, dies of a heart attack at the Palace Hotel, San Francisco. Marcus Garvey sends his condolences from jail. Vice President Coolidge, the man who made his name in the Boston police strike of 1919, takes over.

Sixty-six-year-old Woodrow Wilson is in better health than for years. He resumes regular visits to the theatre with Edith. After one play, several hundred fans gather by the stage door. Woodrow is serenaded with the Marseillaise. 'There's the man you can't forget', cries a well-wisher. A curious thought enters Woodrow's mind. The White House seems wide open again.

LAUSANNE: The Turkish delegates wear top hats for the occasion. After six months of negotiation – and the dramatic failure of the previous attempt – a treaty is finally signed between Mustafa Kemal's Turkey and the victors of the Great War (albeit without the United States).

Obstinacy has paid off. The Turks achieve sovereignty within the country's borders. There is no mention of an independent Kurdistan or Armenia. The Straits are governed by another international agreement. The compulsory exchange of Greek and Muslim populations is ratified by both sides, with an exception made for the Greeks of Istanbul.

A little glimmer of peace in a continent still torn apart by conflict.

DEARBORN: Henry Ford grants an interview. He has still not said whether or not he will run for President in 1924, but he allows speculation to continue. 'I certainly couldn't run the government the way I run my business', he says, with obvious regret. There is too much waste; too few facts. Perhaps industry will take over government in the future, he says. 'The industrial organism has more life flowing through it, more energy.'

Whereas industry understands the need to serve the consumer – it is a question of survival – politicians seem to know only how to serve themselves. 'Would you substitute autocracy?' the journalist asks. No, he wouldn't – but personally he would be prepared to wipe the slate clean somehow: 'I'm sure we're going to get rid of all these dead cells as soon as the time comes to get rid of them.'

BERLIN – THE RUHR: A new German Chancellor is appointed at the head of a left–right coalition to try and manage the worst crisis in Germany since the war.

He faces an impossible task. Passive resistance has yielded nothing. France seems to be in no mood to negotiate except on its own terms, and only once passive resistance is called off. The economy is collapsing. By the end of August the price of *Simplicissimus* has reached eighty thousand marks.

On the face of it, the country is awash with money, more money than anyone has ever seen. Over the summer, the central Reichsbank starts printing banknotes worth one hundred million marks. Before 1914, that sum would have bought three Dreadnought battleships, the most powerful and most expensive weapons in the world; now a shop-keeper might make the same amount in a quiet morning selling a few dozen loaves of bread. The boss of the Reichsbank boasts that, armed with enough zeroes, paper and ink, the bank will soon be able to issue, almost every day, banknotes of a value equal to the entire current stock in circulation.

But despite – or because of – this ever-increasing flood of money, no one ever seems to have enough. Each banknote printed reduces the value of the rest. Local communities try to escape the madness by creating their own currencies pegged to something – *anything* – which can still be trusted as a store of value. Some become fantastically rich in these months; most become poor. They look for scapegoats.

PAMPLONA, SPAIN – PARIS: While André Breton is fishing in Brittany, and Albert and his son are sailing in the Baltic, Hadley Hemingway is five months pregnant and Ernest has a new hobby.

It began earlier in the summer, when Hemingway travelled to Spain with a few friends, stayed in a bullfighters' pension in Madrid, and got hooked on the idea of bull and man, the grandeur and the tragedy of the struggle of life and death represented by the *corrida*. 'It's just like having a ringside seat at the war with nothing going to happen to you', he writes to his friend Bill.

Ernest decides that he will return with Hadley. On the advice of Gertrude Stein, the two of them attend the Fiesta of San Fermin in Pamplona, renting a room in an old house for five dollars a night, with walls as thick as those of a fortress. Neither Hadley nor Ernest speaks much Spanish. They do not meet a native English-speaker for a week. But in Pamplona, Hemingway feels more alive than he has in years. The two of them are up at dawn every morning, roused by military music and by the prospect of seeing the bulls run through the cobblestone streets. Fireworks, drums, drink and music fill their days. And blood, of course. By mid-July, Hemingway claims he has seen twenty fights at least. They fill his writing, offering precisely the kind of short, sharp encounter which suits the style he has been trying to develop for the last year: stark, precise, momentary – like a flash photograph.

When the two of them get back to Paris, as pregnant Hadley's demands for different kinds of exotic food become more and more exacting, and the date of their return to America to have the baby comes closer and closer, Hemingway's thoughts turn back to Spain and freedom. He can barely believe that he is on the point of leaving it all behind. On the morning of 5 August, the proofs come in for Hemingway's first book – a few poems and a couple of short stories in a volume so thin it has to be filled out with blank pages. 'No body will buy a book if it is too goddam thin', Ernest writes to his publisher.

Two weeks later, Mr and Mrs Ernest M. Hemingway, lately of Paris, France, sail to Canada aboard the SS *Andania*.

BOUILLON, BELGIUM: Captain de Gaulle, now halfway through his training to be a senior officer in the French army, decides to take some leave with his wife Yvonne in Belgium. Together, they visit the town and fort of Bouillon in the Ardennes, which Charles proclaims should by rights really be part of France rather than Belgium.

Another day, Charles returns to the battlefield of Dinant, where he was wounded in August 1914. Like Hemingway's return to Fossalta, the visit is an anticlimax. De Gaulle finds himself in a group of thirty men of whom he is the only one who fought in the war. It is strange for the conflict to seem already so far away, and yet so close. In his notebook, de Gaulle jots down the latest aphorism he has picked up from his reading: 'Peace is the dream of the wise, but war is the history of humanity.'

DRESDEN: In the state opera house in Dresden, Thomas Mann's brother Heinrich addresses an assembly on the fourth anniversary of Germany's new Weimar constitution. '1919 is long ago', he says with a mournful shake of the head. In the Germany of 1923 the power of capital has become overwhelming. Capital is the insatiable beast whose needs drive everything else now. The spirit of 1919 has been distorted and nationalism has returned. 'A country on whose soil stand the armies of foreign powers can never know domestic peace', Heinrich declares. Germany's children are starving. Its people are emotionally exhausted. The Ruhr is being bled dry so foreign companies can boost their profits. 'The German world is being bought up piece by piece.'

But, he warns, 'to blame everything on blind fate and a cruel enemy is cheap talk, too cheap for these expensive times'. But what else is there? The Reichstag has become a conference of ghosts, unable to manage the crisis, floating in thin air.

ENNIS, CO. CLARE, IRELAND: The Feast of the Assumption of the Virgin Mary. A couple of thousand people come from all over the country to this small village to see a miracle, a divine apparition. The sceptical and the simply curious jostle with the fanatical.

The apparition arrives in a small, open-top car. Out steps Éamon de Valera wearing a blue overcoat and soft hat. No beard now. This is the old de Valera – the President of the republic, as some would have it. He mounts the platform to give a speech and has barely opened his mouth before an armoured car roars up. Free State soldiers fire in the air. Panic ensues amongst the crowd. De Valera falls. Has he fainted – or has he been shot?

He is arrested that day and taken into Free State custody. Now they will have to decide what to do with him. Putting him on trial is one possibility – but on trial for what? Too dangerous, politically speaking. Éamon de Valera might welcome an opportunity to play the martyr, to present his cause as that of the heroic underdog against an overbearing state. He is already halfway to being considered a saint amongst republican devotees. He must not be allowed to garner further public sympathy.

Pending a final decision on his fate, de Valera is sent to jail – one he remembers from when it was run by the British – and placed in solitary confinement.

GORKI: His room is as it was before. The pictures are taken off the wall. A chair is put by the window. Vladimir enjoys sitting here, looking out over the park towards the town.

A therapist is employed to try and restore Vladimir's faculty of speech. One day he is highly enlivened when he is visited by an acquaintance he has not seen since the 1890s, a man with whom he once debated the merits of Marxism. Conversation is animated in facial expressions and intonation, but limited in vocabulary. 'Look', 'what', 'go' – each word a fragment of a thought that no one can decipher. Vladimir starts learning to recite the alphabet again. On good days, he is able to half mumble his way through the Internationale or 'In a Valley of Dagestan'.

Nadya tries to teach him to write again, with his left hand, but without success. He attempts to read *Pravda*, but finds it hard to get beyond the headlines. He is frustrated, frequently depressed and cries when he thinks no one is looking. Once, Nadya is so angry and upset that she begins to weep herself. Vladimir instantly produces his handkerchief to help her wipe her eyes.

Some days in September, when he is feeling a little better, Vladimir and Nadya are driven out into the countryside to feel the thrill of the air rushing past them. At other times, Vladimir goes out into the forests with the male staff of the estate. They take guns to do a little shooting. They never go very far.

LONDON: Clare Sheridan publishes her memoir of 1922. She pokes fun at Mussolini and declares she has definitively fallen out with fascism. 'My own impression of fascism is that if it were to succeed internationally it would turn the whole world into the conditions of Mexico and Ireland,' she writes, 'where every young man, instead of thinking of work, says: "Give me a gun".' Her cousin Winston, she suggests, thinks fascism is merely the shadow of Bolshevism, and he would prefer to be ruled by the former than the latter. Clare hints that some people think Churchill would make a good fascist leader himself.

MUNICH: 'Democracy is a joke', Hitler tells an American reporter from the *New York World*. 'Just as Americans call for America for the Americans', he says, 'so we call for Germany for the Germans.' It is not material factors, but psychological ones that truly matter: 'What Germany really lacks is not guns – but will'.

THE ALBANIAN–GREEK BORDER: Benito gets his pretext. An Italian general working with a League commission to demarcate the brigand-infested Albanian–Greek border is murdered one morning on the road to the border post at Kakavia.

The basic outline of the ambush is all too familiar: a roadblock in remote countryside, in an area from which there is no easy escape and where the victims can be attacked without difficulty. But the motives are unclear. Who would have done such a thing? No one claims responsibility. Investigators find that no personal valuables have been removed. If it was a political murder, was the Italian the intended victim or was it Greeks who were supposed to die that morning? The order of vehicles in the convoy was changed at the last minute when the Ford carrying the Greek party broke down and the Italian Lancia was sent on ahead. Coincidence or conspiracy?

The answer to such questions does not matter much in Italy. Spontaneous anti-Greek riots break out across the country. Demonstrators urge swift action against the perpetrators – whoever they may be – or, if they cannot be identified, against the Greek government (held responsible for the murder because it occurred on Greek territory). Benito prepares an ultimatum. The terms are deliberately harsh, if not impossible. Greece is given five days to conclude its investigation. As an act of penance, Athens is required to organise a state funeral for the slain Italian general in the Greek capital's Catholic cathedral. The Greek navy must pay homage to the Italian fleet. An indemnity of fifty million lire is demanded, to be paid within five days.

Full acceptance of the ultimatum is demanded within twenty-four hours. It is assumed that the Greeks will reject these terms. What sovereign nation could accept them? But Benito calculates that he wins either way. If his terms are accepted, he will have shown that, under his leadership, Italy protects its own and will not be pushed around. If Italy's terms are rejected, Benito will have a pretext for some short, sharp military action in an operation that his military has assured him they can pull off without much difficulty. Gabriele D'Annunzio's Fiume adventure will soon be a distant memory. Italians will have a new military hero. Mussolini's political position will be unassailable. In order to avoid any last-minute snafus, Italy's diplomats consult with their British and French counterparts. Rome rapidly concludes that Paris and London will do nothing material to prevent Italy dealing with the Greeks exactly as she pleases.

The clock ticks down towards the expiry of the ultimatum. Athens protests its innocence of any involvement in the murder of the Italian general and accepts some of Rome's terms – but not all. It's not enough. Within three days of the ambush on the windy mountain road to Kakavia – and within hours of Athens's partial rejection of the ultimatum – Italian forces land on the island of Corfu. Italy has a new daring hero to admire, and the world has a full-blown international diplomatic crisis on its hands. Although the Italian occupation of the island is supposed to be peaceful, a delay in the landing means the Italian officers in charge have to rely on brute force to ensure their troops are in full control by nightfall. The warning given to Greek authorities (and foreign representatives) is cut from two hours to thirty minutes. Thirty-five shells are fired at Corfu's old hilltop fortress, now a refugee camp for Armenians and Greeks expelled from Anatolia following Mustafa Kemal's triumph. Sixteen are killed. Many more are wounded.

The Greeks take the matter to the League of Nations. The new world order is being tested.

WESTERHAM, KENT – BAYONNE, FRANCE: One rainy English summer's day, still suffering from a persistent sore throat, Clementine is in a philosophical mood. Reports suggest that an earthquake in Japan has just killed tens of thousands of people in and around Tokyo and Yokohama. 'The Kaiser and Mussolini seem quite benevolent & humane compared to the Almighty when he lays about Him', she writes to her husband, currently gambling and yachting in France with a friend. 'In one day He kills as many people as in six months of the Great War.'

Both Clementine and Winston find their attention drawn to Corfu. The Greeks have asked the Council of the League of Nations to intervene. Rome has rejected internationalisation, arguing that the matter should be determined by the Great Powers alone. (It assumes that France – not wanting the League on its back in the Ruhr – will back up Italy on the matter.) But how can anyone have faith in a new world order, if only the strong get to decide how it works?

'The poor League of Nations is on trial', Clementine writes. 'I hope it prevails & is not made a laughing stock.' But what can it do? It has no army or navy of its own. The League is only as strong as the resolve of its members.

If the Great Powers abandon it when it comes to the crunch (or when their own interests are at stake), it can do nothing. 'Poor devil,' Winston replies sympathetically to his wife, 'it is life or death for it now.'

ROME: A talkative group of Americans from Cincinnati engage a German couple – a man in his late sixties and a woman who appears to be his daughter – in an unwanted conversation on the train from Florence to Rome. As they approach the city, one of the Americans mistakes the Apennines for the Urals. Another asks the Germans (who they mistake for being Italian) about where to buy pearls in Rome. Sigmund Freud groans inwardly. Americans!

For the next three weeks the recovering patient is indefatigable in taking his daughter around the city. Every day is packed with sightseeing. On one afternoon alone Freud takes his daughter to see Michelangelo's statue of Moses in the church of San Pietro in Vincoli, the Bocca della Verità, two Roman temples and a Roman victory arch. On another they walk out along the Via Appia Antica to visit the catacombs where Rome's dead used to be buried. Not bad for a recovering cancer patient. Only once is Anna able to escape from her father's punishing schedule, to go to the cinema with the daughter of the owner of their hotel. Italy revives Freud. Can it be that he has cheated death?

The rumble of the international crisis over Corfu does not disturb their fun. Nor does it disturb their business. In amongst all the sight-hopping, Sigmund finds time to compose a brief letter to his nephew Edward in New York complaining about late royalty cheques from America, and appointing him his agent.

MUNICH – NUREMBERG: Ludendorff has fallen in love again. Erich has eyes only for Mathilde, a psychiatrist who was supposed to help his wife with her morphine addiction but ended up charming the general instead. Under Mathilde's guidance the general, who once believed his July 1918 offensive failed because he recited the wrong prayer, is coming around to the startling conclusion that Christianity, with its glorification of the weak rather than the strong, is the spiritual ballast holding Germany back from its true potential. The country does not just need a new politics, Mathilde tells him, it needs a new religion.

In Nuremberg, Germany's nationalist groups hold a large rally. The French are still in the Ruhr and the German mark is worth virtually nothing any more. But there is a sense that the world is going their way. A national mood is sweeping Europe. The defeated are rising up again. Events in Corfu have energised things. The peace of 1919 is under fire from all sides. 'The fate of Turkey shows extraordinarily many similarities to our own', reads an article in a nationalist newspaper. 'If we want to be free then we will have no choice but to follow the Turkish example in one way or another.'

A huge field Mass is held. Tens of thousands of grizzled veterans of the Great War and the Freikorps are joined by those too young to have fought, but infected by their elders' stories of heroism and betrayal from France to the Baltic to the fight against Luxemburg and Liebknecht in Berlin. A Protestant clergyman gets the audience to swear they will not rest till the French have been thrown out of the Ruhr. Then they sing 'Deutschland über Alles'.

The Nuremberg gathering brings together all the strands of the German nationalist movement. Hitler attends with five hundred members of the SA. But his name is far from the most prominent. Ludendorff is the most senior soldier on display. A nationalist admiral – once Kaiser Wilhelm's top naval man and a firm advocate of unrestricted submarine warfare in 1917 – reminds the audience of the global ambitions represented by the imperial fleet. Several members of Germany's royal families are present. The seventeen-year-old son of Hermine, the Kaiser's wife, goes down on one knee to receive a silver chalice of wine from Ludendorff. It is as if 1918 never happened.

Adolf gives a firebrand oration claiming that only violence can help Germany defeat its external and internal enemies. Such a statement is bound to stir things up. An American journalist reports his words back to the United States. 'We need another revolution', Hitler says: 'not that socialist, bourgeois and Jewish revolution of 1918, but a nationalist revolution.' The only way to save Germany, he announces, is through 'blood and sword'.

In the middle of festivities, an alliance is struck between a local Freikorps group called the Bund Oberland, active during the crushing of the Bavarian Soviet in 1919 and then again in Silesia in 1921, and the Nazi Party's SA. The two groups (along with a third splinter group) agree a manifesto. They declare eternal opposition to the Weimar constitution, reparations, international capital and the 'nation-destroying' dogma of class warfare. They claim to be the embodiment of the fighting spirit of 1914. They take Leo Schlageter – the martyr of the Ruhr – as their model.

The manifesto is mostly conservative, demanding better treatment of war veterans and confirming private property (a far cry from Adolf's early speeches). It requires that henceforth all German art – film, painting, theatre – should be mobilised for Germany's national renewal. The national interest must determine everything. The alliance calls itself the Kampfbund, the Battle League.

Adolf is delighted. The Kampfbund can call on thousands of members, many of them with war experience. It is a far cry from the few hundred SA heavies in Austrian ski-hats training outside Munich at the beginning of the year, or the loose nationalist alliance of May. Though not under his sole command, Hitler now has the beginnings of a real army. The question now is, what to do with it?

MONZA – ROME: There is another German besides Freud who shows up in Italy during the glorious late summer of 1923. Former jailbird Kurt Lüdecke bears a slip of paper signed by Hitler which declares him to be the Nazi Party's official representative on the Italian side of the Alps.

Benito is in Monza for the start of the European Grand Prix, where he is photographed talking seriously – as one daredevil to another – to the racing-car drivers. He later gives an interview to the influential British *Daily Mail*, a newspaper quite sympathetic to the virile blackshirts. Lüdecke (arriving in Italy via meetings with anti-Versailles groups in Budapest) tries to catch up with Mussolini in Milan. He accosts him on the steps of the offices of *Il Popolo d'Italia*. When that fails to produce much more than a vague nod of the head from Benito – who *is* that man? – the German follows him on to Rome, hoping for an audience there. It seems much harder to meet Benito now that he is premier.

Mussolini is wary. 'The fall of the Empire has left a void in the German mind', he writes in the preface to a new book about Germany that September. The political consequences of this upheaval will not be decided by whether there are machine guns hidden in forest caves, 'but the mood of the new German generation'. The current situation is hard to read. Benito will always have time for emulators and admirers from abroad, but is too savvy to get himself mixed up too deeply in their intrigues. Germany has never been a country he has had much fondness for. In its current state he views it as dangerous and unpredictable. Why meet with a Munich emissary who, not being in power, can make no concrete promises in the way of territorial concessions, but whose mere presence in Italy will raise question marks about Benito's diplomacy?

Premier Mussolini has more immediate matters to think about: whether France and Britain will back him on Corfu or let the League of Nations become involved.

MADRID, SPAIN – DOORN: A coup d'état in the Spanish capital brings a right-wing military government to power. General Primo de Rivera proclaims himself dictator. The King of Spain offers his support. (A nationalist army officer serving in Morocco – Francisco Franco – is doubtful of the new man.) On the day of his coup Primo de Rivera composes a message to be sent over the Mediterranean. 'Please convey to His Majesty the King of Italy, to Mussolini, and to the Italian navy my sympathy for the example they have set to all the peoples who know how to save and redeem themselves'.

Clare Sheridan races to Madrid to add Europe's latest strongman to her tally. She is not impressed. Primo de Rivera is no Trotsky, Mussolini or Kemal. He seems a copy rather than a true original. But if he is something of a low-grade dictator, imagine what this says about the King of Spain who has called on him to rule the country. Madrileños call the King 'Secondo de Rivera' now. He responds by calling his general-dictator *'mon petit Mussolini'*.

In Doorn, the latest right-wing coup convinces the Kaiser that his time is finally coming. After the false dawn of 1920, he now pins his hopes on 1923. Italy and Spain are blazing a trail for Germany. Democracy is played out. What the world needs now is an iron hand in a velvet glove, military might and monarchy. Wilhelm expects the call from Berlin at any moment. Hermine is less sure: she finds herself cold-shouldered on a trip home. The Kaiser's son is the more popular monarchist choice now.

MUNICH: Adolf asks his secretary to get in touch with the author of several recent articles about Mustafa Kemal. He wants advice. 'What you have witnessed in Turkey', his secretary writes on Hitler's behalf, 'is what we will have to do in the future as well in order to liberate ourselves.'

Hitler now has a series of takeover models to choose from. There is the Ankara model: secure a minor city as your base and then use populist appeal and a national army to take over the rest of the country. There is the Rome model: a theatrical march on the capital backed up by paramilitary force and completed with co-option of the existing order. Now there is the Madrid model: military coup d'état sanctified by royal blessing. He seems to be edging towards the Ankara template. First Bavaria, then Germany – then the world.

AUTUMN

HOF, GERMANY – BERLIN – MUNICH: Adolf holds another German Day gathering, this time in the north Bavarian town of Hof. Seventy thousand members of southern Germany's nationalist groups march through town. The Nazi leader arrives in a shiny new red Mercedes-Benz.

Immediately afterwards, Hitler is driven in secret to fundraising meetings in Berlin, travelling through Saxony with handguns drawn, in case of a repeat of the incident earlier in the year. They reach the capital around two in the morning and tour the city. Hitler points out the royal palace and the Reichstag to his driver. 'When we have our swastika flying over those two beautiful buildings,' Adolf shouts over the automobile engine, 'I will be the Führer of the entire nation.'

In Berlin, it is now clear that passive resistance against the occupation of the Ruhr has failed. The Chancellor tries a last roll of the diplomatic dice, offering all kinds of temptations to Paris and Brussels to get them to negotiate, from a long-term security deal to a share of German businesses. A French diplomat worries about the impact on international public opinion should France refuse to even discuss matters. But in Paris, the reasoning which applied in the autumn of 1918 remains strong: if the enemy is about to crack, stand firm to secure total victory. French support for Italy over Corfu is answered by Italian support for France over the Ruhr.

At the end of September, the Germans break. One Monday around midday the German Chancellor meets a delegation of one hundred and fifty representatives from the Ruhr. They are unanimous that the situation is untenable. On Wednesday, Berlin bows to the inevitable: 'To secure the life of our people, we are today required, out of bitter necessity, to interrupt this fight.' It is as if the country has been defeated a second time: first on the battlefield, now on the field of high politics and high finance. War, peace – what is the difference?

Back in Bavaria, Berlin's decision to call off passive resistance brings matters to a head. After feeding the black crocodile of Germany's radical right for so many years in an attempt to try and tame it, the authorities fear the beast may be about to bite them. They hoped that by allowing Munich to become the capital of Germany's far right they would inoculate Bavaria against communism. They turned a blind eye to far-right infiltration of local army units, thinking this would buy the troops' loyalty to the government in Munich. They allowed paramilitaries to acquire semi-official status as a last line of defence against the Communists. They allowed plotting against Berlin to take place under their noses. They coddled the black crocodile, they let it live. Now the beast is fat, and strong, and angry.

In the wake of the decision to abandon passive resistance in the Ruhr, Hitler is made political leader of the Kampfbund. A new raft of Nazi rallies are announced. Speculation mounts that they might be cover for a putsch attempt. In an act of desperation, the Bavarian establishment decide to pre-empt this by installing their own dictator. A hard-line, self-confident, anti-Semitic conservative named Gustav von Kahr is handed executive power by the authorities with a mandate to secure law and order. Troublemakers are to be deported. All political meetings are made subject to a stringent new system of approval, intended to prevent Nazis, Communists and even Bavarian nationalists from whipping things up.

The decision in Munich fractures relations with Berlin. But the situation demands action. The counter-coup seems to be working. Kahr suppresses the left and tries to woo the more traditional elements of the nationalist right. There are signs the Kampfbund may split.

CORFU, GREECE: After several weeks of diplomatic crisis played out between Rome, Paris, London, Athens and Geneva, the Italians consent to leave Corfu on terms agreed amongst the major powers. The League of Nations is sidelined.

As the date for Italian withdrawal nears, no one is the wiser about who actually murdered the general whose death caused the invasion in the first place. A commission comprising British, French, Italian and Japanese delegates is sent to investigate. Whether on his own initiative or on instructions from Rome, the Italian representative goes out of his way to disrupt anything which might portray the Greek response to the killing in a positive light. He imperiously takes charge of questioning the Greek officer who found the bodies, as if cross-examining him for murder. When the investigators visit the site of the attack he constantly interrupts proceedings to cast doubt on Greek honesty. There is only time to interview a few witnesses: a border guard, the local telephone operator, a shepherd and some goatherds.

The commission of inquiry makes a preliminary report to the major powers with some light criticism of Greek police work. The Italians – working on terms of reference that state that Greek culpability will be assumed unless proven otherwise – insist this is enough for Greece to be forced to pay fifty million lire, as demanded in Italy's original ultimatum. The French back up the Italians. The British are unhappy with the Italian insistence, but accept it. The Greeks have no choice but to give in. This is not the high-minded embrace of international political principles that Woodrow had in mind when the League of Nations was founded. It is the acceptance of power as the true determinant of affairs, dressed up to look like ethical diplomacy. The British Ambassador in Paris is disgusted. Given the grubby reality of international affairs, it is only natural that the United States 'enveloped in her white robe of virtue does not wish to soil it by rubbing shoulders with such an unclean crowd', he writes.

Athens gives instructions to the Swiss National Bank to transfer fifty million lire to the Bank of Italy in Rome. Benito Mussolini claims victory. The hero of Fiume has been eclipsed by the hero of Corfu.

DOORN: Wilhelm is excited by the visit of a German cultural anthropologist, just returned from Africa. Under his spell, the Kaiser becomes an enthusiastic convert to the idea that Germany's true destiny is not, as he had previously thought, to be the bulwark of the West against the various racial and political perils from the east, but to be natural leader of the Orient.

It is as if the scales have been lifted from his eyes, the Kaiser says. The British and the French, he has now realised, are not even white. They are 'negroes and berbers' masquerading as whites. Meanwhile, it is Germany's purity of race which will make a natural leader of those other eastern nations who respect that kind of thing. It all clicks into place. So taken is the Kaiser by this latest visitor (and his latest theories) that he decides to give him a signed photograph the next day, scrawling grandly on it that 'while the West may go under, Germany never will'. Germany's true enemy is not the Bolsheviks. It is the same as it ever was – England!

BONN, GERMANY: 'The Lower Rhine is wonderful despite the gloomy sky, the threatening level of the dollar, and the occupation', Einstein writes to his new secretary, Betty, twenty years his junior. He has fallen in love with her. He writes her poems. Perhaps it is all part of Albert's mid-life crisis, alongside the search for a perfect unified theory. To his wife, Albert writes in rather darker tones. He tells Elsa to hide the silver, in case the unstable situation in Germany leads to a fresh revolution, and advises her to use up a little Czech money they have at the bank.

MUNICH: Adolf gives an expansive interview to an American journalist explaining that while Germany could once have shared the world with England, those days are gone. 'Now, we can stretch our cramped limbs only towards the east', he says. 'The Baltic is necessarily a German lake.'

He talks freely about his racial policies. 'The fact that a man is decent is no reason why we should not eliminate him', Hitler says, reminding his interviewer that hand grenades and artillery shells during the war made no moral distinction between the pure and the impure.

He advocates patriotic ruthlessness. Syphilitics and alcoholics must not be allowed to reproduce. 'The preservation of a nation is more important than the preservation of its unfortunates', Adolf declares. 'That, to me, is the essence of humanity.'

VIENNA: An Austrian surgeon, known for his ground-breaking work on the war wounded, writes up his case notes. 'Operation at the Sanatorium Auersperg. Assistants: Dr Hofer and Dr Bleichsteiner', he begins. 'Cut through the middle of the upper lip, then around the nose till half height', he scrawls, 'after that broad cut around the buccal mucous membrane.' Like a geologist, the surgeon records cutting through bone and chiselling teeth before he can get at what he needs to remove: 'finally pulling forward the tumour and severing the nervus pterygoideus internus', a nerve at the very back of the mouth, where the jaw meets the skull. Where the cancer has been cut out, a prosthesis is fitted. There is relatively little bleeding. The patient's pulse is recorded as good: sixty-four. He must be fed through his nose. He is given injections of camphor for the pain.

It is a week before the patient writes a letter to his mother explaining his absence and warning that she may not see him for some time. When he returns home three weeks after his operation he admits to feeling 'broken and enfeebled'. Not more than a month later, he must submit to the surgeon's scalpel a second time. And then a third, this time to undergo a fashionable operation believed to boost his chances of recovery: the severing of his spermatic duct.

Freud avoids his friends. He cannot work. His speech recovers slowly, and when at last it does come back it sounds different, with the air whistling past his ill-fitting prosthesis as if between two reeds. His hearing is impaired. Is he half alive or is he half dead? Sometimes he does not know.

BAYREUTH, GERMANY: Houston Stewart Chamberlain, the well-known racist, Wagner family member and sometime correspondent of the Kaiser, is delighted that Bavaria's nationalists have chosen Bayreuth, once home of Richard Wagner, as a site for one of their famous rallies. 'Preparations for the German Day bring the house to life', he writes in his diary: 'wheel-chair ride through the flag-strewn town gave me a good deal of pleasure.' Red, white and black flags of the empire are flown rather than the black, red and yellow of the republic. The purpose, a local newspaper explains, 'is to show un-German elements that the time of hiding German patriotism in one's heart, and not showing the German blood that runs in German veins, is over'.

Adolf arrives at a quarter past eleven on Saturday evening to be greeted with the rolling of drums and the sounding of trumpets. The following morning, festivities begin at six-thirty: 'much activity from dawn till dusk', Chamberlain notes. An open-air religious service evokes the spirit of 1914, followed by a march-past of the SA and other nationalist militias (estimates of the numbers involved vary wildly). Police patrol the event with rubber truncheons, on the lookout for left-wing protesters. Someone who shouts 'Heil Moscow!' is quickly bundled away. Cosima Wagner, the great composer's widow, watches the procession from the terrace of the Wagner residence, Wahnfried.

That evening Adolf speaks at an indoor riding-arena. He is one of several nationalist speakers addressing the crowds around the city. The Bavarian authorities have warned them to avoid political controversy by criticising Kahr. They decide to court controversy instead. That night, Adolf visits Chamberlain, the idol of his youth. The old racist and young Nazi are both moved by their encounter. For Hitler, the meeting amounts to holy unction.

The next morning at ten-thirty, Chamberlain waits in his wheelchair outside Wahnfried to give Adolf a tour of the house and introduce him to the Wagner family: Cosima, her son Siegfried, and Winifred, Siegfried's English-born wife. Adolf shows up in short Bavarian leather trousers, a check shirt and thick woollen socks. Cosima is unimpressed (she has seen more dramatic figures in her time). Siegfried, a composer like his father, is much keener on the visitor. Winifred, originally from the English coastal town of Hastings, is keenest of all. Adolf weeps at Wagner's grave. He was twelve when he saw his first Wagner opera, *Lohengrin*, he remembers. The press are informed about Adolf's meeting with the Wagners. It is another step in the creation of the Hitler myth, a symbolic fusing of Nazism with the traditions of high German Romanticism. It gives Nazism a cultural pedigree.

A week later, the emotion has still not worn off for Houston Stewart Chamberlain. Meeting you, he writes to Adolf, was like feeling the spirit of August 1914 all over again: 'You have transformed the state of my soul'. 'That Germany can produce a Hitler in its moment of direst need, is proof that it still lives.' The letter feeds Adolf's sense of himself as a national Messiah. Germany must be saved and he is its saviour.

DÜSSELDORF: The same day that the Nazis march through Bayreuth, a quite different sort of demonstration takes place in Düsseldorf, in the French zone of the occupied Rhineland.

Hundreds of green, white and red flags – the colours of those who want an independent Rhineland – flutter in the air. Thousands of activists gather to hear their political leaders. French observers watch proceedings at a discreet distance, not wanting the rally to look too much like a front for their own interests.

A little before four in the afternoon, having heard the rumour that the separatists are about to formally declare an independent Rhenish republic, members of the local German police sally forth to break things up, swords flashing, guns out. The demonstrators race into nearby alleyways to take cover. The Rheinlandschutz, a pro-separatist militia, fires at the police. A battle develops near the railway station. French troops restore order. The German police are disarmed. Three hundred protestors are locked up. There are numerous casualties on all sides: two hundred have been wounded, a dozen killed.

Some separatists claim that they have been betrayed by Paris. Others see the bloodshed as a stepping stone, proving the bloodthirstiness of the Prussian authorities and making the case for independence impregnable.

TORONTO: 'It was a bad move to come back', Ernest writes to his old Paris pal Gertrude Stein: 'I have understood for the first time how men can commit suicide simply because of too many things in business piling up ahead of them.'

Hemingway is working for the *Star* again. He is not enjoying it. It seems like a step back into the past. Ernest hates his boss, Mr Hindmarsh, with a passion. There is no one he can talk to about serious writing other than a kid at the paper who is working his way through college. He misses Paris and finds Toronto duller than he remembered. Everyone he meets in North America seems so boring, a cardboard cut-out of a human being, compared to the strange and wonderful characters he came across every day in Europe.

When Hadley gives birth to a little baby boy at two o'clock in the morning on 10 October 1923 Ernest is travelling for work on a train somewhere in upstate New York. When he gets back he decides that their son bears a strong resemblance to the King of Spain. Ernie and Hadley decide to give their newborn the middle name Nicanor, after a famous Spanish matador, in addition to John (and the nickname Bumby).

It is a flash of the Hemingway bravado. But Hadley is worried. 'I think we are going to leave here as soon as I am safely strong again', she writes to a friend. 'He is almost crazy and our hearts are heavy, heavy just when we ought to be so happy.'

Hemingway still dreams of being a literary writer. He keeps copies of his first collection of poems and short stories – only three hundred have been printed – in a cupboard ready to send out to any potential reviewers. At the *Star*, he boasts that his friend Ezra Pound told him his writing is 'the best prose he has read in forty years'. In New York, Hemingway is able to lay his hands on a rare copy of a Paris literary journal, several months late, in which six of his short sketches are printed. Life is elsewhere.

PARIS: The latest edition of *Littérature* comes out in October, but its publishers worry about its long-term profitability. (The next edition will not come out until 1924.) Breton earns a crust working for a well-known art collector – who secretly he despises – and helping him expand his collection. He is a regular visitor to Picasso's studio to see what the Spaniard is working on. Over the autumn, he starts writing poetry again.

MUNICH: Hitler's *Bildverbot* – the ban on people taking pictures of him – is lifted. A Nazi photographer who has been begging Adolf to let him take his portrait for years suddenly finds his wish granted. A small picture of Hitler appears for the first time in the German press in the *Berliner Illustrierte* (alongside a feature on Germany's most famous lion tamer and a picture of Soviet gymnasts formed into a five-pointed Soviet star). Postcards of Adolf Hitler are also produced. They catch the Nazi leader in a haughty, dynamic pose, sometimes in a dark suit, other times in a beige raincoat. His hair is brilliantined back. His toothbrush moustache – the same as Chaplin in his early films – suggests a man who looks forward into the twentieth century, rather than back to the Kaiser.

Adolf tries another tack to boost his image. With Ludendorff's help, he hires someone to write a book about him. (In fact, Adolf writes most of it himself.) The task of being Hitler's amanuensis falls on a young, blonde-haired, blue-eyed Prussian aristocrat with impeccable military credentials. Unlike the mangy field-runner, the young aristocrat actively helped crush the Munich Soviet Republic in 1919. He participated in the Kapp putsch, rather than flying in when it had already failed. He has just returned from an extended trip to Finland to study how the White Finns defeated the Reds. He is the perfect choice: another bridge between old-school conservatism and the Nazis.

The resulting tract – *Adolf Hitler: His Life, His Speeches* – is a modern hagiography. Hitler is described as a present-day Christ, whose suffering will expiate the sins of the nation. The gas attack of 1918 becomes a moment of spiritual awakening when a humble patriot realises his extraordinary fate. 'This man, destined to eternal night', reads one passage, 'who during this hour endured crucifixion on pitiless Calvary, who suffered in body and soul – in the ecstasy that is only granted to the dying seer, his dead eyes shall be filled with new light, new splendour, new life!' Seventy thousand copies are printed. 'One can surely expect that this book will find its way into the hands of all party comrades', the *Völkischer Beobachter* notes confidently. It is on sale for only a few weeks before it is banned by the Bavarian authorities.

PARIS: Final preparations are made for a ballet premiere. Just a week of rehearsals before the opening night. How could it fail to succeed? The style is jazz. The writer is a long-expatriated white American called Cole Porter. The name of the show is *Within the Quota*. The subject is something of which many Europeans dream: emigration to America.

An immigrant arrives wide-eyed in America. He encounters all kinds of characters: a lady millionaire, a black vaudeville performer, a cowboy, a jazz-crazed youth, a sheriff, a Puritan. Eventually, of course, the immigrant becomes a movie star, just like Rudolph Valentino, the man who has begun to catch up with Charlie Chaplin in the American celebrity stakes. The message is clear: America, despite being a much harder country to emigrate to these days, is still a place where an outsider can become an insider, where a foreigner can make it, where what matters is who you want to be not who you are.

Ironic, then, that so many Americans should choose to leave. 'It's easier to write jazz over here than in New York', Porter explains, freed from the influence of popular music. What's more, in Europe, jazz does not belong to only one section of the population – here, jazz belongs to everyone.

MUNICH: 'How can we measure the greatness of a man?' Hitler asks a Nazi meeting. 'A feeling for the heroic', he answers. There have been three truly great German heroes, Adolf contends: Martin Luther, Frederick the Great and Richard Wagner. Is Kahr such a hero? At a rally in Nuremberg, Hitler calls the Bavarian leader a 'decent chap' and an 'able civil servant'. But true heroes must have a hero's instincts, they must have a hero's will. 'Kahr does not have such a will', the mangy field-runner tells the Nuremberg Nazis.

Adolf declares himself personally unambitious. But he has sworn an oath of loyalty. 'If everything were to fall apart,' he says, 'if others were to break their oaths of allegiance, if you yourselves deserted me one by one, and I were left quite alone in the world, know this: I will for all eternity be faithful to the German people'. Hitler portrays himself in terms Wagner would readily have understood: a figure upon a mountaintop who believes he has the power to bend nature to his will. Adolf has come to believe that he embodies Germany's rebirth. All he needs now is the right moment to prove it.

AACHEN – SPEYER – HAMBURG: You wait for a putsch for months. Then several come at once.

At two o'clock in the morning of 20 October there is a clatter of boots in Aachen, in the Belgian zone of occupation in the Rhineland. Without a shot being fired, the city's municipal buildings are occupied by a few hundred Belgian-backed Rhenish separatists. The following morning, a Sunday, they declare the Rhineland's independence from Berlin. Separately, self-appointed Rhenish authorities also pop up across the French zone. At the same time, politicians in a wine-growing area known as the Bavarian Palatinate (a portion of Bavaria clustered around the Rhine and physically separated from

the rest of the state) declare autonomy from Munich. Having already peacefully entered government in Saxony and Thuringia, the Communists now
launch their own revolutionary putsch in Hamburg, taking over thirteen of
the city's police stations and holding them for two days against the police
at the cost of forty lives. (Communist HQ tries to call off the rising at the
last minute; word does not get through in time.) Germany's political order
is disintegrating.

Events in the Rhineland are opaque. The separatists themselves are badly
split. Paris and Brussels rightly suspect each other of manipulating local
sentiment to their own ends. London views the putsches and mini-coups
along the Rhine as an attempt to revise the terms of the Treaty of Versailles
by the back door, creating breakaway German states permanently independent of Berlin.

GORKI – MOSCOW: Vladimir sits in his motor car and demands to be taken
to Moscow. His sister Maria remonstrates with him that he does not have
the right permits any more. This produces a guffaw. Vladimir, Nadya, Maria,
the doctors and some bodyguards eventually depart for Moscow, driving
at much lower speed than the impatient revolutionary would like. On
arrival, he goes to his old rooms in the Kremlin. He takes a mournful look
at the Sovnarkom table around which he used to hold cabinet meetings.
He seems emotional. There is talk about going to an agricultural exhibition.
But the rain is too heavy. The group head back to Gorki. Vladimir will not
return to Moscow.

Civil war is raging in Vladimir's Communist Party. For months, a bloc in
the Politburo has been manoeuvring to undermine Trotsky, worried that Lenin's
departure from the scene will turn his Napoleonic ambition into reality unless
it is checked. He has more prestige than any other Politburo member. To many,
he is Lenin's natural heir. He expects his point of view to carry in debate,
even when he is absent from the relevant discussions. His high-handed treatment of his colleagues, always willing to display his intellectual self-
assurance in pointing out the mistakes of others, wins him few friends.
Other Politburo members meet without Leon to caucus against him. The
sniping is incessant.

In October, Leon finally strikes back. His supporters circulate a letter
suggesting the party bureaucracy has become too strong, stifling open
discussion and leading the country into an economic malaise in urgent need
of correction. Greater freedom of expression is demanded for dissenters.

Trotsky's opponents accuse him of factionalism. To ask for a revision of party rules is to violate them. They cry heresy, disloyalty, treachery.

The Red Tsar has departed from the scene, but the soldier-prince is no longer assured a smooth succession. Then, out duck-hunting one Sunday, Trotsky catches cold after walking through a freezing bog back to his automobile. He cannot shake the illness off.

Istanbul – Ankara – Berlin – Munich: In Istanbul, a British army band plays 'Long Live Mustafa Kemal Pasha' (originally written during the war as 'Long Live Enver Pasha'), Turkish troops enter the city and Mustafa Kemal's national victory is sealed.

Within a matter of weeks, Turkey's official capital has been shifted to Ankara, a republic has been proclaimed, with Islam as the state religion, and Kemal has been confirmed as head of both the executive and legislative branches of government. 'We are returning to the days of the first Caliphs', one conservative cleric declares, hopefully. That is not how Kemal sees it, of course. He wants to reform Turkey, not to govern it in the name of God. He does not intend to share power with the last Ottoman in Istanbul, even if he is now only Caliph and no longer Sultan.

The *Berliner Illustrierte* publishes pictures of Kemal's troops parading through Istanbul for its cover in the autumn. On the inside pages a long article discusses the merits of dictatorship, illustrated with snaps of great authoritarian leaders of past and present from Julius Caesar and Napoleon to Mussolini, Lenin, the Chinese warlord Wu Peifu and Kemal. The implication is clear: sometimes, in times of crisis, only a strongman will do.

In Bavaria, the *Heimatland* newspaper demands 'an Ankara government'. Bavarian army divisions should march on Berlin to proclaim a national revolution, it demands, just as Kemal marched from Ankara to Istanbul. The scheme is not so fantastical. Bavaria's top general privately tells nationalist associations that a march on Berlin is 'the first possibility' to save the country. But the window of opportunity is brief. It must happen in the next two weeks.

Milan: Benito Mussolini, the hero of the hour, finds himself amongst friends and colleagues, talking to an association of fellow journalists.

He explains to them his vision of their role in Italian society. 'Journalism', the former editor of *Il Popolo* explains, 'is above all else, an instinct.' You have to be born a journalist; it is very hard to become one. Journalists need to recognise the importance of, as Benito puts it, 'collaborating with the nation'.

A few days later, from a balcony in Milan, he gives a forty-minute speech celebrating the first anniversary of the march on Rome, that by-now mythical event. It has been conveniently forgotten that Benito himself did not march at all, only joining his black-shirted legions once the gamble had been won. The gathered Fascists interrupt every second sentence of Mussolini's speech with loud applause. He reminds them – and all of Italy – just how responsible they have been over these past twelve months. 'We have not invaded or closed parliament', he tells the baying blackshirts, 'in spite of the inevitable nausea it has provoked in us.' But such restraint might end if Benito's enemies do not play along. 'We have not created special tribunals', he notes, 'though they might have been useful to deliver a necessary dose of lead once in a while'.

Mussolini is the master of the crowd. Italy's old bosses thought we would not last a week in office, Benito reminds the blackshirts, and yet they have already been in power for a year. 'Do you think', he asks, plucking numbers out of the air, 'that our rule will last for ... twelve years multiplied by five?' 'Yes, yes!' the crowd replies. He talks about the 'resurrection of the race': the audience laps it up. He talks about national expansion: the blackshirts can hardly contain their enthusiasm. To those who still think that fascism created Mussolini, rather than the other way around, Benito has a message: I am the boss now and I will use my power as I like. 'If tomorrow I told you that it was necessary to continue the march, and sent you off in ... another direction, would you march?' Il Duce bellows. The response is deafening.

Benito laps up the adulation. *Viva il re! Viva il fascismo! Viva l'Italia!* He is about to turn back inside. But he can't resist an encore. He leans out over the balcony balustrade and silences the crowd with a single gesture of his hand.

'To whom does Rome belong?' he asks. 'To us!' the blackshirts reply.

'To whom does Italy belong?' – 'To us!'

'To whom does victory belong?' – 'To us!'

AACHEN – BERLIN – MUNICH: There is more chaos in the Rhineland. Now French-backed Rhenish separatists march into the Belgian zone of occupation, from whence the Belgian-backed putschists of a few weeks ago flee to safety. German police reoccupy Aachen's town hall, defending it with fire hoses. The French-backed Rhenish separatists force them out. Belgian troops arrive to disarm them.

In Berlin, the Chancellor loses his majority in the Reichstag and the mark plunges to its lowest level yet. A few days later, anti-Semitic riots break out in the city, sparked by rumours that immigrants from the east are taking money destined for Germany's unemployed. Jewish shop windows are smashed, tinkling onto the pavement like shattered dreams.

As the riots are in full swing, Einstein is forced to deny media reports that he is planning a trip to Soviet Russia. There are rumours that an attempt on his life is imminent. He decides to get out of town, taking a train to Holland, where he has a teaching position at Leiden. He writes to Betty suggesting that perhaps they should move to the United States together with his wife Elsa, living as a happy threesome somewhere in upstate New York. He pictures a little clapboard house somewhere, spacious enough for them all.

In Munich, Ludendorff and Hitler plot away. They are not the only conspirators. Almost everyone has their plan for a putsch – some seeking to co-opt Kahr, others to displace him, some intending to bring in the Nazis, others to exclude them. In this atmosphere, ears are cupped over neighbours' walls to find out what is going on next door. Kahr orders enhanced surveillance of telephone, post and telegram networks.

'There is no going back now, there is only forwards', Adolf tells another rally. 'We can all feel the moment coming. Only when a black, white and red swastika flag flies over the royal palace in Berlin will the German question have been resolved.'

TORONTO: Ernest's newspaper articles look fondly back across the Atlantic to the Continent he has left behind. This autumn he writes one article on game-shooting in Europe, another on trout-fishing, several on Spain, one on Germany. Most read more like short stories than journalism: a literary escape from the drudge of the family and a job he does not care for any more.

It is hard to find inspiration in Toronto. Hemingway visits the offices of a newly founded League of Young Communists where an enthusiastic former suffragette is teaching her wards the difference between the communal life of bees and human beings. 'The bees kill their non-producers', the kindly Mrs Custance points out, admiring their apian good sense.

Ernest writes a poem entitled 'I Like Americans' for the newspaper. 'They would like to have Henry Ford for president', it suggests, 'but they will not elect him.'

MUNICH: 4 November. Now here is a plan that cannot fail. Following a ceremony attended by local army units to dedicate a monument to Munich's war dead, Adolf is to bound up the stairs of the army museum, confront Kahr and harangue him about the city's food situation. Meanwhile, Ludendorff is to persuade the army to arrest the government.

Ludendorff does not turn up. The car meant to collect him did not arrive, he says. Hitler calls it off. That night, one of the conspirators attends a Breton-style seance to summon the spirits of the netherworld to tell them the future. The dead are sadly unavailable to help.

KILMAINHAM JAIL, DUBLIN: The prisoner asks for mathematical texts to pass the time. He takes an interest in the work of Albert Einstein.

Someone inscribes a name in capital letters above his prison door, using their bayonet point to score the paint: 'MICK COLLINS'. Éamon de Valera is saddened when he sees what the vandals have done. The capital I is dotted; the N and the S are reversed.

He decides to have a word with the prison staff.

MUNICH: 8 November. Another day, another plan. Bavaria's political elite are gathering in a respectable little beer hall by the river Isar to discuss the political situation and hear Kahr speak. A golden opportunity for the unscrupulous to strike.

Ludendorff double-checks that Bavaria's senior army commander will be coming to the Bürgerbräukeller meeting that evening. To make sure that the Munich garrison is as dispersed as possible when the moment comes to launch the putsch, a number of officers are invited to a party that will never happen by putschists who will never show up. That evening, most of the army's top brass are either in the beer hall or at home in civilian clothes. One senior officer is attending a lecture on trade with the United States.

Meanwhile, the putschists prepare. Members of the Kampfbund assemble in their favourite bars and bowling alleys. A little after eight a contingent is bussed to the Bürgerbräukeller. The police guarding Bavaria's political elite are outnumbered. They soon give way. SA men surround the building. The moment has arrived.

Adolf Hitler theatrically throws away a pint of beer (which his friend Putzi has just bought him – for one billion marks) and elbows his way to the front of the hall. Clambering up onto a chair, he shoots into the ceiling with a pistol to get everyone's attention and declares that a national revolution has begun. Hitler invites Kahr, Bavaria's senior general and Munich's police chief to parley in an adjoining room. He tries to persuade them to go along with the putsch rather than fight it.

In the beer hall, there is uproar. Hermann Göring, the air ace turned SA leader, calls for calm. Cries of 'Mexico' and 'South America' go up, likening the Bavarian putschists to bandits. Adolf gives an update from the negotiations. Kahr and the others have not yet been fully persuaded. But they will be. 'Either the German revolution begins tonight', he says, 'or tomorrow we will all be dead.' Ludendorff arrives in full dress uniform to apply pressure on Kahr and his associates. Who can say no to the man who lost the war? Kahr returns to the beer hall to announce that he is prepared to act as regent for the monarchy in a new government. Hitler is to be in charge of propaganda. He clasps Kahr's hand to thank him for his words. While Adolf is off dealing with other matters, Ludendorff lets Kahr, the general and the police chief go.

In Munich, confusion reigns. Nobody is clear about the actual state of affairs between the army, the police and the putsch. Confusion leads to delay in the conspirators taking over vital buildings. And delay saps momentum. At one point, cadets who support the putsch and police who support Kahr face each other across the street outside Kahr's headquarters. There is uncertainty about who is on whose side, or whether they are all in fact on the same side. A shoot-out seems imminent. Then an order comes in, supposedly from Ludendorff, countermanding earlier instructions to take the building.

At midnight, the putschists are still confident. They have the promises of Kahr, the army commander and the police chief. The odd miscommunication is to be expected. By four the next morning, the truth begins to dawn: they have been betrayed. Kahr and the others have decided to oppose Hitler and Ludendorff. A promise extracted at gunpoint is no promise at all. Munich army headquarters has already been in touch with other garrisons in Bavaria to ensure their loyalty. By eight, the Kampfbund members in the Bürgerbräukeller realise that they are not the vanguard of a national revolution, but the isolated remnants of a putsch which has failed before it even got off the ground. Ludendorff, having changed into civilian clothes, sips red wine. Someone orders the beer hall's band to play some marching tunes. Putzi Hanfstaengl is engaged on liaison duties with the foreign press.

The putsch has lost momentum. But no counter-punch has knocked it out. Ludendorff goes back to his creed of 1918: it is a matter of nerves. Show the enemy one's own defiance, and they will crack. 'The heavens will fall before the Bavarian Reichswehr turns against me!' he exclaims. A column of pro-putsch militia is organised, arranged a dozen abreast as if on a German Day march-past. On its way towards the city centre, the Kampfbund column sweeps through a line of armed police guarding one of the bridges, beating them up as it does.

A few minutes later, at the entrance to the Odeonsplatz, more armed police bar the way. The putschists – some armed, some not – are confident these police will be no different. Many are Nazi sympathisers, after all. Then the bullets start flying. It is a little after midday. There are snow flurries in the air. For twenty or thirty seconds, chaos reigns. There is firing in both directions. Machine guns are brought up. Most Kampfbund members hit the ground to avoid the bullets whizzing around. Adolf is pulled down by a Baltic Freikorps man, dislocating his shoulder in the process. Ludendorff keeps walking towards the police, arriving at their lines unscathed.

Fourteen bodies lie on the ground. Göring, wounded in the leg, takes cover behind a stone lion before limping away from the scene of the shooting as fast as he can. Hitler is carried to safety by a doctor and a medical orderly. He is then whisked off in an automobile – destination Austria.

'It sounds very funny,' Hemingway writes about the events in a letter to his pal Gertrude in Paris, 'the early dispatches so far'. He is not the only one. 'Ludendorff may never live down the laughter', says the *New York Herald*. One wit calls the general's gang so hopeless they would have been 'repulsed by "Keep off the grass" signs'. In Paris, they laugh out loud at the putsch's 'vaudeville ending' with everyone backstabbing everyone else. 'An idol has fallen', notes *Le Matin*, declaring Ludendorff irretrievably damaged and the entire revanchist movement leaderless. In Rome, Benito receives an account from the Italian consul in Munich describing the putchists as '*buffoni*' – 'clowns'. It has been a giant farce from start to finish.

In Germany, the putsch is treated as the natural result – understandable and perhaps even forgivable – of months and months of stretched nerves. 'It was almost a mathematical inevitability', notes the *Berliner Illustrierte*. When the moment of explosion finally comes, some find it almost a relief.

DOORN: Wilhelm follows events in Munich from a safe distance in Holland. His adjutant rushes over the latest newspapers for the Kaiser to look at while taking a break from wood-chopping. His entourage debates the merits and drawbacks of a civil war. Amongst the dispatches from Bavaria, the Kaiser also learns, to his dismay, that his son the Crown Prince has gone back to Germany without his father's permission. 'The stupidity of youth', the Kaiser roars. 'What was he thinking?'

Wilhelm seems almost relieved when the putsch fails. 'Thank God, the whole stupid story has come to an end', he tells his equerry. After all, while he is as happy as anyone to see the republic he hates take a black eye, what role would there have been for him if the putsch had been a success? 'The new Reich', Wilhelm writes to an old supporter a little later in the year, 'will not come from a beer joint.'

He will just have to wait a little longer for his moment, the Kaiser tells himself. It is safer that way – look at what happened to stupid Charles in Budapest. Occasionally he contemplates a more dramatic course of action. If the French go any further, he tells a startled adjutant, then he will have to return whatever the cost, first to take up the sword against the Fatherland's domestic enemies (the socialists) and then against the French. His advisers know better than to take such outbursts too seriously.

AMERICA: Through the hisses, haltingly, a voice. Apart from those who have attended the man's speeches, America has not heard Woodrow Wilson before. Now, the day before Armistice Day 1923, the ex-President speaks over the airwaves. It is the voice of another age, the voice of a nineteenth-century Southern gentleman.

To some, Woodrow Wilson's words sound suspiciously like a campaign speech. Does he still entertain political ambitions? President Coolidge and the Republicans are weighed down by rumours of wrongdoing under his predecessor's administration. A scandal around the leasing of some oilfields back in 1921 and 1922 is brewing in Washington, with stories of 'loans' which were really kickbacks. The sage of Dearborn – if he were to stand as an independent – would be likely to further weaken the Republicans. Might a Democrat with experience manage to come through the middle?

Though delivered slowly and deliberately, Woodrow's speech crackles with partisan indignation. The voice coming out of radio-sets across the country attacks the 'sullen and selfish isolation' into which America has retreated since the war. The Republicans, Woodrow claims, have no answers to America's economic and social challenges. France and Italy, meanwhile, have made 'waste paper' of the Versailles Treaty. 'The affairs of the world can be set straight only by the firmest and most determined exhibition of the will to lead', he warns. He does not need to remind America that 1924 will be election year.

America hears the voice – but does not see the man. Wilson delivers his speech in his dressing gown. Though a table is set up in the library for him, he insists on standing behind the microphone, resting on a cane. Edith holds a carbon copy of the speech in case her husband should require a prompt. His eyesight in his good eye is failing. He can barely read. His mind is more one-tracked than it used to be.

INNSBRUCK AND KUFSTEIN, AUSTRIA – UFFING-AM-STAFFELSEE, GERMANY: The former air ace Hermann Göring escapes from Germany to Innsbruck, in terrible pain from the bullet wounds to his leg. Morphine is used to dull the pain during an emergency operation. (Göring develops a lifelong addiction as a result.) Putzi Hanfstaengl is helped across the Austrian border to Kufstein and spends the first night after the putsch attempt on the tiled floor of a flower shop.

Hitler does not make it so far. His escape vehicle breaks down halfway to the border and he seeks refuge in the Hanfstaengls' country house in the foothills of the Alps. Covered in mud from racing along country roads and hiding in a nearby wood till dark, he does not look like anyone's idea of the Messiah. Helene gives him her husband's blue bathrobe to wear. His dislocated shoulder makes it impossible for him to wear anything else.

The next morning, Hitler sends word to allies uncompromised by the Munich fiasco that he needs another car. Two-year-old Egon Hanfstaengl watches Uncle Dolf pace up and down as he waits. What is taking them so long? At five that afternoon, Helene's mother-in-law calls. The police are nearby. Hitler grabs his Browning revolver as if to take his own life. Helene calmly disarms him and hides the gun in a flour jar. Adolf issues instructions for what to do if he is taken. Helene makes notes.

The police arrive an hour later. Hitler is taken into custody dressed in the oversized clothes of another man, covered by a raincoat pinned with his war medals. The Nazi leader briefly harangues the police, as if he were at one of his meetings again. Then he is led away – bedraggled, depressed, beaten.

On the way to Landsberg Fortress, where he is to be incarcerated pending trial, Adolf learns that Ludendorff has already managed to talk his way out of custody, claiming to be an innocent bystander caught up in someone else's plan. It is exactly five years since the armistice of 1918.

MOSCOW – PETROGRAD – BERLIN: Clare Sheridan returns to Russia for the first time since 1920. The romance has gone. Enthusiasm turns to disillusionment.

The promise of the communist revolution once seemed so great, Clare remembers. Back then, utopia was something almost tangible. Now she feels that conviction has turned into cynicism. Clarity has become compromise. History used to gallop; now it seems to crawl. Under the skin, the new bureaucrats are the same as the old. The same instincts – greed, lust, love, hate – rule Russia as they do the rest of the world. Clare telephones one of the Bolshevik leaders she used to dine with, expecting to be invited back into their confidence, to start again where she left off. She is told bluntly: 'You are not the type of newspaper correspondent we are accustomed to.'

Moscow is not a place for romantics like Clare Sheridan. What can they offer the Union of Soviet Socialist Republics? Moscow needs money, not sympathy. Instead of being put up in a VIP guesthouse in an old palace, Clare is forced to stay in a characterless hotel filled with tawdry British and American concession-hunters. Clare suspects the place is bugged.

She suggests a trip to the Caucasus. The authorities say no. Perhaps to Saratov? Too cold, the authorities respond. The Communists do not want foreigners roving around the country. Clare is finally given permission to visit Petrograd, and assigned a minder. To awaken her charitable instincts – a good use for Western journalists, this – Clare is shown around new hospitals which have no medicines and orphanages where she is asked for money. Another day, she is escorted to the former imperial palace of Tsarskoe Selo. Rasputin once walked here. Tsar Nicholas once slept there. Now the place is a museum. Groups of proletarians tramp through to gawp at the tastelessness of the Romanovs (and be told how much better off they are as a result of their removal).

Clare finds herself bored and frustrated. Her thoughts become disjointed. She feels alienated from her surroundings, alienated from her own past. Russia once seemed to throw up dynamic and imaginative revolutionary leaders by the dozen. But who is running Russia today? The country is crawling with capitalists, gamblers, men in sharp suits with rolls of cash. There are new Lenins now, and they are nothing like the old Lenin. They are functionaries, not revolutionaries.

Clare is distraught. It is one thing not to have ever believed in something, quite another to have believed and been disappointed. She decides to give up journalism entirely.

LEIDEN, THE NETHERLANDS: Albert decides to keep out of Germany for the moment. The situation there is too unsettled. He is working on a new theory, trying to address the quantum problem. His stomach problems have returned – nerves, a friend thinks. He has taken to writing aphorisms: '*Children do not learn from the life lessons of their parents. Nations learn nothing from their history. Bad experiences must always be made anew.*'

Albert reads books about Japan and prepares for a talk he is to give at an incandescent lamp factory in Eindhoven. Betty sends him photographs of herself to cheer him up.

ROME: A new political axis is being formed in southern Europe. 'Excellency,' Miguel Primo de Rivera tells Benito over lunch at the Palazzo Venezia in Rome, 'your figure is not just an Italian one, but a global one; you are the chief apostle of the campaign against dissolution and anarchy afflicting Europe.' Glasses of sparkling wine are raised for the Spanish leader's toast.

'From Mussolini-ism', the general says, 'a belief, a doctrine of redemption is forming, with admirers and advocates all around the world.' In a newspaper interview, he goes even further, declaring his hope that Spain follows in the footsteps of Italian fascism, which he calls a 'universal phenomenon' and a 'living gospel'. In return, Benito conveys the fraternal greetings of all Italians now 'marching along the open road of Fascist revolution'.

BERLIN – LANDSBERG FORTRESS: A magazine runs a cartoon showing two smartly dressed bourgeois men meeting on the street. One wears a strange badge on his lapel, multicoloured and multi-form. 'What is it?' his friend asks. 'A swastika inside a Soviet star', the man replies: 'One never knows from which side a putsch will come.'

In the autumn, a new German currency is introduced. Prices begin to stabilise. *Simplicissimus* now sells for thirty pfennigs. By December, the movement for the independence of the Rhineland has lost any support it once had.

Visitors to Landsberg Fortress note how much weight Hitler has lost. He refuses the prison food. The Wagners send him care packages. He is overjoyed when his dog Wolf is brought to see him. Politically, the Nazi Führer is reduced to writing angry letters to the authorities through his lawyer. He rages to the prison psychologist about how Germany is not worth a damn: 'Let them see how well they will do without me.'

GORKI: 'Every day he makes a conquest', Nadya writes to Inessa's daughter, 'but they're all microscopic.' Vladimir sits through a film of the sixth anniversary of the revolution, unable to say more than a few words. Nadya does all the talking now. An artist visits with the thought of doing a portrait of Lenin. But he finds a man in a wheelchair who looks nothing like the dictator he used to know.

Trotsky writes articles for *Pravda* and essays warning of an old revolutionary guard – Stalin and his cronies – unwilling to revise their past and of a new culture of servility in the party. 'Any man trained merely to say "yes, sir" is a nobody'. The party must free itself from its own bureaucracy. Leon is desperately ill. He comes home exhausted every night. The doctors advise him to take a rest by the Black Sea.

TORONTO: A batch of copies of Ernest's second book – called *in our time*, modishly printed out all in lower case – arrives in Canada in December. They contain a dozen literary sketches (some about bullfighting) to add to the six printed in the *Little Review*. Hemingway's sister Marcelline orders a few copies as Christmas presents. Later, she decides that they are not quite right as family gifts. She sends them back to Paris where such literary creations belong.

Hemingway cannot bear it any longer. He hands in his resignation to the *Star*, effective 1 January 1924. The young journalist, still only twenty-five, has made a decision: the Hemingways are going back to Europe and he is going to become a full-time writer.

LAKE GARDA: Gabriele D'Annunzio donates his house, the Vittoriale, to Italy at the end of December. Benito sends a telegram to his old rival to thank him for his gift on behalf of 'THE ITALY OF *VITTORIO VENETO*' (that is to say, the Italy of the glorious final battle of 1918).

'IN THE TOUGH DAILY WORK OF GOVERNMENT', Mussolini continues, 'I FEEL THAT YOUR DREAM OF VICTORY HAS BECOME THE DREAM OF THE ENTIRE ITALIAN PEOPLE.' He promises to live up to it. It is a message from the man of the present to the man of the past.

VIENNA: Still weak from his ordeals, Sigmund Freud receives an early Christmas present, and a token of his growing fame: a copy of an unsolicited biography, the first to be written about him in any language. 'I need hardly say that I neither expected nor desired the publication of such a book', Freud writes back. He sends a list of corrections, in case there is a second edition.

EPILOGUE

1924

For the first time in years, a treat: *Schlagobers* – cream whipped into dreamy Alpine peaks – reappears in Vienna's coffee houses. Sigmund Freud has started work again, 'with downright animalistic satisfaction'. His speaking voice, while less strong than it was, is now intelligible. Smoking cigars, however, has become more difficult. To insert one, his mouth must be held open with a wooden clothes peg.

*

'One has even long since become accustomed to the insecurity about the future and thinks as little of that as of one's own death', Albert Einstein writes. 'It all comes along under its own steam without us doing anything ourselves.' He promises himself to live life more quietly this year. Less travel. At forty-four, he is no longer a young man. He is aware of younger physicists who may yet outshine him.

*

Nadya reads her husband short stories by Jack London about gold prospectors in the Klondike. She lies about the splits at a party conference where Trotsky is accused of 'petty-bourgeois deviation' and the party leaders organise a resolution against him.

On 21 January 1924, Vladimir is given coffee and bouillon and confined to bed. Later that day, Nadya hears a strange gurgling in his chest. That evening, the dictator dies. Trotsky is given the news at a railway station in the Caucasus on his way to the Black Sea. 'Lenin is no more', he writes; 'these words fall upon our mind as heavily as a giant rock falls into the sea.' He decides not to return to Moscow.

The GPU is told to brace for trouble. In life the dictator's health was kept a secret; in death, the published autopsy report turns his final illness into a heroic struggle against fate. A death mask is made. Lenin's brain is removed for special scientific investigation and found to be heavier than average, supposedly a mark of his great intelligence.

His funeral takes place on the coldest day of the year. Thousands queue for hours to walk past his coffin. Portraits are held up like icons. Stalin is in the honour guard. In Petrograd, now renamed Leningrad, three quarters of a million participate in commemorations. Medical stations are set up to take care of frostbite victims.

Russia's radios fall silent. Then a new message pulses across the Red empire the dictator has bequeathed: 'Lenin has died – but Leninism lives'. Against Nadya's wishes, a decision is taken to preserve his body rather than to bury it. It is the revolution's property now.

Trotsky spends long days looking at the sea through palm trees.

Mayakovsky begins to write a poem.

*

Winston Churchill greets the news that Britain will have a Labour Prime Minister with horror. Socialism is the kind of awful thing that usually happens after a country has been defeated in war, not if it is the victor. He writes the new PM a letter of congratulation nonetheless.

*

An agreement is struck for Fiume to be finally annexed to Italy. Shortly thereafter, on his own suggestion, Gabriele D'Annunzio is made a Prince.

*

Woodrow jots down some thoughts for his 1924 presidential nomination acceptance speech. 'Overwhelming honour', he begins. Two weeks later, he is dead. As in Moscow when Vladimir passed, radio shows are cancelled across America. The only embassy in Washington that does not fly its flag at half-mast is that of Germany.

*

The trial of General Ludendorff and Adolf Hitler begins in Munich. Once the mangy ex-field-runner starts talking, no one can shut him up. He launches into an explanation of his political philosophy. There are times when only fanaticism – 'intense, ruthless, brutal fanaticism' – can save a country from slavery, he declares. There can be no treason against the traitors of 1918.

*

André Breton, the sometime Dadaist provocateur, magazine editor, art aficionado, psychiatric doctor and now – tentatively – surrealist, publishes his latest book: *Les Pas Perdus*, or *The Lost Steps*. He sends a copy to Tristan Tzara. He makes it out to 'the swindler-of-all-trades, the old parrot, the police informant'. He returns to automatic writing. He decides he needs a manifesto.

*

Mustafa Kemal cements his power. In March, the Caliphate is abolished and the last Caliph sent off into exile on the Orient Express. Religious schools are closed. Religious courts are shut down.

Kemal's jilted girlfriend Fikriye makes an unauthorised trip from Istanbul to Ankara to try and see the man she loves. She is refused access to the presidential palace in which she once lived. She shoots herself with a handgun and dies from complications soon after.

*

Up early to prepare formula for his son Bumby. Then perhaps some boxing in the gym on the Rue de Pontoise. Relying on Hadley's dwindling inheritance for funds, Ernest takes an unpaid position as assistant editor on the city's latest literary magazine, a rag called the *transatlantic review* (note the lower case). The April issue of the magazine reviews some of his own work.

*

Hitler gives his final court address. 'When is treason really treason?' he asks. In the end, there is only patriotism and betrayal. Bismarck once broke the rules of the Prussian constitution to advance the cause of German unity. Was that treason? Mustafa Kemal disobeyed the Sultan to fight for his people's freedom. Was that treason? Was Mussolini's march on Rome an act of treason before it became an act of national salvation?

He recalls the bright promises made at the end of the war – of peace, freedom, self-determination – and the awful reality of hunger, humiliation and national disintegration which came instead. 'My noble lords, if the next five years are like the last five, will there be any Germany left for our children at all?' The verdict of history is all that really matters, Hitler says: no one will remember what some judge said in 1924.

The judge duly awards Adolf five years in jail. Ludendorff is let off.

*

Benito announces that the works of Machiavelli are now more relevant than ever. The April elections are a triumph. The Fascists – under a list which co-opts figures of influence up and down the country – win two thirds of the national vote. The King salutes the 'generation of victory which now controls the government'. Italy's Great War has come to an end at last.

*

One day in May, in the Sheraton Hotel, Cincinnati, those old rivals William Du Bois and Marcus Garvey finally meet. Garvey is stepping out of the hotel elevator. Du Bois is going in. He pretends not to notice his enemy, about whom he has just published another article. He claims the twitching of his nose was to do with the smell of breakfast and nothing more.

*

The surrealist rush is on. Breton's rivals criticise him for his proprietorial ambitions. 'Mr Breton, get used to it: you will never be the Pope of Surrealism', one writes. 'Surrealism belongs to everyone and will not be monopolised.'

*

In America, the name 'Teapot Dome' becomes a byword for corruption. The country's leading oil baron testifies that one hundred thousand dollars was indeed paid to the former Secretary of the Interior – delivered by his son, in cash, in a black satchel. This was a loan, and not a bribe, he explains. To a man as rich as him, a hundred thousand is a 'mere bagatelle' – equivalent to twenty-five bucks to a mere mortal. America seems full of gangsters and prospectors and men on the make. The nation is obsessed with the stock market.

Henry Ford does not run for the presidency.

*

In jail, Adolf receives food packages from admirers and the prisoners are allowed a pint of beer with dinner every night. While some chop wood for recreation or engage in various athletic activities, Hitler prefers to play the referee. 'A leader cannot afford to be beaten at games', he explains. He takes particular pleasure watching a bloody boxing match.

On the feast day of St Adolf, a revue is organised in his honour. One inmate dresses up as Charlie Chaplin; another pretends to be a gypsy, reading men's fortunes from grains of coffee. Occasionally Hitler relives his war experiences for his followers, jumping around the room gesticulating wildly, making all the sound effects himself, like a Futurist poetry recital or a piece of Dadaist theatre.

He starts writing his autobiography, banging it out day after day on an American-made Remington typewriter. Adolf wonders if he could write a book as great as Henry Ford's bestseller *My Life*. He talks with a new (male) secretary called Rudolf Hess about the possibilities of space travel, discusses his views on astrology and shows him his most recent architectural sketches: a huge domed building in which national festivals will be celebrated in the future, plans for a gigantic new Great War museum, stage designs for operas by Wagner and Puccini.

One day he reads out a passage of his book, recalling how in France the sounds of battle used to mix with young men's voices singing 'Deutschland, Deutschland, über alles'. Adolf starts to cry.

*

The Ku Klux Klan claims four million members across the United States, with Senators at its beck and call. Neither Democrats nor Republicans condemn it.

*

A court in London determines that Grand Duke Michael, Nicholas Romanov's younger brother, must be dead by now. (He was shot in 1918.) A fight breaks out amongst the Romanov family over who is now the rightful Tsar.

In Moscow, Lenin's funeral commission is repurposed as a commission for the immortalisation of his memory. Scientists work on a secret embalming fluid. His body is to be mummified. Stalin delivers lectures on Leninism at Sverdlov University.

The most explosive of Lenin's dictations from two winters ago remain unpublished. Some are read out in a secret party meeting. Stalin admits to being rude. 'We are not frightened by rudeness', a stooge in the audience interjects. Trotsky admits that it is impossible to be right against the party. Even Nadya rebukes him.

*

At the Venice Biennale, works of Russian artists are displayed for the first time since 1914. Following Lenin's death, even Fascist Italy has accorded diplomatic recognition to the Soviets. The centrepiece of the Italian contribution to the exhibition is a white marble bust of Mussolini – not by Clare Sheridan – his neck as thick as a bull's, his brow furrowed in an expression of stern, almost angry, determination. It is Benito's preferred look to keep the masses on their toes – the ancient Roman style updated to reflect a cruder and more energetic age.

No one quite knows whether Mussolini himself is to blame for the bungled kidnapping and murder of the leader of Italy's Socialists that summer. Several Fascist thugs are arrested; there is as yet no bloodied body to shock the nation. 'Let him who is without sin cast the first stone', preaches the Vatican newspaper. The stock market flutters but does not crash. Italy's old elites may not like the rougher side of fascism, but they are prepared to live with it. The Socialists boycott parliament. The King refuses to fire Mussolini.

*

The Kaiser receives a letter from one of his few remaining supporters, an old Prussian general. He is only waiting for the signal to fall behind the Kaiser and his restoration, the general writes. Wilhelm is dismissive. 'Who is going to call?' he asks. 'There are no leaders ... just non-entities.'

*

Armed with three Kodak cameras, two air-beds, four suitcases (one containing evening wear), all strapped to the back of a motorcycle called Santanella, Clare Sheridan sets off on her latest adventure: a trip across

Europe with her brother in his sidecar. Holland whizzes past. In Germany, people ask Clare why she didn't take the train.

In Czechoslovakia she notes pictures of Woodrow Wilson hanging side by side with portraits of Masaryk, the charming Czech gentleman who was so helpful to Jessie Kenney and Emmeline Pankhurst in Petrograd back in 1917. Clare finds Warsaw a disappointment. In Brest-Litovsk, she poses for a photograph outside the fortress where Trotsky declared 'neither war, nor peace'. It seems such a long time ago now. In Kiev, there is a Communist procession on the tenth anniversary of the outbreak of war, complete with clowns playing the capitalists. But the city is quite different from Moscow last year. Communism is only skin deep here. Christian pilgrims still walk the ancient pathways to the old monasteries. Clare meets a few local Jewish traders who would like to emigrate to Palestine.

In Crimea, Clare sees two great naval guns set up by General Wrangel to defend his last redoubt against the Red Army. A guide takes Clare and her brother around the Romanovs' summer palace. In Odessa, Clare is confronted with the strangest thing of all: an actor dressed in black tails and a top hat who is the spitting image of the new British Labour Prime Minister. Clare is told they are making a film about him.

*

'Keep Cool with Coolidge', advises the Republican Party in the hot summer of 1924, ahead of the presidential elections in the autumn. The prospect of a Henry Ford candidacy is now completely forgotten.

*

Adolf Hitler continues to work on his book. He pushes the ideas of others to absurd, hateful conclusions. He does not pause to question his own thinking. He discovers he was right all along, without even knowing it. His own fantasy narratives become a sort of holy gospel. He is his own God, the source of his own revelations. His thoughts only tend in one direction: towards the extremes.

'Yes, it is quite true,' Adolf tells a Nazi from Bohemia, 'I have changed my mind on the best means of fighting the Jews.' He was too soft in the past. 'In the course of writing my book, I have come to the conclusion we must only use the harshest means in the future.'

*

With Germany at the negotiating table and the Americans dangling the mighty dollar before their eyes, the French accept a Wall Street compromise. German reparations will be spread out over decades. France will lose the ability to sanction Germany if payments are not made. The country will be rehabilitated economically, with a huge loan secured against the nation's assets. French troops will be out of the Ruhr within a year. The British Prime Minister calls it the first real peace treaty, 'because we sign it with a feeling that we have turned our backs on the terrible years of war and war mentality'.

*

A new play catches the eye of the *New York Times*'s theatre critic in September. The plot is ridiculous (it centres on the horse races), the set is colourful, the songs are hummable (courtesy of Sissle and Blake of *Shuffle Along* fame). It is called *The Chocolate Dandies*. All the actors are black. One of them steals the show. For most of it she is dressed in a ragged cotton dress. Not much to look at, with a certain slapstick charm. At one point she imitates a saxophone and crosses her eyes while doing so. The audience roars with laughter. Then she dances, and they are mesmerised by her unearthly fluidity.

The *New York Times* calls her a 'freak'. But what does that matter? There it is: Josephine Baker's name in print. The girl from St. Louis has become a star.

*

A commission of twenty-six lawyers starts work on adapting the Swiss civil code for Turkey. Polygamy will be outlawed. Men will lose the right to divorce their wives at will. 'Countries vary,' Mustafa Kemal says, 'but civilisation is one, and for a nation to progress it must take part in this single civilisation.'

*

Despite recognition of his good behaviour by the prison warder, Adolf Hitler's request for parole – after just six months of his five-year sentence for high treason – is turned down.

*

A storm blows in from the Gulf of Finland and Leningrad is flooded. The old wooden block pavements of the city float off into the sea like pieces of an enormous jigsaw puzzle. Students work waist-deep to save Russia's historic treasures from destruction. Tsar Peter the Great's slippers are amongst the casualties. At the Institute of Experimental Medicine, Pavlov's dogs are saved from the drowning. As the flood-waters recede, hundreds of blue-and-gold chairs are set out to dry outside the Mariinsky theatre alongside scenic backdrops from past productions from another age.

Those left homeless will find it easy to secure alternative accommodation somewhere in the city. So many of its people have moved to the country-side, or to Moscow, or abroad. Leningrad is a shadow of what imperial Petrograd once was.

*

One Friday afternoon in the autumn, a new research institute opens its doors in Paris. It is called the Bureau of Surrealist Research. Its director is André Breton. Opening hours to the public are 4.30 p.m. to 6 p.m. every day except Sunday. A new magazine is planned, called *La Révolution Surréaliste*.

The battle for the surrealist name is not yet finished. Now André produces a new weapon: a surrealist manifesto. It bears little relation to Tzara's Zurich text, with its zingy contradictions and jokey tone. Surrealism is serious. Rationalism is dying, Breton writes, 'trapped in a cage of its own making, unable to escape'. The surrealist manifesto is rationalism's epitaph and a slingshot into a new world: an instruction manual, a polemic, a kind of poem, a roll-call of current adherents and past forebears. (Dante and Shakespeare were both surrealists *avant la lettre*, apparently; André claims Picasso for the cause as well.) At its centre, of course, is the rediscovery of the subconscious, and a fascination with the power of dreams.

Breton recalls the impression made on him by the rapid-fire 'spoken thought' of shell-shock victims during the war. He remembers the awe he felt, in 1917, when watching Babinski diagnose patients at La Salpêtrière. Though nameless, they too are the forebears of surrealism. It is in the state of dreaming, the manifesto reads, that the human spirit is at its most unbounded, where humans become superhuman, where 'one can kill, fly faster, love as much as one wants to'. Humankind has been projected into a new world, where the unbounded and irrational can at last be given their proper due. Putting his embarrassing Vienna interview to one side, André makes clear it is Freud who has cleared the way.

'Surrealism is the "invisible ray" which will one day enable us to win over our enemies', he writes: 'This summer the roses are blue; the wood is made of glass. The earth, draped in green, makes no more impression on me than a ghost. It is living and ceasing to live which are imaginary solutions. Existence is elsewhere.'

*

Einstein is unsure. Should he break it off with Betty, or should he embrace the gift he has been given? Two voices compete inside him. He puts them both down in a letter to Betty. 'First voice: You are a degenerate chap for allowing yourself to play with a young creature's future for your own pleasure', he writes. Then: 'It's deplorable if you abandon her against her will for the sake of an uncertain fate.' In mathematics, and in physics, there are answers. Why is it that in love there are only probabilities and uncertainties? Einstein continues working on his unified field theory. It never comes off.

*

The boom is on. Soviet industrial production is growing faster than anyone expected (in a few years it might even pass the level Tsarist Russia reached before the war). On Wall Street, stock prices are double what they were in 1921, when Henry Ford was blaming Jewish financiers for all the world's ills. Millions of dollars in debt repayments, the financial sting in the tail of the Great War alliance, flow across the Atlantic from London and Paris to the money men of New York. Millions flow back as American loans and investment abroad. A loan of eight hundred million goldmarks to Germany is over-subscribed in fifteen minutes.

America's corporations are in expansive mood, buying up the world's oil and rubber, taking control of Spain's telephone and telegraphs, setting up new automobile factories in Copenhagen, Antwerp and London. There is no escaping it, Europe is fast becoming a wholly owned subsidiary. The Continent is flooded with American movies. American culture is surging across the world. In October, the *New York Age* reports negotiations for *The Chocolate Dandies* to go abroad. Above the article, the newspaper runs a picture of Josephine Baker, the star of the show. The twenties have finally begun to roar.

*

A few days before the third election in a year, a letter purporting to come from the Comintern surfaces in London suggesting that Moscow is trying to influence British politics, and that Labour is aware of it. The scandal causes a swing to the right. Winston is elected with Conservative support and given a plum job in the new government. Political resurrection has come early.

*

In October, France accords diplomatic recognition to the USSR (now only the United States does not). In Bizerte, Tunisia, the consequences are immediate. White Russian sailors are ordered off the ships they arrived on from Crimea in Wrangel's retreat. The naval school becomes an orphanage. A Soviet delegation is invited to decide what to do with the sad remainder of the imperial fleet. Wrangel calls it a betrayal, 'an insult to Russian national honour'. The ships are ultimately scrapped.

*

'It is the duty of the Party to bury Trotskyism as an ideological trend', Stalin announces. His enemy is made into an -*ism*, an impersonal tendency which can be censored and removed. 'We did not want and did not strive for this literary discussion', Stalin says. 'Trotskyism is forcing it upon us by its anti-Leninist pronouncements: well, we are ready, comrades.'

In *Pravda* the Georgian reverses the praise he once gave Leon for his contribution to the revolution of 1917. Now, he says the opposite. 'Comrade Trotsky played no particular role in the party or the October insurrection and could not do so, being a man comparatively new to our party in the October period.'

Within a couple of months, Trotsky's long retreat to Mexico has begun, and Stalin's rise has become inexorable.

*

On the cover of *Time* magazine, a pencil sketch, taken from a photograph, shows a man in late middle age, wearing a Western-style bow tie. The high forehead and kindly demeanour suggest perhaps an inventor or a professor of engineering. The viewer's eyes linger for a while on this face, not exactly good-looking, but nonetheless a picture of confident, masculine bourgeois respectability. Then they see a name they recognise: Sigmund Freud.

The new world takes to Sigmund more than the old world ever did. America is infatuated. The country is abuzz with his theories. To 'be psyched' enters common parlance. Freud's open coldness towards America seems to have produced the opposite effect to that one might expect. Perhaps America wants to be dominated after all.

*

Investigations into the murder of Italy's Socialist leader point towards orders from on high. Mussolini's tyrannical impulses provoke acts of rebellion. In La Scala, Toscanini refuses to play the Fascist anthem, declaring the opera house is 'not a beer garden'. But Benito plays his cards slowly and deliberately. By the New Year, his rivals have to acknowledge that they cannot remove him. He now assumes the role of dictator.

*

Mayakovsky starts reciting a poem he has written – his longest yet – praising the dictator who never liked his work, and warning against his deification while contributing to it at the same time.

> I am worried that
>> processions
>>> and mausoleums,
> celebratory statues
>> set in stone,
> will drench
>> Leninist simplicity
> in syrup smooth balsam –

It is far too late for that. By the end of 1924, the Lenin Institute has already become so full of papers and books that a new building is planned for it to move into, with a large new library. The wooden mausoleum on Red Square is already six months old and new editions of Lenin's works are being prepared in haste. The Soviet system is hardening like Lenin's arteries before his death. The lifeblood of revolution is slowing.

*

In December, the Hollywood film producer Samuel Goldwyn departs on a business trip to Europe. He tells reporters that there is one man he is particularly keen to meet, 'the greatest love specialist in the world': the father of psychoanalysis, Sigmund Freud. With Freud as a collaborating screenwriter, the producer explains, films can be made which have 'audience appeal far greater than any productions made today'. He is perfectly serious.

*

A few days before Christmas, the Bavarian Supreme Court decides Adolf Hitler should be released from prison after all. The man can be no harm. Germany is stabilising. The Nazis did not do well in recent elections.

Adolf is picked up at the fortress gates. He rejects the notion of going to see Ludendorff. No time for old generals now. Instead, he visits his only friends. He asks Putzi to play some Wagner on the piano. He talks about the war. And then he talks about the putsch last year. 'It's all been a terrible disappointment, dear Frau Hanfstaengl', he tells Helene. 'The next time I promise you I will not fall off the tight-rope.'

ACKNOWLEDGEMENTS

This book took far longer to write than I ever imagined, with the consequence that my debts to my publishers, to my friends and to those I love most of all are far greater than I ever intended or would have ever wanted them to be.

The patience of Stuart Williams at the Bodley Head and Clive Priddle at Public Affairs commends them as candidates for the high priesthood of a new Zen-inspired sect of publishers, omming through the ether to their frantic writers. My agents Karolina Sutton and Jennifer Joel have been there when I needed them most, which was more than I should have. I could not have asked for a better editor than Jörg Hensgen at the Bodley Head, whose historical expertise, sense of narrative and unstinting humanity have made the process of getting the book into its current shape as much of a pleasure as any difficult process can be. Mary Chamberlain's eye has improved the faults of my writing while being generously indulgent of my stylistic oddities. Alison Rae has lasered textual errors out of existence. I take all responsibility for those that remain.

Through the writing process, I have had the good fortune to have been able to work with several researchers and translators: Sofia Gurevich and Inga Meladze (on Russian language documents), Dr Tomasz Gromelski (on Polish sources) and Zehra Haliloğlu (particularly on Mustafa Kemal's trip to Karlsbad). Eleanor Watson's voice and humour and intelligence and inspiration run through every page of this book from beginning to end, between and under and behind all the words that I have written. Without her, everything would be less good, less bright and less funny. In fact, I am not sure there would be anything to publish at all.

In turning the manuscript into what you are holding in your hands I am indebted to the whole team at the Bodley Head in the UK and Public Affairs in the US. We got there in the end. In London, my thanks are due to Lauren Howard and Eoin Dunne. The cover of the book was designed by Sophie Harris. Lucie Cuthbertson Twiggs has helped get the book to the market which it deserves (and hopefully much more than it deserves). In New York, my thanks go to Jaime Leifer, Jocelyn Pedro, Melissa Raymond, Olivia Loperfido and Pete Garceau, the very patient jacket designer and art director.

I have not been much separated from my laptop since I started writing this book. I have lugged it from archive to archive and library to library, and other places when I really should have left it at home. It is true that some of this book was written by a pool in the south of France, some of it on a Greek island and some of it in a barn in Wales, but the vast bulk of it was written in the Humanities 2 Reading Room of the British Library. I thank the staff of the BL (and its baristas) who probably thought I somehow lived there, under a desk, surviving on energy bars. Some of the best moments of the past three years have been those shared fleetingly over a coffee in the BL stone circle, talking about something just learned, or laughing about one of the many foibles of the all-too-human characters who inhabit this book. Those moments gave joy and impetus to the rest of the work.

Friends old and new have provided me with comradeship, inspiration and home cooking during the writing of this book. We have swum, feasted and laughed together. And that has made everything else all right. Thank you, Hugo, Lottie, Catherine B., Alex McB., Eugenio, Erin, Ginny, Nick, Alissa, Dario, Danae, Teresa, Ron, Mara, George, Camilla P., Valeria C.K., Ali, Hema, Robin, Gina, Soraya, Vali, Amrita, Vivek, Yolanda, Dagna, Alex B., James, Leo, Sarah, Ingrida, Ben, Tobie, Michael, Matt, Andrew, Stian, Nick, Alex v. T., Rajesh, Svenja, Henry, Layli, Lilly, Cic and Ed, Daphna, Danny, Georgie and Hans (and of course my Nina, Billie and Hubert). My family has been wonderful throughout: my father David, who has pointed out the odd slip-up on ancient history and been kind enough to assume it was a typo; my sister Chloe; Robert and Pirjo; JB, Theo and Genevieve. Troilus and Cressida have been particularly unstinting in their moral support, as well as their demands for food and affection, which no human being of feeling could deny them, and certainly not me.

To those I love most, I wish with all my heart that 'the book' had not made me, at times, the unbearable, single-minded, difficult person that I know it did, and distanced me from you. All these words on a page are so unimportant to me compared with your wonderful and joyous reality in front of my eyes. Forgive me.

Charles Emmerson
Easter 2019

NOTES AND SOURCES

Crucible has been swirling around in my mind as an idea for a book for several years, as a way of telling a story about the momentous period at the end of the Great War which goes beyond the memorialisation of the years 1914–1918 and gets into the disorder and the dynamism of the years which followed.

In 1917, with revolution in Russia and the entry of America into the war, Europe passed a point of no return. Things would never go back to how they were before; the social and political order of the Continent was no longer tenable. In 1924, long after the Great War itself had formally ended, a superficial sense of orderliness returned, with peace across the Continent and economic recovery across the world. But in between, everything seemed up for grabs. These were years of extraordinary violence, marked by revolutions, civil wars, lynch mobs, putsches and famines. From that violence, from the ruins of the old world, new ideologies emerged: fascism, communism and a virulent strain of anti-Semitism. But these were also the years of Dadaism and surrealism, when relativity was accepted and the psychoanalytical account of the human mind flourished, the years which re-energised the civil rights movement in the United States and produced the first nationwide successes of the suffragette movement in Europe and America. The tragic and the heroic, the absurd and the comical, the good and the evil: all life is here.

My intention with this book has been to trace trajectories, rather than portray static sets of ideas or completed historical processes. *Crucible* is about movement: rises and falls, arrivals and departures. Hopefully the use of the present tense conveys a sense of immediacy, as if the moments described in the book are like scenes in a moving picture which we have not yet seen to the end. *Crucible* is also about how those trajectories intersected. It is perhaps these intersections which give the true, unsettling and eclectic flavour of the times, one of those rare and 'terribly thrilling' moments in history, as Freud described it in 1918, when 'the old has died, but the new has not yet replaced it.'

This was a world in which Benito Mussolini, the bowler-hatted former socialist, could tout Italian fascism as the most relativist phenomenon of the age (without mentioning Albert Einstein by name). André Breton's surrealism drew on his experiences working in a psychiatric hospital during the war and his veneration of Freud (until he met him). German nationalists saw Mustafa Kemal's success in rejecting a peace imposed by the victorious powers of the war as a token for what they might achieve themselves. Marcus Garvey saw a relationship between his fight for worldwide black empowerment and the struggle of Éamon de Valera to achieve recognition for an independent Ireland.

Adolf Hitler looked admiringly over the Atlantic Ocean at Henry Ford, the American automobile manufacturer who helped popularise a conspiratorial anti-Semitic slander cooked up in the last days of the Russian Empire, a slander finally proven as fake by a British journalist in Istanbul, aided by an American diplomat who once refused a meeting with Lenin in Switzerland in 1917 because he had a tennis date. Emmeline Pankhurst spent several months of that revolutionary year not campaigning in Britain for women's suffrage at home, but in Petrograd, visiting battalions of women soldiers sent to fight for democratic (non-Bolshevik) Russia against the Kaiser's Germany. Years later, her daughter Sylvia was back in Russia, the Bolsheviks now having taken over and ruling a resurrected Red empire from Moscow, arguing with Lenin about how quickly Britain should move to full-on proletarian revolution (Pankhurst was more extreme).

Fascism and communism both emerged in these tumultuous years, each proclaiming itself the sworn enemy and polar opposite of the other. But Mussolini was perhaps more honest when he expressed his admiration for the scale of the Bolshevik experiment in Russia, and spoke about the affinities between the two movements. (Lenin, when he heard about the March on Rome, chuckled that it was 'a merry story', and reflected that the experience of having men like Mussolini in charge might finally awaken the Italian proletariat to the need for communism.) Both political creeds found their footing in Europe at the same time, and developed side by side, evolving and mutating in response to and occasionally in emulation of the other.

Coincidence is not causality, and certainly not equality; but nor is it entirely innocent of meaning. When the old order collapses, the new order does not emerge fully formed, and every experience, every prejudice, every idea floating around the world outside – even those of one's enemies – becomes a potential source of inspiration, for good and for ill. It is in such times, when established hierarchies are collapsing and people are searching for new meaning in the world, that the most unlikely characters – a field-runner from the Bavarian army, a professional revolutionary in exile in Zurich, a mushroom-picking Austrian doctor – are given their chance. Which comes first: the character or the times?

There is a huge amount of historical scholarship and writing which has shaped my own approach to these years, and which I hope readers of Crucible will be encouraged to explore after reading this book. The recognition that the Great War did not end neatly in 1918 with the armistice in the West, nor in 1919 with the signing of the Versailles Treaty, is the underpinning thesis of Robert Gerwarth's *The Vanquished: Why the First World War Failed to End, 1917–1923* (2016), showing how the violence continued across Europe, from Ireland to the Baltic, in Russia and in Turkey, long after the guns had fallen silent on the Western Front. Jay Winter's seminal *Sites of Memory, Sites of Mourning: The Great War in European Cultural History* (1995) reminds us that, for those societies which had lived through war, the absence of military conflict did not bring a full sense of peace for years afterwards. The scars remained, and they were deep.

Paul Fussell's *The Great War and Modern Memory* (1975) made the link between the experience of the war and the birth of modernist literature in what he called the 'dynamics of hope abridged'. Other historians, less focused on the direct links between the war's specific impact on cultural history, have written about the raucous, riotous onset of modernity with similar verve. Peter Conrad's *Modern Times, Modern Places: Life and Art in the Twentieth Century* (1998) is an endlessly fascinating vision of the cultural history of the bloodiest century of human existence. Kevin Jackson's *Constellation of Genius: 1922, Modernism and All That Jazz* (2012) provides a diaristic account of the cultural happenings of that seminal year, which offered a partial inspiration for the approach taken in *Crucible*. Philipp Blom charts the social and cultural history of the interwar period in the twenty-one kaleidoscopic chapters of *Fracture: Life and Culture in the West, 1918–1938* (2015).

At the centre of *Crucible* is the story of the collapse of four European or Eurasian empires: German, Austro-Hungarian, Ottoman and Russian (though the Soviet Union ended up resurrecting the last under the guise of world communism). While hinted at here, another book would be needed to describe the erosion of assumptions of European superiority which followed the Great War, and the global conflicts and anti-colonial movements which emerged from its ashes. David Fromkin, Sean McMeekin, Eugene Rogan and James Barr have all written on the consequences of the war for the shape of the Middle East – consequences which resonate down to today. But the change went far wider than that, to India and China and beyond. As the Chinese intellectual Yan Fu wrote after the war, 'the European race's last three hundred years of evolutionary progress have all come down to four words: selfishness, slaughter, shamelessness and corruption'.

Margaret MacMillan's brilliant *Peacemakers* (2001) inspired in me a fascination with the world in which the peace was made after 1918, and the constraints under which the peacemakers were operating – they acted like gods, but were they really in control? Adam Tooze's *The Deluge: The Great War and the Remaking of Global Order* (2015) broadens and reshapes that story of how the world was remade, as does Robert Boyce's *The Great Interwar Crisis and the Collapse of Globalization* (2009). William Mulligan's *The Great War for Peace* (2014) takes a refreshingly different view of the role of the war in early twentieth-century history. David Reynolds' book *The Long Shadow: The Great War and the Twentieth Century* (2013) widens the frame to the whole of the century. There is an increasing interest, sparked by Ernst Nolte and others, in the notion of a 'European civil war', running from 1917 (or earlier) to 1945. In reality, of course, no periodisation really fits. All history is the story of lives and ideas which meet for an instant, connect, transform each other and eventually dissipate back into the flow of time. There are no breaks; just influences, consequences and memories.

Almost every character in this book has multiple biographies written about them, most of which I have dug into at some point during the research for this book. Among the most enjoyable are Robert Service's trilogy on Lenin, Stalin and Trotsky, Lucy Hughes-Hallett's wonderful *The Pike: Gabriele D'Annunzio: Poet, Seducer and Preacher of War* (2013), John Röhl's epic biography of Kaiser Wilhelm, Colin Grant's *Negro with a Hat: The Rise and Fall of Marcus Garvey and His Dream of Mother Africa* (2008) and Andrew Mango's *Atatürk* (1999). Tim Snyder's *The Red Prince: The Fall of a Dynasty and the Rise of Modern Europe* (2009) is a gem, as is Tim Butcher's unusual *The Trigger: The Hunt for Gavrilo Princip: The Assassin who Brought the World to War* (2014). Tim Pat Coogan's twin biographies of de Valera and Michael Collins are to early twentieth-century Irish history what Robert Service's books are to early Soviet history, giving a human shape to the politics.

And behind all the biographers are those who have collated, edited and translated the sources on which the labours of the later historian depend: the editors of Lenin's *Collected Works* (whose memorialisation of the dictator began before he was even dead and buried), the historians who have collected the papers of the UNIA so that its story can be told, or those engaged in the ongoing and colossal project of collecting and translating the papers of Albert Einstein. Writing a book feels like a solitary task sometimes. In fact, writing a history book is a collective one, where you are constantly thankful for the work that others have done, sometimes years or decades before, in a dusty archive somewhere, without which you would have nothing to say at all.

NOTES ON NAMES, LANGUAGE AND DATES

My guiding principle in decisions on names and language has been immediacy of description and readability for a current audience, while trying to avoid anachronisms and achieve consistency across what was a tumultuous period of historical change, during which names and language were often contested, as they are today.

In descriptions of ethnicity and race I have eschewed terminology which might be used nowadays, such as African American, but which would be anachronistic for the period. I have preferred the phraseology in common parlance at the time. The use of collective nouns for groups of people in the text – such as 'the Jews' – reflects the tendency of the times to identify whole communities by the (real or perceived) actions and beliefs of a few individuals (or simply by generalised prejudice against those communities). In this book, it is normally a paraphrase of the character speaking in the text. Judgements on the basis of sex, race, ethnicity or religion were commonplace in this period, based on lazy, age-old cultural assumptions and the more recent popularisation of false scientific theories. But this was also a time when the challenge to those assumptions and theories began to take flight.

The question of place names was of huge relevance in this period. Borders and populations shifted. Empires ruled by one (or in the case of the Austro-Hungarian Empire, two) population group collapsed; new states arose. In this book I have placed intelligibility and consistency above other considerations. Where they exist, I have used common English names (Salonika rather than Thessaloniki, Warsaw rather than Warszawa). For well-known places I have generally used the most easily intelligible place name for a modern English-speaking audience (Kiev rather than Kyiv and, with a couple of exceptions, Istanbul rather than Constantinople). If the place named is generally less well known, I have had to make a choice about using the administrative name or the name used locally. I have opted for Smyrna rather than Izmir, which is the name which would have been used by the majority of the city's population up to the early 1920s. For Lviv/Lvov/Lemberg/Lwów I have chosen Lviv as the modern and most recognisable name of the city, even though it was controlled by the German-speaking Habsburgs at the beginning of the period (Lemberg), was essentially ruled from Moscow at the end (Lvov), had a Polish majority at one time (Lwów) and now a Ukrainian one (Lviv).

For proper names I have generally used spellings from the original language (Dáil rather than Dail, Friedrich rather than Frederick) except where a name may be mispronounced (Djemal rather than Cemal). With Russian names and with transliteration from Russian in general I have used whatever is most intelligible to a modern English-speaking audience even if that means some inconsistencies (Nicholas rather than Nikolai, Tsarskoye Selo rather than Tsarskoe Selo, Mogilyov rather than Mogilëv).

Except where otherwise indicated, translations are my own. I was helped in Russian translation by Sofia Gurevich and Inga Meladze, Polish translation by Tomasz Gromelski and Turkish translation by Zehra Haliloğlu. I have abbreviated original quotations for readability on a handful of occasions.

In February 1918, the Bolsheviks changed the calendar in use in Russia from the Julian to the Western Gregorian, which is thirteen days ahead in this period. This explains why the 1917 Bolshevik revolution generally described as the 'October Revolution' took place in November according to the Western calendar and why I count Rasputin's burial as taking place at the start of 1917 though according to the Julian calendar in use in Russia it was still 1916. In the endnotes, I have used Old Style dates when citing documents from Russians up to February 1918 and Western calendar dates for documents from non-Russians (in other words, using the dates the writers themselves would have employed).

SOURCES

Libraries and Online Resources

This book has mostly been written at the British Library in London. Parts of the book have also been written and researched at the New York Public Library, the library of the London School of Economics, and the Bibliothèque Sainte-Geneviève and Deutsches Historisches Institut in Paris. In addition to the material in these libraries and the archives listed below (many of which are themselves partly or wholly digitised), a huge amount of primary material is now available online:

www.archive.org for memoirs from the period

www.britishpathe.com is a great source for newsreels of the times

http://www.bureauofmilitaryhistory.ie – for the Bureau of Military History covering material of Irish history from 1913 to 1921

https://gallica.bnf.fr/html/und/presse-et-revues/les-principaux-quotidiens for French newspapers

http://germanhistorydocs.ghi-dc.org – for a selection of German primary sources

https://einsteinpapers.press.princeton.edu – for the collected papers of Albert Einstein

www.marxists.org for the works of Vladimir Lenin and Rosa Luxemburg

https://monoskop.org – for materials relating to Dada

www.newspapers.com for American and British newspapers

https://www.oireachtas.ie – for the proceedings of the Dáil

www.onb.ac.at – for Austrian newspapers

http://sdrc.lib.uiowa.edu/dada/index.html – for the International Dada Archive at the libraries of the University of Iowa

https://wdc.contentdm.oclc.org/digital/collection/russian/search – Warwick University digital collection on the Russian revolution and Britain

zefys.staatsbibliothek-berlin.de for German newspapers

Archival Sources

AWD	Allen W. Dulles Papers, Mudd Manuscript Library, Princeton
BL	British Library, London
BMH	Bureau of Military History, Ireland
EHC	Ernest Hemingway Collection, John F. Kennedy Library, Boston
FHA	Fritz Haber Archives, Max-Planck Gesellschaft, Berlin
HFA	Henry Ford Archives, Benson Ford Research Centre, Dearborn
HIA	Hoover Institution Archives, Stanford
	Frederiksen Letters
	Lockhart Papers
	Luxemburg Jacob Papers
	M. J. Larsons Papers
	Paul Levi Papers
	Register of the Russia. Posol'stvo (U.S.) Records
	Vrangel Collection
	Vrangel Family Papers
JKP	Jessie Kenney Papers, Women's Library, London School of Economics
JRL	Freud Collection, John Rylands Library, Manchester
JRP	John Reed Papers, Houghton Library, Harvard
LOC	Library of Congress, Washington DC
	National Endowment for the Advancement of Colored People
	Sigmund Freud Collection
NA	National Archives, Kew, London
RL	Royal Library, Windsor
WEB	W. E. B. Du Bois Papers, University of Massachusetts at Amherst
USNA	U.S. National Archives, College Park, Maryland

Published Documents

In the endnotes published documents are cited by abbreviation or by title followed by the volume in Roman numerals, and then the page references for the cited document followed by the page number for the individual citation if the document is of considerable length.

CI	*The Communist International, 1919–1943: Documents*, 3 volumes, 1956–1965 (ed. Jane Degras)
DBFP	*Documents on British Foreign Policy*
DIFP	*Documents on Irish Foreign Policy*
DÖZ	*Dokumentation zur österreichischen Zeitgeschichte 1918–1928*, 1984 (eds. Christine Klusacek and Kurt Stimmer)
FRUS	*Papers Relating to the Foreign Affairs of the United States*
GFA	*L'Allemagne et les problèmes de la paix pendant la première guerre mondiale: Documents extrait des archives de l'Office allemand des affaires étrangères*, 4 volumes, 1962–1976 (eds. André Scherer and Jacques Grunewald)
IDDI	*I Documenti Diplomatici Italiani*
MG	*Marcus Garvey and Universal Negro Improvement Association Papers*, 10 volumes, 1983–2006 (ed. Robert A. Hill)
PBL	*Proceedings of the Brest-Litovsk Peace Conference: The Peace Negotiations between Russia and the Central Powers, 21 November 1917 – 3 March 1918*, 1918
ROM	*The Fall of the Romanovs: Political Dreams and Personal Struggles in a Time of Revolution*, 1995 (eds. Mark D. Steinberg and Vladimir M. Khrustalëv)
RPG	*The Russian Provisional Government 1917: Documents*, 3 volumes, 1961 (eds. Robert Paul Browder and Alexander F. Kerensky)
RSS	*The Russian Revolution and the Soviet State, 1917–1921*, 1975 (ed. Martin McCauley)

- *Address of the President of the United States at the Semicentennial of the Founding of the City of Birmingham, Alabama*, 1921
- *Albert Leo Schlageter: Seine Verurteilung und Erschießung durch die Franzosen in Düsseldorf am 26. Mai 1923*, 1938
- *Arbeiterklasse siegt über Kapp und Lüttwitz*, 2 volumes, 1971 (eds. Erwin Könneman, Brigitte Berthold and Gerhard Schulze)
- *Attorney General A. Mitchell Palmer on Charges Made Against Department of Justice by Louis F. Post and Others, Hearings before the Committee on Rules, House of Representatives, Sixty-Sixth Congress, Second Session*, 1920
- *Aus Kaiser Karls Nachlass*, 1925 (ed. Karl Werkmann)
- *Bolshevik Propaganda: Hearings before a Subcommittee of the Committee on the Judiciary, United States Senate, Sixty-Fifth Congress*, 1919
- *Congress of the Peoples of the East: Stenographic Report*, 1977 (trans. Brian Pearce)
- *Der Hitler-Putsch: Bayerische Dokumente zum 8./9. November 1923*, 1962 (ed. Ernst Deuerlein)
- *Der Waffenstillstand, 1918–1919: Das Dokumenten-Material der Waffenstillstands-Verhandlungen von Compiègne, Spa, Trier und Brüssel*, 3 volumes, 1928 (eds. Edmund Marhefka, Hans von Hammerstein and Otto von Stein)

- *Deutsche Parteiprogramme 1861–1954: Quellensammlung zur Kulturgeschichte*, Vol. 3, 1954 (ed. Wolfgang Treue)
- *Die Entwicklung der deutschen Revolution und das Kriegsende in der Zeit vom 1. Oktober bis 30. November 1918*, 1918 (ed. Kurt Ahnert)
- *Documents and Statements Relating to Peace Proposals and War Aims, December 1916 – November 1918*, 1919 (ed. G. Lowe Dickinson)
- *Dokumente zur deutschen Verfassungsgeschichte*, 3 volumes, 1961–1966 (ed. Ernst Rudolf Huber)
- *The Fall of the German Empire, 1914–1918*, 2 volumes, 1932 (ed. Ralph Haswell Lutz)
- *Germany and the Revolution in Russia, 1915–1918: Documents from the Archive of the German Foreign Ministry*, 1958 (ed. Z. A. B. Zeman)
- *Intervention, Civil War, and Communism in Russia, April–December 1918: Documents and Materials*, 1936 (ed. James Bunyan)
- *Official German Documents Relating to the World War*, 2 volumes, 1923 (ed. James Brown Scott)
- *Politische Reden*, 4 volumes, 1994 (eds. Peter Wende and Marie Luise Recker)
- *Riot at East St. Louis, Illinois: Hearings before the Committee on Rules, House of Representatives, Sixty-Fifth Congress, First Session, on H.J. Res. 118, August 3, 1917*, 1917
- *Theses, Resolutions and Manifestos of the First Four Congresses of the Third International*, 1980 (ed. Alan Adler; trans. Alix Holt and Barbara Holland)
- *To the Masses: Proceedings of the Third Congress of the Communist International, 1921*, 2015 (trans. John Riddell)
- *Urkunden der Obersten Heeresleitung über ihre Tätigkeit 1916/8*, 1920 (ed. Erich Ludendorff)
- *What Happened at Leeds*, 1919 (Council of Workers and Soldiers Delegates)

Collected Papers, Speeches and Published Writings

These documents are cited either by the abbreviations below or by the surname of the author. In cases where there are several works by the same author, or there are several authors of primary or secondary sources with the same surname, I have used the author's surname and an abbreviation of the title of the work.

CDG	*Charles de Gaulle: Lettres, notes et carnets*, 3 volumes, 2010 (ed. Philippe de Gaulle)
CPAE	*The Collected Papers of Albert Einstein*, 14 volumes, 1987–2015
CW	Vladimir Lenin, *Collected Works*, 47 volumes, 1960–1980
LS	*Leninskii Sbornik*, 40 volumes, 1924–1985

OO	*Opera Omnia di Benito Mussolini*, 44 volumes, 1951–1980 (eds. Diulio and Edoardo Susmel)
PSS	*Polnoe Sobranie Sochenii*, 55 volumes, 1961–1965
SA	Adolf Hitler, *Sämtliche Aufzeichnungen, 1905–1924*, 1980 (eds. Eberhard Jäckel and Axel Kuhn)
SE	*The Standard Edition of the Complete Psychological Works of Sigmund Freud*, 24 volumes, 1953–1974 (ed. James Strachey)
TMW	*How the Revolution Armed: The Military Writings and Speeches of Leon Trotsky*, 5 volumes, 1979–1981 (ed. Brian Pearce)
TP	*The Trotsky Papers*, 2 volumes, 1964–1971 (ed. Jan M. Meijer)
WSC	*The Churchill Documents*, 17 volumes, 2006–2014 (ed. Martin Gilbert)
WW	*The Papers of Woodrow Wilson*, 69 volumes, 1966–1994 (ed. Arthur S. Link)

ADLER, Friedrich, *Friedrich Adler vor dem Ausnahmegericht. Die Verhandlungen vor dem §-14-Gericht am 18. und 19. Mai 1917 nach dem stenographischen Protokoll*, 1919

D'ANNUNZIO, Gabriele, *Fante del Veliki è del Faiti*, 1932 (ed. Saverio Laredo de Mendoza)

    Prose di Ricerca, 3 volumes, 1962–1968 (ed. Egidio Bianchetti)

    La Scrittura nel Vento: Gabriele d'Annunzio e il volo su Vienna. Immagini e documenti, 1999 (ed. Giorgio Evangelisti)

BRETON, André, *Manifestes du surréalisme*, 1972 (ed. Jean-Jacques Pauvert)

CHURCHILL, Winston, *Winston S. Churchill: His Complete Speeches, 1897–1963*, Vol. 3, *1914–1922*, 1974 (ed. Robert Rhodes James)

    Winston Churchill's Speeches: Never Give In!, 2003 (ed. Winston S. Churchill)

DE GAULLE, Charles, 'La bataille de la Vistule', *Revue de Paris*, No. 6, 1920, 35–53

DE VALERA, Éamon, *Speeches and Statements by Éamon de Valera, 1917–1973*, 1980 (ed. Maurice Moynihan)

FEDERN, Paul, *Zur Psychologie der Revolution: Die Vaterlose Gesellschaft*, March 1919

FITZGERALD, F. Scott, *This Side of Paradise*, 1920

FRAENKEL, Théodore, *Carnets 1916–1918*, 1990

GRAVES, Philip, *The Truth about 'The Protocols': A Literary Forgery*, 1921

HEMINGWAY, Ernest, *The Wild Years*, 1962 (ed. Gene Z. Hanrahan)

    Ernest Hemingway, Cub Reporter: Kansas City Star Stories, 1970 (ed. Matthew J. Bruccoli)

    Dateline: Toronto / The Complete Toronto Star Dispatches, 1920–1924, 1985 (ed. William White)

    Conversations with Ernest Hemingway, 1986 (ed. Matthew J. Bruccoli)

JOHNSON, James Weldon, *The Selected Writings of James Weldon Johnson*, Vol. 2, 1995 (ed. Sondra Kathryn Wilson)

KEMAL, Mustafa, *Atatürk'ün bütün eserleri*, 1998–2009

    Mustafa Kemal Atatürk'ün Karlsbad Hatıraları, 1999 (ed. Ayşe Afet İnan)

KEYNES, John Maynard, *The Economic Consequences of the Peace*, 1920

KOLLONTAI, Alexandra, *Selected Writings of Alexandra Kollontai*, 1977 (trans. Alix Holt)

LENIN, Vladimir, *On Literature and Art*, 1967

    The Unknown Lenin: From the Soviet Archive, 1996 (ed. Richard Pipes)

LUXEMBURG, Rosa, *The Rosa Luxemburg Reader*, 2004 (eds. Peter Hudis and Kevin B. Anderson)

MAYAKOVSKY, Vladimir, *Selected Poems*, 2013 (trans. James H. McGavran III)

MORDEL, Albert, *The Erotic Motive in Literature*, 1919

REED, John, *Ten Days that Shook the World*, 1919

    The Education of John Reed: Selected Writings, 1955 (ed. John Stuart)

    John Reed and the Russian Revolution: Uncollected Articles, Letters and Speeches on Russia, 1917–1920, 1992 (eds. Eric Homberger and John Biggart)

STALIN, Joseph, *Works*, 13 volumes, 1952–1955

Collected Letters

With collections of letters between two known individuals or collections where all the letters relate to one individual I have only listed the sender or recipient, as relevant.

AN/MUSS	*Carteggio d'Annunzio–Mussolini (1919–1938)*, 1971 (eds. Renzo de Felice and Emilio Mariano)
CH/CH	*Speaking for Themselves: The Personal Letters of Winston and Clementine Churchill*, 1998 (ed. Mary Soames)
FR/AB	*The Complete Correspondence of Sigmund Freud and Karl Abraham, 1907–1925*, 2002 (ed. Ernst Falzeder; trans. Caroline Schwarzacher)
FR/EIT	Sigmund Freud and Max Eitingon, *Briefwechsel 1906–1939*, 2 volumes, 2004 (ed. Michael Schröter)
FR/FER	*The Correspondence of Sigmund Freud and Sándor Ferenczi*, 3 volumes, 1993–2000 (eds. Ernst Falzeder and Eva Brabant; trans. Peter T. Hoffer)
FR/FR	Sigmund Freud and Anna Freud, *Correspondence, 1904–1938*, 2014 (ed. Ingeborg Meyer-Palmedo; trans. Nick Somers)
FR/PF	*Psychoanalysis and Faith: The Letters of Sigmund Freud and Oskar Pfister*, 1963 (eds. Heinrich Meng and Ernst L. Freud; trans. Eric Mosbacher)
FR/SAL	Sigmund Freud and Lou Andreas-Salomé, *Letters*, 1972 (ed. Ernst Pfeiffer; trans. William and Elaine Robson-Scott)
HSC	Houston Stewart Chamberlain, *Briefe, 1882–1924, und Briefwechsel mit Kaiser Wilhelm II*, 2 volumes, 1928

LEH	*The Letters of Ernest Hemingway*, 4 volumes up to 1931, 2011–2017 (eds. Sandra Spanier and Robert W. Trogdon)
LRL	Rosa Luxemburg, *The Letters of Rosa Luxemburg*, 2013 (eds. Georg Adler, Peter Hudis and Annelies Laschitza; trans. George Schriver)
LSF	*Letters of Sigmund Freud, 1873–1939*, 1961 (ed. Ernst L. Freud; trans. Tania and James Stern)

HESS, Rudolf, *Briefe: 1908–1933*, 2002 (ed. Wolf Rüdiger Hess)
VACHÉ, Jacques, *Lettres de Guerre*, 1919

Memoirs and Diaries

AXSON, Stockton, *Brother Woodrow: A Memoir of Woodrow Wilson*, 1993 (ed. Arthur S. Link)

BALABANOFF, Angelica, *Impressions of Lenin*, 1964 (trans. Isotta Cesari)

BALLA, Erich, *Landsknechte wurden wir … Abenteuer aus dem Baltikum*, 1932

BÉASLAÍ, Piearas, *Michael Collins and the Making of a New Ireland*, 1926

BENTINCK, Norah, *The Ex-Kaiser in Exile*, 1921

BERKMAN, Alexander, *The Bolshevik Myth*, 1925

BERNAYS, Edward L., *Biography of an Idea: The Founding Principles of Public Relations*, 1965

BOTCHKAREVA (Bochkareva), Maria and LEVINE, Isaac Don, *Yashka: My Life as Peasant, Officer and Exile*, 1919

BRECHT, Arnold, *Aus nächster Nähe: Lebenserinnerungen 1884–1927*, 1966

BRETON, André, *Nadja*, 1960 (trans. Richard Howard)
    Selections, 2003 (ed. Mark Polizzotti)

BUCHANAN, George, *My Mission to Russia and Other Diplomatic Memories*, 2 volumes, 1923

BUCHANAN, Meriel, *The City of Trouble*, 1918
    Dissolution of an Empire, 1932

BUNIN, Ivan, *Cursed Days*, 1998 (trans. Thomas Gaiton Marullo)

CZERNIN, Ottokar, *In the World War*, 1919

DAVIS, Arthur N., *The Kaiser I Knew: My Fourteen Years with the Kaiser*, 1918

DORTEN, J. A., *La Tragédie Rhénane*, 1945

DUKES, Paul, *Red Dusk and the Morrow*, 1922

EDIB, Halidé, *The Turkish Ordeal*, 1928

ELIZAROVA, Anna Ilinichna, *Reminiscences of Lenin by his Relatives*, 1956

FIGGIS, Darrell, *A Second Chronicle of Jails*, 1919

FOKKE, Ivan, 'Na stsene i za kulisami brestkoi tragikomedii: Memuary uchastnika Brest-Litovskih mirnykh peregovorov', *Arkhiv Russkoi Revolutsii*, 1930

FOTIEVA, L. A., *Iz Zhizni Lenina*, 1956

FRANCIS, David, *Russia from the American Embassy, April 1916 – November 1918*, 1921

FRÖHLICH, Paul, *Rosa Luxemburg: Ideas in Action*, 1972 (trans. Joanna Hoornweg)

GIL, Stepan, *Shest' let s V. I. Leninym. Vospominaniya lichnogo shofera Vladimira Il'ina Lenina. Izdaniye vtoroye, pererabotannoye i dopolnennoye*, 1957

GILLIARD, Pierre, *Thirteen Years at the Russian Court*, 1921 (trans. F. Appleby Holt)

GITLOW, Benjamin, *The Whole of Their Lives*, 1948

GOLDMAN, Emma, *My Disillusionment in Russia*, 1923

    Living My Life, 1932, 2 volumes, 1932

GREW, Joseph C., *Turbulent Era: A Diplomatic Record of Forty Years, 1904–1945*, 1953

HABER, Charlotte, *Mein Leben mit Fritz Haber*, 1970

HANFSTAENGL, Ernst, *Hitler: The Missing Years*, 1957

HARRISON, Marguerite E., *Marooned in Moscow*, 1921

HEMINGWAY, Ernest, *A Moveable Feast*, 1964

HILL, George, *Go Spy the Land: Being the Adventures of I.K.8 of the British Secret Service*, 1932

HITLER, Adolf, *Mein Kampf*, 1939 (trans. Chamberlain, Fay, Hayes, Johnson *et al.*)

    Adolf Hitler: Monologe im Führer-Hauptquartier, 1941–1944, 1980

HOFFMANN, Heinrich, *Hitler was My Friend*, 1955 (trans. R. H. Stevens)

HOFFMANN, Max, *The War of Lost Opportunities*, 1924

    War Diaries and Other Papers, 2 volumes, 1929 (trans. Eric Sutton)

HOUSTON, David F., *Eight Years with Wilson's Cabinet, 1913–1920*, 2 volumes, 1926

ILSEMANN, Sigurd von, *Der Kaiser in Holland. Aufzeichnungen des letzten Flügeladjutanten Kaiser Wilhelms II.*, 2 volumes, 1967 (ed. Harald von Koenigswald)

JACOB, Mathilde, *Rosa Luxemburg: An Intimate Portrait*, 2000 (trans. Hans Ferbach)

JOHNSON, James Weldon, *Along This Way: The Autobiography of James Weldon Johnson*, 1945

JONES, Thomas, *Whitehall Diary*, Vol. 3, *Ireland 1918–1925*, 1971 (ed. Keith Middlemas)

JOSEPHSON, Matthew, *Life Among the Surrealists: A Memoir by Matthew Josephson*, 1962

KALLENBACH, Hans, *Mit Adolf Hitler auf Festung Landsberg*, 1939

KANTAKAUZEN, Julia, *Revolutionary Days*, 1920

KARDINER, Alfred, *My Analysis with Freud*, 1977

KERENSKY, Alexander, *The Prelude to Bolshevism*, 1919

    The Catastrophe: Kerensky's Own Story of the Russian Revolution, 1927

KESSLER, Harry, *The Diaries of a Cosmopolitan, 1918–1937*, 2000 (ed. Charles Kessler)

    Das Tagebuch, 1880–1937, 9 volumes, 2004–2018 (eds. Roland S. Kamzelak und Ulrich Ott)

KING, Martin Luther (Sr.), *Daddy King: An Autobiography*, 1980

KRUPSKAYA, Nadezhda, *Memories of Lenin*, 2 volumes, 1935

    Reminiscences of Lenin, 1959

        'Poslednie polgoda Vliadmira Il'icha', *Izvestiya TSK KPSS*, 4, 1989

LÜDECKE, Kurt, *I Knew Hitler: The Story of a Nazi Who Escaped the Blood Purge*, 1937

LUDENDORFF, Erich, *Kriegführung und Politik*, 1922

LUDENDORFF, Margarethe, *Als ich Ludendorffs Frau war*, 1929

LURKER, Otto, *Hitler hinter Festungsmauern: Ein Bild aus trüben Tagen*, 1933

MATTIOLI, Guido, *Mussolini Aviatore*, 1933

MÜLLER, Alexander Georg von, *The Kaiser and His Court: The Diaries, Notebooks and Letters of Admiral George Alexander von Müller, Chief of the Naval Cabinet, 1914–1918*, 1961 (ed. Walter Görlitz)

MÜLLER, Karl-Alexander, *Mars und Venus: Erinnerungen 1914–1919*, 1954
 Im Wandel einer Welt: Erinnerungen, 1919–1932, 1966

MULZAC, Hugh, *A Star to Steer By*, 1963

MUSSOLINI, Benito, *Il Mio Diario di Guerra, 1915–1917*, 1923

NIEMANN, Alfred, *Kaiser und Revolution: Die entscheidenden Ereignisse im Grossen Hauptquartier*, 1928

PALÉOLOGUE, Maurice, *An Ambassador's Memoirs*, 3 volumes, 1925 (trans. F. A. Holt)

PERSHING, John J., *My Experiences in the Great War*, 2 volumes, 1931

RANSOME, Arthur, *Russia in 1919*, 1919

RECK-MALLECZEVEN, Friedrich Percyval, *Diary of a Man in Despair*, 2000 (trans. Paul Rubens; original German 1947)

ROBIEN, Louis de, *The Diary of a Diplomat in Russia, 1917–1918*, 1969 (trans. Camilla Sykes)

ROY, M. N., *Memoirs*, 1964

RUSSELL, Bertrand, *The Autobiography of Bertrand Russell, 1914–1944*, 1968

SCHEIDEMANN, Philipp, *Memoirs of a Social Democrat*, 2 volumes, 1929 (trans. J. E. Michell)

SEBOTTENDORF, Rudolf von, *Bevor Hitler kam*, 1934

SERGE, Victor, *Memoirs of a Revolutionary*, 2012

SHAKESPEARE, Geoffrey, *Let Candles Be Brought In*, 1949

SHERIDAN, Clare, *Mayfair to Moscow: Clare Sheridan's Diary*, 1921
 My American Diary, 1922
 Naked Truth, 1928

SHOTWELL, James T., *At the Paris Peace Conference*, 1937

SHULGIN, V. V., *Dni*, 1925

SISSON, Edgar, *One Hundred Red Days: A Personal Chronicle of the Bolshevik Revolution*, 1931

SNOWDEN, Ethel, *Through Bolshevik Russia*, 1920

STANLEY, Edward Villiers, *Paris 1918: The War Diary of the British Ambassador, the 17th Earl of Derby*, 2001 (ed. David Dutton)

STERBA, Richard F., *Reminiscences of a Viennese Psychoanalyst*, 1982

STUMPF, Richard, *The Private War of Seaman Stumpf: The Unique Diaries of a Young German in the Great War*, 1969 (trans. Daniel Horn)

SUKHANOV, N. N., *The Russian Revolution 1917*, 1984 (ed. Joel Carmichael)

THAER, Albrecht von, 'Generalstabdienst an der Front und in der O.H.L.', *Abhandlungen der Akademie der Wissenschaften in Göttingen*, No. 40, 1958

TOLLER, Ernst, *I Was a German: The Autobiography of Ernst Toller*, 1934

TOYNBEE, Arnold, *The Western Question*, 1922

TROTSKY, Leon, *My Life: An Attempt at an Autobiography*, 1960

ULYANOV, Dmitri, *Ocherki raznykh let: Vospominaniya, perepiska, stat'i*, 1984

ULYANOVA, Maria, *O V. I. Lenine i sem'ye Ul'yanovykh*, 1989

    'O Vladimire Il'iche (Posledniye gody zhizni)', *Izvestiya TSK KPSS*, 1–6, 1991

WELLS, H. G., *Russia in the Shadows*, 1921

WILLIAMS, Albert Rhys, *Journey into Revolution: Petrograd, 1917–1918*, 1969

WILSON, Edith Bolling, *My Memoir*, 1939

WRANGEL, Baron N., *From Serfdom to Bolshevism: The Memoirs of Baron N. Wrangel, 1847–1920*, 1927 (trans. Brian and Beatrix Lunn)

WRANGEL, Pyotr, *The Memoirs of General Wrangel: The Last Commander-in-Chief of the Russian National Army*, 1929 (trans. Sophie Goulston)

ZETKIN, Clara, *Reminiscences of Lenin*, 1929

SELECTED BIBLIOGRAPHY

AARONOVITCH, David, *Voodoo Histories: The Role of the Conspiracy Theory in Shaping Modern History*, 2009

ACKERMAN, Kenneth D., *Young J. Edgar: Hoover, the Red Scare, and the Assault on Civil Liberties*, 2007

    Trotsky in New York, 1917: A Radical on the Eve of Revolution, 2016

ALATRI, Paolo, *Gabriele D'Annunzio*, 1983

ALVERADO, Rudolph and ALVERADO, Sonya, *Drawing Conclusions on Henry Ford*, 2001

ARMBRUSTER, J., 'Die Behandlung Adolf Hitlers im Lazarett Pasewalk 1918: Historische Mythenbildung durch einseitige bzw. spekulative Pathographie', *Journal für Neurologie, Neurochirurgie und Psychiatrie*, 10/4, 2009, 18–22

ASHLEY, Jeffrey S. and JARMER, Marla J. (eds.), *The Bully Pulpit, Presidential Speeches and the Shaping of Public Policy*, 2016

AUERBACH, Hellmuth, 'Hitlers politische Lehrjahre und die Münchener Gesellschaft, 1919–1923', *Vierteljahrshefte für Zeitgeschichte*, 25/1, 1977, 1–45, 22

AVRICH, Paul, *Kronstadt 1921*, 1970

BADGER, Reid, 'James Reese Europe and the Prehistory of Jazz', *American Music*, 7/1, 1989, 48–67

    A Life in Ragtime: A Biography of James Reese Europe, 1995

BAERLEIN, Henry, *The March of the Seventy Thousand*, 1926

BAIRD, Jay W., *To Die for Germany: Heroes in the Nazi Pantheon*, 1992

BAKER, Carlos, *Ernest Hemingway: A Life Story*, 1969

BAKER, Jean-Claude and CHASE, Chris, *Josephine: The Hungry Heart*, 1993

BAKER, Josephine and BOUILLON, Jo, *Josephine*, 1978 (trans. Mariana Fitzpatrick)

BALDWIN, Neil, *Henry Ford and the Jews: The Mass Production of Hate*, 2003

BARNES, Harper, *Never Been a Time: The 1917 Race Riot that Sparked the Civil Rights Movement*, 2008

BARNETT, Vivian Endicott, 'The Russian Presence in the 1924 Venice Biennale', in Paul Wood, Vasilii Rakitin, Jane A. Sharp and Aleksandra Shatskikh (eds.), *The Great Utopia: The Russian and Soviet Avant-Garde, 1915–1932*, 1992, 467–473

BARR, James, *A Line in the Sand: Britain, France and the Struggle that Shaped the Middle East*, 2011

BARROS, James, *The Corfu Incident of 1923: Mussolini and the League of Nations*, 1965

BARRY, John M., *The Great Influenza: The Story of the Deadliest Pandemic in History*, 2005

BAUMGART, Winfried, 'Die Mission des Grafen Mirbach in Moskau April–Juni 1918', *Vierteljahrshefte für Zeitgeschichte*, 16/1, 1968, 66–96

BAYERLEIN, Bernard H. (ed.), *Deutscher Oktober 1923: Ein Revolutionsplan und sein Scheitern*, 2003

BEIERL, Florian and Plöckinger, Othmar, 'Neue Dokumente zu Hitlers Buch "Mein Kampf"', *Vierteljahrhefte für Zeitgeschichte*, 57/2, 2009, 261–295

BECKER, Annette, 'The Avant-Garde, Madness and the Great War', *Journal of Contemporary History*, 35/1, 2000, 71–84

BENNETT, Gill, *The Conspiracy that Never Dies: The Zinoviev Letter*, 2018

BERGMANN, Carl, *The History of Reparations*, 1927

BERNAYS, Edward L., 'Uncle Sigi', *Journal of the History of Medicine and Allied Sciences*, 35/2, 1980, 216–223

BESSEL, Richard, *Germany after the First World War*, 1993

BISKUPSKI, M. B., 'Re-creating Central Europe: The United States "Inquiry" into the Future of Poland in 1918', *International History Review*, 12/2, 1990

BLYTHE, Sarah Ganz and POWERS, Edward D., *Looking at Dada*, 2006

BOGOUSSLAVSKY, Julien and TATU, Laurent, 'Neurological Impact of World War I on the Artistic Avant-Garde: The Examples of André Breton, Guillaume Apollinaire and Blaise Cendrars', *Frontiers of Neurology and Neuroscience*, 38, 2016, 155–167

BORSÁNYI, György, *The Life of a Communist Revolutionary: Béla Kun*, 1993

BOSWORTH, R. J. B., *Mussolini*, 2010

BOYCE, Robert, *The Great Interwar Crisis and the Collapse of Globalization*, 2009

BRADFORD, Richard, *The Man Who Wasn't There: A Life of Ernest Hemingway*, 2018

BREUCKER, Wilhelm, *Die Tragik Ludendorffs: Eine kritische Studie auf Grund persönlicher Erinnerungen an den General und seine Zeit*, 1953

BROOK-SHEPHERD, Gordon, *The Last Habsburg*, 1968

    November 1918: The Last Act of the Great War, 1981

    The Last Empress: The Life and Times of Zita of Austria–Hungary, 1892–1989, 1991

BROPHY, Alfred, *Reconstructing the Dreamland: The Tulsa Riot of 1921*, 2002

BROVKIN, Vladimir, *Behind the Front Lines of the Civil War: Political Parties and Social Movements in Russia, 1919–1922*, 2015

BROWN, Matthew Cullerne and TAYLOR, Brandon (eds.), *Art of the Soviets: Painting, Sculpture and Architecture in a One-Party State, 1917–1992*, 1993, 16–32

BRUCCOLI, Matthew J. (ed.), *Conversations with Ernest Hemingway*, 1986

BUSE, D. K., 'Ebert and the German Crisis, 1917–1920', *Central European History*, 5/3, 1972, 234–255

BUTCHER, Tim, *The Trigger: The Hunt for Gavrilo Princip: The Assassin who Brought the World to War*, 2014

BYERLY, Carol S., 'The U.S. Military and the Influenza Pandemic of 1918–1919', *Public Health Reports*, 125, Supplement 3, 2010, 82–91

CAMPBELL, F. Gregory, 'The Struggle for Upper Silesia, 1919–1922', *Journal of Modern History*, 42/3, 361–385

CAMPT, Tina M., *Other Germans: Black Germans and the Politics of Race, Gender and Memory in the Third Reich*, 2004

CANALES, Jimena, 'Einstein, Bergson and the Experiment that Failed: Intellectual Cooperation at the League of Nations', *Modern Language Notes*, 120/5, 1168–1191

CARTER, William, *Marcel Proust: A Life*, 2002

CARWELL, David H., 'Warren G. Harding: Return to Normalcy', in Jeffrey S. Ashley and Marla J. Jarmer (eds.), *The Bully Pulpit, Presidential Speeches and the Shaping of Public Policy*, 2016, 41–51

CECIL, Lamar, *Wilhelm II*, 2 volumes, Vol. 2, *Emperor and Exile, 1900–1941*, 1996

CHAMBERLAIN, Lesley, *Lenin's Private War: The Voyage of the Philosophy Steamer and the Exile of the Intelligentsia*, 2006

CHAMBERLIN, William Henry, *The Russian Revolution, 1917–1921*, 2 volumes, 1935

CHAPON, François, *Mystère et splendeurs de Jacques Doucet*, 1984

CHERNEV, Borislav, *Twilight of Empire: The Brest-Litovsk Conference and the Remaking of East-Central Europe, 1917–1918*, 2017

CHICKERING, Roger, 'Sore Loser: Ludendorff's Total War', in Roger Chickering and Stig Förster (eds.), *The Shadows of Total War: Europe, East Asia and the United States, 1919–1939*, 2003, 151–178

CLANCY, Louise and DAVIES, Florence, *The Believer: The Life of Mrs. Henry Ford*, 1960

CLARK, Christopher, *Kaiser Wilhelm II: A Life in Power*, 2009

CLARK, Martin, *Mussolini*, 2014

CLARK, Ronald, *Freud: The Man and His Cause*, 1980

COCKFIELD, Jamie H., *With Snow on Their Boots: The Tragic Odyssey of the Russian Expeditionary Force in France During World War I*, 1999

COFFEY, Thomas M., *The Long Thirst: Prohibition in America, 1920–1933*, 1975

COHN, Norman, *Warrant for Genocide: The Myth of the Jewish World-Conspiracy and the Protocols of the Elders of Zion*, 1967

COLES, Peter, 'Einstein, Eddington and the 1919 Eclipse', https://arxiv.org/abs/astro-ph/0102462

CONRADI, Peter, *Hitler's Piano Player: The Rise and Fall of Ernst Hanfstaengl, Confidant of Hitler, Ally of FDR*, 2004

COOGAN, Tim Pat, *Michael Collins*, 1990
    De Valera: Long Fellow, Long Shadow, 1993/1995

COOPER, John Milton, *Breaking the Heart of the World: Woodrow Wilson and the Fight for the League of Nations*, 2001
    Woodrow Wilson: A Biography, 2011

CRAWFORD, Rosemary and CRAWFORD, Donald, *Michael and Natasha: The Life and Love of the Last Tsar of Russia*, 1997

CRELINSTEN, Jeffrey, *Einstein's Jury: The Race to Test Relativity*, 2006

CRISS, Nur Bilge, *Istanbul under Allied Occupation, 1918–1923*, 1999

CROSBY, Alfred W., *America's Forgotten Pandemic: The Influenza of 1918*, 2003

DANTO, Elizabeth Ann, *Freud's Free Clinics: Psychoanalysis and Social Justice*, 2005

DARMON, Pierre, 'Une Tragédie dans la tragédie: la Grippe Espagnole en France (Avril 1918–Avril 1919)', *Annales de Démographie Historique*, 2, 2000, 153–175

DAVIS, Ryan A., *The Spanish Flu: Narrative and Cultural Identity in Spain, 1918*, 2013

DEAN, John W., *Warren G. Harding*, 2004

DEARBORN, Mary V., *Queen of Bohemia: The Life of Louise Bryant*, 1996

   Ernest Hemingway: A Biography, 2017

DE FELICE, Renzo, *D'Annunzio Politico, 1918–1938*, 1978

DE GRAZIA, Victoria and LUZZATTO, Sergio (eds.), *Dizionario del Fascismo*, 2 volumes, 2002

DE LIMA, Marcelo C. and CRISPINO, Luís C. B., 'Crommelin's and Davidson's Visit to Amazonia and the 1919 Total Solar Eclipse', *International Journal of Modern Physics*, 25/6, 2016, 1641002-1–1641002-5

DEUERLEIN, Ernst, 'Hitlers Eintritt in die Politik und die Reichswehr', *Vierteljahrshefte für Zeitgeschichte*, 7/2, 1959, 177–227

   Der Aufstieg der NSDAP in Augenzeugenberichten, 1974

DEUTSCHER, Isaac, *The Prophet Armed: Trotsky, 1879–1921*, 1954

   The Prophet Unarmed: Trotsky, 1921–1929, 1959

DONALDSON, Scott (ed.), *The Cambridge Companion to Hemingway*, 1996

DOUDS, Lara, *Inside Lenin's Government: Ideology, Power and Practice in the Early Soviet State*, 2018

DOUGLAS, A. Vibert, *The Life of Arthur Stanley Eddington*, 1956

DOVE, Richard, *He was a German: A Biography of Ernst Toller*, 1990

DRAPER, Theodore, *The Roots of American Communism*, 1957

DRAY, Philip, *At the Hands of Persons Unknown*, 2002

DUGGAN, Christopher, *The Force of Destiny: A History of Italy since 1796*, 2007

DUNNE, Declan, *Peter's Key: Peter Deloughry and the Fight for Irish Independence*, 2012

EASTON, Laird M., *The Red Count: The Life and Times of Harry Kessler*, 2002

EDMUNDSON, Mark, *The Death of Sigmund Freud: Fascism, Psychoanalysis and the Rise of Fundamentalism*, 2008

EGREMONT, Max, *Siegfried Sassoon: A Biography*, 2005

EISSLER, Kurt Robert, *Freud as an Expert Witness: The Discussion of War Neuroses Between Freud and Wagner-Jauregg*, 1986

EKINS, Ashley, *1918: The Year of Victory*, 2010

ELLIS, Mark, 'J. Edgar Hoover and the "Red Summer" of 1919', *Journal of American Studies*, 28/1, 1994, 39–59

ELTON, Lewis, 'Einstein, General Relativity, and the German Press, 1919–1920', *Isis*, 77/1, 1986, 95–103

ELWOOD, Ralph Carter, *Inessa Armand: Revolutionary and Feminist*, 1992

   'The Sporting Life of V. I. Lenin', *Canadian Slavonic Papers*, 52/1, 2010, 79–94

ENGELSTEIN, Laura, *Russia in Flames: War, Revolution and Civil War, 1914–1921*, 2018

ENGLEMAN, Edmund, *Sigmund Freud: Berggasse 19, Vienna*, 2015

EPSTEIN, Klaus, 'Adenauer and Rhenish Separatism', *Review of Politics*, 29/4, 1967, 536–545

ERGER, Johannes, *Der Kapp-Lüttwitz-Putsch. Ein Beitrag zur deutschen Innenpolitik 1919/20*, 1967

ERKOREKA, Anton, 'Origins of the Spanish Influenza Pandemic (1918–1920) and its Relation to the First World War', *Journal of Molecular and Genetic Medicine*, 3/2, 2009, 190–194

FALASCA-ZAMPONI, Simonetta, *Fascist Spectacle: The Aesthetics of Power in Mussolini's Italy*, 1997

FANNING, Ronan, *Éamon de Valera: A Will to Power*, 2015

FELSHTINSKY, Yuri, *Lenin and his Comrades*, 2010

FERGUSSON, Adam, *When Money Dies: The Nightmare of the Weimar Hyperinflation*, 1975

FIGES, Orlando, *A People's Tragedy: The Russian Revolution, 1891–1924*, 1996

FISCHER, Conan, *The Ruhr Crisis, 1923–1924*, 2003

FISCHER, Louis, *The Life of Lenin*, 1964

FISHMAN, Sterling, 'The Rise of Hitler as a Beer Hall Orator', *Review of Politics*, 26/2, 1964, 244–256

FITZPATRICK, David, 'De Valera in 1917: The Undoing of the Easter Rising', in John P. O'Carroll and John A. Murphy (eds.), *De Valera and His Times*, 1983, 101–112

FOERSTER, Wolfgang, *Der Feldherr Ludendorff im Unglück: Eine Studie über seine seelische Haltung in der Endphase des ersten Weltkriegs*, 1952

FOLEY, Robert T., 'From Victory to Defeat: The German Army in 1918', in Ashley Ekins (ed.), *1918: The Year of Victory*, 2010, 69–88

FÖLSING, Albrecht, *Albert Einstein: A Biography*, 1997 (trans. Ewald Osers)

FORESTER, Margery, *Michael Collins: The Lost Leader*, 1971

FOSTER, R. F., *W. B. Yeats: A Life*, Vol. 2, *The Arch-Poet, 1915–1939*, 2003

FRAME, Murray, KOLONITSKII, Boris, MARKS, Steven G. and STOCKDALE, Melissa K. (eds.), *Russian Culture in War and Revolution*, 2014

FRANK, Philipp, *Einstein: His Life and Times*, 1948

FREEMANTLE, Michael, *The Chemists' War: 1914–1918*, 2014

FRIEDRICH, Thomas, *Hitler's Berlin: Abused City*, 2012 (trans. Stewart Spencer)

FROMKIN, David, *A Peace to End All Peace: Creating the Modern Middle East, 1914–1922*, 1989

GAGE, Beverly, *The Day Wall Street Exploded: A Story of America in its First Age of Terror*, 2009

GAUTSCHI, Willi, *Lenin als Emigrant in der Schweiz*, 1973

GAY, Peter, *Freud: A Life for Our Time*, 1988
    Reading Freud: Explorations and Entertainments, 1990

GELDERN, James von, *Bolshevik Festivals, 1917–1920*, 1993

GELFAND, Toby and KERR, John (eds.), *Freud and the History of Psychoanalysis*, 1992, 341–355

GENTILE, Emilio, *Le origini dell'ideologia fascista, 1918–1925*, 1975
'Paramilitary Violence in Italy: The Rationale of Fascism and the Origins of Totalitarianism', in Robert Gerwarth and John Horne (eds.), *War in Peace: Paramilitary Violence in Europe after the Great War*, 2012, 85–106
Mussolini contro Lenin, 2017

GERWARTH, Robert, *The Vanquished: Why the First World War Failed to End, 1917–1923*, 2016

GERWARTH, Robert and HORNE, John (eds.), *War in Peace: Paramilitary Violence in Europe after the Great War*, 2012

GETZLER, Israel, *Kronstadt 1917–1921: The Fate of Soviet Democracy*, 1983

GEYER, Michael, 'Insurrectionary Warfare: The German Debate about a Levée en Masse in October 1918', *Journal of Modern History*, 73/3, 2001, 459–527

GIETINGER, Klaus, *Eine Leiche im Landwehrkanal: Die Ermordung der Rosa Luxemburg*, 2009

GIFFIN, Frederick C., 'Leon Trotsky in New York City', *New York History*, 49/4, 1968, 391–403

GILBERT, Martin, *Sir Horace Rumbold: Portrait of a Diplomat, 1869–1941*, 1973
World in Torment: Winston S. Churchill, 1917–1922, 1975
Prophet of Truth: Winston S. Churchill, 1922–1939, 1976

GILL, Graeme, *The Origins of the Stalinist Political System*, 2010

GINGERAS, Ryan, *Fall of the Sultanate: The Great War and the End of the Ottoman Empire*, 2016

GLICK, Thomas (ed.), *The Comparative Reception of Relativity*, 1987

GORDON, Harold J., *Hitler and the Beer Hall Putsch*, 1972

GORDON, Linda, *The Second Coming of the KKK: The Ku Klux Klan of the 1920s and the American Political Tradition*, 2018

GRANT, Colin, *Negro with a Hat: The Rise and Fall of Marcus Garvey and His Dream of Mother Africa*, 2008

GREENHALGH, Elizabeth, *The French Army and the First World War*, 2014

GROSE, Peter, *Gentleman Spy: The Life of Allen Dulles*, 1995

GROSSKURTH, Phyllis, *The Secret Ring: Freud's Inner Circle and the Politics of Psychoanalysis*, 1991
'The Idyll in the Harz Mountains', in Toby Gelfand and John Kerr (eds.), *Freud and the History of Psychoanalysis*, 1992, 341–355

GRUNDMANN, Siegfried, *Einsteins Akte: Einsteins Jahre in Deutschland aus der Sicht der deutschen Politik*, 1998

GUMBRECHT, Hans Ulrich, 'I redentoria della vittoria: On Fiume's Place in the Genealogy of Fascism', *Journal of Contemporary History*, 31/2, 1996, 253–272

GUNDLE, Stephen, 'Mass Culture and the Cult of Personality', in Stephen Gundle, Christopher Duggan and Giulana Pieri (eds.), *The Cult of the Duce: Mussolini and the Italians*, 2013

GUTSCHE, Willibald, *Ein Kaiser im Exil: Der letzte deutsche Kaiser Wilhelm II. in Holland. Ein kritische Biographie*, 1991

HAGEDORN, Ann, *Savage Peace: Hope and Fear in America, 1919*, 2007

HAMANN, Brigitte, *Winifred Wagner, oder Hitlers Bayreuth*, 2002

HAMMOND, Bryan and O'CONNOR, Patrick, *Josephine Baker*, 1988

HANEY, Lynn, *Naked at the Feast: A Biography of Josephine Baker*, 1981

HANNOVER, Heinrich and HANNOVER-DRÜCK, Elisabeth, *Der Mord an Rosa Luxemburg und Karl Liebknecht: Dokumentation eines politischen Verbrechens*, 1996

HARDING, James M., *The Ghosts of the Avant-Garde(s): Exorcising Experimental Theater and Performance*, 2013

HART, Peter, *The IRA and its Enemies: Violence and Community in Cork, 1916–1923*, 1998
    Mick: The Real Michael Collins, 2005

HASEGAWA, Tsuyoshi, *The February Revolution: Petrograd, 1917*, 1981

HASTINGS, Derek, *Catholicism and the Roots of Nazism: Religious Identity and National Socialism*, 2010

HAYNES, Robert V., 'The Houston Mutiny and Riot of 1917', *Southwestern Historical Quarterly*, 76/4, 1973, 418–439

HIGHAM, John, *Strangers in the Land: Patterns of American Nativism, 1860–1925*, 2002

HOFFMAN, Louise E., 'War, Revolution and Psychoanalysis: Freudian Thought Begins to Grapple with Social Reality', *Journal of the History of Behavioural Sciences*, 17, 1981, 251–269

HOLMES, Larry E. and BURGESS, William, 'Scholarly Voice or Political Echo? Soviet Party History in the 1920s', *Russian History*, 9/2–3, 1982, 378–398

HOMBERGER, Eric, *John Reed*, 1990

HORSTMANN, Bernhard, *Hitler in Pasewalk: Die Hypnose und ihre Folgen*, 2004

HOUSSIER, F., BLANC, A., BONNICHON, D. and VLACHOPOULOU, X., 'Between Sigmund Freud and Paul Federn: Culture as a Shared Path of Sublimation', *Scandinavian Psychoanalytic Review*, 39/1, 2016, 61–69

HUGHES-HALLETT, Lucy, *The Pike: Gabriele D'Annunzio: Poet, Seducer and Preacher of War*, 2013

IALONGO, Ernest, *Filippo Tommaso Marinetti: The Artist and His Politics*, 2015

IHRIG, Stefan, *Atatürk in the Nazi Imagination*, 2014

ILLY, József, *Albert Meets America: How Journalists Treated Genius during Einstein's 1921 Travels*, 2006

İNAN, Ayşe Afet, *Mustafa Kemal Atatürk'ün Karlsbad Hatıraları*, 1999

ISAACSON, Walter, *Einstein: His Life and Universe*, 2007

JACKSON, Julian, *A Certain Idea of France: The Life of Charles de Gaulle*, 2018

JANGFELDT, Bengt, *Mayakovsky: A Biography*, 2014 (trans. Harry D. Watson)

JEANNESSON, Stanislas, *Poincaré, la France et la Ruhr, 1922–1924: Histoire d'une Occupation*, 1998

JEFFERY, Keith, *Field Marshal Sir Henry Wilson: A Political Soldier*, 2008
    'The Road to Asia, and the Grafton Hotel, Dublin: Ireland in the "British World"', *Irish Historical Studies*, 36/42, 2008, 243–256

JOACHIMSTHALER, Anton, *Hitlers Weg begann in München, 1913–1923*, 2000

JOHNSON, J. H., *1918: The Unexpected Victory*, 1997

JONES, Ernest, *Sigmund Freud: Life and Work*, 3 volumes, 1953–1957

JONES, Mark, *Founding Weimar: Violence and the German Revolution of 1918–1919*, 2016

JONES, Nigel H., *Hitler's Heralds: The Story of the Freikorps, 1918–1923*, 1987

　　'The Assassination of Walter Rathenau', *History Today*, 63/7, July 2013

KATKOV, George, *The Kornilov Affair: Kerensky and the Breakup of the Russian Army*, 1980

KAYE, Howard L., 'Why Freud Hated America', *Wilson Quarterly*, 17/2, 1993, 118–125

KELLOGG, Michael, *The Russian Roots of Nazism: White Émigrés and the Making of National Socialism, 1917–1945*, 2005

KENNEALLY, Ian, 'Truce to Treaty: Irish Journalists and the 1920–1921 Peace Process', in Kevin Rafter (ed.), *Irish Journalism before Independence: More a Disease Than a Profession*, 2011, 213–225

KENNEFICK, Daniel, 'Testing Relativity from the 1919 Eclipse – a Question of Bias', *Physics Today*, 62/3, 2009, 37–42

KEOGH, Dermot, *The Vatican, the Bishops and Irish Politics, 1919–1939*, 1986

KEOWN, Gerard, 'The Irish Race Conference, 1922, Reconsidered', *Irish Historical Studies*, 32/127, 2001, 365–376

KERSHAW, Ian, *Hitler: Hubris, 1889–1936*, 1998

KHLEVNIUK, Oleg V., *Stalin: New Biography of a Dictator*, 2015 (trans. Nora Seligman Favorov)

KING, Charles, *Midnight at the Pera Palace: The Birth of Modern Istanbul*, 2014

KINNAMON, Keneth, 'Hemingway and Politics', in Scott Donaldson (ed.), *The Cambridge Companion to Hemingway*, 1996, 149–169

KINVIG, Clifford, *Churchill's Crusade: The British Invasion of Russia*, 2006

KIRMIZI, Abdulhamit, 'After Empire, Before Nation: Competing Ideologies and the Bolshevik Moment of the Anatolian Revolution', in Stefan Rinke and Michael Wildt (eds.), *Revolutions and Counter-Revolutions: 1917 and its Aftermath from a Global Perspective*, 2017, 119–140.

KISSANE, Bill, *The Politics of the Irish Civil War*, 2005

KLEIN, Gary A., 'The American Press and the Rise of Hitler, 1923–1933', unpublished PhD thesis, London School of Economics, 1997

KLEINERT, Andreas and SCHÖNBECK, Charlotte, 'Lenard und Einstein: Ihr Briefwechsel und ihr Verhältnis vor der Nauheimer Diskussion von 1920', *Gesnerus*, 35, 1978

KNOX, MacGregor, *To the Threshold of Power, 1922/33: Origins and Dynamics of the Fascist and National Socialist Dictatorships*, Vol. 1, 2007

KOTKIN, Stephen, *Stalin: Paradoxes of Power, 1878–1928*, 2014

KREISER, Klaus, *Atatürk: Eine Biographie*, 2011

KRUGLER, David F., *1919, the Year of Racial Violence: How African Americans Fought Back*, 2015

KUN, Miklós, *Stalin: An Unknown Portrait*, 2003

KURLANDER, Eric, 'Hitler's Monsters: The Occult Roots of Nazism and the Emergence of the Nazi "Supernatural Imaginary"', *German History*, 30/4, 2012, 528–549

LACOUTURE, Jean, *De Gaulle: Le Rebelle, 1890–1944*, 1984

LAHAIE, Olivier, 'L'épidémie de grippe dite "espagnole" et sa perception par l'armée française (1918–1919)', *Revue historique des armées*, 262, 2011

LARGE, David Clay, *Where Ghosts Walked: Munich's Road to the Third Reich*, 1997
    '"Out with the Ostjuden": The Scheunenviertel Riots in Berlin, November 1923', in Christhard Hoffmann, Werner Bergmann and Helmut Walser Smith (eds.), *Exclusionary Violence: Antisemitic Riots in Modern German History*, 2002, 123–140

LAYTON, Ronald V., 'Kurt Lüdecke and "I Knew Hitler": An Evaluation', *Central European History*, 12/4, 1979, 372–386

LEESON, D. M., *The Black and Tans: British Police and Auxiliaries in the Irish War of Independence, 1920–1921*, 2011

LEFFLER, Melvyn P., *The Elusive Quest: America's Pursuit of European Stability and French Security, 1919–1933*, 1979

LESLIE, Anita, *Clare Sheridan*, 1977

LEWIS, Bernard, *The Emergence of Modern Turkey*, 2002

LINK, Arthur S. (ed.), *Woodrow Wilson and a Revolutionary World, 1913–1921*, 1982

LLOYD, Nick, *The Amritsar Massacre: The Untold Story of One Fateful Day*, 2011
    Hundred Days: The End of the Great War, 2014

LODDER, Christina, 'Lenin's Plan for Monumental Propaganda', in Matthew Cullerne Brown and Brandon Taylor (eds.), *Art of the Soviets: Painting, Sculpture and Architecture in a One-Party State, 1917–1992*, 1993, 16–32

LOEWENBERG, Peter, 'L'aggresivité pendant la Première Guerre Mondiale: l'auto-analyse approfondie de Sigmund Freud', *Revue Germanique Internationale*, 14, 2000, 53–63

LOEZ, André, *14–18. Les refus de la guerre. Une histoire des mutins*, 2010

LOWRY, Bullitt, *Armistice 1918*, 1996

LUTZ, Ralph Haswell, *The German Revolution, 1918–1919*, 1922

LYANDRES, Semion, 'The 1918 Attempt on the Life of Lenin: A New Look at the Evidence', *Slavic Review*, 48/3, 1989

McAULEY, Mary, *Bread and Justice: State and Society in Petrograd, 1917–1922*, 1991

McCARTNEY, Laton, *The Teapot Dome Scandal: How Big Oil Bought the Harding White House and Tried to Steal the Country*, 2008

MACDONALD, J. N., *A Political Escapade: The Story of Fiume and D'Annunzio*, 1921

McDOUGALL, Walter A., *France's Rhineland Diplomacy, 1914–1924: The Last Bid for a Balance of Power in Europe*, 1978

McLAUGHLIN, Malcolm, 'Reconsidering the East St Louis Race Riot of 1917', *International Review of Social History*, 47, 2002, 187–212

McMEEKIN, Sean, *The Ottoman Endgame: War, Revolution and the Making of the Modern Middle East, 1908–1923*, 2015

MacMILLAN, Margaret, *Peacemakers: Six Months that Changed the World*, 2001

McNEAL, Robert H., *Bride of the Revolution: Krupskaya and Lenin*, 1973
    Stalin: Man and Ruler, 1988

MACHTAN, Lothar, *Die Abdankung: Wie Deutschlands gekrönte Häupter aus der Geschichte fielen*, 2008

MAMATEY, Victor S., 'The Establishment of the Republic', in Victor S. Mamatey and Radomír Luža (eds.), *A History of the Czechoslovak Republic, 1918–1948*, 1973, 3–38

MAMATEY, Victor S. and LUŽA, Radomír (eds.), *A History of the Czechoslovak Republic, 1918–1948*, 1973

MANCHESTER, William, *The Last Lion: Visions of Glory, 1874–1932*, 1983

MANGO, Andrew, *Atatürk*, 1999

MANSEL, Philip, *Constantinople: City of the World's Desire, 1453–1924*, 2006

MANSERGH, Nicholas, *The Unresolved Question: The Anglo-Irish Settlement and its Undoing 1912–1972*, 1991

MARKS, Sally, '"My name is Ozymandias": The Kaiser in Exile', *Central European History*, 16/2, 1983, 122–170

MARKS, Steven G., 'The Russian Experience of Money, 1914–1924', in Murray Frame, Boris Kolonitskii, Steven G. Marks and Melissa K. Stockdale (eds.), *Russian Culture in War and Revolution*, 2014, 121–150

MASER, Werner, *Die Frühgeschichte der NSDAP: Hitlers Weg bis 1924*, 1965

MAWDSLEY, Evan, *The Russian Civil War*, 2008

MAYER, Arno J., *Politics and Diplomacy of Peacemaking: Containment and Counter-Revolution at Versailles, 1918–1919*, 1967

MEISEL, James H., *Counter-Revolution: How Revolutions Die*, 1966

MENEGALDO, Hélène, 'Les russes à Bizerte: de la Tunisie à la France, les étapes d'une intégration contrariée', *Mémoire(s), identité(s), marginalité(s) dans le monde occidental contemporain*, 13, 2015.

MERRIDALE, Catherine, *Lenin on the Train*, 2016

MEYERS, Jeffrey, *Hemingway: A Biography*, 1985
    Scott Fitzgerald: A Biography, 1994

MEYNELL, Hildamarie, 'The Stockholm Conference of 1917: Part I', *International Review of Social History*, 5/1, 1960, 1–25
    'The Stockholm Conference of 1917: Part II', *International Review of Social History*, 5/2, 1960, 202–225

MILLER, Martin A., *Freud and the Bolsheviks: Psychoanalysis in Imperial Russia and the Soviet Union*, 1998

MILLER, Paul, 'Yugoslav Eulogies: The Footprints of Gavrilo Princip', *Carl Beck Papers in Russian and East European Studies*, 2304, 2014

MILTON, Giles, *Paradise Lost: Smyrna 1922: The Destruction of Islam's City of Tolerance*, 2008

MITCHELL, Allan, *Revolution in Bavaria, 1918–1919: The Eisner Regime and the Soviet Republic*, 1965

MONTEFIORE, Simon Sebag, *Stalin: The Court of the Red Tsar*, 2003
  Young Stalin, 2007

MOSER, Charles A., 'Mayakovsky's Unsentimental Journeys', *American Slavic and East European Review*, 19/1, 1960, 85–100

MOSSE, G. L., 'The Mystical Origins of National Socialism', *Journal of the History of Ideas*, 22/1, 1961, 81–96

MSTISLAVSKII, S., *Five Days which Transformed Russia*, 1988

MULLIGAN, William, *The Great War for Peace*, 2014

MURPHY, Gerard, *The Year of Disappearances: Political Killings in Cork, 1921–1922*, 2010

MURRAY, Robert K., *The Harding Era: Warren G. Harding and his Administration*, 1969

NASAW, David, *The Patriarch: The Remarkable Life and Turbulent Times of Joseph P. Kennedy*, 2012

NEBELIN, Manfred, *Ludendorff: Diktator im Ersten Weltkrieg*, 2010

NETTL, J. P., *Rosa Luxemburg*, 2 volumes, 1966

O'BRIEN, Paul, *Mussolini in the First World War: The Journalist, the Soldier, the Fascist*, 2005

O'CALLAGHAN, Sean, *Execution*, 1974

O'CARROLL, John P. and MURPHY, John A. (eds.), *De Valera and His Times*, 1983

O'CONNOR, Emmet, 'Communists, Russia and the IRA, 1920–1923', *Historical Journal*, 46/1, 2003, 115–131

OKRENT, Daniel, *Last Call: The Rise and Fall of Prohibition*, 2010

ORLEDGE, Robert, 'Cole Porter's Ballet "Within the Quota"', *Yale University Library Gazette*, 50/1, 1975, 19–29

ÖZSU, Umut, *Formalizing Displacement: International Law and Population Transfers*, 2015

PAKENHAM, Frank, *Peace by Ordeal: An Account, from First-hand Sources, of the Negotiation and Signature of the Anglo-Irish Treaty 1921*, 1962
  Éamon de Valera, 1970

PALMER, Niall, 'More than a Passive Interest', *Journal of American Studies*, 48/2, 2014, 417–443

PATENAUDE, Bertrand M., *The Big Show in Bololand: The American Relief Expedition to Soviet Russia in the Famine of 1921*, 2002

PAXTON, Robert O., *The Anatomy of Fascism*, 2005

PEDRONCINI, Guy, *Les Mutineries de 1917*, 1967

PETHYBRIDGE, Roger, *The Spread of the Russian Revolution: Essays on 1917*, 1972

PHELAN, Mark, '"Prophet of the Oppressed Nations": Gabriele d'Annunzio and the Irish Republic, 1919–1921', *History Ireland*, 21/5, 2013, 44–48

PHELPS, Reginald, '"Before Hitler Came": Thule Society and Germanen Orden', *Journal of Modern History*, 25/3, 1963, 245–261
  'Hitler als Parteiredner im Jahre 1920', *Vierteljahrshefte für Zeitgeschichte*, 11/3, 1963, 274–330

PINI, Giorgio and SUSMEL, Duilio, *Mussolini: l'uomo e l'opera*, Vol. 2, 1954

PIPES, Richard (ed.), *The Unknown Lenin: From the Soviet Archive*, 1996
  Russia under the Bolshevik Regime, 1919–1924, 1997
POLIZZOTTI, Mark, *Revolution of the Mind: The Life of André Breton*, 1995
PROSACCI, Giovanna, 'Italy: From Interventionism to Fascism, 1917–1919', *Journal of Contemporary History*, 3/4, 1968, 153–176
PUGH, Martin, *The Pankhursts: The History of One Radical Family*, 2001
RABINOWITCH, Alexander, *The Bolsheviks in Power: The First Year of Soviet Rule in Petrograd*, 2007
  The Bolsheviks Come to Power: The Revolution of 1917 in Petrograd, 2017
RAFTER, Kevin (ed.), *Irish Journalism before Independence: More a Disease than a Profession*, 2011
RANGE, Peter Ross, *1924: The Year that Made Hitler*, 2016
RAPPAPORT, Helen, *Conspirator: Lenin in Exile*, 2012
  Caught in the Revolution: Petrograd 1917, 2016
RAUCHENSTEINER, Manfried, *The First World War and the End of the Habsburg Monarchy, 1914–1918*, 2014
READ, Anthony, *The World on Fire: 1919 and the Battle with Bolshevism*, 2008
READ, Christopher, *Lenin: A Revolutionary Life*, 2005
READ, Peter, *Picasso and Apollinaire: The Persistence of Memory*, 2008
REEVES, Barbara J., 'Einstein Politicized: The Early Reception of Relativity in Italy', in Thomas Glick (ed.), *The Comparative Reception of Relativity*, 1987, 189–229
REYNOLDS, David, *The Long Shadow: The Great War and the Twentieth Century*, 2013
RHODES, Benjamin D., 'A Prophet in the Russian Wilderness: The Mission of Consul Felix Cole at Archangel, 1917–1919', *Review of Politics*, 46/3, 1984, 388–409
RIBUFFO, Leo P., 'Henry Ford and "The International Jew"', *American Jewish History*, 69/4, 1980, 437–477
RICHTER, Hans, *Dada: Art and Anti-Art*, 1965 (trans. David Britt)
RIGBY, T. H., 'Staffing USSR Incorporated: The Origins of the Nomenklatura System', *Soviet Studies*, 40/4, 1988, 523–537
RINKE, Stefan and WILDT, Michael, *Revolutions and Counter-Revolutions: 1917 and its Aftermath from a Global Perspective*, 2017
RIORDAN, James, *Sport in Soviet Society: Development of Sport and Physical Education in Russia and the USSR*, 1977
ROGAN, Eugene, *The Fall of the Ottomans: The Great War in the Middle East*, 2015
RÖHL, John, *Wilhelm II: The Kaiser's Personal Monarchy, 1888–1900*, 2004 (trans. Sheila de Bellaigue)
  Wilhelm II: Into the Abyss of War and Exile, 1900–1941, 2014 (trans. Sheila de Bellaigue and Roy Bridge)
  Kaiser Wilhelm II, 1859–1941: A Concise Life, 2014 (trans. Sheila de Bellaigue)
ROSE, Norman, *Churchill: An Unruly Life*, 1994, 149
ROSETTE, Bennetta Jules, *Josephine Baker in Art and Life: The Icon and the Image*, 2007
ROSSI, A., *The Rise of Italian Fascism, 1918–1922*, 1938 (trans. Peter and Dorothy Wait)
RUDWICK, Elliot M., *Race Riots at East St. Louis, July 2 1917*, 1972

RUITENBEEK, Hendrik M., *Freud as We Knew Him*, 1973

SAMMONS, Jeffrey T. and MORROW, John H. Jr, *Harlem's Rattlers and the Great War: The Undaunted 369th Regiment and the African American Quest for Equality*, 2014

SANOUILLET, Michel, *Dada in Paris*, 2009 (trans. Anne Sanouillet)

SCHATTKOWSKY, Ralph, 'Separatism in the Eastern Provinces of the German Reich at the End of the First World War', *Journal of Contemporary History*, 29, 1994, 305–324

SCHRAMM, Martin, '"Im Zeichen des Hakenkreuzes": Der Deutsche Tag in Bayreuth am 30. September 1923', *Jahrbuch für Fränkische Landesforschung*, 65, 2005, 253–273

SCHUKER, Stephen, *The End of French Predominance in Europe: The Financial Crisis of 1924 and the Adoption of the Dawes Plan*, 1978

SCHUMANN, Dirk, *Political Violence in the Weimar Republic, 1918–1933: Fight for the Streets and Fear of Civil War*, 2009 (trans. Thomas Dunlap)

SCHUR, Max, *Freud: Living and Dying*, 1972

SCHURER, H., 'Some Reflections on Rosa Luxemburg and the Bolshevik Revolution', *Slavonic and East European Review*, 40/95, 1962

SEBESTYEN, Victor, *Lenin the Dictator*, 2017

SERVICE, Robert, *Lenin: A Political Life*, 3 volumes, 1985–1995

    Lenin: A Biography, 2000

    Stalin: A Biography, 2005

    Trotsky: A Biography, 2009

    Spies and Commissars: Bolshevik Russia and the West, 2011

    The Last of the Tsars: Nicholas II and the Russian Revolution, 2017

SILVESTRI, Michael, '"The Sinn Fein of India": Irish Nationalism and the Policing of Revolutionary Terrorism in Bengal', *Journal of British Studies*, 39/4, 2000, 454–486

SINGERMAN, Robert, 'The American Career of the *Protocols of the Elders of Zion*', *American Jewish History*, 71/1, 1981, 48–78

SMELE, Jonathan, *Civil War in Siberia: The Anti-Bolshevik Government of Admiral Kolchak, 1918–1920*, 1997

    The 'Russian' Civil Wars, 1916–1926: Ten Years that Shook the World, 2015

SMITH, Arthur L., 'Kurt Lüdecke: The Man Who Knew Hitler', *German Studies Review*, 26/3, 2003

SMITH, Dennis Mack, *Mussolini*, 1983

SMITH, Paul, '1924: Hemingway's Luggage and the Miraculous Year', in Scott Donaldson (ed.), *The Cambridge Companion to Hemingway*, 1996, 36–54

SMITH, Steven, *Russia in Revolution: An Empire in Crisis, 1890–1928*, 2017

SNYDER, Timothy, *The Red Prince: The Fall of a Dynasty and the Rise of Modern Europe*, 2009

SOBEL, Robert, *The Big Board: A History of the New York Stock Market*, 1965

SOUDAGNE, Jean-Pascal, *L'histoire incroyable du soldat inconnu*, 2008

SPENCE, Richard B., 'Interrupted Journey: British Intelligence and the Arrest of Leon Trotskii, April 1917', *Revolutionary Russia*, 13/1, 2000, 1–28

    'Hidden Agendas: Spies, Lies and Intrigue Surrounding Trotsky's American Visit of January–April 1917', *Revolutionary Russia*, 21/1, 2008, 33–55

SPILKER, Annika, *Geschlecht, Religion und völkischer Nationalismus: Die Ärztin und Antisemitin Mathilde von Kemnitz-Ludendorff*, 2013

SPIRO, Jonathan, *Defending the Master Race: Conservation, Eugenics and the Legacy of Madison Grant*, 2009

SPOTTS, Frederic, *Bayreuth: A History of the Wagner Festival*, 1994

STEINER, Zara, *The Lights that Failed: European International History, 1919–1933*, 2005

STERN, Fritz, *Einstein's German World*, 2000

STEVENSON, David, 'The Failure of Peace by Negotiation in 1917', *Historical Journal*, 34/1, 1991, 65–86

    Cataclysm: The First World War as Political Tragedy, 2004

STOCKLEY, Grif, *Blood in their Eyes: The Elaine Race Massacres of 1919*, 2001

STOFF, Laurie S., *They Fought for the Motherland: Russia's Women Soldiers in World War I and the Revolution*, 2006

STRACHAN, Hew, *Financing the First World War*, 2004

    The First World War, 2014

SZÖLLÖSI-JANZE, Margit, *Fritz Haber, 1868–1934: eine Biographie*, 1998

TATLIN, V., DYMSHITS-TOLSTAIA, S. and BOWLT, John, 'Memorandum from the Visual Arts Section of the People's Commissariat for Enlightenment to the Soviet of People's Commissars: Project for the Organization of Competitions for Monuments to Distinguished Persons', *Design Issues*, 1/2, 1984, 70–74

THOMPSON, John M., *Russia, Bolshevism and the Versailles Peace*, 1967

TOOZE, Adam, *The Deluge: The Great War and the Remaking of Global Order*, 2014

TOWNSHEND, Charles, *The Republic: The Fight for Irish Independence, 1918–1923*, 2013

TUCHMAN, Barbara, *The Zimmermann Telegram*, 1959

TUMARKIN, Nina, *Lenin Lives!: The Lenin Cult in Soviet Russia*, 1997

TURTON, Katy, *Family Networks and the Russian Revolutionary Movement, 1870–1940*, 2018

ULLRICH, Volker, *Hitler: A Biography*, Vol. 1, *Ascent*, 2013

VÁCHA, Dalibor, 'Tepluskas and Eshelons: Czechoslovak Legionaries on their Journey across Russia', *Czech Journal of Contemporary History*, 1/1, 2013, 20–53

VALLI, Roberta Suzzi, 'The Myth of Squadrismo in the Fascist Regime', *Journal of Contemporary History*, 35/2, 2000, 131–150

VAN GINNEKEN, Jaap, 'The Killing of the Father: The Background of Freud's Group Psychology', *Political Psychology*, 5/3, 1984, 391–414

VLASOV, Sergey, *Uzniki Bizerty: dokumental'nye povesti o zhizni russkikh moriakov v Afrike v 1920–25*, 1998

VOLKOGONOV, Dmitri, *Lenin: Life and Legacy*, 1994

    Trotsky: The Eternal Revolutionary, 1996

VOLKOV, S. V. (ed.), *Iskhod Russkoi armii Generala Vrangelia iz Kryma*, 2003

WAGNER, Kim, *Amritsar 1919: An Empire of Fear and the Making of a Massacre*, 2019

WALSH, Maurice, *Bitter Freedom: Ireland in a Revolutionary World, 1918–1923*, 2015

WATSON, Alexander, *Ring of Steel: Germany and Austria–Hungary at War, 1914–1918*, 2014

WAZECK, Milena, 'Einstein in the Daily Press: A Glimpse into the Gehrcke Papers', in A. J. Kox and Jean Eisenstaedt (eds.), *The Universe of General Relativity*, 2005, 339–356

    'The 1922 Einstein Film: Cinematic Innovation and Public Controversy', *Physics in Perspective*, 12/2, 2010, 163–179

    Einstein's Opponents: The Public Controversy about the Theory of Relativity in the 1920s, 2014 (trans. Geoffrey S. Koby)

WEBER, Gerda and Hermann, *Lenin: Life and Works*, 1974 (trans. Martin McCauley)

WEBER, Thomas, *Hitler's First War: Adolf Hitler, the Men of the List Regiment, and the First World War*, 2010

    Becoming Hitler: The Making of a Nazi, 2017

WHEELER-BENNETT, John, *Brest-Litovsk: The Forgotten Peace, March 1918*, 1963

WHITE, James D., 'Early Historical Interpretations of the Russian Revolution, 1918–1924', *Soviet Studies*, 37/3, 1985, 330–352

    Lenin: The Practice and Theory of Revolution, 2001

WHITE, Stephen, 'Communism and the East: The Baku Congress, 1920', *Slavic Review*, 33/3, 1974, 492–514

    'Soviets in Britain: The Leeds Convention of 1917', *International Review of Social History*, 19/2, 1974, 165–193

    'British Labour in Soviet Russia, 1920', *English Historical Review*, 109/432, 1994, 621–640

WILLIAMSON, D. G., 'Great Britain and the Ruhr Crisis, 1923–1924', *British Journal of International Studies*, 3, 1977, 70–91

WINTZ, Cary D. and FINKELMAN, Paul, *Encyclopedia of the Harlem Renaissance*, 2004

WOJDECKI, Waldemar, *Arcybiskup Antoni Szlagowski, kaznodzieja Warszawy*, 1997

WOLFE, Bertram D., 'Lenin and Inessa Armand', *Slavic Review*, 22/1, 1963, 96–114

    'Krupskaya Purges the People's Libraries', *Survey*, 72, 1969, 141–155

WOODHOUSE, John, *Gabriele d'Annunzio: Defiant Archangel*, 1998

WRIGHT, Patrick, *Iron Curtain: From Stage to Cold War*, 2007

YATES, W. E., *Theatre in Vienna: A Critical History*, 1996

YOUNG-BRUEHL, Elisabeth, *Anna Freud: A Biography*, 2008

ZAMOYSKI, Adam, *Warsaw 1920: Lenin's Failed Conquest of Europe*, 2008

ZDRAL, Wolfgang, *Die Hitlers: Die Unbekannte Familie*, 2005

ENDNOTES

Books and articles are listed in full form for the first mention and subsequently by the author's name, or by the abbreviations as listed in the notes above and the volume number in Roman numerals (e.g. *CW* XXXV, is Lenin's *Collected Works*, Vol. 35). Where there are several works in the bibliography by the same author or an author with the same surname, then an abbreviated title is also used for subsequent mentions. I have generally provided page references for the whole text, and additionally referenced specific pages where the text is longer than a few pages in order to guide the reader to the exact source of a quotation or detail.

Winter 1917

Mayakovsky quotation from 'To Account', 1917. All of Mayakovsky's poems can be found here: http://www.feb-web.ru/feb/mayakovsky/default.asp

PETROGRAD: for the definitive account of Rasputin's murder see Douglas Smith, *Rasputin*, 2016, 590–614. For Nicholas II see Robert Service, *The Last of the Tsars: Nicholas II and the Russian Revolution*, 2017. *'price of bread'*: Tsuyoshi Hasegawa, *The February Revolution: Petrograd, 1917*, 1981, 200. *'plans to assassinate'*: Maurice Paléologue, *An Ambassador's Memoirs*, 3 volumes, 1925 (trans. F. A. Holt), Vol. 3, 12 January 1917, 162. • **ZURICH**: the best biographies of Lenin are Robert Service, *Lenin: A Political Life*, 3 volumes, 1985–1995, and *Lenin: A Biography*, 2000; Dmitri Volkogonov, *Lenin: Life and Legacy*, 1994; Louis Fischer, *The Life of Lenin*, 1964; Christopher Read, *Lenin: A Revolutionary Life*, 2005. For a briefer account, James D. White, *Lenin: The Practice and Theory of Revolution*, 2001. For readability, Victor Sebestyen, *Lenin the Dictator*, 2017. For a day-by-day calendar, Gerda and Hermann Weber, *Lenin: Life and Works*, 1974 (trans. Martin McCauley). For an account of Lenin's pre-revolutionary life, Helen Rappaport, *Conspirator: Lenin in Exile*, 2012. For his time in Switzerland, Willi Gautschi, *Lenin als Emigrant in der Schweiz*, 1973. For a personal account, Nadezhda Krupskaya, *Memories of Lenin*, 2 volumes, 1935, and the one-volume *Reminiscences of Lenin*, 1959, which incorporates a third section covering the years after 1917. For

Krupskaya's own biography see Robert McNeal, *Bride of the Revolution: Krupskaya and Lenin*, 1973. 'questionnaire': Gautschi, 180. 'spartan existence': Krupskaya, *Memories*, Vol. 2, 175–197. 'horsemeat': McNeal, *Bride*, 236. 'chocolate': Krupskaya, *Memories*, Vol. 2, 195. 'goes to the theatre': Anna Ilinichna Elizarova, *Reminiscences of Lenin by his Relatives*, 1956, 201–207. 'quite a sportsman': Ralph Carter Elwood, 'The Sporting Life of V. I. Lenin', *Canadian Slavonic Papers*, 52/1, 2010, 79–94. 'It's the brain': Service, *Lenin: A Biography*, 158. 'cat after lard': Krupskaya, *Memories*, Vol. 2, 187. 'dress made with a special pouch': to Inessa Armand, 16 January 1917, *CW* XLIII, 603. 'pump him for his impressions': Krupskaya, *Memories*, Vol. 2, 205–206. 'Nadya notes a thinning out': 182–183. 'we of the older generation': lecture on the 1905 Revolution, 22 January 1917, *CW* XXIII, 236–253. There are different interpretations of this speech: see Service, *Lenin: A Biography*, 235; and Read, *Lenin*, 139–141. • **THE FRONT LINE**: there is an extensive literature on the way the Great War forced all sides to mobilise their scientific, civilian and financial resources for war with major long-term consequences. See Hew Strachan, *Financing the First World War*, 2004; Adam Tooze, *The Deluge: The Great War and the Remaking of Global Order*, 2014; David Reynolds, *The Long Shadow: The Great War and the Twentieth Century*, 2013; and William Mulligan, *The Great War for Peace*, 2014. On science see Michael Freemantle, *The Chemists' War: 1914–1918*, 2014. The best overall political history of the war is David Stevenson, *Cataclysm: The First World War as Political Tragedy*, 2004. 'infinite boredom': diary entry for 27–28 January 1917, Benito Mussolini, *Il mio diario di Guerra, 1915–1917*, 1923, 207. 'panettone': 25 December 1916, 197–198. 'government of national impotence': 30 January 1917, 207–208. For Mussolini's growing disenchantment and the condition of the troops over the winter of 1916–1917 see Paul O'Brien, *Mussolini in the First World War: The Journalist, the Soldier, the Fascist*, 2005, 107–122. • **BUDAPEST**: for the Austro-Hungarian Empire during the war, see Manfried Rauchensteiner, *The First World War and the End of the Habsburg Monarchy, 1914–1918*, 2014. For Emperor Charles see Gordon Brook-Shepherd, *The Last Habsburg*, 1968. 'cameras whirr and click': footage is available online. 'too much pomp': *Stimmungsberichte aus der Kriegszeit*, V, 4 January 1917, available at https://www.digital.wienbibliothek.at/wbrobv/periodical/pageview/609419. 'lack of funds': 'Charles Brings Peace Nearer, Austrian View', *Chicago Sunday Tribune*, 26 November 1916. 'adopted children': Phyllis Grosskurth, *The Secret Ring: Freud's Inner Circle and the Politics of Psychoanalysis*, 1991, 52 (quoting a letter from Freud to Ferenczi in 1913). 'stream of letters': *FR/AB* and *FR/FER*. 'Emperor Charles's cousins': Timothy Snyder, *The Red Prince: The Fall of a Dynasty and the Rise of Modern Europe*, 2009, 90–91. 'revolution's latest front': 'A Difficulty in the Path of Psychoanalysis', *SE* XVII, 143–144. • **STOCKHOLM**: reference to letter from Arthur Haas to the Royal Swedish Academy of Sciences, dated 7 January 1917, in *CPAE* VIIIB, 1006. • **PLESS CASTLE**: for an account of Germany's war see Alexander Watson, *Ring of Steel: Germany and Austria–Hungary at War, 1914–1918*, 2014. For Wilhelm II see John Röhl, *Kaiser Wilhelm II, 1859–1941: A Concise Life*, 2014 (trans. Sheila de Bellaigue), and, for a fuller version of the second half of the Kaiser's life, Röhl, *Wilhelm II: Into the Abyss of War and Exile, 1900–1941*, 2014 (trans. Sheila de Bellaigue and Roy Bridge). Also: Christopher Clark, *Kaiser Wilhelm II: A Life in Power* 2009; and Lamar Cecil, *Wilhelm II: Emperor and Exile, 1900–1941*, 1996. *'lies, betrayal, deceit'*: HSC, Vol. 2, from Wilhelm II, 15 January 1917, 250–251. *'may now come to pass'*: Wilhelm to Charles, 4 January 1917, *GFA* I, 660–661. *'children are starving'*: Watson, 416–417. *'cannot be worse'*: protocol of meeting on 8 January 1917, *Official German Documents Relating to the World War*, 1923 (ed. James Brown Scott), 1317–1319. *'last card'*: protocol of meeting on 9 January 1917, 1320–1321. *'strange insouciance'*: diary entry 9 January 1917, Alexander Georg von Müller, *The Kaiser and His Court: The Diaries, Notebooks and Letters of Admiral George Alexander von Müller, Chief of the Naval Cabinet, 1914–1918*, 1961 (ed. Walter Görlitz), 229–231. • **VIENNA**: for Freud's life see Ernest Jones, *Sigmund Freud: Life and Work*, 3 volumes, 1953–1957; Peter Gay, *Freud: A Life for Our Time*, 1988, and *Reading Freud: Explorations and Entertainments*, 1990; Ronald Clark, *Freud: The Man and His Cause*, 1980; and Hendrik M. Ruitenbeek, *Freud as We Knew Him*, 1973. For his relationships with his colleagues see Phyllis Grosskurth, *The Secret Ring: Freud's Inner Circle and the Politics of Psychoanalysis*, 1991. For an interesting view of the relationship between Freud and the politics of his time see Mark Edmundson, *The Death of Sigmund Freud: Fascism, Psychoanalysis and the Rise of Fundamentalism*, 2008. *'outward style of life'*: Jones, *Freud*, Vol. 2, 423–483. *'Notre Dame'*: from a letter to Minna Bernays when Freud was in Paris in the 1880s, in Jaap van Ginneken, 'The Killing of the Father: The Background of Freud's Group Psychology', *Political Psychology*, 5/3, 1984, 391–414, 393. *'recommend a good read'*: Gay, *Freud*, 95–124. *'inveterate hoarder'*: Edmund Engleman, *Sigmund Freud: Berggasse 19, Vienna*, 2015, contains a remarkable selection of pictures of Freud's apartment as it was before he left Vienna in May 1938. *'America'*: Howard L. Kaye, 'Why Freud Hated America', *Wilson Quarterly*, 17/2, 1993, 118–125. *'Gettysburg Address'*: Edward L. Bernays, 'Uncle Sigi', *Journal of the History of Medicine and Allied Sciences*, 35/2, 1980, 216–223. *'filth'*: Clark, *Freud*, 369–370. *'better not to think in advance'*: to Abraham, 13 January 1917, FR/AB, 342. *'dream of his son Martin's death'*: Peter Loewenberg, 'L'aggressivité pendant la Première Guerre Mondiale: l'auto-analyse approfondie de Sigmund Freud', *Revue Germanique Internationale*, No. 14, 2000, 55–66. *'Hamlet'*: Jones, *Freud*, Vol. 3, 408. *'seance in his own home'*: to Ferenczi, 23 November 1913, FR/FER I, 523. • **THE BRONX**: for Trotsky's time in New York see Frederick C. Giffin, 'Leon Trotsky in New York City', *New York History*, 49/4, 1968, 391–403; Kenneth D. Ackerman, *Trotsky in New York, 1917: A Radical on the Eve of Revolution*, 2016; and Richard B. Spence, 'Hidden Agendas: Spies, Lies and Intrigue Surrounding Trotsky's American Visit of January–April 1917', *Revolutionary Russia*, 21/1, 2008, 33–55. For Trotsky's life in general see Isaac Deutscher's 3-volume biography of Trotsky beginning with *The Prophet Armed: Trotsky, 1879–1921*, 1954, and continuing with *The Prophet Unarmed: Trotsky, 1921–1929*, 1959. See also Robert

Service, *Trotsky: A Biography*, 2009; Dmitri Volkogonov, *Trotsky: The Eternal Revolutionary*, 1996; and Trotsky's own account, *My Life: An Attempt at an Autobiography*, 1960. *'always the same'*: Volkogonov, *Lenin*, 250. *'my young friend'*: originally in *Kievskaya Mysl*, quoted in Paul Miller, 'Yugoslav Eulogies: The Footprints of Gavrilo Princip', *Carl Beck Papers in Russian and East European Studies*, 2304, 2014, 15. *'three-piece suit'*: reproduced in Ackerman, *Trotsky*. *'telephone'*: Trotsky, 271. • **THE VATICAN**: Pope Benedict XV to Wilhelm, 16 January 1917, *GFA* I, 676–677. • **WASHINGTON DC**: for the life of Woodrow Wilson see John Milton Cooper, Jr, *Woodrow Wilson: A Biography*, 2011. For more personal accounts see Stockton Axson, *Brother Woodrow: A Memoir of Woodrow Wilson* 1993 (ed. Arthur S. Link); and Edith Bolling Wilson, *My Memoir*, 1939. *'crime against civilization'*: diary of Colonel House, 4 January 1917, *WW* XL, 409. *'suicide on a gigantic scale'*: Madison Grant, *The Passing of the White Race*, 1916, 200. *'mechanical slaughter'*: draft speech, November 1916, quoted in Cooper, *Wilson*, 363. *'American principles, American policies'*: address to the Senate, 2 January 1917, *WW* XL, 533–539. *'greatest message of the century'*: 'Scene in the Senate as President Speaks', *New York Times*, 23 January 1917. *'sacrifices of others'*: 'Message du Président Wilson au Sénat Américain', *L'Action française*, 23 January 1917. • **LA SALPÊTRIÈRE**: for André Breton see Mark Polizzotti, *Revolution of the Mind: The Life of André Breton*, 1995; and André Breton, *Selections*, 2003 (ed. Mark Polizzotti). For Babinski's life and technique see François Clarac, Jean Massion and Allan M. Smith, 'History of Neuroscience: Joseph Babinski (1857–1932)', *IBRO History of Neuroscience*, 2008, online. Breton's description of Babinski's diagnosis is in the 1924 Surrealist Manifesto. For an overview of the impact of the war on the artistic avant-garde, see Annette Becker, 'The Avant-Garde, Madness and the Great War', *Journal of Contemporary History*, 35/1, 2000, 71–84. *'terrifying cannon burst'*: phrase used by Breton's friend Théodore Fraenkel to describe Breton's fear that the psychiatric patients were better poets than him: 19 August 1916, Théodore Fraenkel, *Carnets 1916–1918*, 1990, 56. *'Nantes'*: Polizzotti, 38–43. *'obsession with poetry'*: ibid., 51, which results in the work 'Sujet', in which one patient claims the war itself is make-believe. *'thesis on Freud'*: Julien Bogousslavsky and Laurent Tatu, 'Neurological Impact of World War I on the Artistic Avant-Garde: The Examples of André Breton, Guillaume Apollinaire and Blaise Cendrars', *Frontiers of Neurology and Neuroscience*, 38, 2016, 155–167, 160. • **UNDER THE ATLANTIC OCEAN**: *'suggestions impracticable'*: telegram on 28 January 1917, *Official German Documents* II, 1115. *'out of radio contact'*: Joachim Schröder, *Die U-Boote des Kaisers: Die Geschichte des deutschen U-Boot Krieges gegen Großbritannien im Ersten Weltkrieg*, 2000, 314. *'heraldic beast'*: diary entry 31 January 1917, Müller, *Kaiser and his Court*, 237. *'Not sure of that'*: Cooper, *Wilson*, 374. *'madman that should be curbed'*: diary of Colonel House, 1 February 1917, *WW* XLI, 87–88. *'wonders if the Japanese'*: Cooper, *Wilson*, 375. *'anything so trivial'*: diary of Colonel House, 1 February 1917, as before. *'top-secret German telegram'*: for the full story see Barbara Tuchman, *The Zimmermann Telegram*, 1959. • **VIENNA**: *'stifled expectations'*: to Ferenczi, 16 February 1917, *FR/FER* II, 182. *'ground chestnuts'*: Rauchensteiner, 660. • **MOGILYOV**: *'letter home'*: from Nicholas to

Alexandra, 23/24 February 1917 (dates used are Old Style until changeover in early 1918), *ROM*, 67–69. (I have replaced 'the domino' in Steinberg and Khrustalëv's translation with 'dominoes' for intelligibility). *'Caspian fishermen'*: Paul Wharton, 'The Russian Ides of March', *Atlantic Monthly*, July 1917. *'army morphine'*: diary entry 3 March 1917, Paléologue, Vol. 3, 212. *'Rasputin's ghost'*: Julia Kantakauzen, *Revolutionary Days*, 1920, 110. • **THE ITALIAN–AUSTRIAN FRONT LINE**: for Mussolini's life see R. J. B. Bosworth, *Mussolini*, 2010; and Dennis Mack Smith, *Mussolini*, 1983. *'my best wishes for the day'*: diary entry 21 February 1917, Mussolini, 214. *'crossed paths in Switzerland'*: Emilio Gentile, *Mussolini contro Lenin*, 2017, 3–12. *'not so well'*: diary entry 7 March 1917, Mussolini, 221–224, 222. • **PETROGRAD**: for a detailed account of the February revolution see Tsuyoshi Hasegawa, *The February Revolution: Petrograd, 1917*, 1981. For an account of the revolution in a longer sweep of history see Orlando Figes's modern classic, *A People's Tragedy: The Russian Revolution, 1891–1924*, 1996 (in particular, 307–353); or Steven Smith, *Russia in Revolution: An Empire in Crisis, 1890–1928*, 2017. For an eyewitness account, see N. N. Sukhanov, *The Russian Revolution 1917*, 1984 (ed. Joel Carmichael), 3–135. For the experiences of foreigners see Helen Rappaport, *Caught in the Revolution: Petrograd 1917*, 2016. *'German spy'*: Hasegawa, 220. *'award for best dancer'*: diary entry 8 March 1917, Paléologue, Vol. 3, 214. *'dressing gown'*: Alexandra to Nicholas, 24 February 1917, *ROM*, 69–70. *'they would probably stay indoors'*: Alexandra to Nicholas, 25 February 1917, *ROM*, 73–74. *'uncontrollable anarchy'*: telegram from Rodzianko to Nicholas, 26 February 1917, *ROM*, 76–77. *'not even reply'*: Hasegawa, 275. *'like hedgehogs'*: Maxim Gorky's observation in Figes, 316. *'chimney sweep'*: Baron N. Wrangel, *From Serfdom to Bolshevism: The Memoirs of Baron N. Wrangel, 1847–1920*, 1927 (trans. Brian and Beatrix Lunn), 270. *'Astoria hotel'*: Rappaport, *Caught in the Revolution*, 109–116. *'British Ambassador'*: Meriel Buchanan, *Dissolution of an Empire*, 1932, 170. *'French Ambassador'*: diary entry 13 March 1917, Paléologue, Vol. 3, 225. *'palace lift'*: Alexandra to Nicholas, 2 March 1917, *ROM*, 95. *'all have betrayed me'*: Hasegawa, 505. *'time to shave'*: V. V. Shulgin, *Dni*, 1925, 250. *'coffee and brandy'*: Alexander F. Kerensky, *The Catastrophe: Kerensky's Own Story of the Russian Revolution*, 1927, 21. *'telephone directory'*: Kerensky, *Catastrophe*, 68. *'long and soundly'*: diary of Nicholas, 3 March 1917, *ROM*, 108. *'Georgian bank-robber'*: Stephen Kotkin, *Stalin: Paradoxes of Power, 1878–1928*, 2014, 173. *'cockade or armband'*: diary entry 18 March 1917, Paléologue, Vol. 3, 247. *'orders of the new regime'*: Douglas Smith, *Rasputin*, 2016, 650–654. • **BERLIN**: diary entry 24 March 1917, Müller, *Kaiser and his Court*, 250.

Spring 1917

ZURICH: *'heard the news'*: Krupskaya, *Memories*, Vol. 2, 199. *'staggering'*: Figes, 185. *'simply shit'*: Catherine Merridale, *Lenin on the Train*, 2016, 132. *'slogans remain the same'*: to Alexandra Kollontai, 16 March 1917, *CW* XXXV, 295–296. *'no trust in'*: telegram to Bolsheviks leaving for Russia, 19 March 1917, *CW* XXIII, 292. *'put on a wig'*: to V. A. Karpinsky, 19 March 1917, *CW* XXXV, 300. *'fools'*: to Inessa Armand, 19 March 1917, *CW* XLIII, 616–618. *'Mensheviks in your dreams'*: Krupskaya, *Memories*, Vol. 2, 200–201. *'administrative deposit'*: Gautschi, 260. • **HALIFAX**: for a full account see Richard B. Spence, 'Interrupted Journey: British Intelligence and the Arrest of Leon Trotskii, April 1917', *Revolutionary Russia*, 13/1, 2008, 1–28. *'Following on board'*: ibid., 4. *'punches British naval officer'*: Trotsky, 280. *'Prince George Hotel'*: Service, *Trotsky*, 159. • **ZURICH**: for Lenin's journey back to Russia see Merridale. For an eyewitness account see Karl Radek, 'V plombirovannom vagone', *Pravda*, 20 April 1924. *'James Joyce'*: Merridale, 142. *'young American diplomat'*: Peter Grose, *Gentleman Spy: The Life of Allen Dulles*, 1995, 27. *'confiscated by Swiss customs'*: Merridale, 148. *'seasick'*: Service, *Lenin*, 259. • **WASHINGTON**: *'no quarrel'*: address to joint session of Congress, 2 April 1917, *WW* XLI, 519–527. *'thirty-two minutes'*: diary of Colonel House, 2 April 1917, *WW* XLI, 529. *'Mrs Wilson stands'*: diary of Thomas W. Brahany, 5 April 1917, *WW* XLI, 549. *'not my war'*: Eric Homberger, *John Reed*, 1990, 122. *'James Reese Europe'*: Jeffrey T. Sammons and John H. Morrow, Jr, *Harlem's Rattlers and the Great War: The Undaunted 369th Regiment and the African American Quest for Equality*, 2014, 126. • **MILAN**: for the life of D'Annunzio see Lucy Hughes-Hallett, *The Pike: Gabriele D'Annunzio: Poet, Seducer and Preacher of War*, 2013; John Woodhouse, *Gabriele D'Annunzio: Defiant Archangel*, 1998; and Paolo Alatri, *Gabriele D'Annunzio*, 1983. *'Now the group of stars'*: English text of D'Annunzio's message is taken from 'D'Annunzio Acclaims our Entry into the War', *New York Times*, 8 April 1917; the Italian can be found in Gabriele D'Annunzio, *Fante del Veliki è del Faiti*, 1932, 52–54. *'Chicago Tribune'*: 'Hails America as Beacon Light Pointing Peace', *Chicago Tribune*, 8 April 1917. • **BERLIN**: *'American dentist'*: Arthur N. Davis, *The Kaiser I Knew: My Fourteen Years with the Kaiser*, 1918, 2. *'neither sweets nor potatoes'*: diary entry 5 April 1917, Müller, *Kaiser and his Court*, 254. *'Never before'*: *Dokumente zur deutschen Verfassungsgeschichte*, Vol. 2, 1961 (ed. Ernst Rudolf Huber), 467–468. • **WRONKE**: for Luxemburg's life and work see J. P. Nettl, *Rosa Luxemburg*, 2 volumes, 1966; Paul Fröhlich, *Rosa Luxemburg: Ideas in Action*, 1972 (trans. Joanna Hoornweg); and Rosa Luxemburg, *The Letters of Rosa Luxemburg*, 2013 (eds. Georg Adler, Peter Hudis and Annelies Laschitza; trans. George Schriver) – here abbreviated as *LRL*. *'Rosa's cat'*: to Kostya Zetkin, March 1911, *LRL*, 296. *'finer points'*: H. Schurer, 'Some Reflections on Rosa Luxemburg and the Bolshevik Revolution', *Slavonic and East European Review*, 40/95, 1962, 356–372. *'on leave from World History'*: to Luise Kautsky, 15 April 1917, *LRL*, 392. *'slit each other's throat'*: Rosa Luxemburg, 'Rebuilding the Internationale', *Die Internationale*, No. 1, 1915. *'small overture'*: to Clara Zetkin, 13 April 1917, *LRL*, 390. *'plutonic forces'*: to Luise Kautsky, 15 April 1917, *LRL*, 392. *'notes down'*: daily calendars from this period are available at HIA, Luxemburg Jacob Papers, Box/folder 4. *'dear little bird'* and *'squeeze of the hand'*: to Sophie Liebknecht, 19 April 1917, *LRL*, 399, and to Mathilde Wurm, 16 February 1917, 377. *'two young sycamores'* to *'a mouse finds its way'*: slightly paraphrased from letter Clara Zetkin, 13 April 1917, *LRL*, 389–391, 390. *'For three years'*: Rosa Luxemburg, 'Der alte Maulwurf', *Spartakusbrief*, No. 5, May 1917. • **VIENNA**: *'The world* *is not the same'*: Czernin to Charles, 14 April 1917, *GFA* II, 103–108, 105. *'Wilhelm takes a month'*: Wilhelm to Charles, 11 May 1917, *GFA* II, 191. *'question of nerves'*: Grünau to the Foreign Office, 19 April 1917, *GFA* II, 130–131. *'war aims'*: Watson, 460–468, and Grünau to Bethmann Hollweg, 24 April 1917, *GFA* II, 149–151. For a wider description of war aims up to 1917 see Stevenson, *Cataclysm*, 101–123. • **PETROGRAD**: for an eyewitness account of Lenin's return see Sukhanov, 269–292. For a general account of his reception and next moves see Merridale, 217–226; and Service, *Lenin*, 261–269. • **CHICAGO**: for Hemingway's extraordinary life see Jeffrey Meyers, *Hemingway: A Biography*, 1985; and Carlos Baker, *Ernest Hemingway: A Life Story*, 1969. For more recent biographies, see Richard Bradford, *The Man Who Wasn't There: A Life of Ernest Hemingway*, 2018; and Mary V. Dearborn, *Ernest Hemingway: A Biography*, 2017. *'a poem'*: poem by Marcelline Hemingway, 17 April 1917, EHC, Series 5, Box NC01, EHPP-NC01-002–002. *'Miss Dixon'*: Meyers, *Hemingway*, 19. • **VIENNA**: *'frightful consequences'*: to Ferenczi, 30 April 1917, *FR/FER* II, 198. *'No Nobel prize'*: *Prochaskas Familien-Kalender 1917*, 25 April 1917, LOC, Sigmund Freud Collection, Subject File, 1856–1988, mss39990, box 48. • **THE WESTERN FRONT**: on the French army see Elizabeth Greenhalgh, *The French Army and the First World War*, 2014. On the 1917 mutinies see André Loez, *14–18. Les refus de la guerre. Une histoire des mutins*, 2010; and Guy Pedroncini, *Les Mutineries de 1917*, 1967. *'refuse to swear'*: Jamie H. Cockfield, *With Snow on Their Boots: The Tragic Odyssey of the Russian Expeditionary Force in France During World War I*, 1999, 121. *'Shoot me if you like'*: Loez, 9. • **PETROGRAD**: *'I was born'*: 'An Unfinished Autobiography', 17 May 1917, *CW* XLI, 430. *'caution, caution, caution'*: report to a Bolshevik party conference, 24 April 1917, *CW* XXIV, 228–243, 237. • **HOMBURG PALACE**: *'received a letter'*: diary entry 11 May 1917, Müller, *Kaiser and his Court*, 268–269. *'long list'* to *'Every week will be more expensive'*: Grünau to the Foreign Office, 13 May 1917, *GFA* II, 194–195. • **THE WESTERN FRONT**: for the life of Churchill in these years see Martin Gilbert, *World in Torment: Winston S. Churchill, 1917–1922*, 1975. *'new game'*: ibid., 18–19. • **TSARSKOYE SELO**: diary of Nicholas, April/May 1917, *ROM*, 159–160. • **PETROGRAD**: for the formation and history of Maria Bochkareva's battalion see Laurie S. Stoff, *They Fought for the Motherland: Russia's Women Soldiers in World War I and the Revolution*, 2006; and Maria Botchkareva (Bochkareva) and Isaac Don Levine, *Yashka: My Life as Peasant, Officer and Exile*, 1919. *'wrong cause'*: order from Kerensky, 14 May 1917, *RPG* II, 935–936. *'an offensive, an offensive!'*: 'The Virtual Armistice', original article in *Pravda*, 9 May 1917, *CW* XXIV, 375–377.

Summer 1917

PARIS: *'Sur-realisme'*: Polizzotti, 59. • **VIENNA**: *'Albert Einstein'*: to Emperor Charles, mid-February to 29 April 1917, *CPAE* X, 73–74. *'Freud'*: to Abraham, 20 May 1917, *FR/AB*, 348–350. *'become suffocating'*: Friedrich Adler, *Friedrich Adler vor dem Ausnahmegericht: Die Verhandlungen vor dem §-14-Gericht am 18. und 19. Mai 1917 nach dem stenographischen*

Protokoll, 1919, 127. 'what I had to do': ibid., 194. 'We live in a time': ibid., 196. 'Long live': ibid., 200. • **Tsarskoye Selo**: 'exactly three months' and 'lamp and the window': diary of Nicholas, 9 June 1917, ROM, 160. • **Leeds**: quotations from What Happened at Leeds, 1919. For context see Stephen White, 'Soviets in Britain: The Leeds Convention of 1917', International Review of Social History, 19/2, 1974, 165–193. • **Lewes**: for critical accounts of Éamon de Valera's life see Tim Pat Coogan, De Valera: Long Fellow, Long Shadow, 1993; and Ronan Fanning, Éamon de Valera: A Will to Power, 2015. For the official account see Frank Pakenham (Earl of Longford), Éamon de Valera, 1970. For an overall history of Ireland through the period see Charles Townshend, The Republic: The Fight for Irish Independence, 1918–1923, 2013. For de Valera's speeches see Speeches and Statements by Éamon de Valera, 1917–1973, 1980 (ed. Maurice Moynihan). 'calmly ignores': Fanning, 51. • **The Western Front**: 'spring has been stretched': see the report of Lieutenant-Colonel Chanson of the 358th Infantry Regiment, in Loez, annex online at http://www.crid1418.org/doc/mutins, 66–69. 'start marching towards Paris': Pedroncini, 150–152. 'singing the Internationale': 135–136. • **Vienna**: 'government posters': available electronically from the Vienna public library, https://www.onb.ac.at. 'chief of a primitive tribe': to Abraham, 21 August 1917, FR/AB, 355. • **East St. Louis**: for the riots and their consequences see Elliot M. Rudwick, Race Riots at East St. Louis, July 2 1917, 1972; Malcolm McLaughlin, 'Reconsidering the East St Louis Race Riot of 1917', International Review of Social History, No. 47, 2002, 187–212; and Harper Barnes, Never Been a Time: The 1917 Race Riot that Sparked the Civil Rights Movement, 2008. For eyewitness testimony see Riot at East St. Louis, Illinois: Hearings before the Committee on Rules, House of Representatives, Sixty-fifth Congress, First Session, on H.J. Res. 118, August 3, 1917, 1917. For the long and twisted tale of lynching in the United States, see Philip Dray, At the Hands of Persons Unknown, 2002. For Josephine Baker see Josephine Baker and Jo Bouillon, Josephine, 1978 (trans. Mariana Fitzpatrick); Lynn Haney, Naked at the Feast: A Biography of Josephine Baker, 1981; Bryan Hammond and Patrick O'Connor, Josephine Baker, 1988; Jean-Claude Baker and Chris Chase, Josephine: The Hungry Heart, 1993; and Bennetta Jules Rosette, Josephine Baker in Art and Life: The Icon and the Image, 2007. 'stares back in terror': Josephine Baker remembered the sight in February 1952 on returning to St. Louis, where she gave a speech. 'pull for East St. Louis': 'Post-Dispatch Man, an Eye-Witness, Describes Massacre of Negroes', St. Louis Post-Dispatch, 3 July 1917. 'not dead yet' and 'that kind of advertising': '24 Negroes Killed in St. Louis', St. Louis Post-Dispatch, 3 July 1917. 'ringing the bells': 'Address on the Conspiracy of the East St. Louis Riots', 8 July 1917, MG I, 213. 'safe for democracy': picture in Barnes. 'Houston': Robert V. Haynes, 'The Houston Mutiny and Riot of 1917', Southwestern Historical Quarterly, 76/4, 1973, 418–439. • **Petrograd**: this account is drawn from Jessie Kenney's typed manuscript of the Pankhurst mission to Russia, in the Jessie Kenney Papers at the Women's Library of the London School of Economics: 'The Price of Liberty', JKP, 7/JKE5. The original diary was smuggled out at the end of Kenney's visit. For Emmeline Pankhurst and her daughters Sylvia and Christabel see Martin Pugh, The Pankhursts: The History of One Radical Family, 2001. 'It is the men': 'The Price

of Liberty', 30 June 1917. *'human electricity'*: Trotsky, 295–296. *'predators'*: 'The Petty-Bourgeois Stand on the Question of Economic Disorganisation', original article in *Pravda*, 1/14 June 1917, *CW* XXIV, 562–564. *'at any moment'*: speech on attitude towards the Provisional Government, 4/17 June 1917, *CW* XXV, 15–42. *'grabbing his briefcase'*: Kerensky, *Catastrophe*, 216. *'it is a plot'*: the Menshevik leader Tsereteli in Volkogonov, *Lenin*, 136. *'insinuation'*: 'Insinuations', original article in *Pravda*, 11/24 June 1917, *CW* XXV, 73–74. *'processions'*: speech to Petrograd Bolsheviks, 11/24 June 1917, *CW* XXV, 79–81. *'here come the Cossacks'*: diary entry 24 June 1917, Louis de Robien, *The Diary of a Diplomat in Russia, 1917–1918*, 1969 (trans. Camilla Sykes), 75. • **SARAJEVO**: *'iron and bronze cross'*: photograph of the monument in Miller, 'Yugoslav Eulogies', 11. •
THE RUSSIAN FRONT: *'order to attack'*: order for the offensive, 16 June 1917, *RPG* II, 942. *'before breakfast'*: diary of Nicholas, 20 June 1917, *ROM*, 161. *'Anything is possible'*: diary entry 4 July 1917, Robien, 78. *'new detective novel'*: diary of Nicholas, 27 June 1917, *ROM*, 162. *'British military observer'*: Memorandum from Brigadier General Knox to the War Cabinet, NA, CAB 24/19/88. *'his own son'*: Rauchensteiner, 757. *'Tajik for relaxation'*: George Katkov, *The Kornilov Affair: Kerensky and the Breakup of the Russian Army*, 1980, 41. *'devil brought you'*: Bochkareva, 195–196. *'sex behind a tree'*: ibid., 217. • **TSARSKOYE SELO**: *'bad news from the front'*: diary of Nicholas, 13 July 1917, *ROM*, 163. • **ACROSS EUROPE**: for the diplomatic ballet in 1917 see David Stevenson, 'The Failure of Peace by Negotiation in 1917', *Historical Journal*, 34/1, 1991, 65–86; and *Documents and Statements Relating to Peace Proposals and War Aims*, December 1916 – November 1918, 1919 (ed. G. Lowe Dickinson). For a detailed account of the Stockholm conference see Hildamarie Meynell, 'The Stockholm Conference of 1917: Part I', *International Review of Social History*, 5/1, 1960, 1–25, and 'The Stockholm Conference of 1917: Part II', *International Review of Social History*, 5/2, 1960, 202–225. *'being deliberately prolonged'*: Max Egremont, *Siegfried Sassoon: A Biography*, 2005, 143–144. *'Catholic politician'*: see Matthias Erzberger, *Erlebnisse im Weltkrieg*, 1920, 250–269. *'abdicate straight away'*: Röhl, *Into the Abyss*, 1169. *'reading the newspapers'*: ibid., 1171. *'peace resolution'*: *Dokumente zur deutschen Verfassungsgeschichte*, Vol. 2, 471. *'as I interpret it'*: Watson, 460. • **PETROGRAD**: *'sunflower seeds'* to *'her husband's comrade'*: Krupskaya, *Memories*, Vol. 2, 228–229. • **EAST CLARE**: *'The Spaniard'*: Fanning, 54. *'defended one half'*: David Fitzpatrick, 'De Valera in 1917: The Undoing of the Easter Rising', in John P. O'Carroll and John A. Murphy (eds.), *De Valera and His Times*, 1983, 101–112, 107. • **NEIVOLA**: *'train chugs its way'*: Service, *Lenin*, 283. *'Ambassador's Rolls-Royce'*: diary entry 16 July 1917, Robien, 83. *'front page of Pravda'*: Sukhanov, 439. *'given a good hiding'*: Service, *Lenin*, 284. *'ribbons turned inside'* to *'spilled face powder'*: diary entry 17 July 1917, Robien, 84. *'son of a bitch'*: Israel Getzler, *Kronstadt 1917–1921: The Fate of Soviet Democracy*, 1983, 120. *'declare your will'* to *'Give me your hand'*: Sukhanov, 445–447. *'going to shoot us'*: Kotkin, 202. *'not see each other'*: Krupskaya, *Memories*, Vol. 2, 233. *'Entre nous'*: to Kamenev, 18–20 July 1917, *CW* XXXVI, 454. *'Look in the oven'*: Krupskaya, *Memories*, Vol. 2, 234. *'shave off'*: Service, *Lenin*, 287. • **UPSTATE MICHIGAN**: *'Dad's Ford'*: to Anson T. Hemingway, 6 August 1917, EHC, Series 2, Box OC01, EHPP-OC01-006–005. • **THE VATICAN**: *'Pope

a traitor': Bosworth, 100. *'tide of blood'*: to Walter Hines Page, 27 August 1917, *WW* XLIV, 57–59. • **WILHELMSHAVEN**: *'world is a madhouse'* and *'ought to imitate'*: diary entry for late June or early July 1917, Richard Stumpf, *The Private War of Seaman Stumpf: The Unique Diaries of a Young German in the Great War*, 1969 (trans. Daniel Horn), 339. *'Kaiser suggests'*: diary entry 18 August 1917, Müller, *Kaiser and his Court*, 294. • **WASHINGTON DC**: *'midget submarines'*: Rudolph Alverado and Sonya Alverado, *Drawing Conclusions on Henry Ford*, 2001, 76. *'activist notes'*: James Weldon Johnson, quoted in Colin Grant, *Negro with a Hat: The Rise and Fall of Marcus Garvey and His Dream of Mother Africa*, 2008, 124–125. • **TSARSKOYE SELO**: *'long stay in Livadia!'*: diary of Nicholas, 28 July 1917, *ROM*, 164. *'pleasant to meet'*: diary of Nicholas, 31 July 1917, *ROM*, 165. *'Japanese flag'*: *ROM*, 169. *'Rasputin told them'*: Pierre Gilliard, *Thirteen Years at the Russian Court*, 1921 (trans. F. Appleby Holt), 240. • **MOSCOW**: *'English county'* and following: diary entries 5 August to 2 September 1917, Kenney. *'declare Kerensky's national gathering'*: appeal of the Central Committee, *RPG* III, 1452–1454. *'precautions necessary'*: 'The Atmosphere in Moscow at the Opening of the Conference', *Izvestiia*, 13 August 1917, *RPG* III, 1456–1457. *'Power has passed'*: 'On Slogans', July 1917, *CW* XXV, 185–192. *'needs a disguise'*: full saga in Service, *Lenin*, 287–292. • **RIGA**: *'news is hateful'*: diary entry 4 September 1917, Robien, 101. *'gramophone horns'*: 9 September 1917, ibid., 101. *'finds herself caught'*: diary entry 8 September 1917, Kenney.

Autumn 1917

PETROGRAD: *'lecture on Greek art'*: Sukhanov, 500. *'reality is more devious'*: the details of the Kornilov revolt are contested. For a historian's account see Katkov. For one of the participants see Alexander Kerensky, *The Prelude to Bolshevism*, 1919. *'will not give them the revolution'*: statement by Nekrasov, originally in *Rech'*, 13 September 1917, *RPG* II, 1578–1579. *'operatic arias'*: Katkov, 92. *'regime opposed'*: radio telegram from Kerensky to the country, 27 August 1917, *RPG* II, 1572–1573. *'great provocation'* to *'inevitable ruin'*: Kornilov's response, 27 August 1917, *RPG* II, 1573. *'deathly danger'*: editorial in *Den'*, 28 August 1917, *RPG* II, 1594–1595. *'Shakespearean tragedy'*: diary entry 14 September 1917, Robien, 112. *'vast muddle'*: diary of Nicholas, 5 September 1917, *ROM*, 198. *'Kornilovka'*: Bochkareva, 240. • **SPARTANBURG**: Reid Badger, *A Life in Ragtime: A Biography of James Reese Europe*, 1995, 155–160. • **EASTERN FRONT**: *'Kaiser's knowledge'*: diary entry 29 September 1917, Müller, *Kaiser and his Court*, 303. • **HELSINKI**: *'writes to Nadya'* and description of her trip: Krupskaya, *Memories*, Vol. 2, 238–239. *'into their own hands'* to *'unquestionably'*: letter to the Central Committee, *CW* XXVI, 12–14/25–27 September 1917, 19–21. • **TOBOLSK**: *'Three hundred and thirty-seven'*: recollections of Vasily Pankratov, September–December 1917, *ROM*, 259. • **PETROGRAD**: for Reed's life see Eric Homberger, *John Reed*, 1990. For his writings see John Reed, *John Reed and the Russian Revolution: Uncollected Articles, Letters and Speeches on Russia, 1917–1920*, 1992 (eds. Eric Homberger and John Biggart), and *Ten Days that Shook the World*, 1919.

'джон ридь' to *'observations'* and *'phrases'*: notebooks, JRP, Series V/E, Items 1332–1333. *'black and soggy'* and *'color and terror'*: to Boardman Robinson, 17 September 1917, Reed, *John Reed and the Russian Revolution*, 26–27. *'fake babies'*: notebook, JRP, Series V/E, Item 1333. *'reported speaking'*: David Francis, *Russia from the American Embassy, April 1916 – November 1918*, 1921, 165–168. *'only party with a program'*: ibid., 169. • ROSENBERG FORTRESS: for de Gaulle's life in general up to the end of the Second World War see Jean Lacouture, *De Gaulle: Le Rebelle, 1890–1944*, 1984; and Charles de Gaulle, *Charles de Gaulle: Lettres, notes et carnets*, 3 volumes, 2010 (ed. Philippe de Gaulle) – afterwards *CDG*. For a recent English biography see Julian Jackson, *A Certain Idea of France: The Life of Charles de Gaulle*, 2018. This account of de Gaulle's attempted escape from Rosenberg is drawn from his post-war description submitted in 1927 for the French military medal for POW escapees, reproduced in *CDG* I, 673–685. • LONDON: this section is drawn from the entries from September to November 1917 in *WSC* VIII, 160–196. • VYBORG: for general description see Service, *Lenin*, 302–307. *'positively criminal'*: letter to the Central Committee, 1/14 October 1917, *CW* XXVI, 140–141. • WASHINGTON DC: address to the President by Vira Boarman Whitehouse, 25 October 1917, *WW* XLIV, 440–441. • DUBLIN: for this episode see Coogan, *De Valera*, 95–97; and Fanning, 56–61. • PETROGRAD: *'has finally arrived'*: editorial in *Rabochii Put*, 13 October 1917, *RPG* II, 1763–1764. *'inevitable lutte finale'*: 'Red Russia: The Triumph of the Bolsheviki', written in November 1917 and published in *The Liberator* in March 1918, in Reed, *John Reed and the Russian Revolution*, 83. *'Soviet government will give'*: Sukhanov, 584–585. *'fatal step'*: Kamenev's article was in Maxim Gorky's newspaper *Novaia zhizn*: see Figes, 477. *'not set a date'*: Trotsky's Denial, printed in *Izvestiia*, 18 October 1917, *RPG* II, 1767. *'strike-breaker'*: letter to Bolshevik Party members, 18 October 1917, *CW* XXVI, 216–219. *'general croaking'*: 'Strong Bulls of Bashan Have Beset Me Round', original article in *Rabochy Put*, 20 October 1917, in Joseph Stalin, *Works*, 13 volumes, 1952–1955, Vol. 3, 409–413. • ROSENBERG FORTRESS: see *CDG* I, 673–685. • KARFREIT: for the Caporetto episode see Stevenson, *Cataclysm*, 308–311. For Mussolini's reaction see O'Brien, 141–146. *'blood which moves'*: Mack Smith, *Mussolini*, 29. *'trincerocrazia'*: the word appears in a letter of Mussolini's published in *Il Popolo d'Italia* on 27 December 1916, *OO* VIII, 270–272, 272. *'parasites'*: 'Trincerocrazia', *Il Popolo d'Italia*, 15 December 1917, 140–142, 141. *'touch of an artist'*: 'I Nostri Postulati: Per la Storia di una Settimana', *Il Popolo d'Italia*, 27 November 1917, *OO* X, 86–88, 87. • BERLIN: *'In all my life'* and following: Davis, *Kaiser I Knew*, 20–27. *'spat between'*: Rauchensteiner, 793. *'catches a chill'*: diary entry 15 November 1917, Müller, *Kaiser and his Court*. • PETROGRAD: for general descriptions of the October revolution see Figes, 474–500; and, for a fuller description, Alexander Rabinowitch, *The Bolsheviks Come to Power: The Revolution of 1917 in Petrograd*, 2017. For an eyewitness see Sukhanov, 547–669. For foreign observers see memoirs cited elsewhere in this book, and also Rappaport, 257–301. For Lenin's role see Service, *Lenin*, 306–323. *'on receiving another note'*: Margarita Fofanova in Rabinowitch, *Bolsheviks Come to Power*, 265. *'must not wait!'*: letter to Central Committee, 24 October 1917, *CW* XXVI, 234–235.

'*have gone where you did not want me to go*': note to Margarita Fofanova, 24 October 1917, *CW* XLIII, 638. '*smells terribly*': Trotsky, 338. '*ballet tickets*': Reed, *Ten Days*, 88. '*belonging to the American embassy*': Francis, 179–180. '*Long live the world socialist revolution!*': speech to Petrograd Soviet, 25 October 1917, *CW* XXVI, 239–241. '*es schwindelt*': Trotsky, 337. '*rising of the masses*': Sukhanov, 639. '*candles and torches*': Meriel Buchanan, *The City of Trouble*, 1918, 177. '*women soldiers being thrown out of windows*': Stoff, 160. '*send out our appeal everywhere*': concluding speech at Second All-Russia Congress of Soviets, 26 October 1917, *CW* XXVI, 254–256. '*Ludendorff sends a telegram*': telegram 1628, 9 November 1917, in *Germany and the Revolution in Russia, 1915–1918*, 1958 (ed. Z. A. B. Zeman), 75. '*British Ambassador observes*': George Buchanan, *My Mission to Russia and Other Diplomatic Memories*, 2 volumes, Vol. 2, 1923, 208. '*French diplomat heads*': diary entry 13 November 1917, Robien, 138–139. '*Michael Romanov*': Rosemary and Donald Crawford, *Michael and Natasha: The Life and Love of the Last Tsar of Russia*, 1997, 335–338. • **VIENNA**: '*grumpy and tired*': to Ferenczi, 6 November 1917, *FR/FER* II, 245. '*put Lamarck entirely on our ground*' and '*future is pretty dim*': to Abraham, 11 November 1917, *FR/AB*, 361–362. '*mourning and melancholia*': the paper had been finished two years before; *SE* XIV, 237–260. '*silenced*': Gay, *Freud*, 373, cites the German as 'verschweigen werden' from letter of Freud to Ferenczi, 20 November 1917. • **SIBERIA**: '*spreads by railway and by telegraph wire*': Roger Pethybridge, *The Spread of the Russian Revolution: Essays on 1917*, 1972. '*stop this willfulness?*': recollections of Vasily Pankratov, September–December 1917, *ROM*, 272. '*Kun is busy in the local library*': György Borsányi, *The Life of a Communist Revolutionary: Béla Kun*, 1993, 48. • **BRESLAU**: to Clara Zetkin, 24 November 1917, *LRL*, 444–447. • **BERLIN**: to Heinrich Zangger, 6 December 1917, *CPAE* VIII, 561–563. • **PETROGRAD**: see Service, *Lenin*, 324–337, and *The Russian Revolution and the Soviet State, 1917–1921*, 1975 (ed. Martin McCauley) – afterwards *RSS*. '*highly skilled accountants*': telegram to V. V. Vorovsky, 8 December 1917, *CW* XLIV, 50. '*dirty collar*': Trotsky, 337. '*I felt very hungry*': Nadezhda Krupskaya, *Reminiscences of Lenin*, 1959, 413. '*first official automobile*': Stepan Gil, *Shest' let s V. I. Leninym. Vospominaniya lichnogo shofera Vladimira Il'ina Lenina. Izdaniye vtoroye, pererabotannoye i dopolnennoye*, 1957, 10–13. '*That's Kollontai!*': Simon Sebag Montefiore, *Young Stalin*, 2007, 305, originally from Trotsky. '*bicycle for the journey*' and '*shut up shop*': Trotsky, 341. '*John Reed joins*': Homberger, 158. '*As soon as*': Decree on the Press, 9 November 1917, *RSS*, 190–191. '*Socialism cannot be decreed*': meeting of the Central Executive Committee, 4 November 1917, *CW* XXVI, 285–293. '*thin and gloomy Pole*': *RSS*, 188. '*bourgeoisie are prepared to commit*': note to F. E. Dzerzhinsky, *CW* XXVI, 374–376. '*The following changes*': 'The Tasks of the Public Library', November 1917, *CW* XXVIII, 351. • **KANSAS CITY**: '*All cops love me*': to Marcelline Hemingway, 26 October 1917, *LEH* I, 56. '*enlist in the Canadian Army*': to Marcelline Hemingway, 30 October and 6 November 1917, *LEH* I, 58–60. '*marched and skirmished*': to Clarence and Grace Hemingway, 15 November 1917, EHC, Series 2, Box OC01, EHPP-OC01-008-002. '*unusual sight*': to Clarence and Grace Hemingway, 17 December 1917, *LEH* I, 70. • **JERUSALEM**: for context see Eugene Rogan, *The Fall of the Ottomans: The Great War in the Middle East*, 2015; James

Barr, *A Line in the Sand: Britain, France and the Struggle that Shaped the Middle East*, 2011; Sean McMeekin, *The Ottoman Endgame: War, Revolution and the Making of the Modern Middle East, 1908–1923*, 2015; and David Fromkin, *A Peace to End all Peace: Creating the Modern Middle East, 1914–1922*, 1989. For the life of Mustafa Kemal see Andrew Mango, *Atatürk*, 1999; and Klaus Kreiser, *Atatürk: Eine Biographie*, 2011. *'Christmas present'*: Rogan, 350–352. *'Jews Here Jubilant'*: 'Jerusalem Falls to the British Army, Jews Here Jubilant', *New York Times*, 10 December 1917. *'gives me any pleasure'*: to Ferenczi, 10 December 1917, *FR/FER* II, 363–364. *'got so heated'*: Mango, 171–172, though Mango rather doubts the story. *'stationary train'* to *'get a better view'*: Kreiser, 117–121. • **BREST-LITOVSK**: for an analysis see Borislav Chernev, *Twilight of Empire: The Brest-Litovsk Conference and the Remaking of East-Central Europe, 1917–1918*, 2017; and John Wheeler-Bennett, *Brest-Litovsk: The Forgotten Peace, March 1918*, 1963. For a word-by-word account see *Proceedings of the Brest-Litovsk Peace Conference: The Peace Negotiations between Russia and the Central Powers, 21 November 1917 – 3 March 1918*, 1918 – afterwards *PBL*. For an insider's perspective, other than the main figures who are cited elsewhere here – Czernin, Hoffmann, Trotsky – see Ivan Fokke, 'Na stsene i za kulisami brestkoi tragiko-medii: Memuary uchastnika Brest-Litovskih mirnykh peregovorov', *Arkhiv Russkoi Revolutsii*, 1930. • **INGOLSTADT**: *'My heartache'*: to Jeanne de Gaulle, 19 December 1917, *CDG* I, 337–338. • **BRESLAU**: to Sophie Liebknecht, 24 December 1917, *LRL*, 457. • **WASHINGTON DC**: *'class war'*: memorandum by Lincoln Steffens, 28 December 1917, *WW* XLV, 381–384. *'poem by Wordsworth'*: Cooper, *Wilson*, 421.

Winter 1918

Rosa Luxemburg quotation from 'Der Anfang', *Die Rote Fahne*, 18 November 1918.

BREST: *'tense voyage'*: Badger, *Life in Ragtime*, 162. *'do not recognise'*: Sammons and Morrow, 190. • **STOCKHOLM**: for Einstein's life see Philipp Frank, *Einstein: His Life and Times*, 1948; Albrecht Fölsing, *Albert Einstein: A Biography*, 1997 (trans. Ewald Osers); and Walter Isaacson, *Einstein: His Life and Universe*, 2007. *'milk and sugar'*: to Hans Albert Einstein, 25 January 1918, *CPAE* VIII, 615, note 4. *'torment me'*: from Mileva Einstein-Marić, 9 February 1918, *CPAE* X, 141–143. • **KANSAS CITY**: *'get into aviation'*: to the Hemingway family, 2 January 1918, *LEH* I, 71. *'still a Christian'*: to Grace Hemingway, 16 January 1918, *LEH* I, 76–77. *'more terrestrial matters'* to *'sans use of the eyes'*: to Marcelline Hemingway, 30 January 1918 and 12 February 1918, *LEH* I, 79–80 and 82–83. • **WASHINGTON DC**: *'10.30 on a Saturday morning'*: diary of Colonel House, 9 January 1917, *WW* XLV, 550–559. *'moral climax'*: address to Congress, 8 January 1917, *WW* XLV, 534–539. *'Poland will be free'*: for more on this see M. B. Biskupski, 'Re-creating Central Europe: The United States "Inquiry" into the Future of Poland in 1918', *International History Review*, 12/2, 1990, 221–240. • **BREST-LITOVSK**: *'Austrian Foreign Minister'*: diary entry for 5 January 1918, Ottokar Czernin, *In the World War*, 1919, 231.

'Wilhelm presents a map': Chernev, 64–65; and Max Hoffmann, *The War of Lost Opportunities*, 1924, 214. '*Trotsky, persuaded by Lenin*': Trotsky, 363. '*will not bow its head*': Fokke, 128. '*unnecessarily decorative*': *PBL*, 66. '*master rather than his emissary*' and '*Austrian counterpart*': Trotsky, 367. '*no way compensated*': *PBL*, 62. '*dictates a history*': Trotsky, 369–370. '*taking part with much interest*': *PBL*, 75. '*protest against the tone*': 82. '*Vienna urgently needs*': Czernin, 231. '*bound to raise problems*': Chernev, 120–157. • **VIENNA**: '*Eve of the Austrian Revolution*': Brook-Shepherd, *Last Habsburg*, 122. '*Cold shivers*': to Abraham, 19 January 1918, *FR/AB*, 369–370 (the original German reads 'Kälte Tremor'). • **BERLIN**: '*must now be done in the west!*': Röhl, *Into the Abyss*, 1157. '*Died for the Fatherland*': Davis, *Kaiser I Knew*, 285. • **PETROGRAD**: for the episode of the Constituent Assembly see Alexander Rabinowitch, *The Bolsheviks in Power: The First Year of Soviet Rule in Petrograd*, 2007, 104–131. '*rousing speech to Red Guards*': speech at send-off of troop trains, 1 January 1918, *CW* XXVI, 420. '*collapse of a bluff, which?*': Edgar Sisson, *One Hundred Red Days: A Personal Chronicle of the Bolshevik Revolution*, 1931, 236. '*Ex-poachers*': diary entry 18 January 1918, Robien, 195. '*armed with sandwiches*': Sisson, 242. '*company of corpses*': 'People from Another World', 6 January 1918 (published in 1926), *CW* XXVI, 431–433. '*funereal black*': Rabinowitch, *Bolsheviks in Power*, 110. '*Wild West show*': Albert Rhys Williams, *Journey into Revolution: Petrograd, 1917–1918*, 1969, 198. '*go at it systematically*': ibid., 199. '*hand on heart*': Rabinowitch, *Bolsheviks in Power*, 117. '*majestic air*': Williams, 200. '*Let them just go home*': Rabinowitch, *Bolsheviks in Power*, 122. '*guards are tired*': S. Mstislavskii, *Five Days which Transformed Russia*, 1988, 154. '*not the end*': Rabinowitch, *Bolsheviks in Power*, 124. • **THE WESTERN FRONT**: for Erich Ludendorff's life see Manfred Nebelin, *Ludendorff: Diktator im Ersten Weltkrieg*, 2010. For Adolf Hitler's war see Thomas Weber, *Hitler's First War: Adolf Hitler, the Men of the List Regiment, and the First World War*, 2010. For the biography of Adolf Hitler see Ian Kershaw, *Hitler: Hubris, 1889–1936*, 1998; Volker Ullrich, *Hitler: A Biography, Ascent*, 2013; Thomas Weber, *Becoming Hitler: The Making of a Nazi*, 2017; John Toland, *Adolf Hitler*, 1976. Adolf Hitler, *Mein Kampf*, 1939 (trans. Chamberlain, Fay, Hayes, Johnson et al.), proves some interesting insights, but must be read above all as a propaganda document. '*go under*': Nebelin, 408. • **PETROGRAD**: for the political debate around this question see Service, *A Political Life*, Vol. 2, 317–322. '*human yearning*': Theses on the Question of The Immediate Conclusion &c., 7 January 1918, *CW* XXXVI, 442–450. '*dirty stable*': speech at meeting of the Central Committee, 11 January 1918, *CW* XXXVI, 467–470. '*shot on the spot*': meeting with food supply officials, 14 January 1918, *CW* XXVI, 501–502. • **PARIS**: '*mind bringing me*': Apollinaire to Breton, 6 February 1918, http://www.christies.com/lotfinder/Lot/guillaume-apollinaire-4717464-details.aspx. '*telephone rings*': entry for February 1918, Jessie Kenney. • **TOBOLSK**: '*saws up wood*' to '*greenhouse roof*': diary of Nicholas, 9–26 January 1918, *ROM*, 227. '*a lot of time thinking about*': Alexandra to Anna Vryubova, 9 January 1918, *ROM*, 219–221. '*swastika*': Alexandra to Aleksandr Syroboiarsky, 11 January 1918, *ROM*, 221. '*In other words*': diary of Nicholas, 1/14 February 1918, *ROM*, 227. • **BREST-LITOVSK**: '*demagogic trick*' and following: *PBL*, 143. '*twang of sympathy*': Czernin, 246. '*can only thank the President*': *PBL*, 145. '*requests* *a visa'* and *'refused'*: Trotsky, 375–376; and to Count Czernin, 26 January, 1918, *TP* I, 9–11. *'intellectual combat'*: *PBL*, 148. *'peace without profit'* to *'I wonder if'*: Czernin, 247–249. *'final card'*: *PBL*, 171–173, very slightly paraphrased. *'what is going to happen'*: Fokke, 207. • **PETROGRAD**: *'robbed blind'*: diary entry, 14 February 1918, Robien, 222. *'Hell's fire'*: Patriarch Tikhon anathematises the Bolsheviks, *RSS*, 193–195. • **HASKELL COUNTY**: John M. Barry, *The Great Influenza: The Story of the Deadliest Pandemic in History*, 2005, 91–97. • **BREST-LITOVSK**: *'start hostilities again'*: diary entry 17 February 1918, Max Hoffmann, *War Diaries and Other Papers*, 2 volumes, Vol. 1, 1929 (trans. Eric Sutton), 204–205. *'Stalin is blunt'*: Kotkin, 255. *'most comical war'*: diary entry 22 February 1918, Hoffmann, *War Diaries*, Vol. 1, 207. *'radiant with joy'*: diary entry 21 February 1918, Robien, 229. *'spiky article'*: 'The Revolutionary Phrase', *Pravda*, 21 February 1918, *CW* XXVII, 19–29. • **VIENNA**: *'mutiny breaks out'*: Rauchensteiner, 887–893. *'infuriates the empire's Poles'*: Watson, 500. • **PETROGRAD**: for Lenin's political gamesmanship on Brest-Litovsk and party matters see Service, *A Political Life*, Vol. 2, 322–355. For the life of Stalin see Kotkin; Miklós Kun, *Stalin: An Unknown Portrait*, 2003; and Robert Service, *Stalin: A Biography*, 2005. For Béla Kun see Borsányi. For the move to Moscow and details of living arrangements see Kotkin, 259–264; and Trotsky, 350–353. *'second New York'*: Rabinowitch, *Bolsheviks in Power*, 201. *'Foreign embassies'* to *'glass of fresh milk'*: diary entry 28 February 1918 and 1 March 1918, Robien, 236–241. *'Tsar's brother Michael'*: Crawford and Crawford, 340–341. *'had an affair'*: Simon Sebag Montefiore, *Stalin: The Court of the Red Tsar*, 2003, 24. *'moving in zig-zags'*: 'The Immediate Tasks of the Soviet Government', 23–28 March 1918, *CW* XLI, 682–684. *'dark spy'*: Borsányi, 52. *'kill anyone younger than seven'*: diary entry 20 March 1918, Ivan Bunin, *Cursed Days*, 1998 (trans. Thomas Gaiton Marullo), 65–66. • **NANTES**: for the band's journey across France see Badger, *Life in Ragtime*, 166–173. For the somewhat fluid notion of jazz itself and James Reese Europe's contribution see Badger, 'James Reese Europe'. *'receives a delegation'*: Cooper, *Wilson*, 409.

Spring 1918

THE WESTERN FRONT: for the German offensive, see Robert T. Foley, 'From Victory to Defeat: The German Army in 1918', in Ashley Ekins (ed.), *1918: The Year of Victory*, 2010, 69–88; and Watson, 514–523. *'rumours among troops'* to *'single cigarette'*: Nebelin, 407–412. *'looks like a film'*: letter dated 21 March 1918, extract reproduced in Albrecht von Thaer, 'Generalstabdienst an der Front und in der O.H.L.', *Abhandlungen der Akademie der Wissenschaften in Göttingen*, No. 40, 1958, 170–171. *'lights up his sleeping quarters'*: Gilbert, *World in Torment*, 79. *'push looks awful'*: to Hemingway family, 23 March 1918, *LEH* I, 91. *'always been a carnivore'*: to Abraham, 22 March 1918, *FR/AB*, 374. *'utterly defeated'*: diary entry 23 March 1918, Müller, *Kaiser and his Court*, 344. *'sending King George'*: Gilbert, *World in Torment*, 81. *'begins to wonder'*: diary entry 29 March 1918, Müller, *Kaiser and his Court*, 346. *'crawling through'*: Noble Lee Sissle,

'Memoirs of Lieutenant "Jim" Europe', unpublished manuscript, 1942, LOC, NAACP Papers, Group 1, Boxes J56 and J70, 155–165. *German army that is breaking apart*: Watson, 525–526. *'Oh! Oh! Oh!'*: Gilbert, *World in Torment*, 94. • ZURICH: to Mileva Einstein-Marić, 3 April 1918, *CPAE* X, 154–155. • VIENNA: for this episode see Rauchensteiner, 896–906. See also the German and Austrian correspondence in April/May 1918, in *GFA* IV, 101–168. For the panic in Vienna and at court see Brook-Shepherd, *Last Habsburg*, 142–150. • MAYNOOTH: see Coogan, *De Valera*, 107–109. *'have not met one soldier'*: Minutes of the War Cabinet, Irish Conscription, 6 April 1918, *WSC* VIII, 297–298. *'fit resting place'*: Father Patrick Gaynor quoted in Fitzpatrick, 'De Valera in 1917', 110. • RUSSIA: for histories of the Russian civil war see Evan Mawdsley, *The Russian Civil War*, 1987 (2008 edition cited here); Jonathan D. Smele, *The 'Russian' Civil Wars, 1916–1926: Ten Years that Shook the World*, 2015; and Laura Engelstein, *Russia in Flames: War, Revolution and Civil War, 1914–1921*, 2018. For an older account see William Henry Chamberlin, *The Russian Revolution, 1917–1921*, 1935, 2 volumes. For foreign intervention see Mawdsley, 62–76; and Engelstein, 383–400. For the civil war in the context of other pressures facing the Bolshevik regime in its early years, see Richard Pipes, *Russia under the Bolshevik Regime, 1919–1924*, 1997; and Figes, 555–720. For British involvement see Clifford Kinvig, *Churchill's Crusade: The British Invasion of Russia*, 2006, with 17–71 particularly relevant for this section. For a broader perspective on relations between the Bolsheviks and the West in these years see Robert Service, *Spies and Commissars: Bolshevik Russia and the West*, 2011. For Count Mirbach see Winfried Baumgart, 'Die Mission des Grafen Mirbach in Moskau April–Juni 1918', *Vierteljahrshefte für Zeitgeschichte*, 16/1, 1968, 66–96. *'taken Kharkov'*: diary entry 9 April 1918, Hoffmann, *War Diaries*, Vol. 1, 214. *'diplomatic capital of Russia'*: Francis, 237. *'French diplomat describes'*: diary entries 25 April–15 May 1918, Robien, 251–264. *'discipline must be discipline'*: Kotkin, 297. *'exhilarating game'*: see, for example, George Hill, *Go Spy the Land: Being the Adventures of I.K.8 of the British Secret Service*, 1932; and Paul Dukes, *Red Dusk and the Morrow*, 1922. *'British operative briefly considers'*: Service, *Spies and Commissars*, 147. *'say with confidence'* to *'Furious struggle'*: speech in Moscow Soviet, 23 April 1918, *CW* XXVII, 292–293. *'credentials formally'*: diary entry 26 April 1918, Robien, 252. *'thieving rabble of proles'*: diplomatic report sent by Mirbach, 29 April 1918, Baumgart, 76. *'socialist future!'* to *'We'll see'*: report sent on 30 April 1918, 77–78. *'advertising power'*: 'Political Report No. 3', 12–26 January 1918, prepared by Felix Cole, US Consul in Archangel, USNA, RG84.800 Foreign Service Posts of the Department of State, Archangel, Vol. 14. For an overview of the activities of Felix Cole see Benjamin D. Rhodes, 'A Prophet in the Russian Wilderness: The Mission of Consul Felix Cole at Archangel, 1917–1919', *Review of Politics*, 46/3, 1984, 388–409. *'suction pump'* to *'Baghdad railroad'*: 'The Allies, Archangel and Siberia', report by Felix Cole, 26 April 1918, USNA, RG84.877 Foreign Service Posts of the Department of State, Archangel, Vol. 18. *'time is fast approaching'*: cable from Francis to Washington, 13 April 1918, Rhodes, 'Prophet in the Russian Wilderness', 397. • THERESIENSTADT FORTRESS: Tim Butcher,

The Trigger: The Hunt for Gavrilo Princip: The Assassin who Brought the World to War, 2014, 283. An account of Princip's own view of his situation written by an Austrian, Dr Pappenheim, was published in German in 1926. • **TOBOLSK**: for this period of the Romanovs' incarceration see Service, *Last of the Tsars*, 2017, 152–175. *'rumours the Tsar's daughter'*: newspaper report 23 November 1917, *ROM*, 204. *'the Tsar jokes'*: Gilliard, 255. *'last chance of escape'*: 257–258. *'the baggage'*: Service, *Last of the Tsars*, 174. *'Distraught'*: Gilliard, 260–262. *'I'd rather cut off'*: Service, *Last of the Tsars*, 164. • **MOSCOW**: see Christina Lodder, 'Lenin's Plan for Monumental Propaganda', in Matthew Cullerne Brown and Brandon Taylor (eds.), *Art of the Soviets: Painting, Sculpture and Architecture in a One-Party State, 1917–1992*, 1993, 16–32. • **SPA**: *'taken away my will to live'* to *'would gladly give up'*: Nebelin, 423–424. *'lieutenant visits Ludendorff'*: Thaer, 192–198. • **AMERICAN FRONT LINE**: this account is drawn from Sammons and Morrow, 265–275. *'great Day of Decision'*: 'Close Ranks', *The Crisis*, July 1918. • **CHELYABINSK**: for the role of the Czechoslovak legion in this phase of the Russian civil war see Engelstein, 393–400. The description of conditions is drawn from Dalibor Vácha, 'Tepluskas and Eshelons: Czechoslovak Legionaries on their Journey across Russia', *Czech Journal of Contemporary History*, 1/1, 2013, 20–53. • **NEW YORK**: *'well-wishers crowd'* and following: 'President Leads Red Cross Parade', *New York Times*, 19 May 1918. *'insurance policy'* and *'Woolworth Building'* : to the Hemingway family, 14 May 1918 and 17/18 May 1918, with latter addition, *LEH* I, 97–101. • **CHELYABINSK**: *'telegram from Moscow'*: For the relevant series of documents see *Intervention, Civil War, and Communism in Russia, April–December 1918: Documents and materials*, 1936 (ed. James Bunyan), 88–98. • **THE WESTERN FRONT**: *'wish for peace?'*: General Rees's memoirs quoted in J. H. Johnson, *1918: The Unexpected Victory*, 1997, 70–71. *'discuss evacuating'*: Stevenson, *Cataclysm*, 340. *'city of the dead'*: letter dated 28 May 1918, Edward Villiers Stanley, *Paris 1918: The War Diary of the British Ambassador, the 17th Earl of Derby*, 2001 (ed. David Dutton), 22. • **PETROGRAD**: letter to the workers of Petrograd, 22 May 1918, *CW* XXVII, 391–398.

Summer 1918

LINCOLN: *'singing as we are now'*: Darrell Figgis, *A Second Chronicle of Jails*, 1919, 58. *'Back inside'* to end: Fanning, 67–68; and Coogan, *De Valera*, 112–121, including reference to Machiavelli at 118–121. • **MADRID**: for the origins of the Spanish naming of the flu, Ryan A. Davis, *The Spanish Flu: Narrative and Cultural Identity in Spain, 1918*, 2013. *'El Liberal reports'*: ibid., 44. *'alarmist suggestions'*: *British Medical Journal*, 1/2996, 1 June 1918, 623–628. *'all the armies'*: Anton Erkoreka, 'Origins of the Spanish Influenza Pandemic (1918–1920) and its Relation to the First World War', *Journal of Molecular and Genetic Medicine*, 3/2, 2009, 190–194. • **PARIS**: *'more money'*: Ernest Hemingway, *Ernest Hemingway, Cub Reporter: Kansas City Star Stories*, 1970 (ed. Matthew J. Bruccoli), 10. *'hot poppums'*: to the Hemingway family, 3 June 1918, *LEH* I, 110. *'wonderful time!!!'*: to a friend at the *Kansas City Star*, 9 June 1918, *LEH* I, 112. • **SAMARA**: *'Tsaritsyn'*: Kotkin, 300–307. *'Götterdämmerung'*: report by Mirbach, 1 June 1918, Baumgart, 86–87. • **VIENNA**: *'no relying on the supernatural'*: to Ferenczi, 9 May 1918, *FR/FER* II, 281–282. *'begging letter'*: Charles to Wilhelm, 24 June 1918, *GFA* II, 218–219. • **PERM**: Crawford and Crawford, 353–363. • **GIZAUCOURT**: Noble Lee Sissle, 'Memoirs of Lieutenant "Jim" Europe', 167–170. • **AHRENSHOOP**: *'like a crocodile'*: to Max Born, 29 June 1918, *CPAE* VIIIB, 818–819. *'nice last year'*: from Hans-Albert Einstein, after 4 June 1918, *CPAE* X, 166–168. • **PETROGRAD**: *'new rationing system is introduced'*: Mary McAuley, *Bread and Justice: State and Society in Petrograd, 1917–1922*, 1991, 286. *'so few one-legged'*: ibid., 326. *'no longer give a positive diagnosis'*: report by Mirbach, 25 June 1918, Baumgart, 94–95. *'details of the assassination plot are unclear'*: for a conspiratorial reading see Yuri Felshtinsky, *Lenin and his Comrades*, 2010, 104–135; for a more straightforward version see Figes, 632–635. *'appropriate German word to use'*: Felshtinsky, 117. *'broken glass'*: ibid., 132. • **FOSSALTA DI PIAVE**: for a description of this episode see Meyers, *Hemingway*, 30–44. *'Hemenway'*: '3 Dead, 6 Hurt, 3 Missing, City's Share of Glory', *Chicago Daily Tribune*, 17 July 1918. *'scrapbook'*: from Anson T. Hemingway to Ernest Hemingway, EHC, 19 July 1918, Series 3, Box IC10, EHPP-IC10-048–007. *'sometimes a letter every day'*: letters from Agnes von Kurowsky, 1918 to 1922, EHC. *'Austrian carbines'*: to Hemingway family, 21 July 1918, *LEH* I, 117–119. • **KARLSBAD**: for Mustafa Kemal's diary in Karlsbad see İnan, Ayşe Afet, *Mustafa Kemal Atatürk'ün Karlsbad Hatıraları*, 1999. • **SPA**: for the sequence of events from July see Stevenson, *Cataclysm*, 343–351; and Nick Lloyd, *Hundred Days: The End of the Great War*, 2014, 1–27. *'Baedeker'*: Karl Baedeker, *Northern France from Belgium and the English Channel to the Loire excluding Paris and its Environs: Handbook for Travellers*, 1909, 82. *'several thousand tanks'*: letter dated 20 July 1918, Thaer, 212–215. *'blames his subordinates'*: Nebelin, 438. • **PRESSBURG**: *'all a dream?'*: Brook-Shepherd, *Last Habsburg*, 167. *'flour ration'* to *'Suicides'*: Rauchensteiner, 973. • **EKATERINBURG**: Service, *Last of the Tsars*, 254–257. • **SPA**: *'quiet evening at head-quarters'*: diary entry 23 July 1918, Müller, *Kaiser and his Court*, 374. *'shouldn't have trusted that date'*: Nebelin, 439. • **PARIS**: *Le Matin*, 6 July 1918, in Olivier Lahaie, 'L'épidémie de grippe dite "espagnole" et sa perception par l'armée française (1918–1919)', *Revue historique des armées*, 262, 2011, consulted at http://rha.revues.org/7163. • **WÜLZBURG**: escape narrative drawn from de Gaulle's 1926 account as before. *'been buried alive'* to *'thick of it all along'*: to Jeanne de Gaulle, 1 September 1918, *CDG* I, 421–422. • **NEW YORK**: *'organisation he creates'*: Constitution and Book of Laws, July 1918, *MG* I, 256–280. • **MOSCOW**: *'list of individuals'*: Vladimir Lenin, *On Literature and Art*, 1967, 205. *'attics and dark rooms'*: V. Tatlin, S. Dymshits-Tolstaia and John Bowlt, 'Memorandum from the Visual Arts Section of the People's Commissariat for Enlightenment to the Soviet of People's Commissars: Project for the Organization of Competitions for Monuments to Distinguished Persons', *Design Issues*, 1/2, 1984, 70–74, 73. • **MILAN**: *'changes its masthead'*: Bosworth, 101. *'time for angels'*: 'Una Politica', *Il Popolo d'Italia*, 23 February 1918, *OO* X, 342–343. • **ACROSS RUSSIA**: for an overview for this phase of the civil war see Figes, 555–588. For individual campaigns see

Mawdsley and Engelstein. *'one hundred known kulaks'*: telegram from Lenin to Communists in Penza, 11 August 1918, Vladimir Lenin, *The Unknown Lenin: From the Soviet Archive*, 1996 (ed. Richard Pipes), 50. *'committing a great crime'*: telegram to A.Y. Minkin, 14 August 1918, *CW* XXXV, 352. *'charlatans and fools'*: Service, *Trotsky*, 223. *'bloody reign of terror'*: Kotkin, 300–307. • **CROYDON**: *'wood-carved furniture'*: Gilbert, *World in Torment*, 131. *'ten times as many'*: Hew Strachan, *The First World War*, 2014, 311. *'sturdy lot'*: Gilbert, *World in Torment*, 132. • **VIENNA**: *'flowery prose'*: the manifestos are reproduced in Giorgio Evangelisti, *La Scrittura nel Vento: Gabriele D'Annunzio e il volo su Vienna. Immagini e documenti*, 1999, 78–84. The rest of this book contains a wealth of other detail on the flight and those involved. *'a few minutes'*: 'Italienische Flieger über Wien', *Die Neue Zeitung*, 10 August 1918. *'wonderfully theatrical'* to *'our D'Annunzios?'*: 'Italienische Flieger über Wien', *Arbeiter-Zeitung*, 10 August 1918. • **MOSCOW**: for the thesis of an inside job see Felshtinsky, 136–170; for alternative accounts, see Volkogonov, *Lenin*, 219–229; and Semion Lyandres, 'The 1918 Attempt on the Life of Lenin: A New Look at the Evidence', *Slavic Review*, 48/3, 1989, 432–448. For an eyewitness, see Gil, 13–26. *'victory or death'*: speech at the Mikhelson Works, 30 August 1918, *CW* XXVIII, 51–52. *'buy a lemon'*: Service, *Lenin*, 368. *'What are we going to do?'*: Krupskaya, *Reminiscences*, 480. *'discreetly takes'*: Sebestyen, 413. *'What's there to look at?'*: Krupskaya, *Reminiscences*, 481. *'Trotsky is telegrammed'*: Service, *Trotsky*, 222. *'turns his talents to propaganda'* to *'skull'*: Volkogonov, *Lenin*, 222. *'apostle of the socialist revolution'* and *'systematic terror'*: Kotkin, 287. *'prepare the terror'*: Lenin, *Unknown Lenin*, 56. • **FORT GIRONVILLE**: *'doing his duty in Paris'*: Badger, *Life is Ragtime*, 192. *'Pershing watches'* to *'boys have done'*: John J. Pershing, *My Experiences in the Great War*, Vol. 2, 1931, 266–273. *'savours the victory'*: 'Great Force in Stroke', *New York Times*, 13 September 1918. • **MOSCOW**: *'Recovery proceeding excellently'*: telegram to Trotsky, 6 September 1918, *CW* XXXV, 359. *'no accident'*: speech in Kazan, 12 September 18, *TP* I, 128–131. *'Fewer highbrow articles'*: 'The Character of our Newspapers', originally *Pravda*, 20 September 1918, *CW* XXVIII, 171–178. *'furious note'*: to Y. A. Berzin, V. V. Vorovsky and A. A. Joffe, 20 September 1918, *CW* XXXV, 362–363. *'I reprimand you'*: telegram to A. V. Lunacharsky, 18 September 1918, *CW* XXXV, 360. *'pointed out a thousand times'*: Sebestyen, 428. • **AVESNES-SUR-HELPE**: Wolfgang Foerster, *Der Feldherr Ludendorff im Unglück: Eine Studie über seine seelische Haltung in der Endphase des ersten Weltkriegs*, 1952, 72–79. • **THE BRONX**: for John Reed's return to America see Homberger, 166–174. *'hardrock blasters'*: Reed, *Education of John Reed*, 177. • **GORKI**: Krupskaya, *Reminiscences*, 484–485. • **BUDAPEST**: for a general account see Jones, *Freud*, Vol. 2, 222–223. *'Freud's Cigar'*: Kosztolányi Dezső, 'Freud szivarja', *Pesti Napló*, 1 October 1918. *'only a handful of us'* to *'come to this'*: 'Lines of Advance in Psycho-Analytic Therapy', *SE* XVII, 158–168. *'swimming in satisfaction'* to *'better times approaching'*: to Ferenczi, 30 September 1918, *FR/FER* II, 296. • **BRESLAU**: *'socialism will be decreed'* to *'direct influence'*: 'The Russian Revolution', written in September 1918 and unpublished until 1928, Luxemburg, 281–311, particularly 306–308. *'spineless jellyfish'* to *'compelled to rebel?'*: Rosa Luxemburg, 'Die russische Tragödie', *Spartakusbrief*, No. 11, September 1918. • **SOFIA**: *'We've eaten shit'*: Mango, 185. • **SPA**:

Nebelin, 458–459. • **THE WESTERN FRONT**: *'embalming fluid'*: Alfred W. Crosby, *America's Forgotten Pandemic: The Influenza of 1918*, 2003, 124. • **MUNICH**: for the Thule Society see Reginald Phelps, '"Before Hitler Came": Thule Society and Germanen Orden', *Journal of Modern History*, 35/3, 1963, 245–261. For an eyewitness account see Rudolf von Sebottendorf, *Bevor Hitler Kam*, 1934. For the complex of beliefs on which both the Thule Society and then the Nazi Party drew see Eric Kurlander, 'Hitler's Monsters: The Occult Roots of Nazism and the Emergence of the Nazi "Supernatural Imaginary"', *German History*, 30/4, 528–549; and G. L. Mosse, 'The Mystical Origins of National Socialism', *Journal of the History of Ideas*, 22/1, 1961, 81–96. *'bronze pins'*: Sebottendorf, 52. *'divining rods'*: Phelps, 'Before Hitler Came', 251. *'Race purity'* to *'fertilised it with their blood'*: Sebottendorf, 47.

Autumn 1918

CHICAGO: *'For a few seconds'*: Meyers, *Hemingway*, 38. *'influenza closes everything'*: see www.influenzaarchive.org project. For one particularly striking example of the explosion of influenza see Carol S. Byerly, 'The U.S. Military and the Influenza Pandemic of 1918–1919', *Public Health Reports*, 125, Supplement 3, 2010, 82–91. • **SPA**: principally drawn from diary entry 1 October 1918, Thaer, 234–237. *'worries about the widows'*: Nebelin, 682, footnote 25. *'will be hanged some day'*: ibid., 468. • **GORKI**: *'fires off a note'*: CW XXXV, Note to Sverdlov and Trotsky, 1 October 1918, 364–365. *'finds time to be infuriated'*: 'The Proletarian Revolution and the Renegade Kautsky', 10 October, 1918, CW XXVIII, 104–112. • **WASHINGTON**: for the sequence of events see Stevenson, *Cataclysm*, 384–391. For an alternative reading of Wilson's purposes see Tooze, 222–232. For the documents themselves see *Documents and Statements Relating to Peace Proposals and War Aims*, December 1916 – November 1918, 1919 (ed. G. Lowe Dickinson). For a highly readable account of the last months of the war incorporating diplomatic and military perspectives see Gordon Brook-Shepherd, *November 1918: The Last Act of the Great War*, 1981. *'in order to prevent further bloodshed'*: *Urkunden der Obersten Heeresleitung über ihre Tätigkeit 1916/8*, 1920 (ed. Erich Ludendorff), 535. The armistice request is not included in Lowe Dickinson. • **THE WESTERN FRONT**: *'German army retreats'*: Lloyd, *Hundred Days*, 208–210. *'Wervik'*: Weber, *Hitler's First War*, 220–221; and Hitler, 264. • **MOSCOW**: *'noisy gestures'* to *'no lover of noise'*: Kotkin, 308. *'insist on Stalin's recall'*: to Lenin, 4 October 1918, TP I, 134–137. *'lighten the load'*: Trotsky's explanation, 13 October 1918, TP I, 148–151. • **VIENNA**: for the beginnings of the break-up of the Habsburg Empire see Rauchensteiner, 979–998. *'bankruptcy of the old state'*: 'Die Friedensfrage in Parlament', *Neues Wiener Tagblatt*, 4 October 1918, DÖZ, 15. *'magnificent Duce'*: Bosworth, 100. *'crew for a sinking ship'*: Brook-Shepherd, *Last Habsburg*, 188. • **BERLIN**: *'Woodrow's latest diplomatic note'*: Wilson's reply to the German note of 12 October, 14 October 1918, *Documents and Statements Relating to Peace Proposals*, 250–252. *'Ludendorff is evasive'* and following quotations: Michael Geyer, 'Insurrectionary Warfare:

The German Debate about a Levée en Masse in October 1918', *Journal of Modern History*, 73/3, 2001, 459–527, particularly 503–507. *'dug up and sent home'*: Wilhelm Breucker, *Die Tragik Ludendorffs. Eine kritische Studie auf Grund persönlicher Erinnerungen an den General und seine Zeit*, 1953, 35. • VENICE: Alatri, 199. • MOSCOW: speech at a joint session of the All-Russian Central Executive Committee, 22 October 1918, *CW* XXVIII, 113–126. • VIENNA: see Rauchensteiner, 992–998. *'Fiume'*: ibid., 997. *'Prague'*: Victor S. Mamatey, 'The Establishment of the Republic', in Victor S. Mamatey and Radomír Luža (eds.), *A History of the Czechoslovak Republic, 1918–1948*, 1973, 3–38, particularly 23–38. *'Budapest'*: Rauchensteiner, 1004. *'prevent further bloodshed'*: ibid., 998. *'terribly thrilling'*, to Eitingon, 25 November 1918, *FR/EIT* I, 139–140. *'Withdraw your libido'*: to Ferenczi, 27 October 1918, *FR/FER* II, 304–305. • PASEWALK: on Hitler's time in Pasewalk there is little evidence and much conjecture. See Kershaw, 101–105; and Ullrich, 69–72. For an entirely sceptical approach see J. Armbruster, 'Die Behandlung Adolf Hitlers im Lazarett Pasewalk 1918: Historische Mythenbildung durch einseitige bzw. Spekulative Pathographie', *Journal für Neurologie, Neurochirurgie und Psychiatrie*, 10/4, 2009, 18–22. For a speculative approach, Bernhard Horstmann, *Hitler in Pasewalk: die Hypnose und ihre Folgen*, 2004. Hitler's own account is at Hitler, 264–269 • BERLIN: *'seem to forget'*: diary entry 28 October 1918, Thaer, 246–249. *'Mark my words'*: Bruecker, 61. *'Chile and Argentina'*: letter 26 October 1918, Thaer, 244–245. • WASHINGTON DC: *'Much as I should enjoy'*: Wilson to House, 28 October 1918, *FRUS, The Paris Peace Conference, 1919*: I, 119 • SPA: Röhl, *Concise Life*, 176. • THE AUSTRO-ITALIAN FRONT LINE: Rauchensteiner, 1002–1005. • MOSCOW: 'In Honour of the Austro-Hungarian Revolution', *Pravda*, 5 November 1918, *CW* XXVIII, 130. • THE AUSTRO-ITALIAN FRONT LINE: *'highest mountain'*: Rauchensteiner, 1008. *'macabre Lord's Prayer'*: Woodhouse, 312, original dated 1 November 1918, in Gabriele D'Annunzio, *Prose di Ricerca*, 3 volumes, 1962–1968 (ed. Egidio Bianchetti), Vol. 1, 648–649. *'ministers gather'*: Rauchensteiner, 1010. *'trainload of Austrian soldiers'*: 'Plünderungen durch Soldaten', *Arbeiter-Zeitung*, 3 November 1918, *DÖZ*, 34. • LONDON: *'drizzle of empires'*: Gilbert, *World in Torment*, 158. • KIEL: *'no turning back'*: *Schleswig-Holsteinische Volkszeitung*, 5 November 1918, in *Die Entwicklung der deutschen Revolution und das Kriegsende in der Zeit vom 1. Oktober bis 30. November 1918*, 1918 (ed. Kurt Ahnert), 156–157. *'hussars are said to be on their way'*: Mark Jones, *Founding Weimar: Violence and the German Revolution of 1918–1919*, 2016, 44. • SPA: *'can sign up'*: diary entry 5 November 1918, Thaer, 252. *'not informed'*: Cecil, 289. • THE GHENT ROAD: Gilbert, *World in Torment*, 156–158. • PETROGRAD: description of preparation and events in Petrograd: Rabinowitch, *Bolsheviks in Power*, 353–388. *'Georgian bank-robber writes'*: 'The Role of the Most Distinguished Party Activists', *Pravda*, 6 November 1918. *'Shortly the revolution'* to *'We are strong'*: Rabinowitch, *Bolsheviks in Power*, 377–382. Newspaper description of events in Moscow: 'The Festival of Great Renewal', *Pravda*, 9 November 1918. Also: James von Geldern, *Bolshevik Festivals, 1917–1920*, 1993, 93–97. *'Lenin unveils'*: speech unveiling the plaque, 7 November 1918, *CW* XXVIII, 167–168. *'special visit to Cheka headquarters'*: speech to Cheka staff, 7 November 1918, *CW* XXVIII, 169–170. *'carried out at night'*: Volkogonov, *Lenin*, 239.

• The Western Front: for a general description see Bullitt Lowry, *Armistice 1918*, 1996, 147–162. *'Then we are lost'*: ibid., 158. • Spa: for Kurt Eisner see Allan Mitchell, *Revolution in Bavaria, 1918–1919: The Eisner Regime and the Soviet Republic*, 1965. *'dodges revolutionary roadblocks'*: diary entries 7–8 November 1918, Harry Kessler, *Das Tagebuch, 1880–1937*, 9 volumes, 2004–2018 (eds. Roland S. Kamzelak und Ulrich Ott), Vol. 6, 612–622. *'sidearm'*: 9 November 1918, ibid., 622–627. • Vienna: *'So much is now going on'* to *'Don Quixote'*: to Ferenczi, 9 November 1918, FR/FER II, 310. *'Thousands of Austrian refugees'*: 'Die Vorarlberger streben nach der Schweiz', *Arbeiter-Zeitung*, 6 November 1918, *DÖZ*, 42. • Spa: for the situation in Spa see Sigurd von Ilsemann, *Der Kaiser in Holland: Aufzeichnungen des letzten Flügeladjutanten Kaiser Wilhelms II.*, ed. Harald von Koenigswald, 2 volumes, Vol. 1, 1967, *Amerongen und Doorn, 1918–1923*, 38–43; and Alfred Niemann, *Kaiser und Revolution: Die entscheidenden Ereignisse im Grossen Hauptquartier*, 1928, 132–145. For an account of the fall of monarchs across Germany see Lothar Machtan, *Die Abdankung: Wie Deutschlands gekrönte Häupter aus der Geschichte fielen*, 2008. *'medicated slumber'*: Ilsemann, Vol. 1, 7 November 1918, 35. *'Scheidemann'*: see Philipp Scheidemann, *Memoirs of a Social Democrat*, 2 volumes, Vol. 2, 1929, 580–582. *'disgraceful betrayal!'*: Niemann, 142. • Eijsden: diary entry 10 November 1918, Ilsemann, Vol. 1, 43–48. For the Dutch reception see Sally Marks, '"My name is Ozymandias": The Kaiser in Exile', *Central European History*, 16/2, 1983, 122–170. *'no hope left for me'*: Cecil, 294. *'My conscience is clear'*: diary entry 11 November 1918, Ilsemann, Vol. 1, 53–54. *'letter is read out in German'*: 'Aufzeichnungen über die Schlußsitzung der Waffenstillstandskommission am 11. November 1918, 2.15 nachts in Compiègne', in *Der Waffenstillstand, 1918–1919: Das Dokumenten-Material der Waffenstillstands-Verhandlungen von Compiègne, Spa, Trier und Brüssel*, 3 volumes, 1928 (eds. Edmund Marhefka, Hans von Hammerstein and Otto von Stein), Vol. 1, 61–73. • The Western Front: *'bows at the enemy'*: Brook-Shepherd, *November 1918*, 392. Paris: *'Apollinaire's funeral cortège'*: Polizzotti, 84. *'three hundred Parisians'*: Pierre Darmon, 'Une Tragédie dans la tragédie: la Grippe Espagnole en France (Avril 1918–Avril 1919)', *Annales de Démographie Historique*, No. 2, 2000, 153–175, 158. *'last diary entry'*: Peter Read, *Picasso and Apollinaire: The Persistence of Memory*, 2008, 136. • Vienna: *'sympathetic visitors'* to *'chambermaid'*: Brook-Shepherd, *Last Habsburg*, 212–216. *'excuse me'*: 'Der Tod Dr. Viktor Adlers', *Kronen-Zeitung*, 13 November 1918, *DÖZ*, 37–38. • Europe: *'Finnish diplomat'*: Nebelin, 507. *'come back to power'*: Margarethe Ludendorff, *Als ich Ludendorffs Frau war*, 1929, 209. *'bad dream'*: ibid., 212–213. *'Emil Sebastyen'* to *'loft apartment'*: Borsányi, 77–86. • Milan: *'post-war must be ours'*: Bosworth, 102. • Berlin: for conditions in Germany after the war see Richard Bessel, *Germany after the First World War*, 1993. For the course of political events see Mark Jones, *Founding Weimar: Violence and the German Revolution of 1918–1919*, 2016; and Ralph Haswell Lutz, *The German Revolution, 1918–1919*, 1922. For the role and attitude of Friedrich Ebert see D. K. Buse, 'Ebert and the German Crisis, 1917–1920', *Central European History*, 5/3, 1972, 234–255. *'drawn to a socialist rally'*: Hitler, 731; and Weber, *Becoming Hitler*, 3–4. *'has completed its revolution'*: Lutz, 55. *'chaos, hunger and misery'*: circular 2 November 1918, in Bessel, 70. *'over our ears'*:

to Adolf Warski, November/December 1918, *LRL*, 484–485. • **ISTANBUL**: for Istanbul's final years as the Ottoman capital see Philip Mansel, *Constantinople: City of the World's Desire, 1453–1924*, 2006, 380–414; Charles King, *Midnight at the Pera Palace: The Birth of Modern Istanbul*, 2014; and Nur Bilge Criss, *Istanbul under Allied Occupation, 1918–1923*, 1999. For a Turkish first-hand account see Halidé Edib, *The Turkish Ordeal*, 1928, 1–19. *'Forty-two Allied ships'* to *'Gallipoli'*: 'Allied Fleet at the Dardanelles', *Times*, 13 November 1918. *'Armenian bishop'*: Rogan, 385–387. *'Turkey Overrun by Brigands'*: *Times*, 20 November 1918. *'Kemal arrives at Haydarpaşa'*: Mango, 171–172. • **VIENNA**: *'tries to explain his son's silence'*: to Pfister, 2 January 1919, *FR/PF*, 64–65. *'Limitations and deprivation'*: to Ferenczi, 17 November 1918, *FR/FER* II, 311. *'bar of soap'*: Brook-Shepherd, *Last Habsburg*, 220. • **WASHINGTON DC**: *'document has been circulating'*: see 'Materials on the Protocols of the Elders of Zion', records kept by Leland Harrison, USNA, RG59, Box 1 Entry A1-349; and Robert Singerman, 'The American Career of *The Protocols of the Elders of Zion*', *American Jewish History*, 71/1, 1981, 48–78. *'Supreme Court judge'*: Singerman, 51. • **SOUTHERN RUSSIA**: *'breathing space'*: speech to Fifth All-Russian Central Executive Committee, 30 October 1918, *TMW* I, 512–514. *'Trotsky's train'*: Trotsky, 411–422; and Volkogonov, *Trotsky*, 152–154 and 163–173. *'at his present whereabouts'*: telegrams to Trotsky, 12 December 1918, *CW* XLIV, 170. *'Revolution, the daughter of war'* to *'A formidable blow'*: speech in Voronezh, 18 November 1918, *TMW* I, 515–545. *'Denikin'*: Engelstein, 378–382. *'Yudenich'*: ibid., 308–311. *'Kolchak'*: ibid., 417–444; and more generally Jonathan Smele, *Civil War in Siberia: The Anti-Bolshevik Government of Admiral Kolchak, 1918–1920*, 1997. *'history is now condensed'*: speech in Voronezh, 18 November 1918, *TMW* I, 541. *'finally finishes the pamphlet'*: 'The Proletarian Revolution and the Renegade Kautsky', *CW* XXVIII, 227–325. *'blind puppy'*: ibid., 235. *'particularly ridiculous'*: ibid., 262. *'sheer mockery'*: ibid., 244. *'lynching'*: ibid., 245. *'unrestricted by any laws'*: ibid., 236. *'a million times'*: ibid., 248. • **BLODELSHEIM**: *'tired of the army life'*: letter dated 21 November 1918, Badger, *Life in Ragtime*, 197–198. *'cover of The Crisis'*: *The Crisis*, November 1918. *'The nightmare is over'*: 'Peace', *The Crisis*, December 1918. • **LINCOLN**: see Coogan, *De Valera*, 124–127; and Declan Dunne, *Peter's Key: Peter DeLoughry and the Fight for Irish Independence*, 2012. • **THE ATLANTIC**: *'set of invitation cards'*: diary of Edith Benham, 5 December 1918, *WW* LIII, 319. *'sweetheart'*: diary of Raymond Blaine Fosdick, 11 December 1918, *WW* LIII, 366. *'ice cream'*: 8 December 1918, 341. *'Victrola'*: 'Victrola and Records Bought for President's Ship', *Talking Machine World*, 15 February 1919. *'off-colour jokes'*: diary of Edith Benham, 10 December 1918, *WW* LIII, 358. *'have her sandwich'*: 9 December 1918, 344. *'what sort of a fellow'*: diary of Dr Grayson, 8 December 1918, *WW* LIII, 337. *'Château Thierry'*: diary of William Christian Bullitt, 9/10 December 1918, *WW* LIII, 352. *'lucky number'*: diary of Dr Grayson, 13 December 1918, *WW* LIII, 378. • **AMERONGEN**: *'two dozen'*: Röhl, *Into the Abyss*, 1190. *'who carries the blame'* to *'I would like to give you a kiss'*: diary entry 19 November 1918, Ilsemann, Vol. 1, 58–60. For various escape plans, see diary entries for December – *'damn arm?'* and *'sanatorium'*, 11 and 13 December 1918 respectively, ibid., 72–78. • **BERLIN**: see Jones, *Founding Weimar*, 104–135. *'Ebert worries'*: Bessel, 84–85. *'welcome back to your* *homeland'* to *'Germany's unity'*: 'Ansprache an die heimkehrenden Truppen', 10 December 1918, *Politische Reden,* 4 volumes, 1994 (eds. Peter Wende and Marie Luise Recker), Vol. 3, 94–96. *'current of separatism'*: see Klaus Epstein, 'Adenauer and Rhenish Separatism', *Review of Politics,* 29/4, 1967, 536–545; and Ralph Schattkowsky, 'Separatism in the Eastern Provinces of the German Reich at the End of the First World War', *Journal of Contemporary History,* Vol. 29, 1994, 305–324. *'one enemy above all '*: Buse, 246. *'Freikorps'*: see Nigel H. Jones, *Hitler's Heralds: The Story of the Freikorps, 1918–1923,* 1987; and Robert G. L. Waite, *Vanguard of Nazism: The Free Corps Movement in Postwar Germany, 1918–1923,* 1952. • MOSCOW: for Lenin and the problem of bureaucracy see Read, *Lenin,* 270–276. For the functioning of the early Soviet state see Lara Douds, *Inside Lenin's Government: Ideology, Power and Practice in the Early Soviet State,* 2018. *'Any worker will master any ministry'*: Smith, *Russia in Revolution,* 216. *'deliberately maintained'* to *'register is kept'*: Fischer, *Lenin,* 463–465. *'outskirts of Moscow'* to *'enquiry offices'*: Krupskaya, *Reminiscences,* 517–519. *'sends more immediate complaints'*: to Lenin, 26 December 1918, *TP* I, 210–213. • TRAUNSTEIN-IM-CHIEMGAU: Weber, *Becoming Hitler,* 14–18. • ZURICH: for the Dada manifesto see *Dada* 3, December 1918, available online at https://monoskop.org. For the Berlin manifesto see Hans Richter, *Dada: Art and Anti-Art,* 1965 (trans. David Britt), 107. • BERLIN: for the build-up to the Spartacist coup see Fröhlich, 259–287; and Jones, *Founding Weimar,* 136–172. *'on the edge of the abyss'*: *Vossische Zeitung,* 25 December 1918, in Jones, *Founding Weimar,* 141. *'constantly live like this?'*: Mathilde Jacob, *Rosa Luxemburg: An Intimate Portrait,* 2000 (trans. Hans Ferbach), 97. • VIENNA: *'Just before the end of the year'*: to Ferenczi, 1 January 1919, *FR/FER* II, 320–322. *'few weeks later'*: to Ferenczi, 24 January 1919, *FR/FER* II, 328–329. • DOUAI: the artist was Henri Duhem, 'L'exhumation de l'Eve de Rodin', *L'Illustration,* 28 December 1918. • MOSCOW: to Lenin, 20 December 1918, *LRL,* 486.

Winter 1919

The Gandhi quotation is taken from a pamphlet published in May 1919, reproduced in Mahatma Gandhi, *The Collected Works of Mahatma Gandhi,* Vol. 15, 1958, 268. The quotation from Trotsky is originally from the onboard newsletter of Trotsky's train, entitled *En Route,* in its ninety-third edition of September 1919, reproduced in *TMW* II, 412–414.

A ROAD OUTSIDE MOSCOW: *'running around on all fours'*: Arthur Ransome, *Russia in 1919,* 1919, 58. *'first boatload of Czech troops'*: Henry Baerlein, *The March of the Seventy Thousand,* 1926, 276. *'on their way to visit Nadya'* to *'car is recovered'*: Krupskaya, *Reminiscences,* 493–495; and Gil, 28–34. • PARIS: for the peace conference as a whole see Margaret MacMillan, *Peacemakers: Six Months that Changed the World,* 2001. *'cold as Greenland'*: James T. Shotwell, *At the Paris Peace Conference,* 1937, 95. *'prematurely pronounce'*: Barry, 381. *'Two black American soldiers'*: Sammons and Morrow, 397.

'trap-door': Grose, 43. • **HÄSSLEHOLM**: 'lips quiver': Margarethe Ludendorff, 244. 'stabbed him in the back': Roger Chickering, 'Sore Loser: Ludendorff's Total War', in Roger Chickering and Stig Förster (eds.), *The Shadows of Total War: Europe, East Asia and the United States, 1919–1939*, 2003, 151–178, 154. 'Wild rumours circulate': Nebelin, 507. 'Swedish socialists threaten': Margarethe Ludendorff, 245. • **BERLIN**: for the course of events see Jones, *Founding Weimar*, 172–192; and Lutz, 88–98. For description see Harry Kessler's diaries for early January in the German original or translated and abridged in Harry Kessler, *The Diaries of a Cosmopolitan, 1918–1937*, 2000 (trans. Charles Kessler). For an account from the Spartacist perspective see Fröhlich, 288–297. 'awakened from our dreams' to 'school of action': 'Rede zum Programm', *Politische Reden*, Vol. 3, 142–175. 'reminded of a religious prophet': diary entry 5 January 1919, Kessler, *Tagebuch*, Vol. 6, 77–78. 'further loss of blood': Robert Leinert, a Social Democrat from Hanover, quoted in Jones, *Founding Weimar*, 186. 'books a room' to 'Not since the great days': diary entry 6 January 1919, Kessler, *Tagebuch*, Vol. 6, 79–81. 'Over a thousand': Jones, *Founding Weimar*, 61. • **MILAN**: 'great Republic of the stars': 'Viva Wilson!', *Il Popolo d'Italia*, 3 January 1919, *OO* XII, 107–109, 108. 'heart of America has gone out': diary of Edith Benham, 5 January 1919, *WW* LIII, 619. 'Benito is back': Arno J. Mayer, *Politics and Diplomacy of Peacemaking: Containment and Counter-Revolution at Versailles, 1918–1919*, 1967, 219–221. 'reached its climax': quotes from Hans Ulrich Gumbrecht, 'I redentoria della vittoria: On Fiume's Place in the Genealogy of Fascism', *Journal of Contemporary History*, 31/2, 1996, 253–272, 261. The original 'Letter to the Dalmatians' from 15 January 1919 available in *Prose di Ricerca*, Vol. 1, 803–820. 'confront the new conspiracy': 'D'Annunzio Counsels Bombs for Bissolati', *New York Times*, 15 January 1919. • **PARIS**: 'found dead in a hotel room': Polizzotti, 85–89. 'I rely on you': Jacques Vaché, *Lettres de Guerre*, 1919, 25–27. 'sits alone on a bench': André Breton and André Parinaud, *Entretiens, 1913–1952*, 1952, 57. 'What I loved most': Polizzotti, 91. • **BUDAPEST**: Borsányi, 103–104. • **BERLIN**: for descriptions of the general situation in Berlin see diary entries 7–17 January 1919, Kessler, *Tagebuch*, Vol. 7, 82–101. For a Spartacist perspective see Fröhlich, 288–305. For the collapse of the Spartacist rising see Jones, *Founding Weimar*, 193–220. 'cafés on Potsdamer Platz' to 'cigarettes': diary entry 8 January 1919, Kessler, *Tagebuch*, Vol. 7, 84–86. 'fiery atmosphere of the revolution' to 'Act quickly!': 'Was machen die Führer?', *Die Rote Fahne*, 7 January 1919. 'sick body of the German people': Germania, 9 January 1919, in Jones, *Founding Weimar*, 196. 'Rosa Luxemburg herself': ibid., 212. 'Seven Spartacists': ibid., 213. 'psychosis of the days of August 1914': ibid.,221. 'I wish I were back in jail' to 'fairy tale by Tolstoy': Jacob, 99–100. 'victories will spring' to 'I was, I am, I shall be!': 'Die Ordnung herrscht in Berlin', *Die Rote Fahne*, 14 January 1919. For a detailed account of the murder of Rosa Luxemburg and Karl Liebknecht see Klaus Gietinger, *Eine Leiche im Landwehrkanal: Die Ermordung der Rosa Luxemburg*, 2009, 17–23. For another account, including the media and political reaction, see Jones, *Founding Weimar*, 233–243. For documentation around the murders, see Heinrich Hannover and Elisabeth Hannover-Drück, *Der Mord an Rosa Luxemburg und Karl Liebknecht: Dokumentations eines politischen Verbrechens*, 1996. For the life and career of Waldemar

Pabst, see Gietinger, *Der Konterrevolutionär: Waldemar Pabst. Eine deutsche Karriere*, 2009. *'sanitised version of events'*: the version of the Wolffsche news agency, based on official sources, reproduced in Hannover and Hannover-Drück, 36–38. *'Pabst later claims'*: Gietinger, 24–25. *'victims of their own bloody terror'*: Hannover and Hannover-Drück, 41–42. *'elephant stabbed with a penknife'*: diary entry 17 January 1919, Kessler, *Tagebuch*, Vol. 7, 98–101, 101. • PARIS: *'trumpets and kettle-drums'*: Shotwell, 126–128. *'supreme conference'*: protocol of the plenary session, 18 January 1919, *WW* LIII, 128–132. *'must be in our hearts'*: ibid., 131. • SOLOHEADBEG: for context and immediate consequences see Townshend, 73–83; Maurice Walsh, *Bitter Freedom: Ireland in a Revolutionary World, 1918–1923*, 2015, 70–86; and BMH, Witness Statement 1739, Dan Breen, 19–23. *'meet together publicly for the first time'* to *'in English'*: full proceedings are available at https://www.oireachtas.ie. *'luncheon at the Mansion House'*: 'Sinn Féin Congress', *Times*, 22 January 1919. *'final touches to an escape plan'*: Piearas Béaslaí, *Michael Collins and the Making of a New Ireland*, 1926, 256. *'nations of the world, greeting!'*: see the record of the Dáil. *'most drastic measures'*: 'Ruthless Warfare', *An tOglac*, February 1919, in Townshend, 77. • MOSCOW: *'Our enemy today'*: speech at Communist Party conference, 18 January 1919, *CW* XXVIII, 405–406. *'Death to the butchers!'*: speech to a protest rally, 19 January 1919, *CW* XXVIII, 411. *'Eleventh Army has ceased'*: from Ordzhonikidze to Lenin, 24 January 1919, in Chamberlin, Vol. 2, 146. • BERLIN: *'funeral procession'* to *'scrawled'*: Jones, *Founding Weimar*, 248–249. *'hills of corpses'*: speech given by Paul Levi, reproduced in Jacob, 123. *'commercial shipping fleet'*: Lutz, 115. *'Eisner's political authority'*: Mitchell, 242–272. *'friends abducted me'* to *'hundreds of such places'*: diary entry 9 February 1919, Kessler, *Tagebuch*, Vol. 7, 128–130, 130. *'venereal disease'*: Bessel, 237. • VIENNA: *'accompanied by two baskets'*: to Abraham, 5 February 1919, *FR/AB*, 391–392. *'animal hooves'*: 'Die Lebensmittelmärkte', *Arbeiter Zeitung*, 4 February 1919, *DÖZ*, 125. *'In grateful acknowledgement'*: Edward L. Bernays, *Biography of an Idea: The Founding Principles of Public Relations*, 1965, 179. • LINCOLN: see Coogan, *De Valera*, 124–127; and Declan Dunne. *'broken a key'*: Béaslaí, 267. • AMERONGEN: *'Senator from Tennessee'* to *'Belgian pilot'*: Marks, 'My Name is Ozymandias', 133. *'remained in the open air'*: 'Rumors of Attempts to Deport Ex-Kaiser', *New York Times*, 7 January 1919. *'Kaiser's birthday'* to *'red tulips'*: diary entry of Countess Elisabeth Bentinck, 27 January 1919, Ilsemann, Vol. 1, 90. • PARIS: for an account of the workings of the peace conference see MacMillan 2001. *'recitations of Homer'*: Harold Nicholson quoted in Giles Milton, *Paradise Lost: Smyrna 1922: The Destruction of Islam's City of Tolerance*, 2008, 126. *'And so it goes'*: letter to Edith Dulles, 9 April 1919, AWD, Box 19, Folder 6. *'cannot be at peace'*: notes of a conversation held at the Quai d'Orsay, 22 January 1919, *FRUS, Russia, 1919*, 30–31. *'cordon sanitaire'*: for an exploration of this term see Patrick Wright, *Iron Curtain: From Stage to Cold War*, 2007; for a general discussion of the issue of Russia at the peace conference see John M. Thompson, *Russia, Bolshevism and the Versailles Peace*, 1967; and MacMillan, 71–91. *'British military assessment'*: 'Bolshevik Strength and Weakness', 24 February 1919, NA, WO 32/5680. *'Whites joke'*: Chamberlin, Vol. 2, 162. *'car windscreen'*: MacMillan, 85. *'Many terrible things'*: address to the third plenary session, 14

February 1919, *WW* LV, 177. *'smuggled in'*: John Milton Cooper, *Breaking the Heart of the World: Woodrow Wilson and the Fight for the League of Nations*, 2001, 10. • **WASHINGTON DC**: for an account of the unrest in the United States in 1919, see Ann Hagedorn, *Savage Peace: Hope and Fear in America, 1919*, 2007. *'Senate inquiry'*: *Bolshevik Propaganda: Hearings before a Subcommittee of the Committee on the Judiciary, United States Senate, Sixty-Fifth Congress*, 1919. *'very radical looking'*: 11 February 1919, ibid., 9. *'as many wives as they want?'*: ibid., 35. *'whole day in mid-February'*: for Reverend Simons's full testimony, 12 February 1919, ibid., 141–162. *'looks so Yiddish'*: ibid., 116. *'we ought to know'*: ibid., 136. *'stiff letter of complaint'*: ibid., 378–379. *'slipperiest witnesses'*: for Bryant's testimony, 20–21 February 1919, ibid., 465–561, and for Reed, 21 February 1919, 561–601. *'believe in God'* to *'witchcraft'*: ibid., 465. *'No more than I see'*: ibid., 496. *'professional gambler'*: ibid., 491. *'self-determination'*: ibid., 499. *'present time'*: ibid., 503. *'real butcher'*: ibid., 557. *'even more belligerent'*: ibid., 540. *'club-house bill'*: Russian scrapbook, JRP, Series VI, Biographical Material, Item 1371. *'infamous and anti-constitutional'*: 'Reed Condemns Peace League as Infamous', *New York Times*, 23 February 1919. • **NEW YORK**: *'triumphal epoch'*: Sammons and Morrow, 385. *'Sixteen abreast'*: description drawn from Sammons and Morrow, 386–389. *'impostor'*: ibid., 452. *'Garvey is moved'*: Grant, 112. *'black soldier saved civilization'*: Du Bois, 'The Black Man in the Revolution of 1914–1918', *The Crisis*, March 1919. *'wherever persons of African descent'*: Du Bois, 'The Pan African Congress', *The Crisis*, April 1919. *'world-fight for black rights'*: Du Bois, 'My Mission', *The Crisis*, May 1919. • **LIBAU**: for context see Robert Gerwarth, *The Vanquished: Why the First World War Failed to End, 1917–1923*, 2016, 69–76. *'full Latvian citizenship'*: Waite, 104. *'excellent colonisation opportunities'*: recruitment advertisement quoted at footnote 33 in Waite, 105. *'obscenity of Auschwitz'*: after the Second World War, Rudolf Höss, camp commandant at Auschwitz, wrote in his memoirs of his experiences in Latvia as a Freikorps volunteer, including burning down houses with people trapped inside. For another example of the genre from the 1930s see Erich Balla, *Landsknechte wurden wir ... Abenteuer aus dem Baltikum*, 1932. The British Library copy of this book, acquired from a library in Hamburg, clearly shows the book's popularity. It was borrowed twenty-one times in 1935 alone. *'sprinkling it with the urine'*: David Clay Large, *Where Ghosts Walked: Munich's Road to the Third Reich*, 1997, 103. *'dead are rising up again'*: 'Arbeiter, Proletarier!', *Die Rote Fahne*, 3 March 1919. *'During the past week'*: Laird M. Easton, *The Red Count: The Life and Times of Harry Kessler*, 2002, 293; original from 13 March 1919, Kessler, *Tagebuch*, Vol. 7, 184–185. • **PARIS**: Polizzotti, 94–95. • **MUNICH**: *'his Wittelsbach best'*: Clay Large, 104. *'caught in a snapshot'*: Weber, *Becoming Hitler*, 38–40. *'beer hall meetings'*: Hitler, 820–821. *'old army gas masks'*: Ernst Schmidt quoted in Anton Joachimsthaler, *Hitlers Weg begann in München, 1913–1923*, 2000, 192. • **VENICE**: *'message arrives at the Hotel Danieli'*: the Lisle-Strutt episode is described in some detail in Brook-Shepherd, *Last Habsburg*, 229–247. Here, the quotes are from the original diary consulted in the Royal Library at Windsor. • **DUBLIN**: *'photograph is circulated'* to *'unsubstantiated rumour'*: documents and press cuttings kept by the British secret service in their file on de Valera, NA, KV2/515. *'night in a whiskey* *factory'*: Coogan, *DeValera*, 127. • **WASHINGTON DC**: for the political complexities of the League fight see Cooper, *Breaking the Heart*. *'gala dinner in New York'*: 'League of Nations Fight Opened Here', *New York Times*, 7 March 1919.

Spring 1919

MOSCOW: Miklós Kun, *Stalin: An Unknown Portrait*, 2003, 256. The story is originally from Trotsky. • **OAK PARK**: *'It's hell'*: to William D. Horne, 3 February 1919, *LEH* I, 167–168. *'talk at his high school'*: the original article describing the event from the Oak Park High School *Trapeze*, 21 March 1919, reprinted in *Conversations with Ernest Hemingway*, 1986 (ed. Matthew J. Bruccoli), 3–5. *'allowed a reporter'*: original article is '227 Wounds, but is Looking for Job', *New York Sun*, 22 January 1919, reprinted in Bruccoli (ed.), *Conversations*, 1–2. *'resembles closely'*: 'From Italian Front', *Oak Leaves*, 14 March 1919, EHC, Series 5, Box NC01, EHPP-NC01-005–016. *'if he himself were white'*: Sammons and Morrow, 457. *'She doesn't love me Bill'*: to William D. Horne, 30 March 1919, *LEH* I, 176–178. • **MOSCOW**: *'invitation is issued'*: invitation to first congress of Communist International, 24 January 1919, *CI* I, 1–5. *'room is painted red'*: Ransome, 214. *'Vladimir opens proceedings'*: opening speech, 2 March 1919, *CW* XXVIII, 455–457. *'leather coat and military breeches'* to *'Spring is coming'*: Ransome, 217–218. *'historical imperative'*: Resolution Constituting the Communist International, 4 March 1919, *CI* I, 16–17. *'Internationale sung in a dozen'*: Ransome, 217. *'genuine order, communist order'*: Platform of the Communist International, 4 March 1919, *CI* I, 17–24, 18. *'cloak of the League of Nations'*: ibid., 19. *'white cannibals'*: ibid., 23. *'debris and smoking ruins'*: Manifesto of the Communist International, 6 March 1919, *CI* I, 38–48, 39. *'Alexandra Kollontai puts forward'*: *CI.Th.*, Resolution on the Role of Working Women, 6 March 1919, 46. *'anyone wish to discuss this?'*: The Organisation of the Communist International, 6 March 1919, *Theses, Resolutions and Manifestos of the First Four Congresses of the Third International*, 1980 (ed. Alan Adler; trans. Alix Holt and Barbara Holland), 50. *'victory of the proletarian revolution'*: closing speech, 6 March 1919, *CW* XVIII, 476–477. *'Dictatorship of the Photographer'*: Ransome, 220. *'greatest events in world history'*: Kotkin, 318. *'Pitiable, pitiable'*: Ransome, 227. *'If Russia today'* to *'microbe is already there'*: Ransome, 225–226. • **ECKARTSAU**: *'plays bridge with them'*: apart from the Lisle-Strutt diaries in the Royal Library at Windsor see British diplomatic correspondence for further elements of this story, NA, FO 608/18/27. *'confiscating food'* to *'repatriation'*: 'Report on Situation in Vienna and Budapest', 8 March 1919, NA, FO 608/11/13, and reports from Vienna dated 19 March, 24 March and 31 March 1919, FO 608/27/7. *'I am still Emperor'*: entry for 3 March 1919, Lisle-Strutt diary. • **BOSTON**: Badger, *Life in Ragtime*, 206–211. • **VIENNA**: translation is from Gay, *Freud*, 380. A translation of the whole letter in, to Ferenczi, 17 March 1919, *FR/FER* II, 334–335. • **MOSCOW**: see Service, *A Political Life*, Vol. 3, 75–87. *'childish'*: report of the Central Committee, 18 March, 1919, *CW* XXIX, 146–164, 156. *'notes the persistent misspelling'*: Service, *A Political Life*, Vol. 3, 83.

• **Paris**: *'gold taps'*: Cooper, *Wilson*, 484. *'a broom'* to *'causes are'*: Thompson, 240.
• **Milan**: *'no preconceptions'*: Giovanna Prosacci, 'Italy: From Interventionism to Fascism, 1917–1919', *Journal of Contemporary History*, 3/4, 1968, 153–176, 171. *'assembles his fellow discontents'*: for an account of the San Sepolcro meeting, Bosworth, 108–110; for Mussolini's interventions see *OO* XII, 317–327. For the origins of Italian fascism see Emilio Gentile, *Le origini dell'ideologia fascista, 1918–1925*, 1975; and Roberto Vivarelli, *Storia delle origini del fascismo*, 2 volumes, 1991. For the history of fascism in general see Robert O. Paxton, *The Anatomy of Fascism*, 2005. • **Budapest**: for the treatment of Hungarian issues at the peace conference see MacMillan, 265–278. *'French colony'*: ibid., 270. *'personal influence'*: Borsányi, 144. *'first flash of lightning'*: Manifesto of the ECCI, 28 March 1919, *CI* I, 48–50. • **Eckartsau**: description drawn from Lisle-Strutt's diary entries for 23 and 24 March 1919. Most, but not all, of those are reproduced in Brook-Shepherd, *Last Habsburg*, 243–247. • **Moscow**: *'series of recordings'*: speeches on gramophone records, late March 1919, *CW* XXIX, 239–253. *'no fewer than nine passports'*: Kotkin, 322. *'sell seedlings'*: Krupskaya, *Reminiscences*, 508. • **Amritsar**: for two strongly opposed accounts see Nick Lloyd's apologia, *The Amritsar Massacre: The Untold Story of One Fateful Day*, 2011, and Kim Wagner's more recent *Amritsar 1919: An Empire of Fear and the Making of a Massacre*, 2019. • **Paris**: *'confined to bed'*: diary of Dr Grayson, 6 April 1919, *WW* LVII, 50. *'falls ill at the same time'*: Barry, 383. *'Influenzal psychoses'*: *Policlinico*, 8 February 1919, cited in Barry, 378. *'Woodrow to Jesus'*: Cooper, *Wilson*, 491. *'universal contempt'*: ibid., 487. *'ocean of talk'*: diary of Dr Grayson, 17 April 1919, *WW* LVII, 428. • **Amerongen**: *'Every thousandth log'* to *'move into a hotel'*: diary entry 17 April 1919, Ilsemann, Vol. 1, 94–97. *'writes to Ludendorff'*: Röhl, *Into the Abyss*, 1225.
• **Vienna**: Paul Federn, *Zur Psychologie der Revolution: Die Vaterlose Gesellschaft*, 1919. For more about Paul Federn and how his work relates to Sigmund Freud's thinking, see F. Houssier, A. Blanc, D. Bonnichon and X. Vlachopoulou, 'Between Sigmund Freud and Paul Federn: Culture as a Shared Path of Sublimation', *Scandinavian Psychoanalytic Review*, 39/1, 2016, 61–69; and van Ginneken. *'Volksführer'*: Federn, 28. • **Munich**: *'elected as the Vertrauensmann'*: Thomas Weber notes the overwhelmingly left-wing political orientation of the battalion and the likelihood that Adolf Hitler would hardly have been voted into this position unless he was, at the very least, viewed as being broadly in line with the battalion's general political alignment: Weber, *Becoming Hitler*, 41–43. For the propaganda role of the *Vertrauensmann* position see Joachimsthaler, 201–202. *'Soviet Republic'*: Mitchell, 305–317. *'shaking feverishly'*: Sterling Fishman, 'The Rise of Hitler as a Beer Hall Orator', *Review of Politics*, 26/2, 1964, 244–256, 249. *'barracks is renamed'*: Ernst Toller, *I Was a German: The Autobiography of Ernst Toller*, 1934, 160; Joachimsthaler, 207. The Karl Liebknecht barracks were subsequently renamed the Adolf Hitler barracks. *'marry an Eskimo girl'*: Toller, 171. *'nineteen votes'*: Joachimsthaler, 210. • **Milan**: *'absolutely spontaneous'*: 'Dopo i Fatti del 15 Aprile 1919', *Il Giornale d'Italia*, 17 April 1919, *OO* XIII, 61–63. • **The Ural Mountains**: for the rise and fall of Kolchak see Engelstein, 417–444. *'Lenin calls for total mobilisation'*: On the Situation on the Eastern Front, 1 April 1919, *CW* XXIX, 276–279. *'for every man conscripted'*:

Pipes, *Russia under the Bolshevik Regime*, 59. *'military gamester'*: Norman Rose, *Churchill: An Unruly Life*, 1994, 149. *'nurses' uniforms'*: Chamberlin, Vol. 2, 263–264. *'provide security for those'*: parliamentary report, *Times*, 17 April 1919. *'foe of tyranny in every form'* to *'worst tyranny in history'*: 'Bolshevist Atrocities', 11 April 1919, in Winston S. Churchill (ed.), *Winston Churchill's Speeches: Never Give In!*, 2003, 77–78. *'baboons'*: H. A. L. Fisher to his wife, 8 April 1919, *WSC* VIII, 609. • VIENNA: to Eitingon, 9 May 1919, *FR/EIT*, 152–155. • BUDAPEST: *'hills around Budapest'*: 'The Communist Revolution in Hungary', 31 May 1919, NA, CAB 24/80/86. *'Lenin Boys'*: Gerwarth, 134. *'Your example shows'* to *'don't need instructions'*: Borsányi, 151–156. • PARIS: for the Italian departure see MacMillan, 288–314. *'breaks down in tears'*: ibid., 288. *'fattest and most bourgeois'*: Bosworth, 111. *'tragic gargoyle'*: Walter Starkie quoted in Woodhouse, 318. *'Croatified Quaker'* and *'teeth'*: speech in Rome, 4 May 1919, *Prose di Ricerca*, Vol. 1, 860–877, particularly 870–871 (see also Woodhouse, 318–319). • SEATTLE: *'postal clerk recalls'*: Hagedorn, 184. *'malicious rumour'*: Grant, 151. *'purposeful enterprise'*: Grant, 189–191. • MUNICH: *'bourgeois executioners?'*: message of greetings to the Bavarian Socialist Republic, 27 April 1919, *CW* XXIX, 325–326. *'sabotage'*: Mitchell, 323. *'wear a pretty hat'*: Toller, 175. *'magic lustre'*: Mitchell, 326. *'freshly slaughtered pigs'*: Toller, 200. *'peroxiding his hair'*: Richard Dove, *He Was a German: A Biography of Ernst Toller*, 1990, 86. *'fair share'*: Weber, *Becoming Hitler*, 62. *'mass murder at home'*: Borsányi, 162. • BOSTON: *'Jim Europe is stabbed'*: Badger, *Life in Ragtime*, 215–221. *'Won Fame by "Jazz" Music'*: *New York Times*, 10 May 1919. *'jazzing away the barriers'*: *Chicago Defender*, 10 May 1919, in Hagedorn, 200. *'Roosevelt of Negro musicians'*: 'Lieutenant James Reese Europe Buried with Honors', *New York Age*, 17 May 1919, in Badger, *Life in Ragtime*, 221. *'We return'*: 'Returning Soldiers', *The Crisis*, May 1919. • PARIS: *'horse races'*: diary of Dr Grayson, *WW* LVII, 8 May 1919, 535. *'Germans will make no mistake'*: MacMillan, 469. • WEIMAR: *'verzichtet – verzichtet'*: Scheidemann's speech against the Versailles Treaty, 12 May 1919, *Politische Reden*, Vol. 3, 254–262. *'music on a gramophone'*: MacMillan, 473. • SMYRNA: for a description of the entry of Greek troops into Smyrna see Milton, 135–148. *'Turkish Freikorps'*: Ryan Gingeras, *Fall of the Sultanate: The Great War and the End of the Ottoman Empire*, 2016, 265. *'French general'*: Mansel, 381. *'should be permanently ejected'*: 'Memorandum on the Future of Constantinople', 2 January 1919, records of the India Office, BL, IOR/L/PS/10/623. *'their own passports'*: Mansel, 385. *'only once he has a fetva'*: Mango, 207. *'funeral turns into a nationalist protest'* to *'crush their heads'*: 'Execution of Kemal Bey (Mutessarrif of Bogazian), for responsibility for Armenian massacres, and Demonstrations at funeral', 17 May 1919, NA, FO 608/113/3. *'The fools'*: Mango, 219. *'Swedish marching song'*: Mango, 224. • BERLIN: for the trial and escape see Gietinger, 31–41. *'Mathilde Jacob thinks'*: Jacob, 112. *'she was, she is, she will be again'*: Anthony Read, *The World on Fire: 1919 and the Battle with Bolshevism*, 2008, 203. • BELÉM: Crommelin's account of the trip was published as 'The Eclipse Expedition to Sobral', *The Observatory*, No. 544, October 1919, 368–371. *'local newpaper publishes'*: in Marcelo C. de Lima and Luís C. B. Crispino, 'Crommelin's and Davidson's Visit to Amazonia and the 1919 Total Solar Eclipse', *International Journal of Modern Physics*, 25/9, 2016, 1641002-1–1641002-5.

'team on Principe are similarly worried': A. Vibert Douglas, *The Life of Arthur Stanley Eddington*, 1956, 40. • **MUNICH**: 'always advocated': Joachimsthaler, 212. • **MILAN**: 'Universale Illusione', *Il Popolo d'Italia*, 14 May 1919, *OO* XIII, 120–123. • **DUBLIN**: 'willed into more elaborate form': for the struggle to assert statehood see Townshend, 52–99, and Walsh, 127–144. 'I trust you will not allow yourself': Coogan, *De Valera*, 135. For an account of de Valera's voyage, ibid., 136–137. • **AMERONGEN**: 'doing something useful': diary entry 26 June 1919, Ilsemann, Vol. 1, 106–109, 108. 'suggest the Kaiser might': Röhl, *Into the Abyss*, 1196.

Summer 1919

PETROGRAD: 'Death to spies!': 'Beware of Spies', *Pravda*, 31 May 1919, *CW* XXIX, 403. 'chop down wood': Victor Serge, *Memoirs of a Revolutionary*, 2012, 99. 'swift capture of Gorka': to Lenin, 12 June 1919, Stalin, Vol. 4, 271. 'Gorka was taken by land': Oleg V. Khlevniuk, *Stalin: New Biography of a Dictator*, 2015 (trans. Nora Seligman Favorov), 59. • **WASHINGTON DC**: 'bomb explodes': Read, *World on Fire*, 214–218. 'Pamphlets': the whole pamphlet was reprinted in the following day's newspapers: see 'Palmer and Family Safe', *New York Times*, 3 June 1919. 'John Reed': Hagedorn refers to two articles in the *Liberator* in July and August 1919 in *Savage Peace*, 223. 'Mitchell Palmer promises': for the immediate crackdown, see Kenneth D. Ackerman, *Young J. Edgar: Hoover, the Red Scare, and the Assault on Civil Liberties*, 2007, 25–36. • **ADINKERKE**: descriptions of trip from diary of Dr Grayson, 18 and 19 June 1919, *WW* LXI, 3–8 and 10–16. 'What's done is done': discussion with the American Delegation, 3 June 1919, *WW* LX, 45–71. • **TEREZÍN FORTRESS**: Miller, 'Yugoslav Eulogies'. 'Czech journalist': ibid., 5–6. • **NEW YORK**: for de Valera's time in America see Coogan, *De Valera*, 137–196. 'that's a secret' to 're-juiced': 'De Valera, President of Ireland, Here', *New York Tribune*, 24 June 1919. 'compares Ireland' to 'handed down to them': *Speeches and Statements by Éamon de Valera*, 29–31. 'present unholy alliance': Coogan, *De Valera*, 143. 'you and the children': letter to Sinéad de Valera, 19 July 1919, Coogan, *De Valera*, 154. 'six at home': letter dated 13 August 1919, same page. • **PARIS**: Polizzotti, 104–108. • **SCAPA FLOW**: 'pleasing to know': diary entry 26 June 1919, Ilsemann, Vol. 1, 108–109. • **WASHINGTON DC**: for the Palmer episode see Ackerman, *J. Edgar*, 50–59. 'Round up these men': 'Millions Spent by Bolsheviki to Overthrow U.S.', *Chicago Tribune*, 27 June 1919. • **VERSAILLES**: 'cigarette case': Shotwell, 382. 'souvenir programmes': diary of Colonel House, 28 June 1919, *WW* LXI, 333. 'fountain pen': Shotwell, 385. 'Colmar Cathedral': 'Restoration of Stained Glass Carried Off from Colmar by Austrians in 1815 to the Hofburg in Vienna', 15 July 1919, NA, FO 608/20. 'anything more stupid': MacMillan, 448. 'die or resign': diary of Dr Grayson, 3 July 1919, *WW* LXI, 375. 'franchise to all the world': address to passengers, 4 July 1919, *WW* LXI, 382. • **MODLIN**: 'utmost brutality' and 'only serious military force': to Jeanne de Gaulle, 25 June 1919, *CDG* I, 462. 'without any cachet': to Jeanne de Gaulle, 23 May 1919, *CDG* I, 458–459. 'generation of catastrophes': Lieutenant

Medvecki, quoted in Lacouture, 103. *'very embarrassed'*: 19 July 1919, *CDG* I, 466.
• **URALS**: *'political questionnaire'*: MacMillan, 90. *'Kharkov stands in no greater danger'*:
message to the population of Kharkov, 4 June 1919, in Mawdsley, 236; for a general
assessment of Denikin's offensive see 228–245. *'storms out of a meeting'*: Service, *Trotsky*,
238–239. *'first man to set foot in Moscow'*: Pyotr Wrangel, *The Memoirs of General Wrangel:
The Last Commander-in-Chief of the Russian National Army*, 1929 (trans. Sophie Goulston),
89. *'pull themselves together'* to *'practical proposals'*: All Out for the Fight Against Denikin,
3 July 1919, *CW* XXIX, 436–455. • **MT. CLEMENS**: for the life of Henry Ford see
Steven Watts, *The People's Tycoon: Henry Ford and the American Century*, 2005. For the Mt.
Clemens episode see Watts, 268–270. *'I admit I am ignorant'* to *'I like the banjo'*: Roger
Butterfield, 'Henry Ford, the Wayside Inn, and the Problem of "History is Bunk"',
Proceedings of the Massachusetts Historical Society, Third Series, 77, 1965, 53–66,
55–56. • **MUNICH**: *'propaganda course'*: see Joachimsthaler, 237–244; and Ernst
Deuerlein, 'Hitlers Eintritt in die Politik und die Reichswehr', *Vierteljahrshefte für
Zeitgeschichte*, 7/2, 1959, 177–227. *'one of the lecturers finds him'*: Karl-Alexander Müller,
Mars und Venus: Erinnerungen 1914–1919, 1954, 338–339. • **ERZURUM**: *'Turkish Versailles'*:
Stefan Ihrig, *Atatürk in the Nazi Imagination*, 2014, 19. *'town's bloody occupation'*: Kreiser,
143. *'borrows morning dress'*: Mango, 238. • **UPPER REACHES OF THE VOLGA**: *'Krasnaya
Zvezda'* to *'squarity and sizeability'*: Krupskaya, *Reminiscences*, 524–527. *'our country house'*:
to Nadya, 9 July 1919, *CW* XXXVII, 543–544. *'stick strictly to the rules'* to *'hope there will
be'*: to Nadya, 15 July 1919, *CW* XXXVII, 546. • **FIUME**: drawn from 'Disturbances in
Fiume on the Nights of July 2, 5 and 6 1919', USNA, RG84 Foreign Service Posts of
the Department of State, Vol. 80, Fiume. An alternative rendering of Fiume's summer
of violence is provided by J. N. Macdonald, *A Political Escapade: The Story of Fiume and
D'Annunzio*, 1921, 60–87. • **CHICAGO**: for the Chicago riots see William M. Tuttle, *Race
Riot: Chicago in the Red Summer of 1919*, 1970; and Hagedorn, 312–318. For the race
riots of 1919 in general see David F. Krugler, *1919, the Year of Racial Violence: How African
Americans Fought Back*, 2015. *'searches for evidence to connect'*: Mark Ellis, 'J. Edgar Hoover
and the "Red Summer" of 1919', *Journal of American Studies*, 28/1, 1994, 39–59. *'hunt
for black employees'*: one escapes through a window; another hides in an ice box. 'Loop
Mob Gets on Trail of Negro Toilers', *Chicago Tribune*, 29 July 1919. *'like wartime casualty
lists'*: 'List of Injured in Race Riot', *Chicago Tribune*, 29 July 1919. *'don't see why'*:
Hagedorn, 315. *'As regrettable as'*: 'The Washington Riots', *The Crisis*, October 1919,
reproduced in Sondra Kathryn Wilson (ed.), *The Selected Writings of James Weldon Johnson*,
Vol. 2, 1995, 36–39. • **VIENNA**: *'He swore undying loyalty'* to *'really miss him'*: to Lou
Andreas-Salomé, 1 August 1919, *FR/SAL*, 98–99. *'orchids'*: to Anna, 21 July 1919, *FR/
FR*, 152–153. *'(often violent) dreams'*: to Sigmund, 24 July 1919, ibid., 154–157. *'alpine
roses'*: to Sigmund, 5 August 1919, ibid., 170–171. *'a lot of death in it'*: to Anna, 21 July
1919, ibid., 152–153. *'finds distraction'*: to Pfister, 31 August 1919, *FR/PF*, 72. *'Freud is
a genius'*: Albert Mordell, *The Erotic Motive in Literature*, 1919, 15. • **BUDAPEST**: for the
struggles and ultimate failure of Kun's regime see Borsányi, 160–206. *'celebrations in the
Hungarian capital'*: ibid., 176. *'thrown into the Danube'*: ibid., 195. *'number of shirts'*: ibid.,

198. *'firm handshake'*: letter to Béla Kun, end July 1919, *CW* XLIV, 271. • **UPSTATE MICHIGAN**: *'we're idealists'* to *'We'll live'*: to William D. Horne, 7 August 1919, *LEH* I, 201–202. *'hundred and eighty trout'*: to Clarence Hemingway, 16 August 1919, *LEH* I, 202. *'bring his Italian medal'*: to Clarence Hemingway, 3 September 1919, *LEH* I, 205. *'sleeps with a woman'*: Meyers, *Hemingway*, 49. • **RUSSIA**: *'Afghanistan, Punjab and Bengal'*: political survey written 5 August 1919, *TP* I, 620–629, 625. *'all sides, including the Reds'*: Engelstein, 520–533. *'Cossack method'*: Pipes, *Russia under the Bolsheviks*, 59. *'Kolchak's favourite book'*: Norman Cohn, *Warrant for Genocide: The Myth of the Jewish World-Conspiracy and the Protocols of the Elders of Zion*, 1967, 118. *'anyone with the surname Bronstein'*: Service, *Trotsky*, 263. *'Denikin promptly pushes out'*: Engelstein, 466. *'an unpleasantness'*: in Volkogonov, *Trotsky*, 159. *'Proletarian, to horse!'*: *TMW* II, 412–414. • **WASHINGTON DC**: *'Beyond a doubt'* to *'practice of lynching'*: memorandum for the Director of Military Intelligence, 15 August 1919, *MG* I, 491–493. *'reads the Communist Manifesto'*: Ackerman, *J.Edgar*, 68. • **MUNICH**: *'lectures on war guilt, Goethe'*: Deuerlein, *Eintritt*, 197–198. *'field-runner a natural'*: ibid., 200–201. *'considered anti-Semitic'*: Weber, *Becoming Hitler*, 110. • **VIENNA**: *'people of Austria'* to *'ascendancy and oppression'*: 'Covering Letter to Reply to Observations on Peace Treaty made by Austrian Delegation', 2 September 1919, NA, FO 608/25. • **CHICAGO**: for an account of the meetings in Chicago see Theodore Draper, *The Roots of American Communism*, 1957, 176–187. *'husky Russians'*: Ackerman, *J. Edgar*, 75. • **BERLIN**: *'number of items'*: Willibald Gutsche, *Ein Kaiser im Exil: Der letzte deutsche Kaiser Wilhelm II. in Holland. Ein kritische Biographie*, 1991, 43–44. *'lift and electric lighting'*: ibid., 41. • **FIUME**: for a full account of the Fiume story see Woodhouse, 315–352; Hughes-Hallett, 483–568; Macdonald, *A Political Escapade*; and Michael A. Ledeen, *The First Duce: D'Annunzio at Fiume*, 1977. *'lieutenant colonel'*: Woodhouse, 326. *'American diplomat catches'*: 'Paraphrase of the Cipher Telegram sent to the Department of State', 5 September 1919, USNA, RG84 Foreign Service Posts of the Department of State, Vol. 80, Fiume. *'from a picnic'*: British diplomatic file quoted in Woodhouse, 327. *'Great Poet, I hope that your dream'*: *Il Popolo d'Italia*, 13 September 1919, in Macdonald, 96. *'nothing to show'*: 'Decypher of telegram from Fiume', 13 September 1919, NA, FO 608/36/1. *'first act of revolt'*: 'Gesto di Rivolta', *Il Popolo d'Italia*, 14 September 1919, *OO* XIV, 5. *'I am astonished'* to *'prick the belly'*: Woodhouse, 334; original in *AN/MUSS*, 9–10. *'drops pamphlets'* to *'British are uncertain'*: 'Decypher of telegram from Fiume', 18 September 1919, NA, FO 608/36/1. *'comic element'*: interview in the *Corriere della Sera* in Macdonald, 106. *'truly Futurist'*: letter dated 16 September 1919 in Ernest Ialongo, *Filippo Tommaso Marinetti: The Artist and his Politics*, 2015, 92. • **MUNICH**: *'Capitalism Be Eliminated?'*: Joachimsthaler, 252. • **BERLIN**: *'Joyous news'*: to Pauline Einstein, 27 September 1919, *CPAE* IX, 170–171. *'need to be properly interpreted'*: see Daniel Kennefick, 'Testing Relativity from the 1919 Eclipse – a Question of Bias', *Physics Today*, 62/3, 2009, 37–42; and Peter Coles, 'Einstein, Eddington and the 1919 Eclipse', available online at https://arxiv.org/abs/astro-ph/0102462. • **MUNICH**: *'too lightly characterised'* to *'complete and total removal'*: letter to Adolf Gemlich, 16 September 1919, *SA*, 88–90. • **SOUTHERN RUSSIA**: *'will see in my memo'*: to Lloyd

George, 20 September 1919, *WSC* IX, 865. *'confidently predict'* to *'upsetting your balance'*: from Lloyd George, 22 September 1919, *WSC* IX, 867–869. • ORLY: *'ponder the vast airfield'*: Polizzotti, 113. *'rally a foursome'*: Grose, 65.

Autumn 1919

MOSCOW: *'speaks to a conference of working women'* to *'unproductive work'*: speech to a conference of non-party working women, 23 September 1919, *CW* XXX, 40–46. *'two once fell out'*: Bertram D. Wolfe, 'Lenin and Inessa Armand', *Slavic Review*, 22/1, 1963, 96–114, 108–110. *'Inessa is a frequent visitor'* to *'sits in his kitchen'*: Krupskaya, *Reminiscences*, 539. • ISTANBUL: *'Kemal's influence continuing to spread'*: De Robeck to Curzon sent 30 September 1919 and received the following day, *DBFP* First Series, Vol. 4, 785–786. • FIUME: 'La prima adunata fascista', *Il Popolo d'Italia*, 6 October 1919, *OO* XIV, 43–45. • VIENNA: Jones, *Freud*, Vol. 3, 14–19. • AMERICA: for Wilson's voyage across America see Cooper, *Breaking the Heart*, 158–198. For a personal account see Edith Wilson, *My Memoir*, 275–288. All the speeches are in the Woodrow Wilson Papers, alongside other material, allowing the President's American progress to be followed day by day. Most descriptions here are drawn from those texts. *'moving picture men'*: 'President Starts his Long Tour', *Washington Herald*, 4 September 1919. *'terms of the treaty are severe'* to *'only country in the world'*: address to the Columbus Chamber of Commerce, 4 September 1919, *WW* LXIII, 7–18. *'lifelong reckoning'*: address in Convention Hall in Kansas City, 6 September 1919, ibid., 66–76. *'single whispering gallery?'* to *'blissful peace'*: address in the Des Moines Coliseum, 6 September 1919, ibid., 76–88. *'farmers and ranchers who have come'*: diary of Dr Grayson, 8 September 1919, ibid., 95. *'Henry Ford'*: Cooper, *Breaking the Heart*, 164. *'disciples of Lenin'* to *'chaos and disorder'*: address in the Billings Auditorium, 11 September 1919, *WW* LXIII, 175. *'Trotsky are on their way'*: in Hagedorn, 152. *'American people could really understand'*: Cooper, *Breaking the Heart*, 170. *'handkerchief in lavender'*: Edith Wilson, 282. *'inexpressible weariness'*: *Wyoming State Tribune*, 25 September 1919, *WW* LXIII, 487. *'cabbages and apples'*: diary of Dr Grayson, 25 September 1919, ibid., 488–489. *'mists of this great question'*: address in the City Auditorium in Pueblo, Colorado, 25 September 1919, ibid., 513. *'feel like I am going to pieces'*: diary of Dr Grayson, 26 September 1919, ibid., 513–521. *'Nothing to be alarmed about'*: to Jessie Woodrow Wilson Sayre, 26 September 1919, ibid., 521. • OMAHA: Hagedorn, 376–378. For the violence in Arkansas see Grif Stockley, *Blood in their Eyes: The Elaine Race Massacres of 1919*, 2001. • NEW YORK: *'white man has outraged American civilization'* to *'opportunity presents itself'*: editorial letter, 1 October 1919, *MG* II, 41–44. *'kickback'*: Grant, 205. *'latest in a long line'*: ibid., 206–207. *'Du Bois warns his uncle'*: ibid., 204. • MOSCOW: *'Winston plays with the idea'*: Henry Wilson's diary, 16 October 1919, *WSC* IX, 921. *'Cheka officials sift'*: Pipes, *Russia under the Bolshevik Regime*, 121–122. *'stops going on his walks'*: Krupskaya, *Reminiscences*, 528. *'White general declares'*: Pipes, *Russia under the Bolshevik Regime*, 123. *'retires to the sofa'*: Trotsky, 427. *'let us try'*: ibid., 424. *'metal wagons'*: Pipes, *Russia under the*

Bolshevik Regime, 124. *'stone labyrinth'* to *'cultural treasures'*: 'Petrograd Will Defend Itself from Within as Well', *En Route*, 16 October 1919, *TMW* II, 540–542. • **MANCHESTER**: *'Life is hard'*: Sigmund to Sam, 27 October 1919, JRL, Freud Collection, GB133 SSF 1/1/4. *'pathetic stumps'*: this wording is from Stefan Zweig, quoted in Gay, *Freud*, 380. *'rabble is the worst?'*: ibid., 387. *'sterner'*: Sam to Sigmund, 4 November 1919, JRL, Freud Collection, GB133 SSF 1/2/2. *'countermanding the project'*: the cable Edward sends back to his uncle dated 9 October 1919 is in LOC, Sigmund Freud Collection, Family Papers, 1851–1978, mss39990, box 1. • **PRANGINS**: for the sale of Habsburg jewellery, see annexe to 'Mémoire présenté au nom de S.M. L'Impératrice et Reine Zita', NA, FO 893/20/10. • **WASHINGTON DC**: for an account of Woodrow's confinement see Cooper, *Wilson*, 534–542; and Edith Wilson, 289–293. On prohibition see Thomas M. Coffey, *The Long Thirst: Prohibition in America, 1920–1933*, 1975; and Daniel Okrent, *Last Call: The Rise and Fall of Prohibition*, 2010. *'invading army'*: Ackerman, *J. Edgar*, 100. *'doctor is evasive'*: Cooper, *Wilson*, 540. *'Thanksgiving proclamation'*: memorandum by Robert Lansing, 5 November 1919, *WW* XLIII, 619. • **MUNICH**: *'are we dogs?'*: police notes of a meeting 22 November 1919, in Weber, *Becoming Hitler*, 136–137. *'Instead of the understanding'*: Deuerlein, *Eintritt*, 206. *'compares his technique'*: Fishman, 249. *'bring three friends'*: police report dated 13 November 1919, in Deuerlein, *Eintritt*, 207. *'three hundred in the audience'*: police report dated 26 November 1919, in Deuerlein, *Eintritt*, 208. • **LONDON**: for a full account of the meeting see 'Joint Eclipse Meeting of the Royal Society and the Royal Astronomical Society', *The Observatory*, November 1919, 545, 389–398. For the testing of the results see Kennefick. For the need to seek further proofs see Jeffrey Crelinsten, *Einstein's Jury: The Race to Test Relativity*, 2006. For the media response, see Einstein's biographies. For the German media response, see Lewis Elton, 'Einstein, General Relativity, and the German Press, 1919–1920', *Isis*, 77/1, 1986, 95–103. For controversy see Milena Wazeck, *Einstein's Opponents: The Public Controversy about the Theory of Relativity in the 1920s*, 2014 (trans. Geoffrey S. Koby). *'Revolution in Science'*: *The Times*, 7 November 1919. *'gargantuan headline'*: *New York Times*, 10 November 1919. *'scientist from Yorkshire'*: from Robert W. Lawson, 28 November 1919, *CPAE* IX, 256–257. *'ringing telephones'*: to Adrian D. Fokker, 1 December 1919, *CPAE* IX, 264–265. *'hardly breathe'*: to Max Born, 8 December 1919, *CPAE* IX, 280–281. *'state of unrest'*: 'Jazz in Scientific World', *New York Times*, 16 November 1919. • **ACROSS THE UNITED STATES**: details of the raids from Ackerman, *J. Edgar*, 113–123, unless otherwise stated. *'back to Russia'*: ibid., 117. *'communist meeting in Yonkers'*: 'Patriotic Song Ends Soviet Talk', *New York Tribune*, 10 November 1919. *'Russian Plot Nipped'*: *Wausau Daily Record*, 8 November 1919. *'cartoon of Uncle Sam'*: 'There Seems to be a Comeback', *Brooklyn Daily Eagle*, 10 November 1919. • **IRELAND**: *'In County Clare'*: BMH Witness Statement 1547, Michael Murphy, 11–12. • **MILAN**: *'Neither a victory, nor a defeat'*: 'L'Affermazione fascista', *Il Popolo d'Italia*, 18 November 1919, *OO* XIV, 136–137. *'mock funeral march'*: Giorgio Pini and Duilio Susmel, *Mussolini: l'uomo e l'opera*, Vol. 2, 1954, 45–48. *'Mussolini takes stock'*: Bosworth, 114–115; and A. Rossi, *The Rise of Italian Fascism*, 1938 (trans. Peter and Dorothy Wait), 39–42. • **LONDON**: *'chances of saving the situation'*: Churchill to

Lloyd George, Bonar Law and Curzon, 3 December 1919, *WSC* IX, 970. *'refugees freeze'*: Engelstein, 439–440. *'Can't you understand?'*: Trotsky, 433. • **WASHINGTON DC**: Cooper, *Wilson*, 549. • **AMERONGEN**: *'twelve thousand mark'*: diary of Elisabeth Bentinck, 15 November 1919, Ilsemann, Vol. 1, 124. *'glass of port'* to *'children's playhouse'*: diary of Elisabeth Bentinck, 1 and 2 December 1919, ibid., 127. *'Aged and Melancholy'*: *Dearborn Independent*, 15 November 1919. *'dark musings'*: Kaiser's doctor in Röhl, *Into the Abyss*, 1201. *'died in his arms'*: diary of Elisabeth Bentinck, 12 December 1919, Ilsemann, Vol. 1, 129. *'explains to a bewildered guest'* to *'Russia against England!'*: diary of Wolfgang Krauel, 24 October 1919, in Röhl, *Into the Abyss*, 1232. *'positive disgust'*: ibid., 1202. *'blames the Jews'* to *'exterminated from German soil!'*: letter to General Mackensen, 2 December 1919, in Cecil, 302. *'poisonous mushroom'*: diary of Wolfgang Krauel, 24 October 1919, in Röhl, *Into the Abyss*, 1233. *'they cannot do'*: diary of Elisabeth Bentinck, 31 December 1919, Ilsemann, Vol. 1, 132. *'unmitigated relief'*: Marks, 'My Name is Ozymandias', 149. • **SAGUA LA GRANDE**: *'adventurous'* to *'behaving splendidly'*: Captain Joshua Cockburn to Garvey, 2 December 1919, *MG* II, 157–159. *'Eternal has happened'* to *'steel their souls'*: editorial letter by Garvey, 3 December 1919, *MG* II, 159–161. • **MODLIN**: *'what I intended'*: to Jeanne de Gaulle, 18 November 1919, *CDG* I, 472. • **MOSCOW**: *'banking on the world revolution'* to *'may say without exaggeration'*: report to the All-Russian Congress of Soviets, 5 December 1919, *CW* XXX, 205–252, 208. *'fizzling out'* to *'thrust upon us'*: ibid., 222. *'just try it'*: ibid., 219. *'sphere of peaceful construction'*: ibid., 225. *'if you want free sale'*: ibid., 226. *'Either the lice'*: ibid., 228. • **KIRŞEHİR**: *'Will no one arise'*: Mango, 262. • **MUNICH**: *'black trousers, white shirt'*: Weber, *Becoming Hitler*, 137. *'possible without might?'* to *'soaked in blood'*: party meeting 10 December 1919, *SA*, 96–99. • **VIENNA**: *'seem not to be aware'*: Sigmund to Sam, 17 December 1919, JRL, Freud Collection, GB133 SSF 1/1/7. *'blames strike conditions'* to *'America would listen'*: Edward Bernays to Freud, 18 December 1919, LOC, Sigmund Freud Collection, Family Papers, 1851–1978, mss39990, box 1. *'person of public notoriety'*: Freud to Edward Bernays, 4 January 1920, LOC, Sigmund Freud Collection, Family Papers, 1851–1978, mss39990, box 1. *'finished sowing'*: to Abraham, 15 December 1919, this translation from Jones, *Freud*, Vol. 2, 447; the whole letter in English can be found at *FR/AB*, 411–412. • **NEW YORK**: see Ackerman, *J. Edgar*, 155–163. *'beginning of the end'*: 'Goldman Proud to be First Political Agitator Deported by the United States', *New York Tribune*, 22 December 1919. *'we're coming back'*: 'Soviet Ark to Russia', *Los Angeles Times*, 22 December 1919. *'share out clothing'*: Emma Goldman, *Living My Life*, 1932, Vol. 2, 721. *'latest recipient'*: Homberger, 201. *'too many foreign words'*: 'Stop Spoiling the Russian Language', December 1919, *CW* XXX, 298.

Winter 1920

Fitzgerald's famous quotation can be found in context in F. Scott Fitzgerald, *This Side of Paradise*, 1920, 304. The quotation from Alexandra Kollontai appeared first in an article entitled 'Communism and the Family' in the magazine *Kommunistka* in 1920, reproduced in *Selected Writings of Alexandra Kollontai*, translated from the Russian by Alix Holt, 1977, 250–260.

PARIS: *'better if I'd died'*: from Dr Grayson's diary, in Cooper, *Wilson*, 552. *'blind and deaf Don Quixote'*: John Maynard Keynes, *The Economic Consequences of the Peace*, 1920, 41. • **HAMBURG**: *'had been worried about her'* to *'undisguised brutality'*: to Pfister, 27 January 1920, *FR/PF*, 74–75. *'death-drive'*: for a description of the idea see Gay, *Freud*, 394–396. • **AMERICA**: for a description of the raids and the chaos which ensued see Ackerman, *J. Edgar*, 180–196. *'Los Angeles'*: 'Federal Police Nip Communists', *Los Angeles Daily Times*, 3 January 1920. *'Greatest Raid in History'*: *Ogden Standard*, 3 January 1920. *'play music and learn English'*: Ackerman, *J. Edgar*, 202. *'danger in the dragnet methods'*: *Chicago Daily News*, 6 January 1920, ibid., 205. • **MUNICH**: *'We fight against the Jew'*: meeting in the Kindl Keller, 7 January 1920, *SA*, 101. *'Every drop of our sweat'*: meeting in the Gasthaus Zum Deutschen Reich, 16 January 1920, *SA*, 105. • **SUNDERLAND**: *'ever a more awful spectacle'* to *'this is Utopia!'*: speech in Sunderland, 3 January 1920, in *Winston S. Churchill: His Complete Speeches, 1897–1963*, Vol. 3, *1914–1922*, 1974 (ed. Robert Rhodes James), 2917–2927. *'Trotsky's train is derailed'*: Deutscher, *Prophet Armed*, 496. *'shoved through the ice'*: Engelstein, 442. • **UNITED STATES OF AMERICA**: for descriptions of the first night of prohibition see Coffey, 3–9. *'unceremoniously dumped'*: Grant, 228. • **BERLIN**: *'lady calls on a British military officer'* to *'Winston Churchill'*: 'Notes on an Interview with Enver Pasha', 6 January 1920, NA, WO 32/5620. *'subsequent meeting'* to *'influence and power'*: 'Notes on a second Interview with Enver Pasha', 15 January 1920, NA, WO 32/5620. • **MOSCOW**: *'time to produce a dictionary'*: to Lunacharky, 18 January 1920, *CW* XXXV, 434. *'rather unhappy family'*: for one account see Katy Turton, *Family Networks and the Russian Revolutionary Movement, 1870–1940*, 2018. *'Varya impresses her friends'*: Fischer, *Lenin*, 487. *'what books to remove'*: Betram D. Wolfe, 'Krupskaya Purges the People's Libraries', *Survey*, 72, 1969, 141–155. *'answer should come to me'*: to Skylanksy, 16 February 1920, *TP* II, 44–45. • **NEW YORK**: *'trifle tacky'*: Jeffrey Meyers, *Scott Fitzgerald: A Biography*, 1994, 67. • **MOSCOW**: *'write me what is the matter'* to *'from me'*: Fischer, *Lenin*, 433–434; and Sebestyen, 453. *'evading my questions'*: R. C. Elwood, *Inessa Armand: Revolutionary and Feminist*, 1992, 257. • **BERLIN**: *'like a pagan idol'*: to Heinrich Zangger, 3 January 1920, *CPAE* IX, 338–340. *'Great Man of World History'*: *Berliner Illustrierte Zeitung*, 14 December 1919. *'Prague philosopher'*: Frank, 211. *'tells the Archbishop'*: Isaacson, 279. *'if the aliens'*: calendar entry for 31 January 1921, *CPAE* XII, 430. *'Mayakovsky'*: Bengt Jangfeldt, *Mayakovsky: A Biography*, 2014 (trans. Harry D. Watson), 253. *'Bolsheviks are not so unappealing'*: to Hedvig and Max Born, 27 January 1920, *CPAE* IX, 386–388. *'old-fashioned assimilationists'*: for the relationship between Fritz Haber and Albert Einstein see Fritz Stern, *Einstein's German World*, 2000. For the life of Fritz Haber see Charlotte Haber, *Mein Leben mit Fritz Haber*, 1970; and Margit Szöllösi-Janze, *Fritz Haber, 1868–1934: Eine Biographie*, 1998. *'first German edition of The Protocols'*: Cohn, 133–135. • **PETROGRAD**: *'one hundred and two small diamonds'*: Homberger, 204. *'personal endorsement'*: JRP, MS Am 1091, Series II, 556. • **THURLES**: *'four hand grenades'*: 'Four

Hours' Terror in Thurles', *Guardian*, 22 January 1920. *'new vocabulary of violence'*: for the development of the conflict see Townshend, 113–119; Walsh, 87–103; and Tim Pat Coogan, *Michael Collins*, 1990, 120–156. *'chafe under his presidential pomposity'*: Coogan, *De Valera*, 156–175. • **PARIS**: for Tzara's arrival in Paris to *'too important'*: Polizzotti, 122–123. *'cooing at the baby'*: Germaine Everling, 'C'était hier: Dada ...', *Les œuvres libres*, June 1955, 137–138. *'audience that turns up'* to *'Back to Zurich!'*: Polizzotti, 124–125; and Michel Sanouillet, *Dada in Paris*, 2009 (trans. Anne Sanouillet), 103–105. • **FIUME**: for a general account see Woodhouse, 315–352; and Hughes-Hallett, 483–568; for more detail see Macdonald and Ledeen. *'Irish nationalists and Béla Kun's Hungarian Bolsheviks'*: Mark Phelan, '"Prophet of the Oppressed Nations": Gabriele D'Annunzio and the Irish Republic, 1919–1921', *History Ireland*, 21/5, 2013, 44–48; and Ledeen, 177–186. *'oppressed peoples of the world'*: Woodhouse, 347. *'special steamer'*: Macdonald, 157. *'Guido Keller'*: Hughes-Hallett, 529–531. *'table cloth with a large ink stain'*: Macdonald, 160. • **VIENNA**: *'all my good bringing up'*: Anna to Sam, 9 February 1920, JRL, Freud Collection, GB133 SSF 1/3/1. *'soft Shetland cloth'*: postcard from Sigmund to Sam, 22 February 1920, JRL, Freud Collection, GB133 SSF 1/1/11. • **MUNICH**: for an account of the meeting see Weber, *Becoming Hitler*, 150–155. The police report of the meeting at the Hofbräuhaus, 24 February 1920, *SA*, 109–111, with the shout *'get out'* at 110. For the full twenty-five points of the party programme see Wolfgang Treue (ed.), *Deutsche Parteiprogramme 1861–1954/ Quellensammlung zur Kulturgeschichte*, Vol. 3, 1954, 143–146. *'newspapers barely report'*: Weber, *Becoming Hitler*, 155. *'Secret Jewish Document'*: 'Ein jüdisches Geheimdokument', *Völkischer Beobachter*, 25 February 1920. • **PARIS**: see Polizzotti, 134–137. *'inconsistent farce'*: 'Le Dadaisme n'est qu'une farce inconsistante', *Action française*, 14 February 1920. *'André Gide'*: Gide in the *Nouvelle Revue Française*, in Sanouillet, 143. • **THE HAGUE**: *'Dutch persuade the Kaiser'*: Marks, 'My Name is Ozymandias', 133. *'Wilhelm explains'*: diary entry 10 March 1920, Ilsemann, Vol. 1, 147–148. • **NEW YORK**: *'warm-up speaker'*: Professor William H. Ferris, report of a UNIA event, dated 6 March 1920, *MG* II, 231–233. Garvey's own speech is at 233–238, with the remarks on the UNIA's financial situation over the previous nine months on 236. For a first-hand account of the problems of the *Yarmouth* on these early trips see Hugh Mulzac, *A Star to Steer By*, 1963, 78–80. • **TORONTO**: *'presents a book by D'Annunzio'*: Baker, 580. *'shekels'*: to William D. Horne, 25 March 1920, *LEH* I, 227. *'first signed article for the Star'*: most of these articles are collected in Ernest Hemingway, *Dateline Toronto: The Complete Toronto Star Dispatches, 1920–1924*, 1985 (ed. William White). *'slackers who dodged the draft'*: 'Popular in Peace – Slacker in War', *Toronto Star Weekly*, 13 March 1920, reproduced in White, 10–11. • **ST. LOUIS**: there are different versions of Josephine Baker's cupid episode in St. Louis – one with Josephine suspended, one simply with her dancing. All include the element of initial embarrassment made up for by the alacrity of her switch into performance. See Baker and Bouillon, 13–17, for Margaret Baker's recollection. A somewhat different version is contained in Haney, placing the Cupid episode a little later, 27–31. • **BERLIN**: for the meeting itself, 'Interviews with Field-Marshal von

Ludendorff and General Hoffman', 4 March 1920, NA, CAB 24/100/31. 'Huns are very impudent': H. A. L. Fisher to Lloyd George, 13 March 1920, Gilbert, *World in Torment*, 182. • **DUBLIN**: see Coogan, *Michael Collins*, 120–144, with 'a question of our nerves' at 134. • **MOSCOW**: for Lenin's hunting see Fischer, *Lenin*, 380–383. 'Leon is convinced': Trotsky, 497. 'pins and needles': Service, *A Political Life*, Vol. 3, 259. 'locksmith from Moscow': Dmitri Ulyanov, *Ocherki raznykh let:Vospominaniya, perepiska, stat'i*, 1984, 137–138. 'Why on earth didn't you fire?': Krupskaya, *Memories*, Vol. 1, 33. • **ÅBO**: Homberger, 204–207.

Spring 1920

MONTREUX: for the history of the Kapp Putsch see Johannes Erger, *Der Kapp-Lüttwitz-Putsch: Ein Beitrag zur deutschen Innenpolitik 1919/20*, 1967. 'Kessler is in a bookshop': diary entry 13 March 1920, Kessler, *Tagebuch*, Vol. 7, 290–291. 'quick-thinking civil servant': Arnold Brecht, *Aus nächster Nähe: Lebenserinnerungen 1884–1927*, 1966, 302–307. 'Wilhelm calls for champagne': diary entry 15 March 1920, Ilsemann, Vol. 1, 149. • **PRANGINS**: for Charles's growing doubts about Horthy see Brook-Shepherd, *Last Habsburg*, 253–256. For the sale of Habsburg jewellery, see annexe to 'Mémoire présenté au nom de S.M. L'Impératrice et Reine Zita', NA, FO 893/20/10. • **AMERONGEN**: 'revolution instead of the opera': Grose, 69. • **CORK**: 'prepare for death': Coogan, *Michael Collins*, 123. 'I'll be out': BMH, Witness Statement 1547, Michael Murphy, 18–19. • **BERLIN**: see Erger for the progress and failure of the Kapp Putsch. For Hitler's Berlin excursion see Weber, *Becoming Hitler*, 159–162. 'anti-Semitic propaganda Kapp once supported': Michael Kellogg, *The Russian Roots of Nazism:White Émigrés and the Making of National Socialism, 1917–1945*, 2005, 90. • **ISTANBUL**: 'if I wanted I could give': Mango, 273. 'forcible occupation of Istanbul': Mansel, 392–393. 'seaside town in Italy': for the San Remo conference see Fromkin, 403–404. • **MOSCOW**: 'strikes across the country': Vladimir Brovkin, *Behind the Front Lines of the CivilWar: Political Parties and Social Movements in Russia, 1919–1922*, 1994, 287–299. 'carried out by a dictator': speech on economic development, 31 March 1920, *CW* XXX, 439–490, 476. 'appointed, rerouted and dispatched': Brovkin, 273. • **WASHINGTON DC**: Cooper, *Wilson*, 558–560. • **ACROSS GERMANY**: 'strike must continue': 19 March 1920, *Arbeiterklasse siegt über Kapp und Lüttwitz*, Vol. 1, 1971 (eds. Erwin Könneman, Brigitte Berthold and Gerhard Schulze), 202. 'dictatorship of the proletariat': 20 March 1920, ibid., 764. • **PARIS**: Polizzotti, 129–130. • **MUNICH**: 'turns up wearing gaiters': Friedrich Percyval Reck-Malleczeven, *Diary of a Man in Despair*, 2000 (trans. Paul Rubens; original German 1947), 35. • **SEBASTOPOL**: 'God has not given': Pyotr Wrangel, 140. 'cannot refuse to drink': ibid., 146. 'I'm struggling': Pyotr to Olga Wrangel, 1 April 1920, HIA, Vrangel Family Papers, Box 1, Folder 13. 'If only God helped me': Pyotr to Olga Wrangel, 8 April 1920, ibid. • **COLÓN**: for an account of the voyage see Mulzac, 79–83. 'cartoon in the Negro World': *Negro World*, 13 March 1920, reproduced in *MG* II, 260. 'wanted a place in the sun': report of UNIA Meeting, 13 March 1920, *MG* II, 241–259, 254. 'no power on *earth*': report of UNIA meeting, 29 April 1920, *MG* II, 299–303, 302. • **WASHINGTON DC**: '*looks meaningfully at the door*': David F. Houston, *Eight Years with Wilson's Cabinet, 1913–1920*, 1926, Vol. 2, 69–70. '*This is an experiment*' to '*see red*': from the diary of Josephus Daniels, 14 April 1920, *WW* LXV, 186–187. • **MOSCOW**: for Lenin's birthday see Nina Tumarkin, *Lenin Lives!: The Lenin Cult in Soviet Russia*, 1997, 95–104. '*proposes a newspaper campaign*': note from Lenin to Chicherin, 6 April 1920, Lenin, *Unknown Lenin*, 79–80. '*beating Lenin to the punch*': telegram to Stalin, 14 February 1920, in Lenin, *Unknown Lenin*, 78; see also Adam Zamoyski, *Warsaw 1920: Lenin's Failed Conquest of Europe*, 2008, 1–13. '*drastic measures*': to Lenin, Stalin and others, 26 April 1920, *TP* II, 148–151. • **DOORN**: '*Busts, paintings and etchings*': Gutsche, 45. '*four hundred and seventy imperially felled logs*': ibid., 42. • **WASHINGTON**: '*three hundred and sixty suspected radicals*' and '*Everybody is laughing*': Ackerman, *J. Edgar*, 283. '*only three handguns*': ibid., 291. • **PETROGRAD**: for an account of the spectacle see Emma Goldman, *My Disillusionment in Russia*, 1923, 74–78. '*sheerest fabrication*': speech to departing Red Army soldiers, 5 May 1920, *CW* XXXV 127–128. • **VIENNA**: '*prevents all evening entertainment*': W. E. Yates, *Theatre in Vienna: A Critical History*, 1996, 203. '*must sound rather bad*': Anna to Sam, 7 March 1920, JRL, Freud Collection, GB133 SSF 1/3/2. '*give up tennis*': Anna to Sam, 20 April 1920, JRL, Freud Collection, GB133 SSF 1/3/3. • **MUNICH**: for Hitler's development as a speaker, see Reginald H. Phelps, 'Hitler als Parteiredner im Jahre 1920', *Vierteljahrshefte für Zeitgeschichte*, 11/3, 1963, 274–330. '*mass murder of the intelligentsia*': speech at the Hofbräuhaus, 27 April 1920, *SA*, 127–129, 127. '*talk in Stuttgart*': 7 May 1920, *SA*, 130. '*subjugation of India*': for example, speeches on 11 and 16 June 1920, *SA*, 142–148. '*sun will shine through once more*': speech in Hofbräuhaus, 17 April 1920, *SA*, 122–125, 124. '*need a dictator*': speech at the Hofbräuhaus, 27 April 1920, *SA*, 127–129, 127. '*excerpts of the Protocols*': for example, *Völkischer Beobachter*, 22 and 27 April 1920. '*grasp at the very root*': speech at the Hofbräuhaus, 6 April 1920, *SA*, 119–120. • **LONDON**: '*English version of the Protocols*': Cohn, 152. '*note of prophecy*': 'The Jewish Peril, a Disturbing Pamphlet', *Times*, 8 May 1920. • **BERLIN**: '*tortured by bed bugs*': Frank, 199. • **DEARBORN**: for Henry Ford's anti-Semitism see Neil Baldwin, *Henry Ford and the Jews: The Mass Production of Hate*, 2003. '*winter will not freeze it*': 'Mr Ford's Page', *Dearborn Independent*, 7 February 1920. '*house painter in Oklahoma*': 'The Reminiscences of Mr. Fred L. Black', HFA, *Owen W. Bombard Interview Series*, Accession 65, 8. '*primed for conspiracy theories*': for one take on the psychology and impact of conspiracy theories (including Henry Ford and the *Protocols*) see David Aaronovitch, *The Role of the Conspiracy Theory in Shaping Modern History*, 2009. '*not making as much money*': Baldwin, 96–97. '*Persecution is not a new experience*': this, and following, taken from 'The International Jew: The World's Foremost Problem', *Dearborn Independent*, 22 May 1920. '*case of The Protocols*': 'Does a Jewish World Program Exist?', *Dearborn Independent*, 10 July 1920. '*articles shall continue*': Baldwin, 120. '*supersensitivity*': 'The Jewish Question – Fact or Fancy?', *Dearborn Independent*, 12 June 1920. '*enormity of the injury*': for this episode, see Baldwin, 132–133. • **PETROGRAD**: for an account of the delegation's time in Russia, apart from the accounts written by the participants, see Stephen White, 'British Labour in Soviet Russia, 1920', *English Historical Review*,

109/432, 1994, 621–640. *'their oldest clothes'*: Ethel Snowden, *Through Bolshevik Russia*, 1920, 21. *'peering behind an iron curtain'*: Snowden, 132. • **ÅBO**: Homberger, 204–207. • **PARIS**: *'not a Dadaist'*: Polizzotti, 145.

Summer 1920

KIEV: for a general account see Zamoyski, 48–52. *'former commander-in-chief'*: Figes, 698–699. • **WASHINGTON DC**: *'unconscionable falsehoods'*: Attorney General A. Mitchell Palmer on Charges Made Against Department of Justice by Louis F. Post and Others, *Hearings before the Committee on Rules, House of Representatives, Sixty-sixth Congress, Second Session*, 1 June 1920, 6. *'world is on fire'*: ibid., 18. *'so-called "liberal press"'*: ibid., 34. *'parlor Bolsheviki'*: ibid., 25. *'sly and crafty eyes'* to *'lopsided faces'*: ibid., 27. • **PARIS**: for Berlin Dada slogans see Sarah Ganz Blythe and Edward D. Powers, *Looking at Dada*, 2006, 5. • **PETROGRAD**: *'great international language'*: Snowden, 77. (Trotsky was subsequently upbraided by Lenin for having been seen in the imperial box with the British delegation: Trotsky, 576.) *'girl falls to her knees'*: Snowden, 21. *'reportedly eat moss'*: Smith, *Russia in Revolution*, 227. *'chemist's scales'*: Deutscher, *Prophet Armed*, 501. *'limon'* to *'overcoats bought with firewood'*: Steven G. Marks, 'The Russian Experience of Money, 1914–1924', in Murray Frame, Boris Kolonitskii, Steven G. Marks and Melissa K. Stockdale (eds.), *Russian Culture in War and Revolution*, 2014, 121–150, 130–133. *'lemons hand-delivered'*: M. N. Roy, *Memoirs*, 1964, 332. *'economist proposes a system'*: Marks, 'Russian Experience of Money', 136. *'blasphemous thoughts'*: Service, *Trotsky*, 268–269. *'working title Hunger'*: notebook, JRP, Series V/E, Item 1336. *'use up less wool'*: Snowden, 22. *'vitally necessary operation'*: Wright, 192. *'interminable discussion'*: Bertrand Russell, *The Autobiography of Bertrand Russell, 1914–1944*, 1968, 149. • **TEREZÍN FORTRESS**: Miller, 10. • **MOSCOW**: *'food on allotments'*: to Lydia Fotieva, 27 May 1920, *CW* XLIV, 377. *'by hand'* to *'figure as an example'*: to the fuel department of the Moscow Soviet, 16 June 1920, *CW* XLIV, 387. *'damage to Soviet property'*: 14 June 1920, *CW* XLIV, 196–197. *'Cooking Food Without Fire'*: to the Presidium of the Moscow Soviet, 29 June 1920, *CW* XLIV, 395. *'publish quickly'*: Fischer, *Lenin*, 431. *'order of the day'*: Zamoyski, 53. *'time to encourage revolution in Italy'* to *'Czech lands and Romania'*: Volkogonov, *Lenin*, 388. *'sinful'*: Kotkin, 360. • **MUNICH**: *'warning sign to the Entente'* to *'seek an Anschluss'*: speech in Rosenheim, 21 July 1920, *SA*, 163. *'far-right delegation'*: for this episode and its background, see Kellogg, 110–122. • **BAD GASTEIN**: for Freud's work on the crowd see van Ginneken and 'Group Psychology and the Analysis of the Ego', originally published in German in 1921, *SE* XVIII, 67–143. *'not even an organ grinder'*: to Anna, 1 August 1920, *FR/FR*, 181–182. *'Lenin is an artist'*: 'L'Artefice e la Materia', *Il Popolo d'Italia*, 14 July 1920, *OO* XV, 91–94, 93; see more generally Simonetta Falasca-Zamponi, *Fascist Spectacle: The Aesthetics of Power in Mussolini's Italy*, 1997. **WARSAW**: *'more the danger approaches'*: Anon. (Charles de Gaulle), 'La bataille de la Vistule', *Revue de Paris*, No. 6, 1920, 35–53, 37. *'tragic destiny'*: ibid., 38. • **NEW YORK**: *'accredited spokesman'*: letter to Du Bois, 16 July 1920, *MG* II, 426. *'under no* *circumstances'* to *'public know'*: from Du Bois to Garvey, 22 July 1920, *MG* II, 431–432. • LONDON: letter to Sir Henry Wilson, General Harington and General Macdonogh, 20 July 1920, *WSC* IX, 1145–1146. • PETROGRAD: *'false passports'*: Roy, 308. *'bring their own Chianti'*: ibid., 359. *'group of Irish delegates'*: for an account of the relationship between Irish nationalism and Moscow see Emmet O'Connor, 'Communists, Russia and the IRA, 1920–1923', *Historical Journal*, 46/1, 2003, 115–131. *'infantile'*: for the question of so-called left-wing Communism see Service, *A Political Life*, Vol. 3, 121–125. *'organising a women's conference'*: Elwood, *Armand*, 258–261. *'music of Wagner'*: Geldern, 181. *'produced in four languages'*: Serge, 118. *'Vladimir gives the opening speech'*: report on the international situation, 19 July 1920, *CW* XXXI, 215–234, with *'backward'* at 232. *'capture the moment'*: Serge, 120. *'especially regilded'*: Geldern, 180. *'nearby bedchamber'*: Roy, 372. • DUBLIN: *'new force appears in Ireland'*: for the origins of the Black and Tans, see D. M. Leeson, *The Black and Tans: British Police and Auxiliaries in the Irish War of Independence, 1920–1921*, 2011, 68–95. *'Tuam'* to *'Belgium and France'*: Leeson, 44. *'rumours that he is having an affair'*: Coogan, *De Valera*, 185–187. • UPSTATE MICHIGAN: this account of Hemingway's summer is drawn from his letters. *'gambles at roulette'*: letter to Grace Quinlan, 8 August 1920, *LEH* I, 237–240. *'man named Ponzi'*: Robert Sobel, *The Big Board: A History of the New York Stock Market*, 1965, 224. *'for a job in New York'*: letter to Grace Quinlan, *LEH* I, 8 August 1920, 237–240. *'lazy loafing'*: from Grace Hemingway, 24 July 1920, EHC, Series 3, Box IC11, EHPP-IC11-010–006. • MOSCOW: *'jar of fruit and a bag of flour'*: James Riordan, *Sport in Soviet Society: Development of Sport and Physical Education in Russia and the USSR*, 1977, 79–80. *'threat to resign'*: Homberger, 210. *'as a child accepts'*: Service, *A Political Life*, Vol. 3, 131. *'iron proletarian centralism'*: Theses on the Role of the Communist Party, 24 July 1920, *CI* I, 127–135, 133. *'Internationale three times a day'*: Roy, 330. • NEW YORK: *'striking out for freedom'* to *'from all quarters'*: speech at the opening of the UNIA Convention, 1 August 1920, *MG* II, 476–487. *'Jim Europe's old band'* to *'Africa for the Africans'*: report of UNIA parade, 3 August 1920, *MG* II, 490–494. *'Madison Square Garden'* to *'Palestine and Africa'*: report of Madison Square Garden meeting, 3 August 1920, *MG* II, 497–509. *'Declaration of Rights'*: UNIA Declaration of Rights, *MG* II, 571–580. *'already swept the world'*: report of the convention, 22 August 1920, *MG* II, 614–620, 617. *'we are coming'*: report of the convention, 4 August 1920, *MG* II, 529–538, 538. *'resting back in cushioned chairs'*: report of the convention, 15 August 1920, *MG* II, 583–597, 594. *'updates from its informants'*: these are reproduced in *MG* II. *'fool or a rogue'*: interview with Chandler Owen and A. Philip Randolph by Charles Mowbray White, *MG* II, 609–612, 609. *'more or less a fraud'*: letter from W. E. B. Du Bois to H. L. Stone, 24 July 1920, *MG* II, 435. *'think he is a demagogue'*: interview with Du Bois by Charles Mowbray White, 22 August 1920, *MG* II, 620–621. *'ablest statesman of his race'*: report of the convention, 31 August 1920, *MG* II, 642–651, 649. *'purchase them now'*: editorial letter by Marcus Garvey, 31 August 1920, *MG* II, 654–656. • THE POLISH FRONT: *'sixth year in a row'*: de Gaulle, 45. *'not averse to a temporary alliance'*: Pipes, *Russia under the Bolshevik Regime*, 189–190. *'beautiful plan'*: note from Lenin to Skylansky, August 1920, *TP* II, 278–279. *'Georgian bank-robber bristles'*: Kotkin, 361–363. • **SÈVRES**: for the diplomacy leading up to Sèvres see MacMillan, 438–466; and Fromkin, 403–411. *'sublime principles'*: in Abdulhamit Kırmızı, 'After Empire, Before Nation: Competing Ideologies and the Bolshevik Moment of the Anatolian Revolution', in Stefan Rinke and Michael Wildt (eds.), *Revolutions and Counter-Revolutions: 1917 and its Aftermath from a Global Perspective*, 2017, 119–140, 132. • **DEARBORN**: *'opines innocently'*: 'Mr. Ford's Page', *Dearborn Independent*, 7 August 1920. • **WARSAW**: for the lead-up to the crucial battle and then the so-called miracle on the Vistula, see Zamoyski, 64–109. *'battle for life and death'* to *'determined at this very moment'*: speech of Antoni Szlagowski by the grave of Ignacy Skorupka, 17 August 1920, in Waldemar Wojdecki, *Arcybiskup Antoni Szlagowski, kaznodzieja Warszawy*, 1997, 184–187. *'Poles have grown wings!'*: de Gaulle, 45. • **MUNICH**: all description taken from speech at the Hofbräuhaus, 13 August 1920, *SA*, 184–204. *'Egypt's cultural flowering'*: ibid., 186. *'could not survive without work'*: ibid., 188. *'alleged use of Assyrian stonemasons'*: ibid., 188–189. *'if we are socialists'*: ibid., 200. *'Franz Léhar'*: ibid., 197. *'always ready to rip up'*: ibid., 198. *'lively and enthusiastic crowds'*: Phelps, 'Hitler als Parteiredner', 308. • **MILAN**: *'taking flying lessons'*: Bosworth, 119. For the myth-making of Mussolini and flight see Guido Mattioli, *Mussolini Aviatore*, 1933. For the origins of the *squadristi* see Roberta Suzzi Valli, 'The Myth of Squadrismo in the Fascist Regime, *Journal of Contemporary History*, 35/2, 2000, 131–150; and Emilio Gentile, 'Paramilitary Violence in Italy: The Rationale of Fascism and the Origins of Totalitarianism', in Robert Gerwarth and John Horne (eds.), *War in Peace: Paramilitary Violence in Europe after the Great War*, 2012, 85–106. *'sleeps in his underwear'*: Bosworth, 130. • **MOSCOW**: *'Reed pesters Vladimir'*: Fischer, *Lenin*, 433. For Inessa Armand's trip to Kislovodsk, see Elwood, *Armand*, 262–266. • **BERLIN**: this description is drawn principally from Siegfried Grundmann, *Einsteins Akte: Einsteins Jahre in Deutschland aus der Sicht der deutschen Politik*, 1998, 151–155. *'with or without a swastika'*: 'Meine Antwort ueber die antirelavitätstheoristische GmbH', from the *Berliner Tageblatt*, 27 August 1920, reproduced in *CPAE* VII, 344–349. *'entente of mediocrity'*: from Fritz Haber, 30 August 1920, *CPAE* X, 395–397. *'Stay the holy man'*: from Hedwig Born, 8 September 1920, *CPAE* X, 416–417. *'world is a curious madhouse'*: to Marcel Grossman, 12 September 1920, *CPAE* X, 428–430. • **WALL STREET**: *'Niagara Falls'*: for this description, and following, see Beverly Gage, *The Day Wall Street Exploded: A Story of America in its First Age of Terror*, 2009, 43–49. *'young financier'*: David Nasaw, *The Patriarch: The Remarkable Life and Turbulent Times of Joseph P. Kennedy*, 2012, 69. *'rent asunder'*: headline, *Philadelphia Enquirer*, 17 September 1920. *'relations between capital and labor'*: 'Dynamite for Wall Street', *Wall Street Journal*, 17 September 1920. • **BAKU**: for a general account of the Baku Congress see Stephen White, 'Communism and the East: The Baku Congress, 1920', *Slavic Review*, 33/3, 1974, 492–514. *'pronounced in American?'*: Homberger, 214–215. *'not given a choice'* to *'requirements are taken care of'*: Benjamin Gitlow, *The Whole of Their Lives*, 1948, 32–34. Gitlow specifically refers to booze and women, with the procurement of young girls organised by Radek. *'huddle in linguistic groups'*: *Congress of the Peoples of the East: Stenographic Report* (trans. Brian Pearce), 1977, 70. *'Internationale'*: according to the stenographic record the Internationale was played or sung twenty-three times during the opening ceremony. *'Uncle Sam is not one'*: stenographic record, 4 September 1920, 88. *'fell into a false situation'*: 4 September 1920, ibid., 76. *'oppressed peoples'*: 7 September 1920, ibid., 161. *'Sweep away with fierce will'* and *'Blow up Europe!'*, 5 September 1920, ibid., 113–114. *'Effigies'*: White, 492. *'Béla Kun'*: stenographic record, 6 September 1920, 127. • **THE HAGUE**: *'snippets of Carmen'*: Elisabeth Young-Bruehl, *Anna Freud: A Biography*, 2008, 96. *'German colleague gives a rambling presentation'*: Clark, *Freud*, 403. *'bananas'*: Gay, *Freud*, 393. *'eating sparingly'* to *'pineapple'*: exchange of notes, FR/FR, 199–200. *'canoe trip'*: Jones, *Freud*, Vol. 2, 29. • **KISLOVODSK**: *'living corpse'* to *'needs of the struggle'*: Volkogonov, *Lenin*, 47–48. *'plays the piano for guests'*: Elwood, *Armand*, 265.

Autumn 1920

VIENNA: Wolfgang Zdral, *Die Hitlers: Die Unbekannte Familie*, 2005, 198. • **BAD NAUHEIM**: for the relationship between Lenard and Einstein before Bad Nauheim, see Andreas Kleinert and Charlotte Schönbeck, 'Lenard und Einstein: ihr Briefwechseln und ihr Verhältnis vor der Nauheimer Diskussion von 1920', *Gesnerus*, 35, 1978. *'not yet made it possible'*: Frank, 201. *'avoid the other physicists'*: CPAE X, see notes on 436. *'most romantic point'* to *'even consciousness'*: to Hedwig Born, 10 October 1920, CPAE X, 440–441. *'minds so malleable'*: to Hendrik A. Lorentz, 25 September 1920, CPAE X, 437–438. • **NALCHIK**: for Armand's final days see Elwood, *Armand*, 265–266. In a footnote, Elwood notes the story that Armand was in despair over personal matters and ended her life with poison. For the death of John Reed see Mary V. Dearborn, *Queen of Bohemia: The Life of Louise Bryant*, 1996, 161–163. *'watermelon'*: Serge, 127. *'caught in a trap'*: Goldman, *Living My Life*, Vol. 2, 851. *'the cause goes on'*: Clare Sheridan, *Mayfair to Moscow: Clare Sheridan's Diary*, 1921, 162. *'real American'*: Marguerite E. Harrison, *Marooned in Moscow*, 1921, 222. • **VIENNA**: *'mouldy cheese overwhelms'*: Sigmund to Sam, 15 October 1920, JRL, Freud Collection, GB133 SSF 1/1/19. *'comic poem'*: Sam to Sigmund, 30 October 1920, JRL, Freud Collection, GB133 SSF 1/2/16. *'popularity in itself'*: Sigmund to Sam, 5 November 1920, JRL, Freud Collection, GB133 SSF 1/1/21. *'silly'* to *'Encyclopaedia Britannica'*: Sigmund to Sam, 26 November 1920, JRL, Freud Collection, GB133 SSF 1/1/22. • **MOSCOW**: for Clare Sheridan's trip to Russia see Sheridan, *Mayfair to Moscow*, 1921. *'D'Annunzio'*: ibid., 12. *'most privileged class'*: ibid., 26. *'redacted version of Vladimir's speech'* to *'no way in the slightest'*: Service, *A Political Life*, Vol. 3, 138; the full speech is in Lenin, *Unknown Lenin*, 95–115. *'cannot expect to see a communist society'*: speech to young Communists, 2 October 1920, CW XXXI, 283–299, 298–299. *'scheme for Russia's electrification'*: H. G. Wells, *Russia in the Shadows*, 1921, 134. *'film of the Baku conference'*: ibid., 80. *'At the ballet'*: Sheridan, *Mayfair to Moscow*, 84. *'mistaken for Sylvia Pankhurst'*: ibid., 78. *'don't mind being looked at'* to *'caressing me with tools'*: ibid., 137–138. *'vous êtes encore femme'*: Clare Sheridan, *Naked Truth*, 1928, 196. *'know how to get you to England'*: Sheridan, *Mayfair to Moscow*, 170. • **NEW YORK**: *'masses of the race'*: editorial letter by Garvey, 11 October 1920, MG III, 50–51. *'writes to the shipping* *registers'*: from Du Bois to Lloyd's Register, 6 November 1920, *MG* III, 72–73. • **RIGA:** *'now alone in the struggle'*: Pytor Wrangel, 296. *'Destroy Wrangel!'*: in Engelstein, 557. *'greatest crime'*: telegram to the front, 24 October 1920, *CW* XXXV, 461. • **VIENNA:** *'done it differently'*: Kurt Robert Eissler, *Freud as an Expert Witness: The Discussion of War Neuroses Between Freud and Wagner-Jauregg*, 1986, 92. *'machine gun behind the front'*: ibid., 60–61. *'mendacious spitefulness'* to *'scheissfreundlich'*: to Abraham, 31 October 1920, *FR/ AB*, 432–433. • **WASHINGTON DC:** for Harding and the origins of normalcy see Robert K. Murray, *The Harding Era: Warren G. Harding and his Administration*, 1969; and John W. Dean, *Warren G. Harding*, 2004. For the normalcy speech itself see David H. Carwell, 'Warren G. Harding: Return to Normalcy', in Jeffrey S. Ashley and Marla J. Jarmer (ed.), *The Bully Pulpit, Presidential Speeches and the Shaping of Public Policy*, 2016, 41–51. For Wilson's last days in the White House see Cooper, *Wilson*, 573–578. *'whole world will wait'*: A Statement, 3 October 1920, *WW* XLVI, 183. *'Hemingway casts his vote'*: Keneth Kinnamon, 'Hemingway and Politics', in Scott Donaldson (ed.), *The Cambridge Companion to Hemingway*, 1996, 149–169, 160. *'stopped to get their breath'*: from Norman Hezekiah Davis, 3 November 1920, *WW* XLVI, 314. *'crown will be one of glory'*: from Bainbridge Colby, 3 November 1920, *WW* XLVI, 313. *'not a repudiation'* to *'Nothing can destroy'*: from Eleanor Randolph Wilson McAdoo, 3 November 1920, *WW* XLVI, 315. *'realise their error'*: Axson, 199. *'which she ranks'*: Edith Wilson, 308. • **SEBASTOPOL:** *'cannot be landed here'*: Admiral de Robeck to the Foreign Office, 10 November 1920, *WSC* IX, 1234. • **FORMER BATTLEFIELDS OF NORTHERN FRANCE:** see Jean-Pascal Soudagne, *L'histoire incroyable du soldat inconnu*, 2008, 79–113. *'group trip to a Paris art exhibition'*: Lacouture, 109. • **SEBASTOPOL:** the description of the departure from Crimea is drawn principally from A. Valentinov's account in S. V. Volkov (ed.), *Iskhod Russkoi armii Generala Vrangelia iz Kryma*, 2003, 534–549. • **DUBLIN:** for a full account of Bloody Sunday see Townshend, 201–208. *'copy of Irish Field'* to *'bad mistake'*: BMH, Witness Statement 771, James Doyle, 2. *'Any casualties?'*: Coogan, *Michael Collins*, 160. *'ambushed on a rainswept road'*: whether this was in fact an ambush or an accidental battle, brought on by the need to evade British patrols, is not entirely clear. Some Auxiliaries may have been shot while surrendering (Townshend, 210–215). *'Devil's competition'*: Townshend, 270–271. *'sinking back into barbarism'*: letter dated 11 December 1920 quoted in R. F. Foster, *W. B. Yeats: A Life*, Vol. 2, *The Arch-Poet, 1915–1939*, 2003, 184. • **NEW YORK:** for the exchange of letters dated 2 October and 19 November 1920 see LOC, Sigmund Freud Collection, Family Papers, 1851–1978, mss39990, box 1. • **REVAL:** *'contain the heads'*: Sheridan, *Mayfair to Moscow*, 204. *'old friend from Germany'*: Clara Zetkin, *Reminiscences of Lenin*, 1929, 11–12. *'just limp behind it'* to *'give me no pleasure'*: ibid., 14. *'used to hum arias'*: Elizarova, *Reminiscences of Lenin by his Relatives*, 127–129. *'complain so bitterly'* to *'prevented the mind'*: Zetkin, 15. *'What a waste!'* to *'marriage forms of Maoris'*: ibid., 52–54. *'over-excitement and exaggeration'*: ibid., 55. *'simple as drinking a glass of water'*: ibid., 57–58. *'living to the full'* to *'D'Annunzio'*: ibid., 59–60. *'hardly time to discuss the other matter'*: for this section of their conversation, ibid., 61–71. *'working groups'* to *'expediency'*: ibid., 63. *'must dress more warmly'*: ibid., 71. • **VIENNA:** for these exchanges see cables 27 November and 1 December 1920 and letter 19 December 1920, LOC, Sigmund Freud Collection, Family Papers, 1851–1978, mss39990, box 1. • **DEARBORN**: *'hack who has to write'*: Baldwin, 98. *'collected in a book entitled The International Jew'*: Leo P. Ribuffo, 'Henry Ford and "The International Jew"', *American Jewish History*, 69/4, 1980, 437–477. • **ISTANBUL**: for the Bizerte story see Sergey Vlasov, *Uzniki Bizerty: dokumental'nye povesti o zhizni russkikh moriakov v Afrike v 1920–25*, 1998; and Hélène Menegaldo, 'Les russes à Bizerte: de la Tunisie à la France, les étapes d'une intégration contrariée', *Mémoire(s), identité(s), marginalité(s) dans le monde occidental contemporain*, 13, 2015. • **MUNICH**: *'crazy utopia'*: speech in the Kindl Keller, 5 November 1920, SA, 257–258. *'want to build'*: speech in the Hofbräuhaus, 19 November 1920, SA, 259–263, 260. *'membership cards start at 500'*: Joachimsthaler estimates at 195 at the end of 1919, 1,100 in July 1920, and around 2,000 by the end of 1920. *'between advertisements for hot chocolate'*: *Völkischer Beobachter*, 16 December 1920. • **PARIS**: *'Hold on to your overcoat'*: *Littérature*, No. 17, December 1920, 12. • **LUDWIGSHÖHE**: for Ilsemann's trip to Ludendorff see diary entry 9 November 1920, Ilsemann, Vol. 1, 162–166. For his return to Doorn see diary entry 22 November 1920, Ilsemann, Vol. 1, 166. • **NEW YORK**: 'Marcus Garvey', *The Crisis*, December 1920. • **FIUME**: for an account of the end of the Fiume adventure see Hughes-Hallett, 553–568. *'mock battle with live weapons'*: Woodhouse, 339. *'deserters to the Cause'*: slightly abbreviated Woodhouse, 349. • **CHICAGO**: 'Plain and Fancy Killings, $400 Up', *Toronto Star Weekly*, 11 December 1920, in Hemingway, *Dateline Toronto*, 65–66. • **ANKARA**: *'know how vital'* to *'demolition of capitalism'*: to Stalin, 14 December 1920, Mustafa Kemal, *Atatürk'ün bütün eserleri*, 1998–2009, Vol. 10, 160. *'independence of Dagestan'*: to Lenin, 18 December 1920, Kemal, Vol. 10, 171. *'Autonomy does not mean independence'*: speech to the Congress of the Peoples of Daghestan, 13 November 1920, Stalin, *Works*, Vol. 4, 407–411, 409. • **MOSCOW**: *'zigzag transition'*: report to the 8th All-Russia Congress of Soviets, 22 December 1920, CW XXXI, 487–518, 496. *'we ourselves forget about them'*: speech to Communist delegates, 30 December 1920, CW XXXII, 19–37, 22. *'largest agitational spectacle yet'*: Geldern, 199–207. *'no question of selling out'*: report to the 8th All-Russia Congress of Soviets, 22 December 1920, CW XXXI, 494. *'Sukharevka'* to *'Soviet power plus'*: ibid., 515–516. • **FIUME**: Hughes-Hallett, 564–568 • **DUBLIN**: *'odd shooting'* to *'one good battle'*: Coogan, *De Valera*, 202. *'patrol in Midleton'*: this account is drawn from two sources: 'Weekly Survey of the State of Ireland for Week Ended January 3rd, 1921', NA, CAB 24/118/20; and BMH, Witness Statement 1456, John Kelleher, 22.

Winter 1921

The Lenin quotation is from a speech given on the anniversary of the revolution, 6 November 1921, CW XXXIII, 120. The quotation from Einstein is from a letter to Emmanuel Carvallo, 12 March 1921, CPAE XII, 155–156.

DUBLIN: *'looks ten years older'*: Peter Hart, *Mick: The Real Michael Collins*, 2005, 264. *'Long Whoor'*: Coogan, *De Valera*, 202. • **CHICAGO**: *'lying on an application'*: Hemingway mis-states his age as twenty-four rather than twenty-one, mentions a commission in the Italian army and fails to mention his time in the American Red Cross: to *Chicago Daily Tribune*, 29 November 1920, *LEH* I, 250–251. *'poems of Siegfried Sassoon'*: to Hadley Richardson, 23 December 1920, 258. *'dope on Rooshia'*: to Grace Hemingway, 10 January 1921, EHC, Series 2, Box OC01, EHPP-OC01-013–003. • **LONDON**: Sheridan, *Mayfair to Moscow*, 216–223. • **GORKI**: *'party is sick'*: 'The Party Crisis', article in *Pravda*, written 19 January 1921, *CW* XXXII, 43–53, 43. *'Syndicalist deviation'*: ibid., 53. *'transmission belts'*: speech to Communist delegates, 30 December 1920, *CW* XXXII, 19–37, 21. *'receives maps'*: Pipes, *Russia under the Bolshevik Regime,* 373. • **FIUME**: *'Wagner's wife once played'*: Hughes-Hallett, 572. • **PRAGUE**: for Einstein's visit see Frank, 206–212. *'deliberate poisoning'* to *'psychological illness of the masses'*: speech in Munich, 3 January 1921, *SA*, 283–287, 286. *'should be murdered'*: see entry for 9 January 1921 in the chronology in *CPAE* XII, 424. • **DEARBORN**: *'show business'*: 'How Jews Capitalized a Protest against Jews', *Dearborn Independent*, 22 January 1921. *'prejudice and hatred'*: 'Issue a Protest on Anti-Semitism', *New York Times*, 17 January 1921. • **INÖNÜ**: McMeekin, 451. • **MUNICH**: 'Die Türkei – der Vorkämpfer', *Völkischer Beobachter*, 6 February 1921. • **MOSCOW**: for the visit to Varya, and Lenin's preference for Pushkin over Mayakovsky, see Fischer, *Lenin*, 488–489; and Elizarova, *Reminiscences of Lenin by his Relatives*, 201–207. *'the letters of Marx'* to *'this dirty lot'*: to D. B. Ryazanov, 2 February 1921, *CW* XLV, 80–81. • **CLONMULT**: *'Clonmult'*: Peter Hart, *The IRA and its Enemies: Violence and Community in Cork, 1916–1923*, 1998, 97–98. *'area of active lawlessness'* to *'Catholic reformatory'*: 'Survey of the State of Ireland for the Week Ending February 28th 1921', NA, CAB 24/120/71. *'Irish woman in County Cork'*: the case of Mary Lindsay is briefly described in Townshend, 240, but the story itself has been told and retold many times (for example, in Sean O'Callaghan, *Execution*, 1974) and even spawned a television drama. For a broader view, including the pushing out of Protestants from Cork, see Gerard Murphy, *The Year of Disappearances: Political Killings in Cork, 1921–1922*, 2010. *'house in which Michael Collins was born'*: Collins's own account in Coogan, *Michael Collins*, 177–178. *'train carrying British soldiers'*: Townshend, 241. *'Irish cheddar'*: BMH, Witness Statement 1713, James O'Donovan, 12. • **MUNICH**: *'brass band'*: Joachimsthaler, 282. *'get close to the Communists'*: Ernst Deuerlein, *Der Aufstieg der NSDAP in Augenzeugenberichten*, 1974, 131. *'war wounded go free'*: advertisement for a speech on 2 February 1921, *SA*, 310. *'blue suit and trench coat'*: Hellmuth Auerbach, 'Hitlers Politische Lehrjahre und die Münchener Gesellschaft, 1919–1923', *Vierteljahrshefte für Zeitgeschichte*, 25/1, 1977, 1–45, 22. • **PARIS**: for the play itself: Pierre Palau, *Les Détraquées*, 1958. For Breton's reaction: André Breton, *Nadja*, 1960 (trans. Richard Howard), 40–51. Breton had a signed copy of Babinski's 1917 book on hysteria at home, with a note promising André a great medical career: Polizzotti, 56. • **MOSCOW**: *'Disaster is imminent'*: to the Politburo, 12 February 1921, *CW* XXXII, 134–136. *'proletarian class = the Communist Party'*: Read, *Lenin*, 274. *'soldiers' shoes'*: Figes, 760. *'Kronstadt batteries'*: Paul Avrich, *Kronstadt 1921*, 1970, 96–97. *'proclamation'*:

Figes, 760. 'nerves are kaput': Kotkin, 410. • **BERLIN**: 'whole world looks on you' to 'Jewish faithlessness': from Fritz Haber, 9 March 1921, CPAE XII, 124–127. 'only for my name' to 'seats have already been booked': to Fritz Haber, 9 March 1921, CPAE XII, 127–130. • **CHICAGO**: 'nothing in the wide world': speech, 1 February 1921, MG III, 149–156, 149. 'as long as they understand': report by Bureau of Investigation agent, 10 February 1921, MG III, 173–175. 'carry mortar' to 'build up in Africa': speech, 4 February 1921, MG III, 161–162. 'trying to develop a business relationship': Grant, 280–283. 'in fact steel': the retraction was printed in The Crisis, March 1921. 'temperamental, unscrupulous': speech, 16 February 1921, MG III, 206–218, 206. • **VIENNA**: see Martin A. Miller, Freud and the Bolsheviks: Psychoanalysis in Imperial Russia and the Soviet Union, 1998; Freud's letters to Osipov: 169–175. • **KRONSTADT FORTRESS**: 'exiled leaders': Avrich, 116. 'White plot cooked up in Paris': Pipes, Russia under the Bolshevik Regime, 382. 'bared their fangs': Avrich, 95. 'clemency, Mr Trotsky' to 'shot like partridges': ibid., 145–146. 'issues its own retort': the full statement is in ibid., 241–243. 'a gun': summing-up speech to the Tenth Congress of the Communist Party, 9 March 1921, CW XXXII, 188–207, 206. For Lenin's speech on trades unions jibing Trotsky on 14 March 1921 see CW XXXII, 210–213. 'fetish of democratic principles' to 'temporary vacillations': Deutscher, Prophet Armed, 508–509. 'bureau-cratic distortions': speech as before on 14 March 1921, CW XXXII, 210–213. 'may have made mistakes' to 'no alternative': summing-up speech to the Tenth Congress of the Communist Party on the tax in kind, 15 March 1921, CW XXXII, 229–238, 233–234. 'turning back towards capitalism': report on the tax in kind, 15 March 1921, CW XXXII, 214–229, 218. 'theoretically it is conceivable': ibid., 220. 'must do a bit of starving': Service, Lenin, 426. 'inch of its life' to 'hobble about': report on the tax in kind, 15 March 1921, CW XXXII, 214–229, 224. 'Crocodiles are despicable': ibid., 222. 'pulls off his masterstroke': Service, A Political Life, Vol. 3, 184; for the congress generally, ibid., 176–184. 'temper-amental man' to 'hasn't got a clue': summary of remarks at the Tenth Communist Party Congress, 16 March 1921, Lenin, Unknown Lenin, 123–124. 'Quotation Marks': Avrich, 244–246. 'canned horsemeat': ibid., 201. 'public health risk': ibid., 210. 'notes one revolu-tionary exile': Goldman, Living my Life, Vol. 2, 886. • **NEW YORK**: 'playing charades': Clare Sheridan, My American Diary, 1922, 21. 'force as an element' to 'mind cannot grasp it': ibid., 40. 'made British Ambassador': Service, Spies and Commissars, 276. 'kill off all Bolsheviks' to 'wonderfully emptier world': Sheridan, American Diary, 51. 'Russian cab driver': ibid., 75. • **MOSCOW**: 'very petty incident' to 'butcher generals': remarks to a journalist from the New York Herald, reported in the Petrogradskaya Pravda, 26 March 1921, CW XXXVI, 538. 'hoping for more trade': see Service, Spies and Commissars, 308–317. 'best port wine': Kotkin, 398. • **BERLIN**: for events in Saxony see Dirk Schumann, Political Violence in the Weimar Republic, 1918–1933: Fight for the Streets and Fear of Civil War, 2009 (trans. Thomas Dunlap), 59–76. For Hitler's Bavarian tour see speeches 15–21 March 1921, SA, 353–355. • **PARIS**: Littérature, No. 18, March 1921. • **ISTANBUL**: 'angry and depressed' to 'mad-house': personal letter from Horace Rumbold to Lord Curzon, 23 March 1921, NA, FO 800/157/91. The full official communication is in DBFP, First Series, Vol. XVII, 87–91, with 'Macedonian revolutionary' at 89. • **MUNICH**: 'introduces him to Erich Ludendorff':

Kellogg, 128. See also Weber, *Becoming Hitler*, 225–226. • **MILAN**: *'airplane and the bomb'*: Falasca-Zamponi, 73. *'Mantua'*: Christopher Duggan, *The Force of Destiny:A History of Italy since 1796*, 2007, 428. *'jack-in-the-boxes'* to *'gigantic, barbaric, universal'*: speech in Trieste, 6 February 1921, *OO* XVI, 150–160, 156–157. • **PARIS**: this description is drawn mostly from Brook-Shepherd, *Last Habsburg*, 248–275, which is based principally on Karl Werkmann, *Aus Kaiser Karls Nachlass*, 1925. • **DOORN**: *'give up their art collections'*: the Kaiser's doctor, quoted in Röhl, *Into the Abyss*, 1234.

Spring 1921

MOSCOW: *'peat industry'*: to Lunacharsky, 9 April 1921, *CW* XXXV, 484–485. *'give orders'*: Lenin to Skylansky, 9 April 1921, *TP* II, 444–446. *'harder to concentrate'*: Felshtinsky, 189–190. • **KINGSTON**: *'faces criticism'*: Grant, 289–290. *'good-for-nothing Jamaicans'*: speech by Garvey, 26 March 1921, *MG* III, 280–285, 281. • **INÖNÜ**: *'thunderous majesty'*: Mango, 311. *'hot snow or wooden iron'*: Ihrig, 30. • **PHILADELPHIA**: for an account of the origins of *Shuffle Along* see Cary D. Wintz and Paul Finkelman (eds.), *Encyclopedia of the Harlem Renaissance*, 2004, Vol. 2, 1108–1110. *'too dark'*: Baker and Bouillon, 27. • **NEW YORK**: for an account of Einstein's trip to America and Britain in the spring of 1921 see Fölsing, 495–509. For his media reception see József Illy, *Albert Meets America: How Journalists Treated Genius during Einstein's 1921 Travels*, 2006. *'not finished yet'* to *'political motives'*: 'Professor Einstein Here, Explains Relativity', *New York Times*, 3 April 1921. *'psychopathological'*: 'Psychopathic Relativity', *New York Times*, 5 April 1921. *'handbook'*: Grundmann, 191. *'official is congratulated'*: 'Jewish World Notes', *Dearborn Independent*, 23 April 1921. *'going to respond to every attack'*: 'Fervid Reception to Zionist Leaders', *New York Times*, 11 April 1921. • **DUBLIN**: *'laughs at de Valera'*: Coogan, *Michael Collins*, 208. *'forty-six casualties'*: 'Weekly Survey of the State of Ireland for Week Ended March 28th, 1921', NA, CAB 24/121/83. *'Castleconnell'*: Walsh, *Bitter Freedom*, 257. *'Nemesis may follow'*: 'Fight Between Parties of Police', *Guardian*, 19 April 1921. • **JERUSALEM**: *'All of us here today'*: remarks to a Palestinian Arab delegation, 2 April 1921, *WSC* IX, 1419–1421. *'full of sympathy for Zionism'*: remarks to a Zionist delegation, 2 April 1921, *WSC* IX, 1421–1422. *'moderate, friendly and statesmanlike'*: cabinet memorandum, 2 April 1921, *WSC* X, 1428–1431. • **DOORN**: *'compares his own dear Kaiserin'*: diary entry, 11 April 1921, Ilsemann, Vol. 1, 173–174. *'every common worker'*: letter of Wilhelm dated 17 April 1921, in Röhl, *Into the Abyss*, 1205. *'band of veterans of the war of 1870'*: 'Kaiserin's Body Back in Germany', *New York Times*, 19 April 1921. *'American newspapers estimate'*: 'Extol Hindenburg at Kaiserin's Bier', *New York Times*, 20 April 1921. *'Workers in Potsdam'*: 'Kundgebungen in Potsdam', *Vossische Zeitung*, 20 April 1921. • **ISTANBUL**: *'If it weren't such a tragedy'* to *'family menagerie'*: letter to her parents by Clover Dulles, 4 April 1921, AWD, Subseries 6B, Box 120, Folder 3. For the French offer and Wrangel's response see 'Repatriation of Cossacks in "Rechid Pasha" by French under False Pretences', NA, ADM 137/2500/A 307, and HIA, Vrangel Collection, Box 138, File 10. *'intercepting short-wave radio transmissions'*: Grose, 78–79; a large collection of General Wrangel's intelligence reports are held as part of the Vrangel Collection at the Hoover Institution. • BERLIN: for the Silesia crisis see F. Gregory Campbell, 'The Struggle for Upper Silesia, 1919–1922', *Journal of Modern History*, 42/3, 1970, 361–385. *'well-armed Polish-speaking soldiers'*: 'Allies Fighting Polish Invaders in Upper Silesia', *New York Times*, 5 May 1921. • WASHINGTON DC: *'reminders of his former position'*: details about the house, and a description of how it was purchased and so forth, can be found in Cooper, *Wilson*, 576; and Edith Wilson, 320–324. The house itself is now a museum open to the public. Woodrow's bedroom is just as Edith left it. She died in 1961. One of her last engagements was to invite the wife of newly elected President John F. Kennedy (born 1917) to tea to discuss the job of being the nation's First Lady. *'insists on hanging prominently'*: Cooper, *Wilson*, footnote on 665. *'seems not to want to know'* to *'self-consuming mind'*: diary of Ray Stannard Baker, 25 May 1921, *WW* LXVII, 288–289. *'business partner is duly dispatched'*: the partner is Woodrow Wilson's Secretary of State, Bainbridge Colby, who engages in 'the toils of the plasterers and carpenters' to get things ready. *WW* LXVII, from Bainbridge Colby, 9 July 1921, 347. *'or she did!'*: diary of Ray Stannard Baker, 27 May 1921, *WW* XLVII, 295. • PRINCETON: *'Marx Brothers comedy is enacted'*: 'Princeton Honors Fuss Dr. Einstein: Theory of Relativity Easier for German Scientist Than Getting a Degree – Grins at His Mistakes', *Evening Bulletin*, 10 May 1921, in Illy, 171–172. *'Kinertia'*: 'Kinertia versus Einstein', *Dearborn Independent*, 30 April 1921; for a discussion see Wazeck, 171–175. *'America is interesting'* to *'a wonderful sense'*: to Michele Besso, before 30 May 1921, *CPAE* XII, 182–183. • MUNICH: the letter is from Rudolf Hess, dated 17 May 1921, Deuerlein, *Aufstieg*, 132–133. • ROME: *'Papal letter'*: Dermot Keogh, *The Vatican, the Bishops and Irish Politics, 1919–1939*, 1986, 70. *'the hills of Ireland could be levelled'*: Michael Collins to Kitty Kiernan, 20 June 1921, Coogan, *Michael Collins*, 121. • VIENNA: *'bronze doppelgänger'*: to Ferenczi, 8 May 1921, *FR/FER* III, 55–56. • MOSCOW: *'Aren't you ashamed?'*: to A. V. Lunacharsky, 6 May 1921, *CW* LXV, 138–139. Quotations from *150,000,000* are taken from Vladimir Mayakovsky, *Selected Poems*, 2013 (trans. James H. McGavran III), 196–247. *'Can't we stop this?'*: to M. N. Pokrovsky, 6 May 1921, *CW* LXV, 139. *'Is it being done?'* to *'exact details'*: to Y. A. Litkens, 6 May 1921, *CW* XXXV, 489. • PARIS: for a detailed account of proceedings see Sanouillet, 186–194. • SAINT-CYR: Lacouture, 115. • ROME: Bosworth, 130. • CROTON-ON-HUDSON: Sheridan, *American Diary*, 129–130.

Summer 1921

SMYRNA: *'two topics of conversation'*: letter to her parents by Clover Dulles, 21 June 1921, AWD, Subseries 6B, Box 120, Folder 3. • MOSCOW: *'quick calculation'* to *'circulated widely'*: Lenin to Skylansky, 30 May 1921, *TP* II, 458–461. *'a push'*: report to the Tenth All-Russian Conference of the Communist Party on the tax in kind, 26 May 1921, *CW* XXXII, 402–416, 415. *'long time'* to *'unstable equilibrium'*: closing speech to Tenth All-Russian Conference, *CW* XXXII, 436–437. *'if revolution occurs'* to *'conjectures on that score'*: Robert Service's translation for the first part in *A Political Life*, Vol. 3, 213. *'bandits'* to *'measures are properly enforced'*: Pipes, *Russia under the Bolshevik Regime*, 386–388; Figes, 768–769. • **Washington DC**: for the origins of the 1921 Immigration Act see John Higham, *Strangers in the Land: Patterns of American Nativism, 1860–1925*, 1955, particularly 300–311. *'perverted ideas'* to *'economic parasites'*: Special Session of the Congress, March 1921, in Jonathan Spiro, *Defending the Master Race: Conservation, Eugenics and the Legacy of Madison Grant*, 2009, 226. *'dash into harbour'*: Higham, 312. • **Berlin**: *'Dancing couples'* to *'theory of relativity'*: Wazeck, 71. *'rooms above a bakery'*: Fölsing, 510. *'toy dogs'* to *'magic spell'*: the remarks originally appeared in the *Nieuwe Rotterdamsche Courant*, and were then reported in the *New York Times* in the 8 July 1921 edition. *'accursed Jew'*: from an unknown sender, after 4 July 1921, *CPAE* XII, 214. *'Another person in Mexico'*: Sheridan, *American Diary*, 196. *'several weeks in the German capital'*: Thomas Friedrich, *Hitler's Berlin: Abused City*, 2012 (trans. Stewart Spencer), 28. *'not be able to lie to history'*: postcard to Fritz Lauböck, 25 June 1921, *SA*, 435. • **Istanbul**: Cohn, 71–83. For Dulles, see Grose. • **New York**: *'pre-breakfast whistling tune'*: advertisement for *Shuffle Along* in *New York Herald*, 29 May 1921. *'infectious score'*: 'Shuffle Along Premiere', *New York Times*, 23 May 1921. *'breeze of super-jazz'*: review in the *Evening Journal*, as advertised in the *New York Herald* as above. *'strange workings of the Caucasian mind'* to *'should continue to shuffle along'*: 'Shuffle Along Latest Musical Gem to Invade Broadway', *New York Age*, 4 June 1921. • **Moscow**: for a colourful account of the congress and the characters in Moscow see Serge, 158–171. *'with us in spirit'*: Zinoviev's opening speech on 22 June 1921, *To the Masses: Proceedings of the Third Congress of the Communist International, 1921* (trans. John Riddell), 2015, 74–82. *'Petit bourgeois'*: Serge, 166 (the 2012 version translates to English). *'developing'* to *'ripe'*: 'Theses on Tactics and Strategy', drafted by Karl Radek, in *To the Masses*, as above, 924–950, 924. *'does not develop in a straight line'*: ibid., 925. *'bêtises de Béla Kun'*: Serge, 163 (Lenin spoke in French, though the 2012 version of Serge's book translates into English). *'an émigré myself'*: note to the participants in a sitting of the commission on tactics, 7 July 1921, *CW* XLV, 203–204. *'Whoever arrives in Russia'* to *'our open enemy'*: Trotsky's intervention on a discussion of the Italian question, 29 June 1921, in *To the Masses*, 374–379, 378–379. *'refusing to travel there'*: Kotkin, 415. • **Tulsa**: for a detailed account see Alfred Brophy, *Reconstructing the Dreamland: The Tulsa Riot of 1921*, 2002, 28–65. *'haven't negroes the right'*: 'Thirty Whites Held for Tulsa Rioting', *New York Times*, 5 June 1921. • **Belfast**: *'appeal to all Irishmen'*: Coogan, *Michael Collins*, 214. • **Moscow**: *'latest calculation'*: ideas about a state economic plan, 4 July 1921, *CW* XXXII, 497–498. *'humanitarian appeal'*: Figes, 760. *'free of squeaks'*: Volkogonov, *Lenin*, 410. • **London**: *'more ill-will'*: Coogan, *DeValera*, 230. *'map is of the Mercator type'*: ibid., 231. *'chant the rosary'*: 'The Premier Meets Mr De Valera', *Guardian*, 15 July 1921. • **Rome**: for the pact of pacification see Bosworth, 131–133. *'far horizon'* to *'thousands of local elements'*: 'Fatto Compiuto', *Il Popolo d'Italia*, 3 August 1921, *OO* XVII, 80–83, 83. *'see if D'Annunzio can be persuaded'*: Renzo De Felice, *D'Annunzio Politico, 1918–1938*, 1978, 169; and Hughes-Hallett, 581. • **London**: for an account of the discussions see Frank Pakenham, *Peace by Ordeal: An*

Account, from First-Hand Sources, of the Negotiation and Signature of the Anglo-Irish Treaty 1921, 1962; and Geoffrey Shakespeare, *Let Candles Be Brought In*, 1949. For Lloyd George speaking Welsh and de Valera speaking English, Shakespeare, 83. *'reminded of being on a circus horse'*: Shakespeare, 76. *'draws a diagram'*: Coogan, *Michael Collins*, 231. • ESKİŞEHİR: see McMeekin, 454–455. • NEW YORK: for an account of Garvey's time as the ship's purser see Grant, 295. For Garvey's speech in New York see speech dated 20 July 1921, *MG* III, 532–545. *'conquer Africa'* to *'become so powerful'*: ibid., 540. *'Negro traitors'* to *'like a piece of cotton'*: ibid., 542–543. • LONDON: *'trips on her high heels'*: *CH/CH*, 237. *'dancing in full swing'*: letter from Clementine to Winston Churchill, 9 August 1921, 240. • BERLIN: for the episode with Dickel and Hitler's resignation see Joachimsthaler, 285–287; Weber, *Becoming Hitler*, 263–264; and for a slightly wider view Kershaw, 160–165. *'check these quotes'* to *'iron leadership'*: letter to NSDAP committee, 14 July 1921, *SA*, 436–438. *'pamphlet'*: Deuerlein, *Aufstieg*, 138–140. • DOORN: *'very lively'*: Röhl, *Into the Abyss*, 1207. *'Chamberlain's latest book'*: letter from the Kaiser in August 1921 thanking him for his 'wonderful' book, in *HSC* II, 259. *'order of the decent people'*: Röhl, *Into the Abyss*, 1235. • ACROSS ANATOLIA: *'No one is safe'*: Gingeras, 285–289. *'Foreign observers accuse'*: Arnold Toynbee, *The Western Question*, 1922, 301. *'"subconscious" pre-human animal'*: Toynbee, 263. • LONDON: for Philip Graves's articles from *The Times* demonstrating the falsity of the *Protocols*, see *The Truth about 'The Protocols': A Literary Forgery*, 1921. *'thanked The Times'*: speech in Rosenheim, 9 August 1921, *SA*, 458. • GORKI: *'so tired'*: to Maxim Gorky, 9 August 1921, *CW* XLV, 249. *'disguised interventionists'* to *'capacity for these things'*: to V. M. Molotov, 11 August 1921, *CW* XLV, 250–251. *'neither treatment, nor work'*: to Maxim Gorky, 9 August 1921, *CW* XLV, 249. • DUBLIN: for the exchanges over the summer months see *Official Correspondence Relating to the Peace Negotiations, June–September, 1921*, 1921. *'take to the beaches'*: Walsh, *Bitter Freedom*, 284. *'peaceful and undisturbed'*: 'Weekly Survey of the State of Ireland for Week Ended August 29th, 1921', NA CAB 24/127/94. *'find myself looking at friends'*: letter to Harry Boland dated July 1921, in Coogan, *Michael Collins*, 232. *'argue the matter late into the night'*: Hart, 290–291. • HORTON BAY: *'afternoon swim'*: Baker, 80–81. *'first American killed in Italy'*: Meyers, *Hemingway*, 60. • RIVER SAKARYA: *'three weeks in late summer'*: for an account of the Battle of Sakarya see McMeekin, 456–458. McMeekin calls it 'the last real battle of the First World War'. *'Bon voyage'*: Edib, 288 • NEW YORK: *'messages for various world leaders'*: see *MG* III, 585–587. *'greatest state social event'*: 'First UNIA Court Reception', 27 August 1921, *MG* III, 698–706, 698. *'congress of rats'* to *'disgrace to Harvard'*: ibid., 606. *'tinsel show'*: enclosure dated 23 September 1921, *MG* IV, 74–77, 75. *'sympathetic British politicians'*: 'Treatment of African Natives', *Guardian*, 29 August 1921, and 'The Pan African Manifesto', *Times*, 30 August 1921. For an account of the congress in London and Brussels (including the presence of Belgian officials, and a trip to a museum where Congo's great mineral wealth is advertised), see Jessie Fauset, 'Impressions of the Second Pan-African Congress', *The Crisis*, November 1921. *'Bolshevik talk'*: reproducing article from *La Dépêche Coloniale et Maritime*, 31 August

1921, *MG* IX, 158–159. *'colored American cannot withstand'*: 'Denounce our Haiti Policy', *New York Times*, 6 September 1921; Du Bois subsequently denied having said this: see, 'Africa for the Africans', *The Crisis*, February 1922. For a further account of proceedings in Paris, where a delegate from Guadeloupe declares: 'I consider it a joy to be a member of that nation which made the revolution of 1789', see 'Transcription from Paris Session', 4 September 1921, WEB, Series 1a. For Du Bois's onward trip to Geneva see Fauset's article, as above. • **Moscow**: *'recommendations for improvement'*: for examples of Lenin's hectoring communications from this period, see his notes to M. I. Friumkin and others, 17 August 1921, *CW* XLV, 257, and to V. S. Dovgalevsky, 2 September 1921, *CW* XXXV, 519–520. *'donates all unconsecrated vessels'*: Pipes, *Under the Bolshevik Regime*, 347. • **Hildesheim**: for an account of the gathering see Phyllis Grosskurth, 'The Idyll in the Harz Mountains', in Toby Gelfand and John Kerr (eds.), *Freud and the History of Psychoanalysis*, 1992, 341–355. *'practical joke'*: Jones, *Freud*, Vol. 3, 85. *'expression of the loss of value'* to *'form no estimate'*: 'Psychoanalyis and Telepathy', translated from 1921 manuscript, *SE* XVIII, 175–193, 177. *'if I were at the beginning'*: to Hereward Carrington, 24 July 1921, in *LSF* (ed. Ernst L. Freud, trans. Tania and James Stern), 339–340. • **Doorn**: *'Baroness Sunshine'* and *'hardly anyone left'*: Röhl, *Into the Abyss*, 1207.

Autumn 1921

Munich: *'pacifistic, defeatist thinking'*: Erich Ludendorff, *Kriegführung und Politik*, 1922, 332. *'insufficient race-consciousness'*: ibid., 337. *'uplifting Dutch song'*: ibid., 342. • **Moscow**: for the famine, and American relief efforts, see H. H. Fisher, *The Famine in Soviet Russia, 1919–1923: The Operations of the American Relief Administration*, 1927; and Bertrand M. Patenaude, *The Big Show in Bololand: The American Relief Expedition to Soviet Russia in the Famine of 1921*, 2002. *'first delivery of food aid'*: Fisher, 79–82. *'new cafés for the rich'*: 'Moscow is Buying and Selling Again', *New York Times*, 10 September 1921. *'fresh pastries'* and the reappearance of produce for those that can pay under the New Economic Policy, see in particular Serge, 172; Goldman, *Living my Life*, Vol. 2, 897–899; and Alexander Berkman, *The Bolshevik Myth*, 1925, 319. • **Vienna**: this account is drawn from Alfred Kardiner, *My Analysis with Freud*, 1977. *'Rosenkavalier'*: ibid., 91. *'paper on the spider'*: ibid., 83. *'the imitation Freud'*: ibid., 84. *'American from Atlanta'*: ibid., 75–76. *'desist from writing'* to *'not productive'*: ibid., 85–86. *'unanalysed'*: ibid., 86. *'I take this to be an insult'*: ibid., 87. • **Munich**: *'dragged down from the podium'*: party circular dated 24 September 1921, *SA*, 492–493. *'Just as during the war'*: speech to SA, 5 October 1921, *SA*, 499. *'any Jew takes offence'* to *'Honour these colours'*: party circular dated 17 September 1921, *SA*, 483–484. • **Moscow**: for the growth of different acronyms in the Soviet regime see T. H. Rigby, 'Staffing USSR Incorporated: The Origins of the Nomenklatura System', *Soviet Studies*, 40/4, 1988, 523–537; Graeme Gill, *The Origins of the Stalinist Political System*, 2010. *'Don't economise'*: Angelica Balabanoff, *Impressions of Lenin*, 1964 (trans. Isotta Cesari), 29–30. *'gets* *his wife expelled'*: Robert H. McNeal, *Stalin: Man and Ruler*, 1988, 46. • **DOORN**: *'book by an English guest'*: Norah Bentinck, *The Ex-Kaiser in Exile*, 1921. *'Best of all I'd like'*: diary entry 16 October 1921, Ilsemann, Vol. 2, 191–195, 192. • **LOS ANGELES**: for Clare's time in California see Sheridan, *American Diary*, 299–350. *'apparently read her books'*: ibid., 303. *'ends up being mobbed'*: 'Charlie Chaplin in England', *Guardian*, 12 September 1921, and 'Hope to See Much of England', *Guardian*, 12 September 1921, *'much sadder place'*: Sheridan, *American Diary*, 333. *'not a Bolshevik'*: ibid., 333–334. *'I find him very interesting'*: ibid., 341. *'referred to as "brother"'*: ibid., 343. *'harangues the dunes'*: ibid., 347. • **TARRENZ BEI IMST**: Polizzotti, 160–163. For Breton's account of his meeting with Freud, 'Interview du Professeur Freud à Vienne', *Littérature*, March 1922. • **WASHINGTON DC**: *'national disgrace'*: unpublished statements, 20 October 1921, *WW* LXVII, 428. *'insists on slowing down'*: Axson, 243. *'America First'*: to Louis Dembitz Brandeis, 6 November 1921, *WW* LXVII, 443. • **MOSCOW**: *'Why not begin to prepare'* to *'getting off the track'*: James D. White, 'Early Historical Interpretations of the Russian Revolution, 1918–1924', *Soviet Studies*, 37/3, 1985, 330–352, 344. *'Lenintrotsky'*: James H. Meisel, *Counter-Revolution: How Revolutions Die*, 1966, viii. • **LONDON**: for an overall account see Pakenham, *Peace by Ordeal*. For a shorter and judicious account of the negotiations and de Valera's reaction to the result see Fanning, 108–129. For the letters and notes exchanged on the Irish side see *DIFP*, Vol. 1, 274–361, which lays out the progress of the negotiations in great detail. *'Hans Place'* to *'good-humoured Irishman'*: Walsh, 311. *'place feel less strange'* to *'Inventions of the Devil'*: Margery Forester, *Michael Collins: The Lost Leader*, 1971, 217. *'in the mood for peace'*: Thomas Jones, *Whitehall Diary*, Vol. 3, *Ireland 1918–1925*, 1971 (ed. Keith Middlemas), 123. *'most difficult part'*: Arthur Griffith to Éamon de Valera, 12 October 1921, *DIFP*, Vol. 1, 274. *'never allow myself'*: Hart, 297. *'Fertile in expedients'*: Forester, 219. *'for love of our beautiful eyes'*: Arthur Griffith to Éamon de Valera, 13 October 1921, *DIFP*, Vol. 1, 275. *'Good feelings are better'*: Hart, 298. *'you have made the position'*: Nicholas Mansergh, *The Unresolved Question: The Anglo-Irish Settlement and its Undoing 1912–1972*, 1991, 219. *'the word "adhere"'*: Pakenham, *Peace by Ordeal*, 177. *'matter of drafting'*: Jones, *Whitehall Diary*, Vol. 3, 142. • **BOLOGNA**: *'My little paunch'*: to Ilse Einstein, 9 November 1921, *CPAE* XII, 339–340. *'still very childish'* and *'Another pretty housemaid!'*: to Elsa Einstein, 9 November 1921, *CPAE* XII, 344–346. • **NEW YORK**: *'gray days of the revolution'*: 'Women are Real Equals in Russia, Leader Declares', 11 October 1921, *St. Louis Star and Times*. *'memorial service'*: for details of the service, including Bryant's poem, Souvenir Programme to John Reed Memorial, 17 October 1921, JRP, MS Am 1091, Series VI, 1357. *'Russia is being crucified'*: Dearborn, *Bryant*, 178. *'they find devastation'*: the following descriptions from Fisher, 85–111. *'sixty-eight thousand Russians'*: statistics in Fisher, 556–557. *'Children's flesh'*: Figes, 777. *'had enough of her'*: Fisher, 97–98. *'strategical retreat'* to *'prelude to its victory?'*: report to the Second All-Russia Congress of Political Education Departments, 17 October 1921, *CW* XXXIII, 60–79, 63. *'several doors'*: ibid., 65. *'you will learn'*: ibid., 72. *'number of transitional stages'*: 'Fourth Anniversary of the Revolution', written 14 October 1921, published in *Pravda* 18 October 1921,

CW XXXIII, 51–59, 58. *'wholesale merchant'*: ibid., 59. *'mass of current work'* to *'becoming tired'*: *Lenin: Life and Works*, 186. • **LONDON**: *'spied upon at Mass'*: Jones, *Whitehall Diary*, Vol. 3, 134. *'lonely splendour'*: Forester, 222. *'visits an old friend in jail'*: 'Memorandum/ Michael Collins/Wormwood Scrubs, October 20 1921', NA, HO 532/8. • **NEW YORK**: *'lighten her skin'*: Baker and Bouillon, 28. For Baker's hiring, see Baker and Bouillon, 31; and Haney, 37. • **DUBLIN**: *'no question of our asking the Irish'*: *DIFP*, Vol. 1, 25 October 1921, 291–292. • **BIRMINGHAM**: for the text of Harding's speech quoted here see *Address of the President of the United States at the Semicentennial of the Founding of the City of Birmingham, Alabama*, 1921. *'daredevil pilot'*: 'Crowds Pouring In', *Birmingham News*, 25 October 1921. *'great cheers'*: 'Harding Says Negro Must Have Equality in Political Life', *New York Times*, 27 October 1921. *'Michael King'*: the father of Martin Luther King, Jr.: for this episode see Martin Luther King, Sr., *Daddy King: An Autobiography*, 1980, 69–71. *'Senator from Mississippi'* to *'Supremacist assumptions'*: 'Praise and Assail Harding Negro Talk', *New York Times*, 28 October 1921. *'Marcus Garvey welcomes'*: 'Negroes Endorse Speech', *New York Times*, 27 October 1921. *'man of great vision'* to *'lynch and burn'*: speech dated 30 October 1921, *MG* IV, 141–151, 143. *'If I cannot be'*: ibid., 149. *'bleach up ourselves'* and *'great slap'*: ibid., 150 (see also 144). • **LONDON**: *'great deal of good'* to *'I was happy'*: Forester, 236. *'privately informing the King'*: Jones, *Whitehall Diary*, Vol. 3, 156. *'sits facing the door'*: Forester, 238. • **DÜBENDORF AIRFIELD**: the October restoration attempt is described in Brook-Shepherd, *Last Habsburg*, 281–300. *'time of the Crusades'*: Zita's diary entry date 9 November 1921, ibid., 310. *'Not that it matters'*: Zita's diary 15 November 1921, ibid., 312. • **ROME**: *'reported as news'*: 'Dopo il Duello Mussolini Ciccotti', *Il Popolo d'Italia*, 30 October 1921, *OO* XVII, 201–203. *'more subtle duel'*: Bosworth, 133–135. • **MOSCOW**: *'after trying revolutionary methods'* to *'confined yourselves'*: 'The Importance of Gold Now and After the Complete Victory of Socialism', published in *Pravda*, 6–7 November 1921, *CW* XXXIII, 109–116, 110. *'public lavatories'* and *'kill twenty million'*: ibid., 113. • **KANSAS CITY**: *'America Impresses'*: 'America Impresses the Allied War Chiefs with Youth, Hope, Bigness and Fairness', *New York Times*, 2 November 1921. *'France did not want war'*: 'Foch Says World Must Have Peace', *New York Times*, 5 November 1921. *'carried by telephone cable'*: 'Cities Observe Day from East to West', *New York Times*, 12 November 1921. *'rain of ruin from the aircraft'*: 'President Harding's Address at the Burial of the Unknown American Soldier', slightly abbreviated, *New York Times*, 12 November 1921. *'naval disarmament conference'*: for the importance of the conference see Tooze, 394–407. • **BUKHARA**: for this final adventure of Enver Pasha see Fromkin, 479–490. • **ROME**: for attitudes towards Einstein's theories in Italy see Barbara J. Reeves, 'Einstein Politicized: The Early Reception of Relativity in Italy', in Thomas Glick (ed.), *The Comparative Reception of Relativity*, 1987, 189–229. For Mussolini's article, 'Relativismo e Fascismo', *Il Popolo d'Italia*, 22 November 1921 in *OO* XVII, 267–269. *'super-relativist movement'* to *'intuition and fragments'*: ibid., 267. • **MOSCOW**: for accounts of this episode see McNeal, 47; Kun, 256–258; and Kotkin, 593–594. *'worries about the Georgian's health'*: to Lydia Fotieva, 26 December 1921, *PSS* LIV, 99. *'vacating of the apartment'* to *'obstacles'*: to A. S. Yenukidze, November 1921, *CW* XXXV, 531.

'*Stalin must have a quiet flat*' to '*mint are being selected*': Kun, 258. • **DUBLIN**: '*if you sign this thing*': Pakenham, *Peace by Ordeal*, 260. '*job to be done*': Forester, 247. '*Journalists are told*': Pakenham, 272. '*peace or war?*': Lloyd George gives this word special resonance by rolling the 'r's in the Welsh fashion, as reported in Shakespeare, 53. '*which letter am I to send?*': Pakenham, 298. '*hung from the lamp posts*': this is Barton's recollection reported in Hart, 318. '*suggesting the Black and Tans be assigned a new role*': Jones, *Whitehall Diary*, Vol. 3, 185. '*When you have sweated*' to '*death warrant*': letter to O'Kane quoted in Pakenham, 166. '*no small change*': Shakespeare, 91. '*sits with his entourage*' to '*Dante Alighieri*': Fanning, 122–123. • **NEW YORK**: 'President Harding and Social Equality', *The Crisis*, December 1921. • **SFAYAT**: for the story of the Russians in Tunisia see Hélène Menegaldo, 'Les russes à Bizerte: de la Tunisie à la France, les étapes d'une intégration contrariée', *Mémoire(s), identité(s), marginalité(s) dans le monde occidental contemporain*, 13, 2015, available online at http://journals.openedition.org/mimmoc/2077 ; DOI : 10.4000/mimmoc.2077. '*PrinceYusupov*' and '*British admiral*': HIA, Vrangel Collection, Box 141, File 17. '*long letter to Henry Ford*' and '*Winston Churchill*': HIA, Vrangel Collection, Box 139, File 11. • **MUNICH**: '*professional boxer*': speech to the SA, 30 November 1921, *SA*, 527. '*special camps could be set up*': report of a discussion dated 8 December 1921, *SA*, 530. This trip to Berlin is sometimes dated 1922. For a discussion see Friedrich, 30 and relevant footnotes. • **THE SS *LEOPOLDINA***: '*acquits himself well*': letter to the Hemingway family, 20 December 1921, *LEH* I, 310–311. '*remarkable strength of the old fishermen*': Baker, 83–84. Hemingway turned his trip to Vigo into a newspaper story, 'Tuna Fishing in Spain', in the *Toronto Star Weekly*, 18 February 1922. '*one suitcase*' and '*younger sister*': Paul Smith, '1924: Hemingway's Luggage and the Miraculous Year', in Scott Donaldson (ed.), *The Cambridge Companion to Hemingway*, 1996, 36–54, 39–40; and, for the detail on Miss Beach's younger sister, Polizzotti, 78. • **DEARBORN**: '*As the Jewish propagandists*' to '*tell the truth*': 'The Jewish Associates of Benedict Arnold', *Dearborn Independent*, 8 October 1921. '*fomenting war in Palestine*': 'How the Jews use Power – by an Eyewitness', *Dearborn Independent*, 17 September 1921. '*game of baseball*': 'How the Jews Degraded Baseball', *Dearborn Independent*, 10 September 1921. '*abandoned sensuousness*': 'Jewish Jazz – Moron Music – Becomes Our National Music', *Dearborn Independent*, 10 August 1921. • **MANCHESTER**: '*hope in 1922*': Sam to Sigmund, 29 December 1921, JRL, Freud Collection, GB133 SSF 1/2/23. • **DUBLIN**: '*fitting peace terms*' and '*Well done all*': *Times* and *Daily Mail* quoted in Pakenham, *Peace by Ordeal*, 327. '*full of blessings*': *Freeman's Journal*, 9 December 1921, quoted in Ian Kenneally, 'Truce to Treaty: Irish Journalists and the 1920–1921 Peace Process', in Kevin Rafter (ed.), *Irish Journalism before Independence: More a Disease than a Profession*, 2011, 213–225, 220. '*rejoicing in Melbourne*': 'Prime Minister's Message', *Sydney Morning Herald*, 8 December 1921. '*American Senators*': 'The Peace Celebrated in America', *Guardian*, 10 December 1921. '*Indian nationalists*': there is a long history of these connections with inspiration running both ways; see, for example, Keith Jeffery, 'The Road to Asia, and the Grafton Hotel, Dublin: Ireland in the "British World"', *Irish Historical Studies*, 36/42, 2008, 243–256; and Michael Silvestri, '"The Sinn Fein of

India": Irish Nationalism and the Policing of RevolutionaryTerrorism in Bengal', *Journal of British Studies*, 39/4, 2000, 454–486. *'Garvey sends a telegram'*: reported in speech dated 11 December 1921, *MG* IV, 259–270, 260. *'our own fellows'* to *'good enough for them'*: Forester, 260. *'fiasco'* and *'awful state'*: Kathleen O'Connell's diary in Fanning, 124. *'steps between Ireland and her hopes'*: *Irish Times*, 9 December 1921, in Kenneally, 221. For the Dáil debates see Fanning, 126–129. For the full text of the debates, *Iris Dhail Éireann. Tuairisg oifigiúl. Díosbóireacht ar an glonnradh idir Éire agus Sasana. Do signigheadh i Lundain ar an badh lá de mhí na Nodlag, 1921. Official Report. Debate on the Treaty between Great Britain and Ireland. Signed in London on the 6th December, 1921*, 1922 available online at https://www.oireachtas.ie. *'If I am a traitor'*: *Official Report*, 14 December 1921. *'Michael Collins'* to *'follow him there?'*: Mary MacSwiney, *Official Report*, 21 December 1921. *'gives us freedom'* to *'living approve of it'*: Michael Collins, *Official Report*, 19 December 1921. *'subverting the Republic'*: Éamon de Valera, *Official Report*, 19 December 1921. *'men are bitter'*: letter dated Christmas 1921, in Foster, 204. *'grammarian's formula'*: *Freeman's Journal*, 22 December 1921, in Kenneally, 222. *'the worst day I ever spent'*: Forester, 271. • **ATLANTA**: *'kind gentleman'*: Dean, 151. • **MOSCOW**: *'Cheka in all languages'* to *'stronger than us'*: report to the Ninth All-Russia Congress of Soviets, 23 December 1921, *CW* XXXIII, 143–177, 175. *'accuses the American Relief Administration'*: ibid., 176. *'feed one million'*: Fisher, 556–557. *'closer we approach'*: Lenin's speech as before, 176. • **ZURICH**: *'nice if you could spend Christmas with us'*: from Eduard and Hans-Albert Einstein, 31 December 1921, *CPAE* XII, 402. *'meets a pretty Austrian girl'*: Kardiner, 91–92.

Winter 1922

Mussolini quote is from a speech made in the Chamber of Deputies and produced as 'Per la Vera Pacificazione', 1 December 1921, *OO* XVII, 289–300, 295.

DEARBORN: for the end of Henry Ford's campaign see Baldwin, 164–166. • **KOSTINO**: *'room in one of the secondary properties'*: Ulyanov, 127. *'Krupp'*: to Politburo and others, 23 January 1922, *CW* XXXV, 448–449. *'Soviet film industry'*: directives on the film business, 17 January 1922, *CW* XLII, 388–389. *'not moved ahead one iota'*: to D. I. Kursky, 17 January 1922, *CW* XXXV, 533–534. • **DUBLIN**: *'national theatres'* to *'chrysalis'*: *Official Report*, Piaras Béaslaí, 3 January 1922. *'you all know me'* to *'I know the English'*: Constance Markievicz, 3 January 1922, ibid. *'can have unity by rejecting this thing'*: Liam Mellowes, 4 January 1922, ibid. *'no soft talk'* to *'no union'*: Mary MacSwinney, 7 January 1922, ibid. *'that is tyranny'*: Patrick Hogan, 9 January 1922, ibid. *'Mexican politics'*: Michael Collins, 9 January 1922, ibid. *'will want us yet'* to *'want you now'*: Éamon de Valera and Michael Collins, 9 January 1922, ibid. *'Deserters all!'* to *'Foreigners, Americans ... English!'*: exchanges between Michael Collins, David Kent and others, 10 January 1922, ibid. • **MUNICH**: *'Ernst Toller'* to *'without understanding them'*: Toller, 255–257. *'lock us up'* to '*enriched by the experience*': speech at the Hofbräuhaus, 30 January 1922, *SA*, 558–559. '*Hitler should be treated generously*': Joachimsthaler, 296. • **PARIS**: '*pointless to name more specifically*': Polizzotti, 171. '*After Dada*': 'Après Dada', *Comoedia*, 2 March 1922. '*Leave everything, leave Dada*': André Breton, 'Lâchez Tout', *Littérature*, No. 2 (new series), April 1922. • **NEW YORK**: '*famine relief edition*': as advertised in *Soviet Russia*, 6/2, February 1922. A copy of this edition is available electronically from the University of Michigan library at https://babel.hathitrust.org/cgi/pt?id=mdp.39015069769571;view=1up;seq=5. • **DUBLIN**: '*castle has fallen!*': Forester, 278. '*conference for the worldwide Irish diaspora*': Gerard Keown, 'The Irish Race Conference, 1922, Reconsidered', *Irish Historical Studies*, 32/127, 2001, 365–376. • **PARIS**: for Hemingway's first stint in Paris see Meyers, *Hemingway*, 62–90. Hemingway's *Toronto Star* articles are all available in *Dateline: Toronto*. '*key to Paris*': 'Living on $1,000 a Year in Paris', *Toronto Star Weekly*, 4 February 1922. '*Russian émigrés*': 'Paris is Full of Russians', *Toronto Daily Star*, 25 February 1922. For Russians in Paris from a historical perspective see Robert Johnston, *New Mecca, New Babylon: Paris and the Russian Exiles, 1920–1945*, 1988. '*man with a goatee called Vladimir*': Rappaport, *Conspirator*, 218. '*scum of Greenwich Village*': 'American Bohemians in Paris', *Toronto Star Weekly*, 25 March 1922. '*Paris is so very beautiful*' and '*about 55*': to Grace Hemingway, 14/15 February 1922, *LEH* I, 327–330. '*real writer at last*': by May he has six sentences, which he titles *Paris 1922*; see Baker, *Hemingway*, 90–91. '*The mills of the gods grind slowly*': poem entitled 'Mitraigliatrice', first published in 1923 as part of *Three Stories and Ten Poems*; Carlos Baker notes the poem as being sent for possible publication in Chicago at the end of 1922 in Baker, *Hemingway*, 90. • **ISTANBUL**: '*Sultan shuts his eyes*': Mango, 336. • **MUNICH**: quotations here from speech at the Zirkus Krone, 2 February 1922, *SA*, 565. • **WASHINGTON DC**: '*from a democracy*': John Sandlin, *Congressional Record*, 18 January 1922. '*In Pennsylvania*': Thomas Bell, *Congressional Record*, 18 January 1922. '*public debauchery*' to '*lynching will end*': 'The Lynching Bill', *The Crisis*, February 1922. '*wave of jubilation*': James Weldon Johnson, *Along This Way: The Autobiography of James Weldon Johnson*, 1945, 366. • **GORKI**: '*Stalin's apartment*': to Enukidze, 13 February 1922, *PSS* LIV, 161–162. '*departments are shit*': to A. D. Tsyurupa, 21 February 1922, *CW* XXXVI, 566. '*including the firing squad*' to '*good practices*': letter to D. I. Kursky, 20 February 1922, *CW* XXXVI, 560–565. • **WASHINGTON DC**: '*I love you*': to Edith Wilson, 14 February 1922, *WW* XLVII, 545. The Document: Cooper, *Wilson*, 586–588. • **ACROSS IRELAND**: '*Yard sales*': Walsh, 334. '*wade through Irish blood*': full speech in *Speeches and Statements by Éamon de Valera*, 97–104. '*no republican any more*': Coogan, *Michael Collins*, 316. '*match-and-petrol men*': *Irish News*, 19 April 1922, in Coogan, *Michael Collins*, 358. '*say your prayers*': ibid., 352. • **GORKI**: '*imagines himself somewhere on a mountainside*': 'Notes of a Publicist' (intended for an article which was not published in his lifetime), written end February 1922, *CW* XXXIII, 204–211. '*old Russian fable of the eagle and the hen*': W. R. S. Ralston, *Krilof and his Fables*, 1885, 227–228. '*made to retire at fifty*': Service, *Lenin*, 439. • **BELGRADE**: apart from Wrangel's own memoirs, for the departure of Wrangel's men to Serbia and other places see Bruno Bagni, 'Lemnos: L'Île des Cosaques', *Cahiers du Monde Russe*, 50/1, 2009, 187–230. '*one-eyed Russian*

admiral': 'Wrangel Refugees Arrive in Steerage', *New York Times*, 17 March 1922.
• VIENNA: quotes from letter to Lou Andreas-Salomé, 13 March 1922, *FR/SAL*, 113–114.
For Breton's account of his meeting with Freud, 'Interview du Professeur Freud à
Vienne', *Littérature*, March 1922. • QUINTA DO MONTE: Brook-Shepherd, *Last Habsburg*,
327–330. *'a piece of history'*: 'ExKaiser Karl', 2 April 1922, *Neue Freie Presse*. • MUNICH:
'takes up residence': Joachimsthaler, 298. *'only the leader of the Social Democrats'*: recollections of one of those present at the meeting in Werner Maser, *Die Frühgeschichte der
NSDAP: Hitlers Weg bis 1924*, 1965, 335. • MOSCOW: translation from McGavran III,
85–87, though I have used the Russian terms at the beginning of the acronyms. *'not
an admirer of his poetical talent'*: speech to congress of metalworkers, 6 March 1922,
CW XXXIII, 212–226, 223. *'huge quantities of material'* to *'through it all'*: ibid., 224.

Spring 1922

BERLIN: 'Miscellanea Berlinese (Dal nostro Direttore)', *Il Popolo d'Italia*, 14 March 1922,
OO, XVIII, 94–97. • NEW YORK: *'seven thousand books'*: letter dated 26 April 1922, LOC,
Sigmund Freud Collection, Family Papers, 1851–1978, mss39990, box 1. • KORZINKINO
VILLAGE: letter to Molotov for Politburo, 19 March 1922, Lenin, *Unknown Lenin*, 152–155.
• DOORN: *'like this my whole life!'*: diary entry 13 April 1922, Ilsemann, Vol. 1, 204. *'like
Finnish women'*: 28 April 1922, ibid., 208. *'burgeoning epistolary romance'*: Röhl, *Into the
Abyss*, 1209. • WEXFORD: *'country is now in a more lawless'*: Coogan, *Michael Collins*, 315.
'absolutely independent of Mr de Valera': 'Interview with Leader of the Rebels', *Guardian*,
15 April 1922. *'Yours is the faith'* to *'Take it'*: Coogan, *De Valera*, 314. *'tells an American
journalist'*: interview, 28 April 1922, quoted in Bill Kissane, *The Politics of the Irish Civil
War*, 2005, 154. *'talk, talk, all the time'*: letter to Kitty Kiernan dated 15 April 1922,
Hart, *Mick*, 370. *'worldwide ridicule'*: Coogan, *Michael Collins*, 323. • MUNICH: *'as a human
and as a Christian'* and following: speech in the Bürgerbräukeller, 22 April 1922, *SA*,
607–625, 623. *'dog is named Wolf'*: Joachimsthaler, 298. • PARIS: *'extracting from his throat'*
and Einstein's lecture at the Collège de France: Charles Nordmann, 'Einstein Discute
et Expose sa Théorie', *Revue des Deux Mondes*, May 1922, 129–166. *'stays out till two'* to
'caricaturist': 'Avant de quitter Paris, le Professeur Einstein nous dit ses impressions', *Le
Petit Parisien*, 10 April 1922, reproduced in *CPAE* XIII, 833–835. *'pretty young Frenchwoman'*:
Charles Nordmann, 'Avec Einstein dans les Régions Devastées', *L'Illustration*, 15 April
1922. *'philosopher Henri Bergson'*: Jimena Canales, 'Einstein, Bergson and the Experiment
that Failed: Intellectual Cooperation at the League of Nations', *Modern Language Notes*,
120/5, 1168–1191. *'our inter-stellar visitor'*: 'Einstein à Paris, ou le Roman Cosmique',
Action française, 28 March 1922, and 'Le Relativisme et l'Avenir de la Science', *Action
française*, 30 March 1922. *'students from all over the world'* to end: Charles Nordmann,
'Avec Einstein dans les Régions Devastées', *L'Illustration*, 15 April 1922. • MOSCOW:
'imported German sedatives': letter to Molotov for Politburo, 19 March 1922, Lenin, *Unknown
Lenin*, 158. *'nerves are still hurting'* and for his thoughts about going to the Caucasus:

see note to Ordzhonikidze, 7 April 1922 and 17 April 1922, *LS* XXXV, 344–345. *'slow-working poison'* and for information given to the public: 'How is the health of our dear Il'ich?', *Bednota*, 22 April 1922. *'ostentatiously studying English'*: Kotkin, 414. • CHICAGO: *'postcard arrives'*: to Clarence Hemingway, late April 1922, *LEH* I, 338. For an account of the Genoa conference and general interwar relations see Zara Steiner, *The Lights that Failed: European International History, 1919–1933*, 2005; and Robert Boyce, *The Great Interwar Crisis and the Collapse of Globalization*, 2009. For Hemingway's version including *'Viva Lenin! Viva Trotsky!'* see 'Genoa Conference', *Toronto Daily Star*, 13 April 1922, and other articles in *Dateline Toronto*. *'pays a visit to D'Annunzio'*: Hughes-Hallett, 589. *'hunted, fleeing men'*: 'Well-Guarded Russian Delegation', *Toronto Daily Star*, 4 May 1922. *'Russian Girls'*: 'Russian Girls at Genoa', *Toronto Daily Star*, 24 April 1922. *'What was the use'*: 'Le Coup de Théâtre de Gênes', *Action française*, 18 April 1922. *'clearly sees the dangers of tomorrow'*: 'Un Grand Discours to M. R. Poincaré', *L'Intransigéant*, 25 April 1922. • MOSCOW: *'the present "victors"'*: 'On the Tenth Anniversary of Pravda', written 2 May 1922, published 5 May 1922, *CW* XXXIII, 349–352. *'show trial of fifty Orthodox priests'*: Pipes, *Russia under the Bolshevik Regime*, 354–355. *'wholesale deportation of intellectuals'*: for this subject, see Lesley Chamberlain, *Lenin's Private War: The Voyage of the Philosophy Steamer and the Exile of the Intelligentsia*, 2006. *'Assign all this'*: to F. E. Dzerzhinsky, 19 May 1922, *CW* XLV, 555–556. • VIENNA: *'Beating Fantasies and Day Dreams'*: see Young-Bruehl, 103–107. *'Ambulatorium'*: Elizabeth Ann Danto, *Freud's Free Clinics: Psychoanalysis and Social Justice*, 2005. • AMERICA: *'Some blame the President'*: Niall Palmer, 'More than a Passive Interest', *Journal of American Studies*, 48/2, 2014, 417–443. *'tried to let out a cry'*: R. B. Moseley to Marcus Garvey, 3 June 1922, *MG* IV, 649–650.

Summer 1922

GORKI: *'pebbles at a nightingale'* and following: Maria Ulyanova, 'O Vladimire Il'iche (Posledniye gody zhizni)', in *Izvestiya TSK KPSS*, 1–6, 1991, here No. 2. *'Years, years'*: Ulyanova, No. 3. *'seven multiplied by twelve'*: Volkogonov, *Lenin*, 412. *'being sly'*: Kotkin, 550. *'quite at home at Gorki now'*: ibid., 413. • EICHHOLZ-IN-MURNAU: Karl Alexander von Müller, *Im Wandel Einer Welt: Erinnerungen, 1919–1932*, 1966, 132. Müller dates this encounter as either 1921 or 1922, at the house of Gottfried Feder. Some sources suggest Mathilde von Kemnitz, later Ludendorff's wife, met Adolf Hitler at Murnau in 1922 (according to a deposition from 1949) but elsewhere she places the meeting in February 1923. Annika Spilker, *Geschlecht, Religion und völkischer Nationalismus: die Ärztin und Antisemitin Mathilde von Kemnitz-Ludendorff*, 2013, 166. • ATLANTA: editorial letter, 27 June 1922, in *MG* IV, 681–686. *'In spirit and in truth'* to *'bounds of the empire?'*: ibid., 684. *'living in the air'* to *'Mars is from Jupiter'*: ibid., 682. • BERLIN: this fascinating episode is described by Milena Wazeck in 'The 1922 Einstein Film: Cinematic Innovation and Public Controversy', *Physics in Perspective*, 12/2, 2010, 163–179. • MILAN: *'wolfhound puppy'*: 'Fascisti Party Half-Million', *Toronto Daily Star*, 24 June 1922. *'remove the region's top civil servant'*: Victoria de Grazia and Sergio Luzzatto (eds.) *Dizionario del Fascismo*, 2 volumes, Vol. 2, 2002 , 169–171 and note 95. *'live Mills bomb'*: 'Italy's Blackshirts', *Toronto Star Weekly*, 24 June 1922. *'shattered tragic dignity'* to *'your old front'*: 'A Veteran Visits the Old Front', *Toronto Daily Star*, 22 July 1922. *'lost generation'*: conversation recalled in Ernest Hemingway, *A Moveable Feast*, 1964, 24–25. • **GORKI**: *'simply furnished'*: for these descriptions see L. A. Fotieva, *Iz zhizni V. I. Lenina*, 1967, 167–234. *'carrot juice'* and following descriptions see: Ulyanova, Nos. 3 & 4. *'bans the playing of the piano'*: Service, *Lenin*, 447. • **MUNICH**: *'driver of the getaway car'*: he is later reported to have changed his name, joined the French Foreign Legion, and helped Jews escape Occupied Europe in the Second World War. See Nigel Jones, 'The Assassination of Walter Rathenau', *History Today*, 63/7, July 2013. *'Rising terror'* to *'go on as we did before'*: 235th Session of the Reichstag, 24 June 1922, *Verhandlungen des Reichstages*, Vol. 355, 8037 (first part), and 234th Session of the Reichstag, *Verhandlungen des Reichstages*, Vol. 355, 8035 (second part), available at www.reichstagsprotokolle.de/Blatt2_w1_bsb00000039_00717.html. *'did Rathenau slip?'*: Ulyanova, No. 4. *'front page'*: 'Berlin Assassins Slay Rathenau', *New York Times*, 25 June 1922. *'thrown into the Neckar'*: Frank, 234. *'After a short oration'*: descriptions from 'Rathenau is Buried as Republic Martyr', *New York Times*, 28 June 1922. *'people of poets and thinkers'*: to Hermann Asnchütz-Kaempfe, 1 July 1922, *CPAE* XIII, 383–384. *'Fugitive Relativity'*: *Rheinisch-Westfälische Zeitung*, 5 August 1922, quoted in Milena Wazeck, 'Einstein in the Daily Press: A Glimpse into the Gehrcke Papers', in A. J. Kox and Jean Eisenstaedt (eds.), *The Universe of General Relativity*, 2005, 339–356. *'dangerous mental derangement'*: to Richard B. Haldane, 3 July 1922, *CPAE* XIII, 387–388. • **DUBLIN**: *'retired field marshal'*: Keith Jeffery, *Field Marshal Sir Henry Wilson: A Political Soldier*, 2008, 281–285. *'must not pretend to misunderstand'*: full statement reproduced in *Speeches and Statements by Éamon de Valera*, 105–106. *'Irish Times'*: 'Sir Henry Wilson', *Irish Times*, 23 June 1922. • **NEW YORK**: *'glorifies the creole beauty'*: 'New All Negro Revue', *New York Times*, 20 June 1922. • **DUBLIN**: *'intrepid Clare Sheridan'*: Clare Sheridan, *In Many Places*, 1923, 46. For the assault on the Four Courts see Walsh, 351–360. • **DOORN**: *'good-for-nothing bum'*: diary entry 4 July 1922, Ilsemann, Vol. 1, 228. *'Kaiser's daughter'*: 8 July 1922, ibid., 229. *'matters of the heart'*: 18 June 1922, ibid., 223. • **ISTANBUL**: *'cheek of them!'*: letter written by Lady Rumbold, 30 July 1922, in Martin Gilbert, *Sir Horace Rumbold: Portrait of a Diplomat, 1869–1941*, 1973, 255. • **ACROSS SOUTHERN IRELAND**: *'has come to this'*: letter to Harry Boland, 28 July 1922, in Coogan, *Michael Collins*, 387. • **MOSCOW**: *'retirement'*: Felshtinsky, 201. • **OCCUPIED RHINELAND**: *'delivery of cows'*: Sheridan, *Many Places*, 75. *'swank'*: ibid., 80. *'rumoured backing of Paris'*: documents published in a Munich newspaper in 1922 showed France had been involved in the earlier 1919 attempt; see Walter A. McDougall, *France's Rhineland Diplomacy, 1914–1924: The Last Bid for a Balance of Power in Europe*, 1978, 220. • **FRINTON-ON-SEA**: *'new kitten'*: letter of 8 August 1922, in Mary Soames, *Clementine Churchill*, 2002, 217. *'gaping wound'*: to Clementine Churchill, 14 August 1922, *WSC* X, 1957–1958. • **GORKI**: *'think I'm a fool'*: Ulyanova, No. 3. *'Armand's children'*: Service, *Lenin*, 447–449. *'basket weaving'*:

Ulyanova, No. 3. *'extreme concern'*: letter to Stalin for Politburo, 15 June 1922, Lenin, *Unknown Lenin*, 1996. *'tennis court'*: Ulyanova, No. 3. *'congratulate me'*: to Lydia Fotieva, 13 July 1922, *CW* LXV, 560. *'permitted to read the papers!'*: to Stalin, 18 July 1922, *CW* LXV, 560–561. *'bottle of wine'*: Kotkin, 415. *'must be chucked out'*: Volkogonov, *Lenin*, 362. Volkogonov dates this to the autumn, but it must have been earlier because Lenin refers to the SR trial which ended in August. On this whole episode, see Chamberlain. • SEEFELD: Jones, *Freud*, Vol. 3, 91. • EASTERN TURKESTAN: Fromkin, 486–488. • LAKE GARDA: for this period in D'Annunzio's life see Hughes-Hallett, 580–600. • GORKI: *'oh hell'*: Ulyanova, No. 3. *'feels so good'*: Ulyanova, No. 4. *'Maria experiments'*: these photographs are easily findable online. • BERLIN: *'vehemently criticises the legislation'*: meeting of nationalist groups on the Königplatz, Munich, 16 August 1922, *SA*, 679. *'idea for a putsch'*: Kurt Lüdecke, *I Knew Hitler: The Story of a Nazi Who Escaped the Blood Purge*, 1937, 54–56. • NEW YORK: *'in-depth exposé'*: 'The Black Star Line', *The Crisis*, September 1922. BÉAL NA BLÁTH: for Michael Collins's death, see Coogan, *Michael Collins*, 389–415. *'own fellow countrymen'*: ibid., 400. *'forgive them'*: 'Collins Died Facing Odds of Ten to One', *New York Times*, 24 August 1922. *'sink to their knees'*: Forester, 342. • DUMLUPINAR: *'Forward!'*: Mango, 342. • GORKI: *'ride a horse'*: Ulyanova, No. 5. *'First Ragdoll'*: Ulyanova, No. 4. *'refuses Lenin's offer'*: Deutscher, *Prophet Unarmed*, 35. • BLACK FOREST: *'moustache'*: Baker, *Hemingway*, 132. *'Tales of the Jazz Age'*: F. Scott Fitzgerald's stories in this volume include 'The Diamond as Big as the Ritz', 'The Curious Case of Benjamin Button' and 'May Day'. These and the books in the collection were mostly published earlier, or serialised, in various publications from 1920 on, principally in a magazine called *The Smart Set*. • SMYRNA: for the atmosphere between the Greek defeat and the arrival of the Turkish cavalry see Giles Milton, *Paradise Lost: The Destruction of Islam's City of Tolerance*, 2008, 221–260.

Autumn 1922

MOSCOW: for the photographs and article see *Pravda*, 24 September 1922. • SMYRNA: descriptions and chronology are largely drawn from Milton, 261–371; and Captain A. J. Hepburn, 'Report upon Smyrna to Commander, US Naval Detachment in Turkish Waters', 25 September 1922, USNA, RG45, Box 823. *'hysterical Armenian priest'*: entry for Sunday, 10 September 1922 in Hepburn's report. *'Bring ships and take them out'*: entry for Monday, 11 September 1922, ibid. *'wears a locket'*: Edib, 884. *'why did he bother'*: Milton, 284. *'nothing to fight about any more'*: Milton, 292. *'tonight's holocaust'*: from Ward Price's account in the *Daily Mail*, in Milton, 325. *'final solution'*: entry for Thursday, 14 September 1922 in Hepburn's report, as above. *'must drink with us'*: Edib, 388. • NEW YORK: *'Mustapha Kemal has become'*: speech, 17 September 1922, *MG* V, 19–26, 20. *'holy war'*: ibid., 21. *'tell us that Kemal is a barbarian'* to *'sticks and stones'*: ibid., 22. • SMYRNA: for Sheridan's interview with Kemal see Sheridan, *Many Places*, 155–161. *'Don't go anywhere'*: Mango, 353. *'will come back, my dear'*: Edib, 399. • BERLIN: *'The man Mustafa*

Kemal': Stefan Ihrig, *Atatürk in the Nazi Imagination*, 2014, 58; see also a similar example quoted from *Heimatland* in September 1922, at 75–76. *'all attempts to contain it'* to end: 'La Lune Crescente', *Gerarchia*, 25 September 1922. • **PARIS**: description is drawn from Polizzotti, 178–186, Breton's own description, and quotations, from 'Entrée des Médiums', *Littérature*, No. 6 (new series), November 1922, 1–16, specifically 12–13. *'By this word we mean'*: ibid., 2. • **PETROGRAD**: *'If these people had stayed'*: Chamberlain, 121. *'additional renovations'* to *'inflammation of the gums'*: Ulyanova, No. 5. *'not working, just reading'*: L. A. Fotieva, *Iz Zhizni Lenina*, 1956, 75–79. *'Are you plotting'*: note to Fotieva, October 1922, *LS* XXXV, 356. *'height of stupidity'*: note to Kamenev, July 1922, Lenin, *Unknown Lenin*, 166. Pipes elsewhere describes this as most likely being in October 1922, in response to Trotsky's refusal to take the job offered to him in September. • **MUNICH**: for Kurt Lüdecke, see Arthur L. Smith, 'Kurt Lüdecke: The Man Who Knew Hitler', *German Studies Review*, 26/3, 2003, 597–606; and Lüdecke's memoirs cited above. *'regales Hitler with tales'*: Lüdecke, 16–39. *'sent off to Italy'*: see Lüdecke, 60–73. Lüdecke's reliability as a witness has long been in question, not least given his criminal history and obvious opportunities for enrichment by writing a book in the late 1930s about the German leader (with little downside once he had fallen out of favour with Hitler's court and fled to America). Though his later trips to Italy were picked up by German diplomatic officials in 1923, there is no direct corroboration of this trip to Italy in 1922. It is plausible. But there are strong doubts about the details. See Ronald V. Layton, 'Kurt Lüdecke and "I Knew Hitler": An Evaluation', *Central European History*, 12/4, 1979, 372–386. • **DEARBORN**: Henry Ford (with Samuel Crowther), *My Life and Work*, 1922. • **ISTANBUL**: *'electric tension'* to *'bandit'*: 'Constantinople Cut Throats Await Chance for an Orgy', *Daily Star*, 19 October 1922 (dateline 1 October 1922). *'dance of death'*: '"Old Constan" in True Light; Is Tough Town; Dust and Dirt, Mud and Immorality, Bad Meat and Worse Booze', *Daily Star*, 28 October 1922 (dateline 6 October 1922). *'hate to be Kemal'*: 'Constantinople Cut Throats', as above. *'Ernest scores an interview'*: 'Hamid Bey Wears His Shirt Tucked in When Seen by Star', *Daily Star*, 9 October, 1922. *'Kemal the businessman'*: 'Turks Beginning to Show Distrust of Kemal Pasha', *Daily Star*, 24 October 1922. • **ACROSS IRELAND**: *'just a simple volunteer'*: for de Valera's meeting with Mulcahy, see Coogan, *De Valera*, 333–334. *'Yeats's new home'*: Foster, Vol. 2, 225. *'Vanity, perhaps self-conceit'*: Coogan, *De Valera*, 344. • **BERLIN**: 'The Peril to German Civilization', published in *The New Leader*, October 1922, *CPAE* XIII, 499–501. • **COBURG**: for the context of the Coburg march see Maser, 355–359. For the programme of events see 'Zum Dritten Deutschen Tag in Coburg', *Coburger Zeitung*, 14 October 1922. *'nationalist sing-along'*: Lüdecke, 82. *'main Coburg newspaper'*: 'Dritter Deutscher Tag in Coburg', *Coburger Zeitung*, 15 October 1922. *'ruthless punishment'*: 'Der Deutsche Tag in Koburg', *Völkischer Beobachter*, 18 October 1922. *'democratic poison'*: speech in Coburg, 14 October 1922, *SA*, 700–701. • **PARIS**: for a full account of the build-up to the occupation of the Ruhr see Stanislas Jeannesson, *Poincaré, la France et la Ruhr, 1922–1924: Histoire d'une Occupation*, 1998, 109–147. *'living through an armistice'*: 'Pourquoi il faut occuper la Ruhr', *Action française*, 25 October 1922.

• **Moscow**: *'empty throne at one end'*: Louis Fischer himself was present, and his account is in *Lenin*, 615–617. *'deluge of paper'*: speech to the Central Executive Committee, 31 October 1922, *CW* XXXIII, 390–395, 395. *'special obstacles'* and following: Fischer, *Lenin*, 618. *'leaves after the first act'*: Elizarova, *Reminiscences of Lenin by his Relatives*, 201–207.

• **Naples**: for the lead-up to the march on Rome and the march itself, see Bosworth 136–139; and Martin Clark, *Mussolini*, 2014, 50–65. For the text of Mussolini's 24 October 1922 speech: 'Il Discorso di Napoli', *Il Popolo d'Italia*, 25 October 1922, *OO* XVIII, 453–460. *'wherever there is demand for a speech'*: reports in *OO* XVIII, 469–470. *'return to their families'*: interview given to Luigi Ambrosini on the morning of 30 October 1922 at 3.30 a.m., *La Stampa*, 30–31 October 1922, *OO* XVIII, 468–469. *'florists run out of flowers'*: Smith, *Mussolini*, 1981, 63. *'eyes of Pallas'* to *'blindfold'*: see 31 October 1922 exchange in *AN/MUSS*, 29. • **New York**: *'filled with cheering'*: 'Legions Enter in Triumph', *New York Times*, 1 November 1922. *'had got tired'*: 'Black Shirts Hold a Roman Triumph', *New York Times*, 1 November 1922. *'Mussolini's chin'*: 'Mussolini Wears His First Frock Coat', *New York Times*, 1 November 1922. *'apostle of national regeneration'*: 'A Fascist Premier', *Guardian*, 31 October 1922; and 'Political Notes', *Observer*, 5 November 1922. *'marvellous ability to dominate'*: slightly abbreviated from *St. Galler Tageblatt*, 4 November 1922, in Falasca-Zamponi, 51. *'irresistible reality'*: 'Autour de la victoire du "Fascio"', *Action française*, 31 October 1922. *'in Moscow'*: Kotkin, 550. *'all those field marshals'*: Dr Haehner's diary in Röhl, *Into the Abyss*, 1223. *'not the shadow of the Italian Blackshirts'*: 'Aus der Bewegung', *Völkischer Beobachter*, 4 November 1922. *'name is Adolf Hitler'*: Maser, 356. • **Adrianople**: *'staggering march'*: 'A Silent, Ghastly Procession Wends Way from Thrace', *Daily Star*, 20 October 1922. *'tries to pretend'*: letter of Lady Rumbold, 6 November 1922, in Gilbert, *Rumbold*, 278. • **Washington DC**: *'Activists blame Republicans'*: Johnson, *Along This Way*, 371–373. *'nothing else but the trick'*: speech, 11 December 1922, *MG* V, 155–160, 158. • **Doorn**: *'letter arrives from England'* to *'get the monarchy back'*: diary entry 6 November 1922, Ilsemann, Vol. 1, 250–251. *'husband's design'*: Röhl, *Into the Abyss*, 1211. • **Moscow**: Lenin's speech to the Comintern gathering on 13 November 1922, *CW* XXXIII, 415–432. *'nothing compared with'*: ibid., 430. *'noughts can always'*: ibid., 422. *'will be very useful'*: ibid., 431. *'not only good, but excellent'*: ibid., 432. *'merry story'*: interview with Arthur Ransome, 'Lenin on the State of Russia: A Remarkable Interview', *Guardian*, 22 November 1922 (conducted the previous week). *'no longer a matter of the distant future'*: speech to the Moscow Soviet, 21 November 1922, *CW* XXXIII, 435–443. • **Barcelona**: *'Breton gives a talk'*: Polizzotti, 185–186. For Proust's death see William Carter, *Marcel Proust: A Life*, 2002, 807–808. *'must be brave'*: Errol Morris, 'The Anosognosic's Dilemma: Something's Wrong but You'll Never Know What It Is', *New York Times*, 21 June 2010. *'Mayakovsky'*: see Jangfeldt, 217; and Charles A. Moser, 'Mayakovsky's Unsentimental Journeys', *American Slavic and East European Review*, 19/1, 1960, 85–100, 88. • **Marseilles**: the entire travel diary, from which all the descriptive details here are drawn, is reproduced in *CPAE* XIII, 532–589. *'two most significant people alive'*: the suggestion of Einstein and Lenin came from Bertrand

Russell according to Fölsing, 524. *'Deutschland, Deutschland'*: ibid., 526. *'schmaltzy coffee-house style'*: travel diary, 2 November 1922, ibid., 539. *'sense of belonging together'*: 14 November 1922, ibid., 543. *'I admire you'*: this story is contained in a German diplomatic report from the embassy sent back to Berlin on 3 January 1923, the text reproduced in Grundmann, 225–226. *'worth fifty times'*: calculations in footnote to letter from Henrik Sederholm and Knut A. Posse, 11 December 1922, *CPAE* XIII, 617. • LAUSANNE: *'They All Made Peace'*: first published the following year, in 1923. *'İsmet Pasha'* to *'French–English dictionary'*: 'Mussolini, Europe's Prize Bluffer', *Toronto Daily Star*, 27 January 1923. *'HUSTLE DOWN'*: to Hadley Hemingway, 25 November 1922, *LEH* I, 369. *'Gare de Lyon'*: Baker, *Hemingway*, 103. • LONDON: *'What bloody shits'*: T. E. Lawrence to Edward Marsh, 18 November 1922, *WSC* X, 2125. *'they have many excuses'*: Churchill to H. A. L. Fisher, 18 November 1922, *WSC* X, 2126. *'tennis courts'*: Lady Hamilton's diary, 17 November 1922, *WSC* X, 2123. *'proverbial cat'*: in William Manchester, *Winston Spencer Churchill: Visions of Glory, 1874–1932*, 1983, 745. *'Scotch electorate'*: Lord Stamfordham to Churchill, 22 November 1922, *WSC* X, 2128. • DUBLIN: *'eye for an eye'*: letter to Liam Lynch, 12 December 1922, quoted in Pakenham, 208. *'best man at the wedding'*: Walsh, 385. • MOSCOW: *'day in late November'*: journal of Lenin's duty secretaries, *CW* XLII, 463–494. *'wind up all political work'*: letter to Kamenev and others, 13 December 1922, *CW* XLII, 432–433. • MUNICH: *'Italian diplomatic correspondence'*: report from before 17 November 1922, *SA*, 730–731. *'Duke of Anhalt'*: Lüdecke, 94. *'portrait of Ford'*: 'Berlin Hears Ford is Backing Hitler', *New York Times*, 20 December 1922. *'American military attaché'*: interview with Truman Smith, 20 November 1922, *SA*, 733. *'something to believe in'*: Ernst Hanfstaengl, *Hitler: The Missing Years*, 1957, 31–37. As with Lüdecke's memoirs, Hanfstaengl's need to be treated with care. They are occasionally transparently self-serving. Nonetheless, there is no reason to disbelieve the basic outlines of much of what he writes. For a biography of Hanfstaengl see Peter Conradi, *Hitler's Piano Player: The Rise and Fall of Ernst Hanfstaengl, Confidant of Hitler, Ally of FDR*, 2004. • ROME: for the interview see Clare Sheridan, *Many Places*, 257–266. *'British Secret Intelligence Service'*: Sheridan's file is at NA KV2/1033. *'rejects his violent advances'*: Anita Leslie suggests that Mussolini tried to force himself on Clare, badly bruising her in the process. Anita Leslie, *Clare Sheridan*, 1977, 218. *'J'aime pas'*: Sheridan, *Many Places*, 266. • VIENNA: *'Such important things'*: to Abraham, 11 December 1922, *FR/AB*, 461. *'Vienna is left quiet and lonely'*: Sigmund to Sam, 14 December 1922, JRL Freud Collection, GB133 SSF 1/2/33. • MOSCOW: for the run-in between Krupskaya and Stalin see Service, *A Political Life*, Vol. 3, 286–290; and Volkogonov, *Lenin*, 273. • LAUSANNE: *'bad and vicious solution'*: discussed on 12 December 1922, Umut Özsu, *Formalizing Displacement: International Law and Population Transfers*, 2015, 82. *'passion, not a program'*: Joseph C. Grew, *Turbulent Era: A Diplomatic Record of Forty Years, 1904–1945*, 1953, Vol. 1, 520. *'music box'*: ibid., 525. • MOJI: from Einstein's travel diary in *CPAE* XIII. • WASHINGTON DC: Memorandum by Dr Grayson, 28 December 1922, *WW* LXVIII, 252. • MOSCOW: *'ten million fewer people'*: Gerwarth, 93.

Winter 1923

The Adolf Hitler quotation is from Brigitte Hamann, *WinifredWagner, oder Hitlers Bayreuth*, 2002, 77.

DEARBORN: 'Ford's White House Bee Buzzing Far and Wide', *NewYork Times*, 7 January 1923. • **MOSCOW**: *'Stalin is too rude'*: addition to the letters of 24/25 December 1922, made on 4 January 1923, *PSS* XLV, 343–348. • **ROME**: *'picture is everywhere'*: Stephen Gundle, 'Mass Culture and the Cult of Personality', in Stephen Gundle, Christopher Duggan and Giulana Pieri (eds.), *The Cult of the Duce: Mussolini and the Italians*, 2013, 72–92, 84–85. *'Photographers follow him'*: Falasca-Zamponi, 49. *'restoring the spirit'*: Mussolini to D'Annunzio, 7 January 1923, in *OO* XIX, 386. *'Is it not the case'*: D'Annunzio to Mussolini, 9 January 1923, *AN/MUSS*, 38–40, 38. • **OUTSIDE MUNICH**: Lüdecke, 101–108. • **NEW ORLEANS**: *'I am positive'*: 'Negro Teacher is Shot in Back', *New Orleans Times-Picayune*, 2 January 1923, *MG* V, 161–162. *'Du Bois writes another piece'*: 'The UNIA', *The Crisis*, January 1923. • **CANNES**: *'front-page news in California'*: 'Mussolini Stripped of Pomp by Writer', *San Francisco Chronicle*, 8 January 1923. *'like digging up a cemetery'*: exchange with Paul Maze quoted in Manchester, 746. • **SMYRNA**: Mango, 368–376. • **MOSCOW**: see journal of Lenin's duty secretaries, *CW* XLII, 463–494. • **ESSEN**: for an account of the first few days of the invasion see either Conan Fischer, *The Ruhr Crisis, 1923–1924*, 2003, 39–48; or Jeannesson, 150–160. *'French newspapers emphasise'*: 'Ce matin les troupes françaises on pénétré dans la Ruhr', *Le Figaro*, 11 January 1923. *'claiming an invasion is not an invasion'*: 'Der Einmarsch', *Vossische Zeitung*, 11 January 1923. *'as far reaching in its effects'*: *The Times*, 6 January 1923, quoted in D. G. Williamson, 'Great Britain and the Ruhr Crisis, 1923–1924', *British Journal of International Studies*, 3, 1977, 70–91. *'when the two men meet'* and following: Jeannesson, 155. *'few hundred nationalist youths in Essen'*: ibid., 157. *'quantity of barbed wire'*: Fischer, *Ruhr Crisis*, 46. • **MUNICH**: *'Germany was unconquered'* to *'African colonies'*: speech to NSDAP meeting, 11 January 1923, *SA*, 781–782. Hitler uses the word 'Negerstaat'. *'army of revenge'*: reporting the speech above, *Berliner Tageblatt*, 12 January 1923, *SA*, 786. *'heads will roll'*: speech in the Zirkus Krone, 18 January 1923, *SA*, 794–795. • **VIENNA**: for Freud's discovery see Jones, *Freud*, Vol. 2, 94. *'position at Duisburg'*: Sigmund to Sam, 9 February 1923, JRL, Freud Collection, GB133 SSF 1/2/34. • **ACROSS IRELAND**: for this last phase of the Irish Civil War see Townshend, 441–447; and Walsh, 396–406. • **ESSEN**: *'call for passive resistance is being heeded'*; Jeannesson, 160–166. *'full-page appeals'*: for example, *New York Herald*, 28 January 1923. *'Copenhagen, Oslo and Stockholm'*: Jeannesson, 174. *'presence of African colonial troops in the French army'*: Tina M. Campt, *Other Germans: Black Germans and the Politics of Race, Gender and Memory in the Third Reich*, 2004, 31–37. *'cover of Simplicissimus'*: edition of 5 February 1923. *'He is the saviour!'*: 'An Adolf Hitler', *Simplicissimus*, 5 February 1923. • **SAN SEBASTIAN**: *'house is bought for her'* and other details of her new life: Brook-Shepherd, *The Last Empress:The Life and Times of Zita of Austria–Hungary*,

1892–1989, 1991, 220–221. *'seventy thousand Swiss francs'*: 'Mémoire présenté au nom de S.M. L'Impératrice et Reine Zita' by Oscar de Charmant. This report was partly submitted in November 1922, and then added to in January 1923. It was discussed by the Conference of Ambassadors in March 1923: NA, FO 893/20/10. • **ROME**: *'only people who still wear bowler hats'*: Smith, *Mussolini*, 123. • **LAUSANNE**: *'like to see the United States'*: Grew, Vol. 1, 539. *'Americans work on İsmet'*: ibid., 551–553. • **MUNICH**: for this episode see Harold J. Gordon Jr., *Hitler and the Beer Hall Putsch*, 1972, 185–190. *'last-minute meeting'*: report of an interview with the chief of police, 26 January 1923, SA, 803–804. *'Mexican passport'*: Lüdecke, 115–116. • **JERUSALEM**: *'when Wilhelm visited the place'*: for an account of the Kaiser's voyage to Palestine see John C. G. Röhl, *Wilhelm II: The Kaiser's Personal Monarchy, 1888–1900*, 2004 (trans. Sheila de Bellaigue), 944–954. For Einstein's impressions of Palestine including material quoted here see travel diary, *CPAE* XIII, 558–561. • **CHAMBY**: *'stops shaving'*: to Ezra Pound, 23 January 1923, *LEH* II, 5–8. *'act of God'*: Ezra Pound to Hemingway, 27 January 1923, *LEH* II, 11. *'Ernest feels trapped'*: Gertrude Stein, quoted in Meyers, *Hemingway*, 120–121. • **NEW YORK**: *'unfortunate mulatto'*: editorial letter by Marcus Garvey, 13 February 1923, *MG* V, 232–242, 232. *'little fat black man'* and following: 'Back to Africa', *Century*, February 1923. A digitised version of Du Bois's copy of this article can be found at WEB, Series 3. *'never was a chance'*: Moore v. Dempsey, 261 U.S. 86 (1923). • **MUNICH**: *'History of Erotic Art'*: Hanfstaengl, 48. *'likes his blue eyes'*: Toland, 135–136. Toland interviewed both Ernst and Helene in the early 1970s. *'naughty wooden beast'*: Hanfstaengl, 39. *'Uncle Dolf'*: Toland, 136. *'skyscrapers'*: Hanfstaengl, 41. *'wanted to be a preacher'*: Weber, *Becoming Hitler*, 257–258. *'a neuter'*: Hanfstaengl, 52. *'Gewürztraminer'*: Hanfstaengl, 40. *'artichoke'*: Lüdecke, 96. *'patent-leather shoes'*: Hanfstaengl, 43. *'Benedictine abbot'*: Müller, 129. For the growing proximity between the Nazi Party and the Church in Munich in 1923 see Derek Hastings, *Catholicism and the Roots of Nazism: Religious Identity and National Socialism*, 2010, 117–140. *'This is it, Hanfstaengl'*: Hanfstaengl, 51. • **MOSCOW**: for Lenin's reaction and Stalin's reply see Service, *A Political Life*, Vol. 3, 307. • **ST. LOUIS**: *'four-line entry'*: 'Negro News', *St. Louis Star*, 1 April 1923. *'takes a taxi to her old home'* and following: Haney, 39–40. *'All you can see'*: Baker and Bouillon, 31. In this book, Baker's return – with the taxi and the whiskey, and a trip to see Josephine's new play – are described as taking place around Christmas 1922. Newspaper reports suggest this is incorrect. *Shuffle Along* arrived in St. Louis on Sunday, 18 March 1923. • **MUNICH**: *'wish I could send'*: 'Heinrich Ford Idol of Bavarian Fascisti Chief', *Chicago Tribune*, 8 March 1923. *'American diplomat sent to investigate'*: report from the US Vice Consul, 17 March 1923, SA, 845–846. • **MONAVULLAGH MOUNTAINS**: *'leg in a boghole'*: Coogan, *De Valera*, 352. • **ESSEN**: *'conflicting stories'*: for two accounts of the same incident, as reported in French and German sources see Fischer, *Ruhr Crisis*, 95; and Jeannesson, 202. *'Recklinghausen'*: Fischer, *Ruhr Crisis*, 96. *'raped a young girl'*: ibid., 144. *'like the ancient city of Carthage'*: speech to the SA in the Bürgerbräukeller, 15 March 1923, SA, 848. *'perfectly clear what the French are planning'* and following: speech to NSDAP members at the Gasthaus Prinz Alfons, Munich, 20 March 1923, SA,

846–847. 'horsewhips': Fischer, *Ruhr Crisis*, 139–140. • **PARIS**: 'tries to stab Ezra Pound': Matthew Josephson, *Life Among the Surrealists: A Memoir by Matthew Josephson*, 1962, 222. 'Breton decides to call a halt': Polizzotti, 187–188. 'only spontaneous forces': interview in *Le Journal du Peuple* quoted in Sanouillet, 275–276. • **LONDON**: Bosworth, 151. • **MOSCOW**: 'recalls the time': Maria Ulyanova, *OV. I. Lenine I se''ye U''yanovykh*, 1989, 110–112. 'Swedish specialist': Volkogonov, *Lenin*, 424–429.

Spring 1923

PARIS: 'between articles': 'La Maladie de Lénine' and 'Gabriele d'Annunzio achète la villa de l'ex-Kaiser', *Le Figaro*, 16 March 1923. 'new-found love': 'Savoir dire non', *Le Figaro*, 19 March 1923. 'forbid the offloading': Fischer, *Ruhr Crisis*, 110–111. 'two hundred thousand children': ibid., 117–135. 'Berlin sends in money': ibid., 208–211. 'local citizens are taken hostage': Jeannesson, 202–204. 'French general declares': Fischer, *Ruhr Crisis*, 172. 'Leo Schlageter': Jay W. Baird, *To Die for Germany: Heroes in the Nazi Pantheon*, 1992, 15–22. • **MOSCOW**: for politics: Service, *A Political Life*, Vol. 3, 311–314. For Lenin's declining physical and mental condition see Volkogonov, *Lenin*, 424–430. For the Lenin Institute and the beginnings of the Lenin cult before he was dead, see Tumarkin, *Lenin Lives!*, 123–126. • **LONDON**: 'must confess myself more interested': letter to the Duke of Marlborough, 7 April 1923, quoted in Martin Gilbert, *Prophet of Truth: Winston S. Churchill, 1922–1939*, 1976, 6. 'Remarkably egotistical': review in the *New Statesman* quoted in Gilbert, *Prophet of Truth*, 7. • **AMERICA**: 'have some fun': 'The Reminiscences of Mr. E. G. Liebold', HFA, Owen W. Bombard Interview Series, Accession 65, 508. 'enough and more than enough': Louise Clancy and Florence Davies, *The Believer: The Life of Mrs. Henry Ford*, 1960, 159. 'You got him into it' and following: 'Reminiscences of Mr. E. G. Liebold', 511 and following. • **DELITZSCH**: 'smeared with oil': Hitler's press officer Otto Dietrich quoted in Friedrich, 35. 'my valet': Hanfstaengl, 56–57. 'takes Putzi round': ibid., 58–59. 'tries to smash the camera': the photographer Georg Pahl quoted in Friedrich, 37–38. • **VIENNA**: for this phase of Freud's illness see Max Schur, *Freud: Living and Dying*, 1972, 347–385; and Jones, *Freud*, Vol. 2, 94–106. • **BERLIN**: 'Einstein resigns': there are several letters on this in *CPAE*. Einstein also wrote an article: 'On My Resignation from the Committee on Intellectual Cooperation of the League of Nations', written on 23 April 1923 and published in *Die Friedens-Warte* in June, reproduced in *CPAE* XIV, 43–45. 'may God forgive him': Canales, 1175. 'knee-jerk reaction' and following: Fischer, *Ruhr Crisis*, 168–169. 'gives an interview to Spain's leading newspaper': interview with Antonio Aspeitua for *ABC*, 6 April 1923, *SA*, 863. 'path of the golden mean' and following: speech to an NSDAP meeting in the Zirkus Krone, 10 April 1923, *SA*, 873–876, 873. 'mentor, Dietrich Eckart': Margarete Plewnia, *Auf dem Weg zu Hitler: Der 'völkische' Publizist Dietrich Eckart*, 1970, 89–91. 'Eckart contributes a poem': this is quite a free translation. *Völkischer Beobachter*, 20 April 1923. 'waits for Putzi': Hanfstaengl, 48. • **WASHINGTON DC**: 'Speaking quite frankly': George Creel to Edith Wilson, 19 April 1923,

WW LXVIII, 342. *'done all I can'* and following: Edith Wilson to George Creel, 24 April 1923, *WW* LXVIII, 347–349. • **THE OCCUPIED RUHR**: *'crowds gather in the streets of Essen'*: 'Les obsèques des victimes d'Essen', *Le Figaro*, 11 April 1923. *'Flags with patriotic emblems'*: the Pathé film of the funeral march is available at https://www.britishpathe.com/video/funeral-of-workmen-killed-in-demonstration-at-krup. *'Communist agitator'*: 'Selbst die Franzosen bewundern – nur die Kommunisten stören', *Vossische Zeitung*, 11 April 1923. *'at least fifteen different accounts'*: 'Hate in Occupied Zone a Real, Concrete Thing', *Daily Star*, 12 May 1923. *'France refused in 1917'*: 'A Victory Without Peace Forced French to Undertake the Occupation of the Ruhr', *Daily Star*, 13 April 1923. *'few years earlier'*: letter dated 22 April 1923, *Albert Leo Schlageter: Seine Verurteilung und Erschießung durch die Franzosen in Düsseldorf am 26. Mai 1923*, 1938, 96. • **DOORN**: *'Wilhelm sees a pig'*: diary entry 7 May 1923, Ilsemann, Vol. 1, 275. *'wonder about the possibility'*: Gutsche, 65. *'What thanks do I get?'*: diary entry 9 April 1923, Ilsemann, Vol. 1, 275. • **MUNICH**: *'briefly entertains the idea'*: Wolfgang Zdral, *Die Hitlers: Die Unbekannte Familie*, 2005, 207. *'asks a party member'*: Weber, *Becoming Hitler*, 262. *'six-foot-tall blonde'*: the recollection of Hitler's fondness for Elisabeth Büchner is from a subsequent visit to Berchtesgaden that Hitler took in the early summer of 1923, as described in Hanfstaengl, 82–83. *'wolf is here'*: monologue in the night of 16/17 January 1942, *Adolf Hitler: Monologe im Führer-Hauptquartier, 1941–1944*, 1980 (ed. Werner Jochmann), 203–204. • **MOSCOW**: *'I'm kept alive'*: Volkogonov, *Lenin*, 434. • **MUNICH**: for the May Day event see Gordon, 195–208. *'dictatorship of national will'* and following: speech at an NSDAP meeting in the Zirkus Krone, 4 May 1923, *SA*, 921–924. • **VIENNA**: *'Nothing but visitors'*: Freud to Salomé, 10 May 1923, *FR/SAL*, 124. *'ever experienced such grief'*: letter to Katja Levy on 11 June 1923, in Schur, 358. • **DUBLIN**: *'legion of the rearguard'*: Coogan, *De Valera*, 344–355. • **GOLZHEIMER HEATH**: for an account of Schlageter's execution see Baird, 25. *'lark singing'*: prison chaplain Fassbender's account of the execution is in *Albert Leo Schlageter: Seine Verurteilung und Erschießung*, 58–86, 75. *'accuracy of the French riflemen'*: 'Schlageter a expié', *Le Figaro*, 27 May 1923. *'German accounts'* and *'birch cross'*: Baird, 25. • **LAKE GARDA**: *'nearby hill should be flattened'*: D'Annunzio to Mussolini, 7 May 1923, *AN/MUSS*, 54. *'not so proud'* to *'within my fist'*: speech to a women's congress in Venice, 31 May 1923, *OO* XIX, 226–228.

Summer 1923

ACROSS EUROPE: *'New York has so many Russian nobles'*: 'Inrush of the Russians', *New York Times Magazine*, 10 June 1923. • **MUNICH**: 'Wie sieht Hitler aus?', *Simplicissimus*, 28 May 1923. • **PARIS**: Polizzotti, 189–192, and Sanouillet, 278–282. • **NEW YORK**: *'million other Garveys'*: speech on 20 May 1923, *MG* V, 308–311. 'Letter from W. E. B. Du Bois to Thomas E. Will', 3 July 1923, WEB, Series 1a. • **ESSEN**: *'the name of Schlageter will be'*: Baird, 27. *'Hitler claims that Schlageter's death'*: speech to nationalist groups in the Königplatz, 10 June 1923, *SA*, 934–935. *'Christ-like composure'*: for the interaction between Schlageter's Catholicism and his role as a Nazi martyr see Hastings, 127–131. *'movement is a restless force'*: speech to an NSDAP meeting in Passau, 17 June 1923, *SA*, 937–938. • **PARIS**: for a full account of the event see James M. Harding, *The Ghosts of the Avant-Garde(s): Exorcising Experimental Theater and Performance*, 2013, 56–58. • **ESSEN**: *'using their gardens'*: Fischer, *Ruhr Crisis*, 172. *'Dortmund'*: ibid., 188. *'German government will never recognise'*: Carl Bergmann, *The History of Reparations*, 1927, 200. *'German officials be kept within the blast zone'* and following: Fischer, *Ruhr Crisis*, 175–176. • **GOTHENBURG**: *'nearly goes mad'*: to Max Born, 23 July 1923, *CPAE* XIV, 153–154. *'you're always frustrating and upsetting Mama'*: from Hans Albert Einstein, 9–20 June 1923, *CPAE* XIV, 103–104. *'safety cannot be guaranteed'*: see footnotes to letter to Paul Langevin, 22 July 1923, *CPAE* XIV, 154. • **LAKE GARDA**: for D'Annunzio see Hughes-Hallett. For Mussolini's politicking up to the Acerbo Law and beyond see Bosworth, 155–158. • **BERLIN**: the best account of the extraordinary distorting effects of the German inflation is Adam Fergusson, *When Money Dies: The Nightmare of the Weimar Hyperinflation*, 1975, from which this section is principally drawn. *'porter in Baden railway station'*: 'Quite Easy to Spend a Million, if in Marks', *Daily Star*, 5 May 1923. *'Koblenz'* to *'We are free citizens'*: J. A. Dorten, *La Tragédie Rhénane*, 1945, 149–150. *'Los von Berlin'*: 'Un important discours du Docteur Dorten', *Le Figaro*, 30 July 1923. *'Chancellor makes a speech'*: 378th Session of the Reichstag, 8 August 1923, *Verhandlungen des Reichstages*, Vol. 378, 11749–11755, available at http://www.reichstagsprotokolle.de/Blatt2_w1_bsb00000045_00014.html. • **SAN FRANCISCO**: *'After one play'*: see news report dated 11 August 1923 reproduced in *WW* LXVIII, 494. • **LAUSANNE**: for the text of the treaty see *The American Journal of International Law*, 18/1, 1924, 1–53. • **DEARBORN**: 'If I Were President', *Collier's*, 4 August 1923. The final quote here is slightly abbreviated. • **BERLIN**: see Fergusson. • **PAMPLONA**: *'struggle of life and death'*: 'Bullfighting a Tragedy', *Toronto Star Weekly*, 20 October 1923. *'ringside seat at the war'*: to William Horne, 17–18 July 1923, *LEH* II, 32–38. *'thick as those of a fortress'*: 'Pamplona in July', *Toronto Star Weekly*, 27 October 1923. *'different kinds of exotic food'*: Baker, *Hemingway*, 113. *'too goddam thin'*: to Robert McAlmon, 5 August 1923, *LEH* II, 39–41. • **BOUILLON**: *'really be part of France'*: letter to Henri de Gaulle, 30 August 1923, *CDG* I, 598. *'Peace is the dream of the wise'*: notebook entry August 1923, *CDG* I, 598. • **DRESDEN**: Heinrich Mann, 'Rede zur Feier des Verfassung', in *Politische Reden*, Vol. 3, 391–400. • **ENNIS**: see Coogan, *De Valera*. • **GORKI**: see Nadya Krupskaya, 'Poslednie polgoda Vliadmira Il'icha', *Izvestiya TSK KPSS*, 4, 1989. • **LONDON**: Sheridan, *Many Places*, 268. • **MUNICH**: report in *The World*, 20 August 1923, *SA*, 974–975; and report in the *Bayerische Vaterland*, 22 August 1923, *SA*, 975–976. • **THE ALBANIAN–GREEK BORDER**: for an account of the ambush, see James Barros, *The Corfu Incident of 1923: Mussolini and the League of Nations*, 1965, 20–32. For the terms of the Italian ultimatum, see Barros, 40. For the process of occupation see Barros, 74–80. • **WESTERHAM**: *'Kaiser and Mussolini seem quite benevolent'*: Clementine Churchill to Winston Churchill, 4 September 1923, *CH/CH*, 274. *'League of Nations is on trial'*: Clementine to Winston, 3 September 1923, 274. *'Poor devil'*: Winston to Clementine, 5 September 1923, 275. • **ROME**: *'talkative* *group of Americans*': 'Notes by Anna on return from Rome', *FR/FR*, Appendix 2, 423–424. *'packed with sightseeing*': for everything that Freud dragged his daughter to see, 'Travel Diary, Rome 1923', *FR/FR*, Appendix 1, 411–422. *'brief letter to his nephew Edward*': letter dated 14 September 1923, LOC, Sigmund Freud Collection, Family Papers, 1851–1978, mss 39990. • **Munich**: *'Ludendorff has fallen in love again*': for the relationship with Mathilde see Chickering, 165–167. *'fate of Turkey*' to *'one way or another*': *Heimatland*, 1 September 1923, in Ihrig, 81. For description of Nuremberg events see 'Thousands Hoch der Kaiser in Bavarian Mass', *Chicago Daily Tribune*, 3 September 1923. For the joint manifesto agreed on 2 September 1923, 990–992. • **Monza**: see Lüdecke, 140–141. Lüdecke suggests the trip took place in August. But the mention of Monza (and Mussolini's travel itinerary) suggests that it actually took place in early September, during the Corfu crisis. This is the dating in Alan Cassels, 'Mussolini and German Nationalism, 1922–1925', *Journal of Modern History*, 35/2, 1963, 137–157. Lüdecke's name first appears in Italian diplomatic correspondence in October. Whether Lüdecke actually met Mussolini on this trip is uncertain. What is relatively clear is that his reception was considerably less warm than before. Lüdecke was not the only envoy between German nationalists and Italian nationalists, and the Nazi Party was not the only game in town on the German side. *'left a void in the German mind*' to *'new German generation*': preface to *La Germania Repubblicana* by Roberto Suster, September 1923, *OO* XX, 29–31. • **Madrid**: *'Please convey to His Majesty*': Shlomo Ben-Ami, *Fascism from Above: The Dictatorship of Primo de Rivera in Spain, 1923–1930*, 1983, 71. *'Secondo de Rivera*': Sheridan, *Naked Truth*, 359. *'mon petit Mussolini*': Bosworth, 155. *'Hermine is less sure*': diary entry 1 June 1923, Ilsemann, Vol. 1, 282. • **Munich**: *'What you have witnessed in Turkey*': Ihrig, 88.

Autumn 1923

Hof: *'When we have our swastika flying*': Ulrich Graf, quoted in Joachimsthaler, 314–315. *'French diplomat worries*': Jeannesson, 294. *'secure the life of our people*': ibid., 296. For the general situation in Bavaria see Gordon. • **Corfu**: *'Italian representative goes out of his way*': Barros, 259–264. *'white robe of virtue*': ibid., 287. • **Doorn**: *'cultural anthropologist*': the cultural anthropologist was Leo Frobenius. See Röhl, *Into the Abyss*, 1229–1230. *'negroes and berbers*' to *'Germany never will*': diary entry 7 October 1923, Ilsemann, Vol. 1, 287. • **Bonn**: *'Lower Rhine is wonderful*': to Betty Neumann, 21 September 1923, *CPAE* XIV, 193. *'tells Elsa to hide the silver*': to Elsa Einstein, 16 September 1923, *CPAE* XIV, 189–190. • **Munich**: interview with Geroge Viereck in *The American Monthly*, October 1923, *SA*, 1023–1026. • **Vienna**: *'Operation at the Sanatorium Auersperg*': Dr Pichler's medical notes are reproduced in Jones, *Freud*, Vol. 2, Appendix B, 499–521. *'writes a letter to his mother*': to Amalie Freud, 17 October 1923, *LSF*, 345. *'broken and enfeebled*': Sigmund to Sam, 25 October 1923, JRL, Freud Collection, GB133 SSF 1/1/40. • **Bayreuth**: *'bring the house to life*': Houston Stewart Chamberlain's diary, 29 September

1923, in Hilmes, 302. *'show un-German elements'*: *Bayreuther Tagblatt*, 28 September 1923, in Martin Schramm, '"Im Zeichen des Hakenkreuzes": Der Deutsche Tag in Bayreuth am 30 September 1923', *Jahrbuch für Fränkische Landesforschung*, 65, 2005, 253–273, 258. *'much activity from dawn till dusk'*: Chamberlain's diary, 30 September 1923, in Hilmes, 303. *'estimates of the numbers'*: left-wing newspapers suggested around 5,200 participants in the march-past; the *Völkischer Beobachter* boasted 12,000. Schramm, 263. *'Heil Moscow!'*: ibid., 263. *'court controversy'*: ibid., 262. *'short Bavarian leather trousers'*: ibid., 267. *'transformed the state of my soul'*: letter to Adolf Hitler, 7 October 1923, HSC, Vol. 2, 124–126. • **DÜSSELDORF**: for a description see Jeannesson, 319. For the internal complications of German Rhenish politics see Klaus Epstein, 'Adenauer and Rhenish Separatism', *Review of Politics*, 29/4, 1967, 536–545. • **TORONTO**: *'bad move to come back'*: to Gertrude Stein and Alice B. Toklas, 11 October 1923, LEH II, 53–56. *'King of Spain'* and *'we are going to leave'*: Baker, *Hemingway*, 117. *'best prose he has read in forty years'*: ibid., 121. • **PARIS**: for Breton's relationship to Doucet see François Chapon, *Mystère et splendeurs de Jacques Doucet*, 1984, 262–307. • **MUNICH**: *'finds his wish granted'*: Heinrich Hoffmann, *Hitler was My Friend*, 1955 (trans. R. H. Stevens), 54. *'feature on Germany's most famous lion tamer'*: *Berliner Illustrierte Zeitung*, 16 September 1923. *'writes most of it himself'*: Weber makes the case for Hitler having been the actual author of Koerber's book in *Becoming Hitler*, 273–291. *'destined to eternal night'*: ibid., 286. *'One can surely expect'*: *Völkischer Beobachter*, 23 October 1923. • **PARIS**: see Robert Orledge, 'Cole Porter's Ballet "Within the Quota"', *Yale University Library Gazette*, 50/1, 1975, 19–29. • **MUNICH**: speech to NSDAP meeting in Nuremberg, 14 October 1923, SA, 1031–1034. • **AACHEN**: *'Aachen'*: McDougall, 306–311. *'Hamburg'*: Bernard H. Bayerlein, *Deutscher Oktober 1923: Ein Revolutionsplan und sein Scheitern*, 2003. • **GORKI**: for two English-language accounts see Service, *Lenin*, 476; and Volkogonov, *Lenin*, 432. *'freezing bog'*: Trotsky, 498. • **ISTANBUL**: *'Long live Mustafa Kemal Pasha'*: Mango, 391. *'returning to the days of the first Caliphs'*: ibid., 394. *'a long article discusses'*: *Berliner Illustrierte Zeitung*, 28 October 1923. *'Ankara government'*: *Heimatland*, 27 October 1923, in Ihrig, 88. *'the first possibility'*: report of a conversation on 24 October 1923, Ernst Deuerlein, *Der Hitler-Putsch: bayerische Dokumente zum 8./9. November 1923*, 1962, 257–258. • **MILAN**: *'Journalism'*: speech to the Journalists' Association of Lombardy, 24 October 1923, OO XX, 59–61, 60. *'from a balcony in Milan'* to end: speech on the first anniversary of the march on Rome, 28 October 1923, OO XX, 61–65, 62 and following. • **AACHEN**: *'French-backed Rhenish separatists'*: McDougall, 314–315. *'anti-Semitic riots'*: David Clay Large, '"Out with the Ostjuden": The Scheunenviertel Riots in Berlin, November 1923', in Christhard Hoffmann, Werner Bergmann and Helmut Walser Smith (eds.), *Exclusionary Violence: Antisemitic Riots in Modern German History*, 2002, 123–140. *'Einstein is forced to deny'*: Fölsing, 544. *'writes to Betty'*: to Betty Neumann, 7 November 1923, CPAE XIV, 227. *'ears are cupped'*: Hanfstaengl, 93. *'enhanced surveillance'*: Kahr's instructions dated 22 October 1923, Deuerlein, *Hitler-Putsch*, 253. *'no going back'*: speech on 30 October 1923, SA, 1047–1051, 1050, with reference to the swastika flying over the royal palace at 1051. • **TORONTO**: *'bees kill their non-producers'*: 'Young Communists', *Toronto Star*

Weekly, 22 December 1923. *'would like to have Henry Ford'*: 'I Like Americans', *Toronto Star Weekly*, 15 December 1923. • **MUNICH**: from the memoirs of Tröbst, in Weber, *Becoming Hitler*, 301–302. • **KILMAINHAM JAIL**: Pakenham, *De Valera*, 229. • **MUNICH**: description drawn principally from Gordon, 270–312, unless otherwise indicated. *'Putzi has just bought'*: Hanfstaengl, 96. *'Mexico'* to *'Either the German revolution begins'*: Müller, *Im Wandel einer Welt*, 162–163. *'sips red wine'*: Hanfstaengl, 104. *'heavens will fall'*: Graf Helldorff quoted in Gordon, 351. *'sounds very funny'*: letter to Gertrude Stein and Alice B. Toklas, 9 November 1923 (and mid-December 1923), *LEH* II, 90–93. *'may never live down the laughter'*: cited in Gary A. Klein, *The American Press and the Rise of Hitler, 1923–1933*, Unpublished PhD thesis, London School of Economics, 1997, 18. *'vaudeville ending'*: 'Ludendorff remis en liberté sur parole', *Le Petit Parisien*, 11 November 1923. *'idol has fallen'*: 'Ludendorff a échoué pitieusement', *Le Matin*, 10 November 1923. *'buffoni'*: Durini di Monza to Mussolini, 10 November 1923, IDDI, Series 7, Vol. 2, 315–318. *'mathematical inevitability'*: *Berliner Illustrierte Zeitung*, 25 November 1923. • **DOORN**: *'stupidity of youth'* to *'Thank God'*: diary entry 10 November 1923, Ilsemann, Vol. 1, 291. *'will not come from a beer joint'*: letter from Wilhelm to Mackensen in December 1923, in Cecil, Vol. 2, 334. *'If the French go any further'*: Röhl, *Into the Abyss*, 1227. • **AMERICA**: for the text of the address on 10 November 1923 see *WW* LXVIII, 466–467. *'dressing gown'*: Edith Wilson, 355. • **INNSBRUCK AND KUFSTEIN**: *'flower shop'*: Hanfstaengl, 106. *'Hanfstaengls' country house'*: for an account from interviews with Helene see Toland, 174–177. • **MOSCOW**: Clare Sheridan wrote a series of articles on her trip to Russia in December 1923 from which some of the detail is drawn here. She covered it only very briefly indeed in her autobiography, a sure mark of disappointment from someone generally so keen to share. The articles were originally published in the *New York World*, and serialised in other American newspapers. See, for example, 'New World for Worker in Soviet Russia is Unknown, Writer Holds', *Dayton Daily News*, 24 December 1923. *'not the type of newspaper correspondent'*: Leslie, 228. *'told how much better off'*: Sheridan, *Naked Truth*, 362. *'Russia once seemed to throw up'*: 'Russia Revisited', *St. Louis Post Dispatch*, 28 December 1923. • **LEIDEN**: *'Children do not learn'*: aphorism, November/December 1923, *CPAE* XIV, 231. • **ROME**: *'figure is not just an Italian one'*: Primo de Rivera's speech, 21 November 1923, *OO* XX, 112. *'universal phenomenon'*: in Ben-Ami, 132. *'marching along the open road'*: speech in reply to Primo de Rivera, 21 November 1923, *OO* XX, 112–113. • **BERLIN**: *'cartoon'*: *Berliner Illustrierte Zeitung*, December 1923. *'care packages'*: Hilmes, 304. *'overjoyed when his dog'*: Otto Lurker, *Hitler hinter Festungsmauern: Ein Bild aus trüben Tagen*, 1933, 8. *'Let them see how well they will do without me'*: Alois Maria Ott, letter to Werner Maser, 12 December 1973, quoted in Peter Ross Range, *1924: The Year that Made Hitler*, 2016, 106. • **GORKI**: *'Every day he makes a conquest'*: Volkogonov, *Lenin*, 434. *'film of the sixth anniversary'*: *Lenin: Life and Works*, 198. *'man in a wheelchair'*: Volkogonov, *Lenin*, 429. *'Any man trained merely to say'*: Deutscher, *Prophet Unarmed*, 121. • **TORONTO**: *'Marcelline orders'*: Baker, *Hemingway*, 582. • **LAKE GARDA**: December 1923, *AN/MUSS*, 60. • **VIENNA**: the book was Fritz Wittels, *Sigmund Freud: Der Mann, die Lehre, die Schule*, 1924. *'I need hardly*

say': *LSF*, 345–347. This translation is taken from the 1924 English-language edition
of Wittels's book, 11.

1924

'*Schlagobers*': Richard F. Sterba, *Reminiscences of a Viennese Psychoanalyst*, 1982, 21. '*down-right animalistic satisfaction*': to Ferenczi, 4 February 1924, *FR/FER* III, 122–124.
• '*long since become accustomed*': to Fried Huber, 5 January 1924, *CPAE* XIV, 308–309.
• '*Jack London*': Elizarova, *Reminiscences of Lenin by his Relatives*, 206–207. For the out-manoeuvring of Trotsky see Deutscher, *Prophet Unarmed*, 132–133. '*petty-bourgeois deviation*': ibid., 132. '*Lenin is no more*': ibid., 133. For a description of the funeral, see
Tumarkin, 160–164. *Pravda* reports are rich in further detail. • '*letter of congratulation*':
Gilbert, *Prophet of Truth*, 24–25. • '*D'Annunzio is made a Prince*': Hughes-Hallett, 607.
• '*Overwhelming honour*': notes for an acceptance speech, 21 January 1924, *WW* LXVIII,
541–544. • '*intense, ruthless, brutal fanaticism*': court testimony, 26 February 1923, *SA*,
1061–1106, 1068. • '*swindler-of-all-trades*': Polizzotti, 192. • '*Fikriye*': Mango, 409.
• '*prepare formula for his son Bumby*': Hemingway, *Moveable Feast*, 87. For Hemingway's
literary development see Meyers, *Hemingway*, 124–151. • '*When is treason really treason?*':
court testimony, 27 March 1924, *SA*, 1197–1216, 1198. '*if the next five years*': ibid., 1201.
• '*works of Machiavelli*': 'Preludio al Machiavelli', *Gerarchia*, 4 April 1924, *OO* XX,
251–254. '*generation of victory*': Bosworth, 198. • Article describing the encounter in
the *Cincinnati Union*, 24 May 1924, *MG* V, 598–599. • '*Pope of Surrealism*': Polizzotti,
211. • '*mere bagatelle*': Laton McCartney, *The Teapot Dome Scandal: How Big Oil Bought
the Harding White House and Tried to Steal the Country*, 2008, 203. • '*pint of beer*': for
the conditions of Hitler's imprisonment, see Otto Lurker, *Hitler hinter Festungsmauren:
ein Bild aus trüben Tagen*, 1933; and Hans Kallenbach, *Mit Adolf Hitler auf Festung
Landsberg*, 1939. Kallenbach describes how he was able to use his malaria to persuade
the prison guards to give him cognac, which he proceeded to share with the rest of
the prisoners. '*leader cannot afford to be beaten*': Hanfstaengl, 114. '*feast day of St Adolf*':
Kallenbach, 112. '*relives his war experiences*': Rudolf Hess, *Briefe: 1908–1933*, 2002 (ed.
Wolf Rüdiger Hess), 324. '*Remington typewriter*': Florian Beierl and Othmar Plöckinger,
'Neue Dokumente zu Hitler's Buch "Mein Kampf"', *Vierteljahrshefte für Zeitgeschichte*,
57/2, 2009, 261–295, 268. '*talks with a new (male) secretary*': Hess, 326–327 and, for
the reference to astrology, 338. '*starts to cry*': ibid., 342. • '*Ku Klux Klan claims four
million members*': see Linda Gordon, *The Second Coming of the KKK: The Ku Klux Klan
of the 1920s and the American Political Tradition*, 2018. • '*not frightened by rudeness*':
Kotkin, 547. • '*Venice Biennale*': Vivian Endicott Barnett, 'The Russian Presence in the
1924 Venice Biennale', in Paul Wood, Vasilii Rakitin, Jane A. Sharp and Aleksandra
Shatskikh (eds.), *The Great Utopia: The Russian and Soviet Avant-Garde, 1915–1932*, 1992,
467–473. '*Let him who is without sin*': Bosworth, 198. • '*Who is going to call?*': letter to
Mackensen from July 1924 in Gutsche, 66. • '*why she didn't take the train*': Clare

Sheridan, *Across Europe with Santanella*, 1925, 24. *'Woodrow Wilson hanging side by side'*: ibid., 28. *'Kiev'*: ibid., 88. *'Crimea'*: ibid., 130. • For Hitler's writing of *Mein Kampf* see Beierl and Plöckinger. *'it is quite true'*: talk with Kugler, 29 July 1924, *SA*, 1242. • *'Wall Street compromise'*: Melvyn P. Leffler, *The Elusive Quest: America's Pursuit of European Stability and French Security, 1919–1933*, 1979, 100–112. *'with a feeling that we have turned our backs'*: Stephen Schuker, *The End of French Predominance in Europe: The Financial Crisis of 1924 and the Adoption of the Dawes Plan*, 1978, 383. • Synopses of *The Chocolate Dandies* taken from Stark Young's review, 'The Play', *New York Times*, 2 September 1924. • *'civilisation is one'*: Bernard Lewis, *The Emergence of Modern Turkey*, 2002, 292. • *'Leningrad is flooded'*: see the account in the Frederiksen Papers, HIA. • *'Bureau of Surrealist Research'*: Polizzotti, 212–220. *'cage of its own making'* and following: see 1924 manifesto in André Breton, *Manifestes du surréalisme*, 1972 (ed. Jean-Jacques Pauvert). • *'letter to Betty'*: to Betty Neumann, 10 October 1924, *CPAE* XIV, 527. • *'eight hundred million goldmarks'*: Steiner, 249. *'America's corporations are in expansive mood'*: ITT in Spain, Ford in Copenhagen and Antwerp, General Motors in London; Boyce, 178–189. *'Chocolate Dandies'*: 'Coast to Coast Route with Foreign Booking, for Chocolate Dandies', *New York Age*, 25 October 1924. • *'letter purporting to come from the Comintern'*: for an account of the Zinoviev letter see Gill Bennett, *The Conspiracy that Never Dies: The Zinoviev Letter*, 2018. • *'naval school becomes an orphanage'*: Menegaldo. *'insult to Russian national honour'*: 'Wrangel Protests Surrender of Ships', *New York Times*, 8 December 1924. • *'duty of the Party'* to *'ready, comrades'*: speech (subsequently published in *Pravda*), 19 November 1924, Stalin, *Works*, Vol. 6, 338–373, 373. *'no particular role'*: Volkogonov, *Trotsky*, 79. • *'be psyched'*: Gay, *Freud*, 452. • *'not a beer garden'*: Bosworth, 197. • *'processions and mausoleums'*: quotation from Jangfeldt, 289. *'already become so full'*: Larry E. Holmes and William Burgess, 'Scholarly Voice or Political Echo?: Soviet Party History in the 1920s', *Russian History*, 9/2–3, 1982, 378–398, 382. • *'greatest love specialist in the world'*: 'To Ask Freud to Come Here', *New York Times*, 21 December 1924. • *'not fall off the tight-rope'*: Hanfstaengl, 125.

INDEX

Aachen, Germany 489, 582, 585–6

Abdullah, Emir 391–2

Åbo (Turku), Finland 302, 318

Abraham, Karl 10, 16, 75–6, 195

Action française (magazine) 294, 297, 474, 509, 513

Adinkerke, Belgium 239

Adler, Friedrich 13, 42–3, 154, 162, 227

Adler, Victor 13, 42–3, 149, 158, 162

African Blood Brotherhood 407, 418

Agamemnon, HMS 164

Albert I, of the Belgians 239, 270

Alexander III, of Russia 38

Alexandra Feodorovna, Tsarina 3, 23, 24, 25, 26, 40, 96, 111, 113, 116, 127

Alexei Nikolaevich, Tsarevich 3, 25, 27, 49, 57, 111, 127

Alfonso XIII, of Spain 117, 573

Allenby, General Edmund 80

Alliluyeva, Nadya (Stalin's wife) 101, 119, 289, 425, 443

American Relief Administration (ARA) 415–16, 433–4, 451, 459, 470, 492

Amerongen, The Netherlands 171–3, 195–6, 221, 237, 243, 276–7, 303, 304, 312

Amette, Léon-Adolphe, Archbishop of Paris 351

Amritsar, India 220

Anastasia Nikolaevna, Grand Duchess 43, 110

Anatolia: in disorder 165, 232, 244; emergence of Kemalists in xi, 233, 248–9, 288, 306, 334; a problem 306, 307; incursions by Greek troops 370–71, 401, 411, 461, 495; and Churchill 392; Christians deported 415, 498, 499; under Kemal 383, 441, 499–500, 531–2, 569; and Treaty of Lausanne (1922) 524; *see also* Ismet Pasha; Kemal, Mustafa; Smyrna

Andania, SS 565

Andreas-Salomé, Lou 466, 555

Anhalt, Duke of 521

Ankara 263, 279, 305, 306, 361, 383, 411, 417, 494, 584

Anselm, SS 234

anti-Semitism: in Germany 144, 229, 586; in Ukraine 219, 254; and Hitler 255, 260, 279, 286, 297, 315, 324, 461–2, 473, 522; and Einstein 291, 389, 390; and Kaiser Wilhelm 276–7, 386, 471; Henry Ford's campaign 316–17, 395, 415, 448, 471; *see also Protocols of the Elders of Zion*

Apollinaire, Guillaume 21, 42, 96, 161, 503

Arabs 143, 145, 182, 306, 307, 391, 413, 539

Aragon, Louis 242, 294, 382

Archangel, Russia 108, 110, 131–2, 197

Arditi, the 209, 215, 258

Arkansas 267, 541

Arlington Cemetery, Virginia 441

Armand, Inessa 3, 6–7, 18, 136, 262, 289, 290, 328, 338, 342, 344, 381, 490; children 136, 490, 554, 593, *see also* Armand, Varya

Armand, Varya 262, 289, 290, 338, 371

Armenia/Armenians 126, 164–5, 182, 232, 334, 361, 383, 496, 498–9, 501, 506, 510, 569; pogrom (1895) 248; Turkish massacres 46, 81, 232–3, 382

Armistice (1918): exchanges leading to 78, 99, 146, 147, 148, 150, 154; signing of ix, 157–8, 159–60, 161, 162, 169

Arnold, Benedict 448

Aryan race 144, 335, 336, 396, 550, 554

Atlanta, Georgia 227, 481–2

August Wilhelm, Prince 276

Auguste Viktoria, Kaiserin 172, 243, 277, 392

Australia/Australians 39, 70, 133, 364, 410, 432, 449

Austria/Austrians: in World War I 7–8, 9–10, 12, 13, 50, 56, 70–71, 152; peace negotiations with Russia 82, 88–91, 95, 97; food supply problems 104, 123–4; union with Germany 106–7, 109, 119, 123, 140, 151, 161, 213, 231; sues for peace with Italy 153; and end of war 147, 154; refugees 158; and banning of Habsburgs 222–3; postwar negotiations 256; signs peace treaty

with France 261; economic difficulties 423; and
NSDAP 458; *see also* Adler, Friedrich; Adler,
Victor; Austro-Hungarian Empire; Charles I;
Hitler, Adolf; Vienna
Austro-Hungarian Empire: in World War I 8–11,
13–14, 16, 70, 88, 100, 113, 115, 153, 154, 505;
collapse of x, 145, 149–50, 154, 256, 617, 619; *see
also* Austria; Czechoslovakia; Hungary; Yugoslavia
Avanti (newspaper) 224, 258

Babinski, Dr Joseph 21, 22, 492, 516; *Les Détraquées*
373–4, 605
Bad Gastein, Austria 324, 326, 419
Bad Kreuznach, Germany 81–2, 106
Bad Nauheim, Germany 343–4
Baker, Josephine 46, 213, 299–300, 388–9, 435,
486, 543–4, 604, 606
Baker, Willie 435
Baku, Azerbaijan 340–41, 346, 374
Ballets Russes 42
Bandirma (ship) 233
Barcelona 516
Barrès, Maurice 399, 400, 458
Bavaria 66, 107, 174, 205; as Soviet Republic
(1919) 222–3, 226, 228, 236, 255, 457,
571; and separatism 260, 279, 424, 457,
584; and Kapp putsch 305, 308; Freikorps
and nationalistic associations 372–3, 414,
484, 493, 578; and Nazi Party 396–7, 457,
508, 538–9, 559, 574; Palatinate 582–3;
see also Eisner, Kurt; Toller, Ernst; Leviné,
Eugen; Munich
Bavarian Reserve Infantry Regiment, 16th 94, 148, 481
Bayreuth, Germany 578–9
Beach, Sylvia 448
Béal na Bláth, County Cork 493–4
Beer-hall putsch (1923) *see* Munich
Belém, Brazil: 'Eclipse Exhibition' (1919) 234–5,
260, 272
Belfast 364, 407, 416, 445, 464, 486
Bell, Gertrude 391
Benedict XV, Pope 18, 55–6, 152, 223, 229, 431
Beneš, Edvard, Czechoslovak Foreign Minister 197
Bentinck, Count Godard 160, 171, 196, 221, 237,
257, 277, 312
Berchtesgaden, Germany 491, 554
Bergson, Henri 474, 550
Berlin: Kaiser Wilhelm's extravagant tastes 28, 33,
72; Einstein in 77, 272–3, 338–9; a missing
dog 91; Communist rising (1918–19) ix, 155,
163–4, 177–8, 183–5, 188–91, 193–4, 204;
returning soldiers greeted by Ebert 173–4;
Dada 177, 320; Luxemburg's body found 233–4;
Enver Pasha in 287–8; Kapp putsch (1920) 303,

304, 305; Talaat Pasha murdered 382; Hitler in
404, 413, 550; Mussolini visits 469
Berliner Illustrierte 580–81, 584, 589
Bernays, Edward 195, 270, 280, 325, 356, 570
Bernays-Freud, Minna 16, 324
Bethmann Hollweg, Chancellor Theobald von 12, 51–2
Birmingham, Alabama 436–7
Bizerte, Tunisia 357, 607
'Black and Tans' 329–30, 353, 364, 391, 396, 459, 471
Black Star Line 228, 267, 277, 287, 298, 309–10,
333, 348, 360, 376, 388, 418, 493, 540, 558
Blake, Eubie 388–9, 435, 604; *see also* Sissle, Noble
Bochkareva, Maria 40, 47, 50, 59, 62, 318, 367
Bohemia 110, 123, 151
Bohr, Niels 518
Bologna University 432
Bolsheviks / Bolshevism (Russia): early days 6–7,
29, 36–7, 39, 48; 1917 revolution 53–4, 64, 67,
69, 70, 73–5, 76; and Brest-Litovsk 82, 90–91,
95, 97, 99, 100, 108, 121; in Petrograd 92–4,
98; renamed Communist Party 100; in Moscow
101–2, 108–9, 142–3, 150–51, 155–7; and civil
war 118–19, 121–2, 131–2, 168, 182, 193, 238,
245–6, 254, 262, 268–9; *see also* Comintern;
Communist Party; Politburo
Bose, Dr Girindrasekhar 466
Boston, Massachusetts 213, 229, 241, 265, 286,
310, 349, 395
Boston American 313
Brailsford, Henry 508
Brandner, Mademoiselle (teacher) 125, 126
Breslau, Silesia 76, 82–3, 142
Brest, France 87, 102, 144, 171
Brest-Litovsk: negotiations and peace treaty
(1917–18) 82, 88–91, 96–8, 99–100, 108, 109,
111, 121, 197, 333, 603
Breton, André: and Apollinaire 21, 96, 161; and
Vaché 21, 187; as assistant to Babinski 21–2, 605;
and Dada and Tzara 177, 187, 204, 205; launches
Littérature magazine 204–5, 241; automatic
writing with Soupault 241–2, 261; and Aragon
242; as doctor at Orly Aviation Centre 261; and
Tzara's arrival in Paris 292–3; performs in Dada
poetry reading 293–4; has doubts about Dada
297; allowance cut off by mother 308; meets
future wife 318; holidays in Brittany 320; keeps
off the breadline 358; and Tzara 359, 382, 428;
and Babinski's play 374; and *Littérature* rankings
382; organises theatrical mock trial 399–400; on
honeymoon 427–8; and Freud 428, 466, 605;
accuses Tzara of fraud 458–9; frees himself from
Dada 459; hosts seances 502–3, 545–6; and surrealism 503, 546, 599, 600; tells Dadaists Dada
is dead 516; and Tzara's new show 558, 559–60;

goes fishing 560; works for art collector 580; sees Picasso 480; publishes *Les Pas Perdus* 599; returns to automatic writing 599; opens Bureau of Surrealist Research 605–6

Breton, Simone (*née* Kahn) 318, 320, 358, 427–8, 466, 502

Bridgeport, Connecticut 273

British Labour Delegation to Russia 312, 318, 320–22

Brooklyn Daily Eagle 274

Brugha, Cathal, Minister of Defence 416

Bryant, Louise 65, 94, 200–1, 318, 340, 344, 345, 400, 433

Buchanan, George, British Ambassador 26

Büchner, Bruno 554

Büchner, Elisabeth 554

Buchs, Switzerland 218

Budapest 8–11, 140–41, 149–50, 151–2, 158, 162–3, 215, 226, 229, 252–3, 280, 304, 385–6

Bullitt, William C. 198, 215

Bund Oberland 571

Bureau of Investigation 243, 251, 273–4, 332

Burford, USAT 280–81, 292

Calcutta: 'Eccentric Club' 466

Canada/Canadians 30, 70, 80, 133, 197, 239, 251, 299, 410, 432, 565; *see also* Toronto; *Toronto Star Weekly*

Cannes, France 531

Caporetto (Karfreit), Battle of (1917) 70–71, 72, 80, 152, 337, 491

Carlotti, Andrea, Italian Ambassdor 98

Carnegie, Andrew 171

Chamberlain, Houston Stewart 414, 578, 579;

Chamby, Switzerland 540

Chaplin, Charlie 296, 297, 370, 383, 426–7, 522, 581, 582

Chaplin, Captain Georgi 131–2

Charcot, Jean-Martin 15, 21, 22, 35

Charleroi, Belgium 239

Charles I, of Austria (Charles IV, of Hungary) *see* Habsburg, Charles

Charpy, General Georges 393

Cheka (*later* GPU) 79, 101, 102, 119, 121, 122, 133, 135, 157, 182, 201, 219, 238, 268, 318, 368, 380, 405, 425, 451–2, 463

Chelyabinsk, Russia 113, 114–15

Chernov, Viktor 93

Chicago 37–8, 251–2, 256–7, 268, 286, 287, 313, 331, 361, 367–8, 376, 395

Chicago Daily News 286

Chicago Daily Tribune 122

Chicago Defender 229

Chicago Tribune 32, 55, 79, 251

Chicherin, Gyorgy 477, 524

Chocolate Dandies, The 604, 608

Churchill, Clementine 413, 489–90, 519, 520, 568–70

Churchill, Jennie (*née* Jerome) 412

Churchill, Marigold 413 489

Churchill, Winston: in World War I 40, 66–7, 104, 105, 107, 133–4, 154, 155; and Russian Civil War 197, 198, 225, 261, 268, 275, 278, 287, 327, 380, 447; and Enver Pasha 288; invited to Germany by Ludendorff 301; and Ireland 107, 329, 430, 445, 472, 487, 494; and Clare Sheridan 345, 380, 531, 567; Lenin on 347; Garvey on 377; supports Zionism 391, 413; approves of Abdullah, of Trans-Jordan 391; opposes Lloyd George's pro-Greek line 392; and daughter's death 413, 490; gambles in France 489–90; has appendicitis operation 519; loses Dundee seat 519–20; devotes himself to painting and writing 531; publishes first volume of *The World Crisis* 531, 549; and MacDonald's victory 598; becomes Chancellor of the Exchequer 607

Cincinnati, Ohio 376, 600

Clan na Gael 207

Clarke, Edward Young 482

Clausewitz, Carl von 424, 542

Clemenceau, Georges 191, 220, 244

Cleveland, Ohio 395

Clonmult, County Cork 371

Coburg, Germany 508–9

Collins, Johnny 372

Collins, Michael 68, 69, 107; frees de Valera from prison 192, 195; as Finance Minister 236; forms hit squad 241; and Sinéad de Valera's salary 274, 330; becomes a hero of the cause 301; orders murder of British officers 353; evades capture 354; his guerrilla tactics blasted by de Valera 364; refuses to go to America 367; relations with de Valera deteriorate 390; opposes attack on Dublin Custom House 396; letters to Kitty Kiernan 396–7, 430, 435, 437–8, 451, 472; excluded by de Valera from discussions in London 408; then sent to negotiate peace terms 416–17, 429–31, 435, 436, 438, 444–5, 446; reception in Ireland 449, 450, 451, 456; and Dáil vote on Treaty 456, 457; chairs new provisional government 459; and civil war 463, 464, 471–2, 487, 488; corresponds with Churchill 490; assassination and funeral 493–4

Cologne, Germany 475, 489

Colón, Panama 310

Comintern (Communist International) 209–12, 217, 219, 255, 291, 312, 321, 425; first Congress (1919) 209–12; second Congress (1920) 327–9, 331, 333, 338, 340–41; third Congress (1921) 405–6; Lenin's speech to (1922) 515; and Schlageter 559; and Zinoviev letter 606–7; fourth Congress (1923) 543

Commissariat of Enlightenment (*Narkompros*) 111, 130, 289, 323, 387, 425, 455
Communism/Communist Parties 328; Russia 100, 175, 211, 213, 219, 262, 289, 346, 362, 363, 377–8, 425, 429, 475, 476, 484, 510, 529, 583, 616, *see also* Comintern; Ukraine 131, 603; Hungary 163, 187, 217; Germany and Bavaria ix, 184, 185, 194, 204, 222, 223, 229, 308, 355, 373, 381, 484, 538, 550–51, 554, 562, 575, 583, *see also* Spartacus League; America 256–7, 286, 291; Italy 409, 453, 616; Toronto 586
Communist Labor Party (US) 256–7, 291
Connable, Dorothy 299, 367
Connable, Harriet 298, 299
Constantine, King of Greece 401, 498
Constantinople *see* Istanbul
Constituent Assembly (Russia) 79, 92, 93–4, 118, 131
Coolidge, President Calvin 265, 349, 603
Coppedge, Samuel 46
Corfu 221, 561, 569, 570, 571, 572, 574, 575–6
Cork/County Cork, Ireland 206, 304–5, 353–4, 364, 371, 372, 488, 493–4
Council of People's Commissars *see* Sovnarkom
Cousins, E. W., President of British Phrenological Society 368
Cox, James 349
Crewe, Robert Crew-Milnes, 1st Marquess of 576
Crimea, the 109, 309, 324, 347, 348, 350, 352, 387, 503, 603, 607
Crisis, The (magazine) 113, 169, 230, 327, 360, 376, 419, 493, 531
Croatia/Croatians 8, 250
Croft, William 251
Crommelin, Dr Andrew Claude de la Cherois 234, 235
Croton-on-Hudson, USA 400
Cuba 277, 287, 298, 310
Cuno, Wilhelm, German Chancellor 562–3
Curie, Marie 473
Curzon of Kedleston, George Curzon, 1st Marquess 524, 537–8
Custance, Mrs (suffragette) 586
Czechoslovak Corps 113, 114–15, 118, 127, 131;
Czechoslovakia 47, 113, 151, 197, 240; troops 49, 113, 181, 197–8, 227, 229, *see also* Czechoslovak Corps; Sudeten Germans 256, 458; *see also* Bohemia; Prague
Czernin von and zu Chudenitz, Count Ottokar, Austrian Foreign Minister 88, 91, 97, 106

Dada /Dadists 157, 176–7, 187, 263, 292, 293, 294, 297, 308, 318, 320, 359, 399–400, 458–9, 503, 516, 544; manifestos 85, 176, 177, 292, 359
Dada magazine 176, 177, 187, 204

Dáil, the 192–3, 236, 274, 292, 354, 450–51, 456–7, 472
Daily Express 225
Daily Mail 206, 290, 449, 520, 572
Dalmatia 186, 227, 250, 258
D'Annunzio, Gabriele 32, 205, 215, 399; and America's entry into the war 32–3; and battle of Caporetto 71; drops propaganda leaflets over Vienna 134; loves war 150; and armistice 154; and Mussolini 163, 216, 263, 385, 410, 470, 512, 530, 556; and Italy's claims to Dalmatia 186, 227; and Fiume 257–9, 294, 295–6, 337, 360–61, 363, 384, 470; his faults become obvious 337; and Clare Sheridan 345; moves to Lake Garda 369; ranked by Breton and Tzara 382; visited by Chicherin 477; transforms Lake Garda villa 491, 561; becomes leader of Federation of the Workers of the Sea 491–2, 511; falls out of a window 492; has new mistress 561; donates house to Italy 594; made a prince 598
Danube, River 127, 174, 212, 253, 439, 557
Daudet, Léon 294, 474
Davidson, Randall, Archbishop of Canterbury 290
Davis, Arthur N. 33, 72
Dearborn Independent 276, 316–17, 334, 357, 358, 370, 390, 395, 415, 448, 455, 529
Debs, Eugene 349, 451
Delitzsch, Saxony 549
Denikin, General Anton 119, 131, 168, 182, 193, 198, 211, 224, 246, 254, 260, 263, 268, 269, 275, 278, 309, 557
Des Moines, Iowa 265
Detroit, Michigan 273
de Valera, Brian 117
de Valera, Éamon 44; released from Lewes jail 44; wins Sinn Féin seat 44, 52–3, 68; and Collins 68; elected president of Sinn Féin 69; rearrested 107, 117; escapes to Dublin 169–70, 195, 205–6; visits America 206, 236, 237, 240–41, 292; and Garvey 332, 333, 418; returns to Dublin 363–4; clashes with Collins 364, 367, 390, 408, 463; has talks with Lloyd George 408–9, 410–11; further negotiations 411, 416–17; sends Collins to London 416–17, 431, 436; and signing of the Treaty (1921) 444, 445–6, 449–51, 456–7; resigns presidency 457; on speaking tour 463; and IRA 471; and Irish civil war 471, 472; and Field Marshal Wilson's assassination 486; backs anti-treaty IRA 487; at large 494; 'a simple volunteer' 507; furious with the Church 507; journeys back to Dublin 544; backs IRA ceasefire 555; rearrested 566–7, 587
de Valera, Sinéad 117, 206, 237, 241, 274, 330, 364
Diaghilev, Sergei 516
Dickel, Otto 413

Dickens, Charles: *The Cricket on the Hearth* 510

Dingfelder, Johannes 296

Dixie Steppers 299–300, 543

Dixon, Miss (teacher) 38

Djemal Pasha 81, 125, 124–5, 152, 232–3

Doheny, Edward 600

Dongen, Kees van 351

Doorn, The Netherlands 312–13, 386, 392, 414, 420–21, 426, 470–71, 487, 514–15, 553, 576, 589

Dörpfeld, Wilhelm 221

Dormans, France 474–5

Doyle, Arthur Conan 242

Dresden, Germany 566

Drews, Bill, Prussian Minister of the Interior 153

Drexler, Anton 286, 296, 372, 413, 414, 458

Dublin: guerrilla warfare 301; murder of British officers 353–4; Custom House set on fire 396; and ceasefire (1921) 407; Dublin Castle ceremony (1922) 459; British forces remain in 463; IRA occupy Four Courts 471, 486–7, 520; Kilmainham jail 587; Yeats's house damaged 607, 535; *see also* Dáil, the

Du Bois, William: articles in NAACP magazine 113, 169; Garvey as alternative to 129; goes to Paris peace conference (1918) 169, 170–71; tours French battlefields 202; attends Pan-African Congress 202; his aim for racial equality 230; and Garvey 268, 327, 332–3, 348, 359–60; and Ford's anti-Semitic campaign 370; invited by Garvey to a debate 412; repudiates Garvey's ideas 418–19; successful in Geneva 419; his views on Harding's Birmingham speech 446; and anti-lynching bill 462; publishes exposé of Black Star Line 493; downgrades UNIA 531; relations with Garvey worsen 540; on race war 540–41; and Garvey's trial and sentence 558–9; finally meets Garvey 600

Duisburg, Germany 308, 381, 535, 548

Dulles, Allen 31, 197, 261, 304, 393, 404, 415

Dulles, Clover 393

Duma, the 25, 26, 27

Dumlupinar, Turkey 494

Dundee, Scotland 519–20

Düsseldorf, Germany 381, 548, 579

Dyer, General Reginald 220

Dyson, Sir Frank Watson, Astronomer Royal 272

Dzerzhinsky, Felix, head of Cheka, 79, 201

Dzhugashvili, Yakov (Stalin's son) 442

Eason, Reverend Dr James 531

East St. Louis, Illinois: riots 45–7, 325

Ebert, Friedrich, Chancellor of Germany 150, 159, 163–4, 167, 173–4, 177, 184, 185, 188, 191, 193, 257, 303, 534

Eckart, Dietrich 144, 272, 296, 305, 358, 551–2, 554

Eckartsau, Austria 162, 165, 205, 212, 217–18

'Eclipse Expedition' (1919) 234–6, 260, 272–3, 485

Edib, Halidé 500, 501

Eichholz-in-Murnau, Bavaria 481

Eichhorn, Emil, Chief of Berlin Police 184

Eijsden, The Netherlands 159–60

Einstein, Albert: nominated for Nobel Prize 11, 87, 291; and Friedrich Adler 42; unknown in Berlin 77; and theory of relativity x, 183, 234–5, 272–3, 290, 389, 442; bedridden with stomach ulcer 87; marital problems 87, 106; with Elsa on the Baltic 120; goes to Zurich 183; and 'Eclipse Expedition' (1919) 234, 235, 260, 272–3, 485; fame and controversy 273, 290, 291; political views 290–91; dirty campaign against 316; on Nordic tour with Elsa 316; and anti-relativists 338–9, 343–4, 482; in Prague 369, 370; and American lecture tour 370, 375; invited to America by Zionists 375–6; ranked by Breton and Tzara 382; fêted in New York 389–90, 395; lectures at Princeton 395; on Baltic coast with sons 403; in trouble for reckless remarks 403; in Italy, Zurich and Leiden 432; cancels trip to Munich 433; has wonderful time in Paris 473–4; visits French battlefield 474–5; on current situation in Germany 508; visits Japan 516–18, 524; awarded Nobel Prize 518; in Palestine 539–40; resigns from League of Nations' committee 550; gives Nobel lecture in Sweden 560–61; fights with Mileva and sons over Nobel Prize money 561; at pacifist rally in Berlin 561; sailing with son 564; in love with secretary 576–7; and anti-Semitic riots in Berlin 586; in Leiden 592–3; decides to live more quietly 597; undecided about secretary 606

Einstein, Eduard 344, 403, 432, 452, 561

Einstein, Elsa (*née* Einstein) 87, 106, 120, 183, 316, 376, 389, 432, 433, 516, 577, 586

Einstein, Hans-Albert 120, 344, 403, 432, 561, 564

Einstein, Margot 339, 432

Einstein, Mileva (*née* Maric) 87, 106, 344, 432, 518, 561

Eisner, Kurt 158, 194, 204, 205

Ekaterinburg, Russia 113, 116, 118, 127, 250

Eliot, T. S. 522; *The Waste Land* 503, 522

Elisabeth of Bavaria, Queen of the Belgians 239

Encyclopaedia Britannica 523

Engels, Friedrich 130, 157, 371; *Communist Manifesto* 255, 341

Ennis, County Clare 566

Enver Pasha, Ismael 81, 125, 126, 152, 232–3, 287–8, 334, 341, 411, 441–2, 491

Erzberger, Matthias 414, 484

Erzurum, Ottoman Empire 233, 248–9

Eskişehir, Ottoman Empire 411

Essen, Germany 533–4, 535–6, 544–5, 548, 552–3, 560
Europe, James Reese (Jim) 32, 63, 87, 102, 105, 112, 119–20, 137, 144, 169, 202, 212–13, 229–30

Faisal, King of Iraq 391–2
Fall, Albert 600
Fasci di Combattimento 216, 217, 224, 258, 263, 296, 360, 369, 384, 409–10, 469–70
Fascism/Fascists 326, 336, 337, 360, 361, 369, 384, 400, 439–40, 442, 469, 492, 510–13, 530, 556, 567, 585, 600; see also Fasci di Combattimento
Feder, Gottfried 481
Federn, Paul: On the Psychology of Revolution 222
Ferdinand, King of Bulgaria 143
Ferenczi, Sándor 10, 140, 141, 152, 226
Fikriye, Mustafa Kemal's girlfriend, 498, 501, 532, 599
Fisher, H. A. L. 301
Fitzgerald, F. Scott 283, 289; This Side of Paradise 289; Tales of the Jazz Age 495
Fitzgerald, Zelda 289
Fiume 151, 186, 227, 250–5, 257–9, 263, 275, 294–6, 337, 360–61, 363, 369, 384, 598
Florence, Italy 263
Foch, Marshal Ferdinand 105–6, 160, 182, 230–31, 440–41
Ford, Clara 549
Ford, Henry 57, 245–6, 265, 276, 316–17, 334, 358, 370, 395, 447, 455, 471, 481, 521, 522, 529, 542, 544, 549, 563–4, 586, 590, 603, 606; My Life and Work 506, 601; The International Jew 535
Fortaleza, Brazil 235
Fossalta, Italy 483
Franchet d'Espèrey, General Louis 232
Francis, David R., American Ambassador 108, 110
Franco, General Francisco 573
Franz Ferdinand, Archduke 9, 49, 110, 162, 205, 244
Frederick Douglass (ship) 309–10
Freikorps 174, 185, 188, 189, 191, 194, 203–4, 229, 234, 257, 303, 304, 372, 414, 548, 571
Freud, Amalia (née Nathansohn) 577
Freud, Anna 13, 16, 252, 270, 296, 314, 342, 466, 479, 550, 570
Freud, Ernst 270
Freud, Martha (née Bernays) 16
Freud, Martin 16, 75, 154, 159, 165, 178
Freud, Mathilde 16
Freud, Oli(ver) 13, 16, 270, 535
Freud, Sam 226, 269–70, 280, 296, 314, 342, 345, 448–9, 523, 535
Freud, Sigmund x, 10, 12–17, 21, 22; preoccupied with submarines 23, 38; fails to win Nobel Prize 38; and Friedrich Adler 42; in Hungarian countryside 45; works on new idea 75;

pessimistic 75–6, and angry 81; afraid he will die in his 61st year 91, 100, 119; and food supply problems 104; arranges a summer break 119; at Psychoanalytic Congress in Budapest 140–42; thrilled by end of war 152; on Kaiser Wilhelm 158; worried about son, Martin 159, 165, 178; on shortages in Vienna 165; brought provisions by American visitors 194–5; on Austrian territorial losses 213; writes to cousin Sam for help 226, 269–70, 280, 296, 345, 523; and Tausk's suicide 252; walks in the hills 252; pleased by Mordell's book 252; visited by English colleague 263; his lectures being translated by Edward Bernays 270, 280; and his daughter's death 285; at Bad Gastein with Minna Bernays-Freud 324; writes crowd psychology 324–5, 326; at The Hague psychoanalytic congress 341–2; dislikes comic poem sent by Sam 345; gives evidence at inquiry investigating doctors' methods during the war 348; refuses American lecture tour 356–7; ranked by Breton and Tzara 382; hates sculpture of his head 397; on group holiday in Harz mountains 419–20; on the 'occult' 420; inundated by patients 423; angry with his acolytes 423–4; misses Anna 466; cheered by global growth in psychoanalysis 466; and Breton's visit 428, 466, 605; remains on formal terms with the Committee 491; and Mussolini 513; has growth in mouth removed 535, 550, 555; birthday celebrations 555; and death of grandson 555; in Rome with Anna 570; has two further operations 577–8; receives unsolicited biography from Fritz Wittels 594; starts work again 597; on cover of Time magazine 607–8; and Sam Goldwyn 608–9
Freud, Sophie see Halberstadt-Freud, Sophie
Frobenius, Leo 576
Futurism/Futurists 157, 177, 209, 216, 259, 290, 558

Gandhi, Mohandas ('Mahatma') 179, 220, 418, 419
Garda, Lake 369, 410, 477, 491, 556, 561, 594
Garibaldi, Giuseppe 130
Garvey, Marcus 46; and UNIA 129–30, 298, 311, 327, 331–3, 347, 449, 493; moved to tears by Jim Europe's band 202; denies involvement in bombing 228; and Black Star Line 228, 267–8, 277, 298, 310, 333; and Du Bois 327, 359–60, 412, 418–19, 540, 558–9, 600; on speaking tours 347, 376–7; returns to Jamaica 387–8, 411–12; in Costa Rica and Panama 412; has run-in with African Blood Brotherhood 418; and President Harding 437, 563; and Irish peace treaty 449; on tour again 479; meets with Ku Klux Klan leader 481–2; on Kemal 500; blames

NAACP for death of anti-lynching bill 514; on trial for mail fraud 531, 558; jailed for five years 558; finally meets Du Bois 600

Gaulle, Charles de 66, 70, 82, 128–9, 173, 244–5, 277–8, 326, 333, 335, 351, 399, 400, 474, 565–6

Gaulle, Yvonne de (née Vendroux) 351, 565

Gehrcke, Ernst 338, 339, 482

General Kornilov (cruiser) 352–3

Geneva 419

Genoa 178, 185; confernece (1922) 476–8

George V, of the United Kingdom 44, 105, 212, 407, 418, 431, 438, 520

George Washington, USS 171, 220

'Georgian bank-robber' see Stalin, Josef

German Workers' Party 259–60, 271, 279, 286, 296, 315; see National Socialist German Workers' Party

Gide, André 197

Goethe, Johann Wolfgang von 420

Goldman, Emma 281, 380

Goldwyn, Samuel 608

Golzheimer Heath, Germany 555–6

Göring, Carin 543

Göring, Hermann 543, 588, 591

Gorki, Russia 140, 146–7, 219, 249–50, 289, 323, 368, 405, 408, 452, 455, 480–81, 483–4, 490, 492, 494, 497, 521, 554, 567, 593–4

Gorky, Maxim 408, 415–16

Gothenburg, Sweden 560–61

GPU 425, 463, 470, 479, 491, 598

Graf, Caecilie ('Mausi') 314, 491

Graham, Robert William, British Ambassador to Italy 522, 546

Grant, Madison 19

Graves, Philip 404, 415

Grayson, Dr Cary T. 525

Greece/Greeks xi, 126, 164–5, 186, 196, 231–2, 248, 305, 334, 350, 361, 370–71, 383, 388, 401, 411, 415, 417, 461, 488, 494, 495–6, 497, 498, 499, 506, 507, 518, 524, 563, 568; see also Corfu

Griffith, Arthur 68, 69, 430, 431, 457

Groddeck, Georg 341

Haber, Fritz 291, 339, 376, 395

Habsburg, Charles (Charles I, of Austria; Charles IV, of Hungary): crowned king of Hungary 8–10; and Kaiser Wilhelm 9, 11, 63, 72, 106, 119, 152; Einstein writes to 42; on official visit to Munich 49; prays for peace 50; and naval mutiny 100; and Sixtus affair 106; has minor heart attack 106; greeted enthusiastically in Pressburg 127; peace attempts 147; proposes reforms to win American favour 149–50, 151; and Italy 152; declares he will no longer play a part in the affairs of state 161; leaves Vienna for Eckartsau 162, 165; and Strutt 205, 212; escapes to Lake Constance 217–18; at Prangins, Lake Geneva 270; hopes for restoration of his crown from Horthy 303–4, 385–6, 438–9; exiled to Madeira 439, 466–7; death 467

Hague, The 160, 171, 277, 297–8, 341–2

Halberstadt-Freud, Heinz Rudolf 555

Halberstadt-Freud, Sophie 16, 285, 555

Hamburg 583

Hanfstaengl, Egon 541, 591

Hanfstaengl, Ernst ('Putzi') 522, 541–2, 543, 549, 550, 552, 559, 591, 609

Hanfstaengl, Helene 541, 542, 543, 591, 609

Hanson, Mayor Ole 227

Harding, President Warren 349, 350, 401, 418, 436–7, 441, 446, 451, 479, 563

Harlem 32, 46, 139, 230, 332, 359, 531; infantry regiments 32, 169, 202, 388

Harrer (sports journalist) 144

Harrer, Karl 144, 271

Haskell County, Kansas 98–9

Hässleholm, Sweden 183

Havza, Ottoman Empire 233

Heemstra, Lili van 420–21, 426

Heimatland (newspaper) 584

Helsinki, Finland 59, 64

Hemingway, Clarence 37, 55, 87, 114, 253, 330, 476

Hemingway, Ernest 37–8, 55; as cub reporter 79–80, 104; joins Missouri National Guard 80; plans to fight in Europe 87–8; embarks for France 114; in Paris 118; wounded 122–3, 145; has jaundice 145; home again 208; gives talk at his old school 208–9; Agnes von Kurowsky calls engagement off 209; on fishing trip with old school friends 253; moves to Petoskey 253; employed by Toronto Star Weekly 298–9; home again 330; votes for Debs 349; moves to Chicago 331, 361, 367–8; meets future wife 367; wedding 417; on SS Leopoldina bound for Paris 447–8; in Paris 460, 545; as a man of letters 460–61; as a journalist at Genoa conference 476–7; meets Mussolini 482–3; visits front line 483; grows a moustache in Germany 495; in Istanbul 506–7, 514; writes profile of Kemal 507; at conference in Lausanne 518; meets Ismet Pasha 518–19; has audience with Mussolini 519; his manuscripts lost by wife 519, 540; visits Pound in Rapallo 540; and his wife's pregnancy 540, 565; and Krupp tragedy 553; and German inflation 562; interest aroused in bull-fighting 564–5; sails for Canada 565; works for Star again 579–80, 586; and birth of son 580; his in our time published 594; resigns from the Star 594; joins transatlantic review in Paris 599

Hemingway, Grace 88, 114, 330, 367, 450

Hemingway, Hadley 367, 417, 447, 448, 460, 482,

483, 495, 519, 540, 564, 565, 580, 594, 599
Hemingway, John Nicanor ('Bumby') 580, 599
Hemingway, Marcelline 37, 80, 88, 145, 594
Hermine, Princess 471, 487–8, 514–15, 571, 573
Herzl, Theodore 539
Hess, Rudolf 396, 601
Hildesheim, Germany 419–20
Hindenburg, Field Marshal Paul von 12, 52, 146, 153
Hindmarsh, Harry 580
Hitler, Adolf ix; as 'mangy Austrian field-runner'
    94; in hospital 152; at Berlin socialist rally 163;
    at POW camp 176; on guard duty for Eisner's
    regime 194; has little to do 205; escapes de-
    mobilisation 222, 223, 236, 247; finds a talent
    248; gives political lectures 255–6; a rising star
    at German Workers' Party meetings 259, 260,
    271–2, 279–80, 286; launches his manifesto 286,
    296–7; and Kapp putsch 305; leaves the army
    308–9; delivers anti-Semitic speeches 255, 286,
    287, 315, 335–6, 370, 451–2, 472–3, 534–5;
    hones his speaking technique 314; foresees
    Anschluss with Russia 324; takes his sister shop-
    ping 343; against League of Nations 357; and
    control of Völkischer Beobachter 358; and survival
    of NSDAP 372–3; has a sweet tooth 373; on tour
    in Bavaria 381; meets Ludendorff 383–4; rails
    against German reparations 393–4; a personal
    testimony from Hess 396; on fundraising drive
    in Berlin 404; and struggle for leadership of
    NSDAP 413–14; and Protocols 415; launches the
    SA 424, 447; designs NSDAP armbands 424;
    provokes his enemies 447; given prison sentence
    457, 458; and Toller 457–8; opposes Rathenau
    as Foreign Minister 461; and deportation to
    Austria 467, 472; is given a dog 473; with Feder
    and Müller 481; begins deferred jail sentence
    484; criticises public order legislation 493; has
    idea for a putsch 493; meets Lüdecke 505–6;
    at Coburg festival 508–9; delivers speeches
    throughout Munich 521; interviewed by Truman
    Smith 521–2; meets Hanfstaengl 522; rages
    at occupation of the Ruhr 534, 551; defends
    rights of SA to march 538–9; with Hanfstaengl
    family 541–2, 543, 549–50, 552; sexuality 542;
    meets Benedictine monk 542–3; and Ford 544;
    outraged at being photographed 550; challenges
    Munich authorities 551–2; visits Eckart 554; on
    a future dictator 554–5; cartoons of 557–8; and
    Schlageter's death 559; on democracy 567–8; at
    Nuremberg rally 571; and Kampfbund 571–2,
    575; and Kemal 573; in Hof and Berlin 574;
    gives interview to Viereck 577; meets Wagners
    578–9; lifts ban on photographs 580–81; hires
    biographer 581; and Kahr 578, 582, 586, 587;

and Beer-hall putsch 587–9, 591; jailed 591,
    593, 599–600, 601, 604; starts writing Mein
    Kampf 601, 603; released from prison 609
Hitler, Paula 343, 554
Hochheimer, Dr 139
Hof, Germany 574
Hoffmann, General Max 89, 90–91, 98, 99, 107
Hoffmann, Johannes 222, 228
Hong Kong 517
Hoover, J. Edgar 251, 274, 433
Horne, William D.: Hemingway's letters to 209,
    253, 565
Horthy, Miklós 100, 303–4, 385, 438, 537
Horton Bay, Michigan 417
House, Colonel Edward 19, 22, 23, 88, 153, 182,
    199, 214, 243, 264, 270
Houston, Texas: riots (1917) 47, 80
Hughes, Charles Evans, Secretary of State 418, 441
Hungary 8, 9, 45, 119, 149–50, 151, 152, 154,
    216–17; Communist Party 163, 217; Soviet
    Republic of 217, 226–7, 229, 253; and Charles
    Habsburg 385–6, 438–9, 466–7; see also Austria-
    Hungary; Budapest; Horthy, Miklós; Kun, Béla

Ilsemann, Sigurd von, Kaiser Wilhelm's equerry
    237, 243, 359, 553, 590
'impatient revolutionary' see Lenin, Vladimir Ilyich
India ix, 182, 219–20, 279, 288, 419, 449, 466;
    Muslim Khalifat campaign 341
Indianapolis 440–41
inflation (Germany) ix, 495, 547, 562
influenza epidemic 117–18, 128, 144, 145, 161,
    169, 182, 220, 285
Ingolstadt, Bavaria 82
IRA see Irish Republican Army
Ireland 44, 107, 274, 292, 328, 372, 396, 416,
    430–32, 463–4, 471–2, 488, 507, 535, 555; see
    also 'Black and Tans'; Collins, Michael; Cork;
    Dáil, the; de Valera, Éamon; Dublin; Royal Irish
    Constabulary; Sinn Féin and below
Irish Free State 444, 457, 464, 486, 487, 488, 507,
    520, 535, 566
Irish Republican Army (IRA) 193, 237, 329, 330,
    353–4, 364, 371–2, 391, 396, 411, 416, 450,
    464, 486, 487, 494, 520, 535, 555
Irish Times 450, 486
Irish Volunteers (later Irish Republican Army) 44,
    52–3, 68–9, 192–3, 241, 274
Ismet Pasha, Mustafa 518–19, 524, 537–8
Istanbul (Constantinople) 81, 124, 125, 145,
    147, 164–5, 196, 305–6, 334, 350, 353, 383,
    393, 401, 404, 447, 461, 488, 499, 506–7,
    514, 584
Istpart 429

Izmir *see* Smyrna
Jacob, Mathilde 178, 189, 234
Japan/Japanese 19, 23, 108, 131, 181, 182, 197,
    441, 510, 569; and League of Nations 214;
    Kaiser Wilhelm's views on 276, 359; Einstein in
    433, 516–18, 524
Jerusalem 80, 81, 307, 375, 391, 539; Hebrew
    University 517, 539
Jews *see* anti-Semitism; Zionism
Joachim, Prince 276
Johnson, Harry 112, 113, 182, 202, 209
Josephson, Matthew 545
Joyce, James 31, 459, 460, 516
Jung, Carl 15, 345, 423

Kahn, Simone *see* Breton, Simone
Kahr, Gustav von 575, 578, 582, 586, 587–8
Kamenev, Lev 70, 504
Kampfbund 572, 575, 587, 588, 589
Kansas City, Missouri 79–80, 104, 264
Kansas City Star 79–80, 118
Kapp putsch (1920) 303, 304, 305, 308, 581
Karabekir, Kâzim 249
Kardiner, Alfred 423
Karfreit *see* Caporetto
Karlsbad, Bohemia 123–6, 334, 532
Károlyi, Mihály, Hungarian Minister-President 152, 216
Kautsky, Karl 6, 147, 168, 211
Kazan, Russia 133, 137
Keller, Guido 295
Kemal, Mustafa (Atatürk) xi; visits Kaiser Wilhelm
    81–2; in Karlsbad for medical treatment 123–6;
    in Syria 143; in Istanbul 165; as inspector of the
    9th army 233; leaves army 233, elected head of
    congress in Erzurum 248–9; his influence con-
    tinues to spread 263; wins elections 279; gives
    campaign speech in Kirsehir 279; and Enver 288,
    411, 441–2; as focus of national resistance in
    Ankara 305–6, 341, 371; and Sultan Vahdettin
    306; makes overtures to Soviet Russia 306, 334,
    361–2, 383, 388; and Fikriye 361, 498, 501,
    532, 599; disliked by Vahdettin 383; position gets
    stronger daily 383; and Greco-Turkish war 401,
    411, 417, 461, 488, 494, 495, 497, 498–9, 569;
    as leader in Smyrna 498–500; and Lâtife 498,
    500, 501, 532; interviewed by Clare Sheridan
    500–1; agrees to be sculpted 501; agrees armistice
    with the Great Powers 507; his profile written
    by Hemingway 507; and Conference of Lausanne
    518; and his mother's death 531, 532; rides
    through Anatolia selling his vision 531–2; marries
    Lâtife 532; signs Treaty of Lausanne 563; and
    Hitler 573; confirmed as head of a secular republic
    584, 599; adapts Swiss civil code for Turkey 604

Kennedy, Joseph P. 339–40
Kenney, Jessie 47, 48, 53, 57–8, 59–60, 96, 603
Kerensky, Alexander 27, 29, 40–41, 43, 48, 49, 50,
    51, 52, 53, 54, 55, 57, 58, 61, 62, 64, 65, 73,
    75, 76, 119, 142, 167
Kessler, Count Harry 158, 185, 194, 204, 303
Keynes, John Maynard 285, 323; *The Economic
    Consequences of the Peace* 329
Kharkov, Ukraine 107, 245–6
Kiel, Germany: naval mutiny 154, 164
Kiernan, Kitty 397, 488, 494; Michael Collins'
    letters to 397, 430, 435, 437–8, 444, 451, 472
Kiev, Ukraine 187, 211, 217, 254, 278, 312, 314,
    319, 603
King, Michael 436
King, Senator William H. 200, 201
King George V, HMS 488
Kingston, Jamaica 310, 387–8
Kırşehir, Ottoman empire 279
Kislovodsk, Caucasus: sanatorium 338, 342
Kitano Maru (ship) 517
Koblenz, Germany 489, 562
Kochnitzky, Leon 294
Koerber, Adolf Victor 581; *Adolf Hitler: His Life, His
    Speeches* 581
Kolchak, Admiral Alexander 168, 176, 181, 182,
    198, 211, 224, 225, 245, 249, 250, 254, 261,
    275, 278, 287, 323
Kollontai, Alexandra 78, 210–11, 283, 433, 477
Komissarzhevskaya, Vera 130
Kornilov, General Lavr 50, 58, 61–2, 92, 108, 109
Korzinkino, Russia 470
Kühlmann, Richard von, German Foreign Minister 97
Krasin, Leonid 477
Kronstadt, Russia 53–4, 56, 62, 94, 376, 377–80,
    381, 402
Krupp, Alfred/steelworks 455, 533–4, 548, 550,
    552, 553
Krupskaya, Nadezhda ('Nadya'): and Lenin 3, 4;
    with him in Switzerland 4, 6, 29, 31; busy in
    Petrograd 52; interrogated about Lenin 54; joins
    him in Finland 64; takes train to Moscow 101;
    and assassination attempt on Lenin 135–6; has
    heart disease 138, 475; in Gorki with Lenin 140,
    146; stays in forest school near Moscow 175,
    181–2; and the problem of educating the masses
    175; experiments with kitchen garden 219;
    sent on propaganda mission 249–50; and Inessa
    Armand's visits 262; walks with Lenin curtailed
    268; their Moscow apartment 289; employed by
    Commissariat of Enlightenment 289; amongst
    delegates at Comintern congress 328; greets
    Inessa's coffin 344; joins Lenin and Clara Zetkin
    in the Kremlin 354–5; visits Varya Armand with

Lenin 371; at Gorki 480, 494–5; sees Dickens play 510; abused by Stalin 523, 543; life with Lenin 554, 567, 583, 593, 597; and his death 597, 598; rebukes Trotsky 602
Ku Klux Klan (KKK) 129, 446, 479, 482, 493, 542, 601
Kühlmann, Richard von 89, 90
Kun, Béla 76, 102, 162–3, 187–8, 217, 223, 226, 227, 229, 253, 294, 341, 346, 381, 406

Lamarck, Jean-Baptiste 75
Landsberg Fortress, Bavaria 591, 593, 601
Lansing, Robert, Secretary of State 265–6
Lâtife, Mustafa Kemal's bride, 498, 500, 501, 532
Latvia/Latvians 35, 122, 203–4, 246, 348, 433
Lausanne, Switzerland 153, 518, 524, 532, 537–8, 563
Lawrence, T. E. 391, 520
Lea, Luvi 163, 195–6
League of Nations 170, 191, 196, 197, 198, 202, 206–7, 210, 214, 241, 244, 263, 264, 265, 275, 279, 285, 306, 357, 419, 428, 509, 550, 568, 569–70, 572, 575, 576
le Bon, Gustave 325
Leeds 43–4
Lefebvre, Raymond 328
Léhar, Franz 336
Leiden, The Netherlands 592–3
Lenard, Philipp 338, 343–4, 485
Lenin, Vladimir Ilyich 4, 27; in Switzerland 3–7, 13, 29, 30–31; relationship with Trotsky 17–18, 48, 89, 95, 99, 101, 137, 146, 149, 167, 208, 268, 301, 302, 311, 321, 368, 378, 402, 406, 429, 475, 495, 504, 523; and Rosa Luxemburg 33–4, 142–3, 184; returns to Russia 36–7; starts autobiography 38–9; as Bolshevik leader 39, 41, 48; and Kronstadt insurrection 53–4; goes into hiding 54–5, 58–9; and Bolshevik revolution 62, 64, 67, 73–4, 76, 77–9; governing style of 92, 93, 94, 95–6, 99, 100, 118, 132, 138; articles in *Pravda* 99–100, 346; moves to Moscow 100, 101, 102; and Kornilov's death 109; proposes food dictatorship 116; and death of Count Mirbach 121–2; lists those worthy of a statue 130; survives assassination attempt 135–6, 137, 138; holidays in Gorki 140; and Rosa Luxemburg 142–3, 178, 193, 465; and unrest in Germany 146–7; angered by Kautsky 147, 168–9; relationship with Stalin 149, 443, 480–81, 529, 543, 548–9; gives first speech since assassination attempt 150–51; speculates on course of events 154; at Bolshevik anniversary celebrations 156, 157; frustrated by petty administrative matters 174–5; and education of the masses 175; visits Nadya at her school 181–2; and Béla Kun 187, 217, 227, 253, 406; and defeat of Red forces

193; forms Communist International (1919) 209–12, 210; backs use of military experts 213; and creation of Politburo 214; records speeches 218–19; and anti-Semitism 219; and running of state farms 219; and White offensive 224, 238, 268; sends out furious instructions 246; on emancipation of women 262; his end-of-year report to All-Russia Congress of Soviets 278–9; and the Russian language 281, 288; frustrated by red tape and bureaucracy 288–9, 468; and Inessa Armand's illnesses and death 290, 338, 342, 344; endorses John Reed's book 292; on hunting trips 301, 302; feels his age 301–2; and birthday celebrations 311–12; and Polish advance 312, 314, 319, 323–4; and the economic crisis 321, 322–3, 362–3, 368–9, 374–5, 378–9, 387, 401–2, 407–8, 434, 440; meets British Labour Delegation 322; at second Commintern congress 328–9, 331, 333; and Red Army advance 333, 348; and Clare Sheridan 345, 346–7; and Kemal 361–2; and art students 371; and Kronstadt mutiny 381; ranked by Breton and Tzara 382; and Mayakovsky 397–9, 468; at third Comintern congress 405, 406; and Gorky 415–16; and Cheka 451–2; at Gorki 455–6, 462–3; illness 434–5, 463, 464–5; campaigns against the Church 470, 478–9; has operation 475, 478; health worsens 480–81, 483–4; and Rathenau's murder 485; fails to go to Politburo meeting 489; health improves 490–91; suffers seizure 492; health improves again 494–5; pleased at exile of intelligentsia 503; returns to work 503–4, 515; health worsens again 516, 520–21; dictates notes 523–4, 529, 602, and articles for *Pravda* 532–3; suffers stroke 546, 548, 567, 593–4; death and funeral 597–8
Leningrad 604–5, *see* Petrograd
Leopold II, of the Belgians 418
Leopold, Prince of Bavaria 82
Leopoldina, SS 447–8
Lerchenfeld, Hugo Count von and zu, Prime Minister of Bavaria 395–6
Leviné, Eugen 223, 228, 229
Levine, Isaac Don 367
Lewes, Sussex 44
Liebknecht, Karl 34, 159, 184, 189–91, 193, 223, 233, 571
Lincoln, England 117, 169–70, 195
Lincoln, Abraham 298, 316
Ling, Benjamin 286
Lìpp, Dr Franz, Foreign Minister 223
Littérature (magazine) 204–5, 241, 261, 293, 359, 382, 399, 466, 502–3, 580
Little Review 594
Lloyd George, David 40, 225, 261, 392, 408–9, 410–11,

416, 430, 431, 435, 438, 444, 446, 507, 519, 538
London 96, 105, 156, 172, 225, 315, 408–9, 426–
    7, 429–30, 438; Wilson in 185; Lenin in 211
Los Angeles, California 266, 286, 426
Louvain, Belgium 240
Lüdecke, Kurt 505–6, 530, 539, 541, 572
Ludendorff, General Erich 12; forces out Beth-
    mann-Hollweg 52; and revolution in Petrograd
    75; clashes with Kaiser Wilhelm 89; plans final
    assault 94–5, 105; and peace treaty with Russia
    97; and death of stepson 105, 111–12, 150;
    indecision 126–7, 128; in need of medical help
    138–9, 143; announces need for ceasefire 145–6,
    148; rejects Wilson's demands 150, 152–3;
    resigns 153; escapes to Copenhagen 162; and
    Kaiser Wilhelm 171–2, 221; moves to Sweden
    183; asks the British for new alliance against Bol-
    shevism 300–1; and Kapp putsch 303, 308; and
    Wilhelm's restoration 359; meets Hitler 383–4;
    at Auguste Viktoria's funeral 392; writings 422,
    541; at ceremony for Schlageter 559; in love
    with a psychiatrist 570; at Nuremberg rally 571;
    and Hitler 581, 586, 587; and beer-hall putsch
    588–9, 591; on trial 599, 600
Ludendorff, Margarethe 112, 162, 422, 570
Ludendorff, Mathilde 570
Ludwig III, of Bavaria 158
Ludwigshöhe, Bavaria 359
Lunacharsky, Anatoly 61, 397, 398
Luxemburg, Rosa 33–5, 76–7, 82–3, 85, 158, 164,
    178, 184, 188, 189–91, 193–4, 203, 233–4,
    328, 331, 335, 465, 571
Lviv, Ukraine 312, 334
lynching and anti-lynching legislation x, 46–7, 63,
    255, 267, 407, 437, 462, 463, 479, 482, 493, 514

MacCurtain, Thomas 304
MacDonald, James Ramsay 43, 598, 603, 604
Madeira 439, 466–7
Madrid 117, 573
Maginot, André 351
Manchester 192, 195, 206, 226, 269–70, 280, 296,
    314, 345, 448, 505, 523, 535
Manchester Guardian 292, 448, 513
'mangy field-runner' see Hitler, Adolf
Mann, Heinrich 566
Mann, Thomas 566
Mantua, Italy 384
Maran, René 493
Maria-Josefa, Archduchess of Austria 218
Marinetti, Filippo 209, 216, 223–4, 259, 275, 297, 337
Markievicz, Constance 456
Marx, Karl 5, 6, 37, 130, 138, 147, 156, 157, 168,
    183, 321, 371; Communist Manifesto 255, 341; Das

Kapital 124
Masaryk, Tomáš 47, 603
Matin, Le 589
Matisse, Henri 382
Matteotti, Giacomo, Italian Socialist leader 602, 608
Max von Baden, Prince 146
Mayakovsky, Vladimir 1, 290, 312, 371, 397, 399,
    468, 516, 598, 608; 150,000,000 397–8
Mayer, Al 435
McAdoo, Eleanor Wilson 267, 350
Mehmed V, Ottoman Sultan 124, 125
Mehmed VI Vahdettin, Ottoman Sultan 81, 125,
    165, 232, 233, 248, 249, 305–6, 334, 383, 461,
    488, 514, 532, 584, 599
Melbourne, Australia 449
Menocal, Mario Garcia, President of Cuba 310
Mensheviks 6, 30, 36, 39, 40, 48, 59, 64
Metternich, Prince Klemens von 161
Michael Romanov, Grand Duke 25–6, 27, 57, 75,
    101, 119, 601
Michaelis, Georg, Chancellor of Germany 52
Michigan 253, 330
Midleton, County Cork 364
Milan 163, 185–6, 223–4, 274–5, 369, 482–3,
    492, 501, 511, 584–5
Miner, Dr Loring 98–9
Mirbach, Count Wilhelm von 109, 119, 121
Moji, Japan 524
Monavullagh Mountains, Co. Waterford 544
Monroe Doctrine 206, 214
Montreux, Switzerland 303, 518–19
Monza, Italy 572
Mordell, Albert: The Erotic Motive in Literature 252
Morgan, J. P. 228, 339
Morning World (New York) 404
Moscow: British suffragettes in 58; and Kerensky
    58, 75; under Lenin and Bolsheviks 100, 101–2,
    108–9, 111, 121; Kremlin 101, 138, 175, 289,
    329, 331, 345, 408, 443, 509; statues 111, 130;
    assassination attempt on Lenin 135–6; Bolshevik
    anniversary festivities (1918) 155, 156–7; Krem-
    lin wine shop 208; first Comintern congress
    209–12; panic at Kolchak's approach 224–5;
    and Denikin's advance 260, 263, 268, 269, 275;
    food shortages 290; Lenin's birthday celebra-
    tions (1920) 311, 312; British Labour delega-
    tion's visit 312, 320–22; foraging for firewood
    322–3; second Comintern congress 327, 329,
    331; suppression of the Sukharevka 363; third
    Comintern congress 405–6; repairs to Lenin's
    Kremlin apartment 408, 503–4; imported goods
    from America 422; and use of acronyms 424–5;
    Stalin's apartment 442–3; Psychoanalytic Society
    formed 466; show trial of Orthodox priests

and laymen 478–9; meeting of the All-Russian Central Executive Committee 509–10; Lenin Institute 548, 608

Mount Clemens, Michigan 246–7

Müller, Karl Alexander von 248, 481

Münchener Beobachter (newspaper) 144

Munich: Thule Society formed 144; and Eisner 194, 204, 205; as Soviet Republic 222–3, 228, 236; taken by White army 228–9; army propaganda course 247–8, 255; German Workers' Party meetings 259–60, 271–2, 279, 286; as a magnet for counter-revolutionaries 308; anti-Semitism 315, 335–6; Nazi Party meetings 335, 370, 372–3, 521; Nazi Party Day (1923) 538–9; Hanfstaengl residence 541; Zirkus Krone 373, 534, 542, 551; commemorative ceremony for Schlageter 559; as capital of Germany's far right 575; Beer-hall putsch 586, 587–9, 599

Mussolini, Arnaldo 529

Mussolini, Benito; wounded in World War I 24; editorials in *Il Popolo* 56, 71–2, 130, 131, 149, 185–6, 215, 236; and D'Annunzio 163, 216, 257, 258–9, 337, 369, 384, 385, 492, 512, 530, 556, 594; forms the Fasci di Combattimento 163, 216, 217, 224, 263, 296; and Marinetti's attack on *Avanti* offices 224; and Turin student riots 227; fails in Milan elections 274–5, 297; arrested for hoarding weapons 275; reads about crowd psychology 325–6, 530; takes flying lessons 336, 384; cultivates his image 337, 369, 529–30; and the *squadristi* 384, 439, 440, 506, 537; and Kemal 388; elected to Italian parliament 400; as leader of Fascist movement 337, 409–10, 439–40, 453, 469–70; fights a duel 439; and theory of relativity 442; in Berlin 469; and Hemingway 482–3, 519; and Turkish war 501–2; and Lüdecke 505–6, 572; his March on Rome x, 510–12; and the King 512, 537, 600, 602; as Prime Minister 512, 513, 519, 546, 556, 561; and Lenin 515; interviewed by Clare Sheridan 522–3, 531; British Ambassador's view of 546; and invasion of Corfu 561, 568–9, 572, 575–6; at Monza Grand Prix 572; on journalists' role 584–5; hears of Beer-hall putsch 589; meets Primo de Rivera 593; triumphs in 1924 elections 600; and death of Socialist leader, Matteotti 602, 608

Mussolini, Rachele 275

NAACP *see* National Association for the Advancement of Colored People

Nalchik, Caucasus 381

Nantes, France 102–3

Naples 510–11

National Association for the Advancement of Col-

ored People (NAACP) 113, 252, 255, 388, 514

National Socialist German Workers' Party (NSDAP; Nazi Party; *formerly* German Workers' Party) 315, 358, 372–3, 395–6, 413–14, 424, 447, 457, 458, 467, 521, 530, 534, 549, 559, 575, 579; *see also* SA (Sturmabteilung)

Negro World (newspaper) 129, 228, 310, 333, 418

Neivola, Finland 53–4

Nelson, Senator Knute 199, 200, 201

Neumann, Betty 577, 586, 591, 606

New Orleans, Louisiana 531

Newton, Isaac 234, 235, 272

New York 17; psychoanalysts 15; silent parade (1917) 47; Jim Europe's band 63; Hemingway and Wilson in Red Cross parade (1918) 114; return of Harlem Hellfighters 202; de Valera visits 240–41; Garvey survives assassination attempt 268; Russians rounded up 273–4; foreigners deported from 280–81; radicals arrested 286; and prohibition 287; and the Fitzgeralds 289; Wall Street bomb 339–40; Clare Sheridan visits 380–81; Einstein visits 289–90; new shows 404–5, 486; Garvey's annual convention 331–2, 417–18; Russian immigrants 465; Garvey's trial 558–9; *see also* Black Star Line; Harlem; UNIA

New York Age 202, 230, 606

New York Evening Journal 404

New York Sun 209

New York Times 80, 137, 229, 272, 403, 404, 440, 512–13, 521, 529, 557, 604

New York Tribune 240. 274

New York World 493, 567–8

Nicholas II, Tsar ix, 3, 23, 25, 26–7, 34, 40, 43, 49, 50, 57, 62, 65, 76, 96, 110–11, 113, 116, 127, 131, 208

Nijinsky, Vaslav 42

Nivelle, General Robert 115

Noske, Gustav 189

NSDAP *see* National Socialist German Workers' Party

Nuremberg 508, 570–71, 582

Oak Park, Illinois 38, 104, 114, 122, 208–9

Obregón Salido, Álvaro 403

Odessa, Ukraine 254

Oizaba (ship) 170

Olson, Ragnar 183

Omaha, Nebraska 267

Organisation Consul 414, 484

Orlando, Vittorio Emanuele, Prime Minister of Italy 227, 230

Osipov, NIkolai 377

Overman, Senator Lee 199, 200, 228

Pabst, Waldemar 190, 191, 203, 234, 404

Pacelli, Eugenio (*later* Pope Pius XII) 229
Paléologue. Maurice, French Ambassador 26,27
Palestine 80, 196, 306, 307, 445, 448, 539–40
Palmer, Mitchell 228, 239, 243, 270, 273, 274,
   285, 311, 313, 319–20, 340, 349
Pan-African Congresses: 1919 202; 1921 418–19
Pankhurst, Sylvia 44, 328, 331, 346
Pankhurt, Emmeline 47–8, 58, 60, 328, 603
Paris: La Salpêtrière Hospital 20–22; Ballet Russes
   42; in World War I 96, 115, 118; Jim Europe's
   band plays in 137; armistice 161; Apollinaire's
   funeral 161; Woodrow Wilson's arrival 171, 176,
   191; Dada 177, 187, 204, 292–4, 297, 308, 320,
   359, 399–400, 458–9; as 'capital of the world'
   182–3; Peace Conference (1919) 187, 191,
   196–9, 206, 214–15, 220, 230, 261; Wilson's
   return 214–15, 220, 221; burial of Unknown
   Soldier 351, 382, 399; Babinski's *Les Détraquées*
   opens 373–4; Irish race conference (1922) 459;
   Hemingway in 460–61, 599; Einstein's visit
   (1922) 473–4; Breton's seances 502–3, 545–6;
   Action française 513; death of Proust 516; Russians
   in 557, 558; Tzara's show 558, 559–60; Cole
   Porter's show 581–2
Passau, Germany 559
Pavlov, Ivan 605
Pelly, Frances 514
Perm, Russia 176, 181
Perovskaya, Sophia 130
Pershing, General John J. 137, 171, 182
Petliura, Symon, Ukrainian nationalist leader 278
Petrograd (*later* Leningrad; St Petersburg) ix;
   murder and burial of Rasputin 3, 28; February
   Revolution (1917) 24–8; Lenin's arrival 36–7,
   38; Bolshevik conference 39; provisional govern-
   ment under Kerensky 40–41, 48, 49–50, 61, 73;
   British suffragettes visit 47–8; First All-Russian
   Congress of Soviets 48; Kornilov marches on
   61–2; John Reed in 65–6; Lenin returns to 67;
   Hermitage treasures packed up 69; Trotsky as
   public face of Bolshevism in 69–70; October
   Revolution (1917) 73–5, 78, 92–4, 95–6; anarchy
   98; and removal of capital to Moscow 100–1;
   lack of food 116, 120; anniversary celebrations
   155–6; and White army advances 238, 268–9;
   agitprop performance (1920) 313–14; and British
   Labour delegation 312, 318, 320–22; second
   Comintern congress 327–9; largest agitational
   spectacle put on 362; shops open 422; visited by
   Clare Sheridan 592; renamed Leningrad 598
Philadelphia, Pennsylvania 310, 311, 388–9, 465
Philadelphia Enquirer 340
Picabia, Francis 292–3, 516
Picabia, Germaine 293

Picasso, Pablo 42, 161, 351, 516, 559, 580, 605
Pichler, Dr: *Operation at the Sanatorium Auersperg* 577
Piłsudski, Józef 158, 198, 225, 254, 312, 314, 319,
   334, 335
Pless Castle, Silesia 11–12
Poland/Poles 63, 88, 89, 97, 98, 100, 149, 198,
   225, 244–5, 254, 277–8, 300, 312, 314, 319,
   320, 323–4, 326, 327, 333, 334–5, 342, 345,
   346, 347, 348, 394, 434, 478
Politburo 214, 425, 452, 468, 479, 489, 490, 504,
   516, 521, 523, 533, 583
Polycarp (ship) 235
Ponzi, Charles 330
Popolo d'Italia, Il 122, 130–31, 215, 258–9, 388,
   409, 439, 442, 469, 491, 529, 572
Porter, Cole 581; *Within the Quota* 581–2
Post, Louis 313
Pound, Ezra 460, 540, 544, 580
Prague 113, 149, 151, 280, 369–70, 377, 557
Prangins, Lake Geneva 270, 303–4
Pravda 36, 37, 44, 53, 54, 55, 91, 99–100, 108, 137,
   156, 346, 377, 478, 497, 532, 533, 594, 607
Pressburg, Austro-Hungarian Empire 127
Prévost, Marcel 125
Primo de Rivera, Miguel 573, 593
Princip, Gavrilo 18, 110, 240, 322
Principe, island of 234, 235, 272
'principled non-tipper' *see* Trotsky, Leon
Protocols of the Elders of Zion, The 165–6, 182, 200,
   254, 291, 297, 315, 316, 317, 404, 415, 448
Proust, Marcel 358, 516
Punch (magazine) 345

Quinlan, Grace 330

race/racism 536; and Thule Society 144; and Wilson
   19, 23, 170; Garvey on 310–11; and Hitler 335,
   396; and Harding 402; and Houston Chamberlain
   414, 578; and Kaiser Wilhelm 414, 471; Du Bois
   on 230, 540–41; *see also* anti-Semitism; lynching;
   NAACP; racial violence
racial violence (USA): East St Louis (1917) 46–7;
   Chicago (1919) 252; Omaha (1919) 267; Arkan-
   sas (1919) 267, 541; Tulsa (1921) 406, 418
Radek, Karl 31, 188
Rapallo, Treaty of (1922) 477
Rasputin, Gregorii 3, 24, 28, 47, 57
Rathenau, Walther 291, 461, 477, 484–5, 492
Ravich, Olga 31
Ray, Man 516
Recklinghausen, Germany 545
Reed, James A. 202
Reed, John/Jack 32, 522; in Petrograd 65–6, 69,
   73, 93, 94; heads back to America 98; writes

Ten Days that Shook the World 98, 292, 459; at trial of trade unionists 139; arrested for sedition 140; at Senate inquiry 199, 200, 201–2; blames provocateurs for Washington bombs 239; joins Communist Labor Party 256–7; back in Russia 281; gets support for United Communist Party of America 291–2; arrested in Finland 302, 318; returns to Petrograd 318, 328; starts work on new play 321; in football match 331; and Lenin 338; in Baku 340, 341; meets Clare Sheridan 346; death and funeral 344–5; memorial to 405; memorial service 433

Reims cathedral 475

Renner, Karl, Chancellor of Austria 217

Representation of the People Act (1918) 96

Rhine, River 12, 169, 173, 197, 230–31, 277, 308, 478, 547, 576, 582

Rhineland, the 143, 174, 230, 478, 484, 489, 536, 547, 551, 562–3, 579, 582–3, 585–6, 593

Riga, Latvia 59, 348

Roberts, Needham 112

Robien, Louis de 49

Rockefeller, John D. 228

Rodin, Auguste 382; *Eve* 178

Rome x, 185, 206, 216, 258, 336–7, 384, 400, 409, 439, 442, 511, 512, 522–3, 561, 593

Roosevelt, Franklin D. 239, 349, 429, 522

Rosen, Jack, President of the American Jewish Committee 200

Rosenberg Fortress, Kronach, Bavaria 66, 70

Rosenthal, Dr Tatiana 466

Rote Fahne (newspaper) 178, 188, 190, 204, 234

Roth, Professor 17

Rotterdam, SS 376, 389

Royal Astronomical Society, London 272

Royal Irish Constabulary 192, 236, 241, 274, 329, 354, 391

Ruhr, the 192, 308, 478, 509, 533–4, 535–6, 538, 544–5, 547–8, 550, 552–3, 560, 569, 570, 574, 575

Ruhrort, Germany 381

Rumbold, Sir Horace 383, 514

SA (Sturmabteilung) 424, 447, 508, 530, 538–9, 543, 559, 571, 578

Saint-Cyr, France: officer training school 400

Saint Germain, Treaty of (1919) 256, 261

St. Louis, Missouri 299–300, 462, 543–4

St. Louis Star 544

Sakarya, River, Ottoman Empire 417

Salt Lake city, Utah 266

Samara, Russia 118, 131

Samsun, Ottoman Empire 233

Samuel, Sir Herbert 539

San Diego, California 266

San Remo: conference (1920) 306

San Sebastian, Spain 536–7

Sarajevo, Yugoslavia 9, 18, 49, 212, 240, 322

Sassoon, Siegfried 367

Scapa Flow, Scotland 243

Scheidemann, Philipp 159, 191, 231

Schlageter, Leo 548, 553, 555–6, 559, 571

Schönau, Germany 559

Seattle, Washington: strike (1919) 199, 227

Sebastopol 309, 324, 348, 350, 352

Sedova, Natalya (Trotsky's wife) 18, 30, 77, 289, 443

Sèvres treaty 334, 371, 383, 501

Sfayat, Tunisia 447

Sheridan, Clare: and Churchill 345, 380, 531, 567; visits Moscow 345–6; sculpts Lenin 345–6, 379, and Trotsky 347; returns home 354; visited by phrenologist 368; on US lecture tour 380–81; visits artists' colony 400; in Mexico 403; in Hollywood 426; meets Chaplin 426–7; at the Four Courts, Dublin 486–7; in the Rhineland 489; interviews Kemal 500–1, and Mussolini 519, 522–3, 531; publishes memoir 567; and Primo de Rivera 573; returns to Russia 591–2; tours Europe on motorcycle 602–3

Shotwell, Professor James T. 182

Shuffle Along (show) *see* Sissle, Noble

Silesia 11, 33, 76, 257, 264, 304, 394, 548, 571

Silver, Rabbi 390

Simons, Reverend George S. 200, 201

Simplicissimus (magazine) 536, 547, 557–8, 562, 564, 593

Sinn Féin 44, 68–9, 107, 192, 236, 241, 292, 381, 396, 472

Sissle, Noble 119–20, 213, 388–9, 405, 435, 604; *Shuffle Along* (with Blake) 404–5, 486, 493, 544, 604

Smith, Clara 300

Smith, Thomas 251

Smith, Truman 521–2

Smyrna, Ottoman Empire 196, 231–3, 334, 370, 401, 415, 494, 495–6, 497–500, 501, 502

Snowden, Ethel 312, 318, 321

Sobral, Brazil 235

Social Democrats (Germany) 39, 51–2, 76, 142, 146, 150, 154, 162, 163, 183–5, 191, 193, 205, 303; and Rosa Luxemburg 33, 34, 35; and Spartacists 34, 184, 188, 189; and Kaiser Wilhelm 153; and Hitler 222, 458, 567, 534

Socialist Revolutionaries 27, 36, 39, 40, 48, 54, 59, 64, 79, 92, 93, 108, 118, 121–2, 35, 484; and Kolchak 168, 181

Soupault, Philippe 241, 242, 382, 428

Sovnarkom (Council of People's Commissars) 78, 101, 175, 425, 489, 510, 583

Spa, Belgium 106, 111, 126, 127–8, 145–6, 150,

153, 159

Spartacus League/Spartacists 33, 34, 35, 142, 159, 162, 164, 173, 177, 178, 184–5, 188–91, 193–4, 209, 336

Spartanburg, South Carolina 63

squadristi 366–7, 384, 440, 483, 492, 506, 511–12, 537, 572, 585

Stalin, Josef 27, 340; in Petrograd 27, 36; shaves off moustache and escapes 54–5; attacks intellectuals 70; responsible for nationality issues 74, 101–2; and Trotsky 77–8, 108, 133, 148–9, 156, 208, 238, 268, 275, 523, 607; arrives in Moscow with his new wife Nadya 101; in Tsaritsyn 118–19, 133, 136–7, 213, 214; and the White army attacks 176, 238, 268; given a country house 289; and corruption in the Party 307; praises Lenin at birthday celebrations 312; and Wrangel 319; ordered to break off from assault on Lviv 333–4; and Kemal 361, 362; has appendix out 381, 387; role in Party 425; his apartment in Moscow 442–3, 462; appointed General Secretary 475; called to Lenin's bedside 480–81, 490–91, 492, 497; rows with him 521; abuses Nadezhda Krupskaya 523; orders Lenin's notes to be burned 524; Lenin wants him removed 529; does not trust Lenin 533; apologises for treatment of Lenin's wife 543; and Communist Party congress 543, 548; and Lenin's illness 546; at his funeral 598

Stalingrad 149

Stars and Stripes (army newspaper) 112–13

Stein, Gertrude 448, 460, 483, 565, 579, 589

Strassburg, Germany 81–2

Stravinsky, Igor: *The Rite of Spring* 558

Stresemann, Gustav, German Chancellor 564, 574, 586

Strutt, Miss Lizzie (musical) 486

Strutt, Colonel Edward Lisle 205, 212, 217, 218

suffragettes 44, 47–8, 60, 68, 312, 318, 320–21, 586

Sunderland 287

surrealism 42, 503, 545–6, 599, 600, 605–6

Syria 143, 306, 307, 383, 391, 403

Talaat, Mehmed, Grand Vizier 81, 125, 143, 152, 232–3, 382

Talty, Kathleen 195

Tambov 402

Tarrenz bei Imst, Austria 427–8

Tausk, Victor 252

Taylor, Frederick W. 532

Tel Aviv 539

Teleki, Pái, Minister-President of Hungary 385

Tellini, General Enrico 568, 571

Terezín Fortress/Theresienstadt, Czechoslovakia

240, 322

Thin, Auguste 351

Thule Society 144, 204, 229, 248, 259, 271, 272, 297, 315, 358

Thurles, Co. Tipperary 292

Time magazine 607

Times, The 272, 273, 315, 415, 449

Tirpitz, Admiral von 571

Tobolsk, Siberia 57, 62, 65, 76, 96, 110–11

Toller, Ernst 222, 223, 228, 229, 271, 457–8

Tolstoy, Leo 130

Toronto 298–9, 579–80, 587, 594; League of Young Communists 586

Toronto Star Weekly 298, 299, 330, 460, 483, 580, 587, 594

Toscanini, Arturo 360, 608

Toynbee, Arnold 415

transatlantic review 599

Trotsky, Leon 17, 199, 223, 518; and Lenin *see under* Lenin, V. I.; held in Halifax, Canada 30; his speeches in Petrograd 48; and July Days 54–5; arrested 55; and Bolshevik revolution 67, 69–70, 73, 74, 95, 138, 142, 156, 380; and Stalin *see under* Stalin, Josef; at Brest-Litovsk (1918) 89, 90, 97–8, 99, 100, 148–9; moves into the Kremlin 101; becomes Red Army military supremo 108; armed Czechoslovaks to be shot 115; and assassination attempt on Lenin 136, 137; tours Russia by train 166–7; at Comintern congress (1919) 211; in Russian Civil War 176, 193, 197, 213–14, 224–5, 229, 245–6, 254, 255, 262, 268–9, 275, 287, 312, 324, 348, 402; his house 289; plans for labour battalions 307, 321; trying for fix railway network 311; and British Labour delegation 320–21; and Garvey 332; and John Reed 344; and Clare Sheridan 346, 347; considered a trouble-maker 362; bust studied by phrenologist 368; and Kronstadt uprising 377, 378; ranked by Breton and Tzara 382; illness 387, 480, 584, 595; at Comintern congress (1921) 405; and famine in Ukraine 406; suggestion of publishing collected works 429; fails to attend Lenin's bedside 480, 490; refuses job 495, 497; and intrigue in Moscow and sidelining of Trotsky 504, 533, 583–4; at Congress (1923) 548–9; launches press salvo 594; rests by the Black Sea 584, 598

Tsaritsyn, Russia 118, 133, 136, 149, 213, 224, 246, 433–4

Tuam, County Galway 330

Tukhachevsky, Mikhail ('Misha') 319, 323, 326, 333, 334, 377, 379, 402

Tulsa, Oklahoma 406–7, 418

Turin 227

Turku *see* Åbo

Tzara, Tristan 176–7, 187, 204, 205, 292, 293, 294, 297, 320, 359, 382, 399–400, 428, 458, 459, 503, 558, 559–60, 599

U-boat warfare 22, 23, 33,8, 56, 76, 87, 114, 170
Ufa, Russia 224, 254
Ukraine/Ukrainians 48, 89, 90, 96–7, 99, 100, 102, 107, 131, 181, 193, 211, 216–17, 229, 246, 253, 254, 312, 422; grain 91, 100; anti-Semitism 219, 254
Ulyanov, Dmitri Ilyich 289, 480, 490
Ulyanov, Ilya 435
Ulyanov, Vladimir Ilyich see Lenin, Vladimi Ilyich
Ulyanova, Anna 289
Ulyanova, Maria 101, 181, 387, 408, 480, 484, 490, 492, 543, 546, 583
UNIA see Universal Negro Improvement Association and African Communities League
Union of Russian Workers 273–4
Universal Negro Improvement Association and African Communities League (UNIA) 129–30, 228, 268, 298, 310, 311, 327, 331–3, 347, 360, 376, 412, 418, 449, 479, 482, 493, 531
Ural mountains 111, 176, 214, 224, 245, 268

Vaché, Jacques 21, 187
Vahdettin, Ottoman Sultan see Mehmed VI
Valentino, Rudolph 582
Venizelos, Eleutherios, Prime Minister of Greece 568, 571
Venice 205
Vermer, Dr 123–4, 125
Versailles, Treaty of (1919) 243–4, 257, 279, 285, 297, 307, 314, 328–9, 333, 477, 515, 533, 536, 583, 590, see also Peace Conference under Paris
Victor Emmanuel II, of Italy 24, 506, 510–11, 512, 537, 600, 602
Victoria, Queen 69, 172, 276
Victoria Louise of Prussia, Princess 487
Vienna: Freud's psychoanalysis lectures 10; trial of Friedrich Adler 42–3; black marketeers 45; food and other shortages 91, 104, 127, 165, 195, 280, 296, 314; and D'Annunzio's leaflets 134; provisional German-Austrian National Assembly 151; celebration of Emperor's name day 154; visitors to Emperor Charles 161; occupying Italian forces 212; and collapse of Austrian crown 423; psychoanalytic clinic opens 479; Schlagobers reappearing 597
Viereck, George 577
Vigo, Spain 448
Villers-Cotterêts, France 126
Virden, Henry 251
Vittorio Veneto, Italy 153

Völkischer Beobachter (newspaper) 315, 358, 371, 373, 388, 414, 509, 513, 542, 551, 559, 581
Vologda, Soviet Union 108, 110
Vorwärts (newspaper) 184, 189

Wadley, Frank 46
Wagner, Cosima 369, 578–9, 593
Wagner, Richard 63, 218, 328, 541, 578, 579, 582, 601, 609; Lohengrin 579; Die Meistersinger von Nürnberg 543
Wagner, Siegfried 578, 579
Wagner, Winifred 578, 579
Wall Street Journal 265, 340, 506
Warsaw 158, 245, 304, 324, 326, 329, 333, 334–5, 341, 394, 406, 603
Wausau Daily Record 274
Weizmann, Chaim 196, 376, 390, 490, 517
Wells, H. G. 346
Weyland, Paul 338, 339
Whitehouse, Vira 68
Wiesbaden, Germany 489
Wilhelmshaven, Germany 56, 76
Weelwright, Catherine (née Coll) 140
Wilde, Oscar 382
Wilhelm, Crown Prince 172, 589–90
Wilhelm II, Kaiser: and Charles Habsburg 9, 11, 35, 63, 106, 119, 152; in World War I 11–12, 18, 22, 28, 31, 33, 56, 63–4, 72, 80, 81, 89, 91, 104–5, 106–7, 109–10, 127–8 ; and peace 35–6, 39, 115, 145, 146, 150, 152, 153, 158, 159, 160; under semi-house arrest at Amerongen 171–3, 195–6, 221, 237, 276–7, 297–8, 303; buys Huis Doorn 257; moves in 312–13, 359, 386, 414; ranked by Breton and Tzara 382; and wife's death 392, 414; and Lili van Heemstra 420–21, 426; publishes memoirs 470, 553; surrounded by sycophants 471; anti-Semitism 276–7, 386, 471; remarries 471, 487–8, 514–15; on Italians 513; allowed to take road trip 553; feels his return to Germany is imminent 553, 573, 590; and Frobenius 576; and Beer-hall putsch 589, 590; gives up on Germany 602
Wilhelmina, Queen of the Netherlands 160, 172
Wilson, Edith (née Bolling) 23, 32, 56, 170, 198, 214, 221, 230, 239–40, 265, 266, 270–71, 311, 350, 394, 395, 441, 463, 474, 552, 563
Wilson, Field Marshal Sir Henry 486
Wilson, President Thomas Woodrow x, 19–20; and America First slogan 19, 428; breaks off relations with Germany 22–3; declares war 31–2, 33, 56, 83; and women's suffrage 68; his fourteen points 88, 146; pardons black Houston soldiers 103; and military intervention in Russia 110; leads Red Cross volunteers through New

York 114; and first offensive in France 137; and influenza epidemic 144; and peace terms 146, 147–8, 149, 150, 152, 153,169; crosses Atlantic 170; and race 19, 23, 170; arrives in Paris 171, 178; in Britain 185; meets Mussolini at La Scala 185–6; in Paris 191; and League of Nations 197, 198–9, 202, 207, 214, 220–21, 244, 263, 275, 285, 307–8, 311, 428, 576; sails home 199, 202, 207; returns to Paris 214, 215; has influenza 220; exhausted 220, 221; and Italian premier 227, 230; picnics in France 239; visits Belgium 239–40; returns to America 244; tours America 263–7; illness 266–7, 270–71, 275, 311; and 1920 election 349–50; and Henry Ford 370; as ex-President 394–5, 428–9 441, 463, 544; declines to support anti-lynching bill 463 and Mussolini 525; writes unsatisfactory article 552; health improves and considers return to politics 563; radio broadcast (1923) 590–91; death 598

Wirth, Joseph, German Chancellor 484–5
Wittels, Fritz: *Sigmund Freud ...* 594
Wolcott, Senator Josiah O. 201
Wrangel, Olga 309, 393
Wrangel, General Pyotr 246, 254, 309, 319, 327, 345, 347, 348, 350, 352, 353, 357, 393, 446, 447, 465, 503, 603, 607
Wronke, Silesia 33–5
Wyoming 266

Yarmouth (ship) 287, 298, 309–10
Yeats, William Butler 242, 354, 451, 459, 507, 520, 535, 555
Yudenich, General Nikolai 168, 198, 238, 249, 268, 269, 557
Yugoslavia/Yugoslavs 240, 250–51, 258, 294, 295, 322, 360–61
Yusupov, Prince Felix 3, 47, 447

Zetkin, Clara 34, 354–6, 375
Zinoviev, Grigory 504
Zinoviev letter 606–7
Zionism/Zionists 291, 298, 307, 332, 336, 375–6, 389, 390, 391, 484, 517, 539, 540; *see also Protocols of the Elders of Zion, The*
Zita, Empress 49, 106, 127, 150, 162, 165, 205, 218, 270, 303, 392, 438, 439, 467, 536–7
Zuckerkandl, Professor Otto 123
Zurich 3–4, 5, 7, 29, 30–31, 176–7

Charles Emmerson is a senior research fellow at Chatham House working on resource security, foreign policy, and global geopolitics. He is the author of *The Future History of the Arctic* and *1913: In Search of the World Before the Great War*. He was formerly a writer for the *Financial Times* and continues to publish regularly on international affairs. He lives in London, England.

PublicAffairs is a publishing house founded in 1997. It is a tribute to the standards, values, and flair of three persons who have served as mentors to countless reporters, writers, editors, and book people of all kinds, including me.

I. F. STONE, proprietor of *I. F. Stone's Weekly*, combined a commitment to the First Amendment with entrepreneurial zeal and reporting skill and became one of the great independent journalists in American history. At the age of eighty, Izzy published *The Trial of Socrates*, which was a national bestseller. He wrote the book after he taught himself ancient Greek.

BENJAMIN C. BRADLEE was for nearly thirty years the charismatic editorial leader of *The Washington Post*. It was Ben who gave the *Post* the range and courage to pursue such historic issues as Watergate. He supported his reporters with a tenacity that made them fearless and it is no accident that so many became authors of influential, best-selling books.

ROBERT L. BERNSTEIN, the chief executive of Random House for more than a quarter century, guided one of the nation's premier publishing houses. Bob was personally responsible for many books of political dissent and argument that challenged tyranny around the globe. He is also the founder and longtime chair of Human Rights Watch, one of the most respected human rights organizations in the world.

. . .

For fifty years, the banner of Public Affairs Press was carried by its owner Morris B. Schnapper, who published Gandhi, Nasser, Toynbee, Truman, and about 1,500 other authors. In 1983, Schnapper was described by *The Washington Post* as "a redoubtable gadfly." His legacy will endure in the books to come.

Peter Osnos, *Founder*